ISBN 978-0-331-66391-4
PIBN 11069385

NEW
PROBATE LAW AND PRACTICE

WITH

ANNOTATIONS AND FORMS

FOR USE IN

ALASKA, ARIZONA, CALIFORNIA, COLORADO, HAWAII, IDAHO,
KANSAS, MONTANA, NEVADA, NEW MEXICO, NORTH
DAKOTA, OKLAHOMA, OREGON, SOUTH DAKOTA,
UTAH, WASHINGTON, AND WYOMING.

BY

W. S. CHURCH

OF THE SAN FRANCISCO BAR

AUTHOR OF CHURCH ON HABEAS CORPUS, ANNOTATED SAN
FRANCISCO CHARTER, ETC.

SECOND EDITION
IN THREE VOLUMES
VOLUME TWO

SAN FRANCISCO
BENDER-MOSS COMPANY
LAW PUBLISHERS AND BOOKSELLERS
1920

WILLIAMS PRINTING COMPANY

INDEPENDENT PRESSROOM

PART VII.
CLAIMS AGAINST ESTATE.

CHAPTER I.

CLAIMS AGAINST ESTATE.

§ 469. Judgment as a claim. Execution not to issue after death. If one is levied property may be sold.

§ 470. What judgment is not a lien on real property of estate.

§ 471. Reference of doubtful claims. Effect of referee's allowance or rejection.

§ 472. Form. Reference of claim.

§ 473. Form. Referee's report as to correctness of creditor's claim.

§ 474. Trial by referee, how confirmed, and its effect.

§ 475. Liability of executor, etc., for costs.

§ 476. Claims of executor, etc., against the estate.

§ 477. Executor neglecting to give notice to creditors, to be removed.

§ 478. Form. Order of removal for neglecting to give notice to creditors.

§ 479. Executor to return statement of claims.

§ 480. Payment of interest bearing claims.

§ 481. Manner of closing estates when claims are unpaid and claimant can not be found.

CLAIMS AGAINST ESTATE.

1. Notice to creditors.
  (1) In general.
  (2) When not necessary.
  (3) Time of, dependent on value of estate.
  (4) Additional notice. New notice.
  (5) Publication.
  (6) Decree establishing notice.
  (7) Order vacating decree.
  (8) Decree of no debts.

2. Claims in general.
  (1) Jurisdiction of courts.
  (2) Meaning of terms.
  (3) What is a claim.
  (4) What is not the proper subject of a claim.
  (5) Statement of particulars.
  (6) Affidavit or verification.
  (7) Claim is good in form when.
  (8) Duty of executor or administrator.

3. Presentation of claims.
  (1) In general.
  (2) Necessity of.
  (3) Place. Persons to act.
  (4) Waiver of statutory requirements.
  (5) Absence from state.
  (6) Manner of presentment.
  (7) What does not preclude presentation of claim.
  (8) Amendment of claims.
  (9) What claims must be presented.
  (10) "Contingent claims."

  (11) Claim of executor or administrator.
  (12) What claims need not be presented.
  (13) Same. For funeral expenses.
  (14) Same. For fund misappropriated by guardian.
  (15) Same. Vendor's lien.
  (16) Same. Specific property.
  (17) Effect of presentment.
  (18) Effect of non-presentment.
  (19) Effect of death.
  (20) Presentation after death.

4. Allowance and rejection of claims.
  (1) In general.
  (2) Passing on claims. In general.
  (3) Same. Rejection of claims.
  (4) Right to consider claim rejected.
  (5) Effect of rejection.
  (6) Opening order of rejection.
  (7) Power of court and judge.
  (8) Filing of claims.
  (9) Defective verification.
  (10) Amendment of claim.
  (11) Objections to allowance.
  (12) Effect of allowance. In general.
  (13) Same. In part.
  (14) Same. Presumption. Evidence.
  (15) Judgment of allowance.
  (16) Arbitration. Reference.
  (17) Claims properly allowed.

§ 440. Notice to creditors of decedent's estates.

Every executor or administrator must, immediately after his letters are issued, cause to be published in some newspaper of the county, if there be one, if not, then in such newspaper as may be designated by the judge or court, a notice to the creditors of the decedent, requiring all persons having claims against said decedent to file them, with the necessary vouchers, in the office of the clerk of the court from which the letters were issued, or to exhibit them, with the necessary vouchers, to the executor or administrator, at the place of his residence or business to be specified in the notice; provided, said residence or place of business shall be in the county in which said proceeding is bad. Such notice must be published not less than once a week for four weeks. In case such executor or administrator resigns, or is removed, before the time expressed in the notice, his successor must give notice only for the unexpired time allowed for such filing or presentation.—*Kerr's Cyc. Code Civ. Proc.*, § 1490.

ANALOGOUS AND IDENTICAL STATUTES.

No identical statute found.

Alaska—Compiled Laws of 1913, section 1652.

Arizona—Revised Statutes of 1913, paragraph 879.

Colorado—Laws of 1917, chapter 70, page 218.

Hawaii—Laws of 1917, Act 188, page 347; amending Revised Laws of 1915, section 2493.

Idaho—Compiled Statutes of 1919, section 7578.

Montana—Revised Codes of 1907, section 7522.

Nevada—Revised Laws of 1912, section 5963.

New Mexico—Statutes of 1915, section 2277.

North Dakota—Compiled Laws of 1913, section 8734.

Oklahoma—Revised Laws of 1910, section 6336.

Oregon—Lord's Oregon Laws, section 1238.

South Dakota—Compiled Laws of 1913, section 5787.

Utah—Compiled Laws of 1907, sections 3848, 3849.

Washington—Laws of 1917, chapter 156, page 672, section 107.

Wyoming—Compiled Statutes of 1910, section 5616.

§ 441. Form. Order for publication of notice to creditors.

[Title of court.]

[Title of estate.] $\begin{cases} \text{No. ——.}^1 \quad \text{Dept. No. ——.} \\ \qquad \text{[Title of form.]} \end{cases}$

It is ordered that notice to creditors of said decedent, pursuant to ——,[2] be published once a week for four weeks in the ——, a newspaper of said county.[3]

Dated ——, 19—.   ——, Judge of the —— Court.

Explanatory notes.—[1] Give file number. [2] Refer to the statute providing for notice to creditors. [3] Or, city and county.

§ 442. Form. Notice to creditors.

[Title of court.]

[Title of estate.] $\begin{cases} \text{No. ——.}^1 \quad \text{Dept. No. ——.} \\ \qquad \text{[Title of form.]} \end{cases}$

Notice is hereby given by the undersigned, administrator [2] of the estate of ——, deceased, to the creditors of and all persons having claims against the said deceased, to file them with the necessary vouchers within ——[3] months after the first publication of this notice, in the office of the clerk of the superior [4] court of ——,[5] to exhibit such claims, with the necessary vouchers, within —— [6] months after the first publication of this notice to the said administrator,[7] at the office of ——,[8] which said office the undersigned selects as his place of business in

all matters connected with said estate of ——, deceased.
——, Administrator [9] of the Estate of ——, Deceased.
        ——, Attorney for said Administrator.[10]
Dated and first published at ——,[11] on this —— day of
——, 19—.   ——, Attorney for Said Administrator.[12]

Explanatory notes.—1 Give file number. 2 Or, administrator with the
will annexed; or, executor of the last will and testament, etc. 3 As
indicated by the statute, depending on the value of the estate. 4 Or,
as the name of the court may be. 5 Naming the state and county.
6 Number of months prescribed by statute, depending on the value of the
estate. 7 Or, executor. 8 Describing it, so that it can be easily identified. 9, 10 Or as the case may be. 11 State where. 12 Or, executor.

§ 443. What time must be expressed in the notice.

The time expressed in the notice must be ten months
after its first publication, when the estate exceeds in
value the sum of ten thousand dollars, and four months
when it does not.—*Kerr's Cyc. Code Civ. Proc.*, § 1491.

ANALOGOUS AND IDENTICAL STATUTES.
The * indicates identity.
Arizona—Revised Statutes of 1913, paragraph 880.
Hawaii—Revised Laws of 1915, section 2493.
Idaho—Compiled Statutes of 1919, section 7579.
Montana*—Revised Codes of 1907, section 7523.
Nevada—Revised Laws of 1912, section 5964.
New Mexico—Statutes of 1915, section 2277.
North Dakota—Compiled Laws of 1913, section 8734.
Oklahoma—Revised Laws of 1910, section 6336.
Oregon—Lord's Oregon Laws, section 1238.
South Dakota*—Compiled Laws of 1913, section 5788.
Utah—Compiled Laws of 1907, section 3849.
Washington—Laws of 1917, chapter 156, page 672, section 107.
Wyoming—Compiled Statutes of 1910, section 5616.

§ 443.[1] Filing copy of printed notice to creditors.

Within thirty days after the first publication of notice
to creditors, the executor or administrator must file or
cause to be filed in the court a printed copy of said notice
to creditors accompanied by a statement setting forth
the date of the first publication thereof and the name of
the newspaper in which the same is printed.—*Kerr's
Cyc. Code Civ. Proc.*, § 1491a.

§ 444. Copy and proof of notice to be filed, and order made.

After the notice is given, as required by the preceding section, a copy thereof, with the affidavit of due publication, or of publication and posting, must be filed, and upon such affidavit or other testimony to the satisfaction of the court, an order or decree showing that due notice to creditors has been given, and directing that such order or decree be entered in the minutes and recorded, must be made by the court.—*Kerr's Cyc. Code Civ. Proc.,* § 1492.

ANALOGOUS AND IDENTICAL STATUTES.
The * indicates identity.

Alaska—Compiled Laws of 1913, section 1653.
Arizona*—Revised Statutes of 1913, paragraph 881.
Idaho*—Compiled Statutes of 1919, section 7580.
Montana*—Revised Codes of 1907, section 7524.
Nevada—Revised Laws of 1912, section 5963.
North Dakota*—Compiled Laws of 1913, section 8735.
Oklahoma—Revised Laws of 1910, section 6337.
Oregon—Lord's Oregon Laws, section 1239.
South Dakota—Compiled Laws of 1913, section 5789.
Utah—Compiled Laws of 1907, section 3850.
Wyoming—Compiled Statutes of 1910, section 5617.

§ 445. Form. Affidavit of publication of notice to creditors.

[Title of court.]

[Title of estate.]

{ No. ——.1 Dept. No. ——.
  [Title of form.]

State of ——,
County ² of ——, } ss.

——, of said county ³ and state, having been first duly sworn, deposes and says:

That he is, and at all times embraced in the publication herein mentioned was, the principal clerk of the printers and publishers ⁴ of ——, a newspaper ⁵ printed and published daily (Sundays excepted)⁶ in said county;⁷

That deponent, as such clerk,⁸ during all times mentioned in this affidavit, has had, and still has, charge of all the advertisements in said newspaper; and

That a notice to creditors, of which the annexed is a true printed copy, was published in the above-named newspaper on the following dates, to wit, ——,[9] being for a period of once a week for four (4) [10] weeks; and further deponent saith not. ——

Subscribed and sworn to before me this —— day of ——, 19—.

——, Notary Public in and for the County [11] of ——, State of ——.

Explanatory notes.—1 Give file number. 2, 3 Or, City and County. 4 Or, printer or foreman. 5 "Of general circulation," if the statute requires it. 6 "Sundays excepted," if such is the case. 7 Or, city and county. 8 Or, printer or foreman. 9 Give date of each publication. 10 "Successive" weeks, if such is the fact. 11 Or, city and county.

§ 446. Form. Order fixing time of hearing on application for decree establishing notice to creditors.

[Title of court.]

[Title of estate.] { No. ——.1 Dept. No. ——.
          [Title of form.]

In the above-entitled matter, application having been made to this court for a decree establishing due notice to creditors in said estate,—

It is hereby ordered, That said application be heard at —— o'clock in the forenoon [2] of ——,[3] the —— day of ——, 19— at the court-room of Department No. 4 of said court, in the court-house at ——,[4] and that the clerk of the court give notice thereof by posting notices in three of the most public places in said county [5] for not less than five [6] days before said day of hearing.

Dated ——, 19—. ——, Judge of the —— Court.

Explanatory notes.—1 Give file number. 2 Or, afternoon. 3 Day of week. 4 Name the location. 5 Or, city and county. 6 Or other time fixed by law or rules of court.

§ 447. Form. Affidavit of posting notice of time of hearing of application for decree establishing notice to creditors.

[Title of court.]

[Title of estate.] { No. ——.1 Dept. No. ——.
          [Title of form.]

——, being duly sworn, says: That on the —— day of ——, 19—, he posted correct and true copies of the annexed notice in three of the most public places in said county,² to wit, one of said copies at the place at which the court is held,³ one at ——,⁴ and one at ——,⁵ in said county.⁶

Subscribed and sworn to before me this —— day of ——, 19—.   ——, Deputy County Clerk.

Explanatory notes.—1 Give file number. 2 Or, city and county. 3 Designating it. 4 City hall. 5 United States post-office in the town or city of ——, in said county, designating its location. 6 Or, city and county.

§ 448. Form. Decree establishing notice to creditors.

[Title of court.]

[Title of estate.] {No. ——.¹ Dept. No. ——.
                     [Title of form.]

It appearing to the satisfaction of the court, upon application of the administrator ² of the said estate, that due and legal notice to the creditors thereof has been given, and that notice of the time and place of such application has been given as directed by the court,³—

It is decreed, That the value of the estate of said deceased is less than ten thousand dollars ($10,000);⁴ that due notice to creditors to present their claims has been given herein in all respects as required by law; and that more than four ⁵ months have elapsed since the first publication of notice to creditors.

Dated ——, 19—.   ——, Judge of the —— Court.

Explanatory notes.—1 Give file number. 2 Or, executor. 3 Or, by a copy, and affidavit of due publication of notice to creditors of said deceased, presented and filed in this court, showing the publication of notice ordered by the judge of this court. 4 Or, more than ten thousand dollars ($10,000). 5 Or, ten; or as the case may be. This decree should not be made and entered until after the time allowed for the presentation of claims has elapsed.

§ 449. Time within which claims against an estate must be presented.

All claims arising upon contracts, whether the same be due, not due, or contingent, and all claims for funeral expenses and expenses of the last sickness must be filed or presented within a time limited in the notice, and any claim not so filed or presented is barred forever; provided, however, that when it is made to appear by the affidavit of the claimant to the satisfaction of the court, or a judge thereof, that the claimant had no notice as provided in this chapter, by reason of being out of the state, it may be filed or presented at any time before a decree of distribution is entered. A brief description of every claim filed must be entered by the clerk in the register, showing the name of the claimant, the amount and character of the claim, the rate of interest, if any, and the date of filing.—*Kerr's Cyc. Code Civ. Proc.*, § 1493.

ANALOGOUS AND IDENTICAL STATUTES.

No identical statute found.

Alaska—Compiled Laws of 1913, section 1653.

Arizona—Revised Statutes of 1913, paragraph 882.

Colorado—Mills's Statutes of 1912, sections 7999, 8000, 8008; and Laws of 1915, chapter 173, page 495, amending said section 8000.

Hawaii—Revised Laws of 1915, section 2493.

Idaho—Compiled Statutes of 1919, section 7581.

Kansas—General Statutes of 1915, section 4565.

Montana—Revised Codes of 1907, section 7525.

Nevada—Revised Laws of 1912, sections 5964, 5965.

New Mexico—Statutes of 1915, section 2278.

North Dakota—Compiled Laws of 1913, section 8736.

Oklahoma—Revised Laws of 1910, section 6338.

South Dakota—Compiled Laws of 1913, section 5790.

Utah—Compiled Laws of 1907, section 3851.

Washington—Laws of 1917, chapter 156, page 673, section 107.

Wyoming—Compiled Statutes of 1910, section 5618.

§ 450. Form. Claim of creditor against estate.

[Title of court.]

[Title of estate.]   { No. ——.[1] Dept. No. ——.
                       {   [Title of form.]

The undersigned, a creditor of ——, deceased, presents his claim against the estate of said deceased, with the necessary vouchers for approval as follows, to wit:

Estate of ——, Deceased. To ——, Dr.[2]

Explanatory notes.—[1] Give file number. [2] Give items of claim, including dates, subject-matter, and amounts, with total; and description

of note or mortgage, etc., with place and book of record. This and the
next two forms should be attached to or printed on the same blank.

§ 451. Form. Affidavit to creditor's claim.

[Title of court.]

[Title of estate.]

{ No. ——. Dept. No. ——.
{   [Title of form.]

State of ——,   }
             } ss.
  County ¹ of ——, }

——, whose foregoing claim is herewith presented to
the administrator ² of the estate of said deceased, being
sworn, says: That the amount thereof, to wit, the sum of
—— dollars ($——), is justly due to said claimant; that
no payments have been made thereon which are not credited; and that there are no offsets to the same, to the
knowledge of affiant.   ——.

Subscribed and sworn to before me this —— day of
——, 19—.   ——, Notary Public, etc.³

Explanatory notes.—1 Or, City and County. 2 Or, executor. 3 Or
other officer taking the oath. This form should be attached to the
Creditor's Claim, or be printed thereon.

§ 452. Form. Indorsements on back of creditor's claim.¹

The within claim, presented by ——, a creditor of the
estate of said deceased, is allowed and approved for
$——, this —— day of ——, 19—.

                 ——, Administrator of said Estate.

Allowed and approved for $——, this —— day of
——, 19—.   ——, Judge of the —— Court.

The within claim is rejected this —— day of ——, 19—.

                 ——, Administrator of said Estate.

                 ——, Judge of the —— Court.

Explanatory notes.—1 These indorsements are to be made on the
back of the Creditor's Claim.

§ 453. Form. Affidavit that creditor had no notice.

[Title of court.]

[Title of estate.]

{ No. ——.¹ Dept. No. ——.
{   [Title of form.]

State of ——,
   County ² of ——, } ss.

——, being duly sworn, says: That he is a creditor of the said⁻——, deceased; that he had notice of the death of deceased, or of notice to creditors, until the —— day of ——, 19—, by reason of being out of the state at the time of such death, to wit, in the state of ——; and that a decree of distribution has not yet been entered in the matter of the above-entitled estate. He therefore makes this affidavit, and presents herewith to the administrator ³ of such estate his claim against said estate, and further says, upon his oath, that the amount of said claim, to wit, the sum of —— dollars ($——), is justly due to the said claimant; that no payments have been made thereon which are not credited; and that there are no offsets to the same, to the knowledge of said affiant.

Subscribed and sworn to before me this —— day of ——, 19—.   ——, Notary Public, etc.⁴

Explanatory notes.—1 Give file number. 2 Or, City and County. 3 Or, administratrix, executor or executrix, etc., according to the fact. 4 Or other officer taking the oath.

§ 454. Form. Affidavit to creditor's claim, by one other than the claimant.

[Title of court.]

[Title of estate.]

{ No.——.¹ Dept. No.——.
{   [Title of form.]

State of ——,
   County ² of ——, } ss.

——, being duly sworn, says: That he is the managing agent ³ of ——, whose foregoing claim is herewith presented to the administrator ⁴ of said deceased; that affiant has personal knowledge of all the facts of said claim, and makes this affidavit in behalf of the said claimant, ——, who is absent from the state;[5] that the amount of said claim, to wit, the sum of —— dollars ($——), is justly due to the said claimant; that no payments have been made thereon which are not credited; and that there are no offsets to the same, to the knowledge of affiant.

Subscribed and sworn to before me this —— day of ——, 19—.   ——, Notary Public, etc.[6]

Explanatory notes.—1 Give file number. 2 Or, City and County. 3 Or other capacity in which affiant is acting. 4 Or, administratrix, or administrator or administratrix with the will annexed; or, executor or executrix of the last will and testament of; or the plural of any of these. 5 Or state any other good reason why the claimant can not make the affidavit. 6 Or other officer, according to the fact.

§ 455. Form. Affidavit of corporation to creditor's claim.

[Title of court.]

[Title of estate.]

{ No. ——.[1]   Dept. No. ——.
{   [Title of form.]

State of ——, } ss.
County [2] of ——, }

——, being duly sworn, says: That the —— Company, whose claim is herewith presented to the administrator [3] of said deceased, is a corporation, organized, acting, and existing under the laws of the state of ——; that affiant is the president [4] of such corporation, and has personal knowledge of all the facts of said claim; that the amount of said claim, to wit, the sum of —— dollars ($——), is justly due to the said claimant; that no payments have been made thereon which are not credited; and that there are no offsets to the same, to the knowledge of said affiant.

Subscribed and sworn to before me this —— day of ——, 19—.   ——, Notary Public, etc.[5]

Explanatory notes.—1 Give file number. 2 Or, City and County. 3 Or, administratrix, or administrator or administratrix with the will annexed, or executor or executrix of the last will and testament of; or the plural of any of these, according to the fact. 4 Or, secretary, or other officer, as the case may be. 5 Or other officer taking the oath.

§ 456.   Form.   Affidavit by partnership to creditor's claim.

[Title of court.]

| Title of estate.]

⎰ No. ——.1   Dept. No. ——.
⎱   [Title of form.]

State of ——, ⎰
  County ² of ——, ⎱ ss.

——, being duly sworn, says: That the —— Company, whose foregoing claim is herewith presented to the administrator ³ of said deceased, is a copartnership, composed of ——, ——, and ——,⁴ doing business under the firm name and style of ——; that affiant is a member of such copartnership, and has personal knowledge of all the facts of said claim; that the amount of said claim, to wit, the sum of —— dollars ($——), is justly due to the said claimant; that no payments have been made thereon which are not credited; and that there are no offsets to the same, to the knowledge of said affiant.

Subscribed and sworn to before me this —— day of ——, 19—.   ——, Notary Public, etc.⁵

Explanatory notes.—1 Give file number.   2 Or, City and County. 3 Or, administratrix, etc., according to the fact.   4 Give names of co-partners, and name of firm.   5 Or other officer taking the oath.

§ 457.   Claims to be sworn to, and, when allowed, to bear same interest as judgments.

Every claim which is due, when filed with the clerk, or presented to the executor or administrator, must be supported by the affidavit of the claimant, or some one in his behalf, that the amount is justly due, that no payments have been made thereon which are not credited, and that there are no offsets to the same, to the knowledge of the affiant. If the claim be not due when filed or presented, or be contingent, the particulars of such claim must be stated. When the affidavit is made by a person other than the claimant, he must set forth in the affidavit the reason why it is not made by the claimant. The oath may be taken before any officer authorized to administer oaths. The executor or administrator may also require satisfactory vouchers or proofs to be produced in support of the claim. No greater rate of interest shall be allowed upon any claim after its approval by the administrator or executor and judge than is allowed on judgments obtained in the superior court.—*Kerr's Cyc. Code Civ. Proc.*, § 1494.

ANALOGOUS AND IDENTICAL STATUTES.

No identical statute found.

Alaska—Compiled Laws of 1913, section 1654.
Arizona—Revised Statutes of 1913, paragraph 883.
Colorado—Mills's Statutes of 1912, sections 8002, 8007, 8008.
Idaho—Compiled Statutes of 1919, section 7582.
Kansas—General Statutes of 1915, sections 4568, 4572, 4573.
Montana—Revised Codes of 1907, section 7526.
Nevada—Revised Laws of 1912, section 5965.
New Mexico—Statutes of 1915, section 2277.
North Dakota—Compiled Laws of 1913, section 8737.
Oklahoma—Revised Laws of 1910, section 6339.
Oregon—Lord's Oregon Laws, section 1240.
South Dakota—Compiled Laws of 1913, section 5791.
Utah—Compiled Laws of 1907, sections 3852, 3855.
Washington—Laws of 1917, chapter 156, page 673, section 108.
Wyoming—Compiled Statutes of 1910, section 5619.

§ 458. Superior judge may present claim, and action thereon.

Any judge of a superior court may file or present a claim against the estate of a decedent pending before him, and if the executor or administrator allows the claim, said judge must in writing, designate some other judge of the superior court of the same or an adjoining county, who, upon the presentation of such claim to him, is vested with power to allow or reject it, and the judge filing or presenting such claim, in case of its rejection by the executor or administrator, or by such judge as shall have acted upon it, has the same right to sue in a proper court for its recovery as other persons have when their claims against an estate are rejected.—*Kerr's Cyc. Code Civ. Proc.,* § 1495.

ANALOGOUS AND IDENTICAL STATUTES.

No identical statute found.

· Arizona—Revised Statutes of 1913, paragraph 884.
Idaho—Compiled Statutes of 1919, section 7583.
Montana—Revised Codes of 1907, section 7527.
Nevada—Revised Laws of 1912, section 5966.
North Dakota—Compiled Laws of 1913, section 8739.
Oklahoma—Revised Laws of 1910, section 6341.
South Dakota—Compiled Laws of 1913, section 5793.
Utah—Compiled Laws of 1907, section 3854.
Washington—Laws of 1917, chapter 156, page 674, section 111.

§ 459. Allowance and rejection of claims.

When a claim, accompanied by the affidavit required in this chapter, has been filed with the clerk, the executor or administrator must allow or reject it, and his allowance or rejection thereof must be in writing and filed with the clerk. If the executor or administrator so allow the claim after filing, the clerk must, immediately after the filing of such allowance, present the claim, together with the allowance, to the judge, and must at the time of such presentation indorse on the claim the date thereof. The judge must indorse upon the claim so filed his allowance or rejection, with the date thereof. When a claim, accompanied by the affidavit required in this chapter, is presented to the executor or administrator before filing, he must indorse thereon his allowance or rejection, with the day and date thereof. If he allow the claim so presented, it must be presented to the judge for his approval, who must in the same manner indorse upon it his allowance or rejection, and, if allowed, it must within thirty days thereafter, be filed with the clerk. If, where a claim has been filed without presentation, the executor or administrator refuse or neglect to file such allowance or rejection for ten days after the claim has been filed, or if, where a claim has been presented before filing, the executor or administrator refuse or neglect to indorse such allowance or rejection for ten days after the claim has been presented to him, or if the judge refuse or neglect to indorse such allowance or rejection for ten days after the claim has been presented to him, such refusal or neglect may, at the option of the claimant, be deemed equivalent to a rejection on the tenth day; and if the presentation be made before filing by a notary, the certificate of such notary, under seal, shall be prima facie evidence of such presentation and the date thereof. If the claim be filed with the clerk, or presented to the executor or administrator, before the expiration of the time limited for the filing or presentation of claims, the same is filed or presented in time, though acted upon by the executor or administrator, and by the judge, after the expiration of such time. If the claim be payable in a particular kind of money or currency, it shall, if allowed, be payable only in such money or currency. Every claim allowed by the executor or administrator and approved by the judge shall be ranked among the acknowledged debts of the estate, to be paid in due course of administration. The dates of allowance of every such claim, together with the amount allowed, must be entered in the register by the clerk after the allowance thereof by the judge.—*Kerr's Cyc. Code Civ. Proc., § 1496.*

ANALOGOUS AND IDENTICAL STATUTES.

No identical statute found.

Alaska—Compiled Laws of 1913, section 1655.

Arizona—Revised Statutes of 1913, paragraph 885.

Hawaii—Revised Laws of 1915, section 2495.

Idaho—Compiled Statutes of 1919, section 7584.

Montana—Revised Codes of 1907, section 7528.

Nevada—Revised Laws of 1912, sections 5967, 5968.

New Mexico—Statutes of 1915, section 2279.

North Dakota—Compiled Laws of 1913, section 8740.

Oklahoma—Revised Laws of 1910, section 6342.

Oregon—Lord's Oregon Laws, section 1241.

South Dakota—Compiled Laws of 1913, section 5794; as amended by Laws of 1915, chapter 152, page 329.

Utah—Compiled Laws of 1907, section 3853.
Washington—Laws of 1917, chapter 156, page 673, section 109.
Wyoming—Compiled Statutes of 1910, section 5620.

§ 460.   Form.   Notary's certificate of presentation of claim.

[Title of court.]

[Title of estate.]   { No.——.[1]   Dept. No.——.
                       {   [Title of form.]

I, the undersigned, hereby certify: That on the ——
day of ——, 19—, I presented the annexed claim of ——,
accompanied by the proper affidavit, to —— administrator [2] of the estate of ——, deceased, personally, at ——,[3]
the place mentioned in the notice to creditors heretofore
published; that said presentation was made at the request
of said claimant; that said administrator [4] refused to
indorse on said claim his allowance or rejection thereof;[5]
and that he kept said claim for ten days, when he returned it to me, with his refusal to make any indorsement
thereon.[6]

Witness my hand and official seal this —— day of ——,
19—.

[Seal] ——, Notary Public in and for the County [7] of
——, State of ——.

Explanatory notes.—1 Give file number. 2 Or, executor, etc. 3 Name
the place. 4 Or, executor, etc. 5 Or, that he took the claim and retained possession; or, destroyed it; or, refused to receive it, etc., according to the fact. 6 In case of destruction, a copy of the claim, if one
was taken, may be attached to the certificate. 7 Or, City and County.

§ 461.   Approved claims or copies to be filed.   Claims secured by liens may be described.   Lost claims.

If the claim be founded on a bond, bill, note, or any
other instrument, the original need not be filed or presented, but a copy of such instrument with all indorsements must be attached to the statement of the claim and
filed therewith, and the original instrument must be exhibited, if demanded by the executor or administrator or
judge, unless it be lost or destroyed, in which case the
claimant must accompany his claim when filed or pre-

sented by his affidavit, containing a copy or particular description of such instrument, and stating its loss or destruction.

SECURED CLAIM.—If the claim, or any part thereof, be secured by a mortgage or other lien which has been recorded in the office of recorder of the county in which the land affected by it lies, it shall be sufficient to describe the mortgage or lien, and refer to the date, volume, and page of its record.

WITHDRAWAL OF CLAIM.—If, in any case, the claimant has left any original voucher in the hands of the executor or administrator, or suffered the same to be filed with the clerk, he may withdraw the same, when a copy thereof has been already, or is then, attached to his claim.— Kerr's Cyc. Code Civ. Proc., § 1497.

ANALOGOUS AND IDENTICAL STATUTES.
No identical statute found.

Alaska—Compiled Laws of 1913, section 1655.
Arizona—Revised Statutes of 1913, paragraph 886.
Colorado—Mills's Statutes of 1912, section 8005.
Idaho—Compiled Statutes of 1919, section 7585.
Montana—Revised Codes of 1907, section 7529.
Nevada—Revised Laws of 1912, section 5968.
North Dakota—Compiled Laws of 1913, section 8741.
Oklahoma—Revised Laws of 1910, section 6343.
South Dakota—Compiled Laws of 1913, section 5795.
Utah—Compiled Laws of 1907, sections 3852, 3854.
Wyoming—Compiled Statutes of 1910, section 5621.

§ 462. Rejection of claim. Notice of, and suit.

When a claim is rejected either by the executor or administrator, or a judge of the superior court, written notice of such rejection shall be given by the executor or administrator to the holder of such claim or to the person filing or presenting the same, and the holder must bring suit in the proper court against the executor or administrator within three months after the date of service of such notice if the claim be then due or within two months after it becomes due, otherwise the claim shall be forever barred. If the residence of the claimant is not known, and the same shall be made to appear to the satisfaction of the court, the court shall by its order require the notice to be served on the claimant by filing with the clerk.—*Kerr's Cyc. Code Civ. Proc.*, § 1498.

ANALOGOUS AND IDENTICAL STATUTES.
No identical statute found.

Alaska—Compiled Laws of 1913, section 1655.
Arizona—Revised Statutes of 1913, paragraph 887.
Hawaii—Revised Laws of 1915, sections 2495, 2502.
Idaho—Compiled Statutes of 1919, section 7586.
Montana—Revised Codes of 1907, section 7530.
Nevada—Revised Laws of 1912, section 5968.
North Dakota—Compiled Laws of 1913, section 8742.
· Oklahoma—Revised Laws of 1910, section 6344.
Oregon—Lord's Oregon Laws, section 1241.
South Dakota—Compiled Laws of 1913, section 5796.
Utah—Compiled Laws of 1907, section 3856.
Washington—Laws of 1917, chapter 156, page 674, section 112.
Wyoming—Compiled Statutes of 1910, section 5622.

§ 463.   Allowance of claim, and statute of limitations.

No claim must be allowed by the executor or administrator, or by a judge of the superior court, which is barred by the statute of limitations. When a claim is presented to a judge for his allowance, he may, in his discretion, examine the claimant and others, on oath, and hear any legal evidence touching the validity of the claim. No claim against any estate, which has been filed and allowed, or presented and allowed, is affected by the statute of limitations, pending the proceedings for the settlement of the estate.—*Kerr's Cyc. Code Civ. Proc.*, § 1499.

ANALOGOUS AND IDENTICAL STATUTES.
No identical statute found.

Alaska—Compiled Laws of 1913, section 1655.
Arizona—Revised Statutes of 1913, paragraph 888.
Hawaii—Revised Laws of 1915, section 2494.
Idaho—Compiled Statutes of 1919, section 7587.
Montana—Revised Codes of 1907, section 7531.
Nevada—Revised Laws of 1912, sections 5969, 5970.
North Dakota—Compiled Laws of 1913, section 8743.

Oklahoma—Revised Laws of 1910, section 6345.
Oregon—Lord's Oregon Laws, section 1241.
South Dakota—Compiled Laws of 1913, section 5797.
Utah—Compiled Laws of 1907, section 3857.
Washington—Laws of 1917, chapter 156, page 674, section 113.
Wyoming—Compiled Statutes of 1910, section 5623.

§ 464. Claims must be presented before suit.

No holder of any claim against an estate shall maintain any action thereon, unless the claim is first filed with the clerk, or presented to the executor or administrator, except in the following case: An action may be brought by any holder of a mortgage or lien to enforce the same against the property of the estate subject thereto, where all recourse against any other property of the estate is expressly waived in the complaint, but no counsel fees shall be recovered in such action unless such claim be so filed or presented.—*Kerr's Cyc. Code Civ. Proc.*, § 1500.

ANALOGOUS AND IDENTICAL STATUTES.
No identical statute found.
Arizona—Revised Statutes of 1913, paragraph 889.
Hawaii—Revised Laws of 1915, section 2495.
Idaho—Compiled Statutes of 1919, section 7588.
Montana—Revised Codes of 1907, section 7532.
Nevada—Revised Laws of 1912, section 5970.
North Dakota—Compiled Laws of 1913, sections 8736, 8743.
Oklahoma—Revised Laws of 1910, section 6346.
South Dakota—Compiled Laws of 1913, section 5798.
Utah—Compiled Laws of 1907, section 3858.
Washington—Laws of 1917, chapter 156, page 674, section 114.
Wyoming—Compiled Statutes of 1910, section 5624.

§ 465. Time of limitation.

The time during which there shall be a vacancy in the administration must not be included in any limitations herein prescribed.—*Kerr's Cyc. Code Civ. Proc.*, § 1501.

ANALOGOUS AND IDENTICAL STATUTES.
The * indicates identity.
Arizona*—Revised Statutes of 1913, paragraph 890.
Idaho*—Compiled Statutes of 1919, section 7589.
Montana*—Revised Codes of 1907, section 7533.
Nevada—Revised Laws of 1912, section 5971.

North Dakota—Compiled Laws of 1913, section 8748.
Oklahoma*—Revised Laws of 1910, section 6347.
South Dakota—Compiled Laws of 1913, section 5799.
Utah—Compiled Laws of 1907, section 3359.
Washington*—Laws of 1917, chapter 156, page 674, section 114.
Wyoming*—Compiled Statutes of 1910, section 5635.

§ 466. Claims in action pending at time of decease.

If an action is pending against the decedent at the
time of his death, the plaintiff must in like manner file
his claim with the clerk, or present it to the executor or
administrator for allowance or rejection, authenticated
as required in other cases; and no recovery shall be had
in the action unless proof be made of such filing or presentation.—*Kerr's Cyc. Code Civ. Proc.*, § 1502.

ANALOGOUS AND IDENTICAL STATUTES.
The * indicates identity.

Arizona—Revised Statutes of 1913, paragraph 891.
Idaho*—Compiled Statutes of 1919, section 7590.
Kansas—General Statutes of 1915, section 4566.
Montana—Revised Codes of 1907, section 7534.
Nevada—Revised Laws of 1912, section 5972.
North Dakota—Compiled Laws of 1913, section 8744.
Oklahoma—Revised Laws of 1910, section 6348.
South Dakota—Compiled Laws of 1913, section 5800.
Utah—Compiled Laws of 1907, section 3360.
Washington—Laws of 1917, chapter 156, page 674.
Wyoming—Compiled Statutes of 1910, section 5636.

§ 467. Allowance of claim in part.

Whenever the executor or administrator or the judge
shall act upon any claim that may be filed with the clerk,
or presented to the executor or administrator, and is willing to allow the same in part, he must state in his allowance the amount he is willing to allow. If the creditor
refuse to accept the amount allowed in satisfaction of his
claim, he shall recover no costs in any action therefor
brought against the executor or administrator, unless he
recover a greater amount than that offered to be allowed.
—*Kerr's Cyc. Code Civ. Proc.*, § 1503.

§ 468. Effect of judgment against executor.

A judgment rendered against an executor or administrator, upon any claim for money against the estate of his testator or intestate, only establishes the claim in the same manner as if it had been allowed by the executor or administrator and the judge; and the judgment must be that the executor or administrator pay, in due course of administration, the amount ascertained to be due. A certified transcript of the original docket of the judgment must be filed among the papers of the estate in court. No execution must issue upon such judgment, nor shall it create any lien upon the property of the estate, or give to the judgment creditor any priority of payment.—*Kerr's Cyc. Code Civ. Proc.*, § 1504.

§ 469. Judgment as a claim. Execution-not to issue after death. If one is levied property may be sold.

When any judgment has been rendered for or against the testator or intestate in his lifetime, no execution shall issue thereon after his death, except as provided in section six hundred eighty-six. A judgment against the decedent for the recovery of money must be filed with the clerk, or presented to the executor or administrator, like any other claim. If execution is actually levied upon any property of the decedent before his death, the same may be sold for the satisfaction thereof; and the officer making the sale must account to the executor or administrator for any surplus in his hands. A judgment creditor having a judgment which was rendered against the testator or intestate in his lifetime, may redeem any real estate of the decedent from any sale under foreclosure or execution, in like manner and with like effect as if the judgment debtor were still living.—*Kerr's Cyc. Code Civ. Proc.*, § 1505.

ANALOGOUS AND IDENTICAL STATUTES.
No identical statute found.

Alaska—Compiled Laws of 1913, section 1657.
Arizona—Revised Statutes of 1913, paragraph 894.
Idaho—Compiled Statutes of 1919, section 7593.
Montana—Revised Codes of 1907, section 7537.
Nevada—Revised Laws of 1912, section 5975.
North Dakota—Compiled Laws of 1913, sections 8746, 8807.
Oklahoma—Revised Laws of 1910, section 6351.
Oregon—Lord's Oregon Laws, section 1243.
South Dakota—Compiled Laws of 1913, section 5803.
Utah—Compiled Laws of 1907, section 3863.
Washington—Laws of 1917, chapter 156, page 675, section 119.
Wyoming—Compiled Statutes of 1910, section 5629.

§ 470. What judgment is not a lien on real property of estate.

A judgment rendered against a decedent, dying after verdict or decision on an issue of fact, but before judgment is rendered thereon, is not a lien on the real property of the decedent, but is payable in due course of administration.—*Kerr's Cyc. Code Civ. Proc.*, § 1506.

/ANALOGOUS AND IDENTICAL STATUTES.

The * indicates identity.

Alaska—Compiled Laws of 1913, section 1656.
Arizona*—Revised Statutes of 1913, paragraph 895.
Idaho*—Compiled Statutes of 1919, section 7594.
Montana*—Revised Codes of 1907, section 7538.
North Dakota*—Compiled Laws of 1913, section 8808.
Oklahoma*—Revised Laws of 1910, section 6352.
South Dakota*—Compiled Laws of 1913, section 5804.
Wyoming*—Compiled Statutes of 1910, section 5630.

§ 471. Reference of doubtful claims. Effect of referee's allowance or rejection.

If the executor or administrator doubts the correctness of any claim presented to him or filed with the clerk, he may enter into an agreement in writing with the claimant to refer the matter in controversy to some disinterested person, to be approved by the superior court, or a judge thereof. Upon filing the agreement and approval of such court or judge, in the office of the clerk of the court for the county in which the letters testamentary or of administration were granted, the clerk must enter a minute of the order referring the matter in controversy to the person so selected, or, if the parties consent, a reference may be had in the court; and the report of the referee, if confirmed, establishes or rejects the claim the same as if it had been allowed or rejected by the executor or administrator and judge.—*Kerr's Cyc. Code Civ. Proc.,* § 1507.

ANALOGOUS AND IDENTICAL STATUTES.

No identical statute found.

Alaska—Compiled Laws of 1913, sections 1658, 1659.
Arizona—Revised Statutes of 1913, paragraph 896.
Idaho—Compiled Statutes of 1919, section 7595.
Montana—Revised Codes of 1907, section 7539.
North Dakota—Compiled Laws of 1913, section 8747.
Oklahoma—Revised Laws of 1910, section 6353.
Oregon—Lord's Oregon Laws, section 1244.
South Dakota—Compiled Laws of 1913, section 5805.
Utah—Compiled Laws of 1907, section 3864.
Wyoming—Compiled Statutes of 1910, section 5631.

§ 472. Form. Reference of claim.

[Title of court.]

[Title of estate.]   { No. ——.¹ Dept. No. ——.
                                [Title of form.]

It appearing that ——, the administrator ² of the estate of ——, deceased, doubts the correctness of the claim of ——, for the sum of —— dollars ($——), presented against said est⌐⌐ on the —— day of ——, 19—; that said administrat⌐⌐. has entered into an agreement with said claimant to refer the matter in controversy, the correctness of said claim, to ——, Esq., for investigation; and that the said —— is a disinterested person; this court ⁴ therefore approves of such reference; and said agreement and approval having been filed in the office of the clerk of the court for the county ⁵ in which the letters of administration were granted; —

It is ordered, That the matter in controversy be referred to the person so selected,⁶ and that said referee make to this court a report, with all convenient dispatch, as to whether said claim, or any part thereof, should be allowed or rejected.

Dated ——, 19—.   ——, Judge of the —— Court.

Explanatory notes.—1 Give file number. 2, 3 Or, executor of the last will and testament, etc. 4 Or, the judge of this court. 5 Or, city and county. 6 If the parties consent, a reference may be had in the court.

§ 473. Form. Referee's report as to correctness of creditor's claim.

[Title of court.]

[Title of estate.]   { No. ——.¹ Dept. No. ——.
                                [Title of form.]

To the Honorable the ——² Court of the County ³ of ——, State of ——.

A controversy having arisen between ——, a creditor of said estate, and ——, the administrator ⁴ thereof, as to the correctness of the claim of said —— for the sum of —— dollars ($——), presented against said estate, —

I, the undersigned, referee, to whom such controversy

has been referred to take evidence and report upon the facts respecting the liability of said estate upon such claim, hereby report that I have performed my duties as such referee, and find that all matters stated in said claim are true, and that such claim is just and correct.[5] I therefore recommend that it be allowed and approved, and that a decree be entered to that effect.[6]

Respectfully submitted.

Dated ——, 19—.   ——, Referee.

Explanatory notes.—1 Give file number. 2 Title of court. 3 Or, City and County. 4 Or, executor, etc. 5 Or whatever the finding may be. 6 Or whatever other recommendation may be made.

§ 474. Trial by referee, how confirmed, and its effect.

The referee must hear and determine the matter, and make his report thereon to the court in which his appointment is entered. The same proceedings shall be had in all respects, and the referee shall have the same powers, be entitled to the same compensation and subject to the same control, as in other cases of reference. The court may remove the referee, appoint another in his place, set aside or confirm his report, and adjudge costs, as in actions against executors or administrators, and the judgment of the court thereon shall be as valid and effectual, in all respects, as if the same had been rendered in a suit commenced by ordinary process.—*Kerr's Cyc. Code Civ. Proc., § 1508.*

ANALOGOUS AND IDENTICAL STATUTES.

The * indicates identity.

Arizona*—Revised Statutes of 1913, paragraph 897.
Idaho*—Compiled Statutes of 1919, section 7596.
Montana*—Revised Codes of 1907, section 7540.
North Dakota*—Compiled Laws of 1913, section 8748.
Oklahoma*—Revised Laws of 1910, section 6354.
Oregon—Lord's Oregon Laws, section 1245.
South Dakota*—Compiled Laws of 1913, section 5806.
Wyoming*—Compiled Statutes of 1910, section 5632.

§ 475. Liability of executor, etc., for costs.

When a judgment is recovered, with costs, against any executor or administrator, he shall be individually liable for such costs, but they must be allowed him in his administration accounts, unless it appears that the suit or proceeding in which the costs were taxed was prosecuted or defended without just cause.—*Kerr's Cyc. Code Civ. Proc.,* § 1509.

ANALOGOUS AND IDENTICAL STATUTES.

The * indicates identity.

Arizona*—Revised Statutes of 1913, paragraph 898.
Idaho*—Compiled Statutes of 1919, section 7597.
Kansas—General Statutes of 1915, section 4570.
Montana*—Revised Codes of 1907, section 7541.
Nevada*—Revised Laws of 1912, section 5976.
North Dakota*—Compiled Laws of 1913, section 8749.
Oklahoma*—Revised Laws of 1910, section 6355.
South Dakota*—Compiled Laws of 1913, section 5807.
Utah*—Compiled Laws of 1907, section 3865.
Wyoming*—Compiled Statutes of 1910, section 5633.

§ 476. Claims of executor, etc., against the estate.

If the executor or administrator is a creditor of the decedent, his claim duly authenticated by affidavit shall be filed with the clerk, and must be presented by the clerk for allowance or rejection to the judge, who shall allow or reject it, and its allowance by the judge is sufficient evidence of its correctness, and it must be paid as other claims in due course of administration. If, however, the judge rejects the claim, action thereon may be had against the estate by the claimant, and summons must be served upon the judge, who may appoint an attorney, at the expense of the estate, to defend the action. If the claimant recover no judgment, he must pay all costs, including defendant's reasonable attorney's fees, to be fixed by the court.—*Kerr's Cyc. Code Civ. Proc.,* § 1510.

Alaska—Compiled Laws of 1913, sections 1660, 1661.
Arizona—Revised Statutes of 1913, paragraph 899.
Colorado—Mills's Statutes of 1912, section 8003.
Idaho—Compiled Statutes of 1919, section 7598.
Kansas—General Statutes of 1915, section 4582.
Montana—Revised Codes of 1907, section 7542.
Nevada—Revised Laws of 1912, section 5977.
North Dakota—Compiled Laws of 1913, section 8750.
Oklahoma—Revised Laws of 1910, section 6356.
Oregon—Lord's Oregon Laws, sections 1246, 1247.
South Dakota—Compiled Laws of 1913, section 5808.
Utah—Compiled Laws of 1907, section 3866.
Washington—Laws of 1917, chapter 156, page 675, section 120.
Wyoming—Compiled Statutes of 1910, section 5634.

§ 477. Executor neglecting to give notice to creditors, to be removed.

If an executor or administrator neglects for two months after his appointment to give notice to creditors, as prescribed by this chapter, the court must revoke his letters, and appoint some other person in his stead, equally or the next in order entitled to the appointment.—*Kerr's Cyc. Code Civ. Proc.,* § 1511.

Arizona*—Revised Statutes of 1913, paragraph 900.
Idaho*—Compiled Statutes of 1919, section 7599.
Montana*—Revised Codes of 1907, section 7543.
Nevada—Revised Laws of 1912, section 5978.
North Dakota*—Compiled Laws of 1913, section 8751.
Oklahoma*—Revised Laws of 1910, section 6357.
South Dakota*—Compiled Laws of 1913, section 5809.
Washington—Laws of 1917, chapter 156, pages 655, 661, sections 52, 74.

§ 478. Form. Order of removal for neglecting to give notice to creditors.

[Title of court.]

[Title of estate.]

{ No. ——.1 Dept. No. ——.
{ [Title of form.]

It being shown to the court that ——, administrator[2] of the estate of ——, deceased, has neglected for two months after his appointment to give notice to creditors, as prescribed by law; that a citation has issued for him to show cause for such neglect; that said citation has been served and returned, as provided by law and directed by this court; and that said administrator [3] has made default;—

It is ordered, That the letters of administration [4] heretofore granted to the said ——, as administrator [5] of the estate of ——, deceased, be, and the same are hereby, revoked; that —— be, and he is hereby, appointed administrator of said estate; and that letters of administration [6] issue to him upon his taking the oath, and giving a bond in the sum of —— dollars ($——), with sureties to be approved by the judge of this court.

Dated ——, 19—.   ——, Judge of the —— Court.

Explanatory notes.—1 Give file number. 2, 3 Or, executor. 4 Or, letters testamentary. 5 Or, executor. 6 Or, in the case of an executor removed, that letters of administration with the will annexed issue, etc.

§ 479. Executor to return statement of claims.

At the same time at which he is required to return an inventory, the executor or administrator must also return a statement of all claims against the estate which have been filed with the clerk, or presented to the executor or administrator, if so required by the court, or a judge thereof, and from time to time thereafter he must present a statement of claims subsequently so filed or presented, if so required by the court, or a judge thereof. In all such statements he must designate the names of the creditors, the nature of each claim, when it became due, or will become due, and whether it was allowed or rejected by him, or not yet acted upon.—*Kerr's Cyc. Code Civ. Proc.*, § 1512.

ANALOGOUS AND IDENTICAL STATUTES.
No identical statute found.
Arizona—Revised Statutes of 1913, paragraph 901.
Idaho—Compiled Statutes of 1919, section 7600.
Kansas—General Statutes of 1915, section 4569.

Montana—Revised Codes of 1907, section 7544.
Nevada—Revised Laws of 1912, section 5979.
North Dakota—Compiled Laws of 1913, section 8752.
Oklahoma—Revised Laws of 1910, section 6358.
South Dakota—Compiled Laws of 1913, section 5810.
Utah—Compiled Laws of 1907, section 3867.
Wyoming—Compiled Statutes of 1910, section 5635.

§ 480. Payment of interest bearing claims.

If there be any debt of the decedent bearing interest, whether filed or not, or whether presented or not, the executor or administrator may, by order of the court, pay the amount then accumulated and unpaid, or any part thereof, at any time when there are sufficient funds properly applicable thereto, whether said claim be then due or not; and interest shall thereupon cease to accrue upon the amount so paid. This section does not apply to existing debts unless the creditor consent to accept the amount.—*Kerr's Cyc. Code Civ. Proc.,* § 1513.

ANALOGOUS AND IDENTICAL STATUTES.
No identical statute found.
Arizona—Revised Statutes of 1913, paragraph 902.
Idaho—Compiled Statutes of 1919, section 7601.
Montana—Revised Codes of 1907, section 7545.
North Dakota—Compiled Laws of 1913, section 8753.
Oklahoma—Revised Laws of 1910, section 6359.
South Dakota—Compiled Laws of 1913, section 5811.
Utah—Compiled Laws of 1907, section 3868.
Wyoming—Compiled Statutes of 1910, section 5636.

§ 481. Manner of closing estates when claims are unpaid and claimant can not be found.

Whenever any claim has been filed or presented and shall have been approved by the executor or administrator and by the judge, but the same has not been paid, and the estate is in all other respects ready to be closed, if it be made to appear to the satisfaction of the court or judge, by affidavit, or by testimony taken in open court, that the same can not be, and has not been, paid because the claimant can not be found, the court or judge shall make an order fixing the amount of said claim, with interest, if any, and directing the executor or administrator to deposit the amount with the county treasurer of the county in which the estate is being probated, who shall give a receipt for the same, and who shall be liable upon his official bond therefor. Such executor or administrator shall at once make the deposit in accordance with such order of court and shall forthwith proceed to close up and settle such estate. Upon the final settlement of his accounts, the receipt of such treasurer shall be received as a proper voucher for the payment of such claim, and shall have the same force and effect as if executed by such claimant.

DEPOSIT IN STATE TREASURY.—When the amount so deposited is not claimed within five years the court or judge, upon such showing by the affidavit of the county treasurer, must direct the same to be deposited in the state treasury for the benefit of such claimant, or his legal representative to be paid to him whenever, within five years after such deposit, proof to the satisfaction of the state controller and state treasurer is produced that he is entitled thereto. When so claimed, the evidence and the joint order of the controller and the treasurer must be filed by the treasurer as his voucher, and the amount of the claim paid to the claimant, or his legal representative, on filing the proper receipt.

WHEN AMOUNT OF CLAIM ESCHEATS TO STATE.—If no one claims the amount, as herein provided, the claim devolves and escheats to the people of the state of California and shall be placed by the state treasurer to the credit of the school fund. This section shall be applicable to any and all estates now pending in which a decree of final discharge has not been granted.—*Kerr's Cyc. Code Civ. Proc.*, § 1514.

ANALOGOUS AND IDENTICAL STATUTES.
No identical statute found.
Arizona—Revised Statutes of 1913, paragraph 903.

CLAIMS AGAINST ESTATE.

1. Notice to creditors.

(1) In general.—A notice to the creditors of a decedent, requiring them to present their claims to the executor or administrator, may designate the office of his attorney as the place where he transacts the business of the estate, and as the place for the presentation, although he may be engaged in transacting some kind of business elsewhere.—Bollinger v. Manning, 79 Cal. 7, 13, 21 Pac. 375. But a claim may be presented to him before the publication of notice to creditors.—Janin v. Browne, 59 Cal. 37, 43. In a statute that requires creditors to present their claims to the executor or administrator "at the place of his business," the words "place of his business" should be construed to include the place where the administrator transacts the business of the estate, though he may be engaged in transacting some kind of business elsewhere. He may properly designate the office of his attorney as the place where he transacts the business of the estate, and designate that as the place for the presentation of claims.—Bollinger v. Manning, 79 Cal. 7, 13, 21 Pac. 375. It is unnecessary, under the Nevada statute, that the notice to be given by an executor or an administrator to the creditors of an estate should specify whether the place where the claims are to be presented is his place of residence or is his place of business.—Douglass v. Folsom, 21 Nev. 441, 33 Pac. 660. Where the statute does not expressly require the administrator to sign the notice personally, he may authorize his attorney to sign it in his name and in his behalf.—Meikle v. Cloquet, 44 Wash. 513, 87 Pac. 841, 843. The provision contained in the statute of the state of Washington, for notice to creditors and barring all claims not presented within the year relates to a mere matter of procedure and is not obnoxious to any provision of the constitution of the United States or of the state of Washington, whether the provision be made applicable to estates already in course of administration or to estates to be administered upon in the future.—Strand v. Stewart, 51 Wash. 685, 99 Pac. 1028. The legislature of the state of Washington had power to extend the provisions of the Act of 1897 to non-intervention wills already executed in so far as the requirement of notice to creditors and the barring of claims is concerned, and it is manifest that the legislature intended to do so.—Strand v. Stewart, 51 Wash. 685, 99 Pac. 1028. In the event of the resignation or removal of an executor or administrator, his successor must give a notice to creditors, not for the presentation of claims within the statutory period of four months, but, where his predecessor gave such notice, only for the unexpired portion of that period at the time of his resignation or removal.—In re Jameson's Estate, — Okla. —, 182 Pac. 518, 521. The only valid means of determining whether a decedent left debts outstanding is to have an administrator appointed and a notice to creditors published.—In re Collins' Estate, 102 Wash. 697, 173 Pac. 1016. The notice which, under the statute of South Dakota, must be given to creditors is a notice to the creditors of the decedent, and requires all persons having claims against

the decedent to present them; it does not apply to a claim for an assessment on stock held by the decedent at the time of his death, when such assessment was made after his death by order of a court in another state; the statute has reference to claims against the decedent, not to claims arising against the estate but which never existed against the decedent.—In re Roberts' Estate (S. D.), 170 N. W. 580.

(2) **When not necessary.**—Notice to creditors is not necessary where it can result in no possible good. The law does not require vain things. Hence where the widow is entitled to have the whole estate set apart to her, as where it does not exceed the statutory limit, publication of notice to creditors is not necessary.—Estate of Atwood, 127 Cal. 427, 430, 59 Pac. 770; Estate of Palomares, 63 Cal. 402.

(3) **Time of, dependent on value of estate.**—Under the California statute, if the estate exceeds $10,000 in value the executor or administrator is to call upon the claimants to present their claims within ten months from the date of the first publication of notice. If the estate is less than $10,000, then to present them within four months. But, while he is so called upon to designate the time, his designation is not, of course, a judicial determination of the value of the estate, and is not binding upon any creditor or claimant, if the time limit is not the time prescribed by law according to the value of the estate. A wrong determination, by an executor or administrator, of the value of the estate, and publication of notice accordingly, can not deprive creditors of their rights. From the fact that the notice to creditors must be published immediately after he is appointed, and that the executor or administrator, after his appointment, has three months within which to return the inventory and appraisement, it is plainly observable that the law does not contemplate that he shall obtain information from the appraisements for the purpose of fixing the time specified in the notice in which creditors may present their claims. It would seem, therefore, that he must, for himself, and at his own risk, investigate and determine the time in which creditors may appear and present their claims; and a wrong determination of that fact, by him, may often result in serious consequences, for his decision of the fact is in no sense judicial, and therefore not binding and conclusive upon the creditors. The law, in effect, says that when the estate is of greater value than $10,000 the creditors are entitled to ten months' notice. It does not say that when the executor or administrator determines the value to be greater than $10,000, the notice shall be given for ten months; but it is the fact, and not the executor's or administrator's determination of the fact, that is controlling. The law gives the creditors certain rights as to the time within which they may present their claims, and no executor or administrator, by giving a four months' notice, where he should have given a ten months' notice, can in any way deprive creditors of those rights.—Paterson v. Schmidt, 111 Cal. 457, 458, 44 Pac. 161. The Oklahoma Statutes of 1893, relating to claims against decedents' estates and requiring such to be presented

to the executor or administrator within 6 months after the first publication of notice to creditors, was not repealed by chapter 65 of the Session Laws of 1910, requiring claims to be presented within 4 months; the latter has reference to the settlement of estates of the value of $5000 or under, and the former to estates amounting to a larger sum.—Soliss v. General Electric Co. (Okla.), 213 Fed. 204, 206, 129 C. C. A. 548.

(4) Additional notice. New notice.—When the probate judge makes an order for the publication of notice to creditors, he may also direct additional notice at any time within the period allowed for the presentation of claims.—Johnston v. Superior Court, 105 Cal. 666, 668, 39 Pac. 36. The only effect of giving insufficient notice is to operate as an extension of the time for the presentation of claims, until due and proper notice shall be given.—Pitte v. Shipley, 46 Cal. 154, 161. If the probate judge determines, when proof of publication is made, that the publication did not give notice to creditors, it is his duty to direct notice to be given, as though there had been no previous attempt to do so, and the time for the presentation of claims will begin to run from the time of the giving of the new notice.—Johnston v. Superior Court, 105 Cal. 666, 669, 39 Pac. 36.

(5) Publication.—The court has no power to designate in its original order the newspaper in which the notice to creditors shall be published; this is a function to be performed by the executor or administrator. A provision in the statute, that if there is no newspaper published in the county, the court is to designate the newspaper in which the notice is to be published, implies that the power of the court to designate the newspaper exists only in the case specified.—Brouse v. Law, 127 Cal. 152, 153, 59 Pac. 384. The legal period of publication, however, is to be fixed by the judge. Until he acts, it can not be known whether the period of publication will exceed the statutory minimum or not. Without an order, therefore, there can be no legal period of publication, and consequently no authority for publishing. A publication in advance of the order of the court is of no validity; and the best evidence of publication is the newspaper itself.—Wise v. Williams, 88 Cal. 30, 34, 25 Pac. 1064. The affidavit of publication is only prima facie evidence of the facts therein stated, and may be contradicted by the files of the newspaper in which the notice was published, showing that such notice was not published for the time required by law.—Wise v. Williams, 88 Cal. 30, 34, 25 Pac. 1064. If a publication is to be made not less than once a week for four weeks, and the affidavit of publication shows that it was published on August 7th, 14th, 21st, and 28th, but the files of the newspaper introduced in evidence show that the notice was not published on August 28th, which contradicts the affidavit, it results that there were only three publications after the order for publication was made.—Wise v. Williams, 88 Cal. 30, 34, 25 Pac. 1064. A failure to publish such notice does not dispense with the necessity of presenting claims before suit thereon, but only with the necessity of presenting them within the time prescribed by the statute.—McFarland v. Fairlamb, 18 Wash. 601, 52 Pac. 239, 240. It is only in those cases where the court, in its discretion, by reason of the circumstances, deems it proper to require a more extended publication than the minimum required by the statute that it is necessary to specify the time of publication in the order. In all other instances the order may be silent in that respect, and when it is so, a publication of proper notice thereunder, not less than the minimum number of times required by the statute, is a compliance with the law, and constitutes legal notice to the creditors.—Hensley v. Superior Court, 111 Cal. 541, 542, 44 Pac. 232. The executor or administrator is required to publish the notice to creditors in a newspaper for the length of time directed, calling upon all persons having claims against him to exhibit their claims, with the necessary vouchers, either at his place of residence or business, as specified in the notice; and he is further called upon to prescribe in this notice the time limit within which their claims must be presented.—Estate of Wilson, 147 Cal. 108, 110, 81 Pac. 313. Under section 1491a of the California Code of Civil Procedure, within thirty days after the first publication of notice to creditors of a deceased person, the executor or administrator must file, or cause to be filed, in court, a printed copy of said notice accompanied by a statement setting forth the date of the first publication thereof and the name of the newspaper in which the same is printed.—Hawkins v. Superior Court, 165 Cal. 743, 134 Pac. 327. That section is not merely directory, but is mandatory, and the notice provided for must be filed in the prescribed time; a compliance with the provision of sections 1491 and 1492 alone is not sufficient to entitle a party to a decree establishing due notice to creditors, where the notice prescribed by section 1491a has not been filed in the prescribed time.—Hawkins v. Superior Court, 165 Cal. 743, 134 Pac. 327. The publication of notice to creditors in a probate proceeding is a statutory process, and when it has been given in compliance with the statute, as the proceeding under which it is given is one in rem, it is binding on all the world, including a foreign corporation doing business in California, except as to those who may be entitled to the benefit of the exception under section 1493 of the Code of Civil Procedure of that state.—Tropico Land, etc., Co. v. Lambourn, 170 Cal. 33, 45, 148 Pac. 206. Publication of notice to creditors is not invalidated by the fact that the first publication was made prior to the entry of the order, where the order was actually signed and filed prior to such first publication.—Votypka v. Valentine, — Cal. App. —, 182 Pac. 76, 77. An order of court, in a probate proceeding, is deemed to be entered when formally prepared, signed by the judge, attested by the clerk, and filed in his office; and until all these things have been done, it is ineffective; hence, a first publication of notice to creditors, having been made before the filing of the order of publication, is void.—Union Sav. Assn. v. Somers (S. D.), 166 N. W. 638.

(6) Decree establishing notice.—If legal notice to creditors has been given, and due proof thereof made, it is the duty of the court to make an order or decree showing that due notice to creditors has been given, and directing that such order or decree be entered in the minutes of the court and recorded.—Hensley v. Superior Court, 111 Cal. 541, 543, 44 Pac. 232. But a decree establishing due notice to creditors is not conclusive. It may be shown by proof that the publication of notice to creditors was insufficient.—Wise v. Williams, 88 Cal. 30, 34, 25 Pac. 1064; Estate of Wilson, 147 Cal. 108, 111, 81 Pac. 313. Upon the application of the executor or administrator for a decree declaring that due notice to creditors has been given, the court will examine the character of the publication that has been made, and, if it shall then determine that its character and form have been such as not to give a sufficient notice for the presentation of claims against the estate, it will refuse to make such decree.—Brouse v. Law, 127 Cal. 152, 154, 59 Pac. 384. A failure to file proof of the publication of the notice to creditors within the time prescribed by the statute does not affect the validity of the notice, if it was properly given. The time within which a creditor is required to present his claim begins to run from the first publication of the notice, and not from the filing of the proof thereof with the county clerk. The publication, and not the filing, is therefore the vital fact to be considered, and the date of the filing is not jurisdictional. The statute requiring it to be made within a certain time is directory, and not mandatory.—In re Conant's Estate, 43 Or. 530, 73 Pac. 1018, 1020. The statute contemplates that an executor or administrator may obtain his decree establishing due notice to creditors after the notice has in fact been given, by presenting and filing a copy thereof, with the affidavit of due publication, and upon the production of such other testimony as may be satisfactory to the court. While, in practice, such decrees are taken always as a matter of course upon the presentation and inspection of the statutory proofs, it may sometimes happen that the question of the value of the estate is an exceedingly close one, and that valuable rights may depend on an exact determination of the value. It is not incumbent, therefore, upon the trial judge to make his decree at haphazard, or upon partial, and what may prove subsequently to be most unsatisfactory, proof. The wisest course to pursue in such a case might well be to wait until the time for distribution has arrived, when all the parties are regularly before the court, and when the value of the estate can be accurately determined.—Estate of Wilson, 147 Cal. 108, 110, 81 Pac. 313. In the settlement of the estate of a deceased person the court is not authorized to make the decree establishing due notice to creditors provided by section 1492 of the California Code of Civil Procedure, unless a printed copy of such notice accompanied by a statement setting forth the date of the first publication thereof and the name of the newspaper in which the same is printed, has been filed in court within thirty days after the first publication of the notice as required by

section 1491a of that code, enacted in 1911.—Hawkins v. Superior
Court of Marin Co., 165 Cal. 743, 134 Pac. 327.

(7) Order vacating decree.—The question of the value of an estate
is often a close one, and the order directing publication of notice in
some designated newspaper is made without knowledge of the actual
value of the estate. It follows, therefore, that the order of the trial
court vacating its decree establishing due notice to the creditors is
in no sense a judgment upon the facts, so as to constitute res judicata
between the parties, and has no other or further effect than to clear
the way for a proper determination of the question as to the disputed
value of the estate. If the determination of that question has been
reserved until the time for distribution has arrived, and it has been
made to appear clearly that the estate was of less value than $10,000,
a publication of notice to creditors for four months would be sufficient,
and the court's decree establishing due notice would be in all respects
regular.—Estate of Wilson, 147 Cal. 108, 81 Pac. 313, 314.

(8) Decree of no debts.—A decree that there are no debts can not
be entered until the time limited in the notice to creditors has
expired, and if no such notice has been given, the ex parte affidavits
of persons interested in the estate are not sufficient to prove that
there are no debts outstanding.—In re Higgins' Estate, 15 Mont. 474,
28 L. R. A. 116, 39 Pac. 506, 510.

2. Claims in general.

(1) Heterogeneous questions.—The filing of a claim, secured or unsecured, with an executor or administrator is not an action, within the
meaning of the rule that there is but one method of recovering a debt
or enforcing a right secured by a mortgage upon real estate or personal
property.—Kendrick State Bank v. Barnum, 31 Idaho 562, 173 Pac. 1144.
The term "claim" as used in sections 178 and 180 of the probate code
of South Dakota has reference to debts or demands against the decedent which might have been recovered against him in his lifetime by
a personal action for the recovery of money only.—Kline v. Gingery,
25 S. D. 16, 18, 124 N. W. 958. Creditors of the estate are persons who
are such, or became such, because of dealings with the decedent, and
their claims are obligations with which the personal representatives of
the decedent had nothing to do originally, and obligations properly
incurred in the administration of the estate do not have to be verified
as claims against the decedent's estate and paid in due course of administration, but are payable as expenses of the administration in priority
over the claims of decedent's creditors.—Garver v. Thoman, 15 Ariz.
38, 135 Pac. 724, 725. After an insane ward dies, claims against the
ward's estate must be settled in the due course of administration; this
applies to the claim of the guardian's attorney for a fee that was
allowed to him.—Eisenhower v. Vaughn, 95 Wash. 256, 163 Pac. 758.
In an action brought under chapter 38, Revised Codes of North Dakota,

of 1905, by the guardian of an infant against the administrator of the estate of the man who had killed the infant's mother, for damages for such killing, it was held that the action would not lie inasmuch as the statute being in derogation of the common law must be strictly construed, and it did not give any right of action against the estate of the tortfeasor.—Willard v. Mohn, 24 N. D. 386, 391, 139 N. W. 981. An undertaker, in order to make his charge one that will be enforced as against an estate, must be considerate in preparing it, having in mind, not only what he regards as the worth of his services, but the circumstances of the decedent, so far as reasonable diligence enables him to learn what they were.—Golden Gate U. Co. v. Taylor, 168 Cal. 94, Ann. Cas. 1915D, 742, 52 L. R. A. (N. S.) 1152, 141 Pac. 922. Where the payee, under an instrument of settlement in removal of a loan, files such instrument, and the accompanying agreement, against the estate of the obligated party; held, a preferred claim for the amount thereof, and not a claim only for a deficiency.—Black Hills T. & S. Bank v. Plunkett (S. D.), 166 N. W. 527. A claim against the estate of a decedent, where negotiable paper was held by him to be sold and the proceeds to be turned over as indicated in the receipt given for such paper, is not a claim of the first class under the Colorado statute; the deceased was not a "trustee" under that statute; the term "trustee" in the statute was intended to include only such trustees as hold property under a technical or special trust; it does not include the bailee of chattels, charged with the duty of selling them and accounting for the proceeds.—McCutchen v. Osborne, 61 Colo. 408, 412, 158 Pac. 136.

(2) **Jurisdiction of courts.**—The estate of a deceased person is within the jurisdiction and under the control of the probate court. Executors and administrators are appointed by and render their accounts to that court, and the whole subject-matter of such estates, and their settlement and distribution, comes within its jurisdiction and under its scrutiny.—Dodson v. Nevitt, 5 Mont. 518, 6 Pac. 358. Though county courts are vested with jurisdiction pertaining to courts of probate, the two jurisdictions are as separate and distinct as if conferred upon separate tribunals. While sitting in the transaction of probate business, the nature and jurisdiction of the county court must be sought in the general nature and jurisdiction of the probate courts as they are known in the history of the English law and the jurisprudence of this country. The allowance or ordering of the payment of claims against estates that are in process of administration has always been considered an appropriate subject for the jurisdiction of probate courts. It follows that, although a county court has civil jurisdiction of an amount not exceeding $500, it has, while sitting in the transaction of probate business, jurisdiction to adjudicate and allow a claim for more than $500 against an estate.—In re Morgan's Estate, 46 Or. 233, 77 Pac. 608. The jurisdiction of the superior court, when sitting in a probate proceeding, is that of a court of general jurisdiction; and its order for the pay-

ment of the debts of a decedent's estate, as the circumstances may
require, is within its jurisdiction, and is part of the settlement
of the account; and an objection made after the decree ordering
a claim to be paid has become final that it was not presented to the
administratrix as required by law comes too late.—L. Harter Co. v.
Geisel, 18 Cal. App. 282, 122 Pac. 1094. A claimant against the estate of
a deceased person has no access to a court of equity but only to the
probate court.—Welsh, Driscoll & Buck v. Buck, 48 Utah 653, 161 Pac.
455. Under the Colorado statutes the estate of a decedent is primarily
liable for a reasonable expense lawfully incurred in the administration
and settlement thereof and the county court has jurisdiction to allow
directly to the claimant his demand therefor and order the administrator to pay the same, observing of course the statutory classification
and requirements in so doing. In contracting for or incurring such expenses the administrator acts for the estate, in his official and not in his
private or individual capacity.—U. S. Fidelity & Guarantee Co. v.
People, 44 Colo. 557, 98 Pac. 833. For money actually expended for
legal services, an executrix may have a valid claim against the estate
she represents; this claim she may present for an item of expense
incurred in the dure course of administration; and, if the services were
necessary, and the amount paid was reasonable, and the claim is allowed and approved by the court, and no appeal is taken from the
order allowing it, the executrix may reimburse herself from the funds
of the estate; but, until the attorney's fee has been actually paid by
the executrix, she can not have any claim against the estate therefor;
consequently, the court can not, prior to such payment, have before it
anything upon which to act in determining the reasonableness or necessity of such a claim.—State (ex rel. Eisenhauer) v. Second Judicial
District Court, 54 Mont. 172, 168 Pac. 522. An order made by a district
court, sitting in probate, fixing and allowing the attorney's fee to be
paid out of the funds of the estate of a decedent, by the executrix to
the attorney, for professional services rendered and to be rendered by
the attorney to the executrix, in advance of any payment made by the
executrix to the attorney, which amount so fixed and allowed shall be
included in the final account and be presented for settlement and allowance, is unauthorized and is not binding upon or enforceable against
the executrix or the estate.—State (ex rel. Eisenhauer) v. Second Judicial District Court, 54 Mont. 172, 168 Pac. 522. In settling a non-intervention will, after the initiatory steps have been taken, the court loses
jurisdiction; and this rule is not modified by the statute whereby
executors, when creditors of the estate, are required to present their
claims to the court.—Schubach v. Redelsheimer, 92 Wash. 124, 158 Pac.
739.

(2) Meaning of terms.—The word "due" is sometimes used, in the
statute, in two senses; namely, in the sense of "payable" and in the
sense of "owing." Thus in the clause "if the claim be not due when
presented," etc., and in the clause "if the claim which is due," etc.,

the term is used in the sense of payable; and in the clause "justly due," it is used in the sense of owing.—Crocker-Woolworth Nat. Bank v. Carle, 133 Cal. 409, 411, 65 Pac. 951. The words "claimant" and "claim" are used, respectively, as synonymous with "creditor" and "legal demand for money" to be paid out of the estate.—Gray v. Palmer, 9 Cal. 616, 636; Estate of McCausland, 52 Cal. 568. "Claims against an estate" are those in existence at the date of the death of the deceased. Other claims against the estate are those incurred by the administrator or executor in settling the estate, and are properly denominated "expenses of administration."—Dodson v. Nevitt, 5 Mont. 518, 6 Pac. 358.

(3) What is a claim.—The term "claim," as used in connection with the estate of a deceased person, has reference to such debts or demands against the decedent as might have been enforced against him in his lifetime by personal action for the recovery of money, and upon which a money judgment could have been rendered. A balance struck upon an account between parties is such a demand as would constitute a sufficient cause of action.—Estate of Swain, 67 Cal. 637, 8 Pac. 497, 500; Fallon v. Butler, 21 Cal. 24, 81 Am. Dec. 140; Estate of McCausland, 52 Cal. 568; Stuttmeister v. Superior Court, 72 Cal. 487, 489, 14 Pac. 35. The word "claim" is broad enough to embrace a mortgage or any other lien against the estate.—Ellis v. Polhemus, 27 Cal. 350, 354. All wages due a clerk for services rendered, before as well as during the last allowance of a deceased employer, fall within the second class of claims against his estate, and are included in the term "wages of servants" as used in the Kansas statute respecting executors and administrators and the settlement of estates of deceased persons.—Cawood Bros. v. Wolfley, 56 Kan. 281, 54 Am. St. Rep. 590, 31 L. R. A. 538, 43 Pac. 236. A vendor of real estate has a lien upon the same in the hands of the administrator for the unpaid purchase-money.—Cahoon v. Robinson, 6 Cal. 225, 226. Where an attorney compromises a claim against an estate, on a contract made with the administrator, several years after the intestate's death, the claim of such attorney for services is not a claim against the estate.—Lusk v. Patterson, 2 Colo. App. 306, 30 Pac. 253, 254. A payment made by the heirs of an intestate on the latter's mortgage indebtedness, before one of such heirs is appointed as administrator, is not a claim against the estate; and can not be made such by the heir's subsequent appointment as administrator.—Estate of Heeney, 3 Cal. App. 548, 86 Pac. 842. So if heirs choose to bring suit to remove a cloud from their property, no one can object; but the expenses of such litigation are to be adjusted and paid by the parties to the action, and not by the estate of which the property forms a part.—Estate of Heeney, 3 Cal. App. 548, 86 Pac. 842, 844. If a large amount of the separate funds of the husband is commingled with a comparatively trifling amount of the separate funds of the wife, the husband's separate property is not to be forfeited, but the wife, at most, can have a claim only against the estate of her husband for her

funds so commingled.—Estate of Cudworth, 133 Cal. 462, 468, 65 Pac. 1041. The words "claim" and "demand" are used in section 7891 of the Revised Codes of Montana in their broad, comprehensive sense, and apply to all sorts of causes of action against the estates of decedents, whether for money claims or for property which would belong to the estate, except for the establishment of the claim or demand. Delmoe v. Long, 35 Mont. 139, 152, 88 Pac. 778. (Citing Code Civ. Proc., § 3162.) Where a check or written order on a bank duly authenticated by the maker, stated: "You are hereby authorized to pay out of the funds I now have in your bank, for a valuable consideration, which I have received, five hundred dollars, to Mrs. Maria Nassano, or her order, prior to my death, if countersigned by me across the back, or on due notification of my death, without such countersignature," and the same was first presented to the bank after the maker's death, and payment thereof was refused, the payee is entitled to recover the amount thereof as a claim against the estate of the maker. In effect there was an obligation that the drawer's estate would pay if the bank refused.—Nassano v. Tuolumne County Bank, 20 Cal. App. 603, 130 Pac. 29. When stock owned by a stockholder in his lifetime has become vested in his estate, the estate is liable as a stockholder for its proportion of indebtedness after his death.—Miller & Lux Inc. v. Katz, 10 Cal. App. 576, 102 Pac. 946. Where a husband agreed with his wife pending divorce proceedings to pay a monthly allowance to a child during minority, the obligation continues after his death and is a claim against his estate.—Stone v. Bayley, 75 Wash. 184, 48 L. R. A. (N. S.) 429, 134 Pac. 820, 825. The estate of a deceased holder of stock in a corporation is liable upon stock held and owned by him in the same way and to the same extent that he was liable in his lifetime.—Douglass v. Loftus, 85 Kan. 720, Ann. Cas. 1913A, 378, L. R. A. 1915B, 797, 119 Pac. 74. Under a lease made to two or more lessees the estate of one dying is liable for rent accruing after the death and the executors are properly joined with the surviving lessees in an action to recover such rent.—Brownfield v. Holland, 63 Wash. 86, 114 Pac. 892. Estate held liable for special damages accruing prior to decedent's death, from decedent's obstruction of highway.—Leverone v. Weakley, 155 Cal. 395, 101 Pac. 304. Upon the death of a stockholder, his estate succeeds to his stock and is liable with the other stockholders for corporate debts thereafter arising so long as the stock is part of the estate. Money so paid, in compliance with what the payer thought to be a contract with the deceased obligating her to do so, in consideration of the deceased giving her a lot with a completed building thereon, will not be deemed a voluntary payment, if the payer, at the time of payment, was ignorant of the facts that the building was uncompleted and that no such deed of gift had been made, and the will directed the funeral expenses to be paid from the estate.—Estate of Hincheon, 159 Cal. 755, 36 L. R. A. (N. S.) 303, 116 Pac. 47. Where a devisee of a building in process of erection, upon the refusal of the executor to make proper expenditures from the estate to insure its preservation, individually pays for the same, such payment must be regarded as voluntary, and the devisee can not recover the amount thereof from the estate.—Estate of Hincheon, 159 Cal. 755, 36 L. R. A. (N. S.) 303, 116 Pac. 47. Where a woman intrusts money to her husband and he converts it to his own use, and, after his death, such money can not be traced to any specific part of his property, she is entitled to file a claim as a creditor of the estate.—Marker v. Van Gerpen, 39 S. D. 648, 166 N. W. 151. If an agent, having received money from his principal, to be expended in a purchase for the principal, mingles this with money of his own and then dies without having made the purchase, the principal may file a preferred claim against the agent's estate.—In re Blattner's Estate; Blattner v. Abel, 89 Wash. 412, 158 Pac. 1015. An executor or administrator may, in good faith, make advances to the estate, if suitable and for its benefit; such advances may be allowed and recovered as claims against the estate.—In re Williams' Estate, 47 Mont. 325, 331, 182 Pac. 421. A promise of recompense, made by a decedent to a non-relative performing services for him, or her, during illness, may be the basis of a valid claim against the estate.—Taylor v. Wilder (Colo.), 165 Pac. 766. A promise by a woman to her dying husband, to provide by will for their foster son in a certain amount, renders such a provision a moral obligation upon her and, on her dying without fulfilling the promise, a claim for the amount may properly be presented to the executor of the estate.—Olsen v. Hagan, 102 Wash. 321, 172 Pac. 1173. If a daughter, throughout a period of ten years, pays taxes for her father, maintains a home for him and pays the house rent, all under an express contract that he will make a deed to her of specific property, and the father dies without having made the deed, the daughter may file a claim against his estate for the money she so expended for him.—In re Kirfel's Estate; Crampton v. Kirfel, 37 S. D. 292, 294, 157 N. W. 1057.

(4) **What is not the proper subject of a claim.**—The wood "claim," as used in probate acts, has reference to a debt of, or a demand against, a decedent, which might have been enforced during his lifetime; it will not cover, therefore, a claim or demand for a family allowance.—Estate of Cutting; Cutting v. Cutting, 174 Cal. 104, 161 Pac. 1137; Estate of McCausland, 52 Cal. 568, 577. A widow's allowance which she elected to take in money in lieu of the specific property allowed her by the appraisers is a sufficient claim against the estate to support a proceeding to sell the realty to pay debts.—Pinnacle Gold Mining Co. v. Popst, 54 Colo. 451, 131 Pac. 413, 418. With the exceptions of homesteads set apart and allowances for the family support, all the decedent's estate is equally liable for the payment of debts, the word "debts" including family allowances, expenses of administration, and debts accrued and to accrue.—Plains Land, etc., Co. v. Lynch, 38 Mont. 271, 129 Am. St. Rep. 645, 99 Pac. 847, 850. The claims against a decedent, which the statute requires to be presented against his estate

within a stated period, are confined to those "arising upon contracts"; a claim against a deceased person who, as guardian, appropriated funds belonging to the ward, is not within that description.—Smith v. Smith (Mont.), 210 Fed. 947, 952, 224 Fed. 1, 4, 139 C. C. A. 465. The costs and expenses of contesting the probate of a will are not a claim against the estate. The deceased did not incur them nor can they in any sense be his obligations. They are collectible out of his estate simply because the statute makes them so.—In re Statler's Estate, 58 Wash. 199, 108 Pac. 433. Rule applied though executrix never had possession of, or dominion over, stock nor knew of its existence until after creation of indebtedness sued on.—Miller v. Katz, 10 Cal. App. 576, 102 Pac. 946. Claims for the price of goods purchased by an administrator for the purpose of carrying on the testator's business under order of court are not claims against the estate and the statute of non-claim does not apply.—Gordon Reduction Co. v. Lorimer, 50 Colo. 409, 115 Pac. 719. Demands against the estate of a deceased person do not under the statutes of Colorado include a claim under a contract with decedent to make a particular will or bequest.—Oles v. Wilson, 57 Colo. 246, 255. A contract between the executrix of an estate and an attorney employed by her to conduct the necessary proceedings for administration is a purely personal and private contract between the executrix and the attorney, and with it the probate court has no concern until she has actually paid him his fee, in which event she has a claim against the estate for the actual amount necessarily paid.—State (ex rel. Eisenhauer) v. Second Judicial District Court, 54 Mont. 172, 168 Pac. 522. Where a will directed that certain shares of mining stock belonging to the estate should be held in trust for providing prizes to the pupils of a school district, it was held that the rights of the school district, under the will, did not constitute a claim upon the whole estate, but that they were confined to the specific mining stock named.—School District v. International Trust Co., 59 Colo. 486, 496, 149 Pac. 620.

REFERENCES.

Testamentary libels.—See note 49 L. R. A. (N. S.) 897.

(5) **Statement of particulars.**—It is not required that a claim against an estate should state the facts with all the preciseness and detail required in a complaint, and the sufficiency of such a claim is not to be tested by the rules applicable to pleadings. It should, of course, sufficiently indicate the nature and amount of the demand to enable the executor and judge in probate to act advisedly upon it; and when it does this, it is sufficient. The claimant is not required to show the circumstances in which the claim originated, and the conduct of the parties in reference thereto.—Pollitz v. Wickersham, 150 Cal. 238, 88 Pac. 911, 916. As an illustration of a sufficient statement of particulars of claims, see Mauer v. King, 127 Cal. 114, 116, 59 Pac. 290. It is a sufficient statement of the "particulars" of claims based on contract, if

such statement shows the date of the contract, the names of the parties, the amount to be paid, when it is to be paid, and the kind of money is also stated.—Landis v. Woodman, 126 Cal. 454, 456, 58 Pac. 857. In the case of a simple, plain, ordinary promissory note, there is no necessity for stating any other particulars than those appearing upon its face. The business world would be badly handicapped in dealing with commercial paper if a history of such paper were required to accompany it from its inception throughout its long and devious travels. To obtain such a history would be impossible in numberless cases.—Landis v. Woodman, 126 Cal. 454, 456, 58 Pac. 857. A claim against the estate of a deceased person, for services rendered to him in his lifetime, which were agreed to be paid for out of the proceeds of the sale of certain parcels of real estate, that remained unsold at his death, is not void for uncertainty in not describing such real estate, as the only necessity for any reference to the land arises out of the fact that the claim should show that it was not barred by the statute of limitations, and the description of the land is not essential to that fact.—Thompson v. Orefia, 134 Cal. 26, 29, 66 Pac. 24. Failure of verified claim to give particulars prescribed by statute held not fatal where claim was accompanied by note and mortgage showing such details.—Raggio v. Palmtag, 155 Cal. 797, 103 Pac. 312. Claim for specified sum "& Int." held sufficient to cover interest.—Raggio v. Palmtag, 155 Cal. 797, 103 Pac. 312.

(6) Affidavit or verification.—The affidavit to a claim against the estate of a deceased person must be made before an officer authorized to administer oaths.—Winder v. Hendricks, 56 Cal. 464, 465. If the statute requires creditors, in filing claims against a decedent's estate, to file an affidavit stating that no payments have been made thereon which are not credited, and that there are no offsets to the same to the knowledge of the "affiant," an affidavit, filed by a creditor, that there are no offsets to the same to the knowledge of said "claimant," is sufficient, where the same person was "claimant" and "affiant." The use of one word rather than the other in such a case is wholly immaterial.—Davis v. Browning, 91 Cal. 603, 605, 27 Pac. 937; Dorais v. Doll, 33 Mont. 314, 83 Pac. 884; Warren v. McGill, 103 Cal. 153, 37 Pac. 144, 145. So the verification to a claim against the estate of a decedent is sufficient where it was in substantial compliance with the law in force at the time it was made.—Poncin v. Furth, 15 Wash. 201, 46 Pac. 241, 242. If it is stated in the claim that it is for the sum of $400, but in the affidavit to the claim it is stated "that the amount thereof, to wit, the sum of four hundred, is justly due," etc., the omission of the word "dollars" is not fatal to the affidavit.—Hall v. Superior Court, 69 Cal. 79, 80, 10 Pac. 257. It is not material that the claim is verified, as in the case of a claim based upon a judgment, if the statute does not require it to be verified.—Estate of Crosby, 55 Cal. 574, 578. The verification of a claim against the estate of a deceased person is sufficient if it substantially complies with the statute.—Griffith v. Lewin, 129

Cal. 596, 598, 62 Pac. 172. Thus if the claim contains a copy of the promissory note on which it is founded, and states that no part thereof has been paid, except the specified amount, and that a specified balance is due for principal and interest to a given date, an affidavit to the claim, reciting that the balance is justly due the claimant up to such date; that no payments have been made thereon which are not credited; and that there are no offsets to the same to the knowledge of the affiant,—is good, although the verification was made about two weeks after the date to which such balance referred.—Griffith v. Lewin, 129 Cal. 596, 598, 62 Pac. 172. Surplusage does not vitiate the verification, where it contains all that the statute requires. If the verification states that the sum is justly due to the claimant, and that no payments have been made thereon which are not credited, and that there are no offsets to the same to the knowledge of the claimant or affiant, "except some small items, the exact amount of which is not known to affiant," but which he is willing to have credited when the same is shown by the administrator, such exception does not vitiate the verification.—Guerian v. Joyce, 133 Cal. 405, 406, 65 Pac. 972. Where the statute requires the affidavit to set forth the reason why it is not made by the claimant, when it is not so made, an affidavit, by claimant's attorney, that the claimant is a corporation, and that none of its officers, except said attorney, reside in the county, is a sufficient compliance with the statute.—Empire State Min. Co. v. Mitchell, 29 Mont. 55, 74 Pac. 81, 82. But the affidavit is defective if it does not assign some reason which would relieve the claimant from making it.—Maier Packing Co. v. Frey, 5 Cal. App. 80, 89 Pac. 875, 876. So if the agent of a claimant presents a mortgage note to an executor or administrator of a deceased mortgagor, and makes an affidavit thereto, which fails to give any reason why it was not made by the claimant, and states that there are no offsets, "to the knowledge of the claimant," instead of "to the knowledge of affiant," as required by the statute, and the claim is rejected as a claim against the estate, such presentation is fatally defective, and will not support an action or judgment upon the note.—Perkins v. Onyett, 86 Cal. 348, 350, 24 Pac. 1024. The statute requiring an affidavit to be attached to a claim showing that it is due, and that there have been no payments and no offsets, is not applicable to a judgment. In the case of a judgment, no such affidavit is required.—Cullerton v. Mead, 22 Cal. 95, 99. The demand of an attorney for services rendered an administrator during the progress of the settlement of the estate of a decedent, which has been allowed and approved, is not technically a "claim" against the estate, but will be treated as such.—Stuttmeister v. Superior Court, 72 Cal. 487, 14 Pac. 35. An affidavit in support of a claim against an estate of a deceased person. which recites that the claim, to the best of affiant's knowledge and belief, is just, due, and unpaid, and that there are no offsets or credits against the same, is a substantial compliance with that section of the statute under which it was filed.—Westinghouse E. & M. Co. v. Robison,

42 Okla. 754, 756, 142 Pac. 1105. A claim against the deceased, filed with the executor or administrator, is verified sufficiently if the verification is made in substantial compliance with the statute.—Doolittle v. McConnell, 178 Cal. 697, 174 Pac. 305. In the case of a claim presented against the estate of a decedent where the claimant himself makes the accompanying affidavit, it is sufficient if the affidavit states that there are no offsets to the knowledge of the "claimant," although the statute uses the word "affiant."—Gee Chong Pong v. Harris, 38 Cal. App. 214, 175 Pac. 806. The law requires a claim against the estate of a decedent to be supported by the affidavit of the claimant; if not so supported, the claim can not be recognized.—First Security & L. Co. v. Englehart (Wash.), 181 Pac. 13, 15. An affidavit in support of a claim against the estate of a deceased person, made by one of claimant's attorneys, and stating that claimant is a non-resident of the state of Oklahoma, and that he is not in the state at the time, satisfies the requirements of that section of the statute to the effect that if the affidavit is made by a person other than the claimant, it must set forth the reason why it is not made by the claimant.—Westinghouse E. & M. Co. v. Robison, 42 Okla. 754, 757, 142 Pac. 1105. One filing a claim against an estate within the time fixed by the notice to creditors, but neglecting first to verify the claim as required, can not file a verified claim after the expiration of such time, although he did not know of the publication of the notice, he being a non-resident.—Printz-Biederman Co. v. Torgeson (S. D.), 168 N. W. 796. A claim against an estate filed on behalf of a corporation must be accompanied by an affidavit setting forth the claimant's corporate character and the affiant's official capacity therein, if he have such; if the affiant is not an officer, he should swear that there are, to his knowledge, no offsets and that his connection with the company is such that he would know in case there were.—Automatic Scale Co. v. Torgeson, 36 S. D. 564, 566, 156 N. W. 86. In a statute relating to the filing of claims against estates and requiring a claim to be supported by affidavit that the amount thereof is justly due, the word "due" is used in the sense of "owing."— In re Roberts' Estate (S. D.), 170 N. W. 580. A person in presenting his claim in probate, in Oregon, for allowance by the executor, administrator, or probate judge, must make affidavit that the amount claimed is justly due and subject to no just counterclaim; this includes equitable cross-demands of any sort when adjusted; while the statute of that state seems to contemplate legal demands only, there is no good reason why a demand against which there exists an equitable set-off or counterclaim may not be adjusted in a court of equity before it shall be allowed or paid out of the decedent's estate.—Schwarz v. Harris (Or.), 206 Fed. 936, 939. Where a statute providing for the presentation of claims against an estate requires that the affidavit in support must state among other things that there are no offsets to the claim to the knowledge of claimant, a claim not containing that clause is fatally defective.—Dakota Nat. Bank v. Kleinschmidt, 33 S. D. 132, 144

N. W. 934, 936. The verification of a claim of a corporation by the secretary, reciting that there are no offsets to the claim to the knowledge of the "claimant," instead of to the knowledge of the "affiant," is not fatal to the claim.—Western States Life Ins. Co. v. Lockwood, 166 Cal. 185, 135 Pac. 496. An affidavit that a claim was due and unpaid; and that there were no offsets or credits, held not in compliance with section 1494 of the Cal. Code of Civ. Proc., requiring a statement that the amount is justly due, that no payments have been made which are not credited, and that there are no offsets.—Richards v. Blaisdell, 12 Cal. App. 101, 106 Pac. 732.

REFERENCES.

Statement of claims against a decedent.—See note in 130 Am. St. 311.

(7) **Claim is good in form when.**—A claim against the estate of a deceased person, for services rendered, is sufficient in form, though it is in the form of an account showing the total number of days of service, the rate of payment per day, the amount paid on account, and the balance due.—Duncan v. Thomas, 81 Cal. 56, 57, 22 Pac. 297. Under a statute which provides that claims presented in the probate court for allowance shall be heard summarily, and without the form of pleading, it is not proper practice to interpose a demurrer to a claim therein.—Hayner v. Trott, 46 Kan. 70, 26 Pac. 415. A claim is good in form where it is presented to a probate court for allowance, and alleges that the debtor therein named owes the party presenting it a stated sum for commissions paid upon the sale of certain machines, for which notes were taken that are uncollectable, and copies of said notes are attached, showing the amount of the same, and the amount of the commissions paid thereon is also shown, and said claim is verified, and has attached thereto contracts which provide that, when commissions have been paid on notes that are uncollectable, they shall be refunded. —Hayner v. Trott, 46 Kan. 70, 26 Pac. 415. So a claim based upon a promissory note which has not matured at the time the claim is presented is sufficient, if it is in the usual form and contains a copy of the note, followed by the required statutory affidavit. No other particulars of the claim need be stated where the promise to pay is not contingent, but is absolute, though the time of payment of the note depends upon the completion of another contract.—Crocker-Woolworth Nat. Bank v. Carle, 133 Cal. 409, 410, 65 Pac. 951. A verified claim on a note, setting out a copy of the note, is sufficient without producing the original instrument, if the original is not demanded, particularly if the attorney for the estate afterwards informs the claimant that his claim may be considered as "rejected."—McFarland v. Fairlamb, 18 Wash. 601, 52 Pac. 239, 241. Where a claim against an estate is only verified by a notary public and complies with the law in every respect, but the claimant failed to subscribe his name thereto, such omission is not fatal to its character as an oath.—Tucker v. Tucker, 21 Colo. App. 94, 121 Pac. 127. The claim by those who had indorsed the testator's

notes secured by mortgage for a deficiency paid by them after foreclosure sale is on the notes and not on the judgment in foreclosure, and it is not necessary that an exemplification of the judgment should be filed with the claim against the estate of the maker of the notes.—Cone v. Eldridge, 51 Colo. 564, 119 Pac. 619. The original notes covering a claim against an estate and not a statement of them must be filed in the probate court with the claims under the Colorado statute; otherwise, the statute of non-claim runs against the claims.—Gordon Reduction Co. v. Loomer, 50 Colo. 409, 115 Pac. 719. The claim against an estate should be clear and convincing as to its existence as well as to the amount of the claim.—De Monco v. Means, 47 Colo. 457, 107 Pac. 1108. A claim against the estate of a deceased surety on an administrator's bond is not required to state the facts with all the preciseness of a complaint, and the exact amount of such claim need not be stated where an accounting is pending.—Elizalde v. Murphy, 163 Cal. 681, 126 Pac. 978. The statutes nowhere state in what particular form one deeming himself a creditor of the estate in respect to personal services for the deceased done by him during the latter's lifetime shall set forth his claim to be presented to the executor or administrator, but it need not be drawn with the precision necessary to render a complaint good against special demurrer.—Doolittle v. McConnell, 178 Cal. 697, 174 Pac. 305. A claim presented against an estate in progress of settlement does not need to be phrased or shaped with the particularity called for in a pleading; and, so that it may express clearly the amount owed by the decedent to the claimant and for what, the right of amendment should be given it liberally.—White v. Deering, 38 Cal. App. 516, 179 Pac. 401. Where a father and mother were divorced, and the daughter claims, as executrix and sole legatee under the non-intervention will of her deceased mother, a sum of money alleged by her to have been left in the hands of her deceased father, and undisposed of by the decree of divorce, her claim is sufficient in form, though made by her individually before her appointment as executrix, and she has the right to sue thereon as executrix.—Harvey v. Pocock, 100 Wash. 263, 266, 170 Pac. 545. The claim need not be in any particular form; if it advises the administrator or executor of the nature of the claim, the amount demanded, and shows enough to bar another action for the same demand, it is sufficient.—Hamilton v. Blakeney (Okla.), 165 Pac. 141. The statute does not contemplate that it shall be necessary to employ one learned in the law to prepare a claim to present to an administrator or executor; if from such claim filed the administrator or executor is fairly advised as to the claim and the nature thereof, and the claim is sufficient in its contents to stand as a bar to another claim for the same indebtedness, it is sufficient.—In re Kirfels Estate; Crampton v. Kirfel, 37 S. D. 292, 295, 157 N. W. 1057.

If a widow files a claim against her husband's estate, and swears to the same in such words as "that the annexed account, amounting to $—— besides interest, is justly due her from the estate of ——, de-

ceased," the claim is correct in form.—In re Hawgood's Estate, 37
S. D. 565, 572, 159 N. W. 117. A claim ex contractu for a partnership
debt can not be maintained against the estate of a deceased partner,
in the absence of proof of a final settlement between the surviving
partner and the estate and on showing that the partnership assets are
insufficient to pay the debts.—De Monco v. Means, 47 Colo. 457, 107
Pac. 1107, 1108.

(8) **Duty of executor or administrator.**—It is the duty of an executor to present claims against the estate to the court for allowance, and
to pay as directed.—In re Dolenty's Estate; Mannix v. Dolenty, 53
Mont. 33, 161 Pac. 524. An administrator need not report to the probate court a claim that he has rejected; and he need not file it.—Chandler v. Probate Court for Kootenai County, 26 Ida. 173, 141 Pac. 635.

3. Presentation of claims.

(1) **In general.**—Claims against the estate of a decedent may be presented to the executor or administrator thereof before the publication
of notice to creditors to present their claims, but it is not usual to do
so.—Ricketson v. Richardson, 19 Cal. 330, 3$4; Janin v. Browne, 59
Cal. 37, 43. A claim must be presented within the time prescribed by
the notice.—Davidson v. Rankin, 34 Cal. 503. There is no statute in
California which, in terms, denies to a creditor and resident of a
sister state the right to present his claim in the courts of California,
whether the administration in the courts of that state be primary or
ancillary; and, under the principle of comity, such a claim should be
entertained.—McKee v. Dodd, 152 Cal. 637, 125 Am. St. Rep. 82, 14
L. R. A. (N. S.) 780, 93 Pac. 854, 856. The commencement of a suit,
and the service upon the executor or administrator of a verified complaint, within the time in which a claim could have been properly presented, operates as a presentation of the claim.—Clayton v. Dinwoodey,
33 Utah 251, 14 Ann. Cas. 926, 93 Pac. 723, 726. The commencement
of a suit and its continuous prosecution operates as a presentation of
the claim, and obviates the necessity of presentation.—Clayton v. Dinwoodey, 33 Utah 251, 14 Ann. Cas. 926, 93 Pac. 723, 726. There should
be an actual presentation of the claim within the time prescribed, or
something done by the party equivalent to it. The presentation need
not be in any particular form, but must be sufficient to give such notice
to the executor or administrator of the existence of the debt or demand,
its character and amount, as would enable him with reasonable certainty to provide for its payment. Mere knowledge on the part of the
executor or administrator of the existence of the claim is not enough.
The party holding the claim or demand must pursue some measures
to present his demand, and not remain passive or sleep upon his right.
The bringing of a suit or action at law or in equity, is in some jurisdictions regarded as an actual presentation.—Clayton v. Dinwoodey,
33 Utah 251, 14 Ann. Cas. 926, 93 Pac. 723, 726. That a proper claim
against an estate is not drawn with the precision which would render

a complaint good against à special demurrer, especially in the absence of a demand for further particulars, is not fatal to its presentation.—Western States Life Ins. Co. v. Lockwood, 166 Cal. 185, 135 Pac. 496. Under the statutory rule of classification, all claims against an estate no: presented within a year after the granting of the first letters are to b: assigned to the sixth class, regardless of the class to which they woulc have been assigned if presented within the first year, and all duly exhibited demands of any of the first five classes are entitled to a preference over those of the postponed class.—In re Estate of Keppelman, International Harvester Co. v. Algie, 101 Kan. 654, 658, 168 Pac. 876. General taxes, also assessments for street improvements, may be enforced otherwise than through administration, and, in a case where they did not accrue during the decedent's lifetime, and more than six years have passed since the death, they, if filed as claims against an estate, are properly regarded as stale.—In re Webster's Estate; Luse v. Webster, 74 Or. 489, 145 Pac. 1063. If a party seeks relief by partition proceedings, when claiming property by reason of an agreement with the owner, since deceased, to work for him and care for him during life and to take the property on the owner's death, the court may deny this relief without affecting the party's right to file a claim for the services.—Faler v. Culver, 94 Kan. 123, 146 Pac. 333. If a claim against an estate is properly prepared, and verified by the person interested, and caused by him to be mailed to the executor, as such, the latter can not, after receiving it, withhold payment and then contend that the right of action on it is impaired by want of due presentation.—Gray v. Hickey, 94 Wash. 370, 162 Pac. 564. In order that a claim against an estate may be sued upon, it need not be formally filed as such with the executor; it is sufficient if, having been duly prepared and verified and mailed to the executor, the latter received it.—Gray v. Hickey, 94 Wash. 370, 162 Pac. 564.

(2) Necessity of.—The holder of a claim against the estate of a deceased person can not maintain any action thereon unless the claim has first been presented to the executor or administrator for allowance or rejection.—Dodson v. Nevitt, 5 Mont. 518, 6 Pac. 356, 359; Etchas v. Orefia, 127 Cal. 588, 60 Pac. 45; Morse v. Steele, 149 Cal. 303, 86 Pac. 693. And there is no exception to this rule, except as to one who has been absent from the state. The statute is imperative, and applies to all claims arising upon contracts, and a court is not authorized to make an exception to relieve from hardship or to aid apparent equities. The requirement is a statute of limitations, and the claims that are due or contingent must be presented within the time limited by the notice, and any claim not so presented is barred forever.—Morrow v. Barker, 119 Cal. 65, 66, 51 Pac. 12. All claims, whether due or not due, stand upon the same footing as to the time of presenting the same for allowance.—Estate of Swain, 67 Cal. 637, 639, 8 Pac. 497. The failure to publish notice to creditors, as provided by the statute, does not dispense with the necessity of presenting the claim before suing thereon.

The only effect of such failure is to dispense with the necessity of presenting the claim within the time prescribed by the statute.— McFarland v. Fairlamb, 18 Wash. 601, 52 Pac. 239, 241. Nor does the statute which regulates the presentation of the claim affect the question of the necessity of presenting it.—Pitte v. Shipley, 46 Cal. 154, 161. If any claim is made against the estate of deceased, it is necessary to present the same; otherwise no presentation is necessary.—Sharpstein v. Friedlander, 54 Cal. 58. The law in force at the time governs as to the presentation of all claims to the representative of the estate for allowance.—Hibernia S. & L. Soc. v. Hayes, 56 Cal. 297, 298. A contingent claim and a claim not due must be presented according to the statute after the same becomes due or absolute.—Pico v. De la Guerra, 18 Cal. 422, 428. Claims must be presented, not merely filed with the county clerk. A mere filing with such officer does not make the claim a charge upon the estate.—Pico v. De la Guerra, 18 Cal. 422, 428. It is compulsory upon a claimant to present his claim under oath, stating all offsets and credits, before he can maintain an action or be paid his claim. The purpose of the law is to ascertain the balance existing, and to give to both the claimant and to the estate the benefit of all just offsets, whether the estate be solvent or insolvent.—Ainsworth v. Bank of California, 119 Cal. 470, 476, 63 Am. St. Rep. 135, 39 L. R. A. 686, 51 Pac. 952. If a married woman owns a mine in her own right and as her separate property, and employs an agent to rent such mine for her and to account for the proceeds to her, and she brings an action against him to recover the same, it is no defense to such claim for rents that the agent had expended money for plaintiff's husband, in representing certain quartz-mining claims, which had been conveyed by the husband to such agent for the purpose of sale, where the facts clearly show that the agent held the title to such quartz claims in trust for the deceased husband, in his lifetime, and, after his death, in trust for his estate, and where the estate had not been administered. In such a case, where the plaintiff was appointed administratrix of her husband's estate, claims against it must have been presented to the administratrix for allowance before a suit could be commenced thereon.—Rutherford v. Talent, 6 Mont. 132, 9 Pac. 821. In an action brought by the assignee of a life insurance policy to recover the amount of the policy, the administratrix of the insured's estate having been made a party upon application of the insurance company, it is not necessary that the plaintiff's claims be first presented to the administratrix for allowance.—Haynes v. City Nat. Bank of Lawton, 30 Okla. 614, 121 Pac. 182. No suit can be brought upon a claim, against the estate of a deceased person, that has not first been presented to the executor or administrator; the presentation is a fact essential to the cause of action as much as the instrument sued on.— Harvey v. Pocock, 92 Wash. 625, 159 Pac. 771. The court can not repeal or amend the statute relative to the presentation of claims against the estates of decedents; there must be a substantial compliance with its requirements.—Vanderpool v. Vanderpool, 48 Mont. 448, 452, 138 Pac. 772. An involuntary lien can not be enforced against the estate of a deceased person, arising out of an executory contract with the deceased while living, unless the claim has been first presented to the executor; but a claim so presented by a principal contractor may include the claims of sub-contractors duly employed on the work.—Gray v. Hickey, 94 Wash. 370, 162 Pac. 564. The statutory requirements of presentation and of authentication are mandatory, and this fact is not changed by the provisions of section 173, Probate Code, allowing the administrator, in certain cases to take credit for the amount of a claim paid by him without proper presentation and authentication.—Dakota Nat. Bank v. Kleinschmidt, 33 S. D. 132, 140, 144 N. W. 934. The statute of South Dakota, requiring the presentation of a claim, in order to prevent the barring of a suit to foreclose a mortgage, was not amended by the act of 1913, requiring the filing of a copy of the mortgage with the claim presented to the executor or administrator.—Massey v. Fralish, 37 S. D. 91, 95, 156 N. W. 791. The fact that an action was pending against one at the time of his death does not dispense with due presentation of the claim against his estate.—First Nat. Bank of Denver v. Hotchkiss, 49 Colo. 593, 114 Pac. 812.

REFERENCES.

Necessity of presenting ward's claim against estate of deceased guardian.—See note 58 L. R. A. 86.

(3) **Place. Persons to act.**—Claims against an estate of a deceased person may be legally presented at the place where the notice directs them to be presented, whether the administrator or executor is there to receive them or not. Absence from the state makes no difference in this rule.—Douglass v. Folsom, 21 Nev. 441, 33 Pac. 660. The owner of a claim is the proper person to present it. Thus so long as a note and mortgage remain in the possession of the mortgagee, unassigned, he is the only person that can lawfully present the demand for allowance, and if he fails to present it within the time specified in the notice to creditors, the demand, as a claim against the estate generally, is barred by the statute.—Marsh v. Dooley, 52 Cal. 232, 235. Under the statutes of Nevada, it is not a sufficient presentation of a claim against an estate to hand it to the "attorney for the estate," at least, not without showing that it actually reached the administrator within the proper time for the presentation of claims. There is no such officer as attorney of record, or attorney generally, for an estate. An attorney's employment with reference to the estate must always be in a particular matter, and with that matter his legal connection with the estate ends.—Douglass v. Folsom, 21 Nev. 441, 33 Pac. 660. Even where an attorney is authorized by the executor to receive the presentation of particular claims, that does not authorize the attorney to receive claims generally, and to bind the executor by their presentation, without regard to whether they ever reached him. The attorney is

simply the vehicle through which such claims are conveyed to the administrator, and this no more authorizes him to receive other claims generally than it would have authorized the post-office department to do so, had that been the instrument of conveyance chosen. The presentation of a claim left at the place designated in the notice to creditors is legal, regardless of whether it is ever delivered to the executor or administrator, but a claim against an estate, not presented to the executor, nor presented at the place designated in the notice, but presented to an attorney who is acting for the estate, is not legally presented.—Douglass v. Folsom, 22 Nev. 217, 38 Pac. 111. An executor or administrator can not waive the necessity of presenting a claim against an estate for allowance.—Harp v. Calahan, 46 Cal. 222, 233. An executor or administrator can not waive the statutory regulation of the probate law that imposes the loss of a claim if it is not presented within the time prescribed.—Defries v. Cartwright, 10 Haw. 249, 251. Where the business of a decedent has been conducted by the executor or administrator at a profit, obligations incurred by him for goods furnished in the conduct of the business are claims against the estate, and not against him personally. Such claims may therefore be presented for allowance either by the creditors or by the successor of the executor or administrator.—Fleming v. Kelly, 18 Colo. App. 23, 69 Pac. 272, 273. Where there is both principal and an ancillary administration, creditors may prove their claims in either jurisdiction and it is not always necessary that they should be proved in both.—Dow v. Lillie, 26 N. D. 512, L. R. A. 1915D, 754, 144 N. W. 1082, 1085.

(4) Waiver of statutory requirements.—An administrator can not, in South Dakota, waive the statutory requirements as to proper presentation and authentication of claims against an estate, and when he asks to be permitted to take credit for the amount of a claim paid by him without proper authentication, as permitted by the statute, the burden is upon him to prove the facts which should have been authenticated.—Dakota Nat. Bank v. Kleinschmidt, 33 S. D. 132, 140, 144 N. W. 934. But, in the state of Kansas, an executor or administrator may waive service of the notice of a claim by either a writing or by an appearance in court.—Faler v. Culver, 94 Kan. 123, 125, 146 Pac. 333. The indorsement of the word "disallowed" by the executrix on a claim againt the estate based on a promissory note, did not constitute a waiver of the statutory requirement that the note must be presented and filed in court, or relieve the claimant from the consequences of failing to present and file the note.—First Nat. Bank v. Cone, 57 Colo. 529, 531, 143 Pac. 569.

(5) Absence from state.—When it is made to appear to the satisfaction of the court or judge, by the affidavit of the claimant, or by other proof, that he had no notice requiring him to present his claim against an estate, as provided by the statute, it may be filed after the expiration of the statutory time for the publication of the notice to

creditors, if within the time prescribed by statute specially applicable to such a case; as, before the decree of distribution is entered, or before the filing of the final account.—Cullerton v. Mead, 22 Cal. 95, 99; Morrow v. Barker, 119 Cal. 65, 66, 51 Pac. 12; Pacific States S. L. & B. Co. v. Fox, 25 Nev. 229, 59 Pac. 4. No other proof of absence will be required than the claimant's own affidavit; nor is the time for filing his claim limited by the fact of his return to the state before the expiration of the time within which, by the terms of the notice, claims were required to be presented, for the law extends the time for presenting his claim, he being absent from the state during the time of the publication of the notice to creditors; and the statute requiring that it must appear "to the satisfaction of the executor or administrator and the probate judge" that the claimant had no notice does not give any power or right to say arbitrarily that they are not "satisfied," and therefore to reject the claim. The affidavit must show to the satisfaction of a reasonable, fair, and impartial mind that the claimant had no notice, and that is all that is required.—Cullerton v. Mead, 22 Cal. 95, 99. The requirement of section 1493, Code Civ. Proc., of California, as a showing by affidavit of the absence of claimant from the state is to enable him to present a prima facie right to present a claim after the time fixed in the notice to creditors, but the court is not precluded by such affidavit from taking other evidence to satisfy itself as to whether the claimant is entitled, by reason of such absence from the state, to the benefit of the exception provided for in that section.—Tropico Land, etc., Co. v. Lambourn, 170 Cal. 33, 43, 148 Pac. 206. A claim for damages for breach of a covenant of warranty contained in a deed of conveyance of decedent not presented within the time limit provided in the notice to creditors for presentation of claims against the estate of the warrantor, is barred, unless it is made to appear, as required by section 1493, Code of Civil Procedure of California, by affidavit of the claimant, to the satisfaction of the court or a judge thereof, that the claimant had no notice as provided by statute by reason of being out of the state.—Tropico Land, etc., Co. v. Lambourn, 170 Cal. 33, 41, 148 Pac. 206. An affidavit as to absence from the state made under the provisions of section 1493, Code of Civil Procedure of California, is not conclusive of the fact of absence from the state although sufficient in its averments, the question of such presence or absence being one of fact proof of which general evidence is admissible.—Tropico Land, etc., Co. v. Lambourn, 170 Cal. 33, 41, 148 Pac. 206.

(6) **Manner of presentment.**—The apparent purposes in requiring the presentation of claims accompanied with proper vouchers are: 1. To furnish the administrator with pertinent evidence touching their validity and justness, by means of which he may determine for himself whether they ought to be paid out of the funds of the estate; and 2. To enable him to justify his acts, in some measure at least, in accounting with the probate court.—Willis v. Marks, 29 Or. 493, 45

Pac. 293, 296. The claimant is required to present his claim with the proper voucher. The voucher referred to is undoubtedly the affidavit of the claimant to the effect that the amount claimed is justly due, etc. The claim and the voucher go together, or, rather, the voucher must go with the claim, in order to constitute a valid presentation of the same.—Willis v. Marks, 29 Or. 493, 45 Pac. 293, 296. No presentation of a claim against a decedent, to an executor or administrator, is effective without an affidavit that the claim is justly due.—Pico v. De la Guerra, 18 Cal. 422, 427. A presentation of the claim, accompanied by a copy of the affidavit, instead of the original, is insufficient.—Ash v. Clark, 32 Wash. 390, 73 Pac. 351, 353. The presentation of a claim to an administrator is in many respects analogous to the commencement of an action, but there are some differences, and one difference is important. One can not maintain an action on a claim which will become due only on demand, until demand has been made, because it is unjust to subject a defendant to costs until he has neglected or refused to perform his obligation, but the administrator not only can not perform on demand, but the mere presentation of the claim for an allowance does not subject the estate to payment of costs, and, in reality, the reqirement that claims must be presented before suit can be brought is the statutory mode as well as the statutory requirement for making a demand upon an estate.—Maurer v. King, 127 Cal. 114, 117, 59 Pac. 290. Where a decedent gave certain shares of mining stock in part payment for land purchased by him, and agreed to take back the stock from the vendor at the end of two years if the vendor should hold the stock at that time and so request it, a claim presented against the estate of the deceased purchaser, a few days after the expiration of the two years, by the vendor of the land, for the amount at which he agreed to take back the stock, and an offer to surrender the shares of the stock to the executor or administrator in the same condition in which they were received, accompanied by a copy of the contract attached to the claim, is a good presentation of the same.—Maurer v. King, 127 Cal. 114, 116, 59 Pac. 290. Although an executor or administrator may demand the production, for his examination, of a promissory note which is made the basis of a claim, yet, if he does not do so, the presentation of a verified copy of the note by the claimant is sufficient.—First Nat. Bank v. Root, 19 Wash. 111, 52 Pac. 521, 522. In Colorado, the manner of exhibiting a claim against the estate of a decedent, founded upon a promissory note, is by filing the note itself in the county court, and this must be done within a year from the granting of letters. It is not sufficient to file a copy of the note, and the knowledge of the executor or administrator of the existence of the note furnishes the claimant no excuse for a failure to file a claim as the statute directs.—In re Hobson's Estate, 40 Colo. 332, 91 Pac. 929, 931. Although an executor or administrator knows of the existence of a note, or has it in his possession, yet if the holder asserts it as a claim against the estate, and the executor or administrator neglects to comply with the request of the claimant to present the claim properly and have it allowed, this furnishes no excuse for the claimant's failure to file his claim in the probate court as the statute directs. If the claimant has been injured by the failure of the executor or administrator to carry out a supposed promise, the estate is not answerable therefor.—In re Hobson's Estate, 40 Colo. 332, 91 Pac. 929, 931. Where a married woman rendered services as nurse to a person who afterwards died, her claim for such services is community property, and should be presented to the executor or administrator of the estate of the deceased in the name of her husband.—Smith v. Furnish, 70 Cal. 424, 12 Pac. 392, 393. It is not necessary that a copy of the claim accompany a presentation of the claim, unless the law at the time required such copy, as in the case of a judgment.—Estate of Crosby, 55 Cal. 574. A claim based on an oral agreement does not fall within a statute providing that a copy of the instrument on which the claim is founded must accompany the claim.—Dorais v. Doll, 33 Mont. 314, 83 Pac. 884, 885. Although a document used as a bill of particulars has been presented to an executor or administrator on one occasion, yet it may be proved that the claim therein described was presented to him at another time.—Poor v. Smith, 10 Haw. 467, 468. It is not fatal to the presentation of a proper claim, against an estate that it is not drawn with the precision which would render a complaint good against a special demurrer, especially in the absence of a demand for further particulars.—Western States Life Ins. Co. v. Lockwood, 166 Cal. 185, 135 Pac. 496. Where property situated in another state was mortgaged by a decedent as collateral security for a note executed by him, in presenting the note to the maker's executor or administrator, the mortgage need not be attached. —Denver Stockyards Bank v. Martin, 177 Cal. 223, 170 Pac. 428. The holder of a note made by a decedent must, when filing his claim against the estate, present the note itself.—First Nat. Bank v. Cone, 57 Colo. 529, 531, 143 Pac. 569. Where a decedent was obligated to one person in different amounts and in respect to distinct matters, such person is not required to combine the debts and to present them as a single claim against the estate.—Olsen v. Hagan, 102 Wash. 321, 172 Pac. 1173. A claim is properly presented to an executor if received by the latter, although sent by mail.—Gray v. Hickey, 94 Wash. 370, 373, 162 Pac. 564. In the statutes of Kansas, there is no provision whereby a person in whose favor the testator executed a note, and who has subsequently been appointed sole executor, must present the note like any other claim against the estate, regardless of its not having yet matured.—In re Hoover's Estate, Kirk v. Hoover, 104 Kan. 635, 180 Pac. 275. The statute of Colorado provides the method for exhibiting claims against an estate, and requires the note itself to be presented and filed in court, if the claim is founded upon a note.—First Nat. Bank v. Cone, 57 Colo. 529, 531, 143 Pac. 569. A claim, presented to the executor as an indebtedness of the decedent to the person presenting it, need not recite the facts with the precision necessary in a complaint.—Parker v. Burkhart, 101 Wash. 659, 172 Pac. 908. A claim must be in due form and in order to be "presented," must be handed to, or left with, the executor or administrator.—Sunberg v. Sebelius, 39 N. D. 413, 418, 165 N. W. 564. In view of the special provision made in section 1495 of the Code of Civil Procedure of California, as to the mode of the allowance of a claim against the estate of a deceased person in favor of the judge, it is to be considered that he is not generally disqualified to sit in any matter of the estate which has no reference to his interest as a creditor.—Regents, etc., v. Turner, 159 Cal. 541, Ann. Cas. 1912C, 1162, 114 Pac. 842.

(7) **What does not preclude presentation of claim.**—The fact that one, to whom notes have been given, surrenders the instruments to the maker, on request, because of the worry it costs her to have them outstanding, does not prevent him, on the maker's death, from presenting a claim for the amount to the executor of her estate.—Olsen v. Hagan, 102 Wash. 321, 172 Pac. 1173. The failure of a retiring administrator to include an item of expense in the final account rendered by him to his successor, does not preclude the person, to whom the money is due, from presenting a claim therefor to such successor.— Lamb Davis Lumber Co. v. Stowell, 96 Wash. 46, L. R. A. 1917E, 960, 164 Pac. 593.

(8) **Amendment of claims.**—No substantial change can be made in the claim on file, either by way of amendment or otherwise, after the expiration of the time for the presentation of claims.—In re Sullenberger, 72 Cal. 549, 552, 14 Pac. 513. Where an order has been made directing the sale of decedent's property, upon a consideration of the claims against the estate theretofore allowed, and such order has been confirmed, no amendment of a claim can be made that affects the order of confirmation, or that will take away from it the force of the direction therein to execute a conveyance on payment of the purchase price. No amendment can be allowed that will affect any sale of the property made under such order, because the claim, after its amendment, would still have to be presented to the executor or administrator for allowance before it could become a charge upon the estate.—Estate of Turner, 128 Cal. 388, 393, 60 Pac. 967. A creditor's claim against an estate is, in no sense of the word, a pleading, nor is there any such thing known to our law as the amendment of such a claim.— Pollitz v. Wickersham, 150 Cal. 238, 88 Pac. 911, 915. A mortgagee's claim may be amended by attaching the original note and mortgage thereto.—Kirman v. Powning, 25 Nev. 378, 60 Pac. 834, 838.

REFERENCES.

Amendment of claim.—See head-line 4, subd. (8), post.

(9) **What claims must be presented.**—A claim in favor of the United States, against the estate of a decedent, can not be sued upon until

after its presentation for allowance to the executor or administrator of such estate.—United States v. Hailey, 2 Idaho 26, 3 Pac. 263, 264. Claims not due must be presented, or they are barred.—Pico v. De la Guerra, 18 Cal. 422. No suit can be maintained against the executor or administrator of the estate of a deceased person on a claim for moneys received by the decedent in his lifetime, while acting as guardian of the plaintiff, until after such claim has been presented to the executor or administrator.—Gillespie v. Winn, 65 Cal. 429, 4 Pac. 411, 412. A claim based on the liability of a decedent as a stockholder is a claim upon which no action can be maintained, though the amount, if any, that will have to be paid is not known, unless it has been presented within the time prescribed by the statute.—Barto v. Stewart, 21 Wash. 605, 59 Pac. 480, 482. The word "claim" includes every species of liability that the executor or administrator can be called on to pay, or to provide for the payment of, out of the general fund belonging to the estate.—Barto v. Stewart, 21 Wash. 605, 59 Pac. 480, 482. The word "due" is not used in the sense of "mature," in the statute prescribing the form of an affidavit to a claim, but was intended to apply to all claims, whether due or to become due, or contingent. The object of this provision is to secure good faith in their presentation, and is satisfied by an affidavit stating that the facts out of which the liability is claimed to arise are true.—Barto v. Stewart, 21 Wash. 605, 59 Pac. 480, 482. One who holds a laborer's lien on logs can not bring an action to foreclose the same against the executor or administrator of a deceased person, against whom the lien was acquired, without first presenting his claim to the executor or administrator.—Casey v. Ault, 4 Wash. 167, 29 Pac. 1048. If a purchaser pays taxes on the property bought before the testator's death, by reason of a breach of a covenant in the deed, his claim against the estate is one that requires presentation.—Clayton v. Dinwoodey, 33 Utah 251, 14 Ann. Cas. 926, 93 Pac. 723, 726. A claim arising on contract must be presented to the administrator for allowance or rejection before suit can be maintained thereon, but not so where the claim arises in tort, or other wrongful act of the deceased.—American Trust Co. v. Chitty, 36 Okla. 479, 129 Pac. 52. Where a claimant against an estate has a lien but which lien is not of record, he should present his claim to an administrator before attempting to foreclose.—Brown v. Truax, 58 Or. 572, 115 Pac. 598. If the court allows a sum to an insane person's guardian, as an attorney's fee and payment is not made before the ward's death and the appointment of an administrator, the guardian must present his claim to the latter as being a debt of the estate.—Eisenhower v. Vaughn, 95 Wash. 256, 163 Pac. 758. On the death of a shareholder of a corporation while in debt to the company in respect to calls for unpaid subscriptions of stock, the corporation must, under the statutes, present a claim against the estate within the time allowed to creditors; otherwise, the claim is barred.—Geary St. P. & O. R. Co. v. Bradbury Estate Co., 179 Cal. 46, 175 Pac. 457. A mechanic's lien claim, based on a contract with a person since deceased, requires, like any other claim against the estate, to be presented to the executor or administrator before it can be enforced.—Gray v. Hickey, 94 Wash. 370, 376, 162 Pac. 564. Where costs are awarded a defendant, on his being dismissed from a cause instituted by an administrator, in proceedings to collect such costs, he must file with the administrator his claim therefor like any other claim against the estate.—In re Richardson's Estate, Larson v. Anderson Steamboat Co., 97 Wash. 488, 166 Pac. 776.

(10) "Contingent claims."—If a code of laws designates three classes of claims against an estate, that must be presented:—1. Claims due; 2. Claims not due; 3. Contingent claims,—this implies that the mere fact that a claim is not due does not make it contingent. If the amount of the claim and the date at which it is to become due are certain, it is not contingent, though not due. Therefore a contingent claim is not distinguished from other claims by the qualifying words "not due," but by the words "not absolute." A claim ceases to be contingent when it becomes absolute, though not yet due, as in the case of a contract to pay money after the future occurrence of a contingent event, in which the obligation becomes absolute before due; yet contingent claims may become absolute and due at the same time; and the probate law requires that all contingent claims that are provable and payable at any time shall be presented for allowance within the prescribed statutory time after the publication of notice to creditors, as a condition precedent to the commencement of actions thereon; otherwise, how can any provision whatever be made for them before the estate is settled? Timely notice of all claims that may prejudicially affect an estate should be given to the administrator, so that he may have an opportunity to investigate their merits, and to contest them if advisable, before the evidence of their invalidity shall be lost. That they should be forever barred if not presented to him within the time prescribed by law is surely no greater hardship than that absolute claims should be so barred.—Verdier v. Roach, 96 Cal. 467, 474, 478, 31 Pac. 554; Janin v. Browne, 59 Cal. 37. In Pico v. De la Guerra, 18 Cal. 422, a claim against the estate was predicated upon a guaranty to indemnify a surety upon a promissory note. Before the note became due and payable, the guarantor died, and the surety, before he had paid the note, presented a claim upon the guaranty, which the executor allowed and approved; but the allowance and approval were held unauthorized and void, because, as the claim against the estate was merely contingent upon payment, by the surety, of the promissory note of his principal, no cause of action accrued until the contingency happened, and no recovery could be had against the estate, either by presentation of an immature claim, or by a suit at law against the estate. A judgment obtained against sureties can not be enforced by them after the death of their principal, as a claim against his estate, until they have paid such debt.—Estate of Hill, 67 Cal. 238,

244, 7 Pac. 664. A covenant to indemnify a lessee must be presented as a contingent claim to the administrator of a deceased lessor within the time limited by the notice to creditors, or no action can be based thereon for a breach occurring after the time for presentation of claims has expired.—Verdier v. Roach, 96 Cal. 467, 31 Pac. 554. A mere personal promise of reimbursement, which creates a contingent liability, must be presented to the administrator for allowance as a claim against the estate. If not so presented within the time fixed by statute, it is barred forever; and the executor or administrator has no power, without the authority of the court, to bind the estate by agreeing to delay the collection of the debt due the estate for a period of years, in order to determine whether a contingent right of set-off shall become absolute, when such contingent right has not been presented or allowed as a claim against the estate.—Maddock v. Russell, 109 Cal. 417, 421, 424, 42 Pac. 139. The statute which allows one who has been absent from the state, and has had no notice of the time in which to present his claim against the estate of a decedent, to present it at any time before a decree of distribution is entered upon making an affidavit to the satisfaction of the court or judge thereof that he had no notice, applies alike to all claims, whether absolute or contingent.— Verdier v. Roach, 96 Cal. 467, 469, 470, 31 Pac. 554.

REFERENCES.

Contingency of claim as affecting limitation of time for its presentation.—See note 58 L. R. A. 82-90.

The amount due on a building contract made by a decedent, whether accrued or contingent, is a proper subject of claim against his estate, but the demand, if not presented as a claim within the time limited, is barred,' and no action thereon can be maintained, in the absence of such presentation. Neither he nor a devisee of the building who has assumed to pay for its completion can compel the executor to pay such demand.—Estate of Hincheon, 159 Cal. 755, 36 L. R. A. (N. S.) 303, 116 Pac. 47. A claim payable on the death of another person is not a contingent claim that may never accrue; but is an absolute unconditional claim which accrued when created, the time of payment alone being uncertain, payment being merely postponed until the happening of an event which must surely transpire.—McDaniel v. Putnam, 100 Kan. 550, 554, L. R. A. 1917E, 1100, 164 Pac. 1167, 1169. A claim for damages for breach of a warranty contained in a deed of conveyance by a person afterwards deceased is a claim based upon the covenant of warranty contained in said deed and was contingent upon the breach of said covenant, an event which might never occur, and the only way in which the covenantee could perpetuate its right to recover such damages from the estate of the covenantor in case of breach was by having the claim allowed and established as a contingent claim against the estate, and unless so presented no action could be maintained thereon.—Tropico Land, etc., Co. v. Lambourn, 170 Cal. 33, 41, 148 Pac. 206.

(11) **Claim of executor or administrator.**—All persons having claims against the deceased must present them for allowance; the executor or administrator, to the probate judge alone; other creditors, to the executor or administrator, and if allowed, to the probate judge. If not thus presented within the time prescribed by the statute after the publication of notice for the presentation of claims, they are barred by the express provision of the statute; and the requirement to make the presentation, and the period within which it is to be made, are the same, whether the claims be held by the executor or administrator, or by other creditors of the deceased.—Estate of Taylor, 16 Cal. 434. A claim due to an executor or administrator must be presented to the judge for allowance within the time allowed by law for the presentation of claims, or it can not be allowed to him in his accounts. —In re Hildebrandt, 92 Cal. 433, 28 Pac. 486. The mere fact that the executor or administrator, as such, has in his hands more money belonging to the estate than the amount of his claim does not entitle him to treat it as an offset to his claim, nor prevent him from making the statutory affidavit, "that there are no offsets to the same, to the knowledge of affiant." Money received by him, and that belongs to the estate, is held by him in his official capacity as such administrator, while the debt due him as a creditor of decedent is due to him in his individual capacity.—In re Hildebrandt, 92 Cal. 433, 436, 28 Pac. 486. But an unauthorized appropriation by an executor or administrator of the funds of the estate can not be made the basis of a claim by him against the estate.—Estate of Hill, 67 Cal. 238, 241, 7 Pac. 664. Under the provisions of section 1510, Code of Civil Procedure of California, construed with sections 1490 and 1493 of the same code, the claim of an administrator upon a promissory note, as a creditor of the estate, must be presented to the judge for allowance within the time provided for the presentation of the claims of other creditors against the estate, and, if presented after the expiration of that time, it is barred forever under the terms of the code; and the claim was properly rejected by the judge.—Estate of Long, 9 Cal. App. 754, 100 Pac. 892.

(12) **What claims need not be presented.**—It is not necessary to present to the executor or administrator, for allowance, a judgment against the deceased.—Knott v. Shaw, 5 Or. 482; Estate of Brennan, 65 Cal. 517, 4 Pac. 561; Estate of Page, 50 Cal. 40. A pledgee is not obliged to present his claim to the executor or administrator for allowance, unless he seeks recourse against other property of the estate than that pledged.—Estate of Kibbe, 57 Cal. 407, 408. A distinction is to be made between the debts of deceased, and the expenses incurred or disbursements made by the executor or administrator in his management of the estate.—Deck's Estate v. Gherke, 6 Cal. 666, 669. Claims against an estate, incurred by an executor or administrator in settling the estate, are expenses of administration, which are subject to the objection and exception of those interested in the estate, and are finally passed upon by the probate judge when the administra-

tor or executor renders his accounts.—Dodson v. Nevitt, 5 Mont. 518, 6 Pac. 358, 359. A claim for expenses of administration need not be presented to the executor or administrator for his approval.—Potter v. Lewin, 123 Cal. 146, 147, 55 Pac. 783; or for services rendered and money advanced, at the request of an administrator, for the benefit of the estate.—Gurnee v. Maloney, 38 Cal. 85, 88, 99 Am. Dec. 352. The only claims required to be filed and rejected before suit brought are those arising on contracts. Hence, an action to abate nuisances and for damages caused by obstructing a private way may be maintained against the personal representatives of the deceased without first filing a claim against the estate.—Hardin v. Sin Claire, 115 Cal. 460, 47 Pac. 363, 364. A cause of action in which equitable relief alone is sought is not a "claim" which it is necessary to present against the estate before the action can be maintained.—Toulouse v. Burkett, 2 Idaho 184, 10 Pac. 26, 28. Nor is it necessary, before suit to present against the estate a claim upon a demand for discovery and accounting, as such demand necessarily involves an uncertain amount. Where the demand is merely for equitable relief, or for uncertain and liquidated damages, it is not necessary to present it to the administrator for allowance or rejection; for it is obvious that in all such cases the exhibition would be but an idle ceremony.—Neis v. Farquharson, 9 Wash. 508, 37 Pac. 697, 700. It is not necessary to present a claim against an estate for the amount of an unpaid subscription by the decedent for the stock of a savings bank before bringing a suit in equity against the administrator to recover the amount of such unpaid subscription.—Thompson v. Reno Sav. Bank, 19 Nev. 242, 3 Am. St. Rep. 883, 9 Pac. 121. There is no provision of the California code requiring the presentation of a claim to a guardian as there is in the case of an administrator.—Estate of Breslin, 135 Cal. 21, 66 Pac. 962. A debt secured by a mechanic's lien made of record is not a claim that must be presented to an administrator for allowance or rejection.—Fish v. De Laray, 8 S. D. 320, 59 Am. St. Rep. 764, 66 N. W. 465. Taxes and street assessments paid under authority given in a mortgage are properly allowed upon the foreclosure of the mortgage against the estate of a decedent, if such payments were made after the presentation of the claim upon the note and mortgage. No separate presentation as to taxes and street assessments is required.—German S. & L. Soc. v. Hutchinson, 68 Cal. 52, 54, 8 Pac. 627. A claim for an assessment for the improvement of a street, made after the death of the property owner, need not be presented.—Hancock v. Whittemore, 50 Cal. 522, 523. Taxes assessed against or which are due upon property of the estate of a decedent are not claims against the estate which need to be presented to the executor or administrator for allowance.—Clayton v. Dinwoodey, 33 Utah 251, 14 Ann. Cas. 926, 93 Pac. 723, 725; People v. Olvera, 43 Cal. 492, 494. It is not necessary that a claim by an executor or administrator for his own compensation and the necessary expenses of administration should be presented against the estate, as they are preferential claims and may be retained in the administrator's hands.—In re Murray's Estate, 56 Or. 132, 107 Pac. 21. Where, before decedent's death, execution was levied on debts due him, judgment creditor had lien within section 1500 of the Code of Civil Procedure of California, excepting demands secured by lien from necessity of presentation.—Nordstrom v. Corona City Water Co., 155 Cal. 206, 132 Am. St. Rep. 81, 100 Pac. 242. Presentation of claims, arising against an estate after decedent's death, for allowance, is unnecessary. Rule applied to liability of estate as stockholder for corporate debts.— Miller v. Katz, 10 Cal. App. 576, 102 Pac. 946. The claim under an agreement to bequeath not less than one-third of an entire estate is not such a demand as must be presented against the estate within the period limited by the statute of non-claim.—Oles v. Wilson, 57 Colo. 246, 141 Pac. 489, 492. If personal property, being administered in the county court as the estate of a decedent, is claimed by the plaintiff in an action to recover it, on the ground that he owns it, the fact that he has not filed a claim therefor in the probate court, will not preclude him from recovering, if the evidence supports his contention.—Truman v. Dakota Trust Co., 29 N. D. 456, 463, 151 N. W. 219. An action pending against the grantee of mortgaged property, who holds under a deed assuming the mortgage, the purpose of the action being to recover interest on the mortgage note, does not abate by the death of the defendant; and it is not necessary that any claim be presented to the grantee's guardian or to his executors.—The Home v. Selling, 91 Or. 428, 179 Pac. 261. Where a judgment debtor, at the time of judgment, was the record owner of particularly described property, but died after having made a conveyance thereof, the property so conveyed after the lien of the judgment attached to it was not a part of his estate; hence, if his estate is not sufficient to satisfy the judgment, and action may be brought against the grantee for the enforcement of such lien, without having first presented to the administrator a claim against the estate.—Stephenson v. Lichtenstein, 24 Wyo. 417, 422, 160 Pac. 1170. A claim purely equitable does not need to be presented to the executor or administrator, and a debt secured by mortgage is such a claim.—Smith v. Kibbe, 104 Kan. 159, 178 Pac. 427.

(13) Same. For funeral expenses.—A debt for funeral expenses need not be filed against the estate as a claim, but needs only to be presented to the administrator in due course; the administrator can not ignore or disallow it; a claim for funeral expenses need not, in California, even be presented to the executor or administrator for his approval; such expenses are expenses of administration.—Potter v. Lewin, 123 Cal. 146, 147, 55 Pac. 783; Elton v. Lamb, 33 N. D. 386, 397, 157 N. W. 288. A claim for funeral expenses, although necessarily not a debt contracted by the deceased, must be presented in the state of Washington, to the executor or administrator within one year after the date of the notice to creditors; otherwise, it is barred.—Butterworth

v. Bredemeyer, 74 Wash. 524, 528, 155 Pac. 152. A person having a claim against an estate for funeral expenses may look to the executor or administrator personally for payment, provided he has an agreement made to that effect in writing signed by such executor or administrator.—Butterworth v. Bredemeyer, 74 Wash. 524, 155 Pac. 152. Under the statute of Washington, the liability of a deceased person's estate, for his funeral expenses, is primary, and the creditor must first resort to and exhaust his remedy against the estate, before he can resort to the wife's secondary liability therefor.—Butterworth v. Bredemeyer, 74 Wash. 524, 528, 133 Pac. 1061. As determined in Barto v. Stewart, 21 Wash. 605, 59 Pac. 480, the decision in other states, excepting claims for funeral expenses from those necessary to be presented to the executor or administrator within one year after date of the notice to creditors, do not apply in the state of Washington.—Butterworth v. Bredemeyer, 74 Wash. 524, 155 Pac. 152.

REFERENCES.

Liability of decedent's estate for funeral expenses.—9 Am. Dec. 652, 52 L. R. A. (N. S.) 1153. What items and amounts are allowable as funeral expenses against the estate of a decedent.—28 L. R. A. (N. S) 572.

(14) Same. For fund misappropriated by guardian.—It is not necessary that a claim for a fund wrongfully appropriated by a guardian be presented to the administrator of such guardian before an action for the recovery thereof can be maintained.—Donnell v. Dansby, 58 Okla. 165, 159 Pac. 317. It is not necessary that a claim for a fund misappropriated by a guardian be presented to the administrator of the surety of such guardian before an action for recovery thereon can be maintained.—Asher v. Stull (Okla), 161 Pac. 808.

(15) Same. Vendor's lien.—A vendor of real estate has a lien on the same, in the hands of the executor or administrator of the purchaser, for the unpaid purchase-money.—Cahoon v. Robinson, 6 Cal. 225, 226; and it is not necessary to present a claim for the purchase-money to the executor or administrator, if nothing is asked against the estate.—Kerns v. Dean, 77 Cal. 555, 560, 19 Pac. 817. The lien of the vendor is of so high a nature that it is not extinguished by his death, but passes to his representatives. Nor is it discharged by the death of the grantee, but may be enforced against his estate, or those into whose hands the property may come. If the vendor presents a claim against the estate of the deceased grantee for the amount of the unpaid purchase-money, it is not necessary for him to state that he claims a lien against the grantee's premises for the amount of such claim. It would probably be the better practice to make such statement, but its omission does not constitute a waiver of the lien, nor make it inequitable to enforce it. So long as the debt exists, the courts will not presume that the lien has been waived, except upon clear and convincing testimony. The filing of the claim does not give

the vendor any security upon specific property, nor any lien upon any property. It simply maintains the same general rights which the vendor had before.—Selna v. Selna, 125 Cal. 357, 361, 363, 73 Am. St. Rep. 47, 58 Pac. 16.

(16) **Same. Specific property.**—The claimant of specific property is not a creditor of the estate, and is not bound to present his claim against it.—Gunter v. Janes, 9 Cal. 643, 658. So an adverse claim, based upon a trust, is one which need not be presented against the estate for allowance. Where one seeks to recover from the representatives of an estate specific property, alleged to have been held in trust by the decedent at the time of his death, he is not seeking payment of a claim from the assets of the estate, is not required to present a claim as a creditor, and is not "a creditor of the estate." His action is not founded upon a claim or demand against the estate. There is a clear distinction between a demand for certain specific property on the ground that it is the property of the claimant held in trust by the decedent, and a claim of personal indebtedness on the part of the decedent based upon the fact that he has so mingled the trust property with his own as to make it impossible for the beneficiaries to follow and identify it. The latter may be a proper claim against the decedent upon the ground that there has been a breach of the trust and that a personal liability has therefore arisen, while the former can not possibly be such a claim.—Estate of Dutard, 147 Cal. 253, 256, 257, 81 Pac. 519. A claim upon the estate for certain specific property does not show any personal liability.—Estate of Dutard, 147 Cal. 253, 258, 81 Pac. 519. If an administrator has wrongfully taken possession of certain horses, and the owner presents his claim for them, which is rejected, he is entitled to replevin the animals, though his suit is not brought within the time limited by statute on rejected claims. The plaintiff, in such a case, is not a "creditor" of the estate, and his claim is not within such statute.—Emele v. Williams, 10 Haw. 123, 124. If recovery is sought of specific property alleged to have been held in trust by the decedent at the time of his death, a party seeking such recovery is not asking payment of the claim from the assets of the estate, and is therefore not required to present his claim as a creditor of the estate.—Brown v. Town of Sebastopol, 153 Cal. 704, 19 L. R. A. (N. S.) 178, 96 Pac. 363. The right to sue an executor or administrator for moneys alleged to be due an estate, and to which the executor or administrator asserts title in himself individually, is not conditioned upon the presentation of a claim therefor. The right to sue, in such cases, without presentation arises from the fact that the specific thing sued for is not a part of the decedent's estate, and the action will lie whenever the thing demanded can be identified in specie as the property of another.—Sprague v. Walton, 145 Cal. 228, 235, 78 Pac. 645.

(17) **Effect of presentment.**—The presentation of a claim against the estate of a decedent is not a demand of payment.—Chase v. Evoy, 49

Cal. 467, 469. But it is practically the commencement of a suit upon the claim, and is sufficient to stop the running of the statute of limitations.—Beckett v. Selover, 7. Cal. 215, 241, 68 Am. Dec. 237; Wise v. Williams, 88 Cal. 30, 25 Pac. 1064. A party, by presenting his claim against the estate of a decedent, does not part with his right to enforce it against the person primarily liable.—Thompson v. Bank of California, 4 Cal. App. 660, 88 Pac. 987, 990. The lien of a vendor is not waived by the presentation of his claim against the estate of a deceased vendee. Its only effect is to maintain the same general rights which the vendor had before the death of his grantee, to look not only to the land of the grantee, but also to the property owned by him; and even if he claims a lien against the granted premises, the omission of a statement, in the claim, that he claims a lien against the granted premises for the amount of such claim does not constitute a waiver of the lien, nor make it inequitable to enforce it.—Selna v. Selna, 125 Cal. 357, 362, 73 Am. St. Rep. 47, 58 Pac. 16. Nor, in the case of a conditional sale, does the presentation of the plaintiff's claim for the unpaid purchase-money to the administrator of the purchaser's estate, and its approval by him and by the court, constitute such an election as debars the plaintiff from bringing a subsequent action to recover the possession of the property upon the assumption that the title has never passed to the purchaser.—Holt Mfg. Co. v. Ewing, 109 Cal. 353, 356, 42 Pac. 435. If a party makes an attempt to present a claim to an executor or administrator for allowance, but from some cause fails to do so properly, he is not estopped from again presenting it in due form, if within proper time.—Westbay v. Gray, 116 Cal. 660, 668, 48 Pac. 800. So a devisee is not estopped from claiming under the will by reason of the fact that he presented a claim against the estate, where such claim was presented in ignorance of the value of the property devised, was allowed only in part, was then withdrawn, and a written election made to take under the will.—Estate of Thayer, 142 Cal. 453, 455, 76 Pac. 41. Presentation of a claim to an administrator does not of itself operate as a waiver of a lien upon the estate of the decedent.—Castle Estate v. Huneberg, 20 Haw. 123. Ward's presentation of claims against guardian's executors for funds converted by guardian held not to affect their right to recover against executors, though changing their remedy.—Miller v. Ash, 156 Cal. 544, 105 Pac. 600. A person who files and procures the allowance of claims against the estate of a deceased person, but who at the same time has knowledge that he has another and independent cause of action against the estate and administrator, is not precluded, in Kansas, by such knowledge from recovering on such cause of action.—Ryan v. Myers, 101 Kan. 261, 167 Pac. 1043. The presentation of a claim against an estate in no way changes the nature of the demand nor the form in which the action must be brought; when brought, it must be upon the original claim.—Idaho Trust Co. v. Miller, 16 Ida. 308, 312, 102 Pac. 360.

(18) **Effect of non-presentment.**—The effect of not presenting a claim within the statutory time from the first publication of notice to creditors

is, that it shall be barred forever, provided that if the claim is not then due, or if it is contingent, it may be presented within a specified time after it shall become due or absolute.—Davidson v. Rankin, 34 Cal. 503, 504. A claim not presented is no charge against the estate, though it is verified and filed with the county clerk.—Pico v. De la Guerra, 18 Cal. 422, 428. A mortgage claim upon a homestead can not be foreclosed, unless the claim is presented for allowance against the estate of a decedent within the time limited for the presentation of claims.—Mechanics' B. & L. Assoc. v. King, 83 Cal. 440, 443, 23 Pac. 376. The limitation, however, on the right to enforce a claim or debt, which is not presented to the executor or administrator within the prescribed statutory time after the publication of notice to creditors, is not a general statute of limitations, taking away all remedy as to every person liable, either personally or through his property, for the debt. It arises under a specific act adopted for a particular purpose, and has reference solely to the estates of deceased persons. It applies to no other subject-matter, and in no way affects the validity of the debt as against other persons who are liable for the debt, or whose property is liable.—Sichel v. Carrillo, 42 Cal. 493, 499. Such a limitation does not apply to proceedings under a non-intervention will.—In re Smith's Will, 43 Or. 595, 75 Pac. 133, 137. Hence, if executors are empowered by will to administer an estate without the intervention of the court, the failure of creditors to present their claims within a certain period after publication of a notice to do so does not bar their claims, as probate precedure relative to the administration of estates does not apply in such case.—In re Smith's Will, 43 Or. 595, 75 Pac. 133, 137; Moore v. Kirtman, 19 Wash. 605, 54 Pac. 24, 26; In re McDonald's Estate, 29 Wash. 422, 69 Pac. 1111, 1115. Nor is the claim of the government of the United States against the estate of a deceased surety, on the bond of a collector of internal revenue, barred by its failure to present a claim against such estate within the statutory time, as such government is exempt from all statutes of limitation, and therefore has a right to pursue the property of a deceased debtor into the hands of the distributee of any estate.—Pond v. Dougherty, 6 Cal. App. 686, 92 Pac. 1035, 1037. A promise by executors who were also sole devisees and legatees to pay a note on which their testator was an indorser did not estop them to rely on non-presentation of the claim as a defense, since they could not by their promise estop creditors whose rights might be adversely affected, especially where the claimant did not rely upon the promise, but attempted to present his claim in a legal way.—Seattle Nat. Bank v. Dickinson, 72 Wash. 403, 130 Pac. 372, 374. The failure to present the claim to the executor or administrator in due manner and time defeats the right to a mechanic's lien on the property.—Crowe & Co. v. Adkinson Const. Co., 67 Wash. 420, Ann. Cas. 1913D, 273, 121 Pac. 841, 842. The failure to present a claim in time does not go to the jurisdiction of the court to direct its payment upon final settlement of the account. It is only matter of error to be corrected on appeal, and it can not be otherwise objected to, in the absence of fraud or collusion, which has not been here alleged or claimed. If not legitimately assailed, the order settling the final account and directing payment of the claim is conclusive upon all persons interested in the estate, whether heirs, legatees, or creditors.—L. Harter Co. v. Geisel, 18 Cal. App. 282, 122 Pac. 1094. No action can be maintained upon a claim against a decedent's estate, unless it has been first presented to the executor or administrator for allowance; neither can it be maintained unless the identical claim sued upon is the one that was presented; a party can not present a claim founded upon an open account and then maintain an action upon a promissory note, or vice versa; and, if he attempts to do so, the result is such a variance as amounts to a failure of proof.—Vanderpool v. Vanderpool, 48 Mont. 448, 453, 138 Pac. 772. If the identical claim sued upon was not presented to the executor or administrator, it is forever barred.—Vanderpool v. Vanderpool, 48 Mont. 448, 455, 138 Pac. 772. Any claim against the estate of a deceased person, arising upon contract, is barred if not presented within the time lawfully limited in the notice to creditors, and no action can be maintained thereon.—Blake v. Lemp, 32 Ida. 158, 179 Pac. 737; Lundy v. Lemp, 32 Ida. 162, 179 Pac. 738; Couglin v. Lemp, 32 Ida. 164, 180 Pac. 990. The failure to present a claim secured by a mortgage or other lien on specific property affects only the deficiency arising after applying the mortgaged property to the payment of the claim or debt secured thereby; in no manner does it affect the right of the lien owner to make foreclosure.—Massey v. Fralisch, 37 S. D. 91, 94, 156 N. W. 791.

REFERENCES.

Effect of failure to present claim in due time under law of the domicile as a bar to its allowance in the state of the ancillary administration, or vice versa.—See note 19 L. R. A. (N. S.) 553, 554.

(19) Effect of death.—In an action on a promissory note, the suggestion of the death of the maker of the note, and the substitution of his administrator, and continuance of the suit against the latter, subject the proceedings to such rules of the probate law as are applicable to proceedings for the collection of claims against the estate of a deceased person.—Myers v. Mott, 29 Cal. 359, 363, 89 Am. Dec. 49. The doctrine that when the statute of limitations begins to run, a subsequent disability, as death of the party bound, etc., does not stop it, has no application where a judgment has been obtained against an intestate in his lifetime, but no execution levied. In such a case the judgment creditor being prevented from suing after the death of the debtor, the statute ceases to run until presentation of the claim to the administrator, and the party is not bound to present it until after publication of the notice required by statute.—Quivey v. Hall, 19 Cal. 97, 100. A judgment, whether rendered before or after death of the judgment debtor, must be presented as a claim against his estate. The lien of the judgment rendered against him during his lifetime is not released or affected by

his death, pending the time limited by the statute for the continuance of such lien; and the presentation and allowance of the judgment as a claim does not destroy nor merge the judgment lien; nor do any of the grounds upon which one judgment has been allowed to be merged in another apply to the case of the allowance of a judgment as a claim against an estate, because the allowance of the claim is not, in any true sense, a judgment.—Morton v. Adams, 124 Cal. 229, 230, 232, 233, 71 Am. St. Rep. 53, 56 Pac. 1038. The death of an insolvent before the return-day upon a petition has the effect of abating insolvency proceedings and all the orders therein; but where an execution was levied prior to his death, and the sheriff took the property into his custody under the execution, the property ceased to be subject to any control of the court in the proceedings in insolvency, and a court has no jurisdiction to make an order restraining the sheriff from selling the same.—Vermont M. Co. v. Superior Court, 99 Cal. 579, 582, 34 Pac. 326.

(20) **Presentation after death.**—Litigants must know, at their peril, of the death of an adversary. Negligence can not be attributed to the dead, and though the heirs may sometimes lose by failure to have administration properly made, yet those having claims against the estate acquire no rights by the delay, except the extension of the time to collect their demands. Hence, one who seeks to recover a judgment against the defendant is not entitled to recover a judgment that will bind his estate, unless, within the period allowed by law for the presentation of claims, he makes a presentation of his claim to the representative of the decedent.—Falkner v. Hendy, 107 Cal. 49, 54, 40 Pac. 21, 386. A claim arising upon a contract presented by the administrator of a deceased claimant, after the time for presentation of claims has elapsed, is properly rejected, and an action thereon is barred. In case of the death of the person entitled to bring an action before the expiration of the time limited for the commencement thereof, an action may be commenced by his representatives after that time, and within the specified time from his death; but the first essential of the right to maintain or to prosecute it is the right to bring or to commence it, and the holder of the claim can not maintain any action thereon, unless it shall have first been presented for allowance within the time prescribed by the statute.—Morrow v. Barker, 119 Cal. 65, 66, 51 Pac. 12. In the event of the death of an executor or administrator, the claim which the creditor of the estate had against him, by reason of his acts or omissions as executor or administrator, was one which became fixed in the lifetime of the executor, and was not contingent upon the fact that the estate might prove insolvent on an account taken after the death of the executor or administrator.—Estate of Halleck, 49 Cal. 111, 116. If a person having a claim against an estate dies before the time limited for its presentation, his representative can not maintain an action against the estate of another deceased person on the claim, where it has not been presented to the executor within the time prescribed by the statute for the presentation of claims.—Morrow v. Barker, 119 Cal.

65, 51 Pac. 12. So a broken promise to provide, by will, a compensation for services rendered to the decedent must be presented as a claim against the estate, if reliance was placed thereon as a continuing contract for services up to the time of his death. If not so presented, it can not be relied upon to save the bar of the statute as to part of the rejected claim for services presented against the estate.—Etchas v. Oreña, 127 Cal. 588, 592, 60 Pac. 45.

4. Allowance and rejection of claims.

(1) In general.—If there are two or more executors or administrators, the allowance of a claim by one of them is the act of all, and is binding upon all.—Willis v. Farley, 24 Cal. 490, 501. A claim may be allowed though the executor or administrator has not filed any undertaking.—Estate of Houck, 23 Or. 10, 17 Pac. 461; but an executor or administrator, who is personally interested in a claim against the estate, is disqualified from acting upon it.—Estate of Hill, 67 Cal. 238, 244, 7 Pac. 664; Estate of Crosby, 55 Cal. 574, 578. The allowing or rejecting of a claim is an official act, which the attorneys of the executors or administrators have not the power to perform; but delivery of a rejected claim to the owner thereof, upon demand, is a mere ministerial act, which attorneys of the executors or administrators have a right to perform, when such claim is in their possession, and their action therein will bind the executors or administrators.—Cowgill v. Dinwiddie, 98 Cal. 481, 484, 33 Pac. 439. The purpose and effect of a statute providing that where a claim is presented to an executor or administrator, and he disallows it, the claimant may present the same to the county court for allowance, on giving notice, and that the court is empowered to hear and determine the same in a summary manner, and to direct a concise entry of the order of allowance and rejection to be made on the record, which order shall have the force and effect of a judgment, from which an appeal may be taken, are to afford a summary method for the adjudication of claims by the court against the estates of deceased persons, without the necessity of technical pleadings. The proceeding is in the nature of an action, as contradistinguished from a suit, affording to the parties the right of trial de novo and trial by jury in the appellate court.—Pruitt v. Muldrick, 39 Or. 353, 65 Pac. 20, 21. A claim against the estate of a decedent can be established only by first being presented to and allowed by the executor or administrator, and then being presented to and approved by the county judge; or, secondly, by a judgment thereon in an action against the personal representative in the proper court.—Osborn v. Foresythe, 54 Okla. 40, 153 Pac. 207. An executor or administrator has no authority to settle and pay a claim of more than $50 against the estate of the deceased without an allowance by the probate court, nor is he authorized to bind the estate by an offer to confess judgment for such clause, or an admission of liability therein, and if he does make such an offer or admission it is not competent evidence against the estate in an action on the claim.—Wright v. Stage, 86 Kan. 475, 121 Pac. 491.

(2) Passing on claims. In general.—The executor or administrator is not required, on the presentation of a claim, immediately to indorse it "allowed" or "rejected"; nor must it be so indorsed within "ten days" after it is presented. The executor or administrator is not limited to any specific period in which he must take formal action to indorse his allowance or rejection of a claim. It may be conceded that it is not the duty of the executor or administrator to seek out one who has presented a claim, to notify such person that he—the executor or administrator—has neglected or refused to act on the claim for ten days after its presentation, or that he has indorsed it "rejected." And it may also be conceded that it is the duty of the claimant to inquire of the executor or administrator whether the claim he has presented has been acted upon, and how. But as there is no specific limitation of time within which the executor or administrator must allow or reject the claim, there is none in which the claimant is entitled to be informed of the action or non-action of the executor. If he neglects to inquire within three months after his claim has been actually indorsed "rejected," his suit on the claim will perhaps be barred. Nevertheless, if he can not maintain a suit on his claim until it has been rejected, he has an absolute right to be informed of its rejection by the executor or administrator, who alone knows what formal action has been taken with respect to it. If information with respect to it is refused by the executor or administrator, the claimant may treat the previous presentation of his claim and secret action, if any, of the executor or administrator, as going for naught, and again present the claim.—Steward v. Hinkel, 72 Cal. 187, 189, 13 Pac. 494. But if the statute makes it the duty of the executor or administrator, within a certain specified time, to indorse on a claim his approval or rejection thereof, his failure to indorse it within the time prescribed operates, in Nevada, as an allowance of the claim.—Kirman v. Powning, 25 Nev. 378, 60 Pac. 834, 838. The claimant is entitled to the possession of the claim presented by him, if the executor or administrator has had a reasonable time in which to examine it, and may maintain an action to recover it.—Willis v. Marks, 29 Or. 493, 45 Pac. 293, 296. If a claim, as presented, is allowed in full, the words "approved and allowed," indorsed thereon, without any limitation or reservation whatever, must be taken to refer to the claim on which they were indorsed, and if that purports, upon its face, to be a secured claim, it must be deemed to have been allowed as a secured claim.—Estate of McDougald, 146 Cal. 191, 193, 79 Pac. 878. A money demand upon unpaid accounts against the estate of an intestate must be allowed, if at all, upon legal evidence sustaining the same; and such evidence must be taken and the claim passed upon at a regular session of the probate court. At least, the executor or administrator of the estate against whom the claim is made must either be present in court while the evidence is being taken of the claim passed upon, or he must have an opportunity to be present and to be heard.—Chaves v. Perea, 3. N. M. 71, 2 Pac. 73, 74. The Alaskan code provides that upon the refusal of the administrator to allow a claim, it may be presented to the district court or a judge thereof, who shall have jurisdiction to hear and determine it summarily.—Esterly v. Rua (Alaska), 122 Fed. 609, 611, 58 C. C. A. 548. An administrator's act in passing upon a claim is not res judicata; in allowing or rejecting any claim he acts merely as an auditor; his allowance or rejection simply means that he is or is not satisfied as to the justice of the claim, but it is in no sense a judicial determination, as he is not vested with judicial functions respecting it. —Dow v. Lillie, 26 N. D. 512, L. R. A. 1915D, 754, 144 N. W. 1082, 1085.

(3) Same. Rejection of claims.—The rejection of a claim against the estate of a decedent, either by the executor, administrator, or county judge, is a condition precedent to the right to sue upon it.—In re Smith's Estate, 13 N. D. 513, 101 N. W. 890. A claim against an estate may be rejected by an administrator, either by indorsing his written disallowance on such claims, or by neglecting or refusing to act thereon for a period prescribed by the statute after it is presented, and in either case the rejection is a rejection by the administrator.—Boyd v. Von Neida, 9 N. D. 337, 83 N. W. 329. It is statutory that an executor or administrator may indicate his rejection of a claim presented against the estate either by indorsing "disallowed" on the claim or by leaving it unacted upon for ten days after presentation.—Williams v. Jackson (Okla.), 179 Pac. 603. If an executor or administrator indorses on a claim: "This claim is disallowed," it is sufficient without words specifying the reasons for the disallowance.—First Nat. Bank v. Cone, 57 Colo. 529, 143 Pac. 569. It is only in states where an affidavit of outstanding indebtedness is required to accompany the claim that the executor or administrator must, in rejecting the claim, disclose his grounds for doing so; South Dakota is not one of these states.—Automatic Scale Co. v. Torgeson, 36 S. D. 564, 156 N. W. 86. If the claim is presented at the office of the administrator's attorney, and it is indorsed "rejected" by such attorney, under the direction of the administrator, and such rejection is subscribed by the administrator named, it is a valid rejection of the claim.—Dorais v. Doll, 33 Mont. 314, 83 Pac 884, 885. A note signed by an alleged surety may, after the maker's death, be rejected by the administrator, as a debt of the estate, unless it bears intrinsic evidence of its character and also of the fact that the principal debt is unpaid.—Stockton Sav. Bank. v. McCown, 170 Cal. 600, 150 Pac. 985. The allowance of a claim against a decedent's estate, by an executor or administrator, for a portion of the full amount, is clearly a rejection of the remainder of the claim.—Jones v. Walden, 145 Cal. 523, 78 Pac. 1046, 1047.

(4) Right to consider claim rejected.—The question of reasonable time in which to allow or reject a claim is a matter of law, and should be so declared by the court; and six months is clearly a reasonable length of time in which to determine whether an executor or administrator will allow or reject a claim.—Goltra v. Penland, 45 Or. 254, 77

Pac. 129, 132. If a reasonable time elapses, without action on the part
of the executor or administrator, the claimant is entitled to consider his
claim as disallowed and to maintain an action thereon.—Goltra v. Penland, 45 Or. 254, 77 Pac. 129, 132; Gregory v. Clabrough's Executors, 129
Cal. 475, 480, 62 Pac. 72. Where the statute requires the executor or
administrator to whom a claim is presented to indorse thereon his
allowance or rejection, with the day and date thereof, but does not, in
terms, specify the time within which this must be done, and provides
that if the executor or administrator, or the judge, refuses or neglects
to indorse such allowance or rejection for "ten days" after the claim
has been presented to him, it is optional with the claimant to consider
his claim rejected after the tenth day, if it has not been so indorsed
within ten days, but he need not so deem it unless he chooses.—Cowgill
v. Dinwiddie, 98 Cal. 481, 483, 33 Pac. 439. If the executor or administrator neglects, for more than ten days, to indorse either his allowance
or rejection thereof, the claim, at the expiration of ten days, becomes
a rejected claim by operation of law, and not before.—Rice v. Inskeep,
34 Cal. 224, 226; Bank of Ukiah v. Shoemake, 67 Cal. 147, 148, 7 Pac. 420;
Roddan v. Doane, 92 Cal. 555, 558, 28 Pac. 604. And if the claim was
presented to the administrator at the office of his attorney, the leaving
of the claim at the attorney's office, with the attorney's clerk, in the
absence of the administrator, is a sufficient presentation of the claim,
and if it is not acted upon within ten days, the creditor's right to consider it as rejected is not affected by the fact that the administrator
afterwards demanded proof and vouchers.—Roddan v. Doane, 92 Cal. 555,
558, 28 Pac. 604. There are two methods by which an executor or
administrator may accept or reject a claim; it may be by written indorsement on the claim, or by neglect or refusal, for ten days, to make
such an indorsement; and he is allowed always the ten days in which
to act.—Sunberg v. Sebelius, 38 N. D. 413, 418, 165 N. W. 564. Neglect
to approve a claim, within the time specified, amounts to its rejection.—
Miller v. Lewiston Nat. Bank, 18 Ida. 124, 136, 108 Pac. 901. The neglect
or refusal of an executor or administrator to indorse the acceptance
or rejection of a claim on the claim, within ten days after its presentment, amounts to a rejection.—Sunberg v. Sebelius, 38 N. D. 413, 418,
162 N. W. 564. Where, in the section, as to approval and rejection of
claims against the estate of a decedent, it is said that "if the executor ·
or administrator, or the judge, refuse or neglect to indorse" the allowance or rejection for ten days it is equivalent to a rejection, the word
"refuse" implies action upon a demand made, and "neglect" implies
simply a negligent failure to perform; neither word can apply to a case
where a necessary extension of time for considering the matter is
agreed upon by the parties, or a promise to hold the matter open must
necessarily be inferred from the facts and circumstances.—Powell-
Sanders Co. v. Carssow, 28 Ida. 201, 152 Pac. 1067. The indorsement
required to be made by the executor or administrator is evidence of his
action, necessary to the claimant in bringing and maintaining an action

to establish the claim, and if he secretly rejects the claim, and refuses to deliver it to the claimant, or to inform him of the action taken thereon, it operates, or may operate, as a fraud upon the claimant, and become inoperative as a rejection. Where the executor or administrator not only fails to inform the creditor of his action, but also refuses to do so, it may be considered that he has not acted at all. Secret action, which the creditor has no means of knowing, is equivalent to no action at all.—Cowgill v. Dinwiddie, 98 Cal. 481, 484, 33 Pac. 439.

(5) **Effect of rejection.**—Where a claim has been presented to the administrator and partially rejected the only recourse the dissatisfied claimant has is to the court.—Estate of Bette, 171 Cal. 583, 153 Pac. 949. If a representative refuses to allow a claim against a decedent'e estate, the claimant's remedy is to present it to the county court for allowance; it will there be tried as a law action.—Irvine v. Beck, 62 Or. 593, 596, 125 Pac. 832, 834. For the purpose of authorizing actions on claims, and of limiting the time in which suit must be brought, the constructive rejection which, by statute, follows as a result of ten days' neglect or refusal to allow it is equivalent to a rejection by written indorsement.—In re Smith's Estate, 13 N. D. 513, 101 N. W. 890. The non-action of the administrator, upon a claim presented to him for allowance, for a period of time exceeding ten days next after the claim is filed with him for allowance, operates, under the statute, as a rejection of the claim; and the time limited for bringing suit on the claim begins to run at once after the ten-day period expires.—Farwell v. Richardson, 10 N. D. 34, 84 N. W. 558. The statute contemplates that no claim which has reached the status of a rejected claim will be presented to a county court for its allowance, and where such a claim is in fact presented to such court for allowance, and the same is rejected by the court, such rejection does not operate to fix any new period of time within which an action can be instituted upon the rejected claim.—Farwell v. Richardson, 10 N. D. 34, 84 N. W. 558. In case an administrator withhold's action for a period exceeding ten days upon a claim presented against the estate, the claim is thereby rejected, and the time limited for bringing suit upon the claim begins at once then to run.—Williams v. Jackson (Okla.), 179 Pac. 603. The rejection of a claim against the estate of a decedent, by the probate court, has all the attributes of a judgment.—Ross v. Lewis, 23 N. M. 524, 169 Pac. 468.

(6) **Opening order of rejection.**—If a claim filed against an estate is rejected, a motion may be made, at any time before final distribution, to have an opening of the order rejecting it.—In re Stroup's Estate (S. D.), 166 N. W. 155. If a claimant is misinformed, or not informed, by the administrator's attorney as to the time of hearing of the claim, and so is not present to press its validity, he is entitled afterwards to have the order rejecting the claim opened, if he acts with due diligence after being advised of such rejection.—In re Stroup's Estate (S. D.), 166 N. W. 155.

(7) Power of court and judge.—Probate courts have jurisdiction to correct the classification of claims allowed against the estate of deceased persons at a term of the court subsequent to the allowance and erroneous classification thereof.—McPherson v. Wolfley, 9 Kan. App. 67, 57 Pac. 257. An executor or administrator, by paying a claim after its allowance, does not devest the county court of jurisdiction of claims against the estate.—Clemes v. Fox, 25 Colo. 39, 53 Pac. 225, 228. If a claim has been presented to the administrator, and allowed by him within ten days after its presentation, no action can be maintained thereon until after its presentation to the judge, unless he rejects it within that period.—Nally v. McDonald, 66 Cal. 530, 532, 6 Pac. 390. A claim may be approved and allowed by a county judge after it has been rejected either by non-action or by written indorsement, at any time before it is barred by the special or general statute of limitations. —In re Smith's Estate, 13 N. D. 513, 101 N. W. 890. Where the claim has been lost, after its allowance by the executor or administrator, the judge may approve a copy thereof.—Nally v. McDonald, 66 Cal. 530, 533, 6 Pac. 390. When an executor or administrator rejects a claim, the rejection is complete and final, and can not be changed or in any way affected by any future action of the judge. In such a case there is no reason for presenting a claim to the judge at all. It is only where a claim has been allowed by an executor or administrator that there is a necessity of presenting it to the judge, for he may reject it, notwithstanding its allowance by the executor or administrator. A claim may be conclusively rejected by either the administrator or the judge; and when there is a rejection by either, the statute commences to run from the date of such rejection.—Jones v. Walden, 145 Cal. 523, 525, 78 Pac. 1046. ·When an executor or administrator rejects a claim against an estate, the rejection is complete and final, and can not be changed or in any way affected by any future action of the judge. In such case there is no reason for presenting a claim to the judge at all, and it is only where a claim has been allowed by the executor or administrator that there is a necessity for presenting it to the judge, for he may reject it notwithstanding its allowance by the administrator.—Jones v. Walden, 145 Cal. 523, 78 Pac. 1046, 1047. Although the judge had allowed a claim against the estate of a deceased person, he may, upon an ex parte application, afterwards set such allowance aside without notice to the claimant.—Estate of Sullenberger, 72 Cal. 549, 552, 14 Pac. 513. The superior court has no discretion, in the settlement of an estate, to allow a claim that otherwise is barred.—Estate of Aldersley, 174 Cal. 366, 163 Pac. 206. The district court of Alaska has jurisdiction under the Alaskan Code to determine a claim by a surviving partner against the estate of a deceased partner, which involved an accounting of partnership affairs.—Esterly v. Rua (Alaska), 122 Fed. 609, 611, 58 C. C. A. 548. The judge of a county court has power to approve a claim against the estate of a decedent only where the executor or administrator has already allowed it; an order of the county court, purporting to allow such a claim after the executor or administrator has disallowed it, is void.—Osborn v. Foresythe, 54 Okla. 40, 153 Pac. 207; In re Barnett's Estate, 52 Okla. 623, 627, 153 Pac. 653. Where a claim has been filed against an estate by the decedent's daughter, but the relationship does not appear on its face, if the claim is rejected on the ground of the relationship, the court in approving the rejection, can not go into the record for proof of such relationship and ignore evidence of an express contract which was the basis of the claim.—In re Kirfel's Estate, Crampton v. Kirfel, 37 S. D. 292, 294, 157 N. W. 1057. In making the allowance of a claim against the estate of a deceased person in favor of the judge, it is to be considered that he is not generally disqualified to sit in any matter of the estate which has no reference to his interest as a creditor.—Regents, etc., v. Turner, 159 Cal. 541, Ann. Cas. 1912C, 1162, 114 Pac. 842.

(8) Filing of claims.—When a claim is allowed by the executor or administrator, and approved by the judge of the superior court, it must be filed in the court within the prescribed time, but as to rejected claims there is no such provision. It is the duty of the executor or administrator, on demand, to return rejected claims to claimants with his official action indorsed thereon.—Cowgill v. Dinwiddie, 98 Cal. 481, 484, 33 Pac. 439. The allowance of a claim against the estate prevents the claim from becoming barred by the statute, although it has not been filed in the probate court, especially where the statute requiring it to be so filed does not declare by whom it should be so filed. It is the presentation of the claim that saves the debt from becoming barred.—Willis v. Farley, 24 Cal. 490, 501. The allowance of a contingent claim admits and establishes the validity of the application, and entitles it to be filed in court and to rank among the acknowledged debts of the estate, to be paid in due course of administration, as the circumstances of the estate require.—Verdier v. Roach, 96 Cal. 467, 475, 31 Pac. 554. The statute requiring judgments against administrators and claims against the estate, that have been allowed, to be filed in the probate court are merely directory, where there is no penalty prescribed for a failure to file them within the designated time.—Estate of Schroeder, 46 Cal. 304, 316. Rejected claims need not be filed with the county clerk. It is only the claims that have been allowed that are· to be filed.—Saxton v. Musselman, 17 S. D. 35, 95 N. W. 291, 292. A claim against the estate of a decedent, consisting of an itemized statement of expenditures made by the claimant for and on account of the deceased in his lifetime, with a balance due defendant of a specified amount after deducting a sum named in favor of the deceased from the total amount claimed to have been so expended for the deceased by the defendant, does not carry with it the acknowledgment of any indebtedness to the deceased or to the estate; but, on the contrary, negatives any such inference, and would not, of course, have been filed but for the claim of the claimant that the estate was indebted to him and not he to the estate.—Visher v. Wilbur, 5 Cal. App.

562, 90 Pac. 1065, 1069, 91 Pac. 412. A claim that has been rejected by the administrator need not be reported by him to, or filed by him in, the probate court; it is only claims that have been allowed that must be filed in the probate court.—Chandler v. Probate Court, 26 Idaho 173, 178, 141 Pac. 635. A person with whom an administrator has contracted may file his claim with the successor of the administrator after the latter has been displaced.—Lamb-Davis Lumber Co. v. Stowell, 96 Wash. 46, L. R. A. 1917E, 960, 164 Pac. 593. All claims against the estates of deceased persons not filed in the probate court, and notice given as provided by law, within one year from the date of the appointment of the executor or administrator, are barred.—Buss v. Dye, 21 N. M. 146, 153 Pac. 74. The statute requiring claims against an estate to be filed within a designated time after the date of publication of notice to creditors applies to estates that are being administered under a non-intervention will as well as to estates being administered under other wills.—First Security & L. Co. v. Englehart (Wash.), 181 Pac. 13, 15. A statute which provides that a claim against an estate not filed within a designated time after the date of publication of notice to creditors shall be barred, is mandatory.—First Security & L. Co. v. Englehart (Wash.), 181 Pac. 13, 15.

(9) **Defective verification.**—The allowance of claims upon defective verification does not always render them void. Where claims have been allowed and approved by the administrator and the probate judge, and have been filed among the approved claims against the estate, such allowance prima facie establishes their validity. The heirs have the right to question the allowance at the settlement of the estate, but the burden of showing the invalidity of the allowance is cast upon them. The allowance of a claim, although made upon a defective verification, is a judicial act, which entitles the claim to rank as an acknowledged debt of the estate, to be paid in due course of administration, and if the claim is adjudged to be valid, the defective verification will not invalidate it. The allowance of a mortgage claim entitles it to rank as an acknowledged debt against the estate, to be paid in due course of administration, but because there is a defective verification of a claim upon a note secured by mortgage is no reason why the foreclosure of the mortgage should be denied. A mortgage is a mere incident of the debt it was intended to secure, and passes by the assignment of the debt, is discharged by a payment of the debt, and is barred by the statute of limitations when the debt is barred; and if the allowance of the claim on the mortgage was sufficient to make it an acknowledged debt of the estate, it is also sufficient to keep alive the mortgage, and to entitle the plaintiff to have it foreclosed.—Consolidated Nat. Bank v. Hayes, 112 Cal. 75, 82, 44 Pac. 469; Estate of Swain, 67 Cal. 637, 8 Pac. 497.

(10) **Amendment of claim.**—No substantial change can be made in a claim on file, either by way of amendment or otherwise, after the

expiration of the time for the presentation of claims.—Estate of Sullenberger, 72 Cal. 549, 552, 14 Pac. 513; Dickey v. Dickey, 8 Colo. App. 141, 45 Pac. 228. But the claimant may be permitted to amend his claim as to any technical matter that does not substantially change the nature and character of the same.—Kirman v. Powning, 25 Nev. 378, 60 Pac. 834, 838. If the account of a claimant against the estate of a decedent is contested, the court, upon motion, should allow the claimant to file a more particular account of his claim.—Estate of Hidden, 23 Cal. 362, 363. If by inadvertence a demand against the estate of a decedent was assigned to a lower class than that to which it rightfully belonged the probate court has jurisdiction to correct the error even at a subsequent term, and justice required such correction to be made, upon due application and notice.—Commercial State Bank v. Ross, 90 Kan. 423, 133 Pac. 538, 539.

REFERENCES.

Amendment of claim.—See head-line 3, subd. 6, ante.

(11) Objections to allowance.—An objection that a claim was never presented can not be made after a decree allowing it. Such objections should be made during the pendency of proceedings.—Estate of Cook, 14 Cal. 129, 130. An objection that a claim against a decedent's estate was not presented by the proper person is a matter in abatement only, and is waived by joining issue on the merits without raising it in the county court.—In re Morgan's Estate, 46 Or. 233, 78 Pac. 1029, 1030. Under the Colorado statute, not only an executor or an administrator may object to the allowance of a claim, but also the heirs at law, devisees, legatees, or creditors, or others interested in the estate, may do so.—In re Hobson's Estate, 40 Colo. 332, 91 Pac. 929, 931. Where a claim against an estate has been allowed by the administrator and afterward by the probate judge, after which objections and exceptions are filed by an heir of such estate, the probate judge has power and jurisdiction to set aside his former allowance of such claim, and to hear and determine the objections and exceptions filed.—Estate of Coryell, 16 Idaho 201, 215, 101 Pac. 723. Under the statutes of the state of Idaho, where a claim against an estate has been allowed by the administrator and afterwards by the probate judge, and thereafter objections and exceptions are filed by an heir of such estate, the probate judge has power and jurisdiction to set aside his former allowance of such claim and to hear and determine the objections and exceptions filed.—In re Coryell's Estate, 16 Idaho 201, 101 Pac. 724. When claims are pending against an estate before the probate court upon an order setting aside their former allowance by the administrator and the probate judge, upon objections by the heirs, the probate judge is not required to indorse upon said claims his allowance or rejection of the same within ten days after such order, nor does his failure to do so amount to a rejection of said claims and defeat his jurisdiction to set said claims for hearing upon the objections made by the heirs.—Miller

v. Lewiston Nat. Bank, 18 Idaho 124, 108 Pac. 906. It was sufficient for
the executrix to indorse upon a claim "disallowed," without specifying
the objections thereto, and any objections to the claim's allowance can
be orally interposed at any time before or at the hearing.—First Nat.
Bank v. Cone, 57 Colo. 529, 531, 143 Pac. 569. A charge for a monument
for the grave of a deceased person is not objectionable because of the
fact that such monument was also intended to serve as a monument
for the grave of the father of the decedent.—Estate of Aldersley, 174
Cal. 366, 163 Pac. 206. In the matter of the allowance or rejection of
claims, the intent of the statutes is that any one aggrieved may, on
notice of the hearing of the petition for a final settlement, appear in
the probate court and file exceptions, or make objections; otherwise
laches may be imputed to him.—Chandler v. Probate Court for Kootenai
County, 26 Idaho 173, 141 Pac. 635.

REFERENCES.

Heirs may object to allowance of claim.—See infra, subd. 24.

(12) **Effect of allowance. In general.**—The allowance of a claim,
by an executor or administrator and the probate judge, amounts to a
judgment, not in a general sense, but of a qualified character only.
It is simply a judgment as to the amount due and to whom due, and
by the act of allowance and approval the claim is placed among the
acknowledged debts of the estate; but before payment can be enforced,
it is necessary to obtain a decree of the probate court for that purpose.—Magrow v. McGlynn, 26 Cal. 420, 431; Estate of Hidden, 23 Cal.
362; Pico v. De la Guerra, 18 Cal. 422; Walkerly v. Bacon, 85 Cal. 137,
141, 24 Pac. 638. No claim against any estate, which has been presented and allowed, is affected by the statute of limitations, pending
the proceedings for the settlement of the estate; and such proceedings
are pending until the entry of a decree discharging the executor or
administrator.—Dohs v. Dohs, 60 Cal. 255, 260. When a claim against
an estate has been allowed and approved and filed, it ranks among
the acknowledged debts of the estate to be paid in due course of the
administration.—Estate of Loshe, 62 Cal. 413, 415. A demand of an
attorney for services rendered to an administrator or executor during
the settlement of the estate, and which has been presented, allowed,
and approved, and ordered to be paid out of the estate, in due course
of administration, while not technically a "claim" against the estate,
yet it will be treated as such.—Stuttmeister v. Superior Court, 72 Cal.
487, 489, 14 Pac. 35. The appearance in a probate court, at a hearing
upon a claim against an estate, and consent to the allowance of such
claim, by one of two joint executors, without notice to or the concurrence of the other, is sufficient to bind the estate.—Cross v. Long, 66
Kan. 293, 71 Pac. 524. The admissions of an executor, made in the
allowance of a claim against the estate, although the claim is allowed
only in part, bind the estate.—Meinert v. Snow, 3 Idaho 112, 27 Pac.
677. The presentation and allowance of a claim in part is not material

in determining the question as to whether such claim is barred by the statute of limitations.—Potter v. Lewin, 123 Cal. 146, 147, 55 Pac. 783. The allowance of a claim in part is clearly a rejection of the remainder, though when an administrator rejects a claim, the rejection is complete and final, and can not in any way be affected by any future action of the judge.—Jones v. Walden, 145 Cal. 523, 78 Pac. 1046. A verbal allowance of a claim against an estate is ineffective to give the claimant any cause of action against the estate.—Pitte v. Shipley, 46 Cal. 154, 161. If a claim against an estate has passed beyond the jurisdiction of the administrator to allow the same, and has reached the status of a rejected claim, his indorsement of allowance upon such rejected claim is futile, and does not operate to allow or validate the claim, either in whole or in part, especially where it was outlawed at the time he indorsed his allowance thereon.—Farwell v. Richardson, 10 N. D. 34, 84 N. W. 553. The allowance of such a claim is a judicial act, having the force and effect of a judgment; that is, it is final and conclusive as between the parties until it is reversed or set aside, and can not be collaterally attacked.—Ross v. Lewis, 23 N. M. 524, 169 Pac. 468. An executor's allowance of a claim is only his approval of it, which does not bind the heirs or creditors, who have an opportunity to contest it, upon the settlement of the final account.—Irvine v. Beck, 62 Or. 593, 596, 125 Pac. 832, 834. The allowance of a claim against an estate establishes it as a charge of indebtedness against the estate, subject, however, to the right of heirs and distributees to question it, as they may any other expenditure of the funds, on the hearing of the executor's reports, or at any other due and suitable time.—In re Parkes' Estate, Parkes v. Burkhart, 101 Wash. 659, 172 Pac. 908. If a claim is presented to the administrator and by him allowed, and is afterward presented to the probate judge and by him allowed, the effect of such allowance is merely to rank the claim among the acknowledged debts of the estate to be paid in due course of administration.—Estate of Coryell, 16 Idaho 201, 213, 101 Pac. 723. Under the provisions of the Code of Civil Procedure an allowed claim against an estate of a deceased person does not attain to the dignity and force of an absolute judgment until, upon the settlement of an account, an order is made directing the executor to pay it. Prior to that time it ranks as an acknowledged debt, but it is still subject to contest by the heirs.—Haub v. Leggett, 160 Cal. 491, 117 Pac. 556. A creditor seeking to recover a fund alleged to have been misappropriated by its agent may simultaneously in separate actions proceed against the estate of the misappropriator and other parties alleged to have participated in the misuse of the fund, and, after the full amount of the claim has been allowed against the estate and classified, such creditor is entitled to the same dividend as other creditors of the same class (the estate being insolvent) without regard to the result of pending suits against such other parties.—Sarbach v. Fidelity & Deposit Co., 87 Kan. 774, 125 Pac. 63. Where a claim is presented to the administrator and by him allowed, and afterwards to the probate judge and by him allowed, the effect of such allowance is merely to rank the claim among the acknowledged debts of the estate, to be paid in due course of administration.—In re Coryell's Estate, 16 Idaho 201, 101 Pac. 723. The allowance of a claim of a creditor by the administrator of the estate of the debtor has the same force and effect as a judgment, and gives the claimant the right to maintain an action to set aside fraudulent transfers made by the debtor and to subject the property to the satisfaction of his judgment.—Scholle v. Finnell, 166 Cal. 546, 137 Pac. 241. Allowance of claim of representative by judge of superior court, under Code of Civil Procedure, sec. 1510, is of equal force as judgment in favor of another creditor against representative, and subject to contest same as other allowed claims.—Shiels v. Nathan, 12 Cal. App. 604, 108 Pac. 34.

REFERENCES.

Allowance of claims by executors and administrators, when and against whom conclusive.—See note 65 Am. Dec. 121-127.

(13) **Same. In part.**—The allowance of a claim by the executor and judge for a portion of the amount for which it was presented, and its subsequent filing by the claimant with the clerk of the court, does not constitute conclusive evidence of acceptance by the claimant of the part allowed in full satisfaction of his debt, or operate as a bar to a suit to recover the whole claim.—Haub v. Leggett, 160 Cal. 491, 177 Pac. 556. The creditor may treat a partial allowance by the executor as a rejection of the entire claim and may bring his suit at once without presenting it to the judge at all. But there is nothing in the statute which makes this the only mode of procedure or which declares that he can not sue for the whole, if he first presents it to the judge and files it with the papers after the judge has approved the partial allowance of the executor.—Haub v. Leggett, 160 Cal. 491, 117 Pac. 556.

(14) **Same. Presumption. Evidence.**—The presumption is, where a claim against the estate of a decedent has been allowed and approved as presented, that it was allowed upon vouchers and proof to the satisfaction of the executor or administrator and probate judge.—Estate of Swain, 67 Cal. 637, 8 Pac. 497, 500. Under the statute of Oregon, the mere allowance of a claim by the executor or administrator is not even prima facie evidence in favor of its validity. The claimant must, on the settlement of an account, support his claim by proof of its validity, and by other evidence than the allowance of the administrator. The county court is not bound to approve a claim, simply because it has been allowed by the administrator; for, if such was the case, it would merely sit in a perfunctory manner to enter its approval upon the journal. The court acts judicially, and when objections are interposed to a claim, it must be supported by proof, as in other litigated controversies, or the claim must fail of its establishment, and the simple allowance by the administrator will

not avail to make a prima facie case.—Chambers v. Chambers, 38 Or. 131, 62 Pac. 1013, 1014, 1015. The final recognition of a claim as valid in no way depends upon the question whether the administrator or probate judge allowed it upon insufficient evidence. The law simply makes the allowance evidence, prima facie, of the claim, and casts the onus of proof upon him who contests it.—Estate of Crosby, 55 Cal. 574, 579. The allowance of a claim against an estate by a court having jurisdiction is prima facie evidence of the debt and of its due presentment against the heirs or devisees in a proceeding brought to subject real estate to its payment.—In re Jones' Estate, Thomas v. Williams, 80 Kan. 632, 25 L. R. A. (N. S.) 1304, 103 Pac. 772.

REFERENCES.

Allowance of claim by executor or administrator and when and against whom conclusive.—See note 65 Am. Dec. 121.

(15) Judgment of allowance.—The judgment of a probate court allowing a claim against an estate in the form of a promissory note, which is not sworn to, is erroneous, but not void for want of jurisdiction.— Guiterrez v. Scholle, 12 N. M. 328, 78 Pac. 50, overruling, on this point, Clancey v. Clancey, 7 N. M. 405, 37 Pac. 1105, 1107, 38 Pac. 168. A decree of the probate court, ordering a claim to be paid, at the instance of the administrator, and upon his petition, stating the amount and class of the claim, the person to whom due, and the amount of money in his hands ready to pay out as the court shall direct, is final and conclusive, and can not be collaterally attacked; nor can it be attacked in any other proceeding upon the ground of the insufficiency of the evidence upon which it was rendered.—Estate of Cook, 14 Cal. 129, 130. A judgment of allowance of a claim against the estate of a deceased person is not a complete and effective judgment until an order on the administrator to pay is obtained, and a proceeding to obtain such order is not an action on the judgment of allowance.—Guiterrez v. Scholle, 12 N. M. 328, 78 Pac. 50. The presentation and allowance of a claim based upon a judgment lien, to be paid in due course of administration, is not inconsistent with the continuance of the lien, and such lien ranks with the recognized lien of a mortgage, and is not released or affected by the death of the judgment debtor, pending the time limited by the statute for the continuance of the lien. No difference is perceivable between the allowance of the claim by the administrator, and the judgment of the court allowing the claim, on suit brought after its rejection; the judgment establishes the claim the same as if it had been allowed.—Estate of Wiley, 138 Cal. 301, 306, 71 Pac. 441. See Morton v. Adams, 124 Cal. 229, 71 Am. St. Rep. 53, 56 Pac. 1038. The order or judgment of a probate judge, allowing a claim against an estate upon an ex parte showing, is not a final order or judgment, which binds or affects the heirs of such estate, who have not appeared, objected to, or contested such claim.—Estate of Coryell, 16 Idaho 201, 213, 101 Pac. 723. A claim for the return of forfeited earnest money, filed,

nearly four years after the transaction, against the estate of the person who, in his lifetime, received the payment in an abortive real estate deal, is of so long a standing that it should be allowed only upon strong and convincing proof.—Scott v. Merrill's Estate, Brown v. Merrill's Estate, 74 Or. 568, 146 Pac. 99. Under the statute of Washington, judgment rendered against an administrator establishes the claim for the amount ascertained to be due, but does not "create a lien upon the property of the estate."—Spokane Merchants' Assn. v. First Nat. Bank, 86 Wash. 367, L. R. A. 1918A, 323, 150 Pac. 434. The order or judgment of a probate judge allowing a claim against an estate upon an ex parte showing is not a final order or judgment which binds or affects the heirs of such estate, who have not appeared, objected to, or contested such claim.—In re Coryell's Estate, 16 Idaho 201, 101 Pac. 724. The statutes of the state of Idaho give an heir the right to appear and contest a claim after its allowance by the administrator and the probate judge, and such heir is not concluded by the order or judgment of allowance made in the first instance.—In re Coryell's Estate, 16 Idaho 201, 101 Pac. 624.

(16) Arbitration. Reference.—If an executor or administrator doubts the validity of any claim presented to him, he may agree, in writing, with the claimant that an order of reference be made by the court or judge concerning the same by filing such agreement. The order should be made accordingly. The referee is empowered to hear and determine the matter, and to report thereon to the court, in the same manner and with like effect as if the order were made in an action or suit on the claim.—Chambers v. Chambers, 38 Or. 131, 62 Pac. 1013, 1014. The reference of a claim may be made in court by consent of the parties.—Hall v. Superior Court, 69 Cal. 79, 10 Pac. 257. The referee should report his findings, in writing, to the court, and the facts found and conclusions of law must be separately stated. If the claim is referred to the superior court for its decision, the testimony taken before the judge sitting as a referee, although embodied in his report, is no part of the record, and can not be reviewed upon appeal, unless embodied in a bill of exceptions and filed. It is only the finding of the referee which becomes part of the judgment roll. The court or judge sitting as a referee is as distinct in law from the court acting as such in its own proper sphere as if a different referee had been selected. The code fixes one rule for the guidance of all referees, and they are alike, and, without exception, subject to its provisions.—Lee Sack Sam v. Gray, 104 Cal. 243, 248, 38 Pac. 85. Claims against an estate may, under the approval of the probate court, be submitted by the executor or administrator to a referee.—Unterrainer v. Seelig, 13 S. D. 148, 82 N. W. 394, 396. If a claim in favor of an estate has been referred to arbitrators, who have clearly determined by their award the amount due the estate, the fact that they have included matters, in their award, not submitted to them does not render the award invalid as to the matters properly submitted, as that portion of the award may

be rejected.—Unterrainer v. Seelig, 13 S. D. 148, 82 N. W. 394, 396. An executor or administrator has, at common law, the right to submit any controversies between himself and creditors of or debtors to the estate to arbitration.—Unterrainer v. Seelig, 13 S. D. 148, 82 N. W. 394, 396. The statute of South Dakota does not deprive the executor or administrator of the common-law power to arbitrate claims, either against or in favor of the estate. It provides a certain mode of adjusting a certain class of claims, without the formal proceeding of an action, and leaves it to the option of the parties whether they will avail themselves of its provisions, but it was not intended to restrict or exclude the common-law right of arbitration.—Unterrainer v. Seelig, 13 S. D. 148, 82 N. W. 394, 396.

(17) Claims properly allowed.—Even where there is no testamentary disposition or direction, the court will allow a reasonable sum to be paid out of the funds of the estate for the erection of a monument over decedent's grave, putting the expenditure upon the ground of funeral expenses.—Van Emon v. Superior Court, 76 Cal. 589, 590, 9 Am. St. Rep. 258, 18 Pac. 877; Estate of Koppikus, 1 Cal. App. 84, 81 Pac. 732. The burial of the dead is a necessity that the preservation of the health of the living enjoins, and the reasonable expenses connected therewith constitute a preferred charge upon the decedent's estate. What is a reasonable charge in such a case must be determined by the apparent condition of the estate that is burdened therewith. An estate appraised at two thousand four hundred dollars warrants the administrator in incurring expenses aggregating thirty-one dollars for funeral notices, carriages, and hearse hire.—In re Osburn's Estate, 36 Or. 8, 58 Pac. 521, 523. If a nephew pays out money for traveling expenses prior to the death of his uncle, he can not recover such expenses from the estate of his uncle after the latter's death, by reason of the relation existing between them; but if he incurs traveling expenses for the benefit of the estate, after his uncle's death, he is entitled to be compensated therefor in a reasonable amount.—Estate of McCullough, 31 Or. 86, 49 Pac. 886, 887. The proper amount to allow on a claim against an estate for services rendered in consideration of a conveyance of land which the decedent failed to convey before his death is the value of the land agreed to be conveyed, without other proof of reasonable value.—Estate of Towne, 143 Cal. 507, 510, 77 Pac. 446. The burden to show that a claim was not properly allowed is on contestant.—Shiels v. Nathan, 12 Cal. App. 604, 108 Pac. 34. Same rule applies in action by representative to enforce his own approved claim.—Shiels v. Nathan, 12 Cal. App. 604, 108 Pac. 34.

(18) Claims that will be rejected.—One who renders a kindly and gratuitous service to another, with no intention at the time of asking for or receiving any pecuniary compensation, can not afterwards make such act the subject of a claim. Hence gratuitous services to a decedent, in his lifetime, under such circumstances, can not form the basis

of a charge against his estate after his death.—Estate of Hanson,
133 Cal. 38, 39, 65 Pac. 14. Where a son maintained his aged mother
in his own home as a member of his family, the law will not imply a
promise on her part to pay for her maintenance.—Jones v. Humphrey's
Estate, 10 Kan. App. 545, 63 Pac. 26. So it is proper to reject the
claim of a child against the executor of his parent's estate for services rendered by such child to the parent, unless a clear promise
on the part of the parent to pay therefor appears. Where services are
rendered by one near relative to another, no promise is implied to pay
for the services, and no compensation can be claimed therefor unless
an express agreement, or its equivalent, to pay for the same is shown.
—Wilkes v. Cornelius, 21 Or. 348, 28 Pac. 135. The universally accepted rule is, that the estate of a deceased person is answerable for
the funeral expenses and other debts. This being true, and it not
appearing from the record that the estate of a decedent is insolvent,
the question of the liability of his wife's estate for such expenses
should not arise. If the executor or administrator of the estate of decedent's wife sets up a claim to property standing in the name of the
deceased husband, such claim for funeral expenses can not be allowed
against the estate of the widow.—Hulbert (Burdsal's Estate) v. Walley,
3 Colo. App. 250, 32 Pac. 985, 986. If the sum of two hundred and forty
dollars is an ample and liberal allowance for the purchase of a burial
lot, it is proper to refuse the administrator credit for thirteen hundred
dollars expended in the purchase of such lot, if the estate is insolvent.
—Clemes v. Fox, 6 Colo. App. 377, 40 Pac. 843, 847. A claim by a brother
or sister of the decedent for services rendered in nursing him and
caring for him during a period closing with his death is not valid.—
Estate of Aldersley, 174 Cal. 366, 163 Pac. 206. Where a claim against
an estate is not properly exhibited to the court in compliance with
the provisions of the statute in that behalf within one year from the
granting of letters of administration its allowance by the court is
reversible error.—Alvater v. First Nat. Bank, 45 Colo. 528, 103 Pac.
379. Where the executor fraudulently used a power of attorney given
to him by decedent while he was lying ill near death, which contains
no power to execute a note, to execute his note to himself, and then
transferred the same to his sister-in-law, so as to include a large
amount of interest added to his debt to her, and then approved the
same as a claim against the estate, the case is clearly one of fraud
upon the estate.—In re Newell, 18 Cal. App. 258, 122 Pac. 1099. Claims
barred at the time of their presentation, can not be allowed.—Estate
of Aldersley, 174 Cal. 366, 163 Pac. 206.

(19) Claim of executor or administrator.—If an administrator's claim
against an estate is disallowed by the probate judge, the administrator's only remedy is to resign his trust and to bring suit as any
other creditor of the estate.—Wilkins v. Wilkins, 1 Wash. 87, 23 Pac.
411. If the administrator holds a claim against the estate which
be represents, the county court has power to allow his claim, although

he failed to file his undertaking as administrator.—Estate of Houck, 23 Or. 10, 17 Pac. 461, 463. An executor or administrator can not, under the guise of allowing a claim against himself as such, and in favor of himself as a creditor, be permitted to put the assets of the estate beyond the reach of the rightful claimants, whoever they may be.—Clancey v. Clancey, 7 N. M. 405, 37 Pac. 1105, 1107. An executor or administrator holding a claim against the estate must present the same duly verified, like any other creditor, and, if forced to sue to enforce it, must first resign his office.—In re Parkes' Estate (Wash.), 178 Pac. 830.

(20) **Absence from state.**—While the statute provides that a creditor of the estate of a deceased person, who is absent from the state during the whole period of publication of the notice to creditors, and has no actual knowledge of the publication, may prevent his claim to the administrator at any time before the decree of distribution is entered, yet no other proof of such absence and want of knowledge is required than the affidavit of the claimant; and the statute does not give the executor or administrator, or the probate judge, any power or right to say, arbitrarily, that they are not "satisfied," and therefore reject the claim. All that is necessary is for the affidavit to show, to the satisfaction of a reasonable, fair, and impartial mind, that the claimant had no notice.—Cullerton v. Mead, 22 Cal. 95, 99. But if the claimant returned to the state, and had actual notice of the publication of the notice to creditors for more than one month prior to the expiration of the time for filing his claim, and neglected to do so until long after that date, he does not come within the remedial provision of the statute. Hence, under such circumstances, if he does not present his claim within the time limited, it is barred by the statute.—MacGowan v. Jones, 142 Cal. 593, 596, 76 Pac. 503. When decedent bought goods from plaintiff in New York, and after six-months' absence from the state died one year and twenty-three days from the purchase, without payment, and her executrix received a verified claim for the amount due one month later, and thirteen days before issuance of letters testamentary, and retained the same one year and twenty-eight days thereafter and then rejected the claim as barred in two years from the purchase, an averment in the complaint, filed three months after such rejection, setting up the six-months' absence from the state, to take the case out of the statute of limitations, did not show a change of the cause of action on the rejected claim and the court erred in applying the rule that because the facts pleaded were not set forth in the claim, the plaintiff can not recover upon any cause of action not stated therein and in giving judgment for the estate.—Scott, Stamp & Co. v. Leake, 9 Cal. App. 511, 99 Pac. 731.

(21) **Judgments as claims.**—A judgment may be allowed as a claim against an estate without the affidavit required in other cases showing

that it is due, and that there have been no payments, and that there are no offsets.—Cullerton v. Mead, 22 Cal. 95, 99. The presentation and allowance of a judgment as a claim against the estate of a decedent does not destroy or merge the judgment lien. None of the grounds upon which one judgment has been allowed to merge in another apply to the case of the allowance of a judgment as a claim against the estate.—Morton v. Adams, 124 Cal. 229, 232, 233, 71 Am. St. Rep. 53, 56 Pac. 1038. Where the surety on an appeal bond of the deceased pays the amount, on dismissal of the appeal, and files a claim therefor against the estate, such claim is not on a judgment within the Colorado statute, requiring such a claim to be exhibited by filing an exemplification of the record.—German A. T. Co. v. National Surety Co., 55 Colo. 499, 136 Pac. 457.

(22) Contingent claims.—All contingent claims, which are provable and payable at any time, must be presented for allowance within the statutory time after publication of notice to creditors, as a condition precedent to the commencement of actions thereon. The requirement that an allowed claim shall be ranked "among" debts does not exclude from the ranks all claims which may not properly be termed legal debts. The statute plainly requires contingent claims to be presented for allowance, and that all allowed claims shall be filed in court and ranked "among" the acknowledged (allowed) debts, whether all such allowed claims are technical debts or not.—Verdier v. Roach, 96 Cal. 467, 476, 478, 31 Pac. 554; Pico v. De la Guerra, 18 Cal. 422, 430. If the claim is allowed and approved, the allowance, prima facie, establishes its validity against the estate. If it is due, and is rejected, the claimant is required to establish its validity by suit upon it within the prescribed statutory time after the rejection, or if it is not due, then within a certain time after it becomes due; and if its validity is established by recovery thereon, the judgment entitles the claimant to rank as a creditor of the estate, and to payment in due course of administration; or, if the administrator allows the claim although not due, it entitles the claimant to rank in the same way, and, upon deducting a rebate of interest upon the claim, entitles him to payment of the principal sum, or to share in a distribution of the estate pari passu with creditors whose allowed claims are due.—Estate of Swain, 67 Cal. 637, 640, 8 Pac. 497. That the amount of the liability of a stockholder for corporate debts had not been determined in an action against him did not on revival after his death render the claim a contingent one not presentable until its amount was determined.—First Nat. Bank v. Hotchkiss, 49 Colo. 593, 114 Pac. 312.

(23) Interest.—An allowed claim against an estate draws interest at the legal rate from the date of its approval by the judge.—Estate of Glinn, 74 Cal. 567, 569, 16 Pac. 396; Estate of Olvera, 70 Cal. 184, 11 Pac. 624; and this is true, although the demand on which another claim was founded did not bear interest.—Estate of Olvera, 70 Cal. 184,

185, 11 Pac. 624. A claim against the estate of a decedent for funeral expenses bears interest after its allowance.—Estate of Cummins, 143 Cal. 525, 77 Pac. 479. If a suit on a mortgage claim is not brought within the prescribed statutory time after the rejection of a claim for accrued interest, there can be no foreclosure of the mortgage therefor; but where there has been a stipulation respecting interest, which has been overlooked in drawing a dercee of foreclosure, the judgment should be modified so as to conform with the stipulation.—Consolidated Nat. Bank v. Hayes, 112 Cal. 75, 84, 44 Pac. 469. It is sometimes provided by the statute that, "if the estate be insolvent, no greater rate of interest shall be allowed upon any claim after the first publication of notice to creditors, than is allowed on judgments obtained in the superior court"; but such a statute applies only to claims which must be presented for allowance, or be barred forever, and which, when approved, are filed in the court and become acknowledged debts. It does not. apply to an independent action brought by a mortgagee to foreclose his lien against the property of the estate, where he looks to the mortgaged property alone as security. In such an action the court acts independently of the administration of the estate, and may enforce the lien upon the property by a sale thereof for the full amount of the mortgaged debt, irrespective of the insolvent condition of the estate. The court, in such an action, is not called upon to "allow" a claim against the estate, which is to be paid in the course of administration, but merely determines the amount of the mortgage debt according to its terms, and directs a sale of the mortgaged property.—Visalia Sav. Bank v. Curtis, 135 Cal. 350, 353, 67 Pac. 329; Christy v. Dana, 42 Cal. 174; Richardson v. Diss, 127 Cal. 58, 59 Pac. 197; Estate of McDougald, 146 Cal. 196, 79 Pac. 875. Such a statute, in specially mentioning insolvent estates as subjects of reduction of interest, ex industria excludes all estates not mentioned from the operation of this law reducing interest, and shows, as plainly as anything short of positive enactment can show, that it was the purpose and intention of the legislature that credits against solvent estates should continue after allowance to draw interest at any rate. in excess of the legal rate that the contracts on which they were based will warrant.—Richardson v. Diss, 127 Cal. 58, 60, 59 Pac. 197. Allowance with interest up to the time of the allowance does not preclude the recovery of interest after that time.—Raggio v. Palmtag, 155 Cal. 797, 103 Pac. 812.

(24) Contest of claims. Vacating allowances.—There are at least two points in the administration of an estate at which an approved claim may be contested; namely, when application is made for the sale of property, and when an account is rendered for settlement. But, in making the contest, the contestant has the affirmative, and must show cause.—Estate of Loshe, 62 Cal. 413, 415. Heirs may question the allowance and approval of claims by the administrator and judge.— Beckett v. Selover, 7 Cal. 215, 241, 68 Am. Dec. 237; and minor heirs are not estopped from questioning the correctness of the administra-

tor's account by reason of proceedings in the probate court for a
sale of the property to pay an alleged claim.—Estate of Hill, 67 Cal.
238, 244, 7 Pac. 664. If the account of a claimant is contested, and
he applies for leave to amend by filing a more full and particular
account of his claim, the amendment should be allowed, and the court
errs in refusing to give him an opportunity to prove that his claim
has not been barred by the statute of limitations.—Estate of Hidden,
23 Cal. 362, 363. An order of the probate court allowing a claim
against the estate of a decedent is not open to collateral attack upon
the ground that the statute of limitations had run against such claim
before its allowance.—Van Dusen v. Topeka Woolen Mill Co., 74 Kan.
437, 87 Pac. 74. And it is not sufficient ground for refusing to order
the payment of a claim for professional services rendered the decedent
in his lifetime, that such services were not worth the amount charged
by him, and allowed by the administrator and by the probate judge.—
Estate of McKinley, 49 Cal. 152, 154. Not only may an executor or
administrator object to the allowance of a claim, but the heirs at law,
devisees, or legatees, or creditors, or others interested in the estate,
may do so; and where the holder of a note asserts it as a claim against
the estate, a general objection to it is sufficient, under a statute which
expressly provides that formal pleadings shall not be required, and
that, in case of a contested claim, the issue shall be formed, heard,
and determined in the same manner as in actions before justices of
the peace. Under this procedure, a plea of the statute of limitations,
or that a copy, and not the note itself, was filed, may be orally interposed any time before or at the time of the hearing. The allowance
by a judge, of a claim against the estate of a decedent, made on an
ex parte application, may properly be set aside by him without notice
to the claimant.—In re Sullenberger, 72 Cal. 549, 552, 14 Pac. 513.
Orders approving claims against an estate may be set aside, undoubtedly, upon the ground of fraud or mistake, but, in the absence of proof
of such fraud or mistake, the appellate court will presume that, in
setting aside such orders, the administrator's claim to protection for
making payments under its previous orders was considered by the
lower court, and, in the absence of anything in the record to the contrary, the appellate court will assume that the court below had jurisdiction, and that an approval order was set aside upon the ground of
fraud or mistake, or upon both of these grounds.—Clemes v. Fox, 25
Colo. 39, 53 Pac. 225, 228. A proceeding to vacate the allowance of a
claim against an estate is a direct attack upon the judgment of the
probate court which that court has jurisdiction to entertain.—Lutz v.
Balcom, 59 Kan. 777, 53 Pac. 523. The statutes of this state
give an heir the right to appear and contest a claim after its
allowance by the administrator and the probate judge, and such
heir is not concluded by the order or judgment of allowance made
in the first instance.—Estate of Coryell, 16 Ida. 201, 215, 101 Pac. 723.
Foreign residents, interested in an estate but unaware of a claim filed

with the administrator, until after its approval and an administrator's sale had under order to obtain funds to pay it, may successfully contest the claim even at that late day, if they show fraud.—McLaughlin v. Rote, 62 Colo. 505, 163 Pac. 841.

REFERENCES.

Is an administrator or executor in such privity with a legatee, distributee, or creditor, that he may assert a personal defense of the latter to a claim against the estate.—See note 8 **L. R. A.** (N. S.) 212, 214.

(25) **Same. Jury trial.**—If an allowance of claim is contested by a legatee or other proper person, either he or the person filing the claim may have a jury to pass upon the matter.—Estate of Hellier, 169 Cal. 77, 145 Pac. 1008. On a contest tried before a jury, as provided by the statute of California, of an allowed claim against the estate of a deceased person, which as presented and allowed consisted of several specified amounts claimed to be due for various items of materials furnished and services rendered, a ground of contest that the "claim is not a proper or legal claim against the estate," puts in issue, in the absence of a demurrer to the contest, or other objection to its sufficiency, both the value and the legality of the various items of the claim.— Estate of Weir, 168 Cal. 330, 143 Pac. 612.

5. Suits on claims.

(1) **In general.**—The plaintiff, in his suit upon the claim of a decedent, is not estopped because of the prior presentation of a different claim, which was not approved, although the former claim was for a lesser amount. The doctrine of estoppel can not be invoked in such a case, where the former claim was never read to nor seen by the executor or administrator, and was largely incorrect.—Warren v. McGill, 103 Cal. 153, 155, 37 Pac. 144. The doctrine of estoppel can not be invoked where, to give it effect, there must be an entire disregard of statutory law. Hence, a plea of estoppel can not be invoked against the substituted executors of the deceased member of a copartnership, so as to permit a judgment against them in violation of the statute requiring the presentation of a claim, on the ground that the deceased fraudulently induced plaintiff to believe that he was dealing with a copartnership, and not with him individually.—Frazier v. Murphy, 133 Cal. 91, 98, 65 Pac. 326. So if a portion of a claim which has been filed has been allowed, and the remainder refused, the claimant is not estopped to sue, either at law or in equity, for the portion disallowed.— Walkerly v. Bacon, 85 Cal. 137, 141, 24 Pac. 638. Where the plaintiff had conveyed a mining claim to the decedent before the latter's death, and the deceased failed to make payment therefor, and subsequently the plaintiff agreed to accept a specified sum of money and a farm, and plaintiff did not agree to release his claim for the purchase price of the mining claim until the title to the farm had been cleared and a deed given him, which latter agreement was not in writing, and was

without consideration, such latter agreement was not binding upon either party, at law or in equity, and did not prevent a right of recovery against a representative of the estate for the amount due for the claim. —Bull v. Payne, 47 Or. 580, 84 Pac. 697, 699. In an action against an executor on a claim against his decedent, it is no defense that the payment of such claim would exhaust the assets of the estate.—Grubbe v. Grubbe, 26 Or. 363, 38 Pac. 182, 183, 184. A defendant administrator, in an action upon the claim of his decedent, that has been barred by the statute of limitations, has no power to bind the estate by waiving the defense of such statute. The administrator is prohibited from allowing or paying any claim that is barred, and for him to waive the defense of the statute of limitations would be to allow such a claim to be collected. In other words, the administrator would be fraudulently paying a claim that is barred. No such consent could be given so as to bind the estate. This rule is applicable to all trustees.—Vrooman v. Li Po Tai, 113 Cal. 302, 45 Pac. 470, 472. If a claim against the estate of a deceased person has been presented to the executor or administrator, and allowed by him within the prescribed statutory time after its presentation, no action can be maintained thereon until that time has elapsed after its presentation to the judge, unless he rejects it within that period.—Nally v. McDonald, 66 Cal. 530, 532, 6 Pac. 390.

(2) Construction of statutes.—The statute giving to the owner of a rejected claim the right to bring, within a limited time, an action on the claim, does not restrict the owner to that action, so as to exclude his right to move for an opening of the order by which the rejection was approved.—In re Stroup's Estate (S. D.), 166 N. W. 155. If a person, to whom money is owing from another, dies, and in the settlement of his estate the claim is distributed to an heir or legatee, the latter can not sue the debtor, alleging that he is assignee of a judgment against him.—Lapique v. Plummer, 168 Cal. 310, 142 Pac. 1079. If permission is given to present a claim, as within the exception provided for in section 1493 of the Code of Civil Procedure of California, and such claim is thereafter allowed and approved by the court in probate, it stands as other allowed claims, a legal charge against the estate; but if such permission is denied, it is equivalent to a rejection of the claim, and then takes the position as any rejected claim, and must be established by action, and the claimant must then affirmatively establish all matters which it was essential for him to prove in the first instance to the judge or court to whom application for permission to present the claim was made.—Tropico Land, etc., Co. v. Lambourn, 170 Cal. 33, 43, 148 Pac. 206. Legal presentation of a claim against an estate must be made in the manner prescribed in section 171, Probate Code, and an omission to comply with the requirements of any one of the clauses of that section renders the affidavit materially defective and the presentation itself ineffectual for the purpose of maintaining an action on the claim.—Dakota Nat. Bank v. Kleinschmidt, 33 S. D. 132, 138, 144 N. W. 934. Under the provisions of section 178, Probate

Code, until presented, properly authenticated in the manner prescribed in section 171, Probate Code, and rejected by the administrator, a claim against an estate has no judicial standing and can not be made the foundation for an action having for its purpose the collection of such a claim out of the assets of the estate.—Dakota Nat. Bank v. Kleinschmidt, 33 S. D. 132, 139, 144 N. W. 934. Under the Alaskan code which provides that a claim rejected by the administrator of an estate shall be heard and determined in a summary manner by the district court or a judge thereof, neither party is entitled to a jury trial in the district court, under the seventh amendment to the federal constitution.—Esterly v. Rua (Alaska), 122 Fed. 609, 613, 58 C. C. A. 548. An action required to be brought under the provisions of section 5468, Revised Codes of Idaho of 1909, to recover a rejected claim, if it is a demand for money, is an action at law and the rejection of the same by the administrator does not change the character of the claim or of the action required to be brought.—Idaho Trust Co. v. Miller, 16 Ida. 308, 102 Pac. 360.

(3) **Method of trial.**—One who presents a claim against a decedent's estate in Oregon is entitled to a jury trial; while a probate matter is in the nature of an equity proceeding, the trial of a claim against an administrator is a trial at law, and the statute of that state does not preclude a jury trial in such a case.—In re McCormick's Estate; Branch v. McCormick, 72 Or. 608, 611, 143 Pac. 915, 144 Pac. 425. The method of trial provided in section 1241, L. O. L., is not exclusive; after the claim, or demand upon which it is based, has been presented to the executor or administrator, and by him disallowed, suit thereon may be brought in the circuit court, under section 386, L. O. L.—In re McCormick's Estate; Branch v. McCormick's Estate, 72 Or. 608, 611, 143 Pac. 915, 144 Pac. 425. Where, in the matter of a claim against an estate, the items are submitted to a jury for them to determine whether the claim is a valid one, the question of both the value and legality of the various items of claim is before the jury.—Estate of Weir, 168 Cal. 330, 143 Pac. 612. An instruction that when a party presents to an administrator a claim in proper form, it is necessary for the party to request the administrator either to allow or to reject it, is erroneous.—Spaulding v. Thompson, 60 Okla. 136, 159 Pac. 509.

(4) **Jurisdiction.**—The superior court has no jurisdiction of a suit on a note against the estate of a decedent, where the demand, exclusive of interest, does not amount to $300; and the fact that the claim upon the note, with accrued interest, amounts to over $300 when presented to the administrator, does not change the result. The action is upon the note. It is made necessary, under the statute, to present a claim of this kind to the representative of the deceased before an action can be maintained upon it, but when the action is brought it is upon the original claim or note. The presentation of the claim in no way changes the nature of the demand, nor the form in which the action must be

brought.—Gallagher v. McGraw, 132 Cal. 601, 64 Pac. 1080. If a defendant executor or administrator, in an action upon a claim against the estate, makes a voluntary appearance, the court acquires jurisdiction over him with the same effect as if he had been brought in by a summons upon him at that time.—Union Sav. Bank v. Barrett, 132 Cal. 453, 455, 64 Pac. 713, 1071. The "proper court" is the one that has jurisdiction, under the constitution and laws of this state, to hear and determine a civil action for the recovery of the debt sued on; and, if the amount claimed is within the jurisdiction of a justice's or probate court, an action on the rejected claim may be brought therein; if it is not, the action must be brought in the proper district court.—Idaho Trust Co. v. Miller, 16 Ida. 308, 311, 102 Pac. 360.

(5) **Presentation, when necessary.**—It is a condition precedent to the right to maintain an action on a claim against the estate of a deceased person where recourse is had to such estate alone, that such claim be first presented to the executor or administrator for allowance or rejection.—Dodson v. Nevitt, 5 Mont. 518, 6 Pac. 358, 359; Eustace v. Johns, 38 Cal. 3. Or, as it is sometimes expressed, no action can be maintained upon a simple money demand or claim against an estate, whether such demand or claim be based upon a simple or special contract, or any other legitimate basis for a claim or demand payable out of the general assets, until the same has been duly presented to the executor or administrator for allowance, and by him disallowed or retained for more than the time specified in the statute, without the indorsement of his action thereon.—Eustace v. Johns, 38 Cal. 3, 23. No action can be maintained on a claim if there has been no legal presentation of it within the time prescribed.—Zachary v. Chambers, 1 Or. 321. If the claim has been rejected for want of verification, as not having been made before an officer authoried to administer oaths, no action can be maintained against the executor or administrator upon such claim.—Winder v. Hendricks, 56 Cal. 464. Thus a claim in favor of the United States, against the estate of a decedent, can not be sued on unless it has been properly presented. When the government of the United States is compelled to come into court to enforce its rights, it must come as any other suitor, and the proceeding in such action must be in accordance with the local laws in force when the suit is commenced.—United States v. Hailey, 2 Ida. 26, 3 Pac. 263. No action can be maintained by a ward against the administrator of his deceased guardian to recover a sum of money received by the guardian in trust, where the claim was never presented for allowance, and it is not shown that the money received as the guardian of plaintiff ever came into the hands of defendant as administrator or otherwise.—Gillespie v. Winn, 65 Cal. 429, 430, 4 Pac. 411. And a surviving partner can not bring suit against the administrator of his deceased partner for his interest in the assets of the same, unless he has first presented his claim to the executor or administrator within the time prescribed by the statute.—McKay v. Joy, 2 Cal. Unrep. 639,

9 Pac. 940. An action can not be maintained against the representative of a deceased stockholder of a mining corporation, by reason of his individual liability for its debts, unless the claim arising therefrom was presented to his executors or administrators for allowance within the time prescribed by statute.—Davidson v. Rankin, 34 Cal. 503, 506. And no action can lie to foreclose a laborer's lien on logs, against the executor of a deceased person, unless the claim has first been presented to the executor or administrator of decedent's estate.—Casey v. Ault, 4 Wash. 167, 170, 32 Pac. 294. No action can be maintained upon a claim until it is first presented, save in excepted cases, but the California statute does not require that the executor or administrator must reject the claim before an action can be maintained upon it.—Cowgill v. Dinwiddie, 98 Cal. 481, 486, 33 Pac. 439. Under the Montana statute, both the presentation and the rejection of a claim are necessary before an action can be maintained thereon; and a complaint which alleges a promise to pay, and simply the presentation of a claim against the estate, fails to state a cause of action.—Brown v. Daly, 33 Mont. 523, 84 Pac. 883, 884. In an action against an estate upon a rejected claim the plaintiff can not recover upon any other cause of action than the one set up in the claim which has been presented and rejected.—Bechtel v. Chase, 156 Cal. 707, 106 Pac. 81. If a lunatic, who is a woman, has a claim against an estate, and the person who is her guardian happens to be also the administrator of that estate, the fact that such person suggests that a guardian ad litem be appointed to push the claim by action, after its rejection, is no ground for asking for a dismissal.—Haberly v. Haberly, 27 Cal. App. 139, 149 Pac. 53. Where a woman was a lunatic and a claim by her against the estate of her son was rejected by the court because it was presented by her guardian, who was also the administrator of the estate, this necessarily relegated her to an action upon the claim; the fact that the guardian of her person and estate happened to be at the same time the administrator of the deceased could not deprive her of the remedy that she sought.—Haberly v. Haberly, 27 Cal. App. 139, 149 Pac. 53. A claim against the estate of a deceased person can be established only: (1) by being first presented to and allowed by the executor or administrator, and then presented to and approved by the county judge; or (2), by judgment in an action thereon, against the personal representative in the proper court.—In re Barnett's Estate, 52 Okla. 623, 627, 153 Pac. 653. Section 178, Probate Code of South Dakota, requires the holder of a claim against an estate to present the same to the executor or administrator before an action may be maintained thereon, and such presentation is a fact essential to the jurisdiction of the court and must be alleged in the complaint, and a failure to do so may be taken advantage of at any stage of the proceedings, and on appeal, and such objection is not waived by failure to demur.—Dakota Nat. Bank v. Kleinschmidt, 33 S. D. 132, 138, 144 N. W. 934.

(6) No presentation necessary when.—As the statute which relates to the presentation of claims against estates before actions can be maintained thereon relates to claims arising upon contracts, other actions do not come within the rule. Thus no presentation of a claim is necessary before the bringing of an action to recover damages for wrongful acts.—Hardin v. Sin Claire, 115 Cal. 460, 464, 47 Pac. 363. No presentation need be made in an action which is purely equitable, and in which purely equitable relief is sought.—Toulouse v. Burkett, 2 Ida. 184, 10 Pac. 26, 28; Tyler v. Mayre, 95 Cal. 160, 168, 27 Pac. 160, 30 Pac. 196. A claim in favor of the attorney of an assignor, in trust, against the administrator of the assignee, in trust, need not be presented before suit.—Tyler v. Mayre, 95 Cal. 160, 168, 27 Pac. 160, 30 Pac. 196. So a pledgee is not obliged to present his claim to the administrator of the pledgor, unless he seeks recourse against other property of the estate than that pledged.—Estate of Kibbe, 57 Cal. 407, 408. The death of the grantor in a trust deed does not operate as a revocation of the power of sale contained in the deed, nor in any manner limit the effect of the deed. Hence, a failure to present claims secured by such deed to the administrator of the deceased furnishes no ground for a court of equity to cancel the deed.—More v. Calkins, 95 Cal. 435, 438, 29 Am. St. Rep. 128, 30 Pac. 583. Liens in general may be foreclosed without presentment of a claim against the estate, where no recourse against other property is waived and no deficiency judgment is sought.—Schadt v. Heppe, 45 Cal. 433, 437. Where expenditures have been made for taxes and insurance, for the protection of property, subsequent to the presentation of a mortgage claim to the executor of the deceased mortgagor, they may properly be allowed on the foreclosure without demand or the presentation of a claim therefor.—Humboldt S. & L. Soc. v. Burnham, 111 Cal. 343, 346, 43 Pac. 971. An action may be maintained without the presentment of a claim where the specific thing sued for is not a part of the decedent's estate. An action will lie whenever the thing demanded can be identified in specie as the property of another.— Sprague v. Walton, 145 Cal. 228, 78 Pac. 645, 647. In Colorado, although the estate is in course of administration in the county court, a plaintiff is not for this reason required to present his claim to that court for allowance, but, at his option, may bring a suit thereon in the district court, without first having presented his claim to the county court.— Jones v. Perot, 19 Colo. 141, 34 Pac. 728, 731. An action against a special administrator to recover damages for the maintenance of a nuisance may be maintained without the presentation of a claim against the estate for such wrongful act.—Hardin v. Sin Claire, 115 Cal. 460, 47 Pac. 363, 364. A claim against the estate of a decedent, for property pledged, may be foreclosed without any presentation of a claim against the estate, if all recourse against the estate is expressly waived in the complaint.—Building and Loan Assoc. v. King, 83 Cal. 440, 444, 23 Pac. 376; Estate of Galland, 92 Cal. 293, 294, 28 Pac. 287. A claim for damages against the estate of a deceased person, for special injury caused by the destruction of a public highway maintained by the deceased up to the time of his death, does not arise upon contract, and need not be presented to his personal representative prior to the bringing of suit thereon.—Leverone v. Weakley, 155 Cal. 395, 101 Pac. 304. A deceased wife's administrator may, on the death of the husband, sue the latter's executor to recover her separate estate, without first having presented a claim.—Hatch v. Hatch, 46 Utah 116, 131, 148 Pac. 1096.

(7) **Who may defend.**—The assignee of an heir has sufficient interest in an estate to entitle him to intervene and defend against a claim against the estate.—Gordon Reduction Co. v. Loomer, 50 Colo. 409, 115 Pac. 718.

(8) **Contingent claims.**—A contingent claim against the estate of a deceased person is a claim "not due." An action upon a rejected contingent claim, brought after such rejection, but before the claim has become due, is pemature, and can not be sustained. An action upon a rejected contingent claim must be brought within the prescribed statutory time after it becomes due; and if it never becomes due, no action can be sustained thereon.—Morse v. Steele, 132 Cal. 456, 458, 64 Pac. 690. If a claim presented against the estate of a decedent as a guarantor of the faithful performance of the covenants of a lease is the foundation of an action, the complaint, upon its face, must show a present liability of the guarantor. It must show a presentation and rejection of the claim upon which the action is brought, or a legal reason excusing such presentation and rejection. If the complaint fails to do this, there can be no recovery.—Fratt v. Hunt, 108 Cal. 288, 294, 41 Pac. 12. An action upon a contingent claim is barred, unless the same was presented within the time limited by the notice to creditors.—Verdier v. Roach, 96 Cal. 467, 479, 31 Pac. 554. An action upon a rejected claim against the estate of a deceased person, based upon a promise to pay money when certain land is sold, is upon a contingent claim, and can not be maintained before the land is sold. If any action can be maintained thereon at all, it must be within two months, or other specified statutory time after the claim becomes due.—Brooks v. Lawson, 136 Cal. 10, 13, 68 Pac. 97. The term "any contingent claim," as used in the statute of the state of Nevada, relative to distribution after final account, would, in proceedings in the settlement of the estate of a minor, include the bond given by the guardian of the minor conditioned for the faithful performance of his duties.—Pruett v. Caddigan, 42 Nev. 329, 176 Pac. 787. Where a claim filed against an estate is rejected by the executor because on its face it is yet to become due, the claimant must wait until it is due before bringing action.—Miller v. Miller, 171 Cal. 269, 152 Pac. 728.

child from filing a claim against the estate.—In re Kirfel's Estate, 37 S. D. 292, 394, 157 N. W. 1057. It may be true that a woman, who devotes fifteen years of her life to caring for her mother, is not entitled to file a claim for her services against the estate, on her mother's death; but, if she has believed herself so entitled, the existence of the belief and expectation and the question of her good faith are for the jury to consider, in an action by her to enforce an agreement whereby she was induced to withhold the filing of such a claim.—Norman v. Miller (S. D.), 167 N. W. 391. Where in proceedings to establish a claim against a decedent's estate for services rendered the evidence of the quality and amount of the service are indefinite and there is no evidence of the value of the services, no part of the claim should be allowed.—Carl v. Northcott, 48 Colo. 47, 108 Pac. 994. All contracts for personal services which can be performed only during the lifetime of the party contracting are subject to the implied condition that he shall be alive to perform them, and should he die his executor is not liable in an action for the breach of contract occasioned by his death.— Mendenhall v. Davis, 52 Wash. 169, 17 Ann. Cas. 179, 21 L. R. A. (N. S.) 914, 100 Pac. 336, 338. A contract for personal services did not require the performance by the grantee, personally and individually, of the obligations to occupy, cultivate, and improve the land, within the meaning of the rule that contracts to perform personal acts are discharged by the death or disability of the person who was to perform the acts. That rule does not apply where the services are of such a character that they may be as well performed by others, nor where the contract by its terms shows that performance by others was contemplated. The obligations to occupy, cultivate, and improve the land and to pay the stipulated annual amount could be performed by the surviving members of the family of the grantee. This construction of the contract finds support in the fact that for several years after the death of the grantee the grantor accepted such payments from them.—Husheon v. Kelley, 162 Cal. 656, 124 Pac. 231. Where the only objection made to a claim for services is that the claimant was fully paid in the decedent's lifetime, this is the only issue open for consideration.—Irvine v. Beck, 62 Or. 593, 597, 125 Pac. 832.

(10) Same. Gratuitous.—Where a person, as nurse, companion, etc., rendered services to a decedent before his death, or voluntarily performed work or made voluntary payments, and no express contract to pay therefor appears, the law will not imply a contract to pay therefor, especially where the one who rendered such services or performed such work, or made such payments, is a member of the family of the employer; and, in order to sustain an action therefor, it must be proved, on the presentation of a claim against the estate, that there was an understanding that such services should be paid for. But it is not necessary that such proof be made of a direct and positive contract. It is sufficient that proof be made of words, acts, and conduct of the parties, and circumstances from which the inference may follow that

there was an understanding that the services were not to be rendered gratuitously. When such is the case, there is a contract upon which the value of the services can be recovered, and it is for the jury to say, from all the conduct of the parties, and from the circumstances in evidence, whether there was in fact such an understanding and agreement. In the absence of proof of any such agreement there can be no recovery.—Hodge v. Hodge, 47 Wash. 196, 11 L. R. A. (N. S.) 873, 91 Pac. 764, 765; Lichtenberg v. McGlynn, 105 Cal. 45, 38 Pac. 541; McGlew v. McDade, 146 Cal. 553, 80 Pac. 695. Evidence held sufficient to sustain finding of no implied contract to pay for care and support of mother.—Crane v. Derrick, 157 Cal. 667, 109 Pac. 31.

(11) Same. Not gratuitous.—The mere fact that persons, since deceased, for whom others were put to labor, care, and expense during illness, were relation of such others, does not deprive the latter of the right to file a claim for compensation if there were circumstances from which an implied contract could arise.—Higgs v. Bigelow, 39 S. D. 359, 164 N. W. 89. A woman who, at the request of her aged and infirm grandmother, had taken up her abode with the latter and cared for her until her death, her services in that connection having been unusual, arduous, and disagreeable, in recognition of which the patient had promised to "make it right" to her, may, in case the patient dies without redeeming the promise, recover her compensation from the estate.—Wilkin v. O'Brien (Utah), 176 Pac. 853. An express promise by a sick and infirm parent, made to a child or grandchild, to pay for services performed or to be performed during the last sickness, is not necessary in order that the attendant may afterward recover compensation, but the promise may be inferred.—Wilkin v. O'Brien (Utah), 176 Pac. 853. The fact that the nurse was the wife of a nephew of the deceased, and that she and her husband resided in the home of the deceased during the time the services were rendered, raises no presumption that the services were gratuitous.—Estate of Rohrer, 160 Cal. 574, Ann. Cas. 1913A, 479, 117 Pac. 672. Where father and son made an oral agreement that if the son would take care of the father and his wife (the son's mother) and manage his ranch so long as the father and mother should live, he would leave the ranch to his son at his death and a will was made accordingly and the son performed his part of the agreement, but later, after the death of his wife, the father sold the ranch and left the state and afterwards died, and his will had disappeared, it was held that the son had a claim on quantum meruit against the father's estate for the value of his services.—Pool v. Pool, 21 Wyo. 435, 133 Pac. 372, 374. As a general rule a child who is living with its parents is not entitled to compensation for services rendered to the parent, even though the child be an adult or otherwise emancipated, for such services are presumed to be gratuitous, and a promise on the part of the parent to pay for them will not be implied from their mere rendition. But if from all the facts and circumstances surrounding the parties and under which the services were rendered,

it can be reasonably inferred that the child expected to receive remuneration and the parent intended to pay for the services, a promise to pay therefor may be implied.—Mathias v. Tingey, 39 Utah 561, 38 L. R. A. (N. S.) 749, 118 Pac. 782. Under an oral agreement a girl was received into the home of decedent to live with and work for him until the death of himself and wife, in consideration of which she was to receive the property of decedent at his death. In execution of this agreement she faithfully served decedent for twenty-two and one-half years and until her discharge a few years before his death, when he paid her $200 on account and at the same time fraudulently induced her to sign a receipt containing a provision of which she was not aware, acknowledging payment in full of all debts and demands, and when he died it was found that no provision had been made by will or otherwise to compensate her for her services under agreement. Held (1) that the contract, though not in writing, was enforceable; (2) that as performance of the contract was to be completed and compensation paid at the death of decedent and his wife the statute of limitations would not ordinarily begin to run on her cause of action for her services until that event transpired. The fact that there was a renunciation of the contract by the decedent before his death did not compel her to end the contract relation. She was at liberty to keep the contract alive and await the time for final performance specified therein.—Heery v. Reed, 80 Kan. 380, 102 Pac. 846. The fact that the services to be performed under a contract for personal services were to be, or were, performed in a foreign country, does not affect plaintiff's right to maintain an action in the courts of this state against an administrator appointed here. Where the contract of the deceased is of an executory nature, and the personal representative can fairly and sufficiently execute all the deceased could have done, he may do so, and enforce the contract; e converso, the personal representative is bound to complete such a contract, and if he does not, may be made to pay damages out of the assets of the estate.—McCann v. Pennie, 100 Cal. 547, 551, 35 Pac. 158. The fact that a husband is liable for necessary services rendered to the wife does not preclude her from making any contract which she sees fit in respect to those matters to be compensated out of her estate.—Bonebrake v. Tauer, 67 Kan. 827, 72 Pac. 521. When a daughter nurses and cares for her mother for several years, including her last sickness, under an express contract that payment for such services will be provided for in the will of her mother, who dies intestate, the daughter may recover the reasonable value of such services from the estate of the deceased mother.—Griffith v. Robertson, 73 Kan. 666, 85 Pac. 748. And it is not essential that the evidence in support of such express contract shall consist of a formal offer and acceptance; it may be established, like other disputed facts, by competent testimony.—Griffith v. Robertson, 73 Kan. 666, 85 Pac. 748. A person employed as housekeeper, at an agreed price per week, can not recover from the estate of such employer, who dies during the employment, compensation for services as nurse in addition to her weekly wages as housekeeper, when it does not appear that any agreement was ever made to pay for such extra services, or that the employer had any knowledge that she expected to charge therefor.—Houghton v. Kittleman, 7 Kan. App. 207, 52 Pac. 898. In an action on a claim against the estate of a deceased person for services rendered at his request, the evidence must be confined to proof of services rendered within two years prior to the death of the decedent, as there is no right to allow a claim which has been barred by the statute of limitations.—Etchas v. Oreña, 127 Cal. 588, 592, 60 Pac. 45. If one has rendered services to a deceased person as nurse, and it appears that the decedent, by his will, bequeathed to such person a sum of money in consideration of, and in payment for, services during his last sickness, an action brought by such person to recover the value of such services rendered is a renunciation of the bequest, and an election by the plaintiff not to rely upon it as a payment for such services.—Smith v. Furnish, 70 Cal. 424, 428, 12 Pac. 392. The judgment against the administrator on a claim for services can only have the effect of a claim duly allowed against the estate to be paid in due course, and can not give the creditor any further rights. There is nothing in the mode of allowance which fixes the rank of a claim; and as there is no mode of allowance which can give a claim priority, it must follow that there can be no judgment establishing the validity of a claim which the administrator or court has refused to allow which can have that effect. The priority of claims must be determined by the probate court when the assets are finally marshaled, and the order of payment must be determined by that court. —McLean v. Crow, 88 Cal. 644, 647, 26 Pac. 596. Evidence that a testator desired to make payment for services rendered him by a nurse during his last illness, and to that end left her a legacy, which failed because she became a witness to the will, coupled with evidence that the nurse performed the services in the expectation of receiving compensation after the death of the testator, is sufficient to support a claim of the nurse for the reasonable value of her services.—Estate of Rohrer, 160 Cal. 574, Ann. Cas. 1913A, 479, 117 Pac. 672. It is held that no suspicion can arise as to the claim of the daughter for her services as a nurse to her mother under the facts appearing; and it must be presumed that any unknown circumstances, not disclosed by the record, were such as supported the fairness of the contract, and repelled any suspicion of its not having been made in good faith.—Wood v. James, 15 Cal. App. 253, 114 Pac. 587.

(12) Pleadings. Sufficiency of complaint.—In an action against an administrator upon a claim against the estate of a decedent, it is sufficient to aver non-payment by the deceased, and that the claim has been properly presented to and rejected by the administrator.— Wise v. Hogan, 77 Cal. 184, 188, 19 Pac. 278. A complaint in an action by an administrator upon a claim against the estate of another person is sufficient against the objection that the administrative characters of the plaintiff and defendant are not sufficiently alleged, where, as to the plaintiff, the death of his intestate is alleged, and further, that on a certain day a decree was duly given and made, in a designated court, upon which letters of administration upon the estate of the decedent named were issued by the said court, etc.; where the allegation as to the defendant is in effect the same; and where, as to each, the allegation is, "that he duly qualified and entered upon the discharge of his duties as such administrator, and has ever since been, and now is, the duly qualified and acting administrator," etc.—Wise v. Hogan, 77 Cal. 184, 189, 19 Pac. 278. The complaint in such a case is sufficient if it shows a subsisting liability in favor of the plaintiff, and is verified according to the statute. It is not necessary to set out therein the evidence upon which the claimant expects to recover.—Goltra v. Penland, 42 Or. 18, 69 Pac. 925, 926. The facts constituting the claim need not be set out with the same particularity required in a pleading, but may be stated in general terms; and if the claim is rejected, and an action is brought thereon, it is sufficient, if it appears that it is founded on the same claim or demand as that presented to the erecutor or administrator.—Goltra v. Penland, 42 Or. 18, 69 Pac. 925, 926; Pollitz v. Wickersham, 150 Cal. 238, 88 Pac. 911, 916. Although the details alleged in the complaint are more particular than is necessary, the complaint will support a recovery if it is upon the same cause of action set out in the claim, sets forth the same services, where the action is for the value of services, and states the same agreement referred to in the claim.—Thompson v. Oreña, 134 Cal. 26, 29, 66 Pac. 24. An averment of non-payment is necessary to the sufficiency of a complaint for money claimed to be due on a contract. This is on the ground that the failure to pay constitutes the breach of a contract, and gives a right of action. Hence, in an action on a claim against the estate of a decedent, it is sufficient to allege non-payment by the deceased, and that the claim has been properly presented to and rejected by the administrator. The non-payment by the debtor is a breach of the contract, and gives a cause of action. The subsequent presentation of the claim to the administrator is made necessary by the statute before an action can be maintained, but this does not render it necessary to allege that he has not paid the claim.—Wise v. Hogan, 77 Cal. 184, 188, 19 Pac. 278. A complaint in an action on an account against an executor is sufficient, as against the statute of limitations, where it does not appear upon the face of the complaint that the claim is barred. In such a case, that objection can not be raised by demurrer, and may be determined on the trial.—Wise v. Hogan, 77 Cal. 184, 19 Pac. 278, 280 (reversing Wise v. Hogan, 2 Cal. Unrep. 893, 18 Pac. 784). The complaint, based upon a claim against a decedent's estate, fails to state a cause of action, where it does not allege the due presentation of the claim sued upon.—Vanderpool v. Vanderpool, 48 Mont. 448, 453, 138 Pac. 772. While much liberality may be indulged in in sustaining a claim as not being so defective in

form as to render it void for ambiguity or uncertainty, where suit is
instituted upon such a claim, upon its rejection, the allegations of the
complaint ought to be sufficient to clarify an ambiguous or uncertain
statement contained in the claim as filed.—Hibbard v. Clark, 39 Nev.
230, 233, 156 Pac. 447. The rule that in an action against an individual
defendant a plaintiff is not required to allege facts constituting an
offset or counterclaim, is inapplicable to an action against an administrator upon a rejected claim against the estate, by reason of the
provisions of the statute requiring the claimant to credit upon the
claim all offsets in favor of the decedent known to the claimant.—Hibbard v. Clark, 39 Nev. 230, 233, 156 Pac. 447. A money demand against
the estate of a decedent can not be enforced unless a claim has first
been duly presented to the executor or administrator, and has been
rejected by him; hence, the complaint, in an action to enforce the
claim, must set forth such presentation and rejection.—Reed v. Reed,
178 Cal. 187, 172 Pac. 600. Where a sufficient claim was presented by
plaintiff against the estate of the deceased trustee for the amount of
the trust fund, and was rejected and a sufficient cause of action to
enforce the same was set forth in an amended complaint which re-
veals nothing inconsistent with the acknowledgment of the trust and
shows no laches on the part of the plaintiff, the court erred in sustaining a demurrer thereto and in entering judgment for the defendant,
and it must be reversed with directions to overrule the demurrer.—
Fleming v. Shay, 19 Cal. App. 276, 125 Pac. 761. Where a rejected
claim of a daughter was "for services as nurse for 204 days" between
certain dates "at $2.50 per day, $510," and the complaint therein alleged services between said dates "as nurse to Mary J. James, at her
request and for her use and benefit, performing at such time and times
in said capacity of a nurse all the duties of a nurse, including the cook-
ing, housekeeping, laundering, and caring for the said Mary J. James,
during her last illness, which services were and are reasonably worth
the sum of $2.50 per day," it is held that the duties of a nurse do
not include the particular services specified, but that, in the absence
of a demurrer for uncertainty, and in view of the admission of defendant and the finding of the court that her services as a nurse were
worth $2.50 per day, during the time claimed, the complaint may be
construed as so asserting.—Wood v. James, 15 Cal. App. 253, 114 Pac.
387. The Colorado statute makes formal pleadings in probate matters
unnecessary, so a claim against an estate that decedent "held in trust
and converted the sum of $2000, credit $500 paid on account, balance
$1500," was sufficient.—Brown's Estate v. Stair, 25 Colo. App. 140, 136
Pac. 1005. A complaint, in an action against an executor on a promissory note executed by the decedent, which alleges the non-payment of
the original obligation and its due presentation to and rejection by
the executor, sufficiently states a cause of action, and it is not necessary to further aver that the executor has not paid the claim.—Nicol
Co. v. Cameron, 23 Cal. App. 124, 137 Pac. 270. The claim sued upon

against the estate was properly admitted in evidence over the objection of the defendant. It was not necessary that such claim should
show on its face that it is not barred by the statute of limitations;
and in so far as the objection was directed to the formal sufficiency
of the claim, its general rejection in the first instance, without special
reason assigned, must be deemed a waiver of any formal defects
therein.—E. Martin & Co. v. Brosnan, 18 Cal. App. 477, 123 Pac. 550.

(13) Pleadings. Allegation as to presentation of claim.—In an action
upon a claim against the estate of a decedent, where it was not necessary to present such claim to the executor or administrator for allowance or rejection, it is not necessary that the plaintiff should set forth
in his complaint any presentation of the claim.—Security Sav. Bank v.
Connell, 65 Cal. 574, 4 Pac. 580; Toulouse v. Burkett, 2 Idaho 184,
10 Pac. 26. But in a case where it was necessary for the claimant
to present his claim against the estate, the allegation of presentation
of the claim becomes material to plaintiff's complaint, and must be
made and proved.—Rowland v. Madden, 72 Cal. 17, 20, 12 Pac. 226,
870. The presentation is sufficiently averred where the complaint alleges that the claim sued upon was presented to the administrator
within the time limited in the notice to creditors, and a copy of the
claim presented, with the verification annexed, together with the
indorsement thereon, is attached to the complaint.—Janin v. Browne,
59 Cal. 37, 42. So a general allegation of presentment to the executor
or administrator for the amount due and to become due, that the
claim was duly verified in all respects according to law, and was duly
allowed, and approved by the executor or administrator and judge, and
was duly filed, etc., is a sufficient averment of the ultimate fact of
presentation of the claim, as against a general demurrer, though the
claim is not set out, nor attached to the complaint; such allegation is
sufficient to authorize proof as to whether the claim, as presented,
was sufficient in form or was properly presented.—Humboldt Sav. &
L. Soc. v. Burnham, 111 Cal. 343, 345, 43 Pac. 971. In an action on a
claim against the estate of a deceased person, the complaint must
show that the claim had been first presented to the executor or administrator, in order to state a cause of action.—Foley v. McDonnell, 48
Wash. 272, 93 Pac. 321, 322. In a suit on a claim against the estate
of a deceased person, the complaint, stating a cause of action sound-
ing in contract, fails to state a cause of action if it does not aver
that a claim for the cause of action sued on had been presented to the
administrator.—Burke v. Maguire, 154 Cal. 456, 98 Pac. 21. A failure
to make an averment in the complaint, in an action on a claim against
the estate of a decedent, that it was presented to the executor or administrator and rejected, where presentment is necessary, makes the
complaint demurrable.—Morse v. Steele, 149 Cal. 303, 86 Pac. 693. An
allegation of presentment, though defectively stated, is good as against
a general demurrer for want of facts.—Wise v. Hogan, 77 Cal. 184, 188,
19 Pac. 278; Chase v. Evoy, 58 Cal. 348. Where the complaint alleges.

that the claim was presented in due form, but contains no allegation touching the publication of notice to creditors, the complaint is not demurrable for not alleging that the plaintiff presented his claim within the time limited in the notice to creditors.—McCann v. Pennie, 100 Cal. 547, 552, 35 Pac. 158. It is not necessary, in the complaint on a claim against the estate of a decedent, to allege that notice to creditors has been published. It is not the publication of notice which is the prerequisite to the maintenance of an action on a claim, but the proper presentation of the claim and its rejection.—Harp v. Calahan, 46 Cal. 222, 233; Janin v. Browne, 59 Cal. 37, 43. Hence an allegation, in such complaint, that the executor or administrator had waived the presentation of the claim for allowance is irrelevant and immaterial, as he has no power to waive the necessity of the presentment of the claim for allowance and rejection.—Harp v. Calahan, 46 Cal. 222, 233. Where a person, suing as an executor, alleges, in his complaint against the administrator of another estate, that the plaintiff caused to be presented to this administrator, as such, a claim duly verified, according to the law, claiming the sum of $1500 as a lawful charge against said estate, the allegation is one that the plaintiff presented the claim both individually and as an executor.—Harvey v. Pocock, 92 Wash. 625, 159 Pac. 771. If an executor brings ejectment, and an intervener alleges adverse possession under a mortgage, not suing the decedent's estate upon the mortgage notes, but asking for alternative relief that they be paid as a condition of his surrender of possession such intervener is not required to plead compliance with the statute as to the presentation of claims against the estates of decedents.—Cameron v. Ah Quong, 175 Cal. 377, 165 Pac. 961. The necessity of proving the presentation and rejection of a claim against a decedent's estate, and of suit begun within the statutory time from such rejection, is upon the plaintiff, as a part of the proof of his cause of action, irrespective of defendant's answer pleading the statute of non-claim.—Mann v. Redmon, 27 N. D. 346, 145 N. W. 1031.

(14) **Pleadings. Amendment of complaint.**—In an action against the estate of a decedent, it is error to refuse the plaintiff permission to amend his complaint, if defectively stated, so as to state properly his cause of action.—Cowdery v. McChesney, 124 Cal. 363, 365, 57 Pac. 221; Anglo-Californian Bank v. Field, 146 Cal. 644, 656, 80 Pac. 1080; Vanderslice v. Matthews, 79 Cal. 273, 277, 21 Pac. 748; but the complaint can not be amended so as to set up a new or different cause of action.—Morehouse v. Morehouse, 140 Cal. 88, 94, 73 Pac. 738. The plaintiff should be permitted to amend his complaint by inserting a waiver of all recourse against the property of the estate, other than that described in the complaint.—Anglo-Californian Bank v. Field, 146 Cal. 644, 656, 80 Pac. 1080. The only way in which an action can be brought against an estate is to sue the administrator or executor in his representative capacity; and the rule is, that he can not be sued in the same action upon his individual or personal liability, and in his

representative capacity. Hence, if a complaint has been brought against him in his representative capacity, it can not be so amended as to constitute an action against him individually, as that would be an entire change of the party defendant, and a different suit.—Sterrett v. Barker, 119 Cal. 492, 494, 495, 51 Pac. 695. The plaintiff in an action upon a claim against the estate of a decedent can recover only upon the claim as presented. He can not recover upon any other cause of action.—Lichtenberg v. McGlynn, 105 Cal. 45, 47, 38 Pac. 541; McGrath v. Carroll, 110 Cal. 79, 84, 42 Pac. 466; Barthe v. Rogers, 127 Cal. 52, 54, 59 Pac. 310; Etchas v. Oreña, 127 Cal. 588, 594, 60 Pac. 45; Brooks v. Lawson, 136 Cal. 10, 13, 68 Pac. 97. If the claim is upon a note, the plaintiff can not change the nature of the demand, with reference to the jurisdiction of an action upon the note for the amount of the claim.—Gallagher v. McGraw, 132 Cal. 601, 602, 64 Pac. 1080. No other cause of action can be properly alleged or proved, than that stated in the claim presented and passed upon by the executor.—Etchas v. Oreña, 127 Cal. 588, 592, 60 Pac. 45. If the action is upon an original oral promise, against which the statute of limitations had run before the death of the decedent, the recovery is limited to the claim presented, and the complaint can not be amended to set up a new cause of action upon a subsequent conditional promise.—Morehouse v. Morehouse, 140 Cal. 88, 92, 73 Pac. 738, 739. If the action is upon a claim for certain specified services, for which specific compensation was demanded, he can not recover a greater amount having no foundation in the claim as presented.—Barthe v. Rogers, 127 Cal. 52, 54, 59 Pac. 310.

(15) Pleadings. Answer. Bill of particulars.—In an action upon a claim against an estate, an allegation that the claim, duly verified, had been presented, is sufficiently denied by an affirmative allegation in the answer that the claim was not verified or presented as required by the statute.—Derby & Co. v. Jackman, 89 Cal. 1, 4, 26 Pac. 610; and see Rowland v. Madden, 72 Cal. 17, 20, 12 Pac. 226, 870. Non-payment should be presumed from the alleged fact of the rejection of the claim.—Wise v. Hogan, 77 Cal. 184, 188, 19 Pac. 278. A party suing on an account need not set forth specifically the items of the indebtedness. If the defendant is not satisfied with the general allegation of indebtedness, he may, within a specified time, demand a copy of the plaintiff's account. If he fails to avail himself of the right thus given him, he can not be heard to say that the complaint is insufficient on the ground of uncertainty in that respect, and executors and administrators are governed by this rule of practice.—Wise v. Hogan, 77 Cal. 184, 186, 19 Pac. 278. Where the allegation was that the claim presented "was duly verified by the oath of plaintiff, in the form prescribed by law, an objection that the complaint does not state facts sufficient to constitute a cause of action, because "it fails to show the due presentation of the claim to the administratrix" of the estate of the deceased is untenable.—Chase v. Evoy, 58 Cal. 348, 352; and see Guerian v.

Joyce, 183 Cal. 405, 408, 65 Pac. 972, for a much better allegation as to verification and presentment of the claim than did the complaint in the case last cited. In an action on a claim rejected by an administrator, an answer, pleading the statute of limitations, which alleges that the cause of action therein set forth did not accrue within six years from the commencement of the action is sufficient, without alleging that deceased had been a resident of the state for six years prior to his death.—Saxton v. Musselman, 17 S. D. 35, 95 N. W. 291, 292.

(16) Pleadings. Variance.—If the claim sued upon can be reconciled with the claim as presented to the executor or administrator, the recovery is upon the same cause of action as that set up in the claim; and the fact that plaintiff, in his complaint, has segregated and lumped certain items of the claim, without increasing or diminishing the amount of any item, and without alleging any different contract as to liability on any items other than those that appear on the face of the complaint, does not constitute a material variance.— Enscoe v. Fletcher, 1 Cal. App. 659, 662, 82 Pac. 1075. While the recovery must be had on the same cause of action as that set up in the claim, and while no other or different contract or cause of action can be alleged or proved, yet, where the action is upon the identical notes rejected, and additional facts stated in the complaint are merely explanatory of the demand, and no different contract is stated than that set forth in the claim, the cause of action is upon the claim.—Enscoe v. Fletcher, 1 Cal. App. 659, 82 Pac. 1075. Where the cause of action established by the findings is precisely the cause of action attempted to be set out in the claim and in the complaint, and by all, the claim asserted is one for money advanced by plaintiffs to the use of the decedent, which he had agreed to pay, there is no material variance.—Pollitz v. Wickersham, 150 Cal. 238, 88 Pac. 911, 916. In Cheney v. McGarvin, 7 Cal. App. 71, 93 Pac. 386, 387, an order granting a new trial on the ground of a variance between the claim presented against the estate of a decedent and the proof adduced in an action commenced on the claim by the plaintiff within the statutory time was reversed on the ground that there was no variance. Section 7529, Revised Codes of Montana, provides that if a claim against an estate in probate be founded upon a bond, bill, note, or other instrument, a copy thereof must accompany the claim and the original must be exhibited if demanded, unless it be lost or destroyed, in which case the claim must be accompanied by an affidavit containing a copy or particular description of the instrument, so that where the claim as presented was on an open account for money loaned and was rejected and suit was afterward brought for the same claim as on a note, a copy thereof being set out in the complaint, it was held that there was a fatal variance and the statutes of nonclaim could be successfully set up as a defense to the action.—Vanderpool v. Vanderpool, 48 Mont. 448, 138 Pac. 772, 773. Under section 1500 of the Code of Civil Procedure of California, requiring the presen-

tation of claims to representatives, actions against an estate must be on the same cause of action set up in the rejected claim.—Bechtel v. Chase, 156 Cal. 707, 106 Pac. 81. The plaintiff who had filed a claim for goods sold held not entitled to amend at the trial so as to authorize recovery for fraud inducing an exchange of property.—Bechtel v. Chase, 156 Cal. 707, 106 Pac. 81. Where complaint for services was on a quantum meruit, while the proof was on an express contract, the variance was fatal.—Eidinger v. Swigart, 13 Cal. App. 667, 110 Pac. 521.

(17) Parties. Administrator, only, is necessary when.—In an action to enforce claims of liens against an estate, where the same might have been maintained against the deceased, if living, the only necessary party defendant is the administrator. The heirs of the decedent need not be joined, and this applies to an action to foreclose a mortgage executed by the decedent.—McCaughey v. Lyall, 152 Cal. 615, 93 Pac. 681, 682. An administrator of a co-surety may be joined as defendant with the surviving sureties in an action on an indemnity bond.—City of Spokane v. Costello, 57 Wash. 183, 106 Pac. 764, 767. The joinder of heirs is not necessary in action against executrix to enforce liability of estate as stockholder, such liability being contractual, within the California Code Civ. Proc., section 1532, providing that actions founded on contract may be enforced against representative where they might have been maintained against decedent.— Miller v. Katz, 10 Cal. App. 576, 102 Pac. 946.

(18) Evidence. In general.—The only way that an account can be proved, ordinarily, is by establishing by evidence the several items of the same, and the oral evidence of persons having personal knowledge of the transactions is the best evidence of the items, unless there is something to indicate that such items accrued in pursuance of, or are the result of, a written contract between the parties. The fact that one or both of the parties kept a book-account of their transactions does not affect the rule of evidence, and the oral testimony of eye and ear witnesses to the transactions in which the various items of an account accrued is still primary and not secondary evidence of such items. The books themselves are secondary or supplementary evidence.—Cowdery v. McChesney, 124 Cal. 363, 365, 57 Pac. 221. In an action on a rejected claim against the estate of a decedent, it is proper to admit in evidence, as tending to discredit plaintiff's claim, a letter of the plaintiff to third persons bearing directly upon the transaction in controversy, and showing other unpaid claims in his favor against the estate amounting to a larger sum.—Sanguinetti v. Pelligrini, 2 Cal. App. 294, 296, 83 Pac. 293. Where a daughter gave her father a general power of attorney, authorizing him to sell and convey her lands, and to manage the proceeds without any restrictions whatever, and he sold the land many years prior to his death, without notifying her of such fact, and she presented a

claim against his estate on her demand, which was denied, and afterwards commenced suit upon the claim, in which she alleged and proved the foregoing facts, she is entitled to recover, in the absence of proof by the defense showing that the agency had been terminated more than six years prior to the commencement of the action. The agency was a continuing one, and plaintiff had a right to expect that, in case her property had been sold, the proceeds had been managed by him for her benefit.—Quinn v. Gross, 24 Or. 147, 33 Pac. 535, 536, 537. In an action against the estate of a decedent, evidence that the plaintiff had given the decedent a check, and that the latter had collected it, is not proof of a loan to the decedent, nor sufficient to establish a claim against his estate.—Dickey v. Dickey, 8 Colo. App. 141, 45 Pac. 228. As to what evidence, other than that of plaintiff, is insufficient to establish a claim upon a note given by a decedent, see Harding v. Grin, 25 Or. 506, 36 Pac. 634. The proof of a fact admitted by the pleadings is harmless error. Hence, in a claim against the estate of a decedent, the introduction of his will in evidence is harmless error, where no issue is made upon its provisions.—Bonebrake v. Tauer, 67 Kan. 827, 72 Pac. 521, 522. As to evidence sufficient to sustain a finding that the claim sued on arose from a debt of a firm of which 'the decedent was a partner, see In re Morgan's Estate, 46 Or. 233, 77 Pac. 608. In an action upon a note against the estate of decedent, it is proper to admit the note in evidence, where the holder has testified that no part of the principal or interest coupons attached thereto have been paid, but that decedent had paid other interest coupons amounting to a designated sum, as the payment of interest is prima facie evidence of the execution of the note by decedent, and obviates the necessity of further proof of the genuineness of the signature.—McKay v. Belknap Sav. Bank, 27 Colo. 50, 59 Pac. 745, 747. One who sues to enforce a claim against an estate, that has been rejected by the administrator, need not prove the rejection in case the defendant has not denied in his answer that it was rejected.—Thomas v. Fursman (Cal.), 178 Pac. 870. In an action brought against an administrator for damages arising out of a claim against the decedent on a contract made by him with the plaintiff and unfulfilled, the plaintiff can not introduce evidence of matter not included in the claim as filed against the estate.—Pearson v. Parsons, 173 Cal. 336, 159 Pac. 1173. No demand against a decedent's estate, that has been rejected by the personal representative, can be allowed by a court or jury, where the evidence, other than the testimony of the claimant, is not competent or satisfactory.—Consor v. Andrew, 61 Or. 483, 490, 123 Pac. 46. The law requiring testimony besides that of the claimant, in order to insure the court's allowing a claim for money rejected by an executrix, is satisfied where the claimant only testifies that the money claimed to have been collected by the deceased as his agent, has not been paid to him and other persons testify that the deceased made the collection.—Godfrey v. Howes, 91 Or. 98, 178 Pac. 388. Evi-

dence sufficient to justify a recovery upon a claim against the administrator of a deceased person, for boarding, lodging, and caring for such
deceased person.—Thompson v. Jackson, 85 Wash. 330, 148 Pac. 5.
In an action on a rejected claim against the estate of a deceased person, where the administratrix of the estate was called as a witness
for the plaintiff, was examined and cross-examined without objection
to her testimony as a whole, the defendant can not be heard to complain, after the witness has left the stand, that her evidence was
objectionable as a whole, and a motion then made to strike out all
of her evidence, not based upon any valid objection previously stated,
was properly denied.—E. Martin & Co. v. Brosnan, 18 Cal. App. 477, 123
Pac. 550.   In an action on a claim of $5000 alleged to be due from the
estate of a decedent on account of profits made in the purchase by him
of property as plaintiff's agent, where interested witnesses testified to
the claim, though they were presumed to speak the truth, yet where
there was evidence before the jury, upon which to determine the
weight to be given to their testimony, the jury was entitled to consider their motives and interests, and the conduct of the plaintiff in
failing to speak when the circumstances required in good faith he
should do so and even entitled to discredit their testimony and to
find against the existence of any agency, though there was no direct
testimony in conflict with such witnesses.—Sterling v. Cole, 12 Cal.
App. 93, 106, Pac. 602.   In an action on a note against an executor
of a deceased testator, the testimony of disinterested witnesses
familiar with his handwriting, that the note was in his handwriting, is
sufficient to support a verdict against the executor for the full amount
of the note.—Rooker v. Samuels, 10 Cal. App. 227, 101 Pac. 689.   Under
the provisions of the Probate Code of South Dakota no action can be
maintained against an executor or administrator upon a claim against
the estate of the decedent until the claim has been first presented to
and rejected by the administrator.   Where an action was brought
upon a claim which was filed in the proceedings and indorsed, "The
within claim presented to Garrett F. Johnson, administrator of the
estate of said deceased, is rejected this 26th day of July, 1910. Garrett F. Johnson. Filed August 2, 1910," but no proof of the signature
of the administrator to the rejection was offered. The claim was
offered in evidence as part of the records of the court. The Probate
Code required that allowed claims must be filed but not rejected ones.
A rejected claim is therefore not, in contemplation of law, a record
of the probate court and it was held that the trial court erred in
admitting the claim in evidence without proof of the purported signature of the administrator thereon.—Murray v. Johnson, 28 S. D. 571,
572, 134 N, W. 206. Where it appeared by plaintiff's complaint and
summons and proof of the date of service thereof that the action was
brought more than 90 days after the claim had been rejected by the
administrator, it is held that the necessity of proving the presentation
and rejection of a claim against a decedent's estate and of a suit begun

within 90 days from such rejection, is upon plaintiff, as a part of the proof of his cause of action, and this without regard to whether the defendant has answered pleading the statute of non-claim.—Mann v. Redman, 27 N. D. 346, 145 N. W. 1031, 1032. Though, under section 8028 of the Revised Codes of Montana, the evidence is to be weighed not only according to its own merits but also according to the power of the one side to produce and of the other to refute, an action on a claim against a decedent's estate is governed by the ordinary rules of evidence and procedure.—Ganss v. Trump, 48 Mont. 92, 135 Pac. 912. The statute of Oregon requires that no demand upon a decedent's estate that has been rejected by an administrator or executor shall be allowed by any court or jury except upon some competent or satisfactory evidence other than the testimony of the claimants.—In re Lucke's Estate, Consor v. Andrew, 61 Or. 483, 123 Pac. 48. A claim against a decedent's estate should be supported by stronger evidence than admissions to third persons.—Anderson v. Osborn, 62 Wash. 400, 114 Pac. 161. Where the answer affirmatively admits the presentation and rejection of the claim, no evidence thereof is required, but it is sufficient for the plaintiff to show that the action thereon is founded upon the same claim which was presented to the defendant for allowance.—E. Martin & Co. v. Brosnan, 18 Cal. App. 477, 123 Pac. 550. It is held that the evidence for the plaintiff is amply sufficient to support the verdict, and that, as there was no counter evidence for the defendant, a motion for a nonsuit of the plaintiff was therefore properly denied.—E. Martin & Co. v. Brosnan, 18 Cal. App. 477, 123 Pac. 550.

(19) Evidence. Presentation. Payment. Burden.—In an action on a claim against the estate of a decedent, where recourse is had against the estate, there must be proof of the presentation of the claim to the executor or administrator of the estate before a recovery can be had thereon.—Rowland v. Madden, 72 Cal. 17, 18, 12 Pac. 226, 870. There is no proof of the presentation, where there is no proof of the signature of the executor or administrator to the rejection of the claim.—Bank of Chico v. Spect, 2 Cal. Unrep. 675, 11 Pac. 740. Where there is no issue raised as to the presentation of the claim, it is neither necessary nor proper for the rejected claim to be offered in evidence.—Guerian v. Joyce, 133 Cal. 405, 65 Pac. 972. Where the action is to recover on a promissory note, and plaintiff introduces in evidence the note, with indorsements thereon, proves the signature of the deceased thereto, and the due presentation of the claim and its rejection, he thereby makes out a prima facie case of non-payment. Such evidence on the part of the plaintiff raises a presumption of non-payment, which, in law, entitles him to recover, and, it being thus shown that the note was not paid, the burden is cast upon defendant to prove by competent evidence that it had been paid; and the evidence must be such, whether direct or by raising legal presumptions, as to rebut the prima facie case made by the plaintiff.—Griffin v. Lewin, 125 Cal. 618, 620, 58 Pac. 205. Although due presentation of the claim

is not denied, still it must be proved.—Derby v. Jackman, 89 Cal. 1, 4, 26 Pac. 610. Where the plaintiff charged that a claim, duly verified, was left with the attorney for the administrator, in accordance with the published notice, but that subsequently the claim as made out was lost or destroyed, so that the action of the administrator thereon could not be ascertained, but does not state that the claim was approved by the administrator, the inference is that he neglected to inform himself as to the action taken by the administrator, and a court can not, in aid of the allegations of the complaint, presume that the administrator approved the claim. If any presumption is to be indulged in, it must be that either the claim was rejected or not acted upon, especially where no record appears that the executor or administrator has presented the same to the probate court for the latter's allowance or rejection, as he would have been required to do, where he had taken action thereon. Hence, under a statute requiring suit to be brought upon the claim within three months, no action can be maintained thereon where suit was not commenced until the expiration of eight months from the time of such alleged presentation.—Underwood v. Browne, 7 Ariz. 19, 60 Pac. 700, 701. Proof of the presentation of plaintiff's claim to the executor or administrator, and the rejection thereof by him, though expressly required by the statute, and that prohibits any recovery unless proof of the presentation is made, is not required, if defendant's supplemental answer admits the presentation and rejection as alleged.—Harrington v. Butte, etc., Min. Co., 35 Mont. 530, 90 Pac. 748, 749. Whether a claim, as presented, was sufficient in form, or properly presented, is a matter of evidence, and a general allegation of presentation is sufficient to authorize proof as to such presentation.—Humboldt S. & L. Soc. v. Burnham, 111 Cal. 343, 345, 43 Pac. 971. In an action against the executor or administrator on a claim against the deceased, the burden of proof of showing non-payment does not rest upon the plaintiff, but is upon the defendant to prove payment; and it is error to find payment merely because plaintiff does not prove that the claim is not paid.—Stuart v. Lord, 138 Cal. 672, 674, 72 Pac. 142. The allegation of non-payment of a debt sued on, though necessary to make the complaint perfect, need not be proved; the burden of proof of payment is upon the defendant.— Melone v. Ruffino, 129 Cal. 514, 519, 79 Am. St. Rep. 127, 62 Pac. 93; Hurley v. Ryan, 137 Cal. 461, 462, 70 Pac. 292. In an action by a creditor of a decedent against the administrator of the estate, who has, by representing the latter to be insolvent, purposely prevented plaintiff from filing a claim, the defendant has the burden of proving that the estate is not merely incumbered but actually insolvent.—Kennedy v. Burr, 101 Wash. 61, 171 Pac. 1022. Where an answer admits that a verified claim for the amount sued for has been duly presented to, and disallowed by, the administrator of one of the defendants, the plaintiff is not required to prove the presentation and disallowance.—Harrington v. Butte, etc., Min. Co., 35 Mont. 530, 532, 90 Pac. 748. (Citing Code

Civ. Proc., § 2612.) In a case where an executrix has rejected a claim presented by a person, alleging a collection made for him by the deceased and not handed over, the burden of proof, if the evidence as to the collection is conclusive in support of the allegation respecting it, shifts to the administrator, who must allege and prove that the deceased paid over and fully accounted for the moneys involved.—Godfrey v. Howes, 91 Or. 98, 178 Pac. 388. In a proceeding to compel an executor to act upon a claim against an estate the burden rests upon the petitioner to establish a presentation of the claim, and whether petitioner asserted such presentation or merely assumed it, the assumption was an assertion, and the burden still rested upon her to prove the assertion.—In re King's Estate, Schrader v. Buffum, 102 Wash. 299, 300, 172 Pac. 1167.

(20) **Evidence. Plaintiff's statutory inability to testify.**—Where the statute says that no claim which has been rejected, etc., shall be allowed by any court, referee, or jury, except upon some competent or satisfactory evidence, other than the testimony of the claimant, but says nothing about the proof necessary to establish the preliminary issue of the presentation and rejection of the claim, it is only on the trial of the merits of the rejected claim that the statute can apply. The issue as to whether the claim has been presented or rejected is not within the purpose of the statute or the mischief intended to be remedied. It is an issue to be determined from the testimony of living witnesses, to be tried out as any other question of fact, and decided upon the preponderance of the evidence; but, when it comes to the trial of the merits, the statute applies. It must be first shown, however, that the claim has been presented to the executor or administrator and rejected by him, and this can be done by any evidence satisfactory to the trier of fact.—Goltra v. Penland, 45 Or. 254, 77 Pac. 129, 132. In an action upon a rejected claim against the estate of a decedent, the burden of proof is upon the plaintiff to establish his claim, and the statutory inability on the part of the plaintiff to testify in his own behalf does not relieve him from the necessity of producing sufficient evidence to prove his cause of action. His incompetency to testify may be his misfortune, but the defendant's obligation does not thereby vary.—Barthe v. Rogers, 127 Cal. 52, 54, 59 Pac. 310; Stuart v. Lord, 138 Cal. 672, 677, 72 Pac. 142. As to when plaintiff in an action on a claim against the estate of a deceased person has established his claim by satisfactory evidence other than his own testimony, see Bull v. Payne, 47 Or. 580, 84 Pac. 697, 698.

In an action, brought against an administrator, to enforce a claim on a contract made with the decedent, involving the exercise of an option, the plaintiff can not testify as to the service on the decedent of a notice of intention to exercise the option.—Pearson v. Parsons, 173 Cal. 331, 335, 159 Pac. 1171. An officer or stockholder of a corporation plaintiff in an action on a claim against a decedent's estate defended by the administrator is "a party interested in the event" so as to preclude him from testifying for the plaintiff under the statute of Colorado.—Gilmour v. Hawley Merchandise Co., 21 Colo. App. 301, 121 Pac. 766; Same v. First Nat. Bank, 21 Colo. App. 301, 121 Pac. 767. Under the Utah statute a party plaintiff is not a competent witness in his own behalf as to "any statement by or transaction with" the deceased "or matters of fact whatever which must have been equally within the knowledge of both" the plaintiff and the deceased.—Kislingbury v. Evans, 40 Utah 356, 121 Pac. 571.

REFERENCES.

Competency of witnesses to testify in an action on a claim against the estate of a decedent.—See note § 1107, head-line 2, subd. 2, post.

(21) Evidence. Admissions of decedent.—The general rule that evidence of admissions against interest is admissible applies to a case where one who has presented a bill or demand against the estate of a decedent, embodying certain statements as to the facts upon which it is founded, subsequently seeks to maintain an action utterly inconsistent with the facts previously asserted. In such a case the statements of the superseded pleading are admissible as admissions against interest on the part of the person making them.—Pollitz v. Wickersham, 150 Cal. 238, 88 Pac. 911, 915. As to the insufficiency of admissions of decedent to establish the value of any services rendered for the decedent individually, see Lichtenberg v. McGlynn, 105 Cal. 45, 48, 38 Pac. 541. Where plaintiff suing the estate of a decedent for money advanced and services rendered was the timekeeper and bookkeeper of the deceased and in such capacity kept a journal containing entries, seemingly made in the usual course of business, it is the book of the principal and admissible to show the plaintiff's account.—Roberton v. O'Neill, 67 Wash. 121, 120 Pac. 885. In an action against executors for services rendered testator, where the executors set up a contract and performance of the deceased, testator's declaration to a third and uninterested party, that plaintiff had rendered services but that there was no agreement as to the amount to be paid therefor was admissible in plaintiff's behalf.—Wright v. State, 83 Kan. 445, 111 Pac. 467. An instrument dated and signed by a person since deceased, stating that he has a certain amount of money on deposit at a named bank which at his death he wishes paid to a designated person "for kindness she has shown me during my lifetime, and she is to pay all my funeral expenses and just debts," does not amount to an account stated.—Outwaters v. Brownlee, 17 Cal. App. 145, 135 Pac. 300. Such an instrument is not admissible as evidence, in an action against the administrator of the estate of the deceased to recover for services rendered to him, of an intention on his part to any certain amount; it can do no more than indicate an intention to pay the reasoable value of the services performed.—Outwaters v. Brownlee, 17 Cal. App. 145, 135 Pac. 300.

(22) Interest.—Interest follows the contract according to the law in existence at the time and place of the contract, or of the performance of it. But a subsequent change of the legal rate of interest does not affect the contract.—Aguirre v. Packard, 14 Cal. 171, 172, 73 Am. Dec. 645. If an account presented to an executor or administrator for allowance contains no item for interest, and the face of the paper does not show that interest results necessarily from the facts stated in the claim, interest can not be recovered in the action founded upon such claim.—Aguirre v. Packard, 14 Cal. 171, 172, 73 Am. Dec. 645; Etchas v. Oreña, 127 Cal. 588, 593, 60 Pac. 45. If an executor or administrator, refuses a legal claim against the estate, and the claimant afterwards brings suit thereon, and recovers judgment therefor, he is entitled to interest from the time of the presentation of his claim.—Pico v. Stevens, 18 Cal. 376, 378. The statute which provides that "if the estate be insolvent no greater rate of interest shall be allowed after the first publication of notice to creditors than is allowed on judgments obtained in the superior court" does not apply to the foreclosure of mortgages where no recourse is had against the property of the estate other than that mortgaged. In such a case the estate has no interest in the land, and can in no manner be benefited by a reduction of the interest.—Christy v. Dana, 42 Cal. 174. 178; Visalia Sav. Bank v. Curtis, 185 Cal. 350, 352, 67 Pac. 329.

(23) Set-off. Counterclaim.—An executor or administrator of the estate of a deceased person has no right to set off any claim held by himself individually against a debt due from him as executor or administrator to a creditor of his intestate.—Estate of Watkins, 121 Cal. 327, 328, 53 Pac. 702. But in an action against an executor or administrator for the value of articles pledged, which were not returned upon demand and tender of the amount due, the indebtedness secured by the pledge is a proper subject to set off against the value of the articles.—Vanderslice v. Matthews, 79 Cal. 273, 276, 21 Pac. 748. A person can not avoid the payment of a debt owed to the administrator, by buying at a discount, after the death of the decedent, a claim against his estate, which accrued in his lifetime; and such purchase will not operate as a set-off to the debt.—Van Dusen v. Topeka Woolen Mill Co., 74 Kan. 437, 87 Pac. 74. One who is a creditor and also a debtor of an insolvent estate may have his claim against the estate set off against his debt to the estate, if both accrued during the lifetime of the deceased and are of such character as to constitute proper subjects of set-off in an action by or against the deceased if living.—Helms v. Harclerode, 65 Kan. 736, 70 Pac. 866, 867. In an action to foreclose a mortgage by a distributee of the mortgagee's estate, claims of the mortgagor which must have been presented to the estate of the deceased mortgagee before suit, but were not so presented, can not be pleaded as counterclaims to the mortgage.—Moore v. Gould, 151 Cal. 723, 732, 91 Pac. 616. Under the express language of the code of California, the right of set-off is limited to parties between whom actions are pending; a proceeding for an order directing the payment of an allowed claim is not, strictly speaking, an action; however, for this purpose it is to be regarded as one, and the

administrator contesting such proceeding should be allowed to plead
a set-off to the claim.—Estate of Bell, 168 Cal. 253, 141 Pac. 1179.   In an
action brought by an executor or administrator, a demand against the
estate may be offset to the extent of plaintiff's recovery, without presentation, under the statute of the state of Washington.—Mendenhall v.
Davis, 52 Wash. 169, 17 Ann. Cas. 179, 21 L. R. A. (N. S.) 914, 100
Pac. 336, 339.

(24) Findings.—Where a claim was not presented against an estate
within ten months after the notice to creditors, and an action is brought
to recover the claim, which was disallowed, a finding is necessary from
which it can be seen at what precise time the claim became due, in
order to determine whether the presentation of the claim was made
within the time required by the statute.—Elliott v. Peck, 53 Cal. 84, 85.
A proceeding to compel an executor to act upon a claim against an
estate is one either of equitable cognizance or a special proceeding of a
mandatory nature, and findings of fact and conclusions of law are not
required.—In re King's Estate, Schrader v. Buffum, 102 Wash. 299, 300,
172 Pac. 1167.   A finding that a foreign corporation's contingent claim
against an estate, and its right to establish the same by action against
the estate, was barred by the statute, disposed of the controlling issue
in the case, and findings upon other issues presented by the pleadings
were rendered immaterial.—Tropico Land, etc., Co. v. Lambourn, 170
Cal. 33, 46, 148 Pac. 206.   Evidence that long prior to and during the
publication of notice to creditors all the property of a corporation
claimant was within the state of California; that it transacted all of
its business in that state; that all of its officers and agents were there;
and that all the meetings of its board of directors were held in that
state, was sufficient to support a finding that it was not absent from the
state within the meaning of section 1493 of the Code of Civ. Proc. of
that state, notwithstanding the fact that the claimant was a foreign corporation having its principal place of business in the state of its incor-
poration.—Tropico Land, etc., Co. v. Lambourn, 170 Cal. 33, 44, 148
Pac. 206.   A finding as to an express contract of the sick mother, in this
case, to pay her daughter for her services as nurse, is sufficiently supported by evidence that when the mother became afflicted with paralysis
she requested her neighbor to call a doctor and a nurse, and the
daughter, who lived in another county, was sent for, as a nurse, and
after she came the mother told the neighbor to request her to remain
and she would pay her for her services, and she remained and served
as a nurse until her mother's death.—Wood v. James, 15 Cal. App. 253,
114 Pac. 587.   It is no objection to such finding that the evidence shows
no direct contract between the daughter and her mother, as no such
evidence is admissible under section 1880 of the Code of Civil Procedure
of California, which closes the lips of the plaintiff, and does not permit
her to testify thereto.—Wood v. James, 15 Cal. App. 253, 114 Pac. 587.

6. Limitation of actions. Special statutes of limitation.

(1) In general.—A claim may be conclusively rejected by either the administrator or the judge, and when there is a rejection by either, the statute limiting the time within which suit may be brought commences to run from the date of such rejection.—Jones v. Walden, 145 Cal. 523, 78 Pac. 1046, 1047. That special regulation of the probate law that imposes the loss of a claim if not presented within the time prescribed is a statute of non-claim, frequently called a special statute of limitations. —Defries v. Cartwright, 10 Haw. 249, 251. The general statute of limitations is not affected by the giving, or failure to give, notice to creditors of a decedent. Such notice is simply a matter of probate procedure.—McMillan v. Hayward, 94 Cal. 357, 29 Pac. 774, 775. If the debtor has substituted a new obligation in place of an old one, a claim against his estate must be based on the new obligation. Thus, where a note is extinguished by the substitution of a new obligation in its place, and the maker of the note afterwards dies, the claim must be based on the new obligation and not on the note.—Estate of Sullenberger, 72 Cal. 549, 551, 14 Pac. 513; Etchas v. Oreña, 127 Cal. 588, 593, 60 Pac. 45. So a broken promise to provide, by will, a compensation for services rendered to the decedent, if not presented as a claim against the estate, can not be relied upon to save the bar of the statute as to part of a rejected claim for services presented against the estate.— Etchas v. Oreña, 127 Cal. 588, 592, 60 Pac. 45. Where the statute gives to the plaintiff three years after the commencement of an action in which to make service and the return of summons, and declares, "but all such actions may be prosecuted if appearance has been made by defendant or defendants within said three years, in the same manner as if summons had been issued and served," the necessity of any service of the summons is obviated by the appearance, in the action, of the personal representative within three years. Such voluntary appearance gives the court jurisdiction over this representative, the same as if he had been brought in by the service of summons upon him at that time; and where this jurisdiction is acquired within three years after the commencement of the action, no rights of the estate, or of the person interested therein, are waived by his appearance.—Union Sav. Bank. v. Barrett, 132 Cal. 453, 455, 64 Pac. 713, 1071. The statute of non-claim is a special regulation of probate law; it can not be waived, and need not be specially pleaded.—Kennedy v. Sniffen, 23 Haw. 115, 120. Statutes of non-claim are special in character; they supersede the general statute of limitations; and compliance with thei.· requirements is essential to the foundation of any right of action against an estate, upon a cause of action that sounds in contract.—Vanderpool v. Vanderpool, 48 Mont. 448, 453, 138 Pac. 772. Statutes, such as section 7525, Revised Codes, providing that claims against estates upon causes of action which sound in contract are barred unless presented within the time limited in the notice for their presentation, supersede the general statutes of limitations and compliance with their terms is essential to the maintenance

of actions thereon.—Vanderpool v. Vanderpool, 48 Mont. 443, 138 Pac. 772. The statute making provision for non-liability of the real estate of a deceased person for debts is a statute of limitations.—In re Mason's Estate, Mason v. Mason, 95 Wash. 564, 164 Pac. 205. The provision in the code, barring a claim from presentation against a decedent's estate after a year from the first publication of the notice to creditors, is, in effect, a statute of limitation without any exception therein; and it is an established rule that mere ignorance of the facts constituting the cause of action will not postpone the operation of the statute of limitations.—Harvey v. Pocock, 92 Wash. 625, 159 Pac. 771.

REFERENCES.

Waiver or tolling of the statute of limitations or of non-claim, by personal representative, as to indebtedness of the estate.—L. R. A. 1915B, 1016. Acknowledgment of outlaw debt by devise or legacy reciting a consideration.—See note 1 L. R. A. (N. S.) 1117.

(2) Application of statutes. Special and general.—The special limitations of time within which suit must be brought against the estates of deceased persons are called, in many states, statutes of non-claim or of short or special limitations. These limitations exist independently of and collateral to the general law of limitations. The statute which allows a plaintiff three months after a claim is formally and officially rejected by the executor or administrator in which to bring his action may shorten, but can not lengthen, the general statute of limitations.—Barclay v. Blackinton, 127 Cal. 189, 193, 59 Pac. 834. The right to enforce his claim under statutes of limitation depends upon his own vigilance, and is often lost by his own laches. The policy of the law is to settle up the estates of deceased persons as speedily as possible, to pay the just debts and expenses, and to distribute the property to the rightful heirs or devisees. For this reason, statutes that shorten the period and time of presenting and bringing suits on claims against estates are justified and upheld. After a claim is barred by the general statute of limitations, it can never be allowed or made a valid claim against the estate by any act or neglect of the executor or administrator. —Barclay v. Blackinton, 127 Cal. 189, 194, 195, 59 Pac. 834. If an action is brought more than four years and nine months after the maturity of a written promise of the decedent to pay money, and one year and seven months after the issuance of letters of administration, it is barred by the general statute of limitations.—Barclay v. Blackinton, 127 Cal. 189, 191, 196, 59 Pac. 834. A three months' limitation provided by statute for the commencement of an action upon a rejected claim does not apply to a claim which it is not necessary to present to the executor or administrator, as one for funeral expenses.—Potter v. Lewin, 123 Cal. 146, 55 Pac. 783. An action upon a rejected claim against the estate of a deceased person must be brought, if at all, within the prescribed statutory time after the same becomes due.—Brooks v. Lawson, 136 Cal. 10, 14, 68 Pac. 97; Morse v. Steele, 132 Cal. 456, 64 Pac. 690.

Where an obligation fixes the period of two years within which to exercise an option, a delay of four days after the expiration of the two years in presenting a money demand to the executor or administrator of the decedent is not unreasonable.—Maurer v. King, 127 Cal. 114, 117, 59 Pac. 290. The bar of the statute relates only to claims against the estate; it in no way affects claims against other parties, or against the property of others, or the contracts of other parties, although the same demand may also be a claim against the estate; and where a note was executed by the husband and wife on the separate property of the wife, and where the note and mortgage were not presented for allowance against the estate of the husband within the time fixed by the statute, the bar of the probate act does not apply as to the wife.—Sichel v. Carrillo, 42 Cal. 493. The non-claim section of the practice act, relative to the filing of claims against deceased persons, does not cover a case where the claim, if payable or to be satisfied at a future date, vests in a contingency, and it is uncertain whether any demand will accrue.—Pruett v. Caddigan, 42 Nev. 329, 176 Pac. 787. The statutory provisions regulating the filing of claims against the estates of decedents do not fail to run, as composing a statute of limitations, because of any neglect on the part of the executor to publish a notice of his appointment.—In re Hoover's Estate; Kirk v. Hoover, 104 Kan. 635, 180 Pac. 275. In the absence of some provision in a will requiring the keeping open of an estate longer than two years, a statute of non-claim, requiring demands to be presented within two years shall be forever barred, controls, and a person can not by oral agreement with his creditor establish a different rule as to the time within which his claim may be presented.—McDaniel v. Putnam, 100 Kan. 550, 555, L. R. A. 1917E, 1100, 164 Pac. 1167, 1169. The fact that no order for publication of notice to creditors to present their claims had been made and no such had ever been published does not prevent the running of the three months' limitation of time to bring action after rejection of claim where the claim was presented and rejected without any publication of notice to creditors to present claims.—Singer v. Austin, 19 N. D. 546, 548, 125 N. W. 560. In a proceeding to foreclose a mortgage or in any action asserting an original specific and absolute charge on the land, commenced in the courts of the Indian Territory prior to statehood, the plea of the statute of non-claim is not available. —International Bank, etc., Co. v. Tolbert, 28 Okla. 595, 115 Pac. 601. A creditor, though empowered to do so, is under no obligation to apply for letters of administration of his deceased debtor's estate, and in the event of his not doing so, statutes of limitation do not begin to run against him until after an administrator shall have been appointed.—Robertson v. Tarry, 83 Kan. 716, 112 Pac. 603. Under the statute of Idaho, where a claim has been presented to an administrator and rejected by him, the holder must bring suit in the proper court against such administrator within three months after the date of its rejection if it then be due, or within two months after it becomes due; otherwise, the claim is forever barred.—Idaho Trust Co. v. Miller, 16 Ida. 308, 102 Pac. 360. The limitation of one year after the issuance of letters of administration for filing claims against the estate of a decedent as provided in the statute of Colorado, applies only to those debts or demands which were incurred by the decedent in his lifetime.—United States F. & G. Co. v. People, 44 Colo. 557, 98 Pac. 828, 834.

REFERENCES.

Exceptions to and interruptions of statutes of non-claim.—See note 3 **Am. & Eng. Ann. Cas. 576.** Contingency of claim as affecting limitation of time for its presentation.—See note 58 **L. R. A. 82-90.**

(3) **Barred claims not to be allowed. Exception.**—The statute prohibits the allowance of a claim against the estate of a deceased person, which has been barred by the statute of limitations.—Dorland v. Dorland, 66 Cal. 189, 5 Pac. 77; McGrath v. Carroll, 110 Cal. 79, 42 Pac. 466; Etchas v. Oreña, 127 Cal. 588, 60 Pac. 45; Barclay v. Blackinton, 127 Cal. 189, 59 Pac. 834; Reay v. Heazelton, 128 Cal. 335, 60 Pac. 977; In re Mouillerat's Estate, 14 Mont. 245, 36 Pac. 185. Neither the executor nor the judge has any right to allow any part of a claim against the estate of a decedent, which has been barred by the statute of limitations.—Etchas v. Oreña, 127 Cal. 588, 592, 60 Pac. 45; Farrow v. Nevin, 44 Or. 496, 75 Pac. 711. Where the claim against the estate of a decedent appears to have been barred by limitation, it will not be presumed to have been allowed by the court, unless that fact affirmatively appears by the record; and a mere indorsement upon an account of its approval by some one styling himself "probate judge" is not sufficient evidence of its allowance by that officer.—Janes v. Brunswick, 8 N. M. 345, 45 Pac. 878. Where the claim presented is a simple demand for money lent, accompanied by a demand for legal interest, and there is no hint or suggestion made of a trust, and the debts have long been barred by the statute of limitations, the executor or administrator has no discretion in the matter, but it is his plain duty to reject it.—McGrath v. Carroll, 110 Cal. 79, 84, 42 Pac. 466. Notwithstanding the right to foreclose a mortgage or to collect a debt out of the real property of a deceased debtor is barred by the statute of limitations, the creditor still has the right to have his claim allowed by the administrator to be paid, as other claims of the estate must be paid, out of the personal property in the hands of the administrator belonging to the estate. The statute destroys the lien of the debt at the end of six years upon the deceased debtor's real property, but keeps it alive in so far as his personal property is concerned. The debt should, for that reason, be allowed as a claim against the estate.—Gleason v. Hawkins, 32 Wash. 464, 73 Pac. 533, 534.

(4) **Suits to be commenced when.**—Though the statute provides that if a claim is not presented within a designated time after the first publication of notice to creditors, it shall be forever barred, yet there is no bar if no publication was made.—Smith v. Hall, 19 Cal. 85, 86. A

suit not brought within such specified time after the rejection of the claim is not, of course, in time to avoid the bar of the statute.—Consolidated Bank v. Hayes, 112 Cal. 75, 84, 44 Pac. 469. If the claim is presented to the executor, and allowed by him within the statutory time after its presentation, no action can be maintained thereon until the lapse of such time after its presentation to the judge, unless he rejects it within that period.—Nally v. McDonald, 66 Cal. 530, 532, 6 Pac. 300. Where the statute requires the executor or administrator, to whom a claim is presented, to indorse thereon his allowance or rejection, with the day and date thereof, and provides that if he refuses or neglects to indorse such allowance or rejection for ten days after the claim has been presented to him, such refusal or neglect may, at the option of the claimant, be deemed equivalent to a rejection on the tenth day, but does not require that the executor or administrator shall reject a claim before an action can be maintained upon it, it is optional with the plaintiff, if his claim has not been so indorsed within ten days to deem it rejected, and he may bring an action thereon within three months after notice of such election; and, in the absence of other proof, suit brought is conclusive evidence of such election and notice thereof.—Gowgill v. Dinwiddie, 98 Cal. 481, 483, 33 Pac. 439; Bank of Ukiah v. Shoemake, 67 Cal. 147, 7 Pac. 420. See Rice v. Inskeep, 34 Cal. 224. Where the statute requires one whose claim against the estate of a decedent has been rejected to bring suit within three months after such rejection, he can not maintain a suit brought nearly eight months after the presentation of the claim, in the absence of any showing entitling him to equitable relief.—Underwood v. Brown, 7 Ariz. 19, 60 Pac. 700, 702. If one who has a claim against the estate of a decedent commences an action thereon within the time in which a claim should have been presented, before giving the executor or administrator an opportunity to pass on the claim, such action is, at most, only prematurely brought. A premature insitution of a suit may be ground for a plea in abatement, which, if interposed, has the effect of defeating or suspending the suit for the time being; but it is not ground for a plea in bar, and can not have the effect of impairing or defeating the action altogether.—Clayton v. Dinwoodey, 33 Utah 251, 14 Ann. Cas. 926, 93 Pac. 723, 728.

(5) Statute commences to run when.—The statute of limitations does not begin to run, where no administration exists on the decedent's estate at the time the cause of action accrues.—Heeser v. Taylor, 1 Cal. App. 619, 621, 82 Pac. 977; Estate of Bullard, 116 Cal. 355, 357, 48 Pac. 219; Smith v. Hall, 19 Cal. 85; Danglada v. De la Guerra, 10 Cal. 386. A claim may be conclusively rejected by either the administrator or the judge; and when there is a rejection by either, the statute commences to run from the date of such rejection.—Jones v. Walden, 145 Cal. 523, 525, 78 Pac. 1046; Bank of Ukiah v. Shoemake, 67 Cal. 147, 148, 7 Pac. 420. The statute of limitations does not run against the claim between the date of its presentation

to the executor or administrator and that of its rejection by the judge.—Nally v. McDonald, 66 Cal. 530, 531, 6 Pac. 390. It is only where a claim has been allowed by an executor or administrator that there is any necessity of presenting it to the judge.—Jones v. Walden, 145 Cal. 523, 525, 78 Pac. 1046. A statute which regulates actions upon rejected claims against the estates of deceased persons does not begin to run until a claim has been properly presented and rejected. If a party makes an attempt to present a claim for allowance, but from some cause fails to do so properly, this does not prevent him from subsequently presenting the claim in due form, if within proper time, and the statute of limitations does not begin to run until proper presentation of the claim is made, provided that it is made within the time prescribed by the statute.—Westbay v. Gray, 116 Cal. 660, 668, 48 Pac. 800. The statute which fixes a limitation for the presentation of claims against an estate does not commence to run until a claim becomes absolute.—Gleason v. White, 34 Cal. 258, 265. Where a claim has been twice presented and twice rejected, the statute of limitations commences to run from the date of the first rejection.—Gillespie v. Wright, 93 Cal. 169, 171, 28 Pac. 862. The filing and withdrawal of a claim does not constitute the commencement of an action such as will prevent the statute of limitations from running.—Morse v. Clark, 10 Colo. 216, 14 Pac. 327, 328. The general statute of limitations does not begin to run against a claim until it matures and can be enforced.—Thompson v. Oreña, 134 Cal. 26, 28, 66 Pac. 24. The statute does not run against a trust claim until some repudiation of the trust made by the trustee is brought home to the knowledge of the trustor.—McGrath v. Carroll, 110 Cal. 79, 81, 42 Pac. 466.

(6) Arrest, staying, or suspension of statute.—The time during which a claim is in the hands of the executor or administrator for examination, without notifying the claimant that it has been rejected, should not be taken as a part of the time limited by the statute for the commencement of an action thereon.—In re Morgan's Estate, 46 Or. 233, 77 Pac. 608, 610. The statute of limitations does not run, while the administration is pending and unsettled, as to a claim against the estate that has been allowed.—Estate of Schroeder, 46 Cal. 304, 316; Estate of Arguello, 85 Cal. 151, 153, 24 Pac. 641. Hence the statute of limitations will not disqualify a creditor whose claim has been allowed from petitioning for an order of sale.—Estate of Arguello, 85 Cal. 151, 154, 24 Pac. 641. Nor does the statute of limitations run, while the administration is pending and unsettled, as to a judgment that has been recovered against an executor or administrator for a debt of the estate.—Estate of Schroeder, 46 Cal. 304, 317. When claims have been presented and allowed, none of the statutory limitations run against them.—In re Tuohy's Estate, 33 Mont. 230, 83 Pac. 486. 491. Until the entry of a decree discharging the executor or administrator, the administration of the estate is still pending, and until then no claim against the estate which has been presented and allowed

is affected by the statute of limitations.—Dohs v. Dohs, 60 Cal. 255, 260. The allowance of a claim by an executor or administrator, and its approval by the judge, stops the running of the statute of limitations.—Barclay v. Blackinton, 127 Cal. 189, 194, 59 Pac. 834; Wise v. Williams, 88 Cal. 30, 25 Pac. 1064; Wise v. Williams, 72 Cal. 544, 14 Pac. 204; Willis v. Farley, 24 Cal. 490; and this applies to a claim arising upon a mortgage and notes secured thereby.—Hibernia Sav. & L. Soc. v. Conlin, 67 Cal. 178, 7 Pac. 477; German Sav. & L. Soc. v. Hutchinson, 68 Cal. 52, 8 Pac. 627; Wise v. Williams, 72 Cal. 544, 14 Pac. 204, 88 Cal. 30, 25 Pac. 1064. An executor's repeated promise to pay a claim against an estate which has not been barred by the statute of limitations does not suspend the running of the statute; the creditor is chargeable with knowledge of his legal rights, and is bound to know that the statute of limitations is constantly running against his claim; and if he allows the period of limitation to expire, his claim is thereafter barred, although the executor neglects his duty in failing to proceed with the administration, as that is no reason why the creditor should remain idle and allow the statute to continue to run against his claim.—Bank of Montreal v. Buchanan, 32 Wash. 480, 73 Pac. 482, 484. The time in which a creditor is prohibited from commencing an action upon his claim, either because the statutory time after the granting of letters testamentary or of administration has not expired, or because the question of allowance of the claim is pending before the executor and undecided, will not be deemed a part of the time limited for the commencement of the action thereon. The creditor must, of course, present his claim before it is barred by the statute of limitations; otherwise the executor or administrator is not authorized to allow it. The statute can not be tolled by a mere failure to present the claim. After it has been presented, however, the claimant is prohibited from suing until it is disallowed, and the operation of the statute will be suspended during the time of such prohibition.— In re Morgan's Estate, 46 Or. 233, 77 Pac. 608, 609. An action on a judgment claim against the estate of a decedent is barred, under the general statute of limitations, unless it is brought within six years; but the time intervening between the death of the judgment debtor and the qualification of his executor or administrator may be excluded in the computation of such period.—Whiteside v. Catching, 19 Mont. 394, 48 Pac. 747, 748. When the statute of limitations has commenced to run, it continues to run, notwithstanding the death of defendant or an intervening disability, unless it is expressly provided otherwise in the statute. Disability of the defendant does not, in any case, prevent the running of the statute, nor will ignorance of the creditor as to the residence of the debtor, or that he has property which can be reached, or even of his own right of action, prevent the running of the statute. Whenever the statute has commenced to run, delay in bringing an action is always at the risk of an intervening disability, which may, in the absence of a statutory saving, prevent suit from

being brought at all.—Davis v. Hart, 123 Cal. 384, 388, 55 Pac. 1060.
If not barred by the statute of limitations, the right of action on a
claim against the estate of a decedent can not be lost by reason of
the negligence of the plaintiff in the prosecution of the claim on
which the action is founded.—Nally v. McDonald, 66 Cal. 530, 532, 6
Pac. 390. If a claim against an estate is filed within a year from the
granting of letters, that stops the running of the statute, regardless
of when such claim is called up for allowance.—Milner B. & Trust
Co. v. Estate of Whipple, 61 Colo. 252, 255, 156 Pac. 1098. The statute
of non-claim is highly penal in its nature and must be strictly construed and liberally followed in order to be a bar, and under the
provisions of § 6347, Rev. Laws of Oklahoma, of 1910, it is held that
the statute of non-claim does not run during a vacancy in the administration, and if such a vacancy occurs within four months after
notice to creditors, the statute is tolled until a successor gives the
notice to creditors required by section 6336 of such laws.—In re
Jameson's Estate, — Okla. —, 182 Pac. 518, 520. The mere filing of
a claim against an estate does not arrest the running of the general
statute of limitations in the state of Colorado.—Alvater v. First Nat.
Bank, 45 Colo. 528, 103 Pac. 379. Whenever a person desiring to establish a demand against an estate delivers to the administrator a written
notice containing a copy of the instrument or account on which it is
founded, and stating that he will present it for allowance to the probate court at a time named, an action on the claim is deemed to be
begun so as to stop the running of the statute of limitations. It is
not necessary that the controversy shall be decided, or that it shall
be submitted for decision before the expiration of the period of limitation, or even that the day first set for a hearing shall fall within
that period.—Clifton v. Menser, 79 Kan. 655, 100 Pac. 644.

(7) **Revival of actions. Waiver of statute.**—An executor or administrator will not be permitted to waive either the general statute of
limitations or the failure of a party to present his claim.—Boyce v.
Fisk, 110 Cal. 107, 117, 42 Pac. 473; Reay v. Heazelton, 128 Cal. 335,
60 Pac. 977; Clayton v. Dinwoodey, 33 Utah 251, 14 Ann. Cas. 926, 93
Pac. 723. His waiver of the statute and allowance of a claim barred
thereby are invalid.—Jones v. Powning, 25 Nev. 399, 60 Pac. 833. An
executor or administrator can not, by appearing and answering a
supplemental complaint in an action originally brought against the
decedent, in which the summons was not returned within the time
limited by the statute, waive the statute of limitations.—Vrooman v.
Li Po Tai, 113 Cal. 302, 306, 45 Pac. 470; Reay v. Heazelton, 128 Cal.
335, 60 Pac. 977; Union Sav. Bank v. Barrett, 132 Cal. 453, 64 Pac.
713, 1071. But a testator may express on the face of his will his
intent that all his actual obligations shall be paid without reference
to the law of limitations; and there is no good reason why that testamentary intent should not be carried out by his executors and administrators, as well as any other part of the will.—Glassell v. Glassell,

147 Cal. 510, 512, 82 Pac. 42. If the statute of limitations has run, the debt can not be revived, except by a promise in writing signed by the debtor.—Estate of Galvin, 51 Cal. 215, 217. A plea of the statute of limitations can not be waived or omitted by an executor and neither can he waive the bar of the statute of non-claim as against the estate. —Ward v. Magaha, 71 Wash. 679, 129 Pac. 397.

(8) **Action is not barred when.**—Where it has been agreed, by the terms of a written contract, entered into by defendant's testator and plaintiff's assignor, for the sale of land by the former to the latter, to return a deposit of money in case of failure to make title as agreed upon, the liability is upon the contract, and does not arise by implication. Hence an action to recover the deposit is not controlled by the two-year statute of limitations, and is not barred until the lapse of four years from the accrual of the cause of action.—Melone v. Ruffino, 129 Cal. 514, 525, 79 Am. St. Rep. 127, 62 Pac. 93. Where a daughter executed and delivered to her father a general power of attorney, which authorized him to sell and convey her real property and to manage the proceeds without any restrictions whatever, and he sold the land, and died about seventeen years afterwards, without ever having informed his daughter of the condition of her property, and of his receiving any money on account of its sale, and fraudulently misinformed her concerning the facts, which she did not discover until after her father's death, and hence failed to demand the proceeds of such sale during his lifetime, her claim against his estate is not barred by the statute of limitations. The agency was a continuing one, and the statute would not commence to run until it was terminated, or until the agent had notified the principal that the proceeds of the sale of her property were at her disposal, and then, if she failed to demand them within the statutory period, her right of action would be barred. The agency being general and continuing, the money received by the testator on account of the sale of plaintiff's land must, in the absence of proof of the termination of such agency, be considered as held by him for her use and benefit.—Quinn v. Gross, 24 Or. 147, 33 Pac. 535, 536. The Colorado statute does not prevent a claimant against the estate of a decedent from bringing an action at any distance of time, provided the same is not barred by some other statute, if the creditor can discover property not inventoried or accounted for by the executor or administrator, and such creditor has the right to have his claim passed upon by the court, and recover a judgment presently for the amount due, if any, to be satisfied out of any estate that may be found not inventoried or accounted for by the executor or administrator. Hence, although the claim of the creditor is not sued upon within one year, nevertheless the same is not barred. The only effect of such failure to sue within that time is, that the creditor is deprived of the right to a distributive share in the inventoried assets. The suit may proceed to judgment that, however, must be special in character, and limited to a satisfaction out of the uninventoried property of the

estate.—McClure v. Commissioners, etc., 23 Colo. 120, 46 Pac. 677,
679. In a case where an executor or administrator is empowered by
will to administer an estate without the intervention of the court, the
claim of a creditor against such estate is not barred by the fact that
he did not present his claim within one year from the first publication of the notice to creditors, especially where his claim did not
exist until after the expiration of the year specified in such notice.—
In re MacDonald's Estate, 29 Wash. 422, 69 Pac. 1111, 1115. Where a
creditor presented an amended claim to the executor within due
time after the first publication of notice to creditors, and at a time
when the executor had not acted upon the claim theretofore presented,
as required by law, the creditor's time for commencing an action upon
the claim is governed by the rejection of the claim; if the complaint
is filed within three months after such rejection, the action is not
barred.—Colburn v. Parrett, 27 Cal. App. 541, 150 Pac. 786. To bar a
claim against an estate under what is generally known as the statute
of non-claim, there must be proof that the notice was advertised or
posted, as required by law, containing all the material and essential
matters intended by the statute to be conveyed to the creditor, and
a notice which fails to convey such information is void, and does not
start the statute of limitation.—State (ex rel. Langford) v. Soliss
(Okla.), 152 Pac. 1114, 1115. The statutes of Oklahoma, which provide
for the giving of notice to creditors of the estate of a deceased person,
declare that the notice shall contain substantially the statement that
unless claims are presented within the period named "the same will
be forever barred," and it is held that a notice in which such phrase,
or words clearly and plainly purporting the same meaning to not appear, is void and does not start the statute of limitations or prevent
an action on a claim against the estate.—State (ex rel. Langford) v.
Soliss (Okla.), 152 Pac. 1114, 1115. If a party makes an attempt to
present a claim to an administrator, or executor for allowance, but for
some cause fails to properly do so, he is not estopped from presenting
it in due form if within the proper time.—Patrick & Co. v. Austin,
20 N. D. 261, 267, 127 N. W. 109.

(9) **Action is barred when.**—Under the statute, all claims must be
presented within the time limited in the notice to creditors, or they
are barred forever, except in cases where it is made to appear, by the
affidavit of the claimant, to the satisfaction of the court or judge,
that the claimant had no notice, by reason of being out of the state.
Hence if a claim is not presented within such time, it is barred.—
Melton v. Martin, 28 Mont. 150, 72 Pac. 414; Consolidated Nat. Bank
v. Hayes, 112 Cal. 75, 44 Pac. 469; Morse v. Clark, 10 Colo. 216, 14
Pac. 327; In re Hobson's Estate, 40 Colo. 332, 91 Pac. 929; and the
claimant can not be given relief on the ground of mistake, if the
court is not satisfied that a mistake was ever made, and that the
claimant could have discovered its existence within the time limited
in the notice, by the exercise of reasonable diligence.—Melton v. Mar-

tin, 28 Mont. 150, 72 Pac. 414. Under the Colorado statute of non-claim, a claim that has not been exhibited as the statute requires, within one year from the granting of letters testamentary, is barred except as to property that may be subsequently discovered or inventoried by the executor; and where there is no claim that the is any such property of the estate, the claim is completely barred.—In re Hobson's Estate, 40 Colo. 332, 91 Pac. 929, 931. Where no administrator has been appointed, the claim of a creditor will become barred by limitation at the end of three years after the last date at which the administrator might have been appointed.—Brown v. Baxter, 77 Kan. 97, 94 Pac. 155, 574. A promissory note which has not been presented as a claim against the estate of a decedent is barred by the statute of limitations, where more than six years have elapsed since the note became due.—In re Hobson's Estate, 40 Colo. 332, 91 Pac. 929, 931. In the case of non-intervention wills, creditors must present their claims within one year of the publication of notice, and failure so to do bars such claim.—Foley v. McDonnell, 48 Wash. 272, 93 Pac. 321, 322. A claim against an estate presented more than two years after notice of the appointment of the executor, was barred under the provisions of a statute of non-claim requiring claims against an estate to be presented within two years after notice of the appointment of the executor, otherwise they shall be forever barred, notwithstanding an oral agreement between the claimant and the decedent not to present the claim until the death of the latter's widow, which death occurred more than two years after notice of appointment of the executor.—McDaniel v. Putnam, 100 Kan. 550, 555, L. R. A. 1917E, 1100, 164 Pac. 1167, 1169. If a man departs from this state and dies abroad leaving property here, but more than six years elapse between the death of the decedent and the time when letters of administration are issued in this state, no suit or action for the collection of any claim against the estate of such decedent can be maintained here; such a claim is not only barred, but in equity is a stale claim.—Luse v. Webster, 74 Or. 489, 492, 145 Pac. 1063. Where the complaint, summons, and proof of service affirmatively and conclusively show that an action upon a claim against the estate of a decedent's estate was not commenced until 107 days after its presentment to the administrator, and 97 days after its rejection, the statutory limit of time for suit being three months after the date of the rejection of the claim, judgment of dismissal for want of a cause of action was properly entered therefor based upon the summons, complaint, and proof of service.—Mann v. Redmon, 27 N. D. 346, 145 N. W. 1031.

REFERENCES.

Claims against decedent's estate are barred when.—See note 8 L. R. A. 651, 652.

(10) Pleading. Defense.—As between parties acting in their own right, the plea of the statute of limitations is unquestionably a per-

sonal privilege which may be waived. But an executor or administrator acting for others, and in a trust capacity, is not vested with this privilege, and has no power to waive such a defense. He will not be permitted, by his failure to invoke the plea of the statute of limitations, to suffer judgment upon the claim, which, when presented to him, he was bound by law to reject because of the bar of the statute.—Reay v. Heazelton, 28 Cal. 335, 338, 60 Pac. 977. The failure of the executor or administrator to plead the bar of the statute of limitations can not avail the claimant, since the duty to set up the bar of the statute rests upon the executor or administrator. In pleading the statute of limitations, the facts relied upon, or the facts constituting the defense, should be stated. A defense of the statute of limitations may be presented by demurrer when the pleadings show that the statutory time has elapsed. But the statute of limitations can not be raised under a demurrer that the complaint does not state facts sufficient to constitute a cause of action. The statute must be pleaded.—Fullerton v. Bailey, 17 Utah 85, 53 Pac. 1020. To be raised by demurrer, the bar must affirmatively appear on the face of the petition; otherwise the objection must be taken by answer.—Columbia Sav. & L. Assoc. v. Clause, 13 Wyo. 166, 78 Pac. 708, 709; Wise v. Williams, 72 Cal. 544, 548, 14 Pac. 204; McCann v. Pennie, 100 Cal. 547, 553, 35 Pac. 158. If it does not affirmatively appear upon the face of the complaint that the claim is barred by the statute of limitations, a demurrer based upon such statute is not allowable. The question as to whether the claim is or is not barred is a matter to be determined at the trial, if the claim does not appear on its face to have been barred when presented. The fact that it does not show upon its face whether it was or was not barred would not defeat a recovery.—Wise v. Hogan, 77 Cal. 184, 187, 19 Pac. 278. If the statute provides that suit must be brought upon a rejected claim within three months after its rejection, and that if not so brought it is forever barred, an answer, in an action upon a rejected claim which alleges that the claim was duly presented at a date named, and that the same was not acted on within ten days thereafter, nor at all, and that more than three months after such ten-day period had expired before suit was commenced, states a complete defense.—Boyd v. Von Neida, 9 N. D. 337, 83 N. W. 329. The statute of limitations is a valid defense by an administrator to a suit on a rejected claim, when such suit is not begun within the statutory time after the rejection, whether express or implied; but a rejection is not to be implied when the claim is held open, by arrangement, to enable the administrator to make investigation concerning it.—Powell-Sanders Co. v. Carssow, 28 Idaho 201, 152 Pac. 1067. In an action by a lessor against the administrator of the estate of the lessee for damages for nonperformance of the terms of the lease the complaint set up the presentation of the claim and its rejection. Demurrer was interposed on the ground that the action was not brought within the time limited by the statute of non-claim. Plaintiff moved to strike the demurrer out as "sham and frivolous" and for judgment. Defendant also moved to strike out the complaint and for dismissal of action. The court ordered the demurrer stricken out and gave the defendant leave to answer on any issues other than the statute of limitations. The defendant appealed. The court granted the appeal, giving the defendant leave to set up the defense of the statute of non-claim.—Mann v. Redmond, 23 N. D. 508, 137 N. W. 478.

7. Judgment against executor or administrator.

(1) In general.—It is one of the very elements of the law, that, when a suitor reaches the parting of the ways in the pursuit of inconsistent remedies, he must elect which road he shall follow. The first step taken is an election, and the election, when made, is irrevocable. But this principle has no application to a case where there is no choice between two inconsistent remedies. Thus the mere filing of a complaint, which can not be sustained, and which was abandoned, can not be urged as an estoppel against the assertion of a judgment against the estate which has not been satisfied and still remains in full force and effect. In such a case there is no election of remedies.—Shively v. Harris, 5 Cal. App. 513, 90 Pac. 971, 972. A judgment on a rejected claim against the estate of a decedent is subject to be afterward contested by any person interested in the estate, in the same manner and to the same extent as other allowed claims may be contested. But in all such cases the burden is upon the party contesting to show that the claim was not properly allowed.—Estate of More, 121 Cal. 635, 639, 54 Pac. 148. An undertaker need not petition the probate court to have his claim paid, for services in respect to burying the decedent; but, in order to establish the demand and have judgment therefor, payable in due course of administration, may sue the executor in the latter's representative capacity.—Golden Gate U. Co. v. Taylor, 168 Cal. 94, Ann. Cas. 1915D, 742, 52 L. R. A. (N. S.) 1152, 141 Pac. 922. Where there is no inconsistency between the general and special verdicts of the jury as to the amount awarded by them to the claimant, which was less than the face of the claim, it is error for the court to grant a motion of the claimant for judgment for the full amount claimed, on the theory that the value of the several items were not in issue.—Estate of Weir, 168 Cal. 330, 143 Pac. 612. If the claim presented against the estate of a decedent shows on its face that the claimant has no cause of action, the claim can not be the basis of a successful litigation against the representative of the estate.—Tharp v. Jackson, 85 Or. 78, 165 Pac. 585, 1173. Where, in an action on a claim against an estate, the only question contested is the sufficiency of the verification of the claim, and this court having held that the verification is sufficient, and set aside the judgment appealed from, it is the duty of the court below to render judgment, under the statutes, against the estate.—Westinghouse E. & M. Co. v. Robison, 42

Okla. 754, 759, 142 Pac. 1105. If a part of the plaintiff's claim is admitted by the answer to be justly due, the plaintiff is entitled to judgment for that amount without regard to the value of the evidence as to the remainder of the claim.—Roy v. King's Estate, 55 Mont. 567, 179 Pac. 821. To warrant a recovery upon an account against a deceased person, it is not necessary to prove the separate items of the account where such person had, after examination, approved the account and expressed an intention to pay it; this constituted it an account stated; and proof establishing the account stated is prima facie sufficient to warrant a recovery, though the complaint declares upon an open account.—Roy v. King's Estate, 55 Mont. 567, 179 Pac. 821. In a suit to enforce against an estate a rejected claim, filed by the decedent's son and lessee, under a farm lease, held that, conceding the·merit of the plaintiff's contention that the lease was on a half and half basis, the plaintiff was not entitled to judgment.—Gossard v. Stevens (S. D.), 166 N. W. 233.

(2) **Default. Amendment.**—A judgment by default may be taken against an executor or administrator, as well as any other party. A default must be taken as an admission of all the material allegations of the complaint.—Chase v. Swain, 9 Cal. 130, 137. If a judgment against an executor or administrator is informal, in that it omits the provision that it is to be paid out of the estate "in the due course of administration," such omission may be supplied by an amendment, though made some years after the judgment was rendered, where such amendment is made by the records in the action.—Estate of Schroeder, 46 Cal. 304, 316. Thus it is error to render a personal judgment against him, and such error being apparent on the judgment roll, it may be corrected even on appeal.—Davis v. Lamb, 5 Cal. Unrep. 765, 35 Pac. 306, 307.

(3) **Judgment of dismissal.**—Where plaintiffs could not under any circumstances be entitled to a judgment different from that which defendant as administrator offered them they can not complain that their action was dismissed on their refusal to accept the offer.—First Nat. Bank v. Hotchkiss, 49 Colo. 593, 114 Pac. 312.   .

(4) **Form of judgment.**—Upon the issue as to whether the estate of a decedent is indebted to the plaintiff upon a claim, a judgment in personam can not be rendered against the executor or administrator.—Myers v. Mott, 29 Cal. 359, 363, 89 Am. Dec. 49; Rice v. Inskeep, 34 Cal. 224, 226. A judgment against an executor or administrator should first ascertain the amount due, and adjudge the same to be a valid claim against the estate, and then provide that the same be paid by the defendant "in the due course of administration."—Fisher v. Hopkins (Chadwick), 4 Wyo. 379, 62 Am. St. Rep. 38, 34 Pac. 899; Rice v. Inskeep, 34 Cal. 224, 226; Racouillat v. Sansevain, 32 Cal. 376; Kelly v. Bandini, 50 Cal. 530; Drake v. Foster, 52 Cal. 225. In an action to foreclose a mortgage against the estate of a decedent, brought

after the note and mortgage have been presented to the executor or administrator, and rejected, the judgment for a deficiency should provide that it be paid "in due course of administration."—Moore v. Russell, 133 Cal. 297, 301, 85 Am. St. Rep. 166, 65 Pac. 624. No valid judgment can be entered against a testator after his death, and upon the substitution of the executor or administrator of defendant as defendant, in an action to recover money; and where plaintiff obtains judgment, such judgment should be made payable "in due course of administration," and not otherwise.—Preston v. Knapp, 85 Cal. 559, 560, 24 Pac. 811; Estate of Brennan, 65 Cal. 517, 518, 4 Pac. 561. At common law, there could not be a joint judgment, even on the joint demand against the executor or administrator of a deceased obligor and the surviving obligors, for the reason that, as to the former, the judgment would be payable de bonis testatoris, and as to the latter, de bonis propriis. Nor has the rule been changed by the statute in California. There can not be a joint judgment against all, for the reason stated.—Bank of Stockton v. Howland, 42 Cal. 129, 130, 133. But an error in the judgment as to the executor or administrator does not invalidate the judgment as to the other defendants.—Bank of Stockton v. Howland, 42 Cal. 129, 133; Kelly v. Bandini, 50 Cal. 530. At common law, the rule is absolute that the estate of a deceased joint contractor was not liable to the obligee in the joint contract except in case of the insolvency of the surviving joint obligor. If the survivor was solvent, there was a plain and adequate remedy by action at law against him. In such a case the liability of the estate of the deceased joint obligor was to contribute to him after the debt was collected from or paid by him. In case of his insolvency, the obligee in the joint contract could bring his action in equity against the administrators of the deceased joint obligor. But the English courts no longer follow the old common law, making the solvent surviving joint obligor alone liable to the obligee in the joint contract. They permit the action to be brought against the executors or administrators in the first instance, whether the survivor be solvent or not; and a statute which provides that any person may be made a defendant, who has or claims an interest in the controversy adverse to plaintiff, or who is a necessary party to a complete determination of the question involved does away with the common-law rule, where the petition alleges a joint and several contract, and one of the joint contractors is dead.—Fisher v. Hopkins (Chadwick), 4 Wyo. 379, 62 Am. St. Rep. 38, 34 Pac. 899, 900. The judgment rendered in an action in equity for an accounting against the administrator of a deceased administrator must be made payable out of his estate "in due course of administration."—Vance v. Smith, 124 Cal. 219, 222, 56 Pac. 1031. A judgment against executors on a claim against the estate should be that they pay, "in due course of administration, the amount ascertained to be due." It should not be entered against them personally.—Clayton v. Dinwoodey, 33 Utah 251, 93 Pac. 723, 728. Under the statute of Utah, a judgment against an executor or administrator upon any claim for money against the estate of a deceased person must be, that the executor or administrator pay, in due course of administration, the amount ascertained to be due. No execution must issue upon such judgment, nor shall it create any lien upon the property of the estate or give to the judgment creditor any priority of payment. In such a case it is error to enter a personal judgment against the representative.—Smith v. Hanson, 34 Utah 171, 18 L. R. A. (N. S.) 520, 96 Pac. 1087, 1091. A judgment against an administrator as administrator is against the estate of the deceased and not against the administrator personally.— Collier v. Gannon, 40 Okla. 275, 137 Pac. 1179. A judgment, in favor of one filing a claim against an estate, is not invalidated by its concluding with an authorization of an issue of execution; although, on appeal, it must be amended by striking out the words giving such authority.— Stratton's Estate v. Finnerty, 57 Colo. 413, 140 Pac. 796. A judgment providing that the plaintiff "have and recover" from the defendant, as administratrix, the amount of the verdict and costs, is not in proper form; it should be as directed in this section; but, as no substantial rights are affected, it forms no ground of reversal.—Gauss v. Trump, 48 Mont. 92, 102, 135 Pac. 910. Where a judgment against an administrator is that the plaintiff "have and recover" from him, it is not reversible error, but the judgment may be corrected so as to require payment "in due course of administration."—Gauss v. Trump, 48 Mont. 92, 135 Pac. 913. A judgment against the executrix upon a demand against the estate of her testator should have been made payable in due course of administration.—Nathan v. Dierssen, 164 Cal. 607, 130 Pac. 12, 14. A judgment for mesne profits against the estate of a deceased person should be made payable in due course of administration.—Nathan v. Diersson, 164 Cal. 607, 130 Pac. 12.

(5) Recovery. Costs.—In an action upon a rejected claim against the estate of a decedent, the claimant can recover only upon the cause of action set forth in that claim.—Estate of Dutard, 147 Cal. 253, 81 Pac. 519, 520; Enscoe v. Fletcher, 1 Cal. App. 659, 82 Pac. 1075. If the court finds that the claim has been paid and that nothing is due, no further finding on the evidence concerning the usury law of the place in which the debt was contracted is necessary.—Sanguinetti v. Pelligrini, 2 Cal. App. 294, 83 Pac. 293, 296. A judgment on a claim draws interest at the legal rate.—Estate of Glenn, 74 Cal. 567, 568, 16 Pac. 396; Quivey v. Hall, 19 Cal. 97. If the executor or administrator neglects or fails to indorse his allowance or rejection on a claim within ten days after its presentation, and the claimant elects to consider his claim rejected, but, pending an action thereon, it is approved and filed as an allowed claim, a judgment for costs is the maximum of plaintiff's relief.—Hall v. Cayot, 141 Cal. 13, 16, 74 Pac. 299. In a suit against an administrator on a claim, part of which has been allowed against the estate, the court, on a verdict for the defendant, should enter judgment for the amount so allowed and tax the plaintiff with the costs.—

Selzer v. Selzer, 45 Okla. 142, 145 Pac. 318. A successful claimant against the estate of a deceased person is, under the statute of Colorado, entitled to his costs incurred in establishing the validity of his claim.—Brown v. First National Bank, 49 Colo. 393, 113 Pac. 486. While suit may be brought upon an allowed claim, the plaintiff can not recover costs, as he gets no more than the administrator was willing to allow.—Corbett v. Rice, 2 Nev. 330.

(6) Effect of judgment.—The sole object of an action upon a rejected claim for money is to place it among the allowed claims against the estate. The judgment rendered against an executor or administrator upon any claim for money against the deceased only establishes the claim in the same manner as if it had been allowed by the executor or administrator and the judge, and such judgment is no more effectual as an estoppel than an allowance of a claim would be, for it can be contested by the heirs on the settlement of an account in the same manner as a claim allowed by the executor or administrator and judge can be contested.—Hall v. Cayot, 141 Cal. 13, 16, 74 Pac. 299; Estate of More, 121 Cal. 635, 54 Pac. 148; McLean v. Crow, 88 Cal. 644, 26 Pac. 596; Estate of Glenn, 74 Cal. 567, 16 Pac. 396; Wells, Fargo & Co. v. Robinson, 13 Cal. 133. And a judgment in favor of an executor or administrator upon a claim presented by him and rejected by the judge has no greater force and effect than a judgment upon any other rejected claim. It merely establishes the claim in the same manner and to the same extent as if it had been allowed.—Estate of More, 121 Cal. 635, 638, 54 Pac. 148. A judgment against the estate of a decedent does not have the effect of giving the creditor any further right than if his claim had been allowed, nor does it determine the right of priority over other claims. That must be determined by the probate court when the assets are finally marshaled and the order of payment determined by that court.—McLean v. Crow, 88 Cal. 644, 647, 26 Pac. 596. A judgment at common law was no evidence in an action against the heir.—Beckett v. Selover, 7 Cal. 215, 228, 68 Am. Dec. 237; but in this country, where the real estate is a fund in the hands of the executor or administrator for the payment of debts, a judgment against the estate is prima facie evidence of indebtedness as against the heir.—Estate of More, 121 Cal. 635, 638, 54 Pac. 148; Estate of Schroeder, 46 Cal. 304, 318. A judgment may afterward be contested by any person interested in the estate, but in all cases the burden is upon the contestant to show that the claim is without merit.—Estate of More, 121 Cal. 635, 639, 54 Pac. 148. If one is sued as an administrator, but he is not an administrator, a judgment against him in a representative capacity is void.—Willis v. Farley, 24 Cal. 491, 502. A judgment against an executor, after the resignation of his trust and acceptance thereof by the probate court, and where the heirs were not made parties, does not bind the heirs.—Luco v. Commercial Bank, 70 Cal. 339, 341, 11 Pac. 650. No judgment can properly be rendered against an executor or administrator, pending an appeal from an order removing him, and such judgment should be

vacated, as the appeal does not revive or restore his powers, but he remains suspended from office pending the appeal, and has ceased from the date of the removal to be practically and in effect the executor or administrator of the estate until such time as the order may be reversed.—More v. More, 127 Cal. 460, 463, 59 Pac. 823. As the presentation of a judgment lien as a claim against an estate does not destroy the lien, the recovery of another judgment upon the claim, if rejected, does not merge the original judgment nor destroy its lien. The executor or administrator can not, by rejecting the claim and compelling the creditor to establish it by suit, take from the latter any right that would have attached to the claim had it been allowed without suit; and no difference is observable between the allowance of the claim by the executor or administrator or the court, and the judgment of the court allowing the claim on suit brought after its rejection; the judgment establishes the claim, the same as if it had been allowed. —Estate of Wiley, 188 Cal. 301, 306, 71 Pac. 449. The mere dismissal of an action against an estate of a decedent by the plaintiff, and a judgment entered thereon without prejudice to his right to bring a new action on the same cause of action, is no bar to another action on the same claim.—Moore v. Russell, 133 Cal. 297, 299, 85 Am. St. Rep. 166, 65 Pac. 624. When a judgment lien has attached to land, it continues two years from its inception, whether or not any execution has been levied. The issuance of execution is not necessary to the life of the judgment lien.—Estate of Wiley, 138 Cal. 301, 305, 71 Pac. 441. Where a claim against the estate of a deceased person is based upon a promissory note; where the executor has rejected the claim; where suit has been brought against the executor to establish it; and where the plaintiff obtains judgment, such judgment does not bind a legatee under the will; until a claim has been passed upon on settlement of an account or rendition of an exhibit, or in making a decree of sale, whether the claim be one approved by the executor or administrator and the judge, or one established, after rejection, by a final judgment, it may be contested by the heirs or legatees.—Estate of Hellier, 169 Cal. 77, 80, 145 Pac. 1008. A judgment establishing the validity of a claim against a decedent's estate has no other or greater effect than the allowance of a claim by an executor or administrator, and by a judge of the superior court.—Estate of Hellier, 169 Cal. 77, 145 Pac. 1008. By reason of section 1504 and 1636 of the Code of Civil Procedure of California, a judgment on a claim against an estate for money is an exception to the rule resulting from the provisions of section 1582, that a judgment against an executor or administrator in the actions there enumerated, including those "founded upon contracts" concludes the legatees, devisees, and heirs of testators and intestates.— Estate of Hellier, 169 Cal. 77, 82, 145 Pac. 1008. A claim against a decedent's estate, by passing to judgment, becomes an acknowledged debt of the estate, to be paid in due course of administration.—Miller v. Lewiston Nat. Bank, 18 Ida. 124, 142, 108 Pac. 901. A judgment against an executor or administrator, on a claim for money owed by the estate, only establishes the claim as though allowed, and the judgment must be that the executor or administrator pay the amount in due course of administration.—McElroy v. Whitney, 24 Ida. 210, 213, 133 Pac. 118. A judgment rendered against an administrator only establishes the claim for the amount ascertained to be due; it does not "create a lien upon the property of the estate."—Spokane Merchants' Assn. v. First Nat. Bank, 86 Wash. 367, L. R. A. 1918A, 323, 150 Pac. 434. The effect of a judgment rendered against an estate on a rejected claim is to adjudicate the same as a charge against the estate the same as if it had been allowed by the administrator and the county court, and, when a transcript of such judgment is filed in the probate proceedings, it becomes the duty of the administrator to pay the same in due course of administration.—National L. & C. Co. v. Robison's Estate, 48 Okla. 140, 149 Pac. 1133. In actions to establish rejected claims against estates, the heirs, legatees, and devisees are not concluded by the judgment obtained against the executor or administrator, but may contest the validity of the claim after it has been thus judicially established.—Estate of Hellier, 169 Cal. 77, 145 Pac. 1008. Under the provisions of section 5474, Revised Codes of Idaho, a judgment rendered against an executor or administrator upon any claim for money against the estate only establishes the claim in the same manner as if it had been allowed by the executor or administrator and the probate judge, and the judgment must be that the executor or administrator pay in due course of administration the amount ascertained to be due.—McElroy v. Whitney, 24 Ida. 210, 133 Pac. 118.

(7) Satisfaction of Judgment.—Where an action against an administrator was not brought within the year provided for the exhibition of claims, the satisfaction of the judgment was properly limited to decedent's uninventoried estate.—First Nat. Bank v. Hotchkiss, 49 Colo. 593, 114 Pac. 312.

(8) Interest.—A judgment recovered on a claim filed against an estate in course of administration, bears interest from the presentation of the claim.—White v. Deering, 38 Cal. App. 516, 179 Pac. 401.

(9) Merger.—If the creditor sues for the entire demand, giving no credit for the part allowed, the executor or administrator can set up the allowance in the answer, and the record will then necessarily show whether the judgment given is for the whole claim, or for the balance only. If it is for the whole, the allowance formerly made will be merged in such judgment. If for the balance, only, the former allowance will stand.—Haub v. Leggett, 160 Cal. 491, 117 Pac. 556.

(10) Execution.—After the death of the judgment debtor, no execution can issue; the creditor must then present his claim to the executor or administrator, like any other claim, and if rejected, may bring suit thereon.—Estate of Wiley, 138 Cal. 301, 305, 71 Pac. 441; Rice v. Inskeep, 34 Cal. 224, 226. Upon a judgment rendered against the de-

ceased in his lifetime, no execution can issue; but where an execution is issued before the death of the decedent, and actually levied, the property may be sold under it.—Balloc v. Rogers, 9 Cal. 123, 127. A decree for the payment of money in probate proceedings can not be enforced as for a contempt. The proper process is an execution.— Rostel v. Morat, 19 Or. 181, 23 Pac. 900. Where a statute inhibits an execution to issue upon a judgment rendered on a claim filed against an estate the violation of such inhibition does not justify the reversal of the judgment but same will be amended by striking out the part awarding the execution.—Stratton's Estate v. Finnerty, 57 Colo. 413, 140 Pac. 797. The fact that a judgment rendered against an estate on a rejected claim directs that an execution may issue thereon does not render it void or impair its effectiveness as an adjudicated claim against the estate.—National L. & C. Co. v. Robison's Estate, 48 Okla. 140, 149 Pac. 1133. Where a judgment debtor, at the time of judgment, was the record owner of designated property, but died after having made a conveyance thereof, and an action is brought by the judgment creditor against the grantee and others for the enforcement of a judgment lien, the petition should be construed as an action to enforce the judgment lien against the particular property described in the petition, and not as an action to establish a lien, the statute declaring, in effect, that no execution will issue on a judgment, for the recovery of money, rendered for or against a testator or intestate in his lifetime.—Stephenson v. Lichtenstein, 24 Wyo. 417, 421, 160 Pac. 1170.

8. Enforcement of claims against estates.

(1) In general.—If an administrator uses money belonging to an estate with which to buy property in his own name, and to all appearances in his individual capacity the administrator has the legal title, but he holds it in trust for the heirs, and one who, without notice of the rights of the estate, supplies labor and materials for a building thereon, acquires a mechanic's lien on the building and land, superior to the rights of the heirs.—Seibel v. Bath, 5 Wyo. 409, 40 Pac. 756, 760. A creditor has the right to reduce his collaterals and to pursue his debtor by a judgment and execution until his claim is satisfied, subject to the limitation that the creditor may only have one satisfaction; and if he is a creditor of an insolvent estate of a decedent, who holds collateral security for his claim, but disposes of such collateral security after his claim has been proved, the amount received for the security is a payment pro tanto, and to that extent the debt is extinguished. He is, therefore, entitled to dividends only on the amount remaining due on the claim. He is not entitled to dividends on the whole claim as allowed, though the authorities on this question are divided.—Sullivan v. Erle, 8 Colo. App. 1, 44 Pac. 948, 949, 953. A creditor of an estate which can not pay all claims in full is entitled to come in upon notice at the settlement of the administrator's account, and contest any allowed claim. He is injured by the allowance of a claim, for the reason that it reduces the percentage which he is to receive in case the estate does not pay its debts in full. He is interested in the estate, and there is facing him a final judgment, which is to his injury, given without his knowledge, and without his having a day in court. There has been no hearing to which he has been invited; there has been no adjudication at which he has been notified to appear. Of course, it may be said that he can be present at the probate court, or before the probate judge, during all the period during which claims may be filed, and watch for the presentation of the claim to which he believes he has a valid objection. But the law does not require anything of this sort.—In re Mouillerat's Estate, 14 Mont. 245, 36 Pac. 185, 187. Where the note of a decedent is secured by shares of corporate stock, but the claim is not acted upon within the statutory time by the executor or administrator, and the claimant, deeming his claim rejected, brings suit upon the rejected note and security, he is entitled to enforce both, and to have an order of sale of his stock as against the executor who occupies the same position that the decedent would have occupied had he lived.—Hall v. Cayot, 141 Cal. 13, 18, 19, 74 Pac. 299. A claimant against the estate of a decedent can not recover the amount of his debt from the administrator's bondsmen, where he failed to file his claim against the estate until after the time set therefor, and made no attempt to have its validity determined by the court. The filing of the claim in the county court proves nothing, and, unless there is an allowance and an adjudication, there is no establishment of the debt as against the estate, and no proof of its liability to pay.—Metz v. People, 6 Colo. App. 57, 40 Pac. 51, 53. A judgment obtained against the sureties on the bond of an official can not be enforced by them as a claim against his estate, after his death, until they have paid such bond.—Estate of Hill, 67 Cal. 238, 244, 7 Pac. 664. The holder of a note, delivered to him as the heir of an estate, may maintain an action thereon against the executor, though such note has not been indorsed or assigned to him.—Perry v. Wheeler, 63 Kan. 870, 66 Pac. 1007. A creditor whose claim against the estate of a decedent has been presented, and rejected in whole or in part, may maintain a suit in equity for the enforcement of his rights.— Walkerly v. Bacon, 85 Cal. 137, 141, 24 Pac. 638. In an action to foreclose the lien of a street assessment, after the death of the owner, the personal representatives of the deceased owner are not necessary parties defendant. His heirs or devisees are the only necessary defendants.—Phelan v. Dunne, 72 Cal. 229, 231, 13 Pac. 662. Where a will directed the payment of the testator's debts out of personalty so far as it would go, the creditor could not subject realty in another state without showing that the personalty had been exhausted, the statute requiring testamentary directions in such regard to be observed.— Richards v. Blaisdell, 12 Cal. App. 101, 106 Pac. 732.

(2) By attachment.—A probate judge has no authority to issue an order of attachment in an action pending in the district court upon

a claim not due, and any levy of an order of attachment issued only by the probate judge is void.—Noyes v. Phipps, 10 Kan. App. 580, 63 Pac. 659. Funds in the hands of an executor or administrator of an estate can not be reached by a garnishment proceeding in an action against a distributee, before an order of distribution has been made, and while the estate remains unsettled.—Nelson v. Stull, 65 Kan. 585, 68 Pac. 617, 618; Norton v. Clark, 18 Nev. 247, 2 Pac. 529; but property vested in a non-resident executor or administrator is subject to attachment and other process.—Barlow v. Cogan, 1 Wash. Ter. 257. Even if a lien by execution could be levied upon specific property sold to a person before his death to satisfy a judgment for the purchase price, it does not follow that the proceeds of such property after sale by the administrator could be levied upon to satisfy such judgment, especially if the same has passed into the hands of the administrator, with other property, and has become so mixed that it can not be ascertained how much of the goods sold by the administrator was sold by the plaintiff to the deceased, nor how much such goods brought. If the plaintiff has a right to any lien at all, it is for the specific goods sold to the deceased under and by virtue of the execution. The plaintiff has no legal claim to money in the hands of the administrator, even though the money accrued in part from the sale of the goods which had previously been sold to the decedent.—In re Farmer's Estate, 17 Utah 80, 53 Pac. 972. By the levy of an attachment at the commencement of an action, only a contingent lien upon the land is created; and until it is matured by a judgment the lien can not be enforced against the property; and when judgment is finally obtained the plaintiff acquires no other than a creditor's interest in the land, except the right to enforce the lien by a sale of the land. The rendition of the judgment, and of an order decreeing the sale of the real estate, does not transfer the title thereto, nor give any right of possession to the judgment creditor. Until the sale and conveyance are made, the right of possession remains in the debtor, and until the sale is completed in pursuance of the judgment and decree, neither the plaintiff nor the purchaser at the sale acquires any right to the lands, issues, or profits of the real estate. Hence, where an administrator takes possession of the real estate of an intestate under an order of the probate court, and collects and receives rent for the same, an attaching creditor has no special right to the rents received, and no interest therein beyond that of a general creditor of the estate.—Kothman v. Markson, 34 Kan. 542, 9 Pac. 218, 222. Where the creditor of the devisee attached real property devised before the distribution of the estate, his rights under the attachment levied will in no way be affected by the decree of distribution. He is not required to present his claim to the probate court, and is not entitled to participate in the distribution of the estate, but the propery distributed continues to be subject to the lien of his attachment, if properly levied.—Martinovich v. Marsicano, 150 Cal. 597, 119 Am. St. Rep. 254, 89 Pac. 333. Property of a decedent attached in his lifetime

can not be sold after his death to satisfy a judgment against him.
The death of defendant destroys the attachment lien.—Myers v. Mott,
29 Cal. 359, 367, 89 Am. Dec. 49; Ham v. Cunningham, 50 Cal. 365, 367.
The death of a defendant destroys the lien of an attachment, and the
attached property passes into the hands of the executor or administrator, to be administered upon in due course of administration.—Myers
v. Mott, 29 Cal. 359, 367, 89 Am. Dec. 49. If the defendant died after
the service of summons and the levy of an attachment, and before
judgment, and the executor or administrator is substituted, and the
action is continued against him, it is error for the court to render
a judgment and enforce the lien of the attachment by a sale of the
attached property and an application of the proceeds to the satisfaction
of the demand.—Myers v. Mott, 29 Cal. 359, 367, 89 Am. Dec. 49.

**9. Action pending against decedent at time of his death. Presentation
of claim.**

(1) In general.—The plaintiff in an action pending against a deceased person at the time of his death must present his claim against
the estate to the executor or administrator of the estate of the deceased, where such presentation is necessary under the law, and can
not recover in his action unless proof of such presentation is made.—
Derby & Co. v. Jackman, 89 Cal. 1, 4, 26 Pac. 610; Hibernia, etc., Soc. v.
Wackenreuder, 99 Cal. 503, 507, 508, 34 Pac. 219; Falkner v. Hendy, 107
Cal. 49, 52, 40 Pac. 21, 386; Vermont Marble Co. v. Black, 123 Cal. 21,
22, 55 Pac. 599; Gregory v. Clabrough's Executors, 129 Cal. 475, 479, 62
Pac. 72; Frazier v. Murphy, 133 Cal. 91, 95, 65 Pac. 326. All that is
required of the plaintiff in such a case is simply to present his claim.—
Gregory v. Clabrough's Executors, 129 Cal. 475, 479, 62 Pac. 72. The
presentation of a claim must be proved, although not denied in the
answer, and no judgment for the plaintiff can be properly rendered
upon the pleadings.—Derby & Co. v. Jackman, 89 Cal. 1, 4, 26 Pac. 610.
If the plaintiff fails to make the required proof, upon a trial had, against
the personal representatives of the decedent, he should be nonsuited.—
Vermont Marble Co. v. Black, 123 Cal. 21, 23, 55 Pac. 599. A statute
limiting the commencement of an action upon a rejected claim, which is
past due, to a specified time, has no application to an action already
pending; and the fact that the suit may have been revived against the
executors more than three months after the rejection of the claim
can not affect the cause of action.—Gregory v. Clabrough's Executors,
129 Cal. 475, 479, 62 Pac. 72. Proof of the presentation of a claim to
the executor or administrator of the estate of defendant, where he
died during the pendency of an action against him, and where the
executor or administrator of his estate has been substituted as defendant, is not a fact essential to the validity of the judgment, where no
issue has been made upon that question, but the failure to make the
proof is ground for reversal, when objection is made in the trial court,
and the exception is properly preserved, although the appeal was not

taken within sixty days after the rendition of the judgment.—Falkner v. Hendy, 107 Cal. 49, 53, 40 Pac. 21, 386. The objection must be first made in the court below; it is too late to raise the point for the first time in the supreme court.—Drake v. Foster, 52 Cal. 225, 227. A statute which requires the plaintiff to present his claim to the representative of the estate, where the defendant dies pending the suit, simply means that, when an action is pending against the decedent at the time of his death, the plaintiff therein is not relieved from the duty of presenting for allowance the claim upon which it is based, when the claim is of that character that he would have been required to make such presentation in order to preserve its validity as a claim against the estate if such action had not been brought in the lifetime of the decedent.—Hibernia, etc., Soc. v. Wackenreuder, 99 Cal. 503, 507, 34 Pac. 219; Frazier v. Murphy, 133 Cal. 91, 96, 65 Pac. 326. Where judgment by default was entered against defendant upon a cause of action upon contract, and thereafter erroneously set aside and vacated, it was not necessary that plaintiff should, upon defendant's death, present the same as a claim for allowance as still pending within the meaning of section 1502 of the Code of Civil Procedure of California, the judgment having been rendered within the lifetime of the decedent, and the default upon which the same was entered not having been set aside in a proper proceeding, it fell under the provisions of section 1505, Code Civ. Proc. of that state.—Christerson v. French (Cal.), 182 Pac. 27, 28. Where a statute provides that, when an action is pending against a decedent at the time of his death, the plaintiff must present his claim to the executor or administrator for allowance or rejection, properly authenticated, and that no recovery shall be had in the action unless proof be made of the presentation required, the purpose of such statute is sufficiently complied with where the case has been revived in the name of the administrator, who files an answer, denying liability on grounds other than failure to present the claim, and cross-petition, asking for affirmative relief against the plaintiff within the time allowed for presenting claims.—Coleman v. Bowles (Okla.), 181 Pac. 304, 306.

REFERENCES.

Death of defendant pending action against him; effect of, as to attachment.—See head-line 8, subd. (2), supra.

(2) **Practice. Substitution. Supplemental complaint.**—If a defendant dies pending an action against him, the proper practice is for the plaintiff to file a supplemental complaint, alleging the death, and due presentation of the claim.—Falkner v. Hendy, 107 Cal. 49, 52, 40 Pac. 21, 386; Bemmerly v. Woodward, 124 Cal. 568, 570, 57 Pac. 561. The proper practice on the suggestion of the death of a party after verdict and before judgment is to direct the entry of the judgment provided for in the statute, and then to suspend all further proceedings in the cause until an executor or administrator shall qualify and be substi-

tuted as a party.—Estate of Page, 50 Cal. 40, 42. If the judgment in such a case is entered against the executor by name, payable in due course of administration, instead of being against the testator by name, such error does not render the judgment void, and it is not necessary to present it to the executor for allowance as a claim against the estate, but the executor must pay out of money in his hands applicable for that purpose.—Estate of Page, 50 Cal. 40, 43. If a party against whom a money judgment has been rendered moves for a new trial, but dies before the motion is determined, and his executor is substituted as defendant, and prosecutes the motion, and obtains an order modifying the judgment, but no new judgment is rendered, the judgment as modified is a claim against the estate which should be paid in due course of administration, and no presentation thereof to the executor is necessary.—Estate of Brennan, 65 Cal. 517, 518, 4 Pac. 561. If an appellant dies pending an appeal, a motion by his substituted executors to remand the cause to the lower court upon the ground that the judgment is incapable of enforcement for the reason that there was a want of proper presentation of it as a claim against the estate of the deceased will be denied. The enforcement of a judgment, or the right to withhold its enforcement, is a matter primarily within the jurisdiction of the court by which it was rendered. Upon the death of the appellant, the power of the lower court to enforce its judgment by execution terminated, and the respondent was remitted for its collection to the probate jurisdiction of the court having charge of the administration of the estate of the decedent, and to that court the executors must present any defense there may have been to its payment out of the assets of that estate.—People's Home Sav. Bank v. Sadler, 1 Cal. App. 189, 193, 194, 91 Pac. 1029. Where a judgment had been obtained against a joint debtor in his lifetime, and he died pending his appeal from the judgment, and his executors were substituted pending the appeal, and obtained a reversal of the judgment, the executors are not released because of a failure to present the claims to them.—Megrath v. Gilmore, 15 Wash. 558, 46 Pac. 1032. If a widow has no children, and dies pending her appeal from an order refusing to grant her application to have the whole estate set apart to her, her right does not survive to any one, and the proceedings abate by her death.—Estate of Bachelder, 123 Cal. 466, 467, 56 Pac. 97. Although an order substituting the representative of a deceased person as a party to an action pending an appeal to the supreme court has been made, the regular and orderly method of procedure is to procure upon a proper showing a like substitution in the lower court. The propriety, if not the necessity, of such procedure must become manifest when it is considered that there will be thus avoided vexatious questions of the responsibility for costs and of the effect which a judgment may have as a lien upon the property of the personal representative who may be found chargeable with costs, and whose name does not appear in the judgment-books.—Reay v. Heazelton, 128 Cal. 335, 338,

60 Pac. 977. Where the statute provides that an action shall not abate by the death of a party, and that the same may be continued against his representative, or his successor in interest, the filing of a supplemental complaint, and the bringing in as defendants such executors or administrators is not the commencement of any action against them, but only a step in the progress of the original action to judgment; and where the original action was commenced within the time limited by the statute, the cause of action stated in the supplemental complaint is not barred by the provisions of such statute, though the time therein specified had expired before the filing of the latter complaint.—Hibernia, etc., Soc. v. Wackenreuder, 99 Cal. 503, 510, 34 Pac. 219. In the absence of proof of the presentation of the claim, a judgment against the executor or administrator as a substituted defendant, payable in due course of administration, and against their objection for want of such proof, is erroneous.—Frazier v. Murphy, 133 Cal. 91, 95, 65 Pac. 326.

10. Death of one against whom right of action exists.

(1) Presentation or filing of claim.—A mortgagee, who has assigned the note and mortgage to her brother, under an agreement that he will foreclose, sell the property, and account to her, may, if the brother die, several years after the foreclosure, without ever having accounted to her, present a claim in the form of an account against the estate, the probate court having jurisdiction in such a case.—Eadie v. Hamilton, 94 Kan. 214, 146 Pac. 323. If a person, after obtaining securities from another to sell and return the proceeds to the owner, uses the securities for some purpose of his own and then dies, the owner need not file a claim against the estate as one of the first class; the decedent would not be regarded as a trustee.—McCutcheon v. Osborne, 61 Colo. 408, 412, 158 Pac. 136. The word "trustee," as used in the statute whereby a claim may be filed against an estate as one of the first class when the decedent received money as trustee, includes only trustees under a technical or special trust.—McCutcheon v. Osborne, 61 Colo. 408, 412, 158 Pac. 136.

(2) Right of action preserved.—If a person against whom an action may be brought dies before the expiration of the time limited for the commencement thereof, and the cause of action survives, and the statute provides that an action may be commenced against his executors or administrators after the expiration of that time, and within one year after the issuing of letters testamentary or of administration, such statute applies only to cases where the statute of limitations has commenced to run. The object of the statute is, not to curtail, but to prolong the period for suing in the given category.—Smith v. Hall, 19 Cal. 85, 86; Estate of Bullard, 116 Cal. 355, 357, 48 Pac. 219. The evident purpose of such a statute is to secure to a party, who has a cause of action against a decedent, one year after the appointment of a legal representative within which to bring his action. This may or

may not have the effect of extending the time.—Barclay v. Blackinton, 127 Cal. 189, 192, 59 Pac. 834. A party having a cause of action against the estate of a deceased person is not bound to cause administration to be had because the statute expressly extends his time for one year after the issuance of letters.—Davis v. Hart, 123 Cal. 384, 388, 55 Pac. 1060. Upon the death of a judgment debtor, the plaintiff's right of action ceases; but the statute substitutes the presentation of the claim for suit, allowing the executor or administrator to acknowledge it and place it on the list of recognized debts of the estate. The right to sue does not come from the existence of the claim and the non-payment, but comes from the refusal of the executor or administrator to acknowledge it as a just claim against the estate. This right, therefore, does not accrue until the presentation of the claim, and the party is not bound to present it until after publication of the notice to creditors. It would be unjust to hold that the claim is barred by the statute of limitations when the claimant was in no default.—Quivey v. Hall, 19 Cal. 97, 100. It is a general rule of law, that when a right of action has accrued against a party who may be sued, the statute of limitations begins to run, and its running will not be suspended by the happening of any subsequent event, unless within some saving clause of the statute; and the subsequent death of the debtor or the lapse of time before the appointment of his personal representative is no exception to the rule. And this is true, although the debtor may die within the period fixed by the statute, and, by reason of litigation as to the right to probate, an executor or administrator may not be appointed until after the expiration of the time limited. To avoid the harshness and injustice of this rule, that often barred a cause of action, without any fault or laches on the part of the creditor, statutes have been passed that preserve to a creditor the right to bring an action within a specified time after the appointment of an executor or administrator, when the time limited would otherwise expire subsequently to the death of the debtor, and before the appointment of his personal representative. Hence, under statutes which provide that an action can not be maintained against an executor or administrator until the rejection of the claim and the expiration of six months from the granting of letters testamentary, it is manifest that the allowance of six months after the issuing of letters testamentary, before an executor or administrator can be sued, is a statutory prohibition, and has the effect of suspending the operation of the statute during the time of the continuance of such prohibition.—Blaskower v. Steel, 23 Or. 106, 31 Pac. 253, 254. If a husband and wife, in view of a divorce, agree out of court upon monthly payments to be made by the husband for the support of their minor child of tender years, during her minority, and the husband soon afterwards dies, without having made provision in his will for the support of such daughter during her minority, the obligation of the contract survives the death of the promisor and may be enforced as a claim against his estate.—Stone v. Bayley, 75 Wash. 184, 197, 48 L. R. A. (N. S.) 429, 134 Pac. 820.

3. Effect of, as to statute of limitations.—Where no cause of action accrued to a person in his lifetime, but did accrue after his death, the statute of limitations began to run at the date of accrual, though there was no person in existence competent to sue, and continued to run from such date without cessation; but, where the cause of action has accrued to the testator or intestate in his lifetime, the running of the statute will not be stayed by his death until the grant of administration. "It is not easy," said Sanderson, J., "to perceive why, upon principle, any distinction should be made between the case where the cause of action accrues in the lifetime of the testator or intestate, and where it does not accrue until after his death. The only reason which can be given why the statute should not run in any case is, that there is no person to sue, therefore no person to whom laches can be imputed, but the reason applies to the latter case as well as to the former, and if an exception is allowed in the former, it ought also to be extended to the latter."—Tynan v. Walker, 35 Cal. 634, 638, 95 Am. Dec. 152; Hibernia Sav. & L. Soc. v. Conlin, 67 Cal. 178, 180, 7 Pac. 477; Estate of Bullard, 116 Cal. 355, 356, 48 Pac. 219. If a cause of action accrues after the death of a person, the statute of limitations begins to run at the date of the accrual, though there is no person in existence competent to sue, and the statute continues to run from such date without cessation; and it makes no difference whether the cause of action was one accruing after the death of a person who would, if he had survived the accrual, been plaintiff in the action, or whether it is one where the action would have been against a person as defendant if he had lived until the cause of action came into existence.—Hibernia Sav. & L. Soc. v. Conlin, 67 Cal. 178, 7 Pac. 477, 478. A claim against the estate of a decedent, which did not exist until after the expiration of the year specified in the notice to creditors, could not be affected by such notice, nor be barred because not presented to the executor or administrator within that time.—In re MacDonald's Estate, 29 Wash. 422, 69 Pac. 1111, 1115. The statute of limitations will run upon a demand against the estate of a deceased person after a reasonable time has elapsed after the death of such person, and this, even though no executor or administrator has been appointed.—Black v. Elliott, 63 Kan. 211, 88 Am. St. Rep. 239, 65 Pac. 215. Where the plaintiff has failed to serve summons within the time prescribed by the statute after its issuance, his action must be dismissed, and it is immaterial that the defendant died within less than one year after the commencement of the action. The time, having begun to run during his lifetime, was not suspended by his death, nor by a failure to appoint an administrator of his estate. When once the statute of limitations begins to run, its running is not suspended by any subsequent disability. There is no exception to the bar of the statute, except it is found in the statute itself.—Davis v.

Hart, 123 Cal. 384, 388, 55 Pac. 1060; Union Sav. Bank v. Barrett, 132 Cal. 453, 64 Pac. 713, 1071. But the doctrine that when the statute of limitations begins to run, a subsequent disability, such as death of the party bound, etc., has no application where a judgment is obtained against an intestate in his lifetime and no execution is levied. In such a case, the judgment creditor being prevented by the statute from suing after the death of the debtor, the statute ceases to run until presentation of the claim to the administrator.—Quivey v. Hall, 19 Cal. 97, 100.

11. Foreclosure of mortgages.

(1) In general.—A mortgagee, by filing with an executor or administrator his mortgage debt, without mention of the security, does not necessarily waive his mortgage lien.—Kendrick State Bank v. Barnum, 31 Idaho 562, 173 Pac. 1144. If the mortgagee of a decedent files with the executor or administrator the mortgage debt as an unsecured claim and participates in a partial distribution of assets, he is, after returning to the estate, under order of court, the payment in partial distribution, entitled to proceed by foreclosure and have a decree, but his relief is limited by the security.—Kendrick State Bank v. Barnum, 31 Idaho 562, 173 Pac. 1144. Where a notice to creditors was given in an estate, and no claim was presented on account of a note and mortgage executed by the decedent, as required by section 1475, Code Civ. Proc. of California, a homestead declared, upon the community property covered by said mortgage, by the decedent and his wife subsequent to the execution of said mortgage, is released from the same and no action to foreclose said mortgage can be maintained.—Votypka v. Valentine, — Cal. App. —, 182 Pac. 76, 77.

(2) Presentation of claim.—The presentation and allowance of a mortgage claim against the estate of decedent is to prevent the debt from being barred and the mortgage extinguished by limitation; but it does not preclude a subsequent action for the foreclosure of the mortgage, in which the estate may be subjected to costs and counsel fees.—Moran v. Gardemeyer, 62 Cal. 96, 100, 23 Pac. 6; and, whether the claim be allowed or rejected, the creditor may at once proceed to foreclose his mortgage.—Willis v. Farley, 24 Cal. 490, 499.

(3) Presentation. When necessary.—If a mortgagee relies on the general assets in the hands of the executor or administrator of an estate for the payment of his debt, or any part of it, he must present the same in the manner and within the time required by the statute relating to the presentation of claims; and failing to do this, he is limited to the proceeds arising from the sale of the mortgaged property. In other words, a mortgage, to be available as a claim against the estate, must be presented as other claims.—Estate of Turner, 128 Cal. 388, 392, 60 Pac. 967; Pitte v. Shipley, 46 Cal. 154; Ellissen v. Halleck, 6 Cal. 386; Ellis v. Polhemus, 27 Cal. 350; Andrews v. Morse, 51 Kan. 30, 32 Pac. 640; Reid v. Sullivan, 20 Colo. 498, 39 Pac. 338;

Scammon v. Ward, 1 Wash. 179, 23 Pac. 439. Under the Colorado statute, a foreclosure of a mortgage can be had within one year from the death of the testator or intestate only by permission of the county court; and before a foreclosure can be had in any case, although one year may have elapsed, the debt or claim secured must have been presented and allowed by such court. The time within which such claim may be allowed is not fixed by statute, but where the claim is presented before the discharge of the administrator, and while the estate is still in process of administration, it is a sufficient compliance with the statute.—Sullivan v. Sheets, 22 Colo. 153, 43 Pac. 1012, 1013; Reid v. Sullivan, 20 Colo. 498, 39 Pac. 338. While it is not necessary under the statute of Oklahoma, for any one who holds an indebtedness against the estate of a deceased person, secured by a mortgage, to present his claim to an administrator before bringing suit to foreclose, in order to recover against the estate of decedent for any deficiency there may have been on sale of the mortgaged premises, the claim must have been presented to the administrator as required by law in the case of unsecured debts.—Fawcett v. McGahan-McKee Lumber Co., 39 Okla. 68, 134 Pac. 388.

(4) Presentation. When not necessary.—A mortgagee may foreclose his mortgage against the property of a decedent, described in the mortgage, without presentation of his claim to the executor or administrator of the estate, where he waives all claim to any other property of the estate.—Dreyfuss v. Giles, 79 Cal. 409, 21 Pac. 840; Anglo-Nevada Assur. Corp. v. Nadeau, 90 Cal. 393, 27 Pac. 302; German S. & L. Soc. v. Fisher, 92 Cal. 502, 28 Pac. 591; Heeser v. Taylor, 1 Cal. App. 619, 82 Pac. 977; Security Sav. Bank v. Connell, 65 Cal. 574, 4 Pac. 580; Andrews v. Morse, 51 Kan. 30, 32 Pac. 640; Fullerton v. Bailey, 17 Utah 85, 53 Pac. 1020; Teel v. Winston, 22 Or. 489, 29 Pac. 142; Reed v. Miller, 1 Wash. 426, 25 Pac. 334; Bank of Sonoma v. Charles, 86 Cal. 322, 327, 24 Pac. 1019; Bank of Suisun v. Stark, 106 Cal. 202, 39 Pac. 531. But, to do this, there must be an express waiver in the complaint.—Security Sav. Bank v. Connell, 65 Cal. 574, 4 Pac. 580; Dreyfuss v. Giles, 79 Cal. 409, 21 Pac. 840; Anglo-Nevada Assur. Corp. v. Nadeau, 90 Cal. 393, 27 Pac. 302; Bank of Sonoma County v. Charles, 86 Cal. 322, 327, 24 Pac. 1019. The presentation of a note secured by mortgage as a claim against the estate, without the presentation of the mortgage, does not waive the mortgage, if there was no intention to waive or abandon it.—Bank of Sonoma County v. Charles, 86 Cal. 322, 327, 24 Pac. 1019. The purpose of the statute as to waiving recourse is to require the plaintiff to put his waiver upon record in his complaint, so that there may be no question that he has waived recourse, etc.; and it is immaterial whether or not he made the waiver before his complaint was drawn by failure to present the claim to the executors within the time prescribed by the statute, or otherwise.—Anglo-Nevada Assur. Corp. v. Nadeau, 90 Cal. 393, 396, 27 Pac. 302. It is not essential to a waiver that the

claim of right waived should be enforceable. There may be a waiver or relinquishment of a claim to something without right.—Anglo-Nevada Assur. Corp. v. Nadeau, 90 Cal. 393, 396, 27 Pac. 302. A suit to foreclose a mortgage given by a decedent may be maintained, though it was not due at the time the estate was closed and discharge made, and was not presented as a claim against the estate, where the complaint expressly waives all claim against any other property of the estate except the land described in the mortgage.—Dreyfuss v. Giles, 79 Cal. 409, 21 Pac. 840. With the exception of a deficiency found to exist after a foreclosure sale, it is not necessary to present to an administrator a claim secured by mortgage upon the real property of a decedent.—Kelsey v. Welch, 8 S. D. 255, 66 N. W. 390. A mortgagee need not, on default in payment, present the claim to the administrator before proceeding to foreclose, if the mortgage is one executed by the administrator under order of court, made after the expiration of the time allowed for presenting claims.—Martin v. Saxton, 48 Utah 488, 160 Pac. 441. In foreclosing a mortgage, made by an administrator under order of court, the mortgagee need not allege in his complaint that he waives all recourse to property of the estate not covered by the mortgage.—Martin v. Saxton, 48 Utah 488, 160 Pac. 441. A surety who obtains an indemnity mortgage from his principal may foreclose the mortgage after the death of the principal, though he does not file a claim with the administrator.—MacDonald v. O'Shea, 58 Wash. 169, Ann. Cas. 1912A, 417, 108 Pac. 436, 439.

(5) Distinct proceedings.—Where the statute gives to the holder of the mortgage the right to enforce the same "against the property of the estate subject thereto" without presentation of the claim to the executor or administrator, the holder of a claim secured by mortgage has two modes in which he may enforce its payment. He may institute an action for its foreclosure under such statute, in which the amount of his recovery will be limited to the proceeds of his security; or he may present his claim to the executor or administrator for allowance, and, under another provision of the statute, receive the amount allowed therefor from the proceeds of a sale made under the supervision of the probate court; and, if those proceeds are insufficient therefor, may share equally, with the other creditors, in the general assets of the estate, for the amount of such deficiency. The two proceedings are entirely independent of each other, and may be conducted in different forums. The proceedings to foreclose the mortgage may be taken after the presentation and allowance of his claim, or even after its rejection.—Visalia Sav. Bank v. Curtis, 135 Cal. 350, 352, 67 Pac. 329; Moran v. Gardmeyer, 82 Cal. 96, 23 Pac. 6; Hibernia, etc., Soc. v. Conlin, 67 Cal. 178, 7 Pac. 477. The manifest intention of the California statute is to give to the holder of a mortgage, where he holds a claim against the estate secured by it, that, if allowed, would rank with the acknowledged debts of the estate, an election to present the claim for allowance, have it allowed and proceed to foreclose for

the whole amount due on the claim, including any deficiency arising on the sale of the mortgage premises, or to present no claim, and sue on the mortgage alone, and obtain whatever may be realized on the sale of the mortgaged premises under the decree of foreclosure.— Hibernia, etc., Soc. v. Conlin, 67 Cal. 178, 180, 7 Pac. 477.

(6) **Presentation. Form of.**—Where the statute does not require the presentation of the mortgage to the administrator for allowance as a claim against the estate, as a condition to foreclosure, and the requirement as to filing the mortgage is not mandatory, the filing of a verified claim for the amount due, with the executor or administrator, apprising him of the nature and character of the claim, is a sufficient compliance with the statute relative to filing.—Kirman v. Powning, 25 Nev. 378, 60 Pac. 834, 838. If the holder of a mortgage note seeks judgment against the estate of the decedent upon the debt, he must substantially comply with the provisions of the statute relative to the presentation of claims, and if he makes no attempt to comply with such provisions as to the affidavit, etc., by which a claim may be supported, he can not maintain an action against the estate upon the note secured by his mortgage.—Perkins v. Onyett, 86 Cal. 348, 351, 24 Pac. 1024. In presenting a mortgage claim against the estate of the deceased mortgagor, it is necessary to accompany the claim by a copy of the mortgage, or to describe it by reference to the date, volume, and page of its record. It is not sufficient to present a copy of the note which states that it is secured by mortgage of even date therewith.—Bank of Sonoma County v. Charles, 86 Cal. 322, 327, 24 Pac. 1019. Nor does the mere recital in a promissory note, presented as a claim against the estate of a deceased person, that it is secured by mortgage, constitute a presentation of the mortgage, where no copy of the mortgage is set out in the claim, and no reference is made therein to the date, volume, or page of its record.—Estate of Turner, 128 Cal. 388, 390, 60 Pac. 967. If a note secured by mortgage is presented as a claim against the estate, but no copy of the mortgage is attached to or presented with the note, and the mortgage is not described in the claim, and no reference is made therein to the date, volume, or page of its recordation, there is no presentation of the mortgage.—Evans v. Johnston, 115 Cal. 180, 182, 46 Pac. 906. The presentation of a note secured by mortgage, and a claim against the estate of a decedent, is sufficient in form where there is attached to the claim a copy of the note and mortgage, showing all the indorsements on the mortgage, the date, volume, and page of its record in the recorder's office, and also containing a full and complete copy of the note.—Consolidated Nat. Bank v. Hayes, 112 Cal. 75, 79, 44 Pac. 469. If a widow, who is the administratrix of the deceased, purchased with her own funds a note secured by mortgage upon all the real property of the deceased to preserve it from foreclosure, and took an assignment of the mortgage, the presentation by her of a secured claim against the estate is not based upon the assignment, but upon the note and

mortgage; and if she presents a claim against the estate for the debt, it is a sufficient description of the mortgage to comply with the statute, where it is stated in the claim that the note was secured by a mortgage upon the real property of the deceased described in the inventory on file, to which reference is made for further particulars, where the date of its execution and its acknowledgment is given in the claim, with the volume and page of record where it was recorded, to which reference was also made, and where the mortgage covered all the real property belonging to the deceased at the time of his death, and included all the real property described in the inventory. In such a case there could be no mistake as to the particular mortgage intended to be relied upon, and the only purpose of the required description is to identify the mortgage.—Estate of McDougald, 146 Cal. 191, 193, 79 Pac. 878. The presentation of a claim against the estate of a decedent, founded on a note secured by a mortgage, is sufficient, without a description of the mortgage, if the presentation refers to the date, volume, and page of the record of the mortgage, showing that it is all real property, situated in a county stated, and was given to secure a note a copy of which is contained in the presentation.—Moore v. Russell, 133 Cal. 297, 299, 85 Am. St. Rep. 166, 65 Pac. 624. Where a note given by a deceased chattel mortgagor, is presented as a claim against his estate, the claimant does not lose his right, under the South Dakota statute as amended, to a deficiency judgment in a suit to foreclose the mortgage, because of the fact that he did not present the mortgage to the administrator, or make proof thereof.—Massey v. Fralish, 37 S. D. 91, 94, 156 N. W. 791.

(7) Pleadings. Parties.—In an action to foreclose a mortgage securing a note, the breach of the contract to pay the note is of the essence of the cause of action, and must be alleged; and a failure to aver non-payment of the note is fatal to the complaint, although no demurrer is interposed, and judgment goes by default, as the defect goes to the statement of a cause of action, and such defect is not waived by a failure to demur.—Ryan v. Holliday, 110 Cal. 335, 337, 42 Pac. 891. The foreclosure of a mortgage is a case of equitable cognizance.—Willis v. Farley, 24 Cal. 490. It is not necessary, in an action for the foreclosure of a mortgage, where all recourse against property of the estate, other than that mortgaged, is waived, to allege that the claim has been presented to an executor or administrator for allowance or rejection.—Security Sav. Bank v. Connell, 65 Cal. 574, 4 Pac. 580. So if the mortgage was not executed by the deceased person, though the mortgaged land was afterwards purchased by the decedent in his lifetime, and became a part of his estate, it is not necessary, in an action to foreclose the mortgage, either to aver a presentation of a claim against the estate of the decedent, or an express waiver of any recourse against his general assets.—Ryan v. Holliday, 110 Cal. 335, 338, 42 Pac. 891. The waiver, in an amended complaint in a former action, of all recourse against the estate, except as to the mortgaged

premises, is effectual only in that action, and if the action is dismissed, it ceases to have any efficacy or binding force in a subsequent action, and does not preclude the proper presentation of a claim against the estate, or the enforcement of such a claim in the subsequent action. —Westbay v. Gray, 116 Cal. 660, 669, 48 Pac. 800. In an action to foreclose a mortgage against an estate, the executor represents the estate, and it is not necessary to make the heirs parties to the suit. A judgment against the executor would bind the heirs and devisees, and a sale under the judgment would relate to the date of the mortgage, and cut off the interest of all persons to the suit derived under the deceased mortgagor subsequently thereto.—Dickey v. Gibson, 121 Cal. 276, 278, 53 Pac. 704; Finger v. McCaughey, 119 Cal. 59, 51 Pac. 13. Nor is it necessary that the administrator should be sued individually, in order to bar his right of succession to the mortgaged premises.—Finger v. McCaughey, 119 Cal. 59, 51 Pac. 13.

(8) Presentation. Failure to present.—The mortgagee's failure to exhibit his mortgage debt as a demand against the estate of a deceased mortgagor within the time prescribed by the statute for the presentation of claims after letters of administration have been granted will not ordinarily preclude him from foreclosing his mortgage lien and subjecting the mortgaged property to the payment of the debt.—Andrews v. Morse, 51 Kan. 30, 32 Pac. 640; Reid v. Sullivan, 20 Colo. 498, 39 Pac. 338; Reed v. Miller, 1 Wash. 426, 25 Pac. 334; Scammon v. Ward, 1 Wash. 179, 23 Pac. 439; Teel v. Winston, 22 Or. 489, 29 Pac. 142; Kirman v. Powning, 25 Nev. 378, 60 Pac. 834; Bank of Sonoma County v. Charles, 86 Cal. 322, 24 Pac. 1019; Dreyfuss v. Giles, 79 Cal. 409, 21 Pac. 840. A mortgagee who has failed to present his claim to the administrator of a deceased mortgagor within the time prescribed by the statute does not thereby lose his remedy by foreclosure.—Kaikainahaole v. Allen, 14 Haw. 527, 529. Where a mortgage executed by the deceased in his lifetime was two years past due at his death, and after the appointment of an administrator and notice to creditors, the mortgage note was presented as a claim, but the mortgage was not presented, the statute of limitations as to the mortgage was not suspended, and where the administrator died eight years after his appointment the mortgage was barred before his death, and such bar could not be affected by the subsequent appointment of an administrator of any proceedings attempted by the mortgagee after such appointment.—Regents, etc., v. Turner, 159 Cal. 541, Ann. Cas. 1912C, 1162, 114 Pac. 842.

(9) Effect of allowance. Right to foreclose.—The allowance of a mortgage as a claim against the estate of a decedent does not bar its foreclosure.—German S. & L. Soc. v. Hutchinson, 68 Cal. 52, 8 Pac. 627; Wise v. Williams, 72 Cal. 544, 14 Pac. 204; Moran v. Gardemeyer, 82 Cal. 96, 23 Pac. 6. Contra.—Falkner v. Folsom's Executors, 6 Cal. 412. The allowance and acknowledgment of a debt against the estate

of a decedent is sufficient to keep alive the mortgage securing it, and
to entitle the plaintiff to foreclose such mortgage, without any express
waiver of recourse against the estate.—Consolidated Nat. Bank v.
Hayes, 112 Cal. 75, 82, 44 Pac. 469. Where a claim against a mortgagor, as indorser of a note of a third party, which was purchased by
the mortgagee from the mortgagor, was not presented to the estate
as a secured claim, but was presented and allowed as an unsecured
claim against the estate, to be paid in due course of administration, the
mortgagee is not authorized to buy up notes of a third party upon
which the mortgagor was the simple indorser, and hold the same as
secured by the mortgage.—Moran v. Gardemeyer, 82 Cal. 96, 99, 101,
23 Pac. 6. If an executor or administrator takes a mortgage to secure
himself against a doubtful payment of a claim to the mortgagor, and
the administrator afterwards goes into bankruptcy, a claim by the
mortgagor for the money paid him by the administrator, and for the
payment of which the mortgage was ordered foreclosed, is properly
disallowed.—In re Myer, 14 N. M. 45, 89 Pac. 246, 249. Where appellant
paid a mortgage to prevent a foreclosure thereof, and the mortgage, at
the time of the payment, was a proper claim upon the land and
against the estate of the deceased, but, after appellant had paid the
mortgage, a claim was allowed in favor of the brothers of the deceased,
which absorbed the entire estate, and left the appellant without anything to reimburse him for money paid to satisfy the mortgage, he is
entitled to subrogation to an interest in the land equal to the amount
of the mortgage debt paid.—Fullerton v. Bailey, 17 Utah 85, 53 Pac.
1020. If there has been no contest in the probate court in regard to a
claim against the estate of a decedent upon a note secured by mortgage, the allowance of the plaintiff's claim is sufficient to make it
an accepted debt of the estate, to keep alive the mortgage, and to
entitle the plaintiff to have it foreclosed.—Consolidated Nat. Bank v.
Hayes, 112 Cal. 75, 82, 44 Pac. 469. The presentation or allowance of
a mortgage claim does not affect the running of the statute of limitations against a mortgage, where it is not necessary to present such
mortgage claim.—Hibernia S. & L. Soc. v. Conlin, 67 Cal. 178, 7 Pac.
477. If a mortgagor has no interest in the property mortgaged, the
mortgage creates no lien, and can not properly be foreclosed.—Otto
v. Law, 127 Cal. 471, 59 Pac. 895.

(10) Judgment. Interest.—Where the mortgage claim has been presented to the estate, and allowed, there can be no deficiency judgment. The amount of any deficiency will be payable, if at all, in the
due course of administration, without any judgment to that effect.—
Pechaud v. Rinquet, 21 Cal. 76, 77. Where a mortgage claim was
presented to the executor or administrator of a decedent, and an
action to foreclose the mortgage against the estate has been brought,
a judgment for a deficiency should provide that it be paid "in due
course of administration."—Moore v. Russell, 133 Cal. 297, 301, 85
Am. St. Rep. 166, 65 Pac. 624. Although a mortgage against the prop-

erty of a deceased person provides for a deficiency judgment, the mortgagee's claim is barred, where he did not present it to the executors or administrators within the time limited in the notice to creditors, published by the executors, and did not, after that, and before bringing an action, or at any time, present the notes sued on in the action, or any claim on account thereof, to said executors or their successors. The conclusion that he is not, under such circumstances, entitled to a deficiency judgment is in full accord with the statute requiring the claim to be presented in such cases within one month after the deficiency is ascertained.—Thurber v. Miller, 11 S. D. 124, 75 N. W. 900. A decree of foreclosure in an action brought against an executor or administrator after his discharge, is a nullity, and is no bar to a subsequent suit against the heirs of the deceased to enforce the mortgage and a sale of the mortgaged property.—Willis v. Fárley, 24 Cal. 490, 501. A mortgagee may enforce the lien of his mortgage against the property for the full amount thereof, including the conventional rate of interest. He is not limited to legal interest upon the mortgage debt, notwithstanding the insolvency of the estate.— Visalia Sav. Bank v. Curtis, 135 Cal. 350, 353, 67 Pac. 329.

(11) **Sale. Holder as purchaser.**—While the holder of a mortgage may be come a purchaser at any sale under order of the court of the lands included in the mortgage, yet if, by reason of the failure to have the mortgage allowed as a claim against the estate, the mortgagee has waived his right to have the same considered as a lien upon the property, he is not entitled to demand a conveyance from the executor or administrator, without payment of the price at which such mortgagee had purchased the land. He can not claim an application of the purchase-money as a credit upon the mortgage not presented and allowed as a claim against the estate.—Estate of Turner, 128 Cal. 388, 392, 393, 60 Pac. 967.

(12) **Redemption. Surplus.**—Unless the owner of a mortgage has, within one year, presented his claim against the estate of a decedent, he is not entitled to apply to the probate court to have his mortgage redeemed out of the personal assets of the estate, nor, in the alternative, to have the land sold and the proceeds applied on the debt.— Scammon v. Ward, 1 Wash. 179, 23 Pac. 439, 440. If a mortgage is foreclosed upon an insolvent estate of a deceased mortgagor, the surplus, if any, should be paid to the administrator, and not to the heirs of the mortgagor, when it is required for the payment of debts. The administrator, in such a case, may recover from the assignee of the mortgagee.—Whitney v. Ross, 17 Haw. 453, 454.

12. Foreclosure of mortgages. Limitation of actions.

(1) **In general.**—Where a mortgage claim has been allowed and approved, the right of the mortgagee to maintain an action to foreclose the mortgage is not affected by the statute of limitations, pend-

ing the proceedings for the settlement of the estate of the mortgagor.— German Sav. & L. Soc. v. Hutchinson, 68 Cal. 52, 54, 8 Pac. 627; Wise v. Williams, 72 Cal. 544, 14 Pac. 204; but the assignee of a mortgage has no right to foreclose it against the estate of a deceased mortgagor for the benefit of the assignor, where the mortgagee is administrator of the estate of the mortgagor; and if he commences a suit for foreclosure while the mortgagee is administrator, but such mortgagee, after ceasing to be administrator, is substituted as plaintiff in place of the assignee, the statute of limitations will run against the mortgage debt until the date of the substitution. If the action is then barred, no suit can be maintained.—Brown v. Mann, 71 Cal. 192, 12 Pac. 51. The failure to appoint an administrator of the estate of a deceased mortgagor and debtor does not prevent the statute of limitations from running in favor of the mortgagor's heirs against an action to foreclose the mortgage.—Colonial, etc., Mtge. Co. v. Flemington, 14 N. D. 181, 116 Am. St. Rep. 670, 103 N. W. 929. Where a mortgagor died intestate, seised of the mortgaged land, before the mortgage debt was due, and left four heirs, only one of whom was a resident of the state; where no administrator was ever appointed; and where nearly fourteen years after the debt was due the heirs conveyed the land to defendant,—it was held that an action to foreclose the mortgage was barred as to one-fourth of the land, but was not barred as to the remaining three-fourths.—Colonial, etc., Mtge. Co. v. Flemington, 14 S. D. 181, 116 Am. St. Rep. 670, 103 N. W. 929. Under the California statute, "no claim against any estate, which has been presented and allowed, is affected by the statute of limitations, pending the proceedings for the settlement of the estate," etc. But it has been held, in an action where a husband and wife executed a joint promissory note, secured by mortgage on their community property, where, after the husband died testate, and the claim of the mortgage was filed against his estate, and where the claim was allowed and approved by the administrator, and duly allowed by the judge, that such statute has application alone to claims against the estate, and does not apply to any person who may happen to be jointly or severally indebted with the deceased upon such claim, and that, in such case, the general statute of limitations applies to all obligations of co-mortgagors or co-obligors generally, and in all cases where exception to its operation is not specifically made.—Vandall v. Teague, 142 Cal. 471, 476; see Tynan v. Walker, 35 Cal. 634, 95 Am. Dec. 152. The settlement and distribution of the estate is no bar to the right to foreclose the mortgage against the distributee of the mortgaged property, or the grantee of such distributee. —Dreyfuss v. Giles, 79 Cal. 409, 21 Pac. 840. The fact that the action was not commenced until after the expiration of the time for the presentation of claims against the estate does not bar the right of action.—German Sav. & L. Soc. v. Fisher, 92 Cal. 502, 28 Pac. 591. Where the law as to the presentation of mortgage claims has been amended, after notice to creditors has been given and the time to

present claims has expired, so that claims must be presented which
would not before have to be presented, a mortgage, given by the
deceased, falling due after the amendment is not barred by a failure
to present the claim to the administrator.—Hibernia Sav. & L. Soc.
v. Hayes, 56 Cal. 297, 299.

13. Foreclosure of mortgages. Death of mortgagor.

(1) In general.—If a husband and wife, during the husband's life,
give a mortgage on a tract of land, such mortgage may be enforced,
after the husband's death, against the heirs, but the mortgagee has no
right to a personal judgment against any of the defendants.—Brown
v. Orr, 29 Cal. 120, 122. Where a mortgagor died, and the mortgagee
filed a claim against his estate for the amount of the mortgage debt,
without referring to the mortgage, an allowance of the same as an
unsecured claim is not void, where there was in fact no mortgage.—
Otto v. Long, 127 Cal. 471, 59 Pac. 895. In an action to foreclose a
mortgage executed by a person before his death, and where his widow
was made administratrix of his estate as a party defendant, the
purchaser at the foreclosure sale, after receiving his deed, is entitled
to a writ of assistance against the administratrix for possession of
the premises, where her answer to the application for the writ fails
to show that she claims the property, or the possession thereof, by
any right or title adverse to that of her deceased husband.—Finger
v. McCaughey, 119 Cal. 59, 61, 51 Pac. 13.

(2) Enforcement without presentation.—If the mortgagor dies after
selling land upon which he has given a mortgage, the mortgagee may
enforce the mortgage against the subsequent purchaser, without presenting his claim to the executor or administrator for allowance.—
Christy v. Dana, 42 Cal. 174, 179. The failure to present a claim
against an estate before bringing suit thereon is a mere matter of
abatement, which is waived unless pleaded.—Bemmerly v. Woodward,
124 Cal. 568, 574, 57 Pac. 561. An action to foreclose a mortgage
does not abate by the death of the mortgagor pending the suit, but
survives against his estate, and may be prosecuted against the representative of such estate, with the same effect as if the original defendant had not died.—Union Sav. Bank v. Barrett, 132 Cal. 453, 454, 64
Pac. 713, 1071; Hibernia, etc., Soc. v. Wackenreuder, 99 Cal. 503, 34
Pac. 219. If a married woman, having authority, executes a mortgage
in her own name and afterwards dies, and the mortgagee seeks to foreclose, but does not ask for any judgment against the estate, and the
estate no longer has any interest whatever in the property, it is unnecessary for the mortgagee to present the note and mortgage to the
executor or administrator for allowance, and he can maintain an action
for the foreclosure of the mortgage against the property without
making the executor or administrator a party to the foreclosure suit.—
Rickards v. Hutchinson, 18 Nev. 215, 2 Pac. 52, 54, 4 Pac. 702. If a
mortgage has been given to secure the debt of a third person, and the

mortgagor afterwards dies, no presentation of the mortgage claim need be made to his personal representative.—Hibernia Sav. & L. Soc. v. Conlin, 67 Cal. 178, 7 Pac. 477. If the mortgagor in a chattel mortgage agrees that, upon default, the mortgagee may take possession of the mortgaged property, either preliminary to foreclosure or for preservation, the right of the mortgagee to take possession is not defeated by the death of the mortgagor; his right of possession is good against the mortgagor's administrator; and the mortgagee's claim to such possession is not such a claim as must be presented to the administrator for allowance or rejection.—Purdin v. Archer, 4 S. D. 54, 54 N. W. 1043. Where a mortgage lien was created by the testatrix herself to secure her own debt, it is to be paid, as between executors, devisees, legatees, and heirs, in the same manner as the general unsecured debts of the deceased, in so far as concerns the question from what property it is to be paid, unless the will discloses a different intent. And it is immaterial that the mortgagee does not present his claim, but relies entirely on the future enforcement of his lien against the specific property mortgaged.—Estate of DeBernal, 165 Cal. 223, Ann. Cas. 1914D, 26, 131 Pac. 375. Where a husband and wife mortgaged their homestead, the mortgagee, after the death of both, could foreclose without presenting claim against the wife's estate, the husband having died first and the claim having been presented against his estate and allowed.—Raggio v. Palmtag, 155 Cal. 797, 103 Pac. 312.

(3) Express waiver in complaint.—In an action to foreclose a mortgage against the property of a deceased mortgagor, where the complaint contains a waiver, in the exact language of the statute, against any other property of the estate, the effect of such express waiver is not destroyed by a prayer for relief in which the plaintiff asks for judgment for "the amount due upon the said note and mortgage," and for costs "and counsel fees," and "that a receiver be appointed to take charge of the real estate until the same be sold, and to collect the rents and all the net income therefrom, to be applied on any deficiency which may remain due to plaintiff after said sale."—Hibernia, etc., Soc. v. Wackenreuder, 99 Cal. 503, 509, 34 Pac. 219.

(4) Limitation of actions. In general.—The fact that one of two mortgagors dies does not have the effect of suspending the running of the statute of limitations as to the other mortgagor or as to his grantee. —Hibernia, etc., Soc. v. Boland, 145 Cal. 626, 628, 79 Pac. 365; Vandall v. Teague, 142 Cal. 471, 76 Pac. 35. If a mortgage is given by one person to secure the promissory note of another person, and the payor of the note dies, and the holder thereof fails to present either the note or mortgage to his administrator for allowance within the time prescribed by the statute after publication of notice to creditors, the claim is barred as against the estate, but the mortgage remains in force, and may be foreclosed at any time before it is barred, as against the mortgagor, by the statute of limitations; and this applies to a note

made by the husband for his own debt, and where the wife gives a mortgage on her separate property to secure it, and the husband signs the mortgage to show his assent to it. The wife's liability on the mortgage, in such a case, is not affected by the death of the husband and the failure of the holder of the note to present the claim for allowance to the administrator of his estate.—Sichel v. Carrillo, 42 Cal. 493, 504. A mortgage is capable of enforcement against the mortgaged property, though the mortgagor be deceased, in a direct suit brought for that purpose against the heirs of the mortgagor, or the person or persons in whom the legal title to the mortgaged property is vested at the time of the foreclosure; and such mortgaged property may be subjected to the payment of the debt it is pledged to secure without a presentation of the debt to the executor or administrator in a probate proceeding; but the statute of limitations runs against such right, and the action must be begun within the statutory period.—Gleason v. Hawkins, 32 Wash. 464, 73 Pac. 533, 534; but, notwithstanding the right to foreclose the mortgage, or to collect the debt out of the real property of the deceased debtor, is barred by the statute, the creditor still has the right to have his claim allowed by the administrator to be paid, as other claims of the estate must be paid, out of the personal property in the hands of the administrator belonging to the estate. The statute destroys the lien of the debt at the end of six years upon the deceased debtor's real property, but keeps it alive, in so far as his personal property is concerned. The debt should for that reason be allowed as a claim against the estate.—Gleason v. Hawkins, 32 Wash. 464, 73 Pac. 533, 534. Want of administration does not suspend the running of limitations against a mortgage in favor of the estate.—Sanford v. Bergin, 156 Cal. 43, 103 Pac. 333.

(5) **Limitation of actions. Death before maturity.**—Where a note and mortgage were not mature at the death of the mortgagor, they are not barred by the statute of limitations, although letters of administration were not issued until more than four years after the maturity of the note and mortgage; and the claim thereon, presented to the administrator immediately after the publication of notice to creditors, is properly allowed.—Estate of Bullard, 116 Cal. 355, 356, 48 Pac. 219. If a mortgage debt was not due at the time of the mortgagor's death, the statute of limitations would not begin to run against the mortgagee's right to foreclose while there was no administration on the mortgagor's estate.—Heeser v. Taylor, 1 Cal. App. 619, 82 Pac. 977. Where a decedent had given a mortgage, but died before its maturity, the statute of limitations does not bar a recovery, although more than four years had elapsed from the maturity of the mortgage before foreclosure, if less than one year had elapsed after the issuing of letters testamentary or of administration, before such foreclosure suit was brought.—Heeser v. Taylor, 1 Cal. App. 619, 620, 82 Pac. 977.

(6) **Limitation of actions. Death of defendant pending action.**— The rule that if an action is pending against a decedent at the time

of his death, the plaintiff must present his claim against the estate in order to recover, does not apply to an action for the foreclosure of a mortgage other than homestead premises, though it was commenced before the death of the mortgagor, and was pending undetermined at his death. Such action may be continued against the executors of the deceased mortgagor without presentation of the claim to them for allowance, where the plaintiff expressly waives recourse against all other property of the decedent.—Hibernia, etc., Soc. v. Wackenreuder, 99 Cal. 503, 507, 508, 34 Pac. 219. An action is deemed to be pending until its final determination on appeal, unless the judgment is sooner satisfied.—Vermont Marble Co. v. Black, 123 Cal. 21, 23, 55 Pac. 599. If an action to foreclose a mortgage does not abate by the death of a mortgagor pending the suit, but survives against his estate, and can be prosecuted against the person who shall thereafter be appointed his personal representative, the plaintiff has the same right to proceed against him as he would have to proceed against the original defendant had he not died, and the cause of action is not extinguished or affected by the fact that the summons was not personally served upon the mortgagor, and that the action was begun more than one year prior to his death. The power expressly conferred upon the court to continue the proceeding against the mortgagor's personal representative carries with it an implied power to order a new summons to bring in the executrix as a new party, after the lapse of a year.—Union Sav. Bank v. Barrett, 132 Cal. 453, 455, 456, 64 Pac. 713, 1071.

(7) **Redemption.**—Upon the death of a mortgagor or owner of redemption, his heir at law may redeem. The widow and the administrator may also redeem; but the right of the heirs at law to redeem is independent of that of the widow or administrator, and the exercise of such right by the heirs, in bringing a suit in equity to redeem, is not an interference with the administration of the estate. Such suit may therefore be brought without asking leave of the probate court.—Kahoomana v. Carvalho, 11 Haw. 516, 517.

14. Mortgages on homesteads.

(1) **In general. Parties to foreclosure.**—Where a homestead is mortgaged, or is declared on land subject to a mortgage, it is not the exemption that is mortgaged, but the whole property, and the homestead exemption still exists, and is to be recognized subject only to a reduction in amount to satisfy the just demand of the mortgagee.—White v. Horton, 154 Cal. 103, 18 L. R. A. (N. S.) 490, 97 Pac. 70. In the case of a mortgage against a probate homestead, the executor or administrator of the estate is not a necessary party to the foreclosure of the mortgage, if no present claim is made against the estate.—Schadt v. Heppe, 45 Cal. 433. Where a recorded homestead has been set apart to the widow by the court, the executor or administrator is no longer a necessary or proper party to an action of foreclosure. Nothing being claimed against the estate, it is a matter of no concern to him whether

the mortgage is foreclosed or not.—Schadt v. Heppe, 45 Cal. 433, 437. But if recourse is had to property of the estate other than that mortgaged, the executor or administrator is a necessary party to the suit. —Belloc v. Rogers, 9 Cal. 123, 126. Where the whole estate has been set apart for the use of the family, and the executor or administrator has been discharged, he is not a necessary party defendant to the foreclosure of a mortgage on the real estate set apart to the family as a homestead.—Browne v. Sweet, 127 Cal. 332, 335, 59 Pac. 774.

(2) **Presentation of claim. When necessary.**—No action to foreclose a mortgage on the homestead of a deceased mortgagor can be maintained, unless the claim secured by the mortgage is first duly presented for allowance to the personal representative of the mortgagor, although the estate has no assets other than the mortgaged homestead which can be subjected to the payment of the mortgage debt; and, notwithstanding an action of foreclosure had been commenced and a lis pendens filed prior to the mortgagor's death, and that the plaintiff has expressly waived all recourse against any other property of the estate.—Bollinger v. Manning, 79 Cal. 7, 12, 21 Pac. 375. Liens and encumbrances on the homestead must be presented for allowance against the estate of a decedent of which it forms a part. The purpose in requiring the presentation of liens and encumbrances on the homestead for allowance against the estate is to preserve the homestead, if possible.—Camp v. Grider, 62 Cal. 20, 26. Where an action to foreclose a mortgage given by a husband and wife upon the homestead has been brought, and all recourse against the property of the estate other than the property mortgaged has been waived, such mortgage must, upon the death of the husband, be presented as a claim against his estate, notwithstanding such waiver.—Wise v. Williams, 88 Cal. 30, 33, 25 Pac. 1064. A mortgage given by a husband and wife upon property upon which a homestead is afterwards declared, must, upon the death of the husband, be presented as a claim against his estate, although recourse against any other property of the estate than that mortgaged is waived.—Wise v. Williams, 88 Cal. 30, 33, 25 Pac. 1064. So a mortgage of a homestead on community property must be presented before an action can be brought for its foreclosure, and a judgment of foreclosure without such presentation is erroneous, even if all recourse against other property has been waived in the complaint; and a presentation of a mortgage note without a presentation of the mortgage is insufficient.—Perkins v. Onyett, 86 Cal. 348, 350, 24 Pac. 1024. If the mortgage is upon property which is subject to a claim of homestead, and the statute provides that if there be subsisting liens or encumbrances on the homestead left by a deceased person, the claims secured thereby must be presented and allowed as other claims against the estate, and the plaintiff has failed to present to the executor or administrator of the estate his claim upon the debt set forth in the complaint, he is not only unable to maintain an action for the foreclosure of the mortgage, but is also precluded from maintaining an action on the

note independently of the mortgage. The extinguishment of the mortgage lien by reason of his failure to present his claim does not give him the right to bring an action upon the debt without such presentation.—Hibernia Sav. & L. Soc. v. Laidlaw (Hinz), 4 Cal. App. 626, 88 Pac. 730.

REFERENCES.

Concerning the presentation of mortgage claims against homesteads, before bringing suit.—See note, subd. 19, § 420, ante.

(3) **Presentation of claim. When not necessary.**—If the mortgage covers a homestead upon the separate property of the wife, and the creditor waives all claims against the husband's estate, no presentation of the claim is necessary.—Bull v. Coe, 77 Cal. 54, 11 Am. St. Rep. 235, 18 Pac. 808. A mortgage on a homestead, exceeding the statutory limit in value, need not be presented as a claim against the estate of the deceased mortgagor prior to the commencement of an action to enforce the mortgage against the excess. The rule that a mortgage upon the homestead can not be enforced unless a claim therefor has been duly presented to the executor or administrator does not apply to a probate homestead. Hence, if a part of the mortgaged premises has been apportioned to the widow of a decedent, the mortgagee may, without presenting his claim to the executor or administrator, foreclose as to the other part, where the premises described in the homestead declaration exceed the statutory limit.—Bank of Woodland v. Stephens, 144 Cal. 659, 664, 79 Pac. 379.

(4) **Limitation of actions.**—A mortgage on an antemortem homestead can not be foreclosed, unless the claim is presented for allowance against the estate of the decedent within the time limited for the presentation of claims.—Building and Loan Assoc. v. King, 83 Cal. 440, 23 Pac. 376. Where a husband and wife have mortgaged the homestead selected from the community property, and the husband dies and the wife conveys her interest, an action to foreclose the mortgage on such homestead can not be maintained, unless it is brought within four years from the maturity of the mortgage.—Vandall v. Teague, 142 Cal. 471, 76 Pac. 35, 37. A statute which provides that claims against the estate of a decedent secured by "subsisting liens or encumbrances on the homestead" "must be presented and allowed as other claims against the estate," and that if the funds of the estate are inadequate to pay all claims, the claims so secured must be first paid, does not forbid the commencement of a proceeding to foreclose a mortgage given by a husband and wife upon a homestead selected from community property; and the statute of limitations will bar such action unless it has been commenced within the statutory period of four years.—Vandall v. Teague, 142 Cal. 471, 76 Pac. 35, 37. Where a husband and wife jointly executed a mortgage upon their homestead declared on community property, title to the homestead vests absolutely in the wife upon the husband's death. Hence, the allowance of a claim against the estate

of the deceased husband has the effect only of suspending the statute of limitations as against the estate. It does not have that effect as against the surviving wife. She and her successor in interest may therefore plead the statute of limitations in bar of a foreclosure against them if not brought within the time prescribed by the general statute of limitations after the maturity of the mortgage.—Vandall v. Teague, 142 Cal. 471, 474, 476, 76 Pac. 35.

15. Trusts. Deeds of trust.

(1) In general.—Equity will enforce a trust against the personal representatives of a deceased trustee, and without the presentation of the claim against the estate, when the identical trust property, or its product in a new form, can be traced into the estate, and so into the possession of the representatives. But a beneficiary who is unable to do this must rely upon the personal liability of the trustee, and, so relying, has only a claim against the estate that must be duly presented for allowance. Such a claim, however, is still based upon the trust, whatever that may have been. It had its origin in the trust, and depends for its validity upon the legality and sufficiency of the trust. The fact that the beneficiary is obliged to present his claim, and to look, like a general creditor, to the assets of the estate for payment, does not change the nature of his demand, which is still one for property due under a trust account; it merely has changed his remedy.— McGrath v. Carroll, 110 Cal. 79, 83, 42 Pac. 466. Where deposits in bank are community property, and were made in the name of the husband, and it is found that these deposits would not pass to the wife, either as donee or beneficiary of a trust, they may be recovered, so far as they can be identified, without the presentation of a claim against the estate of the wife. The right to sue an executor or administrator in cases like this, without the presentation of a claim against his decedent's estate, arises from the fact that the specific thing sued for is not a part of decedent's estate, and the action will lie whenever the thing demanded can be identified in specie as the property of another. —Sprague v. Walton, 1-5 Cal. 228, 235, 78 Pac. 645. In an action to enforce a trust against the executor of a deceased trustee, and the due presentation of a proper claim against the estate is averred in an amended and supplemental complaint, but which shows that such presentation and rejection was after the commencement of the action, the failure to present the claim before suit is a mere matter in abatement of the action, which is not favored, and is waived if not set up in answer either to the original or to the supplemental complaint in proper time.—Bemmerly v. Woodward, 124 Cal. 568, 570, 575, 57 Pac. 561.

(2) Presentation is necessary when.—If one of two executors of the estate of a deceased person dies, having in his hands a portion of the estate, which could not be identified as a trust fund, the other executor must present a claim against his estate, and if the time for such presentation has expired, the amount due from the deceased executor to the

estate of the original decedent can not be deducted from his distributive share of that estate.—Estate of Smith, 108 Cal. 115, 122, 40 Pac. 1037. The beneficiary of a trust, who is unable to follow the trust funds through its mutations, is placed, upon the death of the trustee, in the position of a general creditor of the estate.—Byrne v. Byrne, 133 Cal. 294, 299, 45 Pac. 536; Lathrop v. Bampton, 31 Cal. 17, 89 Am. Dec. 141. Whenever a trust fund has been wrongfully converted into another species of property, if its identity can be traced, it will be held, in its new form, liable to the cestui que trust. No change of its state and form can devest it of such trust. So long as it can be identified, either as the original property of the cestui que trust, or as the product of it, equity will follow it; and the right of reclamation attaches to it until detached by the superior equity of a bona fide purchaser for a valuable consideration without notice. The substitute for the original thing follows the nature of the thing itself, so long as it can be ascertained to be such. But the right of pursuing it fails when the means of ascertainment fails. This is always the case where the subject-matter is turned into money, and mixed and confounded in a general mass of property of the same description.—Lathrop v. Bampton, 31 Cal. 17, 22, 89 Am. Dec. 141. Hence, where trust moneys held and used by a deceased person were so commingled that they are incapable of identification as a distinct fund, and no fruit or product thereof is susceptible of identification, the only remedy of a beneficiary is to present a claim for the money so held and used against the estate, and to sue thereon if the claim is rejected; and no suit against the executor or administrator can be maintained to enforce the trust without such presentation. —Orcutt v. Gould, 117 Cal. 315, 316, 317, 49 Pac. 188; Bemmerly v. Woodward, 124 Cal. 568, 573, 57 Pac. 561; Estate of Smith, 108 Cal. 115, 122, 40 Pac. 1037; McGrath v. Carroll, 110 Cal. 79, 83, 42 Pac. 466; Roach v. Caraffa, 85 Cal. 436, 444, 25 Pac. 22; Gunter v. Janes, 9 Cal. 643. Nor can any action against the executor or administrator to recover a trust fund be maintained, unless it is shown that such fund, or some specific property or fund to which it can be traced, has come into the possession of the defendants.—Gillespie v. Winn, 65 Cal. 429, 4 Pac. 411; Rowland v. Madden, 72 Cal. 17, 12 Pac. 226, 870.

(3) **Recovery of specific property.**—Where recovery is sought of specific property alleged to have been held in trust by the decedent at the time of his death, a party seeking such recovery is not asking payment of the claim from the assets of the estate, and is therefore not required to present his claim as a creditor of the estate.—Brown v. Town of Sebastopol, 153 Cal. 704, 19 L. R. A. (N. S.) 178, 96 Pac. 363, 364. One who seeks to recover from the representatives of an estate specific property alleged to have been held in trust by the decedent at the time of his death is not a "creditor of the estate." He is not seeking payment of a claim from the assets of the estate, and is not required to present a claim as a creditor. His action is not founded upon a claim or demand against the estate.—Estate of Dutard, 147 Cal.

253, 256, 81 Pac. 519. The presentation of a claim against the estate of a decedent is not required in order to maintain an action to recover property held in trust by him. It is only where payment of a claim is sought out of the assets of decedent's estate where such presentation is necessary. Property held by the decedent in trust is not a part of his estate, and can not be applied in satisfaction of his debts, or from a portion of his estate to be distributed by his heirs.—Elizalde v. Elizalde, 137 Cal. 634, 642, 66 Pac. 369, 70 Pac. 861. If it appears that a decedent was the sole devisee of an estate that he received on distribution, subject to a parol trust to pay out of the estate a certain sum to the plaintiff, and that a claim against the estate of the decedent was presented by the plaintiff and allowed in part by the executors of the estate, and approved by the judge, a bill in equity will lie against the executors, without a previous demand upon them, to enforce the trust against the estate as to the remainder of the claim.—Walkerly v. Bacon, 85 Cal. 137, 141, 24 Pac. 638. So where a trust fund received by a deceased husband in his lifetime, under the will of his deceased wife, was invested by him as directed by the decree of distribution of her estate, and was kept separate by the husband from his other estate, such fund was no part of his estate, and it was not necessary for the trustees of a Masonic lodge appointed to receive such fund to present a claim against the husband's estate, as a condition precedent to the recovery of such fund from his administrator. It is only where payment of a claim is sought out of the assets of decedent's estate that a presentation of a claim against the executor or administrator is necessary.—Kauffman v. Foster, 3 Cal. App. 741, 743, 86 Pac. 1108.

(4) **Deeds of trust.**—The right to execute powers of sale conferred by a deed of trust, and to apply the proceeds arising therefrom to the payment of debts and charges named in the deed, is not dependent upon a compliance with the statute prescribing the time within which claims must be presented against the estate of a deceased person.— More v. Calkins, 95 Cal. 435, 438, 29 Am. St. Rep. 128, 30 Pac. 583. If a husband executes a deed of trust to secure money loaned to him, and empowers the trustees to sell the land for default in payment, and his wife afterwards declares a homestead upon the property, which is community property, and the husband dies before any sale is made by the trustees, and his widow becomes executrix of his estate, it is not necessary that any presentation of the debt as a claim against the estate of the deceased husband be made as a prerequisite to the execution of the power of sale. Such deed of trust is not a lien or encumbrance requiring presentation or allowance. It passed title to the trustees, and a sale by them under the power would extinguish the homestead which was subject thereto. In legal effect, a deed of trust does not create a lien or encumbrance on the land, but conveys the legal title to the trustee, and if the homestead applies only to the title vested in one or both of the spouses, and does not affect titles vested in third persons, it follows that the legal title thus vested in the trustee forms no part

of a subsequently declared homestead, and that the deed of trust or the title of the trustee is not a subsisting lien or encumbrance upon the homestead interest.—Webber v. McCleverty, 149 Cal. 316, 318, 320, 86 Pac. 706, 708, 709. See, also, Athearn v. Ryan, 154 Cal. 554, 98 Pac. 390. In Colorado, where a claim against the estate of a decedent is secured by a deed of trust, it is error for the court, in entering judgment, to prohibit the claimant from proceeding to sell the property covered by his lien. The statute of non-claim does not apply to a claim secured by a deed of trust; and, after the expiration of one year, the only condition precedent of the claimant's right to a foreclosure is the allowance of his claim.—Townsend v. Thompson, 24 Colo. 411, 51 Pac. 433.

16. Appeal.

(1) Right of appeal.—In the event that a claim filed against the estate of a decedent is disallowed either by the executor or administrator or by the county judge, the remedy is not by appeal.—In re Barnett's Estate, 52 Okla. 623, 627, 153 Pac. 653. An order disallowing a claim against the estate of a decedent is not appealable. The remedy of the claimant is exclusively by suit.—In re Barker's Estate, 26 Mont. 279, 67 Pac. 941; Wilkins v. Wilkins, 1 Wash. 87, 23 Pac. 411. If the claim of an executor or administrator against the estate is disallowed, his only remedy is to resign his trust, and sue like any other creditor.—Wilkins v. Wilkins, 1 Wash. 87, 23 Pac. 411, 412; and a person, in his representative capacity as executor or administrator, can not appeal from an order disallowing his individual claim against the estate.—In re Barker's Estate, 26 Mont. 279, 67 Pac. 941, 943. Where trustees are not named in the will, and claim no rights under it, and have presented no claim against the estate, they are not "aggrieved" persons, and have no right of appeal from a decree distributing the funds of the estate to the heirs.—Estate of Burdick, 112 Cal. 387, 396, 44 Pac. 734. While an appeal does not lie from a decree establishing due notice to creditors, as such, it is otherwise if such decree is embraced in a decree settling the final account of the executor and making final distribution of the estate, and the appellant, in terms, appeals from such decree.—Estate of Wilson, 147 Cal. 108, 81 Pac. 313, 314. The approval or rejection, by the court, of a claim presented against the estate admits of an appeal by an heir or creditor, but not by the administrator.—In re Estate of Gladough, 1 Alaska 649, 651. Construing sections 6375 and 6442, Rev. Laws of Oklahoma of 1910, it is held that the heirs and those interested in the administration of an estate may file a protest against the approval of a claim allowed by the administrator, in the county court, and if approved, appeal from the order of approval; or they may renew their protest at the time the administrator seeks to sell property belonging to the estate to pay such claim, and appeal from the order decreeing such sale.—In re Jameson's Estate (Okla.), 182 Pac. 518, 520.

(2) **Notice of appeal.**—The administrator of the estate of a deceased person, who seeks to appeal from an allowance of a demand against the estate, must give notice of such appeal, either during the term at which the decision is made or within ten days after the date of the allowance.—McIntosh v. Wheeler, 58 Kan. 324, 49 Pac. 77.

(3) **Dismissal of appeal.**—An administrator's appeal from the order of a county court, allowing a claim against an estate, should be dismissed, where the order recites that the administrator "was present, took part in the examination of witnesses, but stated that he declined to regularly appear in person or by attorney."—In re Carver's Estate, 10 S. D. 609, 74 N. W. 1056. In Nevada a person whose claim against the estate of a decedent has been rejected may institute a suit thereon in which there are adverse parties, and, under the statutory rules, reserve all questions affecting his rights for review in the appellate court. Hence, where he has made application to the court for leave to amend a defective affidavit to a claim, which application is refused, an appeal from the order refusing permission to amend will be dismissed.—In re Powning's Estate, 25 Nev. 428, 62 Pac. 235, 236. An executor or administrator who would except to the action of the commissioner, acting as a probate judge, in allowing a claim, presented against the estate, must appeal within thirty days after the entry of the decree or order, otherwise the appeal will be dismissed.—In re Johnson's Estate, 5 Alaska 114, 117. An appeal from an order reversing the allowance of a claim must be dismissed, when there is nothing before .the court to show that there was either a settled record or even a judgment-roll to base it on.—In re Roberts' Estate (S. D.), 168 N. W. 31.

(4) **Review. In general.**—Where the statute prohibits the county court from allowing the claim of an executor or administrator, unless it has been presented to the county judge for allowance before it is barred by the statute of limitations, and a claim is not so presented, the court exceeds its jurisdiction in allowing the executor or administrator credit for the claim on final settlement, and its order allowing the claim is reviewable on a writ of review.—Farrow v. Nevin, 44 Or. 496, 75 Pac. 711, 713; but matters which were properly within the jurisdiction of the county court will not be disturbed on such writ, although the determination of the county court was erroneous.—Farrow v. Nevin, 44 Or. 496, 75 Pac. 711, 713. In New Mexico, the general administration of an estate in the probate court is in the nature of a proceeding in equity, and an appeal from the decision of such court allowing or disallowing a claim is an appeal to the district court sitting as a court of equity, and the action of the latter may be reviewed in the supreme court on appeal.—Clancey v. Clancey, 7 N. M. 405, 37 Pac. 1105, 1106. In the absence of a showing contrary to the validity of a claim the supreme court can not disturb the ruling below allowing the claim.— Estate of Aldersley, 174 Cal. 366, 375, 163 Pac. 206.

(5) Same. Objections not raised below.—Objections to a claim against the estate of a decedent, not raised in the court below, can not be raised for the first time in the supreme court.—Colman v. Woodsworth, 28 Cal. 567, 569; Hentsch v. Porter, 10 Cal. 555; Bank of Stockton v. Howland, 42 Cal. 129, 134.

(6) Same. Evidence. Findings.—On an appeal from an order granting a motion of the claimant for judgment for the full amount claimed, on the theory that the value of several items were not in issue, and from the judgment, the question of the sufficiency of the evidence to support the jury's findings of value will not be considered, where the parties to the contest had stipulated that the motion was to be heard only upon the record consisting of the claim, the contest thereto, and the general and special verdicts.—Estate of Weir, 168 Cal. 330, 143 Pac. 612. The rule of the supreme court that it will not interfere with a finding of the trial court where the evidence is conflicting is applied to a finding in a proceeding to compel an executor to act upon a claim against an estate, that such claim had not been presented.—In re King's Estate; Schrader v. Buffum, 102 Wash. 299, 302, 172 Pac. 1167. A finding in a proceeding to compel an executor to act upon a claim against an estate that such claim was not presented is held to have been sustained by the evidence.—In re King's Estate; Schrader v. Buffum, 102 Wash. 299, 301, 172 Pac. 1167.

(7) Same. Instructions.—Where the plaintiff failed to show legal presentation of a claim against an estate as required by section 178, Probate Code, as a condition precedent to a right of action thereon, errors in instructions will be deemed immaterial and non-prejudicial, and will, under section 1, Laws of 1913, chap. 178, be disregarded on appeal.—Dakota Nat. Bank v. Kleinschmidt, 33 S. D. 132, 141, 144 N. W. 934.

(8) Same. Of allowance.—If the evidence, in a suit against an administrator on a claim against the estate of a decedent, is conflicting but sufficient to induce the jury to believe that the claim, over the amount allowed by the administrator, is not made in good faith, the court will not disturb a verdict in favor of the defendant.—Selzer v. Selzer, 45 Okla. 142, 145 Pac. 318. On an appeal, the court will not disturb an order allowing a claim against the estate of a deceased person, on the ground that it was not timely presented, where there is no evidence showing that fact affirmatively.—Estate of Aldersley, 174 Cal. 366, 163 Pac. 206.

(9) Modification of judgment.—An erroneous judgment against the estate of a decedent may be modified upon appeal.—Preston v. Knapp, 85 Cal. 559, 24 Pac. 811; Moore v. Russell, 133 Cal. 297, 301, 85 Am. St. Rep. 166, 65 Pac. 624; and the judgment, as modified according to directions, is a final adjudication of the rights of the parties to the action, and the lower court is without jurisdiction to make any further judgment or order.—Vance v. Smith, 132 Cal. 510, 511, 64 Pac. 1078.

(10) Affirmance of Judgment.—Where a judgment against executors established a claim against the estate of a decedent, the subsequent affirmance of that judgment in the appellate court would not create a new or different judgment, nor impose upon the plaintiff therein the necessity of "filing among the papers of the estate in court" a certified copy of the transcript of the docket of judgment on the remittitur from the appellate court.—Estate of Kennedy, 93 Cal. 16, 28 Pac. 839.

(11) Reversal of Judgment.—A judgment for defendant in an action on a claim against an estate will not be reversed on appeal, though based on a ground not stated in the pleadings, where the complaint does not state a cause of action, and it is apparent that it can not be amended to do so.—Brown v. Daly, 33 Mont. 523, 84 Pac. 883, 884. If objection is made that a claim against an estate was not properly presented, the objection should be ruled upon by the court at some time during the trial, in order that the required proof may be supplied, if necessary, and a failure to make such ruling is reversible error.— Thurber v. Miller, 14 S. D. 352, 85 N. W. 600, 601. An objection to the recovery on a claim against the estate of a deceased person on the ground that it was not presented to the executor for allowance can not be made for the first time in the supreme court, nor on motion for a new trial.—Clayton v. Dinwoodey, 33 Utah 251, 14 Ann. Cas. 926, 93 Pac. 723, 727. While proof of the presentation of a claim is not a fact essential to the validity of a judgment, where any issue has been made upon that question, failure to make proof is ground for reversal, if an objection is made in the trial court, and an exception is properly preserved.—Falkner v. Hendy, 107 Cal. 49, 40 Pac. 49; Frazier v. Murphy, 133 Cal. 91, 95, 65 Pac. 91. A judgment against the estate of a decedent will not be reversed for a mere informality in the presentation of the claim.—Smith v. Furnish, 70 Cal. 424, 427, 12 Pac. 392.

(12) Costs.—If an appeal is taken from the rejection by the county court of a claim presented against an estate after adjustment day, the costs are to be taxed against the person presenting the claim.—Milner B. & T. Co. v. Whipple's Estate, 61 Colo. 442, 158 Pac. 811.

(13) Appeal from probate court to district court.—In the trial of an action appealed by an administrator from the decision of the probate court in allowing a claim against an estate, the district court sits as a court of probate. In such a case it is incumbent upon the plaintiff to establish his demand by competent testimony, the same as would be required of him in the probate court.—Phillips v. Faherty, 9 Kan. App. 380, 58 Pac. 801. On appeal to the district court from an order of the probate court allowing a claim against the estate of a deceased person, where the case is tried on the appeal upon the transcript from the probate court, without pleadings being filed, a promissory note purporting to have been given by the deceased in his lifetime does not prove itself, the execution thereof not having been denied under oath, under the provisions of the statute.—Haffamier v. Hund, 10 Kan. App.

579, 63 Pac. 659. To give the probate court jurisdiction to hear and determine a claim, it is necessary that such claim be verified. If it is not verified, the claimant can not, on appeal, supply the defect.— Clancey v. Clancey, 7 N. M. 405, 37 Pac. 1105. On appeal to the district court by a creditor, dissatisfied with the allowance made by the county court on his claim as filed, the case is tried de novo.—McAfee v. McAfee's Estate, 56 Colo. 144, 146, 136 Pac. 1051.

PART VIII.
SALES AND CONVEYANCE OF PROPERTY OF DECEDENTS.

CHAPTER I.

SALES IN GENERAL.

§ 482. Estate chargeable with debts; no priority.
§ 483. Validity of sale, confirmation, and passing of title.
§ 484. Petitions for orders of sale.
§ 485. But one petition, order, and sale must be had when.
§ 486. Form. Petition for order of sale of all the property of the estate at one sale.
§ 487. Form. Order of sale of all property of estate at one sale.
§ 488. Form. Objections to sale of decedent's property.

§ 482. Estate chargeable with debts; no priority.

All of the property of a decedent shall be chargeable with the payment of the debts of the deceased, the expenses of administration, and the allowance to the family, except as otherwise provided in this code and in the Civil Code. And the said property, personal and real, may be sold in the manner prescribed in this chapter. There shall be no priority as between personal and real property for the above purposes.—*Kerr's Cyc. Code Civ. Proc.*, § 1516.

ANALOGOUS AND IDENTICAL STATUTES.
The * indicates identity.

Arizona*—Revised Statutes of 1913, paragraph 904.
Idaho—Compiled Statutes of 1919, section 7602.
Montana*—Revised Codes of 1907, section 7546.
Nevada—Revised Laws of 1912, section 5951.
North Dakota—Compiled Laws of 1913, section 8730.
Oklahoma—Revised Laws of 1910, section 6360.
South Dakota—Compiled Laws of 1913, section 5812.
Wyoming*—Compiled Statutes of 1910, section 5637.

§ 483. Validity of sale, confirmation, and passing of title.

The executor or administrator may sell any property of the estate of a decedent without order of court, and at either public or private sale, as the executor or administrator may determine; but no sale of such property is valid unless the same be under oath reported to and confirmed by the court, and the title to the property does not pass until such sale be so confirmed by the court.—*Kerr's Cyc. Code Civ. Proc.*, § 1517.

ANALOGOUS AND IDENTICAL STATUTES.
The * indicates identity.

Alaska—Compiled Laws of 1913, section 1662.
Arizona*—Revised Statutes of 1913, paragraph 905.
Idaho*—Compiled Statutes of 1919, section 7603.
Montana*—Revised Codes of 1907, section 7548.
Nevada—Revised Laws of 1912, section 5980.
North Dakota—Compiled Laws of 1913, section 8764.
Oklahoma—Revised Laws of 1910, section 6361.
Oregon—Lord's Oregon Laws, section 1248.
South Dakota*—Compiled Laws of 1913, section 5813.
Utah*—Compiled Laws of 1907, section 3878.
Washington—Laws of 1917, chapter 156, page 676, section 122.
Wyoming*—Compiled Statutes of 1910, section 5638.

§ 484. Petitions for orders of sale.

All petitions for orders of sale must be in writing, setting forth the facts showing the sale to be necessary, and, upon the hearing, any person interested in the estate may file his written objections, which must be heard and determined. A failure to set forth the facts showing the sale to be necessary will not invalidate the subsequent proceedings, if the defect be supplied by the proofs at the hearing, and the general facts showing the necessity be stated in the order directing the sale.—*Kerr's Cyc. Code Civ. Proc.*, § 1518.

ANALOGOUS AND IDENTICAL STATUTES.
The * indicates identity.

Alaska—Compiled Laws of 1913, section 1662.
Arizona*—Revised Statutes of 1913, paragraph 906.
Colorado—Mills's Statutes of 1912, section 7974.
Idaho*—Compiled Statutes of 1919, section 7604.

Montana*—Revised Codes of 1907, section 7549.
Nevada—Revised Laws of 1912, section 5981.
North Dakota—Compiled Laws of 1913, section 8764.
Oklahoma*—Revised Laws of 1910, section 6362.
Oregon—Lord's Oregon Laws, section 1248.
South Dakota*—Compiled Laws of 1913, section 5814.
Washington—Laws of 1917, chapter 156, page 677, sections 123, 124.
Wyoming*—Compiled Statutes of 1910, section 5639.

§ 485. But one petition, order, and sale must be had, when.

When it appears to the court that the estate is insolvent, or that it will require a sale of all the property of the estate, of every character, to pay the family allowance, expenses of administration, and debts, there need be but one petition filed, but one order of sale made, and but one sale had, except in the case of perishable property, which may be sold as provided in section fifteen hundred and twenty-two. The court, when a petition for the sale of any property for any of the purposes herein named is presented, must inquire fully into the probable amount required to make all such payments, and if there be no more estate than sufficient to pay the same, may require but one proceeding for the sale of the entire estate. In such case the petition must set forth substantially the facts required by section fifteen hundred and thirty-seven.—*Kerr's Cyc. Code Civ. Proc.*, § 1519.

ANALOGOUS AND IDENTICAL STATUTES.

The * indicates identity.

Arizona*—Revised Statutes of 1913, paragraph 907.
Idaho*—Compiled Statutes of 1919, section 7605.
Montana—Revised Codes of 1907, section 7550.
North Dakota*—Compiled Laws of 1913, section 8765.
Oklahoma*—Revised Laws of 1910, section 6363.
South Dakota—Compiled Laws of 1913, section 5815.
Utah—Compiled Laws of 1907, section 3879.
Wyoming—Compiled Statutes of 1910, section 5640.

§ 486. Form. Petition for order of sale of all the property of the estate at one sale.

[Title of court.]

[Title of estate.]

{ No. ——.[1] Dept. No. ——.
[Title of form.]

To the Honorable the ——[2] Court of the County[3] of ——, State of ——.

The petition of ——, administrator[4] of the estate of ——, deceased, respectfully shows:

That said —— died intestate,[5] on or about the —— day of ——, 19—, in the county[6] of ——, state of ——, being at the time of his death, a resident of the said county[7] of ——; and that he left estate, consisting of both real and personal property, in said state;

That your petitioner is the duly appointed, qualified, and acting administrator[8] of the estate of ——, deceased; and

That your petitioner has made and returned to this court a true inventory and appraisement of all the estate of the said deceased which has come to his knowledge, and also published notices to the creditors of said decedent as required by law.

All of which will more fully appear by the papers on file in the clerk's office and the records of said court, in the matter of said estate, to which reference is hereby made.

That the following described personal property has come into the hands of your petitioner: ——;[9] valued at —— dollars ($——);

That ——[10] of said personal property has been disposed of, as follows, to wit: ——;[11]

That ——[12] remains to be disposed of;

That the debts outstanding against the said deceased, as far as can be ascertained or estimated, amount, at this date, to the sum of —— dollars ($——), and are fully set forth in Exhibit A, hereunto annexed and made a part of this petition;

That the amount due upon the family allowance is the sum of —— dollars ($——);

That the amount that will be due upon said family allowance, after the same shall have been in force for one year, is the sum of —— dollars ($——);

That the debts, expenses, taxes, and charges of administration already accrued amount to the sum of —— dollars ($——), and are fully set forth in Exhibit B, hereunto annexed and made a part of this petition;

That the debts, expenses, and charges of administration that will or may accrue during the administration are estimated by your petitioner at the sum of —— dollars ($——), and are set forth in Exhibit C, hereunto annexed and made a part of this petition;

That the total amount of debts outstanding against the deceased; of the amount due and to become due upon the family allowance, of the debts, expenses, and charges of administration already accrued and remaining unpaid, state and county taxes, and of the estimated debts, expenses, and charges of administration that will or may accrue is —— dollars ($——);

That a full description of all the real estate of which the said decedent died seised, or in which he had any interest, or in which the said estate has acquired any interest, and the condition and the value of the ——[13] said real estate are set forth in Exhibit D, hereunto annexed and made a part of this petition;

That all of said real estate was acquired by said deceased after marriage,[14] and is therefore community[15] property;

That the following are the names and ages of the heirs of the said deceased, to wit, —— and ——;

That it is necessary[16] to sell all of the property of the estate, of every character, to pay the family allowance, expenses of administration, and the debts of the estate.

Wherefore petitioner prays for an order directing that

all of the property of said estate, of every character, be sold at public sale, and that only one sale be had.

Dated ——, 19—.

——, Administrator [17] and Petitioner.

[Add usual verification.] [18]

Exhibit A.

The following is an itemized statement of all claims presented against the estate, whether allowed and approved, and an estimate of debts outstanding:

Name of Claimant. Nature of Claim. Amount.
—— —— $——
—— —— ——
——
Total .... $——

Exhibit B.

The following is a statement of debts, expenses, taxes, and charges of administration, already accrued:

Paid clerk's fees, as per voucher No. 1.......... $——
Paid appraisers, as per voucher No. 2........... ——
Paid printer, as per voucher No. 3.............. ——
Paid probate tax, as per voucher No. 4......... ——
Paid taxes for the year 19—, as per voucher No. 5 ——
——
Total .... $——

Exhibit C.

The following is an estimate of the debts, expenses, and charges of administration that will or may accrue:

Attorneys' fees for administrator............... $——
Collateral inheritance tax...................... ——
Commissions upon appraised value of estate..... ——
Other expenses................................. ——
——
Total .... $——

Exhibit D.

The following is a description of each parcel of real estate, with a statement of its condition, whether improved or unimproved, amount of rents received, etc., and its value: ——. Total value,[19] $——.

Explanatory notes.—1 Give file number. 2 Title of court, or name of judge. 3 Or, City and County. 4 Or, executor of the last will and testament of, etc. 5 Or according to the fact. 6, 7 Or, city and county. 8 Or, executor, etc., as the case may be. 9 Give description and value. 10 A portion, or all. 11 State how. 12 As, part thereof, stating it, with value; or, that none of said property. 13 Respective portions and lots of. 14 Or according to the fact. 15 Or, separate property, as the case may be. 16 To show this necessity, the footings of the exhibits must show that the debts, etc., are equal to or greater than the assets. 17 Or, executor. 18 Although section 1519 of California Code of Civil Procedure does not require a verified petition, yet where real estate is to be sold, the petition should be verified as required by section 1537 of the same code. 19 The value of each parcel should be stated separately and the total given at foot of exhibit.

§ 487. Form. Order of sale of all property of estate at one sale.

[Title of court.]

[Title of estate.]   { No. ——.1   Dept. No. ——.
        [Title of form.]

——, the administrator[2] of the estate of ——, deceased, having presented his petition for the sale of all of the property of said estate, of every character, both real and personal, and it appearing to the court that due notice of the hearing of said petition has been given as required by law, the court thereupon finds that it will require a sale of all of the property of the estate, of every character, to pay the family allowance, expenses of administration, and debts.

It is therefore ordered by the court, That said ——, administrator[3] as aforesaid, after due notice given, proceed to sell the whole of the personal property[4] of said estate, and the whole of the real property thereof,[5] at public auction, to the highest bidder, upon the following terms, to wit, for cash, in gold coin of the United States of America; and that but one sale be had for the entire estate.

The personal property to be sold as aforesaid is described as follows: ——.

The following is a description of the real estate to be sold under said order: ——.

Dated ——, 19——.   ——, Judge of the —— Court.

§ 488.   Form.   Objections to sale of decedent's property.

[Title of court.]

[Title of estate.]   { No.——.1   Dept. No.——.
                         {   [Title of form.]

A petition for an order of sale of the property of ——, deceased, having been filed by ——, administrator [2] of the estate of said decedent, ——, one of the heirs at law [3] of said deceased, now comes and files his written objections to said petition, and alleges as follows:

That it is not true, as alleged in said petition, that it is for the best interests of said estate that the property described in such application be sold, because ——;[4]

That the rents and interest, money due the estate, and money on hand, are more than sufficient to pay all debts of the estate and the expenses of administration.

The contestant therefore asks that said petition be denied.

——, Attorney for Contestant.   ——, Contestant.

CHAPTER II.

SALES OF PERSONAL PROPERTY.

§ 489. Perishable and depreciating property to be sold.

At any time after receiving letters, the executor, administrator, or special administrator may sell perishable and other personal property likely to depreciate in value, or which will incur loss or expense by being kept, and so much other personal property as may be necessary to pay the allowance made to the family of the decedent.

The executor, administrator, or special administrator is responsible for the property, unless, after making a sworn return, and on a proper showing, the court shall approve the sale.—*Kerr's Cyc. Code Civ. Proc.,* § 1522.

ANALOGOUS AND IDENTICAL STATUTES.
The * indicates identity.

Arizona*—Revised Statutes of 1913, paragraph 908.
Idaho*—Compiled Statutes of 1919, section 7606.
Montana*—Revised Codes of 1907, section 7551.
Nevada—Revised Laws of 1912, section 5982.
North Dakota*—Compiled Laws of 1913, section 8766.
Oklahoma*—Revised Laws of 1910, section 6366.
South Dakota*—Compiled Laws of 1913, section 5816.
Utah—Compiled Laws of 1907, section 3885.
Washington—Laws of 1917, chapter 156, page 676, section 123.
Wyoming*—Compiled Statutes of 1910, section 5641.

§ 490. Form. Petition for order to sell perishable and other personal property likely to depreciate in value.

[Title of court.]

[Title of estate.]   {No.——.¹ Dept. No.——.
                                   {   [Title of form.]

To the Honorable the ——² Court of the County³ of ——, State of ——.

Your petitioner respectfully represents, That he is the duly appointed, qualified, and acting administrator⁴ of the estate of ——, deceased;

That there is belonging to said estate, at ——,⁵ in the county⁶ of ——, one thousand sacks of potatoes and one hundred barrels of apples;⁷ that said property is of a perishable nature;⁸ and that it is necessary, and for the best interest of said estate, that such property be immediately sold;

That there is belonging to said estate, at ——,⁹ in the said county¹⁰ of ——, two thousand sacks of onions and five hundred head of sheep,¹¹ all of which property will be liable to depreciate in value if not sold without delay;¹² and that it is for the best interest of said estate that such property be sold.

Wherefore your petitioner prays for an order, made

without notice being given, authorizing him to sell all of said property hereinbefore described, and that such other or further order may be made as is meet in the premises.

——, Attorney for Petitioner.   ——, Petitioner.

Explanatory notes.—1 Give file number. 2 Title of court. 3 Or, City and County. 4 Or, special administrator; or, that on the —— day of ——, 19—, letters testamentary of the last will and testament of said deceased were issued to your petitioner, and that he is now the duly qualified and acting executor of said will. 5 Give name of place. 6 Or, city and county. 7 Or, other property of a perishable nature. 8 State cause, briefly, of immediate danger of diminution in value. 9 Give location. 10 Or, city and county. 11 Or other personal property likely to depreciate in value. 12 If keeping and care is expensive, state that fact, or any other fact likely to cause the property to depreciate in value.

§ 491. Form. Order to sell perishable property.

[Title of court.]

[Title of estate.]
{ No. ——.1   Dept. No. ——.
  [Title of form.]

Now comes ——, the administrator [2] of said estate, and presents his application for an order to sell personal property of the estate; and it appearing therefrom, and from proofs taken, that the following described personal property belonging to said estate is by nature perishable; that it is likely soon to depreciate in value; and that the estate will incur loss and expense by said property being kept,—

It is ordered by the court, That the said administrator [3] proceed to sell at public auction,[4] upon —— [5] days' notice, in the manner required by law, all of the following described personal property, to wit: ——.[6]

Dated ——, 19—.   ——, Judge of the —— Court.

Explanatory notes.—1 Give file number. 2 Or, executor of the last will and testament of ——, deceased. 3 Or, executor. 4 Or, at private sale, without notice, all the following described personal property, to wit (giving description). 5 As prescribed by the court or judge. 6 Give description.

§ 492. Form. Return of sale of perishable property.

[Title of court.]

[Title of proceeding.] { No. ——.1 Dept. No. ——.
[Title of form.]

To the Honorable the —— Court of the County [2] of ——.

The undersigned, ——, administrator [3] of the estate of ——, deceased, respectfully makes the following return of his proceedings under the order of this court dated the —— day of ——, 19—, authorizing said administrator [4] to sell certain personal property of said estate, and reports as follows:

That, in pursuance of said order of sale, he gave public notice of the time and place of sale, for at least ten days, by posting [5] notices thereof, as shown by affidavit Exhibit A, hereto annexed and made part hereof;

That, at the time and place specified in said notice, to wit, ——,[6] he caused to be sold at public auction [7] the property in said order and hereinafter described, to the persons and for the sums hereinafter shown, to wit: ——;[8]

——, Administrator [9] of the Estate of ——, Deceased.

Subscribed and sworn to before me this —— day of ——, 19—.   ——, Notary Public, etc.

Explanatory notes.—1 Give file number. 2 Or, City and County. 3 Or, executor of the last will. 4 Or, executor. 5 Or, publishing. 6 Give time and place of sale. 7 Or, sold at private sale. 8 Give names and sums. 9 Or, executor.

§ 493. Form. Exhibit A. Affidavit of posting notice of administrator's sale of perishable property.

[Title of court.]

[Title of proceeding.] { No. ——.1 Dept. No. ——,
[Title of form.]

State of ——, }
   County [2] of ——, } ss.

——, being duly sworn, says, That on the —— day of ——, 19—, he posted full, true, and correct copies of the annexed notice of the time and place of the sale therein mentioned, in three of the most public places in said county,[3] to wit, one copy at ——,[4] one at ——,[5] and one at ——.[6]

Subscribed and sworn to before me this —— day of ——, 19—.

Explanatory notes.—[1] Give file number. [2, 3] Or, City and County. [4, 5, 6] State place at which each was posted.

§ 494. Form. Order confirming sale of perishable property.

[Title of court.]

[Title of estate.]   { No. ——.[1] Dept. No. ——.
                                      {   [Title of form.]

Comes now ——, the administrator [2] of said estate, and presents his sworn report of the sale of perishable property under the order hereinbefore made, showing that in pursuance of said order, and after giving notice as prescribed by law and by the order of the court, he sold said property for the aggregate sum of —— dollars ($——), and he asks that said sales be confirmed. And the court, after hearing the evidence, approves said sales.

It is therefore ordered by the court that said sales be confirmed.   ——, Judge of the —— Court.

Dated ——, 19—.

Explanatory notes.—[1] Give file number. [2] Or, executor of the last will and testament of ——, deceased.

§ 495. Sale of personal property. Notice.

If claims against the estate have been allowed, and a sale of property is necessary for their payment, or for the expenses of administration, or for the payment of legacies, the executor or administrator may sell so much of the personal property as may be necessary therefor. He may also make a sale from time to time, so long as any personal property remains in his hands, and sale thereof is necessary. If it appear for the best interests of the estate, he may, at any time after filing the inventory, in like manner, and after giving notice by publication for two weeks in a newspaper of general circulation, printed and published in the county, sell the whole of the personal property belonging to the estate, whether necessary to pay debts or not; provided, that the court may, by order, shorten the time of notice to like publication for one week.—*Kerr's Cyc. Code Civ. Proc.*, § 1523.

ANALOGOUS AND IDENTICAL STATUTES.
The * indicates identity.
Alaska—Compiled Laws of 1913, section 1663.
Arizona*—Revised Statutes of 1913, paragraph 909.
Idaho*—Compiled Statutes of 1919, section 7607.
Montana*—Revised Codes of 1907, section 7552.
Nevada—Revised Laws of 1912, section 5982.
North Dakota—Compiled Laws of 1913, section 8767.
Oklahoma*—Revised Laws of 1910, section 6367.
Oregon—Lord's Oregon Laws, section 1249.
South Dakota*—Compiled Laws of 1913, section 5817.
Utah—Compiled Laws of 1907, sections 3877, 3880, 3885.
Washington—Laws of 1917, chapter 156, page 676, section 123.
Wyoming—Compiled Statutes of 1910, section 5642.

§ 496. **Partnership interests and choses in action, how sold.**
Partnership interests or interests belonging to any estate by virtue of any partnership formerly existing, interest in personal property pledged, and choses in action, may be sold in the same manner as other personal property, when it appears to be for the best interest of the estate. Before confirming the sale of any partnership interest, whether made to the surviving partner or to any other person, the court or judge must carefully inquire into the condition of the partnership affairs, and must examine the surviving partner, if in the county and able to be present in court.—*Kerr's Cyc. Code Civ. Proc.*, § 1524.

ANALOGOUS AND IDENTICAL STATUTES.
The * indicates identity.
Arizona*—Revised Statutes of 1913, paragraph 910.
Idaho*—Compiled Statutes of 1919, section 7608.
Montana*—Revised Codes of 1907, section 7553.
North Dakota*—Compiled Laws of 1913, section 8768.
Oklahoma*—Revised Laws of 1910, section 6368.
South Dakota*—Compiled Laws of 1913, section 5818.
Probate Law—73

Utah—Compiled Laws of 1907, section 3885.
Washington—Laws of 1917, chapter 156, page 665, section 89.
Wyoming*—Compiled Statutes of 1910, section 5643.

§ 497. Order in which property is to be sold.

In making orders and sales for the payment of debts
or family allowance, such articles as are not necessary
for the support and subsistence of the family of the
decedent, or are not specially bequeathed, must be first
sold.—*Kerr's Cyc. Code Civ. Proc.*, § 1525.

ANALOGOUS AND IDENTICAL STATUTES.
The * indicates identity.

Alaska—Compiled Laws of 1913, section 1663.
Arizona*—Revised Statutes of 1913, paragraph 911.
Idaho—Compiled Statutes of 1919, section 7609.
Montana*—Revised Codes of 1907, section 7554.
Nevada—Revised Laws of 1912, section 5982.
North Dakota*—Compiled Laws of 1913, section 8769.
Oklahoma*—Revised Laws of 1910, section 6369.
Oregon—Lord's Oregon Laws, sections 1249, 1251.
South Dakota*—Compiled Laws of 1913, section 5819.
Utah—Compiled Laws of 1907, sections 3877, 3885.
Washington—Laws of 1917, chapter 156, page 676, section 123.

§ 498. Sale of personal property. How to be made.

The sale of personal property must be made at public
auction for such money or currency as the court may
direct, and after public notice given for at least ten days
by notices posted in three public places in the county, or
by publication in a newspaper, or both, containing the
time and place of sale, and a brief description of the
property to be sold, unless for good reason shown the
court, or a judge thereof, orders a private sale, or a
shorter notice. Public sales of such property must be
made at the court-house door, or at the residence of the
decedent, or at some other public place; but no sale shall
be made of any personal property which is not present
at the time of the sale, unless the court otherwise order.—
Kerr's Cyc. Code Civ. Proc., § 1526.

ANALOGOUS AND IDENTICAL STATUTES.

The * indicates identity.

Alaska—Compiled Laws of 1913, sections 1664, 1665.
Arizona*—Revised Statutes of 1913, paragraph 912.
Idaho—Compiled Statutes of 1919, section 7610.
Kansas—General Statutes of 1915, section 4555.
Montana—Revised Codes of 1907, section 7555.
Nevada—Revised Laws of 1912, sections 5983, 5984.
North Dakota—Compiled Laws of 1913, section 8770.
Oklahoma—Revised Laws of 1910, section 6370.
Oregon—Lord's Oregon Laws, sections 1250, 1251.
South Dakota—Compiled Laws of 1913, section 5820.
Utah—Compiled Laws of 1907, section 3886.
Washington—Laws of 1917, chapter 156, page 676, section 123.
Wyoming—Compiled Statutes of 1910, section 5644.

§ 499. Sale of personal property, for interest of estate, on hearing of application for sale of real property.

Whenever it appears to the court on any hearing of an application for a sale of real property, that it would be for the interest of the estate that personal property of the estate, or some part of such property, should first be sold, the court may decree the sale of said personal property, or any part of it, and the sale thereof shall be conducted in the same manner as if the application had been made for the sale of such personal property in the first instance.—*Kerr's Cyc. Code Civ. Proc.,* § 1527.

ANALOGOUS AND IDENTICAL STATUTES.

The * indicates identity.

Arizona*—Revised Statutes of 1913, paragraph 913.
Montana*—Revised Codes of 1907, section 7651.
Nevada—Revised Laws of 1912, section 5992.
North Dakota*—Compiled Laws of 1913, section 8839.
Oklahoma*—Revised Laws of 1910, section 6445.
South Dakota*—Compiled Laws of 1913, section 5906.
Utah*—Compiled Laws of 1907, section 3887.
Washington—Laws of 1917, chapter 156, page 676, section 123.
Wyoming*—Compiled Statutes of 1910, section 5694.

§ 500.   Form.   Petition for order of sale of personal property.

[Title of court.]

[Title of estate.]   { No. ——.¹   Dept. No. ——.
                                       {   [Title of form.]

To the Honorable ——, Judge of the —— Court of the
County of ——,² State of ——.

The petition of —— respectfully shows:

That he is the duly appointed, qualified, and acting
administrator of the estate ³ of ——, deceased;

That claims against said estate have been allowed,⁴
amounting to —— dollars ($——), and a sale of personal
property of said estate is necessary to provide for the
payment thereof;

That the following described personal property, belonging to said estate, can be sold for that purpose, to
the best advantage for the estate, to wit, ——.⁵

Wherefore petitioner prays that, after due notice given
of the hearing hereof, an order be made authorizing and
directing your petitioner to sell the above-described
property, and for such other or further order as may
be meet.   ——, Petitioner.

Dated ——, 19—.

Explanatory notes.—1 Give file number. 2 Or, City and County. 3 Or,
executor of the last will. 4 Or, expenses of administration have been
incurred and are unpaid; or, legacies are provided for in said will, etc.
5 Give description.

**§ 501.   Form.   Order to show cause on petition for the sale of
personal property.**

[Title of court.]

[Title of estate.]   { No. ——.¹   Dept. No. ——.
                                       {   [Title of form.]

The petition of ——, administrator ² of the estate of
——, deceased, praying for an order to sell so much of
the personal property of said estate as may be necessary
for the payment of claims against said estate, and for the
payment of expenses of administration, and the allowance to the family of said deceased, having been pre-

sented to this court, and it appearing that such sale is necessary for said purposes,—

It is ordered, That all persons interested in said estate appear before the judge of the court, at the court-room thereof, at ——,[3] in said county [4] and state, on the —— day of ——, 19—, at the hour of —— o'clock in the forenoon [5] of said day, and then and there show cause, if any they have, why such order should not be made.

And it is further ordered, That a copy of this order be published in the ——, a newspaper printed in said county [6] and state, for at least five days [7] previous to the time set for the hearing of said order.[8]

Dated ——, 19—.   ——, Judge of the —— Court.

Explanatory notes.—1 Give file number. 2 Or, executor of the last will, etc. 3 State location of court-room. 4 Or, city and county. 5 Or, afternoon. 6 Or, city and county. 7 Or other time prescribed by statute. 8 Or, that notice be given in such other manner as the court may direct.

§ 502. Form. Notice of hearing of petition for sale of personal property at private sale.

[Title of court.]

[Title of estate.]   { No. ——.[1]   Dept. No. ——.
                             {   [Title of form.]

Notice is hereby given, That ——, the executor [2] of the last will and testament of ——, deceased, has filed with the clerk of this court a petition praying that said court grant its order directing the sale, at private sale,[3] of certain personal property belonging to the estate of said decedent, and described in said petition; and that ——,[4] the —— day ——, 19—, at —— o'clock in the forenoon,[5] at the court-room of said court, at ——,[6] in said county [7] of ——, state of ——, has been set for hearing said petition, when and where any and all persons interested may appear and show cause, if any they have, why the said petition should not be granted.   ——, Clerk.

Dated ——, 19—.   By ——, Deputy Clerk.

Explanatory notes.—1 Give file number. 2 Or, administrator of the estate, etc. 3 Or, at public auction, according to the fact. 4 Day of week. 5 Or, afternoon. 6 Give location of court-room. 7 Or, city and county.

§ 503. Form. Objections to sale of personal property.

[Title of court.]

[Title of estate.]   ·· ·   { No.——.1   Dept. No.——.
                                         [Title of form.]

Now comes ——, and alleges that she is the widow of said ——, deceased, and that said deceased left surviving him three minor children, to wit, ——, three years of age; ——, five years of age; and ——, seven years of age;

That she objects to the granting of the petition of ——, administrator [2] of the estate of ——, deceased, filed herein on the —— day of ——, 19—, praying for an order authorizing him to sell the personal property belonging to said estate, for the following reasons: ——;

That a certain portion of said property, which said administrator seeks to sell, which is hereinafter described, and which is mentioned in the inventory made and filed in said estate, is exempt from execution;[3] that the same ought to be set apart by this court for the use of said widow and children; and that said widow has already filed her petition herein, praying that the same be so set apart;

That the property so claimed as exempt, and to the sale of which the undersigned objects, is particularly described as follows, to wit: ——.[4]

Wherefore she objects to an order that the property hereinbefore described, or any part thereof, be sold, for any purpose, and asks that it be set apart for the use and benefit of the family.   ——, Widow of said Deceased.

   ——, Attorney for Widow.

Explanatory notes.—1 Give file number. 2 Or, executor of the last will and testament, etc. 3 Or, state any other reasons why the sale should not be made. 4 Give description.

§ 504. Form. Notice of administrator's sale of personal property.

[Title of court.]

[Title of estate.]

{ No.——.1 Dept. No.——.
[Title of form.]

Notice is hereby given, That, pursuant to an order of the above court made and entered on the —— day of ——, 19—, in the above-entitled proceeding, the undersigned, administrator [2] of said estate, will sell at public auction,[3] to the highest bidder, for cash, on ——,[4] the —— day of ——, 19—, at —— o'clock in the forenoon [5] of that day, at ——,[6] the following described personal property, to wit: ——.[7]

Said sale will be made subject to confirmation by the court.

Dated ——, 19—.

——, Administrator of the Estate of ——, Deceased.

Explanatory notes.—1 Give file number. 2 Or, executor of the last will. 3 Or, private sale; and if at private sale, state time to which and place at which bids will be received. 4 Give day of week. 5 Or, afternoon. 6 Give place of sale. 7 Give description.

§ 505. Form. Order for sale of personal property.

[Title of court.]

[Title of estate.]

{ No.——.1 Dept. No.——.
[Title of form.]

Comes now ——, the administrator [2] of said estate, and presents his petition for the sale of certain personal property of said estate, and it appearing to the court that due notice of the hearing of said petition has been given by posting notices [3] as required by law, and that the said sale is for the best interests of said estate,[4]—

It is ordered by the court, That said —— proceed to sell at public auction, after the notice and in the manner as provided by law, all the following personal property, to wit: ——.[5]

Dated ——, 19—.　——, Judge of the —— Court.

Explanatory notes.—1 Give file number. 2 Or, executor. 3 Or, by advertising. 4 Or, is necessary for the payment of claims, expenses of administration, or legacies. 5 Describe the property.

§ 506. Form. Return of sale of personal property, and petition for confirmation and approval.

[Title of court.]

[Title of estate.]   {No. ——.¹ Dept. No. ——.
                               { [Title of form.]

To the Honorable the ——² Court of the County³ of ——, State of ——.

The undersigned, ——, administrator⁴ of the estate of ——, deceased, respectfully returns the following account of sales made by him under the order of the judge of this court, dated on the —— day of ——, 19—, and reports as follows, to wit:

That in pursuance of said order of sale he gave public notice for at least ten days, by posting notices in three public places in said county,⁵ in which notices were specified the time and place of sale, as will more fully appear by the affidavit marked Exhibit A, hereunto annexed and made a part hereof, and also by publication in the ——, a newspaper published in said county,⁶ in which published notice were specified the time and place of sale, as will more fully appear by the affidavit marked Exhibit B, hereunto annexed and made a part hereof;⁷

That at the time and place specified in said notice, to wit, ——,⁸ he caused to be sold, to the highest bidder for cash, the property described in said notice, and hereinafter mentioned;

That at such sale the persons hereinafter named became the purchasers of the articles, and at the prices set opposite their names, respectively; that all⁹ of the said property was present at the time of selling; that the said sales were fairly conducted and legally made; and that the sums bid were not disproportionate to the value of the property sold.

The following are the names of the articles sold, the names of the purchasers, and the highest bid for each

Article Sold.	Purchaser.	Highest Bid.
———	———	———
———	———	———

Wherefore the said administrator [10] prays that a hearing be had upon this return, and that said sales be confirmed and approved, and declared valid.

———, Administrator [11] of the Estate of ———, Deceased.

Explanatory notes.—1 Give file number. 2 Title of court. 3 Or, City and County. 4 Or, executor of the last will and testament of, etc. 5, 6 Or, city and county. 7 Notice, either by posting or publication, is sufficient, unless both are ordered by the court. 8 State time and designate location of auction salesrooms. 9 Or as the fact may be. 10, 11 Or, executor.

§ 507. Form. Exhibit A. Affidavit of posting notices of administrator's sale of personal property.

[Title of court.]

[Title of estate.]

{ No. ———.1 Dept. No. ———.
[Title of form.]

State of ———, }
  County [2] of ———, } ss.

———, being duly sworn, says: That on the ——— day of ———, 19—, he posted true, full, and correct copies of the annexed [3] notice of the time and place of sale mentioned in said notice, in three of the most public places in said county,[4] to wit, one copy of said notice at ———,[5] one at ———,[6] and one at ———.[7]

Subscribed and sworn to before me this ——— day of ———, 19—. ———, Notary Public, etc.[8]

Explanatory notes.—1 Give file number. 2 Or, City and County. 3 Or, following; ending the form with the words, "said notice is as follows" (giving a copy thereof). 4 Or, city and county. 5 As, at the auction salesrooms of ———. 6 As, at the United States post-office. 7 As, at the sheriff's office of said county, or city and county. 8 Or other officer taking the oath.

§ 508. Form. Exhibit B. Affidavit of publication of notice of administrator's sale of personal property.

[Title of court.]

[Title of estate.]

{ No. ——.[1] Dept. No. ——.
[Title of form.]

State of ——,
  County [2] of ——, } ss.

——, being duly sworn, says: That he is the principal clerk [3] of the ——, a newspaper published in the said county [4] of ——; that a notice of which the annexed [5] is a true copy, was published in said newspaper for at least ten days next before the sale mentioned therein, and as often during the period of said ten days as said newspaper was regularly issued, to wit, daily, commencing on the —— day of ——, 19—, and ending on the —— day of ——, 19—.

Subscribed and sworn to before me this —— day of ——, 19—. ——, Notary Public, etc.[6]

Explanatory notes.—[1] Give file number. [2] Or, City and County. [3] Or, printer, or foreman. [4] Or, city and county. [5] Or, following is a true copy, to wit (inserting such copy). [6] Or other officer taking the oath.

§ 509. Form. Order approving sales of personal property.

[Title of court.]

[Title of estate.]

{ No. ——.[1] Dept. No. ——.
[Title of form.]

——, administrator [2] of the estate of ——, deceased, having duly returned to this court an account and report, verified by his affidavit, of sales made by him under the order of this court dated on the —— day of ——, 19—, and having also filed a petition praying that said sale be confirmed and approved;

And it appearing from said account and report, to the satisfaction of the judge of said court, that, in pursuance of said order of sale, said administrator [3] gave public notice for at least ten days,[4] by posting notices,[5] in which notices were specified the time and place of sale; that at the time and place mentioned in said public notice he sold

to the highest bidders, for cash, the property described
in said notice, and mentioned in said account of sales;
that the said place of sale was a public place; that all of
the said property was present at the time of selling; that
the said sales were legally made and fairly conducted;
that the sums bid were not disproportionate to the value
of the property sold; and that said account and report
are in all respects true; and no exceptions or objections
being made or filed by any person interested in the said
estate, or otherwise, to the granting of the said order
prayed for,—

It is ordered, That the said sales be, and the same are
hereby, confirmed and approved, and declared valid.

Dated ——, 19—. ● ——, Judge of the —— Court.

Explanatory notes.—1 Give file number. 2, 3 Or, executor. 4 Or, as
directed by the court. 5 Or, by publication, etc.

§ 510. **Form. Short form of order confirming sale of personal
property.**

[Title of court.]

[Title of estate.] { No. ——.1 Dept. No. ——.
[Title of form.] }

The administrator [2] of said estate now presents his
sworn report of sales of personal property under the
order hereinbefore made,[3] showing that he has made sales
thereof amounting to —— dollars ($——); and, after
hearing the evidence,—

It is ordered by the court, That said sales be approved
and confirmed.

Dated ——, 19—. ——, Judge of the —— Court.

Explanatory notes.—1 Give file number. 2 Or, executor. 3 Or, under
the terms of the will.

CHAPTER III.

SUMMARY SALES OF MINES AND MINING INTERESTS.

§ 511. Mines may be sold how.

When it appears from the inventory of the estate of any decedent that his estate consists in whole or in part of mines, or interests in mines, such mines or interests may be sold under the order of the court having jurisdiction of the estate, as hereinafter provided.—*Kerr's Cyc. Code Civ. Proc.,* § 1529.

ANALOGOUS AND IDENTICAL STATUTES.
The * indicates identity.

Arizona*—Revised Statutes of 1913, paragraph 914.
Colorado—Mills's Statutes of 1912, section 7978.
Idaho—Compiled Statutes of 1919, section 7611.
Montana—Revised Codes of 1907, section 7556.
Wyoming*—Compiled Statutes of 1910, section 5645.

§ 512. Petition for sale, who may file, and what to contain.

The executor or administrator, or any heir at law, or creditor of the estate, or any partner or member of any mining company, in which interests or shares are held or owned by the estate, may file in the court a petition, in writing, setting forth the general facts of the estate being then in due course of administration, and particularly describing the mine, interest, or shares which it is desired to sell, and particularly the condition and situation of the mines or mining interests, or of the mining company in which such interests or shares are held, and the grounds upon which the sale is asked to be made.—*Kerr's Cyc. Code Civ. Proc.,* § 1530.

ANALOGOUS AND IDENTICAL STATUTES.

The * indicates identity.

Arizona*—Revised Statutes of 1913, paragraph 915.

Idaho—Compiled Statutes of 1919, section 7612.

Montana*—Revised Codes of 1907, section 7557.

Wyoming*—Compiled Statutes of 1910, section 5646.

§ 513. Order to show cause, how made, and on what notice.

Upon the presentation of such petition, the court, or a judge thereof, must make an order directing all persons interested to appear before such court, at a time and place specified, not less than four or more than ten weeks from the time of making such order, to show cause why an order should not be granted to the executor or administrator to sell such mine, mining interests, shares, or stocks, as are set forth in the petition and belonging to the estate.

NOTICE, SERVICE, AND PUBLICATION.—A copy of the order to show cause must be personally served on all persons interested in the estate, at least ten days before the time appointed for hearing the petition, or published at least four successive weeks in such newspaper as such court or judge shall specify; provided, however, that when it appears from the inventory and appraisement that the value of the whole estate does not exceed the sum of two hundred and fifty dollars, the court or a judge thereof, may at his discretion order in lieu of publication that notices of the hearing thereof be posted in at least three public places in the county. If all persons interested in the estate signify in writing their assent to such sale, the notice may be dispensed with.—*Kerr's Cyc. Code Civ. Proc.,* § 1531.

ANALOGOUS AND IDENTICAL STATUTES.

No identical statute found.

Arizona—Revised Statutes of 1913, paragraph 916.

Idaho—Compiled Statutes of 1919, section 7613.

Montana—Revised Codes of 1907, section 7558.
Wyoming—Compiled Statutes of 1910, section 5647.

§ 514. Order of sale, when and how made.

If, upon hearing the petition, it appears to the satisfaction of the court that it is to the interest of the estate that such mining property or interests of the estate should be sold, or that an immediate sale is necessary in order to secure the just rights or interests of the mining partners, or tenants in common, such court must make an order authorizing the executor or administrator to sell such mining interests, mines, or shares, as hereinafter provided.—*Kerr's Cyc. Code Civ. Proc.*, § 1532.

ANALOGOUS AND IDENTICAL STATUTES.
The * indicates identity.

Arizona*—Revised Statutes of 1913, paragraph 917.
Idaho—Compiled Statutes of 1919, section 7614.
Montana*—Revised Codes of 1907, section 7559.
Wyoming*—Compiled Statutes of 1910, section 5648.

§ 515. Further proceedings to conform with what provisions.

After the order of sale is made, all further proceedings for the sale of such mining property, and for the notice, report, and confirmation thereof, must be in conformity with the provisions of article four of this chapter.—*Kerr's Cyc. Code Civ. Proc.*, § 1533.

ANALOGOUS AND IDENTICAL STATUTES.
The * indicates identity.

Arizona*—Revised Statutes of 1913, paragraph 918.
Idaho—Compiled Statutes of 1919, section 7615.
Montana*—Revised Codes of 1907, section 7560.

§ 516. Form. Petition for sale of mining property.
[Title of court.]

[Title of estate.]　　　　　　　　{ No. ——.1　Dept. No. ——.
　　　　　　　　　　　　　　　　　　{ 　　　[Title of form.]

Now comes your petitioner, ——, and alleges:
That he is ——;[2]
That the said —— died intestate, in the county [3] of

——, state of ——, on the —— day of ——, 19—, and was, at the time of his death, a resident of said county;[4]

That —— is the duly appointed, qualified, and acting administrator [5] of said estate;

That a true inventory and appraisement of all of the estate of the said deceased was returned by said administrator, and filed herein on the —— day of ——, 19—;

That due and legal notice to the creditors of said decedent has been published as required by law;[6]

That it appears from said inventory that the whole [7] of decedent's estate consists of mines [8] hereinafter particularly described in Schedule A, annexed hereto, hereby referred to, and made a part of this petition, the same as if incorporated herein;

That the said mine [9] is appraised in said inventory at the sum of —— dollars ($——), and that said amount is now the value of said mine;[10]

That the condition of said mine is as follows, to wit: ——;[11]

That it is for the advantage, benefit, and best interests of the said estate, and of those interested therein, that a summary sale of such mine [12] be made, for the following reasons, namely: ——.[13]

Your petitioner therefore prays that this court issue an order authorizing the said administrator to sell such mine at public auction,[14] after the making and service of an order to show cause, as prescribed by statute.

——, Attorney for Petitioner.　　——, Petitioner.

[Add ordinary verification.]

Exhibit A.

[Give a full and particular description of the mine, or mining interests.]

Explanatory notes.—[1] Give file number. [2] A partner or member of the —— Mining Company, in which said estate owns or holds interests or shares. [3],[4] Or, city and county. [5] Or, executor. [6] State any further facts, so far as administration has progressed. [7] Or, part. [8] Or, mining shares or other interests, as the case may be. [9] Or, mining interests.

10 Or as the case may be. 11 State whether the mine is being worked or is lying idle; whether it is a source of profit or loss to the estate; whether the property is improved or unimproved, etc., so as to enable the court intelligently to exercise its judgment in the selection of the property of the estate which can be most advantageously sold. 12 Or, mining shares or interests. 13 Specify reasons; as, that a sale is necessary to secure the just rights or interests of the mining partners, or tenants in common of the property; or, that, by reason of remoteness of the mine from lines of transportation, it is difficult of access, and can not be worked without great expense, etc. 14 Or as the case may be.

§ 517.   Form. Order to show cause. Sale of mines.

[Title of court.]

[Title of estate.]   { No. ——.1   Dept. No. ——.
                                      {   [Title of form.]

It is ordered by the court, That all persons interested in said estate appear before the —— 2 court of the county 3 of ——, state of ——, in department —— thereof, at the court-house 4 in said county 5 and state, on the —— day of ——, 19—, at —— o'clock in the forenoon 6 of said day, then and there to show cause, if any they have, why an order should not be granted to ——, as administrator 7 of the estate of ——, deceased, authorizing him to sell the mine, mining interests, shares, and stocks belonging to said estate, and set forth in the petition of —— for the sale thereof, filed herein on the —— day of ——, 19—.

Dated ——, 19—.   ——, Judge of the —— Court.

Explanatory notes.—1 Give file number. 2 Title of court. 3 Or, city and county. 4 Designate its location. 5 Or, city and county. 6 Or, afternoon. 7 Or, executor.

§ 517.1   Order for sale of mine. Proceedings to procure.

To obtain an order to enter into an agreement for the sale of, or for an option to purchase, a mining claim, or claims, or real property, worked as a mine, the proceedings to be taken and the effect thereof shall be as follows:

FIRST. PETITION.—The executor, administrator, or guardian of a minor, or of an incompetent person, or any person interested in the estate of such decedents, minors, or incompetent persons, may file a verified petition showing:

1. REQUIREMENTS.—The advantage or advantages that may accrue to the estate from entering into such agreement or option.

2. A general description of the property affected by said agreement or option.

3. The terms and general conditions of the proposed agreement or option.

4. The names of the legatees and devisees, if any, and of the heirs of the deceased, or of the minor, or of the incompetent person, so far as known to the petitioner.

SECOND. ORDER TO SHOW CAUSE.—Upon filing such petition an order shall be made by the court or judge requiring all persons interested in the estate to appear before the court or judge, at a time and place specified, not less than two or more than four weeks thereafter, then and there to show cause why an agreement for the sale, or an option for the purchase, of the realty should not be made, and referring to the petition on file for further particulars.

THIRD. SERVICE OF ORDER.—The order to show cause must be personally served on the persons interested in the estate at least ten days before the time appointed for hearing the petition, or it may be published for four successive weeks in a newspaper of general circulation in the county if there be one, and if there is none then in some newspaper of general circulation in an adjoining county.

FOURTH. HEARING—ORDER OF SALE—REQUIREMENTS.—At the time and place appointed to show cause, or at such other time and place to which the hearing may be postponed the power to make all needful postponements being hereby vested in the court or judge, the court or judge having first received satisfactory proof of personal service or publication of the order to show cause, must proceed to hear the petition, and any objections that may have been filed or presented thereto. If, after a full hearing, the court or judge is satisfied that it will be for the advantage of the estate to enter into the proposed agreement for the sale, or option for the purchase, of the mines or real property, worked as a mine, an order must be made authorizing, empowering, and directing the executor, administrator, or guardian to make such agreement or option to purchase. The order may prescribe the terms and conditions of such agreement or option to purchase. The court or judge may, at the time of making said order authorizing such agreement to sell or option to purchase, fix the amount of bond to be given by the executor, administrator, or guardian, and may provide for the payment into court of the proceeds from said agreement to sell or option to purchase, and that the said executor, administrator, or guardian, shall give the bond required before obtaining an order of the court for the payment to him of such proceeds from said agreement to sell or option to purchase.

FIFTH. AGREEMENT AND CONDITIONS OF SALE.—After making the order to enter into said agreement or option to purchase, the executor, administrator, or guardian of a minor or of an incompetent person shall execute, acknowledge, and deliver an agreement or option to purchase containing the conditions specified in the order, setting forth in the agreement or option to purchase that it is made by authority of the order, and giving the date of such order.

A certified copy of the order shall be recorded in the office of the county recorder of every county in which the land affected by the agreement or option to purchase, or any portion thereof, is situated. If the party of the second part to said agreement to sell or option to purchase neglects or refuses to comply with the terms of the agreement to sell or option to purchase, the court may, on motion of the executor, or administrator, or guardian, and after notice to the purchaser, order such agreement to sell or option to purchase canceled.

SIXTH. RETURN OF PROCEEDINGS.—The executor or administrator, or the guardian, after the terms of said agreement to sell, or said option to purchase, have been complied with by the party of the second part thereto, and all payments mentioned in the same have been made according to the terms of said agreement to sell or option to purchase, must make a return of his proceedings to the court, which must be filed in the office of the clerk at any time subsequent to the compliance with said conditions and the making of said payments. A hearing upon the return of the proceedings may be asked for in the return or by petition subsequently, and thereupon the clerk must fix the day for the hearing, of which notice of at least ten days must be given by the clerk, by notices posted in three public places in the county, or by publication in a newspaper, and must briefly indicate the land or lands mentioned in the agreement to sell or option to purchase, and must refer to the return for further particulars. Upon the hearing, the court must examine the return and witnesses in relation to the same.

CONFIRMATION OF SALE, AND CONVEYANCES.—If it appears to the court that the terms of said agreement to sell or option to purchase, including all payments to be made, have been complied with, the court must make an order confirming the sale, and directing conveyances to be executed. The sale, from that time, is confirmed and valid, and a certified copy of the order confirming it and directing conveyances to be executed, must be recorded in the office of the recorder of the county in which the land sold is situated.

CONVEYANCES must thereupon be executed to the purchaser by the executor or administrator, or the guardian, and they must refer to the orders of the court authorizing and confirming the sale of the property of the estate, and directing conveyances thereof to be executed and to the record of the order of confirmation in the office of the county recorder, either by the date of such recording, or by the date, volume, and page of the record, and such reference shall have the same effect as if the orders were at large inserted in the conveyance. Conveyances so made convey all the right, title, interest, and estate of the decedent, in the premises, at the time of his death; if prior to the sale, by operation of law or otherwise, the estate has acquired any right, title, or interest in the premises, other than or in addition to that of the decedent at the time of his death, such right, title, or interest also passes by such conveyances.—*Kerr's Cyc. Code Civ. Proc.*, § 1580.

ANALOGOUS AND IDENTICAL STATUTES.

No identical statute found.

Arizona—Revised Statutes of 1913, paragraphs 1181-1185.

Utah—Compiled Laws of 1907, sections 3908-3909X2; as amended by Laws of 1913. chapter 67, page 107 (lease or option).

§ 518.   Form. Order for sale of mining property.

[Title of court.]

[Title of estate.]   { No. ——.1 Dept. No. ——.
                                      {   [Title of form.]

It being shown to the court, from the verified petition of ——, now on file herein, that the estate of ——, deceased, consists wholly [2] of mines; and it appearing to the satisfaction of the court that it is to the interest of said estate that such mining property be sold;[3] and that the order to show cause herein made has been personally served by copy, and as required by law,[4]—

It is hereby ordered, adjudged, and decreed, That ——, the administrator [5] of said estate, be, and he is hereby, authorized to sell, at public auction,[6] to the highest bidder, the following described mining property, to wit: ——;[7] the said sale to be made for cash, gold coin of the

United States; ten per cent of the bid to be paid at the time of the sale, and the balance upon confirmation of such sale. ———, Judge of the —— Court.

Explanatory notes.—1 Give file number. 2 Or, in part. 3 Or, that an immediate sale of said property is necessary to secure the just rights or interests of the mining partners, or tenants in common of said property. 4 Or, published, etc. 5 Or, executor. 6 Or, private sale; or, either at public or private sale, as said administrator shall deem most beneficial. 7 Describe it.

CHAPTER IV.

SALES OF REAL ESTATE, INTERESTS THEREIN, AND CONFIRMATION THEREOF.

§ 585. Fraudulent sales.
§ 586. Limitation of actions for vacating sale, etc.
§ 587. To what cases preceding section not to apply.
§ 588. Account of sale to be returned.
§ 589. Form. Order to show cause why letters should not be revoked for failure to return account of sales.
§ 590. Form. Order to show cause why attachment should not issue for failure to return account of sales.
§ 591. Form. Order for attachment for neglecting to return account of sales.
§ 592. Executor, etc., not to be purchaser.

PROBATE SALES.

I. Nature of Jurisdiction. Law Governing.

II. Sales of Real and Personal Property in General.

.V. Appeal.

1. In general.
2. Non-appealable orders.
3. Appealable orders.
4. Parties interested or aggrieved.
5. Parties not interested or aggrieved.

6. Affirming the order of sale on appeal.
7. Record on appeal.
8. Decree. Effect of, on appeal.
9. Res judicata. Law of the case.

§ 519. Executor or administrator may sell property when.

When a sale of property of the estate is necessary to pay the allowance of the family, or the debts outstanding against the decedent, or the debts, expenses, or charges of administration, or legacies; or when it is for the advantage, benefit, and best interests of the estate, and those interested therein, that the real estate, or some part thereof, be sold, the executor or administrator may sell any real as well as personal property of the estate.— *Kerr's Cyc. Code Civ. Proc.,* § 1536.

ANALOGOUS AND IDENTICAL STATUTES.

The * indicates identity.

Alaska—Compiled Laws of 1913, section 1666.

Arizona*—Revised Statutes of 1913, paragraph 919.

Colorado—Laws of 1915, chapter 176, page 503, with a repealing clause. See, also, Laws of 1917, chapter 69, page 216, as to disposition of family allowances.

Hawaii—Revised Laws of 1915, section 2497.

Idaho*—Compiled Statutes of 1919, section 7616.

Kansas—General Statutes of 1915, sections 4598, 4631.

Montana—Revised Codes of 1907, section 7561; as amended by Laws of 1915, chapter 3, page 6. See Supp. of 1915, page 778.

Nevada—Revised Laws of 1912, sections 5985-6004.

New Mexico—Statutes of 1915, sections 2256, 4408, 4409.

North Dakota—Compiled Laws of 1913, section 8771.

Oklahoma—Revised Laws of 1910, section 6371.

Oregon—Lord's Oregon Laws, section 1252.

South Dakota—Compiled Laws of 1913, section 5821.

Utah*—Compiled Laws of 1907, section 3877.

Washington—Laws of 1917, chapter 156, pages 676, 677, sections 123, 124, 126.

Wyoming—Compiled Statutes of 1910, section 5650.

§ 520. Repeal of section.

Section 1537, Kerr's Cyc. Code Civ. Proc., was repealed in 1919. See California Laws of 1919, chap. 538,

p. 1177; but as statutes analogous to the California statute at the time of its repeal may be of some use, the tables of analogous statutes, together with the appropriate forms, have been retained.

ANALOGOUS AND IDENTICAL STATUTES.

No identical statute found.

Alaska—Compiled Laws of 1913, section 1667.

Arizona—Revised Statutes of 1913, paragraph 920.

Colorado—Laws of 1915, chapter 176, page 503, with a repealing clause.

Hawaii—Revised Laws of 1915, section 2498.

Idaho—Compiled Statutes of 1919, section 7617.

Kansas—General Statutes of 1915, sections 4599, 4601.

Montana—Revised Codes of 1907, section 7562; as amended by Laws of 1915, chapter 3, page 6. See Supp. of 1915, page 774.

Nevada—Revised Laws of 1912, section 5986.

North Dakota—Compiled Laws of 1913, section 8771.

Oklahoma—Revised Laws of 1910, section 6372.

Oregon—Lord's Oregon Laws, section 1253.

South Dakota—Compiled Laws of 1913, section 5822.

Utah—Compiled Laws of 1907, section 3888.

Washington—Laws of 1917, chapter 156, page 677, section 124.

Wyoming—Compiled Statutes of 1910, section 5651.

§ 521. Form. Petition for order of sale of real estate for best interests of estate, including application for the sale of personal property.

[Title of court.]

[Title of estate.]   { No. ——.1 Dept. No. ——.
                        {   [Title of form.]

To the Honorable the ——² Court of the County³ of ——, State of ——.

The petition of the undersigned, ——, administrator⁴ 'of the estate of ——, deceased, respectfully shows:

That said —— died intestate,⁵ on or about the —— day of ——, 19—, in the county⁶ of ——, state of ——, being at the time of his death a resident of the said county⁷ of ——; and that he left estate, consisting of both real and personal property, in said state;

That your petitioner is the duly appointed, qualified, and acting administrator⁸ of said estate;

That your petitioner has made and returned to this court a true inventory and appraisement of all the estate of the said deceased, which has come to his possession or knowledge, and also published notices to the creditors of said decedent as required by law;

That the following is a general description of all the real property of which the decedent died seised, or in which he had any interest, or in which his estate has acquired any interest, and the condition and value thereof, to wit: ——;[9] and that all of said real property is the separate property of decedent;[10]

That the names, ages, and places of residence of the heirs of said deceased, so far as known to your petitioner, are as follows, to wit: ——;[11]

That said real estate is expensive to maintain and manage properly; that a portion of the same is planted to vines, which need the constant care and attention of some person qualified to attend to the same; that circumstances require the remainder of said real estate to be cultivated, and the fruit-trees growing thereon to be attended to; that the fences and buildings on said premises will become dilapidated unless properly attended to; that said real estate, by reason of its not being occupied by some person interested therein, will deteriorate and depreciate in value; that said real estate can be sold at the present time for a better price than if sold later; that it will be difficult to lease said premises for a fair compensation, by reason of there being no dwelling-house thereon; that the expense of maintaining and caring for said premises by said administrator, if he is compelled to employ labor and help therefor, will largely exceed the revenues derived therefrom, and, coupled with the taxes to be annually collected on said premises, will be a source of expense, which will be a disadvantage to the parties entitled to said estate; and that it will be for the advantage, benefit, and best interests of the estate, and of those interested therein, that said real estate, and the whole thereof, be sold, for the reasons aforesaid, and the proceeds distributed among the said heirs in accordance with their respective interests;[12]

That the following is the amount of the personal estate of said deceased which has come to the hands of your petitioner, to wit: ——, of the value of —— dollars ($——);

That a portion of said personal property has been disposed of as follows, ——, and the proceeds paid out as follows, ——, leaving in the hands of your petitioner the sum of —— dollars ($——), and the remainder of said personal property;

That the debts outstanding against the said deceased, as far as can be ascertained or estimated, amount, at this date, to the sum of —— dollars ($——);[13]

That the debts, expenses, and charges of administration already accrued are the following: ——;[14]

That an estimate, by your petitioner, of the debts, expenses, and charges of administration which will or may accrue during the administration of the said estate is the following: ——;[15]

That there is now due upon the family allowance the sum of —— dollars ($——);

That the said debts outstanding against the deceased, the said debts, expenses, and charges of administration already accrued and remaining unpaid, and the estimated debts, expenses, and charges of administration that will or may accrue, amount to the sum of —— dollars ($——).[16]

Your petitioner therefore alleges that the personal 'estate in his hands is not sufficient to pay the debts outstanding against the said ——, deceased, and the debts, expenses, and charges of administration.

Wherefore your petitioner prays for an order of this court directing that all persons interested in said estate appear before this court, at a time and place specified, not less than four nor more than ten weeks from the time of making such order, to show cause why an order should not be granted to sell the real estate of deceased for the benefit of all persons interested therein, and to sell the whole of the personal property of said estate to pay the debts outstanding against the deceased, and the debts, expenses, and charges of administration; that, after a full hearing of this petition, and an examination of the allegations and proofs of the parties interested, and due proof of the publication of said order to show cause, an order be made by this court, authorizing and directing your petitioner to sell the whole of said real and personal property, either at public or private sale, as your petitioner shall judge to be the most beneficial for the said estate; and that such other or further order as may be proper be made in the premises.   ——, Petitioner.

——, Attorney for Petitioner.

[Add usual verification.]

Explanatory notes.—1 Give file number. 2 Title of court, or name of judge. 3 Or, City and County. 4 Or, executor of the last will and testament of, etc. 5 Or according to the fact. 6, 7 Or, city and county. 8 Or, executor, etc. 9 Insert description, condition, and value. 10 Or, community property; or as the fact may be. 11 Insert names, etc. 12 Or other reasons. 13 Give list of claims allowed, approved, and filed. 14-16 Give detailed statement. That the statute authorizing a sale of the property of an estate, whether real or personal, when it is for the advantage, benefit, and best interest to do so, is valid, see Estate of Porter, 129 Cal. 86, 79 Am. St. Rep. 78, 61 Pac. 659.

§ 522.   Repeal of section.

Section 1538, Kerr's Cyc. Code Civ. Proc., was repealed in 1919. See California Laws of 1919, chap. 538, p. 1177. But, as statutes analogous to the California statute at the time of its repeal may be of some use, the table of analogous statutes, together with the appropriate forms, have been retained.

ANALOGOUS AND IDENTICAL STATUTES.

The * indicates identity.

Alaska—Compiled Laws of 1913, section 1668.

Arizona—Revised Statutes of 1913, paragraph 921.

Colorado—Laws of 1915, chapter 176, page 503, with a repealing clause.

Idaho*—Compiled Statutes of 1919, section 7618.

Kansas—General Statutes of 1915, section 4602.

Montana—Revised Codes of 1907, section 7563; as amended by Laws of 1915, chapter 3, page 6. See Supp. of 1915, page 775.

Nevada—Revised Laws of 1912, section 5987.

North Dakota—Compiled Laws of 1913, section 8771.

Oklahoma—Revised Laws of 1910, section 6373.

Oregon—Lord's Oregon Laws, section 1254.

South Dakota—Compiled Laws of 1913, section 5823.

Utah—Compiled Laws of 1907, section 3889.

Washington—Laws of 1917, chapter 156, page 678, section 126.

Wyoming—Compiled Statutes of 1910, section 5652.

§ 523. Form. Order to show cause why order of sale of both real estate and personal property should not be made.

[Title of court.]

[Title of estate.]   { No. ——.1 Dept. No. ——.
                            {   [Title of form.]

——, the administrator [2] of the estate of ——, deceased, having presented to this court and filed herein his verified petition, in due form of law, praying for an order for the sale of all the real property and all the personal property of said ——, deceased, for the purposes therein set forth, and it appearing to this court, by said petition, that it would be for the advantage, benefit, and best interests of the estate, and those interested therein, to sell the whole of the real estate, and that it is necessary to sell the whole of the personal property to pay the debts outstanding against said ——, deceased, and the debts, expenses, and charges of administration, —

It is therefore hereby ordered by this court, That all persons interested in the estate of said deceased appear before said court on ——,[3] the —— day of ——, 19—, at —— o'clock in the forenoon [4] of said day, at the courtroom of said court, in the said county [5] of ——, to show cause why an order should not be granted to said administrator [6] to sell the whole of the real estate and the whole of the personal estate of said deceased, at either private or public sale, as said administrator [7] shall judge to be most beneficial for the estate, and that a copy of this order be published once a week for four successive weeks,[8] in a daily newspaper of general circulation printed and published in said county [9] of ——.

The following is a description of the real estate and personal property hereinbefore referred to, and which is sought to be sold under said petition: ——.[10]

Dated the —— day of ——, 19—.

—————, Judge of the —— Court.

Explanatory notes.—[1] Give file number. [2] Or, executor, etc. [3] Day of week. [4] Or, afternoon. [5] Or, city and county. [6,7] Or, executor, etc. [8] Or as prescribed by statute. [9] Or, city and county. [10] Insert description.

§ 524. Form. Order to show cause why order of sale of real estate should not be made.

[Title of court.]

[Title of estate.]   { No. ——.[1]   Dept. No. ——.
                         {   [Title of form.]

It appearing to the satisfaction of the court from the verified petition of ——, administrator [2] of the estate of ——,[3] on file herein, that it is necessary [4] to sell the whole [5] of the estate of said deceased, —

It is ordered by the court, That all persons interested in the estate of said ——,[6] deceased, appear before the ——[7] court of the county [8] of ——, state of ——, at the court-room thereof,[9] in said county [10] and state, on the —— day of ——, 19—, at —— o'clock in the forenoon [11] of said day, then and there to show cause, if any they have, why an order, as prayed for in the petition, should not be granted to the said administrator [12] to sell the real estate [13] of said deceased, at either public or private sale, for the purposes mentioned in the petition, as he shall judge to be for the best interests of said estate and of the parties interested therein;

It is further ordered, That a copy of this order be published at least once a week for four (4) successive weeks,[14] in the ——, a newspaper printed and published in said county.[15]

Dated this —— day of ——, 19—.

—————, Judge of said —— Court.

Explanatory notes.—1 Give file number. 2 Or, administratrix; or, administrator or administratrix with the will annexed; or, executor or executrix of the last will and testament of ——, deceased; or the plural of any of these, as the case may be. 3 Also known as ——, also known as ——, if known by different names. 4 To pay the debts, expenses, and charges of administration of the estate of said deceased, which have already accrued, and which will or may accrue hereafter during the administration of said estate; or, for the payment of legacies in said estate; or, would be for the advantage, benefit, and best interests of said estate, and those interested therein. 5 Or, some portion. 6 Also known as ——, where known by more than one name. 7 Giving title of court, and number of department, in which matter will be heard, and location of the court. 8 Or, city and county. 9 Designate its location. 10 Or, city and county. 11 Or, afternoon. 12 Or, administratrix. 13 Or, some portion of the said real estate. 14 Must be not less than four (4) nor more than ten (10) weeks, or as otherwise provided by the statute. 15 Or, city and county.

§ 525. Repeal of section.

Section 1539, Kerr's Cyc. Code Civ. Proc., was repealed in 1919. See California Laws of 1919, chap. 538, p. 1177. But as statutes analogous to the California statute at the time of repeal may be of some use, the table of analogous and identical statutes has been retained.

ANALOGOUS AND IDENTICAL STATUTES.

No identical statute found.

Alaska—Compiled Laws of 1913, section 1669.

Arizona—Revised Statutes of 1913, paragraph 922.

Colorado—Laws of 1915, chapter 176, page 503, with a repealing clause.

Idaho—Compiled Statutes of 1919, section 7619.

Montana—Revised Codes of 1907, section 7564.

Nevada—Revised Laws of 1912, section 5988.

North Dakota—Compiled Laws of 1913, section 8772.
Oklahoma—Revised Laws of 1910, section 6374.
Oregon—Lord's Oregon Laws, section 1255.
South Dakota—Compiled Laws of 1913, section 5824.
Utah—Compiled Laws of 1907, section 3889.
Wyoming—Compiled Statutes of 1910, section 5653.

§ 526. Repeal of section.

Section 1540, Kerr's Cyc. Code Civ. Proc., was repealed in 1919. See California Laws of 1919, chap. 538,
p. 1177. But, as statutes analogous to the California
statute at the time of repeal may be of some use, the
table of analogous and identical statutes, and appropriate forms, have been retained.

ANALOGOUS AND IDENTICAL STATUTES.
The * indicates identity.

Arizona*—Revised Statutes of 1913, paragraph 923.
Colorado—Laws of 1915, chapter 176, page 503, with a repealing
clause.
Idaho—Compiled Statutes of 1919, section 7620.
Montana*—Revised Codes of 1907, section 7565.
Nevada—Revised Laws of 1912, section 5989.
North Dakota—Compiled Laws of 1913, section 8772.
Oklahoma—Revised Laws of 1910, section 6375.
South Dakota*—Compiled Laws of 1913, section 5825.
Wyoming*—Compiled Statutes of 1910, section 5654.

§ 527. Form. Objection to order of sale of real estate.
[Title of court.]

[Title of estate.]   ⎰No.———.1 Dept. No.———.
                                       ⎱   [Title of form.]

Now comes ———, one of the devisees [2] of said decedent,
and opposes the application herein made by the administrator [3] of the estate of said deceased, for an order of
sale of real estate as prayed for in his petition, on the
following grounds:

That the order to show cause made herein was not published as required by law, and as directed by this court;
nor was it personally served, as required by law, on any
of the persons interested in said estate;

That said estate is not indebted to ———, as set forth

in said application, because his claim was, at the time of its allowance by the administrator, barred by the statute limiting the time within which claims against the estate must be presented.[4]

The contestant therefore asks that said application be denied.   ——, Contestant.

——, Attorney for Contestant.

Explanatory notes.—[1] Give file number. [2] Or, heir at law, or other party interested, according to the fact. [3] Or, executor, etc., as the case may be. [4] Make other objections, if any exist.

§ 528. Administrator, executor, and witnesses may be examined.

The executor, administrator, and witnesses may be examined on oath by either party, and process to compel them to attend and testify may be issued by the court or judge, in the same manner and with like effect as in other cases.—*Kerr's Cyc. Code Civ. Proc.*, § 1541.

ANALOGOUS AND IDENTICAL STATUTES.
The * indicates identity.
Arizona*—Revised Statutes of 1913, paragraph 924.
Idaho*—Compiled Statutes of 1919, section 7621.
Montana*—Revised Codes of 1907, section 7566.
Nevada—Revised Laws of 1912, section 5991.
North Dakota—Compiled Laws of 1913, section 8772.
Oklahoma*—Revised Laws of 1910, section 6376.
South Dakota*—Compiled Laws of 1913, section 5826.
Wyoming*—Compiled Statutes of 1910, section 5655.

§ 529. Repeal of section.

Section 1542, Kerr's Cyc. Code Civ. Proc., was repealed in 1919. See California Laws of 1919, chap. 538, p. 1177. But, as statutes analogous to the California statute at the time of its repeal may be of some use, the table of analogous and identical statutes has been retained.

ANALOGOUS AND IDENTICAL STATUTES.
The * indicates identity.
Alaska—Compiled Laws of 1913, section 1670.
Arizona—Revised Statutes of 1913, paragraph 925.

Colorado—Laws of 1915, chapter 176, page 503, with a repealing clause.

Idaho*—Compiled Statutes of 1919, section 7623.

Kansas—General Statutes of 1915, section 4605.

Montana—Revised Codes of 1907, section 7567; as amended by Laws of 1915, chapter 3, page 6. See Supp. of 1915, page 775.

Nevada—Revised Laws of 1912, section 5992.

North Dakota—Compiled Laws of 1913, section 8772.

Oklahoma—Revised Laws of 1910, section 6377.

Oregon—Lord's Oregon Laws, section 1256.

South Dakota*—Compiled Laws of 1913, section 5827.

Utah—Compiled Laws of 1907, section 3880.

Washington—Laws of 1917, chapter 156, page 678, section 126.

Wyoming—Compiled Statutes of 1910, section 5656.

§ 530. Repeal of section.

Section 1543, Kerr's Cyc. Code Civ. Proc., was repealed in 1919. See California Laws of 1919, chap..538, p. 1177. But, as statutes analogous to the California statute at the time of its repeal may be of some use, the table of analogous and identical statutes has been retained.

ANALOGOUS AND IDENTICAL STATUTES.

The * indicates identity.

Alaska—Compiled Laws of 1913, section 1670.

Arizona—Revised Statutes of 1913, paragraph 926.

Colorado—Laws of 1915, chapter 176, page 503, with a repealing clause.

Idaho*—Compiled Statutes of 1919, section 7623.

Kansas—General Statutes of 1915, section 4604.

Montana—Revised Codes of 1907, section 7568, as amended by Laws of 1915, chapter 3, page 6. See Supp. of 1915, page 775.

Nevada—Revised Laws of 1912, section 5992.

New Mexico—Statutes of 1915, section 2256.

North Dakota—Compiled Laws of 1913, section 8772.

Oklahoma—Revised Laws of 1910, section 6378.

Oregon—Lord's Oregon Laws, section 1256.

South Dakota—Compiled Laws of 1913, section 5828.

Utah—Compiled Laws of 1907, section 3890.

Washington—Laws of 1917, chapter 156, page 678, section 126.

Wyoming—Compiled Statutes of 1910, section 5657.

§ 531. Repeal of section.

Section 1544, Kerr's Cyc. Code Civ. Proc., was repealed in 1919. See California Laws of 1919, chap. 538,

p. 1177. But, as statutes analogous to, or identical with, the California statute at the time of its repeal may be of some use, the table of analogous and identical statutes, together with the appropriate forms, have been retained.

ANALOGOUS AND IDENTICAL STATUTES.
The * indicates identity.

Alaska—Compiled Laws of 1913, section 1670.

Arizona*—Revised Statutes of 1913, paragraph 927.   ·

Colorado—Laws of 1915, chapter 176, page 503, with a repealing clause.

Idaho*—Compiled Statutes of 1919, section 7674.

Kansas—General Statutes of 1915, section 4604.

Montana*—Revised Codes of 1907, section 7569.

Nevada—Revised Laws of 1912, section 5993.

North Dakota—Compiled Laws of 1913, section 8772.

Oklahoma—Revised Laws of 1910, section 6379.

Oregon—Lord's Oregon Laws, sections 1256, 1257.

South Dakota—Compiled Laws of 1913, section 5829; as amended by Laws of 1915, chapter 148, page 325.

Utah*—Compiled Laws of 1907, section 3891.

Washington—Laws of 1917, chapter 156, page 678, section 126.

Wyoming—Compiled Statutes of 1910, section 5658.

§ 532.   Form.   Petition for order of sale of real estate where personal property is insufficient.

[Title of court.]

[Title of estate.]   . $\left\{\begin{array}{l}\text{No. ——.}^1 \text{ Dept. No. ——.}\\ \text{[Title of form.]}\end{array}\right.$

To the Honorable the ——[2] Court of the County [3] of ——, State of ——.

The petition of ——, the administrator [4] of the estate of deceased, respectfully shows:

That said —— died intestate,[5] on or about the —— day of ——, 19—, in the county [6] of ——, state of ——, being at the time of his death a resident of the said county [7] of ——; and that he left estate, consisting of both real and personal property, in the said state of ——;

That on the —— day of ——, 19—, your petitioner was duly appointed administrator of said estate; that on the same day he qualified as such administrator; that letters of administration, signed by the clerk, and under the seal of said court, were thereupon issued to your petitioner, a competent person; that said letters have not been revoked; and that your petitioner is now the duly appointed, qualified, and acting administrator [8] of said estate; and

That your petitioner duly made and returned to this court, within —— days after his appointment, to wit, on the —— day of ——, 19—, a true inventory and appraisement of all the estate of the said deceased, which has come to his possession or knowledge, and also published notices to the creditors of said decedent, as required by law.

All of which will more fully appear by the papers on file in the clerk's office and the records of said court, in the matter of said estate, to which reference is hereby made.

That the following described personal property has come into the hands of your petitioner: ——; [9]

Valued at —— dollars ($——);

That —— [10] of said personal property has been disposed of, as follows, to wit: ——; [11]

That ——[12] remains to be disposed of;

That the debts outstanding against the said deceased, as far as can be ascertained or estimated, amount, at this date, to the sum of —— dollars ($——), and are fully set forth in Exhibit A, hereunto annexed and made a part of this petition;

That the amount due upon the family allowance is the sum of —— dollars ($——);

That the amount that will be due upon said family allowance, after the same shall have been in force for one year, is the sum of —— dollars ($——);

That the debts, expenses, taxes, and charges of administration already accrued amount to the sum of —— dollars ($——), and are fully set forth in Exhibit B, hereunto annexed and made a part of this petition;

That the debts, expenses, and charges of administration that will or may accrue during the administration are estimated by your petitioner at the sum of —— dollars ($——), and are set forth in Exhibit C, hereunto annexed and made a part of this petition;

That the whole amount of debts outstanding against the deceased, of the amount due and to become due upon the family allowance, of the debts, expenses, and charges of administration already accrued and remaining unpaid, state and county taxes, and of the estimated debts, expenses, and charges of administration that will or may accrue, is —— dollars ($——);

That a full description of all the real estate of which the said decedent died seised, or in which he had any interest, or in which the said estate has acquired any interest, and the condition and the value of the ——[13] said real estate, are set forth in Exhibit D, hereunto annexed and made a part of this petition;

That the whole of said real estate was acquired by said deceased after marriage,[14] and is therefore community[15] property;

That the following are the names and ages of the —— heirs of the said deceased, to wit, —— and ——.

Your petitioner therefore alleges that the personal estate in the hands of your petitioner is insufficient[16] to pay the allowance of the family, the debts outstanding against the deceased, and the debts, expenses, and charges of the administration; and that it is necessary to sell the whole[17] of the said real estate for such purposes.

Wherefore your petitioner prays that an order be made by this court, directing all persons interested in said estate to appear before said court, at a time and place specified,[18] to show cause why an order should not be granted to your petitioner to sell so much of the real

estate of the deceased as may be necessary for the purpose aforesaid;

And that after a full hearing of this petition, examination of the proofs and allegations of the parties interested, and due proof of the publication of a copy of said
order to show cause, etc., an order of sale be made,
authorizing your petitioner to sell all, or so much, and
such parts of the said real estate as said court shall judge
necessary or beneficial, at public or private sale, as petitioner shall judge most beneficial for the estate, and that
such other or further order may be made as is meet in
the premises.   ——, Petitioner.

Dated ——, 19—.

Exhibit A.

The following is an itemized statement of all claims
presented against the estate, whether allowed and approved, and an estimate of debts outstanding:

Name of Claimant.	Nature of Claim.	Amount.
——	——	$——
——	——	——

Total .... $——

Exhibit B.

The following is a statement of debts, expenses, taxes,
and charges of administration already accrued:

Paid clerk's fees, as per Voucher No. 1 .... $——
Paid appraisers, as per Voucher No. 2 .... ——
Paid printer, as per Voucher No. 3 .... ——
Paid probate tax, as per Voucher No. 4 .... ——
Paid taxes for the year 19—, as per Voucher No. 5. ——

Total .... $——

Exhibit C.

The following is an estimate of the debts, expenses,
and charges of administration that will or may accrue:

Attorneys' fees for administrator .... $——
Collateral inheritance tax .... ——

Commissions upon appraised value of estate...... ——
Other expenses .... ——
                                              ——
Total .... $——

Exhibit D.

The following is a description of each parcel of real estate, with a statement of its condition, whether improved or unimproved, amount of rents received, etc., and its value: ——. Total value,[19] $——.

Explanatory notes.—[1] Give file number. [2] Title of court, or name of judge. [3] Or, city and county. [4] Or, executor of the last will and testament of, etc. [5] Or according to the fact. [6,7] Or, city and county. [8] Or, executor, etc., as the case may be. [9] Give description. [10] A portion, or all. [11] State how. [12] Part thereof, stating it, and giving value; or, that none of said property. [13] Respective portions and lots of. [14] Or according to the fact. [15] Or, separate property, as the case may be. [16] Real estate may be sold without the personal property being exhausted, and the allegations of a petition for the sale of realty before the personal property is exhausted should, of course, conform to the statute authorizing such a sale. See §§ 519, 520, 521, ante. [17] Or, part thereof. [18] Not less than four (4) nor more than ten (10) weeks from the making of such order. [19] The value of each parcel should be separately stated, and the total given at bottom of exhibit.

§ 533. Form. Verification of petition.

State of ——,   }
    County [1] of ——, } ss.

——, the petitioner above named, being duly sworn, says: That he has read the foregoing petition, and knows the contents thereof, and that the same is true of his own knowledge, except as to the matters which are therein stated on his information or belief, and as to those matters, that he believes them to be true.

Subscribed and sworn to before me this —— day of ——, 19—.   ——, Notary Public, etc.[2]

Explanatory notes.—[1] Or, city and county. [2] Or other officer taking the oath.

§ 534. Form. Order for sale of real estate.

[Title of court.]

[Title of estate.]   No. ——.1   Dept. No. ——.
                                          [Title of form.]

Comes now, ——, the administrator [2] of said estate, by Mr. ——, his attorney, and presents his verified petition for authority to sell the real estate of said decedent, at public or private sale; and it being proved to the satisfaction of the court that due publication of the order to show cause has been made as required by law and by the order of the court,[3] the court proceeds to the hearing of said petition, and from the proofs offered the court finds that a sale of the real property of said estate, as prayed for in said petition, is necessary, in order to raise funds to pay the debts, family allowance, and expenses of administration of said estate;[4] that said real estate is of the value of —— dollars ($——), and is unimproved and unproductive;[5] and that all the allegations of said petition are true; —

It is therefore ordered by the court, That said ——, as administrator [6] of said estate, be, and he is hereby, authorized to sell, in manner and form required by law, all of the real estate hereinafter described, at private sale,[7] to the highest bidder, upon the following terms, to wit: ——;[8]

It is further ordered, That before making the sale the said administrator [9] shall give a bond in the form required by law, in the penal sum of —— dollars ($——).

The real estate hereby authorized to be sold is described as follows, to wit: ——.[10]   ——, County Clerk.

Entered ——, 19—.   By ——, Deputy.[11]

Explanatory notes.—1 Give file number. 2 Or, executor. 3 Or, that all persons interested in said estate have filed their written consent to said sale. If the matter has been continued, say, "and the hearing having been regularly postponed to this day." 4 Or, to pay the lien thereon, if any, described in the petition; or, will be for the advantage, benefit, and best interests of the estate and of those interested therein. 5 Or, is in need of repairs, and produces no income; or other brief

statement of condition. 6 Or, executor. 7 Or, public auction, according
to the fact. 8 Name the terms. 9 Or, executor. 10 Describe the land.
11 See § 77, ante.

§ 535. Form. Order for sale of real estate, in one parcel, or in subdivisions, and at either private or public sale.

[Title of court.]

[Title of estate.] $\begin{cases} \text{No.} \underline{\quad}.1 \quad \text{Dept. No.} \underline{\quad}. \\ \qquad \text{[Title of form.]} \end{cases}$

——, administrator [2] of the estate of ——, deceased,
having on the —— day of ——, 19—, presented to the
judge of said ——[3] court, and filed herein his petition in
due form, verified by his oath, praying for an order
authorizing him to sell so much and such parts of the real
estate belonging to the estate of said deceased, for purposes therein stated, as this court shall deem necessary or
beneficial; and said matter coming on regularly to be
heard this —— day of ——, 19—, it is, upon proof to the
satisfaction of the court of the due publication of a copy
of the order to show cause, as required by law and the
order of this court, and after a full examination, —

Ordered, adjudged, and decreed, That said ——, the
administrator [4] of the estate of said ——, deceased, be,
and he is hereby, authorized to sell, either in one parcel
or in subdivisions, as the said administrator [5] shall judge
most beneficial to said estate, the real estate belonging to
said estate, hereinafter described, at public auction,[6] to
the highest bidder, upon the following terms, to wit:
——.[7]

And it is further ordered, That, before making such
sale, the said ——, administrator,[8] as aforesaid, execute
an additional bond to the state of ——, with two or more
sufficient sureties, in the penal sum of —— dollars
($——), conditioned that the said administrator [9] shall
faithfully execute the duties of his trust according to
law.

The following is the real estate hereby authorized to
be sold, being situate in the said county [10] of ——, state

of ——, and bounded and described as follows, to wit:
——.[11]

Dated ——, 19—.   ——, Judge of the —— Court.

Explanatory notes.—1 Give file number. 2 Or, executor. 3 Title of
court. 4, 5 Or, executor. 6 Or, private sale, the same having been
asked for in the petition. 7 State the terms. 8, 9 Or, executor. 10 Or,
city and county. 11 Describe the land.

§ 536. Interested persons may apply for order of sale.

If the executor or administrator neglects or refuses to
sell the property of the estate when it is necessary or
when it is for the advantage, benefit and best interests of
the estate and those interested therein, that the real
estate or some portion thereof be sold, any person interested may make application to the court, that the executor
or administrator be required to sell, and notice of such
application must be given to the executor or administrator before the hearing.—*Kerr's Cyc. Code Civ. Proc.*,
§ 1545.

ANALOGOUS AND IDENTICAL STATUTES.
The * indicates identity.

Arizona—Revised Statutes of 1913, paragraph 928.
Idaho*—Compiled Statutes of 1919, section 7625.
Montana—Revised Codes of 1907, section 7570, as amended by Laws
   of 1915, chapter 3, page 6. See Supp. of 1915, page 776.
Nevada—Revised Laws of 1912, section 5994.
North Dakota—Compiled Laws of 1913, section 8773.
Oklahoma—Revised Laws of 1910, section 6380.
South Dakota—Compiled Laws of 1913, section 5830.
Utah—Compiled Laws of 1907, section 3888.
Washington—Laws of 1917, chapter 156, page 677, section 124.
Wyoming—Compiled Statutes of 1910, section 5659.

§ 537. Posting of public auction sale notice.

When a sale is to be made at public auction, notice of
the time and place of sale must be posted in three of the
most public places in the county in which the land is
situated, and published in a newspaper, if there be one
printed in the same county, but if none, then in such
paper as the court may direct, for two weeks successively

next before the sale; provided, however, that when it appears from the inventory and appraisement that the value of the whole estate does not exceed five hundred dollars the court, or a judge thereof, may in his discretion dispense with the publication in a newspaper and order notices be posted. The lands and tenements to be sold must be described with common certainty in the notice.—*Kerr's Cyc. Code Civ. Proc.*, § 1547.

ANALOGOUS AND IDENTICAL STATUTES.
The * indicates identity.

Alaska—Compiled Laws of 1913, section 1671.
Arizona—Revised Statutes of 1913, paragraph 929.
Colorado—Laws of 1915, chapter 176, page 503, with a repealing clause.
Hawaii—Revised Laws of 1915, section 2499.
Idaho*—Compiled Statutes of 1919, section 7627.
Kansas—General Statutes of 1915, section 4613.
Montana—Revised Codes of 1907, section 7571.
Nevada—Revised Laws of 1912, section 5996.
North Dakota—Compiled Laws of 1913, section 8774.
Oklahoma—Revised Laws of 1910, section 6381.
Oregon—Lord's Oregon Laws, section 1257.
South Dakota—Compiled Laws of 1913, section 5831.
Utah—Compiled Laws of 1907, sections 3892, 4030.
Washington—Laws of 1917, chapter 156, page 678, section 127.

§ 538. Time and place.

Sales at public auction must be made in the county where the land is situated; but when the land is situated in two or more counties, it may be sold in either. The sale must be made between the hours of nine o'clock in the morning and the setting of the sun on the same day, and must be made on the day named in the notice of sale, unless the same is postponed.- *Kerr's Cyc. Code Civ. Proc.*, § 1548.

ANALOGOUS AND IDENTICAL STATUTES.
The * indicates identity.

Alaska—Compiled Laws of 1913, section 1671.
Arizona*—Revised Statutes of 1913, paragraph 930.
Colorado—Laws of 1915, chapter 176, page 503, with a repealing clause.
Hawaii—Revised Laws of 1915, section 2499.

Idaho*—Compiled Statutes of 1919, section 7628.
Kansas—General Statutes of 1915, section 4615.
Montana*—Revised Codes of 1907, section 7572.
Nevada—Revised Laws of 1912, section 5997.
North Dakota—Compiled Laws of 1913, section 8774.
Oklahoma*—Revised Laws of 1910, section 6382.
South Dakota*—Compiled Laws of 1913, section 5832.
Utah—Compiled Laws of 1907, section 3893.
Washington—Laws of 1917, chapter 156, page 678, section 127.
Wyoming*—Compiled Statutes of 1910, section 5660.

§ 539. Form. Notice of administrator's or executor's sale of
    real estate at public auction.

[Title of court.]

[Title of estate.]   {No. ——.1 Dept. No. ——.
                             {   . [Title of form.]

Notice is hereby given, That, in pursuance of an order
duly made by said court on the —— day of ——, 19—, in
the matter of the estate of ——, deceased, the undersigned, administrator [2] of said estate, will sell at public
auction, to the highest bidder, for cash, in gold coin of
the United States, and subject to the confirmation of said
court, on ——,[3] the —— day of ——, at the hour of twelve
o'clock, noon,[4] at the auction salesrooms of ——,[5] in said
county [6] of ——, all the right, title, interest, and estate of
said ——, at the time of his death, being an undivided
——[7] interest in and to the property hereinafter described, and all the right, title, and interest that the said
estate has acquired, by operation of law or otherwise,
other than or in addition to that of said deceased at the
time of his death, in and to all that certain lot, piece, or
parcel of land situate in said county [8] of ——, and
bounded and described as follows, to wit: ——.[9]

Terms and conditions of sale: Cash, in gold coin of
the United States; ten (10) per cent of the purchase
price to be paid to the auctioneer on the day of sale, and

the balance upon confirmation of sale by said ——[10]
court and the delivery of a conveyance.[11]

Dated ——, 19—.

——, Administrator [12] of the said Estate.

——, Attorney for Administrator.[13]

Explanatory notes.—[1] Give file number. [2] Or, executor. [3] Day of
week. [4] Or according to the fact. [5] State where. [6] Or, city and county.
[7] State fractional part. [8] Or, city and county. [9] Describe the land.
[10] Title of court. [11] Or as the terms may be. [12, 13] Or, executor.

§ 540.   Private sale of real estate. Notice. Bids.

When a sale of real estate is to be made at private sale,
notice of the same must be posted up in three of the most
public places in the county in which the land is situate,
and published in a newspaper, if there be one printed in
the same county; if none, then in such paper as the court
or judge may direct, for two weeks successively next before the day on or after which the sale is to be made, in
which the lands and tenements to be sold must be described with common certainty.   The notice must state a
day on or after which the sale will be made, and a place
where offers or bids will be received.   The day last referred to must be at least fifteen days from the first
publication of notice; and the sale must not be made
before that day, but must be made within six months
thereafter.   The bids or offers must be in writing and
may be left at the place designated in the notice, or delivered to the executor or administrator personally, or
may be filed in the office of the clerk of the court to which
the return of sale must be made, at any time after the
first publication of the notice and before the making of
the sale.   If it be shown that it will be for the best interests of the estate the court or judge may, by an order
shorten the time of notice, which shall not, however, be
less than one week, and may provide that the sale may
be made on or after a day less than fifteen but not less
than eight days from the first publication of the notice

in which case the notice of sale and the sale may be made to correspond with such order; provided, however, that when it appears from the inventory and appraisement that the value of the whole estate does not exceed five hundred dollars, the court, or a judge thereof, may in his discretion dispense with the publication in a newspaper and order notices be posted. The lands and tenements to be sold must be described with common certainty in the notice.—*Kerr's Cyc. Code Civ. Proc.*, § 1549.

ANALOGOUS AND IDENTICAL STATUTES.
The * indicates identity.

Alaska—Compiled Laws of 1913, section 1671.

Arizona*—Revised Statutes of 1913, paragraph 931.

Colorado—Laws of 1915, chapter 176, page 503, with a repealing clause.

Idaho*—Compiled Statutes of 1919, section 7629.

Montana*—Revised Codes of 1907, section 7573.

Nevada—Revised Laws of 1912, section 5997.

North Dakota—Compiled Laws of 1913, section 8774.

Oklahoma*—Revised Laws of 1910, section 6383.

Oregon—Lord's Oregon Laws, section 1257.

South Dakota*—Compiled Laws of 1913, section 5833.

Utah—Compiled Laws of 1907, sections 3894, 4031.

Washington—Laws of 1917, chapter 156, page 679, section 129.

Wyoming—Compiled Statutes of 1910, section 5661.

§ 541. Form. Order for sale of real estate. Private sale (Short notice.)

[Title of court.]

[Title of estate.]   No. ——.1 Dept. No. ——.
                                      [Title of form.]

Comes now ——, the administrator [2] of said estate, by Mr. ——, his attorney, and presents his verified petition for authority to sell the real estate of said decedent at public or private sale. And it being proved to the satisfaction of the court that due publication of the order to show cause has been made as required by law and by the order of the court,[3] the court proceeds to the hearing of said petition, and from proofs offered the court finds that a sale of the real property of said estate, as prayed for in said petition, is necessary in order to raise funds to pay the debts, family allowance, and expenses of administration of said estate;[4] that said real estate is of the value of —— dollars ($——), and is unimproved and unproductive;[5] and that all the allegations of said petition are true, —

It is therefore ordered by the court, That said ——, as administrator [6] of said estate, be, and he is hereby, authorized to sell in manner and form required by law all of the real estate hereinafter described, at private sale,[7] to the highest bidder, upon the following terms, to wit: ——.[8]

It is further ordered, That before making the sale the said administrator [9] shall give a bond in the form required by law, in the penal sum of —— dollars ($——).

It is also ordered, That the time of notice of said sale be shortened so that a sale may be made on or after a day not less than eight [10] days from the first publication of the notice of sale.

The real estate hereby authorized to be sold is described as follows, to wit: ——.[11]   ——, County Clerk.

Entered ——, 19—.   By ——, Deputy.[12]

Explanatory notes.—1 Give file number. 2 Or, executor. 3 Or, that all persons interested in said estate have filed their written consent to said sale. If the matter has been continued, say, "and the hearing having been regularly postponed to this day." 4 Or, to pay the lien thereon, if any, described in the petition; or, will be for the advantage, benefit, and best interests of the estate and of those interested therein 5 Or, is in need of repairs, and produces no income; or other brief statement of condition. 6 Or, executor. 7 Or, public auction, according to the fact. 8 Name the terms. 9 Or, executor. 10 Or, as limited by statute. 11 Describe the land. 12 Orders need not be signed: See note, § 77, ante.

§ 542. Form. Notice of administrator's or executor's sale of real estate at private sale.

[Title of court.]

[Title of estate.]   { No. ——.1 Dept. No. ——.
                          {   [Title of form.]

Notice is hereby given, That, in pursuance of an order of the ——[2] court of the county [3] of ——, state of ——,

Probate Law—76

made on the —— day of ——, 19—, in the matter of the estate of ——,⁴ deceased, the undersigned, the administrator ⁵ of the estate of ——,⁶ deceased, will sell at private sale, in one parcel, to the highest bidder, upon the terms and conditions hereinafter mentioned, and subject to confirmation by said ——⁷ court, on or after ——,⁸ the —— day of ——, 19—, all the right, title, interest, and estate of the said ——, also known as ——, deceased, at the time of his death, which was an undivided one-half ⁹ interest in and to the real property hereinafter described, and all the right, title, and interest that the said estate has, by operation of law, or otherwise, acquired, other than or in addition to that of said deceased, at the time of his death, of, in, and to that certain lot, piece, or parcel of land situate, lying, and being in the county ¹⁰ of ——, state of ——, and more particularly described as follows, to wit: ——.¹¹

Terms and conditions of sale: Cash, in gold coin of the United States; ten (10) per cent of the purchase-money to be paid at the time of sale; balance on confirmation of sale. Deeds and abstract at the expense of the purchaser. The purchaser to assume the payment of, and take the property purchased by him subject to, all the state and county taxes, and all assessments of whatsoever name or nature, which are now or may become hereafter chargeable to or a lien against the property purchased by him.¹²

All bids or offers must be in writing, and may be left at the office of ——, attorney for said administrator,¹³ at ——,¹⁴ or may be delivered to said administrator ¹⁵ personally, in said county ¹⁶ of ——, or may be filed in the office of the clerk of this court, at any time after the first publication of this notice and before the making of the sale.¹⁷

Dated ——, 19—.

——, Administrator [18] of the Estate of ——, also known as ——, Deceased.

——, Attorney for Administrator.[19]

Explanatory notes.—[1] Give file number. [2] Title of court. [3] Or, city and county. [4] Also known as ——; also known as ——. [5] Or, administratrix; or, administrator or administratrix with the will annexed; or, executor or executrix of the last will and testament of ——; or the plural of any of these, as the case may be. If more than one person is acting as administrator or executor, etc., use appropriate verbs and pronouns; and if the administrator or executor, etc., is a woman, change pronouns to correspond. [6] Also known as ——. [7] Title of court. [8] Day of week. [9] Or whatever the interest may be. [10] Or, city and county. [11] Give description. [12] Or whatever the terms and conditions may be. [13] Or, executor. [14] Give definite location of place. [15] Or, executor. [16] Or, city and county. [17] If the land is to be sold either as a whole or in parcels, say here, "The above described property will be sold as a whole or in subdivisions, and bids must be made and will be received and considered accordingly." [18], [19] Or, executor (giving specific address).

§ 543. Ninety per cent of appraised value must be offered.

No sale of real estate at private sale shall be confirmed by the court, unless the sum offered is at least ninety per cent of the appraised value thereof, nor unless such real estate has been appraised within one year of the time of such sale. If it has not been so appraised, or if the court is satisfied that the appraisement is too high or too low, appraisers must be appointed, and they must make an appraisement thereof in the same manner as in case of an original appraisement of an estate. This may be done at any time before the sale or the confirmation thereof.—*Kerr's Cyc. Code Civ. Proc.*, § 1550.

ANALOGOUS AND IDENTICAL STATUTES.
The * indicates identity.

Alaska—Compiled Laws of 1913, section 1671.

Arizona*—Revised Statutes of 1913, paragraph 932.

Colorado—Laws of 1915, chapter 176, page 503, with a repealing clause; see, also, the amendment of 1917, Laws of 1917, chapter 68, page 214.

Idaho*—Compiled Statutes of 1919, section 7630.

Kansas—General Statutes of 1915, section 4614.

Montana*—Revised Codes of 1907, section 7574.

Nevada—Revised Laws of 1912, section 5997.
North Dakota—Compiled Laws of 1913, section 8775.
Oklahoma*—Revised Laws of 1910, section 6384.
South Dakota*—Compiled Laws of 1913, section 5834.
Utah—Compiled Laws of 1907, section 3895.
Washington—Laws of 1917, chapter 156, page 680, section 130.
Wyoming—Compiled Statutes of 1910, section 5661.

§ 544. Purchase-money of sale on credit, how secured.

The executor or administrator must, when the sale is made upon a credit, take the notes of the purchaser for the purchase-money, with a mortgage on the property to secure their payment.—*Kerr's Cyc. Code Civ. Proc.*, § 1551.

ANALOGOUS AND IDENTICAL STATUTES.
The * indicates. identity.

Alaska—Compiled Laws of 1913, section 1671.
Arizona*—Revised Statutes of 1913, paragraph 933.
Colorado—Mills's Statutes of 1912, section 7978.
Idaho*—Compiled Statutes of 1919, section 7631.
Montana*—Revised Codes of 1907, section 7575.
North Dakota—Compiled Laws of 1913, section 8775.
Oklahoma*—Revised Laws of 1910, section 6385.
Oregon—Lord's Oregon Laws, section 1257; as amended by Laws of 1917, chapter 114, page 144 (confirming and approving sales of property previously made by executors and administrators at private sales).
South Dakota*—Compiled Laws of 1913, section 5835.
Utah—Compiled Laws of 1907, section 3896.
Wyoming*—Compiled. Statutes of 1910, section 5662.

§ 545. Return. Notice of hearing. Court may vacate sale and order new one.

The executor or administrator, after making any sale of real estate, must make a return of his proceedings to the court, which must be filed in the office of the clerk at any time subsequent to the sale. A hearing upon the return of the proceedings may be asked for in the return or by petition subsequently, and thereupon the clerk must fix the day for the hearing, of which notice of at least ten days must be given by the clerk, by notices posted in three public places in the county or by publication in a newspaper, and must briefly indicate the land sold, and must refer to the return for further particulars. Upon the hearing the court must examine into the necessity for the sale, or the advantage, benefit and interest of the estate in having the sale made, and must examine the return and witnesses in relation to the sale, and if good reason does not exist for such sale, or if the proceedings for the sale were unfair or the sum bid disproportionate to the value and it appears that a sum exceeding such bid at least ten per cent exclusive of the expenses of a new sale may be obtained, the court may vacate the sale and direct another to be had, of which notice must be given and the sale in all respects conducted as if no previous sale had taken place. If an offer of ten per cent more in amount than that named in the return be made to the court in writing, by a responsible person, it is in the discretion of the court to accept such offer and confirm the sale to such person or to order a new sale.—*Kerr's Cyc. Code Civ. Proc.*, § 1552.

ANALOGOUS AND IDENTICAL STATUTES.

The * indicates identity.

Alaska—Compiled Laws of 1913, section 1672.
Arizona*—Revised Statutes of 1913, paragraph 934.
Colorado—Mills's Statutes of 1912, sections 7982, 7983.
Idaho*—Compiled Statutes of 1919, section 7632.
Kansas—General Statutes of 1915, section 4616.
Montana*—Revised Codes of 1907, section 7576.
Nevada—Revised Laws of 1912, section 5998.
North Dakota—Compiled Laws of 1913, section 8775.
Oklahoma—Revised Laws of 1910, section 6386.
Oregon—Lord's Oregon Laws, section 1258.
South Dakota—Compiled Laws of 1913, section 5836.
Utah—Compiled Laws of 1907, sections 3898, 3899.
Washington—Laws of 1917, chapter 156, page 680, section 181.
Wyoming—Compiled Statutes of 1910, section 5663.

§ 546. Form. Return and account of sale of real estate, and petition for order confirming sale.

[Title of court.]

[Title of estate.]   { No. ——.1   Dept. No. ——.
                                              {   [Title of form.]

To the Honorable the —— ² Court of the County ³ of ——, State of ——.

——, the administrator of the estate of ——, deceased, respectfully makes the following return of his proceedings, under the order of this court dated on the —— day of ——, 19—, authorizing said administrator to sell certain real estate, and reports as follows, to wit:

That, in pursuance of said order of sale, he caused notice of the time and place of holding such sale to be posted up in three of the most public places in the county ⁴ of ——, in which the land ordered to be sold is situated, and to be published in the ——, a newspaper printed and published in the same county,⁵ for three weeks successively next before such sale, in which notice the lands and tenements to be sold were described with common certainty, all of which will also and more fully appear by the affidavits ⁶ marked respectively "Exhibit A" and "Exhibit B," hereunto annexed and made a part of this return;

That, at the time and place of holding such sale specified in such notice, to wit, on ——, the —— day of ——, 19—, between the hour of nine o'clock in the morning and the setting of the sun on the same day, to wit, at —— o'clock in the forenoon ⁷ of said day, and at ——,⁸ in said county,⁹ ——, he caused to be sold in solido, judging it most beneficial to said estate, at public auction, to the highest bidder, upon the following terms, to wit, ——,¹⁰ and subject to confirmation by this court, the real estate described in said order of sale and in said notice;

That, at such sale, —— became the purchaser of the whole of said estate, for the sum of —— dollars ($——), he being the highest and best bidder, and said sum being the highest and best sum bid;

That the said sale was legally made and fairly conducted; that, as said —— believes, the sum bid is not disproportionate to the value of the property sold, and that a sum exceeding such bid by at least ten per cent, exclusive of the expenses of a new sale, cannot be obtained.

The real estate so sold is situated in the county [11] of ——, state of, and is described as follows: ——.[12]

That, before making such sale, to wit, on the —— day of ——, 19—, said ——, as required in and by said order of sale, duly executed an additional bond to the state of ——, with sufficient sureties, duly approved, on the day last aforesaid, by the judge of this court, in the penal sum of —— dollars ($——), conditioned that the said —— faithfully execute the duties of his trust according to law.

Wherefore the said —— prays that a hearing be had upon this return; that this honorable court make an order confirming the said sale, and directing conveyances to be executed to the said purchaser, conveying all the right, title, interest, and estate of said intestate in the said premises at the time of his death, and all the right, title, and interest of said estate in the same; and that such other or further order may be made as is meet in the premises.

And your petitioner will ever pray, etc.

Dated ——, 19—.

——, Administrator of the Estate of ——, Deceased.

Explanatory notes.—1 Give file number. 2 Title of court. 3-5 Or, City and County. 6 Or, if the affidavits are filed separately from the return, say, "by the affidavits of —— and ——, to that effect, this day filed"; or, "filed herein on the —— day of ——, 19—." 7 Or, afternoon. 8 State place. 9 Or, city and county. 10 State the terms. 11 Or, city and county. 12 Give description.

§ 547. Form. Verification of return, and account of sale.

[Title of court.]

[Title of estate.]

{ No. ——. Dept. No. ——,
[Title of form.]

State of ——,
County ¹ of ——, } ss.

——, who, as the administrator of the estate of ——, deceased, has subscribed the foregoing return and account of sales, being duly sworn, says that he has read the said return and account, and knows the contents thereof, and that the same is true of his own knowledge, except as to the matters which are therein stated on his information or belief, and as to those matters that he believes the same to be true.   ——

Subscribed and sworn to before me this —— day of ——, 19—.   ——, Clerk of the —— Court.

By ——, Deputy.

Explanatory note.—1 Or, City and County.

§ 548. Form. Exhibit A to return of sale.¹ Affidavit of posting notices of sale of real estate.

[Title of court.]

[Title of estate.]

{ No. ——.² Dept. No. ——.
[Title of form.]

State of ——,
County ³ of ——, } ss.

——, being duly sworn, says: That he is, and at all times hereinafter named was, a male citizen of the United States, of the age of twenty-one years and upwards, not interested in the estate of ——, deceased, and is competent to be a witness in the matter of said estate; that on the —— day of ——, 19—, he posted correct and true copies of the annexed notice of time and place of sale of real estate in three of the most public places in said county,⁴ to wit: one of said copies at the place at which the court is held,⁵ one at ——,⁶ and one at ——,⁷ in said county.⁸

Subscribed and sworn to before me this —— day of
——, 19—.   ——, Notary Public, etc.

Explanatory notes.—1 This may be used as a separate form, or as an exhibit with the return. 2 Give file number. 3, 4 Or, City and County. 5 State place. 6, 7 United States post-office, city hall, land-office, or sheriff's office, etc. 8 Or, city and county.

§ 549. Form. Exhibit B to return of sale.[1] Affidavit of publication of notice of time and place of sale of real estate.

[Title of court.]

[Title of estate.]   { No. ——.[2]   Dept. No. ——.
                               {   [Title of form.]

State of ——,   }
  County [3] of ——, } ss.

——, of said county,[4] being duly sworn, says: That he is a white male citizen of the United States of America, of the age of twenty-one years and upwards, not interested in the estate of ——, deceased, and is competent to testify in the matter of said estate;

That he is the principal clerk of the printer and publisher [5] of the ——, a newspaper printed and published in said county,[6] and, as such principal clerk,[7] has charge of all advertisements in said newspaper;

That a true, full, and correct copy of the annexed notice of the time and place of holding the sale of real estate ordered by the —— [8] court of the county [9] of ——, in the matter of said estate, on the —— day of ——, 19—, was published in said newspaper, for three weeks successively [10] next before the day of sale mentioned in said notice, and as often during the period of said three successive weeks as the said paper was regularly issued, to wit: ——.[11]

Subscribed and sworn to before me this —— day of ——, 19—.   ——, Notary Public, etc.[12]

Explanatory notes.—1 This may be used as a separate form, or as an exhibit with the return. 2 Give file number. 3, 4 Or, City and County. 5 Or, printer, or foreman. 6 Or, city and county. 7 Or, printer, or foreman. 8 Title of court. 9 Or, city and county. 10 Or as prescribed by statute. 11 Give dates of publication. 12 Or other officer taking the oath.

§ 550. Form. Fixing time for hearing on return of sale.

[Title of court.]

[Title of estate.]   { No.——.1   Dept. No.——.
                             {   [Title of form.]

——, the administrator ² of the estate of ——, deceased, having this day filed with the clerk of this court his return of sale of real estate, under the previous order of this court;³ and a hearing thereon having been asked for in said return,—

Now, I, ——, clerk of said —— court, do hereby fix and appoint ——,⁴ the —— day of ——, 19—, at —— o'clock in the forenoon of said day, and the court-room of said court, at the court-house ⁵ in said county ⁶ of ——, as the time and place for the hearing upon said return.

Dated ——, 19—.   ——, Clerk of the —— Court.

                     By ——, Deputy Clerk.

Explanatory notes.—1 Give file number. 2 Or, executor, etc. 3 Or, under a power, contained in the will of said deceased. 4 Give day of week. 5 Give location. 6 Or, city and county.

§ 551. Form. Order appointing day of hearing return of sale of real estate.

[Title of court.]

[Title of estate.]   { No.——.1   Dept. No.——.
                             {   [Title of form.]

——, administrator ² of the estate of ——, deceased, having this day made a return to this court of his proceedings under the order of sale of real estate heretofore made herein, and filed the said return,—

It is ordered, That the hearing of said return be had before this court on ——, the —— day of ——, 19—, at —— o'clock in the forenoon ³ of said day, in the court-room of said court, at ——,⁴ in the said county ⁵ of ——, state of ——; and that notice of at least ten days ⁶ be

given thereof, by the clerk, by publication [7] in the ——,
a newspaper printed in said county [8] and state.

The said return is referred to for further particulars.

Dated ——, 19—.   ——, Judge of the —— Court.

§ 552. Form. Notice of hearing return of sale of real estate.

[Title of court.]

[Title of estate.]   { No.——.1   Dept. No.——.
                       {   [Title of form.]

Notice is hereby given, That ——, administrator [2] of
the estate of ——, deceased, has made to the said court,
and filed in the office of the clerk thereof, a return of sale
of real estate of the said deceased, made by him on the
—— day of ——, 19—, under a previous order of said
court; [3] and that ——, [4] the —— day of ——, 19—, at ——
o'clock in the forenoon of said day, and the court-room
of said court, at ——, [5] in said county [6] and state, have
been fixed by the clerk of said court as the time and place
for hearing the said return, when and where any person
interested in the said estate may appear and file written
objections to the confirmation of said sale, and may be
heard and may produce witnesses in support of such
objections.

The following is a description of the land sold and the
sum for which it was sold: Said land is situated in the
county [7] of ——, state of ——, and described as follows:
——. [8]

For further particulars, reference is hereby made to
the return on file herein.

——, Clerk of the —— Court.

By ——, Deputy Clerk.

week. 5 Give location. 6, 7 Or, city and county. 8 Give description, and state price for which each parcel sold.

§ 553. Form. Offer of ten per cent advance on sale of real estate.

[Title of court.]

[Title of estate.]   { No. ——.1   Dept. No. ——.
                                        {   [Title of form.]

The matter of the confirmation of the sale of real estate, made by ——, administrator [2] of the estate of ——, coming on this day for hearing, the undersigned, a responsible person, now comes and offers for the property hereinafter described the sum of —— dollars ($——), which is an offer of ten per cent in advance upon the price named in said administrator's [3] return of sale.

The property sold, and for which such advance is offered, is particularly described as follows, to wit: ——.[4]

——

Dated ——, 19.

Explanatory notes.—1 Give file number. 2, 3 Or, executor, etc. 4 Insert description.

§ 554. Form. Order vacating sale of real estate.

[Title of court.]

[Title of estate.]   { No. ——.1,   Dept. No. ——.
                                          {   [Title of form.]

——, administrator [2] of the estate of —— deceased, having made a return of his proceedings on the sale of real property belonging to said estate, and the matter coming on regularly this day [3] to be heard, the court proceeds to hear the same, and finds, upon the allegations made and testimony offered, that the sum bid at the sale returned as aforesaid was disproportionate to the value of the property offered for sale; and that a sum exceeding the sum bid and reported, by at least ten per cent, exclusive of the expenses of a new sale, can be obtained,—

It is therefore ordered, That said sale be, and the same

is hereby, vacated, and it is directed that another sale be had, after proper notice given, to be conducted in all respects as if no previous sale had ever been made. The property sold, as appears by the return aforesaid, and the sale of which is hereby vacated, is particularly described as follows, to wit: ——.

Dated ——, 19—.   ——, Judge of the —— Court.

Explanatory notes.—1 Give file number. 2 Or, executor of the last will and testament of ——, etc. 3 Or, having been regularly continued by the court to the present time.

§ 555. Objections to confirmation of sale. Hearing.

When return of the sale is made and filed any person interested in the estate may file written objections to the confirmation thereof, and may be heard thereon, when the return is heard by the court or judge, and may produce witnesses in support of his objections.—*Kerr's Cyc. Code Civ. Proc.*, § 1553.

ANALOGOUS AND IDENTICAL STATUTES.
The * indicates identity.

Arizona*—Revised Statutes of 1913, paragraph 935.
Idaho*—Compiled Statutes of 1919, section 7633.
Montana—Revised Codes of 1907, section 7577.
North Dakota*—Compiled Laws of 1913, section 8776.
Oklahoma*—Revised Laws of 1910, section 6387.
South Dakota*—Compiled Laws of 1913, section 5837.
Wyoming*—Compiled Statutes of 1910, section 5664.

§ 556. Order of confirmation. Resale.

If it appears to the court that there is reason for a sale upon the grounds set forth in section one thousand five hundred thirty-six of this code and that the sale was legally made and fairly conducted, and that the sum bid was not disproportinate to the value of the property sold, and that a greater sum, as above specified, can not be obtained, or if the increased bid mentioned in section one thousand five hundred fifty-two be made and accepted by the court, the court must make an order confirming the sale, and directing conveyances to be executed. The sale, from that time, is confirmed and valid, and a certified copy of the order confirming it and directing conveyances to be executed must be recorded in the office of the recorder of the county in which the land sold is situated. If, after the confirmation, the purchaser neglects or refuses to comply with the terms of the sale, the court may, on motion of the executor or administrator, and after notice to the purchaser, order a resale to be made of the property. If the amount realized on such resale does not cover the bid and the expenses of the previous sale, such purchaser is liable for the deficiency to the estate.— *Kerr's Cyc. Code Civ. Proc.*, § 1554.

ANALOGOUS AND IDENTICAL STATUTES.

The * indicates identity.

Alaska—Compiled Laws of 1913, section 1673.
Arizona*—Revised Statutes of 1913, paragraph 936.
Colorado—Mills's Statutes of 1912, section 7984.
Hawaii—Revised Laws of 1915, section 2499.
Idaho*—Compiled Statutes of 1919, section 7634.
Kansas—General Statutes of 1915, section 4616.
Montana*—Revised Codes of 1907, section 7578.
Nevada—Revised Laws of 1912, section 5999.
North Dakota—Compiled Laws of 1913, sections 8777, 8778.
Oklahoma*—Revised Laws of 1910, section 6388.
Oregon—Lord's Oregon Laws, section 1260.
South Dakota*—Compiled Laws of 1913, section 5838.
Utah—Compiled Laws of 1907, section 3900.
Washington—Laws of 1917, chapter 156, page 680, section 131.
Wyoming—Compiled Statutes of 1910, section 5665.

§ 557. **Form. Objections to confirmation of sale of real estate.**

[Title of court.]

[Title of estate.] $\left\{ \begin{array}{l} \text{No.——.1 Dept. No.——.} \\ \text{[Title of form.]} \end{array} \right.$

A return of sale of certain real estate belonging to the estate of said deceased having been made and filed by ——, administrator [2] of the said estate, ——, one of the creditors [3] of said estate, now comes and opposes the confirmation of said sale on the grounds:

That no notice of said sale was posted or published, as required by law;

That said sale was not legally made or fairly conducted;[4] and

That the price offered is disproportionate to the value of the property sold; and that a bid therefor of at least ten per cent more than the amount named in the said return, exclusive of the expenses of a new sale, can be obtained therefor.

The contestant therefore asks that said sale be vacated, and that the court direct another sale to be had.

———, Attorney for Contestant.   ———, Contestant.

Explanatory notes.—[1] Give file number. [2] Or, executor of the last will, etc. [3] Or, heirs at law, or residuary legatee under the will of ——, deceased. [4] State wherein this was so; such as misconduct of the auctioneer, or the executor's lack of business methods in advertising the sale, or any other irregularity in the proceedings prior to and leading up to the sale.

§ 558. Form. Order confirming sale of real estate.

[Title of court.]

[Title of estate.]   { No. ———.[1]   Dept. No. ———.
                         {   [Title of form.]

Now comes ——, the —— of said estate, by Mr. ——, his attorney, and proves to the satisfaction of the court that his return of sale of real estate, under the order of sale hereinbefore made, was duly filed in the office of the clerk of this court on ——, the —— day of ——, 19—; that the clerk thereupon fixed ——, the —— day of ——, 19—, as the day for the hearing thereof, and gave due notice of said hearing by posting notices in form and manner as required by law;[2] and thereupon, after examining the return and hearing the evidence, the court finds therefrom that said sale was legally made and fairly conducted; that notice of the time, place, and terms of said sale was duly given in manner and form as prescribed by law and by the order of this court, and that said notices described said land as the same is hereinafter described;[3] that the price obtained thereat was the reasonable value of the property sold, and that no greater sum can be obtained, and no person objecting thereto or offering a higher price,—

It is ordered by the court, That the sale of the real estate, hereinafter described, to —— for the sum of —— dollars ($——), in cash,[4] be, and the same is hereby, confirmed; and upon payment of the price aforesaid,[5] said ——, executor is directed to execute to said purchaser a deed of conveyance thereof.

Said land is described as follows, to wit: ——.[6]

Entered ——, 19—.   ——, County Clerk.

By ——, Deputy.

Explanatory notes.—[1] Give file number. [2] If continued, add, "and the hearing having been regularly postponed to this day." [3] If sale was private, add, "that said property was appraised within one year of said sale, and that the price obtained at such sale is at least ninety per cent of said appraised value." [4] Or, payable as follows (stating terms). [5] Or, upon compliance with the terms of said sale. [6] Give description.

§ 559. **Form. Order confirming sale of real estate on bid in open court.**

[Title of court.]

[Title of estate.]   No. ——.[1] Dept. No. ——.
                                      [Title of form.]

Now comes ——, the administrator [2] of said estate, by ——, his attorney, and proves to the satisfaction of the court that his return of sale of real estate, under the order of sale heretofore made, was duly filed in the office of the clerk of this court on the —— day of ——, 19—; that thereupon the clerk fixed the —— day of ——, 19—, as the day for hearing thereof, and gave due notice of said hearing by posting notices in form and manner as required by law, and the matter having come regularly on for hearing,[3] the court, after examining the return and hearing the evidence, finds that notice of the time, place, and terms of said sale was duly given in manner and form as prescribed by law and by the order of this court; that said notices described said land as the same is hereinafter described;[4] and that said sale was legally made and fairly conducted; and thereupon, in open court, ——, in writing, offered the sum of —— dollars ($——) for said land, upon the terms prescribed in the order of sale, and he being a responsible person, the court accepted said offer and confirmed said sale to him accordingly.

It is therefore ordered by the court, That the sale of said land, so made in open court, to said ——, for the sum of —— dollars ($——), in cash,[5] be, and the same is hereby, confirmed, and upon payment of the price[6] as aforesaid by said purchaser, the said ——, as administrator[7] of said estate, is directed to execute to said purchaser a deed of conveyance of said land, which is described as follows, to wit: ——.[8]

——, Judge of the —— Court.

Dated ——, 19—.

Explanatory notes.—1 Give file number. 2 Or, executor. 3 Or, the hearing having been regularly postponed to this day. 4 If the property was sold at private sale, say, "that said property was appraised within one year of the time of such sale, and that the price obtained at such sale is at least ninety (90) per cent of said appraised value." 5 Or, payable as follows (stating terms). 6 Or, compliance with the terms of sale. 7 Or, executor. 8 Describe the land.

§ 560. Form. Notice of motion to vacate sale of real estate, and for a resale thereof.

[Title of court.]

[Title of estate.]

{ No. ——.1   Dept. No. ——. [Title of form.] }

To ——.[2]

You are hereby notified, That the administrator[3] of the above-entitled estate will move the court, at the time and place hereinafter stated, to vacate, annul, and set aside the sale of certain real property of said estate hereinafter described, heretofore made to you by said administrator,[4] as well as the order confirming the sale of said property, on the ground that you have neglected and refused, and still neglect and refuse, to comply with the terms of sale, in that you have not paid to said adminis-

Probate Law—77

trator [5] the balance of the purchase price due from you
to him for said property.

You are further notified, That said administrator [6] will
move the court, at said time and place, to order a resale
of said property.

The real property sold as aforesaid, the sale of which
is sought to be vacated, annulled, and set aside, is particularly described as follows, to wit: ——.[7]

Said motion will be made on the —— day of ——,
19—, at the hour of —— o'clock in the forenoon [8] of said
day, at the court-room of said court, at ——,[9] in said
county [10] and state; and will be based upon the papers on
file herein,[11] the orders of court in the matter of the
said estate, and upon oral and documentary proofs to be
made on the hearing of said motions.

                    ——, Attorney for Administrator.[12]

Dated ——, 19—.

Explanatory notes.—1 Give file number. 2 Name of purchaser. 3-6 Or,
executor, etc. 7 Give description. 8 Or, afternoon. 9 Give location of
court-room. 10 Or, city and county. 11 The California statute requires
that "if any such paper has not previously been served upon the party
to be notified, and was not filed by him, a copy of such paper must
accompany the notice." See Kerr's Cal. Cyc. Code Civ. Proc., § 1010.
12 Or, executor.

§ 561. Form. Order for resale of real estate.

[Title of court.]

[Title of estate.]   { No. ——.1 Dept. No. ——.
                                      {   [Title of form.]

——, administrator [2] of the estate of ——, deceased,
having filed a motion in this court to vacate, annul, and
set aside the sale of certain real property of said estate,
hereinafter described, and it being shown to the court
that due notice of said motion has been given as required
by law, and served upon ——, the person to whom said
sale was made, and to whom it was thereafter confirmed;
and that said —— has neglected and refused, and still
neglects and refuses, to comply with the terms of said
sale,—

It is ordered, That the sale of said property made by said administrator [3] to —— on ——, the —— day of ——, 19—, as well as the order made on ——, the —— day of ——, 19—, confirming said sale, be, and the same are hereby, vacated, annulled, and set aside; and that said administrator [4] proceed as if said sale and order of confirmation had never been made.

The real property aforesaid, the sale of which is by this order vacated, annulled, and set aside, is particularly described as follows, to wit: ——.

Dated ——, 19—.   ——, Judge of the —— Court.

Explanatory notes.—1 Give file number. 2-4 Or, executor, etc.

§ 562. Conveyances.

Conveyances must thereupon be executed to the purchaser by the executor or administrator, and they must refer to the orders of the court confirming the sale of the property of the estate, and directing conveyances thereof to be executed, and to the record of the order of confirmation in the office of the county recorder, either by the date of such recording, or by the date, volume, and page of the record, and such reference shall have the same effect as if the orders were at large inserted in the conveyance. Conveyances so made convey all the right, title, interest, and estate of the decedent in the premises at the time of his death; if prior to the sale, by operation of law or otherwise, the estate has acquired any right, title, or interest in the premises, other than or in addition to that of the decedent at the time of his death, such right, title, or interest also passes by such conveyances.—*Kerr's Cyc. Code Civ. Proc.,* § 1555.

ANALOGOUS AND IDENTICAL STATUTES.

The * indicates identity.

Alaska—Compiled Laws of 1913, section 1674.

Arizona*—Revised Statutes of 1913, paragraph 937.

Colorado—Mills's Statutes of 1912, section 7985.

Idaho*—Compiled Statutes of 1919, section 7635.

Kansas—General Statutes of 1915, sections 4616, 4617, 4626.

Montana*—Revised Codes of 1907, section 7579.
Nevada—Revised Laws of 1912, section 6000.
New Mexico—Statutes of 1915, section 2264.
North Dakota—Compiled Laws of 1913, section 8779.
Oklahoma*—Revised Laws of 1910, section 6389.
Oregon—Lord's Oregon Laws, section 1261.
South Dakota*—Compiled Laws of 1913, section 5839.
Utah—Compiled Laws of 1907, section 3901.
Washington—Laws of 1917, chapter 156, page 681, section 133.
Wyoming—Compiled Statutes of 1910, section 5666.

§ 563. Form. Administrator's deed.

This indenture, Made on the ―― day of ――, 19―, by
and between ―― as the duly appointed, qualified, and
acting administrator [1] of the estate of ――, deceased, late
of ――, the party of the first part, and ――, of ――, the
party of the second part,—

Witnesseth, That, whereas, on the ―― day of ――,
19―, the ―― court of the county [2] of ――, state of ――,
made an order of sale authorizing the said party of the
first part to sell certain real estate of the said ――, deceased, situate in the county [3] of ――, state of ――, and
particularly described in said order of sale, which said
order is now on file and of record in the said ―― court,
and is hereby referred to for greater certainty; and

Whereas, under and by virtue of said order of sale,
and pursuant to legal notices given thereof, the said party
of the first part, on the ―― day of ――, 19―, at the time
and place and in the manner specified in said notices, did
offer for sale and sell, subject to confirmation by said
court, to the party of the second part, the said real estate
hereinafter particularly described for the sum of ――
dollars ($――), he being the highest and best bidder, and
that being the highest and best sum bid; and

Whereas the said ―― court, upon the due and
legal return of the proceedings under the said order of
sale, made by the said party of the first part on the ――
day of ――, 19―, and after due notice of hearing on said
return given, did, on the day of ――, 19―, make an

order decreeing said sale to be valid and confirming said sale, and directing a conveyance to be executed to the said party of the second part, a certified copy of which order of confirmation was recorded in the office of the county recorder of the county [4] of ——, within which the said land sold is situate, on the —— day of ——, 19—, which said order of confirmation is now on file and of record in said —— court, which said record thereof in said recorder's office is hereby referred to for greater certainty;—

Now, therefore, the said ——, as administrator [5] of the estate of ——, deceased, as aforesaid, the party of the first part, pursuant to the order last aforesaid of the said —— court, for and in consideration of the sum of —— dollars ($——) to him in hand paid by the said party of the second part, the receipt whereof is hereby acknowledged, has granted, bargained, sold, and conveyed, and by these presents does grant, bargain, sell, and convey, unto the said party of the second part, his heirs and assigns forever, all the right, title, interest and estate of the said ——, deceased, at the time of his death, and also all the right, title, and interest that the said estate, by operation of law or otherwise, may have acquired, other than or in addition to that of said intestate at the time of his death, in and to all that certain lot, piece, or parcel of land lying and being in said county [6] of ——, state of ——, and bounded and particularly described as follows, to wit: ——;[7] together with all the tenements, hereditaments, and appurtenances whatsoever to the same belonging, or in any wise appertaining.

To have and to hold, all and singular, the above mentioned and described premises, together with the appurtenances, unto the said party of the second part, his heirs and assigns forever.

In witness whereof, The said party of the first part, as administrator [8] of the estate of said deceased, as afore-

said, has executed these presents the day and year first
above written.   ——, Administrator,[9] etc.   [Seal]

Signed, sealed, and delivered in the presence of ——
and ——.

Explanatory notes.—1 Or, executor of the last will, etc.   2-4 Or, city
and county.   5 Or, executor, etc.   6 Or, city and county.   7 Describe the
land.   8, 9 Or, executor, etc.

§ 564. Form. Acknowledgment of administrator's deed.

State of ——,   }
    County [1] of ——,   } ss.

On this —— day of ——, in the year one thousand nine
hundred and —— (19—), before me, ——, a notary public [2] in and for the said county [3] of ——, state of ——,
appeared ——, personally known [4] to me to be the person
whose name is subscribed to the foregoing instrument as
the administrator [5] of the estate of ——, deceased, and
acknowledged to me that he, as such administrator,[6] executed the same.

In witness whereof, I have hereunto set my hand and
affixed my official seal at the said county [7] of ——, the day
and year in this certificate first above written.

                                    ——, Notary Public, etc.[8]

Explanatory notes.—1 Or, City and County.   2 Or other officer authorized to take the proof of instruments.   3 Or, city and county.   4 Or,
satisfactorily proved to me, by the oath of ——, a competent and cred-
ible witness upon the question of identity, to be the person, etc.
5, 6 Or, executor of the last will, etc.   7 Or, city and county.   8 Or other
officer taking the oath.

§ 565. Form. Administrator's deed to one offering ten per cent advance.

This indenture, Made on the —— day of ——, 19—, by
and between ——, the duly appointed, qualified and acting administrator [1] of the estate of ——, deceased, and
——, both parties of the county [2] of ——, state of ——,—

Witnesseth: That the —— court of the county [3] of ——,
state of ——, having, on the —— day of ——, 19—, made

an order of sale, authorizing the said administrator [4] to sell certain real estate belonging to said estate, being the same as [5] that hereinafter described, which order is now on file and of record in said court and is hereby referred to; that said administrator, [6] under and by virtue of said order of sale, did, on the —— day of ——, 19—, and pursuant to legal notices given therefor, sell said real estate, [7] subject to confirmation by said —— court, to ——, for the sum of twenty thousand dollars ($20,000); that upon the hearing of the return of said sale, which came on regularly for hearing in this court, on the —— day of ——, 19—, the said ——, the grantee herein, made his written offer in due form, of the sum of twenty-two thousand dollars ($22,000) for said realty, and that no further or greater sum was offered; that on the —— day of ——, 19—, said court made an order accepting said written offer, and confirming the sale of said property to said ——, and directing a conveyance to be executed to him; that a certified copy of said order of confirmation of sale was recorded in the office of the county recorder of said county [8] of ——, state of ——, on the —— day of ——, 19—; [9] and that said order of confirmation of sale is now on file and of record in said court, and which said record thereof in said recorder's office is hereby referred to and made a part hereof, the same as if incorporated herein.

The said ——, administrator [10] of said estate, in pursuance of said order confirming the sale and directing a conveyance to be executed to the said ——, and for and in consideration of the sum of twenty-two thousand dollars ($22,000), gold coin of the United States of America, to him in hand paid by the said ——, the receipt whereof is hereby acknowledged, has granted, bargained, sold, and conveyed, etc. [11]

——, Administrator of the Estate of ——, Deceased.

Explanatory notes.—1 Or, executor. 2, 3 Or, city and county. 4 Or, executor. 5 Or, including. 6 Or, executor. 7 Or, hereinafter described.

§ 566. Form. Executor's deed.

This indenture, Made on the —— day of ——, 19—, between ——, the duly appointed, qualified, and acting executor of the last will and testament of ——, deceased, and ——, both of the county [1] of ——, state of ——,—

Witnesseth: That the said —— court of the county [2] of ——, state of ——, having, on the —— day of ——, 19—, made an order admitting a certain instrument, in writing, to probate as the last will and testament of said ——, deceased, which said order is hereby referred to and made a part hereof, the same as if incorporated herein; that, by the terms of said last will and testament, to which reference is hereby made, the real estate hereinafter described was directed to be sold; that, under and by virtue of said authority contained in said last will and testament, the said executor, on the —— day of ——, 19—, sold said real estate, subject to confirmation by said court, to the said ——, for the sum of —— dollars ($——); and that [3] said court, on the —— day of ——, 19—, made an order confirming said sale, and directing a conveyance to be executed to the said ——, a certified copy of which order of confirmation was recorded in the office of the county recorder of the county [4] of ——, state of ——, on the —— day of ——, at ——,[5] and which said order of confirmation is now on file and of record in said —— court, and which said record thereof in said recorder's office is hereby referred to for greater certainty;—

Now, therefore, the said ——, executor of the last will and testament of ——, deceased, pursuant to said order confirming said sale and directing a conveyance to be executed to the said ——, and for and in consideration of the sum of —— dollars ($——), gold coin of the United States of America, to him in hand paid by the said ——, the receipt whereof is hereby acknowledged, has granted, etc.[6] ——, Executor of the Estate of ——, Deceased.

Explanatory notes.—1, 2 Or, city and county. 8 In case it is desired to refer to the return, insert: "on the —— day of ——, 19—, said executor filed, in said court, his verified return of said sale, and, after due notice given of the hearing on said return." 4 Or, city and county. 5 Give exact time, and volume and page of record. 6 Continue as in § 563, substituting "executor," etc., for "administrator."

§ 567. Order of confirmation, what to state.

Before any order is entered confirming the sale, it must be proved to the satisfaction of the court that notice was given of the sale as prescribed, and the order of confirmation must show that such proof was made.—*Kerr's Cyc. Code Civ. Proc.*, § 1556.

ANALOGOUS AND IDENTICAL STATUTES.
The * indicates identity.
Arizona*—Revised Statutes of 1913, paragraph 938.
Colorado—Mills's Statutes of 1912, section 7984.
Hawaii—Revised Laws of 1915, section 2499.
Idaho*—Compiled Statutes of 1919, section 7636.
Montana*—Revised Codes of 1907, section 7580.
Nevada*—Revised Laws of 1912, section 6001.
North Dakota*—Compiled Laws of 1913, section 8780.
Oklahoma*—Revised Laws of 1910, section 6390.
South Dakota*—Compiled Laws of 1913, section 5840.

§ 568. Sale may be postponed.

If at the time appointed for the sale, the executor or administrator deems it for the interest of all persons concerned therein that the same be postponed, he may postpone it from time to time, not exceeding in all three months.—*Kerr's Cyc. Code Civ. Proc.*, § 1557.

ANALOGOUS AND IDENTICAL STATUTES.
The * indicates identity.
Arizona*—Revised Statutes of 1913, paragraph 939.
Colorado—Mills's Statutes of 1912, section 7981.
Idaho*—Compiled Statutes of 1919, section 7637.
Montana*—Revised Codes of 1907, section 7581.
Nevada—Revised Laws of 1912, section 6002.
North Dakota—Compiled Laws of 1913, section 8774.
Oklahoma*—Revised Laws of 1910, section 6391.

South Dakota*—Compiled Laws of 1913, section 5841.
Utah—Compiled Laws of 1907, section 3897.
Washington—Laws of 1917, chapter 156, page 679, section 128.
Wyoming*—Compiled Statutes of 1910, section 5667.

§ 569.   Notice of postponement.

In case of a postponement, notice thereof must be given, by a public declaration, at the time and place first appointed for the sale, and if the postponement be for more than one day, further notice must be given, by posting notices in three or more public places in the county where the land is situated, or publishing the same, or both, as the time and circumstances will admit.—*Kerr's Cyc. Code Civ. Proc., § 1558.*

ANALOGOUS AND IDENTICAL STATUTES.
The * indicates identity.

Arizona*—Revised Statutes of 1913, paragraph 940.
Idaho*—Compiled Statutes of 1919, section 7638.
Montana*—Revised Codes of 1907, section 7582.
Nevada*—Revised Laws of 1912, section 6003.
North Dakota—Compiled Laws of 1913, section 8774.
Oklahoma*—Revised Laws of 1910, section 6392.
South Dakota*—Compiled Laws of 1913, section 5842.
Utah—Compiled Laws of 1907, section 3897.
Washington—Laws of 1917, chapter 156, page 679, section 128.
Wyoming—Compiled Statutes of 1910, section 5668.

§ 569.¹   Commissions on sales of real property.

Any executor or administrator may enter into a contract with any bona fide real estate agent to secure a purchaser for any real property belonging to an estate, which contract shall provide for payment to such agent out of the proceeds of sale to any purchaser secured by him of a commission, the amount of which must be fixed and allowed by the court upon confirmation of the sale. If a sale to a purchaser obtained by such agent is returned to the court for confirmation and said sale be confirmed to such purchaser, such contract shall be binding and valid as against the estate for the amount so fixed and allowed by the court.

By the execution of any such contract no personal liability shall attach to the executor or administrator, and no liability of any kind shall be incurred by the estate unless an actual sale is made and confirmed.—*Kerr's Cyc. Code Civ. Proc.*, § 1559.

§ 570. Payment of debts, etc., according to provisions of will.

If the testator makes provision by his will, or designates the estate to be appropriated for the payment of his debts, the expenses of administration, or family expenses, they must be paid according to such provision or designation, out of the estate thus appropriated, so far as the same is sufficient.—*Kerr's Cyc. Code Civ. Proc.*, § 1560.

ANALOGOUS AND IDENTICAL STATUTES.
The * indicates identity.

Alaska—Compiled Laws of 1913, sections 1675, 1676.
Arizona*—Revised Statutes of 1913, paragraph 941.
Idaho*—Compiled Statutes of 1919, section 7639.
Kansas—General Statutes of 1915, sections 4607, 11812, 11814.
Montana*—Revised Codes of 1907, section 7583.
Nevada—Revised Laws of 1912, section 6005.
North Dakota*—Compiled Laws of 1913, section 8781.
Oklahoma*—Revised Laws of 1910, section 6393.
Oregon—Lord's Oregon Laws, section 1263.
South Dakota*—Compiled Laws of 1913, section 5843.
Washington—Laws of 1917, chapter 156, page 682, section 137.
Wyoming*—Compiled Statutes of 1910, section 5669.

§ 571. Sales without order, under provisions of will.

When property is directed by the will to be sold, or authority is given in the will to sell property, the executor may sell any property of the estate without order of the court, and at either public or private sale, and with or without notice, as the executor may determine; but the executor must make return of such sales as in other cases; and if directions are given in the will as to the mode of selling, or the particular property to be sold, such directions must be observed. In either case no title passes unless the sale be confirmed by the court.—*Kerr's Cyc. Code Civ. Proc.*, § 1561.

ANALOGOUS AND IDENTICAL STATUTES.
The * indicates identity.

Alaska—Compiled Laws of 1913, section 1677.
Arizona*—Revised Statutes of 1913, paragraph 942.
Colorado—Mills's Statutes of 1912, section 7965.
Idaho*—Compiled Statutes of 1919, section 7640.
Kansas—General Statutes of 1915, section 4621.
Montana*—Revised Codes of 1907, section 7584.
Nevada—Revised Laws of 1912, section 6006.
New Mexico—Statutes of 1915, sections 2265, 2266.
North Dakota*—Compiled Laws of 1913, section 8781.
Oklahoma*—Revised Laws of 1910, section 6394.
Oregon—Lord's Oregon Laws, section 1263.
South Dakota*—Compiled Laws of 1913, section 5844.
Utah*—Compiled Laws of 1907, section 3881.
Washington—Laws of 1917, chapter 156, page 684, section 146.
Wyoming*—Compiled Statutes of 1910, section 5670.

§ 572.   Form.   Order confirming sale of real estate under will.
[Title of court.]

[Title of estate.]

{ No. ——.1   Dept. No. ——.
      [Title of form.]

Now comes ——, the executor of said estate, by Mr. ——, his attorney, and proves to the satisfaction of the court that his return of sale of real estate, made under the authority given in the will of said deceased filed in the office of the clerk of this court on ——, 19—; that the clerk thereupon fixed the —— day of ——, 19—, as the day for the hearing thereof, and gave due notice of said hearing by posting notices in form and manner as required by law; and the matter having come regularly on for hearing,[2] the court, after examining the return and hearing the evidence, finds therefrom that said sale was legally made and fairly conducted, and in all respects according to the directions given in the said will as to the mode of selling the same;[3] that notice of the time, place, and terms of said sale was duly given in manner and form as prescribed by law and by the order of this court, and that said notices described said land as the same is hereinafter described; that the price obtained thereat was the reasonable value of the property sold; and that no greater sum can be obtained, and no person objecting thereto or offering a higher price;—

It is ordered by the court, That the sale, so made, of the real estate hereinafter described to —— for the sum of —— dollars ($——) in cash,[4] be, and the same is hereby, confirmed; and upon payment of the price [5] aforesaid, the said executor is directed to execute forthwith to said purchaser a deed of conveyance thereof.

Said land is described as follows, to wit: ——.[6]

Entered ——, 19—.　　　　　　——, County Clerk.
　　　　　　　　　　　　　　　　　By ——, Deputy.[7]

Explanatory notes.—[1] Give file number. [2] If the matter has been continued, say, "the hearing having been regularly postponed to this day." [3] If the property was sold at private sale, say, "that said property was appraised within one year of the time of such sale, and that the price obtained at such sale is at least ninety (90) per cent of said appraised value." [4] Or, payable as follows (stating the terms). [5] Or, compliance with the terms of sale. [6] Describe land sold. [7] Orders need not be signed: See note, § 77, ante.

§ 573. Where provision by will insufficient.

If the provision made by the will, or the estate appropriated therefor, is insufficient to pay the debts, expenses of administration, and family expenses, that portion of the estate not devised or disposed of by the will, if any; must be appropriated and disposed of for that purpose, according to the provisions of this chapter.—*Kerr's Cyc. Code Civ. Proc.,* § 1562.

ANALOGOUS AND IDENTICAL STATUTES.
The * indicates identity.

Alaska—Compiled Laws of 1913, section 1677.
Arizona*—Revised Statutes of 1913, paragraph 943.
Idaho*—Compiled Statutes of 1919, section 7641.
Kansas—General Statutes of 1915, section 11812.
Montana*—Revised Codes of 1907, section 7585.
Nevada*—Revised Laws of 1912, section 6007.
North Dakota—Compiled Laws of 1913, section 8732.
Oklahoma*—Revised Laws of 1910, section 6395.

§ 574. Liability of estate for debts.

The estate, real and personal, given by will to legatees or devisees, is liable for the debts, expenses of administration, and family expenses, in proportion to the value or amount of the several devises or legacies, but specific devises or legacies are exempt from such liability if it appears to the court necessary to carry into effect the intention of the testator, and there is other sufficient estate.—*Kerr's Cyc. Code Civ. Proc.,* § 1563.

ANALOGOUS AND IDENTICAL STATUTES.
The * indicates identity.

§ 575. Contribution among legatees.

When an estate given by will has been sold for the payment of debts or expenses, all the devisees and legatees must contribute according to their respective interests to the devisee or legatee whose devise or legacy has been taken therefor, and the court, when distribution is made, must, by decree for that purpose, settle the amount of the several liabilities, and decree the amount each person shall contribute, and reserve the same from their distributive shares, respectively, for the purpose of paying such contribution.—*Kerr's Cyc. Code Civ. Proc.,* § 1564.

§ 576. Contract for purchase of lands may be sold, how.

If a decedent, at the time of his death, was possessed of a contract for the purchase of lands, his interest in such land and under such contract may be sold by his executor or administrator, in the same manner as if he had died seised of such land, and the same proceedings may be had for that purpose as are prescribed in this chapter for the sale of lands of which he died seised, except as hereinafter provided.—*Kerr's Cyc. Code Civ. Proc.,* § 1565.

§ 577. Form. Order confirming sale of contract to purchase land.

[Title of court.]

[Title of estate.]   {No. ——.1 Dept. No. ——.
                                      {   [Title of form.]

Now comes ——, the administrator [2] of said estate, by Mr. ——, his attorney, and proves to the satisfaction of the court that his return of sale of the contract to purchase land, under the order of sale hereinbefore made, was duly filed in the office of the clerk of the court on ——, the —— day of ——, 19—; that the clerk thereupon fixed the —— day of ——, 19—, as the day for the hearing thereof, and gave due notice of said hearing by posting notices in form and manner as required by law; [3] and the court thereupon, after examining the return and hearing the evidence, finds therefrom that said sale was legally made and fairly conducted; that notice of the time, place, and terms of said sale was duly given in manner and form as prescribed by law and by the order of this court; and that said notices described said contract to purchase land as the same is hereinafter described; [4] that the price obtained thereat was the reasonable value of the property sold; and that no greater sum can be obtained; and no person objecting thereto or offering a higher price; [5]

And the said purchaser having executed a bond to the said ——, as administrator [6] of said estate for the benefit and indemnity of said administrator, [7] and of the persons entitled to the interest of the decedent in the land so contracted for, in the sum of —— dollars ($——), the same being double the whole amount of payments hereafter to become due on said contract, and conditioned as required by law, and the court having approved said bond and the sureties thereon, the said sale is now confirmed;—

It is therefore ordered by the court, That said sale, so made to —— for the sum of —— dollars ($——), of the contract of purchase possessed by said decedent hereinafter described, be in all things confirmed, and that upon payment of said price the said administrator [8] shall execute to said purchaser an assignment of said contract, the same being described as follows, to wit: ——.[9]

Entered ——, 19—.   ——, County Clerk.

By ——, Deputy.[10]

Explanatory notes.—[1] Give file number. [2] Or, executor. [3] If the matter has been continued, say, "and the hearing having been regularly postponed by the court to this day." [4] If sold at private sale, say, "that said property was appraised within one year of the time of such sale, and that the price obtained at such sale is at least ninety (90) per cent of said appraised value." [5] If any payments are to become due, insert, "that said sale was made subject to all payments that may thereafter become due on said contract." [6-8] Or, executor. [9] Describe the contract, according to its legal effect, giving times of payment, amounts of each, etc., with a description of the land. [10] Orders need not be signed: See note, § 77, ante.

§ 578. Same. Conditions of sale.

The sale must be made subject to all payments that may thereafter become due on such contracts, and if there are any such, the sale must not be confirmed by the court until the purchasers execute a bond to the executor or administrator for the benefit and indemnity of himself and of the persons entitled to the interest of the decedent in the lands so contracted for, in double the whole amount of payments thereafter to become due on such contract, with such sureties as the court or judge shall approve.—*Kerr's Cyc. Code Civ. Proc.*, § 1566.

ANALOGOUS AND IDENTICAL STATUTES.

The * indicates identity.

Alaska—Compiled Laws of 1913, section 1680.

Arizona*—Revised Statutes of 1913, paragraph 947.

Idaho*—Compiled Statutes of 1919, section 7645.

Montana*—Revised Codes of 1907, section 7589.

Nevada*—Revised Laws of 1912, section 6011.

North Dakota—Compiled Laws of 1913, section 8784.

Oklahoma*—Revised Laws of 1910, section 6399.

Oregon—Lord's Oregon Laws, section 1267.

South Dakota*—Compiled Laws of 1913, section 5849.

Utah—Compiled Laws of 1907, section 3903.

Washington—Laws of 1917, chapter 156, page 683, section 140.
Wyoming*—Compiled Statutes of 1910, section 5675.

§ 579. Same. Purchaser to give bond.

The bond must be conditioned that the purchaser will make all payments for such land that become due after the date of the sale, and will fully indemnify the executor or administrator and the persons so entitled against all demands, costs, charges, and expenses, by reason of any covenant or agreement contained in such contract.— *Kerr's Cyc. Code Civ. Proc.,* § 1567.

ANALOGOUS AND IDENTICAL STATUTES.
The * indicates identity.

Alaska—Compiled Laws of 1913, section 1680.
Arizona*—Revised Statutes of 1913, paragraph 948.
Idaho*—Compiled Statutes of 1919, section 7646.
Montana†—Revised Codes of 1907, section 7590.
Nevada—Revised Laws of 1912, section 6012.
North Dakota—Compiled Laws of 1913, section 8784.
Oklahoma*—Revised Laws of 1910, section 6400.
Oregon—Lord's Oregon Laws, section 1267.
South Dakota*—Compiled Laws of 1913, section 5850.
Utah—Compiled Laws of 1907, section 3903.
Washington—Laws of 1917, chapter 156, page 683, section 140.
Wyoming*—Compiled Statutes of 1910, section 5676.

§ 580. Form. Bond on sale of contract for purchase of land.

[Title of court.]

[Title of estate.]   No. ——.1   Dept. No. ——.
                                                   [Title of form.]

Know all men by these presents, That —— as principal, and —— and —— as sureties, are held and firmly bound in the sum of —— dollars ($——) unto ——, administrator [2] of the estate of ——, deceased, for the benefit and indemnity of himself and of the persons entitled to the interest of said decedent in the lands contracted for as hereinafter stated, to be paid to the said ——, or his successors, heirs, or such persons interested, or their heirs or assigns, for which payment well and truly to be made we bind ourselves, our and each of our heirs, executors, and administrators, jointly and severally, firmly by these presents. .

The condition of the above obligation is such, that, whereas the·said ——, deceased, was at the time of his death possessed of a contract for the purchase of certain lands, particularly described as follows, to wit: ——; and whereas the said contract has, by order of said court, .been sold to ——; and whereas the said purchaser has agreed to perform all of the covenants in· said contract agreed to be performed by the said ——, deceased, and to make all payments now 'due, or which shall become due thereon;—

Now, therefore, if the said ——[3] will well and truly make all payments for such lands that become due after the date of such sale, namely, the —— day of ——, 19—, and will fully indemnify the administrator,[4] and the persons entitled to the interest of the decedent in the lands so contracted for, against all demands, costs, charges, and expenses, by reason of any covenant or agreement contained in such contract, then this obligation is to be void; otherwise to remain in full force and effect.

Dated, signed, and sealed with our seals this —— day of ——, 19—.   —— [Seal]
                                                      —— [Seal]
                                                      —— [Seal]

Explanatory notes.—1 Give file number. 2 Or, executor. 3 Purchaser. 4 Or, executor.

§ 581. Same. Executor to assign contract.

· Upon the confirmation of the sale, the executor or administrator must execute to the purchaser an assignment of the contract, which vests in the purchaser, his heirs and assigns, all the right, title, and interest of the estate, or of the persons entitled to the interest of the decedent, in the lands sold at the time of the sale, and the purchaser has the same rights and remedies against the vendor of such land as the decedent would have had if he were living.—*Kerr's Cyc. Code Civ. Proc.,* § 1568.

ANALOGOUS AND IDENTICAL STATUTES.
The * indicates identity.

Alaska—Compiled Laws of 1913, section 1681.
Arizona*—Revised Statutes of 1913, paragraph 949.
Idaho*—Compiled Statutes of 1919, section 7647.
Montana*—Revised Codes of 1907, section 7591.
Nevada*—Revised Laws of 1912, section 6013.
North Dakota*—Compiled Laws of 1913, section 8785.
Oklahoma*—Revised Laws of 1910, section 6401.
Oregon—Lord's Oregon Laws, section 1268.
South Dakota*—Compiled Laws of 1913, section 5851.
Utah*—Compiled Laws of 1907, section 3904.
Washington—Laws of 1917, chapter 156, page 683, section 142.
Wyoming*—Compiled Statutes of 1910, section 5677.

§ 582. **Sales of land subject to mortgage or other lien.**

When any sale is made by an executor or administrator, pursuant to the provisions of this chapter, of lands subject to any mortgage or other lien, which is a valid claim against the estate of the decedent, and has been filed and allowed, or presented and allowed, the purchase-money must be applied, after paying the necessary expenses of the sale, first, to the payment and satisfaction of the mortgage or lien, and the residue, if any, in due course of administration. The application of the purchase-money to the satisfaction of the mortgage or lien must be made without delay; and the land is subject to such mortgage or lien until the purchase-money has been actually so applied.

STATUTE OF LIMITATIONS.—No claim against any estate, which has been filed and allowed or presented and allowed, is affected by the statute of limitations, pending the proceedings for the settlement of the estate. The purchase-money, or so much thereof as may be sufficient to pay such mortgage or lien, with interest, and any lawful costs and charges thereon, may be paid into the court, to be received by the clerk thereof, whereupon the mortgage or lien upon the land must cease, and the purchase-money must be paid over by the clerk of the court without delay, in payment of the expenses of sale, and in satisfaction of the debt to secure which the mortgage or other lien was taken, and the surplus, if any, at once returned to the executor or administrator, unless for good cause shown, after notice to the executor or administrator, the court otherwise directs.—*Kerr's Cyc. Code Civ. Proc.*, § 1569.

ANALOGOUS AND IDENTICAL STATUTES.
No identical statute found.

Alaska—Compiled Laws of 1913, section 1684.
Arizona—Revised Statutes of 1913, paragraph 950.
Idaho—Compiled Statutes of 1919, section 7648.
Kansas—General Statutes of 1915, section 4619.
Montana—Revised Codes of 1907, section 7592.
Nevada—Revised Laws of 1912, section 6014.
North Dakota—Compiled Laws of 1913, sections 8757, 8786.
Oklahoma—Revised Laws of 1910, section 6402.
Oregon—Lord's Oregon Laws, section 1273.
South Dakota—Compiled Laws of 1913, section 5852.
Utah—Compiled Laws of 1907, section 3905.
Wyoming—Compiled Statutes of 1910, section 5678.

§ 583. Holder of mortgage or lien may purchase lands; his receipt as payment.

At any sale of lands upon which there is a mortgage or lien, the holder thereof may become the purchaser, and his receipt for the amount due him from the proceeds of the sale is a payment pro tanto. If the amount for which he purchased the property is insufficient to defray the expenses and discharge his mortgage or lien, he must pay the court, or clerk thereof, an amount sufficient to pay such expenses.—*Kerr's Cyc. Code Civ. Proc.*, § 1570.

ANALOGOUS AND IDENTICAL STATUTES.
The * indicates identity.

Arizona*—Revised Statutes of 1913, paragraph 951.
Idaho*—Compiled Statutes of 1919, section 7649.
Montana*—Revised Codes of 1907, section 7593.
North Dakota—Compiled Laws of 1913, section 8787.
Oklahoma*—Revised Laws of 1910, section 6403.

South Dakota*—Compiled Laws of 1913, section 5853.
Utah*—Compiled Laws of 1907, section 3906.
Wyoming*—Compiled Statutes of 1910, section 5679.

§ 584. Misconduct in sale. Liability.

If there is any neglect or misconduct in the proceedings of the executor in relation to any sale, by which any person interested in the estate suffers damage, the party aggrieved may recover the same in an action upon the bond of the executor or administrator, or otherwise.—*Kerr's Cyc. Code Civ. Proc.*, § 1571.

ANALOGOUS AND IDENTICAL STATUTES.
The * indicates identity.

Arizona*—Revised Statutes of 1913, paragraph 952.
Idaho*—Compiled Statutes of 1919, section 7650.
Montana*—Revised Codes of 1907, section 7594.
Nevada*—Revised Laws of 1912, section 6016.
North Dakota—Compiled Laws of 1913, section 8787.
Oklahoma*—Revised Laws of 1910, section 6404.
South Dakota*—Compiled Laws of 1913, section 5854.
Utah*—Compiled Laws of 1907, section 3882.
Wyoming*—Compiled Statutes of 1910, section 5680.

§ 585. Fraudulent sales.

Any executor or administrator who fraudulently sells any real estate of a decedent contrary to or otherwise than under the provisions of this chapter, is liable in double the value of the land sold, as liquidated damages, to be recovered in an action by the person having an estate of inheritance therein.—*Kerr's Cyc. Code Civ. Proc.*, § 1572.

ANALOGOUS AND IDENTICAL STATUTES.
The * indicates identity.

Arizona*—Revised Statutes of 1913, paragraph 953.
Colorado—Mills's Statutes of 1912, section 7987.
Idaho*—Compiled Statutes of 1919, section 7651.
Montana*—Revised Codes of 1907, section 7595.
Nevada—Revised Laws of 1912, section 6017.
North Dakota*—Compiled Laws of 1913, section 8804.
Oklahoma*—Revised Laws of 1910, section 6405.
South Dakota*—Compiled Laws of 1913, section 5855.
Utah*—Compiled Laws of 1907, section 3907.
Wyoming*—Compiled Statutes of 1910, section 5681.

§ 586. Limitation of actions for vacating sale, etc.

No action for the recovery of any estate sold by an executor or administrator, under the provisions of this chapter, can be maintained by any heir or other person claiming under the decedent, unless it be commenced within three years next after the settlement of the final account of the executor or administrator. An action to set aside the sale may be instituted and maintained at any time within three years from the discovery of the fraud, or other grounds upon which the action is based.—*Kerr's Cyc. Code Civ. Proc.*, § 1573.

ANALOGOUS AND IDENTICAL STATUTES.

The * indicates identity.

Arizona—Revised Statutes of 1913, paragraph 954.
Colorado—Mills's Statutes of 1912, section 7988.
Idaho—Compiled Statutes of 1919, section 7652.
Montana*—Revised Codes of 1907, section 7596.
Nevada—Revised Laws of 1912, section 6018.
North Dakota—Compiled Laws of 1913, sections 8788, 8809.
Oklahoma—Revised Laws of 1910, section 6406.
South Dakota—Compiled Laws of 1913, section 5856.
Wyoming*—Compiled Statutes of 1910, section 5682.

§ 587. To what cases preceding section not to apply.

The preceding section shall not apply to minors or others under any legal disability, to sue at the time when the right of action first accrues; but all such persons may commence an action at any time within three years after the removal of the disability.—*Kerr's Cyc. Code Civ. Proc.*, § 1574.

ANALOGOUS AND IDENTICAL STATUTES.

The * indicates identity.

Arizona*—Revised Statutes of 1913, paragraph 955.
Colorado—Mills's Statutes of 1912, section 7988.
Idaho*—Compiled Statutes of 1919, section 7653.
Montana*—Revised Codes of 1907, section 7597.
North Dakota*—Compiled Laws of 1913, section 8810.
Oklahoma*—Revised Laws of 1910, section 6407.
South Dakota*—Compiled Laws of 1913, section 5857.
Wyoming*—Compiled Statutes of 1910, section 5683.

§ 588. Account of sale to be returned.

When a sale has been made by an executor or administrator of any property of the estate, real or personal, he must return to the court, within thirty days thereafter, an account of sales, verified by his affidavit, or in case of his absence from the county, or other inability, by the affidavit of his attorney. If he neglects to make such return, he may be punished by attachment, or his letters may be revoked, one day's notice having been first given him to appear and show cause why such attachment should not issue, or such revocation should not be made. —*Kerr's Cyc. Code Civ. Proc.,* § 1575.

ANALOGOUS AND IDENTICAL STATUTES.
No identical statute found.
Alaska—Compiled Laws of 1913, section 1672.
Arizona—Revised Statutes of 1913, paragraph 956.
Colorado—Mills's Statutes of 1912, section 7982.
Idaho—Compiled Statutes of 1919, section 7654.
Montana—Revised Codes of 1907, section 7598.
Nevada—Revised Laws of 1912, section 6019.
New Mexico—Statutes of 1915, section 2287.
North Dakota—Compiled Laws of 1913, section 8789.
Oklahoma—Revised Laws of 1910, section 6408.
Oregon—Lord's Oregon Laws, section 1258.
South Dakota—Compiled Laws of 1913, section 5858.
Utah—Compiled Laws of 1907, sections 3883, 3898.
Washington—Laws of 1917, chapter 156, p. 680, section 131.
Wyoming—Compiled Statutes of 1910, section 5684.

§ 589. Form. Order to show cause why letters should not be revoked for failure to return account of sales.
[Title of court.]

[Title of estate.]   {No. ——.1   Dept. No. ——.
                                      {   [Title of form.]

It being shown to the court [2] that the administrator [3] of the above-entitled estate has sold property of such estate, and has neglected, for more than thirty (30) days [4] after the making of such sale, to return an account thereof, —

It is ordered, That the clerk of this court give the said ——, administrator [5] as aforesaid, notice [6] to appear before this court on ——,[7] the —— day of ——, 19—, and show cause, if any he can, why his letters [8] should not be revoked for such failure.

——, Judge of the —— Court.

Explanatory notes.—[1] Give file number. [2] By the affidavit of ——. [3] Or, executor, etc., according to the fact. [4] Or other time prescribed by statute. [5] Or as the case may be. [6] One day's notice, at least, is required. [7] Day of week. [8] Of administration, or letters testamentary, according to the fact.

§ 590. Form. Order to show cause why attachment should not issue for failure to return account of sales.

[Title of court.]

[Title of estate.] { No. ——.[1] Dept. No.——.
                     [Title of form.]

It being shown to the court [2] that the administrator [3] of the above-entitled estate has sold property of such estate, and has neglected for more than thirty (30) days [4] after the making of such sale to return an account thereof, —

It is ordered, That the clerk of this court give the said ——, administrator,[5] as aforesaid, notice [6] to appear before this court, at the court-room thereof,[7] on ——,[8] the —— day of ——, 19—, at —— o'clock in the forenoon [9] of that day, and show cause, if any he can, why an attachment should not issue to compel him to make such return.

Dated ——, 19—.   ——, Judge of the —— Court.

Explanatory notes.—[1] Give file number. [2] By the affidavit of ——. [3] Or, executor, etc., according to the fact. [4] Or other time prescribed by statute. [5] According to the fact. [6] One day's notice, at least, is required. [7] Give number of department, if any, and location of court-room. [8] Day of week. [9] Or, afternoon.

§ 591. Form. Order for attachment for neglecting to return account of sales.

[Title of court.]

[Title of estate.] { No. ——.[1] Dept. No.——.
                     [Title of form.]

It appearing to the court that ——, the administrator [2] of the estate of ——, deceased, has neglected for thirty

(30) days ² to make a return of sale of property of said estate sold by him on the —— day of ——, 19—; that a citation has been issued requiring the said —— to appear and show cause why an attachment should not issue as directed in said citation, and it further appearing that said citation has been served and returned in the manner and form provided by law, and the direction of this court; —

It is ordered, That a warrant of attachment issue, and that the said —— be arrested and brought before this court to show cause, if any he can, why he should not be committed for contempt of court in disobeying said citation.   ——, Judge of the —— Court.

Dated ——, 19—.

Explanatory notes.—1 Give file number. ² Or, executor, etc., according to the fact. ³ Or other time prescribed by the statute.

§ 592. Executor, etc., not to be purchaser.

No executor or administrator must, directly or indirectly, purchase any property of the estate he represents, nor must he be interested in any sale.—*Kerr's Cyc. Code Civ. Proc.*, § 1576.

ANALOGOUS AND IDENTICAL STATUTES.

The * indicates identity.

Alaska—Compiled Laws of 1913, section 1687.
Arizona*—Revised Statutes of 1913, paragraph 957.
Colorado—Mills's Statutes of 1912, section 7981.
Idaho*—Compiled Statutes of 1919, section 7655.
Kansas—General Statutes of 1915, section 4614.
Montana*—Revised Codes of 1907, section 7599.
Nevada—Revised Laws of 1912, section 6020.
New Mexico—Statutes of 1915, section 2256.
North Dakota—Compiled Laws of 1913, section 8789.
Oklahoma*—Revised Laws of 1910, section 6409.
Oregon—Lord's Oregon Laws, section 1276.
South Dakota*—Compiled Laws of 1913, section 5859.
Utah*—Compiled Laws of 1907, section 3884.
Wyoming*—Compiled Statutes of 1910, section 5685.

27. Sales by guardian.
28. Sales by foreign executor. '
29. Exchange is not a sale.
30. Sales without order.
31. Title conveyed by sale.
32. Bona fide purchasers.
    (1) Rights of.
    (2) How affected by adverse possession.
33. Necessary sale is valid when.
34. Voidable sales.
35. Void sales.
36. Vacating sales.
37. Rights of heirs.
    (1) In general.
    (2) Heirs under guardianship.
    (3) Actions by heirs in general to set aside sales.
    (4) Actions by minor heirs to set aside sales.
38. Sales under power in the will.
    (1) In general.
    (2) No implied power when.

    (3) Discretion of executor.
    (4) For best interests of estate.
    (5) Devesting estate.
    (6) Agent to sell. Compensation.
    (7) Purchasers. Estoppel.
    (8) Validity of sale. Notice.
    (9) Equitable conversion. Election for reconversion.
    (10) Devise in trust with power to sell.
    (11) Directions coupled with the trust. Effect of.
    (12) Power passes to administrator with will annexed.
    (13) Particular sales under power in the will.
    (14) Purchase by executor failing to qualify.
    (15) Return of sales under power in will. Confirmation.
39. Sale of pretermitted child's interest.
40. Limitation of actions for vacating sale.

III. Confirmation of Sales and Conveyances.

1. Discretion of court as to confirmation.
2. Authority to confirm, when presumed.
3. When required.
4. When not required.
5. No power to confirm when.
6. Objections to confirmation.
7. Effect of the order.
8. Refusing confirmation. Effect of the order.

9. Refusal to report sale for confirmation. Effect of.
10. Action to set aside confirmation.
11. Conveyance.
    (1) In general.
    (2) May be ordered when.
    (3) Is individual deed when.
    (4) Conditions not to be imposed.
    (5) Title carried by.
    (6) Is void when.
    (7) Mandate to compel.

IV. Direct and Collateral Attack upon Sales.

1. Direct attack in general.
2. Distinction between direct and collateral attack.
3. Collateral attack.
    (1) In general.

    (2) What can not be questioned.
    (3) Presumptions on.
    (4) What is good on collateral attack.

V. Appeal.

1. In general.
2. Non-appealable orders.
3. Appealable orders.
4. Parties interested or aggrieved.
5. Parties not interested or aggrieved.

6. Affirming the order of sale on appeal.
7. Record on appeal.
8. Decree. Effect of, on appeal.
9. Res judicata. Law of the case.

I. NATURE OF JURISDICTION. LAW GOVERNING.

1. Nature of proceedings.

(1) In general.—One prominent purpose of administration is to pay the debts of the estate from the real and personal property of the

deceased. The administrator is, by law, charged with this duty. To sell real estate of the decedent to pay the debts is as plainly a step in the administration as is the sale of personal property for the same purpose. But, although it is within the scope of the administration to sell either real or personal property, the legislature has power to direct how this shall be done.—Burris v. Kennedy, 108 Cal. 331, 338, 41 Pac 458. The application of the executor or of an administrator for the sale of lands belonging to the estate is a special and independent proceeding. The jurisdiction of the probate court depends absolutely on the sufficiency of the petition; in other words, on its substantial compliance with the requirements of the statute. Though the proceeding for a sale occurs in the general course of administration, it is a distinct proceeding in the nature of an action in which the petition is the commencement and the order of sale is the judgment.—Pryor v. Downey, 50 Cal. 388, 398, 19 Am. Rep. 656. What is meant when it is said that an application to sell real estate of a decedent is an independent proceeding is, simply, that it is essential that the application should be made substantially as provided by statute; otherwise the court has no power to order the sale, or the administrator to sell.—Burris v. Kennedy, 108 Cal. 331, 338, 41 Pac. 458. While an application to sell real estate of a deceased person does partake somewhat of the nature of an action, it is not, in any sense of the term, an action to recover real estate, or the possession of it. Nor is it an action arising out of the title thereto, or the rents and profits thereof.—In re Tuohy's Estate, 33 Mont. 230, 83 Pac. 486. In Colorado, the proceeding to sell real estate of a decedent is separate and distinct from the administration of the estate proper, and is a special proceeding recognized by the statute.—Ryan v. Geigel, 39 Colo. 355, 89 Pac. 775. The rule that the application of the administrator for the sale of lands belonging to the estate of a decedent is an independent proceeding; that the jurisdiction of the probate court over such sale does not come from its general jurisdiction over the administration of the estate, but from the petition for the sale; and that the petition must comply with the requirements of the code,—is not changed by the provisions of the present constitution, which give jurisdiction of probate business to a court of general jurisdiction, or by the fact that the code no longer requires a deficiency of personal property to be shown before there can be any valid sale of real property.—Richardson v. Butler, 82 Cal. 174, 176, 16 Am. St. Rep. 101, 23 Pac. 9. So long as the administration of the estate is pending, the executors are at all times subject to the control and direction of the superior court, and that court may at any time order a sale of the lands, if necessary for the payment of creditors, or when it will be for the advantage of those interested in the estate, or when they assent to its sale. There is therefore no point of time at which the beneficiaries under a will may not unite in a conveyance made at a sale under the order of the court, and thus give to the grantee an absolute interest in

possession of the estate of the testator in the property conveyed.—
Estate of Pforr, 144 Cal. 121, 127, 77 Pac. 825. Upon the death of
the wife, the husband, in succeeding to the estate, takes the same
subject to the claims against it; and the only interest in the estate,
therefore, that can be taken at a sale under execution upon a judgment recovered against the husband is the distributive share of the
husband in the estate of the wife after the payment of all debts.—
Nichols v. Lee, 16 Colo. 147, 26 Pac. 157. A proceeding leading up to
the sale of real estate by an administrator is a proceeding in rem.—
Shane v. Peoples, 25 N. D. 188, 194, 141 N. W. 737.

REFERENCES.

Additional bond, when required to be given on sale of real estate.—
See §§ 281, 282, ante.

(2) Proceedings are statutory.—Proceedings for the sale of real
property of a decedent are statutory, and such sale will be void, unless
the requirements of the statute are complied with.—Hellman v. Merz,
112 Cal. 661, 666, 44 Pac. 1079. The provision of the statute declaring that no sale of any property of an estate shall be valid unless
made upon an order of the probate court applies only to sales made
by executors or administrators. It has no reference to judicial sales
under the decrees of the district courts (superseded by the superior
courts, in California), or to sales in pursuance of testamentary authority.—Fallon v. Butler, 21 Cal. 24, 31, 81 Am. Dec. 140. The administration of an estate is a proceeding in rem.—See Dooly v. Russell, 10
Wash. 195, 38 Pac. 1000.

(3) Policy of law as to titles.—The policy of the statute is to quiet
titles to real estate sold by order of the probate courts.—Harlan v.
Peck, 33 Cal. 521, 91 Am. Dec. 653.

2. Jurisdiction.

(1) When acquired.—There are three methods, under the California
statute, by which jurisdiction of an application for leave to sell may
be acquired: 1. By a personal service on all persons interested in
the estate; 2. By publication for four successive weeks; 3. By the
assent, in writing, to the order of sale by all persons interested in
the estate.—Pearson v. Pearson, 46 Cal. 610, 636. Where the court
acquires jurisdiction, all parties interested in the estate are bound
by its actions as fully by default, for not appearing, as if they had
appeared and contested the sufficiency of the petition.—Estate of
Couts, 100 Cal. 400, 402, 34 Pac. 865. When the record discloses what
was done to acquire jurisdiction, it will not be presumed that something different was done.—Hahn v. Kelly, 34 Cal. 407, 94 Am. Dec. 742;
Pearson v. Mitchell, 43 Cal. 610, 636. The authority of a court to
order the sale of real property of a decedent's estate is not general,
but limited, is derived from the statute conferring the right, and can be

exercised only in the manner prescribed.—Haynes v. Meeks, 20 Cal. 288, 312; In re Noon's Estate, 49 Or. 286, 88 Pac. 673, 675, 90 Pac. 673. The legislature has prescribed, as a prerequisite to the sale of the property of a decedent, that a petition shall be filed; that notice shall be given; and that an opportunity for a hearing shall be afforded. These acts, therefore, are essential to power on the part of the court to order the sale, and in that sense the petition and the order are jurisdictional.—Burris v. Kennedy, 108 Cal. 331, 339, 41 Pac. 458.

(2) **Nature and extent.**—In proceedings to sell real estate to pay the debts of a deceased person, the decedent's title or interests in the land described in the petition shall not be put in issue, but, otherwise, the jurisdiction of the court extends to the adjudication of all questions, in such proceedings, involving the rights of those before the court, interested in the real estate sought to be sold, whose rights therein will be injuriously affected by a decree of sale. As to such proceedings, the constitutional prohibition that county courts shall not exercise jurisdiction where the value of the property involved exceeds two thousand dollars does not apply.—New York Life Ins. Co. v. Brown, 32 Colo. 365, 76 Pac. 799.

(3) **Basis of jurisdiction.**—The legislature has prescribed that a petition shall be filed, that notice shall be given, and that an opportunity for a hearing shall be afforded. Since the procedure is one in which there are no adversary parties present at all times in court, it is reasonable to hold, as has always been held, that these acts are essential to the power on the part of the court to order the sale. In that sense the petition and notice are jurisdictional.—Burris v. Kennedy, 108 Cal. 331, 338, 41 Pac. 458. In acting upon the petition for an order of sale, the superior court of the state of California is still a court of general jurisdiction, etc.—Estate of Cook, 137 Cal. 184, 186, 69 Pac. 968. The petition for a sale is a necessary prerequisite to the jurisdiction of the court to order a sale.—Burris v. Kennedy, 108 Cal. 331, 345, 41 Pac. 458; Gager v. Henry, 5 Saw. 244, Fed. Cas. No. 5172; Wright v. Edwards, 10 Or. 298, 306. Without jurisdiction, the probate court has no power to confirm the sale or to impart any validity to it.—Gregory v. Taber, 19 Cal. 397, 410, 79 Am. Dec. 219. See Gregory v. McPherson, 13 Cal. 562, 573.

(4) **Not dependent on truth of petition.**—It is immaterial, so far as the question of jurisdiction is concerned, whether the statements of the petition are true or not; the jurisdiction rests upon the averments of the petition, not upon proof of them.—Pryor v. Downey, 50 Cal. 388, 398, 19 Am. Rep. 656; Richardson v. Butler, 82 Cal. 174, 178, 16 Am. St. Rep. 101, 23 Pac. 9. The truth of averments respecting personal property, so far as they affect the validity of the order, is to be determined at the hearing of the petition.—Haynes v. Meeks, 20 Cal. 288, 316.

3. Law governing probate sales.

(1) In general.—A statute in force at the time of the death of an intestate, concerning authority to sell his property, governs the rights of the heirs.—Estate of Porter, 129 Cal. 86, 88, 79 Am. St. Rep. 78, 61 Pac. 659. Upon an application for an order of sale, the court must be governed by the statute in force at the death of the testator, at which time the estate vests in the devisees.—Estate of Roach, 139 Cal. 17, 19, 72 Pac. 393. See Halleck v. Moss, 22 Cal. 266, 276. Such proceedings must be in accordance with local laws in force at the time, in the state or territory where suit is commenced, and this principle applies, though the United States itself is a suitor.—United States v. Hailey, 2 Idaho 26, 3 Pac. 263. It is undoubtedly within the scope of legislative authority to direct that the debts of an estate be paid from the realty instead of the personal property; or (as is done in some states) that the heir need not be made a party to the proceeding to obtain a sale of the real estate; or that the administrator may sell without any order of the court whatever. But all these acts must be for the satisfaction of liens of creditors, or for the support of the family of the deceased, which matters are held to be paramount to the claim of the heirs or devisees.—Brenham v. Story, 39 Cal. 179, 185. The limitation placed upon actions for the recovery of real estate sold by an executor or administrator, under the provisions of the probate law, are not applicable, where the premises in controversy were not subject to sale, and were not sold under the provisions of such law.—McNeil v. Congregational Soc., 66 Cal. 105, 111, 4 Pac. 1096. An order of the probate court, made after the passage of the act of April 22, 1850, authorizing a person, appointed by an alcalde's court as administrator of the estate of a decedent, to sell the real estate of the intestate, was void for want of jurisdiction, because there was no provision for the transfer of such proceeding from the alcalde's court to the probate court.—McNeil v Congregational Soc., 66 Cal. 105, 108, 4 Pac. 1096. The sole effect of an administrator's deed or bill of sale is to convey to the purchaser such title as the decedent had; the administrator does not warrant title, and the purchaser is subject to the rule of caveat emptor.—Payne v. People (Colo.), 173 Pac. 397. A purchaser at an administrator's sale can not hold his vendor for a deficiency in the land sold, such sales being controlled by the rule of caveat emptor.—Moyle v. Thomas, 46 Utah 542, 151 Pac. 361

(2) Statute of frauds.—The statute of frauds does not apply to sales made by executors or administrators under our probate system, inasmuch as such sales are judicial and not ministerial. The administrator is under the control of the court, and the contract for the sale in probate, therefore, need not be in writing, nor is it required to be subscribed by the parties.—Halleck v. Guy, 9 Cal. 181, 195, 70 Am. Dec. 643.

(3) Statute of limitations.—The statute of limitations does not run against an allowed claim of a creditor while the administration is pending and unsettled, and he is not, for that reason, precluded from petitioning for an order of sale.—Estate of Arguello, 85 Cal. 151, 153, 24 Pac. 641; Estate of Schroeder, 46 Cal. 305, 316.

II. SALES OF REAL AND PERSONAL PROPERTY IN GENERAL.

1. Property capable of sale in general.

(1) Rule at common law.—At common law, the representative could sell personal property without restraint, so long as his acts were not fraudulent; but under the code his power to sell is dependent upon the assent of the court.—Wickersham v. Johnson, 104 Cal. 407, 412, 43 Am. St. Rep. 118, 38 Pac. 89; Rankin v. Newman, 114 Cal. 635, 660, 34 L. R. A. 265, 46 Pac. 742; Bovard v. Dickenson, 131 Cal. 162, 164, 63 Pac. 162. The rule at common law with reference to the application of lands and personalty for the payment of debts has been modified by the code provisions. Under our statute, both lands and personalty, as assets in the hands of the executor, are liable for all the debts, and both, if generally devised, are therefore, like specific legacies and devises, chargeable with the same debts, and stand upon precisely the same footing, so far as the reasons for charging them pro rata are concerned.—Estate of Woodworth, 31 Cal. 595, 614. Rule of the common law relating to vesting of legal title.—See Welder v. Osborn, 20 Or. 307, 25 Pac. 715.

(2) Rule under codes and statutes.—There is no priority, under the code, between real and personal property, where a sale of property is necessary for the payment of debts.—Estate of Montgomery, 60 Cal. 645, 647. Under the Washington statute providing for the order of payment of the debts of an estate, including funeral expenses, and further providing that "no real estate of a deceased person shall be liable for his debts unless letters testamentary or of administration be granted within six years from the date of the death of such decedent," the real estate is stamped with the charges and expenses of administration only within the limitation provided, but, after the lapse of that time, purchasers who have taken possession of the real property in good faith, and who have paid taxes thereon, shall not be disturbed in their possession.—In re Smith's Estate, 25 Wash. 539, 66 Pac. 93. It is competent for the legislature to change the rule of inheritance, or to restrict the testamentary power. It may provide that the heir or devisee shall take, subject to certain burdens as the payment of the debts, etc.; but this is far from saying that the legislature may, after the title has vested in the heir, empower the administrator to sell the inheritance for purposes not authorized at the time the title vested, and to which it was not subject when it vested.—Estate of Freud, 131 Cal. 667, 670, 82 Am. St. Rep. 407, 63 Pac. 1080. Upon the death of the ancestor, the heir at once becomes vested with the full property, subject only to liens then existing or created by the statute then in force.—Brenham v. Story, 38 Cal. 177; Smith v. Olmstead, 88 Cal. 582, 586, 22 Am. St. Rep. 336, 12 L. R. A. 46, 26 Pac. 521. See, also, Estate of Packer, 125 Cal. 396, 399, 73 Am. St. Rep. 58, 58 Pac. 59. The entire estate, both real and personal, is liable in the hands of the executor to the charge of all the debts.— Estate of Woodworth, 31 Cal. 595, 614; Murphy v. Farmers, etc., Bank, 131 Cal. 115, 119, 63 Pac. 368. The executor has no more right to sell personal than real estate, unless necessary for its preservation, to pay charges upon it. Personal estate not bequeathed, like real estate, goes to the heir, under our statute, and not to the executor, except for the purpose of settling the estate and paying the debts and charges upon it. The executor no more owns it (as he did at common law), than he does real estate; and he is no more authorized to sell it unless necessary, than he is to sell real estate.—Estate of Woodworth, 31 Cal. 595, 606. The whole property of a decedent, not exempt, both real and personal, is charged with the payment of debts.—McNutt v. McComb, 61 Kan. 25, 58 Pac. 965; Lake v. Hathaway, 75 Kan. 391, 89 Pac. 666. As to the real estate, the title of the decedent upon his death, descends at once to the heir, who is entitled to the possession thereof. No right or title therein goes to the administrator; not even possession.— Black v. Elliott, 63 Kan. 211, 88 Am. St. Rep. 239, 65 Pac. 215; following Bauserman v. Charlotte, 46 Kan. 480, 26 Pac. 1051; and Kulp v. Kulp, 51 Kan. 341, 21 L. R. A. 550, 32 Pac. 1118. The whole of the estate, both real and personal, goes into the possession of the executor or administrator, first for the payment of debts, and then for distribution under the will or the laws of succession.—In re Tuohy's Estate, 33 Mont. 230, 83 Pac. 6. Therefore any question of title to the property belonging to the estate of a deceased person must be settled in an appropriate action brought in the district court as a court of general jurisdiction.—In re Tuohy's Estate, 33 Mont. 230, 83 Pac. 486; Estate of Burton, 63 Cal. 36; Estate of Groome, 94 Cal. 69, 29 Pac. 487; Stewart v. Lohr, 1 Wash. 341, 22 Am. St. Rep. 150, 25 Pac. 457. Upon the appointment of an administrator, the court obtains jurisdiction of the real and personal estate of the deceased, and the administration of the estate is a proceeding in rem.—Furth v. United States, etc., Trust Co., 13 Wash. 73, 42 Pac. 523. Under the rule that prior possession of public lands will entitle the possessor to maintain an action against a trespasser, the right of enjoyment of possession of public lands descends among the effects of a deceased person to the executor or administrator, and may be the subject of a sale under the order of a probate court, entitling the purchaser to be subrogated to the rights of the first holder.—Grover v. Hawley, 5 Cal. 485, 486.

(3) **Rule where personalty is insufficient.**—If there is not. sufficient personalty to pay the aggregate of all classes of claims,—family allowance, debts, expenses, and charges of administration,—be the same more or less, or be it made up of items belonging to one or more

of these classes of charges, real estate may be sold to pay the deficiency left over the amount which the personalty will pay.—Estate of Bentz, 36 Cal. 687, 690. The California statute does not require all of the personal property to be exhausted before an order can be made for the sale of the realty.—Stuart v. Allen, 16 Cal. 473, 503, 76 Am. Dec. 551. The long-established rule of priority in marshaling assets, as between legatees, devisees, and heirs, has not been disturbed by our statute. It follows that, as between a legatee of the personalty and a devisee of the realty, the executor is not authorized to appropriate the rents of real estate, which accrued subsequent to the decease of the testator, to the satisfaction of a mortgage debt in exoneration of the personalty.—Estate of Woodworth, 31 Cal. 595, 609. The title to both real and personal property of one who dies without disposing of it by will passes, under the statute of Idaho, to the heirs of the intestate, subject, however, to the control of the probate court, and to the possession of any administrator appointed by that court for the purpose of administration. This being true, the minor heirs, in a proceeding for the confirmation of a sale of real estate and the conveyance thereof, are adverse parties to said proceeding, and to a proceeding to set aside the sale, and their guardian ad litem should be served with notice of appeal from the order in the premises.—Reed v. Stewart, 12 Idaho 699, 87 Pac. 1002, 1152. It is the duty of the court first to ascertain whether the proceeds of a sale of personal property is sufficient to meet legitimate charges, expenses, and claims, before ordering a sale of the realty.—In re Houck's Estate, 23 Or. 10, 17 Pac. 461. Provision is made in the state of Washington, by the statute, for the sale of real estate for the payment of the debts of decedent only in cases where there is not sufficient personal estate in the hands of the representative for that purpose.—Prefontaine v. McMicken, 16 Wash. 16, 47 Pac. 231. A statute providing that whenever it shall appear, after an inventory and appraisement, that the personal estate of any decedent is insufficient to discharge the just debts, resort may be had to the real estate, can not be regarded as prescribing a condition precedent to the exercise of the right, by the administrator, to resort to the real estate for the satisfaction of the payment of the · debts. The right to resort to the realty is given whenever it appears that the personalty is insufficient for the purpose, independently of whether an inventory of the personal property and its appraisement has been filed or not.—Nichols v. Lee, 16 Colo. 147, 26 Pac. 157. There are two separate and distinct methods in Kansas by which real property in that state may be sold to satisfy the debts of a non-resident testator. One method is as follows: When a will has been duly proved in another state, upon the production, by the executor or other interested person, of an authenticated copy of the will and probate thereof, the probate court of any county in Kansas in which there is property upon which the will may operate may admit it to record; and the executor taking out letters, or the administrator with the will annexed, shall have the same power to sell and convey the real and personal estate, by virtue of the will or the law, as other executors or administrators with the will annexed shall or may have by law. The other method referred to does not contemplate the appointment of a Kansas executor or administrator, or any appointment in Kansas whatever. This latter method merely relates to the recognition, for the purpose of effecting the sale of real estate situated in Kansas, of an appointment made elsewhere.—Albright v. Bangs, 72 Kan. 435, 115 Am. St. Rep. 219, 83 Pac. 1030. The mere fact that there is personal property belonging to the estate does not preclude a sale of realty to pay family allowance, debts, or expenses of administration.—Estate of Pavert, 177 Cal. 353, 170 Pac. 827. The court does not abuse its discretion by ordering a sale of real property to pay debts of an estate owning personalty, if the latter consists of a disputed claim of doubtful value.— Estate of Pavert, 177 Cal. 353, 170 Pac. 827. The administrator who asks power to sell real property, and thereby take it permanently from the control and management of the heirs or devisees, must show good cause therefor.—Estate of Rawitzer, 175 Cal. 585, 166 Pac. 581, 585. Real estate of an intestate goes immediately to the heirs, subject to the right of the administrator to apply to the court to order its sale to supply a deficiency of the personalty to pay the debts of the estate; a sale of realty to pay the debts, when there is no such deficiency is invalid.—Costello v. Cunningham, 16 Ariz. 447, 463, 147 Pac. 701. Where an estate of a deceased person is in process of settlement and there is no claim filed against the estate, nor any debts left by the deceased, there is no occasion for the heirs, to whom the real estate descended, to apply to the probate court for authority to sell it. Such authority is required only where the personal estate is insufficient to meet the indebtedness of the decedent.—Sturgeon v. Culver, 87 Kan. 404, Ann. Cas. 1913E, 341, 124 Pac. 419.

REFERENCES.

Order of sale of personal property for the payment of debts, etc.— See § 497, ante.

2. Particular interests in property.

(1) Sales of mines and mining interests.—No sale of a decedent's estate is authorized, except when it is necessary,—1. To pay family allowance; 2. Debts of the decedent; 3. Expenses of administration; or 4. Legacies. But mines and mining interests belonging to estates of decedents are an exception to this rule. Such interests may be sold, when it is expedient to do so, for the benefit of the estate, although the proceeds are not needed to pay debts, expenses, etc.; and where it is sought to sell mining property for the benefit of the estate, it is not required that the petition shall set forth the condition of any property except that which is to be sold. The manifest reason of this is, that the expediency of such sales is in no wise dependant upon the condition of other portions of the estate.—Smith v. Biscailuz, 83 Cal. 344, 349, 21 Pac. 15, 23 Pac. 314.

(2) Sale of property subject to lease.—The executor may sell property held under a lease, where there is no provision in the lease itself prohibiting a sale of the property during its term, and where the sale is made subject to such lease.—Estate of Brannan, 5 Cal. Unrep. 882, 51 Pac. 320.

(3) Sale of partnership interests.—When a partnership is dissolved by the death of one of the partners, its assets, debts, and credits remain as distinct from those of its late members, until its affairs are wound up, as before the dissolution.—Gleason v. White, 34 Cal. 258. It would seem to be equally clear, that, if all die, (whether within the jurisdiction of the same or of different probate courts), the assets, debts, and credits of the partnership do not become confused with the estate of the last survivor, but continue a separate existence, and that the rights of the representatives or successors of the several partners can only be determined in a court of equity, which has the power and machinery for settling those rights by appropriate decree.—Theller v. Such, 57 Cal. 447, 461.

(4) Sale of community interests.—The interest of the surviving widow in the community property is that of an heir, and her title to one-half of the community property is to be administered as part of the estate of her husband, and is subject to sale for the payment of his debts.—Sharp v. Loupe, 120 Cal. 89, 93, 52 Pac. 134, 586. Section 1402 of the Civil Code of California provides that, "in case of the dissolution of the community by the death of the husband, the entire community property is equally subject to his debts, the family allowance, and the charges and expenses of administration." This is the same rule expressed in different terms by section 1516 of the Code of Civil Procedure of that state. The latter section declares that "all the property of a decedent shall be chargeable with the payment of the debts of the deceased, the expenses of administration, and the allowance to the family, except as otherwise provided in this code and in the Civil Code." The phrase, "all the property of a decedent," in the latter section, is the equivalent of "the entire community property," in the former.—Estate of Burdick, 112 Cal. 387, 399, 44 Pac. 734; Sharp v. Loupe, 120 Cal. 89, 92, 52 Pac. 134, 586.

(5) Homestead under United States land laws.—The homestead law of the United States vests the right in the land in the claimant himself, for his exclusive benefit, and if he dies before patent issues, leaving no widow, then in his heirs, or devisees, if they are at the time citizens of the United States. There is no authority under the land laws for an executor or administrator to consummate the inchoate claim of the decedent's homestead, or to sell his right thereunder, for the benefit of the creditors.—Towner v. Rodegeb, 33 Wash. 153, 99 Am. St. Rep. 936, 74 Pac. 50, 51. If the homestead claimant dies before patent issues, or before the right to demand a patent has accrued, the land does not become a part of his estate. Upon his death,

all his rights under the homestead entry cease, and his heirs become
entitled to a patent, not because they have succeeded to his equitable
interest, but because the law gives them preference as new home-
steaders, and allows them the benefit of the residence of their ancestor upon the land.—Gjerstadengen v. Van Duzen, 7 N. D. 612, 66
Am. St. Rep. 679, 76 N. W. 233; Chapman v. Price, 32 Kan. 446, 4 Pac.
807. The same principle, under similar statutory provisions, is applied in case of the death of a pre-emptor. The subsequently perfected title inures to the benefit of the heirs, and can neither be
devised by the pre-emptor nor sold in satisfaction of his debts or
expenses of administration.—Wittenbrock v. Wheadon, 128 Cal. 150,
79 Am. St. Rep. 32, 60 Pac. 664. Moreover, a homestead can not be
sold for debts contracted before patent issues.—Barnard v. Boller, 105
Cal. 214, 38 Pac. 728; Wallowa Nat. Bank v. Riley, 29 Or. 289, 54
Am. St. Rep. 794, 45 Pac. 766. It follows that such debts can not be
enforced against the homestead by the processes of administration;
and an attempted sale of the inchoate right thereof for the benefit
of the creditors is void.—Towner v. Rodegeb, 33 Wash. 153, 99 Am. St.
Rep. 936, 74 Pac. 50. Where a patent conveys land to the heirs, and
not to the decedent, the heirs have the right to convey and give possession as grantees of the United States, and any attempted sale of
such lands made by the administrator of the estate of the deceased
is in absolute nullity, and no title is communicated thereby to any
purchaser.—Coulson v. Wing, 42 Kan. 507, 16 Am. St. Rep. 503, 22
Pac. 570. Under the Revised Statutes of the United States, directing
that, in case of the death of the claimant before perfecting title, it
shall be competent for his administrator, or one of his heirs, to file the
necessary papers to perfect the same, but that entry in such cases
shall be made in favor of the heirs of the deceased pre-emptor, and
that a patent thereon shall cause the title to inure to such heirs, as
if their names had been specially mentioned, the right of possession of
pre-empted land to which title is inchoate passes, on the death of the
pre-emptor, to his administrator. The right of possession thus acquired
is subject to a trust, which requires the administrator to proceed to
perfect title in favor of the heirs, provided there are heirs and the
estate is in such condition as to enable him to do so, and the interest
of the heirs, all things considered, so demand. But, aside from this
trust, he is free to dispose of the possession for the best advantage of
the estate. No fraud in the premises, on the part of the administrator,
will be presumed; but, when there is no administrator, or, if there is
one, and he consents, an heir may perfect the title. The statute puts
only one limitation upon the administrator in dealing with the possession, which limitation is, that he should, for all purposes of perfecting
the title, stand in possession as representing the ancestor for the
benefit of the heirs and creditors alike; and, aside from such limitation, a salable possessory right passes to the administrator.—Burch v.
McDaniel, 2 Wash. Ter. 58, 63, 3 Pac. 586.

(6) Sale of contracts for purchase of realty.—Contract for purchase of lands may be sold how.—See § 576, ante.

(7) Property under mortgage or other lien.—Where the court has jurisdiction of land, with power to order a sale, and a mortgagee claimant has subjected his mortgage to the jurisdiction of the court, by consent, and the proceedings have been fully carried out, and a deed issued to the mortgagee thereunder, it is thereafter too late to raise any question relating to the regularity of the proceedings, where there are no jurisdictional questions involved.—Dooly v. Russell, 10 Wash. 195, 38 Pac. 1000. When mortgaged property of a decedent is sold at a probate sale, such sale of the decedent's interest in the land does not in any way affect the indebtedness of his widow to the estate, except to alter the security held by the estate for the payment of such debt. Instead of holding her interest as heir in the land of the estate, as security, it thereafter holds her interest as heir in the proceeds of such land.—Estate of Angle, 148 Cal. 102, 82 Pac. 668. Where a mortgage is given by an heir, by which he mortgages his interest in an estate, and where the mortgaged land was subsequently sold by the administrator at probate sale, the mortgagee acquires, upon foreclosure, only a lien on the funds of the mortgagor in the hands of the defendant administrator; and, for the purpose of securing the amount due, is the assignee of the mortgagor's interest therein, with power, as his attorney, to demand and receive the same. The mortgagee is therefore entitled to recover of the administrator, payable out of the share of the mortgagor, the amount due, with costs as found by the court.—Gutter v. Dallamore, 144 Cal. 665, 669, 79 Pac. 383. The purchaser at a mortgage sale, which is void for any reason, becomes the assignee of the mortgage and the debt secured thereby.—Smithson Land Co. v. Brautigam, 16 Wash. 174, 47 Pac. 434; Bryan v. Brasuis, 162 U. S. 415, 40 L. Ed. 1022, 16 Sup. Ct. 803. The heirs and a mortgagor can not recover in an action against the mortgagee, who makes a void foreclosure, and in good faith takes possession under cover of such proceedings, where no claim is made that the debt was ever paid.—Investment Security Co. v. Adams, 37 Wash. 211, 79 Pac. 625.

(8) Same. Application of purchase-money.—Where a bidder has the privilege of paying the whole sum on the date of sale, it is error for the court to direct the entire amount to be credited upon a mortgage held by the purchaser against the property for an amount exceeding the amount of his bid, which mortgage debt was drawing interest at the rate of two and a half per cent per month, whereas, by the terms of the sale, half of the purchase-money was to have been cash in hand, and the remainder in ninety days, with interest from the date of sale, at the rate of one per cent per month.—Halleck v. Guy, 9 Cal 181, 197, 70 Am. Dec. 643. Where property is sold by an administrator, and the purchaser has a mortgage claim against the property, which he presented to the estate, and the claim was allowed by the administrator and by the court, the amount of such claim upon the mortgage is a credit upon the purchase price, and the purchaser will not be compelled to pay such amount to the administrator of the estate in cash, before he is entitled to a conveyance of the property upon the sale and confirmation. It is sufficient, where the purchaser, or, in the event of his death, his administrator, credits the amount due upon the mortgage claim against the estate of the mortgagor, for such credit is equivalent to an actual payment of the amount in cash.—Estate of Lewis, 39 Cal. 306, 309. The provision of the statute, that, "when any sale is made by an executor or administrator of land subject to any mortgage or lien, which is a valid claim against the estate of the deceased, the purchase-money shall be applied, after paying the necessary expense of the sale, first to the payment and satisfaction of the mortgage, and the residue in due course of administration," is not controlled by the general provisions of the statute in reference to the distribution of assets and payment of debts. The creditor merely gets the benefit of the contract made with the deceased, and is under no obligation to pay any other expenses than those incurred in the enforcement of the mortgage security.—Estate of Murray, 18 Cal. 686, 687.

(9) Choses in action.—It was not the intention of legislation, changing the rule at common law, to require an order for the sale of personal property to include choses in action, or to deprive the executor or administrator of the power of disposition over them.—Weider v. Osborn, 20 Or. 307, 25 Pac. 715. In California, choses in action must be sold in the same manner as other personal property.—Bovard v. Dickenson, 131 Cal. 162, 164, 63 Pac. 162. The statute has curtailed the power of the executor or administrator to sell or dispose of the personal property of the decedent, and limited it to such as is visible and tangible, except by an order of the probate court, either at public or private sale, as may be provided therein; but with this difference, the power of disposition of the executor or administrator remains as at common law, and the title of all choses in action is vested in him, with authority to collect and otherwise dispose of them.—Weider v. Osborn, 20 Or. 307, 25 Pac. 715. An executor or administrator may sell or dispose of choses in action by indorsement to another, or to a distributee, without an order of the probate court, and such transfer passes the title, so as to enable the transferee or distributee to maintain an action on them; and the makers, in the absence of fraud, can not abate such an action for a want of authority to make the transfer.—Weider v. Osborn, 20 Or. 307, 25 Pac. 715. An administrator can not sell the property under administration to pay for improvements on land of the heirs, erected by some unauthorized person years after the decedent's death.—Cain Heirs v. Young, 1 Utah 361. A sheriff's certificate of sale is personal property and an executor as such has a right to assign it and a sale regularly so made transfers all the interest therein of the devisees under the will of which he is executor.—Winterberg v. Van De Vorste,

19 N. D. 417, 423, 122 N. W. 866; see, also, Boschker v. Van Beek, 19 N. D. 104, 122 N. W. 338.

3. **When sale is not authorized.**—Before a probate court, in Utah, is authorized to order an administrator to sell the lands of a decedent, two prerequisites must be observed: 1. There must be debts and charges against the estate unpaid; and 2. The personal property of the decedent must be insufficient to pay these debts and charges. Where, therefore, the petition for such a sale did not allege that there existed debts or charges against the estate unpaid, and did not allege that there was no personal property to pay such debts or charges, if any existed, there is no escape from the conclusion that the court had nothing before it to give it jurisdiction, and an order of sale based upon such petition is void.—Needham v. Salt Lake City, 7 Utah 319, 26 Pac. 920.

4. Petition for order.

(1) **In general.**—A petition for the order of sale of the estate of a decedent, for the purpose of paying debts, whether made by the executor, or administrator, or a judgment creditor, must set out all the facts required to be shown by the statute.—Prefontaine v. McMicken, 16 Wash. 16, 47 Pac. 231, 233. A substantial compliance with the statute is sufficient in setting forth the facts in the petition for an order of sale.—Estate of Arguello, 85 Cal. 151, 152, 24 Pac. 641; Richardson v. Butler, 82 Cal. 174, 16 Am. St. Rep. 101, 23 Pac. 9; Silverman v. Gundelfinger, 82 Cal. 548, 549, 23 Pac. 12; Estate of O'Sullivan, 84 Cal. 444, 447, 24 Pac. 281. The court gets jurisdiction, not merely by the actual existence of jurisdictional facts, but by their averment in the petition.—Holmes v. Oregon, etc., R. R. Co., 7 Saw. 380, 387, 9 Fed. 229; Wright v. Edwards, 10 Or. 298, 304. A petition for the sale of real property should show the facts required, since not only the judgment of the court is invoked to determine whether there shall be any sale, but also, if any, what property it is best for the interests of the heir should be sold.—Townsend v. Gordon, 19 Cal. 189, 208. The general rule that matters of substance must be alleged in direct terms, and not by way of recital or reference, much less by exhibits merely attached to the pleading, is applicable with equal force and propriety to petitions for the sale of real estate to pay debts and expenses of administration.—Estate of Cook, 137 Cal. 184, 186, 69 Pac. 968. The sufficiency of the particulars, in a petition for the sale of property, as to the condition of the property, must be determined by the circumstances of each case. Therefore, in a case where it is shown to be necessary to make a sale of some of the property of the estate for the purpose of paying claims against it, and the estate of the decedent consists of a single piece of real property, a court will require less particularity in the petition than where the estate comprises several pieces of property, and only one of such pieces is to be sold.—Estate of Devincenzi, 119 Cal. 498, 501, 51 Pac. 845, 846; Burris v. Kennedy, 108 Cal. 331, 41 Pac. 458. If the

court has, by the petition and notice, acquired jurisdiction, errors afterward made in the exercise of it will not render the decree invalid.—Burris v. Kennedy, 108 Cal. 331, 339, 41 Pac. 458.　The petition is sufficient if it substantially complies with the statute.—Plains L. & I. Co. v. Lynch, 38 Mont. 271, 279, 129 Am. St. Rep. 645, 99 Pac. 847.　The requirement of the Rev. Codes of Montana, that the "condition" and "value" of the real estate be set forth in the petition to sell such real property to pay debts, is not jurisdictional.—Plains L. & I. Co. v. Lynch, 38 Mont. 271, 284, 129 Am. St. Rep. 645, 99 Pac. 847.　In a petition to the probate court for leave to sell real estate, to pay debts, the vital parts are the allegation of the estate's indebtedness, the description of the property to be sold, and the verification.—Yeaton v. Barnhart, 78 Or. 249, 150 Pac. 742, 152 Pac. 1192.　Under the Oregon statute, requiring the petition for an order of sale to give the residences of the heirs and devisees, it is not sufficient to give merely the "address" of nonresident heirs who are served by publication; the term "address" is not equivalent to the term "residence."—Smith v. Whiting, 55 Or. 393, 401, 106 Pac. 791.

(2) Defects.　Mistakes.　Omissions.—A petition for the sale of the property of an estate is defective, and an order based thereon conveys no title, where there is no attempt at a statement of the condition of the property of the estate, nor of the value of the property asked to be sold, except a statement that it is of uncertain value, on account of litigation with reference thereto, and where the defects in the petition itself are not supplied by proofs at the hearing, and where the decree authorizing the sale does not state any general or other facts showing a necessity for the sale.—Estate of Rose, 63 Cal. 346, 348.　There is no difference between no petition at all, and a petition lacking the substantial averments required by statute.—Gregory v. McPherson, 13 Cal. 562, 578.　A petition may set forth inaccurately the amount of the personal property which has come to the hands of the administrator; it may even omit valuable portions thereof: yet, if it purports, on its face, to set forth the whole of such property, and how much of it, if any, remains undisposed of, the order for the sale which may follow can not be attacked by reason of the inaccuracies or omissions.—Haynes v. Meeks, 20 Cal. 288, 315.　When the petition states that the personal property of the estate which will be shown by the inventory is insufficient, this averment, though informal and indirect, is equivalent to saying that the personal estate mentioned in the inventory is still on hand, and therefore undisposed of.　No nice criticism of the mere form of statement for the purpose of ousting a court of jurisdiction will be made, where it is sought to declare its proceedings void.—Stuart v. Allen, 16 Cal. 473, 503, 76 Am. Dec. 551.　A recital in a petition for an order of sale as follows: "This petition respectfully represents that, in order to settle up the business of the estate of said deceased, to pay certain debts and demands due and owing by such estate," etc.,—is not a sufficient allegation that legal debts and legal charges exist

unpaid against the estate.—Needham v. Salt Lake City, 7 Utah 319, 26 Pac. 920. A mistake in the petition, in stating the amount of the estate, is not fatal to the jurisdiction, as not truly setting forth the condition of the estate, or the amount of the property, so as to present to the court the proper data by which it can judge of the portion necessary to be sold.—Fitch v. Miller, 20 Cal. 352, 383. The omission, in a petition for an order to sell real estate of a decedent, to state that the persons who were named in the petition as the devisees and legatees were also the heirs of the deceased, as appears from the order of sale, is not fatal to the validity of the order.—Estate of Levy, 141 Cal. 639, 645, 75 Pac. 317. No sale is invalid on account of the omission to state in the petition any of the matters enumerated in the statute, provided the general facts showing that the sale is necessary are proven and found. The facts showing that the sale is necessary are: that there are debts; that an allowance has been made for the support of the family, or that there are expenses of administration; and that there is not sufficient money in the hands of the administrator to pay them. Where such facts are alleged in the petition, even though erroneous, the decree is not void, nor the sale invalid on that ground.—Burris v. Kennedy, 108 Cal. 331, 340, 41 Pac. 458. Though there is no statement in the petition as to the "condition" of the real estate, such omission does not necessarily render the petition fatally defective; and "value" is sufficiently shown by the statement of a sum at which the property was appraised less than one year prior to the presentation of the petition.—Plains L. & I. Co. v. Lynch, 38 Mont. 271, 284, 129 Am. St. Rep. 645, 99 Pac. 847. The statute of Oregon aids defects in matters of procedure that do not go to the jurisdiction of the county court to make an order for the sale of property.—Howe v. Kern, 63 Or. 487, 498, 125 Pac. 834, 128 Pac. 818.

(3) **May be made when. Laches in filing.**—The administrator is justified in assuming that creditors will exhibit and prove their claims against the estate, and he is not required to wait until they do so before preparing to pay them. When he ascertains that the personal property will not be sufficient to pay the debts, he may then petition the court to sell the real estate.—Randel v. Randel, 64 Kan. 254, 67 Pac. 837. A creditor may petition the court for a sale of the land of the estate, where the administrator neglects to perform his duty, at least within a reasonable time after the claim is presented and filed.—Estate of Wiley, 138 Cal. 301, 307, 71 Pac. 441. An application for an order authorizing the sale of the real estate of a decedent should be refused, where there has been long delay preceding the filing of the petition without any satisfactory explanation.—Estate of Crosby, 55 Cal. 574, 588. The right to sell real property in a proceeding for the payment of expenses and charges of administration accrued and to accrue is not lost by laches, where the application is made upon the double necessity of redeeming the mortgaged premises from an existing lien, and to pay the "debts, expenses, and charges of the adminis-

tration accruing and to accrue."—Estate of Freud, 131 Cal. 667, 673, 82 Am. St. Rep. 407, 63 Pac. 1080. Gross negligence or palpable laches on the part of the executor or administrator is sufficient reason for denying an order of sale in a given case.—Estate of Crosby, 55 Cal. 574. No hard and fast rule has ever been promulgated defining what lapse of time in applying for a license to sell real property will amount to laches, and every case must necessarily be governed by its own particular facts and circumstances.—In re Smith's Will, 43 Or. 595, 75 Pac. 133. The rule that laches will, in some cases, defeat a creditor's application for the sale of property of the estate goes only to the extent that a probate court has discretionary power to deny a petition for the sale of real estate when there has been unreasonable delay without circumstances to excuse it.—Estate of Arguello, 85 Cal. 151, 154, 24 Pac. 641. An objection that there was an unreasonable delay in applying for the order of sale finds no support in facts showing a persistent and long-continued effort, on the part of the creditors, to bring the administrator to an accounting, and where litigation assumed so many phases and had been so protracted as to account for the delay which occurred.—Estate of Schroeder, 46 Cal. 305, 320. Laches in applying for an appointment as administrator, and for a license to sell real property, will not bar the right of the administrator to sell the realty, where delay in applying for letters of administration or license to sell has resulted in no such changes of ownership or physical conditions as to render it inequitable to sell, or where, by analogy to the statute of limitations prescribed in the jurisdiction, sufficient time has not run to bar the relief in the form proposed.—In re Smith's Will, 43 Or. 595, 75 Pac. 133. There is no limitation in the state of Oregon as to the time when a claim against the estate of a deceased person may be presented, nor as to when an application for an order of sale of real property for the purpose of paying debts, etc., may be made.—In re Houck's Estate, 23 Or. 10, 17 Pac. 461. Where a question of laches is in issue, the plaintiff is chargeable with such knowledge as he might have obtained upon inquiry, provided the facts already known to him were such as to put the duty of inquiry upon a man of ordinary intelligence.—Johnston v. Standard Mining Co., 148 U. S. 360, 37 L. Ed. 480, 13 Sup. Ct. 585.

REFERENCES.

Laches of executors or administrators in applying for orders authorizing them to sell property for the payment of debts.—See note 26 Am. St. Rep. 22-29.

(4) Parties to the proceeding.—The creditor of an heir is in no sense a necessary party to a proceeding in an estate for leave to sell.— Nichols v. Lee, 16 Colo. 147, 26 Pac. 157. Under the statute of New Mexico, the surviving wife is a party to the proceeding, where it is sought to sell lands of the decedent in which she has an interest, which are not susceptible of division; but in such case her interest should be ascertained, so that her rights at the sale may be protected without

putting her under the burden of protecting incidentally the rights of the creditors. And the proceedings to sell of real estate be joined in one suit with proceedings for the sale of real estate belonging to the decedent.—First Nat. Bank v. Lee, 8 N. M. 589, 45 Pac. 1114.

(5) **Necessity for sale.**—The necessity for a sale is not a matter for an executor or administrator to determine, but is a conclusion which the court must draw from the facts stated, and the petition must furnish the materials for its judgment.—Pryor v. Downey, 50 Cal. 388, 398, 19 Am. Rep. 656. The executor has no more right to sell personal estate than he has to sell real estate, unless necessary for its preservation, or to pay charges upon it; but there may be as great a necessity for selling it, for the purpose of marshaling the assets between the legatees, heirs, and devisees, as to pay debts.—Estate of Woodworth, 31 Cal. 595, 605. The facts showing that a sale is necessary are: that there are debts; that an allowance has been made for the support of the family, or that there are expenses of administration; and that there is not sufficient money in the hands of the executor or administrator to pay them.—Burris v. Kennedy, 108 Cal. 331, 339, 41 Pac. 458. It is not necessary to the right of the administrator to petition for, or to the power of the court to order, a sale, that there should first be a demand upon the administrator to sell. It is his duty to petition for a sale whenever a necessity arises under the statute. The creditor, or any one interested, may make application, if the administrator neglects to apply for the order.—Estate of Roach, 139 Cal. 17, 19, 72 Pac. 393. The statute in California does not make it necessary that an account of the executor's transactions shall be rendered and a final adjudication had upon it before the court can make an order for the sale of the real estate to meet the expenses of administration. It can not, therefore, be said that where an executor applies for an order apthorizing him to sell real property belonging to the estate of his testator for the purpose of satisfying a claim in his own favor, for services and expenses as executor, that an account should be first presented and settled. It is proper, and not premature, for the court to make an order of sale on finding a legal necessity for such sale.—Abila v. Burnett, 33 Cal. 658, 665. The description and condition of the property quite fully appear, and the necessity for a sale sufficiently appears, when it is shown that there are debts or expenses of administration, and that there is no money, or personal property, or income from which to meet these liabilities.—Estate of Roach, 139 Cal. 17, 21, 72 Pac. 393. A petition which discloses the nature, extent, and value of the personal property belonging to the estate, and contains a detailed statement of facts from which it sufficiently appears that the personal property is not sufficient to meet the claims and costs allowed against the estate, sufficiently shows the necessity for resorting to the real property.—Bateman v. Reitler, 16 Colo. 547, 36 Pac. 548. The question as to whether there was a necessity for a sale is one for the probate court to decide, and its unreversed decision, whether right or wrong,

1262 PROBATE LAW AND PRACTICE.

is absolutely binding upon the parties in a collateral attack thereon.—
Lake v. Hathaway, 75 Kan. 391, 89 Pac. 666. If the debts of the estate
appear to exceed in amount the available means at hand with which to
pay them, it may fairly be said to appear that a sale is necessary; and,
if real estate is to be sold, the court or judge may properly consult the
recitals of the petition as to the condition of the real estate to determine whether all or only a portion should be sold, and, if only a portion, then what particular portion.—Plains L. & L. Co. v. Lynch, 38
Mont. 271, 283, 129 Am. St. Rep. 645, 99 Pac. 847.

(6) Condition of property.—The court should be informed, by the
petition, of the condition of the property; that is, whether the property is improved or unimproved, productive or unproductive, occupied
or vacant, and the like. Such information is necessary to enable the
court to intelligently exercise its judgment in the selection of the property of the estate, which can be most advantageously sold. Where
the condition of the property is not stated, the petition is substantially
defective, and the provision found in the statute, as to supplying defects by proof at the hearing, has no application to a petition, the
sufficiency of which is directly attacked by general demurrer, or by
objection to its sufficiency, taken upon appeal from the order of sale.—
Estate of Smith, 51 Cal. 563, 565. An objection that the petition fails
to state the condition of the property will not be considered on appeal,
where such objection was not made in the court below, where the
petition states the jurisdictional facts required by the statute, and
where the attack is collateral and not direct.—Baum v. Roper, 132 Cal.
42, 48, 64 Pac. 128. In the case of mining property, which a guardian
seeks to sell for the interest of his ward's estate, it is not required that
the petition should set forth the condition of any property except that
which is to be sold. The manifest reason of this is, that the expediency of such sales is in no wise dependent upon the condition of other
portions of the estate.—Smith v. Biscailuz, 83 Cal. 344, 349, 21 Pac. 15,
23 Pac. 314.

(7) Description of property.—The sufficiency of a description of one
parcel of land does not cure defects of description as to other parcels;
for the statute requires that all of the real estate of the deceased
should be described.—Wilson v. Hastings, 66 Cal. 243, 245, 5 Pac. 217.
Where a petition for an order of sale describes the land as in "Township 29 N.," etc., instead of in "Township 25 N.," where the same is situated, and in connection with the statement that the land is in "Township 29 N," is the further statement that it is in "King County,"
in which said township is not situated, the description is fatally defective, and a sale under such petition is void.—Hazelton v. Bogardus, 8
Wash. 102, 35 Pac. 602. Where, in a contract for the sale of land, the
property is described as "the whole of the Redding ranch," purchased
by deed of a certain date, and the place of record of such deed is
specified, the description is sufficient; and where the land, so described

in a decree of distribution, has been distributed to the heirs of a deceased person, they have a marketable title thereto.—Bates v. Howard, 105 Cal. 173, 183, 38 Pac. 715.

(8) **Reference to other papers.**—Reference may be made in the petition to other papers to show the facts.—Wilson v. Hastings, 66 Cal. 243, 246, 5 Pac. 217. The petition may refer to the inventory for the description of the real property, and the inventory thereupon becomes a part of the petition for that purpose.—Richardson v. Butler, 82 Cal. 174, 178, 16 Am. St. Rep. 101, 23 Pac. 9. But a reference to the inventory in the petition for one purpose can not be taken as a reference for any other purpose to supply an omission of some necessary statement.—Townsend v. Gordon, 19 Cal. 189, 208. A petition for an order of sale may refer to the inventory for the description of the real estate to be sold; but where the inventory is deficient as to the description, the petition itself is insufficient to give the probate court jurisdiction to order a sale of the property.—Wilson v. Hastings, 66 Cal. 243, 246, 5 Pac. 217. See Stuart v. Allen, 16 Cal. 473, 76 Am. Dec. 551. Where a petition sufficiently shows to the court what the interest of the deceased in the land was at the time of his death, and contains, by reference to the inventory, a full description of all real property of the estate at the time the sale is asked, and gives to the court all the information on that subject contemplated by the code, the sale can not be held void for want of a sufficient description of the real property in the petition itself, apart from the inventory.—Richardson v. Butler, 82 Cal. 174, 179, 16 Am. St. Rep. 101, 23 Pac. 9. Schedules attached to the petition constitute a part thereof, and if, in the body of the petition, it is stated that the values and conditions of the realty are set forth in a particular schedule, naming it, and the only values there set forth are the appraised values, this, in the absence of special objection, is a sufficient statement as to present value.—Estate of Levy, 141 Cal. 639, 643, 75 Pac. 317. The requirement of the statute, that the facts prescribed shall be stated in the petition, is peremptory. If the petition refers to another paper on file, for the purpose of a more full and explicit statement of facts, that paper might be considered in connection with the petition, and both be taken together as a statement of all the required facts. But it is apparent that no such result can be attained, unless the petition itself make the reference. It is not sufficient for the administrator to file a separate paper, not a part of, nor referred to in, the petition, though this paper contains part of the facts which the statute requires the petition to state.—Gregory v. Taber, 19 Cal. 397, 410, 79 Am. Dec. 219. See Gregory v. McPherson, 13 Cal. 562, 573. A reference, "for greater certainty," without stating for what the reference is made, whether for description, or value, or condition, is an insufficient reference to make the inventory a part of the petition as to description, or value, or condition.—Wilson v. Hastings, 66 Cal. 243, 246, 5 Pac. 217. A reference to an inventory may be construed as justifying the omission to include in the petition a more particular

statement of personal effects than that made in it, but such reference does not make the inventory a part of the petition for any other purpose.—Townsend v. Gordon, 19 Cal. 188, 208. A petition for the sale of mining interests, referring to the inventory for a description of the real property, while sufficient as to the description, is defective in failing to set forth the condition and value of the estate, as required by the statute; if there is nothing in the petition, or the inventory and appraisement referred to therein, which indicates the condition of the mining interests, or of the mining company in which such interests are held, or of the mining claims, or whether they are being worked or are lying idle, or whether they are sources of profit or of loss to the estate.—Estate of Boland, 55 Cal. 310, 314.

(9) Verifying the petition.—A petition lacking a verification is invalid. The description of the property, its condition, value, and character, are jurisdictional facts, which must affirmatively appear in a verified petition, before a probate court can make any valid order for the sale of the real property of an estate to pay debts. These are of the essence of the petition, without which it has no legal existence.—Estate of Boland, 55 Cal. 310, 315. In the state of Washington, it has been held that a failure to verify the petition, which is the foundation of proceedings to sell real estate, is a mere irregularity; for, if the petition is in other respects sufficient, the court is given jurisdiction.—McCoy v. Ayers, 2 Wash. Ter. 203, 3 Pac. 273. Schedules attached to the petition are a part of it, and are included in the verification. An objection that the petition is not properly verified because the certificate of verification is placed before the schedules which were attached to it, is not tenable.—Richardson v. Butler, 82 Cal. 174, 180, 16 Am. St. Rep. 101, 23 Pac. 9.

(10) Amending the petition.—The petition must contain a general description of all the real property of which the decedent died seised; and if it does not contain any such description, it is error to make the order of sale on such petition, though amended, without further notice. The court should treat the petition, when amended, as a new petition, and proceed de novo.—Gharky v. Werner, 66 Cal. 388, 389, 5 Pac. 676. A petition based upon a former petition is, in effect, a continuation of a first application, where there was no revocation of the order made upon such first application, and the statute of limitations can not be considered as barring the subsequent proceeding, where the first application on which it was based is not barred.—Estate of Montgomery, 60 Cal. 645, 648.

(11) Defects cured by the order of sale.—If the petition substantially complies with the requirements of the code, it may be aided by the order of sale as to all the facts showing the sale to be necessary, and giving the court jurisdiction, if the defect is supplied by proofs at the hearing, and the general facts showing such necessity are stated in the decree.—Dennis v. Winter, 63 Cal. 16, 17. A defect in

the petition, which consists in the failure to state whether the real property was separate or community property, is remedied by the fact that it is stated in the order directing the sale that the property was separate property.—Estate of Arguello, 85 Cal. 151, 152, 24 Pac. 641. Under section 1537 of the Code of Civil Procedure of California, although the petition for the sale of the real estate is required to state "the condition and value thereof," yet the failure to make such statement will not invalidate the subsequent proceedings, if the defects be supplied at the hearing, and the general facts showing the necessity for the sale, or that it is for the advantage, benefit, and best interest of the estate and those interested therein, be stated in the decree.—Dane v. Layne, 10 Cal. App. 366, 101 Pac. 1067.

(12) Defects not cured by the order.—If the petition for the sale of real estate does not set forth the value of the real estate sought to be sold, the petition is fatally defective, and can not be cured by recitals in the order of sale, or by inferences to be drawn from the inventory and appraisement of the estate referred to in the petition generally, but not specifically, as to the lands or their value.—Estate of Cook, 137 Cal. 184, 190, 191, 69 Pac. 968. A petition in which the only recital upon the subject of condition and value of the land is, that it was an "unperfected claim under the homestead laws of Congress," and which does not state what the land was worth, whether it was improved or unimproved, productive or unproductive, occupied or vacant, nor any other information by which the court might intelligently have exercised its judgment that the property could be most advantageously sold, is fatally defective, and a sale thereof is void for want of jurisdiction in the court to order it.—Kertchem v. George, 78 Cal. 597, 599, 21 Pac. 372. A petition for an order of sale is fatally defective, where, with reference to personal property, there is no attempt to comply with the statute, and the court is left in entire ignorance as to the condition of the estate with respect to such property, information in respect to which is essential to its jurisdiction, and where, in respect to the real property asked to be sold, the petition does not show the condition of the land, whether it is improved or waste land, or whether it is yielding an income or is burdening the estate with expense, and does not purport to give a description of all the real estate of which the intestate died seised. The condition of the land that it is desired to sell should be stated so that the court may judge of the necessity of its sale.—Haynes v. Meeks, 20 Cal. 288, 317. See Estate of Boland, 55 Cal. 514; Janes v. Throckmorton, 57 Cal. 386.

(13) Creditor's petition.—A creditor of the estate of a decedent, whose claim has been allowed by the court, may petition for the sale of the real estate of such estate.—Estate of Couts, 87 Cal. 480, 481, 25 Pac. 685. When the proceeding for a sale is not instituted by the representative of the estate, but by a creditor, his standing, as

such, must be averred and shown, in order to qualify him to institute the proceeding; but, when the real estate of the decedent is sold under the decree, the proceeds are to be paid over to the executor or administrator for administration under the direction of the probate court. The allowance of an ordinary claim against the estate of a deceased person does not give the creditor any superior right or lien over the real estate, or the proceeds arising from the sale thereof, prior and superior to the rights of any other creditor whose claim against the estate may be allowed.—First Nat. Bank v. Lee, 8 N. M. 589, 45 Pac. 1114. A creditor of an estate, having a valid lien, may petition for an order of sale of the lands covered by the lien, and has the right, upon purchasing the property at the sale, to have the amount of his bid, less the necessary expenses of sale, credited on his claim by reason of his lien upon said lands.—Estate of Wiley, 138 Cal. 301, 303, 71 Pac. 441. The petition of a creditor, whose claim is secured by a lien upon specific property of the estate, to sell the land to enforce payment of the claim and lien, filed before the statute of limitations has expired, has the effect of arresting the further operation of the statute.—Estate of Wiley, 138 Cal. 301, 308, 71 Pac. 441. Where a creditor of the executor files a petition asking for an order requiring the executor to sell so much of the real estate as shall be necessary to pay his claim, and, upon the hearing, evidence upon every material allegation of his petition is introduced, it is error to grant a nonsuit, on motion of the devisees, upon the ground that the claim is against the executor; that, until he pays it and presents it in his account as an expense of administration, the court can not act upon it; that the order allowing the claim is void; and that the claim is barred by the statute of limitations.—Estate of Couts, 87 Cal. 480, 481, 25 Pac. 685.

5. Opposing the application.

(1) **In general.**—A grantee of one of the heirs of the deceased, being entitled, upon distribution of the estate, to the share of the heir so conveyed to him, is a person "interested" in the estate, and is entitled to oppose an application for an order of sale.—Estate of Steward, 1 Cal. App. 57, 60, 81 Pac. 728; Estate of Baum, 92 Cal. 192, 28 Pac. 221. The court is not bound to refuse an order of sale whenever it appears that the required money can be obtained by mortgage. It may inquire into the wisdom of mortgaging the property, and the means of payment thereof possessed by the heirs, and, if it appears that the distributees must inevitably lose the entire property at some time before default and foreclosure, in case a mortgage be made, unless they can make a sale of the property, the court does not err in finding that a sale is necessary.—Estate of Newlove, 142 Cal. 377, 382, 75 Pac. 1083. The provisions of the statute allowing objections to be made to the sale, and requiring, for its efficacy, a confirmation by the court, are intended to secure only such an execution of the order of sale that a just and fair price may be obtained for the

property for the benefit of the estate. The authority of the court is limited to such a supervision and control, that this end may be effected.—Estate of Spriggs, 20 Cal. 121, 126. The pendency of a suit involving title to a part of the real property is not, in itself, sufficient cause for refusing to make an order of sale; especially where the evidence taken concerning the merits of the action tends strongly to show that it was instituted in good faith. Whether a sale would impair the value of the land, under such circumstances, is a matter largely within the discretion of the court to determine.—Estate of Newlove, 142 Cal. 377, 382, 75 Pac. 1083. If one, who is in a position to object to an administrator's sale on the ground of irregularities, does not do so within the time therefor allowed by law, he can not object subsequently, unless the irregularity is one affecting the jurisdiction.— Entiat Delta O. Co. v. Unknown Heirs, 99 Wash. 84, 86, 168 Pac. 1130.

(2) **Demurrer to the petition.**—The point that a statement is insufficient, which is easily understood as an admitted statement of a particular fact, and is merely shadowed by some uncertainty or want of fullness or aptness of expression, can be reached only by a special demurrer or objection in the court below.—Estate of Heydenfeldt, 127 Cal. 456, 458, 59 Pac. 839; Estate of Levy, 141 Cal. 639, 643, 75 Pac. 317. See, also, Silverman v. Gundelfinger, 82 Cal. 548, 23 Pac. 12; Estate of Devincenzi, 119 Cal. 498, 500, 51 Pac. 845. Upon a special demurrer the court might require a little more certainty, where the value is informally alleged; but where there is not such a total want of a statement of values as renders the petition defenseless against a collateral attack, which is in the nature of an objection, in an ordinary civil action, that the complaint does not state facts sufficient to constitute a cause of action, the petition will be held sufficient.—Silverman v. Gundelfinger, 82 Cal. 548, 549, 23 Pac. 12. If a defect of parties plaintiff or defendant does not appear upon the face of the petition filed in a proceeding to sell, the objection may be taken by answer; but if no objection is taken, either by demurrer or by answer, the defendant is deemed to have waived the same.—Coulson v. Wing, 42 Kan. 507, 16 Am. St. Rep. 503, 22 Pac. 570. So far as the question of the insufficiency of the petition is concerned, an appellant occupies a no more advantageous position by reason of the filing of a general demurrer, than he would have occupied had he presented no demurrer and simply appealed from the order of sale. In either event the question for determination is as to whether or not the petition is substantially defective in any of the requirements of the code.—Estate of Levy, 141 Cal. 639, 642, 75 Pac. 317. The provision of the statute, that a failure to set out the necessary facts in the petition will not invalidate the subsequent proceedings, if the defects are supplied by proof at the hearing and stated in the decree, has no applicability to a petition, the insufficiency of which is directly attacked by general demurrer in the probate court, or by objection to its sufficiency taken upon appeal from the order of sale.—Estate of Smith, 51 Cal. 563,

565; Estate of Boland, 55 Cal. 310, 315; Estate of Cook, 137 Cal. 184, 188, 69 Pac. 968.

6. Sale for payment of debts.

(1) In general.—One prominent purpose of administration is to pay the debts of the estate from the real and personal property of the deceased. To sell real estate to pay the debts is as plainly a step in the administration as is the sale of personal property for the same purpose; and while it is within the scope of the administration to sell either real or personal property, yet the legislature has the power to direct how this shall be done.—Burris v. Kennedy, 108 Cal. 331, 338, 41 Pac. 458. An order for the sale of certain personal property to pay debts, set forth in a schedule of claims against the estate, is not a determination that the claim is a valid debt due from the estate.—Estate of Wells, 7 Cal. App. 515, 94 Pac. 856, 858. An executor or an administrator can not be compelled, by a probate court, to sell the real estate of a decedent which has been distributed by order of the proper court, to pay debts established after such distribution. It is only property in the hands of the personal representative that can be sold by him, and such sale must be made in accordance with the statute.—Prefontaine v. McMicken, 16 Wash. 16, 47 Pac. 231, 233. A probate court does not have any authority to order a sale of the homestead for the purpose of paying debts of the deceased, although they are secured by a valid mortgage on the same.—Estate of Orr, 29 Cal. 101, 104. While it is the duty of the administrator to preserve the estate, yet this does not mean that he is, at his discretion, to pay off all incumbrances resting on the property, upon the notion that the property may increase in value, and that thereby a speculation may be made for the estate. He can not advance money to remove incumbrances, unless his intestate was bound to pay the money.— Estate of Knight, 12 Cal. 200, 207, 73 Am. Dec. 531. A sale may be ordered when necessary to meet the prospective charges or expenses, though there be no debts or expenses of administration accrued and unpaid at the time the application is made.—Richardson v. Butler, 82 Cal. 174, 179, 16 Am. St. Rep. 101, 23 Pac. 9; Estate of Freud, 131 Cal. 667, 670, 82 Am. St. Rep. 407, 63 Pac. 1080. The executor or administrator has power to use the money in his hands for the purpose of redeeming property of the estate from liens existing on it.—Estate of Freud, 131 Cal. 667, 671, 82 Am. St. Rep. 407, 63 Pac. 1080. This power arises from the general character of the executor or administrator as a trustee charged with the duty of preserving the property of the estate.—Estate of Smith, 118 Cal. 462, 466, 50 Pac. 701; Estate of Freud, 131 Cal. 667, 671, 82 Am. St. Rep. 407, 63 Pac. 1080; Burnett v. Lyford, 93 Cal. 114, 118, 119, 28 Pac. 855. The same principle applies in the case of taxes, tax sales, etc.—People v. Olvera, 43 Cal. 492, 494; Weinreich v. Hensley, 121 Cal. 647, 657, 54 Pac. 254. And in cases of cattle or horses impounded and held for the expense of pasture.— Estate of Armstrong, 125 Cal. 603, 605, 58 Pac. 183. But the principle

does not apply where the lien is not a charge against the estate, and no part of it could ever be paid out of the estate.—Tompkins v. Weeks, 26 Cal. 50, 60. Under the Washington statute, funeral expenses are a debt against the estate, and may be given preference in payment.—In re Smith's Estate, 25 Wash. 93, 66 Pac. 93. The probate court has no authority to reach out and dispose of property belonging to the heirs of the decedent, which is in no respect subject to the debts or the liabilities of such decedent.—Coulson v. Wing, 42 Kan. 507, 16 Am. St. Rep. 503, 22 Pac. 570. An administrator is not entitled to distribute money received on the compromise of a claim by the estate against another and then have the real estate sold for the payment of debts and expenses.—Randolph v. Prowers, 21 Colo. App. 541, 122 Pac. 804, 808. Where a petition for the sale of the lands of an estate in Kansas showed that the executrix had been appointed more than five years; where the estate had not reached final settlement; and where the petition contained no allegations of unpaid debts, it will not be presumed that the sale of the land was necessary for the payment of debts.—Strom v. Wood, 100 Kan. 556, 561, 164 Pac. 1100, 1102.

REFERENCES.

Order of payment of debts provided for by will.—See § 570, ante. Payment of debts provided for by will, where the fund or estate appropriated therefor is insufficient to pay.—See § 573, ante. Order or resort to the property of the testator for the payment of debts.— See §§ 570, 573, 574, ante.

(2) **Limitations. Contesting debts.**—There being no statute of limitations provided with regard to a proceeding instituted in the probate court for the sale of real estate to pay debts of the testator, the requirement of the law is that such a proceeding can be maintained only if begun within a reasonable time, in view of all the circumstances of the case.—In re Jones's Estate (Thomas v. Williams), 80 Kan. 632, 25 L. R. A. (N. S.) 1304, 103 Pac. 772. Upon an application to sell real estate to pay debts, the heir can dispute the validity of the claims allowed, and to pay which the application is made. The petition to sell the real estate of an intestate is the substitute, under our system, for an action against the heir at common law. The heir is required to be cited, and is allowed to be heard. The hearing amounts to a re-examination of the claim, to test its validity as against the heir, and to produce or to prevent a decree for the sale of the land. If the claim is not valid, then, of course, the land ought not to be sold, if the application is made for the purpose of meeting such claim.— Beckett v. Selover, 7 Cal. 215, 229, 68 Am. Dec. 237. See Estate of Schroeder, 46 Cal. 305, 318. Upon this question, it has been held that the allowance by the administrator, and the approval by the probate judge, of a claim against the estate is a quasi-judgment, and, in attacking it, the burden of proof is on the heir.—Hillebrant v. Burton, 17 Tex. 138; approved in Estate of Schroeder, 46 Cal. 305, 319. "Allow-

ance" is only prima facie proof of the validity of the claim; therefore, on an application to sell, the heir may dispute the claims, upon which the petition is based, although they have been allowed by the executor or administrator and probate judge.—Wingerter v. Wingerter, 71 Cal. 105, 111, 11 Pac. 853. See Beckett v. Selover, 7 Cal. 215, 68 Am. Dec. 237. A judgment, in the state of Kansas, against the executor, in favor of a creditor, although binding upon the personalty, is not necessarily binding upon the heirs to the extent of subjecting the real estate descended to them for the satisfaction of any such judgment. Before there can be a valid order devesting them of their title by a sale for the payment of debts, the heirs must have an opportunity to be heard, and to contest not only the necessity or propriety of the sale, but also the justice and validity of the debts for the payment of which the sale is demanded.—Black v. Elliott, 63 Kan. 211, 88 Am. St. Rep. 239, 65 Pac. 215; following Bauserman v. Charlott, 46 Kan. 480, 26 Pac. 1051, and Kulp v. Kulp, 51 Kan. 341, 21 L. R. A. 550, 32 Pac. 1118. See, also, O'Flynn v. Powers, 136 N. Y. 419, 32 N. E. 1087.

REFERENCES.

Laches in applying for orders to pay debts.—See note, 26 Am. St. Rep. 22.

(3) "Demand." When not a debt or claim.—A demand against an estate, based on an instrument upon which the testator never could be made liable, is not a "claim" against the estate, within the meaning of the statute conferring power upon administrators, with license from the proper court, to sell the real estate of decedents to pay claims against their estates in the event of a deficiency of personal assets.—Weill v. Clark's Estate, 9 Or. 387, 391. See, also, Walker v. Diehl, 79 Ill. 473, and Gray v. Palmer, 9 Cal. 616.

(4) Expenses of administration.—The provisions of the statute which authorizes a sale of the property of a decedent for certain purposes are maintained to afford to creditors of the executors, as well as creditors of the decedent, the means of securing payment of their claims against the estate, and necessarily contemplate expenses of administration which the executor neglects or refuses to pay.—Estate of Couts, 87 Cal. 480, 482, 25 Pac. 685. It is error for the court to order a sale of property to meet expenses, on petition of a local administrator of the estate of a non-resident decedent, when the trustee under the will of such decedent offers to deposit in court sufficient money to meet these expenses.—Estate of Rawitzer, 175 Cal. 585, 166 Pac. 581, 584.

(5) Procedure.—In proceedings to sell the real property of a decedent for the payment of debts, parol testimony is not admissible to prove the personal service of citation upon resident heirs.—Smith v. Whiting, 55 Or. 393, 402, 106 Pac. 791. In a proceeding for the sale of a decedent's real property to pay debts, non-resident heirs or

devisees may be served by publication.—Smith v. Whiting, 55 Or. 393, 401, 106 Pac. 791. In the case of the petition of an executor or administrator for an order to sell real estate to pay debts, it is jurisdictional that the order provide for the heirs and next of kin to be given ten days from the day of the service of the citation to appear and show cause, if any they have, why the sale should not be made.—Stadelman v. Miner, 83 Or. 348, 155 Pac. 708, 163 Pac. 585, 983.

(6) Power to order sale.—An offer to furnish a bond conditioned to pay the debts mentioned in the application for an order of sale for the payment of debts, does not deprive the court of authority to order a sale.—McLeod v. Butts (Butts v. McLeod), 89 Kan. 785, 132 Pac. 1174, 1175. The statutes of Oregon do not do away with the lack of jurisdiction of the court to order a sale of real estate to pay debts of the estate, when the order fails to provide for the giving to the heirs and next of kin ten days from the day of the service of the citation, within which to appear and show cause why the sale should not be made.— Stadelman v. Miner, 83 Or. 348, 155 Pac. 708, 163 Pac. 585, 983. When an administrator's sale of real estate to pay debts is void, for lack of jurisdiction of the court ordering it, the legislature can not transfer to the purchaser, where he is not in actual posession, title by lapse of time alone.—Stadelman v. Miner, 83 Or. 348, 155 Pac. 708, 163 Pac. 585, 983.

7. Sale to pay funeral expenses.—An executor may petition for a sale of the real property in order to meet the expense of erecting a monument over the grave of the deceased person, pursuant to a provision in the will. The expense, in such a case, is included in funeral expenses.—Estate of Koppikus, 1 Cal. App. 84, 81 Pac. 732; Van Emon v. Superior Court, 76 Cal. 589, 9 Am. St. Rep. 258, 18 Pac. 877.

8. Specific devises to contribute to payment of debts.—Under the statute of Oregon, if any article of personal property has been specially bequeathed, it is exonerated from the operation of the order of sale until resort thereto becomes necessary for the payment of claims, by reason of a deficiency, in the proceeds of the sale of other property.—In re Noon's Estate, 49 Or. 286, 88 Pac. 673, 675, 90 Pac. 673. A devise made in the will for the payment of an indebtedness due from the testator is required to contribute with the other devises to the payment of the debts of the estate and charges of administration. There is no exception made in the statute as to such devise.—Estate of Thayer, 142 Cal. 453, 456, 76 Pac. 453. The remedy of a legatee, whose special bequest is applied to the payment of a claim, where there are other special bequests which would bear their proportion in the payment of a debt, is to seek contribution from the legatees of such other bequests.—Estate of Moulton, 48 Cal. 191, 192. Where there is no personal property in an estate and all the real property is specifically devised the rule that such land can not be sold for the payment of debts and expenses of administration has no application.—Howe v. Kern, 63 Or. 487, 128 Pac. 820. If different lots of land have been

specifically devised, without any preference of one over the other, each is exempt from sale, under the Oregon statute, so long as any property not specifically devised remains unsold; but when the property last named is· exhausted, all the lots are equally liable for the funeral expenses, debts of the estate, and expenses of administration, and either may be resorted to for the payment of such claims or liabilities.—Howe v. Kern, 63 Or. 487, 496, 500, 125 Pac. 834, 128 Pac. 818. Where specific devises of different lots of land were of equal rank, and one lot was ordered to be sold for debts for which it was liable, the fact that more property was included in such order than was necessary to pay such debts, or that a part of the proceeds of such sale was applied to claims for which such lot was not liable, does not invalidate the sale.—Howe v. Kern, 63 Or. 487, 497, 125 Pac. 834, 128 Pac. 818. It is not an abuse of discretion to deny an application for a sale of specifically devised real property for the purpose of paying the only claim against the estate of the deceased notwithstanding that there is no other property immediately available for such purpose, where it appears that the result of certain pending litigation for the recovery of property claimed to belong to the estate may be such as to render a sale of such devised land unnecessary.—Estate of Braff, 166 Cal. 103, 134 Pac. 1140.

REFERENCES.

Devises or legacies, when subject to and when exempt from payment of debts of administration.—See § 574, ante. Contribution among legatees for the payment of debts, expenses of administration, etc.— See § 575, ante.

9. Sale to pay legacies.—The probate court is not bound to decree a sale of the assets of an estate for the payment of legacies until there is an ascertained balance of assets, real or personal, in the hands of the executor or administrator. If the assets are merely claimed to exist, and the right to them is involved in litigation, either by an action brought by the executor or administrator to recover them for the estate, or by an action against the executor or administrator to recover them from the estate, then the estate is not ready for distribution, and the probate court, in the exercise of judicial discretion, may delay the distribution until the right to the assets is judicially determined, and the balance for distribution ascertained.—Estate of Ricaud, 57 Cal. 421, 423.

REFERENCES.

Order of resort to the property of the testator for the payment of legacies.—See § 709, post.

10. Sale for best interests of the estate.—The California statute, which authorizes the property of a decedent to be sold, whether real or personal property, where it appears to be for the advantage, benefit, or best interests of the estate, is constitutional and valid.—Estate

of Porter, 129 Cal. 86, 87, 79 Am. St. Rep. 78, 61 Pac. 659. The
provisions of section 1536 of the Code of Civil Procedure of California,
as amended in 1893, in so far as they authorize a sale "for the advantage, benefit, and best interests of the estate," are unconstitutional as
to titles that vested prior to such amendment, but such a sale is valid
as to titles which vested subsequently to that amendment.—Gutter v.
Dallamore, 144 Cal. 665, 668, 79. Pac. 383. An amendment to the code,
authorizing a sale to be made when it appears to be for the advantage, benefit, and best interest of the estate, can not affect the title
to the land vested in the heirs at the death of the decedent, which
occurred prior to the enactment of such amendment; the right of
the heirs is subject only to such powers to order a sale in the course
of administration as were possessed by the court at the time of testator's decease, and are unaffected by subsequent legislation giving the
power of sale for new purposes different from and greater than those
conferred by the law in force at the death of the deceased.—Estate of
Newlove, 142 Cal. 377, 380, 75 Pac. 1083. Whether it be for the advantage, benefit, and best interests of the estate, or those interested
therein, to order a sale of more than one parcel of real estate, is a
question of fact to be determined by the court upon the evidence before it in reference thereto; and to the extent that its decision depends
upon inferences to be drawn from the situation of the property, or
of the parties who are interested therein, it is not open to review.—
Estate of Steward, 1 Cal. App. 57, 81 Pac. 728. Upon the death of the
ancestor, the property of the intestate at once vests in the heir; it
vests subject to conditions imposed by the statute, such as the qualified possession and control of the administrator, under the direction of
the court, for its care and its appropriation to the payment of the
debts of the decedent, expenses of administration, and other liabilities
enumerated in the statute; but, as the right of the heir to inherit the
estate is itself a creature of the statute, there can be no question as to
the power to impose these liabilities upon the estate, subject to which
the property vests in the heir. Directions for the control of the estate
have no other basis than that of the preservation of the best interests
of those in whom the statute vests the right of property. An amendment to a statute adding, as a ground upon which an order of sale
may be made, the following: "Or when it appears to the satisfaction
of the court that it is for the advantage, benefit, and best interests of
the estate, and those interested therein, that the real estate, or some
part thereof, be sold, the executor or administrator may sell any real
as well as personal property of the estate upon an order of the court,"
is not unconstitutional, and where a testator died after the enactment
of such amendment to the code, the court may order a sale, upon the
ground mentioned in such amendment, under such circumstances that
the consent of the owner, if he were capable of giving it, would be
presumed.—Estate of Porter, 129 Cal. 86, 99, 79 Am. St. Rep. 78, 61
Pac. 659. The amendment of 1893 to sections 1536 and 1545 of the

California Code of Civil Procedure, authorizing a sale of the real property forming part of the estate of a decedent, when it is for the best interests of the heirs that a sale should be had, was prospective only in its effect, and did not authorize a sale for this cause of real estate, or interests therein, held by the decedent at his death, where such death occurred prior to the enactment of the amendment.—Estate of Bazzuro, 161 Cal. 71, 118 Pac. 434. This rule is inapplicable as to real property, the title to which was acquired by the administrator of the estate, subsequent to the death of the deceased, under a foreclosure of a mortgage belonging to the deceased at the time of his death. The title to the interest of the heirs in the mortgage indebtedness, which was the consideration for the deed to the administrator, vested in them as personal property, at the death of the decedent, and was then subject to sale as such, under section 1523 of the Code of Civil Procedure of California, if such sale was for the best interest of the estate, whether necessary to pay debts or not.—Estate of Bazzuro, 161 Cal. 72, 118 Pac. 434. The basis and reason of this rule is that the title had vested in the heirs before the law was enacted, and that, because of constitutional limitations to legislative power over vested rights, such title could not be impaired or burdened by subsequent legislation imposing burdens not before existing.—Estate of Bazzuro, 161 Cal. 72, 118 Pac. 434.

11. Order to show cause. Notice of hearing.

(1) In general.—The absence of any order to show cause, and of any service of the notice upon all persons interested in the estate, as provided by statute, is fatal to the validity of the sale.—Campbell v. Drais, 125 Cal. 253, 258, 57 Pac. 994. The court may proceed at once, on completion of the publication of the order, at the time named in the order. It is not required that thirty days shall have elapsed after the completion of publication of the order to show cause before the court has jurisdiction of persons interested in the estate, even though some of such persons reside in a foreign country. There is no analogy between this method of obtaining jurisdiction of the person in probate proceedings, and by the publication of summons in ordinary civil actions.—Estate of Roach, 139 Cal. 17, 21, 72 Pac. 393. The posting of a notice on the twelfth day of July, giving notice of a hearing of the petition on the twenty-second day of the same month, is sufficient as a ten-day notice.—Bates v. Howard, 105 Cal. 173, 182, 38 Pac. 715. An administrator's deed is void, even upon a collateral attack, if there was no notice to the heirs of the time and place at which the application to sell real estate to pay debts could be heard.—Chicago, etc., R. Co. v. Cook, 43 Kan. 83, 22 Pac. 988. See Mickel v. Hicks, 19 Kan. 578, 27 Am. Rep. 161. An order to show cause why a sale should not be granted, directed only "to all persons interested," is not required to be addressed to the heirs of the deceased by name. While it would be proper to name the parties interested, where the same are

known, yet it has been held by the supreme court, in the state of Washington, that it is not essential, under existing legislation.—Furth v. United States, etc., Trust Co., 13 Wash. 73, 42 Pac. 523. Nor is it required, under the Washington statute, that an order for the publication of the notice, with the designation of the particular newspaper, shall be contained in the order to show cause why a sale should not be granted.—Furth v. United States, etc., Trust Co., 13 Wash. 73, 42 Pac. 523. Upon the hearing of a petition by an administrator for an order of sale of real estate to pay judgments, and costs, and expenses of administration, an objection was made to the introduction in evidence of the said judgments, on the ground that they had not been filed in time, and because of omissions which were supplied by amendments made some years after the judgments were rendered, and before the hearing; but it was held that the provision as to the time of filing was merely directory; that the amendments in the judgments were to correct clerical errors and misprisions by the record itself; and that the court did not exceed its powers in permitting the amendments.—Estate of Schroeder, 46 Cal. 305, 316. Under the Kansas statute relating to proceedings of the probate court for the sale of lands of decedents, the court has full authority and discretion to fix the time of the notice as it sees fit, and, in doing so, is in no wise restricted by law. The defect in the notice must have rendered the proceedings void in order to avail the heir, upon collateral attack, in an action of ejectment.—Thompson v. Burge, 60 Kan. 549, 72 Am. St. Rep. 369, 57 Pac. 110. See, also, Wyant v. Tuthill, 17 Neb. 495, 23 N. W. 342. If the clerk enters in the minute-book, at length, an order to show cause why real estate should not be sold, such entry, though the order purports to have been signed by the judge, is evidence that the order was made, as such signature may be treated as surplusage; and there is no requirement that the clerk shall recite that the order was made. —Plains L. & I. Co. v. Lynch, 38 Mont. 271, 285, 129 Am. St. Rep. 645, 99 Pac. 847. An administrator's deed executed by order of the probate court, when made by statute presumptive evidence that the administrator in all respects observed the directions and complied with the requisites of the law, is prima facie evidence that the court made an order, which was complied with, requiring the giving of a notice of the hearing of the application for an order of sale and that in all respects the proceedings on which the deed was based were regular.— Rust v. Rutherford, 101 Kan. 495, 496, 167 Pac. 1056.

(2) Service of notice.—Where objection is made that the order of sale is void because there was no service of the order to show cause entered, after the filing of the petition, upon the minor heirs, and it is urged that the appointment of the guardian ad litem was made on the same day on which the order of sale was entered, the act of the court and of the guardian in making a sale can not be held void, because the statute does not prescribe that service must be made of a copy of the order before such appointment, and the statute is silent as

to the time of the appointment.—Stuart v. Allen, 16 Cal. 473, 504, 76 Am. Dec. 551. The order to show cause must be personally served at least ten days before the hearing, on all persons interested, etc., or be published in some newspaper, as the court may direct. If all persons interested join in the petition for the sale, or assent in writing thereto, the notice may be dispensed with, and the hearing had at any time. The language of the statute, that the appearance of an appointed attorney "is sufficient proof of the service of the notice on the parties he is appointed to represent," implies that there must be notice to the parties and proof of the service of such notice, and merely means that after such service the "appearance" of the attorney, under certain circumstances, may be taken as sufficient proof of the fact of service. But where it affirmatively appears that there was neither notice nor service, there is no jurisdiction. The attorney can not waive both notice and service.—Campbell v. Drais, 125 Cal. 253, 258, 57 Pac. 994. An attorney for minor heirs can represent them only in a proceeding which has been duly inaugurated, and in which the court has already jurisdiction of the minors by such service of summons or notice as the code provides. Therefore he has no authority to represent them in a proceeding to sell the real estate of a decedent until after the court has obtained jurisdiction of their persons by the service of notice upon them. He can not waive such notice, nor by any of his acts invest the court with jurisdiction of their persons, which it has not already acquired.—Campbell v. Drais, 125 Cal. 253, 258, 57 Pac. 994. The statutory provisions of the state of Oregon inhibit the sale of real property of an estate except upon an order made afer a hearing to which the heirs and devisees have been duly cited to appear in the manner and form required, and when, as the result of such hearing, it has been judicially determined and a finding made that the proceeds of the sale of the personal property have been exhausted and there are claims against the estate unsatisfied, rendering the sale necessary. —Smith v. Whiting, 55 Or. 393, 106 Pac. 793.

12. Hearing.

(1) Demand for jury trial of issues.—Where a demand for a trial by jury of the issues raised upon an opposition to the executor's petition to sell real property belonging to the estate to pay debts, etc., was made in the lower court only in the objections filed, and not by a written demand for a trial by jury as required by the statute, and so far as the record shows, the demand was never called to the attention of the court or judge until the hearing began, a trial by jury was properly denied, no matter what the issues were.—In re Tuohy's Estate, 33 Mont. 230, 83 Pac. 486.

(2) Questions not considered.—Upon an application for an order to sell property, the court will not hear and determine a question of heirship. Such fact may be determined at the final settlement of the estate, in proceedings connected therewith. When parties appear,

claiming to be heirs of the intestate, they should be permitted to show any relevant and pertinent cause why a sale of the real property should not be made in accordance with the petition, without questioning their heirship.—In re Houck's Estate, 23 Or. 10, 17 Pac. 461. In the settlement of an estate the widow who with other interested persons has stipulated for the sale of an item of the personalty, and for an order of court directing the sale to be made and the manner thereof, can not complain afterwards that her bid at the sale was not considered, if the sale as made was for a large sum in excess of her bid, and the latter was not submitted in accordance with the directions.—In re Finn's Estate, Finn v. Finn (Wash.), 178 Pac. 449.

(3) **Findings.**—It has never been definitely determined that findings are necessary in probate orders, such as an order for the sale of real property; but where the record does not show that findings were not waived, the error, if any, is immaterial.—Estate of Arguello, 85 Cal. 151, 153, 24 Pac. 641. See Reynolds v. Brumagim, 54 Cal. 258; Estate of Crosby, 55 Cal. 574; Estate of Sanderson, 74 Cal. 199, 15 Pac. 753; Campbell v. Coburn, 77 Cal. 36, 18 Pac. 860. A finding, in a former proceeding, which is not necessary to the judgment in that proceeding, can not operate as an estoppel as against any one in a subsequent proceeding upon an application for an order to sell real estate for the payment of debts and costs of administration.—Estate of Heydenfeldt, 127 Cal. 456, 59 Pac. 839. See Lillis v. Emigrant Ditch Co., 95 Cal. 553, 30 Pac. 1108.

13. Notice after appeal.—After the remittitur of the appellate court has been filed in the probate court, the last-named court is at liberty to hear and dispose of a petition upon such notice as may be provided by its general rules, or as it may deem reasonable in the particular case; and, unless it should be made to appear that it has abused its discretion in this respect, or that the parties entitled thereto have been prevented from having a hearing, its action will not be set aside. It is not necessary for the court below, after reversal of its former order, again to give the notice required by the statute, where it originally complied with the requirements of the statute, and had obtained jurisdiction in the matter and over all persons interested therein. The court's subsequent action upon the petition is a movement within its jurisdiction, to be reversed only for some error in law which might be shown upon a direct appeal.—Estate of Couts, 100 Cal. 400, 403, 34 Pac. 865.

14. Order of sale.

(1) **In general.**—An order of sale, after notice to all parties interested, and after examination of the proofs presented, is an adjudication of the court that the sale of the property described is necessary. From this order the administrator, and any person interested in the estate, may appeal, but, unless taken, the order is conclusive and binding upon them.—Estate of Spriggs, 20 Cal. 121, 125. An order for the

sale of real estate is not one made in the pre-existing proceeding, in which the court has already acquired jurisdiction, but it is in reality a judgment in a new, separate, and independent proceeding; depending for its validity upon the sufficiency of the facts contained in the petition.—Ethell v. Nichols, 1 Idaho 741, 745. It is not necessary to particularize, in an order for the sale of a decedent's property, items constituting the debts and expenses of administration accrued and to accrue.—Estate of Roach, 139 Cal. 17, 21, 72 Pac. 393. The order of sale imports a finding of the truth of the general facts showing that the sale is necessary, and that evidence of that effect was given at the hearing.—Burris v. Kennedy, 108 Cal. 331, 339, 41 Pac. 458. It will be presumed that the evidence sustains the findings and the order, where the court finds that outstanding debts existed, and that there were charges of administration accrued and to accrue.—Estate of Roach, 139 Cal. 17, 21, 72 Pac. 393. The order of sale can not be obviated, nor can its efficacy be impaired, by the fact that it may subsequently appear that too low an estimate was placed by the court upon the value of the property ordered to be sold, or as to the price it would bring.—Estate of Spriggs, 20 Cal. 121, 125. The order for a sale of perishable personal property is not required to state that such property was "perishable property, and liable to assessment and taxation," inasmuch as such statements are not necessary to the order, and are in truth, mere surplusage.—Halleck v. Moss, 22 Cal. 266, 275. The order for the sale and the order of confirmation are both judicial acts. The sale is a judicial sale, and therefore not within the statute of frauds.—Halleck v. Guy, 9 Cal. 181, 196, 70 Am. Dec. 643. The executors of the estate of a deceased person have no authority to sell and transfer notes belonging to the deceased. They are assets of the estate which can be sold only under and by an order of the probate court having jurisdiction of said estate.—Jones v. Wheeler, 23 Okla. 771, 101 Pac. 1112. The court may make its order of sale in the alternative; it may grant authority to sell either at public or private sale. —Plains L. & I. Co. v. Lynch, 38 Mont. 271, 285, 129 Am. St. Rep. 645, 99 Pac. 847.

(2) Validity of.—It would be better practice for the court, in all cases where there are several distinct parcels of property, to insert in its order a direction that the sale cease when the amount required has been obtained; but the omission of such a direction can not invalidate the order or the sales made in pursuance of it.—Estate of Spriggs, 20 Cal. 121, 125. The principle that no sale can be had without the order of the court applies also to claims of causes of action existing in favor of the estate. So where an executrix, appointed in another state, attempted to assign and transfer to the plaintiff, by an instrument in writing executed by her as such executrix, presumably in such foreign state, all the claim and cause of action of said estate, under instruments of writing held by the estate against the plaintiff, it was held that such transfer and assignment, without authority of the probate

court, was invalid, the presumption being that the laws of such foreign state, prohibiting probate sales without order of court, are the same as the laws of this state, in the absence of evidence to the contrary.—Bovard v. Dickenson, 131 Cal. 162, 164, 63 Pac. 162. See, also, Wickersham v. Johnson, 104 Cal. 407, 43 Am. St. Rep. 118, 38 Pac. 89; Rankin v. Newman, 114 Cal. 635, 660, 34 L. R. A. 265, 46 Pac. 742. The provision of the statute declaring that no sale of any property of an estate shall be valid unless made upon an order of the probate court applies only to sales by executors and administrators. It has no reference to judicial sales under the decrees of the district courts, nor to sales in pursuance of testamentary authority.—Fallon v. Butler, 21 Cal. 24, 31, 81 Am. Dec. 140. See Larco v. Casaneuava, 30 Cal. 561, 567. An order of sale, where it appears that the person applying for the order never had letters issued to him, and never qualified as administrator, is void, and a statute passed for the purpose of curing defects of form, omissions, or errors, etc., is without effect, in so far as it attempts to validate such judgment or order.—Pryor v. Downey, 50 Cal. 388, 398, 19 Am. Rep. 656. Where the order of sale provides "that such sale shall cease when an amount not less than $10,000 and not exceeding $11,000 has been obtained," such provision does not render the whole order void.—Richardson v. Butler, 82 Cal. 174, 180, 16 Am. St. Rep. 101, 23 Pac. 9. An order of sale providing for the sale of other property before a sale is made of a particular lot or tract described therein, is in conformity with the requirements of the Washington code, and a sale of the property that was last to be resorted to will not be set aside, where it appears that the administrator complied with the order by first offering the other property for sale in the manner provided.—In re Bryant's Estate, 38 Wash. 337, 80 Pac. 555. Under section 1537 of the Code of Civil Procedure of California, a sale is not invalid for failure of the petition to state the "condition and value" of the property or any other matters enumerated to be stated, provided facts showing the necessity of a sale are proved and found.—Dane v. Layne, 10 Cal. App. 366, 101 Pac. 1067. The misnumbering of the "Range" in which the section lies, in an order for a license to sell real estate, is not a jurisdictional defect, so as to render the sale void, the correct number having been given in the petition, the order, and notice of hearing on petition, the report of sale, and in the order confirming the sale, and the error having been formally corrected after due notice to all persons concerned.—Cathro v. McArthur, 30 N. D. 337, 340, 152 N. W. 686. An administrator's sale, valid under the statute, does not contemplate any sort of a condition annexed to the payment; the latter must be absolute.—Estate of Bradley, 168 Cal. 655, 144 Pac. 136. A mere clerical error in writing in the wrong range in a description of land in the order of sale, is to be disregarded, where but one piece of land is involved, where no one was misled by the mistake, and where the heirs reaped the benefit.—Plains L. & I. Co. v. Lynch, 38 Mont. 271, 289, 129 Am. St. Rep. 645, 99 Pac. 847. The service of a citation upon the heirs and devisees is mandatory, before the real property of a decedent can be sold, where the proceeds of the sale of personal property have been exhausted and the charges, expenses, and claims specified in the statute have not all been satisfied; such service is essential to the validity of the order of sale, and, if not made, the order and proceedings thereon are void.—Smith v. Whiting, 55 Or. 393, 399, 106 Pac. 791.

15. Notice of sale.

(1) In general.—A sale upon insufficient notice is at least voidable, if not absolutely void.—Haynes v. Meek, 10 Cal. 119; Halleck v. Moss, 17 Cal. 340, 344. The probate court, in its order confirming a sale, declared that the notice of sale had been posted in three public places. Evidence was introduced with the intent to show that one of the places was not a "public" place, within the meaning of the code. It was held that the court, having jurisdiction of the proceeding, could, within that jurisdiction, find the fact that the place was a public place, and that such finding could not be attacked collaterally.—Richardson v. Butler, 82 Cal. 174, 180, 16 Am. St. Rep. 101, 23 Pac. 9.

(2) Publication.—Under the California statute, notice of a sale must be published "for two weeks successively next before the day on or after which the sale is to be made," and the publication must be "as often, during the prescribed period, as the paper is regularly issued." This means that the publication must be for two successive weeks, and in each successive issue of the paper up to the day on or after which the sale is to take place. Under this statute, a notice published on January 27th, February 3d, and February 10th is sufficient for a sale which takes place on February 15th.—Estate of O'Sullivan, 84 Cal. 444, 448, 24 Pac. 281. Where publication of a notice of administrator's sale, under a statute and order requiring publication for "at least four successive weeks," etc., was made for three weeks in a paper, at which time the paper discontinued publication, and the fourth publication was in a paper not mentioned in the order, it has been held that the discontinuance of the paper did not annul the order, nor turn the question of publication, or of further publication, over to the discretion of the administrator, and that the order of sale was void from the beginning, for that reason.—Townsend v. Tallant, 33 Cal. 45, 51, 91 Am. Dec. 617. On an appeal from an order confirming a sale of real property on the ground of insufficiency of the notice of sale, it has been held that where a statute prescribes that the notice shall be published in a newspaper for three weeks successively, etc., the phrase "three weeks successively" has the same meaning as "three successive weeks." It simply indicates the time during which the sale must be advertised, and not the manner of the publication, as that it shall be published successively during the period. The word "successively" refers to weeks, and not to the publications of the paper. Therefore it is not required, where a publication under such an order is had in a daily newspaper, that the

notice be published in each issue of the paper.—Estate of Cunningham, 73 Cal. 558, 559, 15 Pac. 136. Publication, under a statute which requires notice of the sale to be published "for three weeks successively next before such sale," is insufficient, where the notice of sale was published in a weekly newspaper for three successive weeks, but not during the last week next before the day named for the sale, there being an interval of nine days between the completion of the last publication and the day of sale.—Hartley v. Croze, 38 Minn. 325, 37 N. W. 449. So, also, where a notice of sale named April 21, 1892, as the day on or after which the sale would be made, and the notice was published in a daily newspaper from the fifth to the nineteenth day of that month, such publication is insufficient; for if publication in the daily paper may be omitted for one day, it may be omitted for two or more days, and there can, in such case, be no certainty as to when the last publication must be made.—Hellman v. Merz, 112 Cal. 661, 666, 44 Pac. 1079. Where there is nothing in the statute to indicate a legislative intent that the publication of the notice of sale shall be in a daily rather than a weekly paper, the publication in a weekly paper is sufficient to meet all requirements of the law.—Estate of O'Sullivan, 84 Cal. 444, 447, 24 Pac. 281. When notice of sale had been given by publication in a newspaper, but it is not shown that it had been so given under the authority of any order directing it to be done, this is a fatal defect of proof in relation to the notice under which the sale was made, and for this reason, and for the additional reason that no notices had ever been posted, the sale was invalid.—Halleck v. Moss, 17 Cal. 340, 344.

16. Ordering resale.—Where no other course is open, it is proper for the court, in its discretion, to order a resale.—Estate of Long, 5 Cal. App. 684, 91 Pac. 169. A resale of real estate, made after annulment of the first sale, but based upon the original unverified petition, is, as was the first sale, void for want of jurisdiction.—Estate of Boland, 55 Cal. 310, 316. Where an executor, upon a resale of property,—directed by the court, at the hearing for confirmation, because of an advanced bid having been made,—contracted with the purchaser at the second sale, after the sale but before confirmation, and received a deed from the purchaser, immediately after confirmation to such purchaser, the executor holds the legal title to the property in trust for the devisees under the will, subject to a proper accounting for money paid on the purchase, for repairs, etc., less rents received, and for any other proper transactions that may exist between the parties.—O'Connor v. Flynn, 57 Cal. 293, 295. Where the executors of a vendor have canceled his contract for the sale of land, for default of the purchaser, and thus regained title, they may sell and convey such real estate, and account to the court of their appointment for the proceeds as personalty, and the title so conveyed is good as against the heirs of the decedent claiming title by succession.—Clapp v. Tower, 11 N. D. 556, 93 N. W. 862.

17. Nunc pro tunc order of sale.—Where, on the return-day mentioned in the order to show cause, a hearing was had and proofs made, and a decree directing a sale was also made on that day; and subsequently, seven days later, another decree or order of sale was made, referring to the same petition, and reciting that the order theretofore made in the matter had been vacated for errors, and where the sale took place under a later order, although the later order was not in form a nunc pro tunc order, it must be so regarded, as it was evidently in lieu of the order made on the first day of the hearing, although, by mistake, a different decree was then entered.—Burris v. Kennedy, 108 Cal. 331, 340, 41 Pac. 458.

18. Public sale.—Under the provisions of the statute of California, all sales must be made at public auction, unless, in the opinion of the court, the best interests of the estate would be subserved by a private sale. When, however, a private sale is asked for, the court may act upon the opinion of the executor or administrator and order such a sale to be made. Where, upon a petition of a creditor for an order of sale at public auction, and where a private sale is not asked for by the administrator, the court does not improperly exercise its judgment in ordering a public sale, although the administrator is present at the hearing of the petition, and objects to having the property sold at public auction, on the ground that a private sale would be most beneficial to the estate and to the creditors thereof.—Estate of Dorsey, 75 Cal. 258, 260, 17 Pac. 209. The duty of an administrator is not, necessarily, inconsistent with an agreement to ask for an order of sale, upon consideration that the purchaser will give an agreed sum at the sale, nor does this amount to a private sale, for the very agreement contemplates that the sale shall be public, and the court has no power to make or to authorize any other sale, or a sale in any other mode. —Stuart v. Allen, 16 Cal. 474, 499, 76 Am. Dec. 551.

19. Private sale.—Where land is sold by the executor at private sale, and return made thereof, and not at public sale, as directed in the order of sale, the court has no jurisdiction to confirm it, and the sale is void on the face of the record.—Schlicker v. Hemenway, 110 Cal. 579, 581, 52 Am. St. Rep. 116, 42 Pac. 1063. Neither an executor nor a legatee can authorize a sale of the property of a decedent, and therefore neither can ratify such sale; nor can an agent, empowered by a decedent in his lifetime to sell certain property, effect a sale thereof after the decease of his principal. The agency is terminated by death, and thereafter the estate acquires the property for purposes of administration, and for the benefit of all classes of creditors, in the manner prescribed by the statute.—Krumdick v. White, 107 Cal. 37, 41 39 Pac. 1066. Under the Oregon statute, the county court is vested with discretion in the matter of ordering private sales of the personal property of an estate, and may allow the administrator compensation for clerk's rent of a store, and other expenses connected therewith, but the court is powerless to authorize the purchase of goods to replenish the stock. As to such expenses, the administrator will be charged on his own account.—In re Osburn's Estate, 36 Or. 8, 58 Pac. 521.

20. **Return of sales.**—At the hearing of a return of sale of certain real estate, made by the administrator, under order of the court, it is within the jurisdiction of the court to postpone a further hearing upon the matter until another day to receive additional bids, even though an offer is made, at the time of the original hearing, of ten per cent more in amount than that named in the return. The provision of the California statute, giving the court discretion to accept the offer of an advanced bid or to order a new sale, does not limit the exercise of that discretion to the alternative of accepting the first offer that may be made or of ordering a new sale. It is authorized to receive as many bids as may be made, and, upon a consideration of all the bids, may then determine whether to accept the highest, or to order a new sale.— Estate of Griffith, 127 Cal. 543, 544, 59 Pac. 988. A recital in the decree confirming the fact that the return of the sale was duly verified by affidavit is conclusive as to that fact, and a finding of fact to the contrary does not in any manner affect the conclusiveness of the recital in the decree. The fact is not a jurisdictional one, and the principle applied to the inconclusiveness of statements or recitals in judgments, conferring jurisdiction, does not apply.—Dennis v. Winter, 63 Cal. 16, 18. The provisions of section 5520, Rev. Codes of Idaho, directed to the court as to accepting a 10 per cent raise in a bid or ordering a new sale, confer a legal discretion on the court, and the provisions of the section clearly contemplate that the offer there referred to must be made in the probate court, at the time of the hearing of the confirmation and not a long time after such hearing and after an appeal has been taken to the district court.—McGregor v. Jensen, 18 Idaho 320, 109 Pac. 731. By statute, in Montana, the court or judge is vested with a discretion to accept an offer of ten per cent more in amount than that made in a return of real estate, but the fact that no such provision is found in the statute as to personal property, does not efface the question of implied discretion.—State v. District Court, 42 Mont. 182, 185, 111 Pac. 717. "Discretion" means a legal discretion.— McGregor v. Jensen, 18 Idaho 320, 325, 109 Pac. 729. Upon the hearing of an administrator's return of a sale of real property, the court has no authority to accept an advance bid, made conditional upon the repayment to the bidder of a sum of money previously paid by him to a real estate broker on account of the purchase price of the property, which sale the heirs have objected to and the court has refused to confirm.—Estate of Bradley, 168 Cal. 655, 144 Pac. 136.

21. **Irregularities in sales. Mutual mistake.**—Informality as to the delivery of personal property upon a probate sale does not make the sale so far void that it can not be ratified by the probate court in some subsequent order.—Brewster v. Baxter, 2 Wash. Ter. 135, 3 Pac. 844.

Irregularities, in no wise fatal to the proceedings, may be subsequently cured by the order of the court confirming the sale.—Furth v. United States, etc., Trust Co., 13 Wash. 73, 42 Pac. 523. Irregularities, defects, and inconsistencies in the proceedings do not necessarily render a decree ordering a sale void, for, where it appears that the court was acting within the scope of its jurisdiction in making its final decree, such inconsistencies, irregularities, and defects may be corrected upon appeal, and the decree will not be nullified in an indirect attack.— Stuart v. Allen, 16 Cal. 474, 499, 76 Am. Dec. 551. Technical objections to sale, where there is no pretense that the sale under which appellants claim was in fact fraudulent, or that it was without adequate consideration, or in any way unfair, will not be regarded as sufficient to overturn, for want of jurisdiction, the judgment of a court, or to destroy a title to realty honestly acquired.—Richardson v. Butler, 82 Cal. 174, 180, 16 Am. St. Rep. 101, 23 Pac. 9. Mere irregularities do not affect the title, and such objections can not prevail in a collateral attack upon the order of sale.—Dennis v. Winter, 63 Cal. 16, 18. See Irwin v. Scriber, 18 Cal. 499; Halleck v. Moss, 22 Cal. 266, 276. The failure of a probate court to require a new or an additional bond from the executor, if any is necessary, with resident sureties, does not render void the sale of real estate which was subsequently confirmed by the probate court.—Higgins v. Reed, 48 Kan. 272, 29 Pac. 389. Though the petition for a sale is irregular and defective, in not stating some of the things that the statute requires it to state, yet if it is sufficient to give the court jurisdiction, questions raised in a collateral proceeding as to the publication of the order to show cause, a failure of the petition to state the amount of the personal estate undisposed of, to state that a sale of the real estate was necessary in the course of administration, or to state whether the deceased left any debts, are defects insufficient to affect the title in the hands of bona fide purchasers.—Ackerson v. Orchard, 7 Wash. 377, 34 Pac. 1106. In a case where there is no misstatement or concealment of any fact, and no misrepresentation as to the law, and which presents only a mutual mistake of the purchaser of certain land sold under the order of the probate court and the administrator as to the law, each believing that, under the facts, the land, was part of the decedent's estate, there can be no estoppel based on such error.—Gjerstadengen v. Van Duzen, 7 N. D. 612, 66 Am. St. Rep. 679, 76 N. W. 233. Irregularities as to amount of land sold and manner of sale held only error of judgment immaterial on collateral attack and remediable only by review as provided by law. —Dane v. Layne, 10 Cal. App. 366, 101 Pac. 1067.

22. Fraud in sales.—If the administrator and another person enter into a contract with the purchaser at a probate sale, after the sale and before confirmation, to purchase the property from the latter, such contract is a violation of the statute which prohibits an executor or administrator from being interested in a sale made by him, and is voidable, at the election of heirs or other persons interested in the

estate, but is not absolutely void.—Burris v. Kennedy, 108 Cal. 331, 341, 41 Pac. 458. In such cases the sale is always virtually to the administrator, and it is that fact which renders it voidable.—Burris v. Kennedy, 108 Cal. 331, 343, 41 Pac. 458. Where, in order to overthrow title to property purchased at a probate sale, by proof of a fraudulent conspiracy between the administrator and the real purchaser, the facts constituting the fraud must be averred; and this rule applies in an action to quiet title, where the only possible defense would be proof of such fraudulent conspiracy. The defendant, in such a case, could not give proof without an averment of the facts constituting the fraud.—Burris v. Adams, 96 Cal. 664, 668, 31 Pac. 565; Wetherly v. Straus, 93 Cal. 283, 28 Pac. 1045. An executor or administrator, as the case may be, who fraudulently sells any real estate of the decedent, is made, by statute, liable in double the value of the land sold, as liquidated damages, to be recovered in an action by the person having an estate of inheritance therein, but this liability does not apply to the sureties, and the statute affords no warrant for an action upon the bond of the administrator for the recovery of double the value of the land alleged to have been fraudulently sold by him.—Welhe v. Statham, 67 Cal. 245, 248, 7 Pac. 673. Where fraud is not established by the record, or the evidence, and the court acquires jurisdiction to order and confirm the sale, the proceedings are not void, and their regularity is not subject to attack in a collateral manner as against a bono fide purchaser.—Ackerson v. Orchard, 7 Wash. 377, 34 Pac. 1106, 35 Pac. 635; McKenna v. Cosgrove, 41 Wash. 332, 83 Pac. 240; Otis Brothers Co. v. Nash, 26 Wash. 39, 66 Pac. 111; Huberman v. Evans, 46 Neb. 784, 65 N. W. 1045; Phillips v. Phillips, 13 S. D. 231, 83 N. W. 94; Hahn v. Kelly, 34 Cal. 391, 94 Am. Dec. 742. Where a sale is brought about by fraud, a judgment or other proceeding may be collaterally attacked in a court of equity, but the bill must charge the purchaser with notice of fraud and there should be an offer to restore the purchase money.—Shane v. Peoples, 25 N. D. 188, 191, 141 N. W. 737. A real estate agent, seeking the authorization of an owner to sell property, or the ratification of a sale already made without authority, is bound to disclose the price actually received or to be received by him on a sale. He has not the right, after making a sale for a given price, to represent that price to be smaller than it is, or to secretly purchase the property himself at a smaller price, in order to make the profit of a resale at a price which he might and should have secured for his principal.—Estate of Bradley, 168 Cal. 655, 144 Pac. 136.

23. Executor purchasing at his own sale.

(1) **Generally prohibited.**—The rule that prohibits an executor from purchasing at his own sale is based upon the principle that a trustee is disabled from purchasing trust property, whether the purchase is made directly by himself or through another.—Webb v. Branner, 59 Kan. 190, 52 Pac. 429. If an administrator purchases property of the

estate at a foreclosure sale, he can not claim title thereto adversely to the estate, but he is a trustee thereof, and will be compelled to reconvey to the estate upon payment to him of the amount equitably due him from the estate.—Smith v. Goeth, 147 Cal. 725, 82 Pac. 384, 387. If two executors lend money of the estate, taking a trust deed on certain real estate as security, and, the money not being paid, a foreclosure is had, and one of the executors bids in the property, taking a deed investing him personally with the title, his creditors, who have attached the land, are entitled to subject it to their claims, where the statute declares that all conveyances or agreements in writing affecting title to real estate shall, when recorded, take effect as to subsequent bona fide encumbrancers without notice. They are supposed to have known that the executor might lawfully purchase for himself at the sale by the trustee, and, finding upon the record a deed from which it appears that he has so purchased, they have the right, in the absence of other knowledge, to regard the property as his.— Perkins v. Adams, 16 Colo. App. 96, 63 Pac. 792, 795. An administrator can not buy, either directly or indirectly, at his own sale, in the absence of a statute authorizing him to purchase, or unless some controlling equity intervenes to bar the cestui que trust.—Stewart v. Baldwin, 86 Wash. 63, 149 Pac. 662. It is true that the act of purchasing property of the estate by the executor or administrator thereof is expressly enjoined by section 1576 of the California Code of Civil Procedure, but it has uniformly been held in this state that the purchase of such property by such officer involves an act which is not void, but only voidable.—French v. Phelps, 20 Cal. App. 101, 128 Pac. 772, 776.

REFERENCES.

Validity of sale to surety on executor's bond.—See note 4 L. R. A. (N. S.) 820. 821. Purchases in the interest of executors or administrators at sale made by them.—See note 12 Am. Dec. 85, 86. An executor or administrator is not permitted to purchase any property of the estate, directly or indirectly, at sales thereof.—See § 592, ante. Validity and enforceability of purchase by executor or administrator of interest of devisee, legatee, or heir, in estate.—See note, Ann. Cas. 1913A, 1115.

(2) Invalidity of such purchase. Remedy.—An executor who bargains with the purchaser of property sold by the estate, after purchase and before confirmation, places his interest in conflict with his duty, and such purchases will be set aside as void, at the instance of the cestui que trust, and a resale ordered.—O'Connor v. Flynn, 57 Cal. 293, 296. Where the agent of the administrator purchases the property at a tax sale, while he or his tenants are in possession, such purchase does not pass, or otherwise affect the title to the property.—Burnall v. Lynch, 36 Cal. 135, 146. While, upon the face of the proceedings, the sale may appear to be a bona fide sale and an actual transfer, yet where it was only a device by which the administrator undertook to acquire,

indirectly, title for himself, as trustee, this is as much a violation of the fiduciary relation, and as great a fraud, in the eye of the law, as though the administrator had made a direct sale to himself.—Webb v. Branner, 59 Kan. 179, 52 Pac. 429. A corrupt agreement entered into by an executrix, while acting as such, with a person, by which, upon a sale of the property of the estate, such person is to purchase the same and share with the executrix the profits of the transaction, is interdicted by the law, and any contract sued upon by such purchaser, as, for instance, for commissions in purchasing and selling the property, and for interest on the advances, etc., can not be enforced in court, either against the representative of the estate or any person who knowingly indorsed instruments relating to the transaction, as such contract is not only contrary to the express provisions of the statute, but is also contrary to public policy, and is void.—Jones v. Hanna, 81 Cal. 507, 509, 22 Pac. 883. If the administrator, in effect, purchases at his own sale, the cestui que trust has several remedies which may afford him adequate relief. He may have the sale set aside and the administrator declared a trustee; he may sue upon the administrator's bond; or he may proceed to recover the penalty of double the value of the land sold, where the statute provides for such penalty.—Boyd v. Blankman, 29 Cal. 20, 35, 87 Am. Dec. 146. Though an heir acquiesced in the settlement of the administrator's accounts, and was paid the amount awarded thereunder, yet, if the administrator failed to act in good faith, and effected a fraudulent and indirect sale to himself, and the heir, by reason of his fraud and concealment, was not aware of the facts in the case, he is not estopped from bringing his action to recover his interest in the property thus fraudulently sold, together with the rents and profits thereof.—Webb v. Branner, 59 Kan. 190, 52 Pac. 429.

(3) **Such purchase is not void when.**—An executor or administrator is prohibited by the statute from purchasing the property of the estate he represents.—Burnett v. Lyford, 93 Cal. 114, 120, 28 Pac. 855; Danielwitz v. Sheppard, 62 Cal. 339. A violation, however, of such prohibition does not render a sale or conveyance to the administrator absolutely void. It is only voidable within a reasonable time, at the election of the heirs or other persons interested in the estate, who must rescind, and, in doing so, restore to the purchaser the money which has been paid as a consideration.—Burris v. Kennedy, 108 Cal. 331, 342, 41 Pac. 458; Burnett v. Lyford, 93 Cal. 114, 118, 28 Pac. 855. If an administrator has, without actual fraud, purchased property of the estate at his own sale, the transaction is not absolutely void, but only voidable, at the suit of the cestui que trust.—Furth v. Wyatt, 17 Nev. 180, 30 Pac. 828. There is nothing in the law to prohibit the executor from becoming interested and acquiring an interest in property after the estate has ceased to have an interest therein. So where an executor acquired an interest after a sale, for its full value, although an interest so acquired may create a suspicion that he was

interested in the first sale, it is, nevertheless, not sufficient to authorize setting the sale aside.—Estate of Millenovich, 5 Nev. 161. Where the administrator, in good faith, and to save the estate from costs, and to preserve the same, purchased a mortgage claim, and such purchase resulted in benefit to the estate, without gain to the administrator, the administrator is entitled to be protected and remunerated.—Furth v. Wyatt, 17 Nev. 180, 30 Pac. 828. An executor or administrator may purchase the property of a decedent he represents, to protect it from a sacrifice by foreclosure at the suit of a mortgagee. In such a case it will be considered that he is acting within the exercise of. his duties as a representative, rather than as a purchaser of the claim for his own benefit.—Burnett v. Lyford, 93 Cal. 114, 118, 28 Pac. 855.

24. Substitution of purchasers.—The mere substitution of one purchaser for another can not affect the validity of the sale. The order directing the sale, and the order confirming it, give vitality to the purchase.—Halleck v. Guy, 9 Cal. 181, 197, 70 Am. Dec. 643.

25. Illegal contracts with executor or administrator.—A contract entered into between the widow of a decedent as administratrix of the estate, and by another person as heir, with a third person, by which it was agreed that all moneys derived from the sale of real property belonging to the estate over and above a stated figure should be paid to such third party for services, etc., is an agreement unauthorized by any provision of the statute, and is contrary to the policy of the law. Hence a judgment recovered by such third person for the amount derived from the property, over and above the amount stated in the contract in such agreement, will not be sustained.—Danielwitz v. Sheppard, 62 Cal. 339, 342. Where one brother and joint heir agreed with another brother who was the administrator selling the land, to bid in the land at the administrator's sale and the agreement was carried out, it was held that the same constituted the bidder a constructive trustee of the land and that it was not such a trust as was required by section 7267, Snyder's Comp. Laws of Oklahoma, to be in writing.—Turner v. Turner, 31 Okla. 272, 125 Pac. 730.

26. Irregularities cured by retroactive acts.—Where the sale is void, merely in consequence of a failure of those having the direction of it to observe conditions imposed by the legislature itself, and which it could have dispensed with in the beginning, and the sale has been otherwise valid, the legislature may, by a retroactive act, cure the defect.—Mitchell v. Campbell, 19 Or. 198, 24 Pac. 455, 457. The title of heirs to the property is subject to the paramount right of the government to direct its disposition, if necessary, for the purpose of liquidating existing claims against the estate of the decedent. The title of the heirs vests in them by operation of law, but is subject to such right of disposition. If, therefore, the property is sold under an order of the probate court, by a duly appointed and qualified executor or adminis-

trator, for the purposes mentioned, and a valuable consideration has been paid therefor by the purchasers in good faith, the heirs are not deprived of any vested right, although the conditions upon which the general statute authorized the sale to be made were not strictly complied with.—Mitchell v. Campbell, 19 Or. 198, 24 Pac. 455. Where a probate court has jurisdiction of an estate and the administrator files a petition for sale of real estate to pay debts and the sale is had after due notice and the sale is confirmed by the court and an administrator's deed duly executed and delivered to the purchaser, the fact that the petition for sale did not set out fully all the circumstances called for by the statute was an irregularity which did not affect the validity of the sale, under the express provisions of the statute in the state of Washington.—Jones v. Seattle Brick & Tile Co., 56 Wash. 166, 105 Pac. 240, 241.

27. Sales by guardian.—The provision of the statute requiring the petition to show the amount of personal estate, and how much remains undisposed of, is inapplicable to a guardian's sale. The reasons requiring that the personal estate of a deceased person should be first sold do not apply to the estates of a ward. In the latter case, the court, in determining whether the real or personal estate should be sold, should ordinarily be governed by the same reasons which would influence a competent adult in disposing of his own property. A determination of what is for the best interest of the ward must control.—Estate of Hamilton, 120 Cal. 421, 424, 52 Pac. 708. The petition for a sale by a guardian is required to state only the condition of the estate to be sold, when the sale is asked upon the sole ground that it is for the benefit of the ward that his real estate, or some part of it, should be sold and the proceeds otherwise invested.—Smith v. Biscailuz, 83 Cal. 344, 351, 21 Pac. 15, 23 Id. 314. The order for a guardian's sale must describe the land to be sold with sufficient certainty, and this must be so without reference to any extraneous matter. The record can not be helped out by reference to a document not found in the order itself. —Hill v. Wall, 66 Cal. 130, 132, 4 Pac. 1139. See Crosby v. Dowd, 61 Cal. 557. Where the statute relating to a guardian's sale provides for the publication of notice, and further provides that the relatives living in the county, if the court thinks proper, shall be given such notice as the court deems reasonable, this clearly implies that the kind or character of the notice to be given is a matter for the judge to determine, and that a personal notice is not absolutely demanded by the statute. Furthermore, it is a matter of discretion, upon the part of the court, whether to give any notice whatever to the relatives residing in the county.—Asher v. Yorba, 125 Cal. 513, 515, 58 Pac. 137. See, also, Burroughs v. De Couts, 70 Cal. 373, 11 Pac. 734. Though a non-resident guardian of non-resident minor devisees assumes to consent to a probate sale in this state on behalf of such minor devisees, such consent is insufficient to give the court here jurisdiction to make an order of sale of their property in this state.

Such guardianship gives no authority here to bind the estate of non-resident minor devisees, that is situated in this state.—Wilson v. Hastings, 66 Cal. 243, 246, 5 Pac. 217. Where a collateral attack is made upon a guardian's sale of the land of a minor, the burden of showing that the sale was not a valid one, or that it was void, is upon the person who attacks the same. The absence of evidence in the record, upon such collateral attack, showing the jurisdictional facts, may be taken as evidence of their existence.—Asher v. Yorba, 125 Cal. 513, 516, 58 Pac. 137. The provisions of the chapters of the code relating to sales of property by administrators, apply to proceedings in sale by guardians as well, unless otherwise specially provided; but it is specially provided by statute that the court may exercise its discretion in ordering a private rather than public sale; but it is only in cases where the guardian has petitioned for an order to sell the ward's property at private sale that the court has jurisdiction to make such an order.—In re Verwoert, 177 Cal. 488, 171 Pac. 105. Evidence, in an action to set aside an executor's sale, held insufficient to show that the executor and the purchaser, who afterwards became the guardian of the testator's minor children, had entered into a conspiracy to defraud the wards; on the contrary, it appeared that the sale was made in good faith, that the guardian accounted for everything and withheld nothing, and that the wards did not lose anything.—Smith v. Smith, 45 Mont. 535, 579, 125 Pac. 987.

28. Sales by foreign executor.—An executor or administrator in another jurisdiction, with power to sell, and having property of his testator or intestate, may sell the same, and vest title in the purchaser. The title of the purchaser is complete, as between the parties, when the property (in this case indorsed certificates of stock) has been delivered. And with reference to such sale and transfer of stock, it is not necessary to have letters of administration issued in this state in order to obtain a transfer on the books of the corporation. Nor is it necessary that the bond provided for in section 326 of the Civil Code of California be required by the corporation from the purchaser of the stock.—Brown v. San Francisco Gas Light Co., 58 Cal. 426, 428. Where a resident of Iowa died in that state and administration of her estate was had, and on such administration a creditor proved his claim and said claim was allowed by the court, but there was not assets in such jurisdiction sufficient to pay the same, and an ancillary administration was had in North Dakota where there was real estate belonging to the estate, but no money or personal property, and there were no debts, and a petition was filed in said ancillary administration by the administrator in the principal administration under the direction of said principal court, asking for the sale of the real estate in North Dakota and the transmission of the proceeds to said principal court for the payment of the debts there proved and allowed, held that such petition should have been granted even though such debts had not been proved in North Dakota in the

said ancillary administration.—Dow v. Lillie, 26 N. D. 512, L. R. A. 1915D, 754, 144 N. W. 1082, 1087. A delay of six years by a foreign executor to petition for the sale of land in the state of Kansas to pay the indebtedness of the testator is not unreasonable, when it is occasioned by the pendency of litigation carried on in good faith to determine the validity and amount of such indebtedness.—In re Jones's Estate (Thomas v. Williams), 80 Kan. 632, 25 L. R. A. (N. S.) 1304, 103 Pac. 772. A foreign executor with testamentary power to sell and convey land in the state of Kansas may make a valid contract to convey before the will has been admitted to record in that state in accordance with the statute. All that the Kansas statute requires in that behalf is that the will shall be of record at the time of conveyance.—Niguette v. Green, 81 Kan. 569, 106 Pac. 270.

29. Exchange is not a sale.—The exchange, by an executor, of one form of currency, belonging to the estate, for another form, can not be treated as a sale.—Estate of Sanderson, 74 Cal. 199, 214, 15 Pac. 753.

30. Sales without order.—Section 1561 of the Code of Civil Procedure of California implies an authority in the testator to confer power on his executor to sell property without the order of the court, and declares that when such authority is given, the executor may sell any "property of the estate" without such order. The "property of the estate" here referred to "must receive the same construction as the same words have when used in other sections of this title, and must include the entire estate and the property of which the decedent died seised, including the interest of the surviving widow as well as that of the other heirs."—Sharp v. Loupe, 120 Cal. 89, 92, 52 Pac. 134, 586. Where an administrator sells property belonging to the estate, without an order of the court authorizing him to do so, and in the absence of any authority under the will, he, in legal effect, converts such property to his own use, and becomes responsible for its value, with legal interest thereon.—Estate of Radovich, 74 Cal. 536, 539, 5 Am. St. Rep. 466, 16 Pac. 321.

31. Title conveyed by sale.—The rule of caveat emptor applies to a purchaser at an administrator's sale.—Towner v. Rodegeb, 33 Wash. 153, 99 Am. St. Rep. 936, 74 Pac. 50; Gjerstadengen v. Van Duzen, 7 N. D. 612, 66 Am. St. Rep. 679, 76 N. W. 233; Smith v. Wildman, 178 Pa. St. 245, 56 Am. St. Rep. 760, 36 L. R. A. 834, 35 Atl. 1047; Lindsay v. Cooper, 94 Ala. 170, 33 Am. St. Rep. 105, 16 L. R. A. 813, 11 So. 325. In the absence of any special agreement as to the title of the property sold, it is incumbent upon the vendee to examine the title for himself, and to point out any objections he may have to the title tendered him by the vendor.—Easton v. Montgomery, 90 Cal. 307, 313, 25 Am. St. Rep. 123, 27 Pac. 280; Estate of Pearsons, 98 Cal. 603, 613, 33 Pac. 431. Sales made under orders of the probate court pass only such title as the decedent had at the time of his death, and such as the estate may have subsequently acquired.—Meyers v. Farquharson, 46

Cal. 190, 200. Under this principle, that a sale by an executor passes only such interest in and title to the property sold as the decedent had at the time of his death, a sale of the interest of the estate in community property, made by the wife in her capacity as executrix, does not affect the wife's one-half interest in the property sold.— Estate of Wickersham, 139 Cal. 652, 656, 73 Pac. 541. No distinction is made between sales of community property to pay debts and to pay expenses of administration. Such a sale passes the wife's title, and also the title of any heir, under the statutory provision declaring that the community property shall be subject to claims against the estate and for purposes of administration.—Sharp v. Loupe, 120 Cal. 89, 93, 52 Pac. 134. If an executor or administrator sells the land of a decedent, under an order of the court, to pay the debts and expenses of administration, the title vests as of the date of the death of the decedent, and devests the lien of a mortgage made thereon by an heir. Hence such mortgage can not be foreclosed as against the purchaser. —Gutter v. Dallamore, 144 Cal. 665, 669, 79 Pac. 383. The statement of a witness regarding the claim of title of the plaintiff, where too indefinite to be the basis of a judgment as to title, can not in any sense be considered as an estoppel.—Wilson v. Hastings, 66 Cal. 243, 246, 5 Pac. 217. The question of the power of the executor to sell any property of the decedent under a power in the will is not involved in proceedings before the court, upon petition filed by the executor, praying for the construction of certain clauses of the will, and for the determination of his duties in reference thereto, prior to the sale of the land. Nor can the purchaser, upon an appeal from an order confirming a sale, urge that, by such proceeding, the executor had doubts as to his power to sell any portion of the estate of the testator, that thereby the title to the land sold by him was rendered uncertain, and therefore that the purchaser ought not to be compelled to take the same, and that the court should not have made a confirmation of the sale.—Estate of Pearsons, 98 Cal. 603, 610, 33 Pac. 431.

32. Bona fide purchasers.

(1) Rights of.—A bona fide purchaser, at a probate sale to pay a mortgage executed, under authority of the court, by the executor, takes the land from the estate free of any claim of lien or charge against it for a personal obligation of the widow.—McKenna v. Cosgrove, 41 Wash. 332, 83 Pac. 240. When one purchases land at a void or voidable judicial sale, in entire ignorance that it is void, and in good faith pays money thereon, which is applied to the satisfaction of a lien or encumbrance on the land, he should be put in the place of the creditor, to the extent, at least, that his money has satisfied the lien.— Russell v. Mixer, 42 Cal. 475; Waldrip v. Black, 74 Cal. 409, 412, 16 Pac. 226; Favill v. Roberts, 50 N. Y. 222. But where the purchaser knew of the want of power of the executor to sell without an order of the probate court, was warned not to purchase without an order and

sanction of said court, but purchased in the face of this knowledge
and caution, he is not an ignorant purchaser in good faith to which
the doctrine of subrogation would, under any circumstances, apply.—
Huse v. Den, 85 Cal. 390, 400, 20 Am. St. Rep. 232, 24 Pac. 790.
Where the sale is a fraud upon the heirs, a purchaser of the property
can only be protected upon the hypothesis that he was a purchaser
for a valuable consideration, in good faith and without notice. Where
the fact of notice is clearly charged in a bill to set aside the sale for
fraud, and a specific denial of such facts, and knowledge thereof, are
not made in the answer, the answer does not contain a sufficient denial
of notice, though it contains affirmative averments to the effect that
the defendant purchased the property for a valuable consideration, in
good faith, and without any knowledge or suspicion, on his part, of
any unfairness, illegality, or wrongfulness on the part of the administrator.—Scott v. Umbarger, 41 Cal. 410, 418. One who buys land in
the state of Kansas from the devisees, seven years after the death of
the testator, while a resident of another state, is not protected as an
innocent purchaser against proceedings thereafter brought to subject
it to the payment of debts of the estate.—In re Jones's Estate (Thomas
v. Williams), 80 Kan. 632, 25 L. R. A. (N. S.) 1304, 103 Pac. 772.
Where decedent's widow and children conveyed land part of the estate and which land was afterward sold by the administratrix under
order of the court to pay decedent's debts, the purchaser from the
administratrix took title as against the grantee from the widow and
children.—Rio Grande Ry. Co. v. Salt Lake Inv. Co., 35 Utah 528, 101
Pac. 589.

(2) **How affected by adverse possession.**—In an action to recover
possession of real property sold at an administrator's sale, adverse possession thereof for the period prescribed by the statute of limitations
vests a perfect title in the possessor as against the former holder of
the title and all the world, and the tenure in the property is as certain
under the proof of an adverse holding during the period prescribed by
the statute of limitations, as it would be under an absolute deed of
conveyance.—Mitchell v. Campbell, 19 Or. 198, 24 Pac. 455, 459. Where
the plaintiff waits for nearly twenty years after reaching her majority
and then institutes proceedings to set aside a sale made to an innocent
purchaser for value by the executors of her father's estate in the utmost good faith and by virtue of a purported power in the will, and
afterward confirmed by a solemn decree of the court, no judicial tribunal, with proper regard for vested interests and that wise public
policy which fosters the stability of titles, should allow her want of
actual knowledge of the adverse claims to operate, under such circumstances, to protect her from the bar of the statute of limitations.—
Bagley v. City and County of San Francisco, 19 Cal. App. 255, 125
Pac. 931, 933.

33. Necessary sale is valid when.—No sale of the real estate of a
decedent, made by an administrator or executor, is invalid on account

of a failure to set forth, in the petition therefor, the facts showing
such sale to be necessary, if the general facts showing the necessity of
the sale are proved and found.—Blackman v. Mulhall, 19 S. D. 534, 104
N. W. 250, 253. A failure to set forth any of the facts enumerated in
section 1537 of the Code of Civil Procedure of California, prescribing
what the verified petition for the sale of real property of a decedent
shall contain, will not invalidate the sale, provided the general facts
showing that a sale is necessary are proved and found.—Burris v. Kennedy, 108 Cal. 331, 339, 41 Pac. 458.

34. Voidable sales.—Where an executor, as a trustee, charged with
the duty of selling the property, purchases the same from his cestui
que trust, and takes a conveyance directly to himself or acts through
the intervention of a third person, the sale is not, as a general rule,
absolutely void.—Blockley v. Fowler, 21 Cal. 329, 82 Am. Dec. 747;
Boyd v. Blankman, 29 Cal. 19, 87 Am. Dec. 146; but is voidable, at
the election of the cestui que trust.—Blockley v. Fowler, 21 Cal. 329,
82 Am. Dec. 747; Guerrero v. Ballerino, 48 Cal. 118; Tracy v. Colby,
55 Cal. 71; and without reference to the question of the adequacy of
the price.—San Diego v. San Diego, etc., R. R. Co., 44 Cal. 106;
O'Connor v. Flynn, 57 Cal. 293. This principle is applicable in a case
where the executors, acting under a power of sale in the will, purchase, from absent devisees, property belonging to the estate, and
convey the same, under their power, to the wife of one of the executors, and, after distribution, obtain the conveyance thereof to themselves, where it is admitted that the wife acted for the executors
throughout the transaction.—Goldson v. Dunlap, 73 Cal. 157, 159, 14
Pac. 576. The legislature itself can not make a void proceeding valid.
It can no more impart a binding efficacy to a void proceeding, than
it can take one man's property from him and give it to another.—
Pryor v. Downey, 50 Cal. 388, 405, 19 Am. Rep. 656. A contract entered
into by an administrator with a prospective purchaser, which is reported to the probate court, with a petition praying the court to confirm the agreement, or if the court should conclude not to confirm
the contract, then that an order for sale be made, is not contrary
to public policy and void; nor is a decree passed thereon void because
the prayer for the petition for an order of sale is in the alternative,
the main object of the petition being to obtain from the court a confirmation of the private agreement. Although the petition is defective in this respect, the decree is not rendered a nullity where the final
decree is made in the usual form.—Stuart v. Allen, 16 Cal. 474, 499,
76 Am. Dec. 551. A mere volunteer, who institutes proceedings in
probate upon an estate in which he has no interest, and for the
ostensible purpose of paying the debts of such estate, but, in fact,
to procure a sale of a part of the estate to himself, and directs, controls, and manages the proceedings in probate successfully to that
end, has no standing in a court of equity. Such a sale is voidable,
and will be set aside at the instance of any one injured thereby.—

Bergin v. Haight, 99 Cal. 52, 55, 33 Pac. 760. Sale of land to appraiser held voidable only.—Dane v. Layne, 10 Cal. App. 366, 101 Pac. 1067.

35. Void sales.—An order of sale upon a defective petition is utterly void.—Pryor v. Downey, 50 Cal. 388, 399, 19 Am. Rep. 656. A conveyance can not be said to be utterly void unless it is of no effect whatsoever and is incapable of confirmation or ratification. The acceptance of the purchase-money, with full notice that the administrator was the purchaser, per interpositam personam, would unquestionably amount to a ratification of the sale.—Boyd v. Blankman, 29 Cal. 20, 35, 87 Am. Dec. 146. Lands acquired under the provisions of a statute of the United States, providing that "no lands acquired under the provisions of this chapter in any event become liable to the satisfaction of any debt contracted prior to the issue of the patent therefor," are subject to such statute. The probate court of a state has no authority to order a sale of such lands for the payment of debts of the patentee, contracted prior to the issuance of the patent, and a sale made under such circumstances is void.—J. B. Watkins L. and Mortgage Co. v. Mullen, 8 Kan. App. 705, 54 Pac. 921. An order of sale is void as to a minor without any guardian at the time, and who was not made a party to the proceeding, where the statute explicitly provides that the order to show cause shall be directed to all persons interested, and if any of the devisees or heirs are minors, that a general guardian shall be appointed before proceeding to act upon the petition.—Fiske v. Kellogg, 3 Or. 503. If the court authorizes and directs an executor to sell certain real estate of a decedent at public auction, but the executor, instead of doing so, negotiates a private sale, and reports it as such to the court, such sale is void, and there is no power to confirm it.—Schlicker v. Hemenway, 110 Cal. 579, 581, 52 Am. St. Rep. 116, 42 Pac. 1063. A probate sale of real estate, made without the required order to show cause, and without the required service or publication of notice, is void.—Campbell v. Drais, 125 Cal. 253, 257, 57 Pac. 994. If the deceased left personal property, not specially bequeathed, which is primarily liable for the payment of his debts, the court is powerless to order a sale of the real estate until the proceeds of the sale of the former class of property is exhausted. Under such circumstances, an order for the sale of any part of the real property would be void; but if such order is not obeyed by the executors, no injury results therefrom.—In re Noon's Estate, 49 Or. 286, 88 Pac. 673, 675, 90 Pac. 673. Where a large part of the purchase money received from a void sale by an administrator was used to pay the debts of the estate which were a charge upon the land heirs are not entitled to recover the land forced from those charges.—Browne v. Coleman, 62 Or. 454, 125 Pac. 280. An attempted sale of land in a probate proceeding is void as to the heirs of the deceased where the heirs were not named in the petition for the sale, were not served, and did not appear in the proceedings.—Marks v. Wilson, 72 Or. 5, 143 Pac. 906. If an executrix makes sales of realty under

an order of court, which sales are void, it is error to treat them as
valid and allow her to charge herself with the proceeds only; such
property is still the property of the estate.—In re Dolenty's Estate;
Mannix v. Dolenty, 53 Mont. 33, 161 Pac. 524. Where the petition for
an order to sell real estate does not follow the letter of the statute,
objection should be made at once; for, if it contains matter of substance
upon which jurisdiction can hinge and, notwithstanding its defects, the
court orders as prayed in it, and the sale is then made and bona fide
purchasers enter into possession of the property, the sale will not be
held void upon application therefor made, after the time for appeal
has passed.—Yeaton v. Barnhart, 78 Or. 249, 150 Pac. 742, 152 Pac. 1192.

REFERENCES.

Sales by executors or administrators are void, because in excess of
the order of sale, when.—See note 37 Am. Dec. 65, 66.

36. Vacating sales.—It has been suggested that the proper procedure
to set aside a sale, void or voidable, would be by a direct proceeding,
for, under our probate system, the true theory is, that both the real
and personal estate of the intestate vest in the heir, subject to the
lien of the administrator for the payment of debts and the expenses of
administration, and with the right in the administrator of present possession. If the sale is void or voidable, the lien of the administrator
continues; and it would seem equitable that the purchaser, who has
paid the debts of the estate, should have a lien upon the estate for
his purchase-money. All the equities of all parties could, it is said, be
better settled in a direct proceeding.—Haynes v. Meeks, 10 Cal. 110,
120, 70 Am. Dec. 703. An action to set aside a fraudulent probate sale
of land, made by an administrator, involves the determination of
a right or interest in real property, and is to be tried where the real
property is situated.—Sloss v. De Toro, 77 Cal. 129, 132, 19 Pac. 233.
A creditor, who accepts payment of his debt out of sales of property
of the estate, knowing that there are no other assets, will not be permitted afterward to attack the validity of the sale under any circumstances; because one who, with full knowledge of the facts, accepts
the benefit of a void judicial sale is thereby precluded from questioning its validity.—Powers v. Scharling, 76 Kan. 855, 92 Pac. 1099. See,
also, Meddes v. Kenny, 176 Mo. 200, 98 Am. St. Rep. 496, 75 S. W. 633.
The district court, considered apart from the probate court, in the
state of Colorado, has jurisdiction to hear and determine a cause
instituted for the purpose of annulling and setting aside a sale made
by an administrator, and for the purpose of quieting the title to the
property sold under the decree of the probate court.—Ryan v. Geigel,
39 Colo. 355, 89 Pac. 775. A sale of the real estate of a decedent will
not be held void because the petition fails to give a description of all
the real estate of which the deceased died seised, or the value or condition of the different parcels.—Burris v. Kennedy, 108 Cal. 331, 339, 41
Pac. 458. A sale can not be treated as invalid because the adminis-

trator received a promissory note from the purchaser for a portion of the price of the property sold, where it appears that the note was in addition to the full cash value of the stock; that the administrator reported that the sale was advantageous to the estate; and that the court, in confirming the sale, determined the sale to be thus advantageous.—Estate of Kibbe, 57 Cal. 407, 408. A contract for the sale of corporate stock, belonging to the estate of a decedent, can not be avoided as against the purchaser, if found to be fair and for the benefit of the estate; and it is "fair" where the value of the stock was purely speculative and the purchaser was willing to take a chance that others would not take.—In re Crim's Estate, 89 Wash. 395, 154 Pac. 811. Where corporate stock, belonging to the estate of a deceased person, was sold by an executor under a non-intervention will, before his appointment, but for the purpose of raising money to save the remainder of the stock and to pay debts of the estate; where such stock was the only asset of the estate; and where it was admitted that the money derived from the sale was used for such purpose, the subsequent probate of the will, in effect, ratified the sale, although the will was afterward set aside on the grounds of testamentary incapacity and undue influence; the sale was therefore valid, and an administrator de bonis non could not, as against the purchaser, avoid it.—In re Crim's Estate, 89 Wash. 395, 154 Pac. 811. The question whether or not the property of an estate was sold for a price disproportionate to its value is addressed to the sound discretion of the court. This court must consider all the facts of the case, including the value and condition of the estate, the necessity for funds, the state of the market, and all other matters bearing on the question.—Estate of Scott, 172 Cal. 485, 152 Pac. 242. Upon the hearing of an administrator's return of sale of real property, it is not necessary, under section 1552 of the Code of Civil Procedure, in order to authorize the court to accept the increased offer of ten per cent, that it should appear that "the proceedings were unfair" or that the "sum bid was disproportionate to the value" of the property; but this unfairness or disproportion must be shown to justify an order vacating the sale.—Estate of Bradley, 168 Cal. 655, 144 Pac. 136. To justify an order vacating an administrator's sale under the California statute, it is necessary for it to appear not only that a sum exceeding the bid by ten per cent may be obtained, but also that "the proceedings were unfair" or that the "sum bid was disproportionate to the value"; but there is no such requirement when, on the hearing of the return of sale, a ten per cent higher bid is made by a responsible person.—Estate of Bradley, 168 Cal. 656, 660, 144 Pac. 136. Where the administrator's attorney had bought at an administrator's sale and conveyed to the administrator less than two years afterwards, and the heirs had thereupon sued to avoid the sale, but the court had adjudged for the defendant, it was held, on appeal, that the evidence was not sufficiently clear to enable the court to vacate the judgment, the judge giving it having had the advantage of observing the demeanor of the witnesses.—Ryan v. Geigel, 25 Colo. App. 122, 136 Pac. 804. A sale of real estate made in the Indian Territory, belonging to the estate of a deceased person, made by a duly appointed administratrix, upon a petition therefor filed, but without notice of the application being given as provided by the statute, and the petition being deficient in form, though in substantial compliance with the statute, and where the sale has been confirmed, is not void, and will not be set aside in a direct proceeding instituted for that purpose, unless it be shown that actual fraud was committed or that there existed some other ground of acknowledged equity jurisdiction.—Steele v. Kelley, 32 Okla. 547, 122 Pac. 934.

37. Presumption and estoppel.—In North Dakota the defense of the statute of limitations can not be raised by demurrer even though the fact is apparent on the face of the complaint. The law is well established that there is a strong presumption in favor of the validity of sales by the court sitting in probate. To subject a judgment to collateral attack the absence of jurisdiction must appear on the face of the judgment. The proceedings leading up to the sale of real estate by an administrator are proceedings in rem. The rule of law is well settled upon principles of public policy, that evidence aliunde the record can not be availed of in a collateral attack upon a judgment of a domestic court of general jurisdiction, regular on its face.—Shane v. Peoples, 25 N. D. 188, 191, 141 N. W. 737. Heirs of a decedent who, with knowledge that the sale of lands by an administrator was invalid, accepted their distributive share of the proceeds of the sale, are estopped from questioning its validity.—Browne v. Coleman, 62 Or. 454, 125 Pac. 280.

38. Rights of heirs.

(1) **In general.**—Upon the death of the ancestor, the heir becomes vested at once with the full property, subject to the liens for the payment of debts, expenses of administration, etc., and, subject to these liens and the temporary right of possession of the administrator, the heir may at once sell and dispose of the property, and has the same right to judge for himself of the relative advantages of selling or holding, that any other owner has.—Smith v. Olmstead, 88 Cal. 582, 586, 22 Am. St. Rep. 336, 12 L. R. A. 46, 26 Pac. 521, quoting from and approving Brenham v. Story, 39 Cal. 188. A special act of the legislature empowering the probate court to order a sale of the property of an estate, either at public or private sale, at the discretion of the administrator, "as in the judgment of the said administrator will best promote the interest of those entitled to the estate," would be to pass beyond the proper functions of the administrator and constitute him the forced agent of the living for the management of their estates.— Brenham v. Story, 39 Cal. 179, 186. While probate proceedings are, at least, quasi proceedings in rem, yet, where the statute provides for the service of notice upon persons, the same rule applies as in ordinary civil actions. Where, therefore, a sale is made without notice to show

cause, as provided by statute, and no service of any kind is made upon the heirs, the court acquires no jurisdiction to make the order of sale, and the sale, if made, is invalid and void.—Campbell v. Drais, 125 Cal. 253, 258, 57 Pac. 994. If there has been a purchase, by an administrator, at his own sale, made by order of the probate court, of land belonging to the estate, it is necessary, in order to cut off the cestui que trust from any recourse upon the land and to restrict him to the proceeds, that there be either some positive act of affirmance of the sale, or such an acquiescence in it, manifested by the receipt of the proceeds, or such a delay, beyond the period fixed by the statute of limitations, in commencing proceedings to set it aside, or in some other manner, that the court will deem it equivalent to and presumptively a ratification of the sale. By disaffirmance, the cestui que trust elects to have the legal title held as it was before the sale, and have the property remain subject to all the trusts with which it was formerly charged.— Boyd v. Blankman, 29 Cal. 20, 32, 87 Am. Dec. 146. Where the court has jurisdiction to appoint an administrator of the estate of a deceased person, and where the letters that issued were duly attested, the heirs, in a collateral proceeding to set aside a probate sale made of the property, will not be permitted to say that there was no administration of the estate at all, and it is unquestionable that, as against any collateral attack, the attestation to the letters will be deemed conclusive evidence of the administrator's due qualification and of his authority to act as such.—Dennis v. Bint, 122 Cal. 39, 42, 68 Am. St. Rep. 17, 54 Pac. 378. A creditor of an heir can acquire no better right in the estate of a decedent than that held by the heir himself. Hence, if the heir owes the estate more than the value of his share, and does not pay his debt, he has no interest in the property of the estate, and it necessarily follows that a creditor of the heir, by a sale and purchase, under judicial process, of his nominal interest, can acquire no right in the property.—Boyer v. Robinson, 26 Wash. 117, 66 Pac. 119, 120. The appointment of "attorneys for absent and minor heirs," prior to the filing of a petition for leave to sell, can not satisfy a statute requiring the appointment of a guardian for minor heirs, to represent them before the petition shall have been acted upon.—Townsend v. Tallant, 33 Cal. 45, 52, 91 Am. Dec. 617. An administrator's sale of real property, under order of court, to raise money to pay off debts of the estate, deprives the heirs of their rights in the property sold; it does not, however, devest the widow of her right of dower.—Yeaton v. Barnhart, 78 Or. 249, 150 Pac. 742, 152 Pac. 1192. Where a creditor secures a lien upon an heir's interest in the real estate of an intestate, the subsequent sale of the property by the administrator, under order of the court, carries the property burdened with the lien; provided, the creditor had no notice of the proceedings at the time they were had.— Yeaton v. Barnhart, 78 Or. 249, 150 Pac. 742, 152 Pac. 1192. Upon the death of the ancestor, title to the personal property passes directly to the personal representatives; hence, the heirs and legatees have no right of possession thereto until the close of the administration, except as otherwise derived throught the personal representatives by distribution, or in some other lawful way.—Smith v. Steen, 20 N. M. 436, 150 Pac. 927, 929.

REFERENCES.

Right of heirs or legatees to enjoin the sale of realty by the executor under power in the will.—See note, Ann. Cas. 1912B, 1019.

(2) Heirs under guardianship.—Where a person unites in himself the capacities of administrator and guardian, although the two, so far as general uses are concerned, are necessarily incompatible, yet, in a special proceeding, set on foot by the person as administrator against his ward, and for the distinct purpose of devesting the ward of his title as heir, the administrator can not represent the ward.—Townsend v. Tallant, 33 Cal. 45, 52, 91 Am. Dec. 617. It was objected that the real estate of certain wards could not be sold by an order of the probate court, because its disposition was controlled by will, under which they held, the provision of the will being that the devisees "may each 'take out' one-half of his share when he comes of age, and the other half not until all the other children come of age." But, whatever effect this provision might have in controlling the use of the property until the devisees were entitled to take its control by the terms of the will, the title to the property, the estate of the devisees, undoubtedly vested in the devisees upon the death of the testator, and a statute authorizing the sale of the estate of any person under guardianship, when necessary, or when for his benefit, in certain cases, is sufficiently comprehensive to authorize the sale of such estate, and if legally made, to transfer whatever estate the wards had to the purchasers.—Fitch v. Miller, 20 Cal. 352, 385.

(3) Actions by heirs in general to set aside sales.—Where an executor or an administrator has sold the real property of a decedent by order of the probate court, the heirs of the decedent are barred from bringing an action to recover the property sold, unless such action is brought within three years next after the sale, or within three years after they attain majority; and this rule applies, whether the invalidity of the sale resulted from an insufficiency in the petition for sale, in the notice of sale, or in the notice for the appointment of an administrator, or other insufficiency in the progress of the administration.—Ganahl v. Soher, 68 Cal. 95, 97, 8 Pac. 650. After an administrator's deed, made pursuant to an order or judgment of the proper court, directing a sale, has been placed on record, heirs, under the Kansas statute, must sue to recover the property within five years, or be deemed to have admitted the validity of the sale and conveyance, whether they had notice of the proceedings or not. After the expiration of that time, the purchaser can not be called upon to vindicate their legality.—O'Keefe v. Behrens, 73 Kan. 469, 9 Ann. Cas. 867, 8 L. R. A. (N. S.) 354, 85 Pac. 555. Compare Gage v. Downey, 94 Cal.

241, 29 Pac. 635. In an action brought by heirs to obtain a decree that the legal title to lands in the estate, sold fraudulently, is held in trust for the plaintiffs, and that defendants convey the same, the answer, in effect, admits that the pretended sale was purely fictitious, and was made for the purpose mentioned in the complaint, where it fails to deny the fraud alleged in the complaint.—Scott v. Umbarger, 41 Cal. 410, 416. The laches of the administrator, who, under our system, represents the heirs, while he holds office as such, must be imputed to the beneficiary, and the remedy of the heir, where the administrator fails to sue to recover land, or to set aside a probate sale, is against the administrator.—Wheeler v. Bolton, 54 Cal. 302; McLeran v. Benton, 73 Cal. 329, 343, 2 Am. St. Rep. 814, 14 Pac. 879. Where the heirs join with the administrator in asking for a sale of real estate in a particular way and after it was made joined in a writing asking that the sale be confirmed and afterward received the purchase money on the distribution of the estate, they are estopped from setting the sale aside on the ground of irregularities.—Cunningham v. Richardson, 68 Wash. 24, 122 Pac. 369.

(4) Actions by minor heirs to set aside sales.—In an action of ejectment, brought by a minor through his guardian ad litem, to recover certain land sold by the administrator of his father's estate, which administrator also represented the minor as guardian, and where such sale was declared void for this and other irregularities, it can not be maintained that the minor is estopped from maintaining the action upon the ground that he, although an infant, received the purchasemoney paid at the probate sale of the land in question, upon a judicial accounting with the administrator, it not appearing that the minor received any money from his guardian on that occasion, or on any other, and where the only questions involved in such accounting were as to receipts and disbursements by the administrator, the final balance being in his favor.—Townsend v. Tallant, 33 Cal. 45, 55, 91 Am. Dec. 617. A person who assumes to act as administrator, who has not given the official bond required by law, and who is not even under the sanction of an oath of office, can not be said to represent the interests of minor heirs, so as to raise the bar of the statute of limitations against them. The principle that the administrator represents the heirs (minors as well as others), and that when he is barred by limitation they also are barred, has no application where the acts of the person assuming to act as administrator can not be sustained, even upon the ground that he is an officer de facto.—Staples v. Connor, 79 Cal. 14, 16, 21 Pac. 380. The limitation reserving to minors, and others under legal disability to sue, the right to commence an action for the recovery of any estate sold by an executor or administrator under the probate law, applies alike to all probate sales of real estate, void as well as voidable, belonging to persons who have died since the passage of the probate act.—Ganahl v. Soher, 68 Cal. 95, 97, 8 Pac. 650. The attorney for minor heirs can represent them only in the proceed-

ing which has been duly inaugurated, and in which the court has already jurisdiction of the minors, by such service of summons or notice as the code provides; he can not waive their rights, nor by any of his acts invest the court with jurisdiction of their persons which it had not already acquired.—Campbell v. Drais, 125 Cal. 253, 258, 57 Pac. 994.

39. Sales under power in the will.

(1) In general.—The power to sell without an order from the court does not apply to nor restrict the statutory powers of the executor or executrix to sell under an order of the court whenever it is shown to be necessary to sell, or beneficial to the persons interested in the estate to do so.—Campbell's Estate, 149 Cal. 712, 87 Pac. 573, 574; Estate of Pforr, 144 Cal. 126, 77 Pac. 825. An administrator can not make investments for the heirs, nor satisfy adverse claims, nor sell because the estate would profit by it.—Brenham v. Story, 39 Cal. 179, 188. A sale by an executor under a power in the will is not a judicial sale, nor does the statutory requirement that no title shall pass until the sale is confirmed give to it the incidents of a judicial sale.—Godell v. Sanford, 31 Mont. 163, 77 Pac. 522, 524. A power of sale given to the creditors as such is not applicable to trust property distributed to them as trustees under the will.—Goad v. Montgomery, 119 Cal. 552, 561, 63 Am. St. Rep. 145, 51 Pac. 681. A sale under a power in a will must be made by the executors in the course of administration; and the court has power at any time to direct a sale, when it is necessary for the purposes of administration, to pay creditors, or when it will be for the advantage of those interested in the estate, or when such interested persons assent to it.—Estate of Pforr, 144 Cal. 121, 126, 77 Pac. 825. When a testator confers upon each one of several executors full power to administer, and gives to each all the power over his property which he himself possesses, power is conferred thereby, not to his executors jointly, but to each of them, and consequently each one is authorized to dispose of the property for the purposes mentioned in the will.—Panaud v. Jones, 1 Cal. 488, 510. The legislature may give to the husband the right to authorize an executor to sell any portion of the community property without obtaining an order of the court therefor.—Sharp v. Loupe, 120 Cal. 89, 91, 52 Pac. 134, 586. The testator has the same right to authorize the executor to determine the portion of his estate which should be sold for the purpose of paying his debts, as he had to designate any portion to be appropriated for their payment.—Sharp v. Loupe, 120 Cal. 89, 93, 52 Pac. 134, 586. There is a clearly marked distinction between a mere executor (whether his power to sell lands is conferred by the will or by the order of the probate court), and an executor to whom the lands are devised in trust to carry into effect the provisions of the will. In the former case he possesses the power of sale, but in the latter he takes the fee, or any less estate which the testator may devise.—Estate of Delaney, 49 Cal. 76, 85. A sale by executors or trustees under a will

is on the same footing as a judicial sale, and where there is jurisdiction or authority to make the sale, the purchaser takes the complete
title of the decedent relieved of all burdens and liabilities of the administration under which the sale is made and that the purchase price or
proceeds of such sale takes the place of the property so disposed of
and which proceeds become liable for the burdens of administration,
for the payment of debts, legacies, etc., and that the heir takes a
distributive share of the proceeds and has no title to the land after the
decease of the ancestor.—Spencer v. Lyman, 27 S. D. 471, 480, 131
N. W. 802. An executor having power, under a will, to sell land,
may sell the whole of it, notwithstanding that it is community property,
if necessary, to pay the charges and expenses of administration.—
Tatum v. Iowa Water Co., 34 Cal. App. 55, 166 Pac. 817. Under a will
directing the executor to sell all the testator's property as soon as
convenient after his death, but giving no directions as to the manner
and terms of sale, the executor can not give a valid option to purchase
real estate without giving notice of the sale as required by section
1257 L. O. L.—Jones v. Ross, 82 Or. 706, 162 Pac. 974. An executor,
directed by will to sell the testator's property, but not so directed as to
the manner and terms of sale, may sell without an order of court, but
must in all the steps save the actual sale itself, follow the statute.—
Jones v. Ross, 82 Or. 706, 162 Pac. 974.

(2) No implied power when.—An executor has no implied power to
sell lands, arising from the mere charge of debts upon it made by the
will. The lands descend to the heir or devisee, subject to the charge,
and the executor has no power to sell them to enforce the charge.—
Worley v. Taylor, 21 Or. 589, 28 Am. St. Rep. 771, 28 Pac. 903, 904.

REFERENCES.

Executor or administrator is vested with power of sale by implication when.—See note 87 Am. Dec. 209-217.

(3) Discretion of executor.—Though executors may have a discretion, under the terms of a will, in making payments for the support of certain designated beneficiaries, yet they have no right to sell
real property belonging to the estate for that purpose without application to and authority from the proper court.—Allen v. Barnes, 5
Utah 100, 12 Pac. 912, 916. The right to determine whether or not
a sale should be made pursuant to a power of sale in the will is
lodged by the testator in the discretion of his executor, who has been
given "full power and authority to grant, bargain, sell, and convey
all property, real or personal, or to pay dividends, without application
to any court for authority to do so." The court will not inquire into
the fairness of the sale, where one is made, or the reasonable adequacy of the purchase price, where such questions are not presented
by averments and proof; and the discretion of the executor, exercised
in good faith, as to whether or not the sales were for the best interests

of the estate, is controlling.—Estate of Wickersham, 139 Cal. 652, 655, 73 Pac. 541. An executrix who, in selling real estate under a will which provided that the property "may be sold when a fair price may be obtained therefor satisfactory to all," used the same judgment in selling such property as she did toward her own, and received the approbation of her two brothers, who were co-owners with her of such property, will be deemed to have used all necessary care, and entitled to commissions on the sale.—Estate of Robl, 163 Cal. 801, Ann. Cas. 1914A, 319, 127 Pac. 55.

(4) For best interests of estate.—A power of sale, given by will to an executor as such, is a limited power, where it manifestly embraces only the right to make a sale for the best interests of the estate.— Cowell v. South Denver Real Estate Co., 16 Colo. App. 108, 63 Pac. 991, 993. A power given in a will to an executor to make a sale for the best interests of the estate, and coupled with a life estate, gives no right to make any sale or disposition of the property, unless such a sale or disposition is necessary to carry out the express provisions of the will, and is essential to the due administration of the estate.— Cowell v. South Denver Real Estate Co., 16 Colo. App. 108, 63 Pac. 991, 995. Where there is a general devise without any specification as to the estate devised, and an absolute power of disposal, the donee may convey a title in fee, although he may be required to account for the proceeds as a trustee; and this applies to a case in which the testator devised and bequeathed to his widow all his property for certain uses and purposes, with power to sell and to dispose of the same for the use and benefit of the estate.—Savage v. Savage, 51 Or. 167, 94 Pac. 182, 184.

(5) Devesting estate.—A clause in a will, which empowers the executor to sell land to pay the testator's debts, can not operate to devest a child's title to the land, though such child was born after the making of the will, if it was not named or provided for therein.— Worley v. Taylor, 21 Or. 589, 28 Am. St. Rep. 771, 28 Pac. 903, 905. An estate which is cast on the heir by the law, or devolved on him by will, can not be devested or taken away by the exercise of the power of sale given in the will to a representative, unless the intention is most clearly and most unmistakably expressed, and the exercise of that power is essential to the execution of the evident purposes of the testator.—Cowell v. South Denver Real Estate Co., 16 Colo. App. 108, 63 Pac. 991, 993.

(6) Agent to sell. Compensation.—A statute which prescribes the compensation of executors does not apply to the compensation of executors making a sale under a power in the will. In such cases the executor has a right to employ an agent to make the sale, and to agree with him as to his compensation.—Ingham v. Ryan, 18 Colo. App. 347, 71 Pac. 899.

(7) Purchasers. Estoppel.—The purchaser from an executor, at a sale under a power in the will, deals with him, in making the purchase, as he would with any other vendor.—Estate of Pearsons, 98 Cal. 603, 612, 33 Pac. 451, 102 Cal. 569, 574, 36 Pac. 934. Purchasers at a sale made by virtue of a power in the will are estopped from saying that they received no title, or that the sale was irregularly made, where they have assented thereto for years, entered into possession of the property, sold portions thereof, made payments on the purchase price and in all respects have ratified the sale until sued for the balance of the purchase price.—Godell v. Sanford, 31 Mont. 163, 77 Pac. 522, 525.

(8) Validity of sale. Notice.—Before a power in a will to make a sale can have any validity, it is essential that the will shall have been admitted to probate.—Estate of Pearsons, 98 Cal. 603, 613, 33 Pac. 451. A person empowered by will to make a sale of property may be vested with a wide discretion in doing so, and the sale will not be disturbed where the donee of a power does not appear to have transgressed his rights under the terms of the will.—Godell v. Sanford, 31 Mont. 163, 77 Pac. 522, 525. Where the intent of the testator was to withdraw his estate from the operation of the probate act, and vest in his executor full power to convert, in his own way, the estate into cash for the benefit of the devisees, it is not essential to the validity of his sale that it should be conducted in the statutory mode. The party, in such case, acts under the will, and, like a power of an attorney, the will is to be looked to and consulted on the question of power, and if found sufficient, the act must be declared valid.—Larco v. Casaneuava, 30 Cal. 561, 569. A sale of the estate of a decedent, by an executor and trustee of the estate with power to sell, but not to mortgage, may be valid, and transfer the estate to the purchaser, although mortgages given to secure the debts for which the property was sold are void. In such a case the purchaser will not hold the property as security for a debt, but as an absolute transfer.—Sprague v. Betz, 44 Wash. 650, 87 Pac. 916, 918. Where a sale was made by an executor, and the deposit and the bid were made for a proposed sale to be authorized by an order of the court, and it was such a sale only which was confirmed, the validity of the sale must be determined by the sale made, and not by the supposed validity of a sale which might have been made under authority given in the will.—Hellman v. Merz, 112 Cal. 661, 667, 44 Pac. 1079. A memorandum of agreement to sell, the sale being under a power in the will, is sufficient, where it contains the names of the parties, a sufficient description of the property for identification, and the price and terms of purchase, and states that the sale is made subject to confirmation by the superior court; and such memorandum can not be said to be insufficient to take the sale out of the statute of frauds.—Estate of Robinson, 142 Cal. 152, 155, 75 Pac. 777. A power of sale in the will does not authorize a conveyance, by the executor, of the wife's share of the community property.—King v. La Grange, 50 Cal. 328. Under the circumstances of this case a sale by the executor named in the will, to whom letters testamentary had been issued, under a power of sale authorizing the executors to sell the real and personal property, is not void because the other executor named in the will renounced his appointment and refused to accept the trust.—Smith v. Steen, 20 N. M. 436, 150 Pac. 927, 928. Where a sale of corporate stock, belonging to the estate of a deceased person, has been sold by an executor under a nonintervention will, before his appointment, but for the purpose of raising money to save the remainder of the stock and to pay debts of the estate; where such stock is the only asset of the estate; and where it is admitted that the money derived from the sale was used for such purpose, the subsequent probate of the will, in effect, ratifies the sale, although the will has since been set aside on the grounds of testamentary incapacity and undue influence; the sale is therefore valid, and an administrator de bonis non can not, as against the purchaser, avoid it.—In re Crim's Estate, 89 Wash. 395, 154 Pac. 811. If there be a construction of a will, by a court having jurisdiction, as giving an executor or administrator authority to sell without notice, and the subsequent order confirming such sale is made without the court's having jurisdiction, the order is not void; and the title of the purchaser is good as against one claiming under the decedent.—Tatum v. Iowa Water Co., 34 Cal. App. 55, 166 Pac. 817. Statutes of 1851, page 470, section 177 of the Probate Act in effect in 1872, provided that notice should be given by an executor of the sale of real estate, unless there was special direction given in the will, in which case the executor should be goverened by such direction. It was held that a sale of real estate under a power given in a will, though made without notice, was not invalid where the will made no specific direction as to whether the sale should be with or without notice, but provided that the executors, within a reasonable time, should sell the property.— Bagley v. City and County of San Francisco, 19 Cal. App. 255, 125 Pac. 931.

(9) Equitable conversion. Election for reconversion.—The question of equitable conversion is a question of intention. If it is apparent from the terms of the will that it was the testator's intention that his estate be sold and the proceeds given to his beneficiaries, an equitable conversion results, even if the direction for the sale is not imperative.— Estate of Pforr, 144 Cal. 121, 128, 77 Pac. 825. As reconversion depends upon an election therefor by the beneficiaries, such election is an affirmative element in the establishment of their right to the land, and must be manifested by some unequivocal act or declaration; and the plaintiff, whose right of action rests upon a reconversion resulting from such election, must not only show this fact by his complaint, but also establish it by proof.—Bank of Ukiah v. Rice, 143 Cal. 265, 101 Am. St. Rep. 118, 76 Pac. 1020, 1022. Until the beneficiaries make an election for reconversion of the estate, and manifest such

intention to the executor, they are not entitled to the possession of the land, nor to exercise any dominion over it. The executor of the will is entitled to the possession of the land until the estate is settled or delivered to the heirs or devisees, "by order of the court."—Bank of Ukiah v. Rice, 143 Cal. 265, 101 Am. St. Rep. 118, 76 Pac. 1020, 1022. Where a testator directs land to be sold, and the proceeds thereof to be distributed between certain designated beneficiaries, such beneficiaries may elect, before the sale has taken place, to take the land instead of its proceeds, and when they have so elected and sufficiently manifested their election, the authority to sell the land can not thereafter be exercised by the executor, but is extinguished. The estate is to be reconverted into real property, and, by reason of such reconversion, the relation of the beneficiaries to the land is the same as if it had been directly devised to them.—Bank of Ukiah v. Rice, 143 Cal. 265, 101 Am. St. Rep. 118, 76 Pac. 1020, 1022. A conveyance by one beneficiary of his undivided interest in land will not operate as a reconversion of that interest.—Bank of Ukiah v. Rice, 143 Cal. 265, 101 Am. St. Rep. 118, 76 Pac. 1020, 1023. The commencement of an action for a partition of land is a positive and unequivocal act, indicating an election to take the land, where, by the terms of the will, land is to be sold and the proceeds divided between certain beneficiaries.—Bank of Ukiah v. Rice, 143 Cal. 265, 101 Am. St. Rep. 118, 76 Pac. 1020, 1023 (showing other positive and unequivocal acts indicating an election for a reconversion). In the case of Wood v. Pohrsson, 21 N. D. 357, 370, 130 N. W. 1010, it is held that where the will directed the executrix to sell on or before a certain date all the testator's real estate and that the proceeds were to be distributed among the children, such provision operated as an equitable conversion of such real property with personalty, from the date of the testator's death, for the purpose of its administration.

REFERENCES.

Equitable conversion.—See note 5 L. R. A. 104. Effect of provisions in will for equitable conversion upon wife's dower or distributive share, where the will makes no provision for her, or she renounces such provision.—See note 22 L. R. A. (N. S.) 285. When there is such a failure of testator's purpose or object as to preclude the application of the doctrine of equitable conversion.—See note 20 L. R. A. (N. S.) 117. When conversion takes place under a direction to sell real property, which postpones the sale to an ascertainable time.—See note 20 L. R. A. (N. S.) 65. Conversion by directing sale after devising land.—See note 39 L. R. A. (N. S.) 817.

(10) **Devise in trust with power to sell.**—By a will devising to the executor the fee of the lands in question, to be held in trust for the purposes mentioned in the will, the testator intended to give and did give the executor the power of sale without requiring a compliance with the provisions of the probate act applicable to the procuring of

orders of sale and confirmations.—Estate of Delaney, 49 Cal. 76, 85.
The renunciation, by the widow of the testator, of her right under the
will, and the order of the probate court setting off to her a portion
of the property as common property, does not extinguish the trust
declared in the will, nor devest the executor of the fee, nor alter his
powers, in the remaining portion of the property.—Estate of Delaney,
49 Cal. 76, 84. It is within the province of the probate court to determine whether a valid trust has been created, but the power to regulate and direct its subsequent administration is in a court possessed
of general equity jurisdiction.—Estate of Hinckley, 58 Cal. 518; Estate
of Thompson, 101 Cal. 349, 353, 35 Pac. 991; Morffew v. San Francisco,
etc., R. R. Co., 107 Cal. 587, 594, 40 Pac. 810. Under a will creating
a trust for the purpose of the preservation of an estate, "with an
ordained succession of trustees," permitting, however, a sale of unproductive property if found desirable, the lands thus delivered into the
hands of a trustee, although he is also executor of the estate of the
deceased, ceases to be part of the estate in the course of administration, and the probate court and its successor, the superior court, in the
exercise of probate jurisdiction, has no further control of the same.—
Morffew v. San Francisco, etc., R. R. Co., 107 Cal. 587, 594, 40 Pac.
810. The circumstance that, at a future time, there is to be a division
of the property among the remaindermen, beneficiaries of the trust,
does not affect the rule.—Estate of Thompson, 101 Cal. 349, 353, 35 Pac.
991, 36 Pac. 98, 508; Morffew v. San Francisco, etc., R. R. Co., 107 Cal.
587, 594, 40 Pac. 810. No ground for an action to declare a trust exists,
where the title to real estate is vested in the heirs under a will giving
to the executor complete power to dispose of the property of the
estate "as to him shall seem best, etc., and without responsibility."—
Augulsola v. Arnaz, 51 Cal. 435, 439. The quantity of interest which
passes to the trustee in case of an express trust is commensurate with
the necessities of his office; the trustee shall have an estate in fee, if
that is necessary, to enable him to perform the duties imposed upon
him, although it is not, in terms, given to him by the instrument
creating the trust. A devise of lands, in trust, to sell, clothes the
trustee with a fee, because that is necessary to the execution of
the trust.—Morffew v. San Francisco, etc., R. R. Co., 107 Cal. 587, 595,
40 Pac. 810; Young v. Bradley, 101 U. S. 787, 25 L. Ed. 1044. A provision in a will, appointing a trustee apparently for the sole purpose of investing the proceeds of the sale of lands, and the payment of
the same to relatives of the decedent, and from which no intention
of the testator is apparent to devise the land directly to the trustee,
does not create a testamentary trust to sell land.—Estate of Walker,
149 Cal. 627, 85 Pac. 310. A life estate in the trustee, being created
by express words in the will, with limitation over, is not enlarged
to a fee by a power of sale.—Morffew v. San Francisco, etc., R. R. Co.,
107 Cal. 587, 596, 40 Pac. 810. The lands of an estate, delivered into
the hands of the executor, as the donee of a power under the will, in

his character as trustee, cease to be a part of the estate in the course of administration; and the probate court, in the exercise of probate jurisdiction, has no further control of the same.—Morffew v. San Francisco, etc., R. R. Co., 107 Cal. 587, 594, 40 Pac. 810. Where a will of a testatrix after providing for the payment of certain special pecuniary legacies, directed that all her real estate, with a specified exception, should be sold by her executors .to the best advantage, and after the payment of such legacies which were expressly charged upon the real estate so to be sold bequeathed "all the rest and residue of the proceeds of said real estate so as to be sold" to certain persons named as trustees in trust, to found and maintain a home for aged and infirm men, and by a residuary clause bequeathed the remainder of her estate to her husband, the only proceeds of her real property passing to such trustees were proceeds of such real property as she owned at her death and which her executors were empowered to sell. The proceeds of a portion of her real estate, sold in her lifetime, under a contract for its sale which had become executed before her death, and which proceeds were collected by her executors after her death, did not pass to such trustees but passed under the residuary clause. There is nothing in the provisions of sections 1301 or 1303 of the Civil Code of California militating against such a construction.—Estate of Dwyer, 159 Cal. 664, 115 Pac. 235.

(11) Directions coupled with the trust.‸ Effect of.—A will which merely gives the executor certain directions to be observed in carrying out its conditions does not create an express trust in the real property to which such directions relate. To the extent that such directions are inconsistent with the law, they are nugatory.—Estate of Pforr, 144 Cal. 121, 125, 77 Pac. 825. A direction, in the will, to the executor to collect the rents and maintain the estate for a definite term, is not a restriction upon its alienation during that period, nor is the provision for its sale at the expiration of such term a prohibition against its sale prior to that time.—Estate of Pforr, 144 Cal. 121, 126, 77 Pac. 825. A provision contained in a will, directing the executor to sell the property within one year, is merely directory, and does not limit the exercise of the power to that period, where power to sell is coupled with, and is subsidiary to, certain express trusts, and is given as the means, and the only means, of carrying out those trusts.—Kidwell v. Brummagim, 32 Cal. 437, 442.

REFERENCES.

Interest in lands is taken by an executor or administrator under the will for the purpose of executing a power when.—See note 12 Am. Dec. 102-104. Right of executor, after discharge, to sell real estate under a direction in the will.—See note 2 L. R. A. (N. S.) 623.

(12) Power passes to administrator with will annexed.—The power to sell as set forth in a will passes to the administrator with the will annexed, as such power is not merely personal, but is given to the

executor, as such, by virtue of his office.—Kidwell v. Brummagim, 32 Cal. 436, 442. A distinction is made, however, between cases where the power to sell under a will passes to the administrator with the will annexed, not as a mere naked power, but a power coupled with various trusts which could only be carried out through an execution of the power, and those cases which clearly show that where the terms made use of in creating the power, detached from other parts of the will, confer merely a naked power to sell.—Kidwell v. Brummagim, 32 Cal. 437, 440. An executor or administrator with the will annexed, where power of sale of real estate has been given by the will, has, as a general rule, considerable discretion as to the manner and conduct of such sale, and may sell at private sale at his discretion, when prudently and honestly exercised.—Bull v. Bal, 17 N. M. 466, 130 Pac. 252.

REFERENCES.

Whether a special power, other than a power of sale, conferred on executor by will passes to an administrator with the will annexed.— See note 29 L. R. A. (N. S.) 264.

(13) **Particular sales under power in the will.**—An executor having moved, before the hearing, to dismiss his own petition for a sale, upon a satisfactory showing that the sale had in fact been made by him in his character of devisee in trust, and no creditor or distributee having objected, the court should have dismissed the proceeding, and left the sale to stand upon the same footing with other sales made by the trustee as such.—Estate of Williams, 92 Cal. 183, 187, 28 Pac. 227, 679.

REFERENCES.

Sales of property of testators under authority of the will generally.— See § 571, ante.

(14) **Purchase by executor failing to qualify.**—The fact that a person is named in the will as executor, and actually applies for letters, but refuses or fails to qualify as executor, does not constitute him a trustee for the estate at the time the contract of sale was made, and at which sale such person becomes a purchaser, where it appears that he paid full consideration for the property purchased by him, and that the estate was in no way injured by his acts.—Bowden v. Pierce, 73 Cal. 459, 464, 14 Pac. 302, 15 Pac. 64.

(15) **Return of sales under power in will. Confirmation.**—While an executor may sell land under a power in the will, his sale thereof must be reported to the court and confirmed, as in other cases of sales of real property by executors or administrators.—Northrop v. Marquam, 16 Or. 173, 18 Pac. 449, 457. The statute contemplates that the same proceedings shall be had with respect to the return of sale, whether the sale is made under a power in the will or under an order of court. If the will creates a naked power,—a power not coupled with an interest,—the executors must give notice of the sale,

return accounts thereof, and, unless there are special directions in the will, must conduct the sale in all respects as if made under an order of the court. If no date was fixed by order of the court or judge, and no notice of the hearing of the report, or the filing thereof, was given by posting or publication, and where it does not appear in the record that the persons interested in the estate were actually present at the hearing, in person or by attorney, the order purporting to confirm the sale is properly set aside, as the probate court may annul it whenever the attention of the judge is called to the circumstance that it was made without the acquisition of jurisdiction over the persons of all interested.—Estate of Durham, 49 Cal. 490, 495; Perkins v. Gridley, 50 Cal. 97, 100. An executor, to whom lands have been devised in trust for sale to pay debts of the estate, can legally sell and convey such lands to a purchaser without confirmation by the probate court.—Estate of Williams, 92 Cal. 183, 185, 28 Pac. 227, 679. If, under a will, the executor is given power, after the expiration of two years from the death of the testator, to sell any portion of his estate at public or private sale, "without any order of court, or being required to account to any court," such will does not have the effect of creating a valid trust in relation to the land, or any other trust than such as pertains to the office as executor, and such sale must be confirmed by the court before title is passed.—Bennalack v. Richards, 116 Cal. 405, 408, 48 Pac. 622, 125 Cal. 427, 432, 58 Pac. 65. If the only persons interested in the proceeds of any sale of the property of the estate have so ratified the contract made by the executor under a supposed power in the will as to estop them from disputing it, the probate court may, upon that ground alone, confirm the sale, and direct the execution of a conveyance on a compliance by the purchaser with the terms of the contract.—Estate of Walker, 149 Cal. 627, 85 Pac. 310.

40. As affecting pretermitted child.—A pretermitted child is not estopped, by the decree of distribution, from claiming any portion of the estate, where the proceedings as to such child are void for want of jurisdiction.—Pearson v. Pearson, 46 Cal. 610, 635. Minor children of the decedent, not provided for in his will, and the will not showing that the omission to provide for them was intentional, succeed immediately, by operation of law, to the same portion of the testator's real property as if no will had been made. As to such portion, the testator is to be regarded as dying intestate, and its succession is directed by law, and not by the will. As a necessary consequence of this construction, it follows that every provision of the will, directly or indirectly attempting to dispose of such portion of the estate, except for the discharge of the decedent's debts, or other charges accruing in due course of administration, is inoperative as against such child. This title of a pretermitted child can not be devested by a sale made by the executrix of his father's will.—Smith v. Olmstead, 88 Cal. 582, 585, 22 Am. St. Rep. 336, 12 L. R. A. 46, 26 Pac. 521; quoting from and approving Brenham v. Story, 39 Cal. 188. See Estate of Wardell, 57

Cal. 439.   The omitted child takes title by descent, and becomes a
tenant in common with the devisees.—Pearson v. Pearson, 46 Cal. 610,
628.   A power of sale in a will does not authorize a sale of the interest
of a child not mentioned in the will.—Smith v. Olmstead, 3 Cal. Unrep.
223, 22 Pac. 1143.   An order of confirmation, in such cases, imparts
no validity to the sale as against such interests; it only adjudicates
that the power contained in the will had been followed, and that the
sale was for a fair price.—Smith v. Olmstead, 88 Cal. 582, 588, 22
Am. St. Rep. 336, 12 L. R. A. 46, 26 Pac. 521. (quoting from and approving Brenham v. Story, 39 Cal. 188).   A recital in the decree, and the
appearance of the "attorney appointed to represent the minor heirs
of said estate," must be construed as an appearance by him only for
the minors whom he had been appointed to represent, and not for a
minor pretermitted child for whom he had no authority to appear.—
Pearson v. Pearson, 46 Cal. 610, 636.   The sale of personal property
by the personal representatives during the pendency of the administration, under power of sale contained in the will, passes good title
thereto as against a pretermitted child.—Smith v. Steen, 20 N. M. 436.
150 Pac. 927, 929.   Under the provisions of the statute of New Mexico,
the ancestor dies intestate as regards a child not named or provided
for in the will and a sale by the executor of real estate of the estate.
under power of sale contained in the will, does not devest the pretermitted child of his interest therein.—Smith v. Steen, 20 N. M. 436,
150 Pac. 927, 929.

41. Limitation of actions for vacating sale.—An application to sell
real estate of a decedent is not, in any sense of the term, an action
to recover real estate or the possession of it; nor is it an action
arising out of the title thereto, or the rents and profits thereof; and,
since the petition for the sale must set forth the debts of the estate,
it would seem that the appropriate limitation may then be invoked in
order to defeat a particular claim, and therefore the sale pro tanto.—
In re Tuohy's Estate, 33 Mont. 230, 83 Pac. 486, 490.   The period of
three years prescribed by the statute within which the heirs of the
decedent may avoid a sale made by an executor or administrator does
not run if it appears that the heirs had no cause of action against
the purchaser.—Campbell v. Drais, 125 Cal. 253, 260, 57 Pac. 994.   The
limitation of the code with reference to actions for the recovery of
any estates sold by an executor or administrator does not affect the
question of title, but simply refers to a right of action.   Hence, if
no title passed at a probate sale, it is in the heirs and their grantees,
and is not affected by the statute of limitations.—Gage v. Downey,
94 Cal. 241, 251, 29 Pac. 635, 79 Cal. 140, 21 Pac. 855.   The law limiting,
to three years after the settlement of the final account, the time within
which one claiming under the decedent may sue to recover property
of the estate sold by the executor or administrator, extends to sales
made without notice by the administrator with the will annexed when
authorized by the will.—Tatum v. Iowa Water Co., 34 Cal. App. 55, 166

Pac. 817. It may ᵢbe that a sale, by an administrator with the will annexed, made without notice, was unauthorized, and that therefore the order confirming it was void; nevertheless a person claiming under the decedent must, if he would recover the property sold, bring his suit within three years after the settlement of the final account.— Tatum v. Iowa Water Co., 34 Cal. App. 55, 166 Pac. 817. The statute whereby a suit to recover real property, sold by an executor or administrator under order of court, must be begun within five years after the recording of the deed, does not bar a suit by a person whose claim arises from a source paramount and superior to the deed of an executor or administrator.—Byerly v. Eadie, 95 Kan. 400, 148 Pac. 757. When a person files on public land and, on his dying before making final proof, the government issues the patent to his heirs, an action by these heirs to quiet title, as against purchasers at a sale by the administrator of the ancestor's estate, may be begun regardless of the statute barring suits on an administrator's deed after five years from its being placed on record.—Byerly v. Eadie, 95 Kan. 400, 148 Pac. 757.

III. CONFIRMATION OF SALES AND CONVEYANCES.

1. Discretion of court as to confirmation.—The court doubtless has the power to confirm or refuse to confirm, but this is not an arbitrary power; it is neither more nor less than a sound discretion, and must be exercised with a just regard to the rights of all concerned, subject to the review of the appellate tribunal, and the propriety of its exercise depends upon the circumstances of each case. A rightful`exercise of this discretion requires due consideration of the rights and interests of all concerned, the purchaser as well as others.—Dunn v. Dunn, 137 Cal. 51, 59, 69 Pac. 847. From the express provisions of section 7548, Rev. Codes of Montana, there is implied authority for the district court or judge to exercise a judicial discretion in determining whether a particular sale of personal property belonging to an estate shall, or shall not, be confirmed and where on application for confirmation a higher bid is made it is not an abuse of that discretion for the court to refuse to confirm the sale and to order a resale.— State v. District Court, etc., 42 Mont. 182, 111 Pac. 719. There is implied authority in the Montana statute for the district court or judge to exercise a judicial discretion in determining whether a particular sale of personal property, belonging to an estate, shall or shall not be confirmed.—State v. District Court, 42 Mont. 182, 187, 111 Pac. 717. "Disproportionate to the value" means disproportionate to the value at the time the bid was made.—McGregor v. Jensen, 18 Idaho 320, 326, 109 Pac. 729. If it appears upon the hearing of a return of the sale of real property by an administrator that the purchaser is acting under the direction and in the interest of a real estate broker who is secretly purchasing the property himself in order to make a profit on a resale, the court is justified in finding the sale is tainted

Probate Law—83

with unfairness within the meaning of sections 1552 and 1554 of the California Code of Civil Procedure.—Estate of Bradley, 168 Cal. 655, 144 Pac. 186.

2. **Authority to confirm, when presumed.**—As the court has power to make an order confirming an administrator's sale of personal assets in a proper case, its authority to act will be presumed, unless the want of such authority is clearly made to appear.—Jerrue v. Superior Court, 7 Cal. App. 717, 95 Pac. 906, 907.

3. **When required.**—The court has no authority or jurisdiction to set aside the order of sale, to refuse to confirm a sale, or to hear any evidence in relation thereto outside of the method provided by statute, and in disregard of the rights of a purchaser after a sale. If the order of sale is regularly made, and it has not been appealed from, it is binding upon all. The purchaser is entitled to have the sale confirmed, if there is no valid reason within the law why this should not be done.—Dunn v. Dunn, 137 Cal. 51, 58, 69 Pac. 847. Upon the court's own finding that the sale "was legally made and fairly conducted"; that due proof was made, to its satisfaction; that the price was not disproportionate to the value of the property; and that a sum exceeding the bid of the appellant (ten per cent, exclusive of the expenses of a new sale) can not be obtained,—it only remains for the court to confirm the sale, where the order of sale has not been vacated, and no appeal has been taken therefrom, even though it is admitted that the court erred in directing too large an amount of the property to be sold.—Estate of Spriggs, 20 Cal. 121, 126. Words in a will, which direct that the executor "shall have the property sold" at the expiration of two years after the testator's death, and shall distribute the proceeds among designated beneficiaries, do not confer upon the executor the power to sell as a trustee. The sale which is thus directed is to be made by the executor as executor of the will, and as a part of his administration of the estate, and not as a trustee of an express trust, and will be ineffectual without a confirmation by the court.—Estate of Pforr, 144 Cal. 121, 126, 77 Pac. 825. Under the statute of Idaho, it is mandatory that all sales be reported, under oath, to the probate court and be confirmed by it, before title to the property sold can pass; and where there is no return of sale, the order confirming a sale is void.—People v. Cunningham, 6 Idaho 113, 53 Pac. 451. If objections are made to the confirmation of the sale and, on a hearing, it appears to the probate court that the sale was fair, and that the sum bid was a reasonable and fair value for the property sold, it is the duty of the probate court to confirm the sale; and, where the case has been tried anew, on its appeal to the district court, it is equally the duty of that court to confirm the sale, where the same elements of fairness appear.—McGregor v. Jensen, 18 Idaho 320, 109 Pac. 729.

4. When not required.—Under a will that creates a trust, with power in the trustee to sell the property without the intervention of any court, no confirmation by the court is required or authorized by law.—Morffew v. San Francisco, etc., R. R. Co., 107 Cal. 587, 595, 40 Pac. 810. If the order of sale is coram non judice, then the "sale" is no sale, and it can not be made valid and binding by any number of so-called confirmations. The sale being void, there is no subject-matter upon which the order of confirmation can act.—Townsend v. Tallant, 33 Cal. 45, 54, 91 Am. Dec. 617.

5. No power to confirm when.—If, at the time an executor or administrator asks for a confirmation of a sale of the real estate of a deceased person, the court is confronted with a valid order by which that sale has been annulled, it is without jurisdiction to grant the application.—Estate of Devincenzi, 131 Cal. 452, 453, 63 Pac. 723.

6. Objections to confirmation.—The provisions of the statute allowing objections to be made to the sale, and requiring for its efficacy a confirmation by the court, are only intended to secure such an execution of the order of sale that a just and fair price may be obtained for the property for the benefit of the estate. The authority of the court is limited to such a supervision and control that this end may be effected. —Estate of Spriggs, 20 Cal. 121; Estate of Leonis, 138 Cal. 194, 199, 71 Pac. 171. At a probate sale the court is regarded as the vendor, and the purchaser who buys property at the sale has the right to a conveyance that will vest in him the title of the property sold. He may present, in objection to its confirmation, any facts that will impair or defeat the title thereby transferred.—Estate of Pearsons, 98 Cal. 603, 612, 33 Pac. 451. An objection to the confirmation of the sale, on the ground that the bond required by the probate judge had not in fact been given, is a valid one, and the objecting party should be permitted to submit his proof in support of his objections.—Estate of Arguello, 50 Cal. 308, 310. Objections may be made to the confirmation of the sale by any one interested.—McGregor v. Jensen, 18 Ida. 320, 109 Pac. 729. The mere filing of objections do not amount to anything unless they are supported by evidence.—Estate of Christensen, 15 Ida. 692, 697, 99 Pac. 829. When return to a probate sale is made and filed, any person interested in the estate may file written objections to confirmation, and a hearing shall be had thereon. The issues formed by the return and the objections present the issues to be tried by the probate court.—Estate of Christensen, 15 Ida. 692, 695, 99 Pac. 829. The successor of the sole heir of the deceased is a party interested in such sale, and entitled to resist the confirmation thereof and appeal from the order of confirmation, and the fact that she was in good faith asserting an adverse title to the land, which was the cause of the low bid, does not estop her from objecting to the confirmation.—Estate of Bazzuro, 161 Cal. 73, 118 Pac. 434.

7. Effect of the order.—The order of confirmation is a final judgment, and, in the absence of an appeal, is as conclusive on the rights of the parties as could be any adjudication by a court of competent jurisdiction.—Lake v. Hathaway, 75 Kan. 391, 89 Pac. 666; Watson v. Trondle, 33 Neb. 450, 29 Am. St. Rep. 492, 50 N. W. 331. The fact that the court confirms a sale upon the return thereof, made by an administrator pursuant to an order of sale, is not an adjudication against the alleged purchaser. He may not have bid at all, or if he did bid, he may have been, by timely withdrawal, or otherwise, legally released from any obligation thereon. In an action to enforce the alleged contract of purchase against him, the proceedings, at most, could constitute evidence only in a prima facie case.—Jerrue v. Superior Court, 7 Cal. App. 717, 95 Pac. 906, 907. Where a sale was made for cash and for more than the appraised value, and confirmed, any irregularity in failing to state the terms of sale, as required by the statute, is cured.—Plains L. & I. Co. v. Lynch, 38 Mont. 271, 285, 129 Am. St. Rep. 645, 99 Pac. 847. It is the order of confirmation which finally operates to devest the heirs of their title and to secure the property to the purchaser; all errors, irregularities, and defects, not jurisdictional, are cured by confirmation.—Plains L. & I. Co. v. Lynch, 38 Mont. 271, 285, 286, 129 Am. St. Rep. 645, 99 Pac. 847. Errors made in the granting of decrees in confirmation of sales should be taken advantage of by appropriate action at the time; otherwise, the confirmation can not be assailed.—Rountree v. Montague, 30 Cal. App. 170, 157 Pac. 623.

8. Refusing confirmation. Effect of the order.—On refusal to confirm the first sale, it is in the discretion of the court either to order a new sale or to accept another bid of an advance of ten per cent and additional costs.—Griffin v. Warner, 48 Cal. 383, 385. Or the court may merely vacate the sale and continue the cause for further proceedings. —Griffin v. Warner, 48 Cal. 383, 385. In a case where confirmation is set aside for insufficiency of notice of the hearing, proceedings for hearing upon the application to confirm may be renewed, and, if the bid be disproportionate to the value of the property in the amount designated by the statute, such sale may be set aside.—Estate of Durham, 49 Cal. 490, 495; Perkins v. Gridley, 50 Cal. 95, 100. It was an abuse of discretion for the court to confirm a sale of real property belonging to the estate of a deceased person, for a price less than one-sixth of its real value, because of supposed defects in its title, where it appears probable that such defects could have been removed by a suit brought for that purpose. The court should have directed suit to that end, and, in the meantime, refused confirmation.—Estate of Bazzuro, 161 Cal. 72, 118 Pac. 434.

9. Refusal to report sale for confirmation. Effect of.—Where the executor refuses to report a sale to the court for confirmation, in violation of a duty imposed upon him by law, and having put the purchaser in possession, and permitted him to make improvements to an amount nearly or quite equal to the value of the property at the time the contract of sale was made, he can not invoke the aid of a court of equity to compel an accounting, or to place the property in the hands of a receiver, until some future order of the court. In making the sale, the executor exercised and exhausted his power to deal with the property, unless, upon reporting to the court, confirmation of the sale was refused.—Bennalack v. Richards, 125 Cal. 427, 433, 58 Pac. 65.

10. Action to set aside confirmation.—No one but parties interested in the estate may object to confirmation. This being true, a complaint does not state facts sufficient to constitute a cause of action, and a demurrer thereto is properly sustained, where the action to set aside a confirmation is brought by parties who allege that they are willing to pay an advance of ten per cent on the price for which the lands were sold, all objections by the heirs and other parties interested to confirmation having been withdrawn or abandoned.—Terry v. Clothier, 1 Wash. 475, 25 Pac. 673.

11. Writ to compel confirmation.—The district court, sitting in probate, has a discretion to refuse to confirm a sale of personal property upon the sole ground that a bid of ten per cent in excess of the former bid, together with the costs of resale, has been received; and, where no abuse of such discretion is shown, an application for a writ of supervisory control to compel the confirmation of the sale will be dismissed.—State v. District Court, 42 Mont. 182, 187, 111 Pac. 717.

12. Conveyance.

(1) In general.—The word "administrator," following the name of a person in a deed, is simply descriptive of the person, and is not entitled to any greater significance.—Love v. Love, 72 Kan. 658, 83 Pac. 201, 202. Where land was purchased from the estate in good faith, and the purchase price thereof was paid into the estate and used in the administration thereof, the administrator's deed should not be set aside without repayment of the purchase price.—Ball v. Clothier, 34 Wash. 299, 75 Pac. 1099, 1104; Wilson v. Morrell, 5 Wash. 654, 32 Pac. 733, 734.

REFERENCES.

Validity of deed by executor or administrator to person other than the purchaser.—See note Am. & Eng. Ann. Cas. 708.

(2) May be ordered when.—The probate court has jurisdiction to order a conveyance by an administrator after confirmation of a sale, in a case where the purchase price of the premises sold was paid by the purchaser in cash, less the amount of the mortgage debt against the premises held by the purchaser, for which he was entitled to a credit.—Estate of Lewis, 39 Cal. 306, 307. Where an executor, in satisfaction of mortgage debts, has accepted conveyances of the encumbered land, and also foreclosed mortgages, and, on the sale of the real property affected thereby, takes deeds therefor to himself as executor,

he will, as a condition precedent to his discharge and liberation of his bondsmen, and in order that any right, title, or interest he may have in such premises may be transferred, be required to execute quitclaim deeds of certain designated property.—In re Roach's Estate, 50 Or. 179, 92 Pac. 118, 127.

(3) Is individual deed when.—An administrator's deed, which recites that it was made by the grantor as "administrator of the estate," etc., but which is acknowledged by him individually, is his individual deed, and not his deed as an administrator, where such deed contains no recital showing that it was intended to be a deed by such person in his official capacity as administrator, except as above indicated.— Estate of Conroy, 6 Cal. App. 741, 93 Pac. 205, 206.

(4) Conditions not to be imposed.—When the sale is confirmed, and a deed is ordered and made, the purchaser, or his assignee, is entitled to the possession of it, on payment of the purchase-money, and neither the administrator nor the court can impose any other condition than the payment of the purchase-money, no matter in whose hands the deed is left for delivery.—Cockins v. McCurdy, 40 Kan. 758, 20 Pac. 470.

REFERENCES.

Effect of covenants in conveyances made by executors or administrators.—See note 17 Am. Dec. 224-228.

(5) Title carried by.—Where a trustee is clothed with the legal title, and is not restrained by the terms of the trust, a conveyance by him, although in violation of the trust, carries the legal title, and the beneficiaries must seek their remedy in equity.—Davidson v. Mantor, 45 Wash. 660, 89 Pac. 167. Though an administrator's deed may be ineffectual to convey the legal title, it may pass to the vendee an equitable title.—Wilson v. Morrell, 5 Wash. 654, 32 Pac. 733, 734. The only effect of an administrator's deed is to convey to the purchaser the title of the deceased. Such a deed can contain no warranty of the title. The purchaser must know the law, the character of the sale, the effect of the deed, and is bound to examine the title for himself. The language of the notice puts him upon his guard. In these sales, caveat emptor is the rule.—Halleck v. Guy, 9 Cal. 181, 197, 70 Am. Dec. 643. The only effect of an administrator's deed or bill of sale is to convey to the purchaser the title of the deceased; it can not contain any warranty of title; the rule of caveat emptor applies to probate sales and, in the absence of any special agreement as to the title of the property sold, it is incumbent on the vendee to examine the title for himself.—Payne v. People, — (Colo.) —, 173 Pac. 397.

(6) Is void when.—A conveyance made by an administrator to himself is ipso facto void, without regard to the statute, for it bears its own invalidity upon its face.—Boyd v. Blankman, 29 Cal. 20, 24, 87 Am. Dec. 146. An administrator's deed is void where it appears that the land was sold without the prescribed order, showing notice of the

time and place of the hearing of the petition to sell, and fixing the length of time and the manner in which notice should be given.— Braden v. Mais, 77 Kan. 702, 127 Am. St. Rep. 456, 95 Pac. 412.

(7) Mandate to compel.—A writ of mandate will lie to compel the administrator to execute a conveyance to which the purchaser is entitled.—People v. Cunningham, 6 Ida. 113, 53 Pac. 451.

REFERENCES.

Effect of qualifying words, "as executor" and "as administrator."— See note 15 L. R. A. 850-852. Form and contents of deed of executor or administrator.—See note 56 Am. Dec. 55-58.

IV. DIRECT AND COLLATERAL ATTACK UPON SALES.

1. Direct attack in general.—If the proceedings on a probate sale were defective or irregular in any way, they can only be attacked by a direct action brought for that purpose. They can not be impeached in any collateral suit.—Irwin v. Scriber, 18 Cal. 499. If the petition upon which the order of sale was made is so defective that the court did not acquire jurisdiction, the order may be assailed at any time upon a collateral as well as upon a direct attack; but if the facts stated in the petition were sufficient to confer jurisdiction upon the court to hear the application, its order directing the sale can not be impeached upon a collateral attack.—Estate of Devincenzi, 119 Cal. 498, 500, 51 Pac. 845. On direct appeal from an order of sale, a substantial compliance with the provisions of the statute is essential to the validity of such order.—Estate of Byrne, 112 Cal. 176, 44 Pac. 467; Estate of Levy, 141 Cal. 639, 643, 75 Pac. 317.

2. Distinction between direct and collateral attack.—An action to enjoin the delivery of a deed executed by the executor, and to set aside the orders of a probate court for the sale, and confirmation of the sale, of land in pursuance of which the deed was executed, is a collateral attack on the proceedings in and decision of a court of record.—Lake v. Hathaway, 75 Kan. 391, 89 Pac. 666; Watson v. Trondle, 33 Neb. 450, 29 Am. St. Rep. 492, 50 N. W. 331. The attack on a probate sale is direct and not collateral, where it is based upon the ground of fraud. The fraud must be, however, a fraud extrinsic or collateral to the questions examined and determined in the action. Among the instances given in the books are such as these: keeping the unsuccessful party away from the court by a false promise of a compromise; or purposely keeping him in ignorance of the suit; or where an attorney fraudulently attempts to represent a party and connives at his defeat, or, being regularly employed, corruptly sells out his client.—Bergin v. Haight, 99 Cal. 52, 56, 33 Pac. 760. See Pico v. Cohn, 91 Cal. 129, 133, 25 Am. St. Rep. 159, 13 L. R. A. 336, 25 Pac. 970, 27 Pac. 537. Proceedings in an application for a probate sale are subject to review and reversal, as in other cases, upon a direct attack made by appeal from the order directing the sale, and upon such review any substantial departure from the statutory requirements compels a reversal; the distinction being that upon a collateral attack the proceedings will be sustained, and the purchaser's title held good, unless it appears that the court did not acquire jurisdiction to order the sale; while, upon a direct attack by appeal from the order, it may be reversed for error, though the court had jurisdiction.—Estate of Cook, 137 Cal. 184, 186, 69 Pac. 968. Suit to quiet title is collateral attack on administrator's sale.—Dane v. Layne, 10 Cal. App. 366, 101 Pac. 1067. Where an administrator sold land of a decedent's estate, an action to quiet title, subsequently brought in the district court, against the purchaser, to avoid the sale and the decree of the county court authorizing it and ratifying it, is a collateral attack upon such sale and decree; wherever the validity of an executed order of sale is drawn in question other than by appeal, writ of error, certiorari, or timely application to the court wherein the order was made, the attack is collateral.—Shane v. Peoples, 25 N. D. 188, 194, 141 N. W. 737. If the petition upon which the order for sale is made is so defective that the court did not acquire jurisdiction, the order may be assailed at any time upon a collateral as well as upon a direct attack; but if the facts stated in the petition are sufficient to confer jurisdiction upon the court to hear the application, its order directing a sale can not be impeached upon a collateral attack.—Plains Land & Imp. Co. v. Lynch, 38 Mont. 271, 129 Am. St. Rep. 645, 99 Pac. 847, 853.

3. Collateral attack.

(1) In general.—Probate sales will not be upheld, even against a collateral attack, when the petition in the proceeding for an order of sale affirmatively discloses an entire want of any statement of facts essential, under the statute, to give jurisdiction.—Wright v. Edwards, 10 Or. 298, 306. A party, in a collateral proceeding to set aside an administrator's sale, is bound by the findings in the judgment of the court in the proceedings resulting in the sale, especially where such party was also a party to such proceedings.—Bateman v. Reitler, 19 Colo. 547, 36 Pac. 548. If a court of general jurisdiction, and particularly charged with the administration of estates, acquires jurisdiction of the subject-matter and of the parties, its orders and judgments are not open to attack in a proceeding brought by the heirs to set aside an administrator's sale and for other relief, the same being a collateral proceeding.—Bateman v. Reitler, 19 Colo. 547, 36 Pac. 548. If the petition for an order of sale sufficiently states the facts necessary to give the court jurisdiction, the order thereon, being a judicial determination in a proceeding of which the court has jurisdiction over the subject-matter and of the parties interested therein, is not subject to a collateral attack.—Estate of Devincenzi, 119 Cal. 498, 501, 51 Pac. 845. The authority of the administrator to sell land of a decedent is not impaired by the absence of the impress of a seal upon his letters

of administration, where his authority is impeached collaterally.—Dennis v. Bint, 122 Cal. 39, 43, 68 Am. St. Rep. 17, 54 Pac. 378. When an order of sale is relied upon as a defense in a collateral proceeding, the authority of the court to make the order must exist; for, if it acted without jurisdiction, its order or decree is a nullity, and confers no right or title, and can not be asserted as a defense to bar a recovery.—Wright v. Edwards, 10 Or. 298, 302. A minor heir, who was four years of age at the time of a probate sale, may commence an action of ejectment within two years after reaching his majority; but irregularities or defects in giving or publishing notice of the pendency of the proceeding for a sale of real property of the deceased can not vitiate the proceedings of the probate court when attacked collaterally in such an action.—Thompson v. Burge, 60 Kan. 549, 72 Am. St. Rep. 369, 57 Pac. 110. A title acquired on a probate sale is not affected by mere irregularities, and, upon collateral attack, such objections can not be made.—Dennis v. Winter, 63 Cal. 16, 18.

(2) **What can not be questioned.**—A finding of the court that a petition for the sale of the land of a decedent was presented by two administrators, and an order of sale made in the name of both, can not be questioned in a collateral proceeding, though there may have been a defect in the appointment of one of the administrators.—Blackman v. Mulhall, 19 S. D. 534, 104 N. W. 250, 254. The publication of an order to show cause why the real property of a decedent should not be sold, for two days less than the time prescribed by statute, does not render the sale void, nor affect its validity, in a collateral proceeding. Where there is some notice, an irregularity or the insufficiency thereof can not be questioned in a collateral proceeding.—Blackman v. Mulhall, 19 S. D. 534, 104 N. W. 250, 255. If a decree ordering the sale of a decedent's real estate states that the same is based upon a verified petition, with certain auxiliary proceedings essential to its validity, and recites all jurisdictional facts, it can not be attacked collaterally on the ground that the petition was not verified, and failed to specify facts sufficient to justify the order granting leave to sell.—Phillips v. Phillips, 13 S. D. 231, 83 N. W. 94, 95. Where a court, having jurisdiction of the subject-matter, orders the real property of a decedent to be sold under the authority of this section, any mere errors, irregularities, or defects in the proceedings leading up to the sale are errors within the jurisdiction; and, in an action by the purchaser to quiet title, the heirs can not collaterally attack the sale because of such errors.—Plains L. & I. Co. v. Lynch, 38 Mont. 271, 289, 129 Am. St. Rep. 645, 99 Pac. 847. A private sale of real estate under a power given by the will to the executors made without notice, which was reported to and confirmed by the probate court, is not subject to collateral attack, as against the purchaser, by an heir, made thirty-three years after the confirmation and nearly twenty years after such heir had ceased to be a minor. A plea of want of actual knowledge of the sale until three years before the commencement of the action can not justify the long

delay of the heir in bringing the action. The statute of limitations embodied in sections 343 and 1573, Cal. Code Civ. Proc., had long run in favor of the purchaser at such sale before such attack.—Bayley v. Bloom, 19 Cal. App. 255, 125 Pac. 931.

(3) **Presumptions on.**—If an order confirming the sale of a decedent's land to pay debts recites that the sale was legally made and fairly conducted, that the amount received is not disproportionate to the value of the land, and orders and decrees that the said sale be and the same is hereby in all things confirmed, it must be assumed on collateral attack, that the probate court had before it the required proof showing that all of the provisions of the statute had been complied with.—Blackman v. Mulhall, 19 S. D. 534, 104 N. W. 250, 255. The same presumption must now attach to decrees in probate proceedings, upon collateral attack, as to judgments in cases at common law or in equity, and the sufficiency of the proceedings, or petition for an order of sale, will be tested by the same liberal rule which applies to the pleadings in an ordinary action upon such attack.—Burris v. Kennedy, 108 Cal. 331, 338, 41 Pac. 458. In a collateral attack upon an administrator's sale of land of a decedent's estate, in a proceeding instituted by a child of an heir at law of the deceased, whose parents in the interim have also died, it will be presumed that the trial court, the district court in this case, did its duty; and that all parties affected by the judgment and decree were properly before it; it will also be presumed, in such a case, that the county court, in which the petition for letters of administration was filed by one of the alleged heirs at law, had jurisdiction and passed upon the question of heirship.—Shane v. Peoples, 25 N. D. 188, 192, 194, 141 N. W. 737.

(4) **What is good on collateral attack.**—Where the petition for a probate sale fails to state the value of the property sought to be sold, but where, following the description of the property in the schedule annexed to the petition, it is stated that "the said one-half interest was appraised at seven thousand dollars," the petition is good, on collateral attack, and is sufficient under the statute, as it fully and fairly answers the purpose of the code.—Silverman v. Gundelfinger, 82 Cal. 548, 550, 23 Pac. 12. Where the petition of the administrator sets forth that there was no personal property belonging to the estate, this is sufficient, upon collateral attack, to warrant an order for the sale of real estate, where the petition is otherwise sufficient.—McKenna v. Cosgrove, 41 Wash. 332, 83 Pac. 240. Though an order to show cause why the sale of a decedent's land should not be made for the payment of debts fails to use the words, "that the party is required to show cause why the sale should not be ordered," it is good, as against a collateral attack, where it substantially complies with the statute by giving notice that application has been made for a sale, and that a hearing will be had at the time designated in the notice, and one of the recitals in the order is that all the proceedings required by the statute have

been complied with, as this is an adjudication that the proceedings prior to the granting of the order were valid.—Blackman v. Mulhall, 19 S. D. 534, 104 N. W. 250, 255. If enough appears upon the face of the petition to show the necessity of a sale, such petition is sufficient when drawn in question by a collateral attack upon the order of sale.—Plains L. & I. Co. v. Lynch, 38 Mont. 271, 279, 129 Am. St. Rep. 645, 99 Pac. 847. If the petition upon which the order of sale was made is so defective that the court did not acquire jurisdiction, the order may be assailed at any time upon a collateral as well as upon a direct attack; but, if the facts stated in the petition were sufficient to confer jurisdiction upon the court to hear the application, its order directing a sale can not be impeached upon a collateral attack.—Plains L. & I. Co. v. Lynch, 38 Mont. 271, 290, 129 Am. St. Rep. 645, 99 Pac. 847. If a petition for the sale of land of a decedent is sufficient to invoke an exercise of jurisdiction, the order based thereon is not void; it can not, therefore, be set aside on collateral attack, though it and all subsequent proceedings might have been vacated if an appeal from such order had been regularly taken.—Yeaton v. Barnhart, 78 Or. 249, 150 Pac. 742, 152 Pac. 1192. A petition for an order of sale of real property, which meets the requisites of the Oregon statute, is sufficient to give the county court jurisdiction of the subject-matter, and its decision, whether right or wrong, is immune from collateral attack.—Howe v. Kern, 63 Or. 487, 496, 504, 125 Pac. 834, 128 Pac. 818. In a collateral attack upon the decree of a county court, authorizing and ratifying an administrator's sale of a decedent's real property, such sale will not be set aside on a mere allegation that the sale was made without notice of any kind to the plaintiff, and that he was not made a party to the proceeding; nor will it be set aside in such attack, upon the ground of alleged fraud, without allegation and proof that the purchaser was a party to the fraud.—Shane v. Peoples, 25 N. D. 188, 196, 141 N. W. 737.

V. APPEAL.

1. **In general.**—If an appeal is taken from an order vacating a sale of the real estate of a deceased person before such order is entered in the minutes of the court, the appeal is premature, and gives the court no jurisdiction of the subject-matter.—Estate of Devincenzi, 131 Cal. 452, 453, 63 Pac. 723. An appeal from an order vacating a sale of the real estate of a deceased person is ineffectual, where there was a want of jurisdiction, whether such appeal was dismissed or not.—Estate of Devincenzi, 131 Cal. 452, 454, 63 Pac. 723. Parties who have been duly notified of the proceedings for the sale of the property of a decedent should be held to have waived all objections to the petition not made in the court below.—Estate of Levy, 141 Cal. 637, 643, 75 Pac. 317. Proof of due publication of notice to interested persons to show as required by statute confers jurisdiction, and court's subsequent action on defective petition is within its jurisdiction and reversible only for error of law on direct appeal.—Dane v. Layne, 10 Cal. App. 366, 101

Pac. 1067. Where the court has jurisdiction to make an order of sale, the remedy for any error committed by it in making such order is by an appeal; such error is not ground for a collateral attack.—Plains L. & I. Co. v. Lynch, 38 Mont. 271, 290, 129 Am. St. Rep. 645, 99 Pac. 847.

2. Non-appealable orders.—An order directing the executor or administrator to make a sale under a previous order is not appealable.—Estate of Martin, 56 Cal. 208, 209. An order of the probate court refusing to set aside an order of sale previously entered is not the subject of appeal.—Estate of Smith, 51 Cal. 563, 565. An order directing the sale of land by an administrator is appealable, and after such order becomes final, matters that were properly justifiable upon the hearing therefor can not be again reopened and litigated upon the hearing of the return of sale.—Estate of Bazzuro, 161 Cal. 72, 118 Pac. 434.

3. Appealable orders.—Writs of error lie from the supreme court of the state of Colorado to every final judgment or decree of the county courts of that state, including a decree in probate for the sale of the lands of an estate of a deceased person. Such cases may be reviewed on the ground that the judgment or decision is final.—Sloan v. Strickler, 12 Colo. 179, 20 Pac. 611; Vance's Heirs v. Rockwell, 3 Colo. 240. Where, on an application for the sale of real estate to pay debts, the matter under adjudication is the construction of the will, and a decree is entered after a full hearing, the same is final and appealable, and can not be set aside unless the statutory steps are instituted for its vacation.—In re Barker's Estate, 33 Wash. 79, 73 Pac. 796. An order refusing to hear evidence or to confirm the sale is, in effect, an order against directing the sale or conveyance of real estate, and is therefore appealable, under the language of the California statute.—Estate of Leonis, 138 Cal. 194, 197, 71 Pac. 171. An order overruling a motion to set aside an order to sell the real estate of a decedent is not subject to appeal.—Estate of McCarty, 169 Cal. 708, 147 Pac. 941. If the order of confirmation directs a broker, with whom money had been deposited by the purchaser named in the return, to pay the money to the administrator, the broker also has a right to appeal from the order.—Estate of Bradley, 168 Cal. 655, 144 Pac. 136.

4. Parties interested or aggrieved.—It is a statutory rule that a litigant can appeal only from an order affecting a substantial right. This rule accords with the fundamental principle, everywhere recognized, that the administrator has no appeal unless aggrieved by the judgment or decree of the trial court.—Hume v. Turner, 42 Or. 202, 208, 70 Pac. 611, 614; In re Smith's Will, 43 Or. 595, 75 Pac. 133. An order confirming a sale and directing a conveyance to be made is appealable. The right of the purchaser at such sale to be heard at the return of sale is implied from the statute, and such person may be a party "aggrieved" by the action of the court, whether he be "interested" in the estate or not.—Estate of Pearsons, 98 Cal. 603, 605, 33 Pac. 451. Where the administrator has allowed claims against the estate, and the law

imposes upon him the duty to sell the real property, and he petitions for leave to sell, the administrator in such proceeding represents the creditor, and has an appealable interest in the order denying him license to sell the real property.—In re Smith's Will, 43 Or. 595, 75 Pac. 133. In a proceeding for the sale of real estate belonging to a decedent's estate, the guardian ad litem of the minor heirs is entitled, as an adverse party, to service of the notice of appeal from an order confirming a sale of such real estate. Under the provisions of the Idaho statute, title descends to the heirs, subject to the control of the probate court for the purposes of administration, etc. The heirs are therefore affected by a modification or reversal of the order or judgment appealed from, and are adverse parties, within the meaning of the provisions of such statute.—Reed v. Stewart, 12 Ida. 699, 87 Pac. 1002, 1152; Aulbach v. Dahler, 4 Ida. 654, 43 Pac. 322; Titiman v. Alamance Min. Co., 9 Ida. 240. 74 Pac. 529. On appeal by a purchaser, at the first sale of property, from an order of the probate court authorizing the administrator to resell the property, which order was made after the court had vacated and annulled the decree of confirmation of the previous sale, although the appellant was in no way a party to the order directing a resale, the court will assume, for the purposes of the decision, that such purchaser at the original sale was a party aggrieved by the order for a resale.—Estate of Boland, 55 Cal. 310, 312. The purchaser named in a return of an administrator's sale of real property is a "party aggrieved" by an order confirming the sale to a person other than himself, and is entitled to appeal therefrom.—Estate of Bradley, 168 Cal. 655, 144 Pac. 136.

5. Parties not interested or aggrieved.—The administrator is not a party aggrieved by an order denying the petition to sell, where none of the parties interested in the property objected to the terms of the order, and the administrator, therefore, is not entitled to an appeal from such order.—Estate of Steward, 1 Cal. App. 57, 81 Pac. 728. A party interested adversely to the estate, as a claimant of the land, is not a party injured or aggrieved by an order authorizing the administrator to mortgage the property of the estate covered by the lien, which will be lost unless redeemed. Such party has no standing in court, and his grievance, if any, in failing to acquire the property of the estate can not be considered.—Estate of Freud, 131 Cal. 667, 674, 82 Am. St. Rep. 407, 63 Pac. 1080.

6. Affirming the order of sale on appeal.—Where an order of sale is made, and the owner, who has succeeded to the title of the sole devisee, has expressly consented to the order of sale, such order must be affirmed, whether it is erroneous or otherwise, if the appellant claims no interest therein.—Estate of Schroeder, 46 Cal. 305, 317.

7. Record on appeal.—Where the record is produced upon the hearing, and it purports to contain a full and detailed statement of everything that occurred in the course of the proceedings on the petition

for leave to sell, there is no room left for presuming that anything more was done than what the record recites, nor anything less, nor anything different.—Townsend v. Tallant, 33 Cal. 45, 53, 91 Am. Dec. 617. Where it appears that an order of sale was not granted on the day the caption would indicate, it will be presumed that there was a mistake in making up the record, rather than that the order was made before the return-day.—Russell v. Lewis, 3 Or. 380, 385. An affidavit purporting to embody the objections of a purchaser, who neglects or refuses to comply with the terms of the sale, to the granting of a motion to set aside a sale of real estate and ordering a resale, and which affidavit was stricken from the files, will not, nor will the ruling of the court thereon, be considered on appeal from the order.—Estate of Long, 5 Cal. App. 684, 91 Pac. 169. The petition, citation, and proof of service are as essential parts of the record in a probate case as are the pleadings, process, and return in proceedings in the circuit court. It has been held, therefore, that where the statute regulating probate proceedings does not contain a provision directing the clerk of the probate court to attach together papers constituting the judgment roll, similar to the provision of the general practice act relating to the judgment roll, that the general act should be construed to include probate cases.—Gilmore v. Taylor, 5 Or. 89, 91. The supreme court cannot act upon a stipulation as a basis for a judgment to be entered in that court, consenting that the order of confirmation be affirmed in part, unless the stipulation be signed by all the parties to the proceeding, either in person or by attorneys.—Estate of Arguello, 50 Cal. 308, 310. It is the duty of the superior court upon an appeal from an order confirming a sale of real property in the matter of the estate of a deceased person, where the appeal is taken under the new method, to certify to the papers requested in the notice to the clerk given under section 953a of the Code of Civil Procedure of California. Such papers, and the reporter's transcript of the testimony and proceedings taken and had at the hearing, constitute the transcript contemplated by section 953a on such an appeal. There is no "judgment-roll," strictly speaking, in proceedings in probate, but, whenever proceedings in probate are so akin to a civil action as to necessitate the "papers" which are declared by section 670 of that code to constitute the judgment-roll in a civil action, they may be held to constitute the judgment-roll referred to in section 661. They are a quasi judgment-roll only, but they will be held equivalent thereto whenever the interests of justice require it in considering the sufficiency of a transcript on appeal.—Going v. Guy, 166 Cal. 279, 135 Pac. 1128.

8. Decree. Effect of, on appeal.—It is not error for an appellate court to go behind the order of sale made in a probate court, and to hear and sustain objections to the order of sale itself, in order to ascertain whether the sale should be approved or not, the objections coming from one who had no opportunity to be heard.—Estate of Gibbs, 4 Utah 97, 6 Pac. 525. Whether a sale will be for the advantage, benefit, and best

interests of the estate, or those interested therein, is a question of fact to be determined by the probate court upon the evidence before it in reference thereto; and to the extent that its decision depends upon inferences to be drawn from the situation of the property, or of the parties who are interested therein, it is not open to review upon an appeal from the order.—Estate of Steward, 1 Cal. App. 57, 60, 81 Pac. 728. If the court finds as an ultimate fact that an estate is indebted to a plaintiff in an action brought to recover a debt, the appellate court will not disturb such finding, where the evidence is not before the court.—Merithew v. Orr, 90 Cal. 363, 364, 27 Pac. 295. On an appeal from an order refusing to confirm a sale, the purchaser can not object that the court had no power to direct a new sale, where such order was made upon the application of the executor, and where a written offer, at the time of the return, was made by the purchaser of a ten per cent advance over the amount named in the return, it being in the discretion of the court, under the provisions of the statute, either to accept such offer and confirm the sale or to order a new sale.—Estate of Reed, 3 Cal. App. 142, 85 Pac. 155.

9. Res judicata. Law of the case.—The doctrine of res judicata applies to the judgments and decrees of a probate court, as well as to those of any other judicial tribunal.—Garwood v. Garwood, 29 Cal. 515, 522. A ruling, given upon a former appeal, construing a will, and holding that it gave no power to the executors to sell the real estate without an order of the probate court, and holding that the sales and conveyances attempted to be made without such order were void, is the law of the case, and conclusive upon the points in subsequent appeals.—Hill v. Den, 54 Cal. 6, 21; Huse v. Den, 85 Cal. 390, 399. 20 Am. St. Rep. 232, 24 Pac. 790.

CHAPTER V.

CONVEYANCE OF REAL ESTATE OR TRANSFER OF PERSONAL PROPERTY, BY EXECUTORS AND ADMINISTRATORS, IN CERTAIN CASES.

(5) Justidiction of equity and at   4. Statute of frauds.
    law.   (1) In general.
(6) Pleading and evidence.   (2) Changes in the law.
(7) Statute of nonclaim, and   (3) Part performance.
    laches.   4. Appeal. Law of the case.
(8) Relief granted.

§ 593. Completion of contracts for sale of property.

When a person who is bound by contract in writing to convey any real estate, or to transfer any personal property, dies before making conveyance or transfer, and in all cases when such decedent, if living might be compelled to make such conveyance or transfer, the court, having jurisdiction of the probate proceedings of the estate of such decedent, may make a decree authorizing and directing the executor or administrator of such deceased person to convey or transfer such real estate or personal property to the person ·entitled thereto.—*Kerr's Cyc. Code Civ. Proc.,* § 1597.

ANALOGOUS AND IDENTICAL STATUTES.
The * indicates identity.
Arizona*—Revised Statutes of 1913, paragraph 977.
Colorado—Mills's Statutes of 1912, sections 7940, 7941.
Idaho—Compiled Statutes of 1919, section 7673.
Kansas—General Statutes of 1915, section 4622.
Montana—Revised Codes of 1907, section 7614.
Nevada—Revised Laws of 1912, section 6032.
North Dakota—Compiled Laws of 1913, section 8792.
Oklahoma—Revised Laws of 1910, section 6410.
South Dakota*—Compiled Laws of 1913, section 5871.
Utah—Compiled Laws of 1907, section 3935.
Washington—Laws of 1917, chapter 156, p. 695, section 188.
Wyoming—Compiled Statutes of 1910, section 5686.

§ 594. Petition for representative to make conveyance and notice of hearing.

On the presentation of a verified petition by the executor or administrator, or by any person claiming to be entitled to such conveyance from an executor or administrator, setting forth the facts upon which the claim is predicated, the court, or a judge thereof, must appoint a.time and place for hearing the petition, and must order notice thereof to be served on the executor or adminis-

Probate Law—84

trator personally when he is not the petitioner, and published at least once a week for four successive weeks before such hearing, in such newspaper in this state as the court may designate; provided, however, that if such contract was of record at the date of the death of the person executing such contract, notice of such hearing shall be served on the executor or administrator personally, when he is not the petitioner, and posted in three public places in the county where the court is held for at least ten days prior to the date of hearing.—*Kerr's Cyc. Code Civ. Proc.*, § 1598.

ANALOGOUS AND IDENTICAL STATUTES.

No identical statute found.

Arizona—Revised Statutes of 1913, paragraphs 977, 978.
Colorado—Mills's Statutes of 1912, sections 7940, 7941, 7942.
Hawaii—Revised Laws of 1915, section 2834.
Idaho—Compiled Statutes of 1919, section 7674.
Kansas—General Statutes of 1915, sections 4622, 4623, 4624.
Montana—Revised Codes of 1907, section 7615.
North Dakota—Compiled Laws of 1913, section 8793.
Oklahoma—Revised Laws of 1910, section 6411.
South Dakota—Compiled Laws of 1913, section 5872.
Utah—Compiled Laws of 1907, section 3936.
Washington—Laws of 1917, chapter 156, p. 696, section 189.
Wyoming—Compiled Statutes of 1910, section 5687.

§ 595. **Form. Petition for order directing administrator specifically to perform contract to convey real estate.**

[Title of court.]

[Title of estate.]   { No. ——.¹   Dept. No.——.
                   {   [Title of form.]

To the Honorable the ——² Court of the County ³ of ——, State of ——.

· This, the verified petition of ——, respectfully shows: That on the —— day of ——, 19—, ——, now deceased, executed and delivered to your petitioner a contract, in writing, a copy of which is hereinafter set forth, wherein and whereby he agreed to sell and convey to your petitioner, for a consideration therein stated, that certain real estate situated in the county [4] of ——, state of ——, particularly described in said written contract;

That the said —— died on the —— day of ——, 19—, without having made such conveyance; but that, prior to such death, petitioner performed all of the matters and things required by said agreement to be performed by him, and by reason of the premises was, and is, entitled to a specific performance of said agreement, according to the terms thereof, to wit: a conveyance of the premises described in said instrument; and said decedent, if living, might be compelled to make such conveyance;

That, subsequent to the death of said decedent, —— was appointed administrator [5] of his estate; that he took the oath and filed a bond as such administrator;[6] and that he is now the duly qualified and acting administrator [7] of said estate.

The following is a full, true, and correct copy of the contract of which specific performance is herein sought: ——.[8]

Wherefore your petitioner prays for an order of this court authorizing and requiring the said administrator [9] specifically to perform said agreement, by executing to petitioner a good and sufficient conveyance of the real estate in said contract specifically described.

——, Attorney for Petitioner. ——, Petitioner.

[Add usual verification.]

Explanatory notes.—1 Give file number. 2 Title of court. 3, 4 Or, city and county. 5-7 Or, executor. 8 Give copy of contract. Under the California statute as it now exists, a copy of the contract is not required: Kerr's Cal. Cyc. Code Civ. Proc. (Kerr's Stats. and Amdts., p. 501), § 1598. If a copy is available, the better practice would seem to be to insert it; but if it is omitted, the petition must be changed, to avoid reference to copy set forth, and a description of the land inserted in its proper place, instead of referring to the contract for description. 9 Or, executor.

§ 596. **Form. Petition for order directing executor specifically to perform contract to convey real estate. (Incomplete transaction.)**

[Title of court.]

[Title of estate.] {No. ——.1 Dept. No. ——.
                     {   [Title of form.]

To the Honorable the ——² Court of the County³ of ——, State of ——.

This, the verified petition of ——, respectfully shows: That on the —— day of ——, 19—, ——, now deceased, executed and delivered to your petitioner a contract, in writing, to convey to your petitioner, for the sum of —— dollars ($——), that certain real estate situated in the county⁴ of ——, state of ——, particularly described as follows, to wit: ——;

That, by the terms of said agreement, the said property was to be paid for in ——⁵ monthly instalments of —— dollars ($——), each, with interest;

That, after the payment of ——⁶ instalments, but before the payment of all thereof, the said —— died, and, after proceedings duly had therefor, the will of said —— has been admitted to probate in this court, and letters testamentary duly issued to ——, who is now the duly qualified and acting executor of said will;⁷

That your petitioner is ready and willing and desires to pay in full the balance owing on said contract of purchase hereinbefore described, and that, upon such payment, your petitioner is entitled to a conveyance of said real estate; and that said decedent, if living, might be compelled to accept such payment and to make such conveyance.

Wherefore your petitioner prays for a decree authorizing and directing the said executor⁸ to execute a conveyance of said property to your petitioner upon pay-

ment of the remaining instalments of money due, with
interest thereon. ——, Petitioner.
——, Attorney for Petitioner.
[Add usual verification.]

Explanatory notes.—1 Give file number. 2 Title of court. 3, 4 Or, city
and county. 5 Give number of instalments, or other terms of contract.
6 State number. 7 Or, letters of administration on the estate of said
—— were duly issued to ——, who is now duly qualified and acting
administrator of said estate. 8 Or, administrator.

§ 597. Form. Order appointing time for hearing petition for
specific performance of contract to convey.

[Title of court.]

[Title of estate.] ⎰ No. ——.1 Dept. No. ——.
⎱ [Title of form.]

——, having filed his verified petition in this court, setting forth facts on which he bases a claim that he is
entitled to the specific performance of a contract, made
with him, by said decedent in his lifetime, to convey
certain real estate, which said contract is set forth in his
petition, and praying for an order requiring the administrator 2 of the above-entitled estate to execute to him a
conveyance of the following described real property, to
wit: ——, —

It is ordered, That ——,3 the —— day of ——, 19—,
and the court-room of said court at ——,4 in the said
county 5 of ——, state of ——, be, and the same are
hereby, appointed as the time and place for the hearing
of said petition; and that notice thereof be served on said
administrator 6 personally, and published in ——, a newspaper published in this state, for at least four 7 successive weeks before said hearing.

Dated ——, 19—. ——, Judge of the —— Court.

Explanatory notes.—1 Give file number. 2 Or, executor. 3 Day of
week. 4 State location of court-room. 5 Or, city and county. 6 Or,
executor (unless petition is filed by him). 7 Or other time prescribed
by statute.

§ 598. Interested parties may contest.

At the time and place appointed for the hearing, or at such other time to which the same may be postponed, upon satisfactory proof by affidavit or otherwise, of the due publication of the notice, the court shall proceed to hear the said petition, and all persons interested in the estate may appear and contest such petition, by filing their objections in writing, and the court may examine, on oath, the petitioner and all who may be produced before him for that purpose.—*Kerr's Cyc. Code Civ. Proc.,* § 1599.

ANALOGOUS AND IDENTICAL STATUTES.
The * indicates identity.

Arizona*—Revised Statutes of 1913, paragraph 979.
Colorado—Mills's Statutes of 1912, sections 7942, 7943.
Idaho*—Compiled Statutes of 1919, section 7675.
Kansas—General Statutes of 1915, sections 4624-4626.
Montana*—Revised Codes of 1907, section 7616.
Oklahoma*—Revised Laws of 1910, section 6412.
South Dakota*—Compiled Laws of 1913, section 5873.
Wyoming—Compiled Statutes of 1910, section 5688.

§ 599. Form. Objections to order directing specific performance, by administrator, of decedent's contract to convey real estate.

[Title of court.]

[Title of estate.]   { No. ——.[1] Dept. No. ——.
                                           {   [Title of form.]

Now comes ——, an heir at law [2] of said deceased, and objects to the granting of the order prayed for in the petition of ——, heretofore filed herein, directing the administrator [3] of said estate to convey to him the land described in his petition; and for cause of contest alleges:

That no notice of the hearing of said petition has ever been published, as required by order of this court;[4]

That the alleged written contract to convey was not binding upon said deceased, for the reason that ——;[5]

That the alleged contract between petitioner and said

deceased was procured from the decedent, in his lifetime, by the duress and fraud of said petitioner, in the following manner, to wit: ——.[6]

Wherefore he prays that the order sought in said petition be denied.　　　　　　　　　　　　——, Contestant.

——, Attorney for Contestant.

Explanatory notes.—[1] Give file number. [2] Or, residuary legatee under the last will and testament of ——, deceased; or otherwise, according to the fact. [3] Or, executor. [4] Or, by a judge of this court. [5] State the facts showing why contract was not binding. [6] State the facts out of which duress and fraud arose, as fully as would be required in a complaint in equity setting up duress and fraud. Set forth, in subsequent paragraphs, any other causes which would have been a defense to decedent in an action for the specific performance of the contract, such as a different contract, rescission, want of title in plaintiff, statute of limitations, want of equity, etc.

§ 600. Conveyance or transfer to be ordered when.

If, after a full hearing upon the petition and objections, and examination of the facts and circumstances of the claim, the court is satisfied that the petitioner is entitled to a conveyance of the real estate described in the petition, a decree authorizing and directing the executor or administrator to execute a conveyance thereof to the petitioner must be made.—*Kerr's Cyc. Code Civ. Proc.,* § 1600.

ANALOGOUS AND IDENTICAL STATUTES.

No identical statute found.

Alaska—Compiled Laws of 1913, section 1674.
Arizona—Revised Statutes of 1913, paragraph 980.
Colorado—Mills's Statutes of 1912, section 7943.
Hawaii—Revised Laws of 1915, section 2835.
Idaho—Compiled Statutes of 1919, section 7676.
Kansas—General Statutes of 1915, section 4625.
Montana—Revised Codes of 1907, section 7617.
North Dakota—Compiled Laws of 1913, section 8793.
Oklahoma—Revised Laws of 1910, section 6413.
South Dakota—Compiled Laws of 1913, section 5874.
Utah—Compiled Laws of 1907, section 3937.
Washington—Laws of 1917, chapter 156, p. 696, sections 191, 193.
Wyoming—Compiled Statutes of 1910, section 5689.

§ 601.   Form. Order for conveyance of land sold by decedent.

[Title of court.]

[Title of estate.]   { No. ——.1   Dept. No. ——.
                                       {   [Title of form.]

Now comes ——, the petitioner herein, by ——, his attorney, and proves to the satisfaction of the court that notice of the time and place of the hearing of the petition herein to obtain an order for the conveyance of land sold by said decedent was duly served on ——, the administrator [2] of said estate, for the time required by law and by order of the court, and was duly published in the ——, a newspaper of general circulation, published in the county [3] of ——, at least four successive weeks before the time fixed for said hearing; and said administrator [4] also appearing by ——, his attorney, and the court, after hearing the evidence, being satisfied that the deceased was bound by a contract, in writing, to convey the property hereinafter described to ——, but that he died before making such conveyance, and that said petitioner is entitled to a conveyance as prayed for in his petition, —

It is therefore ordered, adjudged, and decreed by the court, That the said ——, as administrator [5] of the estate of ——, deceased, be, and he is hereby, authorized and directed to execute forthwith, as such administrator,[6] a deed of conveyance to said —— for the land described as follows, to wit: ——.[7]   ——, County Clerk.

Entered ——, 19—.   By ——, Deputy.[8]

Explanatory notes.—1 Give file number. 2 Or, executor. 3 Or, city and county. 4-6 Or, executor. 7 Describe the land. 8 Orders need not be signed. See note, § 77, ante.

§ 602.   Form. Order for conveyance of land sold by decedent. (Conditional.)

[Title of court.]

[Title of estate.]   { No. ——.1   Dept. No. ——.
                                       {   [Title of form.]

Now comes ——, the petitioner herein, by ——, his attorney, and proves to the satisfaction of the court that notice of the time and place of hearing his petition herein was duly served on ——, the administrator [2] of said estate, in the manner and for the time required by law and the order of court, and was duly published in the newspaper known as ——, a newspaper of general circulation, published in the county [3] of ——; that said publication was made for four successive weeks [4] before the time appointed by the court for said hearing; and said administrator [5] also appearing by ——, his attorney, the court, after hearing the evidence, being satisfied that the deceased was bound by a contract, in writing, to convey the property hereinafter described to the said ——, but that he died before making such conveyance, and that said petitioner is entitled to a conveyance upon the conditions hereinafter stated, —

It is therefore ordered, adjudged, and decreed by the court, That the said ——, as administrator [6] of the estate of said deceased, be authorized and directed to execute, as such administrator,[7] a deed of conveyance to said —— for the land described as follows, to wit: ——.[8]

It is further ordered, That said deed be delivered to said —— only upon the payment by him, to said administrator,[9] of the sum of —— dollars ($——), the said payment and delivery to be concurrent.[10]

Entered ——, 19—. ——, County Clerk.
  By ——, Deputy.

Explanatory notes.—1 Give file number. 2 Or, executor of the will of said deceased. 3 Or, city and county. 4 Or as prescribed by the court. 5-7 Or, executor. 8 Describe the land. 9 Or, executor. 10 Insert other conditions, if any remain unperformed.

§ 603. Execution of conveyance or transfer, and recording of order therefor.

The executor or administrator must execute the conveyance or transfer according to the directions contained in the decree, which decree shall be prima facie evidence of the correctness of the proceedings, and of the author-

ity of the executor or administrator to make the conveyance or transfer. If the transaction relate to real
property a certified copy of the decree must be recorded
with the deed in the office of the recorder of the county
in which the land conveyed is situated.—*Kerr's Cyc.
Code Civ. Proc.*, § 1601.

ANALOGOUS AND IDENTICAL STATUTES.
The * indicates identity.

Arizona*—Revised Statutes of 1913, paragraph 981.
Colorado—Mills's Statutes of 1912, section 7944.
Idaho—Compiled Statutes of 1919, section 7677.
Kansas—General Statutes of 1915, section 4626.
Montana—Revised Codes of 1907, section 7618.
Oklahoma—Revised Laws of 1910, section 6414.
South Dakota—Compiled Laws of 1913, section 5875.
Washington—Laws of 1917, chapter 156, p. 696, section 192.
Wyoming—Compiled Statutes of 1910, section 5690.

§ 604. Right of petitioner to enforce the contract.

If, upon the hearing, as hereinbefore provided, the
right of the petitioner to have a specific performance of
the contract is found to be doubtful, the court must dismiss the petition without prejudice to the rights of the
petitioner, who may, at any time within six months after
such dismissal, proceed by action to enforce a specific
performance thereof.—*Kerr's Cyc. Code Civ. Proc.*,
§ 1602.

ANALOGOUS AND IDENTICAL STATUTES.
The * indicates identify.

Arizona*—Revised Statutes of 1913, paragraph 982.
Hawaii—Revised Laws of 1915, section 2838.
Idaho*—Compiled Statutes of 1919, section 7678.
Montana*—Revised Codes of 1907, section 7619.
North Dakota—Compiled Laws of 1913, section 8796.
Oklahoma*—Revised Laws of 1910, section 6415.
South Dakota—Compiled Laws of 1913, section 5876.
Utah*—Compiled Laws of 1907, section 3938.
Wyoming*—Compiled Statutes of 1910, section 5691.

§ 605. Form. Dismissal of petition for an order directing an administrator to convey land.

[Title of court.]

[Title of estate.]

No. ——.1 Dept. No. ——.
[Title of form.]

The petition of ——, praying for an order directing the administrator [2] of the estate of ——, deceased, specifically to perform the agreement of his decedent, by executing to said petitioner a conveyance of certain real estate described in said petition, coming on regularly this day for hearing,[3] the court proceeds to hear the proofs adduced, and to consider the objections to said petition, and, after such hearing and consideration, finds that the petitioner's right to demand a specific performance of the contract described in his petition is doubtful.

It is therefore ordered, That said petition be, and the same is hereby, dismissed without prejudice to the right of petitioner to proceed, at any time within six months [4] from date hereof, to enforce, by action, a specific performance of said agreement.

Dated ——, 19—.   ——, Judge of the —— Court.

Explanatory notes.—1 Give file number. 2 Or, executor. 3 Or, having been regularly postponed, by order of court, to the present time. 4 Or other time prescribed by statute.

§ 606. Effect of conveyance or transfer.

Every conveyance or transfer made in pursuance of a decree as provided in this chapter, shall pass title to the property contracted for, as fully as if the contracting party himself was still living, and executed the conveyance or transfer.—*Kerr's Cyc. Code Civ. Proc.*, § 1603.

ANALOGOUS AND IDENTICAL STATUTES.
The * indicates identity.
Arizona*—Revised Statutes of 1913, paragraph 983.
Colorado—Mills's Statutes of 1912, section 7945.
Idaho—Compiled Statutes of 1919, section 7679.
Kansas—General Statutes of 1915, section 4627.
Montana—Revised Codes of 1907, section 7620.
Nevada—Revised Laws of 1912, section 6033.

PROBATE LAW AND PRACTICE.

North Dakota—Compiled Laws of 1913, section 8794.
Oklahoma—Revised Laws of 1910, section 6416.
South Dakota—Compiled Laws of 1913, section 5877.
Utah—Compiled Laws of 1907, section 3935.
Washington—Laws of 1917, chapter 156, p. 697, section 697.
Wyoming—Compiled Statutes of 1910, section 5692.

§ 607. Effect of recording copy of decree.

A copy of the decree for a conveyance or transfer as
provided in this chapter, duly certified and recorded in
the office of the recorder of the county in which the property is situated, gives the person entitled to the conveyance or transfer a right to the possession of the property
contracted for, and to hold the same according to the
terms of the intended conveyance or transfer, in like
manner as if the same had been conveyed or transferred
in pursuance of the decree.—*Kerr's Cyc. Code Civ. Proc.*,
§ 1604.

ANALOGOUS AND IDENTICAL STATUTES.
The * indicates identity.
Arizona*—Revised Statutes of 1913, paragraph 984.
Idaho—Compiled Statutes of 1919, section 7680.
Montana—Revised Codes of 1907, section 7621.
Oklahoma—Revised Laws of 1910, section 6417.
South Dakota—Compiled Laws of 1913, section 5878.
Utah—Compiled Laws of 1907, section 3937.
Washington—Laws of 1917, chapter 156, p. 696, section 192.

§ 608. Same. Does not supersede power of court to enforce
decree.

The recording of any decree, as provided in the preceding section, shall not prevent the court making the decree from enforcing the same by other process.—*Kerr's
Cyc. Code Civ. Proc.*, § 1605.

ANALOGOUS AND IDENTICAL STATUTES.
The * indicates identity.
Arizona*—Revised Statutes of 1913, paragraph 985.
Idaho*—Compiled Statutes of 1919, section 7681.
Montana*—Revised Codes of 1907, section 7622.
Oklahoma*—Revised Laws of 1910, section 6418.
South Dakota*—Compiled Laws of 1913, section 5879.

§ 609. Where party entitled to conveyance is dead.

If the person entitled to the conveyance or transfer dies before the commencement of the proceedings therefor under this chapter, or before the completion of the conveyance or transfer, any person entitled to succeed to his rights in the contract, or the executor or administrator of such decedent, may, for the benefit of the person so entitled, commence such proceedings or prosecute any already commenced, and the conveyance or transfer must be so made as to vest the property in the person or persons entitled thereto, or in the executor or administrator, for their benefit.—*Kerr's Cyc. Code Civ. Proc.,* § 1606.

ANALOGOUS AND IDENTICAL STATUTES.

The * indicates identity.

Arizona*—Revised Statutes of 1913, paragraph 986.
Hawaii—Revised Laws of 1915, section 2839.
Idaho—Compiled Statutes of 1919, section 7682.
Montana—Revised Codes of 1907, section 7623.
Oklahoma—Revised Laws of 1910, section 6419.
South Dakota—Compiled Laws of 1913, section 5880.
Utah—Compiled Laws of 1907, section 3939.
Washington—Laws of 1917, chapter 156, p. 696, section 193.
Wyoming—Compiled Statutes of 1910, section 5693.

§ 610. Decree may direct possession to be surrendered.

The decree provided for in this chapter may direct the possession of the property therein described to be surrendered to the person entitled thereto, upon his producing a certified copy of the decree, when, by the terms of the contract, possession is to be surrendered.—*Kerr's Cyc. Code Civ. Proc.,* § 1607.

ANALOGOUS AND IDENTICAL STATUTES.

No identical statute found.

Arizona—Revised Statutes of 1913, paragraph 987.
Idaho—Compiled Statutes of 1919, section 7683.
Montana—Revised Codes of 1907, section 7624.
Oklahoma—Revised Laws of 1910, section 6420.
South Dakota—Compiled Laws of 1913, section 5881.
Utah—Compiled Laws of 1907, section 3940.

EXECUTORY CONTRACTS OF DECEASED. SPECIFIC PERFORMANCE.

1. Contracts of decedent to convey real estate.

(1) Scope and validity of statute.—The power of the legislature
over the succession and conveyance of land is unlimited. Hence it
may authorize an executor or administrator to convey land pursuant
to the contract of his intestate.—Adams v. Lewis, 5 Saw. 229, Fed.
Cas. No. 60. And this special statutory remedy, conferring upon the
probate court administering the estate jurisdiction to grant specific
performance in cases where the right of petitioner in the premises
is free from doubt, would seem to be a wise provision; it evidently
tends to save the expenses and delay that would follow a separate
action in equity for a specific performance. At any rate, the remedy
in California seems to be complete, and it is clearly within the power
of the legislature to prescribe such remedy. In several of the states,
a summary special proceeding is allowed, in which a contract may
be enforced without suit, as a step in the settlement of the deceased
vendor's estate. In such case the statutory method may be followed,
and the probate court having jurisdiction may authorize the administrator or executor of the decedent to make the conveyance which
the vendor himself should have made had he been alive.—Estate of
Garnier, 147 Cal. 457, 459, 82 Pac. 68. The statute does not authorize
the probate court to direct an executor or administrator to perform
specifically a contract for the conveyance of land made by his intestate
unless such contract was in writing.—Cory v. Hyde; 49 Cal. 469, 473;
Wadleigh v. Phelps, 149 Cal. 627, 87 Pac. 93. The statute has no
reference to a suit to compel an executor or administrator to reconvey
certain property to his testator by an absolute deed intended as a
mortgage.—Wadleigh v. Phelps, 149 Cal. 627, 87 Pac. 93, 100. Neither
is the statute applicable to a contract involving property which was
not subject to administration.—Estate of Healy, 137 Cal. 474, 478, 70
Pac. 455. The statute of Washington provinding that the title of a

decedent in realty shall, without any decree of distribution, vest in the heirs, subject to his debts, does not impliedly repeal the statute which provides that, on the death of an owner who had contracted to convey real estate, the court may direct his representative to convey to the purchaser, etc. In that state, where the owner of land has made a contract to convey, he can leave to his heirs only the interest owned at the time of his death, which is virtually but the right to the proceeds, the holder of the contract being entitled to have the land conveyed to him upon paying the purchase price. In such cases the courts treat the property, for purposes of administration, as personal rather than real.—Griggs Land Co. v. Smith, 46 Wash. 185, 89 Pac. 477, 479. The statute of the state of Washington, which provides "that actions for the recovery of any property, real or personal, or for the possession thereof, and of actions founded upon contracts, may be maintained by and against executors and administrators in all cases in which the same might have been maintained by or against their respective testators or intestates," applies to all persons who have contracted in writing to convey real property, whether they have died testate or intestate, and without regard to the conditions of a will.—Hyde v. Heller, 10 Wash. 586, 39 Pac. 249.

(2) Jurisdiction. Probate courts and equity.—The statute provides, in effect, that when a person bound by a contract in writing to make a conveyance of real estate shall die before making the conveyance, in a case where, if the decedent were living, a court of equity would compel him to make such conveyance, the probate court may decree it; but, as the contract must be in writing, it was not intended to confer upon the probate court equity powers in that large class of cases founded on a part performance of verbal contracts for the sale and conveyance of land.—Cory v. Hyde, 49 Cal. 469, 472, 473. The proceeding provided for by the statute is one for a specific performance of a contract in the probate court, but it was not the intention of the statute to vest in the probate court more extensive power than was administered by a court of equity.—Estate of Corwin, 61 Cal. 160, 163. A specific performance is essentially a branch of equity jurisdiction. Under the statute, many deeds have been made in this state by executors and administrators upon orders made by the probate court, and the titles thereby attempted to be made have been acted upon and recognized as valid. Yet the compelling of an executor or administrator, representing a deceased person, who was bound by contract in writing, to execute his deed is a case in equity.—Rosenberg v. Frank, 58 Cal. 387, 416. But, while the probate court has power to decree specific performance of certain written contracts, it has no power, on the petition of an executor, to order him, on the receipt of money loaned, to reconvey real estate conveyed to his testator by a deed absolute on its face, but intended as a mortgage.—Anderson v. Fisk, 41 Cal. 308, 309, 310. The probate court has power to compel

an administrator, as administrator, to convey to himself as an individual.—Estate of Garnier, 147 Cal. 457, 458, 82 Pac. 68.

(3) Evidence.—It is a well established rule that the burden of showing, by clear and satisfactory evidence a contract which it is sought
to have specifically enforced, rests upon the party who sets it up and
asks its enforcement, and unless this is done specific performance will
not be decreed.—Forsyth v. Heward, 41 Nev. 305, 315, 170 Pac. 21.
Evidence in a suit to specifically enforce a contract of adoption and
to leave property by will examined and held insufficient to show more
than adoption, and not to establish a contract to leave property by
will.—Forsyth v. Heward, 41 Nev. 305, 310, 170 Pac. 21.   On a claim
advanced by an agent that his principal, a woman, persuaded him to
marry and to bring his wife to live with her, promising to transfer the
dwelling to them in return for care and support, the court considers
that the facts in the cause support that claim.—Schlussel v. Hays, 89
Or. 463, 174 Pac. 722.   In a suit for specific performance of a promise,
made by a person since deceased, to transfer property in return for
care and support, the plaintiff can not recover, as against the heir,
judgment for money which the deceased left due on the property and
unpaid, unless he shows that there are not sufficient personal assets
to pay the amount, or that he presented a claim against the estate and
that it was refused.—Schlussel v. Hays, 89 Or. 463, 174 Pac. 722.

(4) Petition and discretion of court.—The petition asking for a decree
compelling the executor or administrator to convey must state that the
contract was in writing, in order to give the probate court jurisdiction.
As the probate court has no jurisdiction to decree a conveyance, except when the contract is in writing, the jurisdictional fact must appear on the face of the petition.—Cory v. Hyde, 49 Cal. 469, 470.   An
executor or administrator of an estate has the same right, under the
provisions of the code, to present a petition for the conveyance of real
estate, or for a transfer of personal property, as any other party.
If an executor or administrator petitions for a specific performance,
the court, by analogy, may appoint a separate attorney to represent
the estate, though he is not required to do it if the heirs appear and
oppose the petition.   However that may be, an executor or administrator, under the law, has the same right as an outside party, whether
his claim be a money demand, or for the performance of a written
contract to transfer property, and the law does not require that he
should first resign his position as executor or administrator in order
to have his claim allowed or enforced against the estate.—Estate of
Garnier, 147 Cal. 457, 460, 82 Pac. 68.   Under the statute of Montana,
the petition must also show that the agreement was in writing.   This
fact is jurisdictional.   If the petition fails to show that the contract was
in writing, the court is without power to proceed, and its order is not
effective for any purpose.   There can be no presumption that the contract was in writing.—Bullerdick v. Hermsmeyer, 32 Mont. 541, 81 Pac.

334, 336. A petition, under the statute of Montana, to compel an executor or administrator to convey real estate, is sufficient where it sets forth the contract at length and alleges an adequate consideration; it need not contain all the essential averments of a bill in equity for the specific performance of a contract, nor is it necessary for the allegations of the petition to avoid every negative statement contained in § 6103 of the Rev. Codes of Montana.—In re Grogan's Estate, 38 Mont. 540, 542, 100 Pac. 1044. An application to a court of equity for a decree enforcing the specific performance of a contract is addressed to its sound and reasonable discretion, and is granted or rejected according to the circumstances of each case; the power of the court in such a connection can not be invoked as a matter of right.—Wetherby v. Griswold, 75 Or. 468, 147 Pac. 388.

REFERENCES.

Devolution of vendee's interest under contract for the purchase of real property.—See note 42 L. R. A. (N. S.) 446.

(5) Specific performance may be enforced when.—If the probate court dismisses a petition to compel an executor or administrator to convey lands in accordance with the terms of the contract executed by his decedent, the superior court has jurisdiction of the action, and may decree a specific performance of the contract of the sale and purchase of such lands.—Hall v. Rice, 64 Cal. 443, 444, 1 Pac. 891, 2 Pac. 889. A specific performance of a decedent's contract may be decreed upon the petition of the executor or administrator.—Estate of Garnier, 147 Cal. 457, 82 Pac. 68. In Oregon, where two partners made a verbal contract to convey certain real property, and a portion of the purchase price was paid, but both members of the firm died subsequently to entering into the contract, the purchaser from the firm is entitled to a title free from litigation before he can be required to accept it and to pay the balance of the purchase price.—Wollenberg v. Rose, 45 Or. 615, 78 Pac. 751, 753. A partially executed contract to convey land for a valuable consideration can be enforced by or against the estate of the deceased vendor. Thus where a son received property as heir of his father's estate, and thereafter occupied and cultivated a tract of land that the testate had received as part consideration of his contract to convey certain other lands to which it is found he had no title, the agreement of the son with the vendees therein, made after becoming the owner, by purchase, of the last-named land, to carry out the terms of the contract, is based on a sufficient consideration and is enforceable.—James v. Holanden, 7 Kan. App. 811, 52 Pac. 913. Where a father verbally offered fifty acres of his farm to his son if the latter would work for him until the farm was paid for; where the son accepted and performed the work; and where he then brought suit for a specific performance of the contract, his right to such performance is not affected by the fact that, before commencing his suit, he offered to convey to the defendants his inter-

Probate Law—85

est in the remainder of his father's estate if they would join in
transferring to him all their possible estate in the fifty acres sued for
by him.—Hayes v. Hayes, 89 Or. 630, 174 Pac. 579.

(6) **Specific performance can not be enforced when.**—No specific
performance of the contract of a decedent to convey can be enforced
unless the contract is in writing.—Cory v. Hyde, 49 Cal. 469, 470;
Bullerdick v. Hermsmeyer, 32 Mont. 541, 81 Pac. 334, 336. Nor can
specific performance of such contract be decreed unless it is found
that the intestate had contracted to convey the particular lands described in the complaint. The decedent's agreement to exchange
"some" of his city lots will not be enforced, where no particular lot
is described.—Ferris v. Irving, 28 Cal. 645, 648. Under the statute of
Utah, there can be no specific performance of a written contract of
a deceased husband as against his wife. "The buyer's right," said
the court, quoting from 6 Pomeroy's Equity Jurisprudence, 3d ed.,
section 834, "to specific performance, with compensation, is subject to
certain limitations; as, when it conflicts with the intervening rights
of third parties, an instance of which is the case of the right of a
wife to be protected in her dower interest. Where the wife of the
vendor refuses to convey her inchoate dower interest in the land
which the vendor has contracted to sell, equity, in many jurisdictions,
denies specific performance with compensation, against the vendor for
the deficiency, viz., the dower interest, on the ground that compul-
sion upon the husband would tend to cause him to procure his wife's
conveyance of dower against her will. For that reason, the buyer
must be satisfied to take less than he contracted for, by the amount
of the dower interest, or abandon the contract." The court will not
order a defendant to procure a conveyance or release by his wife,
or require him to furnish indemnity against her right of dower unless
in cases of clear fraud. Hence a suit for the specific performance of
a contract between plaintiff and defendant's ancestors to convey land
is open to the defense that the contract is not enforceable, because of
the law in relation to dower. And in that state, unless a petition
is filed or a claim is made in a court for specific performance within
the time limited to file other claims, the claim for specific performance must be held to be waived or abandoned, unless, as in other
cases, good cause is shown why it could not be filed within the time
allowed for claims to be filed; and such application must be made
before the administration of the estate is closed and distribution is
made, where the applicant knew of the death of the person against
whom he holds a claim, and of the administration of his estate.—
Free v. Little, 31 Utah 449, 88 Pac. 407, 411, 414. In Washington, it
is error for the court to decree the specific performance of a decedent's contract to convey real estate, where no copy of the petition
or notice was served on the executor or administrator; where the
hearing was had at a time later than that fixed in the notice, and
to which no adjournment had been taken; and where the convey-

ance was ordered to be made before the expiration of the time allowed for appeal.—Sander-Boman Real Estate Co. v. Yesler's Estate, 2 Wash. 429, 27 Pac. 269, 270. Under the statute of Montana, requiring the contract to be in writing, before specific performance thereof can be decreed, the probate court has no jurisdiction to direct the specific performance of a verbal contract whereby the deceased in his lifetime agreed to convey certain water rights to his wife.— Bullerdick v. Hermsmeyer, 32 Mont. 541, 81 Pac. 334, 336. Where the decedent was bound by contract to convey real estate, but died before making the conveyance, and a petition is filed for a decree to compel the executor to make the conveyance, and the right to specific performance is doubtful, such petition will be dismissed.—Hartshorn v. Smith, 19 S. D. 653, 104 N. W. 467, 468. If the decree of a probate court for the specific performance of a written contract of a decedent to convey is void for want of jurisdiction in the court at the time of its rendition, a subsequent act of the legislature validating judicial sales by executors and administrators can give such decree no validity. —Bullerdick v. Hermsmeyer, 32 Mont. 541, 81 Pac. 334, 337. It is statutory that no part of an estate of a decedent can be alienated without leave of court first obtained; hence, the promise of an administratrix to convey can not be specifically enforced.—McDermott v. Lindquist (Colo.), 179 Pac. 147.

(7) Nunc pro tunc orders. Costs.—In a proceeding which seeks the specific performance of a contract for the sale and conveyance of land made by deceased with petitioner, and where the judgment is advisedly silent as to costs, the court has no power, at a subsequent time, to enter a judgment nunc pro tunc so as to include costs. The object of entering judgments and decrees as of some previous date is to supply matters of evidence and to rectify clerical misprisions, but not to enable the court to correct judicial errors. If the court has not rendered a judgment that it might or should have rendered, or if it has rendered an imperfect or improper judgment, it has no power to remedy such errors by ordering an amendment nunc pro tunc of a proper judgment.—Estate of Potter, 141 Cal. 424, 426, 75 Pac. 850.

2. Enforcement of other contracts made by decedent.

(1) Obligation to perform contracts of deceased.—Executors are answerable on all the contracts of the testator broken in his lifetime, and there is only one exception with regard to their liability upon contracts broken after his death; and that is, that they are not answerable in those cases where personal skill or taste is required. Executors and administrators, as representatives of the deceased, are charged with the duties of performing his contracts where they involve no special skill or taste. If the complaint alleges that the deceased was the holder of a large tract of land adjacent to and surrounding the land of plaintiff, on which a house was erected, "and was desirous of improving and building up said neighborhood, for the

purpose of attracting purchasers for his said land"; and, with this inducement, he agreed to improve the lands of plaintiff, to superintend the house erected by the expenditure of plaintiff's money, and to guarantee him a certain profit on the investment,—all that required any peculiar skill, taste, or judgment was done by deceased in his lifetime, and the contract and right of action upon it survived.— Janin v. Browne, 59 Cal. 37, 45. Building contracts are binding upon the heirs and executors of a decedent and must be performed, or the estate will be liable in damages for not completing the work.— Exchange Nat. Bank v. Betts's Estate, 103 Kan. 807, 176 Pac. 660.

(2) **What contracts may be enforced.**—Where the contract of the deceased is of an executory nature, and the personal representative can fairly and sufficiently execute all the deceased could have done, he may do so, and enforce the contract. E converso, the personal representative is bound to complete such a contract, and if he does not, may be made to pay damages out of the assets. But where an executory contract is of a strictly personal nature, the death of the party by whom work is to be done before its completion determines the contract, unless what remains to be executed can be certainly done to the same purpose by another.—Janin v. Browne, 59 Cal. 37, 44; McCann v. Pennie, 100 Cal. 547, 551, 35 Pac. 158. A cause of action for personal services performed in a foreign country for a person afterwards deceased is transitory in its nature, and may be maintained in any jurisdiction wherein the executor or the administrator of the deceased may be served with process, without reference to where the contract was made or was to be performed.—McCann v. Pennie, 100 Cal. 547, 552, 35 Pac. 158. As to the conclusiveness, upon administrators and heirs, of decedent's contract to transfer certain bonds, see Jones v. Tallant, 90 Cal. 386, 27 Pac. 305. Where a will authorizes the executor to sell land of the testator, and such representative enters into an executory contract for the sale, specific performance of such contract may be enforced in equity at the suit of the purchaser.—Ingham v. Ryan, 18 Colo. App. 347, 71 Pac. 899, 900.

(3) **What contracts can not be enforced.**—An executory contract, which involves personal service, terminates with death, and no action will lie against his executor or representative to enforce it.—Janin v. Browne, 59 Cal. 37, 44. So with the contract of a decedent which requires skill or taste.—Janin v. Browne, 59 Cal. 37, 45. The contract against a decedent is not enforceable unless it bound decedent in his lifetime. Thus where an agent of the owner entered into a written contract for the sale of real estate, upon the express condition that it was to be subject to the approval of the owner, but the owner died before approving such contract, it can not be enforced against his personal representative.—Estate of Dick, 74 Cal. 284, 286, 15 Pac. 837. Support, which a daughter and son-in-law are already bound to give to the surviving widow of a decedent can hardly form a con-

sideration for the assignment of property by her to them.—Estate of Casner, 1 Cal. App. 145, 147, 81 Pac. 991.

3. Contract to make a will.

(1) In general.—A contract "to leave property" may be performed by deed or will.—Harris v. Morrison, 100 Kan. 157, 163 Pac. 1062. A contract by which the obligor undertakes to make provision at his death for the obligee, although no present title to any property passes, is not required, in order to be valid, to be executed in accordance with the statute relating to wills.—Stahl v. Stevenson, 102 Kan. 844, 848, 171 Pac. 1164, 1168. Where an ancestor promised his presumptive heir to leave her by will the share of his estate to which she would be entitled under the law of descent and distribution if he should die intestate, if she, on her part would sign a release of interest in a life insurance policy on which he wished to realize the cash surrender value, it was held that the signing of the release was a sufficient consideration for the promise, whether the heir had any interest in the policy or its proceeds or not.—Stahl v. Stevenson, 102 Kan. 447, 171 Pac. 1164, 1166. The intent of the testator, in connection with the claim of an oral agreement to make a will, which agreement is sought to be enforced specifically, is to be measured as of the time the agreement was entered into.—Alexander v. Lewes, 104 Wash. 32, 175 Pac. 572. In the absence of fraud or overreaching, a person being of competent mind, may fix upon anything, that is not in itself unlawful, as a consideration for his agreement to make a will favoring the other party thereto.—Alexander v. Lewes, 104 Wash. 32, 175 Pac. 572. A contract to leave by will property to a child in consideration of his living with the promisor, will, when the contract meets all of the requirements, be specifically enforced after the promisor's death, it having been fulfilled on the part of the promisee.—Oles v. Wilson, 57 Colo. 246, 261, 141 Pac. 489. A contract to devise by will a parcel of land free of incumbrance and condition, when properly evidenced, is valid and binding, and may be enforced in equity, unless superior equities intervene.—Rundell v. McDonald — (Cal. App.) —, 182 Pac. 450, 451.

(2) When enforceable.—Contracts providing for the disposition of property by will are clearly enforceable, but the same general principles of equity apply that must be present in the enforcement of contracts to convey during the lifetime of the parties; there must be an adequate consideration; the contract must be just and reasonable as to the party against whom it is to be enforced; the other parties must not have practiced fraud or undue influence in securing the contract; it must be certain and definite, not within the statute of frauds; and its enforcement must not involve an invasion of the legal or equitable rights of an innocent third party.—Stewart v. Smith, 6 Cal. App. 152, 91 Pac. 667, 669. A contract to leave a will in favor of certain parties, in consideration of a conveyance of certain prop-

erty to the testator by the proposed beneficiaries under the will, which contract had been fully performed on the part of such beneficiaries, is not open to attack under the statute of frauds.—Stewart v. Smith, 6 Cal. App. 152, 91 Pac. 667, 670-672. When a definite contract to leave property by will has been clearly and certainly established, and there has been performance by the party asking its enforcement, equity will grant relief, provided the case is free from objection on account of inadequacy of consideration, and there are no circumstances or conditions rendering the claim inequitable.—Anderson v. Anderson, 75 Kan. 117, 9 L. R. A. (N. S.) 229, 88 Pac. 743, 745. A decedent, having a right to dispose of his property as he pleases, his contract to dispose of it, when free from fraud, imposition, or surprise, and being reasonable and moral, will be carried out and enforced by a court of equity.— Burns v. Smith, 21 Mont. 251, 53 Pac. 742, 748. The contract of a decedent to leave the plaintiff a child's share of deceased at his death, if clearly shown, can not be avoided by the heirs on the ground that the plaintiff had not performed her portion of the contract, where no objection had been made by the deceased prior to his death, and no fraud, imposition, or surprise is shown, and the contract was not rescinded.—Burns v. Smith, 21 Mont. 251, 53 Pac. 742, 748. Where a decedent, for an adequate consideration, had agreed to leave a will giving all of his estate to plaintiff, but died intestate, the decedent's failure to leave the will as agreed by him works a fraud upon plaintiff; and, where he can not be placed in statu quo, the agreement will be enforced in equity by declaring the heirs constructive trustees, where the granting of such equitable relief will work no injustice to innocent third parties.—McCabe v. Healy, 138 Cal. 81, 85, 70 Pac. 1008. Specific performance will be decreed where there is present the element of peculiar personal services fully performed under the contract, which are incapable of compensation in money.—Owens v. McNally, 113 Cal. 444, 45 Pac. 710, 33 L. R. A. 369; McCabe v. Healy, 138 Cal. 81, 70 Pac. 1008. A contract by which a party agrees to leave all property of which he dies possessed in a particular manner is not invalid as a sale, although it may include property having neither an actual nor a potential existence at the time.—Stewart v. Smith, 6 Cal. App. 152, 91 Pac. 667, 670. A promise to make a will is enforceable at the suit of the promisee, if the latter, relying upon it, has so changed his position that a failure to redeem such promise virtually works a fraud upon him.—Wolfsen v. Smyer, 178 Cal. 775, 175 Pac. 10. A contract, made by a man with the father of a child he has adopted, for providing for such child by will, is one that seeks to create a contractual relation wholly independent of the law of inheritance and that of adoption.—Oles v. Wilson, 57 Colo. 246, 141 Pac. 489. Where, for a good consideration, two persons enter into an agreement to execute mutual wills and do execute such wills pursuant to such agreement, and one of them dies while both of such wills are in force and effect, the survivor probating the will of the deceased and accepting property under it; and where such agreement is valid and reasonable, and such facts are established by competent evidence, a court of equity will then enforce the specific performance of such agreement on behalf of a third person who is a beneficiary under such mutual wills.— Stevens v. Myers, 91 Or. 114, 177, Pac. 37.

REFERENCES.

Specific performance of contracts against estate of decedent.—See note 14 L. R. A. 860. Specific performance of contract to make will, or to leave property, in consideration of services to continue during the promisor's lifetime, as affected by brevity of period before the promisor's death.—See note 9 L. R. A. (N. S.) 157, 158. Right to recover for services rendered beyond statutory period of limitation upon breach of parol contract to make provision by will.—See note 6 L. R. A. (N. S.) 703, 704. Enforceability of contract to give a child a share of estate in consideration of the surrender of the child to the promisor, as affected by non-compliance with a statute prescribing the mode of adoption.—See note 8 L. R. A. (N. S.) 1130-1132. Specific performance of contract to make a will.—Ann. Cas. 1914A, 399.

(3) **When not enforceable.**—An alleged contract to dispose of property in a particular manner by will can not be enforced in equity, when there is no evidence to sustain an allegation of the existence of such contract.—Ostrom v. De Yoe, 4 Cal. App. 326, 332, 87 Pac. 811. Equity will not enforce specific performance of an alleged agreement to leave property in a particular manner by will, unless the agreement is established by clear and convincing evidence.—Richardson v. Orth, 40 Or. 252, 66 Pac. 925, 931. Before the contract to dispose by will of a part or the whole of the promisor's estate in a particular manner will be enforced in equity, it must be definite, certain, and founded on a valuable consideration. The delivery of a life-insurance policy to the promisor, to which he is already entitled, is not such a consideration.—Schaadt v. Mutual Life Ins. Co., 2 Cal. App. 715, 718-719, 84 Pac. 294. A promise to make a gift of property by will can not be enforced after the death of the party making the promise. Proof of some return or consideration for such promise is necessary to make it enforceable.—Mitchell v. Pirie, 38 Wash. 691, 80 Pac. 774. Although one may make a valid agreement, binding himself to dispose of his property in a particular way by will, and equity will enforce such agreement, in proper cases, yet no agreement may be enforced the terms of which are not sufficiently certain to make the precise act to be done clearly ascertainable. The terms of the agreement must not only be fair, but they must also be free from doubt.—Russell v. Agar, 121 Cal. 396, 398, 53 Pac. 926, 66 Am. St. Rep. 35. Specific performance of a contract to leave property by will may be decreed when no other adequate relief is available, but where the complaint in an action against an executor to compel specific performance of an alleged contract with the testator shows that no services were performed, but, at most,

that plaintiff forbore to press a fixed money demand, the failure of the deceased to deed plaintiff the property, upon his death, according to promise, constitutes a breach of his promise, for which the plaintiff may be compensated by money in an action at law, and hence he is not in a position to apply to a court of equity for specific relief.— Flood v. Templeton, 148 Cal. 374, 83 Pac. 148. Equity, in proper cases, will decree specific performance of a contract to convey property by will; but it does so only upon clear proof of fairness, justness, and adequacy, and where the rights of innocent third parties are not imperiled; and further, where the plaintiff can not be compensated in money.—Flood v. Templeton, 148 Cal. 374, 378, 83 Pac. 148; See Flood v. Templeton, 152 Cal. 148, 13 L. R. A. (N. S.) 579, 92 Pac. 78. The facts in this case considered, and it is held that they do not support a finding that a contract to devise was made, and that at most an inference that the alleged promisor agreed to take plaintiff and treat him as his child, which creates no legal obligation, if true, to give his property by will to such child, and such obligation would not arise from such a contract.—Monsen v. Monsen, 174 Cal. 97, 101, 162 Pac. 90. A promise by a woman, made to a younger woman, to leave to the latter "all of her jewelry, personal effects, and a large part of her personal property," or "all of her jewelry and personal effects," if the younger woman would spend six months with her in Paris, is a promise that is not based on an adequate consideration so as to warrant a decree for specific performance.—Christin v. Clark, 36 Cal. App. 714, 173 Pac. 109. The specific performance an alleged contract to make one an heir can not be decreed where the evidence fails to disclose the fact that any contract between the parties was ever made.—McKeown v. Carroll, 102 Kan. 826, 172 Pac. 525.

(4) Parties. Misjoinder.—In an action for the specific performance of a contract to make a will in favor of the plaintiff, the executor of a will made in violation of the contract is not a necessary party.— Stewart v. Smith, 6 Cal. App. 152, 91 Pac. 667, 669. Nor is the administrator of a decedent, who dies intestate, a necessary party to such an action.—McCabe v. Healy, 138 Cal. 81, 89, 70 Pac. 1008. In an action for the specific performance of a contract to devise property, there is no misjoinder of parties when all are interested in the same subject of enforcing the contract, though all may not be interested to the same extent.—Stewart v. Smith, 6 Cal. App. 152, 91 Pac. 667, 669. In a suit for specific performance of an express contract, made by a testator with the father of child he had adopted, for providing for such child by will, all the legatees under the will are proper parties but only the residuary legatee is a necessary party.—Oles v. Wilson, 57 Colo. 246, 273, 141 Pac. 489.

(5) Jurisdiction of equity and at law.—It is recognized as within the equity jurisdiction of courts to compel specific performance of a promise to devise land, given in consideration of a parol agreement, which

has been already proved and partly performed.—Worden v. Worden, 96 Wash. 592, 165 Pac. 501. The purpose of an action against the executor of the estate of a deceased person to compel specific performance of a contract with decedent to make a particular will or bequest is to impress a trust upon the real and personal property of such decedent after his debts and the costs of administration are paid, and it must be prosecuted, if at all, in a court of original and equitable jurisdiction and powers.—Oles v. Wilson, 57 Colo. 246, 256, 141 Pac. 489. One may make a valid contract with another to devise or bequeath property in a certain specified way, and, in the event of a breach of such a contract this other has an action at law for the damage caused by such breach. In some cases, this, by reason of the circumstances may be his only remedy; for a resort to any equitable remedy can be had only where the circumstances are such as to make the case one within the well settled principles relative to the proper exercise of equitable jurisdiction.—Morrison v. Land, 169 Cal. 580, 147 Pac. 259. A person to whom another, since deceased, made a promise to leave property to him by will, and who, relying on the promise, has changed his course of life, is entitled to have the promise enforced in equity, as though seeking relief as against a fraud practiced upon him.—Wolfsen v. Smyer, 178 Cal. 775, 175 Pac. 10. Under the statutes of Colorado the district court has jurisdiction of a suit to enforce specific performance of a contract to make a particular will or bequest, made by a deceased person, against his executor.—Oles v. Wilson, 57 Colo. 246, 257, 141 Pac. 489. But a suit to enforce specific performance of a contract to leave property by will, brought against the executor of a deceased person, can not be said to relate to probate matters or proceedings therein, within the meaning of the statutes of Colorado requiring suits relating to such matters to be brought in the county court.—Oles v. Wilson, 57 Colo. 246, 256, 141 Pac. 489. When services have been performed in pursuance of a contract to leave property by will to the one rendering the service, and the promisor fails to comply with the agreement, a recovery may be had at law against his estate for the reasonable value of his services; but the complaint in such a case must allege that a claim has been presented to the executor or administrator.—Morrison v. Land, 169 Cal. 580, 585, 147 Pac. 259.

REFERENCES.

Enforcement of agreements in equity.—See note on Trusts, post.

(6) Pleading and evidence.—An amendment of a complaint in a suit for specific performance of an agreement to devise by will, showing ratification of such contract does not set up a new cause of action.—Steinberger v. Young, 175 Cal. 81, 165 Pac. 432, 436. To warrant specific performance of a contract to make a certain will or to make a person one's heir, the proof must be clear, definite, and certain. —Steinberger v. Young, 175 Cal. 81, 165 Pac. 432, 433. A suit to have enforced specifically a parol agreement to make a will in the

plaintiff's favor may be entertained in a case where the agreement
is reasonably definite and certain, is established by clear, full, and
irrefragable evidence, and has been performed to such an extent and
in such manner that the beneficiary can not be compensated properly
in damages.—Price v. Wallace (Or.), 224 Fed. 576, 578. Specific performance of a parol agreement to provide by will for the plaintiff will
be decreed only when the contract itself, as well as the terms thereof
have been clearly proved.—Forsyth v. Heward, 41 Nev. 305, 170 Pac.
21. Where there is evidence to establish clearly the fact that the
plaintiffs went into possession of particular land, and made valuable
improvements thereon, in consideration of the execution of a will by
an uncle, the owner of the land, assuring him of title on the testator's
death, a decree for specific performance may be rendered.—Worden v.
Worden, 96 Wash. 610, 612, 165 Pac. 501. Suits to enforce specifically a
promise alleged to have been made by a person, since deceased, to
execute a will in favor of the plaintiff, are not favored, and when the
promise rests in parol, are regarded with suspicion; hence, the
strongest evidence must be produced, as there having been a valuable
consideration for the promise, and that the latter was deliberately
entered into.—Alexander v. Lewes, 104 Wash. 32, 175 Pac. 572. An
agreement by a person, since deceased, to devise land to the plaintiff
must, in order that the courts may enforce it specifically, be proved by
sufficient evidence, and be in all respects fair and equitable.—James
v. Lane, 103 Kan. 540, 175 Pac. 387. A contract by a decedent to
make a will in the plaintiff's favor may, like any other fact, be established by circumstantial evidence, but this must be of so strong a
character as to raise a convincing implication that the contract was
made; such claims can not rest on merely doubtful proof, for it is
easy to color testimony or to fabricate evidence, wholly in control
of persons testifying, as to casual statements made by a decedent in
his lifetime.—James v. Lane, 103 Kan. 540, 175 Pac. 387. The fairness
and justness of an alleged agreement, by a person since deceased to
make a will favoring the plaintiff, must be determined by resort to
the relations of the parties, their relations to each other, and the circumstances prevailing at the time of the making of such agreement.—
Alexander v. Lewes, 104 Wash. 32, 175 Pac. 572. Where a contract
to devise by last will and testament, resting in parol, and sought to
be enforced after the death of the promisor, comes before a court of
equity for review, it is scrutinized, and should be scrutinized, with particular care; and, applying section 3390 of the California Civil Code,
it is only upon a satisfactory showing that it is definite, certain, and
just, that the court will enforce it.—Monsen v. Monsen, 174 Cal. 97, 99,
162 Pac. 90. Courts of equity will not require of the plaintiff in a
suit to enforce specific performance of a contract to make a particular will or bequest, brought against the executor of the deceased promisor, more than reasonable certainty as to the material terms of the
contract, particularly where the contract has been fully performed

on plaintiff's part, and the impossibility in such a case of measuring the value of his acts in that behalf by any money standard.—Oles v. Wilson, 57 Colo. 246, 265, 141 Pac. 489. Evidence of ratification by a married woman of a previous agreement to devise after the passage in 1874 of the amendment to section 167, Civil Code of California, removing the last restriction upon the power of a married woman to contract with respect to her separate property was held sufficient to establish the fact of ratification.—Steinberger v. Young, 175 Cal. 81, 165 Pac. 432, 435. Declarations made by a decedent against her interest, were, under the provisions of section 1853, Code of Civil Procedure, admissible in a suit for specific performance of a contract to devise against her personal representative.—Steinberger v. Young, 175 Cal. 81, 165 Pac. 432, 436.

(7) Statute of nonclaim, and laches.—The statute of nonclaim, relating to "demands" upon estates of minors, deceased persons, and persons mentally incompetent, and limiting the time within which they may be presented, does not contemplate such a demand as one for the specific performance of an express contract, made by a decedent with the father of a child he had adopted, for providing for such child by will.—Oles v. Wilson, 57 Colo. 246, 255, 141 Pac. 489. Where plaintiff's suit to specifically enforce an agreement to devise by will was brought within a reasonable time after she learned that decedent had failed to perform her agreement, she was not guilty of laches.—Steinberger v. Young, 175 Cal. 81, 165 Pac. 432, 436.

(8) Relief granted.—A man may make a valid contract binding himself to dispose of his property in a particular way by last will and testament, and a court of equity will enforce such agreement specifically by treating the heirs as trustees and compelling them to convey the property in accordance with the terms of the contract.—Monsen v. Monsen, 174 Cal. 97, 98, 162 Pac. 90. A contract to devise by will, if clearly and satisfactorily shown, if clear, certain, and definite in its terms, and if specific performance thereof would not be harsh or oppressive, or unjust to innocent third parties, even if such contract rest in parol, will be enforced, not by ordering a will to be made, but by regarding the property in the hands of the heirs, devisees, assignees, or representatives of the deceased promisor, impressed with a trust in favor of plaintiff.—Rundell v. McDonald (Cal. App.), 182 Pac. 450, 451. In a suit for specific performance of a contract to make a particular will or bequest brought by the promisee against the executor of the deceased promisor, relief is afforded by declaring the legatees named in the will trustees for the plaintiff to the extent of her right.—Oles v. Wilson, 57 Colo. 246, 269, 141 Pac. 489. If a girl of nineteen is, when preparing to go away to make her own living, persuaded by an aged uncle to live with him and his wife until they should die, and promised, as a reward for so doing, the devise of certain real estate, she is, after living with such uncle twelve years, entitled

to a decree for the specific performance of the promise, on his surviving his wife and then dying, neither of them making any conveyance
to her by will or otherwise.—Clow v. West, 37 Nev. 267, 280, 142 Pac.
226. In a suit by a son to enforce specifically a contract with his
parents for the ownership of the land by him in return for giving them
support, relief in full as prayed should be denied, on a showing that,
after supporting the parents for seventeen years, the plaintiff drove
the survivor of them off the premises; however, a sale of the land to
persons other than to the plaintiff should be enjoined until the plaintiff
be reimbursed for the support given.—Holland v. Holland, 97 Kan. 169,
155 Pac. 5.

4. Statute of frauds.

(1) In general.—When a contract to make a will, resting in parol,
is sought to be enforced and comes before a court of equity for review,
it is scrutinized and should be scrutinized, with particular care, and is
enforced only upon a satisfactory showing that it is definite and certain and just, and the proofs of the contract should be clear and the
acts of the claimant referable alone to the contract.—Blanc v. Conner,
167 Cal. 719, 723, 141 Pac. 217. An oral contract to dispose of property upon death in a particular way may, under proper conditions, be
specifically enforced.—Steinberger v. Young, 175 Cal. 81, 165 Pac. 432,
433. A promise of an ancestor that he will leave by will to an heir
presumptive the share of his estate to which the heir would be entitled, if he should die intestate, under the statutes of descents
and distributions, is not a contract for the sale of an interest in land
within the meaning of the statute of frauds, notwithstanding such
ancestor was the owner of real estate at the time the promise was
made and at his death.—Stahl v. Stevenson, 102 Kan. 447, 171 Pac.
1164. A promise of an ancestor to leave by will to an heir presumptive
the share of his estate to which such heir would be entitled under the
statutes of descent and distribution, in the event he should die intestate,
is not a contract, not to perform within a year, within the meaning of
the statute of frauds.—Stahl v. Stevenson, 102 Kan. 447, 171 Pac. 1164,
1165. A promise made by a person since deceased, to devise property
as a reward for the plaintiff's devoting herself during twelve years to
caring for the person making the promise, is not within the statute of
frauds.—Clow v. West, 37 Nev. 267, 273, 142 Pac. 226.

(2) Changes in the law.—Sections 1624, Civil Code of California, as
amended in 1905, and 1973, Code of Civil Procedure of that state,
as amended in 1907, provide that an agreement to devise or bequeath
property, or to make provision for any person by will, is invalid unless
it is in writing, and it is held here that an oral agreement to devise by
will (made in contemplation of and in consideration of a marriage, subsequently fully consummated) could not be enforced.—Trout v. Ogilvie
(Cal. App.), 182 Pac. 333, 334. Prior to the amendments of 1905 and
1907 to section 1624 of the Civil Code of California, and section 1973 of
the Code of Civil Procedure of that state, an agreement to dispose of

property upon death in a particular way was not required to be in writing.—Steinberger v. Young, 175 Cal. 81, 165 Pac. 432, 433. An oral agreement by a married woman to devise her separate property was not absolutely void under the law of 1850 as amended in 1858 and 1862, and such agreement might be validated by ratification after 1874, when the amendment to section 167 of the Civil Code of California was adopted, removing all restrictions upon a married woman's right to contract with respect to her separate property.—Steinberger v. Young, 175 Cal. 81, 165 Pac. 452, 435. An agreement to devise made by a married woman is one "concerning or relating" to her separate property within the meaning of Stats. 1850, chap. 103, p. 254, section 6, as amended by Stats. 1858, p. 22, and by Stats. 1862, p. 518, requiring such contracts to be executed in writing.—Steinberger v. Young, 175 Cal. 81, 165 Pac. 432, 434. The amendments to sections 1624, Civil Code of California and 1973 Code Civ. Proc. of that state, bringing agreements to devise within the scope of the statute of frauds have no application of such an agreement made long prior to their adoption, and the validity of such an agreement is not affected by them.—Monsen v. Monsen, 174 Cal. 97, 98, 162 Pac. 90. Under the law, as existing prior to 1905, an oral promise to convey an estate by will, under certain circumstances was enforceable in equity, and is so still, provided the promise was made before that date.—Walfsen v. Smyer, 178 Cal. 775, 175 Pac. 10. The provision of the statute of frauds requiring written evidence of a contract "for the sale of lands . . . or any interest in or concerning them," does not apply to all contracts which in any way concern lands.—Stahl v. Stevenson, 102 Kan. 844, 845, 171 Pac. 1164, 1167. An oral contract, made prior to 1905, to dispose of property in a particular way on death, may be enforced without regard to the time elapsing between the making of the contract and the bringing of the suit.—Doolittle v. McConnell, 178 Cal. 697, 174 Pac. 305.

(3) Part performance.—An oral contract to make a will is obnoxious to the statute of frauds of the state of Washington, unless the testator in his lifetime did something substantial in pursuance of it.—Alexander v. Lewes, 104 Wash. 32, 175 Pac. 572. In a suit for the specific performance of a verbal contract to convey realty, the possession relied upon to take the contract out of the statute of frauds must be marked and certain, and referable only to such a contract.—Hayes v. Hayes, 89 Or. 630, 174 Pac. 579. To compel the specific performance of a verbal contract to convey realty, the contract itself must be clearly proved, and there must be a sufficient showing of part performance to take the contract out of the statute of frauds.—Hayes v. Hayes, 89 Or. 630, 174 Pac. 579. The mere payment of the consideration is not a sufficient performance to take out of the statute of frauds a parol agreement for the purchase of land; nevertheless, where a property owner makes a young man his companion, and for many years has him attending on him and nursing him continually, and tells him, and persons who know both, that he will leave property to him as payment for these services, evidence to this effect will support the enforcement of such a promise.—Velikanje v. Dickman, 98 Wash. 584, 168 Pac. 465.

5. Appeal. Law of the case.—An order directing, or refusing to direct, a conveyance of real estate, by an executor or administrator, under the statute relative to the conveyance of real estate and transfer of personal property by executors and administrators in certain cases, is appealable.—Estate of Corwin, 61 Cal. 160, 163. If the court decrees specific performance of a contract for the sale and conveyance of land, made by deceased with petitioner, and the decree is silent as to costs, but the court afterwards makes an unauthorized amendment and modification of the decree so as to include costs, an appeal will lie, if taken within sixty days from such judgment.—Estate of Potter, 141 Cal. 350, 74 Pac. 986, 141 Cal. 424, 75 Pac. 850. The rule of the "law of the case," where the specific performance of the contract of a decedent is sought, is applicable only where the same matters which were determined in the previous appeal are involved in the second appeal.—Flood v. Templeton, 152 Cal. 148, 13 L. R. A. (N. S.) 579, 92 Pac. 78, 83. In an action for specific performance of a contract to devise, where the pleadings and proof are based upon the theory that such a contract was made, the theory that a resulting trust arising from a transfer of an interest in the property to be devised by quitclaim can not be raised for the first time on appeal.—Blanc v. Conner, 167 Cal. 719, 726, 141 Pac. 217. Evidence of oral declaration of the decedent and her husband, supported by other evidence and by inferences drawn from the entire conduct of the plaintiff and the above who were her foster parents, is held sufficient to support a finding that decedent contracted to will her property to plaintiff.—Steinberger v. Young, 175 Cal. 81, 165 Pac. 432, 434.

PART IX.

MORTGAGES AND LEASES OF REAL ESTATE.

CHAPTER L

MORTGAGES AND LEASES.

MORTGAGES AND LEASES.

1. Mortgages.
    (1) Construction and validity of statute.
    (2) Authority to mortgage. Jurisdictional facts.
    (3) Purpose to be shown.
    (4) Sufficiency of petition.
    (5) Validity of mortgage.
    (6) Presumptions. Creditor's right.
    (7) Procedure. Practice. Collateral attack. Appeal.
    (8) Foreclosure. Title of purchaser.

2. Leases.
    (1) Power of executor or administrator to lease.
    (2) Validity of lease.
    (3) Power of court to revoke or modify order authorizing lease.
    (4) Power of representative to alter or modify existing lease.
    (5) Indian lands. In general.
    (6) Same. Power and approval of Secretary of Interior.
    (7) Same. Leases by guardians of minors. Approval.

§ 611. Mortgage of real property of decedent, minor, etc.

Whenever, in any estate now being administered, or that may hereafter be administered, or in any guardianship proceeding now pending, or that may hereafter be pending, it shall appear to the superior court, or a judge thereof, to be for the advantage of the estate to raise

(1359)

money upon a note or notes to be secured by a mortgage of the real property of any decedent, or of a minor, or an incompetent person, or any part thereof, or to make a lease of said real property, or any part thereof, or to agree to sell or to give an option to purchase a mining claim, or mining claims, or real property worked as a mine, or an undivided interest in real property, the court or judge, as often as occasion therefor shall arise in the administration of any estate, or in the course of any guardianship matter, may on a petition, notice, and hearing as provided in this article authorize, empower and direct the executor or administrator, or guardian of such minor or incompetent person, to mortgage such real property, or any part thereof, and to execute a note or notes to be secured by such mortgage, or to lease such real estate, or any part thereof, or to enter into an agreement to sell such real estate, or any part thereof, or to give an option to purchase such real estate or any part thereof.

PROCEDURE.—The proceedings to be taken to obtain an order to enter into an agreement for the sale of or for an option to purchase a mining claim or claims or real property worked as a mine, and the effect thereof shall be as provided in section one thousand five hundred eighty of this code, and the provisions of said section in so far as applicable shall also govern the proceedings to be taken to obtain an order to enter into an agreement for the sale of or for an option to purchase an undivided interest in real property and the effect thereof.—*Kerr's Cyc. Code. Civ. Proc.,* § 1577.

ANALOGOUS AND IDENTICAL STATUTES.

No identical statute found.

Arizona—Revised Statutes of 1913, paragraph 958.

Colorado—Laws of 1915, chapter 176, p. 503; and Laws of 1917, chapter 68, p. 214, repealing sections 7168-7178, 7182, 7196-7204, Rev. Stats. of 1908, being sections 7967-7977, 7981, and 8055-8063, Rev. Stats. of 1912. Power to lease estate property, see Laws of 1915, chapter 173, p. 491; amending Mills's Statutes of 1912, section 7947.

Idaho—Compiled Statutes of 1919, section 7668.

Kansas—General Statutes of 1915, sections 5050, 6117.

Montana—Revised Codes of 1907, sections 7600, 7778.

New Mexico—Statutes of 1915, section 4406.

North Dakota—Compiled Laws of 1913, sections 8710, 8790.

Oklahoma—Revised Laws of 1910, section 6364; Laws of 1913, chapter 66, p. 103; as amended by Laws of 1915, chapter 11, p. 9.

Oregon—Lord's Oregon Laws, section 1278.

South Dakota—Compiled Laws of 1913, section 5767, and volume II, p. 529, section 408.

Utah—Compiled Laws of 1907, sections 3908-3909X2; as amended by Laws of 1913, chapter 67, p. 107, and by Laws of 1917, chapter 10, p. 29.

Washington—Laws of 1917, chapter 156, p. 676, sections 122-146.

§ 612. Proceedings to obtain order to mortgage.

To obtain an order to mortgage such realty, the proceedings to be taken and the effect thereof shall be as follows:

FIRST. WHAT PETITION MUST SHOW.—The executor or administrator of any estate, or guardian of any minor or incompetent person, or any person interested in the estates of such decedents, minors, or incompetent persons, may file a verified petition showing:

1. PARTICULAR PURPOSES.—The particular purpose or purposes for which it is proposed to make the note or notes and mortgage, which shall be either to maintain the ward and his family or to maintain and educate the ward when a minor, or to pay the debts, legacies, or charges of administration, or to pay, reduce, extend, or renew some lien or mortgage already subsisting on said realty or some part thereof; or, if the application be made by the guardian of any minor or incompetent person, to erect, alter, or repair buildings or other structures upon, or otherwise to improve, the realty proposed to be mortgaged, or some part thereof.

2. STATEMENT OF FACTS, ETC.—A statement of the facts and circumstances showing the insufficiency of the income of the estate under guardianship to maintain the ward and his family or to maintain and educate the ward when

Probate Law—86

a minor and the debts, legacies, charges of administration, liens or mortgages to be paid, reduced, extended, or renewed, as the case may be; or, if the application be made by the guardian of any minor or incompetent person for the purpose of improving the realty or some part thereof, the condition and value of all the real and personal property then belonging to the estate, a statement of all debts and obligations secured or unsecured outstanding against the estate, and the character and estimated cost of the buildings, structures, or other improvements proposed to be erected, altered, or repaired with the proceeds of the mortgage.

3. ADVANTAGES THAT MAY ACCRUE.—The advantage that may accrue to the estate from raising the required money by note or notes and mortgage or providing for the payment, reduction, extension, or renewal of the subsisting liens or mortgages, as the case may be; or, if the application be made by the guardian of a minor or incompetent person for the purpose of improving the realty belonging to the estate or some part thereof, the advantage that will accrue to the estate by the making of such improvements.

4. AMOUNT TO BE RAISED.—The amount to be raised, with a general description of the property proposed to be mortgaged; and,

5. NAMES OF LEGATEES.—The names of the legatees and devisees, if any, and of the heirs of the deceased, or of the minor, or of the incompetent person, as the case may be, so far as known to the petitioner.

SECOND. ORDER TO SHOW CAUSE.—Upon filing such petition, an order shall be made by the court or judge, requiring all persons interested in the estate to appear before the court or judge, at a time and place specified, not less than four nor more than ten weeks thereafter, then and there to show cause why the realty (briefly indicating it), or some part thereof, should not be mortgaged for the amount mentioned in the petition (stating such amount), or such lesser amount as to the court or judge shall seem meet, and referring to the petition on file for further particulars.

THIRD. SERVICE OF ORDER.—The order to show cause may be personally served on the persons interested in the estate, at least ten days before the time appointed for hearing the petition, or may be published for four successive weeks in a newspaper of general circulation, published in the county.

FOURTH. HEARING OF PETITION.—At the time and at the place appointed in the order to show cause, or at such other time and place to which the hearing may be postponed (the power to make all needful postponements being hereby vested in the court or judge), having first received satisfactory proof of personal service or publication of the order to show cause, the court or judge must proceed to hear the petition and any objections that may be filed or presented thereto.

TESTIMONY OF WITNESSES. ORDER OF COURT DIRECTING LOAN.—Upon such hearing, witnesses may be compelled to attend and testify, in the same manner, and with like effect, as in other cases; and if, after a full hearing, the court or judge is satisfied that it will be for the advantage of the estate to mortgage the whole or any portion of the real estate, an order must be made authorizing, empowering, and directing the executor or administrator, or the guardian of such minor or incompetent person, to make such mortgage, and a promissory note or notes to the lender, for the amount of the loan, to be secured by said mortgage; the order may direct that a lesser amount than that named in the petition be borrowed, and may prescribe the maximum rate of interest and period of the loan, and may direct in what coin or currency it shall be paid, and require that the interest and the whole or any part of the principal be paid, from time to time, out of the whole estate or any part thereof, and that any buildings on the premises to be mortgaged shall be insured for further security of the lender, and the premiums paid from such income.

FIFTH. DUTY OF EXECUTOR, ADMINISTRATOR, ETC.—After the making of the order to mortgage, the executor, administrator, or guardian of a minor or of an incompetent person shall execute and deliver a promissory note or notes for the amount and period specified in the order, and shall execute, acknowledge, and deliver a mortgage of the premises, setting forth in the mortgage that it is made by authority of the order, and giving the date of such order. A certified copy of the order shall be recorded in the office of the county recorder of every county in which the encumbered land, or any portion thereof, lies. The note or notes and mortgage shall be signed by the executor, administrator, or guardian as such, and shall create no personal liability against the person so signing.

SIXTH. EFFECT OF SUCH NOTE AND MORTGAGE.—Every note or notes and mortgage so made shall be effectual to mortgage and hypothecate all the right, title, interest, and estate which the decedent, minor, or incompetent person had in the premises described therein at the time of the death of such decedent, or at the time of the appointment of the guardian of such minor or of such incompetent person, or prior thereto, had any right, title, or interest in said premises acquired by the estate of such decedent, minor, or incompetent person, by operation of law or otherwise, since the time of the death of such decedent, or the appointment of the guardian of such minor or incompetent person.

JURISDICTION OF THE COURT to administer the estate of such decedent, minor, or incompetent person shall be effectual to vest such court and judge with jurisdiction to make the order for the note or notes and mortgage, and such jurisdiction shall conclusively inure to the benefit of the mortgagee named in the mortgage, his heirs and assigns. No irregularity in the proceedings shall impair or invalidate the same or the note or notes and mortgage given in the pursuance thereof, and the mortgagee, his heirs and assigns, shall have and possess the same rights and remedies on the note or notes and mortgage as if it had been made by the decedent prior to his death, the minor after reaching the age of maturity, or the incompetent person when legally competent;

No DEFICIENCY JUDGMENT.—Provided, however, that upon any foreclosure, if the proceeds of the encumbered property are insufficient to pay the note or notes, and mortgage, no judgment or claim for any deficiency or such proceeds to satisfy the note or notes and mortgage, or the costs or expenses of sale, shall be had or allowed, except in cases where the note or notes and mortgage were given to pay, reduce, extend, or renew a lien or mortgage subsisting on the realty, or some part thereof, at the time of the death of the decedent, and the indebtedness secured by such lien or mortgage was an allowed and approved claim against his estate or a lien upon the interest of the minor in said real estate at the time it vested in him, or upon the estate of the incompetent at the time the incompetency of the incompetent person was so declared by the court;

How UNSATISFIED INDEBTEDNESS IS TO BE PAID.—And provided also, that in cases affecting the estate of the deceased persons, the part of the indebtedness remaining unsatisfied must be classed and paid with other demands against the estate, as provided in article three, chapter ten, of title eleven, part three, of this code, with respect to mortgages subsisting at the time of death.—*Kerr's Cyc. Code Civ. Proc.*, § 1578.

ANALOGOUS AND IDENTICAL STATUTES.

No identical statute found.

Arizona—Revised Statutes of 1913, paragraph 959.

Colorado—Laws of 1915, chapter 176, p. 503, and Laws of 1917, chapter 68, p. 214, repealing sections 7168-7178, 7182, 7196-7204, Rev. Stats. of 1908, being sections 7967-7977, 7981, and 8055-8063, Rev. Stats. of 1912. Redemptions. See Laws of 1917, chapter 112, p. 426.

Idaho—Compiled Statutes of 1919, section 7669.

Kansas—General Statutes of 1915, sections 5052, 6109, 6110, 6111, 6119.

Montana—Revised Codes of 1907, sections 7601, 7778.

New Mexico—Statutes of 1915, section 4406.

North Dakota—Compiled Laws of 1913, sections 8790, 8791.

Oklahoma—Revised Laws of 1910, section 6365.

Oregon—Lord's Oregon Laws, section 1278.

South Dakota—Compiled Laws of 1913, volume II, p. 505, section 241, and volume II, p. 529, section 409.

Utah—Compiled Laws of 1907, sections 3908, 3909.

Washington—Laws of 1917, chapter 156, pp. 677, 682, sections 124, 135.

§ 613.   Form.   Petition for leave to mortgage realty.

[Title of court.]

[Title of proceeding.]

No. ——.[1]   Dept. No. ——.
[Title of form.]

To the Honorable the —— Court of the County [2] of ——.

The petition of —— respectfully shows:

That he is, and has been since the —— day of ——, 19—, the duly qualified and acting administrator [3] of the estate of ——, deceased; and

That the inventory and appraisement of said estate have been duly made and filed herein, —

Wherefore petitioner hereby asks leave of the court to borrow money, and to make a note or notes and mortgage, on the real property of said estate hereinafter described; and the particular purpose or purposes for which it is proposed to make said note or notes and mortgage are as follows: ——.[4]

That the following is a statement of the debts, ——,[5] which are to be paid with the proceeds of said proposed mortgage;[6]

That the advantages that may accrue to the estate by

raising the required money by note or notes and mortgage are as follows: ——;[7]

That the amount which petitioner proposes so to raise by mortgage is —— dollars ($——); and a general description of the property proposed to be mortgaged is as follows: ——;[8]

That the names of the heirs [9] of said deceased, so far as known to petitioner, are as follows: ——.[10]

Wherefore petitioner prays that an order be made requiring all persons interested in said estate to appear and show cause, at a time and place therein fixed, why the realty herein described should not be mortgaged for the amount herein specified; and that, after due notice and hearing, an order be made authorizing and directing petitioner as such administrator [11] to make such note or notes and mortgage, and for such other and further order as may be meet in the premises.   ——, Petitioner.

——, Attorney for Petitioner.

Explanatory notes.—[1] Give file number. [2] Or, City and County. [3] Or, executor of the will, or guardian, etc. [4] Set forth particular purposes, which must be those prescribed by statute. [5] Or, legacies or expenses of administration, etc.; or, in case of guardianship, the facts and circumstances showing the insufficiency of the income to maintain the ward, etc. [6] In case of guardianship, if the application be made for the purpose of improving realty, the condition and value of all real estate must be stated, with a statement of the debts outstanding, etc., and the character, cost, etc., of the proposed improvements, and all matters required by statute. [7] Set forth the advantages expected to accrue. [8] Give description of property sought to be mortgaged, and interest therein. [9] And of the devisees and legatees, if any. [10] Give names. [11] Or, executor, or guardian.

§ 614. Form. Order to show cause on petition to mortgage.

[Title of court.]

[Title of proceeding.]   { No.——.[1]   Dept. No.——.
                            {   [Title of form.]

——, administrator [2] of the estate of ——, deceased,[3] having filed herein his petition, duly verified by affidavit, praying for an order of this court authorizing, empowering, and directing him, as such administrator,[4] to mortgage the real property of said deceased therein, and hereinafter described, for the purpose set forth in said petition; and it appearing that it will be of advantage to said estate that said mortgage be made, —

It is ordered by the court, That all persons interested in the estate of ——, deceased, do appear before this court on the —— day of ——, 19—, at —— o'clock in the forenoon [5] of said day, then and there to show cause, if any they have, why the real property of said estate, described below, or some part thereof, should not be mortgaged for the sum of —— dollars ($——), as prayed for in the petition of ——, the administrator,[6] this day filed, or for such lesser amount as to the court shall seem meet. Reference is made to said petition for further particulars. Said real estate, the property to be mortgaged, is situated in the county [7] of ——, state of ——, and is more particularly described as follows, to wit: ——.[8]

It is further ordered, That this order to show cause be published once a week for four successive weeks before the day of hearing, in ——, a newspaper of general circulation, published in said county [9] of ——.

Dated this —— day of ——, 19—.   ——, Judge.

Explanatory notes.—[1] Give file number. [2] Or, executor of the last will; or, guardian of the estate, etc. [3] Or, minor or incompetent person. [4] Or, executor, or guardian. [5] Or, afternoon. [6] Or, executor, or guardian. [7] Or, city and county. [8] Give description of property, and interest therein. [9] Or, city and county.

§ 615. Form. Order authorizing mortgage.

[Title of court.]

[Title of estate.]   { No. ——.[1] Dept. No. ——.
                 [Title of form.]

Comes now ——, the administrator [2] of the estate of said deceased, by Mr. ——, his attorney, and presents his petition for authority to mortgage the real estate of said deceased, and proves to the satisfaction of the court that the order herein made, requiring all persons interested to show cause why said estate should not be mortgaged, has been duly and personally served on all persons interested in said estate at least ten days before the time appointed for this hearing,[3] and the matter coming on regularly this day to be heard,[4] the court thereupon proceeds to hear the said petition, and, after hearing the evidence, the court being satisfied that the same is for the advantage of said estate, grants said petition.

It is therefore ordered by the court, That said ——, as administrator [5] of the estate of said deceased, be, and he is hereby, authorized to borrow the sum of —— dollars ($——), and to execute his promissory note therefor, and a mortgage in form as mentioned in said petition, to secure the payment thereof, on the property hereinafter described, said notes to be payable ——[6] from date, in gold coin of the United States, and to bear interest from date, not exceeding —— per cent per annum,[7] and attorneys' fees not exceeding —— per cent on principal, if suit is brought to foreclose said mortgage, and the building on said property shall be insured for the further security of the lender.

The property to be mortgaged is situated in the county [8] of ——, state of ——, and is described as follows, to wit: ——.[9]   ——, Judge of the —— Court.

Dated ——, 19—.

Explanatory notes.—1 Give file number. 2 Or, executor. 3 Or, was duly published four successive weeks before the time appointed for this hearing, in a newspaper of general circulation, published in said county. 4 Or, if the matter has been continued, say, "and the matter having been regularly postponed by the court to this time." 5 Or, executor. 6 State time. 7 The said interest to be paid solely out of the income of said property; or as otherwise directed. 8 Or, city and county. 9 Describe the property, and interest therein.

§ 616. Form. Mortgage of decedent's real estate.

This indenture, Made on the —— day of ——, 19—, between ——, the duly appointed, qualified, and acting

administrator [1] of the estate of ——, deceased, and ——,
both parties being of the county [2] of ——, state of ——, —

Witnesseth: That the —— court of the county [3] of ——,
state of ——, having, on the —— day of ——, 19—, made
an order, which is now on file and of record in said court,
and a certified copy of which order is duly recorded in
the office of the county recorder of the county of ——,
and which is hereby referred to and made a part hereof,
the same as if incorporated herein, authorizing, empowering, and directing the said administrator [4] to mortgage
certain realty of said estate; and that said administrator [5] has, under and by virtue of said order, agreed to
mortgage the said real estate to said —— to secure the
sum of —— dollars ($——), which said —— has agreed
to loan to the said administrator [6] for the use and benefit of said estate, —

The said administrator,[7] in consideration of said loan,
hereby mortgages to said —— all that certain real property situated in the county [8] of ——, state of ——, particularly described as follows, and which is the same land as
that described in said order, to wit: ——;[9] said mortgage being given as security for the payment, on the
—— day of ——, 19—, to said mortgagee, of the said sum
of —— dollars ($——), gold coin of the United States of
America, with interest thereon from date hereof until
paid.[10]

It is agreed between the mortgagor and the mortgagee,
that the former shall keep the buildings upon said land
insured for the sum of —— dollars ($——), and will
have the policies of insurance made payable to the mortgagee, for the latter's further security.

In witness whereof, The said mortgagor hereunto sets
his hand and seal this —— day of ——, 19—.

——, Administrator,[11] etc.   [Seal]

Explanatory notes.—1 Or, executor of the last will, etc. 2, 8 Or, city
and county. 4-7 Or, executor. 8 Or, city and county. 9 Insert description. 10 If it is deemed desirable to provide against default in the

payment of principal or interest, or both, etc., proceed as in an ordinary mortgage. If the mortgage is given to secure the payment of a note given by the administrator or executor, as such, insert copy thereof, as, "said mortgage being given as security or the payment of the promissory note of ——, given and signed by him as administrator [or executor] of the estate of ——, deceased, and in the words and figures as follows, to wit: ——." 11 Or, executor of the last will, etc.

§ 617. Proceedings to obtain lease of realty.

To obtain an order to lease the realty, the proceedings to be taken and the effect thereof shall be as follows:

FIRST. PETITION.—The executor, administrator, guardian of a minor or an incompetent person, or any person interested in the estates of such decedents, minors, or incompetent persons, must file a verified petition showing:

a. REQUIREMENTS.—The advantage or advantages that may accrue to the estate from giving a lease.

b. A general description of the property proposed to be leased.

c. The term, rental, and general conditions of the proposed lease.

d. The names of the legatees and devisees, if any, and of the heirs of the deceased, or of the minor, or of the incompetent persons, so far as known to the petitioner.

SECOND. ORDER OF COURT TO SHOW CAUSE.—Upon filing such petition an order shall be made by the court or judge requiring all persons interested in the estate to appear before the court or judge, at a time and place specified, not less than two nor more than four weeks thereafter, then and there to show cause why the realty (briefly indicating it) should not be leased for the period (stating it), at the rental mentioned in the petition (stating it), and referring to the petition on file for further particulars.

THIRD. SERVICE OF ORDER.—The order to show cause may be personally served on the persons interested in the estate at least ten days before the time appointed for hearing the petition, or it may be published for two successive weeks in a newspaper of general circulation in the county.

FOURTH. HEARING. WITNESSES. APPRAISERS. MINIMUM RENTAL.—At the time and place appointed to show cause, or at such other time and place to which the hearing may be postponed (the power to make all needful postponements being hereby vested in the court or judge), the court or judge having first received satisfactory proof of personal service or publication of the order to show cause, must proceed to hear the petition, and any objection that may have been filed or presented thereto. Upon such hearing witnesses may be compelled to attend and testify in the same manner and with like effect as in other cases, and the court may, in its discretion, appoint one or more, not exceeding three, disinterested persons to appraise the rental value of the premises, and direct that a reasonable compensation for the services, not exceeding five dollars per day, be paid by the estate.

ORDER TO MAKE LEASE.—If, after a full hearing, the court or judge is satisfied that it will be for the advantage of the estate to lease the whole or any portion of the real estate, an order must be made authorizing, empowering, and directing the executor, administrator, or the guardian, to make such lease. The order may prescribe the minimum rental or royalty to be received for the premises, and the period of the lease, which must in no case be longer than for ten years, and may prescribe the other terms and conditions of such lease; provided that, for the purpose of exploiting for minerals, or mineral oils or petroleum and extracting minerals therefrom, the period of the lease may be for twenty years.

FIFTH. CONDITIONS OF LEASE.—After the making of the order to lease, the executor, administrator, or guardian of a minor or of an incompetent person, shall execute, acknowledge, and deliver a lease of the premises for the term and period and with the conditions specified in the order, setting forth in the lease that it is made by authority of the order, and giving the date of such order. A certified copy of the order shall be recorded in the office of the county recorder of every county in which the leased land or any portion thereof lies.

SIXTH. EFFECT OF LEASE. ERRORS AND OMISSIONS.— Every lease so made shall be effectual to demise and let, at the rent, for the term, and upon the conditions therein prescribed, the premises described therein. Jurisdiction of the court to administer the estate of the decedent, the minor, or of the incompetent person shall be effectual to vest such court and judge with jurisdiction to make the order for the lease, and such jurisdiction shall conclusively inure to the benefit of the lessee, his heirs and assigns. No omission, error, or irregularity in the proceedings shall impair or invalidate the same, or the lease made in pursuance thereof.—*Kerr's Cyc. Code Civ. Proc.,* § 1579.

ANALOGOUS AND IDENTICAL STATUTES.
No identical statute found.

Arizona—Revised Statutes of 1913, paragraph 966.
Colorado—Mills's Statutes of 1912, section 7947.
Idaho—Compiled Statutes of 1919, section 7671.
Kansas—General Statutes of 1915, sections 5052, 6109, 6110-6119.
Montana—Revised Codes of 1907, section 7602.
New Mexico—Statutes of 1915, section 4407.
North Dakota—Compiled Laws of 1913, section 8710.
South Dakota—Compiled Laws of 1913, section ——.
Utah—Compiled Laws of 1907, sections 3908-3909X2; as amended by Laws of 1913, chapter 67, p. 107, and by Laws of 1917, chapter 10, p. 29.

§ 618. Form. Petition for leave to lease realty.
[Title of court.]

[Title of proceeding.] { No. ——.1 Dept. No.——.
{ [Title of form.]

To the Honorable the —— Court of the County [2] of ——.

The petition of —— respectfully shows:

That he is, and has been since the —— day of ——,

19—, the duly qualified and acting guardian [3] of the estate of ——, a minor; [4] and

That the inventory and appraisement of the said ward has been duly made and filed.

Wherefore petitioner hereby asks leave of the court to execute, on behalf of said ward, a lease on the real estate of his ward hereinafter described; and shows that the advantages that may accrue to said ward and his estate therefrom are as follows: ——. [5]

That the property of said ward proposed to be leased is described as follows: ——; [6]

That the term, rental, and general conditions of the proposed lease are as follows: ——; [7]

That the names of the heirs [8] of said ward are: ——. [9]

Wherefore petitioner prays that an order be made requiring all persons interested in said estate to appear and show cause, at a time and place to be fixed in said order, then and there to show cause why the realty above described should not be leased as above proposed; and that, after due notice and hearing, an order be made authorizing and directing your petitioner, as guardian as aforesaid, to execute a lease of the above-described premises, at the rental, for the period, and on the terms and conditions above set forth; and for such order or further order as to the court shall seem meet.

——, Attorney for Petitioner.   ——, Petitioner.

[Add usual verification.]

Explanatory notes.—1 Give file number. 2 Or, City and County. 8 Or, administrator of the estate, or executor of the last will of ——, deceased. 4 Or, an incompetent person. 5 Set forth the advantages. 6 Give description of property, and interest of ward. 7 State duration, rental, and general conditions of the proposed lease. 8, 9 Give names of heirs of ward, or names of heirs and of devisees and legatees, if any, of deceased.

§ 619. **Form. Order to show cause on petition to lease realty.**

[Title of court.]

[Title of proceeding.]   { No.——.¹ Dept. No.——.
                         {   [Title of form.]

——, the guardian² of the estate of ——, a minor,³ having this day filed a verified petition for authority to lease the real property belonging to said estate hereinafter described, for the period and at the rental hereinafter stated, and it appearing that the giving of said lease will be advantageous to said estate, —   .

It is ordered, That all persons interested in said estate be, and they are hereby, required to appear before this court on ——,⁴ the —— day of ——, 19—, at —— o'clock, — m., at the court-room of said court, then and there to show cause, if any they have, why an order should not be made authorizing and directing said ——, as such guardian,⁵ to execute a lease of the real property belonging to said estate hereinafter described for the period of ——⁶ years, at the ——⁷ rental of —— dollars per ——, as mentioned in said petition.

Said real property is situated in the county⁸ of ——, state of ——, and is described as follows: ——.⁹

For further particulars, reference is hereby made to the above petition on file.

It is further ordered, That a copy of this order be published once a week for two successive weeks in ——, a newspaper of general circulation in said county.¹⁰

Dated ——, 19—.   ——, Judge of the —— Court.

Explanatory notes.—1 Give file number. 2 Or, administrator of the estate, or, executor of the last will of ——, deceased. 3 Or, an incompetent person. 4 Give day of week. 5 Or, administrator or executor. 6 Give period of proposed lease. 7 Give rental as stated in petition. 8 Or, city and county. 9 Give description of property, and interest therein. 10 Or, city and county. Authority may be given to lease land located in another county. See Kerr's Cal. Cyc. Code Civ. Proc., § 1295. Persons interested may be required to show cause why the administrator should not be authorized to lease the building he proposes to construct on the property belonging to the estate of said deceased, and situated in the county of ——, for a term of —— years from and after the full completion of said building, in accordance with certain plans, and tendered possession thereof to the lessee; such lessee to pay a rental, based so that the estate of said deceased derive —— per cent per annum upon all the moneys that may be expended in the construction of the said building, plus the value of the real estate fixed, at —— dollars ($——), such annual rental to be paid in —— equal monthly instalments, commencing at the date of the completion of said building, the lessee also to pay the premiums on the fire insurance for said building, taxes, and all costs and expenses of keeping said building in good and substantial repair during the term of the lease; the rental and covenants of the lessee to be guaranteed by a bond not exceeding in amount one year's rental, "as will fully appear by reference to the petition on file herein, for full particulars," where such is the nature of the petition. Or, persons interested may be required to show cause why an order should not be granted to the said executors, authorizing them to lease for one to three years, with or without temporary improvements, such parts or portions of said real estate as may be to the benefit and advantage of said estate, at the best rental they can obtain, but not below the minimum, to be named by the court.

§ 620. Form. Affidavit of publication of order to show cause.

[Title of court.]

[Title of estate.]

{ No. ——.1   Dept. No. ——.

[Title of form.]

State of ——, } ss.
County [2] of ——,

——, of the said county [3] and state, having been first duly sworn, deposes and says:

That he is, and at all times embraced in the publication herein mentioned was, the principal clerk [4] of the printers and publishers of the ——, a newspaper of general circulation, printed and published daily (Sundays excepted) in said county;[5]

That deponent, as such clerk, during all times mentioned in this affidavit has had, and still has, charge of all the advertisements in said newspaper; and

That an order to show cause, of which the annexed is a true printed copy, was published in the above-named newspaper on the following dates, to wit, ——,[6] being as often as said newspaper was published during said period; and further deponent saith not. ——

Subscribed and sworn to before me this —— day of
——, 19—.   ——, Notary Public, etc.[7]

Explanatory notes.—1 Give file number. 2, 3 Or, City and County.
4 Or, the printer; or, the foreman of the printer. See Estate of Melone,
141 Cal. 331, 334, 74 Pac. 991. 5 Or, city and county. 6 Put in each
date. 7 Or other officer taking the oath.

§ 621. Form. Order authorizing lease.

[Title of court.]

[Title of estate.]   { No.——.1 Dept. No.——.
                                      {   [Title of form.]

Now comes ——, the administrator [2] of said ——, by
Mr. ——, his attorney, and presents his petition for
authority to let, lease, and demise certain real estate of
said deceased; and, having proved to the satisfaction of
the court that the order herein made requiring all persons interested to show cause why said real estate should
not be leased has been duly and personally served on all
persons interested in said estate at least ten days [3] before
the time appointed therein for this hearing,[4] the court
thereupon proceeds to the hearing of said petition, and,
after hearing the evidence, the court, being satisfied that
the same is for the advantage of the estate, grants said
petition as follows, to wit: —

It is ordered by the court, That ——, as administrator [5] of the estate of ——, be authorized, empowered, and
directed to make a lease of the land herein described for
a period not less than ——[6] nor more than ——,[7] at a
rental of not less than —— dollars ($——) per ——[8]
nor more than dollars ($——) per ——,[9] and upon the
terms and conditions following, to wit: ——.[10]

Said real property is described as follows, to wit:
——.[11]   ——, County Clerk.

Entered ——, 19—.   By ——, Deputy.[12]

Explanatory notes.—1 Give file number. 2 Or, executor. 3 Or, was
published in a newspaper of general circulation in this county [or city
and county] for two successive weeks. 4 If the matter has been continued, say, "and the hearing having been regularly postponed to this

Probate Law—87

time"; and if objections are made, say, "and —— having appeared and filed objections to the granting of said petition." 5 Or, executor. 6, 7 Months or years. 8, 9 Month or year. 10 State terms and conditions of petition, or other terms and conditions, if any. 11 Describe the land. 12 Orders need not be signed. See note, § 77, ante.

§ 622. Form. Lease of decedent's real estate.

This indenture, Made on the —— day of ——, 19—, between ——, the duly appointed, qualified, and acting administrator [1] of the estate of ——, deceased, and ——, both parties of the county [2] of ——, state of ——,——

Witnesseth: That the —— court of the county [3] of ——, state of ——, having, on the —— day of ——, 19—, made an order, which is now on file and of record in said court, and a certified copy of which order was duly recorded in the office of the county recorder of the county of —— on the —— day of ——, 19—, and which is hereby referred to and made a part hereof, the same as if incorporated herein, authorizing, empowering, and directing the said administrator [4] to lease certain realty of said estate; and that said administrator [5] has, under and by virtue of said order, agreed to lease the said real estate, on the terms and conditions hereinafter stated, to the said —— for the term of —— years;

That said administrator,[6] in consideration of the premises, has demised and let, and by these presents does demise and let, unto the said ——, that certain real property situated in the county [7] of ——, state of ——, particularly described as follows, and which is the same land as that described in said order, to wit: ——; with the appurtenances, for the term of —— [8] from the —— day of ——, 19—, at the —— [9] rental or sum of —— dollars ($——), payable in gold coin of the United States of America, in advance, on the —— day of each and every month during said term.[10]

In witness whereof, The said parties have hereunto

set their hands and seals the day and year first above
written. [Seal]
——, Administrator,[11] etc. ——, Lessee. [Seal]

Explanatory notes.—1 Or, executor of the last will, etc. 2, 8 Or city
and county. 4-6 Or, executor. 7 Or, city and county. 8 Years or
months. 9 Yearly or monthly. 10 As to any further agreements, follow
the form of an ordinary lease. 11 Or, executor of the last will, etc.

MORTGAGES AND LEASES.

1. Mortgages.
  (1) Construction and validity of
     statute.
  (2) Authority to mortgage. Ju-
     risdictional facts.
  (3) Purpose to be shown.
  (4) Sufficiency of petition.
  (5) Validity of mortgage.
  (6) Presumptions. Creditor's
     right.
  (7) Procedure. Practice. Collat-
     eral attack. Appeal.
  (8) Foreclosure. Title of pur-
     chaser.

2. Leases.
  (1) Power of executor or admin-
     istrator to lease.
  (2) Validity of lease.
  (3) Power of court to revoke or
     modify order authorizing
     lease.
  (4) Power of representative to
     alter or modify existing
     lease.
  (5) Indians lands. In general.
  (6) Same. Power and approval
     of Secretary of Interior.
  (7) Same. Leases by guardians
     of minors. Approval.

1. Mortgages.

(1) Construction and validity of statute.—The court has, undoubtedly, in a proper case, power to authorize the mortgaging of estates
of decedents; and, within the limitations placed by law upon the power
to sell to pay charges against the estate, if the law existed at the
decedent's death, the court may, on cause shown, as required by the
statute, authorize such mortgage, whether the decedent died before or
after passage of the act of 1887, the time at which sections 1577 and
1578 of the Code of Civil Procedure of California were originally
enacted.—Murphy v. Farmers, etc., Bank, 131 Cal. 115, 120, 63 Pac. 368;
Howard v. Bryan, 133 Cal. 257, 259, 65 Pac. 462. To authorize the
mortgaging of such property for the express purpose of raising money
with which to pay charges or liens resting upon it is but to change
the form of the lien, and adds no new burden not already borne by the
property, or to which the property may be subjected under the law as
it existed when the testator died; and even if the mortgage, under the
statute, may bear a greater rate of interest than the legacies may bear,
that fact does not affect the question of power, nor can it reasonably be
said to be a new burden, as the increased rate of interest allowed by
law is but an incident of the power by which the burden or lien already
on the property may be changed by changing the form of the statutory
burden to a mortgage lien.—Murphy v. Farmers, etc., Bank, 131 Cal.
115, 119, 63 Pac. 368. For cases where probate mortgages given under
said sections 1577 and 1578 have been upheld, see Thomas v. Parker, 97

Cal. 456, 32 Pac. 562; Stow v. Schiefferly, 120 Cal. 609, 52 Pac. 1000; Weinreich v. Hensley, 121 Cal. 647, 54 Pac. 254; Fast v. Steele, 127 Cal 202, 59 Pac. 585. The authority of the court to order a mortgage for the purpose of paying liens on the realty of a decedent's estate, or to pay debts, legacies, or expenses of administration, is expressly given by the provision of the statute; and it is not essential to the jurisdiction of the court that the order shall include the payment of all debts. —Estate of Freud, 131 Cal. 667, 674, 82 Am. St. Rep. 407, 63 Pac. 1080; Stambach v. Emerson, 139 Cal. 282, 285, 72 Pac. 991. The statute of Oregon does not, in express terms, authorize the borrowing of money with which to redeem real property, belonging to the decedent's estate, that may have been sold under a decree or judgment; but, as a lien of this character is an indebtedness against said estate, the right to borrow money for the purpose of funding such indebtedness necessarily carries with its exercise a grant of power to borrow money to be used in redeeming real property from such sale.—Lawrey v. Sterling, 41 Or. 518, 69 Pac. 460, 462. The statute of Oregon authorizing an executor or administrator to borrow money upon any property belonging to the estate of his decedent for the purpose of funding the indebtedness against the estate is not unconstitutional because of the title of the act containing more than one subject. The subject of the act is the granting of power by the county court to an executor or administrator to borrow money, and the incident to the exercise of such power is the right to use the money so borrowed in paying the indebtedness against the estate of a decedent, including the redemption of the real property, though that may be sold under a decree or judgment. The purpose for which the money may be used is properly connected with an exercise of the power to borrow it.—Lawrey v. Sterling, 41 Or. 518, 69 Pac. 460, 462.

(2) Authority to mortgage. Jurisdictional facts.—A mortgage or sale of the real estate of a deceased person is in derogation of the common law, and is authorized, if at all, by statute. And when authorized by statute, the statute must, in substance at least, be complied with.— Wallace v. Grant, 27 Wash. 170, 67 Pac. 578, 579. In the statute of Washington the basis of the statutory provision is the exhaustion of the personal estate in the hands of the executor or administrator, and it is only when the personal estate in the hands of the executor or administrator shall be insufficient to pay the debts of the administration that the executor or administrator may sell or mortgage the real estate. There must be a showing that the personal property is insufficient to pay the expenses of the estate.—Wallace v. Grant, 27 Wash. 170, 67 Pac. 578, 579. The foundation of jurisdiction in cases of this sort is the petition filed by the applicant for leave to mortgage; and the essential fact to be found by the court, under the present statute of California, as the basis of its order is, that it will be for the advantage of the estate to raise money by a loan, and the statute prescribes the matters which must be set forth in the petition as a basis for the

judgment of court.—Howard v. Bryan, 133 Cal. 257, 260, 263, 65 Pac. 462. Where a petition to mortgage real estate was not verified, and failed to show that the personal estate was exhausted, or that the same was insufficient to pay the debts of the administration, the probate court would not acquire jurisdiction to make an order to mortgage.—Wallace v. Grant, 27 Wash. 170, 67 Pac. 578, 580. Where a will indicates by its language the testator's intent to create a trust in his wife, executrix of the estate, for the benefit of their children and, in a residuary sense, in favor of her, this confers upon her no authority to borrow money and to give her individual note therefor, secured by mortgage on real property belonging to the estate.—Beakey v. Knutson, 90 Or. 574, 174 Pac. 1149, 177 Pac. 955.

(3) **Purpose to be shown.**—The first requisite of the petition is that it must disclose the particular purpose for which the money is to be used. And, in the case of a minor's estate, that purpose must be either to pay debts or charges of administration, or to pay, reduce, extend, or renew some lien or mortgage already subsisting on the realty which it is proposed to mortgage.—Howard v. Bryan, 133 Cal. 257, 263, 65 Pac. 462. A petition which shows that the purpose is to obtain the money wherewith to pay a debt of the deceased sufficiently shows a purpose authorized by statute to clothe the court with jurisdiction to make the order. The language of the statute, providing that the petition shall state the particular purposes, and which enumerates them, was intended simply to designate the various objects for which a mortgage, binding the property of the estate, may be given, to the end that the court should not impose a lien for some purpose not included within the proper functions of the administration of the estate. It is necessary, before there can be any final distribution of the realty, that the expenses of administration, debts of deceased, and legacies be paid. It was to confine the authority to mortgage to these general purposes that the language of the statute was used, and subdivision one of section 1578 of the Code of Civil Procedure of California should be read precisely as if the word "the" were omitted, and the statute was, "which shall be either to pay debts, legacies, or charges of administration."—Stambach v. Emerson, 139 Cal. 282, 284, 72 Pac. 991.

(4) **Sufficiency of petition.**—To mortgage the land of a decedent, a verified petition, in substantial conformity with the statute, must be filed to give the court jurisdiction to proceed. The omission to file it would be more than a mere irregularity; and the petition must disclose the particular purpose for which the money is to be used.—Howard v. Bryan, 133 Cal. 257, 263, 265, 65 Pac. 462; Stambach v. Emerson, 139 Cal. 282, 284, 72 Pac. 991. In the state of Washington the petition to mortgage the realty of a decedent is insufficient unless it shows that there is not enough personal property to pay the expenses of the estate, and such petition must be verified by the oath of the party presenting the same.—Wallace v. Grant, 27 Wash. 170, 67 Pac. 578, 579, 580. The

county court in Oregon, in the administration of estates, exercises its powers by means of an affidavit, or the verified petition or statement of a party, and this applies to an application for an order to mortgage the real estate of a decedent.—Lawrey v. Sterling, 41 Or. 518, 69 Pac. 460, 463.

(5) Validity of mortgage.—The power to borrow money, conferred upon an executor or administrator by the statute of Oregon, evidently carries with it, by implication, authority to execute promissory notes evidencing the loan, expressing the rate of interest stipulated for, and fixing the day of payment, and also the right to execute an instrument in common form, and containing the provisions in common use. It is the common practice, in that state, to include in a promissory note a stipulation for the payment of such sum as the court may adjudge reasonable for attorney's fees in case suit or action is instituted to collect the sum specified in the note, or any part thereof; and this being so, the executor or administrator is authorized to include such a promise in the note.—Lawrey v. Sterling, 41 Or. 518, 69 Pac. 460, 464. A power to mortgage, given in general terms, without specifying what provisions the deed shall contain, includes the power to make it in the form and with the provisions customarily used within the state or county where the land is situated.—Lawrey v. Sterling, 41 Or. 518, 69 Pac. 460, 464. Under the California statute, no irregularity in the proceedings impairs or invalidates the note or notes, or the mortgage given in pursuance thereof. Hence, if the executor follows the statute, and executes a promissory note for the money borrowed, though the order made by the court omitted the direction to execute a promissory note, such omission is a mere irregularity, whether such irregularity consists in the omission of the court to direct the execution of the note, or in the action of the executor in giving it. In any event, no injury is done, and the proceedings are not affected by such irregularity. Neither does the fact that the note and mortgage were made payable on or before one year after their date, while the order directed that the mortgage should be made payable "on or before two years" after its date "impair or invalidate" the note or mortgage. Such departure from the order is a mere irregularity. Nor will an oral direction of the judge to the executor to pay, or individually secure to the mortgagee the whole of the interest which was to become due on the note, which was to be secured by the mortgage, and that the executor, in order to secure to the mortgagee one year's interest, assigned to him his commissions as executor to the extent of one year's interest, affect the rights of the mortgagee. He is charged with notice of all that the order contains, but is not bound by such oral direction of the judge to the executor.— Fast v. Steele, 127 Cal. 202, 205, 59 Pac. 585. A mortgage is sufficient to show that it was intended as a mortgage of property belonging to the estate of which the mortgagor was administrator, and was executed by him in his character as administrator in pursuance of law, and the order of the court directing its execution, where it refers to the order

of the court authorizing its execution, and recites that "the said mortgagor, pursuant to the order," mortgages to the mortgagee, etc.—Thomas v. Parker, 97 Cal. 456, 457, 32 Pac. 562. Where a testator has given his executors certain directions to be observed in carrying out the provisions of his will, such directions are nugatory, to the extent that they are inconsistent with law. The executors, as such, are not trustees of an express trust in such a case, and the authority which the testator gives them creates only such a trust as pertains to the office of executor, where he has not conferred upon them the power to make any sale or disposition of his estate other than that they "shall have the property sold" at the expiration of two years after his death, and shall distribute the proceeds among his designated beneficiaries. The sale which is thus directed is to be made by them as executors of his will, and as a part of their administration of the estate, and not as the trustees of an express trust, and will be ineffective without a confirmation by the court. In such a case, a mortgage, by them, of the property of the estate will not be effective unless made by an order of the court as prescribed by the statute. Otherwise they would be able to transfer the estate without the approval of the court, and thus to do indirectly what they are forbidden to do directly, since the right to mortgage includes a right in the mortgagee to have a sale of the remainder in satisfaction of the obligation for which the mortgage was given.—Estate of Pforr, 144 Cal. 121, 125, 77 Pac. 825. The law can not be construed to authorize the mortgage of a minor's estate to pay any debt but his own. It must be such a mortgage as he can discharge by paying what he is individually bound for, and such as will admit of a redemption by the payment of that which is due from him on his own account. Hence, if a court authorizes a mortgage of the interest of five minors to secure a sum in excess of their aggregate indebtedness, or to mortgage their separate interests for their aggregate debt, it exceeds its jurisdiction, however advantageous it may seem to pursue that course. The proceeding can not be sustained without establishing a dangerous precedent, from which serious abuses would be certain to flow.—Howard v. Bryan, 133 Cal. 257, 264, 65 Pac. 462. No bond is required as a condition to the making of a mortgage upon the estate of a decedent.—Howard v. Bryan, 133 Cal. 257, 265, 65 Pac. 462. A mortgage executed by the survivor of two parties, husband and wife, where the other died on the 16th day of September, 1909, intestate and leaving issue, was a nullity, so far as it purported to cover the interests of the children, and did not create any lien thereon.—Ewald v. Hufton, 31 Ida. 373, 173 Pac. 247. Where the proceedings for the sale of the allotted lands of a minor Choctaw allottee and the deed issued pursuant thereto are set aside for fraud, and pending the suit, the grantee in the deed set aside executes a mortgage upon the land described in the deed and the mortgagee is made a party defendant, the refusal of the court to set aside both deed and mortgage was error.—Bridges v. Rea (Okla.), 166 Pac. 416, 419. Where all the proceedings are regular on their face, and the purchaser at a guardian's sale executes a mortgage upon the lands purchased, the lien of the mortgagee may not be defeated for fraud affecting the sale, where the mortgagee did not participate therein or have notice or knowledge thereof.—Langley v. Ford (Okla.), 171 Pac. 471, 472.

(6) **Presumptions. Creditor's right.**—In examining the record of a mortgage authorizing the sale of a decedent's property, the same presumptions are indulged in view of the regularity and validity of the proceeding as those which govern the construction of the record in an ordinary action.—Howard v. Bryan, 133 Cal. 257, 262, 65 Pac. 462. Presumably the mortgaged property has a market value greater than the mortgage debt, for the lender would rarely lend up to the full cash value. But the mortgage is not a sale, and the creditors may at any time petition to sell, and pay the mortgage, and they will thus have an opportunity to realize the margin of value above the mortgage debt; and if a sale can not be made for an amount in excess of the loan, it will show that the estate has realized on the mortgage all the property is worth in the market, and creditors would have no cause of complaint, for no deficiency judgment can be entered. The mortgagee must look alone to the property.—Murphy v. Farmers, etc., Bank, 131 Cal. 115, 120, 63 Pac. 368.

(7) **Procedure. Practice. Collateral attack. Appeal.**—An order to show cause why the real estate of a decedent should not be mortgaged, having been duly published, is not insufficient because it does not direct or require personal service on minor heirs.—Thomas v. Parker, 97 Cal. 456, 458, 32 Pac. 562. And the non-appointment of a guardian ad litem is merely an irregularity. The statute does not require any guardian ad litem to be appointed, and provides that if the court has jurisdiction to administer the estate of decedent, it has jurisdiction to make the order for the mortgage.—Thomas v. Parker, 97 Cal. 456, 458, 32 Pac. 562. In making an order directing that the estate of a decedent shall be mortgaged, the interest of one who is seeking to acquire title to the property adversely to the estate can not be considered.—Estate of Freud, 133 Cal. 667, 674, 82 Am. St. Rep. 407, 63 Pac. 1080. If, by mistake, the court authorizes a mortgage to be given on property which is subject to a probate homestead, such mortgage should be paid out of moneys realized from the sale of other property belonging to the estate, where it is solvent.—Estate of Shively, 145 Cal. 400, 402, 78 Pac. 869. The statute controls the probate court in the exercise of its jurisdiction in the matter of the payment of debts of the estate, and a disregard thereof would be error reviewable on appeal taken by any person interested. But the court has jurisdiction to make an order erroneously preferring one creditor to another, and its action in so doing is only error in the exercise of jurisdiction, and can not be collaterally attacked. If the effect of an order authorizing the mortgage of decedent's property is to prefer erroneously certain creditors of the estate, the action of the

court can be reviewed only on appeal from the order.—Stambach v. Emerson, 139 Cal. 282, 284, 72 Pac. 991. In a collateral attack upon an order authorizing the estate of a decedent to be mortgaged, only those facts and matters appearing upon the face of the record are to be considered; and if they show no excess or defect of jurisdiction, no mere error of the court in the exercise of its jurisdiction, or irregularity in the proceeding, will invalidate the order.—Howard v. Bryan, 133 Cal. 257, 262, 65 Pac. 462. A mortgagee may, after the death of the mortgagor, not only establish his claim but pursue it to a satisfaction of the judgment, by a sale under the ordinary processes prevailing on the equity side of the court; in so proceeding, however, he is held to have waived his right to satisfy any deficiency that may arise on the sale, out of the unincumbered property of the estate.—Denton v. Maple, 92 Wash. 290, 158 Pac. 1001. A husband, acting as the administrator of his wife's estate, may petition the court for a sale of community land to pay off a mortgage on such land, but where no sale can be made except to himself; or in such a way as merely to change the form of the mortgage, equity requires that he report that fact to the court and take an order allowing him to remortgage the property.—Stewart v. Baldwin, 86 Wash. 63, 149 Pac. 662. The county court has no jurisdiction under the laws of this state or the acts of congress to determine whether the allotted lands of a Cherokee minor should be mortgaged for more than the amount of the indebtedness subject to be paid or secured, under the provisions of such laws and acts of congress, with interest thereon, and an order made on the application of the guardian of such minor authorizing such mortgage for any excess of such amount, as well as the mortgage given in pursuance thereof is, to the extent of such excess, void and subject to collateral attack, without allegation or proof of fraud.—Roth v. Union Nat. Bank (Okla.), 160 Pac. 505, 511. Where the proceedings of the county court appointing a guardian for certain minors and thereafter ordering a sale of the lands of said minors, are regular, the record can not be collaterally attacked in an action to foreclose a mortgage upon said lands, executed by the purchaser at the guardian's sale, in the absence of fraud.—Langley v. Ford (Okla.), 171 Pac. 471, 472.

(8) **Foreclosure. Title of purchaser.**—Where an order authorizing the mortgaging of a decedent's property declares that it was made and entered upon a verified petition, it will be presumed, if a verification to the petition was essential to jurisdiction, that such verification appeared upon the original as filed. The court must assume the fact to be as stated in the complaint and in the order, although the verification does not appear on the exhibit. It is not necessary to a good complaint, that all the proceedings leading to the mortgage should be set out in the complaint. It is only necessary to set forth the mortgage in hæc verba or in substance; it is not necessary to set out the petition or order; both of these exhibits may be wholly disregarded, and there will remain a good complaint.—Stone v. Schiefferly, 120 Cal. 609,

612, 52 Pac. 1000. If the purpose of the mortgage authorized is to pay an indebtedness of the estate, but such mortgage is executed in part for a private debt of the executor or administrator, and in part for money loaned to the estate, the title obtained by the mortgagee under foreclosure is not void, but the application of the mortgage-money to pay the personal debt of the executor or administrator is a breach of trust on the part of the representative, and if the mortgagee became a party to the violation of the trust, such mortgagee acquired no right to the money received from the representative, so far as a minor heir is concerned, and the minor heir's right to the money is unaffected by the mortgage, or by the payment to the representative.—Murphy v. Farmers, etc., Bank, 131 Cal. 115, 118, 63 Pac. 368.

2. Leases.

(1) **Power of executor or administrator to lease.**—An administrator has the right to lease the property in his possession, as such, to a third person.—Boyer v. Anduiza, 90 Or. 163, 175 Pac. 853. An executor or administrator of the estate of the deceased person has authority to lease the real property of the estate during the period of administration; but any lease for a term definite is subject to be terminated by final distribution of the estate and the discharge of the representative. —Doolan v. McCauley, 66 Cal. 476, 6 Pac. 130. A resident of Ohio, owning, in Kansas, a farm that had never been used for other than agricultural purposes, executed a will in Ohio, providing that the executor and trustee should take charge of said premises, and "lease and maintain the same in repair and good condition, with a view to obtaining the best income therefrom without permitting the same to deteriorate in value or quality." It was held that the executor and trustee was not, by said will, authorized to execute an oil and gas lease granting to the lessee all the oil and gas under said premises and bind the legatees thereby. Where an executor and trustee, without having sufficient authority under the will to bind the legatees thereby, executed an oil and gas lease on a farm that had never been used for other than agricultural purposes; but, prior to the execution of the lease, he had individually acquired the interest of one of the legatees in the premises, and soon thereafter acquired the interest of another of the legatees, he is estopped, in an action of partition, under such circumstances, from denying that the interest acquired by him was not subject to the lease.—Lanyon Zinc Co. v. Freeman, 68 Kan. 691, 1 Ann. Cas. 403, 75 Pac. 995.

REFERENCES.

Power of executor to make oil and gas lease.—See note 1 Am. & Eng. Ann. Cas. 406. Right to rents on lease of intestate's property.—See note 40 L. R. A. 321-345.

(2) **Validity of lease.**—Under the statutes of Utah, requiring a lease for more than one year to be in writing, if one of six duly qualified executors of the estate of a decedent, having no written authority from

the others, or any of them, who are all within that jurisdiction, and free from any disability, executes a lease for more than one year, such lease is not valid, where the statute requires the act of a majority, if there are more than two executors or administrators.—Utah L. & T. Co. v. Garbutt, 6 Utah 342, 33 Pac. 758. The proceedings to obtain an order to lease the realty of a decedent, in Montana, are set out at length in State v. Second Jud. Dist. Court, 24 Mont. 1, 60 Pac. 489, 491. In that state, the order may prescribe the minimum rental to be received for the premises, and the period of the lease, which must in no case be longer than for five years, and may prescribe the other terms and conditions of such lease. The notice to be given must contain mention of the term and rental contemplated by the proposed lease. The lease may also be conditioned upon the furnishing of security for the faithful performance thereof, as there may be circumstances indicating that rents will fluctuate during the term, and it may fix a rental for the time being, with provisions for the payment of a greater or less amount upon the happening of certain contingencies, but never a less amount than a specified minimum. A verified petition by some authorized person, and notice to all parties interested, can not be dispensed with. It has no power to authorize the execution of a lease to parties who are not before it, and where no one is petitioning for them. If the court could grant them the lease, it could, of its own motion, without any application, or notice, or hearing, grant a lease to any person making it known that a lease was desired. This the court can not do.—State v. Second Jud. Dist. Court, 24 Mont. 1, 60 Pac. 489, 493.

(3) Power of court to revoke or modify order authorizing lease.— Under the statute of Montana, the court has power to make an order modifying its former order authorizing a lease, where the lessees and executors agree to the modification; and it is also the duty of the court to refuse to revoke an order authorizing a lease, without the consent of the lessees, after they have accepted its terms, and complied with them on their part. After this has been done, the court has no authority to revoke it.—State v. Second Jud. Dist. Court, 24 Mont. 1, 60 Pac. 489, 493.

(4) Power of representative to alter or modify existing lease.—The representative of a deceased lessor has no power to alter or modify a lease, which would be, in effect, making a new lease, without an order of the probate court under proceedings had for that purpose; nor can he compromise or reduce the rent provided for in the lease without the approval of the probate court, on a showing that it is for the best interest of the estate, or that the lessee is not abundantly able to pay the full sum stipulated in the lease as rent.—Brosnan v. Kramer, 135 · Cal. 36, 40, 66 Pac. 979.

(5) Indian lands. In general.—The heirs of a full-blood Indian allottee step into such allottee's shoes upon her death, so far as a lease of the allotted lands, made in her lifetime, is concerned, and they are

estopped, as she is estopped, by the lease, from revoking it or conveying the land free from it, and the lease being made upon the sole condition of the approval of the Secretary of the Interior, the estoppel
becomes absolute upon all alike, upon the allottee if the approval occurs prior to her death, and upon her heirs after that event.—Anchor
Oil Co. v. Gray (Okla.), 257 Fed. 277, 280. The restrictions as to the
alienation of surplus lands under the Osage allotment act of congress
of June 28, 1906, do not follow the land into whosoever hands they may
pass, but it does not follow that a non-competent Osage Indian who
may succeed to or acquire title to such land, may lease the same, and
the government, through its powers and duty of wardship over a people
in a state of pupilage, retains its control for their protection in the
disposition of their lands, no matter from what source those lands may
come.—La Motte v. United States (Okla.), 256 Fed. 5, 12. Although a
lease made by an Indian allottee contains a condition precedent, such
allottee may waive the condition and thereby make the lease effective;
but this question of waiver is a question for the jury.—Rogers v.
Maloney, 85 Or. 61, 165 Pac. 357. A clause in a lease made by an
Indian allottee, providing that the lease shall be binding only after approval by the superintendent of the Indian reservation, or by the Secretary of the Interior, is a "condition precedent."—Rogers v. Maloney, 85
Or. 61, 165 Pac. 357. Evidence sufficient to show the waiver of a
condition precedent, in a lease made by an Indian allottee, which contained a clause that such lease should not become binding until it
had been approved by the superintendent of the Indian reservation,
or by the Secretary of the Interior.—Rogers v. Maloney, 85 Or. 61, 165
Pac. 357.

(6) Same. Power and approval of Secretary of Interior.—The requirement that leases of the lands of Osage Indians are subject to the
approval of the Secretary of the Interior means that such leases require such approval to make them valid, and this provision taken in
connection with the power given him to do all things necessary to carry
into effect the provisions of the Osage Allotment Act of Congress of
June 28, 1906, the Secretary of the Interior is empowered to prescribe
the form of the lease to be executed.—La Motte v. United States
(Okla.), 256 Fed. 5, 13. The only restrictions on alienation removed
by the death of a full-blood Indian allottee by section 9 of the Act of
May 27, 1908, are the restrictions on the alienation of the rights in the
land that descend on such death to the heirs of such allottee, and those
rights are subject and inferior to the rights of the lessees of such
allottee to the full benefit of the lease, subject to the subsequent approval of the lease by the Secretary of the Interior.—Anchor Oil Co.
v. Gray (Okla.), 257 Fed. 277, 280. The true construction of section
9 of the act of May 27, 1908, is that it is prospective and not retrospec-
tive, and that it applies to conveyances and leases made after its
passage and not to those made prior thereto, and that the Secretary
of the Interior had plenary power to approve and validate a lease made

prior to the enactment of said section, by a full-blood Indian allottee, although such approval was actually given subsequent to the said enactment and to the death of the lessor.—Anchor Oil Co. v. Gray (Okla.), 257 Fed. 277, 279. A lease of the lands of a full-blood Indian allottee, when approved by the Secretary of the Interior after the death of such allottee, relates back and takes effect as of the date of its execution, and the heirs of such allottee and those claiming under them, with notice of such lease, are estopped from denying, revoking, or avoiding it, except for fraud or mistake.—Anchor Oil Co. v. Gray (Okla.), 257 Fed. 277, 280.

(7) Same. Leases by guardians of minors. Approval.—The right to enter into a lease contract affecting the restricted lands of a minor Indian rests solely in his guardian, and not in the Secretary of the Interior under act of congress; and the only actual authority of the Secretary in such cases is, either to approve the contract entered into by the guardian, or disapprove it.—Crosbie v. Brewer (Okla.), 158 Pac. 388, 395. The provision of the act of congress of June 28, 1898, that "every lease which is not recorded in the clerk's office of the United States court for the district in which the land is located within three months after the date of its execution, shall be void," should be construed in the case of a guardian's lease of allotted lands to mean three months from the date of approval by the court having jurisdiction of the proceedings.—Walker v. McKemie, 44 Okla. 468, 471, 145 Pac. 359. The act of congress of March 3, 1905, required the approval of all guardian's leases to allotted lands of minor members of the Five Civilized Tribes, and that without such approval by the United States court having jurisdiction of the guardianship proceedings no guardian's lease should be valid or enforceable.—Walker v. McKemie, 44 Okla. 468, 470, 145 Pac. 359. The act of congress of May 27, 1908, authorizes the guardians of Indian minors to make certain lease contracts, subject to the approval of the Secretary of the Interior. Held, that where a guardian, under proper probate procedure made a lease contract under the authority of said act, and the same was duly approved by the Secretary of the Interior, the lessee was bound by such contract.—Crosbie v. Brewer (Okla.), 173 Pac. 441. The act of congress of May 27, 1908, removing restrictions from part of the lands of allottees of the Five Civilized Tribes held to completely remove all restrictions on alienation from all lands of mixed-blood Indians, having less than half-blood, including minors formerly provided under certain Indian treaties and acts of congress, and that leases of minors of the class named do not have to be approved by the court having jurisdiction of guardianship, nor do such leases have to be recorded to make them valid and binding, when otherwise made and executed according to law.—Bailey v. King, 57 Okla. 528, 157 Pac. 763. Under the Osage Allotment Act of Congress of June 28, 1906, the approval of the Secretary of the Interior is required to leases of land held by minors or other incompetent Indians, whether the land covered thereby came to such Indians through

allotment, descent, or devise, provided the land was allotted under the
above act.—La Motte v. United States (Okla.), 256 Fed. 5, 10, 11.
Under section 6569, Rev. Laws of 1910, the legally qualified and acting
guardian of a minor allottee of the Chickasaw tribe of less than one-
half blood is authorized, under the direction and with the approval
of the county court having jurisdiction of such minor's estate, to give
an agricultural lease on the allotted lands of said minor for a fixed
term during his minority, although such lease runs for more than five
years from its date.—Coleman v. Davis (Okla.), 180 Pac. 381, 382. The
approval of a guardian's lease to the allotted lands of minor members of
the Five Civilized Tribes being necessary to its validity and enforceability, such a lease is not fully executed within the meaning of the act
of congress of June 28, 1898, until its approval as required by the act
of congress of March 3, 1905.—Walker v. McKemie, 44 Okla. 468, 471,
145 Pac. 359. After a contract has been entered into with the guardian
of a minor Indian for an oil land lease upon the latter's restricted
lands, the lessee can not voluntarily withdraw therefrom, pending the
action thereon of the Secretary of the Interior, without the consent of
the guardian, unless notified by said Secretary, or his agent, that the
terms of the contract were rejected.—Crosbie v. Brewer (Okla.), 158
Pac. 388, 396. A communication of the Indian Commissioner to the
lessees of an oil lease of the restricted lands of a minor Indian entered
into with the guardian of such minor, to the effect that a deposit of
cash for the bonus provided in said lease instead of the certified check
which accompanied the lease, is held to have been, in effect, a notice
of the disapproval of such lease, and the lessees were thereby privileged
to withdraw therefrom and after so notifying the superintendent to
that effect were no longer bound by the contract.—Crosbie v. Brewer
(Okla.), 158 Pac. 388, 396. Where the records of the county court show
every jurisdictional fact in the matter of the appointment of a guardian for a certain minor, an action on a note given in payment of a
lease of the minor's land made the said guardian on the ground of the
want of validity of his appointment as such is a collateral attack upon
such appointment, and is not permissible.—Crosbie v. Brewer (Okla.),
158 Pac. 388, 395. The recitals contained in an order approving a
guardian's lease to allotted lands, made by the United States court in
the Indian Territory, together with the recitals in the lease, and the
court's approval indorsed thereon, and which recitals appear to have
been regularly made in a pending proceeding, and recite the fact of
the guardianship, and direct the entering into of a lease, are, in the
absence of the entire record, admissible as prima facie evidence that
the lessor was duly appointed guardian.—Walker v. McKemie, 44 Okla.
468, 474, 145 Pac. 359. Where an Indian minor died in October, 1908,
leaving a father and mother surviving, and in 1910 the mother and a
sister executed a lease to plaintiff, on which he predicated his right
to possession, it was error to instruct the jury to find for the plaintiff,
in the absence of evidence of the father's death.—Aldridge v. Whitten,
56 Okla. 694, 156 Pac. 667.

PART X.

POWERS AND DUTIES OF EXECUTORS AND ADMINISTRATORS, AND MANAGEMENT OF ESTATES.

CHAPTER I.

POWERS, DUTIES, AND MANAGEMENT.

(1391)

§ 645. Form. Notice of hearing of petition for leave to invest moneys of estate.

§ 646. Form. Order directing investment of moneys of estate in United States bonds.

POWERS AND DUTIES OF EXECUTORS AND ADMINISTRATORS. ACTIONS. MANAGEMENT OF ESTATES. PARTNERSHIP ESTATES.

I. Powers and Duties of Executors and Administrators.

1. Administration of estates in general.
2. Title to property.
3. Become trustees when.
4. Administrator de bonis non.
5. Executors de son tort.
6. Property and other rights.
7. Duties of executors and administrators.
8. Power of executors and administrators.
    (1) In general.
    (2) Notice of scope of power.
    (3) To dispose of personal property.
    (4) To compound or compromise, in general.
    (5) Same. Restrictions. Approval of court.
    (6) Same. Distinction.

(7) To bind estate.
(8) Not to purchase claims against estate.
(9) Not to purchase estate.
(10) Can not do what. In general.
(11) Same. Can not sell to wife.
(12) With respect to leases and mortgages.
(13) Can not litigate what claims.
(14) In judicial proceedings.
9. Joint administrators and co-executors.
    (1) In general.
    (2) Obligations and liability. Bond.
    (3) Same. Foundation of liability.
10. Foreign and ancillary administration.
    (1) Foreign administration.
    (2) Same. Ancillary administration.

II. Actions by Executors or Administrators.

1. In general.
2. Abatement. Discontinuance.
3. Parties.
4. By ancillary administrators.
5. By foreign executors.
6. Executor or administrator as representative.
7. By a co-executor.
8. Intervention.
9. Substitution. Survival and revival of action.
10. Pleading. In general.
11. Same. In action to recover value of land.
12. Evidence.
13. Judgment.
14. Costs.
15. To recover possession.
16. On contracts.
    (1) In general.
    (2) Fire insurance policies.
    (3) Promissory notes.
    (4) Personal services.

17. Conversion.
    (1) In general.
    (2) What is a conversion.
    (3) Suits in individual capacity.
    (4) Action must fail when.
18. For damages in causing death.
    (1) Right of action. In general.
    (2) Same consideration of statutes.
    (3) Employers' liability act.
    (4) Abatement of action.
    (5) Pleading and evidence.
    (6) Measure of damages.
    (7) Assets of estate.
    (8) Action by infant.
19. Ejectment.
20. Trusts and trustees.
21. To recover excessive fees charged.
22. On foreign judgments.
23. Gifts.
24. For injunction.
25. For life insurance, and sick benefits.
26. For dividends on stock.
27. On mortgages.

Probate Law—88

§ 623. Possession to be taken of entire estate.

The executor or administrator must take into his possession all the estate of the decedent, real and personal, and collect all the debts due to the decedent or to the estate. For the purpose of bringing suits to quiet title, or for partition of such estate, the possession of the executors or administrators is the possession of the heirs or devisees; such possession by the heirs or devisees is subject, however, to the possession of the executor or administrator, for the purposes of administration, as provided in this title.—*Kerr's Cyc. Code Civ. Proc.*, § 1581.

ANALOGOUS AND IDENTICAL STATUTES.
The * indicates identity.

Arizona*—Revised Statutes of 1913, paragraph 967.
Colorado—Mills's Statutes of 1912, section 7939.
Idaho*—Compiled Statutes of 1919, section 7656.
Kansas—General Statutes of 1915, section 4546.
Montana*—Revised Codes of 1907, section 7603.
Nevada—Revised Laws of 1912, section 6021.
New Mexico—Statutes of 1915, section 2257.
North Dakota—Compiled Laws of 1913, section 8797.
Oklahoma—Revised Laws of 1910, section 6301.
South Dakota—Compiled Laws of 1913, section 5860.
Utah—Compiled Laws of 1907, sections 3912, 3913.
Wyoming*—Compiled Statutes of 1910, section 5561.

§ 623.[1] Deposits of deceased persons may remain in savings banks.

Where a decedent, at the time of his or her death, left moneys on deposit with a savings bank, it shall be lawful for any public administrator, who shall become the administrator of the estate, to allow such deposit to remain in said savings bank, and also, it shall be lawful for him to deposit therein to the account of said decedent, any and all moneys of said estate not required for the current expenses of administration. Such deposit, whether made by the decedent or a public administrator, shall relieve the public administrator from depositing the same with the county treasurer. Moneys so deposited, whether by the decedent or by a public administrator, may be drawn upon demand without notice, upon the order of said administrator, countersigned by a judge of a superior court, when required for the purpose of administration or otherwise.—*Cal. Stats.* 1911, ch. 494, new section 68½ added, p. 1007.

§ 624. Form. Petition for a patent.

[Title of court.]

[Title of estate.] ⎰ No.——.1 Dept. No.——.
⎱ [Title of form.]

To the Commissioner of Patents, Washington, D. C.

Your petitioner, ——, administrator [2] of the estate of ——, deceased, as will more fully appear by reference to the duly certified copy of letters of administration [3] hereto annexed, prays that letters patent may be granted to him for the invention of the said ——,[4] set forth in the annexed specification.   ——, Petitioner.

Explanatory notes.—[1] Give file number. [2] Or, executor of the last will, etc. [3] Or, of letters testamentary. [4] Deceased.

§ 625. Representative may sue and be sued.

Actions for the recovery of any property, real or personal, or for the possession thereof, or to quiet title thereto, or to determine any adverse claim thereon, and all actions founded upon contracts, may be maintained by and against executors and administrators in all cases in which the same might have been maintained by or against their respective testators or intestates.—*Kerr's Cyc. Code Civ. Proc.*, § 1582.

ANALOGOUS AND IDENTICAL STATUTES.
The * indicates identity.

Colorado—Mills's Statutes of 1912, sections 7939, 7949, 8047.
Idaho—Compiled Statutes of 1919, section 7657.
Montana—Revised Codes of 1907, section 7604.
Nevada—Revised Laws of 1912, section 6022.
North Dakota—Compiled Laws of 1913, section 8798.
Oklahoma—Revised Laws of 1910, section 6302.
South Dakota—Compiled Laws of 1913, section 5861.
Utah*—Compiled Laws of 1907, section 3914.
Washington*—Laws of 1917, chapter 156, p. 685, section 148.
Wyoming—Compiled Statutes of 1910, section 5562.

§ 626. May maintain actions for waste, conversion, or trespass.

Executors and administrators may maintain actions against any person who has wasted, destroyed, taken, or carried away, or converted to his own use, the goods of their testator or intestate, in his lifetime. They may also maintain actions for trespass committed on the real estate of the decedent in his lifetime.—*Kerr's Cyc. Code Civ. Proc.*, § 1583.

ANALOGOUS AND IDENTICAL STATUTES.
The * indicates identity.

Arizona*—Revised Statutes of 1913, paragraph 968.
Colorado—Mills's Statutes of 1912, sections 7949, 8047.
Idaho*—Compiled Statutes of 1919, section 7658.
Montana—Revised Codes of 1907, section 7605.
Nevada*—Revised Laws of 1912, section 6023.
North Dakota—Compiled Laws of 1913, section 8800.
Oklahoma*—Revised Laws of 1910, section 6303.
South Dakota*—Compiled Laws of 1913, section 5862.
Utah*—Compiled Laws of 1907, section 3915.
Washington*—Laws of 1917, chapter 1917, p. 685, section 149.
Wyoming*—Compiled Statutes of 1910, section 5563.

§ 627. May be sued for waste or trespass of decedent.

Any person or his personal representatives may maintain an action against the executor or administrator of any testator or intestate who in his lifetime has wasted, destroyed, taken, or carried away, or converted to his own use, the goods or chattels of any such person, or

committed any trespass on the real estate of such person.
—*Kerr's Cyc. Code Civ. Proc.,* § 1584.

§ 628. Surviving partner to settle up business. Appraisement. Accounting.

When a partnership exists between the decedent, at the
time of his death, and any other person, the surviving
partner has the right to continue in possession of the
partnership, and to settle its business, but the interest of
the decedent in the partnership must be included in the
inventory, and be appraised as other property. The
surviving partner must settle the affairs of the partnership without delay, and account with the executor or administrator, and pay over such balances as may from
time to time be payable to him, in right of the decedent.
Upon the application of the executor or administrator,
the court, or a judge thereof, may, whenever it appears
necessary, order the surviving partner to render an account, and in case of neglect or refusal may, after notice,
compel it by attachment; and the executor or administrator may maintain against him any action which the
decedent could have maintained.—*Kerr's Cyc. Code Civ.
Proc.,* § 1585.

Montana—Revised Codes of 1907, section 7607.

Nevada*—Revised Laws of 1912, section 6025.

New Mexico—Statutes of 1915, section 2269.

North Dakota—Compiled Laws of 1913, sections 8711, 8801.

Oklahoma—Revised Laws of 1910, section 6305.

Oregon—Lord's Oregon Laws, sections 1166, 1168, 1171, 1172.

South Dakota—Compiled Laws of 1913, section 5864.

Utah—Compiled Laws of 1907, section 3918.

Washington—Laws of 1917, chapter 156, p. 664, sections 88-91.

Wyoming—Compiled Statutes of 1910, section 5565; Laws of 1917, chapter 97, p. 132, section 25, subd. d.

§ 629. Form. Petition that surviving partner render an account.

[Title of court.]

[Title of estate.]   { No. ——.¹ Dept. No. ——.
                      { [Title of form.]

To the Honorable the ——² Court of the County ³ of ——, State of ——.

The undersigned, ——, administrator ⁴ of the estate of ——, deceased, respectfully represents:

That, at the time of the death of said deceased, to wit, on the —— day of ——, 19—, and for a long time prior thereto, there was a partnership existing between deceased and ——, who were doing business, in said county ⁵ and state, as wholesale liquor dealers, under the firm name and style of ——;

That the surviving partner, the said ——, continued in possession of the effects of the said partnership, and is still in such possession, for the purpose of settling up the business thereof;

That the interest of the decedent in the partnership property was included in the inventory heretofore filed herein, and was appraised as other property, and that more than —— months have elapsed since the said inventory was filed, but that said surviving partner has neglected and refused, and still neglects and refuses, to account ⁶ with said administrator,⁷ or to give any information as to the affairs of the said partnership, and has never paid over any such balances as may, from time to time, have been payable to said administrator [8] in right of the decedent;

That the deceased owed many debts, and that it has become essential to determine the value of said partnership interest in order to determine whether a sale of real estate is necessary to pay said debts, and the debts, expenses, and charges of administration.

Wherefore your petitioner prays for an order directed to the said ———, requiring him to render an account of the said partnership, and of his dealings with the same, showing a full statement of its affairs, property, and effects at the time of and since the death of the deceased, including a statement of the true value and condition of the interest of said deceased, and of the moneys, if any, due and owing to your petitioner as the administrator [9] of said estate.

———, Administrator [10] and Petitioner.

———, Attorney for Administrator [11] and Petitioner.

Explanatory notes.—1 Give file number. 2 Title of court. 3 Or, City and County. 4 Or, executor of the last will and testament of ———, deceased. 5 Or, city and county. 6 Or, that said surviving partner has promised to account, but has neglected and refused, and still neglects and refuses to do so. If he has rendered an unsatisfactory account, say, "that said surviving partner has rendered to your petitioner what purports to be a full account of the affairs of said partnership, but your petitioner is informed and believes that said account does not exhibit a full, true, and particular statement of all the affairs, property, effects, and assets of said partnership, and of such surviving partner's dealings therewith; that it does not show the true value and condition of decedent's interest at and subsequent to the time of his death; and that it does not contain a full and true statement of all moneys due and owing to petitioner as administrator, or executor, of said estate." 7-11 Or, executor.

§ 630. Form. Alternative order that surviving partner account to administrator, or show cause.

[Title of court.]

[Title of estate.] { No. ———.1 Dept. No. ———. [Title of form.] }

It being shown by the application of ———, administrator [2] of the estate of ———, deceased, filed herein, that

——, the surviving partner of said deceased, has delayed, and is delaying, settlement of the partnership affairs, and neglects and refuses to render an account to said administrator,[3] —

It is ordered, That ——, the said surviving partner, be cited to render an account of the partnership existing at the time of the death of said deceased, and to file the same herein [4] within ——[5] days from this date, or show cause, within that time, why he should not account.

Dated ——, 19—.   ——, Judge of the —— Court.

Explanatory notes.—1 Give file number.   2 Or, executor of the last will, etc.   3 Or, executor.   4 Or, render to, and serve the same upon, the administrator, or executor.   5 As fixed by the court.

§ 631.   Form.   Order for attachment to compel surviving partner to render an account.

[Title of court.]

[Title of estate.]   { No. ——.1   Dept. No. ——.
                                      {   [Title of form.]

It appearing to the court that ——, surviving partner of deceased, has neglected to make settlement of the partnership affairs, and to account with the administrator [2] of said estate; that a citation has been issued requiring the said —— to appear and show cause why an attachment should not issue to compel him to render an account of the affairs of the partnership existing between him and the deceased at the time of the latter's death; that said citation has been served and returned in the form and manner provided by law; and that the said —— has failed to appear and render said account, or to show cause why an attachment should not issue as directed in said citation, —

It is ordered, That a warrant of attachment issue, and that said —— be arrested and brought before this court to show cause why he should not be committed for contempt of court in disobeying said citation.

Dated ——, 19—.   ——, Judge of the —— Court.

Explanatory notes.—1 Give file number.   2 Or, executor.

§ 632. Action on bond of one administrator may be brought by another.

An administrator may, in his own name, for the use and benefit of all parties interested in the estate, maintain actions on the bond of an executor, or of any former administrator of the same estate.—*Kerr's Cyc. Code Civ. Proc.,* § 1586.

ANALOGOUS AND IDENTICAL STATUTES.
The * indicates identity.

Alaska—Compiled Laws of 1913, section 1620.
Arizona*—Revised Statutes of 1913, paragraph 971.
Idaho*—Compiled Statutes of 1919, section 7661.
Montana*—Revised Codes of 1907, section 7608.
Nevada*—Revised Laws of 1912, section 6026.
New Mexico—Statutes of 1915, section 2302.
North Dakota—Compiled Laws of 1913, section 8802.
Oklahoma*—Revised Laws of 1910, section 6306.
South Dakota*—Compiled Laws of 1913, section 5865.
Utah*—Compiled Laws of 1907, section 3919.
Washington*—Laws of 1917, chapter 156, p. 685, section 151.
Wyoming*—Compiled Statutes of 1910, section 5568.

§ 633. What executors are not parties to actions.

In actions by or against executors, it is not necessary to join those as parties to whom letters were issued, but who have not qualified.—*Kerr's Cyc. Code Civ. Proc.,* § 1587.

ANALOGOUS AND IDENTICAL STATUTES.
The * indicates identity.

Arizona*—Revised Statutes of 1913, paragraph 972.
Idaho*—Compiled Statutes of 1919, section 7662.
Montana*—Revised Codes of 1907, section 7609.
Nevada*—Revised Laws of 1912, section 6027.
Oklahoma*—Revised Laws of 1910, section 6307.
South Dakota*—Compiled Laws of 1913, section 5866.
Utah—Compiled Laws of 1907, section 3920.
Wyoming*—Compiled Statutes of 1910, section 5569.

§ 634. May Compound.

Whenever a debtor of the decedent is unable to pay all his debts, the executor or administrator, with the approbation of the court, or a judge thereof, may compound with him and give him a discharge, upon receiving a fair and just dividend of his effects. A compromise may also be authorized when it appears to be just, and for the best interest of the estate.—*Kerr's Cyc. Code Civ. Proc.,* § 1588.

ANALOGOUS AND IDENTICAL STATUTES.

The * indicates identity.

Alaska—Compiled Laws of 1913, section 1703
Arizona*—Revised Statutes of 1913, paragraph 973.
Colorado—Mills's Statutes of 1912, section 7960.
Idaho*—Compiled Statutes of 1919, section 7663.
Kansas—General Statutes of 1915, sections 4547, 4552.
Montana*—Revised Codes of 1907, section 7610.
Nevada*—Revised Laws of 1912, section 6028.
North Dakota*—Compiled Laws of 1913, section 8814.
Oklahoma*—Revised Laws of 1910, section 6308.
Oregon—Lord's Oregon Laws, section 1294.
South Dakota*—Compiled Laws of 1913, section 5867.
Utah*—Compiled Laws of 1907, section 3921.
Washington—Laws of 1917, chapter 156, page 686, section 152.
Wyoming*—Compiled Statutes of 1910, section 5570.

§ 635. Form. Petition for authority to compromise debt.

[Title of court.]

[Title of estate.]   { No. ——.1   Dept. No. ——.
                 [Title of form.]

To the Honorable the ——² Court of the County ³ of ——, State of ——.

The undersigned, your petitioner, respectfully represents:

That he is the duly appointed, qualified, and acting administrator ⁴ of the estate of ——, deceased;

That there is owing from —— a debt to said estate, of the sum of —— dollars ($——), which debt was appraised at said amount in the inventory and appraisement on file herein;

That said debtor declines to pay said debt in full, but does offer to pay ——⁵ thereof in liquidation of the whole demand; that, in view of all the circumstances that would surround the enforcement of such demand, the said offer appears to be just; and that it is for the best interest of said estate that such offer be accepted.

Your petitioner therefore prays that he may be authorized to compromise said debt by accepting the said amount in liquidation of the whole sum due.

——, Attorney for Petitioner.　　——, Petitioner.

Explanatory notes.—1 Give file number. 2 Title of court. 8 Or, City and County. 4 Or, executor. 5 State what part of percentage.

§ 636. Form. Order approving administrator's agreement to compromise with debtor.

[Title of court.]

[Title of estate.]　　　　　{No. ——.1　Dept. No. ——.
　　　　　　　　　　　　　　{　　　[Title of form.]

It being shown to this court[2] by ——, administrator[3] of the estate of ——, deceased, that there is owing from —— a debt to said estate, of the sum of —— dollars ($——), which debt was appraised at said amount in the inventory and appraisement on file herein; that said debtor is unable to pay all his debts; that he has made an assignment of all his property, in manner and form provided by law, for the benefit of creditors; that said administrator[4] has accepted a payment of —— dollars ($——) in satisfaction of said debt due said estate; that other creditors of the said —— have agreed to accept a like amount in satisfaction of their respective demands; and that it is not probable that any greater amount can be obtained on said debt, due the estate from said ——, as aforesaid, —

The court hereby approves of the aforesaid compounding of said debt, and orders that the said ——, as administrator[5] of said estate, give the said —— a discharge in full of said debt.

Dated ——, 19—.　　——, Judge of the —— Court.

Explanatory notes.—1 Give file number. 2 Or, to the judge of this court. 8.5 Or, executor.

§ 637.   Recovery of property fraudulently disposed of by testator.

When there is a deficiency of assets in the hands of an executor or administrator, and when the decedent, in his lifetime, has conveyed any real estate, or any rights or interests therein, with intent to defraud his creditors, or to avoid any right, debt, or duty of any person, or has so conveyed such estate that by law the deeds or conveyances are void as against creditors, the executor or administrator must commence and prosecute to final judgment any proper action for the recovery of the same; and may recover for the benefit of the creditor all such real estate so fraudulently conveyed; and may also, for the benefit of the creditors, sue and recover all goods, chattels, rights, or credits, which have been so conveyed by the decedent in his lifetime, whatever may have been the manner of such fraudulent conveyance.—*Kerr's Cyc. Code Civ. Proc.*, § 1589.

ANALOGOUS AND IDENTICAL STATUTES.

The * indicates identity.

Alaska—Compiled Laws of 1913, sections 1688, 1689.
Arizona*—Revised Statutes of 1913, paragraph 974.
Idaho*—Compiled Statutes of 1919, section 7664.
Montana*—Revised Codes of 1907, section 7611.
Nevada—Revised Laws of 1912, section 6029.
North Dakota*—Compiled Laws of 1913, section 8811.
Oklahoma*—Revised Laws of 1910, section 6309.
Oregon—Lord's Oregon Laws, sections 1279, 1280.
South Dakota*—Compiled Laws of 1913, section 5868.
Utah*—Compiled Laws of 1907, section 3922.
Washington*—Laws of 1917, chapter 156, page 686, section 153.
Wyoming*—Compiled Statutes of 1910, section 5571.

§ 638.   When executor to sue, as provided in preceding section.

No executor or administrator is bound to sue for such estate, as mentioned in the preceding section, for the benefit of the creditors, unless on application of creditors, who must pay such part of the costs and expenses of the suit, or give such security to the executor or administra-

tor therefor, as the court, or a judge thereof, shall direct.
—*Kerr's Cyc. Code Civ. Proc.*, § 1590.

ANALOGOUS AND IDENTICAL STATUTES.

The * indicates identity.

Alaska—Compiled Laws of 1913, sections 1688, 1689.
Arizona*—Revised Statutes of 1913, paragraph 975.
Idaho*—Compiled Statutes of 1919, section 7665.
Montana*—Revised Codes of 1907, section 7612.
Nevada*—Revised Laws of 1912, section 6030.
North Dakota*—Compiled Laws of 1913, section 8812.
Oklahoma*—Revised Laws of 1910, section 6310.
Oregon—Lord's Oregon Laws, sections 1279, 1280.
South Dakota*—Compiled Laws of 1913, section 5869.
Utah*—Compiled Laws of 1907, section 3923.
Wyoming*—Compiled Statutes of 1910, section 5572.

§ 639. Form. Creditors' application that suit be brought to recover property fraudulently disposed of by decedent.

[Title of court.]

[Title of estate.]   { No.——.1   Dept. No.——.
                              {   [Title of form.]

This, the application of the undersigned, respectfully shows:

That they are creditors of said estate; that their respective claims have been duly presented, allowed, approved, and filed; and that the aggregate amount of said claims is —— dollars ($——);

That there is a deficiency of assets in the hands of the administrator [2] of said estate to pay the claims of applicants, as is shown by a copy of the inventory and appraisement on file herein, marked "Exhibit A," and by a copy of the account of the administrator [3] of said estate filed herein, marked "Exhibit B," which said copies and exhibits are hereby referred to, and made a part of this application, the same as if the originals of said papers were incorporated herein;

That decedent, in his lifetime, was possessed of the following described real estate, particularly described as follows, to wit, ——; and also of certain goods and chattels, particularly described as follows, to wit, ——;

That said decedent, in his lifetime, to wit, on the —— day of ——, 19—, conveyed all of the property hereinbefore described to ——; and your applicants are informed and believe, and therefore allege the fact to be, that said conveyance was made by the said ——, now deceased, with intent to defraud his creditors; and that said conveyance was accepted by the said ——[4] wilfully, knowingly, and fraudulently, and with intent, both on the part of the grantor and of the grantee, to defraud the creditors of ——, now deceased, and to hinder and delay said creditors from collecting the amounts justly due them;

That, in law and in equity, said property should now be in the hands of the administrator [5] of said deceased, to be applied toward payment of the debts aforesaid;

That said applicants have requested said administrator [6] to sue for the property hereinbefore described for the benefit of creditors of said estate, and have offered, and now offer, to pay such part of the costs and expenses of such suit, or to give security to the administrator [7] therefor, as this court shall direct, but that said administrator [8] has wholly neglected and refused, and now neglects and refuses, to bring such suit.

Said applicants therefore pray that a citation issue to said administrator,[9] requiring him to show cause why he should not bring said suit upon payment by applicants of costs as aforesaid, or giving security therefor.

——}Applicants.

——, Attorney for Applicants.

Exhibit A.

[Give copy of inventory and appraisement.]

Exhibit B.

[Give copy of administrator's account.]

Explanatory notes.—1 Give file number. 2, 3 Or, executor. 4 Grantee. 5-9 Or, executor.

§ 640. Form. Order that administrator bring suit to recover property fraudulently disposed of by decedent.

[Title of court.]

[Title of estate.] 　　　　　{No. ——.1 Dept. No. ——.
　　　　　　　　　　　　　{　　[Title of form.]

It appearing from the application of —— and ——, filed herein, that said decedent, in his lifetime, fraudulently disposed of certain property, hereinafter described, with intent to defraud his creditors, and that said —— and —— have heretofore applied to the said administrator [2] to bring suit to recover said property for the benefit of creditors of said estate, but that said administrator [3] has neglected and refused, and still neglects and refuses, to do so; and it further appearing that a citation has issued to said administrator [4] requiring him to show cause why he should not bring such suit, and the matter now coming regularly on for hearing at the time and place appointed in said citation to show cause, —

The court proceeds to hear the proofs adduced, and, after such hearing, finds that said citation was served and returned as required by law; that said applicants are creditors of the estate of said deceased; that the assets in the hands of said administrator [5] are not sufficient to pay the debts due to said applicants; and that the allegations of said application as to the fraudulent disposition of said property by decedent are true.

It is therefore ordered, That said administrator [6] forthwith institute suit to recover said property, and that he prosecute the same to final decree.

It is further ordered, That said applicants give to said administrator [7] a bond, to be approved by this court,[8] in the sum of —— dollars ($——), conditioned that they will, from time to time, pay to said administrator,[9] on his demand, a sum sufficient to pay the costs and expenses of such suit, and save said administrator [10] and said estate harmless from all expense by reason of said suit; and that, in the event of a recovery of said property, said administrator [11] will refund to said applicants, out of the property so recovered, all costs and expenses of suit, which may have been paid by them.

The property hereinbefore referred to, and which the said administrator [12] is ordered to bring suit to recover, is particularly described as follows, to wit: ——.[13]

Dated ——, 19—.   ——, Judge of the —— Court.

Explanatory notes.—1 Give file number. 2-7 Or, executor. 8 Or, a judge thereof. 9-12 Or, executor. 13 Give description.

§ 641. Disposition of estate recovered.

All real estate so recovered must be sold for the payment of debts, in the same manner as if the decedent had died seised thereof, upon obtaining an order therefor from the court; and the proceeds of all goods, chattels, rights, and credits so recovered must be appropriated in payment of the debts of the decedent in the same manner as other property in the hands of the executor or administrator. The remainder of the proceeds, after all the debts of the decedent have been paid, must be paid to the person from whom such property was recovered.—*Kerr's Cyc. Code Civ. Proc.*, § 1591.

ANALOGOUS AND IDENTICAL STATUTES.

No identical statute found.

Alaska—Compiled Laws of 1913, section 1690.
Arizona—Revised Statutes of 1913, paragraph 976.
Idaho—Compiled Statutes of 1919, section 7666.
Montana—Revised Codes of 1907, section 7613.
Nevada—Revised Laws of 1912, section 6031.
North Dakota—Compiled Laws of 1913, section 8813.
Oklahoma—Revised Laws of 1910, section 6311.
Oregon—Lord's Oregon Laws, section 1281.
South Dakota—Compiled Laws of 1913, section 5870.

Utah—Compiled Laws' of 1907, section 3924.
Washington—Laws of 1917, chapter 156, page 686, section 153.
Wyoming—Compiled Statutes of 1910, section 5573.

Note.—At first blush the last sentence of this section seems to place a premium upon fraud; and one might be inclined, without due consideration, to imagine that the section is unconstitutional, on the ground that it takes the property of the heirs without due process of law, that is, without giving them their day in court. But a man may do what he will with his own property, and, unless his heirs take by will or the law of succession, they have no interest in it, and they can not take in either way where the ancestor has conveyed it. If the conveyance was fraudulent, it could be fraudulent only as to creditors, for no one else was, at the time, interested. And it is only the executor or administrator, who can attack the deed as fraudulent, and even this must be for the benefit of the creditors. No other person is authorized to sue. As said in Campbell v. Whitson, 68 Ill. 240, 18 Am. Rep. 553: "It is well settled and familiar doctrine, that, although voluntary conveyances are or may be void, as to existing creditors, yet they are valid and effectual as between the parties, and can not be set aside by the grantor if he should become dissatisfied with the transaction; the law regards it as his own folly to have made such a conveyance, and leaves him to bear the consequences without means of redress. 'They are,' says Story, 'not only valid as to the grantor, but also as to his heirs, and all other persons claiming under him in privity of the estate with notice of the fraud. A conveyance of this sort (it has been said with great truth and force), is void only as against creditors, and then only to the extent in which it may be necessary to deal with the conveyed estate for their satisfaction. To this extent, and to this only, it is treated as if it had not been made. To every other purpose it is good. Satisfy the creditors, and the conveyance stands.'—1 Story's Eq. Jur., § 371, and cases cited in notes." If a grantor, since deceased, conveyed his property in fraud of creditors, and the assignee of money demands against his estate brings suit to have the deed declared fraudulent as against the plaintiff "the judgment," said McFarland, J., in Emmons v. Barton, 109 Cal. 662, 668, 42 Pac. 303, "should be that the property fraudulently conveyed, or so much thereof as is necessary, be applied to the satisfaction of the debts, and that the residue, if any, go to the grantee. It is not to go into the assets of the estate for any purpose other than the payment of the debts. The residue does not go to the heir; for he stands in the shoes of the fraudulent grantor." See, also, Tully v. Tully, 137 Cal. 60, 66, 69 Pac. 700; Burtch v. Elliott, 3 Ind. 99, 101; showing that the residue after satisfying creditors, goes to the grantee or the latter's heirs. Where the invalidity of a mortgage has been established, as to creditors, the surplus, if any, may be paid to the mortgagee.—Fleischner v. First Nat. Bank, 36 Or. 553, 61 Pac. 345, 346. In case of a gift fraudulent as to creditors, the surplus, upon settlement of the doner's

Probate Law—89

estate, goes to the donee, not to the heirs.—Abbott v. Tenney, 18 N. H. 109, 114; Williams v. Avent, 40 N. C. 47. A conveyance, though fraudulent as to creditors, passes title to the grantee against all except such creditors.—Mellen v. Ames, 39 Iowa 283, 286.

§ 642. Pending settlement, court may order moneys to be invested.

Pending the settlement of any estate, on the petition of any person interested therein, and upon good cause shown therefor, the court may order any moneys in the hands of the executors or administrators to be invested for the benefit of the estate in securities of the United States or of this state. Such order can only be made after publication of notice of the petition for not less than ten days in some newspaper, to be designated by the court or a judge thereof.—*Kerr's Cyc. Code Civ. Proc.*, § 1592.

ANALOGOUS AND IDENTICAL STATUTES.
No identical statute found.

Arizona—Revised Statutes of 1913, paragraph 1015.
Colorado—Laws of 1915, chapter 175, page 501; amending Mills's Statutes of 1912, section 7946.
Idaho—Compiled Statutes of 1919, section 7709.
Montana—Revised Codes of 1907, section 7652.
North Dakota—Compiled Laws of 1913, section 8840.
Oklahoma—Revised Laws of 1910, section 6446.
South Dakota—Compiled Laws of 1913, section 5907.
Utah—Compiled Laws of 1907, section 3925.

§ 642.[1] Money in estates of deceased persons' fund to be invested in bonds.

Whenever and as often as there is in the state treasury to the credit of the estates of deceased persons' fund (in excess of the retention hereinafter provided for) the sum of ten thousand dollars or more, the board (state board of examiners), must invest the same in the bonds of this state, or in the bonds of the United States, or in the bonds of the several counties, city and county, permanent road districts, cities and towns, or school districts of this state; the investments to be made in such manner and on such terms as the board shall deem best for the

fund. No investment shall be made which, with the
amounts previously vested shall reduce the uninvested
portion of the fund below the amount of ten thousand
dollars, and whenever a demand presented against said
fund will reduce the amount of cash therein below the
specified amount of ten thousand dollars, it shall be the
duty of the board to sell such bonds belonging to said
fund as they may deem proper, for the purpose of making good the cash retention of ten thousand dollars.

Bonds purchased by the board under the provisions of
this section must be delivered to the state treasurer, who
shall keep them as a portion of said estates of deceased
persons' fund, and the interest upon such bonds shall be
paid into the state school fund and apportioned like other
moneys employed for the support of common schools.—
Kerr's Cyc. Pol. Code, § 677.[1]

[1] Transfer of moneys from the general fund to the fund of the estates
of deceased persons. See Cal. Stats. 1909, ch. 45, p. 38.

§ 643. Form. Petition for leave to invest moneys of estate in
United States bonds.

[Title of court.]

[Title of estate.]

{ Department No. ——.
{ [Title of form.]

To the Honorable the ——[1] Court of the County[2] of
——, State of ——.

The petition of —— and ——, executors of the last
will and testament of ——, deceased, respectfully represents:

That said executors now have on deposit in the ——, a
commercial bank of said county,[3] over forty thousand
dollars ($40,000) of the moneys belonging to said estate;
that said moneys are not drawing any interest, nor producing any revenue or income to said estate; that all of
said moneys are not required for the ordinary expenses
and disbursements of said estate, and that said executors
deem it for the best interest of said estate that, pending

the settlement thereof, the sum of thirty-five thousand dollars ($35,000), or thereabouts, or such other sum as may be advised, be invested for the benefit of said estate, in bonds of the government of the United States, pursuant to ——.[4]

Wherefore the said executors pray that, upon the filing of this petition, an order be made fixing a day for the hearing thereof, and for the publication of notice thereof for not less than ten (10) days in some newspaper to be designated in said order by the court, or a judge thereof; and that after such hearing the court make an order authorizing said executors to invest said sum of thirty-five thousand dollars ($35,000), or such other sum as this honorable court may determine upon, for the benefit of said estate, in bonds of the government of the United States, pending the settlement of said estate; and that such other and further order be made in the premises as is meet and proper. ——, Executor.

Dated ——, 19—. ——, Executor.

——, Attorney for Executor ——.[5]

——, Attorney for Executor ——.[6]

Explanatory notes.—1 Title of court. 2, 3 Or, city and county. 4 Section of code authorizing such investment. 5, 6 Give names, where two or more executors are represented by different attorneys.

§ 644. Form. Order directing publication of notice of petition for leave to invest.

[Title of court.]

[Title of estate.]

{ No. ——.1 Dept. No.——.
  [Title of form.]

—— and ——, executors of the last will and testament of ——, deceased, having this day filed their petition for an order authorizing them to invest moneys of the above-entitled estate in bonds of the government of the United States, and good cause appearing therefor, —

It is hereby ordered, That notice of such petition be given by publishing said petition in the ——, a daily newspaper published in the county [2] of ——, state of ——, for —— days previous to the hearing thereof.

——, Judge of the —— Court.

Explanatory notes.—1 Give file number. 2 Or, city and county.

§ 645. Form. Notice of hearing of petition for leave to invest moneys of estate.

[Title of court.]

[Title of estate.] {No. ——.[1] Dept. No. ——.
                     { [Title of form.]

—— and ——, executors of the last will and testament of ——, deceased, having this day filed their petition for an order authorizing them to invest moneys of the above-entitled estate in bonds of the government of the United States, —

The hearing of said petition is hereby set for ——, 19—, at the court-room of said court,[2] at the hour of —— o'clock in the forenoon [3] of said day, at which time and place objections, if any, may be interposed to the making of such order.

Dated ——, 19—.

[Seal] ——, Judge of the —— Court.[4]

Explanatory notes.—1 Give file number. 2 State location of court-room. 3 Or, afternoon. 4 Or, clerk of the court.

§ 646. Form. Order directing investment of moneys of estate in United States bonds.

[Title of court.]

[Title of estate.] {No. ——.[1] Dept. No. ——.
                     { [Title of form.]

Now come —— and ——, executors of the last will and testament of ——, deceased, and show to the court that on the —— day of ——, 19—, they filed a petition for an order authorizing them to invest moneys of the above-entitled estate in bonds of the government of the United States; that publication of notice of such petition has been made as required by law and the order of this court; and that due and legal notice of the time and place of the hearing of said petition has been given; and it appearing that there is a large amount of money, to wit, the sum of —— dollars ($——), now on deposit in the —— bank of this county,[2] which is not drawing any interest; and that it will be for the benefit of such estate that such money be invested in bonds of the government of the United States, —

It is therefore ordered, That said money be invested in ——[3] bonds of the United States.

Dated ——, 19—.　　——, Judge of the —— Court.

Explanatory notes.—[1] Give file number. [2] Or, city and county. [3] Designate the kind of bonds; as, three-per-cent, etc.

POWERS AND DUTIES OF EXECUTORS AND ADMINISTRATORS. ACTIONS. MANAGEMENT OF ESTATES. PARTNERSHIP ESTATES.

I. Powers and Duties of Executors and Administrators.

1. Administration of estates in general.
2. Title to property.
3. Become trustees when.
4. Administrator de bonis non.
5. Executors de son tort.
6. Property and other rights.
7. Duties of executors and administrators.
8. Power of executors and administrators.
   (1) In general.
   (2) Notice of scope of power.
   (3) To dispose of personal property.
   (4) To compound or compromise, in general.
   (5) Same. Restrictions. Approval of court.
   (6) Same. Distinction.
   (7) To bind estate.
   (8) Not to purchase claims against estate.
   (9) Not to purchase estate.
   (10) Can not do what. In general.
   (11) Same. Can not sell to wife.
   (12) With respect to leases and mortgages.
   (13) Can not litigate what claims.
   (14) In judicial proceedings.
9. Joint administrators and co-executors.
   (1) In general.
   (2) Obligations and liability. Bond.
   (3) Same. Foundation of liability.
10. Foreign and ancillary administration.
    (1) Foreign administration.
    (2) Same. Ancillary administration.

II. Actions by Executors or Administrators.

1. In general.
2. Abatement. Discontinuance.
3. Parties.
4. By ancillary administrators.
5. By foreign executors.
6. Executor or administrator as representative.
7. By a co-executor.
8. Intervention.
9. Substitution. Survival and revival of action.
10. Pleading. In general.
11. Same. In action to recover value of land.
12. Evidence.
13. Judgment.
14. Costs.
15. To recover possession.
16. On contracts.
    (1) In general.
    (2) Fire insurance policies.
    (3) Promissory notes.
    (4) Personal services.

I. POWERS AND DUTIES OF EXECUTORS AND ADMINISTRATORS.

1. Administration of estates in general.—Numerous sections of the Rev. Codes of Montana, relating to probate matters, show a clear purpose to place, in the hands of the court, authority sufficient to secure a just administration of the estate, to the end that creditors may be protected and the heirs receive the largest amount of the property compatible with an economic but complete administration of the estate.—State v. District Court, 42 Mont. 182, 185, 111 Pac. 717. The administration of the estate of a decedent is an entirety, and extends to the whole of the estate so far as its assets are within the jurisdiction where the appointment is made, and the administrator, whether general or special, has the exclusive right of control, subject to the orders of the court for the purpose of administration.—Murphy v. Nett, 51 Mont. 82, L. R. A. 1915E, 797, 149 Pac. 713. The administration of an estate, in a judicial district of Alaska, in which sessions of the court depend upon the pleasure of the court itself to direct, may be reason for extending indulgence to an administrator for delay in respect to a matter for which an order of court is necessary.—In re Delaney's Estate, 41 Nev. 384, 389, 171 Pac. 383.

2. Title to property.—At common law, the legal title to all personal property of the deceased is vested in the executor or administrator, with absolute power to dispose of it.—Weider v. Osborn, 20 Or. 307, 25 Pac. 715. The real estate descends directly to the heirs of the deceased, subject to the payment of the debts of the deceased. The administrator has no title or interest in the real estate, except the rents thereof, and then only when it becomes necessary to have recourse to the real estate to pay the debts of the deceased.—Adams v. Slattery, 36 Colo. 35, 85 Pac. 87, 88. The right of possession of pre-empted land to which the title is inchoate, passes, on the death of the pre-emptor to his administrator.—Burch v. McDaniel, 2 Wash. Ter. 58, 3 Pac. 586. Title to personal property of an intestate vests in the administrator immediately upon his qualification, and it is the administrator's duty to protect it.—In re Tamer's Estate, Clayton v. Elea (Ariz.), 179 Pac. 644, 645. The legal title to money received by an administrator in the course of administration is vested in him to enable him to pay the expenses of administration, to liquidate claims against the estate, and to deliver the remainder, if any, together with other assets, to the heirs.—Thorsen v. Hooper, 57 Or. 75, 78, 109 Pac. 388, 50 Or. 497, 93 Pac. 361. An executor or administrator, as such, has no title to the real estate of the decedent, and can not, by reason of the provisions of the statutes of Wyoming sue to establish a resulting trust and compel the conveyance of land.—Cook v. Elmore, 25 Wyo. 393, 405, 171 Pac. 261. An administrator's title to property is an official title which ordinarily can not be affected to the prejudice of the estate by any acts of his prior to his appointment.—First State Bank v. Braden, 39 S. D. 53, 55, 162 N. W. 929. Under the laws of Arkansas in force in the Indian Territory at the time of the death of the intestate, neither an executor nor administrator has, as such, any interest in, title to, or control over, the real estate of the decedent except for the purpose of the payment of debts.—Moseley v. McBride, 40 Okla. 270, 138 Pac. 138. The only effect of an administrator's deed or bill of sale is to convey to the purchaser the title of the deceased; it can not contain any warranty of title; the rule of caveat emptor applies to such sales; in the absence of any special agreement as to the title of the property sold, it is incumbent on the buyer to examine the title for himself.—Payne v. People (Colo.), 173 Pac. 397. A purchaser at an administrator's sale of the allotted land of a minor Creek freedman, takes the title subject to all the restrictions, conditions, or limitations, imposed thereon by the acts of congress relating thereto, and such a sale is subject to collateral attack.—Barnard v. Bilby (Okla.), 171 Pac. 444, 446. Acts done by an administrator in his individual capacity can give rise to no estoppel to affect his title in property of the estate, except in cases where the estoppel is based upon and can be supported by equities against the estate.—First State Bank v. Braden, 39 S. D. 53, 55, 162 N. W. 929.

3. Become trustees when.—In a general sense, every executor is a trustee for the legatees and next of kin.—In re Roach's Estate, 50 Or. 179, 92 Pac. 118, 121. One who qualifies as trustee under a will becomes the trustee of an express trust.—Fox v. Tay, 89 Cal. 339, 349,

23 Am. St. Rep. 474, 24 Pac. 855, 26 Pac. 897. If an administrator, by false representations, procures the heir of his estate to convey to him all of the heir's interest in the estate, the administrator becomes an involutary trustee of the property conveyed for the benefit of the heir, though such representations were not made with a fraudulent intent.—Wingerter v. Wingerter, 71 Cal. 105, 11 Pac. 853, 855. If an executor or administrator purchases real property from the funds of the estate in his hands, a trust in the property results to the heirs, though the representative added funds of his own to the purchase-money.—Merket v. Smith, 33 Kan. 66, 5 Pac. 394, 396. And an administrator who becomes a trustee can not defeat heirs by afterwards becoming a guardian.—Merket v. Smith, 33 Kan. 66, 5 Pac. 394, 396. The right of possession of pre-empted land, acquired by an administrator, is subject to a trust which requires the administrator to proceed to effect title in favor of the heirs, provided there are heirs, and the estate is in such a condition as to enable him to do so, and the interest of the heirs, all things considered, so demand.—Burch v. McDaniel, 2 Wash. Ter. 58, 3 Pac. 586, 588. An executor is a trustee for the heirs and in no sense stands in the shoes of the deceased; he is bound by the statute, and can not waive as against the heirs or devisees any requirement of the statute.—Ward v. Magaha, 71 Wash. 679, 129 Pac. 397. An administrator stands in a fiduciary relation to those beneficially interested; he is subject to the universal rule that a trustee is bound to do that which will best serve the interests which for the time are intrusted to his care; his own good faith is not enough.—Stewart v. Baldwin, 86 Wash. 63, 149 Pac. 662. Executors hold all property of the estate for purposes of administration, including not only the rents and profits of lands specifically devised, but the land itself, and all of this property is subject, if necessary, to disposition for the payment of expenses and debts.—Estate of DeBernal, 165 Cal. 223, Ann. Cas. 1914D, 26, 131 Pac. 375.

4. **Administrator de bonis non.**—Upon the death of an administrator, the administrator de bonis non becomes vested with the title to such assets of the estate as remain unadministered and unconverted; and it is for him, and not the administrator of the administrator, to administer these assets.—Griffith v. James, 91 Wash. 607, 158 Pac. 251.

5. **Executors de son tort.**—There is no such office recognized under the probate practice of California as an executor de son tort.—Bowdon v. Pierce, 73 Cal. 459, 463, 14 Pac. 302, 15 Pac. 84. Such an executor was regarded by the common law as an intermeddler and a wrongdoer. He had no rights, but there is no doubt that his acts, for some purposes, were regarded as valid.—De la Guerra v. Packard, 17 Cal. 182, 192. It was formerly considered that if an individual interfered with the property of the deceased, he thereby made himself an executor in his own wrong, or, as it is generally termed, an executor de son tort. This rule has long been modified, if not abolished, by the statute; and whoever intermeddles with an estate, without rightful authority

so to do, is answerable to the rightful executor or administrator. The
statutory change, however, produced some important consequences. It
takes away the remedy the creditor before had to charge the intermeddler as an executor de son tort. He can no longer proceed against
him in that character, but must procure the appointment of an administrator, and have suit instituted in his name to recover the property
from such person, who has converted it to his own use. In a word, he
is merely sent to the rightful representative of the estate, and can not
pursue his action against an executor de son tort. The rightful executor or administrator is constituted the trustee of the assets of the deceased, whose duty it is to receive and hold them in his hands as a
fund to be disposed of in the best manner for the benefit of creditors.
The person who intermeddles with the goods of the deceased is now
answerable only to the rightful executor or administrator, in an action
brought by the representative. The fiction of office may be gone, but
the unauthorized act of intermeddling remains to be dealt with judicially, according to the principles of right and justice as applied by
the law in such a case.—Rutherford v. Thompson, 14 Or. 236, 12 Pac.
382, 383. Under our system, there is probably no such thing as an
executor de son tort; at all events, no man can be executor de son tort
in regard to land.—Pryor v. Downey, 50 Cal. 388, 399, 19 Am. Rep.
656.

REFERENCES.

Executors de son tort.—See notes 98 Am. St. Rep. 190-205, 85 Am.
Dec. 423-427, 17 Am. Dec. 561, 562.

6. Property and other rights.—Executors and administrators are entitled to the possession and control of the property, both real and
personal, of estates while being administered by them, as against
heirs and devisees, as well as against all other persons.—Bishop v.
Locke, 92 Wash. 90, 158 Pac. 997. At common law, the liability of an
heir and devisee is confined to the real estate descended; with which
property the administrator or executor has nothing to do.—Rainey v.
Rudd, 82 Or. 461, 160 Pac. 1168. An administrator, as such, has no
greater concern in a contest over a right to the residue of an estate
remaining after administration by virtue of an agreement between
claimants and deceased in the latter's lifetime than he has between
various parties claiming to be entitled by succession. (Citing Estate
of Healy, 137 Cal. 474, 70 Pac. 455, and McCabe v. Healy, 138 Cal
81, 70 Pac. 1008, as foreclosing the argument.)—In re Ross' Estate,
179 Cal. 358, 182 Pac. 303, 304. It is settled law in this state that the
administrator or executor has no right to take a part in litigation
between various parties asserting conflicting rights as heirs, and that
he has no right to engage attorneys for either claimant, or to bind
the estate in any manner on that behalf.—In re Ross' Estate, 179 Cal.
358, 182 Pac. 303, 304. An executor or administrator, in the absence
of a showing that there is a necessity for his interference for some
purpose of administration recognized by statute, has nothing to do

with the decedent's real estate; such estate is the absolute property of the heir.—Malagamba v. McLean, 89 Or. 307, 161 Pac. 560, 173 Pac. 1175.

REFERENCES.

Right of personal representative of lessee to possession of leased premises under a lease to commence in futuro.—See note 22 L. R. A. (N. S.) 301. Right of continuing or surviving executor or administrator against former co-executor or administrator or latter's representative.—See note 47 L. R. A. (N. S.) 995.

7. **Duties of executors and administrators.**—An executor or administrator, while he must act in the utmost good faith, and must strictly perform his official duties, is bound to perform only such duties as are imposed upon him by statute.—Royce v. Hampton, 16 Nev. 25; but he is presumed to have done his duty until the contrary appears.— Territory v. Mix, 1 Ariz. 52. An executor or administrator is not clothed, under the statute, with discretion in any case to determine whether or not it is necessary and proper that he should take possession of the real estate. It is his duty to take charge of the entire estate of the deceased.—Balch v. Smith, 4 Wash. 497, 30 Pac. 648, 650. The measure of an administrator's duty is to act with fidelity and with that degree of prudence and diligence which a man of ordinary judgment would be expected to bestow upon his own affairs of a like nature.—Elizalde v. Murphy, 4 Cal. App. 114, 117, 87 Pac. 245, 246; and it is his duty to settle and to distribute the estate with as little delay as possible.—McNabb v. Wixom, 7 Nev. 163, 171. The duties of an executor or administrator are active, and not passive. He can not be permitted to neglect those things which are plainly required at his hands, by law or the order of the court, and when complaint is made of such neglect, excuse himself by alleging that such delay or omission was for the benefit of the estate.—In re Holladay's Estate, 18 Or. 168, 22 Pac. 750. The duties of the executor are to preserve the estate, pay the indebtedness of the deceased, the charges of administration, and to put the estate in such condition that distribution may be had to those entitled to it under the will; and they have no right to go outside of their duties.—Estate of Willey, 140 Cal. 238, 241, 73 Pac. 998; O'Neile v. Ternes, 32 Wash. 528, 73 Pac. 692, 696. It is the duty of the executor to give the decedent a decent burial, and he can not be absolutely limited in the performance of such duty by the provisions of a will.—Estate of Galland, 92 Cal. 293, 295, 28 Pac. 287. Under the provisions of a will, directing that the body of the testator be buried in a certain cemetery, and that a monument be erected over the grave, the executor is obliged to erect a monument over the place of burial, though the body has been removed.—Estate of Koppikus, 1 Cal. App. 84, 81 Pac. 732, 733. The doctrine that officers and directors of a corporation are trustees of the stockholders applies only in respect to their acts relating to the property or business of the corporation. It does not extend to their private dealings with

stockholders or others, though in such dealings they take advantage of knowledge gained through their official position. Hence where corporate stock has been bequeathed, as a specific legacy, by the terms of a will, the legatee has the right to sell it to whomsoever he pleases, and the executor or administrator has the right to purchase it; and the executor is under no duty to give to the legatee information as to the value of corporate stock bequeathed to such legatee and bought by the executor.—O'Neile v. Ternes, 32 Wash. 528, 73 Pac. 692, 696. If an executrix holds a mortgage on the estate, it is her duty to list her mortgage interest for assessment, and not to allow the land to be taxed in the same manner as if there were no mortgage thereon. The taxes consequently levied on that interest would therefore be her individual debt, and not the debt of the estate; and if the debt is greater than the value of the land, there can be no excess on which the estate could be taxed. The mortgage debt would cover it all. Equity will regard that done which ought to have been done, and the matter must be adjusted by requiring her to bear the burden of the taxes which she should have paid, as fully as she would have borne it had she listed her mortgage interest for taxation, as she ought to have done.—Estate of McDougald, 146 Cal. 196, 198, 79 Pac. 875. And it is her duty to pay taxes on the estate, though she is not in possession.—Stanford v. San Francisco, 131 Cal. 34, 36, 63 Pac. 145. It is the duty of an executor to retain moneys received by him until they can be applied and distributed in the order and mode provided by law. —Magraw v. McGlynn, 26 Cal. 420, 429. It is the duty of the administrator to take possession as soon as he is appointed, and to make and return to the court an inventory and appraisement of all the property which comes into his hands.—In re Colbert's Estate, 44 Mont. 259, 266, 119 Pac. 791. An executor or administrator must take into his possession all the estate of his decedent, real and personal, and collect all debts due to the estate.—In re Dolenty's Estate, Mannix v. Dolenty, 53 Mont. 33, 161 Pac. 524. Executors and administrators have statutory power, as well as a duty, to take into possession the realty and personalty of the decedent, and sue for the possession thereof, and they are subjected to suits to which the decedent would be liable if alive.—Litzell v. Hart, 96 Wash. 471, 165 Pac. 393. The executor or administrator has a right, conferred by statute, to the possession of all the decedent's real and personal property and all the rents and profits of the realty, until the settlement of the estate.—Cook v. Elmore, 25 Wyo. 393, 171 Pac. 261. It is the duty of the administrator not only to conserve the property of the estate, but to protect it against all claims deemed by him either fraudulent or unjust.—In re Estate of Gladough, 1 Alaska 649, 651. The duty and interest of an administrator extends solely to seeing that the estate is preserved for the creditors; he is not legally concerned in the interests of the heirs.—Dunn v. Wallingford, 47 Utah 491, 155 Pac. 347. The duty imposed upon an administrator to ascertain the property of the estate and defend the latter's rights therein, extends to property assigned to him personally, by the decedent; and he should, in case of doubt as to the validity of the assignment, consult the court, and not rely on his own determination.—In re Picot's Estate (Utah), 178 Pac. 75.   An administrator is a mere officer of the court, holding the estate for delivery in accordance with the court's order of distribution; he therefore has no interest in a controversy to determine rights of inheritance.—Estate of Walker, 176 Cal. 402, 168 Pac. 689.   An executor is a person appointed to carry the will into effect or execution after the death of the testator, and to dispose of the estate according to the tenor of the will.—Shufeldt v. Hughes, 55 Wash. 246, 104 Pac. 256.   It is the duty of an administrator with the will annexed to examine and if necessary oppose the accounts submitted for settlement by his predecessor in office.   If technical or expert knowledge is necessary to make a proper examination, it is his duty to employ an expert accountant, and the expense of such employment is a proper charge against the estate.—Estate of Broome, 162 Cal. 258, 122 Pac. 470.   Where the executors of a will are also appointed trustees of a portion of the estate, their duties as executors and trustees are separate, distinct, and independent of each other; and until the estate is settled or distributed, in whole or in part, their duties as executors continue as to the part not distributed and as to such part they do not assume the duties of trustees.—Jones v. Broadbent, 21 Ida. 555, 123 Pac. 476.   Where the decree of final settlement of the claim and directing its payment has become final and conclusive as to all parties interested in the estate, it then becomes the final official duty of the administratrix to comply with the order directing her to pay the same, and the breach of such official duty is a breach of official trust which is not only conclusive upon the administratrix, but also, in the absence of fraud or collusion, is conclusive against the surety upon her official bond, who, by the terms of the bond is liable therefor. —L. Harter Co. v. Geisel, 18 Cal. App. 282, 122 Pac. 1094.   Executor of administratrix does not succeed to her duties or powers as such.— Sanford v. Bergin, 156 Cal. 43, 103 Pac. 333.

REFERENCES.

Duty of executor or administrator to retain from his distributive share of estate the amount of his debt to the estate.—See note 6 Am. & Eng. Ann. Cas. 810.

8. Power of executors and administrators.

(1) In general.—Where the statute does not expressly require the administrator to personally sign the notice to creditors, he may authorize his attorney to sign it in his name and in his behalf.—Meikle v. Cloquet, 44 Wash. 513, 87 Pac. 841, 843.   One who is not qualified as an executor is free to make contracts with the executor or administrator, although they redound to his benefit.—Bowden v. Pierce, 73 Cal. 459, 14 Pac. 302, 304.   If an executrix is also a residuary devisee, and does not appear and contest a petition by legatees for partial dis-

tribution, except in her capacity as executrix only, she is as fully concluded, with respect to her rights as devisee in such proceeding, as are the other devisees. Her appearance as executrix gives her no standing to claim rights which she possesses solely as devisee. As such devisee, she must, under such circumstances, be considered as one who has suffered default.—Estate of Murphy, 145 Cal. 464, 78 Pac. 960, 962. After the distribution of an estate, the persons appointed as executors have a discretion to increase an annuity out of the estate of the residuary legatee, where such discretion has been vested in the executors, although they have also been appointed guardians of the estate of the testator's minor child, a residuary legatee under the will.—Elmer v. Gray, 73 Cal. 283, 14 Pac. 862. The code provides for an appeal from an order of revocation of the probate of a will and of letters testamentary, and therefore the statute keeps alive, ad interim, appellant's character as executor for the purposes of appeal. But, in all other respects, the powers and functions of the other executor are suspended when the revocation is entered.—Estate of Crozier, 65 Cal. 332, 4 Pac. 109, 110. An agreement, by an administrator, to delay the collection of a debt due the estate for years, simply to see if a contingent right of set-off in the defendant, which had not been presented as a claim, would become absolute, is unwarranted, and does not bind the heirs or those interested in enforcing collection of the debt.—Maddock v. Russell, 109 Cal. 417, 424, 42 Pac. 139. A person nominated as executor by a will probated in the state of Utah, and appointed as such in that state, and afterwards appointed administrator with the will annexed in this state, represents said estate in both jurisdictions, and occupies the same position with reference to all controversies and suits by or against said estate, and in that respect, and to that extent, is the same person for both states.— Hilton v. Stewart, 15 Ida. 150, 128 Am. St. Rep. 48, 96 Pac. 579. If the administrator of an estate desires to donate his fees for services as such to a third party, the execution and delivery of a written assignment thereof is a delivery of the property itself.—Luther v. Hunter, 7 N. D. 544, 75 N. W. 916. An executor or administrator, if empowered by the will, may, after the distribution of an estate, increase the annuity of a residuary legatee.—Elmer v. Gray, 73 Cal. 283, 284, 14 Pac. 862. If a testator directs his wife to educate, maintain, and nourish their three children until the youngest shall reach maturity, and, to effectuate the desire, makes a devise to her as executrix, she can act in the premises only in her official capacity.—Beakey v. Knutson, 90 Or. 574, 174 Pac. 1149, 177 Pac. 955.

REFERENCES.

Administrators pendente lite.—See note 6 Am. & Eng. Ann. Cas. 263. Appointment and powers of administrators de bonis non.—See note 24 Am. Dec. 379-390. Care and skill required of executors and administrators.—See note 12 Am. St. Rep. 311-316. Common-law powers of executors.—See note 78 Am. St. Rep. 171-207. Powers and duties of ancillary administrators, and necessity for ancillary administration.—See note 35 Am. Dec. 483-490. Power of executor or administrator to revive debts.—See note 12 Am. Dec. 659-661. Power of executors.—See note 55 Am. Dec. 436-439. Powers and duties of executors and administrators respecting property outside of the state. —See note 45 Am. St. Rep. 664-674. Collateral attack on right of acting executor or administrator.—See note 81 Am. St. Rep. 535-562. Letters of administration are void for want of jurisdiction when.— See note 33 Am. Dec. 239-243.

(2) Notice of scope of power.—Where the scope of the power of an executor and the manner of its exercise are prescribed by the will, any one dealing with or for the assets of the estate is bound to take notice thereof.—Beakey v. Knutson, 90 Or. 574, 174 Pac. 1149, 177 Pac. 955. A person dealing with an executor or administrator is presumed to be aware of the limitations upon that official's authority.—Taylor v. Sanson, 24 Cal. App. 515, 141 Pac. 1060.

(3) To dispose of personal property.—At common law, the legal title to all personal property of the estate vested in the executor or administrator, with absolute power to dispose of it, and, in the absence of fraud or collusion between him and the person to whom he transferred it, the creditors or next of kin could not follow it into the hands of the alienee. But, under the statutes of Oregon, the power is not conferred on the executor or administrator to sell or to dispose of visible, tangible personal property, except by an order of the probate court, either at public or private sale, as may be provided therein. The administrator's power of disposition, however, over his intestate's choses in action remains unaffected by legislation. An executor or administrator is, with respect to choses in action, vested with power and authority to sell and to dispose of them by indorsement to another, or to a distributee, without an order of the probate court. Such transfer is valid, and passes the title, so as to enable the transferee or distributee to maintain an action thereon, and the payers or makers of them, in the absence of fraud or collusion between the administrator and the person to whom he transfers them, can not abate the action on the ground of the want of authority to make such transfer.—Weider v. Osborn, 20 Or. 307, 25 Pac. 715, 717. The right of possession of preempted land, to which the title is inchoate, passes, on the death of the pre-emptor, to his administrator, subject to a trust requiring the administrator to proceed to perfect the title in favor of the heirs, provided there are any, but, aside from this trust, he is free to dispose of the possession to the best advantage of the estate.—Burch v. McDaniel, 2 Wash. Ter. 58, 3 Pac. 586, 588.

REFERENCES.

Deposit of trust funds in bank by an executor or administrator.— See note 98 Am. St. Rep. 371-377.

(4) To compound or compromise, in general.—Executors and administrators have the legal right to compound and discharge debts due to their testator or intestate.—Moulton v. Holmes, 57 Cal. 337, 343; Estate of Dunne, 58 Cal. 543; Denney v. Parker, 10 Wash. 218, 38 Pac. 1018; Estate of Irvine, 102 Cal. 606, 36 Pac. 1013. The authorities are to the effect that an administrator has authority to compound or compromise with a debtor of his decedent when it is to the interest of the estate, irrespective of any statutory power conferred upon him.—Mulville v. Pacific Mut. L. Ins. Co., 19 Mont. 95, 47 Pac. 650, 652. This right exists independently of the statute, the object of which is to afford executors and administrators additional protection, when acting in good faith in the exercise of their common-law powers. Although they may compromise a claim or compound a debt without the aid of the statute, still they may perhaps be held answerable for any serious error in judgment in so doing. The statute enables them to obtain the sanction of the judgment of the probate court in addition to their own, and thus affords them additional protection, if their conduct is fair and honest.—Moulton v. Holmes, 57 Cal. 337, 344. Such a power belongs to all trustees for the benefit of the trust estate, and they have the right to assume the responsibility of judging of the necessity for its exercise. The circumstances which may render it necessary are presumably better known to them than to any one else. Executors and administrators have therefore never been required to obtain preliminary authority for that purpose from the probate court, although the judgment must be ultimately approved by the court, when they come to render an account of their trust.—Moulton v. Holmes, 57 Cal. 337, 343. Conceding that executors and administrators have the legal right to compromise and discharge debts due the estates which they represent without the approbation of the court, or a judge thereof, when it appears to them to be just and for the best interest of the estate, still it has been held in California that a payment of a part of the amount due upon a money judgment under an agreement that it shall operate as a satisfaction in full will not discharge the judgment, and that an agreement to discharge a judgment for a sum less than the amount for which it was rendered is void. . Hence an agreement on the part of an administratrix to accept a note to take the place of and to be a substitute for a judgment, where the amount of the note is for a sum less than the amount for which the judgment was rendered, and where the attempted compromise was never authorized or approved by the probate court, or a judge thereof, is null and void, especially where the note was executed without any special consideration therefore.—Siddall v. Clark, 89 Cal. 321, 323, 26 Pac. 829. Where an executor claims that certain money is an asset of the estate, and trustees claim that it is not, it is the duty of the executor to get it for the estate, and he has no right to compromise the claim of the estate by consenting that the trustees shall have the money, provided they shall pay the debts and expenses of administration out of it; and if he has been permitted to inventory the money as assets of the estate, and administer it as such, the executor can not return the surplus to the trustees, as this would be to assume the responsibility of maintaining the title of the trustees against the estate, and the executor is not at liberty to assume such a position.— Estate of Burdick, 112 Cal. 387, 392, 44 Pac. 734. At common law, the executor or administrator has an absolute power of disposal over the whole of the personal effects of the decedent, with full power to compromise or accept any composition, or otherwise settle any debt, claim, or thing whatsoever.—Olston v. Oregon, etc., Ry. Co., 52 Or. 343, 20 L. R. A. (N. S.) 915, 96 Pac. 1095, 1096, 97 Pac. 538. In Oregon, the powers of an administrator, as to an unliquidated claim for damages, remain the same as at common law, and he may liquidate and accept settlement of such a claim without special authority from the county court.—Olston v. Oregon, etc., Ry. Co., 52 Or. 343, 20 L. R. A. (N. S.) 915, 96 Pac. 1095, 1096, 97 Pac. 538. An administrator may compromise with an heir without his agreements being void as against public policy.—Dunn v. Wallingford, 47 Utah 491, 155 Pac. 347. Under the California statute, an executor, or administrator, is not required to obtain authority from the probate court before compromising with a debtor of the estate, provided that is for the best interests of the estate, but his action needs to be approved by the court afterwards.—Taylor v. Sanson, 24 Cal. App. 515, 141 Pac. 1060. In cases where a compromise is made with a debtor of the estate, by the executor or administrator, the act is justified by a reasonable showing that the debtor was, at the time, either insolvent or about to become so, or that in all reasonable probability the money could not be collected by suit.—Taylor v. Sanson, 24 Cal. App. 515, 141 Pac. 1060. Where an agreement in relation to mining claims has been made by rival claimants, who have since died, and where their personal representatives have arranged a compromise and settlement, which has been approved and confirmed by. the probate court, the order is final until reversed or vacated, notwithstanding an alleged discovery of fraud on the part of the attorney employed by the deceased parties to the agreement in respect to his compensation.—Costello v. Cunningham, 16 Ariz. 447, 462, 147 Pac. 701. The law favors compromises of disputed claims affecting the settlement of estates, when their tendency is to preserve harmony among relatives.—Norman v. Miller (S. D.), 167 N. W. 391.

REFERENCES.

Release of debt by one of several executors or administrators.—See note 14 Am. Dec. 157, 158. Compromise or release by personal representative of claim due the estate.—See note 14 L. R. A. 414-417.

(5) Same. Restrictions. Approval of court.—An executor, without the advice of the court, has no right to make a compromise of a suit pending against the estate.—Lucich v. Medin, 3 Nev. 93, 93 Am. Dec. 376. Under the present statute of California the right of an executor

or administrator to compound with a debtor, and to give him a discharge, is subject to the approbation of the probate court, or a judge thereof.—Hartigan v. Southern Pac. Co., 86 Cal. 142, 144, 24 Pac. 851. In Kansas, the provisions of the statute are held to restrict the powers of administrators under the common law, and do not simply afford them additional protection in the exercise of those powers; and it is there held that no authority is given administrators to do anything in the way of compromising claims, debts, or demands belonging to the estate of an intestate, and accruing in the lifetime of such intestate, without the order or consent of the probate court.—Ætna Life Ins. Co. v. Swayze, 30 Kan. 118, 1 Pac. 36, 38, 40. In that state, an administrator has no authority to accept less than the full amount of a demand in satisfaction thereof, where such demand accrued in the lifetime of his decedent, except by the consent of the probate court.—Van Dusen v. Topeka Woolen Mill Co., 74 Kan. 437, 87 Pac. 74. In Nevada, an executor may pay money to compromise a suit pending against an estate; but he can not lawfully make such payment without the previous consent of the probate court.—Lucich v. Medin, 3 Nev. 93, 93 Am. Dec. 376. An executor has authority, with the approval of the probate court, to compromise an action for damages for injuries resulting in the wrongful death of his testator.—Hartigan v. Southern Pac. Co., 86 Cal. 142, 144, 24 Pac. 851. In Montana, a public administrator, as well as a general administrator, may be authorized to compromise an action brought to recover the amount of an accident-insurance policy, when it is to the interest of the estate to do so.—Mulville v. Pacific Mut. L. Ins. Co., 19 Mont. 95, 47 Pac. 650, 652.

(6) Same. Distinction.—In Washington, a distinction is drawn between the compromise of a claim out of court and the conduct of a litigated claim in court. The statutes of that state require the action of the representative of an estate, in compromising claims in favor of or against the estate, to be subject to the approval of the probate court, but it is said that, in the conduct of a litigated case in court, the representative is often called upon to act at once, and without any opportunity of consulting the probate court, and that his action, once taken, and acted upon by the court in which the action is pending, is generally beyond recall, should the probate court thereafter disapprove of the course taken; and that it must follow, from the very necessities of the case, that such representative has to act without consulting the probate court; that, under such circumstances, his action will be final without its approval; and that if, during the progress of the trial, an opportunity to compromise is offered, the representative should have power to act in reference thereto without the consent of the probate court. "It may well happen, in the conduct of the case, that a favorable compromise will be offered to the representative of the estate; and to give it the benefit of the compromise, he must reject or accept it at once, and if he has not the power to act until he can consult with the probate court, the opportunity to accept the advantageous

compromise may be entirely lost. The interests of the estate are necessarily committed almost entirely to the administrators, so far as they may be affected by issues joined in an action; and, within those issues, he should be given full power to adjust matters as between the estate and the other party to the action. By his neglect of the interests of the estate, in the prosecution or defense of the action, his rights could be lost beyond the power of the probate court to save them, and as its rights can be affected by the negative action of the administrator in the case, there is no reason why he should not have the right to effect them by his positive action as to such matter in litigation. Taking into consideration all of our statutes in reference to the settlement of an estate, we feel compelled to hold, in an action prosecuted in good faith by a representative thereof, that he has power to adjust its rights with the contending parties so far as they might be affected in the action, if prosecuted to judgment. And we can see no good reason for limiting such rights to cases not involving real estate. If the power to compromise exists, it should only be limited by the issues made by the pleadings."—Denney v. Parker, 10 Wash. 218, 38 Pac. 1018, 1019.

(7) **To bind estate.**—The rule is, that executors and administrators can not, by virtue of their general powers as such, make any contract which will bind the estate and authorize a judgment de bonis decendentis.—Remwick v. Garland, 1 Cal. App. 237, 238, 82 Pac. 89. But on contracts made by them on necessary matters relating to the estate, they are personally liable, and must see to it that they are reimbursed out of the assets.—Sterrett v. Barker, 119 Cal. 492, 495, 51 Pac. 695, citing Schouler on Executors and Administrators, sec. 256; Miller & Lux v. Gray, 136 Cal. 261, 264, 68 Pac. 770. There are doubtless exceptions to this rule, such as funeral expenses, clerks' fees, etc.; but neither an executor nor an administrator can borrow money on the credit of the estate. He can not, except when expressly authorized by the will or statute, create an obligation which will give a right of action against the estate.—Sterrett v. Barker, 119 Cal. 492, 495, 51 Pac. 695; Miller v. Gray, 136 Cal. 261, 264, 68 Pac. 770. An executor or administrator can not, without authority of the court, bind the estate by agreeing to delay the collection of a debt due the estate for a period of years in order to determine whether a contingent right of set-off shall become absolute, when such contingent right has not been presented or allowed as a claim against the estate.—Maddock v. Russell, 109 Cal. 417, 424, 42 Pac. 139. Nor has he any authority to pledge the personal property of the estate as surety for money borrowed by him for the purpose of paying debts against the estate.—Parks v. Mockenhaupt, 133 Cal. 424, 425, 65 Pac. 875. Without any showing of authority by the will or otherwise, the executor of the estate of a deceased person will not be held authorized to bind the estate by a new contract for the completion of a building, for the erection of which the deceased had contracted, but the executor, being also an heir, and interested in the property, may bind himself personally by any contract he authorizes.—

Lumber Co. v. Tomlinson, sub nom. Chicago Lumber Co. v. Tomlinson, 54 Kan. 770, 39 Pac. 694. There is no privity between the administrator of one state and a foreign administrator; and an administrator has no authority to act or bind the estate outside of the jurisdiction of his own state.—Braithwaite v. Harvey, 14 Mont. 208, 43 Am. St. Rep. 625, 27 L. R. A. 101, 36 Pac. 38. The estate of a decedent is not answerable for a tort committed by an administrator or executor.—Sterrett v. Barker, 119 Cal. 492, 494, 51 Pac. 695. Authority to an administrator to execute a trust deed does not authorize him to stipulate therein for the payment of an attorney's fee, in case such deed is foreclosed.—Pershing v. Wolfe, 6 Colo. App. 410, 40 Pac. 856, 860. No one, even an executor or administrator, can bind an estate by an agreement to settle a claim against it on condition that the personal property shall amount to a specified sum.—Dunn v. Wallingford, 47 Utah 491, 155 Pac. 347. An executor can not bind the estate by an executory contract and thus create a liability not founded upon a contract or obligation of the testator.—Lawson v. Cobban, 38 Mont. 138, 99 Pac. 130. Where an administrator with others signed a contract to convey at a future time land belonging to the estate, he is personally liable for the breach of such contract whether he be regarded as having acted in his personal or representative capacity.—Lawson v. Cobban, 38 Mont. 138, 99 Pac. 130. It is proper to disallow charges for money paid by executor for work done after decedent's death under a contract which terminated at the time of such death and also charges for work on a road after the owner's death, the work being unauthorized.—In re McPhee's Estate, 156 Cal. 335, Ann. Cas. 1913E, 899, 104 Pac. 455. Fifty dollars' damages awarded in favor of children and against executrix personally.—In re Snowball's Estate, 156 Cal. 235, 104 Pac. 446. Executrix held not entitled to allowance for expense of unjustifiable appeal from order making family allowance to minor beneficiaries.—In re Snowball's Estate, 156 Cal. 235, 104 Pac. 446. An executor or administrator can not create any liability against the estate by the employment of the services of attorneys, brokers, or others, to assist him in the performance of his duties. The attorney, broker, or other person employed has no action or claim against the estate.—Hickman-Coleman Co. v. Leggett, 10 Cal. App. 29, 100 Pac. 1072. Executor's contract employing brokers to sell realty of estate as authorized by will held his own individual contract.—Hickman-Coleman Co. v. Leggett, 10 Cal. App. 29, 100 Pac. 1072. Court could not allow broker's commission for selling land under contract with executor.—Hickman-Coleman Co. v. Leggett, 10 Cal. App. 29, 100 Pac. 1072. A representative can not create any direct liability against the estate of a decedent by the employment of attorneys, brokers, or others to assist him in the performance of his duties.—Hickman-Coleman Co. v. Leggett, 10 Cal. App. 29, 100 Pac. 1072. A broker's right to commission was held not to be affected by the fact that the court confirmed to the purchaser a sale produced by other brokers who bid a higher sum, such brokers not having been employed by the executor, and plaintiffs having fully performed.—Hickman-Coleman Co. v. Leggett, 10 Cal. App. 29, 100 Pac. 1072. Under the California Code of Civil Procedure, section 1619, to warrant allowance to representative for attorney's fees in litigation, such litigation must have been necessary to prosecute or defend.—In re Higgins' Estate, 158 Cal. 355, 111 Pac. 8. A finding below on the question of such necessity is not conclusive on appeal.—In re Higgins' Estate, 158 Cal. 355, 111 Pac. 8. The mere fact that the statute authorizes an executor to resist opposition to the probate of a will does not entitle him to attorney's fees.—In re Hite's Estate, 155 Cal. 448, 101 Pac. 448. Where, though under the statute the executor could defend a will, his defense was solely for his own benefit and against other beneficiaries of the estate so as to be of no benefit to the estate, he was required to pay his own expenses and charges, and attorney's fees in such contest could not properly be allowed against the estate.—In re Higgins' Estate, 158 Cal. 355, 111 Pac. 8. The Code of Civil Procedure of California, section 1616, entitles an attorney only to such fees as are properly allowable to the representative, and not to fees in a will contest of no benefit to the estate but merely for the executor's advantage. —In re Higgins' Estate, 158 Cal. 355, 111 Pac. 8. Executor's attorney held not entitled to fees out of estate for resisting contest of codicils where estate had no interest in contest and certain legatee was only person benefited by sustaining of codicils.—In re Hite's Estate, 155 Cal. 448, 101 Pac. 448. Executor held not entitled to counsel fees incurred in unsuccessful attempt to prove a will.—In re Hite's Estate, 155 Cal. 448, 101 Pac. 448.

REFERENCES.

Allowance to representative of attorneys' fees.—See note post, following the table after § 655, on liabilities and compensation of executors and administrators, including attorneys' fees.

(8) Not to purchase claims against estate.—The statute forbids an administrator from purchasing a claim against the estate he represents, but a mortgage lien is not a "claim" against the estate.—Fallon v. Butler, 21 Cal. 24, 32, 81 Am. Dec. 140. Nor is the lien of a mechanic a "claim" against an estate.—Booth v. Pendola, 88 Cal. 36, 44, 23 Pac. 200, 25 Pac. 1101. The term "claim," as used in the code, in reference to estates of deceased persons, has reference to such demands or debts against the decedent as existed, and, if due, might have been enforced against him in his lifetime by proper action. The liabilities of the administrator or executor, included in the management of the estate or in administering the trust, stand upon a different footing.—Stuttmeister v. Superior Court, 72 Cal. 487, 489, 14 Pac. 35. If the executor or administrator, for the purpose of protecting the estate, advances money of his own to secure the transfer of a mortgage upon decedent's land, where he has no funds of the estate in his hands, and procures the assignment to be made either to himself or to a third party for the purpose of enabling him to protect the property from a sacrifice by

foreclosure at the suit of the mortgagee, he is acting within the line of his authority as representative, and his act is not to be construed as a "purchase" of the claim for his own benefit, in violation of the statute.—Burnett v. Lyford, 93 Cal. 114, 118, 28 Pac. 855; Estate of McDougald, 146 Cal. 191, 192, 79 Pac. 878. The contract between an executrix and third persons, who have full knowledge of the facts, whereby such third persons are to purchase personal property, at a probate sale thereof for the benefit of such executrix, she agreeing to advance the purchase price, and to guarantee the buyers against loss or damage and to give them possession of the goods until other security is furnished, and to pay them interest on the amount advanced, is an unlawful and void transaction, because it is in aid of an act expressly prohibited by law, and because it is contrary to the policy of express law, for the reason that it is indirectly a purchase by the executrix of the property of the estate she represented.—Jones v. Hanna, 81 Cal. 507, 508, 509, 22 Pac. 883. In Nevada, the purchase, by an executor or an administrator, of a claim against the estate which he represents is not absolutely void. Hence, if he purchases a mortgage in good faith, and with no design to injure the estate, the purchase will be sustained, where the estate has been benefited by the delay in foreclosure.—Furth v. Wyatt, 17 Nev. 180, 30 Pac. 828, 829. A surety on an administrator's bond is not precluded from purchasing claims against the estate; and, when the estate is insolvent, and pays only a percentage of the claims against it, and when this percentage was received by such bondsman on a claim which he undertook to purchase, but did not in fact own, and an action is brought against him by the true owner for money had and received, the recovery must be limited to the amount actually received.—Luther v. Hunter, 7 N. D. 544, 75 N. W. 916. An executor or administrator can not buy a claim against the estate at less than its face value, and then pay himself its face value out of the estate.—McFadden v. Jenkins (N. D.), 169 N. W. 151, 163. Though an administrator can not be allowed to acquire any interests inconsistent with the representative capacity he sustains nor be permitted to make a personal profit out of dealings with the property of the estate, yet he is not prevented from buying a legatee's interest in the estate so long as the transaction is fair and equitable and the administrator does not use the estate's money therein.—In re Goss' Estate, 73 Wash. 330, 132 Pac. 410.

(9) Not to purchase estate.—An executor or administrator of an estate of a deceased person has no authority to bid in for the estate, at execution sale, real or personal property levied upon to satisfy an execution issued upon a judgment in favor of the estate.—Sedgwick v. Sedgwick, 2 Cal. Unrep. 363, 4 Pac. 570. A statute which expressly declares that no executor shall, directly or indirectly, purchase any property of the estate he represents, and which prohibits him from being interested in any sale, simply declares, in the case of executors and administrators, an already existing rule in equity, to wit, that

contracts in which a trustee both buys and sells to himself are void. But a contract to purchase the interest of an heir in an estate by an executor does not come within the letter or spirit of either the statute or this equitable rule. The executor has no authority, as such, to sell the interest of an heir in the estate. Such interest is not, in any sense, property of the estate; it is the property of the heir, and he alone can sell it. Owing to the advantage that might be taken of heirs by executors or administrators, the court would, if it were called upon to pass upon such a sale, where the heir was claiming that he had been overreached or wronged, scrutinize the matter, and, if unfair in its terms, would not hesitate to set such contract aside, but not because it is in violation of the statute referred to. In other words, these sales by an heir to an executor are not within the statute at all. If they are fair in themselves, they should be upheld, the same as other contracts.—Haight v. Pearson, 11 Utah 54, 39 Pac. 479, 480. After one has ceased to be an administrator, and the administration has been closed, he has a perfect right to purchase from the purchaser at a probate sale, and there is nothing on the face of the business that is irregular or improper.—Burris v. Adams, 96 Cal. 664, 668, 31 Pac. 565. An administrator can not directly or indirectly purchase the property of the estate he represents or be interested in any sale thereof.—Vaughan v. Vaughan (Okla.), 162 Pac. 1131. Long acquiescence by the parties interested will preclude them from objecting to the purchase by an administrator of property of the estate which purchase would have been improper if objected to promptly.—Lewis v. Hill, 61 Wash. 304, 112 Pac. 375.

(10) Can not do what. In general.—An executor or administrator, being a representative of the estate, can not represent a claimant against the estate.—In re Hobson's Estate, 40 Colo. 332, 91 Pac. 929, 931. He has no power to receive, in full satisfaction of a judgment in favor of the estate, an amount less than that due thereon.—Siddal v. Clark, 89 Cal. 321, 26 Pac. 829, 830. He has no power to relieve a bank, which is an involuntary trustee, of money belonging to the estate, from its trust relation to the estate.—First Nat. Bank v. Wakefield, 148 Cal. 558, 83 Pac. 1076, 1077. He has no power to bind the heirs by consenting to the laying out of a highway across the estate, whereby such heirs are devested of their estate in the land.—Rush v. McDermott, 50 Cal. 471, 473. He has no power to convey a part of the estate to an attorney as a contingent fee for his services in recovering it.—Estate of Page, 57 Cal. 238, 241. He is not authorized to loan funds of the estate, as that, of itself, would be a breach of trust.—Estate of Clark, 53 Cal. 355, 357. He is not authorized to extend the time of payments to the estate.—Maddock v. Russell, 109 Cal. 417, 424, 42 Pac. 139. Whenever an executor or administrator undertakes to go beyond the strict line of his duty, he acts upon his own responsibility.—Estate of Rose, 80 Cal. 166, 172, 22 Pac. 86; Estate of Knight, 12 Cal. 200, 208, 73 Am. Dec. 531. An executor or admin-

istrator can not convey the estate he represents to pay his own debts. Such a conveyance would be a misappropriation and waste of the property of the estate.—Horton v. Jack, 126 Cal. 521, 58 Pac. 1051. Executors or administrators are not authorized to erect a dwelling-house with the funds or assets of the estate to be occupied by one of them; nor can they involve the estate by borrowing money with which to pay for material and labor performed in the construction of such house.—Rolfson v. Cannon, 3 Utah 232, 2 Pac. 205. An executor or administrator can not give a right of lien against the property he represents, without an order of court.—San Francisco Pav. Co. v. Fairfield, 134 Cal. 220, 224, 66 Pac. 255; Fish v. McCarthy, 96 Cal. 484, 31 Am. St. Rep. 237, 31 Pac. 529; Chapplus v. Blankman, 128 Cal. 362, 68 Pac. 925. An executor, not authorized by the will, can not pay a mortgage indebtedness on property conveyed by the testator to another.—Estate of Wells, 7 Cal. App. 515, 94 Pac. 856, 858. An executor or administrator has no power to sign a petition for the opening of a street fronting the property of the estate he represents, unless authorized by the law under which he is acting.—Kahn v. Board of Supervisors, 79 Cal. 388, 398, 21 Pac. 849. An executor or administrator can not, where the estate is insolvent, retain money thereof for a debt due to himself.—De la Guerra v. Packard, 17 Cal. 182, 192. An executor can not, in any case, litigate the claim of one legatee as against the others at the expense of the estate.—Estate of Marrey, 65 Cal. 287, 3 Pac. 896. An executor or administrator has no general authority to borrow capital or funds with which to carry on or complete a contract made by the decedent.—Exchange Nat. Bank v. Betts's Estate, 103 Kan. 807, 176 Pac. 660. Where a testator entered into a contract to convey certain lots, but died before payment in full was made, no claim for money against the estate arose, in favor of the purchaser, out of the action of the executor in failing and refusing to make a deed upon the purchaser's offer to pay the amount still due upon his contract; the purchaser should have obtained a decree of conveyance from the probate court; nothing in the statute authorized the executor to make a deed in the absence of an order of the probate court directing him to do so.—Blake v. Lemp, 32 Ida. 158, 179 Pac. 737; Couglin v. Lemp, 32 Ida. 164, 180 Pac. 990. An executor or administrator has no right to speculate with or use the funds of an estate in his own business; if he does, he and his bondsmen are answerable for any loss occurring, unless such use is made with the consent of or by agreement with those entitled to the estate; and, where he relies upon such consent as a defense, the burden of proof is upon him to show that he acted in good faith by fully and fairly representing the circumstances and communicating all the facts attending the risk to such funds, and of the proposed investment; in no other way can he be protected in deviating from the line of his fiduciary duty.—In re Spann, 51 Okla. 309, 152 Pac. 68. An executor or administrator has no power to consent that a decree be made reforming a deed executed by his decedent, and the title to the property is not affected by his so consenting.—Fickes v. Baker, 36 Cal. App. 129, 171 Pac. 819. The executor or administrator can not bind the estate by a new contract, and the only effect of such, made by him for the completion of a building in progress as the result of a contract made by his decedent, is that he is bound personally.—Exchange Nat. Bank v. Betts's Estate, 103 Kan. 807, 176 Pac. 660.

(11) Same. Can not sell to wife.—The administrator of an estate can not legally sell the same to his wife.—Chastain v. Pender, 52 Okla. 133, 135, 152 Pac. 833. The statutes of Oklahoma prohibit the administrator of an estate from selling the same to his wife even though she is one of the heirs to the estate.—Chastain v. Pender, 52 Okla. 133, 138, 152 Pac. 833. A purchase of real estate by the wife of an administrator, at the administrator's sale, is held to be void as against the heirs of the estate; but such a deed may be made effective, as against the heirs, by ratification, estoppel, or limitation; and, where this occurs, the title does not pass by virtue of the original transaction, but passes by virtue of the ratification, or is founded on estoppel, or is set at rest by the lapse of time.—Chastain v. Pender, 52 Okla. 133, 139, 152 Pac. 833. If, on the setting aside of a purchase by the wife of an administrator of the property of the estate at administrator's sale, it is shown that she and the administrator acted in good faith in making the purchase, and took no unfair advantage therein, that the transaction was free from fraud, and that the proceeds of the sale have been expended in defraying the necessary expenses of administration, or in paying the legal and enforceable indebtedness of the estate, then she should have the purchase money refunded to her.—Chastain v. Pender, 52 Okla. 133, 141, 152 Pac. 833.

(12) With respect to leases and mortgages.—In Colorado, the lands of an intestate descend to the heirs, and not to the administrator. The title vests immediately in the heirs; and the administrator has no control over, or right, title, or interest in, the lands, except the power to harvest growing crops, and to lease, mortgage, or sell in certain contingencies, and under proper order of the court having probate jurisdiction. By special statute, he is empowered to take possession of, sue for, and recover the rents of real property belonging to the estate, but this statute does not give any further power or authority over, or in connection with, the realty, other than the receipt and collection of the rents.—It does not direct nor authorize the administrator to take possession of the lands or tenements. It does not empower him to execute a lease. Neither can the administrator, by virtue of any authority given him in such statute terminate an existing lease, of his own volition.—Rupp v. Rupp, 11 Colo. App. 36, 52 Pac. 290, 291. The administrator can not, without being duly authorized by the probate court, assign to the principal creditor, a mortgage given to the deceased in his lifetime to indemnify

the latter as surety.—Pierce v. Batten, 3 Kan. App. 396, 42 Pac. 924. An estate can not be estopped from pleading the illegality of a mortgage executed thereon by a prior administrator, unless it is shown that the estate was actually the recipient of the money obtained by the administrator.—Wallace v. Grant, 27 Wash. 170, 67 Pac. 578, 580. Where an administrator had given a mortgage to his intestate on certain lots, the administrator has no power to cancel or release, from the lien of the mortgage due to the estate, a portion of the property covered by such mortgage for the purpose of enabling him individually to borrow money thereon. His attempt to do so constitutes a fraud upon the estate, particularly where he does not use the money to make payment of the debt owing by him to the estate.—Eastham v. Landon, 17 Wash. 48, 48 Pac. 729, 740. An administrator receiving, as assets of the estate of his decedent, a promissory note secured by mortgage, and having obtained a judgment on the note, and a decree of foreclosure, may bid in the land at the foreclosure sale, as administrator, in satisfaction of the indebtedness, wholly or in part, and the sheriff's deed will pass the title to him as administrator.—Briggs v. Chicago, etc., R. R. Co., 56 Kan. 526, 43 Pac. 1131.

(13) **Can not litigate what claims.**—Executors and administrators can not litigate the claims of one heir against those of another.—Goldtree v. Thompson, 83 Cal. 420, 422, 23 Pac. 383; Roach v. Coffey, 73 Cal. 281, 14 Pac. 840. An executrix can not litigate the claims of one set of legatees against the others at the expense of the estate, where she has no interest, in her representative capacity, in the matters involved.—Estate of Murphy, 145 Cal. 464, 78 Pac. 960, 961.

(14) **In judicial proceedings.**—An action for divorce is a purely personal action, and where the plaintiff obtained a decree, but died afterwards, his executor has no power to consent to the setting aside of the decree.—Dwyer v. Nolan, 40 Wash. 459, 111 Am. St. Rep. 919, 5 Ann. Cas. 890, 1 L. R. A. (N. S.) 551, 82 Pac. 746, 747. Where judgment was recovered on a note against the estator, who was not in pari delicto with the assignees of the note, his executors are not precluded from denying the validity of the judgment thereon as a claim against his estate.—McColgan v. Muirland, 2 Cal. App. 6, 9, 82 Pac. 1113.

9. Joint administrators and co-executors.

(1) **In general.**—Joint administrators stand on the same footing, and are invested with the same authority, in respect to the administration of the estate, as co-executors, and, like them, are regarded in law as one person, and consequently the acts of one of them, in respect to.the administration, are deemed to be the acts of all, inasmuch as they have a joint and entire authority over the whole property.—Willis v. Farley, 24 Cal. 490, 501. Each is chargeable with the full amount of the assets which may come into his hands, and is entitled to be credited with all disbursements legally made on behalf

of the estate. Each may keep a separate account, and present the same for final settlement. They are entitled to share and share alike only where their liabilities and services have been equal.—Hope v. Jones, 24 Cal. 89. 93. If one of two executors is absent from the state, the other can administer.—Wheeler v. Bolton, 54 Cal. 302. Where it appears from various paragraphs of the will that the intention of the testatrix was simply to make a designated person the attorney and counselor of the executrix, and not to commit to him the administration of the estate, he is not entitled to be appointed as co-executor with the executrix.—Estate of Ogier, 101 Cal. 381, 387, 40 Am. St. Rep. 61, 35 Pac. 900.

(2) **Obligations and liability. Bond.**—The obligations of co-executors arise from their contract, and are several. Although one may, in some cases, make himself liable by placing the other in a position to do wrong, or by aiding him in his acts of misfeasance, the liability is still the several liability of each. And this is so, even if it be conceded that the devisees and legatees may, under some circumstances, claim both to be liable. If an executor stands by and sees a breach of truth committed, or about to be committed, by a co-executor, and does nothing to protect the estate, or to call the defaulting executor to account, he is liable. When an executor is guilty of neglect with reference to assets in the possession of his co-executor, he is not made liable upon the theory that the assets are in the possession of both, which in fact they are not, but for his neglect to deliver them to his co-executor without good cause, or in not seeing to it that they were taken out of the possession of the co-executor, or were not by him misapplied or lost.—Estate of Sanderson, 74 Cal. 199, 211, 213, 15 Pac. 753. The extent of the liability of an executor for the acts of his co-executor will depend very much on the circumstances of each case.—Estate of Sanderson, 74 Cal. 199, 212, 15 Pac. 753. The fact that the testator misplaced his confidence in one executor does not operate to the prejudice of the other.—Estate of Sanderson, 74 Cal. 199, 212, 15 Pac. 753. If one executor merely permits his co-executor to take possession of assets without going further, and does not concur in any misapplication of them, he does not render himself answerable for the receipt of his co-executor.—Estate of Sanderson, 74 Cal. 199, 212, 15 Pac. 753. When two or more persons are appointed executors or administrators, the court must require a separate bond from each of them; and each is chargeable in his account with the whole of the estate which may come into his hands. But when executors give a joint and several bond, the effect is to make them jointly and severally liable on such bond for the misconduct of each.—Estate of Sanderson, 74 Cal. 199, 213, 15 Pac. 753.

(3) **Same. Foundation of liability.**—A wrongful act or omitted duty lies at the foundation of an executor's liability. He has the right to assume, in all cases, that his co-executor is an hones' man. The testator, by his appointment, recommended him as such, and the fact

that he is insolvent should create no suspicion upon which to base a
want of confidence. An honest executor who is poor is as worthy
of confidence and trust as an honest executor who is rich. But where
the estate, or part of it, has been lost through the failure of the executors to perform some duty required of them by the trust, such as to
collect debts before the statute of limitations has barred an action
thereon to preserve the estate, to prevent waste, etc., they are liable
jointly and severally.—Estate of Osborn, 87 Cal. 1, 5, 11 L. R. A. 264
25 Pac. 157. An executor who has money of the estate in his hands,
and turns it over to his co-executor, or who actively assists to put it
into the hands of his co-executor, is generally answerable for any misapplication of it by the latter. There are exceptions to this general
rule; but to avoid liability in such cases, it must appear that good
reasons existed for turning over the money to the co-executor, and
that, in allowing him to keep, control, and disburse it, he acted in
good faith, without notice of any purpose to misapply it, and with
reasonable prudence and discretion.—Estate of Osborn, 87 Cal. 1, 4
11 L. R. A. 264, 25 Pac. 157. When an executor discovers that there
is a shortage in the estate, that his co-executor is not doing right,
and is in failing circumstances, it is his duty to the beneficiaries and
to himself to report the facts to the court, and to procure a settlement
of the estate. This would determine the liability of each, and put all
concerned upon their guard. An executor must be held answerable
when it is apparent that only his own neglect and mistaken idea as
to his liability have occasioned loss.—Estate of Osborn, 87 Cal. 1, 10,
11 L. R. A. 264, 25 Pac. 157. Each co-executor is equally entitled to
the possession of the estate.—Abila v. Burnett, 33 Cal. 658, 667. An
executor who allows his co-executor to handle the money of the estate,
because such co-executor is a lawyer, and knows more about the business, is still jointly and severally answerable with him to the heirs,
if, through his inexcusable neglect, he permits such co-executor to lose
the estate.—Hewlett v. Beede, 2 Cal. App. 561, 83 Pac. 1086, 1087. A co-
executor is properly charged with interest upon a sum which he ap-
propriates as his commissions prior to the final settlement of his
estate.—Estate of Carter, 132 Cal. 113, 114, 64 Pac. 123.

REFERENCES.

Co-executors are considered as one person.—See note 9 L. R. A. 223.
227.

10. Foreign and ancillary administration.

(1) Foreign administration.—It is the duty of a domiciliary executor to gather in and account for the foreign assets of his testator, so
far as he is able to do so.—Estate of Ortiz, 86 Cal. 306, 315, 21 Am. St.
Rep. 44, 24 Pac. 1034. When a court in a foreign jurisdiction has
found, upon the evidence before it, that it has jurisdiction of an estate
and of its settlement, and authority to issue letters of administration therein, this finding necessarily implies that the decedent was

a resident of that place, if that fact was essential to give such jurisdiction to that court.—Collins v. Maude, 144 Cal. 289, 293, 77 Pac.
945. If a foreign executor desires to maintain an action in the courts
of California, his first step is to obtain letters of administration from
the court in that state. He can not maintain an action for a claim
due the testator, without first having obtained ancillary letters testamentary or of administration.—Lewis v. Adams (Cal.), 8 Pac. 619,
620; but a foreign administrator or executor has a right to sue personally, in that state, on a judgment by him recovered as executor
or administrator out of the state.—Lewis v. Adams, 70 Cal. 403, 408,
59 Am. Rep. 423, 11 Pac. 833. And when it is not necessary for a
plaintiff to sue as executor or administrator, all averments in his
complaint in relation to his official capacity may be rejected. Hence
if the plaintiff, who has recovered a judgment as administrator in
one jurisdiction, brings an action on the judgment in another, and
names himself as administrator in the last action, the averment may
be disregarded.—Lewis v. Adams, 70 Cal. 403, 412, 59 Am. Rep. 423,
11 Pac. 833. So an administrator who has, within the jurisdiction
of his appointment, obtained a judgment against a debtor of a foreign
state, or has reduced the personal property of the estate to possession,
so as to acquire the legal title thereto, and it is wrongfully taken
from him and carried to a foreign state, he may, in such foreign
state, maintain an action, not officially, but in his individual capacity,
upon such judgment, or to recover such personal property so wrongfully taken from him.—McCully v. Cooper, 114 Cal. 258, 261, 55 Am.
St. Rep. 66, 35 L. R. A. 492, 46 Pac. 82. If there are no debts owing
by the estate in the jurisdiction where the foreign debtor resides, and
no ancillary administration has been granted there, the principal administrator may, in such foreign state, receive a voluntary payment
from the debtor, which will be a good acquittance to him, even if
an ancillary administrator should be subsequently appointed.—McCully
v. Cooper, 114 Cal. 258, 261, 55 Am. St. Rep. 66, 35 L. R. A. 492, 46
Pac. 82. A certificate of deposit is a negotiable security, and to that
extent is on the same footing as promissory notes; and where a domiciliary administrator, appointed in the state of Indiana, is temporarily
within the jurisdiction of the courts of California, with the evidence
of a simple contract debt, which contract debt is due and owing in
California, the California administratrix may recover from such domiciliary administrator a certificate of deposit which is the evidence of
such debt.—McCully v. Cooper, 114 Cal. 258, 260, 55 Am. St. Rep. 66,
35 L. R. A. 492, 46 Pac. 82.

REFERENCES.

Foreign letters of administration.—See note 9 L. R. A. 244-251. Power
and duty of administrators or executors as to property outside of the
state.—See note 45 Am. St. Rep. 664-674.

(2) Same. Ancillary administration.—The authority of an executor or administrator does not extend beyond the jurisdiction of the

state or government under which the representative is invested with authority; and if there be assets in another state than that in which the principal letters are granted, an administration may be obtained there, and such administration will be regarded as ancillary to the administration of the domicile.—McCully v. Cooper, 114 Cal. 258, 261, 55 Am. St. Rep. 66, 35 L. R. A. 492, 46 Pac. 82. An ancillary administration is recognized by the laws of California.—Estate of Apple, 66 Cal. 432, 435, 6 Pac. 7; McCully v. Cooper, 114 Cal. 258, 55 Am. St. Rep. 66, 35 L. R. A. 492, 46 Pac. 82. Ancillary administration is called such to distinguish it from the administration of the last residence of the deceased, but they are wholly independent of each other. The reason why local administration is provided for is for the protection of local creditors and claimants, and no state should allow property to be taken from its borders until debts to its own citizens have been satisfied. No country will allow a foreign court to exercise its jurisdiction within its borders. For most purposes, a chose in action adheres to the person of the owner, but for the purposes of founding administration, this is not true. For such purpose, the situs is where the debtor resides. The power of a domiciliary executor to assign personal property, which has its situs in another jurisdiction, results from the common-law rule that such assets descend to the personal representative, and not to the heir. That doctrine does not prevail in California. Hence an executor outside of that state has no power, as against an administrator with the will annexed, appointed in the ancillary administration of his property situated in that state, to sell and assign certificates of stock in a national bank located in that state. —Murphy v. Crouse, 135 Cal. 14, 18, 19, 87 Am. St. Rep. 90, 66 Pac. 971. The Kansas statute authorizing foreign executors and administrators with the will annexed to convey real estate in pursuance of power contained in the will is constitutional and valid; and such statute is applicable to all wills which were executed and proved in another state or territory prior to its passage, as well as to those executed and proved after its passage.—Calloway v. Cooley, 50 Kan. 743, 32 Pac. 373. When an executrix is appointed in another state, on the estate of a person dying outside of the state of Kansas, and no executor, executrix, or administrator thereon is appointed in the state of Kansas, the foreign executrix may file an authenticated copy of her appointment in the probate court of any county in the state of Kansas in which there is real estate of the deceased, and then may be authorized, under an order of the court, to sell the real estate for the payment of debts of the decedent and the charges of administration, in the manner and on the terms and conditions prescribed by the statute of Kansas.— Higgins v. Reed, 48 Kan. 272, 29 Pac. 389. Where there is a principal administration in one state and an ancillary administration in another, a creditor may prove his claim in either jurisdiction; the property of a decedent may be likened to a trust fund to be devoted to the payment of his debts wherever they exist; while local creditors are protected, foreign creditors are not to be defrauded; debts must be paid before the assets can be distributed to the heirs, legatees, and devisees, without regard to the place of residence of the creditors; justice requires that creditors should be paid when they have duly established their claims, whether that is done in the principal or in the ancillary administration; they will be paid when established in the ancillary administration, if assets are found within its jurisdiction; if sufficient assets for the payment of debts are not found under the control of the principal administration, and there is under the control of the ancillary administration money assets in excess of the debts proved therein, justice would forbid that such administration should disregard the demands of right, and distribute the assets to the heirs; but as it has not before it the claims of all the creditors, some having been established in the principal administration proceedings, justice demands that the ancillary administration, in response to the demands of comity, transmit the money assets to the principal administrator.— Dow v. Lillie, 26 N. D. 512, L. R. A. 1915D, 754, 144 N. W. 1082. Everything consistent with the probate record of the superior court which would have warranted it in appointing an ancillary administrator will be presumed to have been found and acted upon by the court.— Lincoln Trust Co. of New York v. Gaddis, etc., Co., 15 Ariz. 372, Ann. Cas. 1915D, 1091, 139 Pac. 461. Under section 6 of article 6 of the constitution of Arizona, providing that the superior court shall have original jurisdiction in all matters of probate, and par. 1598, Revised Statutes of Arizona of 1901, providing that wills must be proved and letters testamentary or of administration granted in the county in which any part of the estate may be, the decedent having died out of the state and not resident thereof at the time of his death, the action of the superior court in appointing a foreign corporation, conceding it to be invalid, was ancillary administrator of property in the state of a non-resident decedent dying without the state can not be attacked in a suit by the administrator to recover property of the decedent in the state.—Lincoln Trust Co. of New York v. Gaddis, etc., Co., 15 Ariz. 372, Ann. Cas. 1915D, 1091, 139 Pac. 461. Although the executor or administrator of the domicile can not maintain a suit in another state to recover personal property or to collect a debt due the estate, yet he may take possession of such property peaceably without suit, or collect a debt if voluntarily paid; and, if there is no opposing administration in the state where the property was situated, its courts will recognize his title as rightful, and protect it as fully as if he had taken out letters of administration there; furthermore, the voluntary payment of a debt by the debtor, under such circumstances, would be good, and constitute a defense to a suit by an ancillary administrator subsequently appointed.—Union Trust Co. v. Pacific T. & T. Co., 31 Cal. App. 64, 159 Pac. 820. In the absence of local ancillary administration, the foreign administrator of a decedent is entitled to a transfer of the stock, of a non-resident decedent, in a California corporation, without taking out letters here; and the corporation can successfully defend the surrender of the stock under such circumstances.—Union Trust Co. v. Pacific T. & T. Co., 31 Cal. App. 64, 159 Pac. 820. Courts have jurisdiction to hold assets in ancillary administration, subject to claims proved in such ancillary administration, and to distribute the surplus to legatees and distributees within such administration according to their respective interests in the surplus.—In re Campbell's Estate (Utah), 173 Pac. 688. Where the executor, in domiciliary administration, admits receipts by him of profits of the estate, arising out of an unauthorized proceeding, and betrays an intention that a legatee, residing in the state where letters in ancillary administration have issued, shall not participate in these profits, such legatee should be paid, from the assets of the ancillary administration, a sum equal to his just portion of such profits with interest.—In re Campbell's Estate (Utah), 173 Pac. 688. There is no distinction between creditors, with claims proved in ancillary administration, and legatees and heirs, so far as concerns the rights to be paid out of assets under such administration.—In re Campbell's Estate (Utah), 173 Pac. 688. The appointment of an administrator by order of a court of another state, is, on becoming final, of controlling force in this state, and the acts done under the appointment can not be impeached in a court of this state in a case where the jurisdiction of the appointing court is not brought into question.—Chicago, R. I. & P. R. Co. v. Forrester (Okla.), 177 Pac. 598. If a resident of another state dies there, intestate, owning certificates of deposit issued by a bank in this state, and an administrator is appointed by a probate of such other state, who brings suit in this state against the bank to recover the indebtedness represented by the certificates, and an administrator, appointed by the probate court in this state, intervenes, claiming the right to recover the debt, the administration here is ancillary to the principal administration at the domicile of the deceased, and it is error to render judgment in favor of the ancillary administrator.—Ames v. Citizens' Nat. Bank (Kan.), 181 Pac. 564. If a person dies testate, leaving personalty in another state and realty in this state, administration here must be confined to the realty.—Chandler v. Probate Court, 26 Ida. 173, 180, 141 Pac. 635. It is the spirit and intent of the law, and the proper object and policy of the state courts, in proceedings in ancillary administration of an estate, to take care of the just demands and credits of citizens of the state before transferring money to other states.—In re Campbell's Estate (Utah), 173 Pac. 688.

REFERENCES.

Right of domiciliary executors and administrators or their nominees to ancillary letters.—See note 48 L. R. A. (N. S.) 858. Ancillary letters of administration may be granted when.—See notes 9 L. R. A. 218, 246. Effect of ancillary appointment after commencement of action by foreign executor or administrator.—See note 4 L. R. A. (N. S.) 657, 658.

II. ACTIONS BY EXECUTORS OR ADMINISTRATORS.

1. In general.—If a decedent, in his lifetime, with full knowledge of his rights, transfers personal property to another for an adequate consideration, which he received, his administrator and heirs are bound by his act and can not question the validity of the agreement.—Jones v. Tallant, 90 Cal. 386, 389, 27 Pac. 305. An administrator may maintain an action against the executors of a former administrator to recover moneys received by the testator of the defendant estate, while acting as such former administrator, and for which moneys no accounting had ever been made.—Curran v. Kennedy, 89 Cal. 98, 99, 26 Pac. 64. A widow, who is also executrix, can not, as claimant, sue herself in her representative capacity to recover money paid for funeral expenses of decedent.—Phillips v. Phillips, 18 Mont. 305, 45 Pac. 221. An administrator, who has been appointed under a void order, can not recover fees from the estate.—Slate v. Henkle, 45 Or. 430, 78 Pac. 325, 326. An estate of a decedent would not be entitled to recover the possession of real property on the ground that a sale thereof was made without the confirmation of the court, without returning, or offering to return to the purchaser, the purchase money, after an accounting which would involve the purchase price.—Richards v. Richards, 36 Cal. Dec. 369, 380 (Nov. 4, 1908). If an executor, under a mistake of law, makes a payment of money to a beneficiary under a will, he can not recover the same.—Scott v. Ford, 52 Or. 288, 97 Pac. 99, 100, 101. In an action of assumpsit by an administrator, the defendant can not contest the plaintiff's appointment, or collaterally question its validity. —Magoon v. Ami, 8 Haw. 191, 195. The representative capacity of an executor or administrator and his legal authority to represent the estate for which he is suing goes to the capacity of the plaintiff to maintain the action, rather than to the sufficiency of the facts to constitute a cause of action.—Anthes v. Anthes, 21 Ida. 305, 121 Pac. 534. If an administrator sues to subject equitable interests in land to the claims of creditors, he is not entitled to declare a lien on the land for the sum he intends to advance to the estate to pay the purchase price of the land; equitable liens are not to be declared upon potential events; the court has no power to create a lien dependent upon a contingency that may never arise; the plaintiff's remedy is in the administration proceeding, where the court may, by appropriate order, sanction any advances made by the administrator, and at the same time protect the heirs and others interested in the estate.—Plath v. Mullins, 94 Wash. 154, 156, 161 Pac. 1187. On the death of a ward, an action against the guardian for an accounting must be brought by the ward's representative and not by his heirs.—Miller v. Ash, 156 Cal. 544, 105 Pac. 600. Where, without prior authority being given by the court, an executor or administrator compromises with a debtor of the estate, and the court refuses to approve the compromise, after being made, it is proper for such executor or administrator to bring suit for the excess of the debt over the amount he accepted.—Taylor v. Sanson, 24

Cal. App. 515, 141 Pac. 1060. If an election bet is delivered to a stakeholder, with the express understanding that the widow of the bettor is to be given the money in case he dies before the election, and the bettor does so die and the widow is given the money, the administrator can not recover it from her, inasmuch as, under the law making betting criminal, the bettor, had he not died, could not have recovered it from the stakeholder.—Kelley v. Dirks (S. D.), 167 N: W. 724. Where an unmarried man died as the result of the wrongfull act of some other person, and there has been no administration of his estate, his father, if he has a father living, is the proper plaintiff in an action to recover for the death.—Whitehead Coal Min. Co. v. Pinkston (Okla.), 175 Pac. 364, 366. Under the statute of Oregon, an administratrix, alleging that she is in possession of certain real property belonging to the estate, can not commence a suit against a defendant who claims title to such real property by virtue of a forged deed, purporting to have been executed by the decedent in his lifetime, without leave of the county court upon a proper petition for that purpose.—Butts v. Purdy, 63 Or. 150, 169, 125 Pac. 313, 127 Pac. 25.

The cross-complaint in an action by the decedent's administrator to quiet title, not being a party to the probate proceeding involved, could not be bound thereby. Giving to the order of plaintiff's appointment as administrator the broadest scope possible under the law, it could only be conclusive between parties and their privies in respect of the matters directly adjudged; and those matters could only be those things necessary and essential in conferring jurisdiction and establishing the authority of the court to make the order.—Layne v. Johnson, 19 Cal. App. 95, 124 Pac. 860.

REFERENCES.

Executor or administrator as real party in interest by whom action must be brought.—See note 64 L. R. A. 611. Right of personal representative to bring suit in forma pauperis.—See note 1 Am. & Eng. Ann. Cas. 805. Collateral attack on the right of one acting as executor or administrator.—See note 81 Am. St. 535. Right of domiciliary administrator to sue on judgment in another state.—See note 39 L. R. A. (N. S.) 430.

2. **Abatement. Discontinuance. Survival.**—The statute of Colorado, which extends the time for bringing actions in favor of executors and administrators upon the happening of certain contingencies, is not applicable to a case brought by decedent in his lifetime, and is not abated nor discontinued by his death, or for any other reason enumerated in the statute.—Barlow v. Hitzler, 40 Colo. 109, 90 Pac. 90, 92. Under the common law a cause of action for a wrong does not survive the death of the wrongdoer, and this rule remains unimpaired by the laws of this state.—Clark v. Goodwin, 170 Cal. 527, L. R. A. 1916A, 1142, 150 Pac. 357. Section 385 of the Code of Civil Procedure of California, which provides that an action or proceeding does not abate by the

death of a party if the cause of action survive, refers only to actions or proceedings instituted prior to the death of a party.—Clark v. Goodwin, 170 Cal. 527, L. R. A. 1916A, 1142, 150 Pac. 357. The statute providing when an action shall not abate by reason of certain disabilities, does not apply where the disability occurs after appeal.—Service & Wright Lumber Co. v. Sumpter Valley Ry. Co., 81 Or. 32, 149 Pac. 531, 152 Pac. 262, 158 Pac. 175. "Personal representatives" in the statute providing when an action shall not abate, mean executors and administrators; but the words do not include those who take as sole residuary legatees. —Murphy v. Tillson, 64 Or. 558, 562, 130 Pac. 637.

3. **Parties.**—As the estate is entire, where more than one executor is appointed, they are considered in law as one person, and all of them must join as plaintiffs in bringing an action for an accounting in behalf of the estate; but where no objection was made on account of the non-joinder of two of the executors, and, as they were made defendants in the action in their representative capacity, and remained in the court throughout the proceeding while the accounting was being made, the failure to name them as plaintiffs can not be regarded as a fatal objection.—Insley v. Shire, 54 Kan. 793, 45 Am. St. Rep. 308, 39 Pac. 713. An executrix of a deceased person is the proper party to sue on a fire insurance policy issued on the property of deceased, where the death occurred before the loss; and an allegation that she is the duly qualified and acting executrix is sufficient, without alleging the probate of the will.—German Insurance, etc., Co. v. Wright, 6 Kan. App. 611, 49 Pac. 704. If an administratrix, as an individual, claims adversely to the estate she represents, she can not properly represent the estate in an action relating to property so claimed, and in any such action it is necessary to make all creditors, as well as all heirs, parties.—Byrne v. Byrne, 94 Cal. 576, 581, 29 Pac. 1115, 13 Pac. 196. An action may be maintained by the plaintiff, both in his individual capacity and in his representative capacity, where he has a personal interest in securing the cancellation of a note made by him, and is therefore entitled to an application, on the original debt and interest thereon, of all payments made by him, and where he has, as the executor of another, a like interest in the application of payments made by such other person; and he is a proper party to such suit.— Epping v. Washington Nat. Bldg. Assoc., 44 Or. 116, 74 Pac. 923. In an action by an administrator of a co-surety to recover from the principal a sum paid by such administrator in discharge of the debt, the fact that there was another co-surety does not make the latter's estate a necessary party to the action.—Townsend v. Sullivan, 3 Cal. App. 115, 119, 84 Pac. 435. A bill in equity, by an administrator, to foreclose an equitable interest in lands sold but not conveyed by his intestate, is not objectionable, for nonjoinder of heirs, after answer, if the administrator alleges his readiness to furnish a good deed which would have to be executed by the heirs.—Wollenberg v. Rose, 41 Or. 314, 68 Pac. 804, 805. The surviving husband of a woman, the administrator of

whom sues to have deeds, one executed jointly by herself and husband and the other executed by the grantee of the deed, set aside on the ground that the former deed was induced by undue influence, is a proper and necessary, but not indispensable party to the suit.—Grigsby v. Miller (Or.), 231 Fed. 521, 523, 524.

4. By ancillary administrators.—An ancillary administrator may maintain an action against a foreign domiciliary administrator, who is temporarily in this jurisdiction, to recover possession of a certificate of deposit belonging to the estate, issued by an insolvent bank in this state, which the receiver of the bank had refused to allow.— McCully v. Cooper, 114 Cal. 258, 263, 55 Am. St. Rep. 66, 35 L. R. A. 492, 46 Pac. 82. See, also, Murphy v. Cross, 135 Cal. 14, 19, 87 Am. St. Rep. 90, 66 Pac. 971.

5. By foreign executors.—A foreign executor, who purchased property in his own name as trustee for the estate of which he is an executor, may maintain an action as trustee in respect to such property. —Doe v. Tenino Coal, etc., Co., 43 Wash. 523, 86 Pac. 938, 939. Under the law of Kansas, a foreign executor may sue to foreclose a mortgage in favor of his testator.—Greenwalt v. Bastian, 10 Kan. App. 101, 61 Pac. 513. Foreign executors, to whom, as trustees, a note and mortgage were given for assets of the estate received by the mortgagor, may maintain an action to foreclose the mortgage, without taking out letters testamentary in the state where the land is situated.—Fox v. Tay, 89 Cal. 339, 350, 23 Am. St. Rep. 474, 24 Pac. 855, 26 Pac. 897. A corporation which has been regularly appointed an administrator in another state may bring an action as administrator in this state.—Germantown Trust Co. v. Whitney, 19 S. D. 108, 102 N. W. 304. An assignee of foreign executors may sue on a contract by deceased, if it appears that such executors had authority to make the assignment.—Camp v. Simon, 23 Utah 56, 63 Pac. 332, 335. An action may be maintained by an executor in his individual capacity on a judgment recovered by him in a foreign jurisdiction, in his representative capacity.—Lewis v. Adams, 70 Cal. 403, 411, 59 Am. Rep. 423, 11 Pac. 833. He may also, in Arizona, maintain such an action in his representative capacity.—Arizona Cattle Co. v. Huber, 4 Ariz. 69, 33 Pac. 555. A foreign administrator can not maintain an action for damages in wrongfully causing the death of the deceased, if the law of the state where he was appointed does not authorize such action by him. The powers of the administrator are limited by the laws of the state of his appointment, and can not be changed or enlarged by the laws of another state.—Limekiller v. Hannibal, etc., R. R. Co., 33 Kan. 83, 52 Am. Rep. 523, 5 Pac. 401, 404, 405. An administrator appointed in one state, not being entitled to the possession of land claimed by his decedent in another state, can not sue to redeem said land from a mortgage by setting off waste committed by the mortgagee in possession after the death of his intestate; nor to recover damages for trespasses committed by such mortgagee on said land after the death.—Price v. Ward, 25 Nev. 203, 46 L. R. A. 459, 58 Pac. 849. Where a resident of Illinois dies intestate in Colorado, leaving promissory notes secured by mortgage on land in Kansas, and general administration is had on his estate in Illinois, and administration is also had in Colorado as to property in that state, but no administration is had in Kansas, and the notes and Kansas mortgage come to the hands of the Colorado administratrix, she can not maintain suit thereon as administratrix in Kansas.—Moore v. Jordan, 36 Kan. 271, 59 Am. Rep. 550, 13 Pac. 337, 338. In the state of Washington it is held that if a foreign executor, together with his co-executor and the beneficiaries of the estate, sign a written agreement whereby such foreign executor purchases property in his own name for the benefit of the estate, such purchase has the effect of making him the trustee of an express trust, and that he may, as such trustee, but not as executor, maintain an action in that state concerning the property.—Doe v. Tenino Coal, etc., Co., 43 Wash. 533, 86 Pac. 938, 939. In an action by an executor appointed in a foreign state, all averments in the complaint in relation to the plaintiff's official capacity may be rejected.—Owen v. Frink, 24 Cal. 171; Lewis v. Adams, 70 Cal. 403, 411, 59 Am. Rep. 423, 11 Pac. 833; Biddle v. Wilkins, 1 Pet. (U. S.) 686, 7 L. Ed. 315. A foreign administrator has no authority to sue outside of the state where he receives his appointment, but the objection goes rather to his capacity to sue or maintain an action than to the sufficiency of the cause of action or the jurisdiction of the court.—Whitley v. Spokane & T. Bldg. Co., 23 Ida. 642, 132 Pac. 127. Under letters testamentary issued in another state an executor can not act as such in California, or maintain in court an opposition to a sale of, or otherwise assert as a litigant rights or interests in, the property of a decedent situated in that state. —Estate of Rawitzer, 175 Cal. 585, 166 Pac. 581. The courts of the state of Washington take no notice of foreign administration, and an executor or administrator, as such, can not sue or defend in the courts of that state.—In re Goss' Estate, 73 Wash. 330, 132 Pac. 409. An executor or administrator, under appointment in a sister state, may sue in the state of Colorado, only after filing an exemplification of his letters and bond, but, this being done a failure to set out a copy of the exemplification in the complaint is not demurrable, since the defect can be cured by a filing of the order of appointment, or a copy thereof, at any time before the hearing.—Cordingly v. Kennedy (Colo.), 239 Fed. 645, 649, 152 C. C. A. 479.

REFERENCES.

Assignee of executor or administrator may sue in foreign courts when.—See note 88 Am. Dec. 310, 311. Incapacity of foreign executor or administrator to sue.—See notes 2 L. R. A. 828, 5 L. R. A. 541-543, 9 L. R. A. 244-245.

the estate.—Cunningham v. Ashley, 45 Cal. 485, 493. The administrator is in privity with and represents both heirs and creditors, and a judgment in ejectment recovered by or against an administrator is an estoppel in favor of or against the heirs and those claiming under them.—Cunningham v. Ashley, 45 Cal. 485, 493; McLeran v. Benton, 73 Cal. 329, 342, 2 Am. St. Rep. 814, 14 Pac. 879; Spotts v. Hanley, 85 Cal. 155, 167, 24 Pac. 738. An administrator may maintain an action upon a contract made after the death of the intestate, to which he was not, as such administrator, a party, and of which he had no knowledge at the time it was made, where such contract was made for the benefit of the creditors of the estate. The administrator is the agent of the creditors in marshaling the assets of the estate, and accumulating funds to pay their claims, and .he is, as well, the legal representative of the estate.—Stewart v. Rogers, 71 Kan. 53, 80 Pac. 58, 60.

7. By a co-executor.—A special administrator, under the California statute, may maintain an action to recover what he claims to be property of the estate from the defendant, who asserts that such property belongs to him in his individual capacity and that it is not an asset of the estate. If the alleged cause of action is well grounded, and the property in question ought to be decreed to be the property of the estate, the defendant can not avoid a trial of the merits and hold the property upon the ground that, because he is one of the executors, he can not be sued. The statute providing that one executor can not maintain an action against his co-executor for exclusive possession of property of the estate, etc., does not apply to an action where the defendant is sued in his individual capacity, and this phase of the case is not changed by the fact that the defendant has become an executor.—Stohr v. Stohr, 148 Cal. 180, 82 Pac. 777, 778. An executor can not sue his co-executor on a promissory note given by the latter to the former for money due to the estate.—Taylor v. Minton, 45 Kan. 17, 25 Pac. 222.

8. Intervention.—Executors have a right to intervene in an action brought by a client against her attorneys to set aside an assignment of her interest in the estate of her father upon a contest of his will.—Moran v. Simpson (N. D.), 173 N. W. 769.

9. Substitution. Survival and revival of action.—If an executrix dies and administrators are appointed, who commence an action on a note belonging to the estate, they are the "successors in interest" of the executrix, and may be substituted in her place.—Bunker v. Taylor, 13 S. D. 433, 83 N. W. 555, 557. If an executrix dies, and administrators are substituted, it is correct practice to serve a summons showing the death of the original plaintiff, and the substitution of the administrators as plaintiffs.—Bunker v. Taylor, 13 S. D. 433, 83 N. W. 555, 559. If an action be brought by an administratrix, and another be substituted in her place pending a suit, in the absence of a showing

to the contrary it will be assumed that the substitution was properly made; and an allegation that plaintiff is a stockholder in a designated company is a sufficient allegation that the estate owned stock therein.—Jones v. Pearl Mining Co., 20 Colo. 417, 38 Pac. 700, 702. If a party dies pending his appeal from a judgment against him, and his administrator is substituted as appellant, an affirmance of the judgment makes it a judgment against the administrator, and establishes the judgment as a claim against the estate, which should be paid before distribution.—Green v. Taney, 16 Colo. 398, 27 Pac. 249, 250. Where a judgment has been entered against a party after his death, which is not void on its face, his administrator, subsequently appointed, should procure it to be set aside before applying for mandamus to compel the court to substitute him in the action in place of deceased.—Elliott v. Patterson, 65 Cal. 109, 110, 3 Pac. 493. An action brought by a land-owner in his lifetime, against a railroad company, for damages caused by the company in taking his land, should, after plaintiff's death, be revived in the name of his administrator.—Kansas City, etc., R. R. Co. v. Menager, 59 Kan. 687, 54 Pac. 1043, 1045. Where a plaintiff sues upon a note, having the legal title thereto, but no beneficial interest therein, and upon the death of the real owner executes an assignment of the cause of action to his legatee, and thereafter such plaintiff dies, and the action is revived and prosecuted to judgment in the name of his administrator, no revivor being had in the name of his assignee, the proceeds of such judgment, when collected by the administrator, do not become a part of the assets of the estate, but are held by him in trust for such assignee.—Fischer (Wood) v. Sheidley, 78 Kan. 610, 97 Pac. 800. If an action is brought by a husband and wife, properly joined as plaintiffs, and the husband dies pending the suit, it is proper to substitute his administratrix as a plaintiff.—Gomez v. Scanlan, 2 Cal. App. 579, 580, 84 Pac. 850. Upon the death of a party to an action, the action is suspended until the substitution indicated by the statute is made.—Young's Estate, 59 Or. 348, 363, Ann. Cas. 1913B, 1310, 116 Pac. 95, 1060; and the court has no jurisdiction of the estate, or of its representatives, until the substitution is made and notice given to them.—Oregon Auto-Despatch v. Cadwell, 67 Or. 301, 303, 135 Pac. 880. A cause of suit that inured to a decedent before his death, such as the right to compel specific performance, arising upon a contract made by him, with his parents, for the purchase of land, survives in favor of his personal representatives; hence, the administrator is entitled to maintain suit thereon.—Zeuske v. Zeuske, 62 Or. 46, 51, 124 Pac. 203. If, pending an adverse suit over conflicting mining locations, in aid of an application for the patent in the land office, a defendant dies, there must be a revivor as against both the surviving defendant and other persons interested with him; the proceeding is not one to admit of revival in the name of the administrator.—Fox v. Mackay, 1 Alaska 329, 330. Where an administrator's motion to revive an action was granted, and the court thereafter sustained defendant's motion to vacate the order of revivor, and overruled the administrator's motion for a new trial on motion to vacate, then served notice of motion to revive the action, the vacation of the order was not a final determination of plaintiff's right to revive, and left the motion to revive pending.—Chicago, R. I. & P. Ry. Co. v. Forrester (Okla.), 177 Pac. 593, 597.

10. Pleading. In general.—A complaint by an administrator, containing no allegation respecting his representative character, but in the title of which words showing simply his official capacity are added directly to his name without the word "as," will be deemed a complaint by him in his individual capacity.—Burling v. Tompkins, 77 Cal. 257, 258, 19 Pac. 429. Executors in the state of Washington may sue without alleging that letters testamentary have been granted on a non-intervention will provided for by the statute.—Boyer v. Robinson, 26 Wash. 117, 66 Pac. 119, 120. Where a plaintiff dies pending suit, and the action is revived by an order in favor of his personal representative, the pleadings should be so amended as to show the legal capacity of the representative.—Central Branch U. P. Ry. Co. v. Andrews, 34 Kan. 563, 9 Pac. 213, 216. If the plaintiff sues as administrator, and proves the death of decedent, and issuance of letters of administration to himself, this, in the absence of any proof to the contrary, sufficiently establishes his representative capacity.—Sallazar v. Taylor, 18 Colo. 538, 33 Pac. 369. If representatives allege in their complaint that they sue under authority in a will, which was probated, and their capacity is properly alleged in the complaint, a denial of such allegations on information and belief is insufficient.—Thompson v. Skeen, 14 Utah 209, 46 Pac. 1103. An allegation, in a complaint, that plaintiff was duly appointed administrator, and that he qualified and received letters, is a sufficient statement of his representative capacity as against a general demurrer for want of facts.—Knight v. Le Beau, 19 Mont. 223, 47 Pac. 952; German Fire Ins. Co. v. Wright, 6 Kan. App. 611, 49 Pac. 704; Halleck v. Mixer, 16 Cal. 574, 579. Though a complaint by an administrator may contain redundant matter, and perhaps allegations relating to more than one cause of action, it is the duty of the court to sustain the pleading, if sufficient facts can be found to constitute any cause of action.—Bright v. Ecker, 9 S. D. 192, 68 N. W. 326, 327. Where a cause of action accrues to an executor or administrator after the death of the decedent, he may sue thereon, either in his representative or individual character, and an averment of the representative character may be regarded as surplusage.—Sears v. Daly, 43 Or. 346, 73 Pac. 5, 6; Lewis v. Adams, 70 Cal. 403, 411, 412, 59 Am. Rep. 423, 11 Pac. 833. If an executrix takes notes in her own name for a debt due the estate, she may bring suit in her own name thereon, as well as in her representative character.—Getty v. Larkin, 59 Kan. 548, 53 Pac. 755. A person appointed administrator by an order of court, which was void for want of jurisdiction, can not maintain a bill in equity against the administrator legally appointed for expenses

incurred and fees claimed to have been earned in his alleged administration, where he has an adequate remedy at law for all payments made
by him for the benefit of the estate.—Slate v. Henkle, 45 Or. 430, 78
Pac. 325, 327. An objection to an action brought by an executor, that
the complaint does not show by what court, if any, the plaintiff was
appointed executor, is not good upon general demurrer, where it appears that the defendant contracted with the plaintiff as executor.
This, prima facie at least, would give the executor the right to enforce
or forfeit the contract by suit or otherwise.—Stein v. Waddell, 37 Wash.
634, 80 Pac. 184, 186; Waldo v. Milroy, 19 Wash. 156, 52 Pac. 1012.
An allegation in a complaint in an action by an executor, that the
will authorized and directed said executor to administer upon the
estate, without the intervention, order, or advice of any court, and
to fully execute all its terms and provisions, is sufficient, as against
demurrer, to show that the will under which the executor was acting
at the time dispensed with letters of administration.—Miller v. Borst,
11 Wash. 260, 39 Pac. 662. The statute of Oregon has abolished the
common-law rule which made one who officiously interfered with the
property of a deceased person an executor de son tort, by depriving creditors of the estate and others of the remedy which they
anciently possessed. Such intermeddler is now made answerable only
to the legal representative of the deceased, for the value of all property taken or removed, and for all injury caused by his interference
therewith; and where an adequate remedy in a law action instituted
against such intermeddler may be had to recoup against the claim
for admages caused by his intermeddling, a demurrer to the complaint, in the nature of a cross-bill in equity, should be sustained.—
Slate v. Henkle, 45 Or. 430, 78 Pac. 325, 326. The omission of the
word "as" in the title of an action by an administrator is cured by
clear and distinct averments in the complaint showing that the action
is not brought by the administrator in his individual capacity.—Carr
v. Carr, 15 Cal. App. 480, 115 Pac. 261. Where a daughter seeks to
recover from the estate of her deceased father the share of her deceased mother's interest in the community property of her father and
mother left in his possession undisposed of by the decree of divorce
which dissolved their marriage, an allegation by the plaintiff "that
she is the sole legatee and executrix of the last will of Elizabeth M.
Harvey," her mother, is a sufficient allegation of her being the legally
qualified and acting executrix of her mother's estate; and, in such action, it is of no consequence whether or not she is entitled to sue
individually.—Harvey v. Pocock, 92 Wash. 625, 159 Pac. 771. Jurisdiction of court to appoint the plaintiff an administratrix cum testamento
annexo, suing the administrator of another estate for assets, held not
subject to question where due appointment was alleged in the complaint and was not denied in the answer.—Shiels v. Nathan, 12 Cal.
App. 604, 108 Pac. 34.

REFERENCES.
Effect of qualifying words, "as executor" and "as administrators."—
See note 15 L. R. A. 850-852.

11. Same. In action to recover value of land.—In an action by an executrix who is sole devisee under a will of a testatrix executed several years before her death, to recover the value of land deeded by her while of unsound mind, and conveyed by the grantee, the defendant is estopped by a judgment in probate of the will pleaded by plaintiff, in the proceedings upon which it appears that defendant set up another will executed at the same time as the deed, devising the land to him, which he claimed as a revocation of the prior will, and also set up his deed as evidence of title, whereupon it was adjudged by the court that the first will was valid, and that the second will and deed were executed while the testatrix was of unsound mind and under the undue influence of the defendant, and he can not assert anything to the contrary of such judgment, in the subsequent action by the executrix.—Clapp v. Vatcher, 9 Cal. App. 462, 99 Pac. 549.

12. Evidence.—In an action by an administrator de bonis non against the sureties on the bond of his predecessor, where property is shown to have come to the hands of such predecessor, the burden of proof is on the sureties to show that such property has been properly administered.—Gatch v. Simpson, 40 Or. 90, 66 Pac. 688, 691. If the appointment of an administrator is put in issue by the pleadings, the introduction in evidence of the original judgment signed by the judge, showing the same to have been filed and properly recorded, is prima facie evidence of such appointment.—Daugherty v. Feland, 59 Okla. 122, 157 Pac. 1144. In suit by heirs and executor to recover realty conveyed by decedent shortly before his death, where the evidence showed absence of claims against estate and expiration of time for presenting claims, the executor could not recover unless the decedent at the time of his death had ownership and right of possession and the land was subject to testamentary disposition.—Boye v. Andrews, 10 Cal. App. 494, 102 Pac. 551.

REFERENCES.
Declarations of executor or administrator, when admissible as evidence against the intestate's estate.—See note 25 Am. Dec. 301-303.

13. Judgment.—Judgment in every case commenced by an executor or administrator in which the defendant becomes entitled to costs ought to be entered against such executor or administrator personally. After payment, he may charge the amount in his account of administration, to be allowed or not as it may appear to the judge of the probate court that the suit was discreet or otherwise.—Meyer v. O'Rourke, 150 Cal. 177, 88 Pac. 706, 707. Heirs, legatees, and devisees are privies to judgments, touching the estate, rendered in actions by executors and administrators.—Litzell v. Hart, 96 Wash. 471, 165 Pac. 393. There is no privity between representatives of party of the

same estate in different jurisdictions, and a judgment on a claim
against one is not binding on the other, and has been held not even
evidence against him. This is true whether or not the representatives
are the same person, and applies to an action against any other person
having assets of the decedent in a jurisdiction other than that in which
the letters were granted.—Richards v. Blaisdell, 12 Cal. App. 101, 106
Pac. 732. Full faith and credit doctrine held inapplicable.—Richards
v. Blaisdell, 12 Cal. App. 101, 106 Pac. 732. A judgment providing that
the plaintiff "have and recover" from the defendant, as administratrix, the amount of the verdict and costs, is not in proper form; it
should be as directed in this section; but, as no substantial rights are
affected it forms no ground of reversal.—Gauss v. Trump, 48 Mont. 92,
102, 135 Pac. 910. A judgment in favor of a foreign executor can not
be attacked by a defendant, who was duly served with process and
who contested on the merits, because the plaintiff foreign executor
did not give the required preliminary notice, by publication, of the
pendency of such action; the statutory provision as to notice is not
jurisdictional; neither can the judgment be attacked on the ground
that the bond was insufficient, where the record is silent on that subject; the presumption of regularity and validity attends the conclusion
of the lower court, that the bond was sufficient.—Cordingly v. Kennedy
(Colo.), 239 Fed. 645, 650, 152 C. C. A. 479.

REFERENCES.

Judgment for costs.—See head-line 12, infra. Right of executor or
administrator to have judgment against the decedent set aside.—See
note 54 L. R. A. 761, 762. Power of federal court to enforce its own
judgment against a decedent's estate.—See note 12 L. R. A. (N. S.)
155-157.

14. Costs.—The general rule, subject to certain exceptions, is, that
a personal representative who sues or defends in any proceeding
which he can bring or defend in such capacity is not personally liable
for costs, if he fails in his contest.—De Bow v. Wollenberg, 52 Or. 404,
96 Pac. 536, 544, 97 Pac. 717. An administrator is individually liable for
costs, under a judgment for defendant in an action brought by him as
such administrator, unless the estate is expressly made chargeable.—
Stevens v. San Francisco, etc., R. R. Co., 103 Cal. 252, 254, 27 Pac. 146.
Costs should be imposed upon the executor individually, and not upon
the estate, nor upon him in his representative capacity. He has the
right to seek an allowance from the estate in a proper case. If, however, the litigation has been unjust, or ill-advised, then, to prevent
the dissipation of estates at the hands of careless executors, the executor will be compelled to bear the burden.—Meyer v. O'Rourke, 150
Cal. 177, 88 Pac. 706, 707.

REFERENCES.

Judgment for costs.—See head-line 11, supra. Personal liability of
executor or administrator for costs.—See note 14 L. R. A. 696-699.

15. To recover possession.—An administrator is not only empowered, but it is his duty, to assume the possession of real property of the decedent; if such possession is withheld, he should sue for and recover it; and, if he is in possession, he may sue to quiet the title.—Galligan v. Thomas S. Hayden Realty Co., 62 Colo. 477, 480, 163 Pac. 295. An administrator with the will annexed who has possession of lands belonging to the estate he has in course of administration can maintain a suit against one who forcibly and unlawfully dispossesses him.—Cutburth v. Bell, 55 Okla. 157, 155 Pac. 1136. Although the heir takes title to real estate immediately on the ancestor's death, the administrator has the right of possession and the concomitant right to recover possession, including the right to any and all auxiliary and immediate and permanent equitable relief.—Wendler v. Woodward, 93 Wash. 684, 161 Pac. 1043. The right and duty of an executor or administrator under the statute of Oregon, when directed by the county court in a proper case, to sue to set aside a conveyance made by the decedent in his lifetime, with intent to defraud creditors, does not exclude the right of a personal representative to pursue any remedy afforded him by law or equity to reduce to possession the choses in action surviving to him from the decedent.—Hillman v. Young, 64 Or. 73, 88, 127 Pac. 793, 129 Pac. 124.

16. On contracts.

(1) In general.—An administrator may sue to enforce an agreement to sell corporate stock, which had been sold under a pledge to secure a debt of the deceased before his death, the holder of the stock having agreed to transfer the same to him on certain conditions.—Sayward v. Houghton, 119 Cal. 545, 549, 51 Pac. 853, 52 Pac. 44. An administrator may sue and recover on an oral contract, made after the death of the intestate, in which it is agreed by two creditors of the deceased, that, in consideration of the conveyance of lands of the estate by the heirs to each of said creditors, one of them will release and satisfy a judgment in his favor against the estate, and the other creditor will pay and discharge all debts of the deceased and costs of administration, and cause said estate to be settled solvent, where such contract is shown to have been performed by the heirs and by the former contracting creditor, but the latter creditor refuses to perform after having received the consideration.—Stewart v. Rogers, 71 Kan. 53, 80 Pac. 58, 60. An action may be maintained by an executor on a certificate of deposit issued by a bank to his testator, payable to the order of himself upon the return of the certificate properly indorsed, where a demand of payment by the executor before suit is alleged, without alleging that the certificate was properly indorsed.—Emerson v. Thatcher, 6 Kan. App. 25, 51 Pac. 50, 51. The right to sue on a promissory note belonging to an estate is vested in the personal representatives and not in the heirs of deceased.—Presby v. Pickett, 1 Kan. App. 631, 42 Pac. 405. An action by the executor to compel a specific performance of a contract, by which, as alleged, the defendant became liable to pay the purchase price bid by him at a probate sale of the land of the decedent, will not lie, where the attempted sale was void.—Kertchem v. George, 78 Cal. 597, 600, 21 Pac. 372. The principle that a contract made through a mutual mistake of law may give a right to one of the parties thereto to rescind, or to have some other legal remedy against the other party, does not, in an action by an administrator, apply to a case where property of the estate was used by a former executor to pay an individual debt.—Snyder v. Jack, 140 Cal. 584, 586, 74 Pac. 139, 355. In an action by executors for a debt due the estate, it is no defense that a final account has been rendered and distribution made, if the executors have not been finally discharged.—Denny v. Sayward, 10 Wash. 422, 39 Pac. 119.

(2) Fire Insurance policies.—The right to sue on a policy of fire insurance issued to the decedent is vested in his personal representatives, not in his heirs.—German Fire Ins. Co. v. Wright, 6 Kan. App. 611, 49 Pac. 704.

(3) Promissory notes.—The right to sue on a promissory note belonging to an estate is vested in the personal representatives and not in the heirs of deceased.—Presby v. Pickett, 1 Kan. App. 631, 42 Pac. 405. An action may be maintained by the administratrix of a surety on a promissory note of defendant, which she, as administratrix has been compelled to pay in order to protect the estate.—Townsend v. Sullivan, 3 Cal. App. 115, 118, 84 Pac. 435. In an action by an administrator against a physician on a note, where the defendant sets up payment through medical services rendered the decedent during his lifetime, the question of when the defendant's claim was filed against the estate is immaterial.—Lockard v. Ware, 61 Colo. 354, 157 Pac. 1165. Where a widow, having a life estate only in her husband's personalty, takes, from the maker of a note to her deceased husband a note to replace such note, the fact that the new note is made to her in her private capacity, instead of as executrix, is immaterial in an action on the new note.—Carter v. Karternd (S. D.), 166 N. W. 524. In an action by an administratrix on a promissory note against the maker where the defense was payment where defendant was permitted to testify that he had had a settlement with the payee in the latter's lifetime, conceding without deciding that it was error to admit such testimony over objection, such error was cured by an order striking it out and instructing the jury not to consider it.—Wallace v. Wallace, 101 Kan. 32, 35, 165 Pac. 838, 840. Where an administrator was appointed for the purpose of selecting an allotment for a deceased Choctaw minor; where he soon afterward purchased the land directly from the heirs at law; where he subsequently sold the land, taking a promissory note for its purchase price; and where he brings suit to enforce payment of the note, he is entitled to recover where he shows that he had, prior to the sale, a clear title in himself.—Kelly v. Blackwell (Okla.), 164 Pac. 103.

(4) Personal services.—In an action brought by one administrator against another, involving the right to recover for personal services rendered under an express contract, but which contract does not fix the term of service or the value of the services, the statute of limitations did not begin to run until the services had ended, where the testimony did not show a general custom or usage to the contrary.—Estate of Jewell, In re; Jewell v. Central Trust Co., 103 Kan. 381, 173 Pac. 923. Where one is employed by another, and the term of service and time of payment for the services are not fixed by an agreement, and the employee continues in the service without interruption or payment until the death of the employer, the employment may be deemed to be continuous, in the absence of a general custom or usage, and, in an action brought by one administrator against another, involving the right to recover for such services, it must be held that the statute of limitations will not begin to run against a claim for compensation until the services are ended.—Estate of Jewell, In re; Jewell v. Central Trust Co., 103 Kan. 381, 173 Pac. 923.

17. Conversion.

(1) In general.—An executor may sue for the recovery of converted property of the estate, under the general authority conferred by statute, and needs no special authorization therefor from the court.—Halleck v. Mixer, 16 Cal. 574, 580. An administrator may maintain an action to recover possession of personal property, for the benefit of creditors, from the mortgagee in possession, who had allowed his mortgage to expire by lapse of time.—First Nat. Bank v. Ludvigsen, 8 Wyo. 230, 80 Am. St. Rep. 928, 56 Pac. 994, 1000, 57 Pac. 934. An administrator may maintain an action for the conversion of personal property against one claiming under an alleged sale from decedent, where the evidence shows the sale was not accompanied by immediate delivery and continued change of possession.—Kelly v. Murphy, 70 Cal. 560, 563, 12 Pac. 467. An administrator de bonis non may maintain an action against his predecessor and sureties for assets which have been converted into money, but are still unadministered.—Gatch v. Simpson, 40 Or. 90, 66 Pac. 688, 690; American Surety, etc., Co. v. Piatt, 67 Kan. 294, 72 Pac. 775, 776. At common law, the authority of an administrator de bonis non extended only to such estate as remained unadministered or unconverted by his predecessor. He could not maintain an action to recover converted assets. That right belonged to heirs or others interested in the estate.—Gatch v. Simpson, 40 Or. 90, 66 Pac. 688, 689; Reed v. Hume, 25 Utah 248, 70 Pac. 998, 1000. A complaint in an action in the nature of an action of trover, maintained by the administrator, contained the averment that "said estate was the owner and possessed" of the property, etc. Held, that the allegation was equivalent to an averment that the plaintiff, as administrator, was the owner in possession.—Ham v. Henderson, 50 Cal. 367, 369. If the taking of the property by the defendant was tortious, no demand by the plaintiff, previous to the commencement of the action, is necessary.—Ham v. Henderson, 50 Cal. 367, 369. In an action by an administrator to recover personal property of the estate, which had been sold by the widow, an allegation, in the answer, that the sale was made under a mutual mistake by both parties is no defense.—Snyder v. Jack, 140 Cal. 584, 586, 74 Pac. 139, 355. Whenever a creditor obtains from a personal representative of a decedent's estate, under a mistake of fact, a sum of money on account of his demand which, ex aequo et bono, he ought not to receive, it may be secured in an action instituted for that purpose.—Thorson v. Hooper, 57 Or. 75, 109 Pac. 389. Under the statute of Washington, an administrator de bonis non may maintain an action against the personal representative of a former executor for the conversion of rents and profits by the latter.—Denton v. Schneider, 80 Wash. 506, 519, 142 Pac. 9.

(2) **What is a conversion.**—Where property of the estate has been sold, but the sale was not sanctioned by the probate court, the administrator may treat the property as converted by the purchaser, and sue to recover the same or its value, without regard to the question as to whether it was sold to satisfy a debt.—Horton v. Jack, 115 Cal. 29, 33, 46 Pac. 920. An administrator is absolutely entitled to all personal property of the estate until distribution, and any interference with that property, which deprives him of the possession, is a conversion for which he is entitled to recover, irrespective of whether the estate is indebted or not.—Horton v. Jack, 115 Cal. 29, 34, 46 Pac. 920. If, on the return of an executrix of sales under an order to sell, she reports that she sold the property to satisfy her individual liability to a creditor, and on this showing the court refuses to confirm the sale, and the executrix subsequently files an account, in which she treats the property sold as still on hand, and does not ask for nor receive any credit for the payment of any debt of the estate, title to the property remains in the estate, and the executrix is entitled to treat the property as converted by the individual creditor, and to recover its value from him.—Horton v. Jack, 115 Cal. 29, 33, 46 Pac. 920, 37 Pac. 652.

(3) **Suits in individual capacity.**—The administrator is deemed in law to have possession, or to be entitled to possession, of personal property of the estate from the time of the death of deceased, and may therefore maintain an action in his own name against a person who, after the death and before the issuance of letters, converts any of the personal property of the estate to his use.—Jahns v. Nolting, 29 Cal. 507, 511; Ham v. Henderson, 50 Cal. 367, 369. An executor may sue on a note and mortgage executed to him in either his representative or his individual capacity.—Burrell v. Kern, 34 Or. 501, 56 Pac. 809, 810. The person in possession of personal property as administrator may sue in his individual capacity to recover possession from one who wrongfully takes it from him and converts it to his own

use; and any statement of the representative capacity of plaintiff may be regarded as surplusage.—Munch v. Williams, 24 Cal. 167, 171. Although an administrator may sue in his own name to recover property belonging to the estate, the suit must be brought before he ceases to be administrator.—Afflerbach v. McGovern, 79 Cal. 268, 272, 21 Pac. 837.

(4) Action must fail when.—An action by an executrix for the conversion of property of the estate must fail, where it appears that defendant received the property by direction of the plaintiff to be sold, and that the defendant had sold the same and applied the proceeds in paying debts of the deceased.—Rutherford v. Thompson, 14 Or. 236, 12 Pac. 382.

18. For damages in causing death.

(1) Right of action. In general.—An action for the wrongful death of a deceased husband, though usually prosecuted in the name of the widow and children, may be likewise prosecuted in the name of the personal representative for the benefit of the widow and children.— Archibald v. Lincoln County, 50 Wash. 55, 96 Pac. 831, 832. The statute of Oregon authorizes the personal representative of a deceased person to bring an action for negligence which caused his death; but, the heirs have no remedy for damages occasioned by an injury to the person of the deceased. The fund recovered in such a case is the property of the estate.—Olston v. Oregon, etc., Ry. Co., 52 Or. 343, 20 L. R. A. (N. S.) 915, 96 Pac. 1095, 1097, 97 Pac. 538. A statute creating a cause of action for damages sustained by the relatives or next of kin of the deceased is not penal. Such a cause of action is transitory, and may therefore be enforced in any state or country whose public policy is not opposed to the recognition and enforcement thereof.— Denver, etc., R. R. Co. v. Waring, 37 Colo. 122, 86 Pac. 305, 306. The right given by the statute of one state to recover for the death of a person caused by wrongful act may be enforced in the jurisdiction of another state, through the medium of an administrator appointed by the courts of the latter state for that purpose.—In re Lowham's Estate, 30 Utah 436, 85 Pac. 445, 446; Utah S. & T. Co. v. Diamond Coal, etc., Co., 26 Utah 299, 73 Pac. 524; Stewart v. Baltimore, etc., R. R. Co., 168 U. S. 445, 447, 18 Sup. Ct. 105, 42 L. Ed. 537; Boston and Maine R. R. Co. v. Hurd, 108 Fed. 116, 47 C. C. A. 615, 56 L. R. A. 193. It seems to be the rule in most states, that, unless there is some law of the forum which will prevent the action from being maintained by the person designated by the law of the place where the injury occurred, it may be so maintained. This follows the rule announced by Mr. Justice Miller in Dennick v. Railroad Co., 103 U. S. 11, 26 L. Ed. 429, that actions may be maintained in one state by a personal representative of a decedent, and based upon a liability of the defendant for damages arising out of injuries sustained by the decedent or for death resulting from injuries to the decedent in another state.—Denver, etc.,

R. Co. v. Waring, 37 Colo. 122, 86 Pac. 305, 309. The administrator of the estate of a person who died as the result of the wrongful act of another may sue for damages for the death, notwithstanding that he may have been appointed without reference to his being either a relative or a creditor, or acting by authority of any kin or relative of the deceased.—Caswell v. Copper River & N. W. Ry., 4 Alaska 709, 711. It is well settled that an action for death is statutory; the personal representative of the deceased is permitted to bring the action merely as a statutory trustee for the benefit of the heirs, and in the absence of heirs no action lies. The existence of heirs is an essential element in the cause of action and must be alleged in the complaint.—Slaughter v. Goldberg, Bowen & Co., 26 Cal. App. 318, 147 Pac. 90. The legislature, in providing for the accrual of a right of action to the widow and the lineal heirs of a person, whose life is lost in the course of his employment in coal mines, used the words "lineal heirs" according to the commonly accepted use of them and in accordance with the existing law in regard to descents.—Rocky Mountain Co. v. Kovaics, 26 Colo. App. 554, 556, 144 Pac. 863. If no personal representative has been appointed, the widow may maintain an action for damages for the death of her husband, and if, after commencing such action in due time, she is appointed administratrix of her husband's estate and she amends the petition accordingly, more than two years after the death, her action as administratrix is not barred by the two year statute of limitations.—Mott v. Long, 90 Kan. 110, 132 Pac. 998. An action for the wrongful death of a non-resident may still be brought by the Kansas administrator of his estate under the original act conferring that authority, notwithstanding the passage of the supplemental act authorizing his widow or next of kin to bring the action.—Cox v. Kansas City, 86 Kan. 298, 120 Pac. 553. The commencement and maintenance of an action to recover damages for wrongful death should be held to be within the scope of the powers and duties of a special administrator, as such powers and duties are defined by our statute. Although the moneys recovered in such an action do not constitute assets of the estate, they do constitute property which it is the right and duty of the personal representative of the deceased to collect for the benefit of the heirs, and the right to maintain an action for the recovery of the same is expressly conferred upon such personal representative.—Ruiz v. Santa Barbara G. & E. Co., 164 Cal. 188, 128 Pac. 330, 332. Actions by the executor or administrator for damages sustained by a deceased employee, and resulting in his death, must be brought by and in the name of the party designated by the statute of the state or country in which the cause of action arose, even though a similar statute of the forum provides that the action shall be brought by some other party.—Denver, etc., R. R. Co. v. Waring, 37 Colo. 122, 86 Pac. 305, 306. An administrator may bring an action to recover damages for the death of a decedent whom he represents, but the action is for the benefit of the heirs, and an allegation that there are heirs is necessary to maintain the action.—Webster v. Norwegian Min. Co., 137 Cal. 399, 400, 92 Am. St. Rep. 181, 70 Pac. 276. The power of an administrator to sue for damages sustained by causing death will be upheld, where the record of the probate court shows that it had jurisdiction to issue letters.—Union Pac. Ry. Co. v. Dunden, 37 Kan. 1, 14 Pac. 501, 502.

(2) Same. Consideration of statutes.—Section 377 of the Code of Civil Procedure of California gives a right of action for damages for the death of a person not a minor, caused by the wrongful act or neglect of another, to the "heirs or personal representatives" of the deceased. Section 1970 of the Civil Code of that state, as amended in 1907 (Stats. 1907, p. 119), purports to give a right of action for and on behalf of "the widow, children, dependent parents, and dependent brothers and sisters," against an employer, for damages resulting from the death of an employee in certain cases, to "the personal representative of such employee." It is settled by the decisions that an action of the character authorized by the said section 377 of the Code of Civil Procedure is one solely for the benefit of the heirs, by which they may be compensated for the pecuniary injury suffered by them by reason of the loss of their relative, that the money recovered in such an action does not belong to the estate but to the heirs only, and that an administrator has the right to bring the action only because the statute authorizes him to do so, and that he is simply made a statutory trustee to recover damages for the benefit of the heirs.—Ruiz v. Santa Barbara Gas & Electric Co., 164 Cal. 188, 128 Pac. 330, 331. By passing the act permitting a widow to bring an action for damages for the death of her husband as the result of the negligence of another, the legislature did not mean to take away the right to sue, in such circumstances, from the administrator of the decedent.—Robinson v. Chicago, R. I. & Pac. R. Co., 96 Kan. 654, 153 Pac. 494. Inasmuch as it is "the heirs or personal representatives" of a deceased person who are authorized by section 4100 of the Revised Codes of Idaho to prosecute an action against a person wrongfully causing the death of such person and any judgment obtained in such action inures to the benefit of the "heirs" of the decedent and in no case becomes a part of the assets of the estate of the deceased, when there are no heirs the action can not be maintained.—Whitley v. Spokane, etc., Ry. Co., 23 Ida. 642, 132 Pac. 123. Under the statute whereby recovery may be had for death by wrongful act, it is not required that collateral heirs, who have suffered substantial injury through the loss of the companionship and society of the deceased, shall, where suit is brought by them, show specific pecuniary damage coming to them, nor that the court shall instruct the jury that no damages can be recovered for the loss of the comfort and protection of the deceased.—Kelly v. Lemhi Irr. & Orchard Co., 30 Ida. 778, 168 Pac. 1076. Under the Oregon statutes, a libel in rem may be maintained in a court of admiralty, by the representative of a deceased person, to recover damages for his wrongful death, attributed to the negligence of the ship on which he was em

ployed.—The General Foy, 175 Fed. 590, 594; Aurora Shipping Co. v. Boyce, 191 Fed. 960, 970, 112 C. C. A. 372. Although the Oregon act of 1911 apparently limits the right of action to recover damages for the wrongful death of an employee to a relative of the deceased, the administrator of the deceased can, under this section, maintain an action for such death; that act is not inconsistent with this section.—Statts v. Twohy Bros. Co., 61 Or. 602, 607, 123 Pac. 909. Under section 1970, Civil Code of California, which provides a right of action for wrongful death of an employee by the negligence of the employer in certain instances, the phrase "received as aforesaid" coming in the third clause of the statute has reference to each of the foregoing clauses, and includes the negligence of a fellow-servant as well as defective appliances, etc.—Pritchard v. Whitney Estate Co., 164 Cal. 564, 129 Pac. 989. Although a right of action by the heirs for damages for the wrongful death of deceased was provided by section 377, California Code of Civil Procedure, this right is limited by the provisions of section 1970 of the Civil Code of that state, which is the last declaration of the legislature on the subject, and by this latter section such right of action is limited to the widow, children and dependent brothers and sisters, wherein it will be seen that there survives no right of action to a nephew of the deceased.—Pritchard v. Whitney Estate Co., 164 Cal. 564, 129 Pac. 989. An action for damages, for the death of a person, not a minor, by falling from a building he was engaged in constructing, as servant of a contractor, is properly brought under the statute relating to death by unlawful act, and not under that relating to the indemnification of employees by employers for sufferings incident to the risks of the employment; hence, such an action may be brought by the decedent's wife and children.—Valentine v. Hayes (Cal. App.), 173 Pac. 410.

(3) Employers' liability act.—The employers' liability act of Oregon, of 1910, Laws of 1911, p. 16, authorizes but one action for an injury caused by a violation of the law, in case of death; if there is any one of the beneficiaries named living and in a position to bring the action, it can not be brought by the personal representative of the decedent, under section 380, L. O. L.—McClaugherty v. Rogue River Electric Co., 73 Or. 135, 136, 140 Pac. 64, 144 Pac. 569. The employers' liability act of Oregon, of 1910, did not repeal section 380 of Lord's Oregon Laws; the two acts, being directed to one common object, namely, to provide a statutory action for the death of a person resulting from the wrongful act or omission of another, are to be construed together, and, as far as possible, effect must be given to the provisions of each act.— Niemi v. Stanley Smith Lumber Co., 77 Or. 227, 149 Pac. 1033; Evansen v. Grande Ronde Lumber Co., 77 Or. 1, 149 Pac. 1035. The provisions of the employers' liability act, enumerating the persons who are entitled to sue for the wrongful acts or omissions named therein, are exclusive of section 380, L. O. L., as long as any one of the beneficiaries named therein survives, but, if all are dead, the representatives of a

person, whose death was caused by the wrongful act of another, would be entitled, it seems, to sue therefor under section 380, L. O. L.—Niemi v. Stanley Smith Lumber Co., 77 Or. 227, 149 Pac. 1033. If an action is brought by the administrator of the estate of a deceased employee for the benefit of the surviving parents, on the theory that such representative is the trustee of an express trust, it is proper to deny a motion made by him to substitute the parents as parties; such a substitution would be a clear departure in the proceedings, clearly changing the action in material matters, and amounting in effect to the commencement of a new and materially different action.—Bryan v. Inspiration Consol. Copper Co. (Ariz.), 181 Pac. 577, 578. If the employer, under the liability act, is declared by the statute, where death ensues from an accident to an employee, to be answerable to the personal representative of the deceased for the benefit of the surviving widow or husband and children of such employee, but, if none, then to such employee's parents; and the liability under such statute accrues to the parents of the deceased, they are the real parties in interest, and the personal representative of the deceased has no authority under the act to represent such parents and to maintain an action to recover damages because of such liability; such action must be brought in the name of the parents; it can not be brought in the name of the administrator on the ground that he is a trustee of an express trust.—Bryan v. Inspiration C. Copper Co. (Ariz.), 181 Pac. 577, 578. So much of section 7349, L. O. L., as conflicted with the dispensation of damages to the persons declared to be entitled thereto by the employers' liability act, was impliedly repealed by that act.—McFarland v. Oregon Elec. Ry. Co., 70 Or. 27, 41, Ann. Cas. 1916B, 527, 138 Pac. 458. The employers' liability act dispenses with the necessity of an administrator's being appointed to conduct an action, when, in a case covered by the act, the servant's injuries have proved fatal.—McClaugherty v. Rogue River Electric Co., 73 Or. 135, 144 Pac. 569.

(4) **Abatement of action.**—Section 377 of the Code of Civil Procedure of California, whereby the heirs or personal representatives of a person whose death has been caused by the wrongful act of another may maintain an action for the death against the wrongdoer, does not affect the well-settled common law rule as to the abatement of personal actions by death.—Clark v. Goodwin, 170 Cal. 527, L. R. A. 1916A, 1142, 150 Pac. 357. Where a person is aggrieved by the destruction of, or injury to, his automobile in a collision with the automobile of another, to whom he imputes negligence, he may sue such other; and if the defendant die pending the action, the action does not abate under section 1584 of the California Code of Civil Procedure.—George v. McManus, 27 Cal. App. 414, 150 Pac. 73.

(5) **Pleading and evidence.**—The complaint in an action for wrongful death fails to state a cause of action, where it fails to allege that the deceased left any heir, an allegation absolutely essential in an action of this character.—Ruiz v. Santa Barbara Gas & Electric Co.,

164 Cal. 188, 128 Pac. 330, 331. Where the complaint in an action to recover for wrongful death fails to allege that the deceased left any heirs, and a demurrer thereto is sustained, an amended complaint, not purporting to contain a new cause of action, but merely showing that the deceased left surviving him a widow as his heir, may be filed after the statute of limitations has run against the cause of action.—Barr v. Southern Cal. Edison Co., 18 Cal. App. 279, 140 Pac. 47. An amended complaint in an action for wrongful death, brought by the widow of the deceased as administratrix, which alleges "that the deceased left at the time of his death surviving him his widow, who, as the administratrix of his estate and as his personal representative and as plaintiff, brings this action; that by reason of the premises the plaintiff as such administratrix has sustained damages in the sum of one hundred thousand dollars," is not subject to general demurrer because it does not allege that the suit is brought for the benefit of heirs or that there is any heir of the deceased; since not only is the widow an heir, but section 1970 of the Civil Code of California expressly provides that the personal representative of the deceased may recover damages for the benefit of the widow.—Barr v. Southern Cal. Edison Co., 18 Cal. App. 279, 140 Pac. 47. Nor is such complaint subject to general demurrer because it does not allege that the suit is brought for the benefit of the widow, for she could not maintain the action other than for the benefit of the heirs, for whom she acts as statutory trustee.—Barr v. Southern Cal. Edison Co., 18 Cal. App. 279, 140 Pac. 47. The failure of such complaint to allege in terms that the widow has sustained pecuniary damages does not render it subject to general demurrer, for the statute gives her the right to such damages as under the circumstances are just.—Barr v. Southern Cal. Edison Co., 18 Cal. App. 279, 140 Pac. 47. The failure of such complaint to allege the amount of damages is not fatal, if it alleges facts from which damages must necessarily follow, and the prayer of the complaint is for a specific sum.—Barr v. Southern Cal. Edison Co., 18 Cal. App. 279, 140 Pac. 47. The allegation in such complaint that the plaintiff has suffered damage as administratrix should be disregarded as surplusage.—Barr v. Southern Cal. Edison Co., 18 Cal. App. 279, 140 Pac. 47. In an action for wrongful death, it is proper to admit in evidence a map to locate the premises and as a diagram of the scene of the accident.—Foley v. Northern California P. Co., 165 Cal. 103, 130 Pac. 1183.

(6) Measure of damages.—In an action for wrongful death under the Alaskan Code of Civil Procedure, section 353, providing that the amount recovered should be exclusively for the use of decedent's husband, wife, or children, and in default thereof to be administered as other personal property of a deceased person, the damages recoverable for wrongful death in the absence of wife or children, is the value of the decedent's life to the estate, measured by his earning capacity, thriftiness, and probable length of life.—Jennings v. Alaska Treadwell Gold Mining Co., 170 Fed. 151, 95 C. C. A. 388.

(7) **Assets of estate.**—Money recovered for wronful death is not an asset of the estate of deceased.—Jones v. Leonardt, 10 Cal. App. 284, 101 Pac. 811; Ruiz v. Santa Barbara G. & E. Co., 164 Cal. 188, 128 Pac. 330, 332. While a claim for damages for death by wrongful act is not a general asset of the estate, under the provisions of the Wyoming statute, yet, under the provisions of that statute, it has been held, in an action in the state of Utah, construing said statute and the right of an administrator thereunder, that such claim is a sufficient asset of the estate for the appointment of an administrator to bring suit to recover damages for such death.—In re Lowham's Estate, 30 Utah 436, 85 Pac. 445, 446. The statutes of Arizona create a right of action for the benefit of the estate, the damages recoverable to be distributed as assets of the estate, not subject, however, to debts.—Southern Pac. Co. v. Wilson, 10 Ariz. 162, 85 Pac. 401, 403.

(8) **Action by infant.**—The contract of an infant with an attorney to recover for him damages for a personal injury is not a contract for necessaries.—Plummer v. Northern Pac. Ry. Co., 98 Wash. 67, 167 Pac. 173. After an attorney has contracted with a minor to conduct a damage suit for him and accept a specified portion of the damages for his compensation, the minor may repudiate the contract.—Plummer v. Northern Pac. Ry. Co., 98 Wash. 67, 167 Pac. 73. If a minor, after contracting with an attorney to sue in damages for a personal injury he has suffered and to take part of the damages as a fee, proceeds to have a general guardian appointed, with authority to settle for the injury, this is sufficient notice to the attorney that he has repudiated the contract.—Plummer v. Northern Pac. Ry. Co., 98 Wash. 67, 167 Pac. 73. A guardian ad litem is not qualified to contract with an attorney to conduct a damage suit for his ward and retain part of the damages for his fee; if both the guardian's appointment and the contract is effected without consulting a court of equity.—Plummer v. Northern Pac. Ry. Co., 98 Wash. 67, 167 Pac. 73.

REFERENCES.

Actions for wrongful death.—See note 70 Am. St. 669. Administrator's right to sue for the wrongful death of his intestate.—See note 3 L. R. A. (N. S.) 473, 474.

19. **Ejectment.**—A patent to land, issued to an administrator, vests the legal title in him, and entitles him to recover in ejectment.—Burling v. Tompkins, 77 Cal. 257, 262, 19 Pac. 429. Under the statutes of Washington, an administrator appointed within the time limited for the presentation of claims against the estate, may bring an action to recover possession of land of the intestate held by one claiming adversely, even though such adverse claimant be an heir.—Gibson v. Slater, 42 Wash. 347, 84 Pac. 648, 651. An administrator may bring ejectment in his own name as an administrator for the possession of land of the deceased.—Black v. Story, 7 Mont. 238, 14 Pac. 703, 704. An executor or administartor can, in behalf of the estate and all of the heirs at

law, maintain an action for the possession of real estate against a person who, whether he is one of the heirs or not, has wrongfully seized such real estate and retained the possession under an adverse claim of title, thus depriving both the administrator and the heirs at law of the enjoyment of their rights.—Gibson v. Slater, 42 Wash. 347, 84 Pac. 648, 651. The right of possession resting in an executor or administrator is barred in the same way as the right of possession in any other trustee, and his right to maintain ejectment for lands claimed by the estate may be barred by adverse possession.—Webb v. Winter, 135 Cal. 455, 457, 67 Pac. 691. An executor of a deceased tenant in common may join with his co-tenants in bringing ejectment.— Touchard v. Keyes, 21 Cal. 202, 209. An administrator can not maintain ejectment for land, the legal title to which vested in the heirs of his intestate after his death.—Emeric v. Penniman, 26 Cal. 119, 123, 124. A judgment in an action of ejectment, brought by an administrator, where the title of the decedent is put in issue, binds the heirs and all claiming under the decedent.—Cunningham v. Ashley, 45 Cal. 484, 485, 494. And a judgment in favor of the administrator would inure to the benefit of the heir and of his grantee, to whom he had conveyed prior to the recovery of the judgment.—Spotts v. Hanley, 85 Cal. 155, 167, 168, 24 Pac. 738.

REFERENCES.

Right of an executor or administrator to maintain ejectment regarding the lands of the deceased.—See note to Mayer v. Kornegay, 136 Am. St. 81-86. Ejectment by executor or administrator.—See note 18 L. R. A. 789.

20. **Trusts and trustees.**—An administrator is not a proper party to bring an action to establish a trust and to compel a conveyance of the legal title of land to himself.—Janes v. Throckmorton, 57 Cal. 368, 387; Field v. Andrada, 106 Cal. 107, 108, 39 Pac. 323. An administrator can not maintain an action against a trustee under a trust created by deceased in his lifetime, where neither the trust property nor its proceeds constitute a part of the estate.—Barrette v. Dooly, 21 Utah 81, 59 Pac. 718. Without showing that an alleged trust fund is mingled with some part of a decedent's estate into which it can be traced, no action in equity can be maintained to have it declared a lien thereon and to have it or its equivalent paid over to the beneficiary; and, without averments of a conversion, or some other breach of trust by the representative of the estate, no action at law can be sustained against the estate without averring a presentation of a claim for the fund claimed.—Burke v. Maguire, 154 Cal. 456, 98 Pac. 21. An action may be maintained by an administrator to charge defendants as involuntary trustees of his intestate and to redeem from such persons, who hold a deed of trust executed by the deceased in his lifetime, etc.—Smith v. Goethe, 147 Cal. 725, 730, 733, 82 Pac. 384. In a suit by the administrator of a deceased locator of a mining claim to have the patentee declared a trustee for the estate, on the ground of

fraud, the burden is on the plaintiff of proving the alleged fraud.—Scott v. Crouch, 24 Utah 377, 67 Pac. 1068, 1070. Trustees who are also executors may maintain a suit in equity for the judicial construction of the trusts of the will instead of leaving the matter to be disposed of by the probate court on the distribution of the estate.—Knox v. Knox, 87 Kan. 381, 124 Pac. 410. One who sells before his grantor's death after having become grantee by reason of his promise to hold in trust for the grantor for life and at his death sell the property and share the proceeds with the heirs, commits a breach of trust and may be sued therefor by the administrator.—Pearl v. Pearl, 177 Cal. 303, 177 Pac. 845. A plaintiff administrator sets out a good cause of action by alleging that the defendant accepted a deed from the decedent, and gave no consideration, but promised to hold for him in trust and to convey as he might direct, and at the grantor's death to sell the property and share the proceeds equally with the heirs; and that the defendant defaulted in his promise; that he converted the property; and that he will not account for the proceeds.—Pearl v. Pearl, 177 Cal. 303, 177 Pac. 845.

21. To recover excessive fees charged.—An action may be maintained by an executor to recover from a public officer excessive fees charged for filing papers in the estate, under circumstances showing that the payment was compulsory and not voluntary; and it is none the less compulsory that the party could have procured a writ of mandate compelling the officer to file the papers without the fees demanded.—Lewis v. San Francisco, 2 Cal. App. 112, 82 Pac. 1106. Administrator's assignments of claims against city and county for illegal fees exacted for filing papers held not within the California Code of Civil Procedure, section 1517, requiring an order of court to validate any sales of estate property, it being presumed that the probate court did not give them credit for such payments so that they were charged to them individually, giving them the right to recover from the city and county in their individual capacities.—Trower v. San Francisco, 157 Cal. 762, 109 Pac. 617.

22. On foreign judgments.—If a judgment debtor removes to another jurisdiction, administration may be there granted, and the administrator appointed may maintain an action upon such judgment.—Law v. Horner, 10 Haw. 531, 539. An action may be maintained in the state of California by an executor appointed in a foreign state, upon a judgment obtained in such foreign state, as upon a debt at law due to the plaintiff personally.—Lewis v. Adams, 70 Cal. 403, 411, 59 Am. Rep. 423, 11 Pac. 833.

23. Gifts.—If an action brought by an administrator is one to recover a gift in view of death, the complaint sufficiently shows, if that is necessary, that there are creditors interested in having the property recovered, where it alleges that there are outstanding and unpaid claims which have been duly presented, allowed by the administrator,

and approved by the county judge, to a specified amount, and that there is no property other than that in possession of defendants out of which they can be satisfied.—Bright v. Ecker, 9 S. D. 192, 68 N. W. 326, 327. In an action by an administrator to recover a bank deposit of decedent, a claim of gift from the decedent, by a third party, supported only by the oath of the claimant, should be received with caution, and even with suspicion, in order to prevent frauds.—Freese v. Odd Fellows' Sav. Bank, 136 Cal. 662, 665, 69 Pac. 493. If it is shown, in an action by the executor of a deceased husband to recover bank deposits of community property from the executor of the wife, who died after drawing and transferring them to her own account, that the husband had done everything necessary to a valid gift to his wife, and so intended, the gift was complete.—Spring v. Walton, 145 Cal. 228, 233, 79 Pac. 645. And oral declarations by the donor at the time are admissible to show the husband's intent to make a gift.— Spring v. Walton, 145 Cal. 228, 234, 78 Pac. 645. If such deposits did not pass as a gift, they may be recovered without presenting a claim against the estate of the deceased wife.—Spring v. Walton, 145 Cal. 228, 233, 78 Pac. 645.

24. For Injunction.—An administrator is entitled to bring an action against a county, county judge thereof, and others, to enjoin and restrain the prosecution of a proceeding instituted by the county, for his removal as such administrator, where it appears, among other facts, that the action or proceeding sought to be enjoined was instituted in pursuance of a conspiracy entered into by the county judge, and the attorneys for the county, upon false charges of misconduct against the administrator, filed in the name of the county by certain of the defendants.—Alderman v. Tillamook Co., 50 Or. 48, 91 Pac. 298.

25. For life insurance, and sick benefits.—In an action on a policy of life insurance, which does not contain the name of any beneficiary, but is payable subject to the will of the insured, and where the insured died, leaving a will, by which he gave all his estate to a person named, after payment of his debts, and appointed another person executor, the latter is the proper party to recover on the policy.—Winterhalter v. Workmen, etc., Fund Assoc., 75 Cal. 245, 250, 17 Pac. 1. An action to recover sick benefits due the deceased during his lifetime, from a defendant voluntary beneficial association, is properly brought by and in the name of the personal representative.—Pearson v. Anderburg, 28 Utah 495, 80 Pac. 307, 308. This right to maintain an action against a voluntary benefit association is not lost by stipulations made by the deceased in his application to become a member, to the effect that, "I will seek my remedy for all legal rights on account of said membership or connection therewith, in the tribunals of the order only, without resorting for their enforcement, in any event, or for any purpose, to the civil courts." This stipulation does not go to the extent of affecting a property right created by, and growing out of, a contract with the association.—Pearson v. Anderburg, 28 Utah 495, 80 Pac. 307,

309. An action may be maintained by an administrator against the executor of a deceased predecessor in administration to recover the proceeds of a life insurance policy on the life of the intestate, collected but not accounted for by the deceased administrator.—Curran v. Kennedy, 89 Cal. 98, 26 Pac. 641. If the constitution and by-laws of a fraternal insurance brotherhood provide that, if a member dies without having a legally designated beneficiary, the beneficiary shall be his widow if he leaves a widow, the administrator of the widow's estate is entitled to collect on the beneficiary certificate, where the widow died before she had time or opportunity to collect it herself.—Beeson v. Lotz, 101 Kan. 399, 166 Pac. 466. If the widow of a deceased husband dies intestate before she actually gets possession of her share of the proceeds of certificate of insurance belonging to his estate, her administrator has the right to sue for and to collect the same.—German American Trust Co. v. Ten Winkel, 62 Colo. 96, 99, 160 Pac. 188.

26. For dividends on stock.—In a suit by an executor for dividends on stock, pledged to the defendant by the testator in a transaction of loan,.it is not essential to the defense to show by the answer that a claim, based on the non-payment of the loan has been presented to the executor.—Savings Union B. & T. Co. v. Crowley, 176 Cal. 543, 169 Pac. 67. Evidence examined in a controversy, as to who, as between an executor and the testator's widow, was entitled to dividends on corporation stock, the certificates for which had been given her by her husband, along with his notes, as collateral for a loan; held sufficient to support findings establishing a valid pledge, and the fact that the full principal and interest of the notes were in default.—Savings Union B. & T. Co. v. Crowley, 176 Cal. 543, 169 Pac. 67.

27. On mortgages.—In an action by an administrator to obtain a decree to the effect that the intestate was, at the time of his death, the owner of certain lands; that an accounting be had to determine the amount due to defendant upon a mortgage; that defendant has no right, title, or interest in the land, except as a mortgage thereof; and that, upon the payment to defendant of such sum as may be found due him (if any), he be required to satisfy the mortgage,—the proper judgment to be rendered is that, upon the failure of plaintiff to pay the amount found due, within the time specified by the court, the action be dismissed.—Boyce v. Fisk, 110 Cal. 107, 116, 42 Pac. 473; Booth v. Hoskins, 75 Cal. 271, 17 Pac. 225. In an action by an administrator to foreclose a mortgage, the defendant is not permitted to plead a note held by him against the testator, as a counterclaim, where such note is barred by the statute of limitations at the commencement of the action upon the principal claim, inasmuch as the same did not constitute a cause of action existing at the commencement of the action, or upon which a counterclaim was maintainable.—Lyon v. Petty, 65 Cal. 322, 325, 4 Pac. 103. The answer in such an action should set forth the fact as to when the note pleaded as a counterclaim was assigned to defendant. It is not sufficient to aver that the assignment was before the death of the maker. It must appear whether such assignment was before or after the maturity of the note itself. If the note was assigned before maturity, it would have constituted the subject-matter of a counterclaim if a cause of action could have been predicated upon it at the commencement of the plaintiff's action; but, if after maturity, the assignee took it subject to all existing equities between the maker and the payees. Under such circumstances it would not be the subject of a counterclaim, and could not be pleaded as such.—Lyon v. Petty, 65 Cal. 322, 325, 4 Pac. 103. An action to foreclose a mortgage given to secure a debt due to the deceased should be brought by the administrator. The heirs are not proper parties.—Grattan v. Wiggins, 23 Cal. 16, 29. An executor of the mortgagee of land must bring suit to foreclose before the statute of limitations has run against the mortgage, or the grantee of the mortgagor may plead the bar of the statute.—California Title, etc., Ins. Co. v. Miller, 3 Cal. App. 54, 58, 84 Pac. 453.

28. Partition.—An administrator has no such interest in the land of an estate as entitles him to sue for a partition.—Ryer v. Fletcher Ryer Co., 126 Cal. 482, 485, 58 Pac. 908.

29. To quiet title, or to determine adverse claims.—An executor or administrator is authorized, by the statute of North Dakota, to bring an action to quiet title to real estate belonging to a decedent, pending administration of the estate.—Blakemore v. Roberts, 12 N. D. 394, 96 N. W. 1029. Actions to quiet title, or determine any adverse claim to property of an estate, may be brought by an administrator, and a suit to set aside a deed on the ground of incapacity of the grantor is clearly within this provision.—Collins v. O'Laverty, 136 Cal. 31, 33, 60 Pac. 327. The sole test of the right of action is the right of the estate to the possession of the property.—Collins v. O'Laverty, 136 Cal. 31, 35, 60 Pac. 327. A suit to determine adverse claims to property of the estate is rightly brought in the name of the administrator, and is prosecuted for the benefit of the estate.—Curtis v. Sutter, 15 Cal. 259, 264; Pennie v. Hildreth, 81 Cal. 127, 130, 22 Pac. 398. Under the statute of Colorado, an administrator is not authorized to sue to remove a cloud from a leasehold interest held by his intestate, where there is no allegation that a sale of the land is necessary to pay debts, etc.—McKee v. Howe, 17 Colo. 538, 31 Pac. 115, 116. Nor can he sue to quiet title to a water right appurtenant to land.—Travelers Ins. Co. v. Childs, 25 Colo. 360, 54 Pac. 1020, 1023. Although an administrator has no legal title to the real property of a decedent, yet, as he is entitled to possession thereof, he has such an interest as entitles him to maintain suit to determine an adverse claim thereto.—Ladd v. Mills, 44 Or. 224, 75 Pac. 141, 142. In an action by an administrator to quiet title, where the complaint is unverified, a general denial puts in issue the fact that he is administrator.—Pennie v. Hildreth, 81 Cal. 127, 132, 22 Pac. 398. Under the statutes of Colorado, an administrator can maintain an action to quiet title to the real property of his intestate.—

Galligan v. Thomas S. Hayden Realty Co., 62 Colo. 477, 163 Pac. 295. An administrator has sufficient interest in the property of the decedent to entitle him to bring an action to quiet title, under section 738, Code of Civil Procedure of the state of South Dakota.—Berry v. Howard, 26 S. D. 29, Ann. Cas. 1913A, 994, 127 N. W. 526. The statute of South Dakota, however, does not vest in an executor or administrator appointed in some other state such an interest in real property situated in South Dakota as would authorize him to maintain an action to quiet title to land in the state last named.—Colburn v. Latham, 32 S. D. 310, 143 N. W. 278. The rule established by section 1589 of the Code of Civil Procedure of California, whereby the right of the executor or administrator to avoid the fraudulent transfer of the decedent is conditioned upon there being a deficiency of assets, has no reference to actions by executors and administrators to recover property or quiet title thereto, or determine an adverse claim thereon.—Rice v. Carey, 170 Cal. 748, 151 Pac. 135. A foreign administrator has not such an interest in the real estate of the decedent as will entitle him to maintain an action to determine an adverse claim thereto as required by section 675 of the Code of Civil Procedure and section 252, Probate Code.—Colburn v. Latham, 32 S. D. 310, 143 N. W. 278. No adverse possession can ever be acquired as against a remainderman, so long as the life tenant or party who holds the conditional fee is in possession or has not been ousted for condition broken.—Martin v. City of Stockton (Cal. App.), 179 Pac. 894. In an action by an administrator and heirs of a decedent to quiet title to land, where the defendant, cross-complainant, pleaded a former judgment of the same superior court quieting his title by publication against Bartels and the other defendants upon constructive service ordered by the court, it is held that the court properly excluded evidence of the appointment of the administrator, in order collaterally to assail the former judgment by showing that deceased was dead when the former suit was commenced. It is held that the exact date of his death was not essential to the order of appointment and was not concluded thereby.—Layne v. Johnson, 19 Cal. App. 95, 124 Pac. 860. Suits for the recovery of real property, to remove a cloud therefrom, and to quiet title thereto may be maintained by and against administrators and executors; and in such suits the heirs of the decedent or intestate are not necessary parties, either in the court below or on appeal.—Jameson v. Goodwin, 43 Okla. 154, 141 Pac. 767.

REFERENCE.

Right of the personal representative to maintain action to quiet title to the decedent's real estate.—See note Ann. Cas. 1913A, 996.

30. Replevin.—An action to recover personal property of the estate may be maintained by the administrator, against one who claims title thereto, without a previous demand.—Knight v. Tripp, 5 Cal. Unrep. 735, 49 Pac. 838, 839. In an action by an administrator to recover assets claimed to belong to his intestate's estate, the plaintiff's own

affidavit, and a prior citation issued by the county judge, requiring defendant to appear and be examined, and the order of the county court made on such hearing, requiring defendant to disclose his knowledge of assets of the estate appropriated by him, and to deliver such assets to plaintiff, are competent evidence, and it is error to sustain an objection to it.—Bright v. Ecker, 9 S. D. 192, 68 N. W. 326, 327. If an executor borrows money to pay debts of the estate, and pledges the personal property thereof to secure its payment, he may sue in replevin to recover such pledged property.—Parks v. Mockenhaupt, 133 Cal. 424, 425, 65 Pac. 875. An administrator, under the Kansas statute, may maintain any possessory action to enforce his right to the possession of the personal estate.—Black v. Elliott, 63 Kan. 211, 88 Am. St. Rep. 239, 65 Pac. 215; following Bauserman v. Charlotte, 46 Kan. 480, 26 Pac. 1051, and Kulp v. Kulp, 51 Kan. 341, 21 L. R. A. 550, 32 Pac. 1118.

31. To set aside fraudulent conveyances.

(1) In general.—Where a complaint, by an administrator, to set aside a conveyance for the benefit of creditors charges actual fraud on the part of the deceased grantor, and the evidence shows the conveyance to have been voluntary; that the deceased was indebted at the time, and conveyed all his property subject to execution; that the conveyance was kept secret; that the grantor continued to use the property as his own until the time of his death; and that there were other circumstances of a want of good faith; and there is no substantial contradiction,—a finding which negatives the charge of fraud is unwarranted by the testimony.—Daugherty v. Daugherty, 104 Cal. 221, 223, 37 Pac. 889. An executor or administrator may maintain an action necessary either to protect his possession or reduce into possession property of the estate held by others.—Collins v. O'Laverty, 136 Cal. 31, 35, 68 Pac. 327. Where the husband fraudulently conveyed land to his wife, but the deed was not recorded, and he continued to exercise acts of ownership, and had it assessed to himself until his death, a judgment creditor of the husband may pursue the land to enforce his judgment lien thereon without joining the executrix of the deceased husband as a defendant and without having presented his claim to the estate within the time limited by statute.—O'Doherty v. Toole, 2 Ariz. 288, 15 Pac. 28. Where an estate is insolvent, and there is reason to believe that a conveyance of land executed by decedent was fraudulent, the creditors have the right to insist that the administrator endeavor to recover it for their benefit, and if he refuses to do so, or his personal interest tends to prevent him from doing his duty in this regard, he should be removed.—Marks v. Coats, 37 Or. 609, 62 Pac. 488. If the pleader, in an action to recover property embezzled or alienated before the granting of letters of administration, desires to show that there are acknowledged debts against the estate, it is appropriate for him to allege that the claims have been "approved" by the county judge, where

the statute provides that claims against an estate "allowed by the executor or administrator, and approved by the judge," etc., shall be filed in the county court, and be ranked among the acknowledged debts of the estate to be paid in due course of administration.—Bright v. Ecker, 9 S. D. 192, 68 N. W. 326, 327. In a suit by an administrator to recover, for the benefit of creditors, property fraudulently conveyed by the deceased, he is entitled to recover only the decedent's interest in the property fraudulently conveyed. If it had been previously mortgaged, and the fraudulent grantee discharged that mortgage, he is entitled to be subrogated to the rights of the mortgagee.— Ackerman v. Merle, 137 Cal. 169, 171, 69 Pac. 983. In an' action by an administrator to recover, for the benefit of creditors, property fraudulently conveyed by the deceased, he may recover all the property so conveyed, if his complaint is otherwise sufficient, without a direct allegation that all is necessary to pay debts.—Ackerman v. Merle, 137 Cal. 157, 158, 69 Pac. 982. A judgment in ejectment against an executor, in favor of the grantee in a fraudulent deed of a deceased person, is not a bar to a suit in equity, brought either by the executor or by a creditor of the testator, to set aside such fraudulent deed, on which the judgment in ejectment was obtained, and to apply the property in payment of his claim.—Hills v. Sherwood, 48 Cal. 386, 392. Where land was fraudulently conveyed by a grantor, since deceased, it is not necessary, in a suit by his administrator to subject such land to the debts and expenses of the estate, for the complaint to allege the names of creditors who would have been defrauded by the transfer.—Peterson v. Tull, 85 Wash. 546, 148 Pac. 598. An alleged transfer of a mortgage and notes by a feeble woman, near the time of her death, to a brutal son who threatened her, there being no proof of such transfer save the son's word and there having been no delivery during the woman's life, should set aside.—Peterson v. Lindquist (N. D.), 169 N. W. 76.

(2) **Duty and authority.**—It is the duty of an executor or administrator to invoke the aid of equity to set aside fraudulent transfers of property made by his testator or intestate, when the same is necessary for the protection of creditors.—Hillman v. Young, 64 Or. 73, 80, 127 Pac. 793, 129 Pac. 124. The administrator has power, and statute makes it his duty, to "sue for, recover and preserve the estate both real and personal"; he may properly therefore sue to have a deed set aside, that, having been made by the decedent, is alleged to be void as against lawful claims against the estate.—Grover v. Clover (Cal.), 169 Pac. 578. Where a decedent in his lifetime, conveyed property in fraud of his creditors, the executor or administrator is expressly authorized by statute to sue in equity to avoid the conveyance, in case of a deficiency of assets to pay the debts of the estate.—Dirks v. Union Sav. Assn. (S. D.), 168 N. W. 578. An executor may, under the provisions of sections 1589-1591, Code Civ. Proc. of California, without obtaining an order from the probate court, sue to set aside a convey-

ance made by the decedent on the ground that it was void as made to defraud creditors.—Adams v. Prather, 176 Cal. 33, 167 Pac. 534, 538.

(3) May be brought by special administrator when.—If suit be brought by a special administratrix to set aside a deed and to recover property for the estate, and a will is afterward probated, and both plaintiff and defendant in that action are appointed and qualified as executors, the executrix, who was the special administratrix and the original plaintiff, is the proper party to prosecute the action, and the defendant should retain his individual character therein.—Stohr v. Stohr, 148 Cal. 180, 182, 82 Pac. 40, 777. Where there is a deficiency of assets, an action may be maintained by a special administrator to recover property, for the benefit of creditors, which had been fraudulently conveyed by decedent in his lifetime.—Forde v. Exempt Fire Co., 50 Cal. 299, 302. The statute of limitations does not afford a defense to an action brought by a special administrator to set aside a fraudulent conveyance made by the deceased, where, by the complaint, it appeared that the conveyance was made with the intent to defraud the creditors, and that there was a deficiency in the assets of the decedent's estate, and that some of the creditors obtained judgment against the estate within three years next before the filing of the complaint.—Forde v. Exempt Fire Co., 50 Cal. 299, 302. Under the California statute, it is the duty of a special administrator, where there is a deficiency of assets, to maintain an action to recover real estate conveyed by the decedent, in his lifetime, with the intent to defraud his creditors.—Forde v. Exempt Fire Co., 50 Cal. 299, 302.

(4) May be brought by creditor when.—If it is made the duty of an executor or administrator to sue to recover property fraudulently conveyed by the deceased, when there is a deficiency of assets, such action by a creditor will not ordinarily lie, at least until he has exhausted all means to procure action by the representative; but where the representative is also the fraudulent grantee, it may be maintained by the creditor or his assignee.—Emmons v. Barton, 109 Cal. 662, 668, 42 Pac. 303. A statute empowering the executor or administrator to prosecute an action to set aside a fraudulent conveyance of the personalty or realty by the testator or intestate does not necessarily preclude the creditors from bringing such action, if they are authorized so to do by the general law.—Hills v. Sherwood, 48 Cal. 386, 393. A creditor has, under the general laws, the right to pursue property fraudulently conveyed by the debtor, in the hands of the vendee, without joining the executor of the deceased debtor. The statute gives the executor or administrator the right, when the assets are not sufficient to pay the debts of the estate, to bring suit to set aside a fraudulent conveyance of the testator or intestate; but he is not the only party who has that right. The right is given for the protection of creditors, and a creditor himself may, in equity, pursue the remedy.—O'Doherty v. Toole, 2 Ariz. 288, 15 Pac. 28. The statute providing for the filing of claims against an estate within a specified period, while barring the creditor from collecting his debt against the estate proper (in this instance an insolvent estate), does not preclude the creditor from bringing an action to recover property fraudulently conveyed by a deceased debtor.—O'Doherty v. Toole, 2 Ariz. 288, 15 Pac. 28. Claims against an estate, which have been allowed, may be assigned to one of the creditors for the purpose of bringing an action to set aside a fraudulent conveyance of property by the decedent; and where the grantee of such a conveyance is executrix, the action may be brought by the assignee creditor.—Emmons v. Barton, 109 Cal. 662, 667, 668, 42 Pac. 303. An action to set aside a fraudulent conveyance made by a decedent in his lifetime may be maintained by a creditor of the estate, where the administrator occupies a position hostile to the creditor and refuses to act at his request.—Barker v. Battey, 62 Kan. 584, 64 Pac. 75. It has been held, in Utah, that a creditor can not maintain an action to set aside a fraudulent conveyance by a deceased debtor without first demanding that the administrator bring such suit and being met by a refusal to comply on the part of the latter.—Fehringer v. Commercial Nat. Bank, 23 Utah 393, 64 Pac. 1108. An administrator of a deceased creditor may prosecute an action commenced by his intestate against the widow of a deceased debtor to set aside an alleged fraudulent conveyance by the latter.—Perea v. De Gallegos, 3 N. M. 151, 3 Pac. 246, 248. A judgment in an action by a creditor to set aside a fraudulent conveyance of real property made by an intestate proves the indebtedness prima facie in favor of the plaintiff as against the grantee of the intestate.—Hills v. Sherwood, 48 Cal. 386, 393. See McLaughlin v. Bank of Potomac, 7 How. (U. S.) 221, 12 L. Ed. 675. The holder of a claim against an estate, which has been disallowed by the administrator, is not a creditor who may compel the administrator to sue for property alleged to have been fraudulently conveyed by the deceased.—Ohm v. Superior Court, 85 Cal. 545, 548, 20 Am. St. Rep. 245, 26 Pac. 244. But an order that the administratrix allow her name to be used in a suit for the recovery of such property for the benefit of creditors is not appealable.—Estate of Ohm, 82 Cal. 160, 161, 163, 22 Pac. 927. Where a debtor conveyed property in alleged fraud of creditors, creditors can not, after his death, bring an action to set aside the conveyance without first having applied to the court for an order directing the administrator to bring the action, as provided by sections 1589 and 1590, Code of Civil Procedure of California.—Beswick v. Churchill Company, 22 Cal. App. 404, 132 Pac. 771.

(5) Elements necessary to maintain.—The administrator of a deceased person can not maintain any claim against a surviving wife, for whom provision had been made by the deceased, while solvent, in the setting apart to her of property, upon which a large sum constituting community property had been expended, that the deceased himself could not have successfully asserted in his lifetime; and this applies also to the creditors, who, like the administrator, are limited by the

Probate Law—93

lines bounding the rights of the husband, except in cases of a disposition of his property for the purpose of defrauding them.—Peck v. Brummagim, 31 Cal. 440, 450, 89 Am. Dec. 195. In an action by an administrator to set aside a conveyance of land by the deceased, on the ground that it was in fraud of creditors, it must appear that there are creditors and that there is an insufficiency of assets to meet their demands.—Field v. Andrada, 106 Cal. 107, 110, 39 Pac. 323. In an action by an administrator to subject to administration certain property alleged to have been conveyed by the decedent in his lifetime, in fraud of creditors, where there is neither a claim nor a pretense that the decedent, in making the conveyance in question, had any intent to defraud any one, and where a conveyance by gift is not made, it can not be said that the conveyance is fraudulent as a matter of law. The question of fraudulent intent is one of fact and not of law.—Brown v. Pereault, 5 Ida. 729, 51 Pac. 752. In an action by an administrator against the wife of a decedent to recover property alleged to have been fraudulently conveyed to her, the fraudulent intent of the grantor must be alleged.—Threlkel v. Scott, 89 Cal. 351, 353, 26 Pac. 879. In an action by a legatee against the administrator of a deceased executor to compel the application of property, alleged to have been fraudulently concealed and misapplied by such deceased executor, in payment of a legacy to plaintiff, the complaint should show proper diligence in discovering the alleged fraud; and if more than three years have elapsed after the perpetration of it, the facts and circumstances should be stated which would excuse delay in its discovery.—Burke v. Maguire, 154 Cal. 456, 98 Pac. 21. On the trial of an action by an administrator to recover, for the benefit of creditors, personal property fraudulently transferred by a deceased debtor, evidence that there were creditors to be defrauded, and that the transfer was made with intent to defraud them, would be material, and its exclusion is reversible error.—Harris v. Harris, 59 Cal. 623. It is only in a case where there are no funds otherwise available for paying creditors of the estate that the administrator may sue to have a fraudulent transfer set aside that his decedent made. —Holland v. Kelly, 177 Cal. 43, 171 Pac. 421. An administrator of an insolvent estate has no authority, in Hawaii, to bring a suit to set aside a conveyance of real estate made by the decedent in fraud of creditors.—Estate of Lopez, 19 Haw. 620.

REFERENCES.

The right of executors or administrators to set aside conveyances made by the deceased in fraud of creditors.—See comprehensive note to the case of Sifford v. Cutler, 135 Am. St. 329-341. Constitutionality of statute, authorizing disposition of surplus, after the setting aside of a sale fraudulent as to creditors.—See note § 641, ante.

32. Set-off and counterclaim.—In a suit by an administrator, a defendant having a set-off may plead and prove the same without showing that it has been presented as a claim against the estate, and

this, notwithstanding the amount of the set-off exceeds the sum sued
for, though in such case no judgment for the surplus should be rendered against the estate.—Murphy v. Colton, 4 Okla. 181, 44 Pac. 208,
209; Fishburne v. Merchants' Bank, 42 Wash. 473, 7 Ann. Cas. 848,
85 Pac. 38, 40; Talty v. Torling, 79 Minn. 386, 82 N. W. 632. In an
action by an executrix to recover a deposit of her testator from a
bank, the latter may plead as a counterclaim the application of the
amount in part payment of a promissory note of the testator held by
it for a larger amount, which fell due after his death, but before
suit was brought.—Ainsworth v. Bank of California, 119 Cal. 470, 474, 475,
63 Am. St. Rep. 135, 39 L. R. A. 686, 51 Pac. 952. Under the Washington statute, a set-off may be interposed by the defendant in an
action by an executor or administrator, and it is not required that
such set-off claim shall be first presented to the executor or administrator.—Fishburne v. Merchants' Bank, 42 Wash. 473, 7 Ann. Cas. 848,
85 Pac. 38, 40. A note may be interposed as a set-off in an action by
an administrator, where such note had matured before the commencement of the action. A note maturing after death, and before the commencement of the action, may be properly interposed by way of
counterclaim in an action by the executor or administrator.—Fishburne
v. Merchants' Bank, 42 Wash. 473, 7 Ann. Cas. 848, 85 Pac. 38, 40;
Ainsworth v. Bank of California, 119 Cal. 470, 39 L. R. A. 686, 63 Am.
St. Rep. 135, 51 Pac. 952. The code provision concerning set-off
relates to the situation of the parties "at the commencement of the action,"
and the death of one of the parties to the demand, though such death
occur before the maturity of the demand, does not change the relative
rights of the parties in pleading a counterclaim, or in compensating
the claims so far as they equal each other, provided the set-off be due
when the action is commenced.—Ainsworth v. Bank of California, 119
Cal. 470, 474, 63 Am. St. Rep. 135, 39 L. R. A. 686, 51 Pac. 952.
If a patient of a physician has transferred all of his property, which
fact is known to the physician, who delays for a number of years,
after the patient's death, to assert his rights in the estate, such
physician can not, when sued on an individual claim by the administrator of the decedent, and which administrator was the transferee of
the decedent's property, counterclaim for his services on the ground
of a trust imposed on the plaintiff to pay the decedent's debts when
the property was conveyed to him.—Lauridsen v. Lewis, 50 Wash. 605,
97 Pac. 663, 665. In an action by an administrator to recover upon
a promissory note executed by the defendant to the intestate, the
defendant can not set up, by way of counterclaim, his share of an
indebtedness alleged to be due to him from the intestate, because of
partnership moneys misappropriated by the latter, where there is no
averment in the counterclaim that any claim had ever been presented
to the representative of the estate of the deceased, or any allowance made.—Reed v. Johnson, 127 Cal. 538, 541, 59 Pac. 986. The
cross-demand must have been an existing demand against the testator

or intestate at his death. It is not necessary that the cross-demand thus existing should have become due at the time of the testator's death. It is sufficient if it becomes due and payable in time to be pleaded as a set-off in the same manner as if the testator or intestate had lived to bring the action.—Ainsworth v. Bank of California, 119 Cal. 470, 475, 63 Am. St. Rep. 135, 39 L. R. A. 686, 51 Pac. 952. The statute of the state of Washington, relating to counterclaims for betterments, in actions for the possession of real estate, is not sufficiently broad to create a liability for improvements in one who has inherited a community interest through the death of his mother, as against his father's administrator.—In re Mason's Estate, Mason v. Mason, 95 Wash. 564, 164 Pac. 205. In a cause pending, for having a bank declared insolvent and for the appointment of a receiver, an administrator may file a petition in intervention, to the end that funds deposited in the bank by the petitioner may be set off against an indebtedness to the bank, contracted by the decedent during his lifetime; such facts present a situation wherein an exception to the general rule of mutuality of claims in set-off should be applied and the set-off allowed.—People v. California S. D. & T. Co., 168 Cal. 241, L. R. A. 1915A, 299, 141 Pac. 1181.

REFERENCES.

Right of persons sued by an executor or administrator to set off a claim against the deceased not presented within the statutory period.— See note 7 Am. & Eng. Ann. Cas. 850. Right of personal representative to set off, against joint debt of estate, legacy or distributive share due to one of joint debtors.—See note 21 Ann. Cas. 812.

33. For trespass on land.—An administrator is a proper party to sue for damages to land of the deceased, which accrued in the lifetime of the latter.—Hanlen v. Baden, 6 Kan. App. 635, 49 Pac. 615, 616. As to the sufficiency of allegations that plaintiffs are qualified administrators, see Central Branch, etc., R. R. Co. v. Andrews, 37 Kan. 162, 14 Pac. 509. A sole devisee in possession, who is also executrix, may sue for damages to property of the estate, and a recovery by her as devisee would bar a recovery by her for the same cause as executrix.—Colton v. Onderdonk, 69 Cal. 155, 159, 58 Am. Rep. 556, 10 Pac. 395. A cause of action for trespass or injury to land, occurring after the death of a decedent, does not pass to the executor or administrator, but to the heir or devisee. An executor who has no estate in the premises, except the right to lease the same, can not, therefore, maintain an action for trespass or waste.—Adams v. Slattery, 36 Colo. 35, 85 Pac. 87, 88. An action brought by testamentary executors and trustees for damages to land of the estate in which, under the law of Kansas, the widow has a right, must fail for want of joinder of the widow as a necessary party, unless it is shown that she consented to the will, or elected to take under it.—Atchison, etc., Ry. Co. v. Davenport, 65 Kan. 206, 69 Pac. 195, 199.

34. Unlawful detainer.—Actions to recover both real and personal estate may be maintained by an administrator or executor; hence, a proceeding may be successfully urged by an administrator de bonis non for forcible entry and detainer, even against those claiming the property as heirs or devisees.—Griffith v. James, 91 Wash. 607, 158 Pac. 251. Executors of a deceased lessor may give the necessary notice and maintain an action in unlawful detainer against lessees of the deceased, who hold after rent due and demand made.—Knowles v. Murphy, 107 Cal. 107, 112, 40 Pac. 111.

35. Limitation of actions.—The statute of limitations does not commence to run upon a contract until the plaintiff can maintain an action thereon. Hence an administrator may maintain an action upon a contract made eight years prior to the commencement of the action, where it appears that the contingency on which payment depended happened within the period of the statute.—Noyes v. Young, 32 Mont. 226, 79 Pac. 1063, 1066. An action by an executor of a deceased husband is not barred by limitation against the administratrix of his deceased widow, where the latter was appointed less than two years before action was commenced.—Sprague v. Walton, 145 Cal. 228, 236, 78 Pac. 645. If an executor or administrator makes a void sale of the land of a decedent, and fails to sue for the recovery of the land, or to set aside the sale, the three years' statute of limitations begins to run after the administrator has had a reasonable time in which to obtain settlement of his final account, and what is such reasonable time must depend, in general, on the circumstances of each estate.—Dennis v. Bint, 122 Cal. 39, 44, 45, 68 Am. St. Rep. 17, 54 Pac. 378. Under a statute by which, upon the death of a plaintiff, an order to revive the action in the names of his representatives or successors may be made, but shall not be made without the consent of defendant after the expiration of one year from the time the order might have first been made, the statute of limitations is not suspended until the appointment of a representative, but begins to run after the expiration of a reasonable time from the death in which a representative might have been appointed, and parties seeking to avail themselves of its benefit must use diligence and strictly comply with its terms.—Glazier v. Heneybuss, 19 Okla. 316, 91 Pac. 872. Under the California statute, the executors or administrators of a deceased judgment creditor may, by motion and order, obtain and enforce execution upon a judgment in favor of their decedent after the lapse of five years from the date of its entry.—Weldon v. Rogers, 151 Cal. 432, 435, 90 Pac. 1062. Suit brought by the assignee of a mortgage to foreclose the same for the benefit of the assignor, who is administrator of the mortgagor's estate, may be disregarded in considering whether the action is barred by limitation.—Brown v. Mann, 71 Cal. 192, 193, 12 Pac. 51. If an administratrix, because of lapse of time, can not maintain an action to recover property of the estate sold by her under proceedings alleged to be defective, the right of the heirs to maintain such action is also barred.—Dennis v. Bint, 122 Cal. 39, 47, 68 Am. St. Rep. 17, 54 Pac. 378; McLeran v. Benton, 73 Cal. 329, 342, 2 Am. St. Rep. 814, 14 Pac. 879; Jenkins v. Jensen, 24 Utah 108, 91 Am. St. Rep. 783, 66 Pac. 773, 778. A letter by a debtor of a decedent to plaintiff, before the latter became administrator, although an heir, could not revive a right of action barred by limitation.—Visher v. Wilbur, 5 Cal. App. 562, 90 Pac. 1065, 91 Pac. 412. An administrator will not be permitted to waive the statute of limitations.—Boyce v. Fisk, 110 Cal. 107, 117, 42 Pac. 473.

REFERENCES.

The statute of limitations begins to run in favor of an executor or administrator when.—See note 99 Am. Dec. 394-396.

36. Termination of right to sue.—If it is conceded that an administrator, at the time suit was brought, had ceased to be the administrator, no cause of action can be maintained by him as such. But if it appears on retrial that a bill of sale for the property in controversy should have been to the plaintiff individually, and not as administrator, the reference to him as administrator should be regarded as merely descriptive of the person.—Afflerbach v. McGovern, 79 Cal. 268, 272, 21 Pac. 837. If a testator dies seised of certain land, leaving a will under which his administratrix is the sole residuary legatee. and it appears that she has made an agreement to sell the property after the time for presentation of claims has passed, and all debts and legacies have been paid, leaving in her hands money much more than sufficient to pay all costs and expenses of administration, she thus becomes the sole beneficiary of the land in question, and not having been empowered by the court to sell the land, her contract to sell it is binding on her personally, and operates as an equitable transfer of the ownership of the property. The purchaser must therefore be regarded in equity as the real owner of the land, and, after the estate has been fully settled, leaving nothing to be done except the entry of the decree, which it is the duty of the executrix to apply for and of the court to enter the power of the executrix to maintain a suit against such purchaser must be regarded as having terminated.—Moffitt v. Rosencrans, 136 Cal. 416, 418, 69 Pac. 87. The right of an executrix to maintain suit against one holding under her personally must be regarded as terminated when the estate has been fully settled, except as to costs of administration, for which she has ample funds; and a person in possession of land, under a contract of purchase not authorized or ratified by the court, will be regarded as holding under her personally.—Moffitt v. Rosencrans, 136 Cal. 416, 418, 419, 69 Pac. 87.

III. ACTIONS AGAINST EXECUTORS OR ADMINISTRATORS.

1. In general.—Section 1582 of the Code of Civil Procedure of California providing for action against executors and administrators "in all cases in which the same might have been maintained by or against their respective testators or intestates" is limited by its terms to actions for the recovery of property or the possession thereof or to quiet title thereto, or to determine any adverse claim thereto, and all actions founded on contracts.—Clark v. Goodwin, 170 Cal. 527, L. R. A. 1916A, 1142, 150 Pac. 357. A third party can not maintain a proceeding to require the executor of a non-intervention will to come into a probate court, but the executor himself may invoke the jurisdiction of such court.—Bayer v. Bayer, 83 Wash. 430, 145 Pac. 433.

2. **Parties.**—In an action in equity to adjudge as null and void a note purporting to have been given by a deceased husband and by the plaintiffs, as joint makers, and which was alleged to have been a false, fraudulent, and forged instrument, the personal representatives of the deceased husband of a co-plaintiff are not necessary parties to the adjudication.—Ritterhoff v. Puget Sound Nat. Bank, 37 Wash. 76, 107 Am. St. Rep. 791, 79 Pac. 601. Where a complete determination of the controversy can not be had without the presence of the administrator, the court has the right to order him to be brought in as a party, upon the application of the plaintiff, through the filing of a supplemental complaint, and summons may be issued and served upon such administrator after the expiration of one year from the commencement of the action, where summons had been issued against the original defendants within the year, as provided by statute. The plaintiff, in such case, was under no obligation to procure the appointment of an administrator at an earlier time.—Churchill v. Woodworth, 148 Cal. 669, 84 Pac. 155, 113 Am. St. Rep. 324. The plaintiff in an action to have a deed absolute in form declared to be a mortgage, and to foreclose the same, may bring his action against the heirs of the mortgagor, and subsequently, upon the appointment of an administrator, the latter should be joined in the action as a necessary party. The plaintiff does not waive his right to bring his action against the administrator within a year after the issuance of letters, by commencing the action against the heirs of the deceased, before the appointment of such administrator. —Churchill v. Woodworth, 148 Cal. 669, 84 Pac. 155, 113 Am. St. Rep. 324. No action will lie against an administrator to set aside a decree between parties, where one of the parties to the suit is dead, and the administrator is brought in, in a representative capacity, and the action concerns rights other than those affecting property as to which the administrator stands only in a representative capacity.—Smith v. Smith, 13 Colo. App. 295, 57 Pac. 747, 748. It is no valid objection to an order substituting an executor or administrator in place of a deceased party to an action, that it was made on the day notice of the application therefor was served.—Skinner v. Lewis, 40 Or. 571, 62 Pac. 523. Under the law of Colorado, where an attempt has been made to revive an action in the name of an administrator which was pending against his decedent at his death, if the administrator has no notice of the proceeding, and did not appear in the action, a judgment against him is void for want of jurisdiction.—Symes v. Charpiot, 17 Colo. App. 463,

466, 69 Pac. 311, 312. Inasmuch as the executor or administrator may, in a proper case, convey real estate in furtherance of the terms of a land contract or a bond for a deed given by the deceased, he is a proper party defendant to a suit to enforce an oral contract of that sort alleged to have been made with the plaintiff by the deceased.— Goff v. Kelsey, 78 Or. 337, 153 Pac. 103. In an action against the estate of a deceased person, the administrator is a necessary party to the proceeding in the trial court, and also to an appeal from an order or judgment denying the application of a judgment creditor for an order directing the administrator to sell real estate.—In re McCann's Estate, 51 Okla. 240, 151 Pac. 887. A cause of action against the executor of an estate, based upon a breach of warranty executed by the decedent, and a cause of action against a devisee of the land affected by the warranty to recover to the extent of the land for the loss suffered by the breach of warranty, can not be joined in the same complaint, and there would result also a misjoinder of parties defendant by reason of the absence of unity of interest.—Tropico Land, etc., Co. v. Lambourn, 170 Cal. 33, 46, 47, 148 Pac. 206.

3. Death and substitution.—In the case of the death of a party defendant, where the action survives, personal representatives may be substituted as defendants, but the action is suspended by the death of the party until an order is made by the court continuing the action against the representatives, and the time during such suspension is no part of the time within which an appeal may be taken.—Oregon Auto-Despatch v. Cadwell, 67 Or. 301, 303, 135 Pac. 880. An action for money had and received may, on the death of the defendant during its pendency, be maintained against his executor.—Selkregg v. Thomas, 27 Colo. App. 259, 149 Pac. 273. If, pending an action against him, a man dies, the court does not lose jurisdiction of the case by the plaintiff's not filing the subject-matter, as a claim, with his executor.—Selkregg v. Thomas, 27 Colo. App. 259, 149 Pac. 273. Death of an administrator defendant, and delay in appointing a successor to him until after the beginning of the five year period to run, does not mark an exception to the statutory rule whereby the court, in its discretion, may, on the defendant's motion, dismiss an action on failure to bring it to trial within five years after the defendant has answered.—Larkin v. Superior Court, 171 Cal. 719, Ann. Cas. 1917D, 670, 154 Pac. 841.

4. By distributees.—An action for the distributive share of an estate by a distributee, after final distribution, should be brought against the administrator in his individual and not in his representative capacity, and it is unnecessary to allege a demand before suit.—Malone v. Davis, 67 Cal. 279, 282, 7 Pac. 703. An action by a legatee against an executor or administrator to recover his share of an estate is an action against the executor or administrator individually, and not against him in his representative capacity. It is not an action against the estate. As against the estate, the rights of the distributee are fully adjudicated by the decree of distribution.—St. Mary's Hospital v. Perry, 152 Cal.

338, 92 Pac. 864, 865. In an action to recover a distributive share of an estate, as fixed by the decree of distribution, for refusal to pay over moneys which, under the decree, it was the duty of the executrix to pay, the words "as executrix," in the title of the action, should be held to be merely descriptive.—St. Mary's Hospital v. Perry, 152 Cal. 338, 92 Pac. 864, 865. In an action to recover plaintiff's share of an estate, distributed to the plaintiff legatee in trust, it is not proper for the judgment against the executrix to specify the terms of the trust.—St. Mary's Hospital v. Perry, 152 Cal. 338, 92 Pac. 864, 866.

5. Against foreign executor or administrator.—A foreign executor, who comes into this state to reside, and brings with him property belonging to the estate, can not be made liable in this state, upon the suit of a local creditor of the testator, to the extent of the property brought here, but may be to the extent of the property already here.— Falke v. Terry, 32 Colo. 85, 75 Pac. 425. Under the statute of Kansas, a foreign executor or administrator may be sued in an action on a contract for the recovery of money, and service may be obtained by attachment and publication.—Cady v. Bard, 21 Kan. 667; Donifelser v. Heyl, 7 Kan. App. 606, 52 Pac. 468. Courts of a state, other than that of the domiciliary jurisdiction, can not try the title of real estate situate in the latter, where the action is one between legatees under a will and a foreign executor, who is charged with the wrongful application of the personal assets of the estate.—Falke v. Terry, 32 Colo. 85, 75 Pac. 425. An administrator de bonis non, appointed in Illinois, may be authorized to sell real estate in Kansas, in the same manner and upon the same terms and conditions as are prescribed in the case of an executor or administrator appointed in the latter state; but, to procure an order for that purpose, it is essential that he should give notice. If he sells property in Kansas without giving notice, the deed is void, and constitutes no defense to an action of ejectment brought by the owners of the land.—Albright v. Bangs, 72 Kan. 435, 115 Am. St. Rep. 219, 83 Pac. 1030. Where a defendant dies pending suit, and his executors, appointed in another state, who are also legatees, appear as such executors in the action, without ancillary administration, and adopt the answer of their testator, and judgment is rendered against them, not payable in course of administration, the validity of such judgment can not be denied by them in an action thereon against them as executors de son tort in the state of their appointment, although it can not there be enforced against the estate.—First Nat. Bank v. Lewis, 12 Utah 84, 41 Pac. 712. Where an action is brought against a non-resident executor of a foreign estate to recover commissions for the sale of lands in Kansas belonging to such foreign estate, and the lands in which the defendant has no interest other than as executor are attached and service obtained upon the executor by publication, and he files an answer defending for the estate, the court acquires no jurisdiction to render a judgment against him individually.—Edwards v. Puterbaugh, 86 Kan. 758, 121 Pac. 1116.

There is no distinction between an executor or administrator cum testamento annexo and general administrator respecting the effect of a foreign allowance or judgment and it is immaterial whether the proceeding on the claim is in personam or in rem.—Richards v. Blaisdell, 12 Cal. App. 101, 106 Pac. 732.

REFERENCES.

Attachment against foreign executor.—See headline 42, post.

6. Pleadings.—A suit against an administrator in his representative capacity is simply an action against the estate, and a complaint in such a suit should state a cause of action against the estate.—Nickals v. Stanley, 146 Cal. 724, 727, 81 Pac. 117. In an action brought against a defendant as an executor, the probate of the will and the executorship of defendant are sufficiently pleaded, where it is alleged that the will "was duly admitted to probate"; that "letters testamentary were thereupon issued to him"; and that "he has been and now is the duly appointed, qualified, and acting executor" of the said will of, etc.—Kirsch v. Derby, 96 Cal. 602, 604, 31 Pac. 567. A gift by a decedent to his daughter, who is administratrix of his estate, can not be set aside as fraudulent by a creditor without appropriate pleading in which the fraudulent intent is alleged as a fact.—Estate of Vance, 141 Cal. 624, 627, 75 Pac. 323. Where a plaintiff sues in a representative capacity, he must allege matters showing his appointment, but such is not the case as to defendants who are sued as executors or administrators. It is sufficient to allege, simply, that they are such executors or administrators.—Wise v. Williams, 72 Cal. 544, 14 Pac. 204. An administrator is bound by the rule of practice that a party suing on a contract need not set forth specifically the items of the indebtedness. If the defendant is not satisfied with the general allegation of indebtedness, the code specially provides a remedy. He may, within five days, demand a copy of the plaintiff's account; and if he fails to avail himself of the right thus given him, he can not be heard to say that the complaint is insufficient on the ground of uncertainty in that respect.—Wise v. Hogan, 77 Cal. 184, 186, 19 Pac. 278. In an action against a representative to recover an alleged indebtedness due from the defendant's testator, and based upon separate counts, and where, following the main allegations, there is an allegation of the death of the testator and of the proceedings in probate, the complaint is sufficient against the objection that the allegations as to the death of the testator and as to the proceedings in probate are not separately stated in each count, as such allegations may be considered as referring to either or both of the counts.—Moseley v. Heney, 66 Cal. 478, 6 Pac. 134. A cause of action is not shown in a complaint against an administrator and his sureties, brought by alleged heirs to recover a sum equivalent to the plaintiff's alleged interest in the estate of a decedent, where it is averred that no mention of the two alleged heirs was made in the proceedings for the sale of the real estate of the decedent, or of their claims to heirship, and where it appeared that at no time had either of the alleged heirs, or their assignees, appeared in the probate court to have his or her status as heir adjudicated. An administrator, at his peril, declares persons to be interested as heirs, or other claimants, before such persons have been formally declared by the court, in probate proceedings, to be such.—Kirk v. Baker, 26 Mont. 190, 66 Pac. 942, 943. .In a suit brought by a creditor against an executor de son tort, in Colorado, the complaint, though inartificial, will be deemed to state a cause of action, where it alleges that the defendant was an executor de son tort of the estate of the deceased, and that, as executor, the defendant took charge, without authority, of the property of decedent, which consisted of a large sum of money, house and lot, and personal property, if such allegations are followed by other allegations relating to the employment of the plaintiff by the decedent, the agreed compensation therefor, that decedent died without paying, and that demand had been made upon the defendant and payment refused.—Ebbinger v. Wightman, 15 Colo. App. 439, 62 Pac. 963. Consent given by an executor to the filing of a substituted complaint after an action accrued upon a claim based upon a promissory note, and answering such substituted complaint, does not constitute an estoppel from invoking the premature bringing of the action as a defense, where such action was instituted before the cause of action accrued.—Radue v. Pauwelyn, 27 Mont. 68, 69 Pac. 557. An allegation, in a complaint, that on a stated day letters testamentary were duly and regularly issued to the defendant executor, who has ever since and now is the duly qualified and acting executor of the will in the estate of a named decedent, is sufficient in the absence of a special demurrer.—Vraguizan v. Savings Union, etc., Co., 31 Cal. App. 709, 161 Pac. 507. An allegation in a complaint, which is open to a special demurrer as being a conclusion of law, is, if not demurred to and is admitted in the answer, equivalent to a stipulation of the fact by force of the admission, thus rendering the allegation of more specific facts unnecessary.—Vraguizan v. Savings Union, etc., Co., 31 Cal. App. 709, 161 Pac. 507. Where an administrator petitions the court having jurisdiction of the estate for an order directing certain parties or persons to turn over to him as such administrator certain funds, which order is granted and the administrator receives and accepts the funds as such administrator, neither he nor the sureties on his bond will be permitted thereafter, in a suit against them to recover such funds, to deny that the funds were received by the administrator in his fiduciary capacity, nor will they be permitted in such a proceeding, under such circumstances, to deny that the administrator was legally appointed.—Boudinot v. Locust (Okla.), 151 Pac. 579. The general rule that, where an action is brought against an executor or administrator to recover upon a claim for which he is or may be liable individually, the use of the words "executor" or "administrator" in the pleadings will be regarded as words of description and rejected as surplusage, has no application to a case where it conclusively appears that the action was brought against the person in his representative capacity alone.—Edwards v. Peterbaugh, 86 Kan. 758, 121 Pac. 1116.

7. Evidence. Stipulations.—In an action against an administrator, wherein the plaintiff claims ownership of certain mining lands, and seeks to quiet the title against the administrator and other defendants, declarations of a deceased person, as to the identity of the lands, made after conveyance, are admissible against the personal representative in the action.—Collins v. McKay, 36 Mont. 123, 122 Am. St. Rep. 334, 92 Pac. 295, 298. A will is not admissible in evidence in an action against the executor to recover money paid to the decedent by the plaintiff, where such will did not contain any statements of the deceased concerning his receipt of the money, nor any denial of his obligation to repay it, nor in any manner tend to contradict any fact to which the plaintiff or any of her witnesses, or any of his witnesses, had testified in support of the action. The admission of the will in evidence, injecting collateral facts into a case, and diverting the jurors from the real question in issue, is, where no opportunity was given to rebut it, reversible error.—Grubbe v. Grubbe, 26 Or. 363, 38 Pac. 182, 184. A stipulation, in an action against an administrator upon a promissory note, that the claim sued upon had been disallowed by the administrator, as well as by the probate court, and that the action be tried upon the issues made upon the pleadings, etc., does not estop the defendant, as administrator, from offering evidence to show that the claim was not presented, and does not have the effect of shifting the burden of proof in the action.—Logan County Bank v. Beyer, 17 Okla. 156, 87 Pac. 607. If an administrator, defending an action on a promissory note alleged to be that of his decedent, asserts that such decedent was a mere surety, he has the burden of proof.—Milner B. & T. Co. v. Estate of Whipple, 61 Colo. 252, 254, 156 Pac. 1098. In an action involving the necessity of construing a decree of distribution, a will and an agreement incorporated therein were admissible as a part thereof, and their admission was not as evidence of matters extraneous to the terms of the decree for the purpose of modifying its terms.— Horton v. Winbigler, 175 Cal. 149, 165 Pac. 423, 427. Declarations of a deceased person to the effect that her interest in the property in controversy was only a life interest are admissible under subdivisions 2 and 4, section 1870, Code of Civil Procedure of California, as declarations against interest, in a suit against her personal representative to reform the instrument under which she acquired the property so as to show that she held only a life estate instead of a greater estate.— Horton v. Winbigler, 175 Cal. 149, 165 Pac. 423, 427. In an action for commissions brought by a broker against a landowner and tried after the latter's death, his executor having been substituted as defendant, the court should sustain the plaintiff's objection to witnesses who testify that the original defendant prior to his death and shortly after the institution of the action told them, in conversation with him, that the plaintiff had nothing to do with the sale; such testi-

mony is hearsay and self-serving merely.—Roth v. Thomson (Cal. App.), 180 Pac. 656. Sufficiency of evidence, justifying a recovery for the plaintiff, in an action against an administratrix, sued on a quantum meruit for services rendered to the decedent as stenographer. —Tharp v. Jackson, 85 Or. 78, 165 Pac. 585, 1173.

8. Judgments.

(1) In general.—Where an action was brought against a person who refused, as executor, to turn over to a distributee, after a decree of distribution, a legacy charged with a trust, without first receiving from the legatee an agreement to perform the trust, and this constituted the only defense, it was proper to render a judgment upon the pleadings in favor of the distributee, inasmuch as the duty appertaining to the trust is another and subsequent matter with which the executor or administrator has nothing to do.—St. Mary's Hospital v. Perry, 152 Cal. 338, 92 Pac. 864. See Melone v. Davis, 67 Cal. 279, 7 Pac. 703; Le Mesnager v. Variel, 144 Cal. 463, 103 Am. St. Rep. 91, 77 Pac. 988. A creditor of an estate has the right to inquire into the legality of a judgment against the administrator, such as a judgment rendered for the foreclosure of a mortgage, and for judgment for attorneys' fees and a deficiency, as a judgment for a deficiency arising upon the sale must, of necessity, swell the liabilities of the estate, and leave a smaller amount to be distributed.—O'Keefe v. Foster, 5 Wyo. 343, 40 Pac. 525. If an administrator, believing that he has assets sufficient for the payment of all debts, suffers judgment to be entered against him, he will be relieved in equity, if the assets become insufficient through an unexpected depreciation of their value. So, too, if the act done or the judgment suffered is made under a mistake, or through ignorance of a material fact, and without fault on his part, it is relievable in equity. But if an executor confesses judgment against himself, for a debt of his testator, upon a miscalculation of the amount of assets in his hands, and it appears afterward that the assets are insufficient to satisfy it, he will not be relieved in equity against the judgment.—Brenner v. Alexander, 16 Or. 349, 8 Am. St. Rep. 301, 19 Pac. 9. Where, under the statute, the entire estate has been set aside to the widow, she can not be made a party to a suit against the representative of the deceased, or be bound by any judgment which may thereby and therein be obtained, where she had nothing to do with the making or indorsing of the note upon which the action was based.—Wills v. Booth, 6 Cal. App. 197, 91 Pac. 759. Judgment against the executor of one estate, as well as against the administrator de bonis non of another state, has the effect, only, of establishing the claims of the plaintiff against such estates in the same manner as if they had been presented to and allowed by the executor of the one, and the administrator de bonis non of the other, and by the court. No execution can issue on such a judgment, and it is not even a lien on the property of the estate.—Prefontaine v. McMicken, 16 Wash. 16,

47 Pac. 231. Where an agreement is entered into between a prospective purchaser and an executor, and a deposit is made in advance of the order of the court authorizing the sale of the property, the deposit to be returned if the sale is not a good one, such prospective purchaser is entitled to recover such deposit, where the sale is irregular and invalid, and the deed to the property would pass no title. The executor, in such case, can not recover the loss incident to a resale of such property, or retain such deposit, or apply the same in payment of the deficiency resulting therefrom. In an action to recover the deposit, a judgment in favor of the plaintiff will not be reversed, because it was entered against the defendant individually, where no objection to the action on the ground that defendants were sued as individuals and not as executors, was raised by demurrer or answer.— Hellman v. Merz, 112 Cal. 661, 668, 44 Pac. 1079.

(2) Must be payable in course of administration.—A judgment in an action against an administrator should be against him de bonis testatoris.—Jones v. Perot, 19 Colo. 141, 34 Pac. 728. A judgment against executors or administrators should be made payable in due course of administration.—Atherton v. Fowler, 46 Cal. 323, 327; Kelly v. Bandini, 50 Cal. 530, 532; Drake v. Foster, 52 Cal. 225, 227; Lawrence v. Doolan, 68 Cal. 309, 315, 5 Pac. 484, 9 Pac. 159. So in Colorado, a judgment in an action against an executor or an administrator should be, that it be payable out of the estate of the deceased in due course of administration; and a provision in the judgment, in that state, that the plaintiff have costs and that he have execution therefor, is erroneous.—Kilpatrick v. Haley, 14 Colo. App. 399, 60 Pac. 261. If a party to an action dies after a cause is tried, and submitted to the court for its decision, and a written opinion announcing the court's conclusion is filed, and before judgment is entered, the court may order judgment entered nunc pro tunc as of the date of the submission and filing of its decision. In such case it is proper that judment be directed against the decedent payable in the course of administration on his estate.—Fox v. Hale and Norcross S. M. Co., 108 Cal. 478, 41 Pac. 328. An action may be maintained against the administrator of a tax-collector and the sureties on the official bond of the deceased official to recover money of the plaintiff received by the deceased in his official capacity, but which money was neither paid to the treasurer nor to the plaintiff; and the judgment against the representative must provide that it be paid by him in due course of administration.—Lawrence v. Doolan, 68 Cal. 309, 313, 5 Pac. 484, 9 Pac. 159. If an action is instituted against an executor as such, and the court has acquired no jurisdiction of him in his personal capacity, the proceedings can not be amended so as to permit a personal judgment to be entered.—Renwick v. Garland, 1 Cal. App. 237, 82 Pac. 89. A judgment on a demand arising out of a transaction, with one who has died since the transaction, if recovered against the executor or administrator of such per-

son, must be made payable out of the assets of the estate.—Reed v.
Reed (Cal.), 172 Pac. 600.

(3) **Foreign judgments.**—A judgment recovered against the administrator of a deceased person in one state is no evidence of debt in
a subsequent suit by the same plaintiff in another state, either against
an administrator, whether the same or a different person appointed
there, or against any other person having assets of the deceased.—
Braithwaite v. Harvey, 14 Mont. 208, 43 Am. St. Rep. 625, 27 L. R. A.
101, 36 Pac. 38.   Johnson v. Powers, 139 U. S. 156, 35 L. Ed. 112, 11
Sup. Ct. 525.

REFERENCES.
Foreign judgment against executor or administrator.—See note 27
L. R. A. 101-117.

(4) **Void if made after termination of office.**—A judgment recovered against an executor, upon a contract made by the testator in
his lifetime for the conveyance of an interest in real estate, to compel the execution, by the executor, of a deed according to the terms of
the contract, is not binding upon the heirs and devisees, where such
judgment was obtained against the executor after his resignation, and
the approval and settlement of his account.—Luco v. Commercial Bank,
70 Cal. 339, 11 Pac. 650. No judgment can properly be entered against
an administrator, as such, after his removal from office, although he
may have an appeal pending from the order for his removal.—More
v. More, 127 Cal. 460, 463, 59 Pac. 823.

(5) **Collateral attack.**—There can be no collateral attack made upon
a judgment directing the conveyance of real property by an administrator, acting under the direction of the superior court exercising its
probate jurisdiction, after letters have been issued to him.—Baxter
v. Boege, 173 Cal. 589, 160 Pac. 1072.

9. Costs.—In an action against an executrix to recover plaintiff's
distributive share of an estate, costs are allowable as in other cases,
and both costs and interest are chargeable only against the executrix as an individual, and not against the estate.—St. Mary's Hospital
v. Perry, 152 Cal. 338, 92 Pac. 864, 866.

10. Actions on accounts.—In an action against an executor to recover a balance due on a mutual account, the finding of the trial
court as to the amount due upon the account, which was less than
the amount claimed, will be treated as conclusive by the appellate
court.—Merithew v. Orr, 80 Cal. 363, 364, 27 Pac. 295. An administrator defendant may demand a copy of the account sued on, in
an action against him, where the complaint is on an account, without
specifying the items, and is bound by the rule that if he fails so
to do, he can not object to the complaint for uncertainty in that
respect.—Wise v. Hogan, 77 Cal. 184, 186, 19 Pac. 278.

11. Attachment, execution, and garnishment.—An attachment suit may be maintained against a foreign executor to enforce a contract made by his testator, who died owning property in Kansas.—Manley v. Mayer, 68 Kan. 377, 1 Ann. Cas. 825, 75 Pac. 550. Where an action was commenced and an attachment levied in the lifetime of the defendant therein, and the property sold and the proceeds deposited in court to await the result, pending which defendant died and his administrator was substituted, it was proper, upon judgment against the latter, under the statutes of Colorado, to award a special execution directing the sheriff to take and apply the proceeds of the attached property to the satisfaction of the judgment.—Catlin v. Vandegrift, 58 Colo. 289, 294, 144 Pac. 894. The statute whereby a creditor may proceed by garnishment against a person indebted to, or having in his possession or under his control property belonging to, the debtor, contemplates, as such a person, an executor or administrator after final distribution.—Sherman v. Havens, 94 Kan. 654, Ann. Cas. 1917B, 394, 146 Pac. 1030.

REFERENCES.

Garnishment of executor or administrator.—See note 47 L. R. A. 345-365. Right of creditor to levy attachment on property of decedent's estate under a writ against the executor or administrator.—See note 5 Am. & Eng. Ann. Cas. 912.

12. Actions on contracts.

(1) Of decedent. In general.—The executor is in privity with the decedent and is estopped to deny a contract shown to have been made by such decedent and with which the conduct of the latter throughout thirty years was consistent.—Dawley v. Dawley's Estate, 60 Colo. 73, 83, 152 Pac. 1171. An action may be maintained against the administrator of a deceased person to enforce a verbal agreement by the decedent to share in discharging a mortgage on the land of plaintiff, where decedent had received the full consideration for such agreement.—McDowell v. Miller, 1 Kan. App. 666, 42 Pac. 402.

(2) Same. Services.—In an action against an executor or administrator, for services rendered to the decedent, it is not necessary for the plaintiff to set up in his claim the evidence on which he relies to support it.—Tharp v. Jackson, 85 Or. 78, 165 Pac. 585, 1173. If an administratrix is sued, on a quantum meruit, for services rendered to the decedent as stenographer, evidence of a contract between the plaintiff and the defendant is admissible, but is not indispensable to a recovery; the plaintiff is entitled to have the jury consider other testimony bearing on the reasonable value of the services sued for.—Tharp v. Jackson, 85 Or. 78, 165 Pac. 585, 1173. If an administratrix is sued, on a quantum meruit, for services rendered to the decedent as stenographer, testimony that there was an agreement between the plaintiff and the decedent is admissible as material to the measure of damages.—Tharp v. Jackson, 85 Or. 78, 165 Pac. 585, 1173. To enable a granddaughter to recover against the executor of her grandmother's estate, for services as nurse and for medicine furnished, it is unnecessary that there should have been an express contract or a promise to pay to overcome the presumption, if such exists, that such services were gratuitous, the promise to pay being inferable from circumstances.—Wilkin v. O'Brien, — (Utah) —, 176 Pac. 853, 854. In an action for services by a granddaughter against the executor of her grandmother's estate, it is held that on the evidence before the court and the rulings of this court, a motion for a nonsuit at the conclusion of plaintiff's evidence was properly denied.—Wilkin v. O'Brien, — (Utah) —, 176 Pac. 853, 854. To recover in an action against an estate in assumpsit on a quantum meruit for services rendered by a wife to the decedent, the plaintiff must prove a contract, either express or implied, and that services were rendered under such contract, and the value thereof. Assumpsit does not necessarily imply a contract, but may lie where some duty would justify the court in imputing a promise to perform it.—Snowden v. Clemons, 5 Colo. App. 251, 38 Pac. 475. An action brought against the estate of a decedent for services rendered in discovering ore on mining property belonging to the estate, and based upon the promise of the testator to pay the claimant therefor, is sufficiently supported by the testimony of two witnesses to the facts and circumstances, the weight and credibility of whose testimony is for the jury.—Titus v. Bernard, 20 Colo. App. 104, 77 Pac. 256. In an action by the daughter against the estate of her deceased mother, for services rendered the mother in her lifetime, while it is presumed that such services are gratuitous, the plaintiff may show, and the burden is upon her to show, in such case, an express contract or a mutual meeting of minds upon a matter of contract; but it is not essential that a formal offer and acceptance, in writing or otherwise, be shown.—Griffith v. Robertson, 73 Kan. 666, 85 Pac. 748. In an action by a daughter to recover from the estate of her deceased mother, for services rendered during the mother's lifetime, the daughter is competent to testify to conversations had between her mother and another, which took place in her presence, tending to show that the mother had agreed to pay for the services, and that such payment was to be made by the provisions of a will.—Griffith v. Robertson, 73 Kan. 666, 85 Pac. 748; Bonebrake v. Tauer, 67 Kan. 827, 72 Pac. 521. If personal services are performed by one person for another under a contract or mutual understanding that compensation is to be made therefor in the will of the party receiving the benefit, or by some instrument to become absolute upon his death, and the party dies without making such provision, an action will lie against his estate to recover the actual value of the services. If the question arises as to whether or not the services were gratuitous, the plaintiff is entitled to recover on a quantum meruit. It is not necessary to predicate the action on a breach of the agreement.—Pelton v. Smith, 50 Wash. 459, 97 Pac. 460, 461. An action may be maintained against the administrator of a deceased person on a contract for services, notwithstanding the services were to be rendered in a foreign jurisdiction, as the cause of action is transitory.—McCann v. Pennie, 100 Cal. 547, 552, 35 Pac. 158. An action may be maintained against the representatives of a deceased person for the value of property of which the decedent received the benefit in his lifetime.—Fox v. Hale and Norcross S. M. Co., 108 Cal. 478, 483, 41 Pac. 328. An action can not be maintained against executors for services gratuitously rendered to a decedent during her life without request.—Dallman v. Frank, 1 Cal. App. 541, 545, 546, 82 Pac. 564. In an action against an administrator for services rendered to a decedent during life, a finding that the services were rendered at an agreed price is sustained by proof of admissions by plaintiff to that effect; but a finding that such services were wholly paid for is not sustained by evidence showing only partial payment; and the burden of proving payment is on the defendant.—Stuart v. Lord, 138 Cal. 672, 674, 72 Pac. 142. If a physician performs a surgical operation upon a person who is unconscious as the result of a physical injury, and also renders other professional services to such person, all during his last illness, he has a right to recover upon his claim against the estate of such injured person in case of the latter's death, not by reason of any contract with the injured person, either express or implied, but by virtue of the statute, which gives a preference right of payment of expenses of the last sickness over all ordinary debts out of the estate of the decedent.—Cunningham v. Lakin, 50 Wash. 394, 97 Pac. 447. Where a woman resided with her daughter and the latter's husband, and performed household services while so residing, it will be presumed that the services were gratuitous.—Zuhn v. Horst, 100 Wash. 359, 170 Pac. 1033.

(3) Same. Promissory notes.—In an action against an administrator of an estate on a promissory note, an entire failure, to state a fact in the complaint essential to the jurisdiction of the court, or to state a cause of action, may be urged at any stage of the proceedings or on appeal, and such an object is not waived by a failure to demur.—Dakota Nat. Bank v. Kleinschmidt, 33 S. D. 132, 138, 144 N. W. 934. In a suit against an administrator of an estate on a promissory note, the burden is upon the plaintiff to allege and prove every fact essential to maintain the action, and the allegation and proof of a legal presentation of the plaintiff's claim is a necessary condition precedent to the right to maintain the action.—Dakota Nat. Bank v. Kleinschmidt, 33 S. D. 132, 137, 144 N. W. 934. In an action against the administrator of an estate on a promissory note the proper presentation of the same is a condition precedent to the right of action, and the issue of such presentation is raised by the general denial, and upon a failure of plaintiff to show statutory presentation, the court should dismiss the action.—Dakota Nat. Bank v. Kleinschmidt, 33 S. D. 132, 140, 144 N. W. 934. An action against an executor upon a promissory note executed by a deceased person was prematurely brought, where it was commenced prior to the maturity of the note, although subse-

quent to the presentation of the claim based thereon, and the rejection thereof by the executor. Such rejection did not constitute any breach of the contract giving a right of action before maturity.— Radue v. Pauwelyn, 27 Mont. 68, 69 Pac. 557. In an action against an executor, to enforce the payment of a note executed by the testator when he was nearly eighty years of age, decrepit in body and with a mind impaired, the question whether the note was made by a person competent to transact business, is one of fact.—Rietz v. Crutcher, 103 Wash. 702, 175 Pac. 293. No liability attaches to an administrator on a joint promissory note made by his decedent, and he is not open to an action to enforce it.—McLaughlin v. Head, 86 Or. 361, 168 Pac. 614. In an action to enforce a joint note, if one of the defendants die shortly after the trial the cause may properly be revived against his administrator. —Gordon v. Russell, 98 Kan. 537, 158 Pac. 661.

(4) Made by representative.—As executors and administrators can not, by virtue of their general powers as such, make any contract which will bind the estate and authorize a judgment de bonis decendentis, an action can not be maintained against an estate to recover a balance due on a contract made by the plaintiffs with the defendant, as executrix, by which the plaintiffs agreed that they "would drill a well for defendant on the property of said estate," etc.—Renwick v. Garland, 1 Cal. App. 237, 82 Pac. 89. Where an action is brought in assumpsit against an administrator as such, to recover upon a note signed by him, and default is taken, the only judgment that can be rendered against the administrator is for whatever can be made by a levy against the goods of the deceased in his hands, and if such property is not sufficient to satisfy the judgment, costs can be levied only de bonis propriis. Generally, a judgment by default against an administrator is an admission of assets to the extent charged in the proceedings against him; but where there is no allegation in the declaration that the administrators had assets in their hands, default can not admit what is not charged.—Senescal v. Bolton, 7 N. M. 351, 34 Pac. 446. An administrator can not be sued in his representative capacity for attorney's fees for services rendered in the administration of the estate.—Torrenson v. Bowman, 26 Nev. 369, 68 Pac. 472. See Briggs v. Breen, 123 Cal. 657, 56 Pac. 633, 886. Upon contracts made by an administrator to pay an attorney in property out of the estate for services rendered the estate, the administrator personally, and not the estate, is liable. Such fees, to bind the estate, must be fixed and allowed by the court.—Estate of Page, 57 Cal. 238, 241. Where a lessee takes an administrator's lease of property, he is bound to take notice of the title, and he can not sue the administrator to recover rent paid, should the title fail as to part of the leased property.—Miller v. Gray, 136 Cal. 261, 264, 68 Pac. 770. One who renders services and expends moneys for the benefit of an estate, at the request of the executor or administrator, is entitled to recover the same in an action against the representative. Such services rendered and moneys expended

are "expenses of administration."—Gurnee v. Maloney, 38 Cal. 85, 87, 99 Am. Dec. 352.

(5) Suit to reform contract.—A complaint to reform a contract by incorporating therein a portion of the agreement omitted by mistake therefrom, sufficiently alleges that the portion to be included had been agreed upon to be included, by an allegation that it was intended at the time that the contract should contain the omitted portion, where the property which was the subject of the contract was shown by appropriate allegations to have been purchased with moneys of an estate in which the parties had an interest consistent with such intention, the word "intention" in such a case being held equivalent to "agreement."—Horton v. Winbigler, 175 Cal. 149, 165 Pac. 423, 425. In a suit to reform a contract brought by one of the parties against the administrator of the estate of the other, it was proper to admit in evidence plaintiff's testimony that his intention was that deceased should have only a life estate in the property, where it appeared that the money with which the property was purchased belonged to an estate in which deceased had only a life interest, in view of the fact that deceased, by consenting to the investment of money in which she had only a life interest, could acquire no greater interest in the property purchased.—Horton v. Winbigler, 175 Cal. 149, 165 Pac. 423, 425.

13. For conversion.—The administrator is a trustee for those entitled to succeed to the property, and where he converts the property to his own use, the cestuis que trustent are injured, and become invested with a cause of action against him; but no action for the conversion by the administrator can be sustained against him or his sureties until an accounting is had in the probate court.—Reed v. Hume, 25 Utah 248, 70 Pac. 998. See Beall v. New Mexico, 16 Wall (U. S.) 535, 21 L. Ed. 292. In Oregon, a claimant in an action against an estate, for conversion by the testator, is a competent witness in his own behalf, but his testimony is not, of itself, sufficient to establish his claim.—Goltra v. Penland, 45 Or. 254, 77 Pac. 129. If an administrator or executor applies to the use of the estate money or the proceeds of property belonging to a third person, he is liable in both his individual and representative capacity, and the injured party may elect whether he will hold him in the one capacity or in the other. If, however, a party elects to sue the executor in his representative capacity, he can only take such judgment as the law authorizes in such cases; that is, one which is the same, in effect, as a claim established against the estate.— Collins v. Denny Clay Co., 41 Wash. 136, 82 Pac. 1012. In an action against an administrator for property of a plaintiff alleged to have been converted to his own use by the intestate, a finding that the intestate refused to recognize the right of plaintiff to redeem the property, which had been pledged to him, obviates the necessity of averring a tender of the debts secured.—Lowe v. Ozmun, 3 Cal. App. 387, 395, 86 Pac. 729. If a person defends, in an action brought against him for conversion, upon the ground that the property is held by him as administrator, this defense must be by certain and positive averments show-ing,—1. His appointment and qualification as administrator, together with the facts that he is possessed of or entitled to such property, and is chargeable therewith as administrator; and 2. His intestate's right, title, or interest in and to such property. Unless the defense is un-equivocal in this respect, advantage can not be taken of the statutory rule which precludes parties and persons interested in an action from testifying therein when the opposite party sues or defends as an admin-istrator.—Prewitt v. Lambert, 19 Colo. 7, 34 Pac. 684. The executor of a deceased administrator may be sued by his successor in administration for the proceeds of a policy of life insurance collected by his testator in his former representative capacity, but not accounted for.—Curran v. Kennedy, 89 Cal. 98, 99, 26 Pac. 641. Where an action by a partner is commenced against the estate of his deceased partner for a conver-sion of property alleged to belong to the firm, and the complaint is amended after the statute of limitations has run against the cause of action, the statute bars any new cause of action brought in by way of amendment. In this case the claimant did not assert his right to recover under a claim of joint ownership for more than a year after letters testamentary had been issued to the executor.—Schwartz v. Stock, 26 Nev. 155, 65 Pac. 357. See Atkinson v. Canal Company, 53 Cal. 102.

14. To recover deposit on void sale.—An action to recover money paid as a deposit on a probate sale of land, which was void as not hav-ing been made in accordance with the order of sale, should not be brought against the executor in his representative capacity, unless it appears that the money has actually been made a part of the assets of the estate.—Schlicker v. Hemenway, 110 Cal. 579, 582, 52 Am. St. Rep. 116, 42 Pac. 1063.

15. Ejectment.—Ejectment may be maintained against the repre-sentative of a deceased person.—Barrett v. Birge, 50 Cal. 655, 658.

16. Eminent domain.—Proceedings to condemn land for public use may be maintained against an executor; and the word "recovery," in the statute authorizing suits by and against the estates of a deceased person, includes condemnation for public use.—Monterey County v. Cushing, 83 Cal. 507, 512, 23 Pac. 700.

17. To declare and enforce trust.

(1) In general.—Where, under an agreement with the creditors of an estate, approved by the county court, an administrator purchased all the property of the estate, and instead of satisfying a mortgage on certain realty thereof, permitted such mortgage to be foreclosed and with money derived from the estate purchased the same at foreclosure, it is held that, in a suit by the heirs against such administrator, the district court had jurisdiction to declare a trust as to such property, and that the administrator held such property as trustee for the heirs.—

Vaughan v. Vaughan (Okla.), 162 Pac. 1131. A trust, attempted to be created by a void instrument is also void and can not be given life by estoppel.—Niccolls v. Niccolls, 168 Cal. 444, 143 Pac. 712. A suit in equity to enforce a trust against a specific fund may be maintained against an administrator, where the fund is capable of identification, notwithstanding plaintiff's cause of action may have some elements of an ordinary claim against the estate.—Dunham v. Siglin, 39 Or. 291, 64 Pac. 662, 663. In an action against an administrator to enforce a trust, if the trust property can be traced and identified, the action may be maintained by the beneficiary; for he is seeking his own property only, and does not seek to enforce a claim against the property of the estate of decedent.—Roach v. Caraffa, 85 Cal. 436, 444, 25 Pac. 22. Where the title to land stood in the name of a deceased person, and the purchase price therefor had been paid one-half by decedent and one-half by another person, the latter may enforce his resulting trust in one-half of the property against both the administrator and general creditors of the estate.—Murphy v. Clayton, 113 Cal. 153, 159, 45 Pac. 267. The fact that plaintiff, in an equitable action to recover trust property held by an administrator, had recovered a money judgment against the same administrator will not be regarded as an election to rely on his legal remedy, unless it appears that he made such election with full knowledge of all the facts.—Wells Fargo Co. v. Robinson, 13 Cal. 133, 141, 143. If the holder of a promissory note, pending suit thereon, assigns the same in trust, to pay from the proceeds the fees of his attorney in prosecuting an action thereon, a suit may be maintained by such attorney against the administrator of the trustee to enforce the trust.—Tyler v. Mayre, 95 Cal. 160, 168, 27 Pac. 196. In a suit in equity, relating to a trust fund, against an administrator of a trustee, the statement that the trust fund must be capable of identification does not mean that it must be kept as a separate fund, or in a special account. If the trustee mingle it with other funds, so long as there is in the mass an amount greater than the trust fund, it will be presumed, in the absence of a contrary showing, to include the trust fund; and if, after such mingling, the trustee has withdrawn any portion of the mass, it will be presumed to have been his own, rather than from that held by him in trust.—Elizalde v. Elizalde, 137 Cal. 634, 641, 66 Pac. 369, 70 Pac. 861. Where a decedent had abandoned his wife and family in another state, eloped with another woman and lived with her under a fictitious name in Utah unknown to his said wife and family until his death, the representations under which said woman obtained letters of administration of his estate, under said fictitious name, and as his wife, are held to be extrinsic fraud upon the rights of his said wife and his heirs, and ground for relief in equity in their favor against orders and decrees of the probate court, and against the sureties on the administratrix's bond to the extent of the value of property obtained by her as such.—Weyant v. Utah Sav. & Trust Co. (Utah), 182 Pac. 189, 197. All courts of record, including probate courts, have inherent power to make their judgments correspond with the real judgment intended, notwithstanding lapse of time, where other rights do not intervene; under this rule a final decree may be rectified nunc pro tunc when 'it has erroneously vested a legal estate in the beneficiary of a trust instead of in the trustee.—In re Loevinger's Estate (S. D.), 167 N. W. 726. A plaintiff, who would charge an executor or administrator as trustee of specific property, must allege in his complaint that such officer came into possession of the property, and was charged with a trust in the plaintiff's favor in regard to it.—Reed v. Reed (Cal.), 172 Pac. 600.

(2) Estoppel.—The presence of an executor at a sale by a trustee under a trust deed made by the testator, and the conduct of the executor in failing to object when the trustee read the conditions showing that the title would be certified to the purchaser free and clear of encumbrances, do not conclusively establish an estoppel against him as executor from defending an action brought to charge the estate with liability for a deficiency resulting from the sale.—Crisman v. Lanterman, 149 Cal. 647, 87 Pac. 89, 117 Am. St. Rep. 167.

(3) Presentation of claims.—A suit in equity may be maintained against the executors of a deceased person to enforce an oral trust, notwithstanding the plaintiff has presented his claim to them for the subject of the trust, which claim was allowed in part by them, and was approved by the court, and filed.—Walkerly v. Bacon, 85 Cal. 137, 141, 24 Pac. 638. If an administrator comes into possession of trust funds held by the decedent, which constitute no part of the assets of the estate, he may be sued therefor in equity without presenting a claim against the estate.—Gunter v. Janes, 9 Cal. 634, 658. But this right to proceed in equity exists only so long as the trust property, or the product of it, can be identified.—Lathrop v. Bampton, 31 Cal. 17, 22, 23, 89 Am. Dec. 141. If a trust fund created by the will of the testator has been distributed and invested under the will, but not yet delivered to the ultimate trustee, and the distributee dies after such investment, the ultimate trustee may maintain suit against his administrator for the securities representing the investment without presenting a claim against the estate.—Kauffman v. Foster, 3 Cal. App. 741, 743, 86 Pac. 1108.

(4) Action by creditors.—The creditors of an insolvent estate of a deceased person can not maintain an action against the administrator of such an estate and others, pending administration, to compel him and them to transfer to the estate real property to which he has, for himself and them, obtained the legal title in such a way as to raise a constructive trust in favor of the estate. If the defendant administrator is sued, in such action, both in his representative and personal capacity, there is a misjoinder of parties defendant in the one case, coupled with an incapacity to sue as to the plaintiffs; and a demurrer to the complaint is properly sustained.—Mesmer v. Jenkins, 61 Cal. 151, 153.

(5) Collateral attack.—An action may be maintained against an executor to recover moneys that had constituted a part of the estate, but which are claimed to be due to the plaintiff, as a trustee for certain beneficiaries. But such action, where it exceeds the jurisdictional amount of the justice's court, can be maintained only in the superior court. And where a subsequent action is maintained to obtain a decree vacating and setting aside a judgment rendered against the executor, such subsequent action, even though denominated a direct attack, is in the nature of a collateral attack, and will not warrant the assumption of a jurisdiction to review the proceedings in the original action.— LeMesnager v. Variel, 144 Cal. 463, 467, 103 Am. St. Rep. 91, 77 Pac. 988.

18. For fraud.—An action may be maintained against the executor of a deceased person to set aside a judgment obtained by the decedent against the plaintiff, where such judgment was obtained through fraud of an extrinsic character. Such fraud operates, not upon matters pertaining to the judgment itself, but to the manner in which it was procured. Equity will give relief from a judgment for such fraud practiced on the plaintiff against whom the judgment was obtained, where there was no adverse trial of the issues in the action, and where the plaintiff was prevented, through fraudulent acts of his adversary, and without any fault on his own part, from presenting a meritorious defense to the action brought against him.—Flood v. Templeton, 152 Cal. 148, 13 L. R. A. (N. S.) 579, 92 Pac. 78. An action by an heir is authorized and proper to charge a defendant as an involuntary trustee for the benefit of the plaintiff, where the defendant, while acting as administrator, fraudulently and wrongfully acquired the property by taking advantage of his position in inducing the heir to convey his interest in the estate.—Wingerter v. Wingerter, 71 Cal. 105, 11 Pac. 853. If there is not a deficiency of assets in the hands of the administrator to meet the demands of creditors, he can not maintain an action to recover any property transferred by the decedent in his lifetime, or defend an action for its recovery.—Murphy v. Clayton, 114 Cal. 526, 536, 43 Pac. 613, 46 Pac. 460. Where a decedent had abandoned his wife and family in another state, eloped with another woman and lived with her under a fictitious name in Utah, unknown to his said wife and family until his death, a suit in equity against said woman as administratrix and against her sureties as such, on the ground of fraud, is a direct and not a collateral attack upon the administration of such estate.— Weyant v. Utah Sav. & Trust Co. (Utah), 182 Pac. 189, 197. Where an administrator obtained a fraudulent decree of distribution, by false statements that he and others were next of kin, and suit is brought in a federal court to have the administrator declared to be a trustee, the case is one of fraud by a trustee, and, though the complainants have allowed eight or nine years to elapse before commencing suit, after learning of the death of the decedent, they will not be denied relief upon the ground of laches, where they are illiterate, and made a mistake, bring suit within three years after discovery of the fraud and

show sufficient reasons for their mistake, and for not having made an earlier discovery of the fraud that had been practiced upon them.—Diamond v. Connolly, 251 Fed. 234. A federal court will not disturb the decree of a state probate court by annulling or supervising the same, but it may declare, as a court of equity, in a proceeding properly before it, that an administrator, who had obtained a decree of distribution of the property of the estate to himself and others by false statements, is a trustee; that false representations by him that he was next of kin were a breach of his trust as administrator; and that he be deprived of any benefit or fruits of the fraudulent judgment.—Diamond v. Connolly, 251 Fed. 234.

REFERENCES.

Right of executors or administrators to defend or to impeach on the ground of fraud.—See note 3 Am. St. Rep. 740-745.

19. **On mortgages.**—The administrator being entitled, under the statute, to the possession of the decedent's real property, he must be made a party to all suits affecting it. If, therefore, an action is instituted to foreclose a mortgage, and the administrator of the mortgagor's estate is not made a party, the complaint is defective for want of proper parties.—Harwood v. Marye, 8 Cal. 580, 581. In a suit to foreclose a mortgage made by a deceased mortgagor, it is not necessary to make the heirs parties. The executor represents the state, and a judgment against him binds the heirs and devisees.—Dickey v. Gibson, 121 Cal.. 276, 278, 53 Pac. 704; Bayly v. Muehe, 65 Cal. 345, 348, 3 Pac. 467, 4 Pac. 486. The administrator is a necessary party to an action brought to foreclose a mortgage, where the testator, as mortgagee, dies before judgment.—Belloc v. Rogers, 9 Cal. 123, 126. Where a mortgage can not be foreclosed, by reason of the bar of the statute of limitations, against the grantee of the mortgage, no recovery can be had against the administrator of the deceased mortgagor. The only right of action against the grantee of a mortgage is one to secure a sale of the mortgaged premises, and the application of the proceeds of the debt and costs. This right of action exists against the grantee as soon as the debt falls due. The statute begins to run against this right of action at the same time, and the running of the statute is not interrupted by the death of the mortgagor.—California Title, etc., Co. v. Miller, 3 Cal. App. 54, 84 Pac. 453. An action may be maintained against an executor to have certain deeds of conveyance, absolute in form, decreed to be in fact only mortgages, the amount due thereon ascertained, and conveyances of the property therein described ordered to be executed upon the payment of the amount adjudged to be due. In such a case the grantee, as plaintiff, is competent to testify as to any matter of fact occurring before the death of the decedent grantor.—Wadleigh v. Phelps, 149 Cal. 627, 87 Pac. 93. In a suit against the executor of a grantor to declare a deed a mortgage and to foreclose it, where a claim has been presented to the estate and rejected, but no judgment for a deficiency is demanded, the fact that more than the statutory time had

elapsed after rejection of the claim before suit is immaterial.—Fox v. Bernard, 29 Nev. 127, 85 Pac. 351, 352.

20. To quiet title.—In an action to declare a deed to a decedent a mortgage, and to quiet title to the land so conveyed, both the administrator and heirs of such decedent are proper parties defendant.— Louvall v. Gridley, 70 Cal. 507, 509, 11 Pac. 777.

21. Replevin.—In an action of replevin against an administrator, if the facts would not warrant a recovery in an action by him, they constitute no defense in an action against him.—Murphy v. Clayton, 114 Cal. 526, 536, 43 Pac. 613, 46 Pac. 460. If an administrator is sued to recover property, claimed adversely to the estate, he can not unite with his defense of title in his intestate a claim of lien on the property in favor of himself personally.—Gardner v. Gilliham, 20 Or. 598, 27 Pac. 220, 221. If the taking of possession of personal property by the administrator, after the decease of the intestate, and before her appointment, was lawful, and for the benefit of the estate, the title which the administrator subsequently secured to the property, relates back to the intestate's death, and such title may be pleaded as a defense to an action of replevin, not because of the newly acquired title after the action was commenced, but because of the right and legality of the taking in the first instance.—Casto v. Murray, 47 Or. 57, 81 Pac. 883. An action of replevin or of claim and delivery, to recover personal property, can be maintained by a plaintiff against the executrix of an estate, where the evidence shows that the sole ownership and right of possession was in him, and that the property was converted by the deceased, or wrongfully taken by such estate.—Truman v. Dakota Trust Co., 29 N. D. 456, 151 N. W. 456. Damages, in an action of replevin against a personal representative, date from the time of the taking, not from the date of the presentation of the claim required as a condition precedent to action.—MacKenzie v. Steeves, 98 Wash. 17, 167 Pac. 50.

22. For torts.

(1) Acts done by the executor or administrator.—It is a general rule of law, that no action will lie against an executor or administrator to which his testator or intestate was not liable; hence, where the foundation of plaintiff's demand is the personal tort of the defendant, and not that of his testator, as for damages for personal injuries sustained by the plaintiff in consequence of the neglect of the defendant to keep in repair that portion of the street fronting a lot belonging to the testator, such defect not being alleged to have existed anterior to the death of such testator, and therefore, no obligation having been incurred by the testator in his lifetime, in respect thereto, which could serve as a basis for a valid claim against his estate, or a right of action against the administrator of his estate, an action will not lie against the administrator as such.—Eustace v. Jahns, 38 Cal. 3, 21. As a general principle, an estate can not be held liable for a tort committed by an administrator or executor.—Nickals v. Stanley, 146 Cal. 724, 81 Pac. 117. A personal injury resulting from neglect of the duty devolving upon an administrator, or other person in the representative relation to the estate of his testator, renders him personally liable for a tort; but under no principle of the law can the estate be charged with the result of such negligence. It can not be sustained upon the principle of respondeat superior, or principal and agent, for the simple reason that no such relation exists between heirs, legatees, or creditors of the estate and the administrator. The administrator is not in the employ or subject to the control of any superior, other than the probate court, in the performance of any duty imposed upon him as such by law.—Eustace v. Jahns, 38 Cal. 3, 22. The only way in which an action can be brought against an estate is to sue the administrator or executor in his representative capacity. The estate can not be held liable for a tort committed by the representative, nor can it be held liable for damages for a breach of contract by him.—Sterrett v. Barker, 119 Cal. 492, 494, 51 Pac. 695. An action can not be maintained against an executor or administrator, as such, on a penal statute; nor when the cause of action is founded upon malfeasance or misfeasance, or when the complaint imputes a tort done to the person or goods of another by the testator or intestate.—Eustace v. Jahns, 38 Cal. 3, 23. Tortious acts by an administrator are outside of his authority, and the estate can not be held liable for the consequences thereof. This being so, it has been held that, under a statute providing that the party in interest, or to the record, shall not be allowed to testify, the heir and distributee is not disqualified as a witness, and should be allowed to testify on behalf of the defendant in an action brought against him for an alleged conversion of moneys and chattels.—McCoy v. Ayers, 2 Wash. Ter. 307, 5 Pac. 843.

REFERENCES.

Tortious or negligent acts, personal liability of executor or administrator to third person for.—See note 21 Ann. Cas. 355. In what capacity may an executor or administrator be sued for his personal tort.—See note 51 L. R. A. 266-268.

(2) **Acts commenced before decedent's death.**—An action may be maintained against an executor to recover damages for the wrongful acts of the testator in maliciously, and without cause, procuring an action to be brought against another person, and committing acts whereby the business of such other person was destroyed, and his property, goods, accounts, and bills receivable were lost.—Thornton, etc., Co. v. Bretherton, 32 Mont. 80, 80 Pac. 10, 11. A special administrator may be sued for maintaining an obstruction to a right of way, notwithstanding it was created by a decedent whose estate he represents.—Hardin v. Sin Claire, 115 Cal. 460, 463, 46 Pac. 363. An action may be maintained against a special administrator to abate an obstruction to a private way, and for such damages as the special administrator, by his wrongful acts, had caused the plaintiff to suffer, where it is

alleged that the nuisance was maintained by the special administrator, as it was by the decedent, and such action for abatement and for damages may be maintained without having presented a claim against the estate of decedent, there being nothing in the statute requiring the presentation of claims for damages caused by wrongful acts.—Hardin v. Sin Claire, 115 Cal. 460, 463, 47 Pac. 363. A personal right of action dies with the person, unless the right of action has been kept alive by some statute. It has been held, under a statute providing that a person "may maintain an action against the executor or administrator, or any testator or intestate, who, in his lifetime, has wasted, destroyed, taken, or carried away, or converted to his own use, the goods or chattels of any such person," that an action for false imprisonment by the testator is not maintainable against his administrator.—Harker v. Clark, 57 Cal. 245, 246.

23. Unlawful detainer.—The executor of the will of a deceased tenant can not be sued in unlawful detainer.—Martel v. Meehan, 63 Cal. 47, 50.

24. To vacate sale.—An action commenced against an administrator to vacate and annul an order of sale, that the sale thereunder be declared void and set aside, and that the defendants be enjoined from disposing of the proceeds thereof until a further order of the court, is an action requiring the determination of a right or interest in real property, and a motion for a change of place of trial from the county wherein the land is situated to the county wherein the defendants reside is properly denied.—Sloss v. De Toro, 77 Cal. 129, 132, 19 Pac. 233.

25. For waste.—In an action brought against the administrator and his sureties for waste, or a misapplication of the assets of the estate, it is not necessary, as formerly, that the devastavit be previously established, in order to charge the principal and sureties on the bond, but the action can not be maintained against the sureties unless the facts alleged, if proved, amount to and establish the devastavit.—Howe v. People, 7 Colo. App. 535, 44 Pac. 512. An administrator can not be liable for a devastavit of the estate to an amount greater than the estate has lost, or that has been wasted; and no action can be maintained therefor against him or his bondsmen until his liability has been fixed by a proceeding in the probate court.—Territory v. Bramble, 2 Dak. 189, 5 N. W. 945, 948. Co-executors are to be treated as one individual, and the acts of each are to be taken as the acts of all; and, although there are cases in which one is not answerable for the misconduct of others, still where one, by his negligence, suffers another to waste the estate, when it could have been prevented by reasonable diligence, he is answerable for the loss.—Insley v. Shire, 54 Kan. 793, 45 Am. St. Rep. 308, 39 Pac. 713, 716. In an action by an executor against a co-executor, in his representative capacity, charging waste and asking for his removal, no judgment should be entered against him individually for the value of property lost to the estate.—Insley v. Shire, 54 Kan. 793, 45 Am. St. Rep. 308, 39 Pac. 713, 715.

26. On street assessments.—An action on a street assessment can be maintained against the executor of a deceased person.—Parker v. Bernal, 66 Cal. 113, 114, 4 Pac. 1090. But he is not a necessary party, as the suit may be brought against the successors to the title.—Phelan v. Dunne, 72 Cal. 229, 230, 13 Pac. 662. And where there is no allegation in the complaint touching the estate of the decedent, or as to the representative character of the defendant, and he is sued also as an individual, a judgment against the defendant in his representative capacity must be reversed.—Flinn v. Gouley, 139 Cal. 623, 624, 73 Pac. 542.

27. Claims against estates.—A claim against the estate of a deceased surety on a supersedeas bond, must, like any other claim against an estate, be verified by the oath of the claimant and be presented to the executor or administrator, before it can be made the subject of an action against such officer.—Empson v. Fortune, 102 Wash. 16, 172 Pac. 873. Before an action on a supersedeas bond can be maintained against the executor of a deceased surety's estate, an appropriate claim must be presented; and this formal requirement is not satisfied by the presentation of an abstract of the judgment, recovered against the principal, although it be certified by the clerk of the court out of which the judgment proceeded.—Empson v. Fortune, 102 Wash. 16, 172 Pac. 873. An action at law against an executor or administrator, on a claim against the decedent's estate, must be based on the same claim as that presented to the personal representative of the deceased. —Tharp v. Jackson, 85 Or. 78, 165 Pac. 585, 1173. The proper presentation of a claim is a fact to be proved, as being essential to the cause of action; and the effect is that an executor or administrator is, by the mandatory provisions of the claims statute, prevented from waiving the presentation, so as to estop himself from defending on the ground of the formality's having been neglected.—Empson v. Fortune, 102 Wash. 16, 172 Pac. 873. Neither an executor or administrator, nor an attorney for the estate, can waive any substantial right affecting the interests of the heirs or creditors, nor can either be estopped by his conduct to their prejudice; hence, an executrix was not estopped to contest a claim because of alleged misleading statements and assurances made by the attorney of the estate, which induced the claimant to omit compliance with the provisions of the statute prescribing the manner of presenting the claim.—Vanderpool v. Vanderpool, 48 Mont. 448, 138 Pac. 772.

REFERENCES.

Claims against estate.—See extended note ante, following § 481.

27. Limitation of actions and laches.—The statute of limitations in Kansas runs against the claim of a mortgage creditor as against the estate of the mortgagor, during the time there was no administrator, where an unreasonable time had elapsed before making the claim,—in this case eight years,—and where the debt was renewed by a new note executed by all of the heirs of the deceased mortgagor except one.—

Black v. Elliott, 63 Kan. 211, 88 Am. St. Rep. 239, 65 Pac. 215, following Bauserman v. Charlott, 46 Kan. 480, 26 Pac. 1051, and Kulp v. Kulp, 51 Kan. 341, 21 L. R. A. 550, 32 Pac. 1118. An action by a widow to set aside deeds made by her deceased husband, on the ground that they were made upon trusts which are alleged to be invalid, is barred by the same limitation of time from the date of the execution of the deeds as would have bound the decedent.—Page v. Page, 143 Cal. 602, 604, 77 Pac. 452. Where a statute provides that if a person against whom a right of action exists dies, and the cause of action survives, an action may be brought against his representative within six months after the issuing of letters testamentary or of administration; such provision may prolong, but does not shorten, the time within which an action is barred by the general statute of limitations; and in case there is a statutory provision that when the commencement of an action is stayed by statutory prohibition, the time of the continuance of the prohibition shall not be a part of the time limited for bringing an action, and a further provision that an action can not be maintained until after the rejection of a claim and the expiration of six months from the granting of letters, the allowance of six months before the administrator may be sued is a statutory prohibition, and suspends the general statute of limitations during that time.—Blaskower v. Steel, 23 Or. 106, 31 Pac. 253, 254. The statute of limitations does not run against a judgment recovered against an executor or administrator pending the administration of the estate.—Shively v. Harris, 5 Cal. App. 513, 90 Pac. 971. The statute of limitations can not be pleaded in bar of an action against an administrator, as against an amended complaint stating no new cause of action, where such statute is not a bar to the original complaint.—Vanderslice v. Matthews, 79 Cal. 273, 277, 21 Pac. 748. See Easton v. O'Reilly, 63 Cal. 308; Cox v. McLaughlin, 76 Cal. 60, 9 Am. St. Rep. 164, 18 Pac. 100. An administrator will not be permitted to waive the statute of limitations.—Boyce v. Fisk, 110 Cal. 107, 117. Where the testator, by will, requests executors to pay obligations without reference to any law of limitations, which he positively repudiates and waives, the executors can not urge the statute of limitations against such an obligation of the testator.—Glassell v. Glassell, 147 Cal. 510, 511, 82 Pac. 42. The statute of limitations that reads, "no claim against any estate, which has been presented and allowed, is affected by the statute of limitations, pending the proceedings for the settlement of the estate," etc., is a special statute having application alone to claims against the estate, and can not be held to apply to any and every person who may happen to be jointly or severally indebted with the deceased as to such claim. On the other hand, the statute of limitations is a general statute, and must be applied generally, and in all cases where an exception to its operation is not specifically made.—Tynan v. Walker, 35 Cal. 634, 95 Am. Dec. 152; Vandall v. Teague, 142 Cal. 471, 474, 76 Pac. 35. The provision of the California statute, limiting the time within which an action may

be commenced on a rejected claim, has no application where the
action was already pending when the claim was presented.—Gregory
v. Clabrough's Executors, 129 Cal. 475, 479, 62 Pac. 72. In an action
against the administrator, where the statute of limitations is set up
as a defense, the burden is upon the defendant to show that the plaintiff's cause of action is barred.—Wise v. Williams, 72 Cal. 544, 14 Pac.
204. The exception in the Montana statute of limitations, that the
running of the statute shall not begin, or shall be suspended, during
the time the defendant is absent from the state is not confined to the
absent debtor against whom the action originally accrued; it applies
to a cause of action against a personal representative.—Smith v.
Smith (Mont.), 224 Fed. 1, 5. In a suit to establish a stockholder's
liability in respect to stock in an insolvent corporation, held by a person at the time of his death, the administratrix is a necessary party,
and the statute of limitations is tolled while the person liable is out of
the state; hence, the continued absence of the administratrix from the
state tolls the statute.—Schwartz v. Loftus (Kan.), 216 Fed. 320. An
administrator, not being liable on a joint promissory note made by
his decedent, can not, by a partial payment of the same, toll the statute
of limitations; the payment is the mere act of a volunteer.—McLaughlin
v. Head, 86 Or. 361, 168 Pac. 614. One who sues an executor for an
accounting, the suit being virtually a will contest, can not have relief,
if he has delayed suing for more than a year after probate.—Davis v.
Seavey, 95 Wash. 57, Ann. Cas. 1918D, 314, 163 Pac. 35. An administrator has no power, under the statutes of Idaho, to waive the bar of
the statute of limitations, so as to set a new date for the statute to
begin to run.—Dern v. Olsen, 18 Ida. 358, 369, Ann. Cas. 1912A, 1,
L. R. A. 1915B, 1016, 110 Pac. 164. An executrix is not estopped to
plead the statute of limitations declared in section 7206, Rev. Stat. of
Colorado, to a claim against the estate founded on a promissory note,
by admitting the execution of the note in a separate suit and by admitting the filing of the claim, the note itself on which the claim was
founded not having been presented and filed in court as the statute
requires, within the statutory period of one year after the granting of
letters testamentary.—First Nat. Bank v. Cone, 57 Colo. 529, 531, 143
Pac. 569. Where a dying wife executed a deed of gift to her husband,
upon his promise that he would in turn execute a conveyance of the
property involved to one of her relatives, to be delivered upon the
grantor's death, and the husband afterward's died, and an action is
brought against his administrator to enforce such promise, the case is
one to recover real property, and is governed by the five-year statute
of limitations.—Hillyer v. Hynes, 33 Cal. App. 506, 165 Pac. 718.

REFERENCES.

Waiver of statute of limitations by personal representative.—Ann.
Cas. 1912A, 6. Waiver or tolling of the statute of limitations or of non-
claim, by personal representative, as to indebtedness of the estate.—
L. R. A. 1915B, 1016.

28. Appeal.—Where a mutual benefit association is not legally liable to pay money due upon a certificate issued by it to anybody; where the association institutes an action against the executor of an estate and the heirs thereof for the purpose of determining to whom the moneys due upon the certificate shall be paid; where the association is liable only to the nominee of a deceased member; and where there is no nominee, the policy having remained unchanged at the time of the deceased member's death, the heirs of the deceased wife of the member who took out the certificate are not "aggrieved" parties on appeal from the order of the court directing payment of the amount of the policy to the executor of the estate, where the decedent left a surviving wife, and by will had bequeathed the insurance-moneys to such surviving wife, directing therein that the officers of the order substitute her name in the certificate for the name of the deceased wife, and pay the amount thereof to the surviving wife.—Order of Mutual Companions v. Grist, 76 Cal. 494, 497, 18 Pac. 652. In an action against an executor, where a personal judgment is rendered against him for costs, he is not entitled to review the judgment if he failed to make himself individually a party to the litigation.—Meyer v. O'Rourke, 150 Cal. 177, 88 Pac. 706. Where, on appeal from an order or judgment denying the application of a judgment creditor for an order directing an administrator to sell real estate, no summons in error is served upon the administrator and no appearance or waiver is entered by him or on his behalf, and the case-made is not served upon him, and the time for correcting such error has expired, the appeal will be dismissed.—In re McCann's Estate, 51 Okla. 240, 151 Pac. 887. Where the objections on an appeal from the district court are purely technical, such as that the claim before an administrator was not verified, or that it differed from the claim presented to the court, or that the heirs have not been made parties, and there are no specifications of the grounds in the assignments of error, and such grounds can not be ascertained without searching the record, the circuit court of appeals will not consider the objections.—Esterly v. Ruan (Alaska), 122 Fed. 609, 611, 58 C. C. A. 548. As in other actions, so in one against the estate of a deceased person, the jury are the judges of the weight of the testimony and the credibility of the witnesses, and the supreme court in passing upon the sufficiency of the evidence to support the verdict in such a case will be guided by the same canons of review which obtain in other actions at law.—Gauss v. Trump, 48 Mont. 92, 135 Pac. 910. In an action against an administrator to reform a contract of purchase so as to show that the decedent acquired only a life estate in the property, a finding for plaintiff was held by the court to be supported by the evidence.—Horton v. Winbigler, 175 Cal. 149, 165 Pac. 423, 428.

IV. MANAGEMENT OF ESTATES.

1. In general.—It is no part of the duty of an executor or administrator to manage the estate he represents for the benefit of the estate or of the heirs. So far as they are concerned, it is his duty, simply, to preserve the estate until distribution. He can not make investments for them, or satisfy adverse claims, or sell because the estate would profit by it.—Brenham v. Story, 39 Cal. 179, 188. It is his duty to administer and turn over the estate as soon as possible, and not to speculate with it, or to carry on business on its account, or to improve it for the benefit of heirs.—Estate of Moore, 72 Cal. 335, 342, 13 Pac. 880. If he has money of the estate in his custody, he should deposit it for safe-keeping in a bank of good standing and credit, as this is what prudent and judicious men ordinarily do with such of their own funds as the exigencies of their business require them to keep on hand.—McNabb v. Wixom, 7 Nev. 163, 171. It is his duty to pay all taxes imposed upon the estate; for distribution thereof among the heirs and devisees is forbidden until all taxes are paid.—People v. Olvera, 43 Cal. 492, 494; and the court has power to order the payment of assessments on mining stocks held by the estate.—Estate of Millenovich, 5 Nev. 161. An executor or administrator is affected with notice of unpaid taxes on property of the estate which was owned by or in which the deceased had an interest at the time of his death, and of which the executor or administrator was entitled to the custody for administration and distribution.—Clayton v. Dinwoodey, 33 Utah 251, 14 Ann. Cas. 926, 93 Pac. 723, 726. An executor derives his authority from the will, and confirmation by the court, followed by the filing of his bond, is equivalent to taking out letters testamentary, the letters being but the authentic evidence of the power conferred by the will.—Bank of Montreal v. Buchanan, 32 Wash. 480, 73 Pac. 482, 484. Whether the administrator should be allowed for payments made for the services of a bookkeeper depends upon the circumstances of the estate, and is a matter properly left to the discretion of the probate judge.—Estate of More, 121 Cal. 609, 54 Pac. 97, 99. But if he improperly withdraws money of the estate and pays the same out to a bookkeeper, he is answerable for interest on the sum paid, at the legal rate.—Estate of Scott, 1 Cal. App. 740, 83 Pac. 85, 87. Where an executor fraudulently induces an heir to lend to him a sum of money, bequeathed to her, but to which she is not entitled until she reaches twenty-one years of age, and the evidence shows that the executor procured the loan by concealing from the heir his failing financial condition, and by misleading her in other respects, the transaction is not only questionable, but absolutely void.—Ehrngren v. Gronlund, 19 Utah 411, 57 Pac. 268. An executor or administrator, where the estate consists of an apple orchard in full bearing, can, as a necessary expense, contract for apple boxes in which to ship apples, to further the handling and marketing of the crop, and charge the estate therefor.—Lamb Davis Lumber Co. v. Stowell, 96 Wash. 46, L. R. A.

1917E, 960, 164 Pac. 593. Although one who pays money on a legitimate transfer of property by an executor or trustee is not bound to see that it is rightly applied, on the other hand, he can take nothing by his participation in a transaction which appears by the record to have been unauthorized.—Beakey v. Knutson, 90 Or. 574, 174 Pac. 1149, 177 Pac. 955.

2. Power of executor or trustee named in will. In general.—The executor in a non-intervention will is in fact a "trustee"; he derives his powers not from the court but from the will.—Bayer v. Bayer, 83 Wash. 430, 145 Pac. 433. When a will provides for the payment of debts, legacies, and other charges, and the estate can not be administered without the realization of funds, or can not be fairly distributed unless it is sold and turned into money, the power of the executor or trustee named in the will is commensurate with the objects of the trust; in such cases, the trustee has power, without an order of court, to sell and convey the real and personal property of the testator, where the will authorizes him to do so.—Fulmer v. Gable, 73 Wash. 684, 687, 132 Pac. 641.

3. Same. Intervention of court.—The statute of the state of Washington provides that certain estates "may be managed and settled" without the intervention of the court; it does not provide that they "must" be managed by the executor without the intervention of the court.—Bayer v. Bayer, 83 Wash. 430, 145 Pac. 433. Under the former law, all estates, whether solvent or insolvent, could be administered without the intervention of the court, other than to admit the will to probate; now, no other estates than solvent ones can be settled without the intervention of the court.—Fulmer v. Gable, 73 Wash. 684, 687, 132 Pac. 641. Upon a showing that an estate is solvent, it passes from the immediate jurisdiction of the court, which then has no power to enter an order of sale; and it can not assume jurisdiction unless there is a showing of failure to execute the trust faithfully.—Fulmer v. Gable, 73 Wash. 684, 686, 132 Pac. 641.

4. Discovery of assets.—A summary proceeding in the probate court, for the discovery, and to compel the delivery, of property or effects of an estate, suspected of having been concealed, embezzled, or conveyed away, is not a proper remedy to enforce the payment of a debt to the estate, or to try contested rights to property as between the representative of the estate and others. If, on the hearing of a charge that a person who had given a promissory note, an asset of the estate, was concealing it, it develops that there was in fact no concealment of the note, the court is justified in closing the investigation and discontinuing the proceeding, where it is proposed to extend the inquiry as to the maker's liability upon the note.—Humbarger v. Humbarger, 72 Kan. 412, 115 Am. St. Rep. 204, 83 Pac. 1095. See note to § 385, ante.

5. Advances by administrator.—The administrator, in the absence of special authority, must administer the estate as he finds it, paying taxes and other necessary expenses, and doing such other acts as are necessary to preserve it as left; he can not advance money to remove encumbrances, unless his estate was bound to pay the money. If he takes the responsibility of improving the estate, or bettering the title in this way, it must be at his own risk. The loss can not be visited on the heirs who gave him no authority to cause it. Nor can he ask legal protection when he has himself, though with the best motives, gone beyond the provisions of the law.—Tompkins v. Weeks, 26 Cal. 50, 63. If the executor or administrator does not have on hand, and is not chargeable with, any funds of the estate whatever, no duty rests on him, under such circumstances, to advance money to the estate, or to buy claims against it and to discharge them.—Smith v. Goethe, 147 Cal. 725, 82 Pac. 384, 387. The only right of an administrator, who anticipates distribution to the widow or heirs, and pays in advance of such distribution, is, when distribution is ordered, to have such payments retired therefrom, and receive a credit on account thereof from the distributive share so to be charged. It is not material in such a case, what property may have been distributed to the widow. Whatever may be the rights of subrogation to which the defendant is entitled, the same can only be worked out upon the final decree of distribution.—Elizalde v. Murphy, 4 Cal. App. 114, 116, 87 Pac. 245, 246. If, however, an administrator has made advances for the benefit of the estate, he may be allowed credit therefor as so much money advanced on account of the distributive shares of the heirs, but he is not entitled to charge such advancement as expenses of administration.—Estate of Rose, 80 Cal. 166, 180, 22 Pac. 86. If all interests in an estate are owned by an administrator and another person, who enter into a verbal agreement, whereby the commissions of the administrator, as well as moneys advanced by the administrator, shall be a lien on the property, and whereupon the administrator enters into possession with the verbal understanding that the profits of the estate shall be divided between the owners according to their respective interests, such agreement is within the statute of frauds and void. The administrator, therefore, can not, in equity, enforce his lien against the estate, although there has been a part performance.—Tucker v. S. Ottenheimer Estate, 46 Or. 585, 81 Pac. 360, 362. While it is not in the power of an executor or administrator by advances made by him to the estate to thereby make the estate his debtor regardless of the character or equity of his claim, yet advances made suitably and in good faith for the benefit of the estate may be allowed as a claim against the estate, and section 7542, Revised Codes of Montana, provides the method of allowing such a claim.—In re Williams' Estate, 47 Mont. 325, 132 Pac. 423. While an executor or administrator is to be reimbursed for payments made upon distributive shares, the credits therefor are not to be given upon the settlement of accounts, but are to be retired therefrom, and considered only upon the distribution of the estate. This rule will apply to all advancements made to the heirs by the administrator.—In re Loheide, 17 Cal. App. 475, 120 Pac. 56. Where court could have granted administrator permission to pay out money to complete purchase of realty, such payment without permission was not improper, but merely left propriety open on settlement of account.—In re Bottom's Estate, 156 Cal. 129, 103 Pac. 849. Payment by administratrix of share of amount necessary for administration expenses on death of vendor of realty, in order to secure conveyance of land contracted for by her decedent instead of proceeding to compel conveyance by vendor's administrator, held justifiable and properly allowable as a credit.—In re Bottom's Estate, 156 Cal. 129, 103 Pac. 849. Advancements by the administrator to a beneficiary in the nature of personal loans are chargeable only against the distributive portion of the estate found to be due to such beneficiary.—Elizalde v. Murphy, 163 Cal. 681, 126 Pac. 978, 981. An advancement to a tenant in common operates so that what he receives he receives in severalty, for the time being; but the obligation is on him to account for it later, on there being a partition, at which time there will be coming to him only his due proportion of what remains to be paid over.—Cooley v. Miller & Lux, 168 Cal. 120, 142 Pac. 83.

6. Making Improvements.—It is no part of the duty of an executor or administrator to improve the property he represents for the benefit of the heirs.—Estate of Moore, 72 Cal. 335, 342, 13 Pac. 880; Tompkins v. Weeks, 26 Cal. 50, 63. Administrators are not authorized to erect a dwelling-house with the funds or assets of the estate, to be occupied by one of them, or for any other use or purpose; neither can they involve the estate by borrowing money with which to pay for material and labor performed in the construction of such house. They do not have authority to charge the estate with the repayment of the money by them borrowed for such purpose.—Ralfson v. Cannon, 3 Utah 232, 2 Pac. 205, 206. An administratrix, as a tenant in common with the other heirs of the deceased, has no right to make extensive and costly improvements upon the estate, and charge the expense thereof, or any portion of the same, to her co-tenants, in the absence of an agreement, express or implied, upon the part of the latter to pay therefor. But if she makes the improvements with the consent of her co-tenants, and the same are beneficial to the estate, the co-tenants ought not to complain of her action in that regard, or to refuse to pay their just proportion of the expense, especially where the administratrix did what she believed to be for the best interests of the estate.— In re Alfstad's Estate, 27 Wash. 175, 67 Pac. 593, 598. It is within the province of an executor to make such expenditures on a building which was being erected by the decedent at the time of his death as may be reasonably necessary to preserve it pending administration. It is not his duty to complete the building.—Estate of Hincheon, 159 Cal. 755, 36 L. R. A. (N. S.) 303, 116 Pac. 47. A devise of real property, described in the will as being property on which "is situate a cottage in course of construction," can not be construed as a direction

by the testator that the completion of the building should be a charge upon his estate.—Estate of Hincheon, 159 Cal. 755, 36 L. R. A. (N. S.) 303, 116 Pac. 47. While it is the duty of executors to perform valid and uncompleted contracts which have been entered into by their testator, they are not called on, nor have they the right, to expend the funds of the estate for the doing of new work which the testator himself was not bound to do. Such expenditure, unless incurred for the preservation of the property of the decedent, is not a charge upon the estate. This rule applies to a building which was being erected by the testator by day's labor, as to which there were no unfinished contracts outstanding. The fact that the testator believed that the building was substantially completed is immaterial.—Estate of Hincheon, 159 Cal. 755, 36 L. R. A. (N. S.) 303, 116 Pac. 47.

REFERENCES.

Right of devisee or heir to completion of improvements at the expense of the estate.—See note 36 L. R. A. (N. S.) 303.

7. **Investment of funds.**—In the investment of trust funds, though an executor is not an insurer, he is nevertheless required to exercise that degree of care and discretion which an intelligent person of ordinary prudence and judgment would observe in the management of his own affairs. In lending money on mortgages of real estate, a degree of care is necessary, which, if omitted, will render the executor liable personally. If an executor lends funds on real estate, he must use care as to the title, and ascertain that the value of the premises mortgaged is such as will, in all probability, be adequate security for repayment whenever the money shall be called in. The criterion of value, in such cases, is the opinion or estimate of men of ordinary prudence, who would deem it safe to make a loan of the like amount of their own money on the same property.—In re Roach's Estate, 50 Or. 179, 92 Pac. 118, 123. In the absence of statutory provisions touching the method of investment, executors and administrators are bound to employ, in the investment of funds of the estate, such prudence and diligence as, in general, prudent men of discretion and intelligence employ in their own affairs.—In re Roach's Estate, 50 Or. 179, 92 Pac. 118, 125. The loss of trust funds by an executor or administrator, in consequence of an omission to take adequate security, is negligence, and an executor is personally liable for a failure to obtain a repayment of money of the estate loaned without any security, whether or not the loan was made before or after the passage of an act prescribing the manner of investing funds by a trustee.—In re Roach's Estate, 50 Or. 179, 92 Pac. 118, 126. There is no statutory requirement that an administrator must keep the funds in his hands profitably invested, and he is not ordinarily chargeable with interest unless he has actually received it.—Estate of Davis, 35 Mont. 273, 286, 88 Pac. 957. A representative who invests funds of the estate in his own name instead of collecting securities representing such funds thereby creates himself

a debtor to the estate, and as bearing on his liability it is immaterial
whether he was or was not negligent in collecting the securities taken
in his own name.—Elizalde v. Murphy, 11 Cal. App. 32, 103 Pac. 904.
Rule applied where he took note in his own name in lieu of notes
belonging to estate.—Elizalde v. Murphy, 11 Cal. App. 32, 103 Pac. 904.

8. Effect of chattel mortgage.—Chattels under mortgage constitute
an asset of the estate, subject to the preferential claim of the mortgagee, and the devolution of the decedent's title in no wise affects or
impairs the right of the mortgagee. His right of property remains as
distinct and as sacred as theretofore, and is a lien which can not be
lessened or impaired by the occurring of general expenses in the
course of administration. After the chattels are sold, his right extends
and attaches to the money derived from the sale, and this right is
exclusive of that claimed by the administrator to apply any portion of
the money toward the expenses of administration.—Horsfall v. Royles,
20 Mont. 495, sub nom.; In re Horsfall's Estate, 52 Pac. 199. Where
certain cattle of an estate were, at the time they were sold by an
administrator, encumbered by a chattel mortgage, the proceeds of
such sale should be withdrawn from the general assets of the estate
for the purpose of discharging the mortgage upon the cattle.—Baker v.
Becker, 67 Kan. 831, 72 Pac. 860, 861. Where a decedent, prior to his
death, executed a chattel mortgage to secure the payment of money,
and the property afterwards passed into the hands of the decedent's
administrator and the chattel mortgage was not renewed as required
by law, such mortgage ceased to be valid as against creditors of
the mortgagor, who became such before as well as after the default
in the renewal, and the creditors of the decedent are in a position to
take advantage of the invalidity of the mortgage, and the administrator, as a representative of the creditors of the estate, occupies the
same position as the creditors themselves in respect to the avoidance
of the mortgage, which is void because it was not filed or renewed.—
First Nat. Bank v. Ludvigsen, 8 Wyo. 230, 80 Am. St. Rep. 928, 56
Pac. 994, 997, 999. Where a chattel mortgage provided that on condition broken the mortgagee might take possession of the property; on
refusal to yield possession replevin will lie against the administrator
of the mortgagor.—Western Newspaper Union v. Thurmond, 27 Okla.
261, Ann. Cas. 1912B, 727, 111 Pac. 204.

9. Paying off liens. Redemption.—An executor or administrator
has the power to use the money in his hands for the purpose of
redeeming property of the estate from liens existing on it, when it is
necessary for the preservation of the property of the estate. This
power, however, is subject to the contingency of the expense being
disallowed by the court.—Estate of Freud, 131 Cal. 667, 673, 82 Am.
St. Rep. 407, 63 Pac. 1080. And in cases where the administrator
is otherwise without power to redeem, authority may be given him by
the court to do so.—Estate of Freud, 131 Cal. 667, 673, 82 Am. St. Rep.
407, 63 Pac. 1080. Under the existing law of California, where, in

the course of any regular proceeding, the relief becomes appropriate, resort may now be had to the court in which the administration is pending.—Toland v. Earl, 129 Cal. 148, 79 Am. St. Rep. 100, 61 Pac. 914; Estate of Freud, 131 Cal. 667, 673, 82 Am. St. Rep. 407, 63 Pac. 1080. Where the executors have sufficient funds in their hands to enable them to redeem certain land from a foreclosure sale, they may be ordered to make such redemption by the probate court.—Estate of Heydenfeldt, 117 Cal. 551, 49 Pac. 713. But an executor is not bound by the duties of his office to pay bankers, brokers, and other persons a bonus above legal interest to secure a loan of money to redeem property, belonging to the estate of his testator which has been sold under the decree of a court having jurisdiction to order the sale, nor is he bound to pledge his own securities or to use his own credit to secure such loan.—In re Holladay's Estate, 18 Or. 168, 22 Pac. 750. The estate has a cause of action to redeem from sales under a mortgage and a trust deed, upon a proper accounting, and, in enforcing the right of the estate of the deceased to redemption from such sales, the court has a discretion in the matter and may make a final decree without an interlocutory decree. It is not imperative upon the court, in all actions to redeem, to make the interlocutory order so as to give the opportunity to appeal.—Smith v. Goethe, 147 Cal. 725, 736, 82 Pac. 384. While a creditor holds collateral, he may collect dividends upon his entire claim, even to the extent of payment in full, in which case the security would inure to the benefit of the unsecured creditors; or, if insufficient to pay the claim in full, and the dividends reduce the claim to less than the value of the security, the fiduciary must redeem it for the benefit of the estate; yet if, before or after the claim is proved, he disposes of the security, and realizes thereby a partial payment of the claim, he has derived all the benefit that it was intended to give, and all that, under his contract, he is entitled to receive and it no longer exists for any purpose. In other words, if he disposes of the collateral, and puts it out of his power to return it in case the debt is paid from other sources, it ceases to be collateral, and the sum realized operates as a payment and reduces his claim pro tanto.—Erle v. Lane, 22 Colo. 273, 44 Pac. 591, 594.

10. **Other questions relating to mortgages.**—If an executor or administrator has no funds of the estate in his hands, and desires to protect the property of the estate from a sacrifice under a foreclosure sale, he may purchase the mortgage himself, without going outside of the line of his duties as administrator.—Burnett v. Lyford, 93 Cal. 114, 28 Pac. 855. A purchase of assets by the executor or administrator, or his taking and accounting for the same at their appraised value, may often be really advantageous to the estate, "and such advantage is, after all, the main thing to be considered; and when it becomes necessary to save the estate from loss, it is right, and even obligatory, for the executor or administrator to purchase or to take possession of land, on the foreclosure of a mortgage belonging to the estate, and to

hold the title for the benefit of the estate."—Dusing v. Nelson, 7 Colo. 184, 2 Pac. 922, 924, citing Shouler on Executors and Administrators, secs. 323, 358. It is the duty of an administratrix, who holds a mortgage against the estate she represents, to list such mortgage for taxation.—Estate of McDougald, 146 Cal. 196, 79 Pac. 875, 876. The foreclosure proceedings had by the administrator subsequent to the death of the deceased, whereby the mortgage indebtedness was converted into real estate and title vested in him, did not relieve it of the burden of being sold, as provided in section 1523 of the Code of Civil Procedure of California, and the amendment of 1893, imposing the same burden upon the land did not impair any vested rights that the heirs had therein.—Estate of Bazzuro, 161 Cal. 72, 118 Pac. 434.

11. Continuing business of decedent.

(1) In general.—Generally speaking, an executor or administrator has no power to carry on the business of the decedent, yet he may do so, if necessary to preserve the property.—Estate of Rose, 80 Cal. 166, 172, 22 Pac. 86; Estate of Smith, 118 Cal. 462, 466, 50 Pac. 701; Estate of Freud, 131 Cal. 667, 671, 82 Am. St. Rep. 407, 63 Pac. 1080. As a rule a personal representative has no power to continue the business of a decedent unless under express authority of a will, a statute, or an order of court.—In re Ennis' Estate, Love, W. & M. Co. v. Ennis, Sumner Co. v. Ennis, 96 Wash. 352, 358, 165 Pac. 119. It is the duty of the executor, without special direction of the court, to preserve the property of the estate. He does not require leave of the court so to do, and it is a question how far an order so obtained will protect an administrator either in doing or omitting to do something which might be deemed important. When the court is so consulted, the heirs are not specially cited, but, on the settlement of the accounts of an executor, they are called in, and have an appeal to the supreme court from any determination which may be made. The previous consent of the acts of the executor can not limit their inquiry as to the lawfulness of the acts done or the duty of the executor to do that which has been omitted. Ordinarily, it would determine a question of good faith, and quite often that is the only matter in issue. Hence it is always an advantage to have such permission. Still, the failure to obtain it does not render the expenditures made improper.. The only result is that the matter is yet to be passed upon.—Estate of Smith, 118 Cal. 462, 466, 50 Pac. 701. If an administrator elects to carry on the business of an estate, he is to be charged with gains and credited with expenses.—Estate of Rose, 80 Cal. 166, 178, 22 Pac. 86. And a person who is employed by him in such business is the employee of such administrator, and not the employee of such estate. Such employee must therefore look to the administrator, and not to the estate, for his pay.—Estate of Rose, 80 Cal. 166, 176, 22 Pac. 86. The executor or administrator is chargeable with loss arising from his carrying on of the decedent's business, but where it is found that a

distinct gain has been made in such business, and he has been charged with such gain, the judgment will not be disturbed, notwithstanding alleged losses which have not been satisfactorily accounted for.—Estate of Gianelli, 146 Cal. 139, 141, 79 Pac. 841. If the heirs and devisees desire to continue the business of the ancestor undivided, they should first have the estate closed, as provided by law, and take over the business individually. It is not the affair of the administrator to continue the business as a part of the administration, and the court has no authority to authorize or permit him to do so.—In re S. Marks & Co.'s Estate, 66 Or. 340, 133 Pac. 778. See, also, In re Marks & Wollenberg's Estate, 66 Or. 347, 133 Pac. 779. It is no part of the duty or authority of an administrator with the will annexed to manage the property of the estate for the benefit of the heirs. So far as they are concerned it is simply his duty to preserve the estate until distribution.—Estate of Broome, 162 Cal. 258, 122 Pac. 470. Where, by agreement of all the heirs, one of them continues to carry on the dry goods store of which the decedent had been the proprietor, and, in the proceedings in settlement of the estate, the administrator is, by order of court, authorized to sell the stock of goods at private sale, this gives the administrator no power to purchase goods to replenish the stock.—In re Ennis' Estate, Love, W. & M. Co. v. Ennis, Sumner Co. v. Ennis, 96 Wash. 352, 165 Pac. 119. In case an executor or administrator elects to carry on a transaction arising out of a contract made by the decedent, all persons dealing with him are charged with knowledge of the law, to the effect that the estate is interested only so far as profits are concerned.—Exchange Nat. Bank v. Betts' Estate, 103 Kan. 807, 176 Pac. 660.

(2) **Exception to the rule.**—While it is not permissible, as a general rule, for an executor or administrator to engage in trade with the assets of the estate, or to carry on the business of the decedent, unless expressly so directed by the will, or authorized by the court which has charge of the administration of the estate, this rule is not without exceptions; and where the executor or administrator finds it necessary, in a mercantile business, or in a manufactory, to dispose of and to realize upon the assets of the business to the best advantage, and not for the mere purpose of making profits upon sales, as in the ordinary course of business, it is not regarded, in law, as the carrying on of the trade or business, but simply as the winding up of the affairs.—Fleming v. Kelly, 18 Colo. App. 23, 69 Pac. 272. Where the estate consists of several thousand head of animals, it is the duty of the executor or administrator to care for them until they are sold, and in so doing he is not carrying on the business of the intestate in any sense other than that he is caring for the personal property of the estate until it can be advantageously sold.—Estate of Fernandez, 119 Cal. 579, 585, 51 Pac. 851.

(3) **Individual liability.**—An executor or administrator is not authorized or required by law to continue to carry on the business in

which the decedent had been engaged. If he does so he acts upon
his own responsibility. He can derive no profit from the success of
his venture, and must bear the loss of a failure. Expenses incurred
in carrying on such business are not debts of or claims against the
estate, nor are they "charges or expenses of administration," within
the meaning of the probate law. The items of increase and items
of expenses of such business are not matters that come within the
purview of the itemized account of an administrator, as such, subject
to the rules of audit and allowance.—Estate of Rose, 80 Cal. 166, 173,
22 Pac. 86; Estate of Straus, 144 Cal. 553, 559, 77 Pac. 1122. The
liabilities growing out of the management of a decedent's estate, by
an executor or administrator, are his liabilities. He has a right to
pay them out of the increase of the business, but if by so doing a
loss is sustained to the estate, he must make the loss good. Protected from loss and from liability at all times, the estate is interested in the business only to the extent of its profits; and in them,
not because it is the business of the estate, but because the administrator is using the property of the estate in a way he is not authorized
to do, and consequently is required to account for all the profit made
by its use.—Estate of Rose, 80 Cal. 166, 173, 22 Pac. 86; Estate of
Straus, 144 Cal. 553, 559, 77 Pac. 1122. In the absence of a testamentary direction, an administrator of the estate of a deceased person can not carry on the business of the decedent without being
individually answerable for the conduct of the business. The law
charges him with all losses thereby incurred, without, on the other
hand, allowing him to receive the benefit of any profits that he may
make; the rule being that the persons beneficially interested in the
estate may either hold the representative liable for the amount so
used, with interest, or, at their election, take all the profits which the
representative has made by such unauthorized use of the funds of the
estate.—Campbell v. Faxon, 73 Kan. 675, 5 L. R. A. (N. S.) 1002, 85
Pac. 760, 762. If an administrator continues the business of his decedent, under the sanction of the court, and with the consent of the
parties interested, but is held individually answerable to a vendor of
goods, which goods the administrator purchased in good faith and used
to keep up the stock in trade of such business, justice requires that
he should be reimbursed from the estate.—Estate of Akana, 11 Haw.
420, 423. If an administrator continues to operate the business that
the decedent was engaged in at the time of his death, he, and not the
estate, must bear the burden of such debts of the business as are not
covered by the profits.—Estate of De Rome, 175 Cal. 399, 165 Pac.
919. Where an administrator, without authority of law, carries on
the business of the deceased, he is chargeable with all the losses
thereby incurred.—Western Newspaper Union v. Thurmond, 27 Okla.
261, Ann. Cas. 1912B, 727, 111 Pac. 205.

(4) **Liability created by court.**—If the probate court, in the exercise of its incidental powers, orders the administra

the business of the decedent, and the business results in a profit to
the estate, expenses incurred in the conduct of the business are claims
against the estate, and not against the administratrix personally. The
liability for such obligation incurred by the express order of the court
is not a debt incurred upon the credit of the administratrix, but a
liability created by the court itself.—Fleming v. Kelly, 18 Colo. App.
23, 69 Pac. 272, 273.

(5) Administrator's report and account.—If the executor or administrator elects to carry on the business in which the decedent had
been engaged, he is bound to report to the court, as money or property coming into his hands as administrator, the true net gains or
profits derived from the business in money or kind, but the detailed
account of the management or conduct of the business is no part
of his accounts as administrator. If he reports them into the court
at all, it should be done in a separate paper, perhaps as an exhibit
attached to his official report or account. And when so done, it simply
serves the purpose of showing his good faith in the premises, and is
not a matter for audit by the court. The probate jurisdiction of the
court is separate and distinct from its jurisdiction in ordinary civil
actions. To the extent that the court, in the exercise of its probate
jurisdiction, undertakes to audit the account and control the conduct
of that business, to that extent it also, as well as the administrator,
assumes to make a speculative and hazardous use of the property of
deceased persons not authorized by law. If the administrator fails
to honestly account to the estate for the profits, or to make good the
loss of his acts ultra vires, he is guilty of a fraud, for which he may
be proceeded against in a civil action, as in any other case of fraud,
and then, and in that proceeding, those accounts of the business which
he conducted with the property of the estate, without authority of law,
will become the subject of investigation, item by item, and their investigation will be governed by the same rules of evidence as apply in
the examination of other disputed accounts.—Estate of Rose, 80 Cal.
166, 173, 22 Pac. 86; Estate of Straus, 144 Cal. 553, 559, 77 Pac. 1122.
Where the sons of a decedent, managing the estate, much involved, so
as to clear off all indebtedness, were themselves creditors and paid
off their debt in good faith out of the assets, the report of their action
being approved by the county court, they should not be made to refund
the amount merely because they did not satisfy a technical requirement under the law as to procedure.—Conant v. Machen, 27 Colo. App.
310, 315, 148 Pac. 872. A man's note to a bank was taken up by the
sons of the man, who gave their own note instead and, after repeated
renewals paid off the debt at last. Meantime the father had died, testate, the sons being named as executors, without bond and without
compensation, but the will was not probated at once, the sons being
requested by all concerned, including the creditors, to manage the
estate and pay off the debts. However the will was probated at last
and an administrator appointed cum testamento annexo, the sons waiv-

ing their right. The court, by order, then required the sons to file a report of their management, and, on their complying, the item as to their being repaid in the note transaction was rejected on the ground that the original note of the testator to the bank was not presented within the year allowed for the presentation of claims with vouchers thereof. Held, on appeal, that such presentation was not essential.—Conant v. Machen, 27 Colo. App. 310, 315, 148 Pac. 872.

12. Appeal.—An unsatisfied creditor, of a business carried on by an administrator in continuation of the decedent, is not "a party aggrieved," so as to be able to appeal from the order settling the final account; he is presumed to have dealt with knowledge that the administrator, and not the estate, was liable for the debts of the business.—Estate of De Rome, 175 Cal. 399, 165 Pac. 919. Good faith expenditure for benefit of estate and duly allowed will not be reviewed unless there is no ground in record on which it can be supported.—In re Bottom's Estate, 156 Cal. 129, 103 Pac. 849.

13. Advice and Instructions.—Under certain circumstances, an executor or administrator may go into equity to seek advice and instructions; but not where the questions of law asked are such as can be readily answered by an attorney at law, from whom the executor or administrator has the right to obtain the desired advice at the expense of the estate.—Kaikainahaole v. Allen, 14 Haw. 527, 529. Executors and administrators should be guided by the following advice and instructions, viz.:

1. Upon the receipt of letters, take into your possession, immediately, all the estate of decedent, real and personal, and collect all debts due to the decedent or to the estate.—See § 623, ante.

2. Make and return to the court, as soon as practicable, a true inventory and appraisement of "all" the estate, including the homestead, if any, which has come to your possession or knowledge.—See § 356, ante.

3. Make immediate application to the court for an order of publication of notice to the creditors of the estate to present their claims.—See § 440, ante.

4. Upon the expiration of the time for publication of notice to creditors, file a copy thereof, with the affidavit of the printer, showing due publication.—See § 444, ante.

5. Pay no claim until the same has been properly presented, allowed, approved, filed, and ordered paid by the court.—See §§ 457-459, ante. Pay no amount, however small, without taking a receipt in writing.

6. Sell no property, real or personal, of decedent, without an order of the court.—See § 483, ante.

7. Within thirty days after the expiration of the time mentioned in the notice to creditors, within which claims must be presented, render a full account and report of your administration to the court,

and file therewith vouchers for all charges, debts, claims, and expenses which you have paid.—See §§ 662, 671, post.

8. Upon the settlement of your account, obtain an order of the court for the payment of debts which have been allowed.—See § 702, post.

9. All costs incurred by reason of your neglect to comply with your duty, and in enforcing such compliance, will be charged to you, and not to the estate.

10. In case of doubt as to how you should act, apply to your attorney, or to the court, for advice and instructions.

V. ESTATES WHERE PARTNERSHIP EXISTED.

1. Interest of deceased partner. Assets of estate.—Partnership assets, as such, form no part of the individual estate of a deceased partner; the residuum only, after satisfying liabilities and advances, if any, made by the survivor. becomes the property of the estate. The assets which pass to the executor or administrator consist of the individual estate of the decedent.—Andrade v. Superior Court, 75 Cal. 459, 463, 17 Pac. 531; Theller v. Such, 57 Cal. 447, 459. When a partnership is dissolved by the death of one of the partners, its assets, debts, and credits remain as distinct from those of its late members, until its affairs are wound up, as before the dissolution; and if all the members of a firm die, whether within the jurisdiction of the same or different probate courts, the assets, debts, and credits of the partnership do not become confused with the estate of the last survivor, but continue a separate existence.—Theller v. Such, 57 Cal. 447, 461. Partnership property is assets of the firm, and subject to the exclusive management or control of the surviving partner. It is not assets of the estate in the hands of the administrator.—Tompkins v. Weeks, 26 Cal. 50, 66. But the interest of a decedent in a partnership must be included in the inventory of his estate, and be appraised as other property.—Painter v. Estate of Painter, 68 Cal. 395, 396, 9 Pac. 450.

REFERENCES.

Rights of heirs in real estate of deceased partner.—See note 27 L. R. A. 348-354.

2. Presentation of claims.—In general, a creditor can not reach the property of a deceased partner in disregard of the positive statute requiring the presentation of his claim.—Frazier v. Murphy, 133 Cal. 91, 97, 65 Pac. 326; Falkner v. Hendy, 107 Cal. 49, 40 Pac. 21, 386. The surviving partner can not bring suit against the administrator of a deceased partner for his interest in partnership assets until he has presented a claim within the time limited in the notice to creditors.—McKay v. Joy, 2 Cal. Unrep. 639, 9 Pac. 940, 942. For evidence in a proceeding for the establishment of a claim against a decedent's estate which shows that the claim arose from a debt of the firm of which the deceased was a partner, see In re Morgan's Estate, 46 Or.

233, 77 Pac. 608, 609. But an action for an accounting and settling of the affairs of a partnership, and for an accounting with respect to and for the delivery of trust property remaining in the hands of the decedent at the time of his death, may be maintained without first presenting a claim against the estate and property of the decedent, where the trust property can still be "earmarked," traced, and identified.—Roach v. Caraffa, 85 Cal. 436, 444, 25 Pac. 22. So if one of the members of a firm which executed a negotiable promissory note dies before maturity, presentment should be made to and demand be made of the surviving partners, and not the executor of the deceased partner, and suit on such a note against the surviving partner may be maintained without having presented the claim to the administrator for allowance.—Barlow v. Coggan, 1 Wash. Ter. 257, 260, 261. Nor need a claim against joint lessors, who are partners, for overcharged rent be presented as a claim against the estate of a deceased partner, in order to enforce it against the firm, as such claim is not against the estate of the deceased partner, but against the firm of which he had been a member.—Corson v. Berson, 86 Cal. 433, 441, 25 Pac. 7. Where an administrator of a deceased partner sues a surviving partner for an accounting and settlement of the partnership affairs, such surviving partner is entitled to have the accounts adjusted, and an amount claimed by him for sums drawn by the deceased from the partnership during his lifetime allowed as an offset to the claim of plaintiff, although he has not presented a claim to the administrator for the latter's allowance and approval.—Manuel v. Escolle, 65 Cal. 110, 3 Pac. 411. No presentation of a claim against the estate of the deceased partner is necessary, where payment is not sought out of the assets of the estate.—Franklin v. Trickey, 9 Ariz. 282, 11 Ann. Cas. 1105, 80 Pac. 352, 353.

REFERENCES.

Presentation of claims against estates of deceased persons.—See note to § 481, head-line 3, ante.

3. **Jurisdiction. Probate court. Equity.**—If questions arise in the course of the settlement of partnership affairs, which can not be adjusted without recourse to the courts, the probate court is not the forum in which such questions can be solved, but, like other questions cognizable in courts of equity, they must be determined in the last named courts.—Andrade v. Superior Court, 75 Cal. 459, 463, 17 Pac. 531. If all the members of a partnership die, whether within the jurisdiction of the same or of some different probate court, the rights of the representatives or successors of the several partners can be determined only in a court of equity, which has the power and machinery for settling those rights by an appropriate decree. Where none of the partners are surviving, no one has a better right to the partnership property than those who had received it colore officii, as executors of him who held it, and who have an interest in the residuary rights of his estate.—Theller v. Such, 57 Cal. 447, 460, 461. If the

existence of a partnership between a decedent and a survivor is denied by the latter, the probate court can not adjudicate the question, and decree the existence or non-existence of the relation.—Andrade v. Superior Court, 75 Cal. 459, 463, 17 Pac. 531; Wright v. Wright, 11 Colo. App. 470, 53 Pac. 684; In re Alfstad's Estate, 27 Wash. 175, 67 Pac. 593, 597. The probate court has no authority to settle and adjust accounts between a surviving partner and the representatives of a deceased one. Its power is limited to requiring a survivor to account. If the status of partnership is admitted, the court may call upon a survivor to render an account.—Andrade v. Superior Court, 75 Cal. 459, 462, 463, 17 Pac. 531. As ancillary to the right of the court to enforce an accounting by the surviving partner, and to enable it to determine whether what purports to be an account is such in reality, or whether another and further account is requisite, the court has the right to examine the surviving partner under oath, or any other witness or witnesses who may possess information germane to the question.—Andrade v. Superior Court, 75 Cal. 459, 563, 17 Pac. 531. The probate court, in settling the accounts of executors or administrators, has no jurisdiction to determine the administrator's claim, as a partner of the decedent, to one-half of his estate.—In re Alfstad's Estate, 27 Wash. 175, 67 Pac. 593, 597. It is not error for a probate court to refuse to confirm a sale of the personal property of a deceased partner, which was in the possession of the surviving partner, and which constituted a part of the partnership property, where the court had no jurisdiction to order the sale.—In re Auerbach's Estate, 23 Utah, 529, 65 Pac. 488, 490. The fact that an executor under a non-intervention will applied to the court for leave to sell the interest of the deceased in partnership property, and to be discharged from his trust, does not indicate that the estate was either managed or settled under the supervision and control of the probate court. The probate court is without power, except such as is especially conferred upon it by the statute, to control the administration of the estates under wills of this character.—In re MacDonald's Estate, 29 Wash. 422, 69 Pac. 1111, 1115. The probate court has full power to try the issue of partnership or no partnership when raised on an application by one claiming as surviving partner, the right to administer the partnership estate under the provisions of the statute of the state of Washington.—State v. Superior Court, 76 Wash. 291, 136 Pac. 152. Under the Alaskan Code, the administration of estates is in the nature of a suit in equity.—Esterly v. Rua (Alaska), 122 Fed. 609, 611, 58 C. C. A. 548. But, while the settlement of the affairs of a partnership is a proper subject for the exercise of general equity jurisdiction, where a partnership has been dissolved by the death of one of the partners, the settlement of its affairs must be in the probate court.—Esterly v. Rua (Alaska), 122 Fed. 609, 612, 58 C. C. A. 548.

4. Bequest of interest in firm. Payment of partnership debts.—A partner can not bequeath any specific article of firm property, for he

has no absolute title to any part of it. It is all subject to the payment of partnership debts, and then to an adjustment of the interests of the partners. It is the duty of the surviving partner to apply the partnership money on hand at the time of the death of the testator, and all sums collected on notes and accounts, to the payment of the partnership debts, and to pay the deficiency out of the proceeds of the partnership goods. Whatever remains is subject to division, and the portion belonging to the testator's estate passes to his beneficiaries. The partnership property is primarily liable for partnership debts, and the beneficiaries have no right to have the testator's individual property applied to the payment of the partnership debts.—Brady v. Foley, 59 Kan. 778, 53 Pac. 761, 762.

5. Authority of executor or administrator.

(1) In general.—The executor or administrator has no authority to intermeddle at all with the partnership affairs, except so far as he is entitled to call upon the surviving partner to proceed and close up the partnership affairs, and to account to him for the share of the surplus belonging to the estate. The authority of the executor or administrator extends only to settling up the affairs of the estate, sharing the debts, and distributing the remainder, under the direction of the probate court, to the parties interested.—Tompkins v. Weeks, 26 Cal. 50, 66. He is not authorized to advance money or to use funds belonging to the estate for the purpose of carrying on business with the surviving partner of his intestate.—Tompkins v. Weeks, 26 Cal. 50, 65. A court, even upon the application of an executor or administrator, can not order a summary sale of the joint personal property, upon the dissolution of a partnership, by the death of one or more of the partners, for it becomes immediately vested in the survivor as trustee, and it is thereupon his duty to dispose of it in good faith for the best interests of decedent's estate and all concerned. The court has no jurisdiction to make such an order, and no executor or administrator has authority to execute it. Neither has a court jurisdiction to state or to settle a disputed account between an executor and a surviving partner, although it may order the latter to "render an account." No court, in the absence of any breach of duty on the part of a surviving partner, can, by ordering a sale of the decedent's share in the partnership, deprive the surviving partner of his possession and control of the joint property.—In re Auerbach's Estate, 23 Utah 529, 65 Pac. 488, 490. Neither the executor nor the administrator of a partnership has any power, nor can a probate court authorize him, to partition real property.—Burnside v. Savier, 6 Or. 154.

(2) Inventory and appraisement.—An administrator, having reason to believe the decedent to have had a partnership interest, should inventory this and, if necessary, sue for its recovery; if unwilling to do so, he should resign.—Hadley v. Hadley, 73 Or. 179, 144 Pac. 80. Under the Alaskan Code, the administrator of the estate of a deceased

partner is required to include the whole property of the partnership in the inventory, and that if the surviving partner fails to apply for administration within five days after the filing of the inventory the administration of the partnership affairs shall devolve upon the general administrator.—Esterly v. Rua (Alaska), 122 Fed. 609, 611, 58 C. C. A. 548. In the administration of a deceased partner's estate, the interest such partner had in the firm must in all cases be appraised as a single item, and so appear in the inventory; it is to be regarded as personalty and may be sold as such.—Cooley v. Miller & Lux, 168 Cal. 120, 142 Pac. 83.

(3) **Necessary delay.**—On the death of a member of a partnership, the settlement of his estate is delayed necessarily by the winding up of the partnership affairs, this being in the hands of the surviving partner, only on the conclusion of which the administration by the executor can proceed; it follows that, if a distributee has assigned his share in part,· the assignee must, as well as he, wait for the enjoyment.—Cooley v. Miller & Lux, 168 Cal. 120, 142 Pac. 83.

(4) **Actions.**—An administrator may maintain, against a surviving partner, any action which the decedent could have maintained; in the matter of relief the personal representative of the decedent occupies the same relative position with reference to the surviving partners, that the deceased, if alive, would sustain to his co-partners.—Boehme v. Fitzgerald, 43 Mont. 226, 228, 115, Pac. 413.

(5) **Sale to pay debts.**—Although the title to lands, owned by a partnership is in the name of the individual members of the firm, the administrator of the partnership estate is authorized to sell such lands for the payment of partnership debts.—Gregory v. Keenan (Or.), 256 Fed. 949, 956.

REFERENCES.

Rights of administrator of deceased partner.—See note 7 L. R. A. .792. Position of executor or administrator as to real estate of deceased partner.—See note 27 L. R. A. 340-353.

6. Surviving partner as executor or administrator.—Although a surviving partner was appointed executor of a deceased partner's will, wherein the testator waived the giving of a bond by the surviving partner, such executor may still be required to give bond as administrator of the partnership estate, which he must first settle up, and afterwards settle the individual estate of the testator.—Palicio v. Bigne, 15 Or. 142, 13 Pac. 765. Section 1365 of the Code of Civil Procedure of California provides that "if the decedent was a member of a partnership at the time of his decease, the surviving partner must in no case be appointed administrator of his estate"; and, under this provision, one who had formerly been a partner, and between whom and the deceased there were unsettled partnership accounts, is not eligible· as an administrator.—Estate of Garber, 74 Cal. 338, 16

Pac. 233. But section 1350 of that code does not prohibit a surviving partner from being one of the executors of the estate of the deceased partner; and the fact that the surviving partner is also one of the executors of the estate of the deceased partner is not any reason for refusing to settle his accounts as an executor because of the absence of a statement showing the condition of the partnership affairs. Of course, when any portion of the assets of a partnership has come into the hands of an executor, as such, he must charge himself therewith in his accounts.—Miller v. Lux, 100 Cal. 609, 614, 35 Pac. 345, 639. An executor who is also the surviving partner of the deceased can not, on appeal from an order of the probate court settling the account of said executor, and from an order denying his motion for a new trial in the matter of said order, contend that the account involved is his account as surviving partner, and that the probate court has no jurisdiction to settle such an account, especially where the account is, upon its face, the account of appellant, not as surviving partner,. but as executor.— Estate of Sylvester, 105 Cal. 189, 190, 38 Pac. 648. The surviving partner, if he makes timely application therefor, and is a person qualified and competent to act as a general administrator, has the right to administer the partnership estate.—State v. Superior Court, 76 Wash. 291, 304, 136 Pac. 147. The time limit fixed in the statute of the state of Washington, within which the application for administration of the partnership estate may be made, is simply to fix a limit beyond which application may not be made unless an extension of time be granted; it was never intended to prohibit the consideration of such an application, if made before the filing of the inventory.—State v. Superior Court, 76 Wash. 291, 305, 136 Pac. 147. Where a surviving partner petitions for letters of administration upon the partnership estate, the superior court, sitting in probate, has power to determine, at the outset, whether or not there was a partnership, if that fact is denied.— State v. Superior Court, 76 Wash. 291, 305, 136 Pac. 147. The statute of Washington would be of little utility if the superior court had no power, at the outset, to determine whether or not there was a partnership.—State v. Superior Court, 76 Wash. 291, 304, 136 Pac. 147. Where the business of a partnership is conducted by the administrator of a deceased partner, the surviving partners acquiescing, they can not complain afterwards.—In re Campbell's Estate, 98 Wash. 295, 167 Pac. 905. Where the business partner of the decedent was the executor of the estate, and, the testator having made a bequest to his mother, payable out of his separate property, which included his interest in the partnership business, contracted with the legatee to buy up the separate property and pay her the bequest, the contract was held to be without consideration and not enforceable against the executor.—Gates v. Herr, 102 Wash. 131, 172 Pac. 912 The administrator of the liquidating partner of a firm, which was dissolved by mutual consent, such partner having died during the progress of the liquidation, becomes, along with others, who with him form a corporation to continue the business of the deceased, trustees for liquidating the

.business; and for the heirs of the deceased after the accomplishment
of the liquidation, which heirs are entitled to the balance.—McFadden
v. Jenkins (N. D.), 169 N. W. 151. 161. Death of a partner terminates
the partnership, it devolving upon the surviving partner to wind up
the firm's affairs; such partner may, in liquidation, dispose of the
partnership property.—Cooley v. Miller & Lux, 168 Cal. 120, 142 Pac.
83. The method provided by chapter 81, session laws of 1901, of New
Mexico, for winding up partnership affairs on the death of a partner,
is exclusive, and until the appointment and qualification of an administrator of the partnership, the surviving partners have no power to
sell or dispose of the partnership assets.—Dow v. Jimpson, 17 N. M.
357, 132 Pac. 568. If an administrator is appointed and fails to file
an inventory of the partnership estate as required by the law of New
Mexico the surviving partner can compel him to do so.—Dow v. Jimpson, 17 N. M. 357, 132 Pac. 568. Where death has dissolved a partnership, neither the executor nor the heirs of the deceased partner have
any right of possession of the partnership property until the surviving
partner has proceeded to its liquidation and has delivered it over to
them; the executor or administrator has only the right to demand, and
enforce settlement and payment and delivery over, such part thereof
as may remain after final settlement by the surviving partner of the
partnership affairs; the surviving partner is the only legal representative of the partnership, at least between him and the heirs and legal
representatives of the deceased member.—Cooley v. Miller & Lux, 168
Cal. 120, 137, 142 Pac. 83. The failure of a surviving partner to give
the bond required by the statute does not affect his right to the possession of the firm property, or defeat his right to maintain any appropriate action concerning it; the bond is merely to protect the interest of
the deceased partner.—Silver v. Eakins, 55 Mont. 210, 175 Pac. 876.
A surviving partner may be required to make known the amount of
partnership debts and the amount of firm assets in his possession,
to the end that the court may determine whether the possession of
firm property held by the estate of the deceased partner is necessary,
in order that the surviving partner may discharge the duties imposed
upon him by the statute.—Silver v. Eakins, 55 Mont. 210, 175 Pac. 876.
Under the statute, the interest of each partner extends to every portion of the firm property; therefore, neither partner is entitled, as
against the other, to the exclusive possession of the whole or of any
specific part of the partnership assets; this rule, however, ceases
immediately upon the death of one partner.—Silver v. Eakins, 55 Mont.
210, 175 Pac. 876. The death of a partner dissolves the partnership, and
the surviving partner thereupon becomes entitled to the possession of
sufficient firm property to enable him to perform his statutory duties.—
Silver v. Eakins, 55 Mont. 210, 175 Pac. 876. A surviving partner has
the right to continue in possession of the partnership property and to
settle the partnership business.—Weiss v. Hamilton, 40 Mont. 99, 108,
105 Pac. 74. Where death dissolves a general trading partnership, the

surviving partners are entitled to continue in possession and to settle
the partnership affairs; it is their duty to account to the deceased
partner's estate, and, upon failure to do so, they may be compelled by
summary proceedings.—Boehme v. Fitzgerald, 43 Mont. 226, 227, 115
Pac. 413.

7. Surviving partner. Rights and powers.—A surviving partner, in
the absence of statute, has exclusive control of partnership effects.—
Barlow v. Coggan, 1 Wash. Ter. 257; In re Auerbach's Estate, 23 Utah
529, 65 Pac. 488, 490; Allen v. Hill, 16 Cal. 113; Gray v. Palmer, 9
Cal. 616; McKay v. Joy, 2 Cal. Unrep. 639, 9 Pac. 940; Miller v. Lux,
100 Cal. 609, 614, 35 Pac. 345, 639. A surviving partner, if he deems
it advisable and for the interest of the concern, may sell the entire
partnership's stock of goods at auction, or otherwise, within a month
after the dissolution of the partnership; and it is within his discretionary power to continue to dispose of the stock to the customers of
the concern in the ordinary way, if that is deemed more beneficial to
the interest of all parties concerned, and, for that purpose, to employ
the necessary salesmen and other agents.—Louis v. Elfelt, 89 Cal. 547,
551, 26 Pac. 1095. When the partnership has been carried on for some
time, after dissolution by death, and such continuance has proved
beneficial to the parties, it is but just and proper that the surviving
partner should receive a reasonable allowance for his skill and industry
in conducting the business, for, during that time, the business has not
received the care and labor of the deceased partner as an equivalent for such services. While all the parties are living, each is
under obligation to devote his time and services to the partnership
business, and there is, therefore, good reason for holding that neither
should receive a compensation for such service. But when, in consequence of the death of one partner, this equality no longer exists, it is
but equitable that the surviving partner should be compensated for
such services as he may have rendered in the business after the
death of the deceased partner, to be deducted out of the profits realized
by the continuance of the business; the overplus of such profits,
after deducting such compensation, to be divided between the partners.
This principle does not justify the court in holding that the surviving
partner is entitled to compensation merely for services rendered in
winding up the affairs of the firm, but should be applied where the
partnership business has been continued for a considerable time in
order that the affairs of the partnership may be advantageously wound
up.—Griggs v. Clark, 23 Cal. 427, 430; Louis v. Elfelt, 89 Cal. 547, 551,
26 Pac. 1095. A surviving partner may have partition of the real estate belonging to the partnership, standing in the name of his deceased partner, and he has an equitable lien upon partnership real
estate for his indemnity against the debts of the firm and for the
balance due him.—Gray v. Palmer, 9 Cal. 616, 639. A contract, however, made between a surviving partner, a widow of the deceased
partner, who left minor children, and a part of the individual creditors

of the deceased partner, that the surviving partner should pay a proportionate share of the individual indebtedness of the deceased partner and retain all the partnership property, is against public policy, and therefore illegal and void. So a promise made by the surviving partner to a creditor of a deceased partner, in pursuance of such an agreement, to pay such creditor a proportionate share of the individual debt is also illegal and void. No contract can be made respecting the assets of a deceased person's estate except by the authority, and with the approval, of the probate court and then only to the extent authorized or permitted by the laws of the state.—Cox v. Grubb, 47 Kan. 435, 27 Am. St. Rep. 303, 28 Pac. 157. A surviving partner can not collect from the general assets of his deceased partner's estate a debt due by the decedent to the partnership without first complying with the statute relative to his settling up the affairs of the partnership, and ascertaining whether the partnership assets will pay the partnership debts.—Painter v. Estate of Painter, 68 Cal. 395, 397, 9 Pac. 450.

REFERENCES.

Respective rights of surviving partner and heirs of deceased partner.—See note 7 L. R. A. 793, 794. Position of surviving partner in partnership real estate.—See note 28 L. R. A. 129-137.

8. Surviving partner. Settlement of partnership affairs.—A surviving partner is entitled to continue in possession of the partnership for the purpose of settling up its business; and this, in the absence of any statutory provision directing otherwise, he must do without delay, and account for and pay to the executor or administrator of the deceased partner, from time to time, any balance payable in right of the decedent. He may be required to give bond, and for any failure in the performance of his duty is amenable to any action, at the instance of the executor or administrator, which the decedent could have maintained. This is simply declaratory of the common law, and does not change the common-law doctrine that a surviving partner is entitled to the management and possession of the joint property for the purpose of winding up the affairs of the partnership and paying its debts.—In re Auerbach's Estate, 23 Utah 529, 65 Pac. 488, 490; Gleason v. White, 34 Cal. 258, 263; Tompkins v. Weeks, 26 Cal. 50, 56. The power of the surviving partner to settle partnership affairs gives full authority to the surviving partner to do everything that may be necessary to wind up the affairs of the partnership, but he can do nothing that is not indispensable to this end.— Berson v. Ewing, 84 Cal. 89, 94, 23 Pac. 1112. He must settle affairs of the partnership without delay, and account to the executor or administrator, and pay over such balances as may, from time to time, be payable to him in right of the deceased.—Painter v. Estate of Painter, 68 Cal. 395, 396, 9 Pac. 450. When the partnership is dissolved by the death of one of the partners, its assets, debts, and claims remain as distinguished from those of its late members, until its affairs are wound up, as before the dissolution. The surviving partner is to proceed and wind up the affairs of the partnership, pay its debts out of the assets, if sufficient, and divide the residue, if any, among those entitled to it.—In re Auerbach's Estate, 23 Utah 529, 65 Pac. 488, 491. Partnership debts can not be collected out of the assets of an estate of a deceased partner until the firm property is exhausted.—Barlow v. Coggan, 1 Wash. Ter. 257. If the surviving partner has been appointed executor of his deceased partner's will, the partnership estate must be first settled, and next the individual estate.—Palicio v. Bigne, 15 Or. 142, 13 Pac. 765, 767. That the surviving partner may be required to give a bond, see Palicio v. Bigne, 15 Or. 142, 13 Pac. 765, 766; In re Auerbach's Estate, 23 Utah 529, 65 Pac. 488, 490. A delay of five years in winding up the affairs of a partnership, occasioned by a provision of the will of deceased that his interests in the concern should be liquidated and wound up and divided among his "residuary legatees within the period of five years from and after" his death, furnishes no reason that will justify the executors in intervening with the surviving partner and invoking the aid of a court of equity to sell the property, nor can such delay give the court jurisdiction to do so.—In re Auerbach's Estate, 23 Utah 529, 65 Pac. 488, 491; nor does the fact that the surviving partner submitted a bid for the property justify the inference that he had any intention to waive his standing as such partner, particularly where he expressly reserves his legal rights as a surviving partner.—In re Auerbach's Estate, 23 Utah 529, 65 Pac. 488, 491. When the affairs of the partnership are wound up, and, upon striking a balance, it is found that one partner has drawn out more than he was entitled to, or that one partner has paid more than his portion of the debts, if there is a deficiency of assets, then the relation of debtor and creditor between the surviving partner and the representative of the deceased partner arises. There is but one balance between them, as there is but one settlement of the partnership business. There is no such thing as a partial balance as between the partnership and its late members. The surviving partner may, from time to time, divide between the executor or administrator of the deceased partner and himself, and pay over such sums as he may have on hand, which are not needed for the payment of the partnership debts. But there is only one settlement, one balance of account, between the partnership and the partners or their representatives. Until that is struck, the surviving partner can not be said to be either the debtor or creditor of the deceased partner on account of the partnership dealings, though the surviving partner or the estate of the deceased may be either a debtor or creditor of the partnership while it is being wound up, as it may have been before its dissolution.—Gleason v. White, 34 Cal. 258, 263. The surviving partner must settle the business and affairs of the partnership without delay, and account to the executor or administrator of the estate of the deceased partner, paying over to him such balance as may, from time to time, be payable.—Jones v. Marshall, 24 Ida. 678, 682, 135

Pac. 841. One partner can not maintain an action at law against his copartner, until an accounting is had and a balance determined.—Silver v. Eakins, 55 Mont. 210, 175 Pac. 876. If partnership assets in the possession of a surviving partner are sufficient to pay the partnership debts, any balance due him by reason of his partnership interest can be recovered by him only on a settlement of the firm account.—Silver v. Eakins, 55 Mont. 210, 175 Pac. 876. On the death of a surviving partner before settlement of partnership business, the duty devolves upon his legal representative, and it is only after the partnership debts and liabilities have been paid and discharged that the remainder goes to the heirs and devisees of the partner; hence, in a proceeding to partition the estate the court must, so as to do complete justice, order that there first be an accounting of partnership affairs.—Sharp v. Sharp (Utah), 180 Pac. 580.

REFERENCES.

Accounting by surviving partner.—See infra, head-line 10.

9. Surviving partner. Completion of executory contracts.—It is a well-settled rule that the surviving partner must complete all executory contracts of a firm which remain in force after the death of a partner, and must settle the business of the partnership without charge against the partnership for his personal services. And there is no distinction in this respect between commercial partnerships and those entered into by attorneys for the practice of their profession. This obligation of the surviving partner is one of the risks assumed by him in entering into the partnership, unless otherwise specifically agreed. In the discharge of this obligation or duty in relation to the unsettled and unfinished business of the firm, the surviving partner occupies the position of a trustee, and, while he may compromise disputed debts or modify an existing contract by releasing the other party thereto from some of its obligations, when in the exercise of an honest judgment the best interest of the partnership seems to him to require such action, still, in doing so, he can not be permitted to make gain for himself at the expense of the estate of a deceased partner by consenting to the extinguishment of a contract belonging to the partnership, and the substitution therefor of another relating to the same subject-matter, and in the profits of which he alone is to participate. Whatever may be the effect of such new or substituted contract as between the immediate parties to it, a court of equity, in settling the accounts of the partnership, will not treat it as an entire extinguishment of the original contract, nor deny the rights of the representatives of the deceased partner to an equitable participation in the profits realized from the latter contract, and it may be regarded, so far as concerns the partnership, as only a modification of the former contract. This rule is particularly applicable in the settlement of the partnership accounts of attorneys at law when the firm has been dissolved by the death of one member, leaving contracts not fully performed, often constituting a large part of the assets of the partnership, and which it is the duty of the surviving partner, as far as possible, to complete and preserve for the benefit of the firm.—Little v. Caldwell, 101 Cal. 553, 560, 40 Am. St. Rep. 89, 36 Pac. 107.

10. Surviving partner. Accounting.

(1) In general.—The surviving partner must settle the affairs of the partnership without delay, and account with the executor or administrator, and pay over such balance as may, from time to time, be payable to him in right of the decedent.—In re Auerbach's Estate, 23 Utah 529, 65 Pac. 488, 490. He is a trustee for the purposes of winding up the affairs of the firm, and is accountable for the profits of the realty, as well as the personalty, or the value of the use and occupation.—Smith v. Walker, 38 Cal. 385, 389, 99 Am. Dec. 415. After the partnership affairs are all wound up, but not before, a balance is to be struck. As said in the preceding section, there is only one settlement, one balance of account, between the partnership and the partners or their representatives.—Gleason v. White, 34 Cal. 258, 263. A final settlement in the probate court, between the administrator and a surviving partner, bars an action by the heirs to compel the administrator to make full discovery and settlement of the business of the copartnership, and for a judgment for moneys due to the estate.—Kingsley v. Miller, 45 Cal. 95, 96.

REFERENCES.

Settlement of partnership affairs by surviving partner.—See supra, head-line 8.

(2) Court may compel accounting.—The court may, upon application of the executor, compel the surviving partner to render an account of the partnership business, and the executor, in a proper proceeding, may doubtless, if good cause appear therefor, be required to demand an accounting from the surviving partner and return the same into court.—Miller v. Lux, 100 Cal. 609, 614, 35 Pac. 345, 639. The court has no authority to settle and adjust the accounts between the surviving partner and the representative of the deceased, but it does have power to require the surviving partner to file his account of the partnership affairs.—Andrade v. Superior Court, 75 Cal. 459, 17 Pac. 531.

(3) Actions for accounting.—No action can be maintained by a surviving partner against the administrator of his deceased partner for an accounting of the partnership affairs, as the surviving partner has ample power to take possession of the partnership property and to wind up its affairs.—McKay v. Joy, 70 Cal. 581, 582, 11 Pac. 932. But the widow of a deceased partner may sue to compel the surviving partner of a firm to account to her respecting the partnership accounts of attorneys at law, when the firm has been dissolved by the death of one member, leaving contracts not fully performed, and where the executor fails to sue.—Little v. Caldwell, 101 Cal. 553, 40 Am. St. Rep. 89, 36 Pac. 107. The right of action in such cases is fixed by the duty

of a surviving partner. The surviving partner is required to account, not with the heirs, but with the executor or administrator. This duty of the surviving partner is the correlative of the right of the personal representative, and fixes the person in whom the right of action exists. If he is to account with the administrator, the administrator it must be who has the right to call him to account. The heirs have no legal capacity to require the surviving partner to account to them.—Robertson v. Burrell, 110 Cal. 568, 574, 42 Pac. 1086. In an action to obtain an accounting of a partnership business in which the estate is interested, all of the executors should join as plaintiffs; but where such action is brought by one alone, and the other executors are made defendants, and no question is raised on account of the misjoinder, before judgment is rendered, the failure to name them as plaintiffs is not a fatal objection.—Insley v. Shire, 54 Kan. 793, 45 Am. St. Rep. 308, 39 Pac. 713. An action by an executor against a co-executor, charging maladministration, and asking for a removal from the trust, can not be properly joined with an action for an accounting of a partnership in which the estate has an interest with another person not connected with the estate.—Insley v. Shire, 54 Kan. 793, 45 Am. St. Rep. 308, 39 Pac. 713. If an action is brought by an administrator of a deceased partner, to obtain an accounting and settlement of partnership affairs, sums drawn from the partnership by the plaintiff's intestate during his lifetime may be offset against the plaintiff's claim.—Manuel v. Escolle, 65 Cal. 110, 3 Pac. 411.

11. Accounts of executors may be settled, regardless of order.—The failure of the executor to apply for an order requiring the surviving partner to account is no reason why the court should refuse to settle an annual account of the executor; and the fact that the surviving partner is also one of the executors of the estate of a deceased partner is not any reason for refusing to settle his accounts as an executor because of the absence of a statement of the condition of the partnership affairs.—Miller v. Lux, 100 Cal. 609, 614, 35 Pac. 345, 639.

12. Actions by or against surviving partners, and by or against executors or administrators.

(1) **Actions by or against surviving partners.**—Suits may be brought by or against a surviving partner for partnership demands and liabilities.—Barlow v. Coggan, 1 Wash. Ter. 257; Gray v. Palmer, 9 Cal. 616; In re Auerbach's Estate, 23 Utah 529, 65 Pac. 488. But partnership debts can not be collected out of the assets of the estate of a deceased partner until the partnership property is exhausted.—Barlow v. Coggan, 1 Wash. Ter. 257. If the administrator has taken possession of the assets of the deceased partner, the surviving partner can not sue him for his interest in such assets without first having presented his claim to the administrator.—McKay v. Joy, 2 Cal. Unrep. 639, 9 Pac. 940.

(2) **Actions by or against executors or administrators.**—In case of a disputed account between a surviving partner and the representative

of a deceased partner, the representative may maintain any action against the surviving partner which the decedent could have maintained.—Theller v. Such, 57 Cal. 447, 459. In Colorado, authority to proceed against the estate of a deceased partner for a firm debt, whether the debt is evidenced by writing or rests in parol, is strictly equitable in character, and, to maintain it, the plaintiff, by allegation must aver, and by proof show, the facts which, in equity, make the individual estate of a deceased partner liable for firm debts.—Thompson v. White, 25 Colo. 226, 54 Pac. 718, 723. Where two partners are dead, the administrator of the first deceased partner is entitled, without the presentation of his claim, to maintain a suit for an accounting against the administrator of the surviving partner, who died before the partnership affairs were adjusted, as no presentation of a claim is necessary where the demand is not against the estate.—Franklin v. Trickey, 9 Ariz. 282, 11 Ann. Cas. 1105, 80 Pac. 352, 353. The executors of a deceased partner may not be joined as parties to an action to enforce a claim for overcharged rent against joint lessors who were partners, where such claim is made against a firm.—Corson v. Berson, 86 Cal. 433, 441, 25 Pac. 7. An action in which an accounting is demanded, respecting partnership property, must be commenced within ten years after the cause of action accrued, but in case of the dissolution of a partnership by death, neither the representative of the deceased partner, nor his successor in interest, is entitled to sue for a settlement of the partnership affairs before making a demand, or receiving notice of the surviving partner's renunciation of his trust.— McPherson v. Swift, 22 S. D. 165, 133 Am. St. Rep. 907, 116 N. W. 76, 82. Where a partnership existed, between the plaintiff and the defendant administrator's intestate, and the administrator collects funds belonging to the partnership, an action may be maintained by the surviving partner against the administrator to recover the amounts so collected. As to such amounts, the representative of the deceased partner has no right thereto, either in his representative or individual capacity. If, on the other hand, there was no partnership, and the representative collected, either in his individual or representative capacity, more than the share which belonged to the intestate, suit may, nevertheless, be maintained against the representative for moneys received which should have been paid to the plaintiff.—Bales v. Cannon, 42 Colo. 275, 94 Pac. 21.

13. Purchase of deceased partner's interest.—It is competent for articles of copartnership to provide for a sale, on the death of one of the partners, of his interest to the survivors, and to give the surviving partners an option to continue the partnership with the estate of the decedent as a member; and no question of indefiniteness or uncertainty as to the amount of the purchase price, or the manner or mode in which such price is to be arrived at, in any way affects the right of the surviving partner, under the contract to buy. Such conditions, if they exist, only result in casting the burden upon the trial court to

take an accounting and to fix the price. If the amount of the purchase price of the deceased partner's interest in the business is fixed by the articles with sufficient certainty, this simply precludes the right of the court to hold a general accounting. If the making of an inventory and appraisement forms the basic element in fixing the purchase price, the transaction should be upheld, in the absence of a showing of fraud. Upon the purchase, by surviving partners, of the interest of the deceased partner, the good will of the business passes to the surviving partners, and in no case forms an asset of the estate. But when a partnership is dissolved by death, the survivors are absolved from all obligations, except to close out the partnership affairs and to account to the estate. They do not owe a duty to the estate of the deceased to abstain from business, even in the same line as that in which the partnership was engaged.—Rankin v. Newman, 114 Cal. 635, 649, 665, 34 L. R. A. 265, 46 Pac. 742.

14. **New partnership. Carrying on decedent's business.**—Where the testator was in partnership with another person, and there was a provision in his will authorizing the executors "to continue my present business as long as they may deem best," and the executors determined to continue the partnership business in accordance with the will, and do carry on the business upon the same terms as it was·during the lifetime of the testate, the effect of the arrangement is to create a new partnership, composed of the executors of the estate on one side and of the surviving partner on the other.—Insley v. Shire, 54 Kan. 793, 45 Am. St. Rep. 308, 39 Pac. 713, 716. An executor or administrator, who advances money to his loss for the purpose of carrying on a business with the surviving partner of the intestate, can not be allowed to charge such loss in his account. He has no authority to intermeddle with the partnership affairs, except to call upon the surviving partner to close up the same and account to him.—Tompkins v. Weeks, 26 Cal. 50, 66.

15. **Conveyances by one partner to another. Death before payment.**—If one partner conveys his undivided interest in certain land to his copartner, who dies before making payment, the grantor is a creditor of the deceased partner's estate, and, on general principles, has a lien on the property sold, as security for the debt.—Reese v. Kinkead, 18 Nev. 126, 1 Pac. 667.

16. **Certiorari.**—Certiorari lies to review an order refusing to appoint an administrator of partnership property, where the remedy by appeal is inadequate; as, where the purpose and subject-matter of the alleged partnership will have largely ceased to exist before an appeal can be prosecuted to final determination.—State v. Superior Court, 76 Wash. 291, 296, 136 Pac. 147.

PART XI.

LIABILITIES AND COMPENSATION OF EXECUTORS AND ADMINISTRATORS. ATTORNEYS' FEES. ACCOUNTING AND SETTLEMENTS. PAYMENT OF DEBTS.

CHAPTER L

LIABILITIES AND COMPENSATION OF EXECUTORS AND ADMINISTRATORS. ATTORNEYS' FEES.

LIABILITIES AND COMPENSATION OF EXECUTORS AND ADMINISTRATORS. ATTORNEYS' FEES.

I. Liability of Executors and Administrators.

II. Compensation of executors and administrators.

§ 647. Personal liability of representative.

No executor or administrator is chargeable upon any special promise to answer in damages or to pay the debts of the testator or intestate out of his own estate, unless the agreement for that purpose, or some memorandum or note thereof, is in writing or signed by such executor or administrator, or by some other person by him thereunto specially authorized in writing.—*Kerr's Cyc. Code Civ. Proc.,* § 1612.

ANALOGOUS AND IDENTICAL STATUTES.

No identical statute found.

Arizona—Revised Statutes of 1913, paragraph 988.
Colorado—Mills's Statutes of 1912, section 8040.
Idaho—Compiled Statutes of 1919, section 7684.
Montana—Revised Codes of 1907, section 7627.
Nevada—Revised Laws of 1912, section 6034.
North Dakota—Compiled Laws of 1913, section 8815.
Oklahoma—Revised Laws of 1910, section 6421.
South Dakota—Compiled Laws of 1913, section 5882.
Washington—Laws of 1917, chapter 156, page 686, section 154.
Wyoming—Compiled Statutes of 1910, section 5574.

§ 648. Executor to be charged with all estate, etc.

Every executor and administrator is chargeable in his account with the whole of the estate of the decedent which may come into his possession, at the value of the appraisement contained in the inventory, except as provided in the following sections, and with all the interest, profit, and income of the estate.—*Kerr's Cyc. Code Civ. Proc.,* § 1613.

ANALOGOUS AND IDENTICAL STATUTES.

The * indicates identity.

Alaska—Compiled Laws of 1913, section 1697.
Arizona*—Revised Statutes of 1913, paragraph 989.
Colorado—Mills's Statutes of 1912, section 7964.
Idaho*—Compiled Statutes of 1919, section 7685.
Kansas—General Statutes of 1915, section 4640.
Montana*—Revised Codes of 1907, section 7628.
Nevada*—Revised Laws of 1912, section 6035.
New Mexico—Statutes of 1915, section 2291.
North Dakota*—Compiled Laws of 1913, section 8816.
Oklahoma*—Revised Laws of 1910, section 6422.
Oregon—Lord's Oregon Laws, section 1288.
South Dakota*—Compiled Laws of 1913, section 5883.
Utah*—Compiled Laws of 1907, section 3929.
Washington—Laws of 1917, chapter 156, page 686, section 155.
Wyoming*—Compiled Statutes of 1910, section 5575.

§ 649. Not to profit or lose by estate.

He shall not make profit by the increase, nor suffer loss by the decrease, or destruction, without his fault, of any part of the estate. He must account for the excess when he sells any part of the estate for more than the appraisement, and if any is sold for less than the appraisement, he is not responsible for the loss, if the sale has been justly made.—*Kerr's Cyc. Code Civ. Proc.,* § 1614.

ANALOGOUS AND IDENTICAL STATUTES.

The * indicates identity.

Alaska—Compiled Laws of 1913, section 1698.
Arizona*—Revised Statutes of 1913, paragraph 990.
Idaho*—Compiled Statutes of 1919, section 7686.
Kansas—General Statutes of 1915, section 4641.
Montana*—Revised Codes of 1907, section 7629.
Nevada*—Revised Laws of 1912, section 6036.
North Dakota*—Compiled Laws of 1913, section 8817.
Oklahoma*—Revised Laws of 1910, section 6423.
Oregon—Lord's Oregon Laws, section 1289.
South Dakota*—Compiled Laws of 1913, section 5884.
Utah*—Compiled Laws of 1907, section 3930.
Washington—Laws of 1917, chapter 156, page 686, section 155.
Wyoming*—Compiled Statutes of 1910, section 5576.

§ 650. Debts uncollected without fault.

No executor or administrator is accountable for any debts due to the decedent, if it appears that they remain uncollected without his fault.—*Kerr's Cyc. Code Civ. Proc.*, § 1615.

ANALOGOUS AND IDENTICAL STATUTES.

The * indicates identity.

Alaska—Compiled Laws of 1913, section 1698.

Arizona*—Revised Statutes of 1913, paragraph 991.

Idaho*—Compiled Statutes of 1919, section 7687.

Kansas*—General Statutes of 1915, section 4642.

Montana*—Revised Codes of 1907, section 7630.

Nevada*—Revised Laws of 1912, section 6037.

North Dakota*—Compiled Laws of 1913, section 8818.

Oklahoma*—Revised Laws of 1910, section 6424.

Oregon—Lord's Oregon Laws, section 1289.

South Dakota*—Compiled Laws of 1913, section 5885.

Utah*—Compiled Laws of 1907, section 3932.

Washington—Laws of 1917, chapter 156, page 686, 687, sections 155, 157.

Wyoming*—Compiled Statutes of 1910, section 5577.

§ 651. Compensation of representative and attorney. Appeal.

The executor or administrator shall be allowed all necessary expenses in the care, management, and settlement of the estate, and for his services such fees as provided in this chapter; but when the decedent, by his will, makes some other provision for the compensation of his executor, that shall be a full compensation for his services, unless by a written instrument, filed in the court, he renounces all claim for compensation provided for in the will. At any time after one year from the admission of a will to probate, or the granting of letters of administration, any executor, or administrator, may, upon such notice to the other parties interested in the estate as the court shall by order require, apply to the court for an allowance to himself upon his commissions, and the court shall on the hearing of such application make an order allowing such executor or administrator such portion of his commissions as to the court shall seem proper, and the portion so allowed may be thereupon charged against the estate. Any attorney who has rendered services to an executor or administrator may at any time during the administration, and upon such notice to the other parties interested in the estate as the court shall by order require, apply to the court for an allowance to himself of compensation therefor, and the court shall on the hearing of such application make an order requiring the executor or administrator to pay to such attorney out of the estate such compensation on account of services rendered by such attorney up to the date of such order as to the court shall seem proper, and such payment shall be forthwith made.

APPEAL.—Any attorney making such application to the court for compensation and all other persons interested in the estate may appeal from any order made by the court fixing the amount of such compensation, and ordering the same paid.—*Kerr's Cyc. Code Civ. Proc.*, § 1616.

ANALOGOUS AND IDENTICAL STATUTES.

No identical statute found.

Alaska—Compiled Laws of 1913, section 1699.
Arizona—Revised Statutes of 1913, paragraph 992.
Idaho—Compiled Statutes of 1919, section 7688.
Kansas—General Statutes of 1915, section 4650.
Montana—Revised Codes of 1907, section 7631.
Nevada—Revised Laws of 1912, section 6038.
New Mexico—Statutes of 1915, sections 2293, 2299-2301.
North Dakota—Compiled Laws of 1913, section 8821; as amended by Laws of 1915, chapter 2, page 3.
Oklahoma—Revised Laws of 1910, section 6425.
Oregon—Lord's Oregon Laws, section 1290.
South Dakota—Compiled Laws of 1913, section 5886; as amended by Laws of 1915, chapter 188, page 374.
Utah—Compiled Laws of 1907, section 3933.
Washington—Laws of 1917, chapter 156, page 687, sections 156, 158.
Wyoming—Laws of 1911, chapter 16, page 17.

§ 652.   Not to purchase claims against estate.

No administrator or executor shall purchase any claim against the estate he represents; and if he pays any

claim for less than its nominal value he is only entitled
to charge in his account the amount he actually paid.—
Kerr's Cyc. Code Civ. Proc., § 1617.

ANALOGOUS AND IDENTICAL STATUTES.

The * indicates identity.

Alaska—Compiled Laws of 1913, section 1698.
Arizona*—Revised Statutes of 1913, paragraph 993.
Idaho*—Compiled Statutes of 1919, section 7689.
Montana*—Revised Codes of 1907, section 7632.
Nevada*—Revised Laws of 1912, section 6039.
New Mexico—Statutes of 1915, sections 2292, 2299-2301.
North Dakota*—Compiled Laws of 1913, section 8819.
Oklahoma*—Revised Laws of 1910, section 6426.
Oregon—Lord's Oregon Laws, section 1289.
South Dakota*—Compiled Laws of 1913, section 5887.
Utah*—Compiled Laws of 1907, section 3931.
Washington—Laws of 1917, chapter 156, page 687, section 157.
Wyoming*—Compiled Statutes of 1910, section 5579.

§ 653. Executor, commission allowed. Administrator. Extraordinary services.

When no compensation is provided by the will, or the
executor renounces all claim thereto, he must be allowed
commissions upon the amount of estate accounted for by
him, as follows: For the first thousand dollars, at the
rate of seven per cent; for the next nine thousand dollars,
at the rate of four per cent; for the next ten thousand
dollars, at the rate of three per cent; for the next thirty
thousand dollars, at the rate of two per cent; for the next
fifty thousand dollars, at the rate of one per cent; and
for all above one hundred thousand dollars, at the rate
of one-half of one per cent. If there are two or more
executors the compensation shall be apportioned among
them by the court according to the services actually rendered by them respectively. The same commissions shall
be allowed to administrators. In all cases, such further
allowances may be made as the court may deem just and
reasonable for any extraordinary service, but the total
amount of such extra allowance must not exceed one-half
the amount of commissions allowed by this section.

Probate Law—97

Where the property of the estate is distributed in kind, and involves no labor beyond the custody and distribution of the same, the commission shall be computed on all the estate above the value of twenty thousand dollars, at one-half of the rates fixed in this section. Public administrators shall receive the same compensation and allowances as are allowed in this title to other administrators. All contracts between an executor or administrator and an heir, devisee or legatee, for a higher compensation than that allowed by this section, shall be void.—*Kerr's Cyc. Code Civ. Proc.*, § 1618.

ANALOGOUS AND IDENTICAL STATUTES.
No identical statute found.

Alaska—Compiled Laws of 1913, section 1701.
Arizona—Revised Statutes of 1913, paragraph 994.
Colorado—Mills's Statutes of 1912, section 8032.
Idaho—Compiled Statutes of 1919, section 7690.
Nevada—Revised Laws of 1912, section 6040.
New Mexico—Statutes of 1915, sections 2299, 2301.
North Dakota—Compiled Laws of 1913, section 8822.
Oklahoma—Revised Laws of 1910, section 6427.
Oregon—Lord's Oregon Laws, section 1292.
South Dakota—Compiled Laws of 1913, section 5888.
Utah—Compiled Laws of 1907, section 3934.
Wyoming—Laws of 1911, chapter 16, page 17.

§ 654. Form. Executor's renunciation of compensation.

[Title of court.]

[Title of estate.]   { No.——.1   Dept. No.——.
                                      {   [Title of form.]

Provision having been made in the last will and testament of ——, deceased, for the compensation of the executor therein named for his services as such executor,—

I, the undersigned, named as executor in said will, have elected to receive, in place of such compensation, the commissions allowed by law for such services, and hereby renounce all claim to the compensation provided for in said will.   ——, Executor, etc.

Dated ——, 19—.

Explanatory note.—1 Give file number.

§ 655. Allowance of fees for attorneys. Extraordinary services.

Attorneys for executors and administrators shall be allowed out of the estate as fees for conducting the ordinary probate proceedings the same amounts as are allowed by the last section as compensation for executors and administrators for their own services. In all cases such further allowance may be made as the court may deem just and reasonable for any such extraordinary services such as sales or mortgages of real estate, contested or litigated claims against the estate, litigation in regard to the property of the estate, and such other litigation as may be necessary for the executor or administrator to prosecute or defend.—*Kerr's Cyc. Code Civ. Proc.,* § 1619.

ANALOGOUS AND IDENTICAL STATUTES.

No identical statute found.

Alaska—Compiled Laws of 1913, section 1699.

Arizona—Revised Statutes of 1913, paragraph 992.

Kansas—General Statutes of 1915, section 4650.

Washington—Laws of 1917, chapter 156, page 687, section 153.

Wyoming—Laws of 1911, chapter 16, page 17.

LIABILITIES AND COMPENSATION OF EXECUTORS AND ADMINISTRATORS. ATTORNEYS' FEES.

I. Liability of Executors and Administrators.

1. In general.
2. Personal liability.
3. Instances of liability.
   (1) For entire estate.
   (2) Liability in general.
   (3) In what capacity.
   (4) Liability for costs.
   (5) Contracts.
   (6) Mingling trust funds.
   (7) Rents, issues, and profits.
   (8) Bad loans.
   (9) Failure of bank.
   (10) Failure to collect.
   (11) Losses through neglect.
   (12) Personal injuries. Conduct of decedent's business.
   (13) Liability for taxes.
4. Instances of non-liability.
5. When chargeable with interest.
   (1) In general.
   (2) Delay in settlement of estate.
   (3) Simple interest.
   (4) Compound interest.
6. Not to profit or lose by estate.

II. Compensation of executors and administrators.

1. Provision for, in will.
2. Statutory allowance.
3. Basis. Computation.
4. Validity of agreements as to.
5. Not allowable until final settlement.
6. Renunciation. Waiver.
7. What should be allowed.
8. What should not be allowed.
9. Further allowance. Extra services.
10. Co-executors.

I. LIABILITY OF EXECUTORS AND ADMINISTRATORS.

1. In general.—An executor or administrator is chargeable not only with the assets which come into his possession, but also with those which, by negligence, he has failed to collect.—Estate of Kennedy, 120 Cal. 458, 461, 52 Pac. 820. He is prima facie liable for such assets of the estate as come into his possession.—Wheeler v. Bolton, 92 Cal. 159, 171, 28 Pac. 558. His liability can only terminate after compliance with the statute, and after a settlement approved by the court has been made, and after discharge and delivery has been ordered by the court.— In re Higgins' Estate, 15 Mont. 474, 28 L. R. A. 116, 39 Pac. 506, 517. One who takes charge of an estate as administrator, and takes possession of the assets of the estate of his decedent and administers thereon, can not escape liability by reason of his having failed to take the oath and to file the bond required by law. If he is not an administrator de jure, he is de facto, and may settle the estate, if neither creditors nor heirs object.—Harris v. Coates, 8 Ida. 491, 69 Pac. 475. If an executor, who has money of the estate in his hands, turns it over to his co-executor, and leaves the estate for an indefinite length of time, he is answerable for any misapplication of it by the latter.—Estate of Osborn, 87 Cal. 1, 4, 25 Pac. 157, 11 L. R. A. 264. An administrator de bonis non is answerable only for what he receives. He is not liable for a misappropriation of the moneys received for land sold by a former administrator.—Dray v. Bloch, 27 Or. 549, 41 Pac. 660. The right which the law confers upon an administrator to take and hold the possession of the goods and chattels of a decedent's estate is in the nature of a trust and an administrator is authorized to enforce all the rights and is subject to all the remedies, incident to an ordinary trustee. He is not a trustee in the strict sense of the term, but he exercises a statutory power pursuant to the orders of a probate court.—Thorson v. Hooper, 57 Or. 75, 109 Pac. 389.

REFERENCES.

General nature of the liability of executors or administrators.—See note to the case of Bannigan v. Woodbury, 133 Am. St. Rep. 873.

2. Personal liability.—If an executor, aware that the decedent's mercantile business is being conducted in the name of the estate, proceeds in furtherance of such conduct and lends his official position thereto, he becomes personally liable for the debts of the concern, although his intentions may have been of the best, and his action the result of ignorance.—Martin Brothers Co. v. Peterson, 38 S. D. 494, 496, 162 N. W. 154. Where the law imposes a duty on an administrator or an executor, and he neglects to discharge the obligation thus enjoined, whereby another sustains an injury, the personal representative is personally liable therefor.—Fetting v. Winch, 54 Or. 600, 21 Ann. Cas. 352, 38 L. R. A. (N. S.) 379, 104 Pac. 723. The general rule applicable to personal liability of an administrator or executor to distribute for interest, when there has been delay in closing up the estate, is that it depends upon the reasonableness or unreasonableness of the delay under all the circumstances of the particular case.—In re Delaney's Estate, 41 Nev. 384, 388, 171 Pac. 383. If an administrator makes an agreement with another person, in reference to the estate, he may become personally liable but does not bind the estate.—Dunn v. Wallingford, 47 Utah 491, 155 Pac. 347. An executor or administrator who represents to a creditor of the estate that the estate is bankrupt, and succeeds thus in a purpose to prevent the filing of a claim, is personally liable to the creditor.—Kennedy v. Burr, 101 Wash. 61, 171 Pac. 1022. The collection by a widow and administratrix of her husband's entire estate and her removal of it out of the state and it being more than amply sufficient to pay all debts renders her personally liable in an action by a creditor of the estate.—Brown Eastes v. Walley, 51 Colo. 166, 117 Pac. 138. In the making of payments in anticipation of the decree of distribution, the administrator acts at his peril, and if it turns out upon distribution that the payee is not entitled to receive any part of the residue the administrator must look for reimbursement to the person to whom payment was made.—In re Ross' Estate (Cal.), 182 Pac. 303, 305.

REFERENCES.

Personal liability of executor, administrator, or trustee on covenant in deed executed by him.—See note 43 L. R. A. (N. S.) 377.

3. Instances of liability.

(1) For entire estate.—An executor or administrator is to be charged with all estate coming into his hands, real as well as personal, and at the value of the appraisement.—Wheeler v. Bolton, 92 Cal. 159, 174, 28 Pac. 558; Estate of Fernandez, 119 Cal. 579, 584, 51 Pac. 851. The statute makes no distinction between real and personal estate, and the rule applicable in the case of loss by him of personal estate should have equal application to the loss of real estate; and if a liability for the loss of personal property is fixed at the date of the loss, so it must be for the loss of real estate.—Wheeler v. Bolton, 92 Cal. 159, 174, 28 Pac. 558. An administratrix of the estate of her deceased husband, such estate being wholly community property, is liable to the extent of such an estate to creditors of the community.—Carpenter v. Lindauer, 12 N. M. 388, 78 Pac. 57. The executor or administrator is chargeable with all moneys coming into his hands.—Magraw v. McGlynn, 26 Cal. 420, 429; Estate of Sanderson, 74 Cal. 199, 203, 15 Pac. 753. As to making settlement by legal tender, see Estate of Den, 39 Cal. 70; Magraw v. McGlynn, 26 Cal. 420. An administrator exchanging currency for gold is liable only for the gold received.—Estate of Sanderson, 74 Cal. 199, 15 Pac. 753.

(2) Liability in general.—As a general rule, one executor is not answerable for the neglect or bad faith of a co-executor, but where one, by his own negligence, suffers another to waste the estate, when, by the exercise of reasonable diligence, he could have prevented it, he will be held answerable for the loss.—Insley v. Shire, 54 Kan. 793, 45 Am. St. Rep. 308, 39 Pac. 713. An executor or administrator is answerable for an unauthorized expenditure of money. If there is any question of the legality of the outlay, he should protect himself by obtaining an express authorization for the expenditure from the parties in interest.—Estate of Kennedy, 120 Cal. 458, 52 Pac. 820. He is answerable for selling property of the estate under an alleged mutual mistake of law.—Snyder v. Jack, 140 Cal. 584, 74 Pac. 139, 355. He is also answerable in damages where he makes a fraudulent sale of the decedent's real estate. He is liable in double the value of the land sold, as liquidated damages, to be recovered in an action by the person having an estate of inheritance therein, but his sureties are not so liable.—Weihe v. Statham, 67 Cal. 245, 7 Pac. 673, 676. If an executor expends money in a suit which he commences to recover certain personal property, which he thinks belongs to the estate, and abandons the suit, he is not entitled to reimbursement for such expenditure.—Estate of Pease, 149 Cal. 167, 169, 85 Pac. 149. If an executor wrongfully pays the shares of certain distributees to their pretended attorney, he is answerable for such wrongful payment, notwithstanding a judgment or decree discharging him from all liability to be incurred thereafter.—Bryant v. McIntosh, 3 Cal. App. 95, 84 Pac. 440. If he sells certain cooperage at private sale, at a price in excess of the appraisement, without any order of court, or notice of sale, or order of confirmation, he is chargeable with the excess in actual value at the time of the sale, regardless of the amount received.—Estate of Scott, 1 Cal. App. 740, 83 Pac. 85. He is also chargeable with money given him by decedent, just before the latter's death, and which was not given as a present.—Estate of Pease, 149 Cal. 167, 170, 85 Pac. 149. If a broker is employed to procure a loan for an estate, or to effect a sale of its property, and does all that he was required to do under the contract, and procures a party who is willing and ready to make the loan or to purchase the property, he is entitled to the commission agreed upon; but the executor or administrator of the estate is personally liable therefor, unless there has been an express stipulation that the broker shall be paid only out of the estate.—Maxon v. Jones, 128 Cal. 77, 81, 60 Pac. 516. An executor de son tort is subject to all the liabilities of an ordinary executor without

being entitled to any of his privileges.—Slate v. Henkle, 45 Or. 430, 78 Pac. 325, 326. An executor or administrator, as such, has no authority over property that is not assets of the estate; but he is answerable as an individual for wrongfully retaining it.—Lazarus v. Carter, 11 Haw. 541, 543. An executor or administrator is liable for the acts, defaults, or devastavits of a fellow executor or administrator in case only that he has in some manner aided him in them or knowingly profited by them.—In re Hagerty's Estate (Wash.), 178 Pac. 644.

REFERENCES.

Liability of one executor or administrator for the acts and defaults of another representative.—See note 42 Am. Dec. 288-293. Liability of co-executor for default of one permitted to manage estate.—See note 11 L. R. A. (N. S.) 296-352. Liability of executor or administrator in a foreign jurisdiction for the property of decedent.—See note 32 Am. Dec. 632-633. Liability of executor or administrator for funeral expenses.—See note 33 L. R. A. 663-664. Liability of infant as executor or administrator.—See note 57 L. R. A. 688-689. Liability of estates of decedents for contracts and torts of executors and administrators.— See note 52 Am. St. Rep. 118-135. Liability for the debt of an executor or administrator owing to the estate.—See note 112 Am. St. Rep. 406-414. Liability of administrator and his sureties for a debt owing by the former to the estate of his intestates, where the administrator is hopelessly insolvent.—See note 61 L. R. A. 313-317.

(3) In what capacity.—An executor or administrator can not bind the assets of the deceased by his promissory note. If he executes a note, and adds to his signature, "as executor for" the deceased, he will nevertheless be personally liable. Yet, while the executor or administrator will be personally and alone bound upon the note, if that for which it was given was legally a claim against the estate, the giving and accepting the note will not, without more, discharge the estate. In general, an executor or administrator, like an agent, must expressly limit his promise to payment out of the estate represented, in order to avoid individual liability on it.—First Nat. Bank v. Collins, 17 Mont. 433, 52 Am. St. Rep. 695, 43 Pac. 499, 500. Where the statute does not authorize the administrator either to take possession of the real estate of the intestate, or to collect the rents and profits, but he takes possession thereof, he is not answerable therefor in his fiduciary or representative capacity to the estate.—Head v. Sutton, 31 Kan. 616, 3 Pac. 280, 283. But if an executor or administrator applies to the use of the estate money or the proceeds of property belonging to a third person, he is answerable in both his individual and representative capacity, and the injured party may elect whether he will hold him in the one capacity or in the other; but, having elected to pursue the executor or administrator in his representative capacity, he must take such judgment as the law authorizes in such cases.—Collins v. Denny Clay Co., 41 Wash. 136, 82 Pac. 1012, 1015. An administrator is chargeable in his capacity

as administrator with the amount received by him prior to his appointment as administrator.—Head v. Sutton, 31 Kan. 616, 3 Pac. 280, 282.
A person's liability as an individual, as determined by a judgment for
use and occupation, is not his in his capacity of administrator.—Estate
of Piercy, Piercy v. Piercy, 168 Cal. 750, 753, 145 Pac. 88. The indebtedness of the administrator to the estate, when he is also an heir, and as
such interested in the estate, may be deducted from his distributive
share. It can not be applied to the detriment of the estate or to the
rights of other heirs or distributees. Where new notes were given
by the administrator to a company representing the heirs upon distribution to keep them from outlawing against the estate, they are to be
treated as his personal debt, and not intended or received as an advance
upon the distributive shares of any other heirs, but as being only a
charge upon his distributive share where there is nothing to indicate
a contrary intent.—In re Loheide, 17 Cal. App. 475, 120 Pac. 56.

(4) **Liability for costs.**—The statute provides that when a judgment
is given against an executor or administrator, he shall be individually
liable for the costs. This provision was adopted by the legislature for
the purpose of preventing executors or administrators from wasting the
property of estates in speculative or unnecessary litigation, by making
them, in every case, individually answerable for the costs recovered
against them, and permitting them to recover from the estate only such
costs as shall appear to have occurred in the bona fide discharge of
their trust.—Hicox v. Graham, 6 Cal. 167, 169. Costs in a probate proceeding can not be allowed to counsel; if allowed at all, they must be
awarded to the parties themselves.—Henry v. Superior Court, 93 Cal.
569, 29 Pac. 230, 231. If a judgment for costs is recovered in an action
against an executor or administrator, but such costs are not, by the
judgment, made chargeable only upon the estate, the defendant is
individually liable for the costs, and plaintiff is entitled to execution
therefor.—McCarthy v. Speed, 16 S. D. 584, 94 N. W. 411, 413. Where
plaintiff, in an action against an executor or administrator as such,
recovers costs, and has execution issued therefor, the defendant, in his
individual capacity, may move the court to vacate and set aside sales
made under such execution.—McCarthy v. Speed, 10 S. D. 584, 94 N. W.
411, 414.

REFERENCES.

Personal liability of executors and administrators for costs.—See
note 14 L. R. A. 696-707. Liability for costs.—See note to § 646, division
II, head-line 12, and division III, head-line 8, ante.

(5) **Contracts.**—An executor or an administrator is, in ordinary cases,
personally liable upon contracts made by him in his representative
capacity, after the death of the person whom he represents, and which
are supported by some new consideration.—Estate of Page, 57 Cal. 238,
242; Dwinelle v. Henriques, 1 Cal. 387, 392. In an action brought by an
executrix to recover the possession of land as property of the estate,
where it appears that the defendant is in possession under a written

lease, executed to him by the plaintiff,—therein described as "the executrix of the will of James Moffitt, deceased," and signed "Mrs. M. M. Moffitt, Etx.,"—giving him the option to purchase the land during the term for the sum of $1,575; and that he afterwards elected to purchase, and paid to the plaintiff, on account, the sum of five hundred dollars, and tendered the balance before the expiration of the term; that, on the faith of the contract, he made permanent improvements on the land, etc.; that plaintiff's testator died seised of the land in question, leaving a will, under which she was the sole residuary legatee; and that, at the time of her agreement to sell the property to the defendant, the time for presentation of claims had passed and all debts and legacies had been paid, leaving in her hands money much more than sufficient to pay all costs of administration,—the executrix thus became the sole beneficiary of the land in question; and if she was not empowered by the court to sell the land, her contract with the defendant was binding on her personally, and operated as an equitable transfer of the ownership of the property.—Moffitt v. Rosencrans, 136 Cal. 416, 418, 69 Pac. 87. The rule is, that executors and administrators can not, by virtue of their general powers as such, make any contract which will bind the estate, and authorize a judgment de bonis decendentis, but on contracts made by them for necessary matters relating to the estate they are personally answerable, and must see to it that they are reimbursed out of the estate. On a contract under which an executrix employed the plaintiff to drill a well on the property of the estate, the plaintiffs are not entitled to judgment against the executrix, even in her personal capacity, where the court has acquired no jurisdiction over her. In such a case the proceedings can not be amended and a personal judgment entered against the executrix.—Renwick v. Garland, 1 Cal. App. 237, 82 Pac. 89, 90. The executor or administrator of the decedent has no power to bind the latter's estate by any note or bill he may make in his representative capacity. So, also, is it impossible for the executor or administrator to bind the estate by the acceptance of a bill drawn in settlement of a claim against the estate. In all such cases the executor or administrator is personally answerable, even though his signature is stated in the most explicit manner to have been made in his representative capacity.—First Nat. Bank v. Collins, 17 Mont. 433, 43 Pac. 499. An executor may disburse and use the funds of the estate for purposes authorized by law, but may not bind the estate by an executory contract, and thus create a liability not founded upon a contract or obligation of the testator. Where a complaint charges the execution of the contract by an administrator in his individual capacity, it binds him individually, although it relates to matters connected with the estate; and where he enters into a contract upon a consideration executed subsequently to the death of the decedent, it is deemed his individual contract.—Painter v. Kaiser, 27 Nev. 421, 103 Am. St. Rep. 759, 1 Ann. Cas. 765, 65 L. R. A. 621, 76 Pac. 747, 749 (showing many forms in which this doctrine has been applied).

If complaint is made against an executrix personally, she is liable individually on a contract made by her personally, and before her appointment as executrix, by which she agreed that, after her appointment, she would, without any decree of distribution, pay to the plaintiff, and the other legatees named in the will, the amount of their representative proportions of money which might come into her hands in excess of $5000.—Painter v. Kaiser, 27 Nev. 421, 103 Am. St. Rep. 759, 1 Ann. Cas. 765, 65 L. R. A. 621, 76 Pac. 747, 748. If an executor fraudulently induces an heir to loan him a sum of money bequeathed to her, but to which she is not entitled until she reaches 21 years of age, and the evidence shows that the executor procured the loan by concealing from the heir his failing financial condition, and by misleading her in other respects, the transaction is not only questionable, but absolutely void, and the executor can not obtain his discharge so as to release the sureties on his bond until he has complied with the order of the court to deliver all property of the estate to the parties entitled thereto. —Ehrngren v. Gronlund, 19 Utah 411, 57 Pac. 268.

REFERENCES.

Liability of estate for commissions of broker or agent, who sells property.—See note 64 L. R. A. 555-557. Individual liability of personal representatives under original contracts founded on a new consideration.—See note 1 Am. & Eng. Ann. Cas. 769.

(6) Mingling trust funds.—The mere fact that an executor or administrator mingles the profits of a sale of the estate he represents with his own funds does not justify charging him with interest thereon, because he has a right to their custody, and there is no provision of law which requires him to keep them separate from all other funds.—Estate of Sarment, 123 Cal. 331, 333, 55 Pac. 1015. The limit of the liability of a trustee for mingling trust funds with his own, and for use in his own business, where it is not shown that a larger profit was realized therefrom, is the return of the principal, with legal interest thereon compounded annually. This rule is applicable alike to guardians and executors as to other trust relations.—Estate of Dow, 133 Cal. 446, 450, 65 Pac. 890; Estate of Hamilton, 139 Cal. 671, 73 Pac. 578.

REFERENCES.

Liability for mingling trust funds.—See head-line 5, post.

(7) Rents, issues, and profits.—An executor or administrator is answerable for the rents and profits of decedent's land, where he occupies and uses it as his own.—Walls v. Walker, 37 Cal. 424, 431; Estate of Misamore, 90 Cal. 169, 27 Pac. 68. But he is entitled to receive the rents and profits of the real estate of the decedent, accruing after the latter's death, until the estate is settled, or until delivered by order of the court to the heirs or devisees. Such rents and profits are assets of the estate.—Washington v. Black, 83 Cal. 390, 23 Pac. 300, 301.

(8) **Bad loans.**—In lending money on a mortgage of real estate, a degree of care is necessary, which, if omitted, will render the executor or administrator liable personally. If an executor lends funds on real estate, he must use care as to the title, and ascertain that the value of the premises mortgaged is such as will, in all probability, be adequate .security for repayment whenever the money shall be called in. If this is not done, and loss ensues, the executor or administrator is answerable therefor.—In re Roach's Estate, 50 Or. 179, 92 Pac. 118, 123; Estate of Holbert, 48 Cal. 627, 629 (showing circumstances under which he is and under which he is not answerable for loss, especially where he takes a second mortgage as security for the loan, or no security at all).

(9) **Failure of bank.**—If an executor or administrator deposits the moneys of an estate in a bank, but allows it to remain after the time when, if he had fulfilled his duty, it would have been distributed and in the hands of those entitled, and the money is lost through a failure of the bank, he and his sureties are liable therefor, and the sum lost constitutes the measure of damages.—McNabb v. Wixom, 7 Nev. 163, 171. If an executor or administrator, with moneys of the estate in his hands, deposits them in his own name in a bank or other institution which fails, without in some way designating such moneys as trust property, the loss must fall upon him. And his liability will not depend upon the good faith, prudence, or judgment with which apparently he may have acted, nor upon the fact that he may have disposed of his own funds in the same way.—Estate of Arguello, 97 Cal. 196, 200, 202, 31 Pac. 937. But, under the uniform holding of courts that executors, administrators, and guardians are bound by no greater or higher responsibility than that which is imposed upon any agent or trustee, if such a one, in good faith, deposits money in a bank of good repute to the trust account, he ought not to be held liable for its loss in consequence of the failure of the bank.—In re Kohler's Estate, 15 Wash. 613, 47 Pac. 30, 31; In re Jiskra's Estate (Wash.), 182 Pac. 959, 960.

REFERENCES.

Deposit of trust funds in bank by executors or administrators.—See note 98 Am. St. Rep. 371-377. Liability of executor or administrator for loss of bank deposit.—See note 7 L. R. A. (N. S.) 617-619.

(10) **Failure to collect.**—An executor or administrator is chargeable not only with the assets which come into his possession, but also those which by negligence he has failed to collect.—Estate of Kennedy, 120 Cal. 458, 461, 52 Pac. 820; Maddock v. Russell, 109 Cal. 417, 42 Pac. 139. And he is also personally liable for loss by his purchase of unsecured, uncollectable notes.—In re Roach's Estate, 50 Or. 179, 92 Pac. 118. Where the executor or administrator has a note in his individual possession, and he allows an action on the same to become barred by the statute of limitations, the delay not being in consequence of any mistake in law or of advice given by an attorney, it is a simple failure on the part of the executor or administrator to do his duty, and he is

answerable to the estate for the loss occasioned by his negligence in allowing the note to become outlawed.—Estate of Sanderson, 2 Cal. Unrep. 750, 13 Pac. 497, 498; 74 Cal. 199, 203, 15 Pac. 753. He is not chargeable with a failure to collect, however, unless it is shown that it was possible for him to collect.—Estate of Moore, 72 Cal. 335, 13 Pac. 880. The mere failure to sue upon a note is not, of itself, negligence. It is only the failure to proceed when a reasonable prospect of collection is apparent that constitutes negligence.—Elizalde v. Murphy, 4 Cal. App. 114, 87 Pac. 245, 246. The failure to "push" the collection of a note may be negligence, but it is not necessarily so. The executor or administrator is not answerable with respect to a note uncollected without his fault.—Estate of Moore, 96 Cal. 522, 525, 32 Pac. 584. An executor should make all reasonable exertion to collect even desperate debts due to an estate, but should only be held for moneys uncollected, when it appears that they were lost by his want of proper management or effort; and the burden of proving that debts might, by proper effort, have been collected, lies with those who seek to make the executor liable for the loss.—Estate of Millenovich, 5 Nev. 161, 184.

(11) **Losses through neglect.**—An executor or administrator is chargeable with losses to the estate, occasioned through his neglect.— Estate of Carver, 123 Cal. 102, 104, 55 Pac. 770. Whenever he does what the law prohibits, or fails to exercise reasonable care and dili gence in the endeavor to do what the law enjoins, he and his sure- ties are liable for the damages consequent upon such act or omission.— McNabb v. Wixom, 7 Nev. 163, 171. An administrator is answerable to the heirs of the deceased for money or other property that came into his hands, which, through his act or omission, has been lost to the estate.—Callan v. Savidge, 68 Kan. 620, 75 Pac. 1010. And an execu- tor or administrator is not necessarily to be charged with negligence in paying out more to redeem pledged personal property than the prop- erty is worth. The question of negligence depends upon the proof.— Estate of Armstrong, 125 Cal. 603, 606, 58 Pac. 183. Nor is negligence to be imputed to an administrator for his failure to object to the proof of payment of taxes actually paid by a mortgagee, because the com- plaint did not allege such payment.—Estate of Armstrong, 125 Cal. 603, 606, 58 Pac. 183. An executor or administrator is answerable for a loss to the estate he represents, arising from his failure to foreclose a mortgage taken as security for a loan of moneys of the estate, and allowing the statute of limitations to bar a recovery.—In re Roach's Estate, 50 Or. 179, 92 Pac. 118, 125. An executor or administrator should not be charged with the loss arising from his failure to collect rents, or for his failure to lease lands of the estate for a larger rent, where such failure is not due to the lack of ordinary care and diligence on his part in the management of the business of the estate.—Estate of Moore, 96 Cal. 522, 525, 32 Pac. 584. An administrator who fails, within seven years to file a first account, when the estate is one that might have paid all claims in cash, and files his first and final account

only when ordered by court to do so, renders himself and his bond liable for any injury to the estate resulting from his omission.—In re Delaney's Estate, 41 Nev. 384, 386, 171 Pac. 383.

REFERENCES.

Liability of an executor or administrator for negligence.—See note 14 Am. Dec. 65, 66.

(12) **Personal injuries. Conduct of decedent's business.**—An executor or administrator can not commit a tort in his representative capacity, so as to charge the estate. If he commits a trespass, it is his individual and personal act, and not his representative act. And if he is carrying on the business of the decedent, he is individually answerable to a third person injured through the negligence of his servant employed in the business while acting within the scope of his employment.—Kalua v. Camarinos, 11 Haw. 557, 558, 559. An action can not be maintained against an executor or administrator in his representative character while administering the estate for a wrongful act committed by him whereby a personal injury is inflicted upon another. As the act is beyond the scope of his official authority he must be sued as an individual.—Fetting v. Winch, 54 Or. 600, 21 Ann. Cas. 352, 38 L. R. A. (N. S.) 379, 104 Pac. 723.

REFERENCES.

Personal representative or testamentary trustee carrying on business. —See note 40 L. R. A. (N. S.) 201. Liability of executor or administrator for personal injury resulting from negligence in care or management of property of estate.—See note 38 L. R. A. (N. S.) 379.

(13) **Liability for taxes.**—An executor or administrator is answerable for the value of certain real property lost to the estate by his neglect to pay taxes thereon.—Estate of Herteman, 73 Cal. 545, 546, 15 Pac. 121. The liability of an executor or administrator for taxes due on the estate he represents is official and not personal; and, upon his resignation or discharge, such liability is assumed by his successor in the same manner as is any other obligation of the estate.— San Francisco v. Pennie, 93 Cal. 465, 29 Pac. 66, 69; but the extent of his representative accountability or liability for the property in his official capacity does not affect the question of its being liable to taxation. Though he has not the possession, yet he has a control, in so far that he may pay the lien, and would then be entitled to possession and absolute control.—Stanford v. San Francisco, 131 Cal. 34, 36, 63 Pac. 145. An executor or administrator can not be charged with notice of unpaid taxes on property which the deceased had conveyed in his lifetime, and in and to which he had no interest at the time of his death, and which did not become property of the estate or come into the custody of the executor or administrator.—Clayton v. Dinwoodey, 33 Utah 251, 14 Ann. Cas. 926, 93 Pac. 723, 726.

4. Instances of non-liability.—Under the rule that an executor or administrator is not answerable for the loss of property, so long as he acts in good faith and with ordinary discretion, he is not answerable for money lost to the estate by the death or insolvency of an agent employed in another state to receive and forward to him money belonging to the estate, where such agent came well recommended to him.—Estate of Taylor, 52 Cal. 477, 479. He is not negligent for his failure to have mortgaged property appraised, where it appears that it would be a useless expense.—Estate of Armstrong, 125 Cal. 603, 608, 58 Pac. 183. An executor is not liable in unlawful detainer for rent.—Martell v. Meehan, 63 Cal. 47, 50. Nor is an administrator to be charged with the value of the property sold under an order of the probate court, without proof of any fraud whatever on the part of the administrator.—Richardson v. Sage, 57 Cal. 212, 214. An executor or administrator, in the entire absence of proof, or presumption of advantage to himself, or of want of neglect of official duty, is not liable for punitory damages.—Wheeler v. Bolton, 92 Cal. 159, 174, 28 Pac. 558. An executor or administrator can not impose any liability on the estate by making, drawing, accepting, or indorsing any bill or promissory note, though he has authority to indorse negotiable instruments for the purpose of transferring the decedent's title when a transfer is necessary or proper. But such indorsement operates no further, so far as the estate is concerned, than to effect a transfer of title, and any liability which may arise on the indorsement is the personal liability of the executor or administrator. Where a man, after his wife's death, renewed notes previously executed by him during the lifetime of his wife for their joint debt, he is not liable on such notes in his representative capacity, for the reason that he has no power to bind his wife's estate by the giving of a note.—Bank of Montreal v. Buchanan, 32 Wash. 480, 73 Pac. 482, 483. An oral promise made by an executor to pay at maturity an individual note executed by his co-executrix, who is also a sole legatee of the estate, and which note was payable on or before three years after its date, is void under the statute of frauds, as being an agreement which, by its terms, is not to be performed within a year from the making thereof.—McKeany v. Black, 117 Cal. 587, 591, 49 Pac. 710. And no executor or administrator is chargeable upon an oral promise to pay any debt of the decedent out of his own estate, except under the circumstances provided by the statute.—McKeany v. Black, 117 Cal. 587, 593, 49 Pac. 710. Where a decedent, before his death, had agreed to buy certain bonds, provided their legality was examined into by a lawyer whose judgment was wanted, but death occurred before the bonds were tendered, such death operated to terminate the offer to buy, and it became a nullity. A subsequent tender to the administratrix was nugatory; and if the refusal of the administratrix to receive the bonds created a liability, it was a new liability incurred after the death of decedent, and while the administration of the estate was in progress.

Such liability is not provable in the probate court where the claim was not a demand against the decedent existing in his lifetime; and the probate court having no jurisdiction, the remedy, if any, must be sought in another tribunal.—Rinér v. Husted's Estate, 13 Colo. App. 523, 58 Pac. 793, 794. If an executor or administrator pays money in good faith, for the purchase of necessities for the support of helpless minor children of the intestate, at a time when they have no guardian, and the purchases are such as a guardian would have made if one had been appointed, such executor or administrator is not answerable for the money so paid in an action by a guardian thereafter appointed. —Calnan v. Savidge, 68 Kan. 620, 75 Pac. 1010, 1012. An executor or administrator is not liable for losses to the estate occurring through no fault of his, and is entitled to compensation for his services.—In re Dolenty's Estate, Mannix v. Dolenty, 53 Mont. 33, 161 Pac. 524. An administrator with the will annexed is not answerable to heirs and legatees for the appraised value of lots irregularly sold, that belonged to the estate, though loss resulted, where, considering the location and character of the property, incumbrances, and condition of the market at the time, it can not be said that the sale was unjustly made; the statute creates liability only when the sale was "unjustly" made, not because of irregularity in making it.—In re Johnston's Estate (Wash.), 181 Pac. 209, 212. Upon the death of one judgment debtor, the other succeeds to the joint obligation of the judgment, and he is liable alone and not jointly with the executors or administrators of the deceased judgment debtor. The executors and administrators are not liable at law in such case.—Smithies v. Colburn, 20 Haw. 138.

REFERENCES.

Instances of non-liability.—See head-line 2, subds. 2, 9, 11, ante.

5. When chargeable with interest.

(1) In general.—Interest on the assets of an estate is not chargeable, as a matter of course, against the executor or administrator, but may be so charged if the circumstances of the particular case require it.—Estate of Holbert, 39 Cal. 597, 601; Wheeler v. Bolton, 92 Cal. 159, 173, 28 Pac. 558. Whether any delay in prosecuting an order for the settlement of an estate could authorize the court to charge the executor or administrator with interest must be determined by the court upon the consideration of all the circumstances of the case, including the character and condition of the estate, the causes of the delay, and whether it has been reasonable or unreasonable; and in any event the burden showing that he should be charged with interest is upon the contestant of his account.—Walls v. Walker, 37 Cal. 424, 99 Am. Dec. 290; Estate of Sarment, 123 Cal. 331, 332, 55 Pac. 1015. Whether, in any instance, the executor is chargeable with even simple interest must be determined by the trial court from all the circumstances of the case. It can not be said as a matter of law that interest is to be added to the value of property that has been lost by his

neglect. The circumstances connected with its loss may so completely exonerate him from any charge of neglect that he would not be held liable for even its value, and his neglect may have been so technical that the court would not feel justified in requiring from him more than a restoration of the value of the property. The rule charging an executor or administrator with interest is limited to cases in which it is either shown or presumed that the representative has himself profited by his acts, or has been guilty of such wilful misfeasance as to justify the court in requiring from him compensation therefor.— Wheeler v. Bolton, 92 Cal. 159, 173, 28 Pac. 558; Estate of Marre, 127 Cal. 128, 132, 59 Pac. 385. In all cases where he applies money of the estate to his own use, he ought to be charged with interest, either simple or compound, as the facts may justify.—Walls v. Walker, 27 Cal. 424, 99 Am. Dec. 290; Estate of Hilliard, 83 Cal. 423, 23 Pac. 393. He is not to be charged with interest where no such claim is stated in the written grounds of contest.—Estate of Sylvar, 1 Cal. App. 35, 37, 81 Pac. 663; In re Roach's Estate, 50 Or. 179, 92 Pac. 118, 123. If he has, before final settlement of his accounts, appropriated money of the estate as commissions, he is not chargeable with interest on the amount from the time of its appropriation to the date of final settlement.—Estate of Carter (Cal.), 64 Pac. 484 (modifying Estate of Carter, 132 Cal. 113, 64 Pac. 123). So while the good faith of the administrator or executor is no defense against the loss of money or other property loaned by him, still he can not be held answerable for the interest stipulated to be paid, unless he has collected or can collect it.—Estate of Moore, 72 Cal. 335, 13 Pac. 880, 884. The general rule is, that an executor or administrator, except where he is charged with a special trust to invest money or interest, is not chargeable with interest unless he has actually received interest, or else, where, from some culpable delay in settling his accounts, it may be fairly inferred that he has made a profit out of the funds in his hands. If he appeals from an order of settlement and distribution, and it does not appear that he made, in the meantime, a net profit out of the fund of the estate in any way, and it does not appear that he could have invested the funds profitably in the meantime, he should not be charged with interest upon the funds in his hands for the time pending the delay occasioned by the appeal.—In re Davis' Estate, 33 Mont. 539, 88 Pac. 957, 960. It is manifest that executors and administrators should not be charged with interest prior to the dates at which they received money.—Estate of Sarment, 123 Cal. 331, 334, 55 Pac. 1015. An executor or administrator is chargeable with interest where he unreasonably and without just excuse retains money in his hands; though he is not, as a general rule, chargeable with interest until the estate is in a condition to be settled.—Estate of Espinda, 9 Haw. 342-344; Estate of Raleigh, 48 Utah 128, 158 Pac. 705. An executor is not in all cases chargeable with interest on money remaining in his hands uninvested, but the question is for the court to decide in its discretion, according to the circumstances.—In re Hagarty's Estate, 105 Wash. 547, 178 Pac.

644. Where an administrator has retained money of the estate beyond the time when, by proper accounting and other. administrative acts required by statute, he could have paid it out and .distributed it by court order, he is chargeable with interest on the same.—In re Delaney's Estate, 41 Nev. 384, 390, 171 Pac. 383.

REFERENCES.

Executor or administrator should be charged with interest when.— See note 99 Am. Dec. 296-299.

(2) Delay in settlement of estate.—In actions for damages for tort or breach of contract, interest as such can not be allowed where the amount of damage is unliquidated and incapable of being made certain, but other considerations must govern a court in fixing the liability of a delinquent trustee. In such cases, the primary consideration is the equitable one that the trustee must be compelled fully to compensate the beneficiary for the unauthorized use of the trust estate. This principle applies where there was a long delay in settling the estate of a deceased person, where the administrator asserted title to certain lands of the estate to be in himself, and where he was otherwise derelict in his duties as representative.—Estate of Piercy, Piercy v. Piercy, 168 Cal. 755, 145 Pac. 91. Where, on the appointment of an administrator, the estate owns non-interest bearing certificates of deposit to the amount of $5000, and about $1200 subject to check, and the estate's indebtedness is trifling, such administrator is liable for interest on the idle money, to the distributees, in case of his unreasonable delay in settling the estate.—In re Delaney's Estate, 41 Nev. 384, 389, 171 Pac. 383. An executor or administrator can not, because of the estate's not having been promptly closed up and the funds distributed, be charged with interest on funds of the estate under his control, unless he has personally profited by the delay, or has been guilty of fraud, or has withheld funds after demand made upon him.—Estate of Raleigh, 48 Utah 128, 158 Pac. 705. When an administrator has acted in good faith, has made prompt report of all sums received and paid out and has moved for an order permitting final settlement and distribution immediately after the time fixed by statute for the presentation of claims, he should not be charged interest on the estate in his hands simply because of a delay not of his own making.—Fogg v. Quackenbush, 27 Colo. App. 480, 150 Pac. 726.

(3) Simple interest.—The mere fact that an executor or administrator withdraws money of the estate from the bank in which it was drawing interest, where there was no apparent necessity for so doing, for the payment of debts or the expenses of administration, is not a reason for charging him with interest. If he decided in good faith, and in the exercise of his discretion that the interest of the estate demanded, that the money should be reduced into his actual possession, he is not liable for interest, merely because the money was withdrawn from the bank, in the absence of any showing that he acted in

bad faith, or used the money in his private business, or mingled it
with his own, or deposited it in bank to his own credit.—Estate of
McQueen, 44 Cal. 584, 588, 590. If he makes a loan in good faith, and
the money is lost, he is not to be charged with the stipulated rate
of interest upon the sum lost, nor even with the statutory rate of
interest, unless it appears that he could with ordinary diligence have
loaned the money to others at the statutory rate.—Estate of Holbert,
48 Cal. 627, 630. He is not to be charged with even simple interest
upon the funds of the estate which may be in his hands, unless it is
made to appear to the court that the estate, or the parties interested
in it, have sustained loss by reason of his negligence or fault.—Estate
of Sarment, 123 Cal. 331, 332, 55 Pac. 1015. Where an administrator filed two accounts, and there was no dereliction of duty as to
the first, but was as to the second, he can be charged with interest
only from the date of any actual dereliction of duty, which may have
caused loss to the estate.—Estate of Marre, 127 Cal. 128, 132, 59 Pac.
385. In a proper case the court may impose upon the executor or
administrator a charge of interest upon a balance in his hands, as
a penalty for delay in the administration.—Estate of Armstrong, 125
Cal. 603, 608, 58 Pac. 183. But a penalty is not to be imposed upon
an executor or administrator for loss arising from his deposit of funds
of the estate with a private banker or with an individual. In many
cases it would be safer, of course, to do so; and especially should he
not be charged with interest where he has received no interest, profits,
or income from the estate.—In all cases where he is called upon to
pay the penalty of his neglect by being charged with interest, it is
incumbent upon the parties alleging such neglect to prove it.—Estate
of Sylar, 1 Cal. App. 35, 37, 81 Pac. 663. An executor or administrator
who uses money of the estate he represents in his own business and
for his own profit is chargeable with interest thereon at the legal rate,
with annual rests.—Estate of Merrifield, 66 Cal. 180, 4 Pac. 1176; Miller
v. Lux, 100 Cal. 609, 615, 35 Pac. 345, 639; Estate of Pease, 149 Cal.
167, 85 Pac. 149, 151. If he keeps money of the estate, to be used by
himself whenever he wants it or needs it, and uses it for his own
purposes, he is liable for interest without any proof that he has derived benefit by the use of the money.—Estate of Hilliard, 83 Cal. 423,
428, 23 Pac. 393; Estate of Gasq, 42 Cal. 288. In cases of mere negligence, no more than simple interest is ever added to the loss or damage resulting therefrom.—Wheeler v. Bolton, 92 Cal. 159, 172, 28 Pac.
558. An executor or administrator is properly charged with legal
interest upon balances, with annual rests, where he is guilty of great
delay in accounting.—Estate of Sanderson, 74 Cal. 199, 215, 15 Pac.
753. An executor is chargeable with legal interest, computed with
annual rests, upon moneys improperly advanced to his co-executor,
as where he pays a sum of money as a family allowance to the widow,
who is also one of the executors, but without any order of the court
therefor.—Miller v. Lux, 100 Cal. 609, 615, 35 Pac. 345, 639. An execu-

tor or administrator is liable for interest at the current rate for his failure to lend money of the estate in accordance with the provisions of the will.—Estate of Holbert, 39 Cal. 597, 601. He is liable for interest on money of the estate which he has drawn and mingled with his own funds and omitted from his account.—Estate of Herteman, 73 Cal. 545, 547, 15 Pac. 121. He is also liable for interest on money of the estate, improperly withdrawn for the purpose of paying a bookkeeper, and such liability continues until the money is repaid to the estate.—Estate of Scott, 1 Cal. App. 740, 83 Pac. 85, 87. Where an administrator neglects and fails to close and settle the estate of a decedent, if the same is ready for settlement and distribution, and thereafter attempts to have the whole of such estate set aside to him as sole heir or legatee, and he fails in such attempt, he must pay legal interest on all money in his hands ready for distribution from the time such distribution ought to have been made by him.—Harris v. Coats, 8 Ida. 491, 69 Pac. 475.

(4) Compound Interest.—The general rule applicable to an executor or administrator, as well as to any other trustee is, that, except in cases in which he has been guilty of some positive misconduct, or wilful violation of duty, he is not to be charged with compound interest.—Wheeler v. Bolton, 92 Cal. 159, 172, 28 Pac. 558; Estate of Casner, 1 Cal. App. 145, 147, 81 Pac. 991; Estate of Sarment, 123 Cal. 331, 333, 55 Pac. 1015. But where he uses the funds of an estate in his own business, or for any purpose of his own, the well-established rule is to charge him with legal interest compounded annually from the date of appropriation, with annual rests, where it is not found that a higher rate of interest was realized from such use.—Miller v. Lux, 100 Cal. 609, 615, 35 Pac. 345, 639; Estate of Clary, 112 Cal. 292, 295, 44 Pac. 569; Merrifield v. Longmire, 66 Cal. 180, 4 Pac. 1176; Estate of Clark, 53 Cal. 355; Estate of Stott, 52 Cal. 403. It is a general rule, applicable to an executor and administrator, as well as to any other trustee, that, where he has been guilty of positive misconduct or a violation of duty, compound interest may be allowed.—Estate of Cousins, 111 Cal. 441, 452, 44 Pac. 182. An executor or administrator is not to be charged with compound interest from the mere fact that he deposited moneys of the estate in a bank managed by his brother, who was a surety on his bond, where there is no proof that the bank made any other use of the funds deposited than that made by banks of deposit in general.—Estate of Sarment, 123 Cal. 331, 334, 55 Pac. 1015. Where the settlement of an estate has been long delayed, and the administrator has himself used funds belonging to the estate, the heirs will not be fully compensated unless they receive compound interest on the property of the estate thus withheld.—Estate of Piercy, Piercy v. Piercy, 168 Cal. 755, 145 Pac. 91.

REFERENCES.

Liability of executor or administrator for compound interest.—See sentative chargeable with compound interest for mingling trust funds. —See head-line 5, infra.

6. Not to profit or lose by estate.—It is a well-established principle that the executor or administrator shall not profit or lose by the estate he represents.—Estate of Holbert, 39 Cal. 597, 601; Walls v. Walker, 37 Cal. 424, 99 Am. Dec. 290; Estate of Rose, 80 Cal. 166, 173, 22 Pac. 86; Firebaugh v. Burbank, 121 Cal. 186, 191, 53 Pac. 560; Magraw v. McGlynn, 26 Cal. 420, 429. The executor can not profit by his trust, except as provided by law; but if he does wrong or commits serious mistakes, he may lose.—Gibson v. Kelly, 15 Mont. 417, 39 Pac. 517. If he diverts the estate to his private business, he incurs the usual risk of loss, but shall have no corresponding hope of profit.— Estate of Holbert, 39 Cal. 597, 601. If he undertakes to go beyond the strict line of his duty, he acts upon his own responsibility. He can derive no profit from the success of his venture, but must bear the loss of failure.—Estate of Knight, 12 Cal. 200, 208, 73 Am. Dec. 531. If he uses the real estate of the estate, he must account for the rental value thereof, and if he makes a profit, he must account to the estate for that also.—Walls v. Walker, 37 Cal. 424, 431, 99 Am. Dec. 290. If he elects to assume the peril of continuing the business of his decedent, and if he is permitted by the court and parties interested, without objection, to conduct and manage such business, the liabilities growing out of the management are not claims which could be enforced against the estate by the owners thereof. They are his liabilities. He has a right to pay them out of the increase of the business, but if by so doing a loss is sustained to the estate, he must make the loss good. Protected from loss and from liability at all times, the estate is interested in the business only to the extent of its profits.—Estate of Rose, 80 Cal. 166, 173, 22 Pac. 86. If he puts the personal estate to his own private use, he is chargeable with the value of its use or with the actual profits, if any, which the administrator has made by its use, at the election of the party interested in the distribution of the estate, and if loss has ensued thereby, he is not only not entitled to be made whole, but is, notwithstanding, liable for use, for so to use the property of the estate is a breach of his trust, and the profits which he may have made are the earnings of the estate, and must go with it.—Walls v. Walker, 37 Cal. 424, 431, 99 Am. Dec. 290. It would be a most dangerous precedent to hold that an executor or administrator may speculate with the funds of the estate, or pay charges not allowed by law, though solely with a view of benefiting the estate, and then throw the loss upon the estate, and assign his good intentions as a defense to the injurious consequences of his acts.—Estate of Knight, 12 Cal. 200, 208, 73 Am. Dec. 531. The rule as to the unlawful employment of the funds of the estate is quite simple. The estate is to suffer no loss, and the executor is to make no gain. This does not mean that the executor is to be charged for all money invested in speculating, and also with all that is received from it, but only that he must make good the loss resulting from the business, or if a profit has been earned, that he must account for it to the estate.—Estate of Smith, 118 Cal. 462, 465, 50 Pac. 701. If the executor or administrator purchases real property of the estate in his own name, with money of the estate, a trust therein results to the heirs.—Merket v. Smith; 33 Kan. 66, 5 Pac. 394, 397. A representative expressly authorized by a will to carry on the business of a testator for a time may do so under the direction of the probate court. One so authorized is not bound to incur the hazard, but if he does, the contracts made will be his own, and he will be individually bound by them.—Campbell v. Faxon, 73 Kan. 675, 5 L. R. A. (N. S.) 1002, 85 Pac. 760, 762. If an administrator buys a claim against the estate, for the benefit of the estate, and to avoid litigation, and it does not appear that such purchase resulted in gain to the administrator, he is entitled to reimbursement.—Furth v. Wyatt, 17 Nev. 180, 30 Pac. 828, 829. If he sells stock in a corporation for more than its appraised value, he is liable for the amount received.—Estate of Radovich, 74 Cal. 536, 5 Am. St. Rep. 466, 16 Pac. 321. In cases where the executor or administrator has mingled moneys belonging to his trust with his own funds, and used them for his own advantage, courts have charged him with compound interest upon the theory that, in the absence of evidence to the contrary, he will be presumed to have received such profits from their use. The rule which makes an executor or other trustee chargeable with compound interest upon trust funds used by him in his own business is not adopted for the purpose of punishing him for any intentional wrong-doing in the use of such fund, but rather to carry into effect the principle enforced by courts of equity, that the trustees shall not be permitted to make any profit from the unauthorized use of such funds. The rule is intended to secure fidelity in the management of trust estates, and where the conventional rate of interest exceeds the statutory rate, the executor should, in such cases, be charged with legal interest, compounded annually, in order to fully reach the profit realized by him from the use of the trust fund.—Miller v. Lux, 100 Cal. 609, 616, 35 Pac. 345, 639; Wheeler v. Bolton, 92 Cal. 159, 172, 28 Pac. 558; Estate of Stott, 52 Cal. 403.

II. COMPENSATION OF EXECUTORS AND ADMINISTRATORS.

1. **Provision for, in will.**—A testator may, by his will, provide compensation for his executor different from that provided by the statute and there appears to be no reason why he may not direct that his executor shall receive a portion of such compensation at stated intervals during the administration of the estate. No allowance, in such a case, can be made without the approval of the court, but, if the court at all times has the estate under its control, it can make such allowance, from time to time, as may be just, in view of the condition of the estate and to the extent that the administration has been completed.— Estate of Ringot, 124 Cal. 45, 48, 56 Pac. 781. Provision for further

compensation may also be made by will. Thus where the amount
of compensation provided in the will was largely in excess of the
commissions to which the executor would have been entitled if no
provision had been so made, it is reasonable to suppose that when the
testator appointed the manager of his farm to be one of his executors,
he had this fact in mind, and made the appointment in order that,
after his death, his estate might continue to receive the benefit of the
services and experience of such manager, and that he fixed the amount
of his compensation in contemplation thereof. The statement, in his
will, that he deemed the commissions allowed by law to be insufficient
compensation implies that they would perform other duties than those
ordinarily required of an executor.—Estate of Runyon, 125 Cal. 195,
196, 57 Pac. 783. In Hawaii, an administrator with the will annexed
is not entitled to commissions, where the devisees under the will,
which directs the sale of real estate, have elected, before any sale
is made, to take the land instead of its proceeds.—Estate of Kraft, 16
Haw. 159, 162. The fees to accrue to an executor, under the terms of
a will, are to be regarded as giving the appointee an interest, to be
considered in weighing his testimony; still, they are but compensation
for services and not a "legacy," or a "devise," or a "beneficial gift,"
within the meaning of the statute making gifts to subscribing witnesses void.—In re Williams' Estate, Williams v. Davis, 50 Mont. 142,
145 Pac. 957.

2. Statutory allowance.—An executor or administrator is not liable
for losses to the estate occurring through no fault of his, and is
entitled to compensation for his services.—In re Dolenty's Estate, Mannix v. Dolenty, 53 Mont. 33, 161 Pac. 524. When no compensation is
provided by the will, the executor is entitled to commissions, at the
rate specified by the statute, on all the estate which comes into his
hands for which he is answerable.—Estate of Isaacs, 30 Cal. 105, 113;
Estate of Simmons, 43 Cal. 543, 550. The commissions to be allowed
to an executor or administrator are fixed by the statute. They are a
designated percentage "upon the amount of the whole estate accounted
for by him"; and the executor or administrator can not be said to
have "accounted for" an estate, in the sense of the statute, unless he
shall have first taken it into his possession.—Estate of Simmons, 43
Cal. 543, 550. The compensation of an executor, whether according to
the rates fixed by the statute or as determined by the testator, is not
a gratuity, but is in consideration of the services he may render, and
the amount fixed by the statute is deemed ample compensation for the
services ordinarily required.—Estate of Runyon, 125 Cal. 195, 57 Pac.
783. Although an executor or administrator may have been guilty of
neglect, or may have wasted, embezzled, or mismanaged the estate,
he is not to be deprived of the compensation provided by law; though in
such cases he will be charged with the loss and credited with his
commission; so that, so far as necessary, his commissions will be
applied to the payment of such losses.—Estate of Carver, 123 Cal. 102,

104, 55 Pac. 770. The probate court has exclusive jurisdiction over the allowance or apportionment of the commissions of executors and administrators.—Hope v. Jones, 24 Cal. 89, 94. Statutory commissions are provided for the faithful and proper performance of trusts. Hence if an administrator does not comply with the duties devolved upon him by his appointment, he is not, in Hawaii, entitled to commissions.— Estate of Akana, 11 Haw. 420, 422. The claim of an executor or administrator to fees allowed by statute is not a contract, within the inhibition of the Federal statute, which prohibits a state from passing a law which impairs the obligation of contracts.—In re Dewar's Estate, 10 Mont. 426, 25 Pac. 1026, 1029. The legislature has no constitutional power to increase fees in probate cases provided by the statute, which increase is based upon an ad valorem theory, and is regulated according to the amount of property owned by an estate.—Fatjo v. Pfister, 117 Cal. 83, 48 Pac. 1012; State v. Case, 39 Wash. 177, 109 Am. St. Rep. 874, 1 L. R. A. (N. S.) 152, 81 Pac. 554. In Hawaii, an administrator is not allowed commissions on specific chattels delivered in kind to an heir or legatee.—Estate of Kraft, 16 Haw. 159, 161. The only purpose of the Cal. Code of Civ. Proc., section 1616, authorizing an attorney to apply for an order allowing compensation for services rendered to the representative, was to enable the attorney to obtain compensation directly, and did not alter the liability of the estate.—In re Hite's Estate, 155 Cal. 448, 101 Pac. 448. That section, as amended in 1911, contemplates an allowance to an executor or administrator on account of his commissions before the administration is completed, and this rule is applicable to an executor who dies or is removed, as well as to one who continues in office.—Estate of Jones, 166 Cal. 147, 135 Pac. 293. Under the language of sections 1618 and 1619 of the Code of Civil Procedure of California, the general administrator of an estate and his attorney are entitled to the fixed percentage therein provided, and the court can not diminish the same by the deduction of any previous allowance made to a special administrator and his attorney.— Estate of Miller, 15 Cal. App. 557, 115 Pac. 329. Whether a will be construed as an ordinary one or a non-intervention one will not affect the right of the executor to the statutory compensation.—Shufeldt v. Hughes, 55 Wash. 246, 104 Pac. 257. An administrator is entitled to statutory fees, though he was guilty of irregularities in performing his duties, where he had to and did show great resourcefulness and ability in handling and conserving the estate, and no fraud or misappropriation is shown.—In re Johnston's Estate (Wash.), 181 Pac. 209, 214.

3. Basis. Computation.—The commissions to which an executor or administrator will be entitled are purely matters of computation, and are based "on the amount of the estate" accounted for by him.—Estate of Straus, 144 Cal. 553, 556, 77 Pac. 1122; Estate of Simmons, 43 Cal. 543, 551. If the executor or administrator is entitled to commissions "upon the amount of the estate accounted for by him," the inventory and appraisement may be looked to for the purpose of

ascertaining the amount of the estate; but it does not necessarily follow that, in any case, the appraisement on file necessarily constitutes the basis upon which the compensation is to be allowed. The valuation of the inventory was evidently not intended to be conclusive for any purpose. The administrator is chargeable, in his account, with the whole estate of the decedent which may come into his possession, and "at the value of the appraisement contained in the inventory"; but if any is sold for less than the appraisement, he is not answerable for the loss, if the sale has been advantageously made. The inventory may or may not afford a basis of calculation for the purpose of allowance of commissions upon property taken into possession and accounted for; but if resorted to in making such allowance, it can not, in any case, amount to more than prima facie evidence of value, and the value should be left open to inquiry, if the inventoried value is not satisfactory to all parties concerned. If the administrator takes possession of the estate, and it is distributed to the heirs, it is to be "accounted for" by him, and if no objection is made by them to the valuation in the inventory, that valuation would form the basis of estimating his commissions. If the administrator sells the estate, or a portion of it, the amount received upon such sale becomes the evidence of its value to the estate, for which he has to account, and upon which his commissions are to be estimated.—Estate of Fernandez, 119 Cal. 579, 584, 51 Pac. 851. In the absence of proof that the valuation of the property of the estate made in the inventory and appraisement is not fair and reasonable, the administrator should be allowed commissions on that valuation at the statutory rates.—Estate of Carver, 123 Cal. 102, 106, 55 Pac. 770. The general rule is, that, where property subject to mortgage is sold, the executor or administrator is entitled only to have commissions on the net purchase price in excess of the encumbrance; but this rule does not apply where the mortgage was presented as a valid claim against the estate, and the sale is made to a third party. In such a case the executor or administrator is entitled to his commissions on the entire purchase price, as he is to be allowed commissions based on the value of the estate which has been taken into possession and accounted for.—Estate of Pease, 149 Cal. 167, 171, 85 Pac. 149. As the appraised valuation of the estate is only prima facie evidence of its value, the court, in determing the compensation to be allowed the executor or administrator, may, if the value of the appraisement is questioned, take testimony as to the value, and base his judgment thereon. The compensation may therefore be computed on the value of the estate at the time of the settlement.— In re Sour's Estate, 17 Wash. 675, 50 Pac. 587, 589; In re Smith's Estate, 18 Wash. 129, 51 Pac. 348; Estate of Coursen, 6 Cal. Unrep. 756, 65 Pac. 965, 986. It is contemplated by the law that an executor or an administrator shall receive, as his compensation for services performed, certain commissions based upon the value of the property which he has taken into his possession, and which, having been so taken into possession, has been "accounted for."—Estate of Davis, 8 Cal. App. 355, 97 Pac. 86. All matters of probate, including rights of inheritance, succession, testamentary disposition of property, and taxes upon inheritances, are subject to statutory control. It is by virtue of the statute that the heir or devisee is entitled to receive any of the estate of the decedent, and the authority which thus regulates the disposition of such property can subject it to any reasonable condition or expense. This is the basic principle that justifies the legislature in providing uniform fees for the services of executors and their attorneys in the proper administration of estates. The statute, in some jurisdictions, prescribes the exact rate of compensation which shall be allowed, and the courts can not vary the amount which may be allowed, except so far as they may be authorized to award special compensation for extraordinary services; and it seems that the language of the statute, in most states, fixing the compensation of executors and administrators, precludes all discretion in this respect. A court can neither add to nor in any wise vary the compensation directed to be allowed by the statute. It can neither allow nor disallow commissions scaled by the degree of skill or of vigilance, of good or bad faith, displayed in the management of the estate, unless such discretion is vested in the court by such statute.— Estate of Goodrich, 6 Cal. App. 730, 733, 93 Pac. 121, 122 (citing and quoting from Woerner on American Law of Administration, § 526). The court may reduce an administrator's commissions for his failure to settle up an estate within a reasonable time.—Estate of Kaiu, 17 Haw. 514, 516. Where an administrator did not fully administer upon the property of an estate, his attorney is not entitled to full commissions; his fees should be based upon the amount of the estate when the account is finally settled.—Estate of Aldersley, 174 Cal. 366, 163 Pac. 206. The appraised value of an estate may be the prima facie value, if nothing to the contrary is shown, but, where there is ample evidence of the real value of the estate, the statutory administrator's fees should be based thereon, not on the appraised value.—In re Johnson's Estate (Wash.), 181 Pac. 209, 214. Although the amount of the property of a decedent appears prima facie from the appraisement filed in the proceedings in settling the estate, the compensation of the executor should be based on the amount disclosed by the final account, as is the inheritance tax.—In re Hagerty's Estate, Hagerty v. Work, 97 Wash. 491, 166 Pac. 1139. An administrator is not entitled to compute his fees upon the value of household furniture that never passed into his possession as administrator of the deceased, but which property belonged to another estate, that of the decedent's husband, and was administered in that estate by the same representative.—In re Johnston's Estate, (Wash.), 181 Pac. 209, 214.

4. Validity of agreements as to.—The provision of the statute which makes void all contracts for higher compensation between an heir and an executor is not limited to contracts made directly between the

executor and heir, but includes all contracts or agreements by which the executor would receive, either directly or indirectly, any greater compensation than has been fixed by the statute, or any compensation other than such as may have been previously ascertained and determined by the court, and applies to every contract which has for one of its objects the payment of such greater compensation, as well as to those which are made solely for such payment. A contract made in violation of this provision is against the policy of the law and is void.—Firebaugh v. Burbank, 121 Cal. 186, 191, 53 Pac. 560.

5. Not allowable until final settlement.—The commissions of an executor or administrator should not be allowed to him in the settlement of his annual account, but only when he has rendered his final accounts and the estate is ready for distribution.—Estate of Miner, 46 Cal. 564, 572; Estate of Barton, 55 Cal. 87, 90; Estate of Levinson, 108 Cal. 450, 41 Pac. 483, 42 Pac. 479; Estate of Rose, 80 Cal. 166, 22 Pac. 86; Estate of Carter, 132 Cal. 113, 64 Pac. 123; and they must be determined by the law then in force.—In re Dewar's Estate, 10 Mont. 426, 25 Pac. 1026, 1029. Commissions based on amount of estate accounted for held not allowable until settlement of final account.—In re Hite's Estate, 155 Cal. 448, 101 Pac. 448. Under the administration laws of the state of Washington the fixing of compensation of executors and administrators is a subject for determination upon settlement of the final account and is appealable on the ground that it is a final adjudication as to such allowance.—In re Doane's Estate, 64 Wash. 303, 116 Pac. 849. An executor is entitled to receive his compensation only on the completion of his service, and if he pays himself meantime out if the funds of the estate in his hands he must, on final settlement, return any excess over the compensation, his by law, with interest.—In re Hagerty's Estate, Hagerty v. Work, 97 Wash. 491, 166 Pac. 1139.

REFERENCES.

Executors' commissions are chargeable when.—See note 5 L. R. A. 74.

6. Renunciation. Waiver.—An executor or administrator may renounce his claim to compensation for the performance of the duties of his trust, and a promise made by him before his appointment, that he will not charge for his services, may be regarded as equivalent to the renunciation of his claim.—Estate of Davis, 65 Cal. 309, 4 Pac. 22. But where the administrator was the agent of the decedent, prior to her death, for the purpose of collecting rents accruing from the real estate, and was also her legal adviser, a statement made by him to the intestate's husband, prior to his appointment as administrator, that he would protect the husband's interest and the interest of the heirs, in the same manner and to the same extent as he had theretofore protected the interest of the intestate, does not waive his right to an allowance of statutory fees for his services as administrator.—Noble v. Whitten, 38 Wash. 262, 80 Pac. 451, 453. The right of an executor or administrator to commissions is not defeated, though he

has waived his right to compensation, if such waiver has been withdrawn by consent of the court and without objection having been made thereto.—Estate of Carver, 123 Cal. 102, 105, 55 Pac. 770. Where the compensation of an executor has been fixed by will, that is in "full compensation" for his services, unless he has renounced such provision.—Estate of Runyon, 125 Cal. 195, 197, 57 Pac. 783. When the compensation of an executor has been provided for by will, and he would claim that his services entitle him to a greater compensation than that allowed by the statute, he must first renounce that provided by the will, and the court can then make him such allowance as will fully compensate him. But, until such renunciation is made, the provision in the will must be held to be "full compensation" for his services.—Estate of Runyon, 125 Cal. 195, 197, 57 Pac. 783.

REFERENCES.

Agreements to relinquish compensation of executors or administrators, whether and when enforceable.—See note 48 Am. Rep. 332, 333.

7. What should be allowed.—On final settlement, an executor or administrator is entitled to commissions upon the whole value of the estate, both real and personal.—Ord v. Little, 3 Cal. 287; Estate of Isaacs, 30 Cal. 105, 113; Estate of Simmons, 43 Cal. 543; Estate of Miner, 46 Cal. 564, 572. The fees of an administrator are expenses of administration, and are to be allowed in preference to funeral expenses.—Estate of Nicholson, 1 Nev. 518. He is entitled to commissions on funds which he is compelled by law to hold, protect, and guard.—Wells, Fargo & Co. v. Robinson, 13 Cal. 133, 145. Under a statute which allows an executor or administrator a commission on the whole estate accounted for by him, at a certain percentage, the value of the real estate in his control should be included in fixing his compensation.—In re Sour's Estate, 17 Wash. 675, 50 Pac. 587, 589; and, in the absence of proof that the appraised value of the real estate of the decedent is not the actual value thereof, he is entitled to the statutory commission on the appraised value.—Wilbur v. Wilbur, 17 Wash. 683, 50 Pac. 589. Where he is, under the statute, entitled to the possession of his intestate's real estate, he is entitled to a commission on the appraised value thereof.—Noble v. Whitten, 38 Wash. 262, 80 Pac. 451, 453. Where a mortgage has been presented as a claim against the estate, an executor is entitled to commissions on the whole amount for which the mortgaged property is sold, where he has charged himself with the sum for which the sale was made.—Estate of Pease, 149 Cal. 167, 85 Pac. 149. Although the statute provides that "where the property of the estate is distributed in kind, and involves no labor beyond the custody and distribution of the same, the commissions shall be computed upon all the estate, above the value of $20,000, at one-half of the rates fixed in this section," yet, where the estate was appraised at a little over $117,000, and the executor accounted for a little over $145,000, the increase being made up of rents, interest, and dividends collected by him, and it appears that "all of the property belonging to said decedent at the time of his death, and then forming part of his estate, and which has not since been disposed of by said executor, is not now in the same form or condition in which the same was in at the time of the death of the said decedent, or at the time when it first came into the possession of said executor, and that all of the same can not now be, and is not, distributed in kind; and that the property of the estate of said decedent, and the care, management, and administration thereof, by said executor, has necessarily involved, and the said executor has properly bestowed and expended thereon, labor beyond the mere custody and distribution of the same,"—it is proper for the court to allow to the executor, in the settlement of his final account, full commissions upon the property accounted for, instead of half commissions on or above the value of twenty thousand dollars, as provided in the statute.—Estate of Cudworth, 133 Cal. 462, 463, 65 Pac. 1041. So, under such a statute, where it appears that the executor had been active in the management and the supervision of the estate, had performed services in collecting moneys due to it from various banks, and had settled the same for something over $26,000, it was proper for the court, in fixing the commissions, to allow the legal rate of three per cent upon the value of the estate over $20,000.—Estate of Town, 143 Cal. 507, 508, 77 Pac. 446. Where the conditions require the continuance of administration over a period of years, an executor or administrator may lawfully be allowed, at the close of each year, on the annual account, the commission provided by statute for the executor or administrator on moneys of the estate actually disbursed during the preceding year, by way of compensation for the care and management of the estate.—In re Ricker's Estate, 14 Mont. 153, 29 L. R. A. 622, 35 Pac. 960, 965. It is a rule that all expenses of ancillary administration shall be paid from the assets within the jurisdiction which granted the ancillary letters. Hence, where such administration is closed, and the assets have been transferred to the domiciliary administrator, it is proper for the court in which the latter administration is pending to allow the ancillary administrator his compensation as fixed by the court having charge of the ancillary administration.—Doss v. Stevens, 13 Colo. App. 535, 59 Pac. 67, 69. An administrator is entitled to credit for reasonable disbursements, costs, and expenses, and for commissions earned in the proper discharge of his trust during the time of his appointment, though such appointment is erroneous and voidable.—In re Owen's Estate, 32 Utah 469, 91 Pac. 283, 285; Rice v. Tilton, 14 Wyo. 101, 82 Pac. 577. There seems to be no fixed rule of compensation where the administrator resigns, or is removed, leaving the administration incomplete.—Ord v. Little, 3 Cal. 287, 289. Usually the only services for which an administrator or executor will be allowed compensation are such as are beneficial to the estate. This, however, does not mean that when the result of services undertaken in good faith is not of pecuniary or other benefit, but rather results in loss, such services should not be compensated.—In re Lichtenberg's Estate, 58 Wash. 585, 109 Pac. 49.

8. What should not be allowed.—No fees or commissions should be allowed to an executor or administrator for property which does not come into his hands, but which is in the possession of other parties, who claim title to it adversely to the estate, although it is appraised, and included in the inventory.—Estate of Simmons, 43 Cal. 543, 551; especially where, at the time, the property is involved in litigation, and a final judgment is subsequently rendered adverse to the estate.— In re Delaney, 110 Cal. 563, 566, 42 Pac. 981; Estate of Ricaud, 70 Cal. 69, 71, 11 Pac. 471. Neither should any fees or compensation be allowed to an executor or administrator for services voluntarily rendered, however great the benefit conferred.—Estate of Davis, 65 Cal. 309, 310, 4 Pac. 22. No commission can be allowed an executor or administrator on property which never came into his possession, nor on property which, although it belonged to the estate, has not been administered on, and is not under the control of the probate court.—Steel v. Holladay, 20 Or. 462, 26 Pac. 562. If letters testamentary are void, the executor is not entitled to commissions, fees, or charges in the settlement of the estate of his decedent.—Estate of Frey, 52 Cal. 658, 661. So where an order appointing an administrator was afterwards reversed on appeal, he is not entitled to anything for attorneys' fees or costs expended by him in the contest.—Estate of Barton, 55 Cal. 87, 88.

9. Further allowance. Extra services.—The commission authorized by the statute to be allowed to an executor or administrator is the compensation fixed by law for his care of the property belonging to the estate, and the court is not authorized to make any additional allowance, unless he shall file a petition therefor, and show that he has rendered some extraordinary services. Hence, the allowance to him, as commissions, of a sum in excess of the statutory percentage to which he is entitled is erroneous, in so far as it exceeds the percentage fixed by statute, where he has not petitioned the court for an extra allowance for extraordinary services, and it does not appear that he has rendered any such services.—Estate of Moore, 96 Cal. 552, 527, 32 Pac. 584; Estate of Delaney, 110 Cal. 563, 566, 42 Pac. 981; and it must further appear to the court that the claim is just and reasonable.—Firebaugh v. Burbank, 121 Cal. 186, 191, 53 Pac. 560. Unusual and extraordinary services of an executor or administrator for which the court is authorized to allow compensation are such as are not ordinarily required of an executor or administrator in the discharge of his trust; and his claim for such services should contain a statement of each special service claimed to have been rendered, with its particular value, and, until such an account is presented, no allowance should be made therefor.— Steel v. Holladay, 20 Or. 462, 26 Pac. 562. A mere change of the character of the property, such as a collection of outstanding claims that had been distributed in kind, or the collection of policies of insurance for property destroyed by fire, does not entitle an executor or administrator to commissions upon the amount so collected, as the property of the estate would thereby only be changed in form but not increased in value, and no additional estate would be accounted for.—Firebaugh v. Burbank, 121 Cal. 186, 190, 63 Pac. 560. Where the executor never applied to the county court for directions as to the manner of lending money of the estate, and for more than eight years made no report to the court of his dealings with such property in his possession, though required by statute to account therefor semiannually, the court will refuse to allow him any extra compensation for office rent or attorneys' fees.—In re Roach's Estate, 50 Or. 179, 92 Pac. 118, 127. An agreement by the heir to compensate the executor or administrator for extraordinary services, or for expenses incurred in employing attorneys, other than may have been previously fixed by the court, is as fully within the prohibition of the statute making void all contracts for higher compensation between an heir and an executor, as an agreement to give him a greater rate of commission than is fixed by the statute. The relation between them is that of a trustee and his beneficiary, and the law presumes that such an agreement by the heir has been obtained by undue influence of the executor or administrator, and will not enforce it against the heir.—Firebaugh v. Burbank, 121 Cal. 186, 191, 53 Pac. 560. When a lawyer becomes a voluntary administrator, he takes the office cum onere, and although he exercises professional skill in conducting the estate, he does not thereby entitle himself to additional compensation. He is entitled only to the usual statutory commissions of an administrator.—In re Young's Estate, 4 Wash. 534, 30 Pac. 643; Noble v. Whitten, 38 Wash. 262, 80 Pac. 451, 454. If the administrator himself is a lawyer, no additional allowance for costs and charges in collecting and defending the claims of the estate can be allowed him for legal services.—Doss v. Stevens, 13 Colo. App. 535, 59 Pac. 67, 70. For the same reason, and the additional reason that the administrator is presumed to have been appointed because of his ability and fitness to attend to and manage the estate, he should be required to exercise his professional skill and to conduct the business of the estate himself, unless there is necessity shown for the employment of legal assistance. Where there is no litigation concerning the administration of the estate, and there are no legal or other complications, and the administrator himself is an attorney, competent to transact all the business connected with the administration, there is no necessity at all for the employment of an attorney to assist him. He should be required to conduct business of the estate without extra compensation.—Noble v. Whitten, 38 Wash. 262, 80 Pac. 451, 454. The fact that during the early years of the administration one acted as attorney and co-executor does not entitle him to extra compensation.—Estate of Coursen, 6 Cal. Unrep. 756, 65 Pac. 965, 968. If an executor undertakes the management of the estate on behalf of the heirs and loss results he is chargeable with that loss. If upon the other hand, profit over and above normal results from his endeavors he is entitled to an allowance from the estate by way of compensation for extraordinary services under section 1618 California

Code of Civil Procedure.—Estate of Broome, 162 Cal. 258, 122 Pac. 470. The compensation of an executor who claims to have performed extraordinary services should in no case exceed double what he would be entitled to in the absence of such a claim.—In re Hagerty's Estate, Hagerty v. Work, 97 Wash. 491, 166 Pac. 1139. The court properly disallowed the account of the administrator and his attorney for extra services. The allowance or disallowance of the same is within the discretion of the court, and its exercise in disallowing the account does not call for any revisory action by this court.—Estate of Miller, 15 Cal. App. 557, 115 Pac. 329.

REFERENCES.

Right of executor or administrator to extra compensation for extraordinary services.—See note in Ann. Cas. 1913A, 1267.

10. Co-executors.—The partnership relation does not exist between co-executors, and they have no joint interest in the commissions allowed by law for services in administering upon the estate. They are not each entitled to an equal share, merely upon the naked ground of their relation to each other. The share to which they are respectively entitled is to be determined on entirely different considerations. In other words, their respective portions are not ascertained by any established rule of law, but on the principle of equality. The ratio of compensation and of services must be the same, or as nearly so as the circumstances of the case will permit. One who takes no care or charge upon himself, touching the estate, or any part thereof, collects no debts, makes no disbursements, and thus renders no service whatever, is not entitled to any share in the commissions.—Hope v. Jones, 24 Cal. 89, 92. The law declares that the commission should be apportioned to each executor in proportion to the labor he has performed.—Estate of Carter, 132 Cal. 113, 114, 64 Pac. 123. The court has power to divide commissions between two joint administrators, and its action will not be disturbed on appeal, where no abuse of discretion or error of law is shown.—Estate of Dudley, 123 Cal. 256, 257, 55 Pac. 897. A contract entered into between executors and devisees, as to the apportionment of commissions between them, can not be considered on the hearing of the final account by the probate court. That is not the place to settle disputes of this character. It is a matter which should be heard in another forum.—Estate of Carter, 132 Cal. 113, 114, 64 Pac. 123. A co-executor is not entitled to his commissions until the settlement of the final account; and if the apportionment of commissions has been made equally to each executor, based upon an implied finding that there was no substantial difference in the amount of services performed by each, and the evidence is fairly conflicting, the apportionment will not be disturbed on appeal.—Estate of Carter, 132 Cal. 113, 114, 64 Pac. 123. Where co-executors render separate accounts, the probate court should fix the compensation of each in proportion to the services rendered.—Hope v. Jones, 24 Cal. 90, 93.

11. Successive administrators.—There is but one aggregate sum to be allowed as commissions, which, in the case of successive administrations, must be apportioned by the court. There is, however, no basis upon which to make an apportionment until the closing of the estate. Sound judgment can not determine how much the first administrator is entitled to, unless the court knows and considers what the successor has done, and what the comparison is between his acts and those of his predecessor. The administration of an estate is an entirety. There may be different persons in office, at different times, or at the same time; but the claim of each to compensation must be considered with reference to each and all of the others.—In re Owen's Estate, 32 Utah 469, 91 Pac. 283, 285; Estate of Barton, 55 Cal. 87, 90; Ord v. Little, 3 Cal. 287. The allowance of commissions to the first of two successive administrators, if made before the closing of the estate, is premature.—In re Owen's Estate, 32 Utah 469, 91 Pac. 283, 285. Where one administrator has resigned, and has been succeeded by another, and some commissions have been paid, the proper time to make an allowance to each, of his reasonable proportion of commissions, is upon the final settlement of the estate.—Estate of Levison, 108 Cal. 450, 41 Pac. 483, 485; Estate of Barton, 55 Cal. 87, 90. Prior to 1911, when the California code was amended in that respect, statutory commissions could not be apportioned between successive administrators of an estate until the estate had been completely administered and was ready for distribution.—Estate of Piercy, Piercy v. Piercy, 168 Cal. 750, 145 Pac. 88. The apportionment allowed between joint or successive administrators and their attorneys under sections 1618 and 1619 of the California Code of Civil Procedure applies only to cases of general administration.—Estate of Miller, 15 Cal. App. 557, 115 Pac. 329. But the act of 1911, amending § 1616 of that code, provides for an application, after the expiration of one year from the grant of letters, for an allowance upon commissions, and this provision is applicable to successive administrators.—Estate of Piercy, Piercy v. Piercy, 168 Cal. 750, 145 Pac. 88. An administrator who has been removed is not entitled to statutory commissions, but, at most, to such part thereof as the court may apportion to him upon a consideration of the respective rights of the successive administrators; his recourse is simply to ask for a partial allowance.—Estate of Piercy, Piercy v. Piercy, 168 Cal. 755, 145 Pac. 91. The statutory commissions of administrators can be allowed but once, and must be divided between administrators if there are more than one.—In re Ross' Estate, 179 Cal. 358, 182 Pac. 303, 305.

12. Trustees.—In the absence of any direction in the will, or any evidence in relation thereto, the duties of a trustee named in the will, even though he be the person named as executor, would not begin until the duties of the executor have terminated; and until he commences to exercise his duties as trustee, he is not entitled to compensation therefor. If such person takes possession of the immediately upon his appointment as executor, and continues to administer the estate until the termination of his trust, the burden is upon him, if he would claim the compensation of a trustee rather than, that of an executor, to establish the point of time at which his official character took place.—Bemmerly v. Woodard, 136 Cal. 326, 331, 68 Pac. 1017. Trustees under a will are entitled to no compensation, commissions, or fees, under the will, for their management and care of property over which they have no control by virtue of any power under the will.—Blackenburg v. Jordan, 86 Cal. 171, 24 Pac. 1061; Berghauser v. Blanckenburg, 86 Cal. 316, 24 Pac. 1062. Where a petition by one of three trustees for a termination of the trust is successfully opposed by others, the action of the resisting trustees must be held to have been the successful defense of the trust, and their legitimate and necessary disbursements in this regard, such as attorney's fees, are chargeable against the trust property.—Estate of Hanson, 159 Cal. 401, 114 Pac. 810. The fact that the court, upon the first accounting by the trustees, allowed them the compensation fixed by the will for a period of time intervening between the date of the rendition of the decree, when the trust actually commenced, and the date of the entry of the decree, is not determinative of their right to future compensation.—Estate of Hanson, 159 Cal. 401, 114 Pac. 810. Under provisions in a will embodied in the decree distributing the testator's estate, directing that the trust estate shall be held by the trustee "for a period of five years from and after the date of the entry of this decree of distribution" and that the trustees shall receive a fixed annual compensation "during the full term of their trusteeship," the trustees are entitled to receive such compensation for the period of five years only. If by reason of the failure to formally enter the decree of distribution immediately upon its rendition, or for other reasons the duration of the trust is prolonged, the right of the trustees to compensation for the additional time should not rest upon the terms of the trust, but upon an award of the court in quantum meruit.—Estate of Hanson, 159 Cal. 401, 114 Pac. 810. If an executor is allowed full commissions, as such, under the law, a claim of his for more, advanced on the theory that he has acted also in the capacity of trustee, will not be considered.—In re Hagerty's Estate, Hagerty v. Work, 97 Wash. 491, 166 Pac. 1139. Where under a non-intervention will executors have a prolonged service as trustees imposed upon them they are allowed compensation by statute.—In re Cornett's Estate, Cornett v. West, 102 Wash. 254, 173 Pac. 44.

13. Special administrators.—Where the statute does not make any special provision for the compensation of a special administrator, but leaves it to the discretion of the court, in the settlement of his account, it is not improper for the court to take the rate of compensation fixed by the statute for an administrator as the standard for determining a proper allowance to be made to him.—Estate of Moore, 88 Cal. 1, 4, 25 Pac. 915.

14. Appeal.—An allowance of $200 for eight months' work in closing out a stock of goods, under the order of the court, will not be disturbed on appeal, where the statute authorized the court to allow an extra amount for extraordinary services.—In re Osburn's Estate, 36 Or. 8, 58 Pac. 521, 523. Neither will an order allowing an administrator a designated sum in addition to his statutory commissions, as a reasonable compensation for extraordinary services, be disturbed on appeal, where the appellant has not shown himself to be entitled to any more.—In re Partridge's Estate, 31 Or. 297, 51 Pac. 82, 83. So where the testator provided, in his will, that "for the purpose of settling my estate my executors shall be deemed executors; and for the purpose of managing my estate as aforesaid, and of investing the income not used for the said support and maintenance, and increasing the capital of my estate, they shall be deemed trustees, and shall be entitled to just compensation for their services," the provision relating to just compensation includes the settlement as well as the management of the estate; and if the court finds that the sum allowed is a just compensation, in addition to allowing it as the percentage provided by the statute on the value of the estate its judgment will not be disturbed on appeal.—In re Smith's Estate, 18 Wash. 129, 51 Pac. 348. Where the appellate court has jurisdiction in all probate matters, and the legislature has authorized an appeal from an order settling the account of an executor, irrespective of the amount involved, the fact that the share of the commissions in excess of the amount which should have been allowed, is less than $300 can not defeat the appellate jurisdiction.—Estate of Delaney, 110 Cal. 567, 42 Pac. 981. The refusal of the court below to allow an executor or administrator extra compensation will not be disturbed upon appeal where the evidence does not disclose any abuse of discretion by the trial court.—Estate of Hedrick, 127 Cal. 184, 188, 59 Pac. 590. In the absence of a showing as to the amount of the estate accounted for, as a basis from which to estimate commissions, it will be presumed, on appeal, that the allowance made by the court below fully meets the statutory requirement, where it does appear that the amount allowed covers the amount of the estate specifically shown.—In re Mason's Estate, 26 Wash. 259, 66 Pac. 435, 437.

III. ATTORNEYS' FEES.

1. In general.—There is no such office or position known to the law as "attorney of an estate." When an attorney is employed to render services in procuring a will to probate, or in settling the estate, he acts as the attorney of the executor or administrator, and not of the estate, and for his services the executor or administrator is personally answerable.—Estate of Ogier, 101 Cal. 381, 385, 40 Am. St. Rep. 61, 35 Pac. 900. While, in the settlement of the account of an executor or administrator, he will be allowed all necessary expenses in the care, management, and settlement of the estate, including reasonable fees paid to attorneys for conducting the necessary proceedings for suits in court, still, such allowance can be made only to him, and not to the attorney. Such allowance does not depend, in any way, upon contract between the administrator or executor and the attorney, but is an allowance made as a necessary expense of administration.—Estate of Ogier, 101 Cal. 381, 40 Am. St. Rep. 61, 35 Pac. 900; Estate of Levinson, 108 Cal. 450, 41 Pac. 483, 42 Pac. 479; Estate of Kruger, 123 Cal. 391, 55 Pac. 1056; Briggs v. Breen, 123 Cal. 657, 56 Pac. 633, 886; McKee v. Soher, 138 Cal. 367, 71 Pac. 438, 649; Estate of Kruger, 143 Cal. 141, 76 Pac. 891; Sullivan v. Lusk, 7 Cal. App. 186, 94 Pac. 91. An attorney's fee may or may not be an expense of administration, according to the circumstances of each case.—In re Nicholson, 1 Nev. 518. As fees of counsel are to be allowed out of the estate to the executor or administrator, it is error to direct that payment be made out of the estate to the attorneys.—Estate of Levinson, 108 Cal. 450, 458, 41 Pac. 483, 42 Pac. 479. An executor or administrator has the right to have the court, in the first instance, determine what amount shall be allowed as an attorney's fee before he pays the same. He is not required to make payment of the fee before an allowance thereof by the court.—Estate of Dudley, 123 Cal. 256, 257, 55 Pac. 897. Where a statute makes void all contracts for higher compensation between heir and executor or administrator, an agreement by the heir to compensate the executor or administrator for expenses incurred in employing attorneys other than such as may have been previously fixed by the court is as fully within the prohibition of the statute as to give a greater rate of commission than is fixed by the statute.—Firebaugh v. Burbank, 121 Cal. 186, 191, 53 Pac. 560. While it is true that the allowance to be made for commissions, attorneys' fees, and charges to close the administration of an estate can not be definitely fixed until the final settlement of the account of the executor, yet where the account filed by the executor immediately prior to the hearing for partial distribution is, for all practical purposes, a final account, and it, together with the accompanying exhibit, the inventory and appraisement, and the general proceedings in the estate, supplemented by the evidence upon the hearing, provides sufficient data from which the court may determine what would be a prudent, safe, and proper amount to be retained by the executor for the payment of his commissions, attorneys' fees, and expenses to be allowed on final settlement, it is proper for the court to determine such amount, where he retains more than the largest amount of commissions which, under any circumstances, the executor or administrator could obtain.—Estate of Straus, 144 Cal. 553, 556, 77 Pac. 1122. An attorney who has been employed by an executor has no lien upon the estate for his services.—Waite v. Willis, 42 Or. 288, 70 Pac. 1034, 1035. If an application for the allowance of compensation for extraordinary services of an attorney for the executor of a will has been denied, with the privilege of renewing the same, a second application for such allowance may be made.—Estate of Riviere, 8 Cal. App. 173, 98 Pac. 46, 47.

REFERENCES.

Allowance of attorneys' fees in suit for administration of decedent's estate.—See note 54 **L. R. A.** 817, 820. Power of administrators to make estates of decedents liable for attorneys' fees.—See note 93 **Am. Dec.** 393-397.

2. Province of court.—An executor or administrator has no power to make a contract with an attorney to give him an interest in the property of the estate as compensation for his services in recovering it.— Estate of Page, 57 Cal. 238, 241. But, whatever the agreement may be between the executor or administrator and the attorney, the sole question for the court in probate in any case is as to the amount that shall be allowed to the executor or administrator for legal services from the funds of the estate, and of this question the court in probate has sole and exclusive jurisdiction. The question as to what the attorney shall receive from the executor or administrator is an entirely different question, one of which the probate court has no jurisdiction, and is dependent altogether for its determination upon the agreement of the parties.—Estate of Kruger, 143 Cal. 141, 145, 76 Pac. 891. Those who render services of any kind to an executor or administrator for the purpose of assisting him in the execution of his trust must look to him alone for their compensation; and while the court in probate has the sole and exclusive jurisdiction to determine what amount shall be allowed to the executor or administrator from the estate for any such services rendered by him through others, it can not adjudicate between him and those whom he employs to assist him.—Estate of Kruger, 143 Cal. 141, 76 Pac. 891. The court has no power, in the absence of a stipulation, to fix an attorney's fee in an estate, but it can, and must, determine whether a fee charged is a reasonable sum to be charged to the estate on account of legal services rendered to the estate.—Estate of Brignole, 133 Cal. 162, 164, 65 Pac. 294. To justify a court in allowing to the executor or administrator a fee for the services of an attorney, the court must find that the services were needed by the estate, and were of advantage thereto, and were not in lieu of the duties imposed upon such executor.—Estate of Brignole, 133 Cal. 162, 65 Pac. 294; Firebaugh v. Burbank, 121 Cal. 186, 191, 53 Pac. 560. It being within the jurisdiction of the court in probate to fix the compensation which shall be allowed to the attorney of the personal representative of the deceased, it not only has jurisdiction to fix the value of services rendered by an attorney to the executor or administrator, on behalf of the estate, as an expense of administration, but has exclusive original jurisdiction to adjust and enforce such demand, and having jurisdiction, it must of necessity have power to do full and complete justice between the parties; and where an attorney contracts with the representative of the estate, knowing that, in law, the value of his services, so far as they are to be a burden upon the estate, is to be fixed by the court in probate, he can not be heard to say, if dereliction is charged against him, that the question is one not cognizable before that court, to which alone he must look for compensation. It is the duty of the court, in determining the compensation, to hear all evidence pertinent to the consideration, and it would indeed be extraordinary if an attorney, in support of his claim for compensation could be heard to urge his faithful performance of duty, and that, in answer, the opposing heirs should not be permitted to show that, by reason of his culpable dereliction, he was entitled to less compensation, or to none at all.—Estate of Kruger, 123 Cal. 391, 394, 55 Pac. 1056. Where the court has before it sufficient data from which to determine what would, in all probability, be a reasonable compensation for an attorney's fee, it is not necessary that any evidence of a professional nature should be introduced upon this subject. The court, of its own knowledge and experience, may determine what would be a reasonable fee, where all the proceedings in the estate, and all matters in which the executor or administrator could have enlisted or required the services of an attorney, are before the court.—Estate of Straus, 144 Cal. 553, 557, 77 Pac. 1122. The court is not bound to fix the amount of the fee in accordance with the opinion of expert witnesses as to the value of the services of an attorney.— Freese v. Pennie, 110 Cal. 469, 42 Pac. 978; Estate of Dorland, 63 Cal. 281. In fixing the compensation of an executor the probate court may take into consideration the fact that he has performed services as a lawyer by which expense to the estate has been saved.—Nelson v. Schoonover, 89 Kan. 779, Ann. Cas. 1915A, 147, 132 Pac. 1184. The proper fee to be awarded attorneys in probate proceedings is a difficult matter to be determined. Hence, it is one of those matters which must rest largely in the sound discretion of the trial court and should not be interfered with except for a manifest abuse of such discretion.— In re Lichtenberg's Estate, 58 Wash. 585, 109 Pac. 49. On application of attorney for compensation for other than ordinary probate services, court has same discretion as in allowing executor for fees by him already paid out.—In re Hite's Estate, 155 Cal. 448, 101 Pac. 448.

3. Statutory provisions.—It is a constitutional exercise of power for the legislature to provide for definite fees to be awarded to executors and administrators for their own services, and also an allowance to be made to them for their necessary expenses in the administration of the estate, including reasonable attorneys' fees; and there seems to be no difference, in principle, between an act establishing certain fees for the services of an executor or administrator, and one providing what he shall be allowed as payment for the services as an attorney. The latter is as much a part of the necessary expenses of administration as is the former. In fact, under our practice, the services of an attorney are not only essential, but the burden and responsibility of his work are usually much greater than those of the executor or administrator. It is competent, therefore, for the legislature to provide, as it has done, for the compensation in each instance, and the court can neither add to nor in any wise vary the compensation directed to be allowed by the statute.—Estate of Goodrich, 6 Cal. App. 730, 733, 93 Pac. 121, 122. The

late California statute modifies the previous law on the subject, authorizing reasonable attorneys' fees, etc., and provides a uniform standard.
And the law is valid, as providing for reasonable attorneys' fees.—
Estate of Goodrich, 6 Cal. App. 730, 732, 93 Pac. 121, 122. There is
nothing in the law to prevent an executor from making a contract with
an attorney to perform legal services for the estate for less than the
fees provided by the statute, and in that event he would obviously be
allowed only his actual expenditure. But where the contract was for
the full amount, and it was actually disbursed by the executors, the
court should not reduce it.—Estate of Goodrich, 6 Cal. App. 730, 734, 93
Pac. 121, 122. If an executor or administrator has been removed, the
expenses incurred by the former executor or administrator for attorneys' fees, in the performance of his duties, and presumably incident
to his trust, is a claim for which his successor becomes liable, and it is
not material whether the former executor or administrator ever filed
any final report, as that is not a prerequisite to the allowance of an
attorney's fee. Attorneys' fees may be allowed prior to final settlement.
—In re Miller's Estate, sub nom. Knight v. Hamaker, 40 Or. 424, 67 Pac.
107, 109. Authority to award costs in probate proceedings comes from
the statute, but this does not include an attorney's fee. They are not,
in any proper sense, a part of the costs.—Estate of Olmstead, 120 Cal.
447, 454, 52 Pac. 804.

4. Estate not chargeable.—It is well settled that an attorney can not
hold an estate liable for services rendered to the executor or administrator. His services are performed for and on behalf of the representative, for the purpose of assisting him in the execution of his trust.
It is true that the executor or administrator shall be allowed all necessary expenses in the care and management of the estate, including
reasonable fees paid to attorneys for conducting the necessary proceedings in suits in court, but such fees are allowed to the executor or
administrator, and not to the attorney. The estate is not liable, but
the executor or administrator is personally answerable.—McKee v.
Soher, 138 Cal. 367, 370, 71 Pac. 438, 649; Estate of Kruger, 143 Cal. 141,
145, 76 Pac. 891; Firebaugh v. Burbank, 121 Cal. 186, 191, 53 Pac. 560.
The attorney employed by an executor or administrator to assist him
in the execution of his trust has no claim that he can enforce against
the estate, either by action or in any other way. His claim is solely
against his client, the executor or administrator.—Estate of Kruger, 143
Cal. 141, 144, 76 Pac. 891. The estate is not chargeable with the claim
of an attorney at law for professional services rendered in pursuance
of a contract between himself and the heirs of a decedent, in compelling
the executor of the decedent to hasten his administration.—Estate of
Stuttmeister, 75 Cal. 346, 348, 17 Pac. 223. An executor or administrator can not charge the estate with expenses incurred in advising with
counsel whom he knows at the time to be representing interests and
demands antagonistic to the claims of the heirs as such, and with
respect to those very interests. He can not, in any case, or in any

manner, either by advice or otherwise, litigate any claim or demand
of one legatee or heir at the expenses of the estate, for this would be
compelling a legatee or heir to pay for the institution and maintenance
of litigation directed against himself; and this principle applies to litigation in matters of difference between parties who are not heirs and
legatees and those who are.—In re Davis' Estate, 31 Mont. 421, 78 Pac.
704, 705. An attorney's fee contracted in prosecuting letters of administration is not a proper charge against the estate. Such a debt is one
contracted in advance of any authority on the part of the representative
to obligate the estate to pay therefor, and is a personal liability only.—
Bowman v. Bowman, 27 Nev. 413, 76 Pac. 634, 636; Wilbur v. Wilbur, 17
Wash. 683, 50 Pac. 589. Whether the application for letters be successful or not, the estate is not to be charged with an attorney's fee
for the applicant.—Estate of Simmons, 43 Cal. 543, 547. The cases,
however, are not harmonious on the question as to whether a counsel
fee can be allowed to the successful applicant for letters of administration. Some of the cases hold that it may be allowed, and others not.—
See cases cited in Bowman v. Bowman, 27 Nev. 413, 76 Pac. 634. If a
person is appointed administrator, and subsequently a document is
found which purports to be a will, and which is offered for probate,
and the administrator, in contesting such probate, incurs an expense
for attorneys' fees for such purpose, the estate can not be charged
with the compensation for the services of such attorneys.—Estate of
Parsons, 65 Cal. 240, 3 Pac. 817. An executor or administrator is
clearly not entitled to reimbursement out of the estate for fees paid
to an attorney for services rendered, not to the estate, but to himself
personally; but where it is clear from the evidence that the fees were
paid out in matters strictly involving business of the estate; that the
services were rendered the administrator in consultation, advice, and
in proceedings relating to the administration of the estate, and that
no charges were made for personal services rendered to the executor
or administrator individually, and the charges are reasonable,—it is
proper for the court to allow his claim.—Rice v. Tilton, 14 Wyo. 101,
82 Pac. 577, 579. Where an administration has extended over a period
of years, and where attorneys were retained generally, and represented the estate in all litigation during that time, an account for services rendered is sufficiently itemized, where such account gives the
date of the commencement and the date of the closing of such services,
with the total amount claimed for the whole period.—In re Davis'
Estate, 31 Mont. 421, 78 Pac. 704, 705. An attorney's fee may or may
not be a proper charge as an expense of administration, dependent
on the necessity for an attorney; it is not incumbent on every administrator to employ an attorney.—Estate of Nicholson, 1 Nev. 518, 521.
The employment of an attorney by an executor or administrator is a
personal matter, in no way binding upon the estate. But if the services are necessary, the executor or administrator may be allowed
out of the estate a sufficient amount to compensate him for such

employment.—Waite v. Willis, 42 Or. 288, 70 Pac. 1034, 1035. A contest between an annuitant and a residuary legatee, as to which one is liable for the payment of an inheritance tax, to which a construction of the will is incidental, is not such a case as warrants the allowance of attorney's fees out of the estate.—In re Estate of Brown, 24 Haw. 573. If an administrator is in no way concerned in the determination of a controversy, the mere fact that the plaintiff brought him into the action could not authorize him to charge the estate with the burden of the expense incurred by him in litigating a controversy which affected the heirs alone.—In re Ross' Estate, 179 Cal. 358, 182 Pac. 303, 305. Money can not be allowed out of an estate for the compensation of a lawyer, employed to conduct a contest between persons claiming, as against each other, the real estate of the decedent as his heirs, even though the executors may have employed him.—Estate of Friedman, 176 Cal. 226, 168 Pac. 21. Inasmuch as an attorney has no demand against an estate for fees for professional services, an estate has none against an attorney for money which the administrator, solely on his own responsibility, has paid him.—State (ex rel. Cohen) v. District Court, 53 Mont. 210, 162 Pac. 1053. Under exceptional circumstances the unsuccessful appellants from a decree of the supreme court of the Territory of Hawaii to the supreme court of the United States were allowed counsel fees and expenses from the estate.—Fitchie v. Brown, 19 Haw. 411.

REFERENCES.

Liability of estate to attorney employed by executor or administrator.—See 25 L. R. A. (N. S.) 72. Right of executor to allowance for attorney's fee for services rendered in attempt to establish, or to resist attack upon, will.—See note 26 L. R. A. (N. S.) 757.

5. Necessity of notice.—The compensation of the attorney of the executor or administrator, while not a claim against the estate, is an expense of administration, allowed to the representative, the amount of which is to be fixed by the court and paid out of the estate; but such an order for the payment of money, by which the property of the heirs, legatees, and devisees is to be taken from them, can not be made without notice, and an opportunity to them to be heard.—Estate of Kruger, 123 Cal. 391, 55 Pac. 1056; In re Sullivan's Estate, 36 Wash. 217, 78 Pac. 945, 947. Ordinarily, the account of the executor or administrator includes the item of attorneys' fees as an expense of administration; and when the notice required by law, of the hearing and settlement of the account, is duly given, the parties in interest are afforded an opportunity of contesting that, with any other items which fail to meet their approval; but where the final account of the executor or administrator contains no hint or suggestion that it was proposed to make any charge on account of the services of an attorney, an order of the court fixing the compensation of the attorney, without notice to the parties in interest, is void, though upon all matters properly embraced within the account due notice is given.—

Estate of Kruger, 123 Cal. 391, 55 Pac. 1056. If an executor or administrator pays money to himself for his own services, or makes payment for attorneys' fees, pending the course of the administration, without due hearing upon notice, he does so at his peril, for the court can enter no orders or judgment that will protect him, until the interested parties are before it, or until they have been properly notified.—In re Sullivan's Estate, 36 Wash. 217, 78 Pac. 945, 946. If the statute authorizes the court to appoint an attorney to represent devisees and legatees who are minors, and have no general guardian, and to fix the fee of the person so appointed, it will be presumed that the order fixing the attorney's fee, under such appointment, to represent the minor heirs, was made on notice; and this presumption prevails, unless the record affirmatively shows notice was not given. The mere fact that there never had been any previous account filed by the executor or administrator, though such fact is shown by the record, does not conclusively establish want of notice to all parties interested of the application for the fixing of the fee.—Estate of Carpenter, 146 Cal. 661, 80 Pac. 1072, 1073.

6. What is no waiver of fee.—The allowance of attorneys' fees, expenses, and for extraordinary services are matters which can only be adjudicated in the probate court in the final or some subsequent account. The mere fact that the executor or administrator made no such claim when filing his previous accounts should not be taken as an absolute waiver. But the reimbursement to which an executor or administrator is entitled, on account of such payments or such services, is a right personal to himself, and one which he may waive; and until it is asserted, either by the administrator, or by his personal representatives, in an account, and upon a petition presented to the probate court, they are not proper subjects of adjudication.—Elizalde v. Murphy, 4 Cal. App. 114, 87 Pac. 245, 246.

7. Personal liability for.—If the attorney has any claim upon the executor or administrator by reason of any contract for compensation, he must look to the executor or administrator as an individual, and not in his representative capacity; and an action to enforce such a contract would not lie against him in the latter capacity.—Sullivan v. Lusk, 7 Cal. App. 186, 94 Pac. 91, 92; Estate of Kruger, 143 Cal. 141, 76 Pac. 891; McKee v. Soher, 138 Cal. 367, 370, 71 Pac. 438, 649; Briggs v. Breen, 123 Cal. 657, 659, 56 Pac. 633, 886; Estate of Ogier, 101 Cal. 381, 385, 40 Am. St. Rep. 61, 35 Pac. 900; Hunt v. Maldanado, 89 Cal. 636, 27 Pac. 56; Estate of Scott, 1 Cal. App. 740, 746, 83 Pac. 85. An executor or administrator is usually, as a matter of fact, protected against any personal responsibility by the agreement of the attorney that he will accept the amount allowed by the court in full compensation for his services, but this is a matter entirely between the attorney and the executor or administrator, and in no way affects the probate proceeding. The effect of such an agreement, so far as the attorney is concerned, is precisely the same as if the attorney

and executor had agreed that the amount to be paid to the attorney by the executor should be fixed by some third party. It may be, where such an agreement is made, that the executor or administrator would be legally bound to submit to the court an application for the allowance of counsel fees, and would be personally answerable to his attorney for the reasonable value of the services, if he failed to do so, but the probate court has sole and exclusive jurisdiction of the question as to the amount that shall be allowed to the executor or administrator for legal expenses from the funds of the estate.—Estate of Kruger, 145 Cal. 141, 145, 76 Pac. 891. The testator's selection, in his will, of an attorney is not binding on his executor, but is simply an advisory provision, which he may disregard if he chooses to do so. The reason for this is, that, if the attorney employed should be derelict in his duty, and should receive and misappropriate funds of the estate, the executor would be liable therefor to the legatees under the will; and this being so, it would not be reasonable or right to hold that the executor of a will must necessarily accept the services of an attorney selected by the testator.—Estate of Ogier, 101 Cal. 381, 385, 40 Am. St. Rep. 61, 35 Pac. 900. If there is no agreement that the attorneys shall look for their fees to the estate, or an allowance therefrom by the court, it follows that the executors or administrators are answerable personally to them for their reasonable compensation.—Briggs v. Breen, 123 Cal. 657, 659, 56 Pac. 633, 886. The determination of the court, in allowing an attorney's fee, is not a determination of the character of the contract made by the executor and attorney as to the amount of the fee the attorney is to be paid for his services. Upon the contrary, it is simply a determination as to the amount of the fee that the estate should be held to pay. If the executor or administrator agreed to pay an amount in excess of that sum, then such excess becomes purely a personal matter between the contracting parties; but if, by special contract with the executor or administrator, the attorney has agreed to perform the services for a specified sum, which is less than the court might deem the services worth to the estate, then another question will be presented. In any event, if, by the contract of the parties, the fee is to be fixed by the court, according to the value of the services rendered, such an agreement is, in effect, a personal release of the executor or administrator from any personal liability whatever for an attorney's fee.—Estate of Kasson, 119 Cal. 489, 491, 51 Pac. 706. An executor or administrator may make himself personally liable for an attorney's fee, but he can not be permitted to charge the same back to the estate.—In re Davis' Estate, 31 Mont. 421, 78 Pac. 704, 705. The employment of counsel for the administrator, and payment for the services of such counsel, is a matter of personal and private agreement between the executor or administrator and counsel, to be reported to the court as any other expense in due course of administration for the allowance or disallowance of the court. Hence if the administrator refuses to pay a sum claimed for attorneys' fees, or any other sum, and has not contracted with counsel to abide by any finding of the court as to the amount, if any, to be paid counsel, the court has no power to order the executor or administrator to include any sum of money in his accounts as due to such counsel, or to segregate or to set aside any sum from the funds of the estate for the use of counsel, and to order the executor or administrator to amend his final account as including such an allowance therein.—State v. Second Jud. Dist. Court, 25 Mont. 33, 63 Pac. 717, 718. The estate of a decedent is not primarily liable for legal services rendered for the benefit of such estate at the request of the personal representative. Such services are performed for and on behalf of the executor or administrator, who is personally liable for the payment thereof, and for all such reasonable expenditures he is entitled to reimbursement from the estate.—Besancon v. Wegner, 16 N. D. 240, 112 N. W. 965. Prior to the amendment of 1905 to section 1616, Code of Civil Procedure of California, the attorney of an executor or administrator was not a party interested in the estate of a deceased person and must look solely to the executor or administrator for his compensation, such officer being allowed credit on his accounting for such reasonable fees as he had paid his attorney.— Estate of Hite, 155 Cal. 448, 101 Pac. 448. Attorneys employed by an administrator to assist him in administering his trust, or to prosecute or defend an action for or against him in his official capacity, have no claim they can enforce directly against the estate. The administrator is individually liable for such services, and upon settlement of his accounts he may be reimbursed out of the estate for attorney's fees necessarily paid out as expenses of administration.—Brown v. Quinton, 80 Kan. 44, 18 Ann. Cas. 290, 25 L. R. A. (N. S.) 71, 102 Pac. 242. There is no law requiring an executor or administrator to employ an attorney, although, if he does employ one, the person employed is, if he renders valuable services, entitled to compensation.—Estate of Murphy, 171 Cal. 697, 154 Pac. 839. Engagements between an administrator and an attorney for services to be rendered the estate are wholly personal, standing entirely on the individual responsibility of the contracting parties, and create no relation between the attorney and the estate.—State (ex rel. Cohen) v. District Court, 53 Mont. 210, 162 Pac. 1053. If an executor engages the services of an attorney for the estate, agreeing that he will advance him money from time to time and that the balance is to be paid on the closing of the administration, this does not negative the presumption that the executor is to be looked to personally for payment.—Wight v. Dolenty, 53 Mont. 168, 162 Pac. 387. In paying an attorney for professional services, without first asking the probate court for an allowance for that purpose, an administrator acts at his peril.—State (ex rel Cohen) v. District Court, 53 Mont. 210, 162 Pac. 1053. An executor or administrator who employs an attorney to perform services for the estate is presumed to have agreed to pay the fee himself; and the burden is on him to show some other agreement.—Wight v. Dolenty, 53 Mont. 168, 162 Pac. 387.

REFERENCES.

Personal liability for attorneys' fees.—See, also, head-line 4, ante.

8. What may properly be allowed.—An executor or administrator, acting in good faith, is entitled to the aid of counsel in all litigation touching the estate, and to be allowed, in his account, the reasonable compensation paid such counsel.—Estate of Miner, 46 Cal. 564, 572. It is his right, and ordinarily his duty, to employ competent counsel to aid him in the management of adversary suits in which the estate may be involved while under his care, and fees for such services may be allowed to him from the assets of the estate.—Estate of Simmons, 43 Cal. 543, 548. An executor or administrator is entitled to a reasonable compensation for attorneys' fees in any necessary litigation or matter requiring legal advice or counsel. It is the duty of an executor to keep and render a just account of his trust, and, if he thinks proper, to keep a clerk for that purpose, but he must do it at his own expense. His claim for attorneys' fees should ordinarily be presented in an itemized form, and not for an aggregate amount by the year, but, under peculiar circumstances, this rule will not be enforced.—Steele v. Holladay, 20 Or. 462, 26 Pac. 562, 564. It is proper for the court to allow an attorney's fee paid by the administrator in defending a suit brought against the decedent in his lifetime to foreclose the lien of a street assessment, where such defense was successful.—Estate of Heeney, 3 Cal. App. 548, 553, 86 Pac. 842. The executor or administrator should also be allowed a reasonable sum on account of an attorney's fee incurred by him on appeal from an order of the probate court settling his account, where he obtains a reversal of the order.—Estate of Moore, 96 Cal. 522, 531, 32 Pac. 584. He is also entitled to the allowance of an attorney's fee for the services and traveling expenses of his attorney, not exceeding a reasonable compensation for the labor actually performed, when the same was necessary to enable him to properly perform the duties of his trust.—Estate of Moore, 72 Cal. 335, 342, 13 Pac. 880; Estate of Rose, 80 Cal. 166, 122 Pac. 86. An attorney, appointed to defend an action upon a claim presented against the estate by an executor, is also entitled to fees for his services rendered in the supreme court on appeal from a judgment against the claimant.—Painter v. Estate of Painter, 78 Cal. 625, 627, 21 Pac. 433. If an executor or administrator pays an attorney's fee without prior order of the court, he takes chances upon the ultimate disapproval, if the court should not agree with him respecting the justness of the account paid. But where the account, as presented, is reasonable in sum, and calculated on a just basis, it should be allowed as filed, though the claim is for a contingent fee. An executor or administrator is entitled to proper credits in his account for all disbursements made in good faith on behalf of the estate, in the course of administration, whether they concern its necessary expenses, or what may be laid out in recovering assets. And this rule extends so far as to justify the representative

In making contracts with counsel for fees, contingent on the recovery of assets, and therefore estimated at a larger figure than would be proper, where the compensation was certain, and dependent on a contract which was enforceable in any event as against the representative. —Filbeck v. Davies, 8 Colo. App. 320, 46 Pac. 214. No fee should be allowed to the attorney of an executor or administrator for traveling expenses in attending the hearing of a contest of letters of administration.—Estate of Byrne, 122 Cal. 260, 261, 54 Pac. 957; but the proper traveling expenses of an attorney employed by the administrator to take an appeal from what was deemed an erroneous order of sale of real estate, such expenses being incurred to enable him intelligently and properly to prosecute the claim, should be allowed, in addition to his fees in the settlement of accounts of the administrator.—Estate of Byrne, 122 Cal. 260, 267, 54 Pac. 957. An attorney can obtain by an application for fees for legal services made under section 1616 of the California Code of Civil Procedure only such sums as are properly allowable to the executor or administrator as necessary expenses in the discharge of his duties.—Estate of Higgins, 158 Cal. 355, 111 Pac. 8. If an administrator pays his attorney, in anticipation of an allowance by the court for attorneys' fees, he acts at his peril; he can be allowed only necessary expenses, in the care, management, and settlement of the estate, and his judgment may be rejected by the court on the score of the amount as well as of necessity.—State (ex rel. Cohen) v. District Court, 53 Mont. 210, 162 Pac. 1053.

9. What can not be allowed.—While the probate court has sole and exclusive jurisdiction to determine what amount shall be allowed to the executor or administrator for the amount of services rendered by him through an attorney, it can not adjudicate questions between him and the attorney.—Estate of Kruger, 143 Cal. 141, 147, 76 Pac. 891. Executors, administrators, receivers, and trustees are, in their official capacity, indifferent persons, as between the real parties in interest. They are appointed by the court, or by will, and act on behalf of all the parties who claim any interest in the estate. They can not, therefore, litigate the claims of one heir against those of another, and they have no concern in the question as to who shall bear the costs of the litigation.—Goldfield v. Thompson, 83 Cal. 420, 422, 23 Pac. 383. If the executors or administrators attempt to create a charge against the estate, under a contract with the heir for a greater compensation for the payment of an attorney's fee than that previously fixed by the court, such contract is void, and no extra allowance should be made.—Firebaugh v. Burbank, 121 Cal. 186, 191, 53 Pac. 560. Parties interested in an estate have the right to show that the services of an attorney have been so negligently performed as to cause damage to the estate, and consequently that the estate should not pay therefor.— Estate of Kruger, 143 Cal. 141, 147, 76 Pac. 891, 130 Cal. 621, 63 Pac. 31. No fee should be allowed to an attorney for services in contesting the probate of a will on behalf of the administrator.—Estate of Par-

sons, 65 Cal. 240, 3 Pac. 817. On the successful contest of the probate of a will, the court has discretionary power to order costs to be paid by any party to the proceedings, or out of the assets of the estate, as justice may require; but, as attorneys' fees are not costs, the court has no power to make such fees payable out of assets of the estate.—Estate of Olmstead, 120 Cal. 447, 453, 52 Pac. 804. Until a will has been admitted to probate, the court has no power to appropriate the funds of the estate, to aid either the proponents or contestants; but, after a will has been admitted to probate, and executors appointed, it is undoubtedly their duty to defend and to uphold the will, and attorneys employed for such purposes are clearly entitled to a reasonable compensation for their services.—Estate of McKinney, 112 Cal. 447, 454, 44 Pac. 743. Unless the statute permits the court to allow to an administrator not only a certain percentage for commissions, but also such other sum as the court may deem reasonable for extra· trouble, no additional allowance for costs and charges in collecting and defending claims against the estate can be made to an administrator, who is also a lawyer, for legal services rendered to the estate.—Doss v. Stevens, 13 Colo. App. 535, 59 Pac. 67, 70. An administrator, who is also a lawyer, is required to exercise his professional skill and to conduct the business of the estate himself, unless there is a necessity shown for the employment of legal assistance; and he should be required to do so without extra compensation, where it is just an ordinary administration with no legal or other complication.—Noble v. Whitten, 38 Wash. 262, 80 Pac. 451, 454. An executor or administrator should not be allowed an attorney's fee concerning matters with which he, as executor or administrator, had nothing to do, as in the matter of procuring the removal of the guardian of minor heirs.—Estate of Rose, 80 Cal. 166, 179, 22 Pac. 86. He is not entitled to an allowance for fees paid to an attorney for his services in resisting the claims of a pretermitted heir.—Estate of Jessup, 80 Cal. 625, 22 Pac. 260. No attorneys' fee should be allowed for services which were rendered for another estate, and which were paid for.—In re Mason's Estate, 26 Wash. 259, 66 Pac. 435, 436. Where counsel have been retained to protect the estate, and no exigency is presented requiring additional counsel, it is wrong for the court to allow anything further in that behalf. While an executor or administrator is allowed counsel, not only to advise him in the management of the affairs of his trust, but also for conducting such litigation as may necessarily arise from time to time, the assets of the estate are not for him to expend as he chooses, or to further his own ends. He must be guided by prudence and the requirements of the estate. It is within the discretion of the court to reimburse him for necessary expenses in this behalf. But the burden is upon him to show that they have been rendered necessary by the requirements of the estate; and if he fails to sustain this burden, the court should disallow any such charge.—In re Davis' Estate, 33 Mont. 539, 88 Pac. 957, 959. No allowance should be made to an executor or administrator for the services of an attorney employed to do work including services for which the executor or administrator receives a commission. Such services should be paid for by the executor or administrator himself.—Estate of Brignole, 133 Cal. 162, 164, 65 Pac. 294; Estate of Moore, 72 Cal. 335, 342, 13 Pac. 880. In an action by an administrator for damages for the death of his decedent, his duties as assistant district attorney are within the scope of his duties as administrator, and he can not make a contract with his attorneys for additional compensation as assistant attorney in the case.—In re Evans, 22 Utah 366, 83 Am. St. Rep. 794, 53 L. R. A. 952, 62 Pac. 913.

REFERENCES.

Attorneys' fees should not be allowed to representative, when.—See note ante, after § 646, on powers and duties of executors and administrators, I, 5, (6), on power to bind estate.

10. Reasonableness of fee.—The question as to what shall be allowed to the executor or administrator from the estate for legal services, as well as all other necessary expenses, is one solely between such executor or administrator on the one side, and those entitled to succeed to the residue of the estate, after the payment of the expense of administration, on the other side.—Estate of Kruger, 143 Cal. 141, 144, 76 Pac. 891. The court must determine whether a fee charged is a reasonable sum to be charged to the estate on account of legal services rendered to it.—Estate of Brignole, 133 Cal. 162, 164, 65 Pac. 294. The administrator's allowance of a claim for an attorney's fee does not make out a prima facie case in favor of its validity, if objected to on the final account, but the claimant must substantiate the reasonableness of the several charges by proof thereof.—In re Mills' Estate, Knight v. Hamaker, 40 Or. 424, 67 Pac. 107, 1010; as to the reasonableness of an attorney's fee under varying circumstances, see In re McCullough's Estate, 31 Or. 36, sub nom.; Muldrick v. Galbraith, 49 Pac. 886; In re Osburn's Estate, 36 Or. 8, 58 Pac. 521; In re Davis' Estate, 31 Mont. 421, 78 Pac. 704; In re Sullivan's Estate, 36 Wash. 217, 78 Pac. 945. An attorney whose services are effective in the settlement, under a non-intervention will, of an estate appraised at $411,000, including over 400 separate pieces of real estate, many of them subject to tax certificates, such to the extent of upwards of $85,000 it was his care to satisfy, is entitled to $6000 as a reasonable fee.—Snook v. Kennedy, 103 Wash. 390, 174 Pac. 643. An allowance to an executor of $2500 for counsel fees in an estate appraised at upwards of $37,000 is not excessive.—In re Witt's Estate, 72 Wash. 172, 132 Pac. 1013. In an estate of $600,000, having regard to the amount and responsibility of the work done, an attorney's ·fee of $13,000 is excessive and $8750 is reasonable and adequate.—Shufeldt v. Hughes, 55 Wash. 246, 104 Pac. 257.

11. Co-executors and special administrators.—If the court allows an aggregate sum to be drawn from court by three executors to pay attorneys' fees, without direction as to apportionment between the attorneys employed by two of them and an attorney employed by the third, it has power, upon the settlement of the final account, to deduct an allowance from the amount paid to the former, and to increase the allowance made to the executors for the latter. The court has no power to fix the attorneys' fees and to apportion the money between the attorneys, but it does have power to allow the executors represented by two of the attorneys a designated sum as attorneys' fees, and the other executor, represented by another attorney, a stated sum incurred as an attorney's fee.—Estate of Scott, 1 Cal. App. 740, 746, 83 Pac. 85; but see Estate of Dudley, 123 Cal. 256, 55 Pac. 897. Where there are several executors or administrators, the act of the majority can not deprive one of the executors or administrators of the assistance or advice of counsel. If there are three executors, it is true that the estate may be put to more expense for attorneys' fees, but that was for the deceased to consider in making his will. Certainly a testator who appoints three friends, in whose judgment and integrity he confides, does not intend that one of them shall be ignored and not allowed expenses which are allowed to the others.—Estate of Scott, 1 Cal. App. 740, 748, 83 Pac. 85. The court has no power to authorize a special administrator to defray the expenses of a controversy over the probate of a will, unless expressly authorized to do so by the statute. Conceding that counsel fees for services rendered the executor or administrator in probating the will may be regarded as "costs," they can not be allowed, except as an incident to some judgment or order of the court. The probate judge is clothed with discretion to order costs to be paid by any party to the proceeding, or out of the assets of the estate, as justice may require; but this discretion can not be exercised until there is something upon which it may be based.— Henry v. Superior Court, 93 Cal. 569, 571, 29 Pac. 230. An allowance may be made to an attorney of an executor and special administrator out of the assets of the estate for compensation on account of extraordinary services rendered by a person as such attorney.—Estate of Riviere, 7 Cal. App. 755, 96 Pac. 16, 17.

12. **Further allowance.**—Where an allowance has been made by the probate court to an attorney for the administrator "on account" of extraordinary services, the court has jurisdiction to construe the words "on account" in its own order to indicate that the allowance made therein was not intended to cover compensation in full for such services, and, where no abuse of discretion appears, a further allowance will be sustained.—In re Ross' Estate, 179 Cal. 358, 182 Pac. 303, 305.

13. **Contracts as to, effect of.**—Where assets of an estate consist of a partnership interest, and the winding up of the partnership affairs involves a change of the concern into a corporation, so that the interest of the decedent is paid to the estate in shares of stock, the attorney for a distributee, if he has contracted with his client

for a portion of his distributive part, by way of compensation, must accept payment in the form that such part is received by the client.— Cooley v. Miller & Lux, 168 Cal. 120, 142 Pac. 83. Where non-residents, who have interests in an estate in course of administration in this state, employ a local attorney to look after such interests agreeing that his compensation shall be so much a share of what they receive, but, pending the administration, cancel this agreement and substitute one making him a present grant of a percentage of their shares, for services rendered up to that time and to be rendered thereafter, the grant is to be regarded as an immediate transfer, rather than a security, even though there be an accompanying provision whereby any allowance made to him by the court should, in the first place, be applied on current outlays in the service and then credited to them on final settlement.—Cooley v. Miller & Lux, 168 Cal. 120, 142 Pac. 83.

14. Recovery of fee.—No action can be maintained against the estate of a deceased person by an attorney for legal services rendered by him for the benefit of the estate at the request of the personal representative.—Besancon v. Wegner, 16 N. D. 240, 112 N. W. 965. If the attorney has any claim upon the executor or administrator by reason of any contract for compensation, he must look to the executor or administrator as an individual, and not in his representative capacity; and an action to enforce such a contract would not lie against him in the latter capacity.—Sullivan v. Lusk, 7 Cal. App. 186, 94 Pac. 91, 92. An executor or administrator is personally answerable to his attorney for the reasonable value of the latter's services, regardless of the amount allowed by the probate court. It follows, therefore, that an allowance made to him for attorneys' fees is not conclusive on the attorneys.—Estate of Scott, 1 Cal. App. 740, 83 Pac. 85; and an adjudication by the court as to the amount which an attorney should receive as an attorney's fee can not be pleaded in bar of any right of action which the attorney may have on any contract made by him with the executor or administrator as an individual.—Sullivan v. Lusk, 7 Cal. App. 186, 94 Pac. 91, 92. If the agreement was that the attorney should receive from the executor or administrator a certain specified sum for his services, the executor or administrator would be personally answerable for that sum, regardless of what the court in probate might allow the executor or administrator; and if the agreement was simply that the attorney should receive from the executor or administrator what his services were reasonably worth, he could recover from the executor, by personal action against him, the sum adjudged therein to be the reasonable value of his services, regardless of the adjudication of the court in probate as to what constituted such reasonable value.—Estate of Kruger, 143 Cal. 141, 146, 76 Pac. 891; Briggs v. Breen, 123 Cal. 657, 56 Pac. 633, 886. In an action to recover the reasonable value of services rendered to co-executors jointly by an attorney, an executor may be joined with the administrator of a deceased executor, but the recovery of the

latter is limited to payment in due course of administration.—Briggs
v. Breen, 123 Cal. 657, 662, 56 Pac. 633, 886. If each of two administrators have severally employed attorneys, and the powers of one
of them is suspended after the settlement of his accounts, and the
fees of an attorney had been paid by the administrator who employed
him, such fee can not be again recovered, although it had been fixed
in the decree settling the final account. Credit, in the account, for
the sum so allowed does not constitute a judgment or adjudication
in favor of the attorney against either the estate or the executor, and
can not be made the foundation of an action by him against either.
The decree only fixes the allowance of an attorney's fee as an expense
of administration, and it could be allowed in the decree after it was
paid as well as before.—McKee v. Soher, 138 Cal. 367, 371, 71 Pac.
438, 649. There is a distinction between a bill of particulars for an
attorney's services, and bills of particulars of accounts generally, and
where the statement, as rendered by an attorney, informs the defendant fully of the character of the services, the manner in which they
were rendered, the transaction out of which the services arose, and
the aggregate value of the whole, nothing more should be required.
He should not be held to that degree of strictness which would be
necessary in a statement of merchandise sold and delivered. Where
the retainer is general, and the attorney advises his client, or performs
services in a number of distinct matters, he may properly be required
to set out his charge for each separate matter; but, when the services
all relate to one subject, it forms no just measure of the services to
separate the services into parts, and to have the attorney state what
charge he makes for each separate part. The only correct method is
to view the service as a whole, since, by no other method, can one of
its most important elements, namely, the result of the service to the
client, be taken into account in estimating the value of the services.—
Moore v. Scharnikow, 48 Wash. 564, 94 Pac. 117, 120. Upon an application to the court to fix the amount of compensation for the services
of an attorney for the executor or administrator, the court has power
to do full and complete justice between the parties, and to consider
any damage that may have occasioned by the negligence of the
attorney in the conduct of litigation on behalf of the estate.—Estate
of Kruger, 123 Cal. 391, 55 Pac. 1056. In an action in equity for
an accounting against the executor of a deceased administrator the
court may, where it has jurisdiction both in equity and in matters of
probate, determine the amount due the attorney of the deceased administrator.—Pennie v. Roach, 94 Cal. 515, 521, 29 Pac. 956, 30 Pac. 106.

15. Recovery of more than amount allowed.—Although the court
allows the executor or administrator an amount which it deems reasonable for the fees of his attorney, such allowance, in the absence of
agreement, is not binding upon the attorney, and he may recover more
than the amount allowed, provided the allowance was not reasonable.—

McKee v. Soher, 138 Cal. 367, 370, 71 Pac. 438, 649; Estate of Scott, 1 Cal. App. 740, 747, 83 Pac. 85.

16. Appeal.—An order allowing an attorney's fee to the attorney of an executor or administrator is an appealable order.—Estate of Kruger, 123 Cal. 391, 392, 55 Pac. 1056. The order made upon an application by an attorney for compensation on account of extraordinary services rendered by him is an appealable order.—Estate of Riviere, 7 Cal. App. 755, 96 Pac. 16, 17. The order directing the administrator of an estate to pay the demand of an attorney for services rendered to the administrator during the progress of the settlement of the estate, while not technically a "claim" against the estate, is appealable.—Stuttmeister v. Superior Court, 72 Cal. 487, 14 Pac. 35. Any person interested in the estate of a decedent has the right to appeal from an order allowing, out of the assets of the estate, compensation to an attorney on account of extraordinary services rendered by him for the benefit of the estate.—Estate of Riviere, 7 Cal. App. 755, 96 Pac. 16, 17. The discretion of the court below in allowing an attorney's fee to an executor or administrator of an estate will not be disturbed on appeal, in the absence of any showing that such discretion has been abused; as, where the allowance made is less than the estimate of any expert witness who testified, and was consented to by the attorney for the sole heir interested in the estate.—Freese v. Pennie, 110 Cal. 467, 470, 42 Pac. 978; Estate of Adams, 131 Cal. 415, 63 Pac. 838; or where there is conflicting evidence as to the value of the services rendered to the estate by the attorneys and the amount allowed by the court finds support in the evidence.—In re Levinson, 108 Cal. 450, 457, 41 Pac. 483, 42 Pac. 479; or where the court has exercised a discretion in apportioning the allowance of counsel fees between joint administrators.—Estate of Dudley, 123 Cal. 256, 257, 55 Pac. 897. The amount fixed by the court as counsel fees for an executor or administrator will not be disturbed, where no abuse of discretion is shown.—Estate of Gasq., 42 Cal. 288, 290. Upon the reversal of an order appointing an administrator, such person is not entitled to the payment of an attorney's fee and costs expended by him in making the contest.—Estate of Barton, 55 Cal. 87, 90. As the court has no jurisdiction of an appeal taken by an attorney from a decree settling the executor's final account, such appeal will be dismissed.—Estate of Kruger, 143 Cal. 141, 147, 76 Pac. 891. So trustees appointed under a will, who have sued to obtain, for their direction, a construction of certain clauses therein, are not aggrieved by an order allowing the attorney and guardian ad litem for the minor heirs a fee for his services, to be paid by the trustees out of the estate, and their appeal from such order will be dismissed.—Goldtree v. Thompson, 83 Cal. 420, 422, 23 Pac. 383. Where the evidence is not set forth in the record upon appeal, error in the allowance of an attorney's fee is not to be presumed, and, in the absence of evidence, the court can not say that the lower court erred in refusing to allow the expenditure

as a charge against the estate.—Estate of Scott, 1 Cal. App. 740, 743, 83 Pac. 85. It is harmless error for the judgment allowing an attorney's fee to direct that the administrator pay out of the estate to the defendant in the action "for the use and benefit of an attorney," or to "said attorney in person," as payment is not required to be made to the attorney in person. Any invalidity or error in specifying such alternative in the judgment may therefore be disregarded.—Pennie v. Roach, 94 Cal. 515, 519, 29 Pac. 956, 30 Pac. 106. Where a case has been appealed by an administrator, his commissions definitely fixed, and the case remanded, the judge below is not authorized to allow a fee to the attorney for the legatees, and to make the same a charge against the administrator's commissions.—Estate of Alina, 13 Haw. 630, 631. Under the California Code of Civil Procedure, section 1616, an attorney may appeal from an order denying compensation for services rendered to an administrator.—In re Hite's Estate, 155 Cal. 448, 101 Pac. 448. An order directing the payment of attorney's fees incurred by an unsuccessful proponent of a will, payable out of the assets of the estate, is an order directing the payment of a claim against the estate, and under subdivision 3 of section 963, or under section 1616, Code of Civil Procedure of California, is an appealable order. Prohibition will not lie to restrain the making of such order.—Mousnier v. Superior Court, 159 Cal. 663, 115 Pac. 221. Where an estate was appraised at upwards of $144,000, but its actual value was hardly more than one-fourth of that amount, an allowance to an attorney, who acted for the executrix, of a fee of $1025, was considered by the supreme court to be too much; from a consideration of the record, $500 was considered an ample allowance for such fee.—In re Johnston's Estate (Wash.), 181 Pac. 209, 214. Where the question of the necessity and reasonableness of the fees of an attorney of the administratrix, employed in the business of the estate, is tried in the district court on appeal from the county court, and on the hearing in the district court evidence was introduced, and the district court refused to allow them, the supreme court can not review the judgment of the district court in the absence of an assignment of error for overruling the motion for a new trial.—In re McGannon's Estate, 50 Okla. 288, 299, 150 Pac. 1109.

CHAPTER II.

ACCOUNTING AND SETTLEMENTS BY EXECUTORS AND ADMINISTRATORS.

ACCOUNTING AND SETTLEMENT BY EXECUTORS AND
ADMINISTRATORS.

§ 656. Exhibit of condition of estate.

When required by the court, either upon its own motion or upon the application of any person interested in the estate, the executor or administrator must render an exhibit under oath, showing the amount of money received and expended by him, the amount of all claims filed or presented against the estate, and the names of the claimants, and all other matters necessary to show the condition of its affairs.—*Kerr's Cyc. Code Civ. Proc.,* § 1622.

ANALOGOUS AND IDENTICAL STATUTES.

No identical statute found.

Arizona—Revised Statutes of 1913, paragraph 995.

Colorado—Mills's Statutes of 1912, section 8019.

Hawaii—Revised Laws of 1915, section 2492.

Idaho—Compiled Statutes of 1919, section 7691.

Montana—Revised Codes of 1907, section 7634.

North Dakota—Compiled Laws of 1913, section 8822.

Oklahoma—Revised Laws of 1910, section 6428.

South Dakota—Compiled Laws of 1913, section 5889.

Utah—Compiled Laws of 1907, section 3941.

Washington—Laws of 1917, chapter 156, page 687, section 159.

Wyoming—Compiled Statutes of 1910, section 5582.

§ 657. Form. Exhibit for information of court.

[Title of court.]

[Title of estate.] {No. ——.1 Dept. No. ——.
[Title of form.]

To the Honorable the —— [2] Court of the County [8] of
——, State of ——.

——, administrator [4] of the estate of ——, deceased,
renders the following exhibit for the information of the
court:

Statement of Moneys Received by Administrator. [5]

[Give items, with date, from whom received, source
from which the money comes, and amount of each item,
with the total amount.]

Statement of Moneys Expended by Administrator. [6]

[Give items, with date, to whom paid, and amount of
each item, with the total amount.]

Balance in hands of administrator, [7] $——.

Amount of Claims, and Names of Claimants.

The following are the names of those who presented
claims against the estate, and the amount of their demands: ——.

The following claims have been presented, but not yet
allowed: ——. All other claims have been approved and
filed.

State all other matters necessary to show the condition
of the affairs of the estate.   ——, Administrator. [8]

——, Attorney for Administrator. [9]

Verification of Exhibit.

State of ——,   }
    County [10] of ——, } ss.

——, administrator [11] of the estate of ——, deceased,
being duly sworn, says that he has read the foregoing
exhibit, and knows the contents thereof, and that the
same is true of his own knowledge, except as to the mat-

ters therein stated on his information and belief, and as to those matters he believes it to be true.

——, Administrator.[12]

Subscribed and sworn to before me this —— day of ——, 19—. ——, Notary Public, etc.[13]

Explanatory notes.—1 Give file number. 2 Title of court. 3 Or, City and County. 4-9 Or, executor. 10 Or, City and County. 11, 12 Or, executor, etc. 13 Or other officer taking the oath.

§ 658. Form. Petition for order to render exhibit.

[Title of court.]

[Title of estate.]   { No. ——.1 Dept. No. ——.
                                     {   [Title of form.]

To the Honorable the ——[2] Court of the County[3] of ——,[4] State of ——.

Your petitioner respectfully represents:

That he is a creditor of said estate, and that his claim of —— dollars ($——) has been duly presented, allowed, approved, and filed in this court, but has never been paid;

That —— was duly appointed administrator of said estate[5] on the —— day of ——, 19—, immediately qualified as such, and entered upon the duties of his trust, but that since said appointment was made said administrator[6] has not rendered, for the information of this court, any exhibit showing the condition of the affairs of said estate.

Wherefore petitioner prays that this court make an order requiring the said administrator[7] to appear and render an exhibit, under oath, showing the amount of money received and expended by him, and all other matters necessary to show the condition of the affairs of said estate.

——, Attorney for Petitioner.   ——, Petitioner.

Explanatory notes.—1 Give file number. 2 Title of court. 3 Or, City and County. 4 Or, the petition may be addressed to the judge. 5 Or, that —— was duly appointed executor of the last will of ——, deceased. 6, 7 Or, executor.

§ 659. Form. Order requiring administrator to render exhibit.

[Title of court.]

[Title of estate.]   {No.——.1 Dept. No.——.
                                            {   [Title of form.]

It being shown to the court [2] from the petition of ——, now on file herein, that ——, the administrator of said estate, appointed on the —— day of ——, 19—,[3] has failed to render an exhibit for the information of the court; and the court being satisfied from the testimony of ——, a witness produced and sworn, that the facts alleged in said petition are true and that good cause exists therefor,—

It is ordered, That ——, the administrator [4] of said estate, be, and he is hereby, required to appear before this court, at the court-room thereof, at ——,[5] on the —— day of ——, 19—, at the hour of —— o'clock in the forenoon [6] of said day, and render such exhibit; and that a copy of this order be served on said administrator [7] at least five [8] days before said —— day of ——, 19—.

Dated ——, 19—.   ——, Judge of the —— Court.

Explanatory notes.—1 Give file number. 2 Or, to the judge thereof. 3, 4 Or, executor. 5 State location. 6 Or, afternoon. 7 Or, executor. 8 Or other time, as the court may direct.

§ 660. Objections to account. Revocation of letters.

When an exhibit is rendered by an executor or administrator, any person interested may appear and, by objections in writing, contest any account or statement therein contained. The court may examine the executor or administrator, and if he has been guilty of neglect, or has wasted, embezzled, or mismanaged the estate, his letters must be revoked.—*Kerr's Cyc. Code Civ. Proc.,* § 1626.

ANALOGOUS AND IDENTICAL STATUTES.
The * indicates identity.
Arizona*—Revised Statutes of 1913, paragraph 999.
Idaho*—Compiled Statutes of 1919, section 7695.
Montana*—Revised Codes of 1907, section 7638.

New Mexico—Statutes of 1915, section 2294.
North Dakota*—Compiled Laws of 1913, section 8827.
Oklahoma*—Revised Laws of 1910, section 6432.
South Dakota*—Compiled Laws of 1913, section 5893.
Washington—Laws of 1917, chapter 156, page 689, section 162.
Wyoming*—Compiled Statutes of 1910, section 5585.

§ 661. Attachment for not obeying citation.

If any executor or administrator neglects or refuses to appear and render an exhibit, after having been duly cited, an attachment may be issued against him and such exhibit enforced, or his letters may be revoked, in the discretion of the court.—*Kerr's Cyc. Code Civ. Proc.*, § 1627.

ANALOGOUS AND IDENTICAL STATUTES.
The * indicates identity.

Arizona*—Revised Statutes of 1913, paragraph 1000.
Idaho*—Compiled Statutes of 1919, section 7696.
Montana*—Revised Codes of 1907, section 7639.
Nevada—Revised Laws of 1912, section 6043.
North Dakota*—Compiled Laws of 1913, section 8828.
Oklahoma*—Revised Laws of 1910, section 6433.
South Dakota*—Compiled Laws of 1913, section 5894.
Washington—Laws of 1917, chapter 156, page 706, section 220.
Wyoming—Compiled Statutes of 1910, section 5586.

§ 662. Account and report of administration.

Within thirty days after the expiration of the time mentioned in the notice to creditors within which claims must be filed or exhibited every executor or administrator must render a full account and report of his administration. If he fails to present his account the court or judge must compel the rendering of the account by attachments, and any person interested in the estate may apply for and obtain an attachment; but no attachment must issue unless a citation has been first issued, served, and returned, requiring the executor or administrator to appear and show cause why an attachment should not issue. Every account must exhibit all debts which have been filed and allowed during the period embraced in the account.—*Kerr's Cyc. Code Civ. Proc.*, § 1628.

ANALOGOUS AND IDENTICAL STATUTES.

No identical statute found.

Alaska—Compiled Laws of 1913, section 1691.
Arizona—Revised Statutes of 1913, paragraph 1001.
Colorado—Mills's Statutes of 1912, sections 8019, 8031.
Hawaii—Revised Laws of 1915, section 2500.
Idaho—Compiled Statutes of 1919, section 7697.
Kansas—General Statutes of 1915, sections 4638, 4646.
Montana—Revised Codes of 1907, section 7640.
Nevada—Revised Laws of 1912, sections 6041, 6043.
North Dakota—Compiled Laws of 1913, section 8829.
Oklahoma—Revised Laws of 1910, section 6434.
Oregon—Lord's Oregon Laws, section 1282.
South Dakota—Compiled Laws of 1913, section 5895.
Utah—Compiled Laws of 1907, section 3941.
Washington—Laws of 1917, chapter 156, p. 687, section 662.
Wyoming—Compiled Statutes of 1910, section 5587.

§ 663. Form. Account current and report of executor or administrator.

[Title of court.]

[Title of estate.] $\begin{cases} \text{No.} \text{———.}^1 \quad \text{Dept. No. ———.} \\ \qquad \text{[Title of form.]} \end{cases}$

———, as administrator ² of the estate of ———, deceased, renders to the court his first account current and report of his administration of said estate up to and including the ——— day of ———, 19—, as follows, to wit:³

Letters of ——— ⁴ upon said estate were duly issued to him on the ——— day of ———, 19—.

Notice to creditors has been duly published, the first publication thereof being on ———, 19—.

An inventory and appraisement of said estate was returned and filed on the ——— day of ———, 19—, showing the total value of said estate to be the sum of ——— dollars ($———).

The following is a statement of the claims presented and allowed against said estate, to wit:

Name of Claimant.   Amount of Claim.   Class of Claim.⁵

———   ———   ———

———   ———   ———

Said administrator [6] is chargeable as follows:

Amount of inventory and appraisement [7] .... \$——

Gain on sales over appraisement: [8]

Parcel 1, appraised at —— dollars (\$——);
sold for —— dollars (\$——); gain........\$——

Parcel 2, appraised at —— dollars (\$——);
sold for —— dollars (\$——); gain [9] .... ——

Interest collected: [10]

On note of ——............................\$——

On mortgage of ——...................... ——

On mortgage of ——...................... ——

Principal collected in excess of appraisement:

On note of ——............................\$——

On mortgage of ——...................... ——

On account of ——........................ ——

Rents collected:

On Parcel 3, [11] from ——.................\$——

Total charges........................ \$——

And he is entitled to credit as follows: [12]

Loss on sales less than appraisement:

Parcel 3, appraised at —— dollars (\$——);
sold for —— dollars (\$——); loss [13] ....\$——

Property set apart to family by order [14] ...... ——

Homestead set apart [15] .... ——

Property lost or destroyed:

Parcel 4, lost by decree in case No. —, —— v.
—— .... ——

Parcel 5, property ——, [16] burned........... ——

Cash paid as follows:

On family allowance, voucher No. —........\$——

To court clerk ——, [17] fees, voucher No. —.... ——

[Insert other cash payments.] [18]

Total credits........................\$——

Balance chargeable to next account....... ——

Total ....

The balance consists of the following items:

Cash on hand...........................$——
Property on hand [19].................... ——
    Total .... $——

The said —— further states to the court: ——.[20]

And said —— asks that said account be approved and settled, and that an order be made for the payment of the claims filed as aforesaid, or for such portion thereof as shall be proper out of the cash balance on hand.   ——

Explanatory notes.—[1] Give file number. [2] Or, executor. [3] No elaborate or verbose statement of the several proceedings that precede the filing of the account should be made. The fact that they have occurred, and the date, is all that need be stated in the report. If fuller information is desired by any one, it would, in any event, be necessary to resort to the papers in the case. [4] Or, letters testamentary. [5] State the name of each claimant, the amount of the claim, and whether of the first, second, third, fourth, or fifth class, under the statute which designates the order in which debts are to be paid. [6] Or, executor. [7] Each parcel of property, real or personal, should be consecutively numbered in the left-hand margin of the inventory. Demands should be described and appraised as demands, although they may have been paid after the issuance of letters and before the appraisement. In such a case the inventory should state the date and amount of the payment. The inventory should be made as soon as possible after the letters are issued, and should describe the property as it was at that time. [8] All sales should be briefly stated in the report; but no sales should be mentioned in the statement of the account, unless the price is either above or below the appraised value. The only purpose of mentioning them in the statement of account is to show the gain or loss as compared with the appraisement, which is the standard. [9] Proceed with other parcels in the same manner. [10] In charging interest collected, care must be taken not to make a double charge. Interest is sometimes included and computed in the appraised value, in which case no additional charge should be made, unless the interest collected exceeds the amount as appraised. So, also, in charging excess of principal, the appraisement is the standard, and not the actual principal of the demand. [11] Proceed with other parcels in the same way. [12] In making out the statement of account, every item as to which there has been a gain or a loss should be mentioned; items as to which there has been no gain or loss should be omitted, as the appraisement, or standard, shows the amount of such items. The court does not want each item of possible loss or gain to be mentioned, with a denial of loss or gain if there be none. This is not required. If the administrator, or executor, is charged with the amount of the inventory and appraisement, with all gains thereon, and is credited with all losses and payments made, letting the other items stand as in the inventory and appraisement, the difference between the debit and credit sides of the account will be the true balance chargeable to the administrator or executor. 13 Proceed with other parcels in the same manner. 14, 15 Give the appraised value. 16 State what was burned. 17 State nature of fees. 18 When there is no voucher for an item, the account must state the date, place of payment, and name of payee. 19 Appraised value. 20 Here give a statement of any further facts necessary to explain any item of the account, or the condition of the estate.

§ 664. Form. Affidavit to account.

State of ——,
  County [1] of ——, } ss.

——, being duly sworn, on oath says: That he is the administrator [2] who makes the foregoing account and report, and that all the statements therein made are true; that each item of expenditure therein set forth, to an amount not over twenty dollars, for which no voucher is produced, was actually paid at the time and place and to the person as therein specifically stated; and that the same contains a full and true statement of all charges against him, and of all credits to which he is entitled, on account of said estate, ——.

Subscribed and sworn to before me this —— day of ——, 19—.   ——

Explanatory notes.—1 Or, City and County. 2 Or, executor.

§ 665. Form. Petition for order requiring administrator to render an account.

[Title of court.]

[Title of estate.] { No.——.1 Dept. No.——.
                     {   [Title of form.]

To the Honorable the ——[2] Court of the County [3] of ——,[4] State of ——.

Your petitioner respectfully represents:

That he is a creditor of said estate, and that his claim of —— dollars ($——) has been duly presented, allowed, approved, and filed in this court, but has never been paid;

That —— was duly appointed administrator of said

estate [5] on the —— day of ——, 19—, immediately qualified as such, and entered upon the duties of his trust, but
that more than thirty [6] days have elapsed since the expiration of the time mentioned in the notice to creditors
within which claims must be exhibited, but that said administrator [7] has failed to render, as required by law, a
full account and report of his administration.

Wherefore petitioner prays that said administrator [8]
be required to render such account and report.

——, Attorney for Petitioner.   ——, Petitioner.

Explanatory notes.—1 Give file number. 2 Title of court. 3 Or, City
and County. 4 Or, the petition may be addressed to the judge. 5 Or,
that —— was duly appointed executor of the last will of ——, deceased.
6 Or other time prescribed by the statute. 7, 8 Or, executor.

§ 666. Form. Order for citation to administrator to render account.

[Title of court.]

[Title of estate.]
{ No. ——.1 Dept. No. ——.
[Title of form.]

It appearing from the petition of ——, filed herein, and
from the papers and records in the above-entitled estate,
that —— was appointed administrator of said estate [2] on
the —— day of ——, 19—, and thereupon duly qualified
as and is now such administrator; [3] that more than thirty
days have elapsed since the expiration of the time mentioned in the notice to creditors within which claims must
be exhibited; and that said administrator [4] has failed to
render and present an account and report of his administration as required by law,—

It is ordered, That a citation issue to said ——, administrator, [5] requiring him to appear before this court, at
the court-room thereof at ——, [6] on ——, [7] the —— day of
——, 19—, at —— o'clock in the forenoon of said day,
then and there to show cause, if any he has, why an attachment should not issue to compel him to render such
account and report.

Dated ——, 19—.   ——, Judge of the —— Court.

Explanatory notes.—1 Give file number. 2 Or, executor of the last will of said deceased. 3-5 Or, executor. 6 Give location of court-room. 7 Day of week.

§ 667. Form. Order to account on failure to show cause.

[Title of court.]

[Title of estate.] {No. ——.1 Dept. No. ——.
[Title of form.]

It being shown to the court [2] that ——, administrator [3] of the estate of ——, deceased, has failed to comply with the citation heretofore issued, herein requiring him to show cause why he should not be required to render a full account and report of his administration concerning said estate,—

It is ordered, That the said administrator [4] render such account, and report within —— [5] days from the date hereof; and that a copy of this order be served on said administrator [6] within —— [7] days from the date hereof.

Dated ——, 19—. ——, Judge of the —— Court.

Explanatory notes.—1 Give file number. 2 Or, judge of this court. 3, 4 Or, executor. 5 As fixed by the court. 6 Or, executor. 7 Give reasonable time between day of service and day for filing account.

§ 668. Form. Attachment to compel rendering of account.

[Title of court.]

[Title of estate.] {No. ——.1 Dept. No. ——.
[Title of form.]

The court, being satisfied [2] that ——, the administrator [3] of the estate of ——, has neglected to render an account and report of his administration within thirty days after the expiration of the time mentioned in the notice to creditors of said estate, within which claims must be exhibited; and it appearing that a citation has issued, requiring the said administrator [4] to appear and show cause why an attachment shall not issue to compel him to render said account; that the said —— has failed to appear and render such account and report, or to show cause why an attachment should not issue as directed in said citation; and that said citation has been

Probate Law—101

served and returned in manner and form prescribed by law, and as directed by this court,—

It is ordered, That a warrant of attachment issue, and that said —— be arrested and brought before this court to show cause why he should not be committed for contempt in disobeying said citation.

Dated ——, 19—.　　　——, Judge of the —— Court.

Explanatory notes.—1 Give file number. 2 Either from the oath of the applicant, who seeks to make the administrator or executor account, or from any other testimony offered. 3, 4 Or, executor, etc., according to the fact.

§ 669.　Executor to account after his authority is revoked.

When the authority of an executor or administrator ceases, or is revoked for any reason, he may be cited to account before the court, at the instance of the person succeeding to the administration of the same estate, in like manner as he might have been cited by any person interested in the estate during the time he was executor or administrator.—*Kerr's Cyc. Code Civ. Proc.,* § 1629.

ANALOGOUS AND IDENTICAL STATUTES.
The * indicates identity.

Arizona*—Revised Statutes of 1913, paragraph 1004.

Idaho*—Compiled Statutes of 1919, section 7698.

Montana—Revised Codes of 1907, section 7641; as amended by Laws of 1913, chapter 122, p. 470.

Nevada*—Revised Laws of 1912, section 6050.

New Mexico—Statutes of 1915, section 2297.

North Dakota—Compiled Laws of 1913, section 8829.

Oklahoma*—Revised Laws of 1910, section 6435.

South Dakota*—Compiled Laws of 1913, section 5896.

Wyoming*—Compiled Statutes of 1910, section 5588.

§ 670.　Authority of executor to be revoked when.

If the executor or administrator resides out of the county, or absconds, or conceals himself, so that the citation can not be personally served, and neglects to render an account within thirty days after the time prescribed in this article, or if he neglects to render an account within thirty days after being committed where the attachment has been executed, his letters must be revoked. —*Kerr's Cyc. Code Civ. Proc.*, § 1630.

ANALOGOUS AND IDENTICAL STATUTES.
The * indicates identity.

Arizona*—Revised Statutes of 1913, paragraph 1005.
Idaho*—Compiled Statutes of 1919, section 7699.
Montana*—Revised Codes of 1907, section 7642.
Nevada—Revised Laws of 1912, section 6043.
North Dakota*—Compiled Laws of 1913, section 8830.
Oklahoma*—Revised Laws of 1910, section 6436.
South Dakota*—Compiled Laws of 1913, section 5897.
Washington—Laws of 1917, chapter 156, pages 655, 661, sections 52, 74.
Wyoming—Compiled Statutes of 1910, section 5589.

§ 671. To produce and file vouchers, which must remain in court.

In rendering his account, the executor or administrator must produce and file vouchers for all charges, debts, claims, and expenses which he has paid, which must remain in the court; and he may be examined on oath touching such payments, and also touching any property and effects of the decedent, and the disposition thereof. When any voucher is required for other purposes, it may be withdrawn on leaving a certified copy on file; if a voucher is lost, or for other good reason can not be produced on the settlement, the payment may be proved by the oath of any competent witness.—*Kerr's Cyc. Code Civ. Proc.*, § 1631.

ANALOGOUS AND IDENTICAL STATUTES.
The * indicates identity.

Alaska—Compiled Laws of 1913, section 1691.
Arizona*—Revised Statutes of 1913, paragraph 1006.
Idaho*—Compiled Statutes of 1919, section 7700.
Kansas—General Statutes of 1915, section 4644.
Montana*—Revised Codes of 1907, section 7643.
Nevada—Revised Laws of 1912, section 6046.
North Dakota*—Compiled Laws of 1913, section 8831.
Oklahoma*—Revised Laws of 1910, section 6437.
South Dakota*—Compiled Laws of 1913, section 5898.
Utah*—Compiled Laws of 1907, section 3943.
Washington—Laws of 1917, chapter 156, page 691, section 170.
Wyoming—Compiled Statutes of 1910, section 5590.

§ 672. Vouchers for items less than twenty dollars.

On the settlement of his account he may be allowed any item of expenditure not exceeding twenty dollars, for which no voucher is produced, if such item be supported by his own uncontradicted oath positive to the fact of payment, specifying when, where, and to whom it was made; but such allowances in the whole must not exceed five hundred dollars against any one estate, provided, that if it appears by the oath to the account and is proven by competent evidence, to the satisfaction of the court, that a voucher for any disbursement or disbursements whatsoever, has been lost or destroyed, and that it is impossible to obtain a duplicate thereof and that such item or items were paid in good faith and for the best interests of the estate, and such item or items were legal charges against said estate, then the executor or administrator shall be allowed such item or items.

ALLOWANCE OF AMOUNTS PAID FOR DEBTS.—If,. upon such settlement of accounts, it appears that debts against the deceased have been paid without the affidavit and allowance prescribed by statute or sections fourteen hundred and ninety-four, fourteen hundred and ninety-five, and fourteen hundred and ninety-six of this code, and it shall be proven by competent evidence to the satisfaction of the court that such debts were justly due, were paid in good faith, that the amount paid was the true amount of such indebtedness over and above all payments or set-offs, and that the estate is solvent, it shall be the duty of the said court to allow the said sums so paid in the settlement of said accounts.—*Kerr's Cyc. Code Civ. Proc.*, § 1632.

ANALOGOUS AND IDENTICAL STATUTES.

The * indicates identity.

Arizona—Revised Statutes of 1913, paragraph 1007.

Idaho—Compiled Statutes of 1919, section 7701.

Kansas—General Statutes of 1915, section 4645.

Montana*—Revised Codes of 1907, section ·7644.

North Dakota—Compiled Laws of 1913, section 8832.

Oklahoma—Revised Laws of 1910, section 6438.
South Dakota—Compiled Laws of 1913, section 5899.
Utah—Compiled Laws of 1907, section 3944.
Washington—Laws of 1917, chapter 156, page 691, section 170.

§ 673. Day of settlement. Notice. Hearing.

When any account is rendered for settlement, the clerk of the court must appoint a day for the settlement thereof, and thereupon give notice thereof by causing notices to be posted in at least three public places in the county, setting forth the name of the estate, the executor or administrator, and the day appointed for the settlement of the account. If, upon the final hearing at the time of settlement, the court, or a judge thereof, should deem the notice insufficient from any cause, he may order such further notice to be given as may seem to him proper.—*Kerr's Cyc. Code Civ. Proc.,* § 1633.

ANALOGOUS AND IDENTICAL STATUTES.
The * indicates identity.

Arizona*—Revised Statutes of 1913, paragraph 1008.
Colorado—Mills's Statutes of 1912, section 8029.
Idaho—Compiled Statutes of 1919, section 7702.
Montana—Revised Codes of 1907, section 7645.
Nevada—Revised Laws of 1912, section 6044.
New Mexico—Statutes of 1915, section 2290.
North Dakota—Compiled Laws of 1913, section 8833.
Oklahoma—Revised Laws of 1910, section 6439.
Oregon—Lord's Oregon Laws, section 1285.
South Dakota—Compiled Laws of 1913, section 5900.
Utah—Compiled Laws of 1907, section 3942.
Washington—Laws of 1917, chapter 156, page 689, sections 162, 163.
Wyoming—Compiled Statutes of 1910, section 5591; Laws of 1915, chapter 62, p. 52 (final settlement of estates).

§ 674. Form. Order appointing day of settlement of account.
[Title of court.]

[Title of estate.] {No. ——.1 Dept. No. ——.
[Title of form.]

——, administrator[2] of the estate of ——, deceased, having this day filed an account of his administration thereof,—

at —— o'clock in the forenoon [4] of said day, and the court-room of this court at ——,[5] in the said county [6] of ——, state of ——, be, and the same are hereby, appointed as the time and place for the settlement of said account; and the clerk of this court is directed to give notice thereof by causing notices to be posted in at least three public places in said county [7] and state at least —— [8] days before the day fixed for such settlement.

Dated ——, 19—.   ——, Judge of the —— Court.

Explanatory notes.—[1] Give file number. [2] Or, executor. [3] Day of week. [4] Or, afternoon. [5] Give location of court-room. [6,7] Or, city and county. [8] Time as fixed by court.

§ 675. Form. Notice of settlement of account.

[Title of court.]

[Title of estate.]   {No. ——.[1] Dept. No. ——.
                                  {   [Title of form.]

Notice is hereby given: That ——, the administrator [2] of the estate of ——, deceased, has rendered and presented for settlement, and filed in said court, his [3] —— [4] account of his administration of said estate, together with a report thereof, and that ——,[5] the —— day of ——, 19—, at —— o'clock in the forenoon [6] of said day, at the court-room of said court, at the court-house [7] in said county [8] of ——, state of ——, has been fixed by the clerk [9] as the time and place for the settlement of said account and the hearing of said report, at which time and place any person interested in said estate may appear and file his exceptions, in writing, to said account and contest the same.   ——, Clerk.

Dated ——, 19—.   By ——, Deputy Clerk.

Explanatory notes.—[1] Give file number. [2] Or, administratrix; or, executor, etc. [3] Or, her. [4] State character of account. [5] Day of week. [6] Or, afternoon. [7] Designate its location. [8] Or, city and county. [9] Or, court or judge.

§ 676. When settlement is final, notice must so state.

If the account mentioned in the preceding section be for a final settlement, and a petition for the final distribution of the estate be filed with said account, the notice of settlement must state those facts, which notice must be given by posting or publication for at least ten days prior to the day of settlement. On the settlement of said account, distribution and partition of the estate to all entitled thereto may be immediately had without further notice or proceedings.—*Kerr's Cyc. Code Civ. Proc.,* § 1634.

ANALOGOUS AND IDENTICAL STATUTES.

No identical statute found.

Alaska—Compiled Laws of 1913, section 1694.

Arizona—Revised Statutes of 1913, paragraph 1009.

Colorado—Mills's Statutes of 1912, section 8029; as amended by Laws of 1917, chapter 70, p. 219.

Hawaii—Revised Laws of 1915, section 2500.

Idaho—Compiled Statutes of 1919, section 7703.

Montana—Revised Codes of 1907, section 7646.

North Dakota—Compiled Laws of 1913, section 8834.

Oklahoma—Revised Laws of 1910, section 6440.

Oregon—Lord's Oregon Laws, section 1285.

South Dakota—Compiled Laws of 1913, section 5901.

Utah—Compiled Laws of 1907, section 3945.

Wyoming—Compiled Statutes of 1910, section 5699; Laws of 1915, chapter 62, page 52 (final settlement of estates).

§ 677. Form. First and final account, report, and petition for distribution.

[Title of court.]

[Title of estate.] $\left\{\begin{array}{l} \text{No. ——.1   Dept. No. ——.} \\ \text{[Title of form.]} \end{array}\right.$

——, as administrator [2] of the estate of ——, deceased, renders to the court his first and final account and report, and presents therewith his petition for distribution of said estate as follows, to wit:

Said administrator [3] is chargeable as follows:

Amount of inventory and appraisement......$——

Parcel ——,[4] appraised at —— dollars ($——); sold for —— dollars ($——); gain [5] .... ——

Interest collected:

On note of —— [6].........................$——

Principal collected in excess of appraisement:

On note of —— [7] ....$——

Rents collected:

On Parcel 3, from —— [8]...................$——

    Total charges................ .... $——

And he is entitled to credits as follows:

Loss on sales less than appraisement:

Parcel 3, appraised at —— dollars ($——);

    sold for —— dollars ($——); loss [9].......$——

Property set apart to family by order, —— [10] ——

Homestead set apart, —— [11]............... ——

Parcel 4, lost by decree in case No. —, —— v.

    —— [12] .... ——

Parcel 5, personal property burned —— [13]... ——

Cash paid out as follows:

On family allowance, voucher No. ——.......$——

To county clerk, fees, voucher No. ——...... ——

To ——, funeral, voucher No. ——.......... ——

To ——, on claim, voucher No. ——......... ——

To ——, legacy, voucher No.. ——.......... ——

Commissions allowed by law on —— dollars

    ($——), the total value of estate adminis-

    tered .... ——

Attorney's fee agreed on, subject to approval

    of court................................ ——

[Add other cash payments.]

    Total credits.......................... $——

Which, when deducted from total charges,

    leaves for distribution a balance of........ $——

The said balance consists of the following

    described property, to wit:

Cash on hand............................$——

And the following described property, to wit:

    —— [14] .... ——

    Total .... $——

Letters of administration [15] were duly issued upon said estate on the —— day of ——, 19—.

Notice to creditors has been duly published, the first publication thereof having been made on the —— day of ——, 19—.

An inventory and appraisement of said estate was duly returned and filed on the —— day of ——, 19—, showing said estate to be of the value of —— dollars ($——).

The following claims have been presented and allowed against said estate, to wit:[16]

Names of Claimants. Amount of Claim. Class.[17]

—— —— ——

—— —— ——

Said estate is now in condition to be finally settled and distributed.

The following named persons are the next of kin and only heirs at law of said deceased, to wit: ——.

[If there is a will, insert the following:] By the terms of the last will of said deceased duly admitted to probate herein on the —— day of ——, 19—, the said deceased devised and bequeathed, in the proportions and manner in said will specified, his whole estate to the following-named devisees and legatees:[18]

There is an inheritance tax of —— dollars ($——) payable on the legacy to ——, and there is also such a tax on the devise to ——, the value of which for that purpose has not been ascertained.[19]

Wherefore said —— asks that said account be approved, allowed, and settled; that the amount of inheritance tax to be paid on the legacies and devises [20] be determined; and that a decree be made for the distribution of all said estate to the persons entitled thereto, and for all other proper relief.

——, Administrator [21] of the Estate of ——, Deceased.

[Add verification.]

Explanatory notes.—1 Give file number. 2, 8 Or, executor. 4 Give number of parcel. 5 Enumerate each parcel on which was any gain, and the amount of gain in the same way. 6 Enumerate each note in the same way. 7 Enumerate each collection in the same way. 8 Show rents collected from each parcel, or from which ones collected. · 9 Designate each parcel sold in the same way. 10, 11 Appraised value. 12, 13 And any other parcels or property lost. 14 Here describe all remaining property, and state its appraised value. 15 Or, letters testamentary. 16 If all claims have been paid, omit this, and say: "All claims presented and allowed against said estate have been fully paid, as shown by the foregoing account." 17 Show whether claim is of the first, second, third, fourth, or fifth class. 18 Give names of devisees, etc. 19 Or, there is an inheritance tax due on the shares of —— and ——, giving names and amount due on each. 20 Or, shares. 21 Or, executor.

Of the general subject of accounts and proper form of petition for distribution, Judge Shaw, of the Superior Court of Los Angeles, now on the supreme bench of California, once said, in substance: The practice of many attorneys in making separate documents of the account, the report, and the petition for distribution, putting each under a separate cover is not to be commended, because it requires much repetition of the same matter. It also adds unnecessary bulk to the package of papers filed, and makes them more inconvenient to examine. Attempts have been made to make a printed blank for such accounts with the items thereof printed therein. It is obvious that such a blank would be worse than useless. Scarcely ever are two accounts alike. In almost every one some of the items in the blank are not called for and should be omitted. No printed blank for accounts is practicable beyond the merest skeleton giving the title of the cause and the verification, and the saving of labor amounts to nothing.

§ 678. Form. Final account, report, and petition for distribution of estate following an account current.

[Title of court.]

[Title of estate.]   { No. ——.1   Dept. No. ——.
            [Title of form.]

——, as administrator 2 of the estate of ——, deceased, renders to the court his final account and report for settlement of said estate, and presents therewith his petition for distribution thereof, as follows, to wit:

Said —— is chargeable as follows:

Balance chargeable on settlement of last
   account current.........................$——

[Here add any other gains to the estate, as in
   account current.]......................... ——

      Total charges........................... $——

He is entitled to credits as follows:

Paid —— on claim, voucher No. ——.......$——

Paid —— on claim, voucher No. ——³........ ——

Commissions allowed by law on —— dollars
($——), the total value of estate adminis-
tered ....✓........ ——

Attorneys' fees agreed on, subject to approval
of court⁴............................... ——

[Add any other credit items.]

  Total credits......................... $——

Which, when deducted from total charges,
leaves for distribution a balance of........$——

The said balance consists of the following
described property, to wit:

Cash on hand...........................$——

And the following described property, to wit:

—— ⁵ .... ——

  Total .... $——

Letters of administration⁶ were duly issued upon said
estate on the —— day of ——, 19—.

Notice to creditors has been duly published, the first
publication thereof having been made on the —— day of
——, 19—.

In accordance with the order for the payment of claims
hereinbefore made, all claims allowed against said estate
have been paid, as shown by the foregoing account, and
said estate is now in condition to be finally settled and
distributed.

Said deceased left as his next of kin and only heirs at
law certain persons, whose names, relationship and residences are as follows, to wit:

Names.	Relationship.	Residences.
——	——	——
——	——	——

[If there is a will duly probated, add the following, or
a similar statement of its terms, viz.:]

By the terms of the last will of said deceased, admitted to probate herein, the said estate is disposed of as follows: He bequeaths specific money legacies as follows: To ——, —— dollars ($——), etc.[7] He made specific devises of land as follows: To ——,[8] etc. And the residue of said estate he devised and bequeathed as follows: ——.[9]

There will be collateral-inheritance taxes payable on the legacy to —— the sum of —— dollars ($——), and on the legacy to —— the sum of —— dollars ($——), and there will also be such taxes to pay on the devise to ——, the value of which for that purpose has not been ascertained.[10]

Wherefore said —— asks that said account be approved, allowed, and settled, and that the amount of collateral-inheritance tax to be paid on the legacies and devises be determined, and that a decree be made for the payment of such taxes and for the distribution of all said estate to the persons entitled thereto, and for all other proper relief.

——, Administrator [11] of the Estate of ——, Deceased.
[Add verification.]

Explanatory notes.—1 Give file number. 2 Or, executor. 3 Etc., enumerating each payment. 4 This item should be omitted, if no agreement has been made as to the amount of attorneys' fees, but the report should show that attorneys' fees have been incurred, and an allowance should be asked therefor. No attorneys' fees can be allowed or fixed by the court, unless they are asked for, in some way, in the account or report: Estate of Kruger, 123 Cal. 391, 55 Pac. 1056. 5 Describe all the remaining property, and state its appraised value. 6 Or, letters testamentary. 7 Enumerate each legacy. 8 Enumerate each devise, and describe the land, and conditions of each devise. 9 State how, and to whom. 10 If there is no collateral inheritance tax, omit the clause as to collateral inheritance taxes. If there is no will, and there are collateral heirs who must pay a tax, insert a statement of the facts here. 11 Or, executor.

§ 679. Form. Final account, report, and petition for distribution. Insolvent estate.

[Title of court.]

[Title of estate.] 　　　　{ No.——.1　Dept. No.——.
　　　　　　　　　　　　　　　 [Title of form.]

——, as administrator [2] of the estate of ——, deceased, renders to the court his first and final account and report, and presents therewith his petition for distribution of said estate as follows, to wit:

Said administrator [3] is chargeable as follows:

Amount of inventory and appraisement.....$——

Parcel ——,[4] appraised at —— dollars ($——); sold for —— dollars ($——); gain [5] ....$——

Interest collected:

On note of —— [6].........................$——

Principal collected in excess of appraisement:

On note of —— [7].........................$——

Rents collected:

On parcel 3, from ——[8]...................$——

　　　Total charges........................ 　$——

And he is entitled to credits as follows:

Loss on sales less than appraisement:

Parcel 3, appraised at —— dollars ($——); sold for —— dollars ($——); loss [9]........$——.

Property set apart to family by order [10]...... ——

Homestead set apart [11]..................... ——

Parcel 4, lost by decree in case No. —, —— v. —— [12] .... ——

Parcel 5, personal property burned [13]........ ——

Cash paid out as follows:

On family allowance, voucher No. ——.......$——

To county clerk, fees, voucher No. ——...... ——

Commissions allowed by law on —— dollars ($——), the total value of estate administered .... ——

Attorney's fee agreed on, subject to approval
of court................................... ——
[Add other cash payments.]
    Total credits........................... $——
Which, when deducted from total charges,
leaves for distribution a balance of........ $——
The said balance consists of the following
described property, to wit:
Cash on hand.............................. $——

Letters of administration [14] were duly issued on said
estate on the —— day of ——, 19—.

An inventory and appraisement of said estate was duly
returned and filed on the —— day of ——, 19—, showing
the value of said estate to be —— dollars ($——).

The following statement gives the name of each creditor whose claim has been presented and allowed against
said estate, the amount now due on his claim, and the
class to which the same belongs, to wit:

Names of Claimants. Amount of Claims.   Claims.

——   ——   ——

——   ——   ——

The names, degree of kin, and residence of the only
heirs at law of said deceased are as follows, to wit: ——
and ——, etc.[15]

All the assets of said estate have been reduced to cash,
and the estate is now in condition to be finally settled.

Wherefore the said —— asks that said account be
approved and settled; that the court direct the apportionment of said balance among the said creditors, and order
payment accordingly; and that the administration be
closed; and for all other proper relief.

——, Administrator of the Estate of ——, Deceased.
[Add verification.]

Explanatory notes.—1 Give file number. 2, 3 Or, executor. 4 Give
number of parcel. 5 Enumerate each parcel on which was any gain,
and the amount of gain in the same way. 6 Enumerate each note in
the same way. 7 Enumerate each collection in the same way. 8 Show

rents collected from each parcel, or from which ones collected. 9 Designate each parcel sold, in the same way. 10 Appraised value. 11 Appraised value. 12, 18 And any other parcels or property lost. 14 Or, letters testamentary. 16 If a will was probated, say, "The names of the legatees and devisees named in the will of said deceased admitted to probate herein are as follows, to wit: ——.

§ 680. Form. Memorandum, by clerk, fixing time for hearing of final account and petition for distribution.

[Title of court.]

[Title of estate.] {No. ——.1 Dept. No. ——.
                     {   [Title of form.]

——, the administrator ² of the estate of ——, deceased, having this day filed and presented for final settlement his final account of his administration of said estate, together with —— report accompanying the same, and his petition for the distribution of the residue of said estate to the persons entitled thereto,—

Now, I, ——, clerk of said —— court, do hereby fix and appoint ——,³ the —— day of ——, 19—, at —— o'clock in the forenoon of said day,⁴ in the court-room of said court, at the court-house in said county of ——, as the time and place for the hearing upon said final account and petition of distribution.

——, Clerk of the —— Court.

Dated ——, 19—.   By ——, Deputy Clerk.

Explanatory notes.—1 Give file number. 2 Or, executor. 3 Give day of week. 4 Or as the case may be.

§ 681. Form. Order appointing day for hearing petition for distribution and settlement of final account.

[Title of court.]

[Title of estate.] {No. ——.1 Dept. No. ——.
                     {   [Title of form.]

——, the administrator ² of the estate of ——, having this day filed for final settlement an account of his administration of the affairs of said estate, accompanied by the filing of a petition for the final distribution of said estate, among the persons entitled thereto,—

It is ordered, That ——,² the —— day of ——, 19—, at —— o'clock in the forenoon ⁴ of said day, and the court-room of said court,⁵ at ——, in the said county ⁶ of ——, state of ——, be, and the same are hereby, appointed as the time and place for the settlement of said account and the hearing of said petition; and that the clerk of this court give notice thereof for at least ten ⁷ days prior to the day of settlement, by posting notices according to law.⁸

Dated ——, 19—.   ——, Judge of the —— Court.

Explanatory notes.—1 Give file number. 2 Or, executor. 3 Day of week. 4 Or, afternoon. 5 Give location of court-room. 6 Or, city and county. 7 Or other time prescribed by statute. 8 Or in such other manner as the court or judge may direct. In case the clerk fixes the day, as required by the statute, no order of court is necessary.

§ 682. Form. Notice of settlement of final account and distribution.

[Title of court.]

[Title of estate.]   { No. ——.1 Dept. No.——.
                          {   [Title of form.]

Notice is hereby given: That ——, administrator ² of the estate of ——, deceased, has rendered and presented for final settlement, and filed in said court, his final account of his administration of said estate, together with his report and a petition for final distribution, and that ——,³ the —— day of ——, 19—, at —— o'clock in the forenoon ⁴ of said day, at the court-room of said court at the court-house in said county,⁵ has been fixed and appointed as the time and place for the settlement of said account and the hearing of said report and petition, at which time and place any person interested in said estate may appear and file his exceptions, in writing, to the said account, and contest the same.

Notice is further given: That said account is for final settlement, and the said estate is ready for distribution, and on confirmation of said final account final distribution of said estate will be immediately had.

Dated this —— day of ——, 19—.   ——, Clerk.

                       By ——, Deputy Clerk.

Explanatory notes.—1 Give file number. 2 Or, executor. 3 Day of week. 4 Or, afternoon. 5 Or, city and county.

§ 683.   Form. Affidavit of posting notice of settlement of final account and distribution.

[Title of court.]

[Title of estate.]

{ No.——.1   Dept. No.——.
    [Title of form.]

State of ——,   { ss.
  County 2 of ——,

——, deputy county clerk of said county,3 being duly sworn, says: That on the —— day of ——, 19—, he posted correct and true copies of the within notice in three of the most public places in said county,4 to wit, one of said copies at the place at which the court is held, one at ——,5 and one at ——,6 in said county.7

Subscribed and sworn to before me this —— day of ——, 19—.   ——, County Clerk.8

Explanatory notes.—1 Give file number. 2-4 Or, City and County. 5, 6 As, at the city hall, land-office, United States post-office, in the ——, in said county. 7 Or, city and county. 8 Or other officer taking the oath.

§ 684.   Form. Order settling final account and for distribution.

[Title of court.]

[Title of estate.]

{ No.——.1   Dept. No.——.
    [Title of form.]

Now comes ——, the administrator of said estate, by ——, his attorney, and proves to the satisfaction of the court that his final account and petition for distribution herein was rendered and filed on the —— day of ——, 19—; that on the same day the clerk of this court appointed ——,2 the —— day of ——, 19—, for the settle-

Probate Law—102

ment and hearing thereof; that due and legal notice of the time and place of said settlement and hearing has been given, as required by law;[3] and said account and petition being now presented to the court, and no person appearing to except to or contest said account or petition,[4] the court, after hearing the evidence, being satisfied that all taxes upon the property of the estate (and any inheritance tax which was due and payable) have been fully paid, settles said account, and orders distribution of said estate as follows:

It is ordered, adjudged, and decreed by the court, That said administrator has in his possession, belonging to said estate, after deducting the credits to which he is entitled, a balance of —— dollars ($——), of which —— dollars ($——) is in cash, and the remainder consists of the property hereinafter described, at the value of the appraisement; that said account be allowed and settled accordingly; that said deceased died intestate, and left surviving, as his only heirs at law, certain persons, whose names and relationship to the deceased are as follows, to wit: ——;[5] that, out of the .residue of cash in his hands, said —— pay —— dollars ($——), hereby allowed as attorneys' fees, and retain —— dollars ($——) as his commission allowed by law for his services; and that the balance of cash in his hands, and all the residue of the property of said estate as hereinafter described, and all other property belonging to said estate, whether described herein or not, be distributed as follows, to wit: ——[6] thereof to ——;[7] ——[8] thereof to ——;[9] and ——[10] thereof to ——;[11] etc.

The property of said estate hereby distributed, so far as the same is known, is described as follows:

1. Balance of cash as aforesaid, —— dollars ($——).

2. ——.[12]   ——, County Clerk.

Entered ——, 19—.   By ——, Deputy.

Explanatory notes.—1 Give file number. 2 Day of week. 3 If the matter has been continued, say, "and the same having been by the court regularly postponed to the present time." ₄ Or, —— having appeared by ——, his attorney, and filed and presented objections and exceptions to said petition. ₅ Give names of widow and children, or other heirs at law. ₆ State fractional part. ₇ Name of heir. ₈ Fractional part. ₉ Name of heir. ₁₀ Fractional part. ₁₁ Name of heir. ₁₂ Describe the other property, with its valuation as stated in the inventory.

§ 685. Form. Another form of order settling final account, and for distribution.

[Title of court.]

[Title of estate.]   No.——.₁   Dept. No.——.
                                              [Title of form.]

——, administrator of the estate of ——, deceased, . having on the —— day of ——, 19—, rendered and filed herein a full account and report of his administration of said estate, which account was for final settlement, and having with said account filed a petition for the final distribution of the estate;

And said account and petition this day coming on regularly to be heard,² and proof having been made to the satisfaction of the court that the clerk had given notice of the settlement of said account and the hearing of said petition, in the manner and for the time heretofore ordered and directed by the court;

And it appearing that said account is in all respects true and correct; that it is supported by proper vouchers; that the residue of money in the hands of the administrator, at the time of filing said account, was —— dollars ($——); that, since the rendition of said account, the sum of —— dollars ($——) has been received by the administrator; that the sum of —— dollars ($——) has been expended by him as necessary expenses of administration, the vouchers whereof, together with a statement of such expenditures and disbursements, are now presented and filed; and that the estimated expenses of closing the estate will amount to —— dollars ($——), leaving a residue of —— dollars ($——);

And it appearing that all claims and debts against

said decedent, all taxes on said estate,[3] and all debts, expenses, and charges of administration have been fully paid and discharged; that said estate is ready for distribution and in condition to be closed;

That the said estate is community[4] property; and

That said —— died intestate, and left as his only heirs, who are entitled to distribution of his estate, the following named persons: ——;[5] —

It is ordered, That said payments are approved, and said statement of expenditures and disbursements is now settled and allowed.

It is further ordered, adjudged, and decreed, That the said final account of the said —— be, and the same is hereby, settled, allowed, and approved, and that the residue of said estate hereinafter particularly described, and any other property which may belong to the said estate, or in which the said estate may have any interest, be, and the same is hereby, distributed as follows: ——.[6]

The following is a particular description of the said residue of said estate referred to in this decree, and of which distribution is now ordered as aforesaid: ——.[7]

Done in open court, ——, 19—.

——, Judge of the —— Court.

Explanatory notes.—1 Give file number. 2 If the matter has been continued, say, "and the hearing having been regularly continued by the court to the present time." 3 If any inheritance tax was due or paid, insert, "and all inheritance taxes which have become due and payable." 4 Or, separate. 5 Give names. 6 State manner, giving names of distributees, and proportion or part of each. 7 Describe the property.

§ 686.　Form. Order settling final account, report, and petition for distribution under will.

[Title of court.]

[Title of estate.] 　　　{ No. ——.1　Dept. No. ——.
　　　　　　　　　　　　{　　[Title of form.]

Now comes ——, the executor of said estate, by ——, his attorney, and proves to the satisfaction of the court that his final account and petition for distribution herein was rendered and filed on the —— day of ——, 19—; that on the same day the clerk of this court appointed the —— day of ——, 19—, for the settlement and hearing thereof; that due and legal notice of the time and place of said settlement and hearing has been given as required by law;[2] and the said account and petition being now presented to the court, and no person appearing to except to or contest said account or petition, the court, after hearing the evidence, being satisfied that all taxes upon the property of the estate (and any inheritance tax which has become due and payable) have been fully paid, settles said account, and orders distribution of said estate as follows:

It is ordered, adjudged, and decreed by the court, That said executor has in his possession, belonging to said estate, after deducting the credits to which he is entitled, a balance of —— dollars ($——), of which —— dollars ($——) is in cash, and the remainder consists of the property hereinafter described, at the value of the appraisement; that said account be allowed and settled accordingly; and that, in pursuance of and according to the provisions of the last will of said deceased, the said property is distributed as follows, to wit: ——.[3]

Dated ——, 19—. ——, Judge of the —— Court.

Explanatory notes.—1 Give file number. 2 If the matter has been continued, say, "and the said matter having been regularly postponed by the court to the present time." 3 State manner of distribution, designating the persons to whom made, and part awarded to each one, and describing the property so far as known, also the share of each distributee in any residue unknown, etc.

§ 687. Interested party may file exceptions to account.

On the day appointed, or any subsequent day to which the hearing may be postponed by the court, any person interested in the estate may appear and file his exceptions in writing to the account, and contest the same.— *Kerr's Cyc. Code Civ. Proc., § 1635.*

ANALOGOUS AND IDENTICAL STATUTES.
The * indicates identity.
Alaska—Compiled Laws of 1913, section 1695.
Arizona*—Revised Statutes of 1913, paragraph 1010.
Idaho*—Compiled Statutes of 1919, section 7704.
Montana*—Revised Codes of 1907, section 7647.
Nevada—Revised Laws of 1912, section 6045.
New Mexico—Statutes of 1915, section 2294.
North Dakota*—Compiled Laws of 1913, section 8835.
Oklahoma*—Revised Laws of 1910, section 6441.
Oregon—Lord's Oregon Laws, section 1286.
South Dakota*—Compiled Laws of 1913, section 5902.
Washington—Laws of 1917, chapter 156, page 689, section 163.
Wyoming*—Compiled Statutes of 1910, section 5592.

§ 688. Form. Exceptions to account.
[Title of court.]

[Title of estate.] $\Big\{$ No. ——.¹ Dept. No. ——.
                                    [Title of form.]

Now comes ——, who is interested in the estate of ——, deceased, being one of his heirs at law,² and files these, his exceptions in writing, to the account of ——, the administrator ³ of the estate of said deceased, filed herein on the —— day of ——, 19—.

He, the said contestant of said account, contests and objects to the allowance of any item therein, on the ground that said account was not made under oath.

Contestant particularly objects to the following claims, to wit, the claim of —— and the claim of ——, on the ground that the deceased did not owe the same, or any part thereof, at the time of his death, the same being, at that time, barred by the statute of limitations.

The contestant particularly objects to the following claims, to wit, the claim of —— and the claim of ——, on the ground that the same were not presented within the time limited in the notice to creditors.

The contestant particularly objects to the following items, to wit, the item —— and the item ——, on the ground that they are not a proper charge against the said estate.

The contestant particularly objects to the following

items, to wit, the item —— and the item ——, on the ground that the charges are exorbitant.

And, finally, contestant particularly objects to each and every item of said account which decreases the value of the homestead set apart for the use of the family of deceased, or which decreases the family allowance made herein.[4]

——, Attorney for Contestant.   ——, Contestant.

Explanatory notes.—1 Give file number. 2 Or, legatee or devisee; or, state other relationship or interest. 8 Or, executor of the last will and testament, etc. 4 Specify items decreasing value of homestead, and show how such value is decreased.

§ 689. Contest by heirs. Hearing. Referee.

All matters, including allowed claims not passed upon on the settlement of any former account, or on rendering an exhibit, or on making a decree of sale, may be contested by the heirs, for cause shown. The hearing and allegations of the respective parties may be postponed from time to time, when necessary, and the court may appoint one or more referees to examine the accounts, and make report thereon, subject to confirmation; and may allow a reasonable compensation to the referees, to be paid out of the estate of the decedent.

JURY. VERDICT. ORDER.—Whenever an allowed claim is contested by any heir, or other person entitled to contest it, either the contestant or the claimant is entitled to a trial by jury of the issues of fact presented by the contest; and it is the duty of the court, at request of either party, to call a jury and submit to them such issues, and, after receiving their verdict, to enter an order disposing of such contest in accordance therewith. —*Kerr's Cyc. Code Civ. Proc.*, § 1636.

ANALOGOUS AND IDENTICAL STATUTES.

No identical statute found.

Arizona—Revised Statutes of 1913, paragraph 1011.

Idaho—Compiled Statutes of 1919, section 7705.

Montana—Revised Codes of 1907, section 7648.

North Dakota—Compiled Laws of 1913, section 8836.
Oklahoma—Revised Laws of 1910, section 6442.
South Dakota—Compiled Laws of 1913, section 5908.
Utah—Compiled Laws of 1907, section 3947.
Wyoming—Compiled Statutes of 1910, section 5598.

§ 690. Form. Order appointing referee of administrator's account and adjourning settlement.

[Title of court.]

[Title of estate.]　　　　{ No. ——.1　Dept. No. ——.
　　　　　　　　　　　　　　　[Title of form.]

——, the administrator [2] of the estate of ——, deceased, having rendered his account for settlement, and notice of such settlement having been duly given as ordered by this court, —

It is hereby ordered, That ——, Esq., be, and he is hereby, appointed a referee to examine the said account, and make report thereon to this court within ——,[3] and that the settlement of said account be adjourned until ——,[4] the —— day of ——, 19—, at —— o'clock in the forenoon [5] of said day.

Dated ——, 19—.　　　——, Judge of the —— Court.

Explanatory notes.—1 Give file number. 2 Or, administratrix. 3 State the time. 4 Day of the week. 5 Or, afternoon.

§ 691. Form. Order referring account to court commissioner for examination and report.

[Title of court.]

[Title of estate.]　　　　{ No. ——.1　Dept. No. ——.
　　　　　　　　　　　　　　　[Title of form.]

In this matter, the hearing of the —— account of ——, administrator [2] of the estate of ——, deceased, coming on regularly to be heard this day, —

It is hereby ordered, That ——, court commissioner of the county [3] of ——, state of ——, examine the said account filed in this court on the —— day of ——, 19—, and report the same to this court with all convenient dispatch.

Dated ——, 19—.　　——, Judge of the —— Court.

Explanatory notes.—1 Give file number. 2 Or, executor. 3 Or, city and county.

§ 692. **Form. Referee's report of examination of account.**

[Title of court.]

[Title of estate.]　　　　　　{ No. ——.1　Dept. No. ——.
　　　　　　　　　　　　　　{ 　　[Title of form.]

In pursuance of an order of this court made and entered on the —— day of ——, 19—, appointing me, the undersigned, a referee to examine the ——2 account of ——, administrator 3 of the estate of ——, deceased, rendered for settlement and filed in this court on the —— day of ——, 19—, and to make report thereon, I now report as follows:

That I have fully and carefully examined said account, and find that it contains a just and full statement of all the moneys received and disbursed by the administrator 4 during the period covered by said account.

I have examined the vouchers in support of said account, and find proper vouchers for all items of expenditure, except as to ——5 items. No vouchers were produced for these said items, but each of said items was proved before me, by the oath positive of said administrator,6 as attached to said account, which oath is uncontradicted, that such items were actually paid by him, on the dates when, at the places where, and to the persons named in said account as having received such payment.

I am satisfied that said account as presented is just, true, and correct. I therefore recommend that it be allowed and approved, and that a decree be entered to that effect.

Respectfully submitted.

Explanatory notes.—1 Give file number. 2 State character of account. 3, 4 Or, executor. 5 Give number of items, with character thereof, and amount; but no item must exceed twenty-dollars ($20), and the whole thereof must not exceed five hundred dollars ($500). 6 Or, executor, etc.

§ 693. Settlement of accounts to be conclusive when, and when not.

The settlement of the account and the allowance thereof by the court, or upon appeal, is conclusive against all persons in any way interested in the estate, saving, however, to all persons laboring under any legal disability, their right to move for cause to reopen and examine the account, or to proceed by action against the executor or administrator, either individually or upon his bond, at any time before final distribution; and in any action brought by any such person, the allowance and settlement of the account is prima facie evidence of its correctness. —*Kerr's Cyc. Code Civ. Proc.*, § 1637.

ANALOGOUS AND IDENTICAL STATUTES.

The * indicates identity.

Alaska—Compiled Laws of 1913, section 1696.
Arizona*—Revised Statutes of 1913, paragraph 1012.
Colorado—Mills's Statutes of 1912, section 8030.
Idaho—Compiled Statutes of 1919, section 7706.
Montana*—Revised Codes of 1907, section 7649.
Nevada—Revised Laws of 1912, section 6048.
North Dakota*—Compiled Laws of 1913, section 8837.
Oklahoma*—Revised Laws of 1910, section 6443.
Oregon—Lord's Oregon Laws, section 1287; as amended by Laws of 1915, chapter 186, p. 224.
South Dakota*—Compiled Laws of 1913, Vol. II, section 5904.
Utah*—Compiled Laws of 1907, section 3946.
Washington—Laws of 1917, chapter 156, page 694, section 180.
Wyoming*—Compiled Statutes of 1910, section 5594.

§ 694. Proof of notice of settlement of accounts.

The account must not be allowed by the court until it is first proved that notice has been given as required by this chapter, and the decree must show that such proof was made to the satisfaction of the court, and is conclusive evidence of the fact.—*Kerr's Cyc. Code Civ. Proc.*, § 1638.

ANALOGOUS AND IDENTICAL STATUTES.

The * indicates identity.

Alaska—Compiled Laws of 1913, sections 1696, 1702.
Arizona*—Revised Statutes of 1913, paragraph 1013.
Idaho*—Compiled Statutes of 1919, section 7707.
Montana*—Revised Codes of 1907, section 7650.
Nevada*—Revised Laws of 1912, section 6049.
North Dakota*—Compiled Laws of 1913, section 8838.
Oklahoma*—Revised Laws of 1910, section. 6444.
Oregon—Lord's Oregon Laws, section 1293.
South Dakota*—Compiled Laws of 1913, section 5905.
Utah—Compiled Laws of 1907, section 4036.

§ 695. Form. Affidavit of posting notice of settlement of account.

[Title of court.]

[Title of estate.]

{ No. ——.1 Dept. No. ——.
  [Title of form.]

State of ——, }
County ² of ——, } ss.

. ——, deputy county clerk of said county,³ being duly sworn, says: That on the —— day of ——, 19—, he posted correct and true copies of the within notice in three of the most public places in said county,⁴ to wit, one of said copies at the place at which the court is held,⁵ one at ——,⁶ and one at ——,⁷ in said county.⁸

Subscribed and sworn to before me this —— day of ——, 19—.   ——, Deputy County Clerk.

Explanatory notes.—1 Give file number. 2-4 Or, City and County. 5 Designate the place. 6 As, city hall. 7 As, the United States post-office, designating its location. 8 Or, city and county.

§ 696. Form. Decree settling account.

[Title of court.]

[Title of estate.]

{ No. ——.1 Dept. No. ——.
  [Title of form.]

Comes now ——, the administrator ² of said estate, by ——, his attorney, and presents to the court for settlement his account, showing charges in favor of said estate amounting to —— dollars ($——), and claiming credits amounting to —— dollars ($——), leaving a balance of —— dollars ($——) in his [3] hands belonging to said estate; and he now proves to the satisfaction of the court that said account was filed on the —— day of ——, 19—; that on the same day the clerk appointed the —— day of ——, 19—, as the day for the settlement thereof; and that notice of the time and place of said settlement has been duly given as required by law and as ordered by the court;[4] and no person appearing to except to or to contest said account,[5] the court, after hearing the evidence, finds[6] that said account is correct and that it is supported by proper vouchers.

It is therefore ordered, adjudged, and decreed by the court, That said account be in all respects as the same was rendered and presented for settlement, approved, allowed, and settled.   ——, County Clerk.

Entered ——, 19—.   By ——, Deputy.

Explanatory notes.—1 Give file number. 2 Or, administratrix; or as the case may be. 3 Or, her. 4 If the matter has been continued, say; "and said settlement having been by the court regularly postponed to this day." 5 Or, and ——, having appeared by ——, his attorney, and filed his exceptions and objections to said account. 6 Or, if corrections are made, say, "corrects and settles the same as follows" (showing the corrections). The order will then run as follows: It is therefore ordered, adjudged, and decreed by the court that the said account be, and the same is hereby, corrected so that the same show charges in favor of said estate amounting to —— dollars ($——), leaving a balance of —— dollars ($——) belonging to said estate; and that, as so corrected, the same be allowed and settled.

§ 697. Deceased executor's accounts.

If any executor, administrator, or guardian dies, his accounts may be presented by his personal representative to, and settled by, the court in which the estate of which he was executor, administrator, or guardian is being administered, and, upon petition of the successor of such deceased executor, administrator, or guardian, such court may compel the personal representatives of such deceased executor, administrator, or guardian to render an account of the administration of their testator or intestate, and must settle such account as in other cases.—*Kerr's Cyc. Code Civ. Proc.*, § 1639.

ANALOGOUS AND IDENTICAL STATUTES.

No identical statute found.

Montana—Revised Codes of 1907, section 7641; as amended by Laws of 1913, chapter 122, page 470.

ACCOUNTING AND SETTLEMENT BY EXECUTORS AND ADMINISTRATORS.

1. In general.
2. Duty to account.
3. Notice of settlement.
4. Account must show what.
5. Order for payment of dividend.
6. Vouchers.
7. Hearing.
   (1) In general.
   (2) Correction of mistakes.
   (3) Matters not to be considered.
8. Exceptions. Contest. Objections. Evidence.
   (1) In general.
   (2) Exceptions as aid to court.
   (3) Right to appear and contest.
   (4) Contest of allowed claim.
   (5) Manner of stating objections. Facts.
   (6) Purpose of statute. Practice. Pleadings. Issues.
   (7) Additional or amended exceptions.
   (8) Untenable objections.
   (9) Evidence. Burden of proof. Presumptions.
   (10) Waiver of written objections.
9. Jurisdiction. Right, power, and duty of court.
   (1) Jurisdiction.
   (2) Right, power, and duty of court in general.
   (3) As to notice.
   (4) To scrutinize accounts.
   (5) In absence of exceptions.
   (6) Report of referee.
   (7) To compel accounting.
   (8) Striking. Combining. Making more specific.
   (9) Want of jurisdiction.
10. Administrator to be charged with what. In general.
11. Administrator not chargeable when.
12. Administrator is entitled to credit for what.
    (1) In general.
    (2) Payments made for preservation or protection of estate.
    (3) Same. Necessary expenditures.
    (4) For costs paid.
    (5) Funeral expenses. Last illness.
    (6) Payment of family allowance.
    (7) Traveling expenses.
    (8) Items for less than twenty dollars.
13. Administrator is not entitled to credit when.
    (1) In general.
    (2) Improper charges.
    (3) Unnecessary expenditures.
    (4) Expenses before administration.
    (5) Repairs. Protection of estate.
14. Final and intermediate accounts.
    (1) Final account. Waiver.
    (2) Intermediate accounts.
15. Failure to settle.
16. Death or absconding before accounting.
17. Insolvent administrators.
18. Actions.
19. Trial by jury.
20. Validity of settlement.
21. Effect of settlement.
22. Conclusiveness of settlement.
    (1) In general.
    (2) Not conclusive, when.
    (3) Fraud. Collateral attack.
    (4) Items included. Items omitted.

23. Vacating account. Collateral at-
    tack. Relief in equity.
   (1) In general.
   (2) Void decree, only, may be
     vacated.
   (3) Can not be set aside for
     "mistake," etc., when.
   (4) Collateral attack.
   (5) Equitable relief. In general.
   (6) Equitable relief for fraud or
     mistake.
24. Appeal.
   (1) In general.

   (2) Appealable orders.
   (3) Non-appealable orders.
   (4) Parties. Representative.
   (5) Notice.
   (6) Findings. Bill of exceptions.
     Record.
   (7) Sufficiency of judge's cer-
     tificate.
   (8) Consideration of case. Re-
     view.
   (9) Affirmance. Remanding. Re-
     versal. Dismissal. Remit-
     titur.

1. In general.—The final settlement of an executor or administrator must precede distribution, whether the petition for distribution is filed with his final account or subsequent to the final settlement.— Smith v. Westerfield, 88 Cal. 374, 379, 26 Pac. 206; Estate of Sheid, 122 Cal. 528, 531, 55 Pac. 328. An order requiring the ancillary administrator to deliver the residum of the assets of the estate to the domiciliary administrator appointed in another jurisdiction should not be granted before the allowance of the final account.—Estate of Youmans, 10 Haw. 207, 208. There is no requirement that payment of claims against an executor or administrator for services rendered or materials furnished to the estate during the administration be made before they can be allowed in the settlement of his account.—Estate of Couts, 87 Cal. 480, 482, 25 Pac. 685; Pennie v. Roach, 94 Cal. 515, 522, 29 Pac. 956, 30 Pac. 106; Estate of Dudley, 123 Cal. 256, 257, 55 Pac. 897. The disposition which the court may make of moneys in the hands of executors or administrators which belong to the estate is immaterial to them. All that they are concerned in upon the settlement of the account is to be credited with the various payments they have made, and to have the accounts settled according to the correct amount in their hands. Whatever disposition the court makes of this amount is no concern of theirs, and if the parties interested therein make no objection to the order, they should be content.—Estate of Sarment, 123 Cal. 331, 335, 55 Pac. 1015. The administrator, on settlement of his accounts, can not set off a debt due him personally against the share of a distributee; but he may redeem the whole or any part of a distributive share in satisfaction of a debt due from the distributee to the estate, including costs charged against him in legal proceedings.—Dray v. Bloch, 29 Or. 347, 45 Pac. 772. For instructive cases on accounting and settlement of executors or administrators, see In re Osburn's Estate, 36 Or. 8, 58 Pac. 521; In re Conser's Estate, 40 Or. 138, 66 Pac. 607; Estate of Adams, 131 Cal. 415, 63 Pac. 838; Estate of Pease, 149 Cal. 167, 85 Pac. 149; In re Roach's Estate, 50 Or. 179, 92 Pac. 118. An accounting is always a necessary preliminary to a final distribution.—Toland v. Earl, 129 Cal. 148, 152, 79 Am. St. Rep. 100, 61 Pac. 914. Appointee of court, to succeed deceased administrator, may have an accounting, as against the estate of the latter, in respect to the assets unadministered.—Galloway v. Freeburg, 97 Kan. 765, 156 Pac. 766. While, in all cases, a reasonable time is allowed executors and administrators for the settlement of the affairs of an estate, the law discourages unnecessary delay in this connection, as tending to waste by needless expense.—In re Dolenty's Estate, Mannix v. Dolenty, 53 Mont. 33, 161 Pac. 524.

2. Duty to account.—It is the duty of every executor or administrator, within six months after notice of his appointment, and every six months thereafter, until the estate is settled, to file a semi-annual account; and the county court must, at the first term after such account is filed, ascertain and determine if the estate be sufficient to satisfy the claims presented and allowed within the first six months, or any succeeding six months thereafter, after paying the funeral charges and expenses of administration, and if so, it shall so order and direct; but if the estate be insufficient for that purpose, it shall ascertain what per centum it is sufficient to satisfy, and direct accordingly.—Rostel v. Morat, 19 Or. 181, 23 Pac. 900. An executor must account, and his responsibilities as executor can terminate only after compliance with the statute, and after a settlement, approved by the court, has been made, and after a distribution and a delivery up have been ordered by the court.—In re Higgin's Estate, 15 Mont. 474, 28 L. R. A. 116, 39 Pac. 506, 517. From the expiration of the time mentioned in the notice to creditors, it is the duty of the executor to account. His obligation to account is continuous, and does not become barred by the statute of limitations. The right to demand an account from him runs with his duty, and can be asserted so long as his duty remains unperformed, and where there is no such laches as a court of equity will consider sufficient reason for dismissing an appeal to its jurisdiction.—Estate of Sanderson, 74 Cal. 199, 215, 15 Pac. 753.—See Irwin v. Holbrook, 26 Wash. 89, 66 Pac. 116. It is the duty of the domiciliary executor to gather in and account for the foreign assets to the extent of his conscious ability to do so, and the court of the domicile has a corresponding authority to compel him to account for wilful neglect to perform such duty. All the authorities agree that the residuum of the foreign assets must finally be collected and distributed by the domiciliary executor.—Estate of Ortiz, 86 Cal. 306, 316, 21 Am. St. Rep. 44, 24 Pac. 1034. A sole legatee may require an executor to account in the probate court at any time after the latter's neglect, whereby a loss has occurred to the estate.— Wheeler v. Bolton, 92 Cal. 159, 175, 28 Pac. 558. An executor, though a trustee under the will, must account to the probate court.—Dougherty v. Bartlett, 100 Cal. 496, 499, 35 Pac. 431. Each co-executor may keep a separate account, and present the same for final settlement. In such a case, each is chargeable with the full amount of assets which has come into his hands, and is entitled to be credited with all disbursements legally made by him on behalf of the estate.—Hope v. Jones, 24 Cal. 90, 93. Where it is not charged that any of the prop-

erty or assets of one deceased person has come into the possession or under the control of an administratrix of another estate, she can not be called upon to file an account, as her trust as administratrix of one estate does not create the duty to file an account in another estate.—Cross v. Baskett, 17 Or. 84, 21 Pac. 47.

3. Notice of settlement.—The manner in which notice of the settlement of the account of an executor or administrator is to be given is prescribed by statute, such as causing notices to be posted, etc., and it is quite apparent that if such notice is not given there can be no valid settlement of the account, and consequently no valid order made for the payment of a claim against the estate for money loaned by the claimant to decedent. The code seems to contemplate an order for the payment of a debt only upon the settlement of the administrator's account, but if it be assumed that such an order could be made before such settlement, still it would clearly be of no force if made without notice.—Estate of Spanier, 120 Cal. 698, 701, 53 Pac. 357. If the account is for a final settlement, accompanied by a petition for distribution, the notice must state those facts, and must be for at least the time prescribed by the statute.—Estate of Grant, 131 Cal. 426, 429, 63 Pac. 731. The efficacy of a notice of settlement of the final account of an administrator is not destroyed by the subsequent removal of the administrator and the appointment of another in his place, and such removal does not render it necessary to give another notice.—State v. O'Day, 41 Or. 495, 69 Pac. 542, 545. It is not a valid objection to the sufficiency of the affidavit of posting the notice of the time fixed for the hearing on settlement of a final account and distribution, that the affidavit was made on the day of posting, instead of being made at the expiration of the time for which the notice was published, especially where the decree recites due service by publication and posting. Such recital is sufficient to prove service, as against a collateral attack, and the presumption is that the notice remained posted during the statutory period.—Crew v. Pratt, 119 Cal. 139, 153, 51 Pac. 38. If all the heirs appear or are represented at the hearing or settlement of a final account and distribution, this is a sufficient answer to any objection to the sufficiency of the notice of the hearing.—Crew v. Pratt, 119 Cal. 139, 153, 51 Pac. 38. Sections 5000 and 5598, Revised Codes of Idaho, clearly provide for the fixing of a day for hearing a final settlement filed by an administrator and require the probate judge to appoint a day for settlement and that notice must be given at which time any person interested in the estate may appear and file exceptions to the account and contest the same.—Kent v. Dalrymple, 23 Ida. 694, 132 Pac. 304. The failure of an administrator to publish notice of final settlement does not affect the right of one appearing without notice.—Emelle v. Spinner, 20 Wyo. 507, 126 Pac. 398. The expression "all others," in the statutory requirement that an executor or administrator shall give four weeks' notice "to all creditors and all others interested in the estate," when desiring to make final settlement of an estate, refers to persons having

claims on the residue after direct creditors are satisfied.—Sarbach v. Fidelity & D. Co., 99 Kan. 29, 32 L. R. A. 1917B, 1043, 160 Pac. 990.

REFERENCES.

Remedy of distributee as to accounting of which he had no notice, and on which he did not appear.—See note 63 L. R. A. 95-108.

4. Account must show what.—The account of an executor or administrator must show the amount of money in his hands belonging to the estate, and if it is a matter of interest to those beneficially interested, it is competent for the court to require a specification of the kind of money received.—Magraw v. McGlynn, 26 Cal. 421, 429. The account should also show that a failure to collect a debt due to decedent was not the result of the negligence of the executor or administrator.—Estate of Sanderson, 74 Cal. 199, 203, 15 Pac. 753. When an estate is fully administered, the executor or administrator is required to file his final account, which must contain a detailed account of moneys received and expended by him, from whom received, and to whom paid, and refer to the vouchers for such payments, and the amount of money and property, if any, remaining unexpended or unappropriated. But where property of an estate was disposed of at public auction, or by private sale, and the administrator shows that it was impossible to check up the sales with the inventory, so as to be able to say with any degree of certainty that any goods remained on hand, or whether they were sold for more or less than their appraised value; that it was impossible to keep an account of what each article sold for at the auction; that it was impracticable and almost impossible to keep an account of the names of the persons to whom the property was sold, whether at the private sale or the public auction,—the court, if satisfied that the administrator made an honest effort to dispose of the property for the best interest of all concerned, will treat his account as final, though it does not appear therefrom from whom the money was received, or what property, if any, remains undisposed of, where a corrected report can not be had, and the ends of justice can better be subserved by treating the account as a final settlement of the estate.—In re Osburn's Estate, 36 Or. 8, 58 Pac. 521, 523. Where the decedent had a possessory right to two ranches and the executor sold the same by a verbal sale and claimed to retain the purchase money as his own on the grounds that the sales were void and that the property still remained to the estate in specie it was held that he must account for the money to the estate.—Candelaria v. Meera, 18 N. M. 107, 134 Pac. 832.

5. Order for payment of dividend.—An order for the payment of a dividend required by the statute is not, strictly speaking, a part of the proceeding for the settlement of the account, or of the adjudication respecting the claims reported therein. It follows thereon, but it is not a part thereof. It may, of course, be made immediately after the account is settled, but this does not make it a part of the proceeding.

On the other hand, it can not be made until after the account is settled, and it may be deferred to a considerable time thereafter, and be made without notice. It is a part of the proceeding for the administration of the estate, considered as a whole, but it is not, specifically, a part of the proceeding for the settlement of the account. The persons in whose favor such order for a dividend is made do not thereby become parties to the proceeding for the settlement of the account in cases where they did not appear or make any objection or contest upon such settlement.— Estate of McDougald, 143 Cal. 476, 480, 77 Pac. 443, 79 Pac. 878, 879.

6. Vouchers.—Where expenditures have been made, and the executor testifies, without opposition, both to the fact of payment and to the contents of letters acknowledging the receipt of payment, the items of the payment thus proved are sufficiently vouched to justify the charges, in the absence of counter-evidence.—Estate of Hilliard, 83 Cal. 423, 425, 23 Pac. 393. But an order settling the final account of an administrator will be reversed for want of proper vouchers, if the proof as to the correctness of the account is too general and indefinite. —Estate of Rose, 63 Cal. 349, 351. Where the statute requires the executor or administrator to produce and file vouchers for all charges, debts, claims, and expenses which he has paid, there ought to be a reasonable effort to comply with the statute, and he is not entitled to credit his payments made without a reasonable explanation why the vouchers are not produced. If the voucher is lost, or for other good reason can not be produced on the settlement, the payment may be proved by the oath of any competent witness, or of the executor or administrator. Items of expenses, not accompanied by the proper vouchers, should ordinarily be disallowed, but it does not follow that they may not afterwards be allowed on a proper showing.—Rice v. Tilton, 14 Wyo. 101, 82 Pac. 581. Where all parties agree that money has been properly expended, and no claim is made on the money paid out, there is no error in allowing the account without vouchers.— Estate of Coursen, 6 Cal. Unrep. 756, 65 Pac. 965, 967. But it is error to allow items in the account aggregating more than fifteen hundred dollars for which no vouchers are produced, and as to which there is no testimony regarding when, where, or to whom the payments were made.—Estate of Van Tassel, 2 Cal. Unrep. 435, 5 Pac. 611. Items rejected in an account may subsequently be allowed by producing proper vouchers.—Walls v. Walker, 37 Cal. 424, 426, 99 Am. Dec. 290; Estate of Adams, 131 Cal. 415, 417, 63 Pac. 838. But an order settling the final account of an executor or administrator will be reversed for want of proper vouchers.—Estate of Rose, 63 Cal. 349, 350. An order for the payment of money is not a voucher. A voucher must tend to show that the items represented in it were included or paid in or about the business of the administration of the estate.—Estate of Rose, 63 Cal. 349, 350. A receipt taken by an administrator, who is an attorney in fact, to himself as administrator, for money due to a claimant against the estate, which receipt is subscribed with the claimant's

name, by the administrator, as attorney in fact, is not a voucher.—
Estate of Watkins, 121 Cal. 327, 53 Pac. 702. The production of a
voucher, purporting to be for a "balance," is prima facie evidence
that no more was unpaid, and throws upon the contestant the burden
of showing the contrary.—Estate of Sarment, 123 Cal. 331, 335, 55 Pac.
1015. Canceled bank checks, although not strictly "vouchers," under
the statute, may, as evidence of payment, be sufficient to support an
administrator's account.—In re Campbell's Estate, 98 Wash. 295, 167
Pac. 905.

7. Hearing.

(1) In general.—Upon the settlement of an account, every creditor,
heir, legatee, or devisee is a person interested, and, as such, has a
right to enter an appearance, to become a party, and to be heard; and
unless they appear, they are to be considered as having no objections to
the account as rendered, and as consenting that it may be settled
accordingly.—Estate of McDougald, 143 Cal. 476, 479, 77 Pac. 443, 79
Pac. 878, 879. The parties interested in the estate are entitled to be
heard upon the propriety of charges against the estate.—Gurnée v.
Maloney, 38 Cal. 85, 88, 99 Am. Dec. 352. Matters which, in the nature
of things, are out of place in the settlement and accounting, however,
should not be considered by the court. The only items which are
properly to be settled in the account of an executor or administrator
are items relating purely to his administration of the estate, charges of
administration, and payment of debts of the decedent.—Estate of
Willey, 140 Cal. 238, 242, 73 Pac. 998. Thus where, in anticipation of
distribution to them as devisees in trust, the executors made certain
payments to those claiming as beneficiaries of the trust, the propriety
of these payments ought not to be determined on the settlement of
their account as executors, for it may appear that the estate may never
be distributed to them, and in that case the allowance to them of such
payments in settlement of their account as executors would be a
wrong to the rightful distributees. If, on the other hand, the estate
is distributed to them, they can protect themselves by simply charging the beneficiaries with the sums paid to them respectively. If
their charges are disputed, the determination of their correctness will
devolve upon the court having jurisdiction of the trust. In case the
estate is not ultimately distributed to the executors as devisees in
trust, but is distributed to some or all of those to whom these payments
have been made, such payments can be deducted from their distributive
shares by the decree of distribution.—Estate of Willey, 140 Cal. 238,
243, 73 Pac. 998. Whether a person claiming to have an interest in
an estate is entitled to any standing is a matter which is to be determined on the hearing of the distribution, rather than upon the settlement of an account, and particularly is this true where the items contained in the account are obviously improper, and it is the duty of the
court, for that reason, and of its own motion, to reject them.—Estate
of Willey, 140 Cal. 238, 243, 73 Pac. 998. Advances by an executor or

administrator are made at his own risk.—Estate of Knight, 12 Cal. 200, 208, 73 Am. Dec. 531; Tompkins v. Weeks, 26 Cal. 50, 61. The question whether the appraisers of an estate are disinterested parties is not necessary to be determined on the settlement of an executor's account, and can not affect his right to have his account settled.—Estate of Millenovich, 5 Nev. 161, 178.

(2) **Correction of mistakes.**—An error in settling the account of an executor or administrator may be corrected at the instance of any one interested.—Estate of Moore, 96 Cal. 522, 524, 526, 32 Pac. 584. Mistakes in settlements of executors' or administrators' accounts, which are open to correction at any time before final settlement, are confined to cases when the settlement has been ex parte, without notice to interested parties and without contest.—Estate of Raleigh, 48 Utah 128, 158 Pac. 705. The statute of Iowa, whereby mistakes in settlements of executors' or administrators' accounts may be corrected at any time before final settlement, has been adopted in Utah, also the Iowa decisions, construing the same, made prior to the adoption.— Estate of Raleigh, 48 Utah 128, 135, 158 Pac. 705.

(3) **Matters not to be considered.**—On the settlement of an account it is improper to consider questions in advance of distribution, that should be determined exclusively upon distribution, such as the rights of legatees and devisees. Such rights are fixed by the decree of distribution, and can only be determined on distribution. It must be apparent that the determination of the validity of the general trust provisions of a will, the validity of particular trusts in favor of various beneficiaries, the net annual income of the trust estate, and the identity of beneficiaries themselves, which matters may so radically affect the rights of beneficiaries under any will, can only be legally and effectively determined upon distribution, and that any effort to have them determined in the settling of an account must, in the nature of things, be out of place.—Estate of Willey, 140 Cal. 238, 242, 73 Pac. 998. In the settlement, whether the account be intermediate or final, advance payments made by the executor or administrator, under his own construction of the terms of the will, to the beneficiaries named therein, and upon his own judgment, without an order of the court, can not be considered. Such items may properly be retired from the account and considered when the petition for the distribution of the estate is heard.—Estate of Willey, 140 Cal. 238, 241, 243, 73 Pac. 998. On final settlement and accounting, the court should not construe the will.—Estate of Willey, 140 Cal. 238, 73 Pac. 998. So where an administratrix received a gift from the decedent, as his daughter, the question whether the decedent, at the time of the transfer to her, was holding the property in question in trust for the estate represented by the contestant of the final account, and whether the daughter is chargeable with the same trust, can not be determined upon the contest of a final account of a daughter as administratrix of the estate of her deceased father. That question can only be determined in a personal action against her to enforce the

trust.—Estate of Vance, 141 Cal. 624, 628, 75 Pac. 323. And the probate court has no jurisdiction to hear and determine the question as to where the real title to property rests.—In re Haas, 97 Cal. 232, 234, 31 Pac. 893. It can not determine disputes between heirs or devisees and strangers as to the title to property.—Buckley v. Superior Court, 102 Cal. 6, 8, 41 Am. St. Rep. 135, 36 Pac. 360. Neither does it have jurisdiction to determine the existence of an alleged partnership, which is denied, especially where one of the alleged partners has not been cited to appear, and is not before the court.—Wright v. Wright, 11 Colo. App. 470, 53 Pac. 684, 686. The question as to what particular contracts may have been entered into between parties as to the apportionment of the executors' commissions is a matter which should be heard in another forum; as where one of two executors claims that it was agreed between them that if one should do all the work, he should receive all of the commissions. The hearing of a final account by the probate court is not a place to settle disputes of this character. Matters of this kind are of no interest to the estate, and must be heard and determined at some other time and in some other proceeding.—Estate of Carter, 132 Cal. 113, 64 Pac. 123, 124. So where an executor has remained in possession of property for twenty years, claiming no right except as executor, and eventually presents his final account as such, asking for a settlement and discharge, he will not be heard in such proceeding to object to the jurisdiction of the court.—In re Moore, 95 Cal. 34, 36, 30 Pac. 106. If a charge for interest against the executor or administrator is not included in the grounds of contest against the account by the creditors, it can not be considered.—Estate of Sylvar, 1 Cal. App. 35, 38, 81 Pac. 663.

8. Exceptions. Contest. Objections. Evidence.

(1) In general.—An exception may be taken to an account on the ground that credits appear therein which are not such as the executor is entitled to as a matter of law; as, if an executor shall attempt to set off, as against money or property of the estate, which has passed into his hands, individual expenditures of his own, from which the estate could receive no benefit, and for which it is in no way answerable.—Estate of Sanderson, 74 Cal. 199, 204, 15 Pac. 753.

(2) Exceptions as aid to court.—Exceptions are permitted in aid of the court, when performing its duty of making the account correct; but they do not affect the power of the court to supervise, in every particular, the accounts of executors and administrators, which power is conferred for the protection of all interested, including infants, and oftentimes adults ignorant of their rights.—Estate of Sanderson, 74 Cal. 199, 210, 15 Pac. 753. It is not improper for the court to listen to objections to the account of an executor or administrator in advance of the filing of written objections.—Estate of Kennedy, 120 Cal. 458, 463, 52 Pac. 820. If a person interested in an estate wishes to contest an account presented for settlement by an executor or administrator,

he must file his exceptions in writing to the account, setting out specifically the grounds of his objections; and, at the hearing, he should be
held limited to the exceptions so presented. But, whether exceptions
are filed or not, the court should carefully examine every account presented for settlement, and be satisfied that it is in every respect practically correct before rendering an order settling it.—Estate of More,
121 Cal. 635, 639, 54 Pac. 148.

(3) Right to appear and contest.—The right to appear and contest
the account of an executor or administrator is restricted to persons
who are interested in the estate, but where there is any doubt as to
the question of interest, it ought to be resolved in favor of petitioner.
In other words, if he has the appearance of interest, his right to contest ought not to be denied.—Garwood v. Garwood, 29 Cal. 514, 519. A
creditor is entitled to appear in the probate court and to file objections
in writing to the account, and to contest the same.—Tompkins v. Weeks,
26 Cal. 51, 58. An administrator may appear and contest the account
of his predecessor. It is his duty to protect the estate against unlawful
claims of creditors; and it is also the duty of the court to do so, at the
suggestion of any person or on its own motion.—Estate of Spanier, 120
Cal. 698, 53 Pac. 357, 359. A guardian of the estate of minors has the
right to appear and contest the account of an administrator in an estate
where his wards are interested; and the appointment of an attorney to
represent the minors does not supersede the guardian's rights.—Estate
of Rose, 66 Cal. 241, 5 Pac. 220. The reversal of a decree of settlement
vacates it, and any person interested in the estate may subsequently
appear in the lower court and file exceptions to the account.—Estate
of Rose, 66 Cal. 241, 242, 5 Pac. 220. The circumstances that attorneys,
suing for professional services rendered, filed exceptions to the executor's account is unimportant. The are not interested in such account.
have no right to contest it, and the filing of exceptions could not give
them any interest.—Briggs v. Breen, 123 Cal. 657, 56 Pac. 633, 635.
The attorney of an executor or administrator can not file exceptions
to an account presented for settlement, for he is not a "person interested in the estate," and it is such persons only who are entitled to file
exceptions to an account. Hence, exceptions filed by such attorney
are ineffectual for any purpose.—Estate of Kruger, 143 Cal. 141, 145,
76 Pac. 891. Any person interested may appear, and, by objections in
writing, contest any account or statement therein.—Estate of Adams,
131 Cal. 415, 417, 63 Pac. 838. When the account is presented for settlement after due notice, any creditor or person interested may contest
the same, and may object to any item of charge, or credits, or to any
claims allowed and not passed upon on the settlement of any previous
account, and may thereupon have his objection settled and determined.
—Estate of McDougald, 146 Cal. 191, 194, 79 Pac. 878. Those interested
in the estate undoubtedly have the right to show that services, for
which the executor or administrator claims that allowances should be
made to him from the estate, have been so negligently performed as to

cause damage to the estate, and, consequently, that the estate should not pay therefor, as in the case of professional services rendered by attorneys.—Estate of Kruger, 143 Cal. 141, 76 Pac. 891, 893. Where the heirs of an estate make conveyances purporting to transfer the legal title to all property of the estate, the grantee is a person "interested in the estate" within the meaning of the Code of Civ. Proc. of California, sections 1635 and 1636, and has the same right to object to the account of the administrator that the grantors would have had as heirs.—In re Ross' Estate, 179 Cal. 358, 182 Pac. 303, 304. Where, in an account filed by an administratrix in the county court in 1909, certain credits are claimed by the administratrix, but it nowhere appears in the record on appeal to this court that the county court has ever approved such account, persons interested in the estate are not estopped from excepting to any item in such account at a future accounting by the administratrix.—In re McGannon's Estate, 50 Okla. 288, 300, 150 Pac. 1109.

REFERENCES.

Right of executor or administrator or his representatives to object to account of co-executor or co-administrator.—See note 22 L. R. A. (N. S.) 1119.

(4) **Contest of allowed claim.**—An allowed claim may be contested at the settlement of a final account of the administrator, if such claim has not already been passed upon on the settlement of a former account, or on rendering an exhibit, or on making a decree of sale, and the party contesting such claim is entitled to an exception to any adverse ruling of the court.—Estate of Hill, 62 Cal. 186, 187. The individual claim of an administrator against the estate is not conclusive, but may be contested by interested parties when the administrator's account is presented.—In re Barker's Estate, 26 Mont. 279, 67 Pac. 941, 942. There are at least two points in the administration of an estate at which an approved claim may be contested; namely, when the application is made for the sale of property, and when an account is rendered for settlement; but, in making the contest, the contestant has the affirmative, and must show cause.—Estate of Loshe, 62 Cal. 413, 415. The allowance of a claim has the effect only of placing the claim among the acknowledged debts of the estate, to be paid in due course of administration. It is not conclusive upon the heirs or others interested in the estate, but the right is still reserved to them, upon presentation of the account, to contest and have it rejected.—In re Barker's Estate, 26 Mont. 279, 67 Pac. 941, 942.

(5) **Manner of stating objections. Facts.**—Objections to an account may be stated in the most general language, although the probate court may require them to be made more specific. Under a general objection to any and all of the items, the court can inquire into and scrutinize the account, and is not bound by the executor's oath thereto, or by the vouchers produced by him; and, in examining it, he

may, for his information, allow any person to point out errors and defects therein.—Estate of Sanderson, 74 Cal. 199, 205, 15 Pac. 753. One who files an opposition to the settlement of the final account of an executor or administrator, and to a decree of distribution, on the ground that he has contingent claims against the estate must state, in his opposition, facts showing that such claim exists.—Estate of Halleck, 49 Cal. 111, 116. Where objections to the account of an administrator are separated into paragraphs, each stating the objection to a simple point or feature of the account, a report of the referee appointed to settle and report on the account, which is also divided into paragraphs, each of which refers to a specified paragraph of the written objections and states the finding with respect thereto and his recommendation concerning it, is sufficient.—Estate of McPhee, 156 Cal. 335, Ann. Cas. 1913E, 899, 104 Pac. 455.

(6) Purpose of statute. Practice. Pleadings. Issues.—The purpose of the statute in allowing any person interested to appear and file his exception in writing to the account, and to contest the same, is, that an issue shall be made in the trial court as to the items contested, or with which it is sought to charge the administrator. It is intended that the administrator shall know the items contested, or the matters in regard to which he is claimed to have been delinquent, so that he may come into court with his evidence, prepared to meet or to explain any exceptions to his account. The issues are thus made by the verified account and the written exceptions filed to it. The method is simple, and is designed to save the time of the court being taken up by uncontested matters.—Estate of Sylvar, 1 Cal. App. 35, 37, 81 Pac. 663. The account, and the objections thereto, represent the pleadings of the parties, and the issues to be tried are to be determined therefrom. The objector is required to specify with convenient detail the particular items to which he takes exception, and to state any matters of fact attending them, upon which reliance is had for attaching liability to the executor; and there is no good reason for going beyond this convenient practice, and requiring a technical reply of the executor or administrator whereby he must deny or avoid a matter stated by the objector, as by the rules of pleading adapted to ordinary suits or actions.—In re Conser's Estate, 40 Or. 138, 66 Pac. 607, 610. The requirement of the statute, that one who objects to a final account shall indicate the precise exceptions relied upon, was evidently designed, in the system of pleading, as an answer controverting the statements of facts contained in the final account, which is treated as a complaint, and such objections are apparently intended to impart notice to the personal representative of the decedent so as to enable him to prepare for a trial of the issues thus framed. The court's examination of the facts challenged by the exception is therefore limited to the particular specifications set forth in the objections interposed.—In re Roach's Estate, 50 Or. 179, 92 Pac. 118, 123. When persons, claiming to be heirs, file objections to the

final account of an executor or administrator, they are entitled to have such objections disposed of in an orderly and legal manner, and not to be summarily dismissed on motion of the administrator on the mere assumption, without proof, that they are not in fact heirs of the deceased. The issue tendered by them is one of fact, and should be so considered and determined by the evidence regularly offered and submitted.—In re Olischlager's Estate, 50 Or. 55, 89 Pac. 1049, 1050.

(7) **Additional or amended exceptions.**—In objecting to the final account of an executor or administrator, the legatees are not limited to their original objections, but may file additional or amended exceptions, at any stage of the proceedings, to modify or enlarge their demand so as to make it correspond with the testimony produced.—In re Roach's Estate, 50 Or. 179, 92 Pac. 118, 126. It is proper practice to extend to contestants the widest latitude in amending and supplementing their exceptions.—Estate of Sanderson, 74 Cal. 199, 210, 15 Pac. 753.

(8) **Untenable objections.**—It is not a valid objection, for an executor or administrator to make, that one of the persons filing objections to his account was not shown to be a "person interested."—Estate of Pease, 149 Cal. 167, 85 Pac. 149, 151. It is not a valid objection, where one claims a legacy, on the final settlement of the account of an executor, that the statute of limitations has run against the claimant, for the reason that he is not named in the will, and that it would require extrinsic evidence to enable the court to recognize him as the legatee. If the legatee is not named or described in the will, then he has no right to the legacy at all, and no amount of extrinsic evidence can create a right to it. On the other hand, if he is named or described in the will, no matter how defective the designation may be, he stands on an equal footing with all other devisees, and any circumstance which will prevent the statute from running as to them will prevent the statute from running as to him.—Reformed Presbyterian Church v. McMillan, 31 Wash. 643, 72 Pac. 502, 503. It is not a valid objection to the validity of the final account of an executor or administrator that certain property belonging to the estate was not appraised by the executor, where it appears that all the property received, or that which would by reasonable diligence have been received, has been accounted for.—In re Conser's Estate, 40 Or. 138, 66 Pac. 607, 610. An objection, urged to the final accounting of the executor, that proof of publication of notice to creditors was made by the publisher, and not the printer of his foreman, and was not filed within six months, is untenable. The statute requiring such notice is for the benefit of those having claims against the estate, that they may be informed of the appointment of the executor or administrator, and of the time and place of the presentation of demands to him. But it is in no sense a prerequisite to his entering upon the discharge of his duties.—In re Conser's Estate, 40 Or. 138, 66 Pac. 607, 609. It is not a matter pertinent for inquiry upon a final accounting, whether the sales of realty

have been authorized and regularly made with a view of determining their validity. The purchaser is not ordinarily a party to the proceeding, nor is there any process by which he may be brought in, and the proceeding is wholly inappropriate for the purpose, so that a suggestion to set aside the sale is without merit.—In re Conser's Estate, 40 Or. 138, 66 Pac. 607, 611. In a proceedings by an administrator de bonis non against the administrator and bondsmen of the first administrator of plaintiff's intestate, to require the production and filing of papers and vouchers in defendant's possession, showing the disbursements made by his intestate, an objection that the petition does not show that such defendant has in his possession property belonging to the intestate is without merit.—In re Herrin's Estate, 40 Or. 90, sub nom. Gatch v. Simpson, 66 Pac. 688, 689, 690.

(9) **Evidence. Burden of proof. Presumptions.**—Upon a contest of the final account of an administrator, where the exceptions are affirmative, and, so far as they relate to matters of fact or to the real objections of the contestant, constitute new and affirmative matter in opposition to the account, it is incumbent upon the contestant to introduce evidence in support of these allegations, and the administrator, in opening his case upon the account, is not required to anticipate the evidence in support of the exceptions, nor to show that the allegations in the exceptions are not true.—Estate of Vance, 141 Cal. 624, 626, 75 Pac. 323. If objections are made to an executor's final account, that certain property sold by him was worth more than he received for it, his failure to reply to such allegation does not preclude him from showing anything to the contrary.—In re Conser's Estate, 40 Or. 138, 66 Pac. 607, 610. If those who contest an administrator's account state, in their exceptions, that they are creditors of the deceased, and there is not proof, the presumption is that they are creditors.—Tompkins v. Weeks, 26 Cal. 50, 57. The burden of showing that an executor or administrator should be charged with interest is upon the contestant of his account.—Estate of Sarment, 123 Cal. 331, 333, 55 Pac. 1015. If an executor's final account is properly challenged, the burden of proving the truth of the item, or the reasonableness of any credit thus objected to, devolves upon him.— In re Roach's Estate, 50 Or. 179, 92 Pac. 118, 124. There is no error in admitting oral testimony as to the payment of taxes where the loss of tax receipts is shown before such oral testimony is received.— Estate of Moore, 72 Cal. 335, 13 Pac. 880, 884. If nothing further appears, the appraised value is the amount with which an executor or administrator should be charged; but it is not conclusive, and it is incumbent upon him, if there has been any loss, to show the cause thereof, so that the court can say that it was incurred without his fault, and thereby be enabled to extend him credit.—In re Conser's Estate, 40 Or. 138, 66 Pac. 610.

(10) **Waiver of written objections.**—Written objections to an account are waived by the administrator, where he went into the hear-

ing some time after oral objections were made in his presence and in the presence of the court, and at no time objected that the objections to the account were not made in writing.—Estate of Marre, 127 Cal. 128, 132, 59 Pac. 385.

9. Jurisdiction, power, and duty of court.

(1) **Jurisdiction.**—Due notice of a proposed final settlement of an estate having been given, the probate court has jurisdiction to make the settlement, to apportion the residue of the estate among those entitled to share in it, and to order distribution.—Lewis v. Woodrum, 76 Kan. 384, 92 Pac. 306; Toland v. Earl, 129 Cal. 148, 155, 79 Am. St. Rep. 100, 61 Pac. 914. In settling the accounts of the administrator, and in ascertaining the distributive shares of those entitled to succeed to the estate of a deceased person, and in adjudging what shall satisfy the decree of distribution, the superior court, in the exercise of its probate jurisdiction, proceeds upon principles of equity, and may so frame its judgments as to do exact justice in regard to all matters properly entering into the account of the administrator, and which, in the application of equitable rules, affect the distributive shares of the estate.—Estate of Moore, 96 Cal. 522, 528, 32 Pac. 584. The superior court, sitting in probate on proceedings for the settlement of the accounts of an executor, has jurisdiction to determine all issues necessarily incidental thereto, including an issue as to the title to a fund in the hands of the executor which he claimed belonged to him in his individual capacity.—Stevens v. Superior Court, 155 Cal. 148, 99 Pac. 512. The jurisdiction granted by section 1639 of the Code of Civil Procedure of California, to the superior court in which the estate was being administered of which the decedent was executor or administrator, is a power which may, under section 5 of article VI of the constitution, be conferred upon the superior court as a "matter of probate."—King v. Chase, 159 Cal. 420, 115 Pac. 407. The probate court has jurisdiction, on the filing of the final account, to enforce an agreement between the administrator and one who is the widow and sole heir of the deceased, whereby, in consideration of a share of the administrator's commissions, the latter has waived administration and procured the former's appointment as administrator.—In re Tachi's Estate, Tachi v. Kent, 90 Wash. 621, 156 Pac. 833, 93 Wash. 700, 161 Pac. 469.

(2) **Right, power, and duty of court in general.**—A probate court can settle the accounts of executors or guardians only in the manner prescribed by the code.—Reither v. Murdock, 135 Cal. 197, 201, 67 Pac. 784. The statute relating to accounting and settlements of executors and administrators applies to special administrators, so that it becomes the duty of the judge to hear the report, and account or exhibit, of the property of the estate received by a special administrator, and of payments made by him as such, and of issues raised by objections thereto.— French v. Superior Court, 3 Cal. App. 304, 306, 85

Pac. 133, 134. The court, in settling the account of an administrator, would not exceed its jurisdiction by requiring him to turn over the property to a special administratrix, where there is a dispute as to who owns the property which the administrator has in his hands at the time he is settling his accounts, but it is not disputed that the property came into his hands by virtue of his appointment as administrator.—State v. District Court, 26 Mont. 369, 68 Pac. 856, 857. A court, in final settlement, does not abuse its discretion, by denying the right of an executor to extra compensation for drawing an answer to the contest of a will, and for appearing at the continuance of hearings.—Estate of Carr, 175 Cal. 387, 165 Pac. 958. Where a son has had relations of the highest confidence with his father, so that at times he has deposited in bank to his private credit large sums collected for the other, and has taken at times in his own name notes and mortgages the consideration for which actually was his father's money; upon the death of the father and upon the son's becoming administrator, the court should, when the administrator's account comes up for settlement, allow a contestant to rigidly inquire into all such transactions.—Estate of Strong, 172 Cal. 441, 447, 156 Pac. 1026. Where an administrator's account purports to be "a full, true, and correct account of all the property which has come into the administrator's hands belonging to the estate," and a contestant would examine him in respect to specific items in that connection, the court should not thwart the effort.—Estate of Strong, 172 Cal. 441, 447, 156 Pac. 1026.

REFERENCES.

Right of court on its own motion to surcharge executor or administrator.—See note 18 L. R. A. (N. S.) 284-286.

(3) As to notice.—It is the duty of the court to ascertain whether proper notice has been given before allowing the account, and the statute directs that the decree shall show that proof thereof was made to the satisfaction of the court; and when proper notice has been given and so shown, the recital thereof in the decree is made conclusive evidence of the fact, subject, of course, to review on appeal in a proper manner.—McClellan v. Downey, 63 Cal. 520, 523. Whether additional notice shall be given or not is a matter within the discretion of the court below, and, in the absence of anything to show that such discretion has been abused, the appellate court will not interfere.—In re Jessup, 81 Cal. 408, 437, 6 L. R. A. 594, 21 Pac. 976, 22 Pac. 742, 1028.

(4) To scrutinize accounts.—It is the duty of the court to scrutinize carefully the account, and to reject all claims of the executors or administrators which are in themselves illegal or unjust in fact.—Estate of Sanderson, 74 Cal. 199, 210, 15 Pac. 753; Estate of Kennedy, 120 Cal. 458, 462, 52 Pac. 820; Estate of More, 121 Cal. 635, 639, 54 Pac. 148; Estate of Franklin, 133 Cal. 584, 587, 65 Pac. 1081; Estate of Willey, 140 Cal. 238, 243, 73 Pac. 998. The probate court has the power

to determine whether items of expenses of administration were properly incurred or not.—Dodson v. Nevitt, 5 Mont. 518, 6 Pac. 358, 360. The court has power to examine, and to allow or to disallow, any items in the account, even though there is no contest; and if it were brought to the knowledge of the court that the executor had failed to charge himself with money or property belonging to the estate, it would be the duty of the judge to examine the matter of his own motion.— Estate of Sanderson, 2 Cal. Unrep. 750, 13 Pac. 497; Estate of Sanderson, 74 Cal. 199, 15 Pac. 753. The court is not bound by the statement, in the petition of an applicant to contest the account, that he has any interest in the estate, but may take testimony as to whether he has any interest.—Garwood v. Garwood, 29 Cal. 514, 520. The court, on a proceeding for the settlement of the account of an executor, has power to examine him touching any and all items of account, and to base its decree of settlement upon such examination, notwithstanding that no person interested in the estate has filed specific exceptions to which the examination is appropriate.—Estate of Sanderson, 74 Cal. 199, 202, 15 Pac. 753. Though there be no objection or exception, the probate court should make careful examination of credits claimed by the representative and reject improper ones.—In re Hite's Estate, 155 Cal. 448, 101 Pac. 448.

(5) In absence of exceptions.—All persons interested have an opportunity, by filing written exceptions, to call the attention of the court to alleged errors or defects in an account presented by an executor or administrator; but, in the absence of exceptions, the court may, and should, inquire into any matter which may seem to it objectionable, and pass judgment thereon.—Estate of Sanderson, 74 Cal. 199, 208, 15 Pac. 753; Estate of Kennedy, 120 Cal. 458, 463, 52 Pac. 820; Estate of More, 121 Cal. 635, 639, 54 Pac. 148; Estate of Franklin, 133 Cal. 584, 587, 65 Pac. 1081; Estate of Willey, 140 Cal. 238, 243, 73 Pac. 998. Even in the presence of specific objections, the court is not limited to the specific objections.—Estate of Sanderson, 74 Cal. 199, 208, 15 Pac. 753. It was the duty of the court correctly to charge the administrator with the notes he ought to have paid, and to satisfy himself as to the correctness of the account, regardless of whether his attention was called to it in exceptions taken thereupon; and even if exceptions so taken were inadvertently disallowed, in connection with other exceptions to the account not approved, such inadvertent ruling is not ground for a reversal of a properly corrected account of the administrator.—Iu re Loheide, 17 Cal. App. 475, 120 Pac. 56.

(6) Report of referee.—The report of the referee of an account of an executor or administrator is merely advisory to the court. If the court is not satisfied from the evidence adduced before the referee that the findings and recommendations of the referee were correct and proper, it may take further testimony, and make its own findings and conclusions. The report and findings of the referee may be adopted, modified, or disapproved altogether, as the court may see fit,

especially where the reference is only for the purpose of examining the account of the executor and objections thereto and making report thereon.—In re Courtney's Estate, 31 Mont. 625, 79 Pac. 317, 319.

(7) To compel accounting.—An executor or administrator may be directed by the probate court to render a full account of his administration, and the authority of the court to enforce obedience to such order is not doubted.—Magraw v. McGlynn, 26 Cal. 421, 430. In a proceeding to compel an executor or administrator to pay to an heir, his distributive share, the power of the court is not limited to the specific property or the amount awarded by the decree. It has jurisdiction to take an account, or to award an interest according to equitable principles.—Estate of Clary, 112 Cal. 292, 294, 44 Pac. 569. The probate court has competent authority to make all necessary orders to compel an accounting of personal property belonging to the estate of the testator, whether it be such as the testator owned at the time of his death, or is the profits of other property of the estate sold by the executor. That court also possesses competent power to compel an accounting in respect to property which it is alleged the executor has converted to his own use.—Auguisola v. Arnaz, 51 Cal. 455, 438. The personal obligation of an executor or administrator, who has been guilty of a devastavit, is to be enforced by a resort to the court which settled the account.—Washington v. Black, 83 Cal. 290, 295, 23 Pac. 300. The court may compel an executor or administrator, even if he has resigned his trust, to account for the estate to the value of personal property converted by him which he had neglected to include in his prior accounts.—Estate of Radovich, 74 Cal. 536, 539, 5 Am. St. Rep. 466, 16 Pac. 321. The probate court has the power, and it is its duty, to require a full and final accounting, and to make a settlement with an executor, who has resigned, been removed, or whose letters have been revoked, and to order him to deliver the personal effects and assets of the estate to his successor.—Hudson v. Barrett, 62 Kan. 137, 61 Pac. 737. The provisions of the statute requiring guardians to account annually, and oftener, if required by the probate courts, clearly refer to accounts to be rendered during the lifetime of the guardian and the minority of the ward; but where the guardian dies before making a settlement, and long after his ward's majority, his executors, having received no assets of the ward, can not be compelled by the probate court to make a settlement of the estate of the said ward. The guardianship has terminated; the probate court has lost its jurisdiction; and the presentation of such settlement is no part of the duties involved in the administration of the testator.—Harris v. Calvert, 2 Kan. App. 749, 44 Pac. 25. The probate court has no authority to cite the administrator of an administrator to settle the account of his intestate with the estate of which he was the administrator.—Bush v. Lindsey, 44 Cal. 121, 124. Since the enactment, in 1905, of section 1639 of the Code of Civil Procedure of California, empowering the superior court, sitting in probate, to compel the personal representatives of a deceased executor or administrator to render an account of the administration of their testator or intestate, and to settle such account as in other cases, an action in equity will not lie to compel the executor or administrator of a deceased executor or administrator to settle the account of his testator or intestate with the estate in which the decedent has been acting.—King v. Chase, 159 Cal. 420, 115 Pac. 207. Prior to the enactment of that section, the power of a court in equity to compel such an accounting was based solely on the lack of any statutory method of accomplishing the same end by a proceeding in probate. Now that this lack has been remedied, the foundation of the equity jurisdiction is gone.—King v. Chase, 159 Cal. 420, 115 Pac. 207. The fact that the superior court exercises both equitable and probate jurisdiction does not warrant the upholding of a judgment for an accounting, rendered against an executor of a deceased executor in an action in equity brought after the enactment of said section 1639, where such executor, at the time he accounted in such action, objected to the jurisdiction of the court to compel him to account therein.—King v. Chase, 159 Cal. 420, 115 Pac. 207.

(8) Striking. Combining. Making more specific.—Where payments have been made to general creditors without authority of the court, they are made at the peril of the administrator. Hence if exceptions are filed to the account, and it appears that the sufficiency of the assets for the payment of all the debts is doubtful, it is the duty of the court to strike out such payments, with leave to charge them in a future account if the estate should prove solvent, or to the extent of their pro rata share if the estate should prove insolvent.— Estate of Fernandez, 119 Cal. 579, 582, 51 Pac. 851. If the first account of an executor or administrator is not sufficiently specific, the court clearly has the power to require the administrator to make it more specific; and if, pending the settlement of such account, the administrator presents a second account, it is not only the right, but it is also the duty of the court to require the two accounts to be combined into one, so as to present a full and complete showing of the administration up to the time of the rendition of such combined account. Where the circumstances of the estate are such that one account will result in saving expenses, and in more clearly presenting the accounts of the representative of the estate, it is not only the right, but it is also the duty of the court to require the one account.— Hirschfeld v. Cross, 67 Cal. 661, 662, 8 Pac. 507. If an account filed is defective, the court may require it to be made more specific.— Hirschfeld v. Cross, 67 Cal. 661, 8 Pac. 507.

(9) Want of jurisdiction.—A court has no jurisdiction to settle prematurely the account of an executor or administrator. It should not attempt to settle such account before the same is filed. If the court undertakes to direct the dismissal of an action brought by the administrator upon a claim alleged to be due the estate, and to find thereupon that there is no property in the hands of the administrator,

it undertakes both to state and to settle his account to that extent. It determines his rights in that regard, and settles, or attempts to settle, his account as effectually as if the order had been made after the administrator had filed an account. This the court can not do.— Estate of Bullock, 75 Cal. 419, 421, 17 Pac. 540. As a probate court has no power to take cognizance of the differences existing between the administrator and heirs and claimants in their individual capacities, the administrator can not claim an offset of a debt due him, against a creditor or distributee of the estate, and the court has no jurisdiction to pass upon the administrator's right to make such a set-off.— Dray v. Bloch, 29 Or. 347, 45 Pac. 772, 774. The probate court has no authority to cite the administrator of an administrator to settle the account of his intestate with the estate of which he was the administrator.—Bush v. Lindsey, 44 Cal. 121, 124. Neither has it power, after the term at which a final order has been made, approving the accounts of the administrator, to confirm a "supplementary account," without notice to the distributees, which supplementary account is in itself a radical modification of the final account.—Dray v. Bloch, 29 Or. 347, 45 Pac. 772, 774. Nor has the court any power to order an administrator to pay the balance of the estate into court, and that he thereupon be discharged.—Estate of Sarment, 123 Cal. 331, 337, 55 Pac. 1015. The administrator is answerable for the assets in his hands, and, so long as he remains in office, is entitled thereto under the directions of the court. Upon the entry of an order for the payment of the claims against the estate, the administrator becomes liable therefor to the creditors, both personally and upon his bond, and each creditor is entitled to an execution against him therefor. He can not escape this liability by complying with an order which the court had no power to make.—Estate of Sarment, 123 Cal. 331, 337, 55 Pac. 1015. A probate court, in the settlement of an account, has no jurisdiction to declare an executor's deed to real estate to be valid, where no proceeding for the confirmation of said sale has ever been made.—Estate of Richards, 154 Cal. 478, 98 Pac. 528.

10. Administrator to be charged with what. In general.—An executor or administrator is chargeable not only with the assets which come into his possession, but also with those which it was his duty to have taken into possession, and which, by negligence, he has failed to collect.—Estate of Kennedy, 120 Cal. 458, 461, 52 Pac. 820. In the settlement of his final account, he is to be charged with a personal debt due from him to the decedent as money on hand.—Estate of Walker, 125 Cal. 242, 249, 73 Am. St. Rep. 40, 57 Pac. 991; Estate of Miner, 46 Cal. 564, 570. Under the statute of Oregon, an executor, though insolvent, is bound to account for a debt due from him to the estate, and shall be charged therewith on the settlement of his final account as for so much money in his hands from the time the claim became due and payable.—Davisson v. Akin, 42 Or. 177, 95 Am. St. Rep. 735, 70 Pac. 507, 508. An executor or administrator has no right to occupy and use

premises belonging to the estate for a series of years for his own profit, and without accounting for the value of such use. It is as much his duty to pay a reasonable rental for the property as it would be his duty to collect and to account for the rent if the property had been leased to a stranger to the estate. Hence if he uses realty of the estate as his own, he must account for rental.—In re Alfstad's Estate, 27 Wash. 175, 67 Pac. 593, 598. An executor or administrator is chargeable with the value of real property lost to the estate by his neglect to pay the taxes thereon.—Estate of Herteman, 73 Cal. 545, 15 Pac. 121, 123. So if he commences a suit to recover property of the estate, but abandons the suit without good reason therefor, and allows the defendant therein to keep the estate on payment to plaintiff of money, which the plaintiff retains for himself, the executor or administrator is chargeable with the value of the property, if lost to the estate.—Estate of Pease, 149 Cal. 167, 85 Pac. 149, 151. An executor or administrator should be charged with interest on money of the estate which he has drawn and mingled with his own funds and omitted from his account.—Estate of Herteman, 73 Cal. 545, 547, 15 Pac. 121. An executor or administrator is chargeable with money lost to the estate through his negligence, though he does not thereby forfeit his statutory right to commissions. He should be charged with such loss in his account, but be credited with his commissions.—Estate of Carver, 123 Cal. 102, 104, 55 Pac. 770. An administrator personally indebted to the estate on promissory notes, which he was able to pay, but who never credited the estate therewith on the insufficient ground that to pay the same would have sacrificed his private business, was properly charged with the amount thereof in his final account as money on hand for distribution. His primary duty was to the trust assumed, and he was not authorized to show favor to himself as a debtor to the estate greater than to any other debtor. He had no right to use the credit of the estate to promote his personal gain, or to maintain a business which might suffer if he drew out of his capital enough to pay what he owed the estate.—Estate of Loheide, 17 Cal. App. 475, 120 Pac. 56. Even if there are no creditors interested in notes due from the administrator to the estate charged in his final account, the heirs are nevertheless entitled to have brought into the estate for distribution all that legally and rightfully belongs to the estate, including such notes, and if the administrator is then personally insolvent, though able to pay the same at any time during his administration, the heirs may look to the sureties on his official bond to enforce his delinquency.—In re Loheide, 17 Cal. App. 475, 120 Pac. 56. Administrator held chargeable with simple interest for the use of money of the estate though the widow consented.—In re McPhee's Estate, 156 Cal. 335, Ann. Cas. 1913E, 899, 104 Pac. 455. Representative may be charged with compound interest in money converted by him as where he delayed settlement for many years and converted funds.—In re McPhee's Estate, 156 Cal. 335, Ann. Cas. 1913E, 899, 104 Pac. 455. Where an administrator has made per-

sonal use of the decedent's real estate in his hands, this, with other
circumstances, justifies the court in charging him with the rental value
of the land for his use and occupation thereof.—Estate of Piercy,
Piercy v. Piercy, 168 Cal. 750, 145 Pac. 88. If an administrator
squanders the estate or fails to properly administer it, parties interested in the estate may surcharge his final account.—In re Marks'
Estate, 81 Or. 632, 160 Pac. 540, 81 Or. 639, 160 Pac. 542. Whatever
indulgence may be allowed an executor who expends money of the
estate for the purpose of preserving the latter until the proper court
orders may be made with reference to its disposition; he can not,
without charging himself, hazard the estate's money on speculative
ventures, in the absence of an order of court.—In re Delaney's Estate,
41 Nev. 384, 171 Pac. 383. An executor or administrator is chargeable,
not only with the assets that actually come into his hands, but also
those that by reason of his negligence have not come into his hands;
this includes rents and profits of real estate which, in the exercise of
ordinary care, he ought to have collected.—In re Dolenty's Estate,
Mannix v. Dolenty, 53 Mont. 33, 161 Pac. 524.

REFERENCES.

Charging administrator with interest.—See note § 655, head-line 4,
ante.

11. Administrator not chargeable when.—An executor or administrator will not be charged with the appraised value, but with the
amount received only, though his final report does not show that he
has disposed of and accounted for all the goods that came into his
possession, if his testimony as a witness shows that he did dispose of
and account for all the property that come into his possession, and
such testimony is corroborated by his final report, which shows that
he received, on account of sales, very nearly the appraised value of
the property.—In re Osburn's Estate, 36 Or. 8, 58 Pac. 521, 524. An
executor or administrator can not be charged with debts or choses
in action, he can not be charged with money retained under a claim
of right, but, of course, if the administrator should lose the right
to recover such money by neglecting to bring an action for its recovery
before the right to do so is barred by the statute of limitations, he
would then properly be chargeable with the loss.—In re Beam's Appeal, 8 Kan. App. 835, 57 Pac. 854, 855. If an executor or administrator uses diligence in trying to collect claims due the estate, but is
unable, owing to the financial condition of the debtors, to collect in
full, and he rebates from a claim by way of compromise, he should
not be charged with the amount rebated, where the debtor is apparently insolvent.—In re Ricker's Estate, 14 Mont. 153, 29 L. R. A. 622,
35 Pac. 960, 967. So where it appears from his final accounting that
he received for a note and mortgage all that it was reasonably worth,
he is not to be charged with the difference between such sum and the
appraised value of the note and mortgage.—In re Conser's Estate, 40

Or. 138, 66 Pac. 607, 610. An executor or administrator should not be charged for the use and occupation of his decedent's land after a sale of the premises by the sheriff under a foreclosure sale; because from that time the purchaser at the sale becomes entitled to the value of the use and occupation, and, after such sale, the estate, and the parties interested therein, have no claim to the value of the use and occupation.—Walls v. Walker, 37 Cal. 424, 431, 99 Am. Dec. 290. A request made by a testator of a third person to remove to his burial plot the remains of certain of his relatives and to erect a monument over his grave, is not binding upon his executors.—Estate of Hincheon, 159 Cal. 755, 36 L. R. A. (N. S.) 303, 116 Pac. 47. Where corporate stock was part of an estate, the administrator with the will annexed is not chargeable with the appraised value of such stock, for the benefit of heirs and legatees, though he was guilty of many irregularities in his acts with reference to such stock, where the stock never was salable, but the administrator actually realized several thousand dollars in cash from it.—In re Johnston's Estate (Wash.), 181 Pac. 209, 213. An administrator with the will annexed is not, in a proceeding by heirs and legatees to set aside, in the court wherein made, an order approving the administrator's final account as well to set aside the decree of distribution, answerable for the amount of claims twice approved by the court below, though such claims were irregularly paid, if there was no question as to the justness or validity of any of the claims.—In re Johnston's Estate (Wash.), 181 Pac. 209, 213.

12. Administrator is entitled to credit for what.

(1) In general.—It is error to reject unchallenged items on the credit side of the final account of an executor or administrator.—In re Roach's Estate, 50 Or. 179, 92 Pac. 118, 123. He is entitled to credit for moneys advanced to distributees and legatees to the full extent of payments made to them, whether ordered by the court or not. These payments should be charged to the distributive shares.—Estate of Moore, 96 Cal. 522, 529, 31 Pac. 584. He may be allowed money paid for releasing animals belonging to the estate, from a lien for pasturage, where he acts in good faith and for what he deems to be the best interest of the estate; and he can not be legally charged with a loss arising from a sale of the animals for less than the amount of the lien paid by him, unless it is made to appear that he has been guilty of negligence, and did not use ordinary care and diligence in connection with the matter.—Estate of Armstrong, 125 Cal. 603, 605, 58 Pac. 183; Estate of Freud, 131 Cal. 667, 671, 82 Am. St. Rep. 407, 63 Pac. 1080. If an executor or administrator carries on his intestate's business, and charges himself with the gross profits of the business, and the court debits him with the amount thereof, he should be allowed money paid out in the course of the business.—Estate of Rose, 80 Cal. 166, 178, 22 Pac. 86. It is proper to allow to an executor or administrator an item of expenses in procuring a surety com-

pany to go upon his bond, though the authority of the executor or
administrator is afterwards revoked for irregularities, where the statute expressly authorizes him to include, as a part of the lawful expenses of executing his trust, such reasonable sum as may be paid
to a company, authorized under the laws of the state to become such
surety.—Rice v. Tilton, 14 Wyo. 101, 82 Pac. 577, 580. If he acts in
good faith, he is entitled to credit for reasonable disbursements and
commissions, although his order of appointment is voidable.—Rice v.
Tilton, 14 Wyo. 101, 82 Pac. 577, 581; In re Owens' Estate, 32 Utah
469, 91 Pac. 283, 285. An executor or administrator may be allowed
reasonable and necessary costs for prosecuting appeals to the supreme
court, where no mismanagement or bad faith on his part is shown.—
In re Davis' Estate, 33 Mont. 539, 88 Pac. 957, 958. If, pending the
administration of an estate, a mortgage is given thereon by authority
of the court, and a part of the land is afterwards sold, and the other
part is set aside as a probate homestead for the minor children, and
the mortgagee demands payment of a certain sum of money before he
will release the tract sold, and the administrator pays the sum demanded, the court, in proceedings for the settlement of the final account, is authorized to make allowance for the payment so made.—
Estate of Shively, 145 Cal. 400, 78 Pac. 869, 870. Although an order
has been made ex parte and without notice, yet, if the items are proper
ones for allowance under the law, a nunc pro tunc order may be made
at the hearing of the objections to such order, covering the same items
included in the former order.—In re Murphy's Estate, 30 Wash. 9,
70 Pac. 109, 110. That which is a proper charge in favor of an administrator can not be collected otherwise than by his retention of the
property until such charge is paid.—Huston v. Becker, 15 Wash. 586,
47 Pac. 10, 11. The fact that heirs, legatees, and creditors are expressly permitted to contest matters not included and passed upon in
any former account necessarily implies that the administrator is not
precluded from going behind a former account, and bringing forward
charges which, through inadvertence or oversight, may have been
omitted.—Walls v. Walker, 37 Cal. 424, 426, 99 Am. Dec. 290.

REFERENCES.

Right of executor or administrator to credit for amount paid to
a surety company for going on an administration bond.—See note 48
L. R. A. 591, 592.

(2) **Payments made for preservation or protection of estate.**—It is
a cardinal principle, that, subject to the contingency of the expense
being disallowed by the court, an executor or administrator may do
whatever is necessary for the preservation of the property of the
estate, and the specific character of the act done is altogether immaterial. For such purpose, he may pay off liens existing on the property; he may also spend money in litigation, either to protect or to
recover property of the estate, or for insurance; and while he may

not expend money in the erection of a new building, yet he may expend it in repairs to any extent necessary to preserve the property; and, in case that may be readily imagined, power to repair might extend even to the erection of a new building; as, in the case of a necessary outhouse destroyed by fire, or of land paying a large rental on which the building had been destroyed by fire, or decayed so as to be no longer available, and where the new building could be paid for in a very short time out of the rental. As trustee for the estate, he may redeem the property thereof from the lien of a mortgage made by decedent, though not presented as a claim against the estate, and may charge the expense to the estate.—Estate of Freud, 131 Cal. 667, 673, 82 Am. St. Rep. 407, 63 Pac. 1080. But the power of the administrator to pay off encumbrances in any case results solely from the necessity of preserving the property, and can be justified only on the ground that the lien is a charge on the estate, and therefore a peril to it; and this is equally true, whether the lien was created by the intestate, or, as in the case of taxes, in some other way.—Estate of Freud, 131 Cal. 667, 672, 82 Am. St. Rep. 407, 63 Pac. 1080. Certain disbursements for the repair of a house should be allowed to an executor or administrator, although, as an heir, the house may become his property, where the property was inventoried and accounted for as property of the estate, and the administrator charged himself with the rents, which amounted to sums at least one-half the sum expended for repairs, and where there has been no order transferring dominion over the property to the administrator individually,. and there has been no distribution of the estate.—Rice v. Tilton, 14 Wyo. 101, 82 Pac. 577, 580. If it is absolutely essential for the protection of an estate, and the preservation of its property, that the representative should advance money as for the expenses of litigation, and he does so, thereby producing benefit to those interested therein, it is only equitable that he should be fully reimbursed.— Estate of Carpenter, 146 Cal. 661, 80 Pac. 1072, 1074. It is proper for an heir to take care of the property of decedent so far as necessary for its preservation, or cause it to be done, until an administrator was appointed, and if expense was incurred therein, the heir is entitled to compensation out of the estate.—In re Murray's Estate, 56 Or. 132, 107 Pac. 21. The fees of an attorney employed by a personal representative of a decedent in the business of the estate, are not strictly debts of the estate, but if such services are necessary and the charges reasonable, for work actually done, they are proper credits to be allowed in the settlement of the accounts of the personal representative. —In re McGannon's Estate, 50 Okla. 288, 299, 150 Pac. 1109.

(3) Same. Necessary expenditures.—An executor or administrator should be allowed, in the settlement of his account, for wages paid for the protection of the estate.—Estate of Miner, 46 Cal. 564. An executor or administrator is entitled to credit for taxes paid on the property of a decedent; and the probate court may, under a proper

petition, adjust the rights of heirs who are equitably entitled to
reimbursement for taxes paid by them, or those under whom they
claim.—Estate of Heeney, 3 Cal. App. 548, 553, 86 Pac. 842. Where
the expenditure is for the benefit of the estate, and is necessary, and
is for services which it is the duty of the administrator to perform,
but which he can not himself perform, it is within the discretion of
the judge to make an allowance to the administrator for such expenditures, as where a broker has been employed on commission to
make a sale of real estate. No rule can be laid down which shall
catalogue the various kinds of these expenses, or classify them. Much
will depend upon the nature of the estate and the character of the
services for which the charge is made.—Estate of Willard, 139 Cal.
501, 506, 64 L. R. A. 554, 73 Pac. 240. While expenditures made by an
executor or administrator upon the estate he represents for permanent
improvements upon the property in the way of erecting new buildings
and structures will not be allowed, yet, if the repairs and improvements
are absolutely necessary to keep the premises in good tenantable condition, it would be very inequitable to hold that the representative
is not entitled to reimbursement.—Estate of Clos, 110 Cal. 494, 42
Pac. 971. An executor or administrator is entitled to credit for rent
paid under a valid agreement with the representative.—Estate of
Dunne, 58 Cal. 543, 548. "Executors and administrators are allowed,
as proper credits in their accounts, all disbursements made in good
faith for any liability of the estate, either arising in the course of
administration, or existing against the deceased at the time of his
death, and paid in the manner prescribed by law."—Estate of Willard,
139 Cal. 501, 506, 64 L. R. A. 554, 73 Pac. 240, quoting from 2 Woerner's
American Law of Administration, section 514. An executor is entitled
to charge the estate with his expenses necessarily incurred in conducting litigation to determine whether certain real property is liable
for the payment of obligations of the estate.—Nelson v. Schoonover,
89 Kan. 779, Ann. Cas. 1915A, 147, 132 Pac. 1183.

(4) **For costs paid.**—An executor or administrator is entitled to
credit for costs paid on the foreclosure of a mortgage given to his
intestate, where he becomes the purchaser at a sum too small to
satisfy the mortgage and costs.—Estate of Miner, 46 Cal. 564, 571.
While an executor or administrator is individually answerable for
costs, where a judgment has been recovered against him, yet they
should be allowed him in his administration accounts, unless it appears
that the suit or proceeding in which the costs were taxed was prosecuted or resisted without just cause.—Hicox v. Graham, 6 Cal. 167, 169;
Estate of Miner, 46 Cal. 564, 570.

(5) **Funeral expenses. Last illness.**—The proper expenses of the
disposition of the body of a deceased person is a proper charge against
his estate, but neither the court in probate nor the personal representative has any right to the body of the deceased, nor any right
to control the manner of disposition of the remains, nor to dictate the

place of interment. The duty and the right of burial are quite different things from the duty and the right of auditing and paying the expenses of such burial.—O'Donnell v. Slack, 123 Cal. 285, 43 L. R. A. 388, 55 Pac. 906, 907. Funeral expenses are proper charges against the distributive shares of an estate coming to adult children, but subject to the debts of the estate. If they have no estate from which the items can be paid until the estate is settled, and their distributive shares are ready to be apportioned, the court should see that the executor or administrator is paid the amount of these items from such distributive shares, if there be such at the final settlement of the estate, especially where the expenditures, being first charges against the respective estates of the children for whom they were made, were advanced by the executor or administrator at the time when humanity demanded it. In such a case he should be reimbursed before the distributive shares are otherwise distributed.—In re Murphy's Estate, 30 Wash. 9, 70 Pac. 109, 111. The courts will allow a reasonable sum to be paid out of the funds of the estate for the erection of a monument, putting the expenditure upon the ground of funeral expenses.— Estate of Koppikus, 1 Cal. App. 84, 81 Pac. 732, 733. With respect to funeral expenses of decedent, courts generally take into consideration all the circumstances of the case, and when executors have acted with ordinary prudence, they are not held personally liable, although the sums paid therefor may seem large.—Estate of Millenovich, 5 Nev. 161, 182. The expenses of the last illness of the decedent can not be regarded as extravagant when they are not in excess of the customary charges therefor.—Estate of Millenovich, 5 Nev. 161, 182. Money paid for the funeral expenses of a decedent, by one not acting officiously, if reasonable, considering the estate of the deceased and the circumstances surrounding the death and burial, should be repaid by the estate to the party paying them.—Estate of Hincheon, 159 Cal. 755, 36 L. R. A. (N. S.) 303, 116 Pac. 47. Where a will expresses the wish of the testatrix for burial in a particular place, but burial is had elsewhere by direction of husband, in accordance with what he states to have been her desire, expressed after the date of the will, the executor is thereby relieved of responsibility in the matter. His duty does not require him to challenge the accuracy of the husband's statement, or to make an issue therein for the determination of a court.—Nelson v. Schoonover, 89 Kan. 779, Ann. Cas. 1915A, 147, 132 Pac. 1184.

(6) **Payment of family allowance.**—In the matter of paying a family allowance, the administrator is not required to wait for an order of court, but may make the necessary expenditures as the exigencies occur, and the court will allow such sums as may be reasonable in the settlement.—Estate of Lux, 100 Cal. 606, 607, 35 Pac. 345, 114 Cal. 89, 90, 45 Pac. 1028; Crew v. Pratt, 119 Cal. 131, 138, 51 Pac. 44. And the fact that the widow received other moneys from other property of the deceased does not preclude the court from sanctioning the disbursements by the executors for her support, where the court finds that,

taking that fact into consideration, the allowance paid by the executors was reasonable, and properly advanced to the widow as a family allowance for her use and support.—Estate of Lux, 114 Cal. 89, 90, 45 Pac. 1028. The production of a voucher from the widow, showing a receipt of the payment of "one thousand dollars, balance payment of the eighteen hundred dollars allowed by the court for widow's allowance," is prima facie evidence that only one thousand dollars of the allowance is then unpaid, and throws upon the contestant the burden of showing the contrary; and, in the absence of counter-proof, and with the testimony of the administrators that the whole has been paid, the court should give credit for the full amount.—Estate of Sarment, 123 Cal. 331, 335, 55 Pac. 1015. Whether a family allowance made to an administratrix should be cut down by reason of her delay in closing the estate is a question for the lower court to determine, and, in the absence of any showing of an abuse of discretion, its decision will not be disturbed on appeal.—Estate of Freud, 131 Cal. 667, 674, 82 Am. St. Rep. 407, 63 Pac. 1080.

(7) Traveling expenses.—An administrator should be allowed all necessary traveling expenses when on business of the estate.—Rice v. Tilton, 14 Wyo. 101, 82 Pac. 577, 580; and an item of traveling expenses should not be rejected in toto because the account does not disclose for what the expense was incurred, but should be retired from the list of items, with leave to bring it forward with the proper proofs in a future account. The administrator is also entitled to credit for payments made for the services and traveling expenses of his attorney, not exceeding a reasonable compensation for the labor actually performed, when the same were necessary to enable him properly to perform the duties of his trust.—Estate of Rose, 80 Cal. 166, 178, 179, 22 Pac. 86; Estate of Moore, 72 Cal. 335, 13 Pac. 880, 884. It is necessary, howin no case should an administrator be allowed to employ a book-keeper. This may properly be left to the probate judge. He may allow it, if proper; but if the services are such as, under the circumstances, the administrator ought to have performed, and for which his commissions are intended to compensate him, such charge should be disallowed.— Estate of Moore, 72 Cal. 335, 13 Pac. 880, 884. It is necessary, however, for him, in order to secure such allowance, to make a proper showing, accompanied by vouchers or a fit explanation of his charges. If he makes a number of trips, and the charge for each trip is made in a lump sum, he should be required to explain and identify the payments entering into the charge. This, doubtless, might be accomplished by the production of vouchers showing each payment, but items for traveling expenses, not accompanied by vouchers, will be disallowed. —Rice v. Tilton, 14 Wyo. 101, 82 Pac. 577, 581. An administratrix is entitled to her traveling expenses necessarily incurred in her legitimate efforts to preserve the estate, and properly incurred in distributing its assets, but an order rejecting such an item will not be disturbed on appeal, except upon a claim showing that the moneys were thus neces-

sarily and properly expended.—Estate of Byrne, 122 Cal. 260, 262, 54 Pac. 957. Traveling expenses connected with the administration of foreign assets should not be allowed out of the assets collected in this state, but out of the foreign assets.—Estate of Ortiz, 86 Cal. 306, 316, 21 Am. St. Rep. 44, 24 Pac. 1034.

(8) **Items for less than twenty dollars.**—If an administrator swears that he has paid an item which amounts to less than $20, and no contradiction to that evidence appears, it ought to be allowed.—Estate of Rose, 80 Cal. 166, 178, 22 Pac. 86. Where the statute provides that an executor or administrator, on the settlement of his account, may be allowed any item of expenditure not exceeding $20, for which no voucher is produced, if such item be supported by his own uncontradicted oath positive to the fact of payment specifying when, where, and to whom it was made, but that such allowance, in the whole, must not exceed $500, against any one estate, the items of expenditure by him, for which no vouchers are produced, but which may be allowed him on his accounting, are expressly limited to items each of which does not exceed $20, and not aggregating over $500. The administrator may support his account as to an item not exceeding $20, for which he has no voucher, "by his own uncontradicted oath to the fact of payment, specifying when, where, and to whom it was made," to the extent, in all, of $500. Beyond that limit he must support the account by vouchers, and no amount of corroboration of his oath to the expenditures, by the testimony of other witnesses, will avail to dispense with vouchers, and as to the $500, he must show when, where, and to whom the disbursement was made.—Estate of Hedrick, 127 Cal. 184, 187, 59 Pac. 590. Under section 1632, Cal. Code Civ. Proc., a charge not in excess of $500 may be allowed the administrator for expenses, when sufficiently supported by the testimony of the administrator, without a voucher therefor, where the amount of the charge may be treated as made up of a series of separate items of less than $20.—In re Ross' Estate, 179 Cal. 358, 182 Pac. 303, 305.

REFERENCES.

Right of executor or administrator to credit for amount paid to a surety company for going on an administration bond.—See note 48 L. R. A. 591-592.

13. Administrator is not entitled to credit when.

(1) **In general.**—An executor or administrator is not entitled to credit for unnecessary expenditures, or for items for payments made by the testator, or made by the executor before his appointment, for which he intentionally presented no claim, or for the costs of a wrongfully abandoned suit, or for a personal debt of the executor, or for a notice of sale of real estate which was published in the wrong county.—Estate of Pease, 149 Cal. 167, 169, 85 Pac. 149. He is not entitled to credit for the rent of a safe-deposit box, on his own testimony that he

kept therein only some papers which he could have kept safely at home.
—Estate of Pease, 149 Cal. 167, 169, 85 Pac. 149. He is not entitled to
expenses incurred in procuring the removal of a guardian of a minor
heir.—Estate of Rose, 80 Cal. 166, 22 Pac. 86. Nor for money paid to a
physician called as a witness in an action instituted by the administrator.—Estate of Levinson, 108 Cal. 450, 41 Pac. 483, 42 Pac. 479. He is
not entitled to credit for expenses incurred by the distributees in defending a decree of distribution.—Firebaugh v. Burbank, 121 Cal. 186,
53 Pac. 560. An item for money paid to the partner of the deceased for
losses incurred in running a hotel is properly disallowed, where there
is no sufficient evidence of the item.—Estate of Herteman, 73 Cal. 545,
547, 15 Pac. 121. So an advancement to a widow should be disallowed.
The executor or administrator should look for reimbursement to the
widow's distributive share on final distribution.—Elizalde v. Murphy,
4 Cal. App. 114, 116, 87 Pac. 245, 246. An allowance for a harvester
used in farming operations, voluntarily carried on by the executor at
a loss, should be disallowed, but if there is no evidence or finding upon
that point, the allowance will not be disturbed for the reason that such
operations were voluntarily carried on by the administrator or executor.
—Estate of Adams, 131 Cal. 415, 418, 63 Pac. 838. If an executor fails to
comply with the terms of the will, expenses of litigation, attorneys' fees,
etc., can not be allowed to him in the settlement of his accounts.—
Estate of Holbert, 48 Cal. 627, 630. If an executor or administrator
fails to apply to the court for advice in the management of the estate,
and for many years makes no report of his dealings, contrary to the
requirements of the statute, it is proper to deny his claim for extra
compensation, office rent, or attorneys' fees.—In re Roach's Estate, 50
Or. 179, 92 Pac. 118, 127. The costs of executors who are also heirs
incurred in defending an action for accounting and partition brought
against them by other heirs involving purely questions of heirship are
not expenses of administration which can be charged against the
estate.—In re Lotzgesell's Estate, 62 Wash. 352, 113 Pac. 1107.

(2) Improper charges.—An executor or administrator is not entitled
to credit for money expended in contesting the probate of a will. Such
an expense is not a proper charge against the estate.—Estate of Parsons, 65 Cal. 240, 3 Pac. 817. An executor or administrator is not entitled to an allowance, in his account, for money paid by him in excess
of the legal rate of interest, unless there is a written agreement to pay
such interest above the legal rate.—Estate of Dunne, 58 Cal. 543, 545,
549. An executor or administrator is not entitled to credit, in the
settlement of his account, for any loss arising by reason of his making
advances to pay off a mortgage debt upon land for which the estate is
not answerable.—Tompkins v. Weeks, 26 Cal. 50, 67. Although, ordinarily, a charge for insurance of the property of the estate is legitimate,
in an administrator's account, still, where a premium is charged
therein amounting to nearly one-fourth of the sum for which the
insured property with the land on which it stood, was sold pend-

ing administration, the court was justified in disallowing the item. —Estate of Nicholson, 1 Nev. 518, 521. If a husband's curtesy estate gives him possession to the exclusion of the administrator, items for fencing land and for insurance an a hop-house, and other expenses for the benefit of the husband, can not be charged to the estate.—Johnson v. Savage, 50 Or. 294, 91 Pac. 1082, 1083. Neither can an estate be charged with the balance of indebtedness claimed to be due to the executrix individually upon a note given to her for property sold by her to a lessee of the estate, who became insolvent, and returned to the property sold by her to him, and who also returned to the estate property sold to him by the estate, where there is nothing in the record to show any liability of the estate for such charge.—Estate of Adams, 131 Cal. 415, 419, 63 Pac. 838. If the administrators of two estates join in one appeal, the expenses necessarily incurred therein are not properly chargeable to one estate. Each of the estates should bear at least one-half of the expenses necessarily incurred.—In re Davis' Estate, 33 Mont. 539, 88 Pac. 957, 959. Moneys advanced by him for the heirs' benefit are not proper charges in the settlement of his account, though they may be allowed as credits upon the distributive share of the heir when a settlement with him is made.—Estate of Rose, 80 Cal. 166, 180, 22 Pac. 86. The assignments made to plaintiff by executors from whom moneys had been illegally exacted upon the filing of inventories and appraisements were not invalid under section 1517 of the California Code of Civil Procedure as sales made without order of the court. That section is inapplicable. It may be assumed that the assignments were made for collection, but it is also to be considered that the money paid was not part of the property of the estate, but was a payment unauthorized by law. It must be presumed that the probate court refused to give the executors credit for said payments in their accounts. The payments were chargeable to them individually, and they had the right to recover them in their individual capacities and the corresponding right to make assignments.—Trower v. City and County of San Francisco, 157 Cal. 762, 109 Pac. 617.

(3) Unnecessary expenditures.—Expenditures made by an administrator will not be allowed to him on the settlement of his final account, where no reasonable necessity for them is shown.—Estate of Kaiu, 17 Haw. 514, 515. Where an executor borrows money for the use of an estate represented by him, without authority of court, and without showing any necessity therefor, it is proper to disallow a charge for interest thereon.—Estate of Millenovich, 5 Nev. 189, 190. When an executor improperly charged in his accounts the cost of an automobile he is entitled to be credited with the amount obtained on its sale when the original cost is disallowed in his accounts.—In re Witt's Estate, 74 Wash. 172, 132 Pac. 1012. Estates of decedents should not be subjected to unnecessary legal expenses and an attempted sale of real estate of minors to pay unnecessary fees is expressly disapproved.—Estate of Kamaipiialii, 19 Haw. 163.

(4) Expenses before administration.—Items for payments made by an executor or administrator before his appointment, and for which he intentionally presented no claim, should not be allowed.—Estate of Pease, 149 Cal. 167, 169, 85 Pac. 149. The law does not contemplate that the claims of an administrator for reimbursement for moneys expended before his appointment, can be established by his uncontradicted evidence, especially when such evidence, and the assignment presented as his voucher, show that, on the face of the record, the legal claim or right is in another, whose rights are not foreclosed.—Estate of Heeney, 3 Cal. App. 548, 553, 86 Pac. 842. Where all the heirs are seeking to prevent probate proceedings, and a payment is made for that purpose, by the heirs of an intestate, on a mortgage indebtedness owed by the latter prior to the appointment of such administrator, such payment should be disallowed, though one of the heirs is afterwards appointed administrator.—Estate of Heeney, 3 Cal. App. 548, 86 Pac. 842. Items of expenses incurred by an executor or administrator, before his application for letters of administration, are not a proper charge against the estate.—Estate of Byrnes, 122 Cal. 260, 54 Pac. 957, 958. In contests between different executors of the same estate as to the right to administer, it is not just nor proper that the estate should be charged with the expense.—Estate of Millenovich, 5 Nev. 161, 187.

(5) Repairs. Protection of estate.—An executor or administrator can not be allowed credit for payments made without the authority of the court, even to protect the estate, where a loss has occurred by the advancement made; as where he has advanced money to pay off a mortgage debt upon land, for which debt the estate is not answerable.—Tompkins v. Weeks, 26 Cal. 51, 60; Estate of Heeney, 3 Cal. App. 548, 86 Pac. 842. A payment made without authority, to release the mortgage, should not be allowed to the administrator.—Estate of Heeney, 3 Cal. App. 548, 86 Pac. 842. Moneys expended by an executor or administrator in the execution of an addition to a hotel belonging to the estate, or to improve it, for the benefit of the heirs, should not be allowed.—Estate of Moore, 72 Cal. 335, 13 Pac. 880, 884. If an executor or administrator is unsuccessful in resisting the revocation of the probate of a will, he is not, as a matter of right, entitled to his costs incurred in that contest. The court is vested with a discretion to determine whether he shall be charged with them, or whether the estate shall bear them. Before the estate can be charged with the costs of the contest, the court should be in a position to know whether or not the contest was waged by the executor in good faith, with a reasonable belief that the attack on the original probate was unjustified. Hence, items of expenses, in his account, for the services of experts in handwriting, to determine the validity of a second will, should not be allowed, and should be retired for future determination, when it can be found whether such costs should be charged against the executors or be borne by the estate.—Estate of Dillon, 149 Cal. 683, 87 Pac. 379, 380.

14. Final and intermediate accounts.

(1) **Final account. Waiver.**—A final account is one made with a view to the immediate distribution of the estate.—Estate of Grant, 131 Cal. 426, 429, 63 Pac. 731. In a case where the widow is the executrix and the sole beneficiary of the estate, and the debts are all paid, there is no necessity for a final accounting, and she is entitled to waive the rendition and settlement of such account; and the statement that she has filed no accounts as executrix, because she is entitled to have the whole of the residue distributed to her, constitutes a waiver of an account.—Middlecoff v. Superior Court, 149 Cal. 94, 97, 84 Pac. 764. Where the widow is sole heir, and she has the business partner of her husband appointed administrator of the latter's estate, under a private agreement whereby she is to be given half the commissions as the consideration for her waiver of the right to administer, effect should be given to the agreement on the filing of the final account.—In re Tachi's Estate, Tachi v. Kent, 90 Wash. 621, 156 Pac. 833, 93 Wash. 700, 161 Pac. 469. Before a final account can be approved the executor must show affirmatively that he has paid all outstanding claims against the estate or that he has exhausted the property available for such purpose.—In re Williams' Estate, 47 Mont. 325, 132 Pac. 423. Under sections 7661, 7662, Revised Codes of Montana, it is very clear that a final account of an administrator or executor can not be settled or approved so long as there are claims outstanding against the estate, if there is any property in the hands of the executor or administrator available for the payment thereof.—In re Williams' Estate, 47 Mont. 325, 132 Pac. 423. It is clear, from the provisions of section 7661 of the Revised Codes of Montana, and of section 7662 of the same codes, that the final account of an administrator or executor can not be settled or approved so long as there are outstanding claims against the estate, which have not been paid, if there is any property in the hands of the representative that is available for the payment of such claims, in whole or in part.—In re Williams' Estate, 47 Mont. 325, 329, 132 Pac. 421. It is error for the court to settle and approve the final account of an administrator, where it appears that claims against the estate for advancements made for its benefit, though properly allowed, are unpaid, and where there is no showing that all property available for their payment has been exhausted.—In re Williams' Estate, 47 Mont. 325, 331, 132 Pac. 421. Final settlement of the estate of a deceased person is not to be made until the estate is fully administered, and the administrator should not be discharged or released until his trust has been fully performed and he has accounted for and paid out all the moneys received by him, as the law requires.—In re Estate of Kappelman, International Harvester Co. v. Algie, 101 Kan. 654, 657, 168 Pac. 876. It is not error for the court, in the final settlement of an administrator's account, to adjudicate upon certain items, such as clerk's fees and the like, in anticipation of payment.—Estate of Parsons, 65 Cal. 240, 241, 3 Pac. 817. The pendency of an action brought

by an attorney for the recovery of his fees is no ground for the court's declining to approve the final report of the executor and ordering his discharge.—Hallett v. Lathrop, 20 Colo. App. 212, 77 Pac. 1096, 1097. Section 92 of the Probate Code of Washington makes provision for a final accounting in court by the executor of a non-intervention will, and that section should be held to govern every case in which the executor or trustee of a non-intervention will had not fully executed the terms of the will and distributed the estate prior to the taking effect of that section.—In re Cornett's Estate, Cornett v. West, 102 Wash. 254, 263, 173 Pac. 44. If it appears that an executor or administrator, on application for the settlement of his final account, has disposed of estate intrusted to him, without authority, the account, as to such property, should be disapproved, and the representative should be charged with the property as part of the assets of the estate.—In re Dolenty's Estate, Mannix v. Dolenty, 53 Mont. 33, 161 Pac. 524. In the final settlement of an estate the court should find only what amount, if any, the executor, or administrator, is to be charged with, in addition to what is disclosed by his final account, and to order this paid into court so that it may be distributed or applied agreeably to law.— Estate of Raleigh, 48 Utah 128, 158 Pac. 705. A paper, issued by the court at the culmination of probate proceedings in the year 1873, indorsed "Opinion-Order," is to be regarded as an order settling the final account of the executors and closing the estate, if at the time the court evidently intended it to be such and it was so accepted by the parties concerned.—Estate of Yorba, 176 Cal. 166, 167 Pac. 854. The failure of an executor or administrator to apply for an order requiring a surviving partner to account is no reason why the court should refuse to settle an annual account of the administrator or executor, which is intended only to show what property has been received by him, and what he has done with it.—Miller v. Lux, 100 Cal. 609, 614, 35 Pac. 345, 639. If the final account of an executor or administrator be disapproved by the court, he may either appeal from the decree disallowing the same, or file another account to meet the objections of the court.— Rostel v. Morat, 19 Or. 181, 23 Pac. 900.

(2) Intermediate accounts.—All intermediate accounts are only to inform the court and interested parties of the receipts and disbursements and changes in the property from time to time, and it is not the intention of the law that the executor or administrator should in every account give a full inventory of the assets of the estate. This properly belongs to the inventory which is filed, except the actual cash on hand, which the law appears to contemplate he should carry forward in his several accounts rendered to the court.—In re Davis' Estate, 31 Mont. 421, 78 Pac. 704. There is nothing which precludes an executor or administrator from bringing forward, in a succeeding annual account, or in his final account, such charges in his favor as may have been refused allowance at some former accounting, merely because the administrator fails, from any cause, to produce the techni-

cal proof required by the statute. He may include, in a subsequent account, charges admitted to be legal, but not allowed, and by producing vouchers have them allowed.—Walls v. Walker, 37 Cal. 424, 426, 99 Am. Dec. 290. The semiannual return required by the statute of a public administrator is not to be treated as an account stated. It is not made to the court; there is no hearing upon it; and no order of the court is required as to it. It is wholly different from the accounts required to be made by an administrator, and for a wholly different *purpose. It is not intended to, and does not, take the place or serve the purpose of the semiannual account required of the executor or administrator after his appointment.—Estate of Hedrick, 127 Cal. 184, 188, 59 Pac. 590. While, under the California Code Civ. Proc., section 1622, an administrator's intermediate account must state all matters necessary to show condition of estate, the court is required to scrutinize account only so far as receipts and disbursements of money are concerned, and hence an intermediate decree need not charge the representative with all the property as disclosed by the inventory and appraisement.—In re Bottom's Estate, 156 Cal. 129, 103 Pac. 849. A decree settling an annual account of the administrator of an estate of a deceased person, filed under section 1622 of the California Code of Civil Procedure, need not charge the administrator with the entire property in his hands, but may simply determine the accuracy of his accounts as to money transactions which he has had with the estate. As to all other items of property belonging to the estate an accounting is to be made upon final settlement.—Estate of Bottoms, 156 Cal. 129, 103 Pac. 849. In proceedings in probate, for approving an administrator's annual account, the court should, for good cause shown, require the executor to account for property disposed of without authority of law, and for rents and profits of real estate in his possession, lost through neglect, and to furnish information in detail as to the condition of the estate.—In re Dolenty's Estate, Mannix v. Dolenty, 53 Mont. 33, 161 Pac. 524. The probate court does not pass upon an item of the administrator's account expressly reserved when presented, merely by approving a subsequent account which does not contain the item otherwise than in a balance shown by the prior account.—In re Ross' Estate, 179 Cal. 358, 182 Pac. 303, 305.

15. Failure to settle.—The obligation of an executor or administrator to account is continuous, and does not become barred by the statute of limitations. The right to demand an account may be asserted as long as the duty to render it remains unperformed.—Estate of Sanderson, 74 Cal. 199, 215, 15 Pac. 753. If he is guilty of great delay, without satisfactory explanation, in accounting, he is properly chargeable with legal interest.—Estate of Sanderson, 74 Cal. 199, 15 Pac. 753; Estate of Hilliard, 83 Cal. 423, 428, 23 Pac. 393. It is the duty of executors and administrators to account within a reasonable, or the statutory time, and a neglect to account which results in waste renders them liable, the same as in case of a failure to collect debts before the

statute of limitations has run against them.—Estate of Osborn, 87 Cal.
1, 8, 11 L. R. A. 264, 25 Pac. 157. The failure, however, of an executor
or administrator to make a final settlement of the estate does not
preclude those who wish to contest his final account from being heard.
—Estate of Misamore, 90 Cal. 169, 171, 27 Pac. 68. Insolvency does not
relieve him of the burden of accounting for the property of the estate
in his possession. He can not repudiate his trust entirely by his mere
failure to account.—Estate of Sanderson, 74 Cal. 199, 216, 15 Pac. 753.
If creditors charge him with neglect for having money on hand for an
unreasonable time, which should have been distributed or paid to
creditors, and it does not appear that he had wilfully or negligently
caused the delay which is occasioned by litigation, and no disobedience
appears to the order of court, all presumptions are in favor of the
regularity of the management of the estate, and it is incumbent upon
the party alleging such neglect to prove it.—Estate of Sylvar, 1 Cal.
App. 35, 37, 81 Pac. 663. The facts that an administrator of a deceased
person filed an inventory of the personal property belonging to the
estate, and failed at any time thereafter to make an annual or final
settlement of the estate prior to his death, which occurred seven years
afterwards, do not alone show a wrongful conversion of such estate, or
any part thereof, by the administrator, to his own use. A failure to
perform an official duty at the precise time required by law is not
necessarily any evidence, much less conclusive evidence, of a purpose
wrongfully to convert and to misapply trust funds.—Allen v. Bartlett,
52 Kan. 387, 34 Pac. 1042, 1043.

16. Death or absconding before accounting.—If an administrator dies,
his accounts as such may be presented and filed by his personal representative.—Estate of Aldersley, 174 Cal. 366, 163 Pac. 206. If an executor or administrator dies before rendering an account, a court of
equity alone, in the absence of any statute on the subject, has jurisdiction of accounts against the administrator of the administrator to settle the account of his intestate with the estate of which he was administrator.—Estate of Curtiss, 65 Cal. 572, 4 Pac. 578; Chaquette v. Ortet, 60
Cal. 594; Wetzler v. Fitch, 52 Cal. 638; Bush v. Lindsey, 44 Cal. 121;
In re Herren's Estate, 40 Or. 90, sub nom. Gatch v. Simpson, 66 Pac.
688. The probate court has no authority to cite the administrator of an
administrator to settle the account of his intestate with the estate of
which he was administrator.—Bush v. Lindsey, 44 Cal. 121, 124; and it
has no jurisdiction to receive or to act upon an account presented by
an executor of an executor against the estate of the testator of the deceased executor.—Wetzler v. Fitch, 52 Cal. 638, 643. Where the same
court has jurisdiction, both in equity and in matters of probate, such
court may, in an action in equity for an accounting against the executor of a deceased administrator, determine the amount due the attorney of the deceased administrator, and may withhold for future determination by the probate court the question as to the amount of
commission due to the deceased administrator on final settlement of

the estate, and may reserve the power to require payment to the executor of such sum as the probate court may award to the deceased administrator for his services.—Pennie v. Roach, 94 Cal. 515, 29 Pac. 956, 30 Pac. 106. If an administrator dies without having paid his attorney for legal services, an allowance may be made for their value in favor of his executor.—Pennie v. Roach, 94 Cal. 515, 29 Pac. 956, 30 Pac. 106. If an administrator dies without rendering an account, a court of equity must take the place of the probate court for the purpose of settling such account, and in directing payment out of the estate of the amount it finds to be due from it; and when it determines that the estate is indebted for moneys received by the deceased administrator and unexpended, and payment thereof is directed, it becomes the duty of the administrator of the estate of the administrator to make the payment, and his failure to do so constitutes a breach of the administrator's bond, for which the sureties are liable. The decree of a court of equity, directing payment out of the estate of the intestate, is to be regarded in the light of a decree of the probate court settling the acccount and directing payment.—Chaquette v. Ortet, 60 Cal. 594, 601. If an executor or administrator dies, leaving the estate unsettled, his sureties must be made parties to a proceeding requiring the defendant to file papers and vouchers in his possession showing the disbursements made by his intestate, and a citation must be issued to them, or the decree will not be binding upon them, or even evidence against them.—In re Herren's Estate, 40 Or. 90, sub nom. Gatch v. Simpson, 66 Pac. 688, 691. Where one of two executors died, having in his hands funds of the estate, which could not be identified as such, it is necessary that a claim be presented against the estate of the deceased executor.—Estate of Smith, 108 Cal. 115, 122, 40 Pac. 1037. If an executor or administrator or guardian dies or absconds, or is beyond the jurisdiction of the court, the proper method, in order to ascertain whether he is liable, and to what extent, so as to bind the sureties on his official bond, is by a proceeding in the nature of a civil action, wherein the sureties are made parties and have an opportunity to be heard.—Reither v. Murdock, 135 Cal. 197, 201, 67 Pac. 784. An administrator with the will annexed died in office without having accounted for moneys which he had collected belonging to the testator's estate. His successor obtained judgment in the district court against his administrator for the sum found to be due. The judgment was presented, allowed, and classified in the probate court as a claim against the estate, but no order was issued upon his administrator for its payment and it was not paid. Held such an order is not a condition precedent to recovery against the sureties on his bond.—Toffler v. Kessinger, 80 Kan. 549, 102 Pac. 1097.

REFERENCES.

Method of compelling settlement of accounts of deceased executor or administrator.—See note 8 Am. St. Rep. 684. That, in case of the death of an executor or administrator, his personal representative is to present his account.—See Kerr's Cal. Cyc. Code Civ. Proc., § 1639.

17. Insolvent administrators.—A debt due the estate from an insolvent administrator is not, for all purposes, regarded as money on hand, but is so regarded only by a fiction of law. The administrator should be charged with the entire sum, including the debt due from himself, and the decree should then show what portion of that amount consists of debts due from the administrator which he reports as cash on hand. Of course, if it appears that he actually has the money this formula would be unnecessary. The sureties do not agree to augment the estate, but that the executor will not waste it or be in default. Hence, where he has all that comes to his hands, and all that by the greatest diligence he can get, there is no default, and no deficiency to make good. If he is ready to distribute this, he can not do more, unless he can make something out of nothing.—Estate of Walker, 125 Cal. 242, 245, 247, 249, 73 Am. St. Rep. 40, 57 Pac. 991. In an application by persons interested in the ultimate accounting of an administrator or executor, the petition therefor must aver that the decedent's estate is ready for final settlement.—In re Morrison's Estate, 48 Or. 612, 87 Pac. 1043, 1044.

18. Actions.—An allegation in a complaint that an administrator has failed to account for money of the estate means not only that he has failed to file the exhibit required by section 1622, Cal. Code Civ. Proc., but also that he has failed to pay over the money as required by sections 1613, 1697, Cal. Code Civ. Proc.—Moody v. Pacific Surety Co. (Cal. App.), 182 Pac. 802. Where a person, suing as an executor, alleges, in his complaint against the administrator of another estate, that the plaintiff caused to be presented to this administrator, as such a claim duly verified, according to law, claiming the sum of $1,500 as a lawful charge against said estate, the allegation is one that the plaintiff presented the claim both individually and as an executor.—Harvey v. Pocock, 92 Wash. 625, 159 Pac. 771. A judicial adjusting of the amount due an attorney for his services to an estate, in the settlement thereof under a non-intervention will, where such amount is in dispute, can be invoked only in a direct proceeding.—Snook v. Kennedy, 103 Wash. 390, 174 Pac. 643. An executor or administrator is to be recompensed for advances made under the direction of, or when ratified by, the court sitting in probate, but it is beyond the power of the court, in an independent action brought by the administrator, to create, against lands in which the estate is interested, a lien in his favor, upon a contingency that may never arise; his remedy is in the administration proceeding.—Plath v. Mullins, 94 Wash. 154, 161 Pac. 1187. In Kansas the statute of limitations applies equally to legal and equitable cases.—Pickens v. Campbell, 98 Kan. 518, 159 Pac. 21.

19. Trial by jury.—Mere exceptions to an accounting do not create "issues of fact joined," such as must be submitted to a jury on demand

of a party in interest.—Estate of Sanderson, 74 Cal. 199, 209, 15 Pac.
753. But there may be cases in which it is very desirable to submit an
issue arising on the settlement of an account to a jury. If no jury is
demanded under the statute, the court must try the issues joined, but
it was not really intended that every possible disputed fact in any step
of the administration of the estate might, as a matter of right, be
made an issue to be tried by a jury. The statute should not be construed as granting an absolute right to a jury trial, in which, according
to the course of the common law, a jury trial was denied as inappropriate, especially in the settlement of accounts of administrators and
executors, where so much is left to the mere discretion of the judge.—
Estate of Moore, 72 Cal. 335, 13 Pac. 880, 882.—See Estate of Mullins,
47 Cal. 450.

20. Validity of settlement.—A settlement of the accounts of an executor or administrator, without notice, is void.—Estate of Aveline, 53
Cal. 259. It is also void where the executor had in his hands a large
amount of money that belonged to the estate, but took no account of
this money in his inventory, and did not account for it in any manner
whatever. A final settlement of his accounts as executor, under such
circumstances, is a fraud.—Perea v. Barela, 5 N. M. 458, sub nom.
Garcia y Perea v. Barela, 23 Pac. 766, 772. But if he has accounted for
all the property that he has received, or that by reasonable diligence
should have been received, the fact that certain property belonging to
the estate was not appraised by the executor can not affect the validity
of his final account.—In re Conser's Estate, 40 Or. 138, 66 Pac. 607, 610.
A contract for the settlement of an estate out of court is void. No
contract can be made regarding the assets of a deceased person's
estate, except by the authority and with the approval of the probate
court, and only then to the extent authorized or permitted by the laws
of the state. In the absence of administration, no heir can make a
contract that will be binding. No stipulation can be entered into by
the widow that would bind the minor heirs in any manner respecting
the settlement of the estate, or its property, or its debts. The law
fixes the manner of administration. It imposes certain restrictions
upon the sale of the assets of an estate, and even when the sale is
authorized by law, and ordered by the probate court, the sale, and its
terms and its methods, are still subject to the approval of the court
ordering it. No person interested in the estate can, by contract, assent,
or by silence create other methods of selling the assets of the estate,
than those prescribed by the law. To permit this in any one instance
would withdraw all the safeguards and beneficent restrictions that the
law imposes for the protection of the minor and non-resident heirs.
The widow can not make any contract that will bind the minor heirs;
she can make no contract pledging the course of the administration
of the law respecting the settlement of the estate of a deceased person.
—Cox v. Grubb, 47 Kan. 435, 27 Am. St. Rep. 303, 28 Pac. 157, 158. A
final settlement is not invalidated by the fact that proof of the publica-

tion of notice to creditors was not filed within the time provided by the statute, if the notice was properly given. The time within which a creditor is required to present his claim begins to run from the first publication of the notice, and not from the filing of the proof thereof with the county clerk. The publication, and not the filing, is, therefore, the vital fact to be considered, and the date of the filing is not jurisdictional. The statute requiring it to be made within a certain time is directory, and not mandatory.—In re Conant's Estate, 43 Or. 530, 73 Pac. 1018, 1020. Where the executor is found to be personally answerable for part of the loss occasioned by his purchase of unsecured promissory notes, the decree requiring him, in the settlement of his final account, to account for the sum so found to be due the estate must necessarily be based upon the allegations and proof.—In re Roach's Estate, 50 Or. 179, 92 Pac. 118, 126. An order that the account of an executor or administrator "be, and the same is hereby, allowed and approved, except as to the matters following," etc., is sufficient as an order settling the account.—Estate of Sanderson, 74 Cal. 199, 216, 15 Pac. 753. A fraud committed upon the court renders the orders of said court in settling the final account of an administrator, and in discharging him and his bondsmen and declaring heirship, void.—Caulk v. Lowe (Okla.), 178 Pac. 101. Conclusions and findings in a contested proceeding for settlement of an administrator's account are not neces-· sary.—In re McPhee's Estate, 156 Cal. 335, Ann. Cas. 1913E 899, 104 Pac. 455.

21. Effect of settlement.—In the settlement of the accounts of an executor or administrator, if the statute requires notice to be served upon him as to such settlement, a settlement without such citation, and in his absence, does not bind him or his sureties.—Estate of Aveline, 53 Cal. 259, 261. Though a decree of distribution and a decree settling a final account are sometimes embraced in one decree of court, the decree settling a final account need not necessarily, in any way, affect the manner of the distribution of the estate.—Estate of Thayer, 1 Cal. App. 104, 106, 81 Pac. 658; but a decree of settlement and distribution is binding upon the administrator.—McNabb v. Wixom, 7 Nev. 163, 173. A final account decreeing that certain property is in the hands of the representative for distribution is an adjudication between the representative and the heirs and devisees fixing the status and character of that property.—Estate of Young, 123 Cal. 337, 347, 35 Pac. 1011. Where the statute requires notice of the final account, and of the day for hearing objections to it, ex parte orders of the court, directing the administrator to' pay unauthorized bills, affords no protection to him on his final account.—In re Osburn's Estate, 36 Or. 8, 58 Pac. 521, 524. As claims allowed against an estate by the administrator and probate judge have the force and effect of judgments, it is error, upon the final settlement of the administrator's account, to reject sums paid by him on claims so allowed.—Deck's Estate v. Gherke, 6 Cal. 666, 669. If, upon the allowance of the administrator's account, the "balance"

in his hands is ordered to be paid, and that is done, it is presumed that all debts of the estate have been settled.—Lethbridge v. Lauder, 13 Wyo. 9, 76 Pac. 682, 685. That portion of an order, upon the settlement of an account of an executor or administrator, which operates as a rejection of a claim, is a separate and distinct act from the order allowing the account; and the same may be said of that portion of the order which decrees the delivery of certain shares of corporate stock to the special administratrix.—In re Barker's Estate, 26 Mont. 279, 67 Pac. 941, 942. The settlement of the accounts of an executor or administrator, though sometimes spoken of as an "order," is, in effect, a judgment.—Miller v. Lux, 100 Cal. 609, 613, 35 Pac. 345, 639; Estate of Levinson, 108 Cal. 450, 454, 41 Pac. 483, 42 Pac. 479; Estate of Walker, 125 Cal. 242, 249, 73 Am. St. Rep. 40, 57 Pac. 991. The allowance of a claim against the estate of a deceased person is only a qualified judgment.—Selna v. Selna, 125 Cal. 357, 362; 73 Am. St. Rep. 47, 58 Pac. 16. The allowance of a claim has the same effect as a judgment upon the claim; and as a judgment draws interest, an allowed claim therefore draws interest.—Estate of Glenn, 74 Cal. 567, 568, 16 Pac. 396. After an administrator has filed his final account, showing that he has administered upon the estate, he is estopped from denying his representative character, or his liability to act accordingly. —In re Osburn's Estate, 36 Or. 8, 58 Pac. 521, 522. The allowance of the final account of an executor or administrator is not a decree of distribution, nor the legal equivalent of such a decree.—McCreay v. Haraszthy, 51 Cal. 146, 151. The settlement of a final account of an executor or administrator bars the heirs from recovering property alleged to have been wrongfully omitted from the inventory; but the probate court has power to enforce the terms of a stipulation entered into by parties litigant before it respecting such property, and of which the court has jurisdiction.—Grady v. Porter, 53 Cal. 680, 685; Tobelman v. Hildebrandt, 72 Cal. 313, 315, 14 Pac. 20. An administrator can not be garnished before final settlement of the estate or some order of distribution is made.—Clark v. Kraig, 21 Colo. App. 196, 120 Pac. 1044. The fact that on the same day as that of the settlement of the account of the administrator, the petition of an heir to require him to give further security was heard, and a contemporaneous order was made requiring further security to be given within ten days, in default of which his letters were to be revoked, does not imply that the orders are inseparable, or that the order requiring further security is dependent upon the order settling the account.—Estate of McPhee v. Corrigan, 10 Cal. App. 162, 101 Pac. 530.

REFERENCES.

Effect of annual settlements of executors and administrators as res judicata.—See note 86 Am. Dec. 143-146.

21. Conclusiveness of settlement.

(1) In general.—A determination in the settlement of the final account of an executor or administrator, if clearly within the jurisdiction of the court, is final, unless an appeal has been taken from the decree.—Estate of Burdick, 112 Cal. 387, 391, 44 Pac. 734. An order settling an administrator's account, and discharging him, is conclusive against his liability.—Reynolds v. Brumagim, 54 Cal. 254, 258; Grady v. Porter, 53 Cal. 680, 685. No action can be brought, after an account is settled, against the administrator or executor for his neglect to bring an action for the recovery of land in the possession of adverse claimants. The order settling the account is conclusive against all persons interested.—Reynolds v. Brumagim, 54 Cal. 254, 258. An order settling the account of an executor or administrator is conclusive of the amount with which he was at the time chargeable, and against every one interested, except those laboring under disability.—Estate of Stott, 52 Cal. 403, 406; Estate of Couts, 87 Cal. 480, 482, 22 Am. St. Rep. 265, 26 Pac. 92. At the proper time, upon the settlement of the account of an executor or administrator, the legality of his disposition of every dollar of the moneys he has expended is open to attack by the parties interested.—Estate of Bell, 142 Cal. 97, 101, 75 Pac. 679. If an administrator purchases a claim against the estate he represents, and such claim is allowed as a secured claim in his first settled account, and creditors who have a right to object, but who do not object, to the settlement at that time, can not afterwards object to its validity in the settlement of his final account.—Estate of McDougald, 146 Cal. 191, 194, 196, 79 Pac. 878. Claims against the estate, which have been allowed by the administrator and the probate judge, have the force and effect of judgments; but this rule applies only to such claims as were debts against the deceased, and not to the expenses incurred or disbursements made by the administrator in his management of the estate, which latter claims are conclusive only after having been allowed by the probate court upon settlement of the account, after notice to the parties interested.—Deck's Estate v. Gherke, 6 Cal. 667, 669; Gurnee v. Maloney, 38 Cal. 85, 88, 99 Am. Dec. 352. The allowance and settlement of an intermediate account, after due notice, conclusively establishes a claim formerly allowed and presented therein as required by section 1628 of the Code of Civil Procedure of California, as against all persons interested in absence of timely appeal or attack thereon under section 473 of that code.—Kowalsky v. Superior Court, 13 Cal. App. 218, 109 Pac. 158. Where a party's claim against a decedent's estate has been rejected by operation of law, and he has had the proper statutory notice to appear in the probate court, file his exceptions in writing, and contest the final settlement of the administrator's account, and the final distribution of the estate, and he fails to do so, he can not have the order settling the final account, and the decree of final distribution, set aside, because of his "excusable neglect," or otherwise; on the contrary, he is guilty of laches, and the

settlement and decree are conclusive as to him.—Chandler v. Probate Court, 26 Ida. 173, 178, 141, Pac. 635. An administrator's final account can only be rendered after notice to all concerned; but when made and approved it is conclusive and final unless set aside on an appeal, or in a direct proceeding therefor, or is impeached for fraud.—Estate of Davis, 22 Haw. 436, 440. A decree duly entered on a final accounting by a county court, in the absence of mistake or fraud, and from which no appeal has been taken, is conclusive on the administrator and the sureties on his bond.—Shipman v. Brown, 36 Okla. 623, 130 Pac. 603. When in the settlement of an annual account of an executor, investments upon notes and mortgages taken by him in his own name, without an order of court, were reported to the court and found to be for the benefit of the estate, and were assigned to the estate, so long as they were treated as the property of the estate, the settlements of annual accounts based thereon are conclusive against all persons interested in the estate not under disability.—Estate of Richmond, 9 Cal. App. 402, 99 Pac. 554. Where the account of an administratrix has been settled, and it has been adjudged that the estate is indebted to her for moneys advanced by her for the benefit of the estate, the order of court settling such account is, in the absence of an affirmative showing on the face of the claims for money so advanced, conclusive, both on the estate and on all persons interested therein, who, at the time of settlement, were not laboring under any legal disability.—In re Williams' Estate, 47 Mont. 325, 330, 132 Pac. 421. Under the statute, rendering conclusive the settlement of an executor's account and its allowance by the court, and that requiring the court to name, in the order or decree of distribution, the persons entitled and the parts or proportions each is entitled to, the order settling the final account and decreeing distribution stands on like footing with an ordinary judgment in a civil action.—Benning v. Superior Court, 34 Cal. App. 296, 167 Pac. 291.

(2) **Not conclusive when.**—The settlement of the account of an administrator and the allowance thereof by the county court is not conclusive, under the statute of Oklahoma, against one laboring under any legal disability, but such person may, at any time before final distribution of the estate, proceed by action against the administrator, either individually or upon his bond.—Butts v. Larison (Okla.), 170 Pac. 500. An annual or intermediate accounting, had ex parte and without notice, is for the convenience of the executor or administrator, is not final, and is subject to modification or annulment by the circuit judge sitting in probate, at any time before final distribution.—Estate of Davis, 22 Haw. 436, 439. The law's intolerance of repeated litigation, between the same parties in respect to the same subject of controversy, does not extend to a cause in which an administrator, called upon to account, has, by concealing facts concerning the estate, prevented there being an adversary trial or decree upon the issues.—Pickens v. Merriam (Cal.), 242 Fed. 363, 372.

(3) Fraud. Collateral attack.—A decree approving the final account of an executor or administrator is only primary evidence of the correctness of the account as thereby settled and allowed. Such decree is not conclusive, but is only prima facie evidence.—Cross v. Baskett, 17 Or. 84, 21 Pac. 47, 49. A wife's receipt to the executor of an estate whereby she releases all claims against the estate, does not bind her, where it appears that the executor had in his hands a large amount of money that belonged to her at the time of settlement, but did not account for it in any manner whatever. The final settlement of his accounts as executor, under such circumstances, is a fraud upon her rights, and is null and void.—Perea v. Barela, 5 N. M. 458, sub nom. Garcia v. Perea, 23 Pac. 766. If the report of an executor is so imperfect, partial, and misleading as to amount to a fraud in law, the items of such report may be re-examined by a court of equity notwithstanding the prior approval of the probate court.—Candelaria v. Miera, 18 N. M. 107, 134 Pac. 829. A decree settling the final account of an administratrix and directing the payment of a settled claim against the estate, the time for appeal from which has elapsed, is conclusively binding upon the surety of the administratrix, in case of her final non-compliance therewith, and the surety can not collaterally attack the decree by showing that the claim was forever barred by reason of the fact that it had not been presented within the time limited by law and by the notice to creditors.—L. Harter Co. v. Geisel, 18 Cal. App. 282, 122 Pac. 1094. An order of the county court settling the final account of a guardian is a final judgment, and in the absence of fraud, lack of jurisdiction to make the order not appearing in the record, no question of fact not in issue or issuable in the hearing, may be the subject of attack except in a direct proceeding; and in a suit on the guardian's bond, a defense which controverts the existence, correctness or validity of any such issuable question or fact, the existence, correctness or validity of which is necessary to support such final order, is a collateral attack on the same.—Southwestern Surety Ins. Co. v. Richard (Okla.), 162, Pac. 468, 470.

(4) Items included. Items omitted.—After proper notice has been given, an order settling the account of an executor or administrator is conclusive as to all items contained in it, except as to persons laboring under some legal disability; and, in this respect, there is no difference between a final account—that is, one made with a view to the immediate distribution of the estate—and any other account.—Estate of Grant, 131 Cal. 426, 429, 63 Pac. 731. It is to be noticed that courts have fallen into the habit of calling accounts filed prior to the account on final settlement "annual" accounts, although the code does not use that word.—Estate of Grant, 131 Cal. 426, 429, 63 Pac. 731. Though an accounting or settlement is conclusive as to the matters adjudicated, it is not conclusive as to matters omitted from the account, and such matters may therefore be surcharged in a subsequent settlement.—Estate of Adams, 131 Cal. 415, 418, 63 Pac. 838. The decree of the probate court settling the accounts of the executor or administrator, and fixing the amount of his liability, is conclusive upon all persons interested in the estate who are not under disability.—Washington v. Black, 83 Cal. 290, 23 Pac. 300. Items in a final account which were allowed in previous accounts, and which were settled after due and sufficient notice of the filing of said accounts, and of the time and place of hearing the same had been given, are conclusive, and can not be re-examined upon the settlement' of the final account.—Estate of Marshall, 118 Cal. 379, 381, 50 Pac. 540; Guardianship of Wells, 140 Cal. 349, 353, 73 Pac. 1055. It has been said, in a late case, that a judgment or an order of a court having jurisdiction is conclusive of all matters involved "which might have been disputed" at the hearing, although no objection was in fact made; and that this rule applies to the settling of accounts, the same as to any other proceeding.—Estate of McDougald, 146 Cal. 191, 195, 79 Pac. 878. But the general rule seems to be, that the settlement of the annual account of the executor or administrator is conclusive only as to the items actually included therein, and does not estop him from including in his final account any item not previously included and passed upon in any annual account, though it be for a demand existing prior thereto.—Estate of Adams, 131 Cal. 415, 417, 63 Pac. 838. The settlement of an annual account is not conclusive, even as against the heirs, legatees, or creditors, except as to such matters as were actually included in such former account, and directly passed upon by the court; and the fact that the heirs, legatees, and creditors are expressly permitted to contest matters not included or passed upon in any former account, necessarily implies that the administrator is not precluded from going behind the former account and bringing forward charges, which, through inadvertence or oversight, may have been omitted.—Walls v. Walker, 37 Cal. 424, 426, 99 Am. Dec. 290. The settlement of an account is not conclusive except as to such items as are included in it and actually passed upon by the probate, and the court can not be said to have thus actually passed upon an item by approval, when decision as to the same was expressly reserved, and the same was never again presented in any subsequent account in any form.—In re Ross' Estate, 179 Cal. 358, 182 Pac. 303, 305. The settlement of an administrator's account by the decree of a probate court, is not conclusive as to property accidentally or fraudulently withheld from the account.—Pickens v. Merriam, (Cal.), 242 Fed. 363, 372, 155 C. C. A. 139.

REFERENCES.

Conclusiveness of decrees of distribution, and power of chancery to correct or set aside a settlement of accounts in probate courts. See note 48 Am. Dec. 744-751. Effect of annual settlements of executors and administrators as res judicata.—See note 86 Am. Dec. 143-146.

22. Vacating accounts. Collateral attack. Relief in equity.

(1) In general.—After a court has settled the account of an executor, it has no jurisdiction to set aside the settlement of any previous account, and to reopen the same and to adjudicate against him items which were conclusively adjudicated in his favor in the former order.—Estate of Grant, 131 Cal. 426, 429, 63 Pac. 731. Where accounts have been settled by the approval of the court, and the final decree had, they can not be reopened by a legatee, who was represented by counsel at the allowance of the accounts against the estate, after a lapse of time, on a mere general averment of newly-discovered evidence.—Williams v. Price, 11 Cal. 212, 213. Although a final settlement is made by the administrator or guardian, the owner of land and beneficiary of a trust will ordinarily not be estopped from asserting title to the land wrongfully obtained by a trustee, unless the beneficiary had full knowledge of the wrongs practiced by the trustee, and of the facts upon which the rights of the beneficiary are founded. Nor can the fact that the trustee made improvements on land so obtained during the infancy of the beneficiary, and with her knowledge, prevent her from claiming the land after she attains majority.—Webb v. Branner, 59 Kan. 190, 52 Pac. 429. But the settlement of the account of an administratrix, by the probate court, will not be disturbed on the application of a minor, where twenty years have elapsed, and the records of the probate court show that the minor heir was represented, both upon the allowance and settlement of the first account, and the final settlement and partition of the estate, by a guardian ad litem, a different guardian ad litem being appointed in each instance, and notwithstanding the fact that they now testify that they have no recollection of the circumstances, and where both certified then that they had examined the petitions and accounts filed in the proceedings on behalf of the said minor and consented to the allowance and distribution prayed for.—Bowen v. Hughes, 5 Wash. 442, 32 Pac. 98, 100. It was within the discretion of the court to set aside and vacate the order settling the final account of an administrator with the will annexed, upon the petition of absent heirs who are legatees; and in view of their objections stated in their letters and shown by the affidavit of their attorney, and of the files and records of the court, there was no abuse of discretion of the court in setting aside and vacating such order.—Estate of Miller v. Schlegel, 15 Cal. App. 557, 115 Pac. 329. The court had no power, in 1910, to entertain a motion to vacate an allowance made in 1907.—Kowalsky v. Superior Court, 13 Cal. App. 218, 109 Pac. 158. If an order is made approving the final account of an administrator with the will annexed, and a decree of distribution is rendered, but there were many irregularities in the administration proceedings, heirs and legatees, who are dissatisfied with such order and decree, are not driven to an appeal because such order and decree, being final, are appealable, but they may attack such order and decree, in the court wherein made, by a petition to vacate

them though there was no fraud.—In re Johnston's Estate (Wash,), 181 Pac. 209, 211. The effect of the fraudulent withholding of notice of a petition for letters of administration, and of a petition to have heirship determined, is that the court is without jurisdiction at the hearings thereupon, and its judgment in settling the final account of the administrator, and discharging him and his bondsmen, may be set aside at the suit of a non-resident interested person having no knowledge of the proceedings at the time thereof.—Caulk v. Lowe (Okla.), 178 Pac. 101, 106. If an administrator, by means of false statements as to the local assets of the estate, induce non-resident heirs to sign releases, an order of settlement made thereupon in a probate court of Kansas may be subjected to a suit in one of the district courts of that state to set aside the releases to vacate the settlement, and to restore to the plaintiffs their rights.—Pickens v. Campbell, 98 Kan. 518, 520, 159 Pac. 21. Where an administrator with the will annexed was guilty of irregularity in reporting household property and shares of corporate stock and in claiming administrator's fees thereon, an order of court setting aside the administrator's final account is justified.—In re Johnston's Estate (Wash.), 181 Pac. 209.

(2) Void decree, only, may be vacated.—If the decree of final settlement in the county court is void for want of jurisdiction, that court has a right to vacate and set it aside at any time, and does not err in so doing; but, if the decree is not void, it cannot be disturbed by the court that entered it, after the expiration of the term.—In re Conant's Estate, 43 Or. 530, 73 Pac. 1018, 1019.

(3) Can not be set aside for "mistake," etc., when.—A decree settling the final account of an executor, and discharging him from his trust, if regular upon its face, can not be set aside by the probate court on the ground that it had been inadvertently and prematurely entered, after the expiration of the time limited by statute under which a party or his legal representative may be relieved from a judgment, order, or other proceeding taken against him through his "mistake, inadvertence, surprise, or excusable neglect."—Estate of Cahalan, 70 Cal. 604, 607, 12 Pac. 427. An alleged mistake in an account can not be corrected on a final account, where such mistake was claimed to have been made in an account filed five years before, and there is not sufficient proof of the alleged mistake.—Estate of Herteman, 73 Cal. 545, 15 Pac. 121, 123.

(4) Collateral attack.—The order of a probate court allowing or disallowing a final account, is a final settlement and an adjudication of the matter of which it assumes to dispose, and it can not thereafter be collaterally attacked or impeached in the same or any other court by the parties thereto, or those in privity with them.—Tobelman v. Hildebrandt, 72 Cal. 313, 316, 14 Pac. 20. A judgment entered by a county court of this state upon the final accounting of an executor is of equal rank with judgments entered in other courts of record in

this state, and is conclusive as against collateral attack, except upon jurisdictional grounds and those of collusion and fraud.—Joy v. Elton, 9 N. D. 428, 83 N. W. 875.

(5) Equitable relief. In general.—While the district courts, by virtue of their general equity powers, may nullify orders of final settlement made in the probate courts, yet they will not do so as to orders, provisional and interlocutory in their nature, and which do not finally conclude the rights of the interested parties.—Ladd v. Nystol, 63 Kan. 23, 64 Pac. 985. The annual settlements between administrators and probate courts, while not conclusive adjudications, are prima facie correct. They are in the nature of accounts stated, and can be impeached by proceedings brought therefor in the district court only for fraud or some other inequitable circumstance, and not for mere technical illegality in the conduct of the administration prior to the settlement.—Young v. Scott, 59 Kan. 621, 54 Pac. 670. When a just demand against a decedent's estate is paid by the administrator, without a previous order of allowance by the probate court, but the payment made is credited to the administrator in his annual settlement with the court, a subsequent administrator de bonis non of the estate can not impeach the settlement in a suit against his predecessor, for an accounting, brought in the district court, upon the sole ground that the demand paid had not been previously presented to the probate court and allowed by it.—Young v. Scott, 59 Kan. 621, 54 Pac. 670. But while such a settlement is final, one who was not a party to it may treat it as a nullity, and invoke the aid of a court of equity jurisdiction to compel the administrator to render a full account.—Clarke v. Perry, 5 Cal. 58, 60, 63 Am. Dec. 82. Assuming that the superior court, sitting in probate, has no jurisdiction to compel an administrator to pay to an heir his distributive share, yet, if the petition states all the elements of a bill in equity for an accounting, and is answered on the merits, without objection to the form of the proceeding, the fact that it is entitled in the estate, instead of being in form an independent action, can make no difference. The petition, under these circumstances, may be regarded as a petition in equity, addressed to the equitable powers of the superior court, and the form of its title is immaterial.—Estate of Clary, 112 Cal. 292, 294, 44 Pac. 569. An executor's or administrator's account, that has been allowed can be assailed in equity only and on the same grounds as other judgments.—Estate of Raleigh, 48 Utah 128, 158 Pac. 705.

REFERENCES.

Relief in equity from orders settling the accounts of executors and administrator's.—See note 106, Am. St. Rep. 641. Settlement of decedent's estate in equity.—See note 2 Am. & Eng. Ann. Cas. 870.

(6) Equitable relief for fraud or mistake.—If the settlement of the final account of a guardian has been procured by the employment of fraud and artifice, equity has jurisdiction to afford relief, and to

compel a full and just accounting.—Silva v. Santos, 138 Cal. 536, 541, 71 Pac. 703. It is well established that the settlement of an administrator's account by the decree of a probate court does not conclude as to property fraudulently or accidentally withheld from the account. If the property was omitted by mistake, or has been subsequently discovered, a court of equity may exercise its jurisdiction in the premises and take such action as justice to the heirs of the deceased or to the creditors of the estate may require, even if the probate court might, in such a case, open its decree and administer upon the omitted property. And a fraudulent concealment of property, or a fraudulent disposition, is a general or always existing ground for the interposition of equity.—Lataillade v. Oreña, 91 Cal. 565, 576, 25 Am. St. Rep. 219, 27 Pac. 924. A decree approving and settling the final account of an administrator is a final adjudication, and if it was procured by fraud, a court of equity has jurisdiction of the cause, although distribution has not been made and the administrator has not been discharged.— Froebrich v. Lane, 45 Or. 13, 106 Am. St. Rep. 634, 76 Pac. 351, 353. Where a decree approving and settling the final account of an administrator is attacked for fraud, the fact that the suit was not instituted until more than eight months after the entry of final settlement does not constitute such laches as to preclude plaintiff from insisting upon the remedy invoked.—Froebrich v. Lane, 45 Or. 13, 106 Am. St. Rep. 634, 76 Pac. 351, 354. If, however, the heirs of the decedent have knowledge of the fraudulent conduct of the executor prior to the settlement of his account, in omitting to include in the inventory of the estate, or to charge himself in his final account with, an indebtedness due from himself to the decedent, and the account is settled by the court, as presented, they are concluded by the decree, and can not afterwards maintain an action against the executor to recover the indebtedness.—Tobelman v. Hildebrandt, 72 Cal. 313, 316, 14 Pac. 20. A court of equity will review and enjoin or annul decrees of probate courts upon the final settlements of executors and administrators, upon the application of injured parties, for fraud, and in some cases for mistake, or where the matter complained of may have arisen either from fraud or mistake, or constitutes constructive fraud.—Froebrich v. Lane, 45 Or. 13, 106 Am. St. Rep. 634, 76 Pac. 351, 352; Tobelman v. Hildebrandt, 72 Cal. 313, 316, 14 Pac. 20; Lataillade v. Oreña, 91 Cal. 565, 576, 25 Am. St. Rep. 219, 27 Pac. 924. An action for fraud, however, in making such a settlement can not be maintained where the allegations of the petition fail to state a case of fraud.—Ladd v. Nystol, 63 Kan. 23, 64 Pac. 985, 986; In re Conant's Estate, 43 Or. 530, 73 Pac. 1018. A court of equity has jurisdiction to set aside the decree of a county court, approving and settling the final account of an administrator, procured by fraud, notwithstanding the existence of a statute giving such last-named court exclusive jurisdiction, in the first instance, to settle such accounts. Neither does the existence of a statute under which a party may obtain relief from a judgment rendered against him through his "mistake, inadvertence, surprise, or excusable neglect" preclude the proceeding in equity where the remedy under such statute has not been invoked. The equitable remedy, however, has its just limitations, and can not be utilized for the correction of errors or irregularities; and where the party has had an opportunity to be heard in the original proceeding, and to have the matter revised on appeal, but has neglected to avail himself thereof, he is not entitled to redress in the equitable forum.—Froebrich v. Lane, 45 Or. 13, 106 Am. St. Rep. 634, 76 Pac. 351, 353. After an executor's or administrator's account has been allowed an attack can not be made upon it by reference merely to items in the objections filed to the allowance of the final account; it must be made as in other cases where a judgment is assailed for fraud, etc.—Estate of Raleigh, 48 Utah 128, 158 Pac. 705.

24. Appeal.

(1) In general.—Whether an order is appealable is to be determined by what it purports to determine, not by what may be its actual operative effect.—Estate of Bullock, 75 Cal. 419, 421, 17 Pac. 540. Before an appeal can be taken from the action of the probate court on any part of the final settlement of an administrator, it must appear that the probate court has taken final action on the settlement, and has passed on the whole account presented.—Appeal of Biggie, 52 Kan. 184, 34 Pac. 782. Contra: Estate of Rose, 80 Cal. 166, 170, 22 Pac. 86. The right to move for a new trial has been extended in probate matters only to two cases, to wit, a contest over a petition for letters testamentary and a petition for the sale of land. The proceeding is not applicable to the case of an order settling the account of an executor or administrator.—Estate of Franklin, 133 Cal. 584, 587, 65 Pac. 1081. An order settling the account of an executor or administrator is not a final judgment upon which a statement or motion for new trial may be based.—Estate of Franklin, 133 Cal. 584, 587, 65 Pac. 1081. The allowance to an executor or administrator of a sum paid to expert accountants for examining the books of a partnership, of which the decedent was a member, is a matter committed to the sound discretion of the court, and will not be disturbed where no abuse of discretion is shown.—Estate of Levinson, 108 Cal. 450, 457, 41 Pac. 483, 42 Pac. 479. On appeal from a decree made upon a final accounting and settlement of the accounts of an executor or administrator, the petition and account filed with the view to a final settlement, and the written objection filed thereto, constitute a part of the record to be used on appeal without being so made by a bill of exceptions or a statement of facts that constitute the judgment roll.—Estate of Isaacs, 30 Cal. 105, 110; Miller v. Lux, 100 Cal. 609, 613, 34 Pac. 345, 639.

(2) Appealable orders.—An order settling the final account of an executor or administrator is appealable.—Estate of Couts, 87 Cal. 480, 482, 25 Pac. 685. An interlocutory order settling the account of an administrator, but not discharging him from his trust, is not a final

judgment, but such order is appealable.—Estate of Rose, 80 Cal. 166, 170, 22 Pac. 86; Estate of Sanderson, 74 Cal. 199, 15 Pac. 753. Contra: Appeal of Biggie, 52 Kan. 184, 34 Pac. 782. A decree ordering, adjudging and decreeing "that the said final account of said adminis-trator be, and the same is, settled, allowed, and affirmed," is a decree allowing a final account, and such as that from which the statute authorizes an appeal to be taken.—Bowman v. Bowman, 27 Nev. 413, 76 Pac. 634, 635. There is no distinction between orders settling accounts as to their appealability. An order settling an account is appealable, whether it be a final or any other account.—Estate of Grant, 131 Cal. 426, 429, 63 Pac. 731. The omission from an administrator's final account of a claim against the estate leaves to the claimant the right to petition the court for an order directing payment by the adminis-trator, and from a refusal of an order so directing the claimant may appeal.—Benning v. Superior Court, 34 Cal. App. 296, 167 Pac. 291.

(3) Non-appealable orders.—The Montana statute does not permit an appeal from an order directing an administrator to turn over to his successor, upon resignation or removal, the property belonging to the estate, or which has come into his hands as such.—In re Barker's Estate, 26 Mont. 279, 67 Pac. 941, 943. And an order disallowing a claim against an estate is not appealable, where the statute provides that if a claim is rejected the holder must bring suit within a certain time or be barred, as that provides an exclusive remedy.—In re Barker's Estate, 26 Mont. 279, 67 Pac. 941, 942. An allowance of an attorney's fee, upon the settlement of the account of an executor, can not be reviewed on appeal, if no objection thereto was raised in the lower court.—Estate of Rohrer, 160 Cal. 574, Ann. Cas. 1913A, 479, 117 Pac. 672.

(4) Parties. Representative.—Upon the settlement of the account of an executor or administrator, only those parties interested in the estate who appear in the superior court and make some objection or exception to the account, or in some way make themselves parties of record to that proceeding, are necessary parties to an appeal from any order made therein. Having failed to make themselves parties to the proceeding, they must, for the preservation of any advantage to themselves accruing from the order appealed from, depend upon the efforts of those who made the contest for their benefit.—Estate of McDougald, 143 Cal. 476, 482, 77 Pac. 443, 79 Pac. 878, 879. If there is in the hands of the executor or administrator money which he claims does not belong to the estate, he should himself take steps to test the right, if a serious question arises, and if he is improperly charged, his remedy is to appeal from the decree settling his final account.—Estate of Burdick, 112 Cal. 387, 391, 44 Pac. 734. If money belonging to the estate is ordered to be charged to the administrator, though it appears upon the face of the order that the money is in fact in the hands of a third person, the order, if erroneous, must be appealed from; other-wise the administrator is concluded thereby, and is chargeable with the

amount, whether collected or not, if necessary for the payment of creditors.—Estate of Carver, 123 Cal. 102, 106, 55 Pac. 770. But an executor or administrator can not, in his representative capacity, ask for the review of an order disallowing his individual claim against the estate.—In re Barker's Estate, 26 Mont. 279, 67 Pac. 941, 943. Nor can he, in his private capacity, have reviewed an order requiring him, as administrator, to turn over certain property to a special administrator, which has come into his possession in his representative capacity, though there may be a dispute as to the ownership of the property, the administrator claiming it in his private capacity as agent for third persons.—State v. District Court, 26 Mont. 369, 68 Pac. 856, 857. The attorney for the executor or administrator is not "interested in the estate," and is not required to contest the accounts of an executor or administrator, and is not concluded by their settlement.— Briggs v. Breen, 123 Cal. 657, 660, 56 Pac. 633, 886. He has recourse against the executor or administrator personally, and is therefore not entitled to appeal from the settlement of the latter's account.—Estate of Kruger, 143 Cal. 141, 145, 146; 76 Pac. 891. If the claims of a deceased beneficiary are not presented in the settlement of an estate, a creditor of such beneficiary is not "a party interested," so as to be able to appeal from the decree in final settlement.—Estate of Carr, 175 Cal. 387, 165 Pac. 958. A creditor of the personal estate, dependent, for the satisfaction of his claim, on the personal estate's share of the residue of a partnership estate, has such interest in the partnership estate as will entitle him to resist the allowance of a questionable claim in the settlement of the partnership estate in the probate court, and to appeal from the decision of that court.—Sarbach v. Fidelity & D. Co., 99 Kan. 29 L. R. A. 1917B, 1043, 160 Pac. 990.

(5) Notice.—The only parties to the record are those who appear and resist the application for final settlement and accounting; and other persons, equally interested and equally affected by the order, but who do not see fit to make any contest or objection to the account, or to any matter stated therein, need not be served with notice of appeal.— Estate of McDougald, 143 Cal. 476, 482, 77 Pac. 443, 79 Pac. 878, 879. The only parties upon whom it is necessary to serve notice of the appeal, in proceedings for the settlement of the account of an executor or administrator are those who make themselves parties in the court by appearing at the time of the settlement and contesting the account. —Estate of Scott, 7 Cal. Unrep. 187, 77 Pac. 446. Upon an appeal from an order settling the account of an executor or administrator, the executor is the only adverse party upon whom it is necessary to serve notice of appeal.—Estate of Delaney, 110 Cal. 563, 567, 42 Pac. 981. It is not necessary to serve with such notice a creditor whose claim had been allowed, but who did not make any appearance on the settlement of the account.—Estate of Carpenter, 146 Cal. 661, 80 Pac. 1072, 1073. It is not necessary to serve notice of appeal on the attorneys of the executor or administrator, as they are not parties to

the proceeding of settlement of account.—Estate of Carpenter, 146 Cal. 661, 80 Pac. 1072, 1073. A notice of appeal, though not following the exact language of the statute, as being taken from an "order," instead of the decision or decree, is sufficiently descriptive of the document and matter appealed from, where no one can be misled by the notice of appeal.—Bowman v. Bowman, 27 Nev. 413, 76 Pac. 634, 636. If the order settling and allowing the annual account of an executor or administrator recites that the clerk gave due and legal notice in the manner and for the time ordered by the court, such recital is conclusive on the parties on appeal; and if, under the statute, notice required in probate proceedings serves the purpose of a summons in ordinary actions, the giving of the notice in probate proceedings may be rendered useless by the appearaance of the parties and participation in the proceedings. In such a case the purpose of the notice has been served, and one who has taken part in the hearing will not be heard to say that the court had no jurisdiction to determine his right.—In re Davis' Estate, 33 Mont. 539, 88 Pac. 957, 958.

(6) **Findings. Bill of exceptions. Record.**—Express findings are not necessary on the settlement of the account of an executor or administrator.—Miller v. Lux, 100 Cal. 609, 613, 35 Pac. 345, 639; In re Levinson, 108 Cal. 450, 455, 41 Pac. 483, 42 Pac. 479. But when such findings are filed in a contest of this character, they may be considered upon appeal for the purpose of determining the issues upon which such findings were made.—Estate of Adams, 131 Cal. 415, 420, 63 Pac. 838. The settlement of the accounts of an executor or administrator, though sometimes spoken of as an "order," is, in effect, a judgment; and in a proceeding for the settlement of such an account the petition and account and the written objections filed to it are the pleadings, which the clerk of the court is required to attach to the copy of the judgment, and these constitute the "judgment roll"; and while, in such a proceeding, it is not incumbent upon the court to make and file express findings, still, when the account is assailed in any particular for matters not appearing upon its face, the court may properly make express findings upon such issues, and when it does so, such findings become as much a part of the judgment roll as the judgment or order itself, and the account and exceptions thereto constitute the pleadings of the parties.—Miller v. Lux, 100 Cal. 609, 613, 35 Pac. 345, 639. The account of an executor or administrator is itself a bill of items, and specifications of the insufficiency of the evidence to justify a decision setlling the account are stated with sufficient particularity when the evidence is alleged to be insufficient to justify the decision allowing particular items of the account specified in the bill of exceptions.— In re Levinson, 108 Cal. 450, 455, 41 Pac. 483, 42 Pac. 479. In the absence of a bill of exceptions showing the evidence on which an allowance was made to the executor or administrator for advancing funds for the purpose of carrying on litigation relative to

the maintenance of a will, under which minor devisees and legatees claimed, an order allowing him interest on the sums so advanced will not be held erroneous.—Estate of Carpenter, 146 Cal. 661, 80 Pac. 1072. The petition, and especially the account filed and submitted, and the exceptions taken to the account by any person or persons interested, constitute, in part at least, the jurisdictional facts on which the decree is founded, and are necessary on appeal from the judgment or decree, made on the settlement of the executor's account, as are the pleadings in an ordinary civil action upon an appeal from a judgment or order therein.—Estate of Isaacs, 30 Cal. 105, 111. A mere statement in a bill of exceptions, that a party excepted to a decision of the court, does not constitute an exception available on appeal, unless the objection is stated, and also the ground upon which it was made.—Estate of Page, 57 Cal. 238, 239. If the appellant fails to point out why certain items should be allowed, and the attention of the court is not called to the evidence to justify them, it will be presumed that the evidence sustains the finding as to such items, for it is not the duty of the court to search through the record for the necessary evidence.—Estate of Shively, 145 Cal. 400, 78 Pac. 869, 871. The judgment roll on an appeal from an order settling the account of an executor or administrator consists of the petition and account and reports accompanying the same, objections and exceptions thereto, if any, findings of the court, if any, and the order settling the account.—Estate of Thayer, 1 Cal. App. 104, 81 Pac. 658, 659. The filing of an account by an executor or administrator makes the inventory upon which it was predicated a part of the record, and it is properly included in the transcript on appeal without having been offered in evidence.—In re Osburn's Estate, 36 Or. 8, 58 Pac. 521, 522; but the petition for letters of administration, the order appointing the administrator, his undertaking, and the order directing a distribution of the funds of the estate, not being a necessary part of the final report, will not be considered, where they were not offered in evidence.—In re Osburn's Estate, 36 Or. 8, 58 Pac. 521, 522.

(7) **Sufficiency of judge's certificate.**—On appeal from a portion of a decree settling the final account of an administrator fixing and settling his compensation, the judge's certificate is sufficient, where it declares that he has examined the contents "of the within transcript on appeal in said matter," and finds that "the" papers and orders therein set forth and contained are copies of "the" original papers and orders "filed and used" upon the hearing, and in the various proceedings of the said estate. While the certificate does not, in so many words, state that the papers and orders set forth in the transcript are "all" the papers and orders used in the proceeding, it is clear that, by the employment of the definite article "the," as descriptive of the papers and orders thus used, the judge intended to and did certify that said papers and orders were in fact "all" the papers and orders so used.—Estate of Davis, 8 Cal. App. 355, 97 Pac. 86.

(8) Consideration of case. Review.—Upon appeal from an order settling the account of an executor or administrator, all the proceedings leading up to it, including the evidence upon which it is based, are open to review.—Estate of Rose, 80 Cal. 166, 170, 22 Pac. 86. Where, on the final settlement of an estate, a judgment is rendered that the administrator pay to the heir a certain sum, the judgment is the thing necessary to appeal from, and such appeal brings up the whole matter for retrial.—Gunn v. Newcomer, 9 Kan. App. 883, 57 Pac. 1052. If an order is entered settling the account of an executor or administrator, and, more than sixty days after it is signed and filed with the clerk, an appeal is taken, but in less than sixty days after it was entered in the minute-book of the court, the evidence upon which such order was based is open for examination and review by the appellate court, notwithstanding a provision of the code that, upon appeal from a judgment, the evidence can not be reviewed unless the appeal was taken within sixty days after the rendition of the judgment.—Estate of Levinson, 108 Cal. 450, 454, 41 Pac. 483, 42 Pac. 479; Estate of Rose, 80 Cal. 166, 22 Pac. 86. Where exceptions have been taken to items in an annual settlement of an administrator's account, after they have been allowed by the probate judge, and the probate court adheres to its former ruling, and the party excepting appeals to the district court, the allowance of the probate court is prima facie correct, and the burden of showing its incorrectness is upon the party who appeals.—Calnan v. Savidge, 68 Kan. 620, 75 Pac. 1010. The presumption on appeal is, that items disallowed in the account of an executor or administrator were properly disallowed.—Estate of Scott, 1 Cal. App. 740, 83 Pac. 85, 87. Although an order setting aside a decree settling the final account of an executor is not directly appealable, it may be reviewed on appeal from a subsequent decree settling a final account on the ground that it is clearly an intermediate order, which necessarily affects the final judgment from which the appeal is properly taken.—In re Cahalan, 70 Cal. 604, 607, 12 Pac. 427. If the court makes an order respecting the account of an executor or administrator, and afterwards amends it, leaving the original order and the amendment both in the record, their several order may be considered together on a writ of review.—State v. Second Jud. Dist. Court, 25 Mont. 33, 63 Pac. 717, 718. If an appeal is taken from several distinct and separate orders, though embraced in one notice of appeal, the appeals may be treated as separate and distinct.—In re Barker's Estate, 26 Mont. 279, 67 Pac. 941, 942. Although the transcript on appeal from an order settling the accounts of an executor or administrator includes a decree of partial distribution, notice of appeal therefrom and a remittitur can not be considered if they have not been included in a bill of exceptions as required by a rule of court.—Estate of Thayer, 1 Cal. App. 104, 81 Pac. 658, 659. Upon an order simply settling a final account, no matter concerning the distribution of an estate would be necessarily determined, and no error in settling the final account, pending an appeal from a decree of partial distribution, is shown where the account rendered is not in the transcript, and there is nothing to show that the court, by its order settling the final account, determined any matter that it did not have jurisdiction to determine at the time. Under such circumstances, the court must assume that the account did not contain any account of any payment made under or in connection with the order of partial distribution, but only accounts of receipts of payments of debts of decedent and expenses of administration, which are matters proper to be considered in a final account. —Estate of Thayer, 1 Cal. App, 104, 81 Pac. 658, 659. A decree settling the final account of an executor or administrator will not be disturbed upon appeal unless the appellant shows that his interest in the estate has suffered in some way by reason of the findings or the decree of the court. Appellant will not be heard to complain that he has received some part of the estate that should have gone to another person, or to his legal representatives.—Estate of Casner, 1 Cal. App. 145, 147, 81 Pac. 991. In carrying out the decision of the appellate court as to the distribution of real property, the probate in which the proceedings originated, has no power to re-examine the settled account of the executor or administrator, to ascertain whether any part of the moneys included therein represented the net amount of the rents and profits collected by the executor from the real property. The judgment of the appellate court ordering distribution of the realty to the heir at law must be construed as operating upon the estate in its condition at the time of the going down of the remittitur. In other words, the realty of the estate should be distributed to the heir at law.—Estate of Pichoir, 146 Cal. 404, 406, 80 Pac. 512. The petition for letters of administration, the order appointing the administratrix, her undertaking, and the inventory, although properly included in the transcript on appeal, will not be considered where they were not offered in evidence.—In re Osburn's Estate, 36 Or. 8, 58 Pac. 521, 522. On an appeal from an order denying a motion for a new trial, in a proceeding by executors for the settlement of the accounts and for the distribution of the decedent's estate, there being no appeal taken from the decree made in such proceeding, the sufficiency of the findings to sustain the decree can not be reviewed.—Estate of Keating, 162 Cal. 406, 122 Pac. 1079. Where an appeal from an order reducing an allowance to an administrator for attorney's fees, the record contained no testimony as to value of the services, the court's allowance for services, nearly all of which were performed in the course of administration in that court, will not be disturbed in the absence of a clear showing of abuse of discretion.—In re Davis' Estate, 39 Mont. 433, 104 Pac. 522. If an administrator's account is not approved in toto; if claims listed in such account are rejected upon the objection and protest of heirs or creditors of said estate; if such matter is thereafter appealed to the district court; and if a judgment is rendered in favor of the claimant; such judgment establishes the claim in the same manner as if it had been allowed by the executor or administrator and the probate judge; and the judgment must be in the form prescribed by the statute.— Miller v. Lewiston Nat. Bank, 18 Ida. 124, 141, 108 Pac. 901. On an appeal from an order of the district court in a proceeding for the settlement of the accounts of an administratrix upon exceptions filed thereto, where plaintiff in error fails to assign as error the overruling of a motion-for a new trial in the petition in error, no question is properly presented on the appeal to review as errors occurring during the progress of the trial.—In re McGannon's Estate, 50 Okla. 288, 297, 150 Pac. 1109.

(9) **Affirmance. Remanding. Reversal. Dismissal. Remittitur.**— When the decree allowing a final account is found to be erroneous as to any item or items, the appellate court may direct the decree to be corrected, and, as corrected, affirm it.—Estate of Adams, 131 Cal. 415, 420, 63 Pac. 838. But if it appears that, by reason of irregularities in the proceedings, parties in interest were not heard in the settlement, the cause will be remanded for further proceedings, in order that a proper settlement of the account may be had.—Estate of Runyon, 53 Cal. 196. On appeal from an order settling the account of an executor or administrator, such order will not be disturbed, if there is any evidence to sustain the findings of the court, whether the appellate court would have found the same way upon the same evidence or not.—Estate of Rose, 80 Cal. 166, 180, 22 Pac. 86. But an order settling the final account of an executor or administrator will not be reversed for want of proper vouchers and evidence as to the correctness of the account.—Estate of Rose, 63 Cal. 349, 351. As the method of settling final accounts of an executor or administrator does not necessarily involve the method of distribution of the estate, and as distribution to the heirs or legatees may take place upon the settlement of a final account, or at any subsequent time, the settlement of a final account, pending appeal from a decree of partial distribution, will not be disturbed on appeal, where it in no way appears that any payment under the decree of partial distribution, or any expenses incurred therewith, was presented by the final account.—Estate of Thayer, 1 Cal. App. 104, 81 Pac. 658, 659. An appeal, dismissed because there was nothing to appeal from, does not preclude another appeal in the same case, where the record should have been made up from which an appeal can be taken. Hence, the dismissal of an appeal prematurely taken is no bar to a subsequent appeal.—Estate of Rose, 80 Cal. 166, 171, 22 Pac. 86. An appeal from an order settling the annual account of an executor or administrator must be dismissed for failure to file the transcript within the prescribed time; and such dismissal can not be prevented by the pendency of a statement on motion for a new trial, as such a motion is not applicable to an order settling an account.— Estate of Franklin, 133 Cal. 584, 587, 65 Pac. 1081. Although a rule of court requires appellants to print, in their brief, the findings of fact on appeal from an order settling and allowing the account of an execu-

tor or administrator, such failure is not ground for dismissing the appeal, where the court made findings and passed on a large number of separate items, and appellants failed to print such separate findings in their brief.—In re Alfstad's Estate, 27 Wash. 175, 67 Pac. 593, 594. An appeal by a mortgagee must be dismissed where the record does not show that he is an aggrieved party.—Estate of Crook, 125 Cal. 459, 461, 58 Pac. 89. The refusal of the appellate court to dismiss an appeal from an order settling the account of an administrator between contestant parties, because a creditor was not served with notice of appeal, does not determine the question whether the creditor who did not appear has a right of appeal from such order, or from an order for the payment of claims. The rules governing the question who must be served with notice of appeal are not identical with those that control the question who may have the right of appeal.—Estate of McDougald, 143 Cal. 476, 483, 77 Pac. 443, 79 Pac. 878, 879. When the remittitur has been duly and legally issued without inadvertence, the appellate court has no power to recall it. That court thereupon loses jurisdiction of the cause, except in the case of mistake, fraud, or imposition practiced upon the court.—Estate of Levinson, 108 Cal. 450, 459, 41 Pac. 483, 42 Pac. 479. Where a serious question arises, either over the character of value of the service to the estate, rendered by an administrator, the appellant court will be reluctant to disturb the determination of the judge in probate with respect to the allowances made the administrator, or an allowance made where extraordinary services are found to have been rendered. Where, however, the court made a detailed finding of the nature and character of the services, and withheld extra compensation in the mistaken belief that, though they were of great value, and not such as the administrator was bound to render, they still did not come fairly within the category of extraordinary service, the appellate court will revise the order refusing extra compensation, and direct the probate court to fix the amount thereof.—Estate of Broome, 162 Cal. 258, 122 Pac. 470. Where a credit for a commission claimed by an administratrix embraced in an account filed in the county court in 1909 but never approved by that court, it is held that the administratrix is entitled to commissions on the part of the estate fully administered; but the action of the court in failing to adjudge the administratrix not entitled to the same, and leaving the question open to future settlement is held not to have been such an abuse of discretion as to authorize a reversal.—In re Gannon's Estate, 50 Okla. 288, 300, 150 Pac. 1109.

CHAPTER III.

PAYMENT OF DEBTS OF ESTATE.

PAYMENT OF DEBTS.

§ 698. Order in which debts must be paid.

The debts of the estate, subject to the provisions of section twelve hundred and five, must be paid in the following order:

1. Funeral expenses;

2. The expenses of the last sickness;

3. Debts having preference by the laws of the United States;

4. Judgments rendered against the decedent in his lifetime, and mortgages and other liens in the order of their date;

5. All other demands against the estate.

If a debt is payable in a particular kind of money or currency, it must be paid only in such money or currency. If the estate is insolvent, no greater rate of interest must be paid upon any debt, from the time of the first publication of notice to creditors, than is allowed by law on judgments.—*Kerr's Cyc. Code Civ. Proc., § 1643.*

ANALOGOUS AND IDENTICAL STATUTES.
No identical statute found.

Alaska—Compiled Laws of 1913, section 1704.

Arizona—Revised Statutes of 1913, paragraph 1016.

Colorado—Mills's Statutes of 1912, section 7996.

Idaho—Compiled Statutes of 1919, section 7710.

Kansas—General Statutes of 1915, section 4564.

Montana—Revised Codes of 1907, section 7653.

Nevada—Revised Laws of 1912, section 6052.

New Mexico—Statutes of 1915, section 2284.

North Dakota—Compiled Laws of 1913, section 8755.

Oklahoma—Revised Laws of 1910, section 6447.

Oregon—Lord's Oregon Laws, section 1295.

South Dakota—Compiled Laws of 1913, section 5908.

Utah—Compiled Laws of 1907, section 3870.

Washington—Laws of 1917, chapter 156, page 692, section 171.

Wyoming—Compiled Statutes of 1910, section 5595.

§ 699. Where property is insufficient to pay mortgage.

The preference given in the preceding section to a mortgage or lien only extends to the proceeds of the property subject to the mortgage or lien. If the proceeds of such property are insufficient to pay the mortgage or lien, the part remaining unsatisfied must be classed with general demands against the estate.—*Kerr's Cyc. Code Civ. Proc., § 1644.*

ANALOGOUS AND IDENTICAL STATUTES.
The * indicates identity.
Alaska—Compiled Laws of 1913, sections 1705, 1706.
Arizona—Revised Statutes of 1913, paragraph 1017.
Idaho—Compiled Statutes of 1919, section 7711.
Montana—Revised Codes of 1907, section 7654.
Nevada—Revised Laws of 1912, section 6053.
North Dakota*—Compiled Laws of 1913, section 8756.
Oklahoma—Revised Laws of 1910, section 6448.
Oregon—Lord's Oregon Laws, section 1296.
South Dakota—Compiled Laws of 1913, section 5909.
Utah—Compiled Laws of 1907, section 3871.
Washington—Laws of 1917, chapter 156, page 692, section 174.
Wyoming—Compiled Statutes of 1910, section 5596.

§ 700. If estate is insufficient, a dividend must be paid.

If the estate is insufficient to pay all the debts of any one class, each creditor must be paid a dividend in proportion to his claim; and no creditor of any one class shall receive any payment until all those of the preceding class are fully paid.—*Kerr's Cyc. Code Civ. Proc.*, § 1645.

ANALOGOUS AND IDENTICAL STATUTES.
The * indicates identity.
Alaska—Compiled Laws of 1913, section 1707.
Arizona*—Revised Statutes of 1913, paragraph 1018.
Idaho*—Compiled Statutes of 1919, section 7712.
Montana*—Revised Codes of 1907, section 7655.
Nevada*—Revised Laws of 1912, section 6054.
New Mexico—Statutes of 1915, section 2285.
North Dakota—Compiled Laws of 1913, section 8753.
Oklahoma*—Revised Laws of 1910, section 6449.
Oregon—Lord's Oregon Laws, section 1298.
South Dakota*—Compiled Laws of 1913, section 5910.
Utah*—Compiled Laws of 1907, section 3872.
Washington—Laws of 1917, chapter 156, page 692, section 174.
Wyoming*—Compiled Statutes of 1910, section 5597.

§ 701. Funeral expenses and expenses of last sickness.

The executor or administrator, as soon as he has sufficient funds in his hands, must pay the funeral expenses and the expenses of the last sickness, and the allowance made to the family of the decedent. He may retain in his hands the necessary expenses of administration, but he is not obliged to pay any other debt or any legacy until, as prescribed in this article, the payment has been ordered by the court.—*Kerr's Cyc. Code Civ. Proc.*, § 1646.

ANALOGOUS AND IDENTICAL STATUTES.

The * indicates identity.

Alaska—Compiled Laws of 1913, section 1693.
Arizona*—Revised Statutes of 1913, paragraph 1019.
Idaho*—Compiled Statutes of 1919, section 7713.
Montana—Revised Codes of 1907, section 7656.
Nevada—Revised Laws of 1912, section 6055.
New Mexico—Statutes of 1915, section 2283.
North Dakota—Compiled Laws of 1913, section 8759.
Oklahoma*—Revised Laws of 1910, section 6450.
Oregon—Lord's Oregon Laws, sections 1284, 1300.
South Dakota*—Compiled Laws of 1913, section 5911.
Utah*—Compiled Laws of 1907, section 3869.
Washington—Laws of 1917, chapter 156, p. 692, sections 171, 175.
Wyoming*—Compiled Statutes of 1910, section 5598.

§ 702. Order for payment of debts, and final discharge.

Upon the settlement of the account of the executor or administrator, provided for in section sixteen hundred and twenty-eight, the court must make an order for the payment of the debts, as the circumstances of the estate require. If there are not sufficient funds in the hands of the executor or administrator, the court must specify in the decree the sum to be paid to each creditor. If the whole property of the estate is exhausted by such payment or distribution, such account must be considered as a final account, and the executor or administrator is entitled to his discharge on producing and filing the necessary vouchers and proofs showing that such payments have been made, and that he has fully complied with the decree of the court.—*Kerr's Cyc. Code Civ. Proc.*, § 1647.

ANALOGOUS AND IDENTICAL STATUTES.

The * indicates identity.

Alaska—Compiled Laws of 1913, sections 1693, 1694.
Arizona*—Revised Statutes of 1913, paragraph 1020.
Colorado—Mills's Statutes of 1912, section 8020.

Hawaii—Revised Laws of 1915, section 2492.

Idaho*—Compiled Statutes of 1919, section 7714.

Kansas—General Statutes of 1915, sections 4587, 4662.

Montana*—Revised Codes of 1907, section 7657.

Nevada—Revised Laws of 1912, section 6056.

Oklahoma—Revised Laws of 1910, section 6451.

Oregon—Lord's Oregon Laws, sections 1284, 1302.

South Dakota—Compiled Laws of 1913, section 5912; and Laws of 1915, chapter 156, p. 333 (where creditor can not be found).

Utah*—Compiled Laws of 1907, section 3873.

Washington—Laws of 1917, chapter 156, page 690, section 163.

Wyoming*—Compiled Statutes of 1910, section 5599.

§ 703. Form. Decree settling account and for payment of claims.

[Title of court.]

[Title of estate.]   { No. ——.1   Dept. No. ——.
            [Title of form.]

Comes now ——, the administrator [2] of said estate, by ——, his attorney, and presents to the court for settlement his [3] account and report, showing charges in favor of said estate amounting to —— dollars ($——), claiming credits amounting to —— dollars ($——), leaving a balance of —— dollars ($——) in his hands belonging to said estate; and he now proves to the satisfaction of the court that said account was filed on the —— day of ——, 19—; that on the same day the clerk appointed the —— day of ——, 19—, as the day for the settlement thereof; and that notice of the time and place of said settlement has been duly given as required by law;[4] and no person appearing to except to or contest said account,[5] the court, after hearing the evidence, finds said account correct, and that the claims set forth in the accompanying report are justly due and payable out of said estate.

It is therefore ordered, adjudged, and decreed by the court, That said account be in all respects approved, allowed, and settled, and that said administrator [6] forthwith, out of the moneys in his [7] hands belonging to said estate, pay all the debts filed and allowed against the said estate, to wit:

Claim of —— allowed for —— dollars ($——);

Claim of —— allowed for —— dollars ($——).[8]

Entered [9] ——, 19—.   ——, County Clerk.

                              By ——, Deputy.

Explanatory notes.—1 Give file number. 2 Or, administratrix. 3 Or, her. 4 If the matter has been continued, say, "and settlement having been by the court regularly postponed to this day." 5 Or, and —— having appeared by ——, his attorney, and filed his exceptions and objections to said account. 6 Or, administratrix. 7 Or, her. 8 Etc., enumerating each claim. 9 Orders or decrees need not be signed: See note to § 77, ante.

§ 704. Form. Decree settling final account. Insolvent estate.

[Title of court.]

[Title of estate.]   { No. ——.1   Dept. No. ——.
                                   {   [Title of form.]

Comes now ——, the administrator [2] of said estate, by ——, his attorney, and presents to the court for settlement his final account and report, showing charges in favor of said estate amounting to —— dollars ($——), and claiming credits amounting to —— dollars ($——), leaving a balance of —— dollars ($——) in his hands belonging to said estate; and from the proofs offered the court finds that said account was filed on the —— day of ——, 19—; that on the same day the clerk appointed the —— day of ——, 19—, as the day for the settlement thereof; and that notice of the time and place of said settlement has been duly given as required by law;[3] and no person appearing to except to or contest said account,[4] the court, after hearing the evidence, finds that said account is correct, and that the claims set forth in the accompanying report are justly due and payable out of said estate.

It is therefore ordered and adjudged by the court, That said account be in all things approved, allowed, and settled; and that said —— forthwith pay the said balance in his hands upon the claims against said estate, as follows, to wit:

To —— on his claim of —— dollars ($——), the sum of —— dollars ($——);

To —— on his claim of —— dollars ($——), the sum of —— dollars ($——).[5]   ——, County Clerk.

Entered [6] ——, 19—.   By ——, Deputy.

Explanatory notes.—1 Give file number. 2 Or, executor. 3 If the matter has been continued, say, "and said settlement having been regularly postponed to this day." 4 Or, and —— having appeared by ——, his attorney, and filed his exceptions to said account. 5 Enumerating each payment ordered. 6 Orders or decrees need not be signed. See note to § 77, ante.

§ 705. Form. Decree of final discharge.

[Title of court.]

[Title of estate.]   { No. ——.1 Dept. No. ——.
                              { [Title of form.]

It appearing to this court that the above-entitled estate has been fully administered; that the administrator [2] has paid all sums of money due from him; that he has delivered up all property to the parties entitled thereto, and performed all the acts legally required of him in pursuance of the orders and decrees of this court; and that he has filed herein satisfactory vouchers therefor, —

It is ordered, adjudged, and decreed, That said —— be, and he is hereby, discharged from further administering said estate, and that —— and ——, sureties on his bond, are hereby released from any liabilities to be hereafter incurred.

Dated ——, 19—.   ——, Judge of the ——[3] Court.

Explanatory notes.—1 Give file number. 2 Or, executor. 3 Title of court.

§ 706. Provision for disputed and contingent claims.

If there is any claim not due, or any contingent or disputed claim against the estate, the amount thereof, or such part of the same as the holder would be entitled to if the claim were due, established, or absolute, must be paid into the court, and there remain, to be paid over to the party when he becomes entitled thereto; or, if he fails to establish his claim, to be paid over or distributed as the circumstances of the estate require. If any creditor whose claim has been allowed, but is not yet due, appears and assents to a deduction therefrom of the legal interest for the time the claim has yet to run, he is entitled to be paid accordingly. The payments provided for in this section are not to be made when the estate is insolvent, unless a pro rata distribution is ordered.—*Kerr's Cyc. Code Civ. Proc., § 1648.*

ANALOGOUS AND IDENTICAL STATUTES.
The * indicates identity.

Alaska—Compiled Laws of 1913, section 1710.
Arizona*—Revised Statutes of 1913, paragraph 1021.
Idaho*—Compiled Statutes of 1919, section 7715.
Montana*—Revised Codes of 1907, section 7658.
Nevada—Revised Laws of 1912, section 6057.
New Mexico—Statutes of 1915, section 2286.
North Dakota—Compiled Laws of 1913, section 8761.
Oklahoma*—Revised Laws of 1910, section 6452.
Oregon—Lord's Oregon Laws, section 1301.
South Dakota*—Compiled Laws of 1913, section 5913.
Utah*—Compiled Laws of 1907, section 3874.
Washington—Laws of 1917, chapter 156, page 693, section 179.
Wyoming*—Compiled Statutes of 1910, section 5600.

§ 707. Personal liability of representatives to creditors.

When a decree is made by the court for the payment of creditors, the executor or administrator is personally liable to each creditor for his allowed claim, or the dividend thereon, and execution may be issued on such decree, as upon a judgment in the court, in favor of each creditor, and the same proceedings may be had under such execution as under execution in other cases. The executor or administrator is liable therefor on his bond to each creditor.—*Kerr's Cyc. Code Civ. Proc., § 1649.*

ANALOGOUS AND IDENTICAL STATUTES.
The ⁵ indicates identity.

Alaska—Compiled Laws of 1913, section 1711.
Arizona*—Revised Statutes of 1913, paragraph 1022.
Colorado—Mills's Statutes of 1912, section 8022.
Idaho*—Compiled Statutes of 1919, section 7716.

Kansas—General Statutes of 1915, section 4586.
Montana*—Revised Codes of 1907, section 7659.
Nevada*—Revised Laws of 1912, section 6058.
New Mexico—Statutes of 1915, section 2289.
Oklahoma*—Revised Laws of 1910, section 6453.
Oregon—Lord's Oregon Laws, section 1302.
South Dakota*—Compiled Laws of 1913, section 5914.
Utah*—Compiled Laws of 1907, section 3875.
Washington—Laws of 1917, chapter 156, page 693, section 176.
Wyoming*—Compiled Statutes of 1910, section 5601.

§ 708. Claims not included in order for payment of debts, how disposed of.

When the accounts of the administrator or executor have been settled, and an order made for the payment of debts and distribution of the estate, no creditor whose claim was not included in the order for payment has any right to call upon the creditors who have been paid, or upon the heirs, devisees, or legatees to contribute to the payment of his claim; but if the executor or administrator has failed to give the notice to the creditors, as prescribed in section fourteen hundred and ninety-one, such creditor may recover on the bond of the executor or administrator the amount of his claim, or such part thereof as he would have been entitled to had it been allowed. This section shall not apply to any creditor whose claim was not due ten months before the day of settlement, or whose claim was contingent and did not become absolute ten months before such day.—*Kerr's Cyc. Code Civ. Proc.,* § 1650.

ANALOGOUS AND IDENTICAL STATUTES.
The * indicates identity.
Arizona*—Revised Statutes of 1913, paragraph 1023.
Idaho*—Compiled Statutes of 1919, section 7717.
Montana*—Revised Codes of 1907, section 7660.
North Dakota—Compiled Laws of 1913, section 8768.
Oklahoma—Revised Laws of 1910, section 6454.
South Dakota*—Compiled Laws of 1913, section 5915.
Utah—Compiled Laws of 1907, section 3876.
Washington—Laws of 1917, chapter 156, page 693, section 177.

§ 709. Order for payment of legacies and extension of time.

If the whole of the debts have been paid by the first distribution, the court must direct the payment of legacies and the distribution of the estate among the heirs, legatees, or other persons entitled, as provided in the next chapter; but if there be debts remaining unpaid, or if, for other reasons, the estate be not in a proper condition to be closed, the court must give such extension of time as may be reasonable for a final settlement of the estate.—*Kerr's Cyc. Code Civ. Proc.*, § 1651.

ANALOGOUS AND IDENTICAL STATUTES.
The * indicates identity.
Alaska—Compiled Laws of 1913, section 1712.
Arizona*—Revised Statutes of 1913, paragraph 1024.
Colorado—Mills's Statutes of 1912, section 8023.
Idaho*—Compiled Statutes of 1919, section 7718.
Montana*—Revised Codes of 1907, section 7661.
Nevada—Revised Laws of 1912, section 6059.
North Dakota*—Compiled Laws of 1913, section 8762.
Oklahoma*—Revised Laws of 1910, section 6455.
Oregon—Lord's Oregon Laws, section 1303.
South Dakota*—Compiled Laws of 1913, section 5916.

§ 710. Final account, when to be made.

At the time designated in the last section, or sooner, if within that time all the property of the estate has been sold, or there are sufficient funds in his hands for the payment of all the debts due by the estate, and the estate be in a proper condition to be closed, the executor or administrator must render a final account, and pray a settlement of his administration.—*Kerr's Cyc. Code Civ. Proc.*, § 1652.

ANALOGOUS AND IDENTICAL STATUTES.
The * indicates identity.
Alaska—Compiled Laws of 1913, sections 1694, 1702.
Arizona*—Revised Statutes of 1913, paragraph 1025.
Colorado—Mills's Statutes of 1912, section 8030 (Rev. Stats. 1908, sec. 7241); as amended by Laws of 1913, chapter 81, page 274 (relating to settlement of estates of deceased persons); see, also, Laws of 1917, chapter 70, page 219.
Hawaii—Revised Laws of 1915, section 2500.
Idaho*—Compiled Statutes of 1919, section 7719.

Montana*—Revised Codes of 1907, section 7662.
Nevada*—Revised Laws of 1912, section 6060.
Oklahoma*—Revised Laws of 1910, section 6456.
Oregon—Lord's Oregon Laws, section 1285.
South Dakota*—Compiled Laws of 1913, section 5917.
Utah—Compiled Laws of 1907, section 3952.
Washington—Laws of 1917, chapter 156, page 688, section 161.

§ 711. Neglect to render final account. How treated.

If he neglects to render his account, the same proceedings may be had as prescribed in this chapter in regard to the first account to be rendered by him; and all the provisions of this chapter relative to the last-mentioned account, and the notice and settlement thereof, apply to his account presented for final settlement.— *Kerr's Cyc. Code Civ. Proc.*, § 1653.

ANALOGOUS AND IDENTICAL STATUTES.

The * indicates identity.

Alaska—Compiled Laws of 1913, section 1702.
Arizona*—Revised Statutes of 1913, paragraph 1026.
Colorado—Mills's Statutes of 1912, section 8031.
Idaho*—Compiled Statutes of 1919, section 7720.
Montana*—Revised Codes of 1907, section 7663.
Nevada*—Revised Laws of 1912, section 6061.
Oklahoma*—Revised Laws of 1910, section 6457.
Oregon—Lord's Oregon Laws, section 1293.
South Dakota*—Compiled Laws of 1913, section 5918.

PAYMENT OF DEBTS.

1. In general.
2. Order of payment can not be changed.
3. Preference.
4. Payment of claims prior to settlement.
5. Premature or unauthorized payments. Advancement.
6. Funeral expenses. Monuments, etc. Expenses of administration.
   (1) Burial.
   (2) Funeral expenses.
   (3) Expenses of administration.
7. Property available for payment of debts.
   (1) In general.
   (2) Community property.
   (3) Rents and profits.
   (4) Property bequeathed or devised.

(5) Exempt property.
(6) Proceeds of life insurance policies. In general.
(7) Same. When not liable.
(8). Same. When liable.
8. Marshaling of assets.
9. Decree or order for payment.
   (1) In general.
   (2) Application for order.
   (3) Duty of court. Granting of order.
   (4) Validity of order. Effect of.
10. Payment of interest-bearing claims.
11. "Contingent" claims.
12. Deficiency. Part payment. Disputed claims.
13. "Dividends."
14. Mortgages and judgments.
15. Enforcement of payment.
16. Appeal.

Probate Law—107

1. In general.—It is declared by section 1497 of the Code of Civil Procedure of California that a claim allowed and approved and filed shall "rank among the acknowledged debts of the estate, to be paid in due course of administration."—Estate of Loshe, 62 Cal. 413, 415. The words "claim" and "demand," in the statute respecting the settlement of the estates of deceased persons, are synonymous.—Estate of McCausland, 52 Cal. 568, 577. It has been held that an executor or administrator may lawfully make payment of a debt, although a claim therefor has not been filed against the estate, as such payment, although made in an irregular manner, releases the estate from a legal charge.—Adams v. Smith, 19 Nev. 259, 9 Pac. 337, 339; but the statute of California does not allow an executor or administrator to pay even the debts due by an intestate, except in a particular way.—Tompkins v. Weeks, 26 Cal. 50, 62. No executor or administrator is chargeable upon any oral promise to pay any debt of the decedent out of his own estate, except some note or memorandum of the agreement be made in writing, etc.—McKeany v. Black, 117 Cal. 587, 593, 49 Pac. 710. The presumption of regularity of proceedings in the district court of Wyoming applies to its proceedings in probate matters. If, upon the allowance of an administrator's account, the balance in his hands is ordered to be paid to the person entitled thereto, both individually and as a guardian, the presumption is, that all debts of the estate have been settled.—Lethbridge v. Lauder, 13 Wyo. 9, 76 Pac. 682, 685. An administrator is at all times entitled to retain in his hands ample funds to meet the claims and expenses of administration, and the expenses of the funeral and last sickness of the deceased and the allowance to his family.—Walls v. Walker, 37 Cal. 424, 428, 99 Am. Dec. 290. The provision of the statute authorizing the executor to retain money, in certain cases, without paying debts or legacies, is to authorize him to refuse payments of debts and legacies when due, and it is because they are due that it was necessary so to provide.—Estate of Williams. 112 Cal. 521, 527, 53 Am. St. Rep. 224, 44 Pac. 808. If a guardian's claim against his ward's estate has been allowed, he may, upon being appointed administrator of the ward's estate, pay the claim to himself. —Reed v. Hume, 25 Utah 248, 70 Pac. 998, 1000. The title of the heirs is subject to the performance by the administrator of all his trusts, and the heirs finally come into the possession and enjoyment of only such portion of the estate as may remain after the execution of such trusts by the administrator. One of these trusts is the payment of the debts of the decedent. Hence, where the testator bound himself either to pay a sum of money, or to transfer certain shares of stock, both the money and the stock passed to his legatee charged with the burden of the performance of this obligation. One or the other was to pass from the estate, according to the exercise of the option by the executrix; and whatever title the legatee took, it was subject to the exercise of this option.—Estate of Vance, 152 Cal. 760, 93 Pac. 1010, 1011. The equitable title to the personal estate of an intestate descends to his heirs at law, subject only to the debts of the decedent. The legal title to the estate passes to the administrator, when appointed, for the purpose of enabling him to pay the debts due from the estate.—Brown v. Baxter, 77 Kan. 97, 94 Pac. 155, 574. A proceeding to subject the real property of a decedent to the payment of his personal debts is statutory; it could not be maintained under the common law; such a proceeding is not one in rem.—Stadelman v. Minor, 83 Or. 348, 155 Pac. 708, 163 Pac. 585, 983. A sale by an administrator of a decedent's real property to pay the debts of the estate, without legal notice to the heirs is tantamount to taking the heirs' property without due process of law; such a sale is nugatory and void, and one that can not be cured by subsequent legislation.—Gregory v. Keenan (Or.), 256 Fed. 949, 958. No duty is imposed upon an executor or administrator to have a creditor accept less than his full claim, if just.—Estate of Pillsbury, Pillsbury Title I. & T. Co., 175 Cal. 454, 166 Pac. 11.

2. **Order of payment can not be changed.**—Neither the executor, nor administrator, nor the probate court has any authority to change the order of payments prescribed by statute.—Tompkins v. Weeks, 26 Cal. 50, 66. Hence, an order directing partnership debts to be paid before the debts of the estate are paid is void, and if the representative obeys the order, the sums paid under it can not be allowed to him until all debts of the estate are paid. In such a case, if any loss results, it must fall upon the administrator.—Tompkins v. Weeks, 26 Cal. 50, 67.

3. **Preference.**—No preference is given to any debt of a particular class over others of the same class, for the statute provides that if the estate be insufficient to pay all the debts of any one class, the fund must be distributed pro rata among all the debts of that class. It follows that, as the death of the defendant destroys the lien of an attachment, the debt secured thereby is not, in such a case, entitled to a preference over other debts of the same class.—Myers v. Mott, 29 Cal. 359, 369, 89 Am. Dec. 49. A judgment against an administrator can have the effect only of a claim duly allowed against the estate, to be paid in due course, and can not give the creditor any further rights. A claim bay, on its face, be plainly a funeral expense, or an expense of the last sickness, and if allowed at all, be manifestly a preferred claim; but there is nothing in the mode of allowance which fixes its rank; and as there is no mode of allowance that can give a claim priority, it must follow that there can be no judgment establishing the validity of a claim, which the administrator or court has refused to allow, that can have that effect. Therefore, if the administrator is satisfied that a claim for medical services is valid, though not for services rendered during the last illness, and therefore not entitled to rank as a preferred claim, his allowance does not give it such rank, although on its face it purports to be for such services. It would still be an open question.—McLean v. Crow, 88 Cal. 644, 648, 26 Pac. 596. Money expended by an administrator for insuring the property of an estate, which contract of insurance was made after the death of decedent, is

not properly a claim against the estate, being an item of expense incident to preserving the property during the course of administration, and is entitled to payment prior to the payment of debts, and its allowance as a debt can not be prejudical to the estate.—Enscoe v. Fletcher, 1 Cal. App. 659, 666, 82 Pac. 1075. A percentage allowed for collecting and disbursing the estate is a proper allowance to be made as an expense of administration, and may be paid in preference to funeral expenses.—Estate of Nicholson, 1 Nev. 518, 520. In the absence of statute, the expenses of the last sickness have no priority over ordinary debts.—Grace v. Smith, 14 Haw. 144. Funeral expenses are chargeable against the estate, the same as the expense of administration, and must be paid next after necessary expenses of administration, being a preferred charge.—Elton v. Lamb, 33 N. D. 388, 396, 157 N. W. 288. A claim for funeral expenses is a preferred one, and is of the first class, payable as soon as the executor has in hand funds sufficient to meet it.—Golden Gate U. Co. v. Taylor, 168 Cal. 94, Ann. Cas. 1915D, 742, 52 L. R. A. (N. S.) 1152, 141 Pac. 922. Section 1643 of the Code of Civil Procedure of California makes funeral expenses rank as a debt of the estate similar in character to other debts in many respects, but payable in preference to others.—Estate of Magorty, 169 Cal. 163, 146 Pac. 430. Under section 1647, Code of Civil Procedure, the court has control of the matter of the administrator's commissions, and may order payment of debts as the circumstances of the estate may require. This would give the court authority to direct the payment of money for funeral expenses prior to the allowance or payment of the commissions.—Estate of Magorty, 169 Cal. 163, 146 Pac. 430.

4. **Payment of claims prior to settlement.**—There is nothing in the statute which requires payment of claims against the executor for services rendered or materials furnished to the estate during administration, before they can be allowed in the settlement of his account.— Estate of Couts, 87 Cal. 480, 482, 25 Pac. 685. The code provides that "upon the settlement of the accounts of the executor or administrator," the court must make an order for the payment of the debts, as circumstances of the estate may require. It also provides that notice of the day of settlement of any account to be heard must be given in the manner prescribed; and it is quite apparent that if such notice is not given, there can be no valid settlement of the account, and consequently that there can be no valid order made for the payment of the claim, especially where a portion of it is disputed. The code seems to contemplate an order for the payment of the debt only upon the settlement of the administrator's account, but if it be assumed that such an order could be made before such settlement, still it would clearly be of no force if made without notice.—Estate of Spanier, 120 Cal. 698, 701, 53 Pac. 357. With the exception of interest-bearing claims, provided for in section 1513 of the Code of Civil Procedure of California, there can be no valid order for the payment of a claim until after an order for the settlement of an account, in which the validity, right, and

the amount of the claims, and the balance on hand, has been adjudicated; and the notice required is notice of the time and place of settling the account.—Estate of McDougald, 143 Cal. 476, 483, 77 Pac. 443, 79 Pac. 878, 879. An administrator is not authorized to pay a claim that has not been presented according to law.—Estate of Kaiu, 17 Haw. 514, 515.

5. Premature or unauthorized payments. Advancement.—By paying claims in advance of an order by the court, an executor or administrator takes the risk of securing the approval of his act by the court when his accounts and vouchers shall have been presented.—Rostel v. Morat, 19 Or. 181, 23 Pac. 900. Where payments are not authorized by present order of the court, they are made at the peril of the executor or administrator, and, to the extent that they are not approved by the subsequent order of the court, constitute a wrongful use of the money of the estate for the personal advantage of one of the executors, or all of the executors consenting to such use.—Miller v. Lux, 100 Cal. 609, 615, 35 Pac. 345, 639. But, though, debts are paid without any order or direction of the court, the court has power to allow them as claims upon the settlement of the annual account, and though such allowance is ill-advised or erroneous, it is conclusive upon the estate, if no appeal has been taken from the order approving the account.—Estate of Fernandez, 119 Cal. 579, 583, 51 Pac. 851. If payments have been made by an executor before his appointment, and he did not at the time intend to charge the deceased, and did not afterwards present a claim to the court against the estate, the item should be disallowed in the settlement of his account.—Estate of Pease, 149 Cal. 167, 85 Pac. 149, 150. See, also, Estate of Heeney, 3 Cal. App. 548, 86 Pac. 842. If an executor or administrator pays his attorney, without any authority of the court, out of funds belonging to the estate, and his claim therefor against the estate is disallowed, no order to compel the attorney to make restitution will be granted, as the representative himself is personally answerable for the amount paid.—Estate of Sullivan, 36 Wash. 217, 78 Pac. 945, 948. There may be cases in which the conclusion reached will operate as a hardship to the executor or administrator, who, in perfect good faith, pays out money under the orders of the court. Thus if, in his haste to pay a widow, he draws his check in her favor two days before the court directs him to do so, and two days before she elects to waive her right to specific property, and in lieu thereof to accept its value in money, and the payments made to her by the representative are made with knowledge of the power of the court, for good cause shown to annul and set aside the orders, under which the representative acted, it has been held that where such orders were improperly obtained through mistake, or by means of fraud perpetrated upon the creditors or upon the court, it was entirely within the jurisdiction and power of the court to vacate them, and that under such circumstances it would vacate them and declare them void notwithstanding the payment made by the representative.—Clemes v. Fox, 2 Colo. 39, 53, Pac. 225, 229.

An executor or administrator, who has been removed, has no right to pay debts or claims against the estate he represented.—Rutenick v. Hamakar, 40 Or. 444, 67 Pac. 196. And an executor or administrator has no right, after notice, to pay a claim to the assignor thereof.—Estate of Cummins, 143 Cal. 525, 77 Pac. 479. The unauthorized payment of a debt due to an estate does not absolve the debtor from liability to such estate.—McCoy v. Ayers, 2 Wash. Ter. 307, 5 Pac. 843. If a father voluntarily pays a mortgage on his daughter's lands for her benefit, and takes an assignment in blank of the mortgage and note to be secured to hold for her benefit, and keeps them in his possession until his death, such payment will be deemed an advancement out of his estate to her.—Johnson v. Eaton, 51 Kan. 708, 33 Pac. 597. If the administrator pays claims against the estate without a prior order of court establishing the order of preference, he is personally liable.—Elton v. Lamb, 33 N. D. 388, 396, 157 N. W. 288. The payment of claims in excess of fifty dollars by an administrator before presentation to and allowance by the court is illegal and at his own risk.—In re Estate of Kappelman, International Harvester Co. v. Algie, 101 Kan. 654, 658, 168 Pac. 876.

REFERENCES.

Right of executor or administrator to recover back from creditor excessive payments made under the mistaken belief that the estate was solvent.—See note 28 L. R. A. (N. S.) 440.

6. Funeral expenses. Monuments, etc. Expenses of administration.

(1) Burial.—It is the duty of an executor, or of an administrator, to give a decedent a decent burial, and he can not be absolutely limited in the performance of such duty by the provisions of a will.—Estate of Galland, 92 Cal. 293, 295, 28 Pac. 288. But, though he is required by law to pay the funeral expenses, he is not, as against the objections of the persons entitled to the custody of the body of the decedent for the purpose of burying it, entitled, in this country (though he is in England), to the custody and possession of the body of his decedent, until it is properly buried. The custody of the corpse and the right of burial do not belong to the executor or administrator, but to the next of kin, and the court possesses the power to protect such next of kin in the exercise of such rights.—Enos v. Snyder, 131 Cal. 68, 71, 82 Am. St. Rep. 330, 53 L. R. A. 221, 63 Pac. 170. Services in respect to the burying of a dead person, performed by an undertaker at the instance and request of the executor, imposes an obligation upon the executor, and not the estate, to pay for them; although the executor may, of right, look to the estate to credit him with the amount in the settlement.—Golden Gate U. Co. v. Taylor, 168 Cal. 94, Ann. Cas. 1915D, 742, 52 L. R. A. (N. S.) 1152, 141 Pac. 922. It was the duty of the executors, under the circumstances appearing, to initiate and prosecute appropriate proceedings providing for final and permanent disposition of the remains of their testator, and equally the duty of the court upon a proper showing, which we must presume to have been made, to make an order

authorizing the executors to execute that duty. The wish of the deceased and his widow can not affect or interrupt the court's power of jurisdiction to make the order.—Estate of Seymour, 15 Cal. App. 287, 114 Pac. 1023.

(2) Funeral expenses.—At common law the husband was bound to bury his deceased wife in a suitable manner, and was bound to defray the necessary funeral expenses. Although the rule is not universal in this country, it prevails in most of the states. The duty is one which is involved in the obligation of the husband to maintain the wife, while living. He has the control of the body of his deceased wife, and must care for the same, and must select a proper place for her interment, regardless of the wishes of her parents or other relatives. And whether or not the administrator ought to be allowed anything on account of the monument erected over her grave depends on circumstances. Included in the obligation to give the deceased wife a decent burial, is the duty of placing some mark of identification over her last resting-place. If the husband be poor, and the deceased leave a considerable estate, the former ought not to be expected to contribute much to a monument, and it would be proper, in such a case, for the court to fix a reasonable amount to be allowed for that purpose. The amount allowed for the expenses of a funeral and a monument should be governed by the custom of the people of like rank and condition in society. A distinction is made in this respect, however, between solvent and insolvent estates.—Estate of Weringer, 100 Cal. 345, 346, 34 Pac. 825. The expenses of erecting a monument at the grave of a deceased person is part of the funeral expense, and properly payable out of the estate.—Van Emon v. Superior Court, 76 Cal. 589, 590, 9 Am. St. Rep. 258, 18 Pac. 264, 877. Even where there is no testamentary disposition or, direction that a monument be erected over the grave of the testator, the courts will allow a reasonable sum to be paid out of the funds of the estate for the erection of such a monument, putting the expense on the ground of funeral expenses.—Estate of Koppikus, 1 Cal. App. 84, 87, 81 Pac. 732. The word "monument," in common usage, when it relates to a memorial for the dead, means shaft, column, or some structure more imposing than a mere gravestone. It is not understood to be a memorial building. Hence, if a testator leaves funds to be used by his executors for funeral expenses, and for the proper interment of his remains, and "for a suitable monument to his memory," a memorial building is without the purview of the testator's bequest.—Fancher v. Fancher, 156 Cal. 13, 19 Ann. Cas. 1157, 23 L. R. A. (N. S.) 944, 103 Pac. 206. A claim for funeral services is not based on a contract or debt made or incurred either by the decedent before the death or the personal representative, as such afterward; it is a statutory demand arising immediately on death but before administration begins, and is properly chargeable in some form of procedure against the assets of the estate.—Golden Gate U. Co. v. Taylor, 168 Cal. 94, Ann. Cas. 1915D, 742, 52 L. R. A. (N. S.) 1152, 141 Pac. 922. In the absence of an express promise

by a wife, to pay for the funeral expenses of her deceased husband, her liability therefor is secondary, and can not be enforced against her until the creditor has exhausted his remedy against the estate.—Butterworth v. Bredemeyer, 74 Wash. 524, 529, 133 Pac. 1061. The necessities of the case make funeral expenses a legal charge upon the estate, and even an outside person, if he pays them, may be reimbursed on filing his claim with the executor.—Dunn v. Wallingford, 47 Utah 491, 155 Pac. 347. The effect of section 1646, Code of Civil Procedure of California, is that as soon as the executor, or administrator, has sufficient funds in his hands, applicable for the payment of the funeral expenses, expenses of the last illness, and allowance made for the family of the deceased, he must pay them out for those purposes.—Estate of Magorty, 169 Cal. 163, 146 Pac. 430.

REFERENCES.

Liability of separate estate of wife for her funeral expenses.—See note 6 L. R. A. (N. S.) 917, 918. Liability of decedent's estate for funeral expenses.—See note 33 L. R. A. 660, 669. Funeral expenses as a preferred charge.—See supra, subd. 3.

(3) Expenses of administration.—Claims against an estate are those in existence at the death of deceased. Other claims against the estate are those incurred by the administrator or executor in settling the estate, and are properly denominated "expenses of administration."—Dodson v. Nevitt, 5 Mont. 518, 6 Pac. 358, 38 Cal. 85, 99 Am. Dec. 352. The fees of an administrator or executor are expenses of administration, to be allowed in preference even to funeral expenses.—In re Nicholson, 1 Nev. 518, 520. Insurance-money paid on the property of the estate is also an expense of administration, unless it was paid under circumstances showing recklessness and a want of proper care and prudence.—In re Nicholson, 1 Nev. 518, 521. Expenses incurred by executors, in proceedings to contest the will of a decedent, are, if reasonable, expenses of administration.—Notley v. Brown, 16 Haw. 575, 577. Taxes are an expense in the care and management of an estate.—People v. Olvera, 43 Cal. 492, 494. Repairs to the roof of a dwelling-house where the widow resided, after it was consumed by fire, and which were made, at the request of the widow, by order of the probate court, are a necessary expense in the proper administration of the estate to preserve the dwelling from ruin and decay.—In re Thorn's Estate, 24 Utah 209, 67 Pac. 22, 23. Cropping expenses may be, by reason of circumstances, regarded as expenses of administration.—Elton v. Lamb, 33 N. D. 388, 396, 157 N. W. 288. The words, "He may retain is his hands the necessary expenses of administration," in section 1646 of the Code of Civil Procedure of California, qualify what precede them, and allows the administrator—subject to the power and discretion of the court to order him to the contrary effect—to retain enough to pay his expenses of administration until it becomes due under an order of the court; but this does not mean that he may in all cases

hold out enough to pay his commissions, for the court has control of that matter, under section 1647 of that code.—Estate of Magorty, 169 Cal. 163, 146 Pac. 430.

7. Property available for payment of debts.

(1) In general.—Moneys in the hands of an executor or administrator are not assets applicable to the payment of a claim against the estate of a decedent until its payment has been directed by a court of probate. —United States v. Eggleston, 4 Saw. 199, Fed. Cas. No. 15,027. If a testator dies, leaving one-half of his property not disposed of by will, and without having made any provision for the payment of debts and expenses, such debts and expenses of administration are properly chargeable against the property undisposed of by will.—Estate of Travers, 145 Cal. 508, 78 Pac. 1058, 1060. The fair meaning of the language of section 1562 of the Code of Civil Procedure of California, that "if the estate appropriated therefor is insufficient to pay the debts, expenses of administration," etc., resort shall be had to that portion of the estate undisposed of for their payment, is, that, where no estate is appropriated by will, or that which is appropriated is inadequate, such resort shall be had. Where a will fails to make any appropriation to pay the debts and charges against the estate, there is clearly an insufficient appropriation for that purpose. The absence of all appropriation is certainly an insufficient one.—Estate of Travers, 145 Cal. 508, 78 Pac. 1058, 1060. The word "estate" is used in sections 1645 and 1648 of the Code of Civil Procedure of California as signifying all the decedent's property.—Estate of Hinckley, 58 Cal. 457, 515. All of the estate of the testator is made assets in the hands of the administrator for the payment of all debts of every kind, whether simple contract debts, specialty debts, or otherwise, or whether charged upon particular estates or not. One class of creditors is not to look to the executor alone, and another class, in default of the assets in the hands of the executor, is not obliged to follow the heir, devisee, or specific legatee. The entire estate, real and personal, is liable in the hands of the executor to the charge of all the debts.—Estate of Woodworth, 31 Cal. 595, 613. The court has power to set aside a homestead upon property to the value of thirty or forty thousand dollars, and in some instances it has done so. It might be that this was all the property of the estate, but it would not only be an anomaly, but a great injustice, if the creditors were to be left remediless because the court had set aside such a homestead to the widow during her widowhood. It is certainly more in consonance with natural justice and with a spirit of our jurisprudence to say that when the dependent family have been protected in their needs the law will next consider the claims of bona fide creditors, and that only after this is done shall the heirs take. Even so, they get all the deceased could have given them had he lived; that is to say, the residue of his property after the payment of his just debts.—Estate of Tittel, 139 Cal. 149, 152, 72 Pac. 909. The interest of

a deceased person, by virtue of his contract for the purchase of real property, is available for the satisfaction of claims against his estate.— Zeuske v. Zeuske, 62 Or. 46, 51, 124 Pac. 203. When property fraudulently transferred by a decedent has been recovered, the creditors must first be satisfied; but, after that is done, the transfer, as to the residue of the property or the remainder of the fund arising from a sale thereof, is good as between the parties and their privies, and binding upon all persons but creditors.—Hillman v. Young, 64 Or. 73, 81, 127 Pac. 793, 129 Pac. 124. The title conveyed by the heirs of a non-resident intestate leaving real property in another state, is incomplete and imperfect only from the fact that it will always be subject to the right of possession in a local administrator for the payment of the claims of local creditors.—Phelps v. Grady, 168 Cal. 73, 75, 141 Pac. 926.

(2) Community property.—The property of the community is undoubtedly liable for the payment of its debts.—Packard v. Arrelanes, 17 Cal. 535, 538. Community property, however exempt from liability for the separate debt of a member of the community during his or her lifetime, is no longer exempt, under the statute of Washington, upon the death of such member; it is then subject to the separate debts of each spouse.—Crawford v. Morris, 92 Wash. 288, 158 Pac. 957.

(3) Rents and profits.—If a testator bequeaths all shares of stock of a corporation, standing in his name at the time of his death, to trustees to hold for a specified term, and to distribute dividends arising from the stock semiannually among the beneficiaries named, and there is no doubt that it was the testator's intention to vest the trustees named with the title to the stock mentioned, the bequest is specific where the description is particular enough to identify the subject-matter of the testamentary gift. Hence, the corpus of the shares of stock is exonerated from liability on account of the debts of decedent's estate, until a resort thereto becomes necessary by reason of a failure to discharge such obligations from the proceeds of the sales of the remaining property, not specifically devised or bequeathed; and the conclusion reached in regard to the shares of stock also applies to the profits accruing from conducting the business of the corporation.—In re Noon's Estate, 49 Or. 286, 88 Pac. 673, 676, 90 Pac. 673. For circumstances under which it is the duty of the executor or administrator to apply rents accruing from property of the estate to its debts, see Smith v. Goethe, 147 Cal. 725, 82 Pac. 384, 390. If it beccomes necessary to resort to the realty for the payment of debts, the rents collected from it should first be exhausted before the sale of the realty itself. As between the legatees of the personalty and the devisees of the realty, the executor is not authorized to appropriate the rents of the real estate accrued subsequent to the decease of the testator, to the satisfaction of a mortgage debt in exoneration of the personalty.—Estate of Woodworth, 31 Cal. 605, 609.

(4) Property bequeathed or devised.—Section 1822 of the Civil Code of Montana provides: "The property of a testator, except as otherwise specially provided for in this code and the Code of Civil Procedure, must be resorted to for the payment of debts in the following order: 1. The property which is expressly appropriated by the will for the payment of the debts. 2. Property not disposed of by will. 3. Property which is devised or bequeathed to a residuary legatee. 4. Property which is not specifically devised or bequeathed; and 5. All other property ratably." No distinction is made in this section between devises for charitable purposes and those made upon consideration. They are placed upon the same footing. If the property mentioned in the first four classes designated by the statute is not sufficient, specific devises, no matter for what purpose, are to be resorted to ratably; for such devises clearly fall within the fifth class in the enumeration. Devisees have no right to have property devised to them for a valuable consideration, no matter what that consideration may have been, exempted from sale for the payment of debts, or the sale of it postponed until other property specifically devised has been resorted to for that purpose. No distinction is made among specific devises, but all must bear the burden ratably.—In re Tuohy's Estate, 33 Mont. 230, 83 Pac. 486, 490. If the law, at the time of a testator's death, provided that his personal property, not specifically bequeathed, should be primarily liable for the payment of his debts, etc., but such law is changed, pending administration of his estate, so as to authorize a sale of his real property for the payment of debts before disposing of the personal property, where the interest of the parties would be subserved by such sale, the rights of devisees are not impaired by such change in the law. Hence, if the testator left personal property not specifically bequeathed, the court has no power to order a sale of the real property until the proceeds of a sale of the personal property are exhausted. The devisees become seised of the real property devised to them upon the death of the decedent, and their rights thereto can not be defeated or impaired by subsequent legislation attempting to subject their land to a liability not imposed thereon when they become invested with the legal title thereto.—In re Noon's Estate, 49 Or. 286, 88 Pac. 673, 675, 90 Pac. 673. See, also, head-line 7, subd. 3, supra. Where a bequest by a wife to her husband was modified by a subsequent gift of the unexpended portion to another, although the husband was given absolute control and might use the whole if he chose, the unused or unexpended portion is not subject to the payment of the husband's debts, although he might voluntarily use the property for that purpose, the mere contracting of debts not amounting to an expenditure within the meaning of the gift. —Adams v. Prather, 176 Cal. 33, 167 Pac. 534, 538.

(5) Exempt property.—A testator will not be deemed to have appropriated exempt property to the payment of his debts, by a general direction in his will to pay debts; an intention to so appropriate it must appear by clear and apt language.—German-American State Bank v.

Godman, 83 Wash. 231, 145 Pac. 221. If a husband and wife are residing and living upon a homestead, the legal title of which is in the
husband at the time of his death, the widow, after the death of the
husband, may continue to reside upon such homestead, as defined by
law, so long as she does not again marry; in addition to this, the
widow is entitled, as an exemption, to personal property to the extent
of $1500; and none of such property shall be liable for any of the debts
which the deceased owed at the time of his death; the law is mandatory, requiring the administrators of such estate to set aside such
exempt property for the use and benefit of the widow; but the residue
of such property or estate, exclusive of all such exemptions, is chargeable with the debts owing by the decedent at the time of his death.—
Brudevold v. Waldorf, 37 N. D. 516, 164 N. W. 154.

(6) **Proceeds of life insurance policies. In general.**—Policies of life
insurance, three of which are payable to the "executors, administrators, or assigns" of the insured, one to his "estate," and another to
"the legal representatives of the insured," are subject to testamentary
disposition to the extent of the testator's community interest in them.—
German-American State Bank v. Godman, 83 Wash. 231, 145 Pac. 221.
The direction, in a will, to the executrix to "pay all my lawful debts
and the expenses of my funeral" does not appropriate to such payment
the proceeds or avails of insurance on the life of the testator, even if
the executrix is given these proceeds or avails and there are no other
assets.—German-American State Bank v. Godman, 83 Wash. 231, 145
Pac. 221. The Washington statute (of exemptions) has no application
to the proceeds or avails of life insurance policies that have been bequeathed to a designated legatee.—German-American State Bank v.
Godman, 83 Wash. 231, 145 Pac. 221.

(7) **When not liable.**—The statute whereby the avails of a life insurance policy, made payable to the "heirs," "personal representatives,"
or "estate" of the insured, are not subjected to the debts of the decedent, is not an exemption law.—Farmers State Bank v. Smith, 36 N. D.
225, 228, 162 N. W. 302. The law does not differentiate between policies
of insurance payable to the "executors, administrators, or assigns," and
policies payable to "the estate," of the insured.—German-American
State Bank v. Godman, 83 Wash. 231, 145 Pac. 221. In Washington the
proceeds or avails of a life insurance policy are not applicable to the
funeral expenses of the insured even though his "estate," his "executors, administrators, or assigns," or his "legal representatives" may
be designations used in such policies to indicate the beneficiaries.—
German-American State Bank v. Godman, 83 Wash. 231, 145 Pac. 221.
The effect of the Washington statute, as to exemption of the proceeds
and avails of life insurance policies from liability for the debts of the
insured, is to extend the principle even to policies made out for the
benefit of the insured's "estate," or his "legal representatives," or his
"executors, administrators, or assigns."—German-American State Bank
v. Godman, 83 Wash, 231, 145 Pac. 221. The proceeds and avails of life

insurance policies are exempt from the expenses of administration, the funeral expenses, and the expenses of the last sickness.—German-American State Bank v. Godman, 83 Wash. 231, 145 Pac. 221. Avails of a life insurance policy payable to "heirs," "personal representatives," or "estate" of the insured, are not subject to the decedent's debts.—Farmers' State Bank v. Smith, 36 N. D. 225, 230, 162 N. W. 302.

REFERENCES.

Exemption of proceeds of life insurance, after loss, from beneficiary's debts.—L. R. A. 1915A, 1201. Who are heirs within the meaning of life insurance policies.—30 L. R. A. 593. Who are "legal representatives" within the meaning of life insurance policies.—30 L. R. A. 609; 32 L. R. A. (N. S.) 247.

(8) Same. When liable.—The statute, securing the proceeds · or avails of life and accident insurance policies from liability for debt, must be read in connection with that other statute which confines this exemption from liability to the proceeds and avails of policies made out in favor of a beneficiary other than the insured, or his legal representatives; the legislative intention was that the proceeds of policies payable to an estate should be liable to the creditors of the estate.—In re Blattner's Estate, Blattner v. Abell, 89 Wash. 412, 154 Pac. 796. If a policy of life insurance is made payable to the insured, or to his estate, or to "his legal representatives," the proceeds thereof are not exempt, but are available to the creditors of his estate.—In re Blattner's Estate, Blattner v. Abell, 89 Wash. 412, 154 Pac. 796. A life insurance policy payable to the estate of a deceased person is not exempt from the payment of the debts of the estate.—Elsom v. Gadd, 93 Wash. 603, 161 Pac. 483, 162 Pac. 867.

REFERENCES.

In connection with this subdivision, read the next preceding subdivision (7).

8. Marshaling of assets.—Under the common law, where no different order is prescribed or indicated in the will, as between executors, devisees, and heirs, the assets of the deceased, for the purpose of paying the debts of the estate, will be marshaled, and the debts paid out of them, in the following order: 1. The general personal estate,—that is to say, personal estate not specifically bequeathed, or expressly or by implication excepted. 2. Lands expressly devised for the payment of debts. 3. Lands descended to the heir. 4. Lands devised. It is also the settled rule of English and of American law that this order is not to be disturbed by the fact that lands are devised subject to a mortgage or incumbrance thereon. The personal estate is first to be applied and exhausted, even for the payment of the debts charged upon the real estate by mortgage or other incumbrance, if the debt so charged upon it was the personal debt of the testator; for the mortgage is regarded merely as a personal security. And when the

testator devises lands expressly subject to a mortgage, he is considered as using the terms merely as descriptive of the incumbered condition of the property, and not for the purpose of subjecting his devisees to the burden. It requires express words, or an intent clearly manifest upon an examination of the entire will, to disturb this order. There must be a manifest intent, not merely to charge the real estate, but to discharge the personalty.—Estate of Woodworth, 31 Cal. 595, 599. Where the entire estate, both real and personal, has been devised without any provision in the will as to the payment of debts, and the will contains no specific devises or legacies, it results that the devisees under the will, or rather their respective shares, must contribute to the payment of the debts and expenses in proportion to their value.— Estate of Woodworth, 31 Cal. 595, 619. In case of doubt as to a claim for services rendered during the last illness of deceased, the administrator may refuse to pay until required by an order of the court. When the assets are at last marshaled, the order of payment must be determined by the probate court, when other creditors may be heard.— McLean v. Crow, 88 Cal. 641, 22 Am. St. Rep. 341, 26 Pac. 596. The debts of a testator are payable primarily out of his personalty, unless it is otherwise specified in the will; the realty is resorted to for that purpose only in case the personalty is not sufficient.—Smith v. Kibbe, 104 Kan. 159, 178 Pac. 427. The exoneration provided by statute for the protection of devisees has reference to cases where the testator has not required the appropriation of a particular part of his estate to the payment of his debts.—Smith v. Kibbe, 104 Kan. 159, 178 Pac. 427. If there is nothing in an estate from which to pay debts other than legacies, resort must be had, under the statute of South Dakota, first to the residuary legacies; next to general legacies ratably; and, if necessary, to specific and demonstrative legacies ratably; on abatement, different classes of legacies do not prorate between each other, but each class in its order must be exhausted before abatement can take place in the next higher class; and, as to abatement, legacies given to minors are subject to the same rule as that applying to adults. —In re Hawgood's Estate, 37 S. D. 565, 583, 159 N. W. 117.

9. Decree or order for payment.

(1) In general.—An executor or administrator may be required by the decree of the probate court to pay over to creditors or legatees the kind of money received by him.—Magraw v. McGlynn, 26 Cal. 420, 428. In Colorado, the district court is not authorized to decree that a judgment rendered by it against an executor or administrator shall be allowed as a claim of a designated class, as this is a usurpation of the province of the probate court.—Hotchkiss v. First Nat. Bank, 37 Colo. 228, 85 Pac. 1007, 1008. A decree of the probate court for the payment of creditors binds the executor or administrator personally for the amount of the claim of each creditor, or the dividend thereon; and the decree is a judicial determination of the rights of the parties, and

possesses all the elements of a final judgment. Such decree, like the judgment of any other court rendered in the exercise of competent jurisdiction, can not be assailed in a collateral proceeding, or in any other proceeding on the ground of the insufficiency of the evidence upon which it was rendered.—Estate of Cook, 14 Cal. 129, 130.

(2) Application for order.—When the administrator finds himself with funds not needed for the purpose of paying the expenses of the funeral and last sickness of the deceased, the allowance to his family, and the necessary current and prospective expenses of administration, . he ought to report that fact to the court at his next annual settlement, and obtain an order to apply them in payment of debts, though he is at all times entitled to retain in his hands ample funds to meet the claims and expenses above mentioned.—Walls v. Walker, 37 Cal. 424, 428, 99 Am. Dec. 290. If he neglects to apply for an order of sale when it is necessary, any person may make application therefor, in the same manner as the executor or administrator. The law affords to creditors of the executor or administrator, as well as to the creditors of the decedent, the means of securing payment of their claims against the estate, and necessarily contemplates expenses of administration which the executor neglects or refuses to pay.—Estate of Couts, 87 Cal. 480, 482, 25 Pac. 685.

(3) Duty of court. Granting of order.—If the representative of the estate has a doubt as to the legality of a claim presented, or the amount that should be paid for services rendered, or materials furnished, in the course of administration, it is proper for his own protection, as well as for the protection of the heirs, that the court should determine, after notice to all persons interested, whether the estate is liable at all, and if so, in what amount.—Estate of Couts, 87 Cal. 480, 482, 25 Pac. 685. The law provides that upon the settlement of the accounts of executors or administrators the court must make such an order for the payment of the debts as the circumstances of the estate require; and it is the duty of the court, when there is money on hand, to make an order for the payment of debts. If there are not sufficient funds on hand with which to pay the debts, the court must specify the sum to be paid to each creditor. Where creditors in a large amount ask for an order directing the executor or administrator to pay debts of the estate, and there is money on hand, they are entitled to such order, or to an order directing a dividend to the extent that the funds on hand will justify.—Estate of Sylvar, 1 Cal. App. 35, 81 Pac. 663, 664. Though claims against an estate were irregularly paid, some of which bear no indorsement of approval of either the administrator or the judge, and there is not contention that any one of the claims was unjust or invalid, or that the creditors were not morally entitled to their money, the court will not take from the creditors that which was rightfully theirs, though irregularly received, and give it to one who has no right thereto; it will not compel an administrator, who has irregularly paid a just debt, simply because of such

irregularity, to again pay the money, not to the creditor, but to one who has no right thereto, either legally or morally.—In re Johnston's Estate (Wash.), 181 Pac. 209, 213.

(4) Validity of order. Effect of.—Where the executors received legal-tender notes in payment for property sold by them for the benefit of creditors, it was held to be error for the probate court to order payment to the creditors to be made in gold coin.—Estate of Den, 39 Cal. 70, 71. An order for the payment of a debt, made without notice of the settlement of the administrator's account, is of no force.—Estate of Spanier, 120 Cal. 698, 701, 53 Pac. 357; Estate of McDougald, 143 Cal. 476, 483, 77 Pac. 443, 79 Pac. 878, 879. A valid order for payment of a particular creditor's claim, whether or not his claim be a pre-ferred claim, can not, at least in the case of an insolvent estate, be made except upon the settlement of an account of the administrator after notice, given as prescribed by the code. Otherwise the other creditors would not be bound by the order; and if the administrator should obey it, he would do so at his peril.—Estate of Smith, 117 Cal. 505, 508, 49 Pac. 456. The executor or administrator is answerable for the assets in his hands, and, so long as he remains in office, is entitled to retain them in his possession until disposed of, to the party entitled thereto, under the directions of the court. Upon the entry of an order for the payment of the claims against the estate, the administrator becomes answerable therefor to the creditors, both personally and upon his bond, and each creditor is entitled to an execution against him therefor. He can not escape this liability by complying with an order which the court has no power to make, such as an order to pay the balance of the estate into court, and that he thereupon be discharged.—Estate of Sarment, 123 Cal. 331, 337, 55 Pac. 1015. If an order directing the payment of debts is based upon an erroneous order of settlement of accounts, both orders must fall together.—Estate of Grant, 131 Cal. 426, 430, 63 Pac. 731. The court has no authority to order a real estate broker, who has been interested in making a sale of the real property of an intestate, to make a payment to the administrator, without some proceeding in which the broker has been made a party, and where there have been no pleadings presenting the issue of his indebtedness to the estate.—In re Bradley's Estate, 168 Cal. 655, 144 Pac. 136.

10. Payment of interest-bearing claims.—Section 1513 of the Code of Civil Procedure of California, which provides for the payment of interest-bearing claims, is not designed for the benefit of creditors, but for the benefit of the estate. It affords no right to the owner of a debt, although it is a preferred claim bearing interest, to compel an advance payment of it. The order directing the administrator to pay should be, in its form, not compulsory, but permissive merely. Then he may pay or not, as his discretion suggests, and if the condition of the estate warrants. If he does not pay, he can not be compelled to do so by the creditor, but will be answerable to the estate for the interest

accruing thereafter, if he can not show that his refusal was based on sound reasons.—Estate of Hope, 106 Cal. 153, 155, 39 Pac. 523.

11. "Contingent" claims.—The court has no power to order a contingent claim paid, unless it has been presented within the time prescribed by law.—Verdier v. Roach, 96 Cal. 467, 479, 31 Pac. 554. A matured mortgage indebtedness against an estate before foreclosure is not a "contingent" claim, within section 1648 of the Code of Civil Procedure of California. That section contemplates that an amount shall be paid into court for the benefit of such contingent claim equal to the amount that would be payable thereon if the whole of it were established as absolute. The court is not authorized, under such section, to make testimony to ascertain the probable deficiency which might arise on foreclosure.—Estate of McDougald, 146 Cal. 196, 201, 79 Pac. 875.

12. Deficiency. Part payment. Disputed claims.—The Kansas statute is construed to mean that judgments which are liens upon real estate of the deceased, where the estate is insolvent, shall, to the extent of the lien, be paid without reference to classification, with the exception therein stated, but the deficiency shall only be paid as other judgments rendered against the deceased in his lifetime are paid.—Wolfe v. Robbins, 10 Kan. App. 202, 63 Pac. 278. When the court orders creditors to be paid, the decree determines the amount to be paid. This amount is ascertained by reference to the money of the estate in the hands of the executor. If there is sufficient funds in his hands for the payment in full of the creditor's demand, or only enough to pay a portion of the dividend, the decree is made according to the truth of the case, and the executor or administrator is required to make payment as directed by the decree from the money of the estate in his hands, or presumed to be there.—Magraw v. McGlynn, 26 Cal. 420, 431. If there are not sufficient funds in the hands of the executor or administrator, the court shall specify in the decree the sum to be paid to each creditor.—Pico v. De la Guerra, 18 Cal. 422, 431; Rostel v. Morat, 19 Or. 181, 23 Pac. 900; Estate of Sylvar, 1 Cal. App. 35, 38, 81 Pac. 663; In re Osburn's Estate, 36 Or. 8, 58 Pac. 521. Whenever some of the creditors of an estate, whose claims have been allowed, are paid any proportion of their claims, a like proportion must be paid into the court to await the final determination of actions commenced and pending against the administrator, or claims disallowed by him.—Estate of Sigourney, 61 Cal. 71, 72. If a claim is disputed, and is allowed in part, but is rejected in part, the court has no power to order payment of the allowed part of such disputed claim in advance of the settlement of the administrator's account, in the absence of notice of such settlement.—Estate of Spanier, 120 Cal. 698, 701, 53 Pac. 357.

13. "Dividends."—It is error for the court to order a dividend, in excess of the amount in the hands of the executor or administrator, to be paid to the creditors. In such event, the case will be remanded,

with instructions to correct the error.—Estate of Dorland, 63 Cal. 281, 282. The order for the payment of the dividend required by section 1647 of the Code of Civil Procedure of California is not, strictly speaking, a part of the proceeding for the settlement of the account, or of the adjudication respecting the claims represented therein. It follows thereon, but is not a part thereof. It may, of course, be made immediately after the account is settled, but this does not make it a part of the proceeding. On the other hand, it can not be made until after the account is settled, and it may be deferred to a considerable time thereafter, and may be made without notice. It is a part of the proceeding for the administration of the estate, considered as a whole, but it is not specifically a part of the proceeding for the settlement of the account. The persons in whose favor such order for a dividend is made do not thereby become parties to the proceeding for the settlement of the account, in cases where they did not appear or make any objection or contest upon such settlement. Notice must be given of the time and place of settling the final account of the executor or administrator, but the notice of the time of making the order for a dividend is not required.—Estate of McDougald, 143 Cal. 476, 480, 483, 77 Pac. 443, 79 Pac. 878, 879. Though it be conceded that the claim on a mortgage debt, which is due, and the amount thereof not disputed, is contingent, to the extent that the amount of the "proceeds" of the property mortgaged is not ascertained, and can not be determined until there is a sale thereof, and hence that the balance that would remain after the application of such proceeds thereon is uncertain and indeterminable, still, there is nothing in the statute that warrants the taking of testimony by the court, to ascertain the probable deficiency, or the determination by the court of the probable deficiency, in any manner. The court, therefore, has no statutory authority for directing that a contingent dividend thereon be retained until the deficiency shall be determined.—Estate of McDougald, 146 Cal. 196, 201, 79 Pac. 875. In calculating the dividend to be paid out of general assets of the estate, where there has been no sale of property mortgaged, the mortgage debt must be classed as a claim of the fifth class, and allowed a dividend estimated upon the full amount of the claim, without any deduction for the probable proceeds of a future sale.— Estate of McDougald, 146 Cal. 196, 202, 79 Pac. 875. After the property mortgaged has been sold, and its proceeds applied to the debt, leaving a balance unpaid as to that balance, the creditor is no longer a mortgage creditor, but is entitled only to have the same paid from the fund realized from the general assets of the estate pro rata with other creditors. This rule recognizes the rights of a secured creditor to avail himself of the full benefit of his security, and also places him on an equality with the unsecured creditors as to other property of the estate, and is eminently just, because it in no way impairs the secured creditor's legal or contract rights, and affords him an equal remedy with other creditors against the general estate, thereby preserving to him the same remedy that he had against his debtor during his lifetime. Hence if a creditor holds collateral, he may collect dividends upon his entire claim, even to the extent of payment in full, in which case the security would inure to the benefit of the unsecured creditors.—Erle v. Lane, 22 Colo. 273, 44 Pac. 591, 593.

REFERENCES.

Deferring order for dividend until time for appeal from order settling a contested account has expired.—See head-line 16, post. Payment of legacies.—See note § 956, head-line 7, post.

·14. **Mortgages and judgments.**—A mortgagee is under no obligation to pay any other expenses than those incurred in the enforcement of the mortgage security. He can not be subjected to any general expenses of administration.—Estate of Murray, 18 Cal. 686, 687. After payment of the debt for which the mortgage was given, the mortgagee becomes, by operation of law, a trustee of the surplus for the mortgagor.—Pierce v. Robinson, 13 Cal. 116, 133. Where there is a large amount of personal property of the estate in the hands of the executor or administrator applicable to payment of the debts, the debts secured by mortgage, as between the legatee and devisees, is not all payable out of the rents of the real estate mortgage.—Estate of Woodworth, 31 Cal. 595, 615. Although the statute authorizes an executor to retain expenses of administration in preference to any claim or charge against his testator's estate, this does not give him a lien superior in right to a mortgage on the land of the deceased, although such expenses may take precedence in order of payment over charges and claims against the estate. The justice of the rule is manifest. A mortgage would be a thing of uncertain and precarious value if the costs and expenses of administration of a deceased person were advanced to a prior right of payment over a mortgage lien.—Shepard v. Saltzman, 34 Or. 40, 54 Pac. 883, 884. The preference of a mortgage debt is limited to the proceeds of the property, and where there are no proceeds, there can be no preference, and the mortgage debt, in such circumstances, ranks as an unsecured claim, and stands in the fifth class as to the general assets. The effect of sections 1643, 1644, and 1645 of the Code of Civil Procedure of California is, that, with respect to the proceeds of the mortgaged property, the mortgage debt shall have the preference and be first paid, and that where there are no proceeds before the court upon which such preference can operate, the claim has no preference at all, and must be classed among other demands of the estate in the fifth class. The word "proceeds" does not include the rents of property accruing before the sale, at least where they are not included in the mortgage. The rents are general assets of the estate on which the mortgage is not a lien, and in which it is entitled to no preference.—Estate of McDougald, 146 Cal. 201, 202, 79 Pac. 875. In section 1643 of that code, wherein provision is made for the payment of debts, there is given to "judgments rendered against the decedent in his lifetime" the same preference against the general assets which is given to mortgages against the particular property covered by the lien of the mortgage. The payment of judgments "in the order of their dates" is the enforcement of their liens.—Morton v. Adams, 124 Cal. 229, 230, 71 Am. St. Rep. 53, 56 Pac. 1038. Alimony accrued under the order of a court is a judgment, and, after the death of the judgment debtor, such judgment is a preferred claim against his estate.—Estate of Smith, 122 Cal. 462, 55 Pac. 249. A grantee under a deed of gift can not require payment of a mortgage debt on the property conveyed, out of the estate of the grantor, by reason of the implied covenant against incumbrances, unless provision therefor can be found in the will of the deceased grantor.—Estate of Wells, 7 Cal. App. 515, 94 Pac. 856. A debt of a testator, to secure which a mortgage has been given, falls within the class of debts payable out of the personalty.—Smith v. Kibbe, 104 Kan. 159, 178 Pac. 427. Where an executor has assigned his commissions, to satisfy a judgment under a mortgage foreclosure, and, after the filing of the final account, the court has, on the assignee's petitioning therefor, made its order directing this executor to show cause why he should not sell or mortgage sufficient property of the estate to pay the judgment, the order is to be construed as contemplating the executor's taking such valid steps as the statute provides for the purpose.—In re Ferguson's Estate, Gill v. McFarland, 102 Wash. 148, 172 Pac. 812. A mortgagee who complies with the request of an administrator to allow the property to be sold, and relies on his promise that the mortgage note shall be paid out of the proceeds, does not need to file his claim formally, but the same must be paid as a preferred claim.—In re Spark's Estate, Sugg v. Gridley, 101 Wash. 462, 172 Pac. 545. Under the statute of Oregon, the debts of a decedent's estate, secured by mortgage, must first be satisfied out of the mortgaged property, unless some other provision has been made in the will, or by order of court.—Howe v. Kern, 63 Or. 487, 496, 125 Pac. 834, 128 Pac. 818.

15. Enforcement of payment.—After the court has decreed that the creditors of the estate be paid, the executor or administrator at once becomes individually and personally answerable for payment so decreed to be made.—Magraw v. McGlynn, 26 Cal. 420, 432. Upon the entry of an order for the payment of the claims against the estate, the executor or administrator becomes liable therefor to the creditors, both personally and upon his bond, and each creditor is entitled to an execution against him therefor.—Estate of Sarment, 123 Cal. 331, 337, 55 Pac. 1015. A decree for the payment of money in probate proceedings can not be enforced as for a contempt. The proper process is an execution.—Rostel v. Morat, 19 Or. 181, 23 Pac. 900. Where there has been no administration of the estate, and no ascertainment of the assets and liabilities, a creditor is not entitled to have property of the estate, or any portion of it, applied to the discharge of his

claim, in whole or in part, except in due course of administration.—
Peabody v. Hutton, 5 Wyo. 102, 37 Pac. 694, 39 Pac. 980.

16. **Appeal.**—Although the probate court makes an order adjudging
that a claim against the estate is a preferred claim, and that such
claim be paid in due course of administration, and no appeal is taken
from such order, the executor or administrator is entitled to appeal
from a second order directing payment of the claim as a preferred
claim, where such second order was made before the amount of the
distributable estate was ascertained, and the accounts of the administrator settled, and without notice of the settlement of the account of
the administrator, as he is a party aggrieved by such premature order.
—Estate of Smith, 117 Cal. 505, 507, 49 Pac. 456. The decisions do
not declare that the order for a dividend must be made at the same
time as the order settling the account. In substance, they decide that
the first-mentioned order must follow the latter. Doubtless the order
for a dividend is, in practice, usually included in the same entry in the
minutes with the order settling the account, and immediately following, and this is proper when the order is made on the same day. But
there may be reason for delay in ordering the dividend, and the court
has as much power to make it on a subsequent day as it has on the
day the account is settled. It is evident that the order for a dividend
is, in many respects, dependent on the order settling the account, so
that if an appeal is taken from the latter it must, perforce, suspend
the effect of the former, and prevent its enforcement against the will
of the administrator until the latter becomes final. Hence there will
be no impropriety in deferring the making of an order for a dividend
until the time for appeal settling a contested account has expired, or
if an appeal has been taken, until such appeal is determined.—Estate
of McDougald, 143 Cal. 476, 483, 77 Pac. 443, 79 Pac. 878, 879. Where
the court has settled the administrator's account and ordered that
a dividend be declared upon the claims reported, and that the administratrix pay the same out of the balance adjudged to be on hand,
and the administratrix takes separate appeals from these orders,—
one in her capacity as administratrix of the estate, and the other as
a creditor—and only one of the creditors files any objection to the
account, it can not be contended, on appeal, that the creditors who
did not appear, nor make any objections to the account as rendered
are directly interested in the result of the appeal; nor can it be urged
that, under section 1649 of the Code of Civil Procedure of California,
an order for the payment of a dividend has the effect of a several
judgment in favor of each creditor against the administratrix, and that
this makes each creditor a party of record to the proceedings. The
word "party" should not be given so broad a meaning. That a person
interested in an estate, although his name and his interest are disclosed on the face of the record, is not necessarily a party to the cause
or proceeding, is manifest from a consideration of the different cases
where persons interested may or may not appear, at their option,

In a proceeding to probate a will, any person interested, whether a devisee, legatee, or heir, may appear and contest the probate. The petition for probate must show the names of the heirs and devisees, and hence their interest must always appear in the record. Yet, it would not be contended that an heir, devisee, or legatee who fails to appear at the time of the hearing of the petition is, in any sense, a party to such proceeding. So, with the petition for administration, there may be many persons who are entitled to letters and who are interested in the matter of the appointment. But if they fail to appeal or contest the right of the petitioner, it is manifest that they can not be considered parties. Upon the settlement of an account, every creditor, heir, legatee, or devisee is a person interested, and as such has a right to enter an appearance and become a party. The names of these persons generally appear upon the face of the account, or upon some of the documents referred to therein, but the giving of notice of the settlement and the statement of their rights or claims does not, ipso facto, make them parties to the proceeding. The only effect of notice is to give them an opportunity to become parties, so that, if they desire, they may appear and make themselves parties in some appropriate manner.—Estate of McDougald, 143 Cal. 476, 478, 479, 77 Pac. 443, 79 Pac. 878, 879.

PART XII.

PARTITION, DISTRIBUTION, AND FINAL SETTLEMENT OF ESTATES. ABSENT INTERESTED PARTIES, ACCOUNTS OF TRUSTEES.

CHAPTER I.

PARTIAL DISTRIBUTION PRIOR TO FINAL SETTLEMENT.

PARTIAL DISTRIBUTION.

§ 712.   Payment of legacies.

At any time after the lapse of four months from the issuing of letters testamentary or of administration, any heir, devisee, legatee (or his assignee, grantee, or successor in interest) may present his petition to the court for the legacy or share of the estate to which he is entitled, or any portion thereof, to be given to him upon his giving bonds, with security, for the payment of his proportion of the debts of the estate.—*Kerr's Cyc. Code Civ. Proc.*, § 1658.

ANALOGOUS AND IDENTICAL STATUTES.
No identical statute found.
Alaska—Compiled Laws of 1913, section 1714.
Arizona—Revised Statutes of 1913, paragraph 1027.
Colorado—Mills's Statutes of 1912, section 8026.
Idaho—Compiled Statutes of 1919, section 7724.
Montana—Revised Codes of 1907, section 7664.
Nevada—Revised Laws of 1912, section 6064.
North Dakota—Compiled Laws of 1913, section 8841.
Oklahoma—Revised Laws of 1910, section 6458.
Oregon—Lord's Oregon Laws, section 1305.
South Dakota—Compiled Laws of 1913, section 5919.
Utah—Compiled Laws of 1907, section 3948.
Washington—Laws of 1917, chapter 156, page 694, section 184.
Wyoming—Compiled Statutes of 1910, section 5695; as amended and re-enacted by Laws of 1911, chapter 37, page 48.

§ 713.   Notice of application for legacies.

Notice of the application must be given to the executor or administrator, personally, and to all persons interested in the estate, in the same manner that notice is required to be given of the settlement of the account of an executor or administrator.—*Kerr's Cyc. Code Civ. Proc.*, § 1659.

ANALOGOUS AND IDENTICAL STATUTES.
The * indicates identity.
Alaska—Compiled Laws of 1913, section 1715.
Arizona*—Revised Statutes of 1913, paragraph 1028.
Idaho*—Compiled Statutes of 1919, section 7725.
Montana*—Revised Codes of 1907, section 7665.
Nevada—Revised Laws of 1912, section 6065.
North Dakota—Compiled Laws of 1913, section 8842.
Oklahoma*—Revised Laws of 1910, section 6459.

Oregon—Lord's Oregon Laws, section 1306.
South Dakota*—Compiled Laws of 1913, section 5920.
Utah—Compiled Laws of 1907, section 3948.
Washington—Laws of 1917, chapter 156, page 694, section 182.
Wyoming*—Compiled Statutes of 1910, section 5696.

§ 714. Executor or other person may resist application.

The executor or administrator, or any person interested in the estate, may appear at the time named and resist the application.—*Kerr's Cyc. Code Civ. Proc.,* § 1660.

ANALOGOUS AND IDENTICAL STATUTES.

No identical statute found.

Arizona—Revised Statutes of 1913, paragraph 1029.
Idaho—Compiled Statutes of 1919, section 7726.
Montana—Revised Codes of 1907, section 7666.
Nevada—Revised Laws of 1912, section 6066.
North Dakota—Compiled Laws of 1913, section 8843.
Oklahoma—Revised Laws of 1910, section 6460.
South Dakota—Compiled Laws of 1913, section 5921.
Utah—Compiled Laws of 1907, section ——.
Washington—Laws of 1917, chapter 156, page 694, section 183.
Wyoming—Compiled Statutes of 1910, section 5697.

§ 715. Order. Legatee's bond. Delivery. Partition.

If, at the hearing, it appears that the estate is but little indebted, and that the share of the party applying may be allowed to him without loss to the creditors of the estate, the court must make an order in conformity with the prayer of the applicant requiring:

1. LEGATEE'S BOND.—Each heir, legatee, devisee (or his assignee, grantee, or successor in interest) obtaining such order, before receiving his share or any portion thereof, to execute and deliver to the executor or administrator, a bond, in such sum as may be designated by the court, or a judge thereof, with sureties to be approved by the judge, payable to the executor or administrator, and conditioned for the payment, whenever required, of his proportion of the debts due from the estate, not exceeding the value or amount of the legacy or portion of the estate to which he is entitled. Where the time for filing

or presenting claims has expired, and all claims that have been allowed, have been paid, or are secured by mortgage upon real estate sufficient to pay them, and the court is satisfied that no injury can result to the estate, the court may dispense with the bond;

2. DELIVERY.—The executor or administrator to deliver to the heir, legatee, devisee (or his assignee, grantee, or successor in interest), the whole portion of the estate to which he may be entitled, or only a part thereof designating it.

PARTITION.—If, in the execution of the order, a partition is necessary between two or more of the parties interested, it must be made in the manner hereinafter prescribed. The costs of these proceedings must be paid by the applicant, or if there are more than one, must be apportioned equally among them.—*Kerr's Cyc. Code Civ. Proc.*, § 1661.

ANALOGOUS AND IDENTICAL STATUTES.
No identical statute found.

Alaska—Compiled Laws of 1913, sections 1715, 1716.
Arizona—Revised Statutes of 1913, paragraph 1030.
Colorado—Mills's Statutes of 1912, section 8026.
Idaho—Compiled Statutes of 1919, section 7727.
Kansas—General Statutes of 1915, section 4653.
Montana—Revised Codes of 1907, section 7667.
Nevada—Revised Laws of 1912, section 6067.
North Dakota—Compiled Laws of 1913, section 8844.
Oklahoma—Revised Laws of 1910, section 6461.
Oregon—Lord's Oregon Laws, sections 1306, 1307.
South Dakota—Compiled Laws of 1913, section 5922.
Utah—Compiled Laws of 1907, section 3949.
Washington—Laws of 1917, chapter 156, page 694, section 184.
Wyoming—Compiled Statutes of 1910, section 5698.

§ 716. Form. Petition for share of estate before final settlement.

[Title of court.]

[Title of estate.]   {No. ——.1 Dept. No. ——.
                              {   [Title of form.]

To the Honorable the ——² Court of the County ³ of ——, State of ——.

Your petitioner respectfully represents that he is a ——[4] of ——, deceased, and one of his heirs at law,[5] and is entitled to ——[6] of the residue of said estate, after the payment of debts, costs, expenses, and charges of administration;

That said deceased died intestate; that —— is the administrator of said estate; and that more than four months have elapsed since the issuance of letters of administration of said estate;

That the total value of said estate, as appears by the inventory and appraisement on file in said court, is the sum of —— dollars ($——); that your petitioner is informed and believes, and therefore states, that there are no claims against said estate;[7] that the debts outstanding against said estate, together with the costs, expenses, and charges of administration, will probably not exceed the sum of —— dollars ($——); and that petitioner's[8] share of said estate hereinafter described can be allowed to him without loss to the creditors of the estate;

That the only other heirs[9] of said deceased are ——, ——, and ——, all residents of the said county[10] of ——, state of ——.

The following is a description of the property of which distribution is hereby asked: ——.[11]

Wherefore your petitioner prays that this court cause notice of his application to be given; and that it make an order distributing to him the share of said estate above described to which he is entitled, upon his giving to said administrator the bond required by law, and for such other or further order as may seem meet.

——, Attorney for Petitioner. ——, Petitioner.

Explanatory notes.—1 Give file number. 2 Title of court. 3 Or, City and County. 4 State relationship. 5 Or, devisee or legatee, according to the fact. 6 Give fractional part to which petitioner is entitled. 7 Or, that it is but little indebted, stating the amount of claims. 8 Or, that portion of petitioner's share, etc. 9 Or, devisees or legatees. 10 Or, city and county. 11 Describe the property.

§ 717. Form. Notice of application for share of estate before final settlement.

[Title of court.]

[Title of estate.]   {No. ——.1 Dept. No. ——.
                                   {   [Title of form.]

Notice is hereby given to ——, the administrator [2] of said estate, and to all persons interested therein, That ——, on the —— day of ——, 19—, filed with the clerk of this court his petition praying for an order of said court distributing to him, before final settlement, his legacy or share of said estate, to which he is entitled, upon his delivering to said administrator [3] the bond required by law;

And that ——,[4] the —— day of ——, 19—, at the court-room of said court,[5] in said county [6] of ——, at the hour of —— o'clock in the forenoon [7] of said day, have been fixed by the court as the time and place for the hearing of said petition, when and where any person interested in said estate may appear and resist said application, if he sees fit to do so.

Dated ——, 19—.   ——, Clerk of the —— Court.
                              By ——, Deputy Clerk.

Explanatory notes.—1 Give file number. 2, 3 Or, executor. 4 Day of week. 5 State location of court-room. 6 Or, city and county. 7 Or, afternoon.

§ 718. Form. Memorandum, by clerk, fixing time for hearing for partial distribution.

[Title of court.]

[Title of estate.]   {No. ——.1 Dept. No. ——.
                                   {   [Title of form.]

——, heir [2] of ——, deceased, having this day filed and presented a petition praying for a decree of partial distribution to him of certain —— of said estate described and set forth in said petition,—

Now, I, ——, clerk of said ——[3] court, do hereby fix and appoint ——,[4] the —— day of ——, 19—, at —— o'clock in the forenoon of said day, and the court-room of said court, at the court-house in the county of ——, as the time and place for the hearing upon said petition.

Notice is further given, That —— is the administrator [5] of said estate.　——, Clerk of the —— Court.

Dated ——, 19—.　　　By ——, Deputy Clerk.

Explanatory notes.—1 Give file number. 2 Or, devisee or legatee. 3 Title of court. 4 Give day of week. 5 Or, executor of the last will of said deceased, etc.

§ 719.　Form.　Executor's resistance to application for partial distribution.

[Title of court.]

[Title of estate.]　　　　{ No.——.1　Dept. No.——.
　　　　　　　　　　　　　　[Title of form.]

The application of ——, one of the legatees under the last will and testament of ——, deceased, having been presented to this court, with a prayer that the court make an order distributing to him the share of said estate to which he is entitled, ——, the executor of said last will and testament, now objects to the granting of said petition, on the ground that its allegations are not true, and avers that said estate is deeply in debt,[2] and that the share of petitioner can not be allowed to him without loss to the creditors of said estate. Hence such executor resists said petition, and asks that it be denied.

　　——, Executor of the Estate of ——, Deceased.

　　——, Attorney for Executor.

Explanatory notes.—1 Give file number. 2 And other reasons, if any, specifying each one.

§ 720.　Form.　Order directing executor to pay a legatee his share of an estate.

[Title of court.]

[Title of estate.]　　　　{ No.——.1　Dept. No.——.
　　　　　　　　　　　　　　[Title of form.]

It appearing that ——, a legatee under the last will and testament of ——, deceased, has filed in this court his petition for an order directing ——, the executor of said will, to pay him the legacy of —— dollars ($——) given him by said will, and the matter, after due notice of hearing given as required by law, coming regularly on this day [2] to be heard, and being submitted for decision, the court finds that said estate is but little indebted; and that the share of said petitioner may be allowed to him without loss to the creditors of said estate, —

It is therefore ordered, That ——, the executor of said will, pay the said petitioner, ——, the sum of —— dollars ($——) in full of his legacy, upon delivery to him, the said executor, of a bond in the sum of —— dollars ($——),[3] with sureties to be approved by the judge of this court, payable to said executor, conditioned for the payment, whenever required, of his proportion of the debts of the estate, not exceeding the amount of said legacy.

Dated ——, 19—.   ——, Judge of the —— Court.

Explanatory notes.—1 Give file number. 2 Or, if the matter has been continued, say, "and the same having been by the court regularly postponed to the present time." 3 In such sum as shall be designated by the court, or a judge thereof.

§ 721. Form. Order for partial distribution.

[Title of court.]

[Title of estate.]   {No. ——.1 Dept. No. ——.
                            {   [Title of form.]

Now comes ——,[2] the petitioner herein, by ——, his attorney, and shows to the court that his petition for partial distribution herein was filed on the —— day of ——, 19—; that on the same day the clerk appointed the —— day of ——, 19—, as the day for the hearing thereof; that notice of the time and place of said hearing has been duly given as required by law;[3] and the said petition being now presented to the court, and no person appearing to contest the same,[4] the court, after hearing the evidence, finds that said estate is but little indebted, and that the share of the petitioner asked for may be allowed to him without loss to the creditors of said estate; and grants said petition as follows, to wit:

It is ordered by the court, That the said ——, ——, and ——, shall each, before receiving his interest, or any portion thereof, execute and deliver to the —— of said estate a bond in the penal sum of —— dollars ($——), to be approved by the court or judge, payable to the executor or administrator, and conditioned for the payment, whenever required, of his proportion of the debts due from said estate, not exceeding the value of the portion thereof to which he is entitled; and that the said ——, as administrator [5] of said estate, deliver to the said person so executing said bond the portion of said estate as follows, to wit:

To the said ——, upon the giving by him of the bond required as aforesaid, the following portion thereof: ——.[6]

To the said ——, upon the giving by him of the bond required as aforesaid, the following portion thereof: ——.[7]

And to —— and —— each a ——[8] part thereof, etc. The residue so distributed to said last-named persons is described as follows, to wit: ——.[9]

Dated ——, 19—. ——, Judge of the —— Court.

Explanatory notes.—[1] Give file number. [2] Name the petitioner, observing that the court has no power to order partial distribution upon the petition of an executor or administrator: Alcorn v. Buschke, 133 Cal. 655, 66 Pac. 15. [3] If the matter has been continued, say, "and said hearing having been regularly postponed to the present time." [4] Or, ——, having appeared by ——, his attorney, and filed objections and exceptions to said petition. [5] Or, executor. [6-8] State fractional part thereof. [9] Describe the residue.

§ 722. Form. Bond on distribution before final settlement.

[Title of court.]

[Title of estate.]

{ No.——.[1]   Dept. No.——.
{   [Title of form.]

Know all men by these presents: That we, —— as principal, and —— and —— as sureties, are held and

firmly bound to ——, the administrator [2] of the estate of
——, deceased, in the sum of —— dollars ($——),[3] law-
ful money of the United States of America, to be paid to
the said administrator,[4] for which payment well and truly
to be made we bind ourselves, our and each of our heirs,
executors, and administrators, jointly and severally,
firmly by these presents.

The condition of the above obligation is such that
whereas, on the —— day of ——, 19—, the said administrator [5] was, by order of the ——[6] court of the county [7]
of ——, state of ——, duly made and entered, authorized
and directed to pay over or deliver to ——, one of the
heirs at law of said deceased, the whole of his share of
the property of said estate, upon his executing to such
administrator [8] a bond in said sum, conditioned according to law, —

Now, therefore, if the above-bounden principal shall
well and truly pay, or cause to be paid, whenever required
so to do, his proportion of the debts of said estate, not
exceeding the value or amount of his portion of said
estate, to wit, the sum of —— dollars ($——) so paid or
delivered to him by authority of said order, then this
obligation is to be void; otherwise to remain in full force
and effect.

Dated, signed, and sealed with our seals this —— day
of ——, 19—.

—— [Seal]

—— [Seal]

—— [Seal]

. **Explanatory notes.**—1 Give file number. 2 Or, executor. 3 In such
sum as shall be designated by the court, or a judge thereof. 4, 5 Or,
executor. 6 Title of court. 7 Or, city and county. 8 Or, executor.

§ 723. Form. Justification of sureties.

State of ——, ⎱
    County [1] of ——, ⎰ ss.

—— and ——, the sureties named in the above bond,
being duly sworn, each for himself, and not one for the

other, says he is a householder [2] and resident within said state, and is worth the said sum of —— dollars ($——), over and above all his debts and liabilities, exclusive of property exempt from execution.   ——

Subscribed and sworn to before me this —— day of ——, 19—.   ——, Notary Public, etc.[3]

Explanatory notes.—1 Or, City and County. 2 Or, freeholder. 3 Or other officer taking the oath.

§ 724. Form. Order for partial distribution without bond.

[Title of court.]

[Title of estate.]   { No. ——.[1] Dept. No. ——.
                                      {   [Title of form.]

Now comes ——, the petitioner herein, by ——, his attorney, and shows to the court that his petition for partial distribution herein was filed on the —— day of ——, 19—; that on the same day the clerk appointed the —— day of ——, 19—, as the day for the hearing thereof; and that notice of the time and place of said hearing has been duly given as required by law;[2] and the said petition being now presented to the court, and no person appearing to contest the same,[3] the court, after hearing the evidence, finds that said estate is but little indebted, and that the share of the petitioner asked for may be allowed to him without loss to creditors of the estate, and that no injury can result to the estate therefrom, and grants said petition as follows, to wit:

It is ordered by the court, That the giving of any bond by the said —— before receiving his share of said estate be dispensed with, and that the said ——, as the administrator [4] of said estate, forthwith deliver to said —— as [5] his share of said estate the following-described property, to wit: ——;[6] and that he shall also deliver to the said —— as the whole [7] of his share of said estate, the following-described property, to wit: ——.[8]

Dated ——, 19—.   ——, Judge of the —— Court.

Probate Law—109

Explanatory notes.—1 Give file number. 2 If the matter has been continued, say, "and said hearing having been regularly postponed to the present time." 3 Or, —— having appeared by ——, his attorney, and filed objections and exceptions to said petition. 4 Or, executor. 5 The whole, or a part of. 6 Describe the property. 7 Or, part. 8 Describe the property.

§ 725. Order for payment of money secured by bond. Citation. Action on bond.

When any bond has been executed and delivered, under the provisions of the preceding section, and it is necessary for the settlement of the estate to require the payment of any part of the money thereby secured, the executor or administrator must petition the court for an order requiring the payment, and have a citation issued and served on the party bound, requiring him to appear and show cause why the order should not be made. At the hearing, the court, if satisfied of the necessity of such payment, must make an order accordingly, designating the amount and giving a time within which it must be paid. If the money is not paid within the time allowed, an action may be maintained by the executor or administrator on the bond.—*Kerr's Cyc. Code Civ. Proc., § 1662.*

ANALOGOUS AND IDENTICAL STATUTES.

The * indicates identity.

Alaska—Compiled Laws of 1913, section 1717.

Arizona*—Revised Statutes of 1913, paragraph 1031.

Colorado—Mills's Statutes of 1912, section 8027.

Idaho*—Compiled Statutes of 1919, section 7728.

Montana*—Revised Codes of 1907, section 7668.

Nevada*—Revised Laws of 1912, section 6071.

North Dakota*—Compiled Laws of 1913, section 8845.

Oklahoma*—Revised Laws of 1910, section 6462.

Oregon—Lord's Oregon Laws, sections 1308, 1309.

South Dakota*—Compiled Laws of 1913, section 5923.

Utah—Compiled Laws of 1907, section 3950.

Washington—Laws of 1917, chapter 156, page 695, section 186.

§ 726. Form. Petition for order directing legatee, etc., to refund money for payment of debts.

[Title of court.]

[Title of estate.]   { No.——.1   Dept. No.——.
                            {   [Title of form.]

To the Honorable the ——² Court of the County ³ of ——, State of ——.

Your petitioner respectfully represents:

That on the —— day of ——, 19—, this court, by its order duly made and entered, required him, the said petitioner, as administrator ⁴ of the estate of ——, deceased, to pay to ——, an heir at law of said decedent, the sum of —— dollars ($——) upon the giving of a bond to said administrator ⁵ in the sum of —— dollars ($——),⁶ conditioned according to law;

That said bond, as aforesaid, was subsequently given to the said administrator,⁷ in compliance with said order, and that, in compliance with said order, the said administrator ⁸ paid to the said heir at law the sum of —— dollars ($——);

That the court, in making said order, placed an erroneous estimate upon the debts, costs, charges, and expenses of administration; that such debts, etc., are far in excess of the estimate made at the time of the making of said order; and that the amount thereof, instead of being —— dollars ($——), as estimated at the time said order was made, is more than —— dollars ($——).⁹

Your petitioner therefore submits that it is necessary, for the settlement of the said estate, to require the said —— to refund a portion of the money so paid to him as aforesaid; to wit, the sum of —— dollars ($——).

Wherefore your petitioner prays that the said —— be required to refund to the administrator ¹⁰ of said estate, out of the sum so paid to him as aforesaid, a sum sufficient to liquidate his share of the indebtedness of said estate, to wit, said sum of —— dollars ($——); and for such other or further order as may be meet.

——, Attorney for Petitioner.   ——, Petitioner.

Explanatory notes.—1 Give file number. 2 Title of court. 3 Or, City and County. 4, 5 Or, executor, according to the fact. 6 In such sum as may have been designated by the court. 7, 8 Or, executor. 9 Or state any other facts showing that it is necessary to refund a part of the money. 10 Or, executor.

§ 727. Form. Order that legatee, etc., refund money to pay debts.

[Title of court.]

[Title of estate.]   { No. ——.1   Dept. No. ——.
                    {   [Title of form.]

It being shown to this court that ——, the administrator[2] of the estate of ——, deceased, filed in this court on the —— day of ——, 19—, his petition for an order requiring ——, an heir at law of said decedent, to refund to the said administrator[3] a sufficient sum, out of money theretofore received by him out of said estate under and by virtue of the order of this court, to pay his proportion of the indebtedness of said estate; and that a citation was afterwards duly issued and served on the party bound, requiring him to appear and show cause why said order should not be made; and the matter now coming regularly on for hearing,[4] the court proceeds to hear the allegations and proofs, and the court, after such hearing, being satisfied that no sufficient reason exists why said order should not be made, finds that it is necessary, in order to cancel the indebtedness of said estate, that the said —— should refund to said administrator[5] the sum of —— dollars ($——) out of the money heretofore received by him as aforesaid, —

It is therefore ordered, adjudged, and decreed, That the said —— be, and he is hereby, required to pay to the said administrator,[6] out of said money so received as

aforesaid, the said sum of —— dollars ($——) within
——[7] days from the date of this order.

Dated ——, 19—.   ——, Judge of the —— Court.

Explanatory notes.—[1] Give file number. [2], [3] Or, executor, etc., according to the fact. [4] Or, if the matter has been continued, say, "and the matter having been by the court regularly postponed to the present time." [5], [6] Or, executor, etc. [7] Time fixed by court.

§ 727.[1] Partial distribution, how made.

Where the time for filing or presenting claims has expired, and all claims that have been allowed have been paid, or are secured by a mortgage upon real estate sufficient to pay them, and the estate is not in a condition to be finally closed and distributed, the executor or administrator, or co-executor or co-administrator, may present his petition to the court for ratable payment of the legacies, or ratable distribution of the estate to all the heirs, legatees, devisees, or their assignees, grantees, or successors in interest. Notice of such application must be given to all persons interested in the estate, in the same manner that notice is required to be given of the settlement of the account of an executor or administrator. Any person interested in the estate may appear at the time named and resist the application.

ORDER.—If, at the hearing, it appears that the allegations in the petition of said executor, administrator, co-executor, or co-administrator, are true, and the court is satisfied that no injury can result to the estate by granting the petition, the court must make an order directing the executor or executors, administrator or administrators, as the case may be, to deliver to the heirs, legatees, devisees, or to their assigns, grantees, or successors in interest, the whole portion of the estate to which they may be entitled, or only a part thereof, designating it.

COSTS.—If, in the execution of the order, a partition is necessary between two or more of the parties interested, it must be made in the manner hereinafter prescribed.

The costs of the proceedings under this section must be paid by the estate, excepting that in case a partition is necessary, the costs of such partition must be apportioned amongst the parties interested in such partition.— *Kerr's Cyc. Code Civ. Proc.,* § 1663.

PARTIAL DISTRIBUTION.

1. Power of courts.—Whether there be opposition or not, or whatever the opposition may be, the petitioner for partial distribution must show that the estate is but little indebted, that he is entitled to the share he asks, and what, when the expenses of administration are paid, his share will amount to. The only office of an opposition is to rebut this showing.—Estate of Painter, 115 Cal. 625, 640, 47 Pac. 700. The power of the court to make an order of partial distribution before final settlement is expressly conferred by the statute.—Estate of Crocker, 105 Cal. 368, 371, 38 Pac. 954. The requirement of the statute that the estate shall be but "little indebted" is to be construed relatively, and not absolutely, and merely refers to a condition of things in which the debts are small, when considered in connection with the value of the estate.—Estate of Hale, 121 Cal. 125, 130, 53 Pac. 429. No express authority for decreeing partial distribution of an estate in the hands of a special administrator is found.—Estate of Welch, 106 Cal. 427, 433, 39 Pac. 805. Where a will has been admitted to probate under compromise agreements, the order admitting it becomes the basis of administration, and controlling as to the devolution of the property. The court has power, on petition for a partial distribution of the estate, made by persons who are entitled to fixed shares according to such agreement, to authorize distribution according to the agreement. The court has power, on consent of all the parties interested in a will contest, to enter a decree affirming a compromise thereof, and ascertaining the share to which the parties are respectively entitled.—In re Davis' Estate, 27 Mont. 490, 71 Pac. 757, 759. The fact that writs are pending against an estate, in which plaintiffs are strangers, and the distributees and the administrator are parties, for the purpose of obtaining liens on the interest of the defendants in the estate, furnishes no reason why the court should refuse to order a distribution of the estate, where there is nothing in the record to show that any receiver has been appointed, or that the shares thus sought to be reached are impounded in the hands of the administrator.—In re Davis' Estate, 27 Mont. 490, 71 Pac. 757, 760. In a proceeding for partial distribution, on petition of decedent's widow, the court has no power to distribute any of the property of the estate to a person who claims title thereto as grantee of the widow, where, under the statutes in force for partial distribution, no one other than an heir, devisee, or legatee, having an interest, as such, in the property for which distribution is asked, is authorized to petition for such distribution.—In re Foley's Estate, 24 Nev. 197, 51 Pac. 834, 837, 52 Pac. 649. Nor has the court any power to decree a partial distribution upon the petition of the executor or administrator.—Estate of Letellier, 74 Cal. 311, 312, 15 Pac. 847; Alcorn v. Buschke, 133 Cal. 655, 66 Pac. 15. The executors, while authorized to resist an application for partial distribution, have no interest in having the property go to one rather than another of the contending claimants of the estate.—Estate of Young, 149 Cal. 173, 85 Pac. 145, 146. Such a question does not affect the administrator or executor in his representative capacity. It concerns only the rights of the heirs, devisees, legatees, etc. In such cases the administrator or executor can not litigate the claims of one set of legatees against the others at the expense of the estate.—Estate of Murphy, 145 Cal. 464, 467, 78 Pac. 960. An order of distribution to an incompetent person, who has not appeared by guardian, is erroneous, as there is no competent person asking for a distribution in his behalf. —In re Davis' Estate, 27 Mont. 490, 71 Pac. 757, 760. No suit to determine distributees' shares in an estate is necessary, where the parties have agreed as to the share that each one shall receive.—In re Davis' Estate, 27 Mont. 490, 71 Pac. 757, 760. In a proceeding under section 7669, of the Revised Codes of Montana, for partial distribution, the questions of heirship, amount of distributive estate claimed, etc., can not be considered; those questions are to be determined under the express authority of those codes.—In re Fleming's Estate, 38 Mont. 57, 59, 98 Pac. 648. The superior court in probate has no jurisdiction to entertain a proceeding for partial distribution on the petition of an administrator. A decree so rendered is void, as the statute authorizes the proceeding on the petition of an heir, devisee, or legatee only.— Alcorn v. Gieseke, 158 Cal. 396, 111 Pac. 98. A district court in a proceeding for partial distribution may not determine questions of heirship and upon such a proceeding the distribution can be made only to such persons whose rights as heirs have been established and also the amounts of the estate to which they are entitled.—In re Fleming's Estate, 38 Mont. 57, 98 Pac. 649.

(2) Right to distribution.—Section 7669 of the Revised Codes of Montana, is susceptible of but one meaning, namely, that any heir, devisee, or legatee shown by the record to be such, and concerning whose right to inherit there is no question raised, may ask for distribution

to him of the share of the estate which the record shows he is entitled
to receive, and about which there is no controversy.—In re Fleming's
Estate, 38 Mont. 57, 61, 98 Pac. 648. Where a bequest was made to
brothers and sisters of the testatrix, "living" at the time of the execution of the will, but one of the brothers and one of the sisters died
before the testatrix did, the children of such predeceased brother and
sister are not entitled to take, as "descendants," under section 1310 of
the Civil Code of California, their respective proportions of the legacies
bequeathed to their parents and are not entitled to partial distribution
of such assets; words in a will, referring to survivorship, simply relate,
under section 1386 of that code, to the time of the testator's death.—
In re Rounds' Estate (Cal.), 181 Pac. 638. It is a condition precedent to
the issuance of an order for partial distribution to a legatee, on the
latter's petition, besides the condition of the legatee's filing a bond for
the payment of his proportion of the debts, that the estate be not
largely involved, financially; and, in a case where the legacies must
exhaust the estate, such an order is invalid, if the debts of the estate
and the expenses of administration amount to one-half the assets, and
there must necessarily be an abatement of some of the legacies in order
to pay debts, costs, and expenses of administration.—In re Hawgood's
Estate, 37 S. D. 565, 575, 159 N. W. 117. The question whether an estate
"is but little indebted," so that the statute may be invoked providing
for partial distribution in such a case, is to be determined, not by the
amount of the debts viewed absolutely, but by their relation to the
value of the estate.—Estate of Hinkel, 176 Cal. 563, 169 Pac. 70. Whatever objection there may be to paying, on petition for partial distribution, one residuary legatee and devisee in cash, where this must
result in requiring the others to take their shares in undivided interests in real property, there can be none, where all the real estate must
be sold, the estate is ample to pay all legatees and devisees, and there
are few, if any, debts to be paid.—Estate of Huntoon, 174 Cal. 282, 163
Pac. 52.

3. Petition.—The statute does not attempt to prescribe the form
or contents of a petition for partial distribution. It is clear that
elaborate pleadings are not required or contemplated in the proceeding, and, so far as the executor is concerned, they are not necessary,
as generally, he must have greater knowledge of the value and character of the property, the amount of money on hand, and the amount of
the indebtedness, than any other person. Hence a statement of the
ultimate facts concerning the nature of the estate and the amount of
the debts which, according to the code, the court must find to exist
before making the order will afford sufficient information of the grounds
on which the application will be made to enable the executor, at least,
to make any proper opposition or defense. If it accomplishes this, it
serves the purpose for which pleadings are required.—Estate of Murphy, 145 Cal. 464, 466, 467, 78 Pac. 960. The court is authorized to order
the payment of the legacies upon a petition which shows that the

estate "is but little indebted," and that the payment can be made "without loss to the creditors of the estate."—Estate of Chesney, 1 Cal. App. 30, 34, 81 Pac. 679. A petition for partial distribution is not defective because it describes the petitioners as "heirs at law." This, properly, is but a step in the ordinary course of administration; and the fact that petitioners are described in the petition as heirs at law, instead of devisees and legatees under the will, is entirely immaterial, the court having judicial notice of the will at every stage of the proceeding. Nor is it any objection to such a petition that it was filed by several claimants, instead of one.—Estate of Crocker, 105 Cal. 368, 38 Pac. 954, 955. Even if an order of sale has been granted, the court has power to stay the execution of the order of sale, and to grant a petition for partial distribution.—State v. District Court, 34 Mont. 345, 86 Pac. 268, 269. A partial distribution of personal property may properly be made under the provisions of the will; but a petition by a sole heir for distribution of his share of the entire estate is properly denied, pending an application for the sale of the real estate to raise funds necessary to pay charges and funeral expenses.—Estate of Koppikus, 1 Cal. App. 88, 89, 81 Pac. 733. A question of contested heirship, or right to inherit, may be determined on a petition for partial distribution.—Estate of Jessup, 81 Cal. 408, 415, 6 L. R. A. 594, 24 Pac. 976, 22 Pac. 742, 1028.

4. Notice.—Where a motion has been made to vacate an order denying a petition for partial distribution, and an order has been made granting such petition, but the notice in each case is served only upon the executors, and no notice is given by posting as prescribed by the statute, the court acquires no jurisdiction to make either order, as legatees and creditors, for want of such notice, have been deprived of an opportunity to be heard.—Estate of Mitchell, 126 Cal. 248, 252, 58 Pac. 549. Where the notice expressly required by statute has been given, the question as to whether further notice shall be given or not is a matter within the discretion of the court, and, in the absence of anything to show that such discretion has been abused, the appellate court will not interfere.—Estate of Jessup, 81 Cal. 408, 436, 21 Pac. 976.

5. Bond.—The only circumstances under which the giving of a bond, by an heir, for his proportion of indebtedness may be executed upon partial distribution, is where it appears that the time for presenting claims against the estate has expired, and that all claims that have been allowed have been paid, or are secured by mortgage upon real estate sufficient to pay them, and the court is satisfied that no injury can result to the estate.—Estate of Hale, 121 Cal. 125, 131, 53 Pac. 429; Estate of Mitchell, 121 Cal. 391, 393, 53 Pac. 810. If the evidence shows that a large proportion of the demands are unsecured by mortgage or otherwise, and that such unsecured demands have not been paid, a court is not authorized to dispense with the giving of a bond.— Estate of Hale, 121 Cal. 125, 131, 53 Pac. 429. But the court may order a partial distribution of the estate to devisees and legatees, without requiring them to give bonds, if it reserves from distribution sufficient other property to pay all contested claims, and the court finds that no injury can result to the estate by reason of such partial distribution.— Estate of Crocker, 105 Cal. 368, 371, 38 Pac. 954. It is erroneous to dispense with the bond, upon a partial distribution to legatees, if it appears that unsecured claims allowed have not been paid.—Estate of Mitchell, 121 Cal. 391, 395, 53 Pac. 810; but the fact that a claim has been presented by a legatee against the estate, and has been rejected by the executors, and that a suit thereon is pending, does not preclude the court from making an order for the payment of her legacy, where it is not claimed that there is any indebtedness against the estate other than this rejected claim, and the executors still have in their hands property belonging to the estate many times in value the amount of the rejected claim with which to pay the same, if it shall be adjudged valid.—Estate of Chesney, 1 Cal. App. 30, 34, 81 Pac. 679. Upon a petition for partial distribution of an estate at the expiration of four months, it is erroneous to distribute all of the property of the estate, simply reserving bonds to secure debts. Enough property should be reserved not only to cover the entire debts and expenses of administration, but also to secure payment of the inheritance tax by the distribution under the Act of March 20, 1905.—Estate of Gird, 157 Cal. 534, 137 Am. St. Rep. 131, 108 Pac. 499. The failure to give a bond upon presenting a petition for the payment of a legacy, or of the distributive share of a decedent's estate, and upon a decree ordering payment of the same, does not render a decree of partial distribution void, where the creditors are not complaining and could not possibly be injured.—Wilson v. Linder, 18 Ida. 438, 448, 138 Am. St. Rep. 213, 110 Pac. 274. The bond required of a distributee is not obligatory when at the time of the decree of distribution the time allowed for filing claims has expired.—Estate of Hinkel, 176 Cal. 563, 169 Pac. 70. Where, under the statute, a legatee, after the lapse of four months from the issuing of letters testamentary, would petition for the legacy he is entitled to, the filing by such legatee of a bond for the payment of his proportion of the debts, is a jurisdictional condition precedent to the making of an order for partial distribution.—In re Hawgood's Estate, 37 S. D. 565, 574, 159 N. W. 117.

6. **Hearing.**—While it is true that the allowance to be made for commissions, attorneys' fees, and charges to close the administration can not be definitely fixed until the final settlement of the executor, yet, in ascertaining whether a partial distribution shall be ordered, and for the purpose of fixing the amount thereof, it is necessary for the court to take these matters into consideration, and to determine them upon proper data furnished at the application for the hearing. Hence, when the application comes on for hearing, and the court finds that all the debts of the estate have been paid; that there is at least several thousand dollars remaining in the hands of the executor be-

longing to the estate, and that it has been there for several years; that no distribution of any part of the estate has ever been made to the widow, or to her son as her assignee; that fifteen hundred dollars could be allowed and paid to the son without injury to the estate; and that, after such payment, there would remain in the hands of the executor more than enough money to pay for commissions, together with a reasonable attorney's fee and the charges of closing the estate,—there is no error in distributing the said sum of fifteen hundred dollars. —Estate of Straus, 144 Cal. 553, 556, 77 Pac. 1122. But, in determining the amount of money in the hands of executors available for the payment of a legacy, the court is not required to take into consideration the amount of the collateral-inheritance tax. The tax is computed, not on the aggregate valuation of the whole estate of the decedent considered as the unit for taxation, but on the value of the separate interests in which it is divided by the will, or by the statute laws of the state, and is a charge against each share or interest, according to its value, and against the person entitled thereto. Therefore if the court, in fixing the amount to be paid as a legacy, deducts therefrom the amount of the tax on such a legacy, it is to be assumed that, before paying or delivering to the other beneficiaries under the will any property given to them by the testatrix, the executors either deducted therefrom or collected from the said beneficiaries the amount of the tax on their respective gifts.—Estate of Chesney, 1 Cal. App. 30, 33, 81 Pac. 679. The question as to what property is embraced in an agreement between the widow and the other heirs for a distribution of the estate, whether the separate property only, or both the separate and community property, is one foreign to the subject-matter of partial distribution, and is not properly before the court in such a proceeding.— In re Foley's Estate, 24 Nev. 197, 51 Pac. 834, 837, 52 Pac. 649. In proceedings on a petition for partial distribution the inventory is prima facie evidence of the value of the property of the estate.—Estate of Huntoon, 174 Cal. 282, 163 Pac. 52.

7. **Order.**—No default can be taken upon the hearing of a petition for a partial distribution of the estate of a deceased person. A plenary showing must be made by the applicant at the hearing. If opposition is made, and the grounds of the opposition are stated in writing, that can not limit the inquiry, nor can the court take the admission of contestants, unless it clearly appears that the admission is made by all parties in the proceeding.—Estate of Painter, 115 Cal. 635, 639, 47 Pac. 700. An order for partial distribution may be made after the administrator or executor has presented his final account, but before the same has been allowed, upon the giving of a bond to indemnify the estate. If partial distribution could only be had after final accounts are allowed, there would be no use of the proceeding for partial distribution, and the benefits of the statute might be entirely lost. It was to avoid the hardship often incident to the long delays of the final accounting that, upon a sufficient showing, partial distribution might

be had.—In re Phillips' Estate, 18 Mont. 311, 45 Pac. 222, 224. If certain legatees petition for partial distribution, but other legatees and devisees do not appear at the hearing, or in any manner object to the order in favor of petitioners, and the executor, in his representative capacity, appeals on the ground of the insufficiency of the petition respecting its statements of condition and value of the estate and the amount of the debts, the order of distribution becomes final, in as far as it allowed the legacies.—Estate of Murphy, 145 Cal. 464, 78 Pac. 960, 962. Where legatees apply for partial distribution, and the executor appears and contests the petition in his capacity as executor only, such appearance does not entitle him to claim rights, in such proceeding, which he possessed solely as devisee. As such devisee he must be considered as one who has suffered default.—Estate of Murphy, 145 Cal. 464, 78 Pac. 960, 962. If the sum left in the hands of a widow, as executrix of her deceased husband's estate, after payment to legatees, is sufficient to cover expenses of administration, the amount devised to her as widow, and a reasonable family allowance, she is not prejudiced by an order of partial distribution.—In re Phillips' Estate, 18 Mont. 311, 45 Pac. 222, 224. A decree of partial distribution can not be attacked for fraud, where such decree was in strict accord with the terms of the will, and necessarily followed the decree admitting the will to probate, if the probate of the will can not be successfully attacked in some way.—Tracy v. Muir, 151 Cal. 363, 367, 121 Am. St. Rep. 117, 90 Pac. 832, 833. The better practice is to specify, in the order, the sum to be paid by the executors, and the amount of the collateral-inheritance tax to be deducted therefrom.—Estate of Mitchell, 121 Cal. 391, 53 Pac. 810, 811. Where it is admitted at the hearing of a petition for partial distribution that due notice of the application was given to the executors and all persons interested, this is sufficient to require all those interested, who desire to combat the proceeding, to put in an appearance, and if a motion to set aside an order denying such petition is made, it is sufficient to give notice to the executors, who have appeared through their attorneys.—Estate of Mitchell, 121 Cal. 391, 53 Pac. 810, 811. A decree of partial distribution containing a clause imposing a condition is erroneous.—Estate of Garrity, 108 Cal. 463, 474, 38 Pac. 628, 41 Pac. 485. A decree of partial distribution as modified on appeal, is a conclusive adjudication as to the construction to be given to the will in question and the rights of the parties affected thereby must be measured solely by it.—Hardy v. Mayhew, 158 Cal. 95, 139 Am. St. Rep. 73, 110 Pac. 113. Where the proper notice for a decree of partial distribution has been given, as required by section 1659 of the Code of Civil Procedure of California, and the court has thereunder rendered its decree, such decree will be conclusive of the rights of the legatees and devisees under the will, subject to appeal therefrom; hence, such decree is not open to attack on the ground that the evidence upon which it was predicated was incompetent or insufficient. In order to justify any interference with the result flow-ing from the decree, it would be necessary to charge and prove in a proceeding having that purpose in view some fraud collateral or extrinsic to the matters or questions examined and determined in the proceeding culminating in the decree.—French v. Phelps, 20 Cal. App. 101, 128 Pac. 772, 777.

8. Vacating order.—Application to vacate order of partial distribution held within six months' limitation prescribed in the California Code Civ. Proc., section 473, for relief from orders or judgments generally, such order not having been "taken" until formal signing and filing though previously orally announced and noted on "rough minutes" of clerk.—Brownell v. Yolo County Superior Court, 157 Cal. 703, 109 Pac. 91.

9. Other matters.—If a complaint to quiet title, filed by heirs at law and as grantees of the remaining heir at law, sets up a void decree of partial distribution, made upon petition of the administrator, as being one of the sources of defendant's claim of title to the property in question, and alleges that the plaintiffs were not cognizant of the proceedings for partial distribution, and never consented, agreed to, or approved of the object thereof, and there is nothing whatever to indicate that the plaintiffs actually took any land under said decree, or derived any advantage or benefit thereunder, the question as to whether they are estopped, by taking thereunder, from questioning the validity of such decree is not presented upon a demurrer to the complaint.—Alcorn v. Brandeman, 145 Cal. 62, 65, 78 Pac. 343. There is not an "omission to provide" for children in a will where the children are mentioned by the testator; and where the testator has parted with land devised to the issue of a deceased child, and the grand-children petition for a partial distribution of other estate, claiming as pretermitted heirs, parol evidence is not admissible to show that the land devised to them was not owned by the testator at the time of making the will, or at the time of his death, and that the grand-children had never received any part of the estate of the testator by way of advancement.—Estate of Callaghan, 119 Cal. 571, 573, 39 L. R. A. 689, 51 Pac. 860. Whether the widow is entitled to one-half the community property, and to take under the will also, may be determined upon an application for partial distribution; although, if the judge sees fit, he may defer the distribution and direct suit to be brought to determine the extent of her interest.—Estate of Painter, 115 Cal. 635, 640, 47 Pac. 700. A decree of partial distribution of the estate of a decedent, adjudging that the petitioner has succeeded to all the right, title, and interest of the widow, the sole devisee of deceased, does not confer upon him any greater title than she possesses in law, and makes him only a tenant in common with children of the decedent omitted from the will, though the whole land was devised to the widow. Under such a decree he succeeds only to all of the interests of the devisee in the land described, and, any further than that, the decree is a nullity, so far as the interests of the omitted children are concerned.—Estate of Grider,

81 Cal. 571, 573, 577, 22 Pac. 908. If the successor in interest of one
of the distributees enters into possession of land under a decree of
partial distribution, claiming title to the whole of the land, he can not,
by limitation or adverse possession, as against those who are legally
entitled to claim an interest in the land as tenants in common, acquire
title by limitation or adverse possession, so long as the administration
of the estate remains unclosed, and although he pays taxes on the
property.—Estate of Grider, 81 Cal. 571, 578, 22 Pac. 908. The executrix of an estate can not urge that legatees petitioning for a partial
distribution have forfeited their rights to their legacies because of an
alleged violation of a provision in the will, that, if any one named
therein should contest the same, he or she should take nothing under
it, where that question concerns only the rights of the residuary
devisees. This is a question in which the executrix, as such, has no
interest. She can not litigate the claims of one set of legatees against
the others at the expense of the estate.—Estate of Murphy, 145 Cal.
464, 467, 78 Pac. 960. When any person appears in a proceeding for
partial distribution of the estate of a decedent, claiming to be interested
in the estate as the grantee of an heir, devisee, or legatee, and claiming the property sought to be distributed as his own, and objects to
such distribution being made to his grantor on these grounds, the
distribution should be denied or suspended until the rights of the contestant may be determined on final distribution, or in some other appropriate proceeding.—Griffin v. Foley, 24 Nev. 291, 52 Pac. 1134, 53
Pac. 8. There may be circumstances under which a person would be
estopped from maintaining a suit for partial distribution of an estate,
though he is entitled to it, where its effect would be to injure other
heirs.—Estate of Glenn, 153 Cal. 77, 94 Pac. 230, 232. A chose in
action which the executors were endeavoring to recover should not be
distributed on a partition for partial distribution in opposition to the
wishes of certain of the parties in interest and the executors.—Estate
of Colton, 164 Cal. 1, 127 Pac. 643. On partial distribution on application of heirs, under sections 1658 et seq., of the California Code Civ.
Proc., the court, before final settlement, must retain sufficient assets
to pay debts and past and prospective administration expenses, and
can not distribute the entire estate on the theory that the petitioner's
bonds will protect creditors.—In re Gird's Estate, 157 Cal. 534, 137
Am. St. Rep. 131, 108 Pac. 499. If a debt is amply secured by mortgage,
however, it may be disregarded, land mortgaged remaining subject to
mortgage after distribution under section 1661, Cal. Code Civ. Proc.—
In re Gird's Estate, 157 Cal. 534, 137 Am. St. Rep. 131, 108 Pac. 499.
An agreement between all of the heirs of an estate providing for the
distribution to one of them of a sum of money in excess of his share
"upon the distribution of the estate," may be enforced by him on a
proceeding had for a partial distribution, if the estate has ample funds
with which to pay such sum over and above all contingent or possible
demands upon its moneys.—Estate of Broome, 162 Cal. 258, 122 Pac.

470. Where a promissory note is, among other assets of the estate of a deceased person, distributed to the legatees jointly, it is not essential that there be a partition of their interests before such legatees proceed to enforce payment of the note.—Moore v. Lauff, 30 Cal. App. 452, 158 Pac. 557. Where the vendor of land contracted to be sold to a purchaser, deraigns title under a decree of partial distribution of the estate of her deceased husband, which, in effect, adjudged the sufficiency of her title under the will, and included therein the actual distribution of her title, acquired by purchase and assignment of the interests of all the other heirs and legatees under the will, the title so deraigned is complete, and the purchaser is not justified in rejecting it on the ground that the interest of minors and incompetent persons acquired through their guardians were not legally acquired. The title so decreed by a court of competent jurisdiction is not collaterally assailable.—French v. Phelps, 20 Cal. App. 101, 128 Pac. 772.

10. Embezzlement by executor.—Where the legatee became of age shortly after the filing of the petition for partial distribution, and participated in the proceedings for such partial distribution, she thereby ratified the acts of her attorney who signed the petition and represented her in filing and presenting it, and the decree of partial distribution was properly admitted in evidence upon the prosecution of the executor for embezzlement of legacy, notwithstanding the signing and presenting by the minor legatee's attorney.—People v. Dates, 29 Cal. App. 260, 265, 155 Pac. 112. Since the decree of partial distribution did not determine the legatee's title to her legacy, but only her right to its present possession on a fixed date, the defendant in a prosecution for embezzling such legacy was bound to comply with the decree, and his right of appeal from the order as a devisee himself was not affected any more than it would be in the case of any other judgment or order for the present payment of money, from which the party aggrieved must appeal at once or comply with the judgment or order.— People v. Dates, 29 Cal. App. 260, 265, 155 Pac. 112.

11. Appeal.

(1) In general.—An appeal may be taken from an order of partial distribution of an estate of a deceased person, upon the petition of legatees; and the executors may take such appeal.—Estate of Mitchell, 121 Cal. 391, 393, 53 Pac. 810; Estate of Kelly, 63 Cal. 106, 107. An executrix may appeal from such an order, where she presents for review an issue of law as to the sufficiency of the petition to show that there were sufficient assets to pay the legacies without loss to the creditors. It is a sound proposition that administrators, general or special, like receivers and other trustees, or custodians of funds for designated purposes, are not ordinarily affected by orders in reference to their disposition, and therefore will not be heard on appeal from such orders. But, wherever an order or decree involves a construction of the proper exercise of the duties of the officer, whenever it presents

a question as to the right or power of the trustee to comply with it, whenever obedience to it might subject him to liability, the rule does not operate. Even where the order is one merely for the payment of funds, if any of these questions arise under it, and personal liability may attach, the right of the officer to appeal is recognized and upheld. —Estate of Murphy, 145 Cal. 464, 467, 78 Pac. 960. Persons who claim as devisees under decedent's will, and who appear in that capacity to contest a petition for partial distribution, are "adverse parties," within the meaning of the statute that declares that a draft of the bill of exceptions, or a copy thereof, must, within ten days after notice of the entry of judgment, be served upon the adverse party. So if the devisees move to strike such petition from the files, they are entitled to service of a draft of the bill of exceptions, as they are the only parties to the record having a substantial interest in opposing the distribution sought; and the effect of the failure so to serve them will be that the appellate court can not, for any purpose, consider the bill of exceptions on appeal.—Estate of Young, 149 Cal. 173, 85 Pac. 145, 146. If an order for partial distribution, vacating a previous order denying a petition therefor, is reversed on appeal from the entire order, the order denying the petition is left in full force and effect.—Estate of Mitchell, 126 Cal. 248, 251, 58 Pac. 549. A court has no authority to make an order granting a petition for partial distribution, without having vacated a prior order denying it, though such prior order was made without prejudice to the making of another application; such reservation not being necessary to preserve the right to file a new petition.—Estate of Mitchell, 126 Cal. 248, 251, 58 Pac. 549. In determining whether a partial distribution can be safely made, the probate judge should proceed with great caution, and very much must be left to his discretion. If he decides that the condition of the estate is such that distribution can not be safely made, his conclusion can not well be reversed.— Estate of Painter, 115 Cal. 635, 640, 47 Pac. 700. A decree of partial distribution will not be disturbed upon appeal, where it appears that the estate was but little indebted, and that the property could be distributed without loss to the creditors of the estate, especially where it appears that the appellants are not such creditors.—Estate of Dutard, 147 Cal. 253, 256, 258, 81 Pac. 519. If an executor's appeal from an order directing a partial distribution is frivolous, the court may make him respond in damages for the delay which his appeal has occasioned.— Estate of Straus, 144 Cal. 553, 77 Pac. 1122, 1124. Where no trust or invalidity appears upon the face of the will, it must be given effect in the probate court according to its terms.—In re Sharp, 17 Cal. App. 634, 120 Pac. 1079. There is no legal inconsistency in the assertion of rights to an estate on final distribution proceedings on the theory of the intestacy of the deceased, and the assertion at the same time of rights thereto under the will by the prosecution of an appeal from an order made upon partial distribution proceedings denying the latter rights.— Estate of Spreckels, 165 Cal. 597, 133 Pac. 289. A judge in probate does not show undue bias by protesting against an appeal by an executor from a decree of partial distribution, when the only effect of the appeal can be to delay the enjoyment by deserving parties of the proposed distribution, and the judge has in mind the many precedents questioning whether an executor ought to appeal in such a connection, since his official rights are not involved and no liability can attach to him in complying with the decree.—Estate of Friedman, 171 Cal. 431, 441, 153 Pac. 918.

(2) Right of appeal.—Where contest had arisen over a will, and the distributees thereunder entered into a written agreement providing for distribution of the estate, any one interested in the estate would have the right of appeal from an order of partial distribution in violation of the written agreement.—In re Colton's Estate, 164 Cal. 1, 126 Pac. 643. There can be no doubt of the right of an executor to appeal from any order which is embarrassing to the due administration of the estate.— In re Colton's Estate, 164 Cal. 1, 127 Pac. 643.

(3) Waiver.—Where, pending an appeal from an order denying partial distribution of an estate to the trustees, under a will, as such, on the ground of the invalidity of the trust, they, in their individual capacities as devisees and legatees, make application for final distribution of the estate to themselves on the theory of the intestacy of the deceased and contest the rights of certain heirs to participate in such distribution by reason of alleged advancements, such action on their part does not constitute an election to claim as heirs, nor does it constitute a waiver of the prosecution of their appeal, which deprives the court of jurisdiction upon the reversal of the order to enter into the decree of partial distribution.—Estate of Spreckels, 165 Cal. 597, 133 Pac. 289.

(4) Papers necessary.—An appeal by the administrator with the will annexed from portions of a decree of partial distribution is in effect an appeal from a judgment and may be taken on the judgment-roll alone, consisting of the petitions of the parties, the oppositions thereto, the findings thereon, and the decree based upon those findings. No bill of exceptions or other certification as provided by law and by rule XXIX of the supreme court is necessary. The clerk's certificate to the correctness of the transcript is sufficient.—Estate of Broome, 162 Cal. 258, 122 Pac. 470.

(5) Effect of.—Appeals from an order denying a petition for partial distribution suspend all power of the superior court to distribute the estate during their pendency.—Estate of Spreckels, 165 Cal. 597, 133 Pac. 289.

(6) Harmless error.—In a controversy arising in a proceeding for the partial distribution of an estate, error in admitting in evidence a so-called rough draft of a will which was found in the same envelope with the will that was offered for probate, and in admitting some oral evidence in connection therewith, is harmless where the court can,

upon the record, determine the proper interpretation of the will without reference to the rough draft of it.—In re Seay's Estate, Marsh v. Seay (Cal.), 181 Pac. 58, 59.

(7) Objections not raised below.—Where persons claiming to be heirs of a deceased person presented a petition for partial distribution to them as such, and an answer thereto was filed by the executor and by the devisee and legatee under the will, taking issue upon their alleged heirship, and a trial was had of such issue, and findings made thereupon against the claim of heirship, neither party will be allowed to object upon appeal for the first time, that no issue existed to be tried as to heirship, and that the matter must rest upon the terms of the will.—Estate of Campbell, 12 Cal. App. 707, 108 Pac. 669, 676.

(8) Decision.—Upon appeal from an order denying partial distribution of an estate in remainder after the expiration of a life estate in the widow of the testator, on the alleged ground that the remainder is contingent, the decision of the question whether the remainder is vested or contingent must rest on the intention of the testator, which must be gathered from an interpretation of the language of his last will and testament viewed in the light of established and accepted canons of construction.—In re De Vries, 17 Cal. App. 184, 119 Pac. 109. While the court, by reason of the pendency of an appeal from an order denying partial distribution, might not make a decree of final distribution until the appeal is disposed of, it is not without power to settle, upon initiative of all the parties on petition for final distribution and in advance and in anticpation of an ultimate decree therefor, any questions affecting the rights of the estate.—Estate of Spreckels, 165 Cal. 597, 133 Pac. 289. The decision on appeal from the decree of partial distribution is binding on all the parties in the matter of the construction to be given to the will. The court of last resort having spoken in the matter of the interpretation of the will, the decree which the lower court was bound to enter under that construction must control rather than the language of the will.—Estate of Carothers, Waldron v. Witherspoon, 168 Cal. 691, 144 Pac. 957.

(9) Law of the case.—Where on appeal from a decree of partial distribution, the court interprets the will, the interpretation becomes the "law of the case" on appeal from a subsequent decree of final distribution, notwithstanding any intervening development of new facts and circumstances.—Estate of Carothers, Waldron v. Witherspoon, 168 Cal. 691, 144 Pac. 957. Where a motion to dismiss the appeal of an executor and some of the legatees from that portion of a "judgment," rendered in a proceeding had under this and the two following sections, based on the ground that an appeal does not lie from a part thereof, is denied upon consideration of exhaustive briefs of counsel, the determination will be deemed the law of the case on the submission of the question on its merit.—Estate of Klein, 35 Mont. 185, 202, 88 Pac. 798. (Citing Code Civ. Proc., § 2840.) The interpretation of the will on the

appeal from the decree was a determination of a question of law. All such interpretations must be decisions of the law whether the court construes the will with or without resort to extrinsic facts.— Estate of Carothers, Waldron v. Witherspoon, 168 Cal. 691, 144 Pac. 957.

(10) Affirmance.—Where a decree of partial distribution was made according to the terms of a will, and was contested upon petition of the heirs on the alleged ground that the will was void as imposing a secret invalid trust for the heirs, who have appealed from such decree, it is held that the appellants have mistaken their remedy, which is not in the probate court, by opposition to the bequest under the will, but solely by an independent action in equity to enforce the trust, if it exists, and that the decree of partial distribution appealed from must be affirmed.—In re Sharp, 17 Cal. App. 634, 120 Pac. 1079. Where an independent suit in equity was resorted to and the decree of the court of equity adjudging the non-existence of any secret or invalid trust which could be enforced in favor of the heirs has been affirmed upon appeal, such affirmance is res judicata as to the very matter it was sought to litigate in this proceeding, and it is manifest that a reversal of the decree in partition appealed from could be of no avail to the appellants.—In re Sharp, 17 Cal. App. 634, 120 Pac. 1079.

11. Reversal.—It is held that the appellant, having a vested right in real property described in remainder, is entitled to a partial distribution of his estate therein, and an order refusing the same must be reversed.—In re De Vries, 17 Cal. App. 184, 119 Pac. 109.

CHAPTER II.

PROCEEDINGS TO DETERMINE HEIRSHIP.   DISTRIBUTION ON FINAL SETTLEMENT.

ESTABLISHMENT OF HEIRSHIP, RIGHTS AND LIABILITIES OF HEIRS, AND DISTRIBUTION.

I. Proceedings to Determine Heirship.

§ 728.   Proceedings to determine heirship.

In all estates now being administered, or that may hereafter be administered, any person claiming to be heir to
the deceased, or entitled to distribution in whole or in any
part of such estate, may, at any time after the expiration
of one year from the issuing of letters testamentary or
of administration upon such estate, file a petition in the
matter of such estate, praying the court to ascertain and
declare the rights of all persons to said estate and all
interests therein, and to whom distribution thereof should
be made.

COURT TO MAKE ORDER DIRECTING NOTICE.—Upon the
filing of such petition, the court shall make an order directing service of notice to all persons interested in said
estate to appear and show cause, on a day to be therein
named, not less than sixty days nor over four months
from the date of the making of such order, in which
notice shall be set forth the name of the deceased, the
name of the executor or administrator of said estate, the
names of all persons who may have appeared claiming
any interest in said estate in the course of the administration of the same, up to the time of the making of said

order, and such other persons as the court may direct, and also a

DESCRIPTION of the real estate whereof said deceased died seised or possessed, so far as known, described with certainty to a common intent, and requiring all said persons and all persons named or not named having or claiming any interest in the estate of said deceased, at the time and place in said order specified, to appear and exhibit, as hereinafter provided, their respective claims of heirship, ownership, or interest in said estate, to said court, which notice shall be served in the same manner as a summons in a civil action, upon proof of which service, by affidavit or otherwise, to the satisfaction of the court, the court shall thereupon acquire jurisdiction to ascertain and determine the heirship, ownership and interest of all parties in and to the property of said deceased, and such determination shall be final and conclusive in the administration of said estate, and the title and ownership of said property.

DECREE OF SERVICE. APPEARANCE.—The court shall enter an order or decree establishing proof of the service of such notice. All persons appearing within the time limited as aforesaid, shall file their written appearance in person or through their authorized attorney, such attorney filing at the same time written evidence of his authority to so appear, entry of which appearance shall be made in the minutes of the court and in the register of proceedings of said estate. And the court shall, after the expiration of the time limited for appearing as aforesaid, enter an order adjudging the default of all persons for not appearing as aforesaid, who shall not have appeared as aforesaid.

COMPLAINT SETTING FORTH HEIRSHIP.—At any time within twenty days after the date of the order or decree of the court establishing proof of the service of such notice, any of such persons so appearing may file his complaint in the matter of the estate, setting forth the facts constituting his claim of heirship, ownership, or interest in said estate, with such reasonable particularity as the court may require, and serve a copy of the same upon each of the parties or attorneys who shall have entered their written appearance as aforesaid, if such parties or such attorneys reside within the county; and in case any of them do not reside within the county, then service of such copy of said complaint shall be made upon the clerk of said court for them, and the clerk shall forthwith mail the same to the address of such party or attorney as may have left with said clerk his post-office address.

TIME TO PLEAD TO COMPLAINT OF HEIRSHIP.—Such parties are allowed twenty days after the service of the complaint, as aforesaid, within which to plead thereto, and thereafter such proceedings shall be had upon such complaint as in this code provided in case of an ordinary civil action; and the issues of law and of fact arising in the proceeding shall be disposed of in like manner as issues of law and fact are herein provided to be disposed of in civil actions, with a like right to a motion for a new trial and appeal to the supreme court; and the provisions in this code contained regulating the mode of procedure for the trial of civil actions, the motion for a new trial of civil actions, statements on motion for a new trial, bills of exception, and statements on appeal, as also in regard to undertakings on appeal, and the mode of taking and perfecting appeals, and the time within which such appeals shall be taken, shall be applicable thereto; provided, however, that all

APPEALS herein must be taken within sixty days from the date of the entry of the judgment or the order complained of.

PLAINTIFF, PARTY FILING COMPLAINT.—The party filing the petition as aforesaid, if he file a complaint, and if not, the party first filing such complaint, shall, in all subsequent proceedings, be treated as the plaintiff therein, and all other parties so appearing shall be treated as the defendants in said proceedings, and all such defendants shall set forth in their respective answers the facts constituting their claim of heirship, ownership, or interest in said estate, with such particularity as the court may require, and serve a copy thereof on the plaintiff. Evidence in support of all issues may be taken orally or.by deposition, in the same manner as provided in civil actions.

NOTICE of the taking of such depositions shall be served only upon the parties, or the attorneys of the parties so appearing in said proceeding. The court shall enter a default of all persons failing to appear, or plead, or prosecute, or defend their rights as aforesaid; and upon the trial of the issues arising upon the pleadings in such proceeding, the court shall determine the heirship to said deceased, the ownership of his estate, and the interest of each respective claimant thereto or therein, and persons entitled to distribution thereof, and the final determination of the court thereupon shall be final and conclusive in the distribution of said estate, and in regard to the title to all the property of the estate of said deceased. The cost of the proceedings under this section shall be apportioned in the discretion of the court.

ATTORNEY FOR MINOR.—In any proceeding under this section, the court may appoint an attorney for any minor mentioned in said proceedings not having a guardian. Nothing in this section contained shall be construed to exclude the right upon final distribution of any estate to contest the question of heirship, title, or interest in the estate so distributed, where the same shall not have been determined under the provisions of this section; but where such questions shall have been litigated, under the provisions of this section, the determination thereof as herein provided shall be conclusive in the distribution of said estate.--*Kerr's Cyc. Code Civ. Proc.*, § 1664.

ANALOGOUS AND IDENTICAL STATUTES.

No identical statute found.

Arizona— Revised Statutes of 1913, paragraph 1032.

Colorado--Mills's Statutes of 1912, section 7851; as amended by Laws of 1915, chapter 173, page 487 (where estate is of small value); Laws of 1917, chapter 154, page 550 (issue of heirship in will contest, how tried).

Idaho—Compiled Statutes of 1919, section 7925.

Montana—Revised Codes of 1907, sections 7670, 7671; as amended by Laws of 1913, chapter 54, page 104.

North Dakota—Compiled Laws of 1913, sections 8675, 8676, 8679.

Oklahoma—Revised Laws of 1910, section 6488.

Oregon—Laws of 1913, chapter 331, page 646.

South Dakota—Laws of 1913, chapter 231, page 313 (providing for the determination of heirship where a patent has been issued to the heirs of a deceased person by the government of the United States).

Utah—Compiled Laws of 1907, sections 3980, 3981.

Wyoming—Compiled Statutes of 1910, sections 5704-5707.

§ 729. Form. Petition for ascertainment of rights as heirs.

[Title of court.]

[Title of estate.]   {No. ——.1 Dept. No. ——.
                  [Title of form.]

To the Honorable the ——[2] Court of the County[3] of ——, State of ——.

Your petitioner respectfully represents:

That he[4] is a son[5] of ——, deceased, is one of his heirs at law,[6] and is interested in the estate left by him;

That more than one year has expired since letters of administration[7] were issued upon the estate of said ——, deceased;

That various persons claim an interest in the estate of said deceased; and that their rights have not been ascertained or determined by the judgment, order, or decree of any court of competent jurisdiction.

Wherefore your petitioner prays that an order be made and entered herein, as provided by law, requiring all persons interested in said estate to appear and exhibit, in the manner provided by law, their respective claims of heirship, ownership, or interest in said estate, to said court, on or before a day to be specified in said order;[8] and that this court ascertain and declare the rights of all persons to said estate and all interests therein, and to whom distribution thereof should be made.

—, Petitioner.

—, Attorney for Petitioner.

Explanatory notes.—[1] Give file number. [2] Title of court. [3] Or, City and County. [4] Or, she. [5] Or other relative. [6] Or, is a devisee or legatee under the last will and testament of —, deceased. [7] Or, letters testamentary. [8] Not less than sixty days nor over four months from the date of the making of such order, or otherwise as prescribed by statute.

§ 730. Form. Notice upon filing of petition to ascertain rights as heirs.

[Title of court.]

[Title of estate.]   { No. —.[1] Dept. No. —.
 [Title of form.]

To —, the Administrator[2] of the Estate of —, Deceased, and to — and —,[3] and — and —,[4] — and —,[5] and — and —.[6]

You and each of you are hereby notified:

That on the — day of —, 19—, —, one of the heirs at law of —, deceased, filed his petition in this court praying that the rights of all persons interested in the estate of said —, deceased, be ascertained and declared by this court, and that it be determined to whom distribution should be made;

That, so far as known, the following is a description of the real estate whereof said deceased died seised or possessed, to wit: —;[7]

That the said — and —[8] are the only persons who appeared and claimed any interest in said estate, in the course of the administration of the same, up to the time of the making of said order;

That you, and all other persons not named, who have

or claim an interest in said estate, are cited to appear before this court, at the court-room thereof,[9] in the said county [10] of ——, state of ——, on the —— day of ——, 19—, at the hour of —— o'clock in the forenoon [11] of said day; and exhibit, in the manner provided by law, your respective claims of heirship, ownership, or interest in said estate, and show cause why such petition should not be granted.

[Seal]   ——, Clerk of the —— Court.

                      By ——, Deputy Clerk.

Explanatory notes.—1 Give file number. 2 Or, executor of the last will and testament of ——, according to the fact. 3 Heirs at law of said deceased. 4 Devisees and legatees named in will of said deceased. 5 Names of persons who have appeared and claimed an interest in said estate. 6 Such other persons as the court may direct to be notified. 7 Insert description. 8 Names of persons who have appeared, claiming an interest. 9 Give location of court-room. 10 Or, city and county. 11 Or, afternoon.

§ 731. Form. Order upon filing of petition to ascertain rights as heirs.

[Title of court.]

[Title of estate.]   { No. ——.1   Dept. No. ——.
                                   {   [Title of form.]

It appearing to this court that ——, one of the heirs at law of ——, deceased, has filed herein his petition praying that the rights of all persons interested in the estate of said ——, deceased, be ascertained and declared by this court, and that it be determined to whom distribution thereof should be made,—

It is ordered, That the clerk of this court cause notice to be served upon all persons, named or not named, who have or claim any interest in said estate, to appear before this court, at the court-room thereof, at ——,[2] in the said county [3] of ——, state of ——, on the —— day of ——, 19—, at the hour of —— o'clock in the forenoon [4] of said day, and exhibit, in the manner provided by law, their respective claims of heirship, ownership, or interest in said estate, and show cause why said petition should not be granted.

Dated ——, 19—. ——, Judge of the —— Court.

Explanatory notes.—1 Give file number. 2 Give location of court-room. 3 Or, city and county. 4 Or, afternoon, as the case may be.

§ 732. Form. Order establishing service of notice to determine heirship.

[Title of court.]

[Title of estate.] { No. ——.1 Dept. No. ——.
[Title of form.]

Upon motion of ——, the petitioner herein, by ——, his attorney, and due proof of service having been made, it is adjudged and decreed by the court that due service of the notice and order to show cause, issued upon the filing of the petition of —— for the ascertainment of the rights of the persons interested in said estate as to their heirship has been made as required by law and by the order of the court, upon the persons named in the said order.

Dated ——, 19—. ——, Judge of the —— Court.

Explanatory note.—1 Give file number.

§ 733. Form. Attorney's authority to appear in matters of heirship.

[Title of court.]

[Title of estate.] { No. ——.1 Dept. No. ——.
[Title of form.]

Authority is hereby given to ——, an attorney at law, of the county 2 of ——, state of ——, to appear for and to represent me in all matters of the above-entitled estate in which I am interested, and he is hereby authorized and empowered to do all things necessary to protect my interests in said estate, especially in the matter of determining my rights therein, and of the making of distribution thereof. . ——

ACKNOWLEDGMENT.

State of ——,   ⎫
  County [3] of ——, ⎬ss.

On this —— day of ——, 19—, before me, ——,[4] personally appeared ——,[5] known to me to be the person whose name is subscribed to the foregoing instrument, and who acknowledged to me that he executed the same for the uses and purposes therein mentioned.

——, Notary Public, etc.[6]

Explanatory notes.—[1] Give file number.   [2], [3] Or, city and county. [4] Name and official character of officer.   [5] Name of person.   [6] Or other officer taking the oath.

§ 734. Form. Complaint on claim of heirship.

[Title of court.]

[Title of matter.][1]   ⎧ No. ——.[2]   Dept. No. ——.
                            ⎩   [Title of form.]

The plaintiff complains and alleges:

1. That he has entered his written appearance in the above-entitled matter;

2. That —— [3] days have not elapsed since the date of the order or decree of this court, in the above-entitled matter, establishing proof of service of notice as required by law;

3. That he is —— [4] of said decedent, and one of his heirs at law;

4. That the other heirs at law of said ——, deceased, are ——;[5]

5. That said estate consists of both community property and separate property;

6. That the community property of said estate is particularly described as follows, to wit: ——;[6]

7. That the separate property of the said deceased is particularly described as follows, to wit:——;[7]

8. That plaintiff is entitled to —— [8] of said community property, and is entitled to —— [9] of said separate property.

Wherefore plaintiff prays judgment that he be so entitled to share in said property and estate.

——, Attorney for Plaintiff.

Explanatory notes.—1 As, In the Matter of Ascertaining and Declaring the Rights of the Heirs, and of All Other Persons Who Have or Claim any Interest in the Estate of ——, Deceased, and of Determining to Whom Distribution thereof should be Made. 2 Give file number. 3 Twenty days, or other time prescribed by statute. 4 State relationship. 5 Give names, as of widow and children. 6, 7 Give description. 8, 9 State fractional part of estate to which claim is made.

§ 735. Form. Answer to complaint on claim of heirship.

[Title of court.]

[Title of estate.]1

{ No. ——.2 Dept. No. ——.
[Title of form.]

The defendant answering the complaint herein, admits, alleges, and denies 3 as follows:

1. Admits the facts alleged in the second, fifth, sixth, and seventh paragraphs of said complaint.

2. Alleges that she has entered her written appearance in the above-entitled action.

3. Alleges that she is the widow 4 of said decedent, and one of his heirs at law; and that the other heirs at law of said ——, deceased, are: ——.5

4. Alleges that she is entitled to —— 6 of said community property, and is entitled to —— 7 of said separate property.

Wherefore defendant prays that she be so entitled to share in said property and estate.

——, Attorney for Defendant.

Explanatory notes.—1 As in the complaint. 2 Give file number. 3 Denials, when necessary, should follow the statement of defendant's claims. 4 Or state other relationship. 5 Give names. 6, 7 State fractional part of estate to which claim is made.

§ 736. Form. Entry of default on petition to ascertain heirship.

[Title of court.]

[Title of estate.]　　　　　　{ No.——.1　Dept. No.——.
　　　　　　　　　　　　　　　{ 　　[Title of form.]

The following-named persons, to wit, ——,² who are alleged to have or claim some right or interest in the estate of ——, deceased, having failed to appear in the matter of the petition of —— to have the rights and interests of all persons in said estate declared, and said persons having each been duly served with notice of said petition as required by law and by the order of the court, and the time limited for such appearance having expired,—

It is ordered and adjudged by the court, That said persons so failing to appear as aforesaid, to wit, —— and ——, etc., are in default in said proceedings, and that the same be heard and determined in their absence.

Dated ——, 19—.　　——, Judge of the —— Court.

Explanatory notes.—1 Give file number.　2 Give their names.

§ 737. Form. Decree establishing heirship.

[Title of court.]

[Title of estate.]　　　　　　{ No.——.1　Dept. No.——.
　　　　　　　　　　　　　　　{ 　　[Title of form.]

Comes now ——, the petitioner herein, by ——, his attorney, and also comes ——, complainant herein, by ——, his attorney,² and come not —— and ——³ but herein make default, and each of them having been duly served with process herein, and each of them having failed to answer or to plead to the complaint of —— filed herein, the said —— and —— are each adjudged to be in default accordingly, and the issues being joined, the court proceeds to the trial thereof, and, after hearing the evidence and arguments of counsel, the court makes and renders judgment as follows, to wit:

It is ordered, adjudged, and decreed by the court, That —— died testate ⁴ on the —— day of ——, 19—, leaving surviving as his only heirs at law the persons whose names and relationship to said deceased are as follows, to wit, ——;[5] that said deceased left a will, which has been duly admitted to probate herein, and that by the terms of said will the whole of the said estate is devised and bequeathed as follows, to wit: a specific money legacy of —— dollars ($——) is bequeathed to ——; the following personal property is bequeathed to ——, to wit: ——;[6] the following described real estate is devised to ——, to wit: ——;[7] to be held, etc.;[8] and all the residue of said estate is disposed of as follows: ——;[9] and that upon the distribution of said estate the said devisees and legatees are entitled to the respective portions thereof as above set forth, and that in case the estate is not sufficient to satisfy all the said bequests and devises, the order of priority shall be as follows: ——.[10]

Dated ——, 19—. ——, Judge of the —— Court.

Explanatory notes.—[1] Give file number. [2] Insert other appearances in the same way. [3] Give the names of persons not appearing. [4] Or, intestate, as the case may be. [5] Insert names of heirs and relationship. If the deceased died intestate, proceed thus: "and that thereupon the estate of said deceased descended to his said heirs at law, and is now vested in them, subject to administration, in the following proportions, to wit: The said —— is the owner of an undivided —— [state fractional part] thereof; the said —— is the owner, etc.; and each of said persons is entitled to distribution of said estate according to their respective rights and interests herein set forth." [6] Describe it. [7] Insert description. [8] Give the conditions or limitations imposed, if any. [9] State how. [10] State order of priority.

§ 738. Final distribution of estate.

Upon the final settlement of the accounts of the executor or administrator, or at any subsequent time, upon the application of the executor or administrator, or of any heir, legatee, devisee (or his assignee, grantee, or successor in interest), the court must proceed to distribute the residue of the estate in the hands of the executor or administrator, if any, among the persons who by law are entitled thereto; and if the decedent has left a surviving child, or the issue of a deceased child, and any of them, before the close of the administration, have died while under age and not having been married, no administration on such deceased child's estate is necessary, but all the estate which such deceased child was entitled to by inheritance must, without administration, be distributed as provided in the Civil Code.

ACCOUNTS.—A statement of any receipts and disbursements of the executor or administrator, since the rendition of his final account, must be reported and filed at the time of making such distribution; and a settlement thereof, together with an estimate of the expenses of closing the estate, must be made by the court, and included in the order or decree, or the court or judge may order notice of the settlement of such supplementary account, and refer the same as in other cases of the settlement of accounts.—*Kerr's Cyc. Code Civ. Proc.*, § 1665.

ANALOGOUS AND IDENTICAL STATUTES.
No identical statute found.

Arizona—Revised Statutes of 1913, paragraph 1037.

Colorado—Mills's Statutes of 1912, section 8024.

Idaho—Compiled Statutes of 1919, section 7729.

Montana—Revised Codes of 1907, section 7673; as amended by Laws of 1913, chapter 54, page 104.

Nevada—Revised Laws of 1912, section 6072.

New Mexico—Statutes of 1915, section 1838.

North Dakota—Compiled Laws of 1913, section 8846.

Oklahoma—Revised Laws of 1910, section 6463.

Oregon—Laws of 1913, chapter 331, page 646.

South Dakota—Compiled Laws of 1913, section 5924.

Utah—Compiled Laws of 1907, section 3953.

Washington—Laws of 1917, chapter 156, pages 688, 690, sections 161, 163.

Wyoming—Compiled Statutes of 1910, section 5699.

§ 739. Decree of distribution. Contents, and conclusiveness of.

In the order or decree, the court must name the persons and the proportions or parts to which each shall be entitled, and such persons may demand, sue for, and recover their respective shares from the executor or administrator, or any person having the same in possession. Such order or decree is conclusive as to the rights of heirs, legatees, or devisees, subject only to be reversed, set aside, or modified on appeal.—*Kerr's Cyc. Code Civ. Proc.*, § 1666.

ANALOGOUS AND IDENTICAL STATUTES.
The * indicates identity.

Arizona*—Revised Statutes of 1913, paragraph 1038.

Idaho*—Compiled Statutes of 1919, section 7730.

Montana*—Revised Codes of 1907, section 7674.

Nevada—Revised Laws of 1912, section 6073.

North Dakota—Compiled Laws of 1913, section 8849.

Oklahoma*·—Revised Laws of 1910, section 6464.

South Dakota*—Compiled Laws of 1913, section 5925.

Utah—Compiled Laws of 1907, section 3954.

Washington—Laws of 1917, chapter 156, page 689, section 163.

Wyoming*—Compiled Statutes of 1910, section 5700.

§ 740. Distribution when decedent was not a resident of the state.

Upon application for distribution, after final settlement of the accounts of administration, if the decedent was a non-resident of this state, leaving a will which has been duly proved or allowed in the state of his residence, and an authenticated copy thereof has been admitted to probate in this state, or if the decedent died intestate, and an administrator has been duly appointed and qualified in the state of his residence, and it is necessary, in order that the estate, or any part thereof, may be distributed according to the will, or if the court is satisfied that it is for the best interests of the estate, that the estate in this state should be delivered to the executor or administrator in the state or place of the decedent's residence, the court may order such delivery to be made, and, if necessary, order a sale of the real estate, and a like delivery of the proceeds. The delivery, in accordance with the order of the court, is a full discharge of the executor, or administrator with the will annexed, or administrator, in this state, in relation to all·property embraced in such order, which, unless reversed on appeal, binds and concludes all parties in interest. Sales of real estate, ordered by virtue of this section, must be made in the same manner as other sales of real estate of decedents by order of the court.—*Kerr's Cyc. Code Civ. Proc.*, § 1667.

ANALOGOUS AND IDENTICAL STATUTES.

No identical statute found.

Arizona—Revised Statutes of 1913, paragraph 1039.

Idaho—Compiled Statutes of 1919, section 7731.

Kansas—General Statutes of 1915, section 4661 (administration on estate of non-resident).

Montana—Revised Codes of 1907, section 7675.

North Dakota—Compiled Laws of 1913, section 8861.

Oklahoma—Revised Laws of 1910, section 6465.

South Dakota—Compiled Laws of 1913, section 5926.

Utah—Compiled Laws of 1907, section 3968.

§ 741. Notice must precede decree for distribution.

The order or decree may be made on the petition of the executor, administrator, or of any person interested in the estate. When such petition is filed the clerk of the court must set the petition for hearing by the court, and give notice thereof by causing notices to be posted in at least three public places in the county, setting forth the name of the estate, the executor or administrator, and the time appointed for the hearing of the petition. If, upon the hearing of the petition, the court, or a judge thereof, deems the notice insufficient from any cause, he may order such further notice to be given as may seem to him proper. At the time fixed for the hearing, or to which the hearing may be postponed, any person interested in the estate may appear and contest the petition by filing written objections thereto. If the partition is applied for, as provided in this chapter, the decree of distribution does not devest the court of jurisdiction to order partition, unless the estate is finally closed.— *Kerr's Cyc. Code Civ. Proc.*, § 1668.

ANALOGOUS AND IDENTICAL STATUTES.
No identical statute found.
Arizona—Revised Statutes of 1913, paragraph 1040.
Idaho—Compiled Statutes of 1919, section 7732.
Montana—Revised Codes of 1907, section 7676.
New Mexico—Statutes of 1915, section 1839.
Oklahoma—Revised Laws of 1910, section 6466.
South Dakota—Compiled Laws of 1913, section 5927.
Washington—Laws of 1917, chapter 156, page 689, section 162.
Wyoming—Compiled Statutes of 1910, section 5705; as amended and re-enacted by Laws of 1915, chapter 75, page 73.

§ 742. Form. Petition for distribution of estate.

[Title of court.]

[Title of estate.]   { No. ——.1 Dept. No. ——.
                        {   [Title of form.]

To the Honorable the ——[2] Court of the County[3] of ——, State of ——.

The petition of ——, administrator[4] of the estate of ——, deceased, respectfully shows:

That your petitioner was appointed such administrator[5] by order of this court on the —— day of ——, 19—, and on the —— day of ——, 19—, he duly qualified as such administrator,[6] and thereupon entered upon the administration of the estate of said deceased, and has ever since continued to administer said estate;

That on the —— day of ——, 19—, your petitioner duly made and returned to this court a true inventory and appraisement of all the estate of said deceased which has come to his possession or knowledge;

That on the —— day of ——, 19—, your petitioner duly published notice to creditors to present their claims against the said deceased in the manner and within the period limited by law;

That more than —— has elapsed since the appointment of your petitioner as such administrator,[7] and more than —— months have expired since the first publication of said notice to creditors;

That on the —— day of ——, 19—, your petitioner filed his accounts as such administrator,[8] which said accounts, after due hearing and examination, were finally settled;

That all the debts of said deceased and of said estate, and all the expenses of the administration thereof incurred, and all taxes that have attached to or accrued against the said estate, have been paid and discharged, and that said estate is now in a condition to be closed;

That the —— [9] said estate is —— [10] property;

That the said deceased died intestate,[11] in the state of ——, county [12] of ——, on the —— day of ——, 19—, leaving surviving him the following named heirs,[13] who are entitled to distribution of the entire residue of said estate.

Wherefore your petitioner prays that the administration of said estate may be brought to a close; that he may be discharged from his trust as such administrator;[14] that, after due notice is given and proceedings had, the estate remaining in the hands of your petitioner as aforesaid may be distributed to the said parties entitled thereto as aforesaid, to wit: ——; and that such other or further order may be made as is meet in the premises.

Dated ——, 19—. ——, Petitioner.

Explanatory notes.—1 Give file number. 2 Title of court. 3 Or, City and County. 4-8 Or, executor. 9 Whole of, or part thereof, designating it. 10 Community or separate property, according to the fact. 11 Or, testate. 12 Or, city and county. 13 Give names of heirs. In case of will, after giving names of heirs, and before "who are entitled," etc., insert: "that by will which was duly admitted to probate herein on the —— day of ——, 19—, said decedent devised and bequeathed his whole estate, in the proportions and manner in said will specified, to the following named devisees and legatees: ——." 14 Or, executor.

§ 743. Form. Memorandum, by clerk, fixing time for hearing petition for final distribution.

[Title of court.]

[Title of estate.] { No. ——.1 Dept. No. ——.
                     [Title of form.]

——, the administrator [2] of the estate [3] of ——, deceased, having this day filed a petition praying for a decree of distribution of the residue of said estate to the persons entitled thereto,—

Now, I, ——, clerk of said —— court, do hereby fix and appoint ——,⁴ the —— day of ——, 19—, at —— o'clock, a. m., and the court-room of said court, at the court-house in the county of ——, as the time and place for the hearing upon said petition.

Dated ——, 19—. ——, Clerk of the —— Court.

By ——, Deputy Clerk.

Explanatory notes.—1 Give file number. 2 Or, executor, or heir, etc. 3 Or, last will. 4 Give day of week.

§ 744. Form. Notice of hearing of petition for final distribution. [Title of court.]

[Title of estate.]

{ No. ——.1 Dept. No. ——.
{ [Title of form.]

Notice is hereby given: That ——, the administrator ² of the estate of ——, deceased, has presented to and filed in said court his petition for distribution to the parties entitled thereto, of all of the residue of said estate, and that ——,³ the —— day of ——, 19—, at —— o'clock in the forenoon ⁴ of said day, at the court-room of said court,⁵ in said county,⁶ have been fixed and appointed by the court and clerk thereof as the time and place for the hearing of said petition, when and where any person interested in said estate may appear and file his exceptions, in writing, to the said petition and contest the same.

Notice is further given: That ⁷ said estate is ready for distribution, and on the granting of said petition distribution of said estate will be immediately had.

Dated at —— this —— day of ——, 19—.

——, Clerk of the —— Court.

By ——, Deputy Clerk.

Explanatory notes.—1 Give file number. 2 Or, executor, or heir, etc. 3 Day of week. 4 Or, afternoon. 5 Designate location of court-room. 6 Or, city and county. 7 If application is made by any one except the administrator or executor, insert the name and capacity of such representative.

§ 745.   Form.   Affidavit of posting notice of hearing of petition for final distribution.

[Title of court.]

[Title of estate.] { No. ——.1   Dept. No. ——.
{ [Title of form.]

State of ——, }
County 2 of ——, } ss.

——, deputy county clerk of said county,3 being duly sworn, says: That on the —— day of ——, 19—, he posted correct and true copies of the within notice in three of the most public places in said county,4 to wit, one of said copies at the place at which the court is held,5 one at ——,6 and one at ——,7 in said county.8   ——

Subscribed and sworn to before me this —— day of ——, 19—.   ——, County Clerk.9

Explanatory notes.—1 Give file number.   2-4 Or, City and County. 5 Designate it.   6, 7 As, at the city hall, sheriff's office, land-office, or the United States post-office, designating its location.   8 Or, city and county. 9 Or other official designation.

§ 746.   Form.   Decree of distribution.

[Title of court.]

[Title of estate.] { No. ——.1   Dept. No. ——.
{ [Title of form.]

Now comes ——, the administrator 2 of said estate, by ——, his attorney, and proves to the satisfaction of the court that his petition for distribution herein was filed on the —— day of ——, 19—; that on the same day the clerk of this court appointed the —— day of ——, 19—, for the hearing thereof; and that due and legal notice of the time and place of said hearing has been given as required by law and by the order of the court;3 and said petition being now presented to the court, and no person appearing to contest or object to the same,4 the court, after hearing the evidence, being satisfied that all taxes upon the property of the estate (and any inheritance tax which has become due and payable) have been fully paid, orders distribution of said estate as follows:

It is ordered, adjudged, and decreed by the court, That said deceased died intestate,[5] and left surviving, as his only heirs at law, those certain persons whose names and relationship to said deceased are as follows, to wit:

Names.	Relationship.	Residences.
——	——	——
——	——	——

And that the residue of the estate of said deceased, as hereinafter described, and all other property of said estate, whether described herein or not, be distributed according to law,[6] as follows, to wit: To ——;[7] to ——;[8] and the residue as follows, to —— and —— and —— each a —— [9] part, etc.

The residue so distributed to said last-named persons, so far as the same is known, is described as follows, to wit: ——.[10]

Dated ——, 19—.   ——, Judge of the —— Court.

Explanatory notes.—[1] Give file number. [2] Or, executor. [3] If the matter has been continued, say, "and the hearing having been regularly postponed to the present time." [4] Or, —— having appeared by ——, his attorney, and filed and presented objections and exceptions to said petition. [5] If a will has been probated, say, "that said deceased died testate, and that all of his property is disposed of by his will, as hereinafter decreed"; or, if partially intestate, say, "that said deceased died testate, disposing of only a part of his estate by will; and that all of said part is so disposed of by said will as hereinafter decreed." [6] And the provisions of said will, if any. [7-9] State name and fractional part. [10] Describe the residue.

§ 747. Form. Decree of distribution. (Another form.)

[Title of court.]

[Title of estate.]

{ No. ——.[1] Dept. No. ——.
  [Title of form.]

——, administrator [2] of the estate of ——, deceased, having on the —— day of ——, 19—, filed in this court his petition, setting forth, among other matters, that all accounts have been finally settled; that said estate is in a condition to be closed; and that a portion of said estate remains to be divided among the heirs of said deceased;

and praying that said residue be distributed to the parties
entitled thereto; and said matter coming on regularly to
be heard this ——— day of ———, 19—, this court proceeds
to the hearing of said petition, and it appearing to the
satisfaction of this court that the clerk duly fixed the time
and place for hearing said petition, and gave due notice
thereof as required by law; that said accounts have been
finally settled; that all taxes upon the property of the
estate (and any inheritance tax which has become due
and payable) have been fully paid; and that the residue
of said estate, consisting of the property hereinafter particularly described, is now ready for distribution and that
said estate is now in a condition to be closed;

And it further appearing that the residue of said estate
is community property; that the said ——— died intestate,[3]
in the said county [4] of ———, on the ——— day of ———, 19—,
leaving surviving him those certain persons whose names
and relationship to said deceased are as follows, to wit,
———;[5] that, since the rendition of his said final account,
the sum of ——— dollars ($———) has come into the hands
of said administrator;[6] that the sum of ——— dollars
($———) has been expended by said administrator [7] as
necessary expenses of administration, the vouchers
whereof, together with a statement of such receipts and
disbursements, are now presented and filed, and the payments are approved by this court; that the estimated
expenses of closing said estate will amount to the sum of
——— dollars ($———);[8] and that the following-named per-
sons are entitled to the residue of said estate, to wit, ———
and ——— and ———, —

Now, on this, the said ——— day of ———, 19—, on motion
of ———, Esq., counsel for said administrator,[9] and no
objection being made thereto,—

It is hereby ordered, adjudged, and decreed, That the
residue of said estate of ———, deceased, hereinafter particularly described, and now remaining in the hands of

said administrator,[10] and any other property which may belong to the said estate, or in which the said estate may have any interest, be, and the same is hereby, distributed as follows, to wit: ——.[11]

The following is a particular description of the said residue of said estate referred to in this decree, and of which distribution is ordered, adjudged, and decreed, as aforesaid, to wit: ——.[12]

Done in open court this —— day of ——, 19—.

                  ——, Judge of the —— Court.

Explanatory notes.—[1] Give file number. [2] Or, executor. [3] Or as the case may be. [4] Or, city and county. [5] Designate names and relationship. [6,7] Or, executor. [8] In case of will insert: "that by the will of said decedent, which was duly admitted to probate herein on the —— day of ——, 19—, said deceased devised and bequeathed his whole estate to the persons and in the proportions and manner in said will, as hereinafter, specified." [9,10] Or, executor. [11] Give names of distributees, and proportion of share of each. [12] Give description.

§ 748. Form. Decree of distribution to foreign executor. (To be used for personal property only.)

[Title of court.]

[Title of estate.]
                { No. ——.[1]   Dept. No. ——.
                         [Title of form.]

Now comes ——, the executor of said estate, by ——, his attorney, and proves to the satisfaction of the court that his final account had been theretofore settled; that petition for distribution herein was filed on the —— day of ——, 19—; that on the same day the clerk of this court appointed the —— day of ——, 19—, for the hearing thereof; and that due and legal notice of the time and place of said hearing has been given as required by law;[2] and said petition being now presented to the court, and no person appearing to except to or contest said petition,[3] the court, after hearing the evidence, being satisfied that all taxes upon the property of the estate (and any inheritance tax which has become due and payable) have been fully paid, orders distribution of said estate as follows:

It is determined, adjudged, and decreed by the court,

That said executor has in his possession, belonging to
said estate, after deducting the credits to which he is entitled, a balance of —— dollars ($——), of which ——
dollars ($——) is in cash, and the remainder consists of
the following described personal property at the value
of the appraisement, to wit: ——;[4] that the will of said
deceased has been duly admitted to probate in the —— [5]
court of the county of ——, state of ——; that said state
was the place of residence of said deceased at the time of
his death; that it is necessary, in order that the whole of
said estate may be distributed according to the said will,[6]
that the same be delivered to the executor of said estate
in the said county of ——, state of ——, and it is therefore ordered that the executor herein appointed forthwith
deliver to ——, the executor appointed by the said ——[7]
court of the county of ——, state of ——, the whole of
said estate remaining in his hands as aforesaid.[8]

Dated ——, 19—.   ——, Judge of the —— Court.

Explanatory notes.—[1] Give file number. [2] If the matter has been
continued, say, "and the same having been by the court regularly postponed to the present time." [3] Or, —— having appeared by ——, his
attorney, and filed and presented objections and exceptions to said
petition. [4] Describe the property. [5] Title of court. [6] Or, that a certain part of said estate hereinafter described may be distributed according to the said will. [7] Title of court. [8] Or, the following portion of
said estate, to wit (describing the property).

§ 749. Distribution not to be made until taxes are paid.

Before any decree of distribution of an estate is made,
the court must be satisfied, by the oath of the executor or
administrator, or otherwise, that all state, county, and
municipal taxes, legally levied upon property of the
estate, and any inheritance tax which is due and payable
have been fully paid.—*Kerr's Cyc. Code Civ. Proc.,*
§ 1669.

ANALOGOUS AND IDENTICAL STATUTES.
The * indicates identity.
Arizona—Revised Statutes of 1913, paragraph 1041.
Idaho—Compiled Statutes of 1919, section 7733.

Montana—Revised Codes of 1907, section 7677. See Laws of 1917, chapter 40, page 42; amending section 7731, Rev. Codes, relating to payment of inheritance tax to county treasurers.

North Dakota—Compiled Laws of 1913, section 8848.

Oklahoma—Revised Laws of 1910, section 6467.

South Dakota—Compiled Laws of 1913, section 5928.

Utah*—Compiled Laws of 1907, section 3956.

Wyoming—Compiled Statutes of 1910, section 5701

§ 750. Continuation of administration.

In all cases where a decedent shall have left a will, in and by the terms of which the testator shall have limited the time for administration upon an estate left by him, and the executor, and all of the legatees or devisees named in the will, shall file and present to the court a petition, in writing, representing that it will be for the best interests of the estate, and of the beneficiaries under the will, to have the administration upon the estate continued for a longer period of time than that designated in such will, and that it would be injurious to the estate and to such beneficiaries, to have the administration brought to a close at the date therefor designated in the will, the court shall then set a day for the hearing of said petition; and notice thereof shall be served on all persons interested in the estate, in the same manner that summons in civil actions is served. Upon the day set for such hearing (or upon some other day to which the hearing may have been continued), the court shall proceed to hear proofs touching the representations made in such petition—and any person interested in the estate may also present counter-proofs in opposition to said application; and if, upon such hearing, it be made to appear to the court that the representations made by the petitioners in their said petition contained be true, the court may then, by its order and decree in that behalf, decree and direct that the administration upon the estate continue for and during such further period of time as in its judgment will best subserve the interests of the estate and of the beneficiaries under said will;

SECOND PETITION.—Provided, however, that if, at any time during the period for which the administration upon the estate shall have been thus continued, the executor, or any one or more of the legatees or devisees, shall present to the court his or their petition, representing that it has become necessary for the best interests of the estate, and of the beneficiaries under the will, to have the administration upon the estate closed, the court shall then set a day for the hearing of said last-named petition; and notice thereof shall be given in the same manner, and the same proceedings be had thereupon, as shall have been given for and had upon the hearing of the petition asking for the continuation of such administration. And if, upon such hearing, it shall be made to appear to the court that the representations made by such petitioners or petitioner (as the case may be) are true, the court shall then, by its order and decree in that behalf, decree and direct that the administration upon the estate be closed as soon thereafter as, under the circumstances, shall be practicable.—*Kerr's Cyc. Code Civ. Proc.,* § 1670.

ESTABLISHMENT OF HEIRSHIP, RIGHTS AND LIABILITIES OF HEIRS, AND DISTRIBUTION.

I. Proceedings to Determine Heirship.

1. Jurisdiction of courts.
   (1) In general.
   (2) Limitations of jurisdiction.
2. Procedure.
   (1) In general.
   (2) Parties. Pleadings. Issues.
   (3) Evidence. In general.
   (4) Same. Admissions and declarations.
   (5) Same. Burden of proof.
   (6) Trial. In general.
   (7) Same. Nonsuit.
   (8) Same. Findings.
   (9) Decree.
   (10) Costs.
   (11) Appeal. In general.
   (12) Same. Bond.
   (13) Same. Dismissal.
   (14) Same. Review.
   (15) Same. Remand.

II. Rights and Liabilities of Heirs.

1. Appointment of attorney for heirs.
2. Vesting of property in heirs. Burdens.
   (1) In general.
   (2) Judgment liens against heirs.
   (3) Community property.
3. Rights of heirs.
   (1) In general.
   (2) Under agreements.
   (3) To sell, convey, or lease.
4. Assignment.
5. Actions by heirs.
   (1) In general.
   (2) In ejectment.
   (3) To enforce trust.
   (4) In partition.
   (5) On promissory notes.
   (6) To quiet title.

I. PROCEEDINGS TO DETERMINE HEIRSHIP.

1. Jurisdiction of courts.

(1) **In general.**—If the statute expressly provides that, upon proof of service of notice to the satisfaction of the court, "the court shall thereupon acquire jurisdiction to ascertain and determine the heirship, ownership, and interest of all parties in and to the property of said deceased," and jurisdiction has thus attached, the provisions as to the time of future steps in the proceeding are merely directory, are not to be considered as conditions precedent, and are not of the essence of the proceeding.—Estate of Sutro, 143 Cal. 487, 491, 77 Pac. 402. The court acquires jurisdiction to determine, and it is made its duty to determine, not alone the heirship to deceased, but also the interest of each respective claimant to his estate. That this may, and should, properly be done by a decree establishing the degree of kinship or relation in which the separate claimants stood to the deceased, does not admit of debate; and where a claimant is found to bear no kinship whatsoever to the deceased, a finding and judgment to that effect is properly within the jurisdiction of the court, and within the issues to be determined.—Estate of Blythe, 112 Cal. 689, 694, 45 Pac. 6. Authorized proceedings for the ascertainment of heirship necessarily involve questions of title to the property of the estate, whether real or personal. "How is the court to exercise the jurisdiction given without trying and determining such questions?"—Estate of Burton, 93 Cal. 459, 464, 29 Pac. 36; Blythe v. Ayres, 102 Cal. 254, 258, 36 Pac. 522. A proceeding for the determination of heirship to the estate of a decedent is not a civil action, but a special proceeding, and is embraced within the scope of "matters of probate." It is therefore within the jurisdiction of a court sitting in matters of probate.—Smith v. Westerfeld, 88 Cal. 374, 379, 26 Pac. 206; Estate of Burton, 93 Cal. 459, 463, 29 Pac. 36; Estate of Joseph, 118 Cal. 660, 663, 50 Pac. 768. It is embraced within the scope of "matters in probate," as clearly as is the proceeding for the sale of real property to pay the debts of an estate.—Estate of Blythe, 110 Cal. 226, 228, 42 Pac. 641. No distinct "court of probate" has been created or recognized by the present constitution of California; but the superior court is vested with jurisdiction "in matters of probate"; and such a court, while sitting in matters of probate, is the same as it is while sitting in cases of equity and in cases of law, or in special proceedings; and when it has jurisdiction of the subject-matter of a case falling within either of these classes, it has

power to hear and determine, in the mode provided by law, all questions of law and fact, the determination of which is ancillary to a proper judgment in such case, and this applies to proceedings for the ascertainment of heirship.—Estate of Burton, 93 Cal. 459, 463, 22 Pac. 36. Where questions have been litigated under the provisions of the statute relating to the determination of heirship, and have been determined before an application for distribution is made, the determination of such questions shall be conclusive in the distribution of the estate.—Blythe v. Ayres, 102 Cal. 254, 259, 36 Pac. 522. In a proceeding to determine heirship, an order adjudging the default of persons for not appearing, but adding that it is without prejudice to the rights of persons who have petitions filed for distribution in such proceeding, does not deprive the court of jurisdiction.—Estate of Sutro, 143 Cal. 487, 490, 77 Pac. 402. A court must enter a default against all parties failing to prosecute or to defend their rights, as well as those who fail to appear or plead.—Estate of Kasson, 141 Cal. 33, 40, 74 Pac. 436; and where an order is made by the court, adjudging all persons who did not appear therein to be in default, a subsequent order refusing to open the default at the instance of a non-resident heir, who did not know of the proceeding until after the default, is within the jurisdiction of the court, and will not be disturbed upon certiorari.—Hitchcock v. Superior Court, 73 Cal. 295, 14 Pac. 872. Where, in a proceeding for the establishment of heirship, and after the publication of notice on non-resident persons interested therein, parties appear and file a pleading in which they ask for judgment that the estate be distributed to them, such parties are in no position to attack the court's jurisdiction; voluntary appearance is equivalent to personal service.—Estate of Walden, 168 Cal. 759, 145 Pac. 100. A proceeding for the determination of heirship for the purposes of distribution is not, strictly speaking, a civil action, but a "special proceeding" embraced within the scope of "matters in probate"; but the jurisdiction exercised is that before a court of general jurisdiction, and the jurisdictional requirements of the statute must be strictly complied with.—Carter v. Frahm, 31 S. D. 379, 141 N. W. 370. The pendency of the proceeding instituted under the provisions of section 1664, Cal. Code Civ. Proc., does not require nor authorize the denial of a petition for final distribution presented simultaneously with the final account of the administrator, and such denial, if made, is error, in view of the fact that the court has jurisdiction to hear and determine the entire question of heirship in the hearing of the petition for final distribution as in the special proceeding for that purpose under the section named.—In re Ross' Estate, 179 Cal. 358, 182 Pac. 755, 758. In a proceeding to determine heirship, and who is entitled to distribution, the question as to whether or not letters testamentary were properly issued is not a jurisdictional question, where an order was made admitting the will to probate and such letters were in fact issued; furthermore, the defendants, by appearing, submitting to the jurisdiction of the court, and failing to deny the allegations as to the order admitting the will to probate having been duly given and that such letters were properly issued thereon, waived all objections to the jurisdiction of the trial court.—Estate of Friedman, 178 Cal. 27, 172 Pac. 140.

REFERENCES.

Question of heirship is subsidiary to, and may be considered on, distribution.—See Division III, head-line 8, subd. 2, post.

(2) **Limitations of jurisdiction.**—Where the provisions of the statute are carefully limited to the ascertainment and determination of the rights and interest claimed in privity with the estate, they are not applicable to rights or titles claimed adversely to such estate.—Estate of Burton, 93 Cal. 459, 461, 29 Pac. 36. Such a statute provides no means of determining adverse claims, or what property belongs to the estate. The purpose is to determine heirship and the ownership of property of the estate, and the decree is made conclusive only in distribution and of title to property of the estate.—McDonald v. McCoy 121 Cal. 55, 72, 53 Pac. 421. Neither does such a statute provide for the probate of a will, and the court should not proceed, as a part of an action under such statute, to hear and determine the matter of the probate of a will. It is clearly the law that a will can not be received in evidence to maintain a title founded upon it until it has been admitted to probate.—Estate of Christensen, 135 Cal. 674, 676, 68 Pac. 112. In a proceeding under such a statute, the court has jurisdiction of the claims of assignees of the heir, but it has not been held that its jurisdiction extends to claims of an equitable nature against the legal owner, or in other words, to trusts. A probate court has no equitable jurisdiction beyond what is involved in the exercise of its peculiar functions, which are to administer and to distribute the estate. But where a trust has been created by will, the validity of the trust is necessarily involved in the question of distribution, for, if invalid, the bequest fails. Hence, as necessary to distribution, it is within the province of the probate court to define the rights of all who have legally or equitably any interest in the property of the estate, derived from the will. The probate court has no jurisdiction over trusts, not derived from the will. The jurisdiction of the court, either on distribution, or in a proceeding for the ascertainment of the heirs of an estate, is merely to determine the persons entitled, under the will or by succession, or their grantees; and in neither case are the equitable claims of parties against the heirs, or assignees of heirs, a proper subject for its consideration.— More v. More, 133 Cal. 489, 495, 65 Pac. 1044. Where no proceeding for the determination of heirship can be inaugurated until the expiration of one year after the issuance of letters of administration, no jurisdiction can be acquired by a court where the petition is filed within less than four months after the issuance of such letters.—Smith v. Westerfield, 88 Cal. 374, 380, 26 Pac. 206; but, where the court has clearly acquired jurisdiction, such jurisdiction can not be ousted by a

failure to comply strictly with the subsequent steps in the proceeding, which are merely directory, though the action or proceeding in question be statutory or in rem.—Estate of Sutro, 143 Cal. 487, 492, 77 Pac. 402. The jurisdiction of a superior court in proceedings to determine heirship is limited and special. Whenever its acts are shown to have been in excess of the power conferred upon it, or without the limits of this special jurisdiction, such acts are nugatory, and have no binding effect, even upon those who have invoked its authority, or submitted to its decision.—Smith v. Westerfield, 88 Cal. 374, 379, 26 Pac. 206; Estate of Strong, 119 Cal. 663, 666, 51 Pac. 1078. Where there is a statute providing for the determination of heirship, it would seem that, upon partial distribution, jurisdiction to determine the question of contested heirship, or right to inherit, could only be acquired by proceeding under such a statute, but, in California, it has been held that such question may be determined on such petition, under statutes providing for the partial distribution of an estate.—Estate of Jessup, 81 Cal. 408, 415, 6 L. R. A. 594, 21 Pac. 976, 22 Pac. 742, 1028.

2. Procedure.

(1) In general.—In a proceeding to determine heirship, every party is an independent actor, and is a plaintiff as against all other parties whose claims are adverse. When the pleadings of all the parties are in, the subsequent proceedings shall be the same as in an ordinary civil action, and the provisions regulating the mode of procedure for the trial of civil actions are applicable to this proceeding. If it does not appear that the judge can not fairly and impartially try the cause, a motion to disqualify him for bias and prejudice is properly denied. If a party, who claims to be an heir, fails to appear and introduce any proof in support of his claim, it is proper for the court to enter a nonsuit as to him; and any error in granting such nonsuit, which occurred at the trial, and which should have been excepted to at that time, will not be considered on appeal.—Estate of Kasson, 141 Cal. 33, 40, 74 Pac. 436. Where the law of descent of estates is applicable, on the death of an Indian allottee after the primary patent or certificate is issued, a state court has jurisdiction of the subject-matter, and its decree determining the heirs in such cases is valid. The determination, by a state court, of the heirs of a deceased Indian allottee is not an execution of the trust. The finding of such fact is not an interference with the primary disposal of the soil, but is in aid of the general government in protecting the rights of its cestui que trust.—Kaylton v. Kaylton, 45 Or. 116, 78 Pac. 332, 333. All of the property of one who dies without disposing of it by will passes to the heirs of the intestate, subject to the control of the probate court.—Reed v. Stewart, 12 Ida. 699, 87 Pac. 1002, 1004; and since the title vests in the heir at the time of the decedent's death, he is entitled thenceforth to be heard as to the disposition of the estate.—In re Sullivan's Estate, 36 Wash. 217, 78 Pac. 945, 948;

Reed v. Stewart, 12 Ida. 699, 87 Pac. 1002, 1004, 1152; and the mere fact that a resistance to his claim of heirship may exist does not deprive him of such right. The administrator, who seeks to pay out the funds of an estate for his own and counsel's services must recognize the right on the part of all who claim to be heirs or devisees, and who proceed in a regular way to be heard, until conflicting claims have been finally adjudicated.—In re Sullivan's Estate, 36 Wash. 217, 78 Pac. 945, 948. In Utah, a statutory proceeding, which is in the nature of a special proceeding for the determination of heirship and right of succession, can not be commenced until the expiration of one year after the death of the decedent, and then only in the event that letters of administration have not been applied for. Hence, where the year has not elapsed, and an administrator has been regularly appointed, and the estate is in process of settlement in the probate court, that court has exclusive original jurisdiction to determine all questions of heirship and descent.—Garr v. Davidson, 25 Utah 335, 71 Pac. 481, 482. The proceeding to determine heirship provided for by section 1664, Cal. Code Civ. Proc., is required to be instituted in probate proceedings, and is an ample and exclusive remedy for the purpose; hence, it is not error, in a suit for the specific performance of a contract to make testamentary disposition of property, to refuse to determine who are heirs of a deceased person.—Trout v. Ogilvie, (Cal. App.), 182 Pac. 333, 336. Section 1664, of the California Code of Civil Procedure, was intended to provide the means by which all the conflicting rights to an estate, where there are hostile claimants, may be summarily and finally decided in one proceeding; the alleged right of each party, whether nominally a plaintiff or a defendant, is, in such proceeding, as much before the court for determination as is the alleged right of either of the other parties.—Estate of Friedman, 173 Cal. 411, 160 Pac. 237. The complete procedure for determining rights of persons to estates, and interests therein, and who are the proper distributees must be held, under well known rules of statutory construction, to exclude every other procedure for determining such questions.—In re Colbert's Estate, State v. Bush, 51 Mont. 455, 153 Pac. 1022. Where, on a petition for the determination of heirship and for an order looking to a recovery from the state of the proceeds of escheated property, the court has decided adversely, on the ground that the proceeding is barred by the statute of limitations, the decision is not res judicata so as to prevent the petitioner from instituting a fresh proceeding of the sort after the legislature has enacted a law allowing further time for persons in his situation to seek judicial relief, where there is no identity of issues.—In re Pomeroy, 51 Mont. 119, 151 Pac. 333. Heirship, amount of distributive estate claimed, etc., can not be determined on petition for partial distribution; the clear implication of the Montana statute is that such questions can not be determined in any other proceeding than one instituted under sections 7670-7672 of the Rev. Codes of that state, or in one for final distribution.—In re Fleming's Estate, Lockwood v. Fleming, 38 Mont. 57, 59, 98 Pac. 648. The question of heirship and the interest of any heir may be determined, not only under sections 7669-7671, Rev. Codes of Montana, but also upon a proceeding for the final distribution of an estate.—In re Fleming's Estate, 38 Mont. 57, 59, 98 Pac. 648. Enumeration of steps to be taken under the California statute for the determination of heirship.—See Blythe v. Ayres, 102 Cal. 254, 258, 36 Pac. 522. Inasmuch as no right vests in a presumptive heir until the death of the ancestor, persons entitled to succeed must be ascertained according to the law in force at the date of the death.—Estate of Loyd, 170 Cal. 85, 148 Pac. 522.

(2) Parties. Pleadings. Issues.—Under the California statute, to determine heirship, the one who proceeds first and files a complaint, is, for convenience, treated as plaintiff, and the others as defendants. The plaintiff is to file a complaint setting forth the facts constituting his claim of heirship, ownership, or interest in the estate, with such reasonable particularity as the court may require; and the defendants shall set forth, in their respective answers, the facts constituting their claim of heirship, ownership, or interest in said estate, with such particularity as the court may require. It is thus seen that the pleading of each party, whether plaintiff or a defendant, is to contain exactly the same matter. It is clear, therefore, that the alleged right of each party, whether nominally a plaintiff or a defendant, is as much before the court for final adjudication as is the alleged right of any other party; and it is the plain duty of the court to determine the alleged claims of each party to the proceeding.—Blythe v. Ayres, 102 Cal. 254, 260, 36 Pac. 522; Estate of Kasson, 127 Cal. 496, 505, 59 Pac. 950. The fact that a person is styled a "defendant," in the title of the pleadings in such an action, does not fix his status in the proceeding. In such a proceeding each party is an independent actor, and is a plaintiff as against all other persons whose claims are adverse. When the pleadings of all the parties are in, the subsequent proceedings shall be the same as in an ordinary civil action, and the provisions of the statute which regulate the mode of procedure for the trial of civil actions are applicable to such a proceeding.—Estate of Kasson, 141 Cal. 33, 40, 74 Pac. 436. No party has a standing in the trial court in such a proceeding unless he has averred his claim of heirship, etc., and has set forth the facts constituting such claim, and he will not be heard to contest the right of another claimant if he does not set up any right in himself.—Blythe v. Ayres, 102 Cal. 254, 260, 36 Pac. 522. If proceedings are pending for the settlement of the estate of a deceased testator, one who claims to be an heir at law, who, in case residuary legacies are void, might succeed to some of the estate, can not maintain an action in equity, for the purpose of determining his heirship and having some of the legacies pronounced void, where no reason is shown why this matter should be determined in advance of the decree of final

distribution.—Siddall v. Harrison, 73 Cal. 560, 564, 15 Pac. 130; Gold-tree v. Thompson (Cal.), 15 Pac. 359. In a proceeding to determine heirship under the law of California brought by pretermitted heirs, where one claiming under a devisee in the will had procured a partial distribution of the estate to himself, and asserted possession adverse to the pretermitted heirs as a bar to their rights, but no final distribution had been made, his entry should be held to be that of a tenant in common with the pretermitted heirs, and he could not acquire title by limitation against them, pending administration.—Estate of Grider, 81 Cal. 571, 578, 22 Pac. 908. Where a petition has been filed for the purpose of ascertaining and declaring the rights of all persons to an estate, and to whom distribution thereof shall be made, the administrator of such estate, although made a formal party to the proceeding, has no right to litigate the claim of one alleged heir as against another, where he is not alleged to be a claimant to the estate.—Roach v. Coffey, 73 Cal. 281, 282, 14 Pac. 840. It is not required that a petition for the determination of heirship under the Colorado statute (Rev. Stats., section 7050) shall be answered or met by plea. The decree is simply a determination of who are the heirs of the deceased.—Wilson v. Wilson, 55 Colo. 70, 132 Pac. 67. Where a petition is filed for distribution of the estate of an intestate to persons alleged to be the sole heirs of the deceased and thereafter without formally answering such petition and denying its allegations of heirship, other persons file similar petitions claiming to be the sole heirs, issues of fact on the question of heirship are thereby raised, the determination of which by the trial court is subject to be reviewed on motion for a new trial.—Carter v. Waste, 159 Cal. 23, 112 Pac. 727. In the proceeding to determine heirship each person filing a complaint or answer, and setting up title to the whole estate by distinct line of kinship, is necessarily an actor for himself and against all other persons who also claim the entire estate. His claim is antagonistic to that of all the others, and the claim of each of the others is antagonistic to him.—Estate of Friedman, 173 Cal. 411, 160 Pac. 237.

(3) Evidence. In general.—In a proceeding to establish heirship, the executor of the estate is not to be excluded from active participation, and if the evidence produced by him, adverse to the claims of parties, is relevant and competent, such parties are prejudicial no more than they would be, had such production been by opposing counsel employed for the purpose.—Estate of Friedman, 178 Cal. 27, 172 Pac. 140, 144. In a proceeding for the distribution of the estate of a deceased person, which involves the determination of the question of the survivorship of two persons who were killed in the same calamity, the fact of survivorship must be established by a preponderance of evidence, not because the heirs of one decedent or of another begin a contest, but because it is the duty of the court to determine the matter of heirship and survival.—Estate of Loucks, 160 Cal. 551, Ann. Cas. 1913A, 868, 117 Pac. 673. Testimony to the effect that the witness never heard that a named person was the daughter of the intestate is negative evidence and proves nothing one way or the other.—Lauderdale v. O'Neill (Okla.), 177 Pac. 113. An objection that evidence of statements, made by a decedent, that he had not relatives, tends to rebut the direct testimony of claimants to the estate, goes to the weight of the evidence and not to its admissibility; it should therefore not be sustained.—Estate of Friedman, 178 Cal. 27, 172 Pac. 140. If the testimony of a witness, in relation to pedigree, in a proceeding to determine the right of persons claiming to be heirs or entitled to distribution, is willfully false in part, the whole should be excluded.—Estate of Friedman, 178 Cal. 27, 172 Pac. 140, 143. A recital in a deed to the effect that a person mentioned therein is the sole and only heir of another mentioned person is incompetent to establish heirship, regardless of the character of the deed as to validity.—Lauderdale v. O'Neill (Okla.), 177 Pac. 113. Evidence sufficient to show that B was decedent's niece and that two persons were brothers.—In re Hartman's Estate, 157 Cal. 206, 21 Ann. Cas. 1302, 107 Pac. 105. Language is a personal characteristic, competent to be mentioned, along with other things, for purposes of identification; thus, it is competent, in a proceeding by German heirs to establish heirships, for a witness to state that a person spoke German entirely, or English very brokenly.—In re Colbert's Estate, 44 Mont. 259, 264, 119 Pac. 791; State v. Bush, 51 Mont. 455, 153 Pac. 1022.

(4) Same. Admissions and declarations.—Under sections 7869 and 7887 of the Revised Codes of Montana, in an action to determine the right to a decedent's estate, the declarations and attitude of persons, since deceased or out of the jurisdiction, are admissible to show the relationship of the declarants to each other and to others, not the decedent whose estate is in issue, without any prior showing of relationship to such last named decedent.—In re Colbert's Estate; State v. Bush, 51 Mont. 455, 153 Pac. 1022. In a proceeding under section 7670 of the Revised Codes of Montana, to establish heirship, a declaration of relationship is admissible, under section 7887 of those codes.—In re Colbert's Estate, State v. Bush, 51 Mont. 455, 153 Pac. 1022. In a proceeding to determine the rights of persons claiming to be heirs of a decedent, if, in support of the claim, the evidence relied on consists of declarations of deceased members of such decedent's family, or alleged family, testified to by deposition on written interrogatories through an interpreter, it is not to be rejected; but it is unsatisfactory, for the reason that the witness testified with no fear before him of the penalties of perjury.—Estate of Friedman, 178 Cal. 27, 172 Pac. 140. Declarations relative to pedigree are admissible and competent evidence but such evidence is not entitled to the same weight and consideration that direct and positive testimony would have, and is not of a like satisfactory and conclusive nature.—Lauderdale v. O'Neill (Okla.), 177 Pac. 113. Evidence to the effect that a testator had, during his lifetime, declared that his relatives

were gone and that he had no one left, tends to a showing that every member of such testator's family, to whom he was related by blood or marriage, was dead at the time of the declaration.—Estate of Friedman, 178 Cal. 27, 172 Pac. 140. Declarations of members of the family of the deceased concerning family history and relationship, made after contest to succession of the estate, are inadmissible to prove heirship to the estate.—Estate of Walden (Monro v. Latimer), 166 Cal. 446, 137 Pac. 35. Such declarations are not admissible to prove pedigree or relationship, except when they are made by the members of the family as natural or spontaneous declarations on the subject, and before any dispute has arisen over the question or any claim has been made to the establishment of which the declarations would be material.—Estate of Walden (Monro v. Latimer), 166 Cal. 446, 137 Pac. 35. Statements by members of decedent's family concerning family history and relationship, made after the controversy as to the right of the estate of decedent had arisen and in reply to questions propounded to elicit evidence are inadmissible; such declarations being admissible to prove pedigree or relationship, only when made naturally and spontaneously before any controversy has arisen.—In re Walden's Estate, 166 Cal. 446, 137 Pac. 35. Evidence of admissions and declarations of deceased and of other relatives held sufficient proof.—In re Clark's Estate, 13 Cal. App. 786, 110 Pac. 828.

(5) Same. Burden of proof.—In determining a claimant's right to the estate of a decedent, the burden is on the claimant to show the required relationship.—In re Colbert's Estate, State v. Bush, 51 Mont. 455, 53 Pac. 1022. One claiming as heir must make proof of his relationship to the intestate by sufficient evidence, but a preponderance is sufficient.—In re Clark's Estate, 13 Cal. App. 786, 110 Pac. 828. A woman seeking to establish her position as widow, of a man who has left an estate, has the burden of proving that she was, at the very moment of the death of the man, his wife by virtue of a lawful and subsisting marriage.—Estate of Hughson, 173 Cal. 448, 160 Pac. 548.

(6) Trial. In general.—Under a statute providing for the determination of heirship, each person who appears, and, either by complaint or answer, sets up a claim of heirship, etc., peculiar to himself, is an actor, and has a separate and independent right to conduct his case according to his own judgment, including the right to ask proper questions of witnesses of a hostile party. The averments of the pleadings show which parties are hostile to each other, and each has a right to cross-examine the witnesses of a hostile party.—Estate of Kasson, 127 Cal. 496, 505, 59 Pac. 950. It is entirely proper to submit to a jury issues of fact raised by the petition in a proceeding for the determination of heirship.—Estate of Sheid, 122 Cal. 528, 532, 55 Pac. 328.

(7) Same. Nonsuit.—In a proceeding brought by a charitable corporation, beneficiary under a will, to determine the rights of all persons claiming to be heirs, or entitled to distribution, the court will

not grant a nonsuit on failure of the plaintiff to prove that there are no persons so entitled; since, if there are such persons, the plaintiff would still have, under the will, a right to the excess of two-thirds of the estate.—Estate of Friedman, 178 Cal. 27, 172 Pac. 140.

(8) **Same. Findings.**—In a proceeding between the heirs of a deceased husband and those of his deceased wife to determine heirship to his estate, finding that a certain tract of land was the separate property of the husband, and not the property of the community is a finding of fact and not a conclusion of law.—Estate of Hill, 167 Cal. 59, 138 Pac. 690. Where, in a proceeding to determine the rights of all persons claiming to be heirs of a deceased person, the claimants seek to establish their relationship to the deceased in the sixth and seventh degrees, the ultimate fact in issue is whether or not the claimants are related to the deceased, and, if so, their degree of kinship; hence, a finding that they are not related to the deceased in any degree is a finding of that ultimate fact and renders unnecessary findings in detail upon the alleged claim of relationship.—Estate of Friedman, 178 Cal. 27, 172 Pac. 140.

(9) **Decree.**—A decree to determine heirship is properly entered when spread at length upon the minute-book of the probate court. It is not necessary that it should be entered in the judgment-book.—Estate of Blythe, 110 Cal. 229, 230, 42 Pac. 642. As a party is concluded by the decree in proceedings to determine heirship, so far as the distribution of the estate is concerned, a party who is found to have no interest in the estate ceases to be a party interested therein, and can not afterward appeal from a decree distributing the estate.—Estate of Blythe, 108 Cal. 124, 128, 41 Pac. 33. One whose claim of heirship or interest in an estate has been decided adversely to him cannot afterwards be heard to affirm the contrary upon appeal from a decree of distribution of the estate.—Estate of Blythe, 112 Cal. 689, 694, 45 Pac. 6. As the statute which authorizes an action to determine heirship and the ownership of property in the estate of a deceased person does not authorize the determination of adverse claims by third persons to the property, a judgment in such action is not conclusive as to persons claiming the property as their own, where they did not appear in the heirship proceedings, though made parties thereto.—McDonald v. McCoy, 121 Cal. 55, 72, 53 Pac. 421. In a proceeding instituted to determine heirship (section 1664, Cal. Code Civ. Proc.), a judgment entered, to the effect that the decedent died without heirs, can not properly be said to determine the relative rights of any one claimant on the one hand and of the other claimants on the other, but to determine rather that each unsuccessful claimant is without right.—Estate of Friedman, 173 Cal. 411, 160 Pac. 287.

(10) **Costs.**—In a proceeding to determine heirship, the court has a discretion to apportion the costs between the parties, where the circumstances call for such action on the part of the court; other-

wise the losing party is liable for the costs, as any other losing party
in a civil action.—Lindy v. McChesney, 141 Cal. 351, 353, 74 Pac. 1034.
Under a statute which gives the court discretion to apportion the
costs of a proceeding for the ascertainment of the rights of persons
claiming as distributees of the estate of a decedent, and where the
claimant claims the entire estate, but is unsuccessful, it is not
improper to tax him with the entire cost of the proceeding, including
the expense of taking depositions, though they were not used on the
trial, unless it be shown that they were unnecessary, or that, for some
special reason, such disbursement should not be allowed.—Lindy v.
McChesney, 141 Cal. 351, 74 Pac. 1034. Where a person has sued to be
admitted to heirship in respect to an intestate's property and has
failed in the suit neither he nor his attorney can claim as a party
interested in the estate, that the latter bear the expenses, on the
theory that they and their witnesses served to establish heirship for
the true heirs.—Estate of Walden, 174 Cal. 776, 164 Pac. 639.

(11) Appeal. In general.—All appeals and proceedings to determine
heirship must be taken within the prescribed statutory time from the
date of the entry of the judgment, or the order complained of. If not
taken within that time, the appeal from the judgment is too late.—
Estate of Grider, 81 Cal. 571, 574, 22 Pac. 908; Smith v. Westerfield,
88 Cal. 374, 381, 26 Pac. 206; Estate of Westerfield, 96 Cal. 113, 30
Pac. 1104. In such a proceeding, a party who does not except to
or attack a finding that he is not akin to the deceased is not a
"party aggrieved," and has no standing as an appellant from the
decision in favor of the person who is found to be the sole heir of
the deceased.—Blythe v. Ayres, 102 Cal. 254, 257, 36 Pac. 522. Under
the laws of Wyoming, a judgment in a proceeding to determine
heirship is appealable.—Weidenhoft v. Primm, 16 Wyo. 340, 94 Pac.
453. A finding of fact by a jury or trial judge in such a proceeding,
which is the result of the consideration of evidence that is really
and materially conflicting, will not be disturbed on appeal.—Blythe v.
Ayres, 102 Cal. 254, 261, 36 Pac. 522. The object of a statute to
determine heirship is to expedite the distribution of the estate, by
enabling persons claiming interests to have their claims determined
in advance of the application for distribution; and, as the question
of heirship may be determined on the hearing of the petition for
distribution, the court has a discretion either to hear and determine
the whole matter, or to postpone it; and this discretion will not be
interfered with on appeal, unless it has been abused.—In re Oxarart,
78 Cal. 109, 112, 20 Pac. 367. A rejected claimant, appealing from a
decree establishing heirship, can not assign error in the admission of
evidence bearing upon the findings, unless he can specify some
insufficiency of evidence to support the finding that he himself is not
related to the decedent, and has no interest in the estate; having no
interest himself, he is not aggrieved by a judgment that others are
entitled to the estate.—Estate of Walden, 168 Cal. 759, 145 Pac. 100.

(12) **Same. Bond.**—An administratrix who, as such, petitions for the determination of heirship, claiming to be sole heir of the decedent, is not relieved, on appealing from an adverse judgment thereupon, of the necessity of filing a bond on appeal.—Redington v. Redington, (Colo.), 180 Pac. 675.

(13) **Same. Dismissal.**—On appeal from a judgment entered in proceedings to determine heirship each appellant may dispute the right of any other person to take an appeal, and may attack the proceedings by which such person has appealed, and obtain the dismissal of the appeal if there be cause.—Estate of Friedman, 173 Cal. 411, 160 Pac. 237.

(14) **Same. Review.**—A finding by the trial court adverse to the kinship to a decedent of persons claiming as heirs, if supported by substantial evidence, in a case where the evidence on the point has been conflicting, should not be disturbed on appeal.—Estate of Friedman, 178 Cal. 27, 172 Pac. 140. In a proceeding to determine the rights of a large number of legatees, wherein the executor and some of the legatees are adjudged entitled to share in the distribution of the estate but move for a new trial of issues found in favor of other claimants, the aggrieved parties may move for a new trial and appeal from an adverse ruling; the contention that the supreme court can not review the order denying a new trial, because of the complications that would arise in the district court, should a new trial of part of the issues be ordered, is untenable.—Estate of Klein, 35 Mont. 185, 201, 88 Pac. 798. In this proceeding to determine the succession to the estate of a deceased person the decision of the trial court upon the conflicting evidence is conclusive; and even if it be conceded that the appellate court may weigh the evidence where all the testimony is given by deposition, the testimony herein is not of such a character as to justify a reversal of the decision upon the ground of abuse of discretion.—Estate of Walden (Monro v. Latimer), 166 Cal. 446, 137 Pac. 35. In proceedings to administer on the estate of a decedent, the parties appearing as heirs failed to identify such decedent with the person, bearing the same name, from whom they descended; held, in view of the evidence and findings that the claimants were not the heirs of the deceased.—In re McClellan's Estate, 38 S. D. 588, 162 N. W. 383. A person whose claim to kinship to a deceased person has been adjudged unfounded can not be heard to urge error in a decree in favor of other claimants, or in the evidence supporting the decree; if he is not entitled to inherit, he is not interested in those questions.—Estate of Friedman, 178 Cal. 27, 172 Pac. 140.

(15) **Same. Remand.**—Where the proof of heirship was insufficient, but it appeared that on a retrial further evidence might be forthcoming and that further opportunity should be given claimants to submit proof of their relationship to deceased, the action was remanded to the

property would escheat in default of heirs would be represented in the retrial.—In re Peterson's Estate, 22 N. D. 480, 503, 134 N. W. 751.

II. RIGHTS AND LIABILITIES OF HEIRS.

1. Appointment of attorney for heirs.—The appointment of an attorney for absent heirs, and the allowance to him of a fee, are matters entirely within the discretion of the probate court, and if such allowance be improvident or indiscreet, the court may vacate it at the suggestion of any one, or upon its own motion.—Estate of Rety, 75 Cal. 256, 258, 17 Pac. 65. Under a statute providing for the appointment by the court of an attorney to represent absent heirs, it will be presumed that the appointment and the allowance made by the trial court for services rendered by such attorney are justified.—Estate of Simmons, 43 Cal. 543, 547.

REFERENCES.

That section of the California code authorizing the court to appoint an attorney for minor or absent heirs, devisees, legatees, or creditors has been repealed.—See Kerr's Cal. Cyc. Code Civ. Proc., section 718, and notes thereto.

2. Vesting of property in heirs. Burdens.

(1) In general.—Real estate acquired by an administrator, in obtaining satisfaction of a judgment, forming a part of the assets of the estate in his hands for settlement, is to be treated, for purposes of administration, as personal property. The heirs do not take title to such real estate by descent from their ancestors, nor until the probate court of proper jurisdiction has exhausted its authority over it by an order of distribution, either general or special, which is final in character.—Weir v. Bagby, 72 Kan. 67, 82 Pac. 585, 7 Ann. Cas. 702. While it is true that the descent is cast, and property of the decedent is vested in the devisees and legatees, or in the heirs, at the moment of the death of the deceased, it is also true that they take the property subject to whatever charges the legislature has seen fit to impose upon it. They take the property subject to the payment of the expenses of administration, subject to charges that the law fixes upon it for the support, maintenance, and comfort of the widow and family of the deceased, and subject to the liability to have these charges enforced by orders of the court, made without notice, in pursuance of the statute, other than that given for the initiation of the administration by the giving of a general notice as prescribed by law; and the enforcement of these charges in the authorized mode is not a violation of any constitutional right of the heir, devisee, or legatee.—Estate of Bump, 152 Cal. 274, 92 Pac. 643, 644. The estate of the heir which vests in him at once on the death of the ancestor subject to the burdens imposed by the law at the time is indefeasible, except in satisfaction of such burdens. The legislature has no more right to order a sale of such vested interest for other reasons than those prescribed by law, than it has to direct the sale of the property of any other person acquired in any other way; and a sale made under authority so conferred by the legislature is invalid.—Brenham v. Story, 39 Cal. 179 180. The principle that, upon the death of the ancestor, the heir at once becomes vested with the full property, subject only to burdens then existing, or imposed by the law then in force, is not affected by an amendment to the statute passed after the death of the ancestor, providing that property may be sold by the representative for other reasons than those prescribed by the statute in force at the time of the ancestors death.—Estate of Packer, 125 Cal. 396, 399, 58 Pac. 59, 73 Am. St. Rep. 58; Estate of Newlove, 142 Cal. 377, 379, 75 Pac. 1083. A statute which authorizes a sale of the property of an estate, when it appears for the advantage of the estate, without reference to the existence of debts, if in force at the time of the death, devests no one of his property.—Estate of Porter, 129 Cal. 86, 90, 61 Pac. 659, 79 Am. St. Rep. 78. The descent of real property is governed by the laws of inheritance in the state where the land is situated. Title to the same can not be affected by the decree of a court of another state.—Cooper v. Ives, 62 Kan. 395, 63 Pac. 434. When a member of a mutual benefit society has made his certificate payable to his heirs, they do not take the fund by descent, but by contract; and the statutes of descent and distribution do not apply when such heirs have been found.—Burke v. Modern Woodmen of America, 2 Cal. App. 611, 84 Pac. 275, 276. Title to the real estate of a deceased intestate vests immediately in his heirs, of a testate in his devisees, and such heirs or devisees, whether domestic or foreign, may convey their said title, without administration, and the title so conveyed is subject only to the claims of the administrator for the payment of debts.—Smith v. Barrick, — Cal. App. —, 182 Pac. 56, 58. An heir takes the title to real estate immediately upon the death of his intestate, and may convey such title by deed, or lose it by adverse possession, but the grantee or the person who takes by adverse possession takes subject to administration and the claims of creditors, just as a grantee would take title.—Smith v. Barrick, — Cal. App. —, 182 Pac. 56, 58.

REFERENCES.

Rights of an heir in the personal property of his ancestor.—See note to 112 Am. St. Rep. 727-735. Right of heirs to exemption of homestead from ancestor's debts contracted prior to its acquisition by him.—See note 4 L. R. A. (N. S.) 544. Right of devisee of incumbered real estate to exoneration at the expense of legatees of personal property.—See note 3 L. R. A. (N. S.) 898-903. Right of devisees of land incumbered by a testator to have such incumbrance discharged out of personalty to the disappointment of legatees.—See note 8 Am. & Eng. Ann Cas. 592.

(2) **Judgment liens against heirs.**—The estate of an heir or devisee vests in him on the death of the decedent, subject to administration,

and a judgment recovered against an heir or devisee, pending administration, becomes a lien on such interest, which lien is not terminated
by the conveyance of the heir or devisee or by distribution to his
grantee.—Martinovich v. Marsicano, 127 Cal. 354, 356, 70 Pac. 459.

(3) Community property.—Where a wife died, leaving an only child
and her husband surviving, and there was no administration upon
her estate, or upon the community property, it will be presumed, in
favor of the child, after the mother has been dead for eight years,
that, as to the community real property, there was no necessity for
administration, and that the right of a child to the possession of
his share in the community real estate as heir of his mother is
complete. It ought to be presumed, in favor of a child, either that
there were no community debts, or that they have been paid or
barred.—Young v. Young, 7 Wash. 33, 34 Pac. 144, 145.

3. Rights of heirs.

(1) In general.—The heir has no vested right to the property of the
ancestor by reason of kinship.—Estate of Martin, 170 Cal. 657, 151 Pac.
138. A devisee of a life estate in the income of property, where there
are no words of explanation or limitation in the devise creating the
estate, is entitled to the income without diminution by the payment
of the debts, funeral expenses, and costs of administration; but, if
he knowingly participates in such payments, he is a volunteer, and
his heirs will not be allowed to question such participation.—Stahl v.
Schwartz, 81 Wash. 293, 142 Pac. 651. If the widow of an intestate
dies leaving a will devising all her property to her heirs, there
existing no progeny of the pair or father or mother of either, and
the property being all of a community character, the brothers and
sisters and the children of deceased brothers and sisters of each are
entitled as distributees.—In re Watt's Estate, 179 Cal. 20, 175 Pac. 415.
A life tenant without power of appointment, or other disposition of the
remainder, can not in any manner affect the rights of those entitled to
the remainder of the estate by consenting to and approving an
unauthorized investment of the estate.—International Trust Co. v.
Preston, 24 Wyo. 163, 178, 156 Pac. 1128. Where one of the heirs of
the decedent died without issue prior to the determination of the
heirship, the other heirs can not acquire her interest in the estate
of the decedent through the probate procedings of the original estate.—
In re Skelly's Estate, 32 S. D. 381, 143 N. W. 274. Heirs and devisees
have no right to a decedent's property until his debts are paid; the
creditors are the preferred parties in interest, and, until they are
satisfied, neither heirs nor legatees have any enforceable interest.—
Dow v. Lillie, 26 N. D. 512, 528, L. R. A. 1915D, 754, 144 N. W.
1082. The heir or legatee has no right to the presonal property of the
estate until the close of the administration, except as derived through
the executor or administrator.—Murphy v. Tillson, 64 Or. 558, 130 Pac.
637. Failure to mention real property in a petition for letters of

administration does not defeat or even cloud the title of an heir under section 1366 of the Code of Washington, which vests the real property of a deceased person immediately in the heirs subject only to an administration.—Buchser v. Buchser, 72 Wash. 675, 131 Pac. 193. The right to cancel a deed obtained from an ancestor by fraud, duress, or undue influence passes to the heirs, provided the ancestor had not committed acts amounting to ratification before his death.—In re Blackinton's Estate, Woodward v. Utter, 29 Ida. 310, 158 Pac. 492.

(2) Under agreements.—If, by a writing, signed by heirs of a decedent in consideration of a sum found to be the full value of property of the estate, title to this property has been secured to the administrator, in his individual capacity, the transaction constitutes a settlement and distribution as to such of the heirs so signing as were of legal age at the time; the heirs so signing, while under age still retain shares in the property, but can not hold their cotenant accountable for past rents and profits.—Highland v. Tollisen, 75 Or. 578, 147 Pac. 558. During the lifetime of their father, an agreement was entered into between children that they should ignore his will in the event that he made one, and then share his estate equally as if he had died intestate, but under this agreement a final distribution of the parent's estate was a condition precedent to an action on the contract; where the executor refused to apply for distribution when the estate was in a condition to be finally closed, it was held that this constituted a breach of contract, giving a right of action to the other children under their agreement, as the terms of the agreement necessarily implied that a general distribution of the estate should be made within a reasonable time, and the executor would not be allowed to interfere with the rights of the other parties to the contract by a refusal to apply for a final distribution of the estate.—Spanzenberg v. Spanzenberg, 19 Cal. App. 439, 126 Pac. 379.

(3) To sell, convey, or lease.—An heir of a decedent has the right to sell and to convey his interest in the estate, but not, thereby to wipe out the right of a surviving spouse of the decedent to occupy the homestead.—Belt v. Bush (Okla.), 176 Pac. 135. An heir or devisee, whether domestic or foreign, may convey immediately, upon the estate's vesting in him, without awaiting administration.—Phelps v. Grady, 168 Cal. 73, 141 Pac. 926. An oil or gas mining lease of land inherited by a minor Indian from an allottee under the act of congress, such lease being executed by a guardian, and the term of which is extended beyond the minority of such heir, is a conveyance of an interest in allotted lands must satisfy the national law in order to be valid.—Hoyt v. Fixico (Okla.), 175 Pac. 517.

4. Assignment.—The right of heirs to make a valid assignment of an interest depends upon whether there are or are not debts against the estate.—In re Collins' Estate, 102 Wash. 697, 173 Pac. 1016. Since the heir takes subject to the claims against the estate,

if he assigns part of or all his interest the assignee can take only
what the heir would have been entitled to, had he remained in possession until after payment of such claims.—Dunn v. Wallingford, 47
Utah 491, 155 Pac. 347.

5. Action by heirs.

(1) In general.—A statute which provides that the heirs or devisees
may maintain an action for the recovery of the real estate, against
any one except the administrator or executor, is not applicable to
a remainderman, although he may have received his estate through a
devise, and therefore is literally in the general category of "devisee."
It means only those heirs and devisees who have a present right of
possession, and therefore a present cause of action as against every
one except the administrator.—Pryor v. Winter, 147 Cal. 554, 109 Am.
St. Rep. 162, 82 Pac. 202, 203. Upon the death of a mother, her property rights go to her legal representatives, and· they alone can bring
suit to establish the validity of a claim against the estate. The
daughter has no legal capacity to maintain a suit "to collect an
undistributed share of an undivided portion of an unsettled estate."—
Hall v. Cowells' Estate, 15 Colo. 343, 25 Pac. 705, 706. Actions in
relation to the real estate of an ancestor can be maintained by the heir
only after the close of administration, unless some special circumstance
appears which takes the case out of the general rule.—Hazelton v.
Bogardus, 8 Wash. 102, 35 Pac. 602, 603. A direction to the executor,
in a will, to convert all property of the testator into money as soon as
practicable after death, is not a devise, and· vests no title in the
executor, nor does it deprive the heir of the right to maintain an
action for the possession of real estate, of which the testator held the
fee, against any person other than the executor.—Estep v. Armstrong,
91 Cal. 659, 663, 27 Pac. 1091. The ordinary and usual way in which
the title of the ancestor descends to the heir, in such shape as
to make it available to him, is by decree of distribution; and he
can not maintain an action with reference thereto until such decree
has been rendered by the probate court, unless special circumstances
are alleged and proved to show that administration of the estate of
the deceased is unnecessary.—Balch v. Smith, 4 Wash. 497, 30 Pac.
648, 650; Lawrence v. Bellingham Bay, etc., R. Co., 4 Wash. 664, 30
Pac. 1099. Where letters of administration have been granted in one
county, the next of kin of decedent have such an interest as to
entitle them to maintain a proceeding for a writ of prohibition to
prevent another court from assuming jurisdiction of the estate.—Dun-
gan v. Superior Court, 149 Cal. 98, 104, 84 Pac. 767, 117 Am. St. Rep.
119. An action for damages to the freehold may be maintained by
the sole devisee in possession, in her individual capacity, and judgment in such action would bar her recovery for the same cause as
executrix.—Colton v. Onderdonk, 69 Cal. 155, 158, 10 Pac. 395, 58
Am. St. Rep. 556. ᐟ The heirs of a deceased partner can not maintain

an action against a surviving partner or his personal representative for an accounting as to partnership affairs. The surviving partner is not required to account with the heirs, but with the personal representative of the deceased partner; and the title of the heirs to partnership assets is subject not only to the settlement of the partnership affairs, but also to the administration of their ancestor's estate.—Robertson v. Burrell, 110 Cal. 568, 574, 42 Pac. 1086. Sufficient complaint showing that plaintiff heirs were the owners of a fund loaned to a mortgagee by the administrator.—See Chaves v. Myer, 13 N. M. 368, 85 Pac. 233, 6 L. R. A. (N. S.) 793. The heirs may bring, against the widow of the deceased, a suit to set aside a deed made by the intestate, alleged to have been executed under undue influence.—Trubody v. Trubody, 137 Cal. 172, 69 Pac. 968. The right of an heir to institute a suit for the possession of real estate is subject to the right of possession by the executor or administrator.—Honsinger v. Stewart, 34 N. D. 513, 519, 159 N. W. 12. It is the right of the heirs, even where an administrator has been appointed and the estate is in course of settlement, to maintain an action as against third persons for the possession of realty.—Wren v. Dixon, 40 Nev. 170, 210, 161 Pac. 722, Ann. Cas. 1918D, 1064, 167 Pac. 324. Heirs are entitled to maintain an action to recover the personalty of an intestate.—First Nat. Bank v. Tevis, 29 Okla. 714, 119 Pac. 218. The rights and duties of the administrator intervene between the vesting of title and the right of possession enjoyed by the heir; hence, until the estate is settled, if the heir would sue in respect to personal property or claims of the estate, he must show by his complaint why the administrator, rather than he, is not the complaining party.—Holland v. Kelly, 177 Cal. 43, 171 Pac. 421.

REFERENCES.

Right of legatee of distributee to sue for assets belonging to decedent's estate.—See note 4 Am. & Eng. Ann. Cas. 193.

(2) In ejectment.—Pending the administration of an estate, the heirs can not recover, in ejectment, the portion inherited by them, as against the administrator, who is entitled to the possession of the whole estate, until it shall have been settled or delivered over by order of the court; and this applies to the executors of a foreign will, as well as to the administrators of a domestic will. Administration of the estate under the will is set on foot at the time the will is admitted to probate; and the administration thus shown to have been instituted will be presumed to have been in progress at the date of the institution of the action, where the action was brought soon after the probating of the will.—Plass v. Plass, 121 Cal. 131, 53 Pac. 448, 450; Dunn v. Peterson, 4 Wash. 170, 29 Pac. 998. But the possession of an executor is that of the heir or devisee, and, as against third persons, the latter can maintain an action of ejectment, as well as the former. Hence one who is in possession of land as a sole devisee, pending settlement of the testator's estate, may maintain an

action for the recovery of damages for a trespass to such land while he is in possession thereof.—Colton v. Onderdonk, 69 Cal. 155, 158, 10 Pac. 395. The right to the possession of the real property of an intestate remains exclusively with the administrator until the estate is settled, or distribution is directed by order of the probate court. Until such time, neither the heirs nor their grantees can maintain ejectment for any portion of such property.—Meeks v. Hahn, 20 Cal. 620, 629. An heir or devisee, or their grantees, are not entitled to the possession of their share of decedent's estate, and can not maintain ejectment therefor until the administration of the estate is closed.—Chapman v. Hollister, 42 Cal. 462; Meeks v. Kirby, 46 Cal. 168. But this principle does not apply to a case where the claim is by one not bearing such a relation to the estate, and who claims the property as his own, and impliedly denies that it is a part of the decedent's estate.—Lamme v. Dodson, 4 Mont. 560, 2 Pac. 298. An heir can not maintain ejectment for the reason that the real estate is in the possession, actual or constructive, of the administrator, and he should not be allowed to maintain an action to quiet title, for the reason that it is the duty of the administrator to take every step necessary to protect the interest of the estate.—Hazelton v. Bogardus, 8 Wash. 102, 35 Pac. 602, 603. As against strangers, the right of the heir to the possession of land belonging to the estate has been expressly recognized.—Berry v. Eyraud, 134 Cal. 82, 83, 66 Pac. 74; McFadden v. Ellmaker, 52 Cal. 348, 350. Where there are no creditors, nor costs or debts of any kind outstanding against the estate, and the administrator has declined to bring suit, and has waived his right to do so, in favor of the heirs, the latter may maintain ejectment in their own names for property which had descended to them from their ancestor.—Gossage v. Crown Point, etc., Co., 14 Nev. 153, 160. Under the statutes of Washington, an heir, as such, without any allegation as to administration, or the want or necessity of it, can not maintain an action for the recovery of property alleged to have belonged to his ancestor.—Balch v. Smith, 4 Wash. 497, 30 Pac. 648. Where no administration has been taken out on the estate of a decedent, the heir or devisee may maintain ejectment for the real estate; but if administration has been granted, and there is a temporary vacancy in the office of the representative, pending administration, the heir or devisee can not maintain ejectment during the vacancy, and his grantee is bound by the same rule.—Chapman v. Hollister, 42 Cal. 462, 464. A person who is the sole heir of his deceased mother, whose estate he represents as administrator is, as such heir, entitled to the possession of the real property of the estate; and, as heir, may prosecute or defend an action of ejectment.—Eggers v. Krueger (Cal.), 236 Fed. 852, 150 C. C. A. 114. A devisee can not maintain ejectment until the estate is settled and the administration closed.—Bilger v. Nunan, 199 Fed. 549, 561, 118 C. C. A. 23.

REFERENCES.

Actions by heirs to recover possession of property before distribution in probate.—See note 23 Am. Dec. 200-203.

(3) **To enforce trust.**—An action to establish a trust and to compel a conveyance of the legal title to real estate is properly brought by the heirs of a deceased beneficiary, and the administrator of his estate is not the proper party to bring such action.—Janes v. Throckmorton, 57 Cal. 368, 387. A suit in equity to set aside conveyances by a decedent and to enforce a constructive trust in the property so conveyed, may properly be brought by one of the heirs for the benefit of himself and co-heirs.—Kimball v. Tripp, 136 Cal. 631, 635, 69 Pac. 428. A mortgagor died leaving the mortgage unsatisfied so that foreclosure proceedings were begun after his death. Some body made an offer to the heirs to purchase of the mortgagee, proceed with the foreclosure suit, having himself substituted as plaintiff, take a default judgment, purchase in his own name at the sale, and then hold for the heirs in trust, it being agreed that they would repay him principal, interest, and costs. But after the foreclosure sale this person affected never to have agreed to hold in trust and claimed the property as his absolute estate. In a suit by the heirs, to have such alleged trust declared and enforced, the defendant was adjudged to be a trustee.—O'Rourke v. Skellinger, 169 Cal. 270, 146 Pac. 633. The San Francisco stock exchange is an unincorporated body, existing and operating under regulations agreed upon by the members; one of these is that the legal title and ownership of all the association's property, etc., shall be held by the officers in trust for the members, no member being deemed to have an individual right to any part thereof, except in case of final dissolution, in which case the effects would be distributed among the membership, but that, in the event of a solvent member's dying, the board shall dispose of his vacant seat to the best advantage for the benefit of his personal representatives. A building was purchased by the association, and this was afterwards sold and the proceeds divided, by agreement of the living members, in shares of $3000 to each of these living members and to certain successors of deceased members. Hassey, a deceased member, had died in good standing, but the share that would have come to him was paid to the president, Ruggles, who professed to hold the money for his creditors. The court held that if Ruggles paid the money to Hassey's creditors it would be an illegal act, and he would not relieve himself of the duty to account to Hassey's heirs.—Hassey v. Ruggles, 30 Cal. App. 19, 156 Pac. 989. The members of an unincorporated association, such as the S. F. Stock and Exchange Board may, by consent of them all and by an appropriate writing, alter the terms of their original articles of association; and, though one of them, or his successor in interest, did not sign the instrument effecting the alteration, the persons so claiming must show that he was offered the opportunity to consent. The representative of a deceased member, who did not sign such

agreement, has an equal advantage with one who did, where it appears that the one who did not sign was not given an opportunity to do so, or to participate in the benefits of the agreement; the fact that the successor sues for benefits under the alteration shows that there was no refusal to consent.—Hassey v. Ruggles, 30 Cal. App. 19, 156 Pac. 989.

(4) In partition.—The title to land descends to heirs at law subject to administration of the testator's estate, and subordinate to the testator's testamentary disposition thereof. The right of the heirs at law to the land may be superseded by the provisions of a will, and a decree directing its sale and a distribution of the proceeds. The heirs, therefore, have no such estate or interest in the land, or right to its possession, as will enable them to maintain an action of partition respecting it.—Bank of Ukiah v. Rice, 143 Cal. 265, 101 Am. St. Rep. 118, 76 Pac. 1020, 1021. A suit for partition of land can not be maintained by an administrator of an estate, and a statutory provision, that, for the purpose of bringing suits for partition, the possession of executors or administrators is the possession of the heirs or devisees, evidently refers to such suits brought by heirs or devisees. The intent is to give them all the rights which actual possession would give them, and to make the possession of the administrator the same as if the heirs or devisees were actually in possession, preserving, however, all the rights of the executor or administrator for the purposes of administration.—Ryer v. Fletcher Ryer Co., 126 Cal. 482, 484, 58 Pac. 908. Heirs suing for the possession and partition of real estate to which they have acquired title by descent are not required to show, as a condition precedent to recovery, that the land is not subject to appropriation for the payment of the decedent's debts.— O'Keefe v. Behrens, 73 Kan. 469, 9 Ann. Cas. 867, 85 Pac. 555.

(5) On promissory notes.—The heir of a deceased indorsee of a promissory note can not maintain an action thereon until the termination of the probate proceedings, and a showing that he became the owner of the note by an order or distribution made by the probate court.—Mears v. Smith, 19 S. D. 79, 102 N. W. 295, 296, 297.

REFERENCES.

Action by heir against executor on promissory note belonging to decedent.—See head-line 4, subd. 2, post. Actions by heirs in respect to personal estate.—See note 112 Am. St. Rep. 731-735.

(6) To quiet title.—The heirs of a decedent may maintain or defend in their own names an action to quiet title to land in which it is claimed decedent was interested.—Tryon v. Huntoon, 67 Cal. 325, 329, 7 Pac. 741. Heirs or devisees of a decedent may properly be joined with a special administrator of the estate in a suit to quiet title to the property of the estate.—Miller v. Luco, 80 Cal. 257, 259, 260, 22 Pac. 195. Actions in relation to the real estate of the ancestor can

only be maintained by the heir after the close of administration, unless some special circumstance appears which takes the case out of the general rule. This principle applies to actions to quiet title, the same as in actions in ejectment.—Hazelton v. Bogardus, 8 Wash. 102, 35 Pac. 602, 603. Knowledge by an heir that real estate of the intestate has not been included in the probate proceedings of the estate, does not preclude such heir, or those claiming under him, from recovering in an action to quiet title as against persons claiming as grantees under deeds inter vivos; real estate descends to heirs immediately on the death of the owner, and, unless it is necessary to sell it to pay debts of the estate, it need not be included in the probate proceedings. —Showalter v. Spangle, 93 Wash. 326, 160 Pac. 1042.

(7) For use and occupation.—An heir can not sue for use and occupation of real estate as for a period prior to the making of the decree of distribution.—Estate of Piercy, Piercy v. Piercy, 168 Cal. 750, 145 Pac. 88. Where an heir conveys his real property to an administrator, but afterwards seeks to set aside his deed, and the administrator individually claims title in himself, the plaintiff, suing as heir of the decedent, can not recover for use and occupation; but a judgment in favor of the administrator individually is not a bar to a charge against him in his account, as representative, for use and occupation.—Estate of Piercy, Piercy v. Piercy, 168 Cal. 750, 145 Pac. 88.

(8) Counterclaim will not be considered when.—If the administrator of an estate refuses to bring an action to recover property from the widow, which is alleged to belong to the estate, and the heirs bring such action, counterclaims as to the widow's allowance, and as to her interest in the estate, will not be considered in an action on an appeal bond given in the first-named action.—Bem v. Shoemaker, 10 S. D. 453, 74 N. W. 239, 241.

(9) Judgment for heirs as an estoppel.—If heirs are permitted to sue on behalf of an estate, a judgment recovered by them will estop the administrator from presenting another claim on account of the same judgment.—Sixta v. Heiser, 14 S. D. 346, 85 N. W. 598, 599. Though judgment estops only as to parties and privies, all the world are parties to regular probate proceedings wherein claim of representative is allowed, and are thus bound, subject to right of interested parties, to have claim set aside for cause.—Shiels v. Nathan, 12 Cal. App. 604, 108 Pac. 34.

6. Actions by heirs against administrators.

(1) In general.—If the administrator of an estate dies, and the heirs bring an action against the administratrix of such deceased administrator, the new administrator of the original estate is a proper, if not necessary, party to the action, where he is hostile to the interests of the heirs.—Sixta v. Heiser, 14 S. D. 346, 85 N. W. 598, 599. Where the heirs of a deceased person, after the estate has been finally

settled in the probate court, bring an action in the district court against the former administrator and others, and set forth in their petition that the defendants, through conspiracy and fraud, procured fraudulent judgments and orders to be entered in the probate court, and committed other wrongs, whereby they cheated and defrauded the heirs out of a large proportion of the estate, and that plaintiff had no knowledge of such wrongs and frauds until after the final settlement in the probate court, and petitioners pray to have the aforesaid judgments and orders set aside, and for other relief, such petition states a cause of action, and only one, and the district court has jurisdiction of the same.—Gafford v. Dickinson, 37 Kan. 287, 15 Pac. 175. A devisee of land, under the will of decedent, can not maintain an action for rents and profits of such land received by the executrix, but not accounted for by the latter, where the devisee has allowed the accounts of the executrix to be settled without objection. The settlement of the accounts is conclusive upon all such parties interested.—Washington v. Black, 83 Cal. 290, 294, 23 Pac. 300. The heirs of a decedent can not maintain an action on the bond of the administrator to recover funds misapplied by the latter until after the settlement of his accounts, and a refusal by him to pay any sum adjudged against him on such settlement.—Weihe v. Statham, 67 Cal. 84, 7 Pac. 143. If an administrator purchases land in his own name, with funds of the estate, the heirs are entitled to have such land adjudged to be trust property.—Merket v. Smith, 33 Kan. 66, 5 Pac. 394. Heirs have the right to sue the administrator and all others interested to recover a debt due to the estate when the administrator has refused to bring suit therefor.—Trotter v. Mutual Reserve Fund, etc., Assoc., 9 S. D. 596, 600, 70 N. W. 843. The administrator of a decedent's estate is entitled to the possession of the property, pending administration, and a judgment in ejectment against him in favor of the heirs is improper.—Burgel v. Prisser, 89 Cal. 70, 72, 26 Pac. 787. Where an heir abandons a homestead, he can not afterwards, in an action against the administrator, recover the proceeds of its sale as exempt to him.—Miller v. Baker, 9 Kan. App. 883, 58 Pac. 1002, 1003. For circumstances under which an agreement by the heirs not to sue one executor does not release his co-executor, see Estate of Sanderson, 74 Cal. 199, 212, 15 Pac. 753. In an action against an administratrix by an heir to compel defendant to turn over to plaintiff one-half in value of certain notes claimed to belong to the estate, the mortgages securing the notes on which were written assignments of the mortgages to testator's widow, the administratrix, were admissible to identify the notes as the notes which were transferred by decedent.—Lane v. Lane, 57 Colo. 419, 140 Pac. 806.

(2) **Against administrators individually.**—An action against an administrator under a statute which authorizes distributees to "demand, sue for, and recover their respective shares from an administrator or executor, or any person having the same in possession," is an

action against the executor or administrator individually, and not against him in his representative capacity. It is not an action against the estate. If against the estate, the rights of the distributee are fully adjudicated by the decree of distribution.—St. Mary's Hospital v. Perry, 152 Cal. 338, 92 Pac. 864, 865. In an action against an executrix in an individual capacity, her refusal to pay over moneys, which, under the decree, it was her duty as executrix to pay, the words "as executrix," etc., in the title of the action, are merely descriptive.—St Mary's Hospital v. Perry, 152 Cal. 338, 92 Pac. 864, 865. An action by a distributee against an administrator for the share distributed to the former may be brought against the latter individually, and no demand is necessary before suit.—Melone v. Davis, 67 Cal. 279, 7 Pac. 703. If a decree of distribution has been made, and the court has ordered a distributee's share in the estate of the decedent to be paid to the heir within a certain time, and such time has elapsed without payment, an action to recover such share should be brought against the administrator individually, and not in his representative capacity; and no demand on the defendant, as administrator, and refusal to pay, need be alleged. The defendant, in such case, is liable in contempt for not making the payment under the decree, and as to him, the suit brought is a sufficient demand.—Melone v. Davis, 67 Cal. 279, 7 Pac. 703, 704. An unauthorized payment of the shares of certain distributees of an estate to an attorney leaves the executor liable therefor, which liability is not affected by the "judgment or decree discharging him from all liability incurred thereafter."—Bryant v. McIntosh, 3 Cal. App. 95, 84 Pac. 440, 441. A suit by heirs against an executor, on a promissory note, alleged to have belonged to the decedent, but fraudulently destroyed by the executor, and omitted from his inventory and accounts, is barred by a decree settling the executor's final account, where plaintiffs appeared at the hearing and filed objections to the account.—Tobelman v. Hildebrandt, 72 Cal. 313, 316, 14 Pac. 20.

7. **Limitation of actions by heirs. Laches.**—The validity of a claim against the estate of a decedent is not necessarily determined by its antiquity, but when the ancestor permits a period exceeding thrice the statute of limitations to go by without an attempt at legal enforcement, the heir should be held to strict proof of whatever may be necessary to take the case out of the operation of the statute, and of what may be essential to a recovery.—Hall v. Cowles' Estate, 15 Colo. 343, 25 Pac. 705, 706. If an administrator or trustee allows the statute of limitations to run so as to bar his rights as such, he lays himself liable to the heir, or any one else injured by his failure to perform his duty.—Jenkins v. Jenson, 24 Utah 108, 91 Am. St. Rep. 783, 66 Pac. 773, 778. The rule that the statute of limitations does not bar a trust estate holds only between cestui que trust and trustee, and not as between the cestui que trust and trustee on the one side, and strangers on the other. Hence, in an action between one claiming

as heir to an estate on the one hand, and strangers to the estate on the other, as where a posthumous heir of the intestate, born after the administrator's appointment, brings suit to quiet title to the estate owned by his ancestor, he can not avail himself of the disability of infancy to stop the running of the statute of limitations, where it had begun to run against the administrator by reason of adverse possession of the land.—Jenkins v. Jenson, 24 Utah 108, 91 Am. St. Rep. 783, 66 Pac. 773, 776, 778. Where purchasers at a void probate sale entered upon and claimed the property purchased by them, the heirs, and those claiming under them, are barred from maintaining any action to recover the same, unless it is commenced within three years next after the sale.—Meeks v. Vassault, 3 Saw. 206, Fed. Cas. No. 9393. A statute which requires actions brought by the heirs of a deceased person for the recovery of real property descending to them, but sold by an administrator of the estate of the decedent upon an order of court directing such sale, to be commenced within five years after the time of the recording of the deed made in pursuance of the sale, applies to sales which are void for want of notice to the heirs of the proceedings upon which the deed is based.—O'Keefe v. Behrens, 73 Kan. 469, 85 Pac. 555. There is no limitation upon the right of heirs, who are unknown, but who are citizens of the United States, to bring an action to recover either real or personal property, until the entry of a judgment in escheat proceedings brought by the state.—Estate of Miner, 143 Cal. 194, 199, 76 Pac. 968. The heir is barred of his action when the executor is barred, although the heir or devisee may be laboring under a disability. The general rule is, that, when a trustee is barred by the statute of limitation, the cestui que trust is likewise barred, even though an infant. The heir or devisee is dependent upon the diligence of the executor for the maintenance of his rights, but is not without a remedy by an action for damages against his executor and his sureties, or by a proper proceeding to compel him to bring suit. Where the administrator neglects to bring an action to recover property of the estate until it is barred under the statute of limitations applicable to the subject, the heir is also barred, even though the heir be a minor at the time the action accrues to the administrator.—McLeran v. Benton, 73 Cal. 329, 2 Am. St. Rep. 814, 14 Pac. 879; Meeks v. Vassault, 3 Saw., 206, 214, Fed. Cas. No. 9393; Meeks v. Olpherts, 100 U. S. 564, 25 L. Ed. 735. Where the purchaser at a probate sale had been in possession of the lands for a period of nineteen years prior to the commencement of an action by the heirs, and for more than fifteen years after the youngest heir became of age, and such possession had been open, notorious, and exclusive, the courts will not interfere in attempts to establish a stale trust, and the laches of the heirs where such circumstances exist, will preclude them from recovering the land.—Loomis v. Rosenthal, 34 Or. 585, 57 Pac. 55. Where a person died intestate, owning community property consisting of town lots, owing no debts, leaving a widow and two minor sons, and where, under the law as it existed at the time of such death, an undivided one-half interest descended to the widow, and the other one-half interest to the minor children, the widow could not legally convey the entire title to such property, but her deed, purporting to do so, would give the grantee color of title, under which he might obtain title by adverse possession; and, where the facts show that the grantee, after the minor children had arrived at majority, did acquire title to the lots by adverse possession, the right of the heirs to any part or interest in said lots, where no constructive fraud, or trust of any kind, is shown, is barred by the statute of limitations.—Coe v. Sloan, 16 Ida. 49, 56, 100 Pac. 354. Section 6462, Rev. Codes of Montana, operates on the remedy alone; it does not create a new cause of action in favor of the heir; it does not operate retroactively, but it does affect rights of action which might have been enforced at the time it took effect.—Haydon v. Normandin, 55 Mont. 539, 179 Pac. 460. Where the property of an intestate passes immediately upon his death to his wife and daughter, subject to the control of the probate court, but no administration is had and the property is converted by another to his own use, the daughter is authorized, under section 6462, Rev. Codes, to maintain an action for her interest in the converted property, at any time within five years after she becomes of age, although more than seven years have elapsed between the date of the conversion and the date of bringing such action.—Haydon v. Normandin, 55 Mont. 539, 179 Pac. 460. Prior to the time that section 6462, Rev. Codes, became effective, July 1, 1895, an heir at law could not maintain an action for the wrongful conversion of property belonging to the estate of a decedent, the right of action was in the personal representative, who was entitled to the possession of the property for the purpose of administration, and until there was a personal representative qualified to act the statute of limitations did not commence to run.—Haydon v. Normandin, 55 Mont. 539, 179 Pac. 460. The devisee in a will probated in 1894 was given real property, provided a life tenant under the will died without leaving issue surviving her. In April, 1898, the devisee, who was then a minor, executed a deed of the property to the life tenant, without consideration. In December, 1898, the devisee attained her majority. In April, 1900, the life tenant died without issue surviving her. In December, 1901, the devisee disaffirmed the deed, and in July, 1914, she commenced action to recover the property from the husband of the life tenant who claimed adverse possession from April, 1898. Held, the action was not barred by either section 15 or section 16 of the Civil Code, and section 16 does not apply by analogy in determining whether or not the deed was disaffirmed within a reasonable time.—Ralph v. Ball, 100 Kan. 460, 461, 462, 164 Pac. 1081. An action by an heir for relief on the ground of fraud must be brought within two years after the discovery of the fraud.—Campbell v. Dick (Okla.), 157 Pac. 1062. In the case of an indemnity contract which has become operative for payment of a surplus after the foreclosure of a mortgage, where the indemnitor has died, a delay of between 7 and 8 years in seeking relief from an only heir is not necessarily laches, if no change has taken place in the property.—Sullivan v. Ellis (Colo.), 219 Fed. 694, 698, 135 C. C. A. 366.

8. Actions between heirs and devisees.—Where a testator, prior to her death, placed a large amount of money in the hands of her son, to be invested and managed by him, and gave money to several of her other children for their own use, and the moneys thus given were evidenced by notes, and it appears that some interest had been paid thereon, but there is no evidence to the effect that those receiving the money should, at some time, and in some appropriate way, account therefor, it must be held, in an action between the heirs at law and devisees of the deceased (the real purpose of which is the settlement of accounts between the parties, growing out of moneys received by them from her), that the moneys so advanced to the other children were received by them as loans, and not as gifts. If one should therefore be credited with his or her distributive share of the assets, and be charged with the money or other property received, or money unaccounted for, as the case may be, the balances thus ascertained will exhibit the account between the parties.—Haines v. Christie, 28 Colo. 502, 66 Pac. 883, 884, 886, 887. In an accounting between the heirs and devisees of an estate to determine their distributive shares, moneys or property received by one of them from the estate, in the nature of advancements, are properly charged against his share, notwithstanding the statute of limitations may have run since the payments or advancements.—Goodnough v. Webber, 75 Kan. 209, 88 Pac. 879, 881. Where, of the several children of a woman decedent, one daughter devoted herself to caring for her mother for the last 15 years of her life, and, entertaining a purpose to file accordingly a claim against the estate for compensation, was induced to forego the purpose by the other heirs agreeing to pay her each a stipulated sum, a good consideration for the agreement can be pleaded by this daughter in an action by her against one of the other heirs who, when it was two late to file a claim, refused to pay the stipulated sum.—Norman v. Miller, 40 S. D. 399, 167 N. W. 391.

9. Right of heirs to attack transfer of property.

(1) For want of jurisdiction.—The superior court may vacate and set aside orders made by it in the course of its probate jurisdiction. Where the superior court is the successor of the probate court, under a former system of laws, it must be held to be the same court; and where the statute requires the appearance of minor heirs by guardian ad litem before the court shall make an order of sale, such appearance is necessary to give jurisdiction, even if the proceedings are in rem. A court must have jurisdiction both of the estate and of the persons of minor heirs to devest them of their title, where the statute expressly requires the minor heirs to be represented. They can not waive this right, and the court can not waive it by non-compliance with the statute. Hence an order of sale made without the appearance of the minor heirs is without authority of law, and is void as to them.—Ball v. Clothier, 34 Wash. 299, 75 Pac. 1099, 1102, 1103. But where property has been sold by order of the court, without the appearance of minor heirs, but the land was purchased from the estate in good faith, and the purchase price thereof was paid into the estate and used in the administration thereof, and such heirs received the benefit, they should not be permitted to avoid the sale without repaying the purchase price.—Ball v. Clothier, 34 Wash. 299, 75 Pac. 1099, 1104. A statute curing irregularities in executors', administrators', or guardians' sales relates to irregularities, and does not go to the jurisdiction of the court. Such a statute can not validate a sale which was void for want of jurisdiction.—Ball v. Clothier, 34 Wash. 299, 75 Pac. 1099, 1103; Dormitzer v. German Sav. & L. Soc., 23 Wash. 132, 192, 62 Pac. 862, 882. If the order of sale is void, the sale may be attacked collaterally by the heirs.—Townsend v. Tallant, 33 Cal. 45, 54, 91 Am. Dec. 620. If the sale is void, it can not be made valid and binding by a so-called confirmation; the sale being void, there is no subject-matter upon which the order of confirmation can act. If the court had no jurisdiction to order the sale, it has none to confirm it.—Townsend v. Tallant, 33 Cal. 45, 54, 91 Am. Dec. 620. Where an administrator files his petition, and commences proceedings for the sale of real estate belonging to his intestate, all of the orders made in such matter are in one proceedings, and such proceeding consists of all orders and things done by the court, in such matter, from the filing of the petition to the confirmation of the sale and delivery of the deed. The heirs, in such cases, are pecuniarily interested in all such property, and are entitled to their day in court in all of the proceedings affecting the title to such property, and are adverse parties.—Reed v. Stewart, 12 Ida. 699, 87 Pac. 1002.

(2) **Mental incapacity or undue influence.**—Where an assignment is questioned, after the death of the assignor, on the ground of the latter's alleged mental incapacity, and that also of undue influence, the court may, without abuse of discretion, rely on the testimony of the assignor's mother, brothers, and sister, who saw him only now and then, rather than that of his wife and nurses who saw him daily.—Dow v. George E. Dow Estate Co., 37 Cal. App. 20, 173 Pac. 406. Where the questions before the court are the mental condition of an assignor, who has died since becoming such, and of whether he was subjected to undue influence, his mother, brothers, and sister are compentent witnesses even though during his latter years they may have been with him but infrequently.—Dow v. George E. Dow Estate Co., 37 Cal. App. 20, 173 Pac. 406. Where a son transfers a one-eighth interest in his father's estate for one-eighth of the stock of the corporation, into which such estate has been converted, there is a change of form only

without altering the extent, and the question of undue influence respecting the transfer does not arise.—Dow v. George E. Dow Estate Co., 37 Cal. App. 20, 173 Pac. 406. If a deed and bill of sale be given by a father to a son, the instruments will not, after the death of the father, be set aside as having been procured by undue influence, unless evidence is produced other than of the mere fact that the son had ample opportunity to exert such influence.—Walsh v. Walsh, 38 S. D. 628, 162 N. W. 398. Evidence examined and held sufficient to sustain the findings of the trial court that the grantor of instruments conveying his real property and assigning his bank stock to defendants, the children of a living sister of the deceased, was mentally incompetent and incapable of making them at the time of their execution and delivery.—Bruington v. Wagoner, 100 Kan. 10, 439, 164 Pac. 1057.

(3) For fraud.—An action in equity, by certain heirs of deceased, to obtain a decree adjudging the defendants to hold certain real property as trustees for plaintiffs, and for an accounting as to the rents and profits thereof, received by defendant, on the ground of the alleged fraud of defendants in procuring the title in the course of the administration of the estate of deceased, is not a collateral attack on the probate orders, but a direct attack thereon.—Campbell-Kawannanakoa v. Campbell, 152 Cal. 201, 92 Pac. 184, 187. Heirs are entitled to equitable relief on the ground of extrinsic fraud, where the trustees of a void trust in a will, planned and carried into execution a scheme whereby a sale of decedent's property was made, and a nominal decree of distribution procured, where there was no necessity for any sale of the property, no intention to sell, no sale, and no proceeds of sale to be distributed or delivered to the trustees named as distributees in the purported decree, but which scheme was all a fraudulent imposition upon the jurisdiction of the superior court, an attempt, by concealing the real facts of the transaction from the court, to use that jurisdiction for the purpose of depriving plaintiffs, without consideration, of the property to which they had succeeded, and a mere cloak to cover what was in fact simply the bodily taking of plaintiff's property without consideration and without any authority of law.—Campbell-Kawannanakoa v. Campbell, 152 Cal. 201, 92 Pac. 184, 186. A sale of real estate belonging to the estate of a deceased testator, made by an executor to the surety on his bond, under the order of the probate court, procured through the fraud of the executor, may be set aside at the suit of a devisee, even though the surety was ignorant of the dishonest conduct of his principal.—Fincke v. Bundrick, 72 Kan. 182, 4 L. R. A. (N. S.) 820, 83 Pac. 403. Relief may be granted in equity, on the application of defrauded heirs, from a sale of property of an estate to which they are entitled, where such sale was made in fraud of their rights, by the executrix, under a power in the will of their ancestor.—In re Johnson, 7 Cal. App. 436, 94 Pac. 592.

10. Estoppel of heirs.—Although plaintiffs, who sue as heirs, and as grantees of another heir of an intestate, to recover certain real estate, may be precluded, by their conduct, from claiming a one-third interest in the property sued for, the complaint is still sufficient to support their claim as heirs at law of the said decedent for the other two-thirds of the land described in it, unless plaintiffs are estopped by a decree of distribution, available on the face of the complaint.—Alcorn v. Brandeman, 145 Cal. 62, 65, 78 Pac. 343. If a timber-culture claimant dies before performing the conditions precedent to obtaining title from the government, and administration is had, and the claim is sold by order of court, the heir is not estopped from asserting title to the claim, after the purchase at the administrator's sale, where it is not shown that he had actual knowledge of the sale, or that he induced the purchaser to make the purchase, although he may have acquiesced in the proceedings of the administrator. Where the owner of land that is offered for sale stands by, and, with knowledge of his title, encourages the sale, or does not forbid it, and thus another person, in ignorance of the true title, is induced to make the purchase under the supposition that the title offered is good, he is bound by the sale, and neither he nor his privies will be allowed to dispute the purchaser's title. But, to justify the application of this principle, it is indispensable that the party sought to be estopped should, by his conduct or gross negligence, encourage or influence the purchase, and that the other party, being at the time ignorant of the actual title, should have been misled by his acts and conduct, and induced thereby to change his position.—Haun v. Martin, 48 Or. 304, 86 Pac. 371, 373. An heir is not, by reason of an unauthorized act by his guardian, estopped to claim his inheritance.—Packard v. Packard, 95 Kan. 644, 149 Pac. 404. If a settler on public land die before the issue of patent leaving by will all his property to the widow for life with remainder to the children, the fact that the children, ignorant that the title of the land is in the heirs regardless of the will, allow the widow to collect the rents and profits during her lifetime, does not estop them from acting on their legal rights thereafter.—Leslie v. Harrison Nat. Bank, 97 Kan. 22, 154 Pac. 209.

11. Liability of heirs.

(1) In general.—The heirs are not bound to pay the debts or to discharge the obligations of the ancestor, unless they have received property from the estate, but if they have received assets, they are answerable for such debts and obligations only to the extent of their inheritance.—Bacon v. Thornton, 16 Utah 138, 51 Pac. 153. If a party seeks satisfaction for debts or obligations of the ancestor, from the heirs, the burden is upon him to show that they inherited assets from the ancestor's estate.—Bacon v. Thornton, 16 Utah 138, 51 Pac. 153, 154. Although, by the common law of England, heirs are not bound by a covenant of warranty of their ancestors, unless expressly named therein, and then only to the extent of the assets received by descent, yet, in this state, when, after all the assets have been converted into money, and distributed to the heirs, an obligation of the ancestor matures, such heirs may be compelled to refund to the claimant so much of what they have received as shall be sufficient to satisfy the obligation.—Rohrbaugh v. Hamblin, 57 Kan. 393, 57 Am. St. Rep. 334, 46 Pac. 705 (reversing Hamblin v. Rohrbaugh, 3 Kan. App. 131, 42 Pac. 834). In any proceeding brought, either in the probate court or in equity, for the purpose of subjecting the land of an heir or devise to the payment of a claim against the ancestor, such heir or devisee, or any person holding under them, may contest the legality or justness of such claim, and that, regardless of whether it has been duly allowed by the probate court as a claim against the estate.—Black v. Elliott, 63 Kan. 211, 88 Am. St. Rep. 239, 65 Pac. 215 (following Bauserman v. Charlott, 46 Kan. 480, 26 Pac. 1051, and Kulp v. Kulp, 51 Kan. 341, 21 L. R. A. 550, 32 Pac. 1118). If the creditor of an insolvent corporation brings an action against the widow and sole heir of a deceased stockholder of such corporation, to enforce a statutory liability, and to charge her as such heir, she is not a necessary party in her representative character as executrix.—Cooper v. Ives, 62 Kan. 395, 63 Pac. 434, 436; and, in such a case, the action can not be defeated by showing that there is sufficient personal property in another state, in the hands of the widow and executrix, for the payment of the creditor's claim.—Cooper v. Ives, 62 Kan. 395, 63 Pac. 434, 436. An action in the nature of a creditor's bill can not be maintained by a judgment creditor of an estate against an heir to enforce the judgment of the former against land which had descended to the latter.—Huneke v. Dold, 7 N. M. 5, 32 Pac. 45. If a claim against the estate of a deceased person, in Oklahoma, does not accrue or become enforceable until after the administration of the estate has been closed, and all the property has been distributed and passed into the hands of the heirs, its collection may be enforced by a direct action, in a district court of that state, against the heirs of the deceased, and they are answerable in such action to the extent of the assets received by them from the estate; a demurrer to the jurisdiction of the district court in such an action should be overruled.—Chitty v. Gillett, 46 Okla. 724, 148 Pac. 1048.

REFERENCES.

Liability of heirs for obligations of ancestor.—See note 21 L. R. A. 84-89. Liability of heir or devisee for debt of ancestor.—See note 112 Am. St. Rep. 1017-1027.

(2) **Limitation of liability.**—A statute which simply declares a remedy which may be pursued upon a claim, upon the covenant or agreement of the ancestor, does not create a new and independent cause of action against heirs, but must be construed with and as supplementary to the general statutory provisions for the establishment of claims against estates. If the ancestor makes a covenant, which is broken when made, and subsequently dies, leaving a large

estate over his debts and liabilities, which, in due course of administration, is distributed among his heirs and legatees, after payment of
all claims presented and allowed, and his executors are discharged, no
claim having been presented or demand made on account of such
broken contract, by reason of which the same is barred as a claim
against the estate, and no facts appear to excuse such non-presentation, no action can be maintained thereon, under such a statute, against
an heir by reason of his having succeeded to a portion of the real
property of said estate.—Woods v. Ely, 7 S. D. 471, 64 N. W. 531.
The right of action against heirs to whom the ancestor's estate has
been distributed under administration proceedings, to compel a refund-
ing to one claiming damages for breach of a covenant of warranty
occurring after such distribution, is not barred until five years after
such breach.—Wood v. Cross, 8 Kan. App. 42, 54 Pac. 12. Where a
husband had acted as the agent of his wife, in the purchase of land
with her separate funds, and had taken the deed in his own name,
without her knowledge, and recorded the same, and afterwards died,
an action to establish and enforce a resulting trust in her favor may
be maintained by her against the heirs of the deceased husband, and
the statute of limitations is not put in motion, in such a case, by the
recording of the deed.—Hinze v. Hinze, 76 Kan. 169, 12 L. R. A. (N. S.)
493, 90 Pac. 762.

12. No allowance to heirs, of costs and expenses, from estate.—An
heir or legatee, who seeks the removal of an executor, has no power
to deal with or to control the assets of the estate, and can not make
contracts which, in any way, will bind the estate. And the fact that
the heir, who, as such, successfully prosecuted an action for the removal of an executor, afterwards became such administratrix, would
not justify payment, out of the assets of the estate, of any item of cost
and expenses incurred by her in the removal of such executor.—Estate of Bell, 145 Cal. 646, 79 Pac. 358, 359. If heirs choose to bring
suit to remove a cloud from title to their property, the expenses of
such litigation are to be adjusted and paid by the parties to the action,
and not by the estate of which the property forms a part. To hold
otherwise would be to make an estate liable for expenses and costs
which could not be controlled or measured by an administrator or
executor; and invite confusion, if not absolute waste, in the settlement of estates.—Estate of Heeney, 3 Cal. App. 548, 553, 86 Pac. 842.
If two of the heirs of an intestate pay a debt, secured by mortgage on
the family home, for the purpose of dispensing with the necessity of
probate proceedings, which all of the heirs are seeking to avoid, and
procure an assignment of the note and mortgage to their sister, and
one of such heirs is subsequently appointed as administrator, he is
not entitled to credit, in his account, as such administrator, for payment of the debt secured by such mortgage. The law does not contemplate that the claim of an administrator for reimbursement for
moneys expended before his appointment can be established by his

uncontradicted evidence, especially when such evidence, and the assignment presented as his voucher, show that, on the face of the record, the legal claim and right is in another, whose right has not been foreclosed.—Estate of Heeney, 3 Cal. App. 548, 86 Pac. 842.

13. Purchasers from heirs.

(1) In general.—A cause of action for a trespass or injury to land, occurring after the death of decedent, does not pass to the executor or administrator, but to the heir or devisee, or purchasers therefrom. To maintain an action to restrain waste, unless complainant is in actual possession, he must establish a valid and subsisting title in himself to the premises.—Adams v. Slattery, 36 Colo. 35, 85 Pac. 87, 89. Where one entered upon land of an intestate, under a deed from persons who in fact had no title, but who are described therein as all of the intestate's heirs, and afterwards purchased the interest of a part of the true heirs, under circumstances tending to show a recognition of their ownership, the fact that he then made unsuccessful efforts, by advertisement in newspapers and otherwise, to ascertain whether there were any other heirs, is a circumstance from which a trial court is justified in finding that the possession of such occupant was not, at that time, adverse to the heirs who had not conveyed their interest to him, notwithstanding he was in complete control of the property, paying the taxes, making improvements, and collecting the income without accounting to any one.—Sparks v. Bodensick, 72 Kan. 5, 82 Pac. 463. If an heir conveys his interest in the estate, or any part thereof, he conveys such interest only as will remain to him after satisfying the objects of administration, unless the deed should expressly cover more; and such objects of administration are: 1. To support the family for a period; 2. To set apart a homestead to the family; 3. To pay the expenses of administration; 4. To pay the debts of the deceased; 5. To distribute the balance of the estate to those who take it by law.—Estate of Moore, 57 Cal. 437, 442. Where a foreign will has made disposition of real estate in this state, in a manner different from what the law would, a purchaser from an heir of the foreign testator, in order to be protected as against one claiming under such will, must show that he procured his title from such heir in good faith, and without knowledge of the existence of the will; but knowledge of the existence of such will may be acquired by other means than the evidence of a properly certified copy thereof, or a duly entered order of admission to record or probate.—Markley v. Kramer, 66 Kan. 664, 72 Pac. 221. A person who acquires title to land of an estate from a devisee, pending administration, must be held to have the same right to have an action to quiet title thereto as is given by statute to his grantor.—Jordan v. Fay, 98 Cal. 264, 266, 33 Pac. 95. A judgment in ejectment, recovered by or against an administrator, is an estoppel in favor of or against the heir and those claiming under him; and such a judgment recovered by an administrator would inure to the benefit

of those to whom the sole heir had conveyed prior to its recovery.—
Spotts v. Hanley, 85 Cal. 155, 167, 168, 24 Pac. 738. If an heir at law
assigns his claim to an interest in an estate, the assignee has no right
of action against the widow, who wrongfully took money of the deceased, his separate property, and deposited it in a bank, and afterwards claimed it as her own, where there has been no administration
on the estate.—Galvin v. Mutual Sav. Bank, 6 Cal. App. 402, 92 Pac.
322. If an heir conveys his interest in any part of the estate of his
ancestor, pending administration, his conveyance is only of such interest as will remain to him after satisfying the objects of administration,
unless his deed expressly covers more. And such conveyance does not
preclude an application for a homestead from the land conveyed, as
the setting apart of a homestead is one of the objects of administration.
—Estate of Moore, 57 Cal. 437, 442; Phelan v. Smith, 100 Cal. 158, 166,
34 Pac. 667. A contract to purchase the interest of minor heirs at a
guardian's sale, conditioned on the conveyance of the interests of the
adult heirs in the property, the sale being duly approved, and the
adult heirs' acquiescence obtained, may be specifically enforced against
the purchaser, and this may be done although the adult heirs were
not parties to the contract.—Rice v. Theimer, 45 Okla. 618, 622, 146
Pac. 702. A creditor of an heir has no rights as against a purchaser
of the intestate's real property, regularly sold by the administrator
under order of court duly made.—Yeaton v. Barnhart, 78 Or. 249, 152
Pac. 1192.

REFERENCES.

Distribution to grantee of heir.—See division III, head-line 12, subdivision 2, post. Validity of transactions between heir and ancestor
relating to former's expectancy.—See note 32 L. R. A. 595. Validity of
sale of expectancy by a prospective heir.—See note 33 L. R. A. 266-287.

(2) Purchaser does not acquire what.—Where a testator devises a
life estate in land, and on a termination of the life estate directs it
to be sold for the benefit of parties named, who are all his heirs, and
a title to the interest of one of such beneficiaries is vested, through
foreclosure proceedings, in a party not otherwise connected with the
original title before the termination of the life estate, the holder of the
title acquired by such foreclosure can not maintain suit for partition,
after the termination of the life estate, against the remaining beneficiaries under the will, and the heirs of such beneficiaries, who died, in
the absence of a showing that all parties interested have elected to
take the land instead of its proceeds.—Bank of Ukiah v. Rice, 143 Cal.
265, 274, 76 Pac. 1020, 101 Am. St. Rep. 118. A deed by the heir to the
wife of the administrator, the subject-matter being part of the estate
in course of administration, is voidable, if not absolutely void.—In re
Blackinton's Estate, Woodward v. Utter, 29 Ida. 310, 158 Pac. 492.

the majority of his youngest son will not prevent a devisee under the
will from making a valid mortgage of his interest before that time.—
Dunn v. Schell, 122 Cal. 626, 627, 52 Pac. 595. Where a devisee, who is
also executrix, has borrowed money for the support of the family, pending administration, and mortgaged her interest in the estate therefor,
and subsequently procured an order for a probate sale of the same
property for the alleged purpose of paying a family allowance, which
included the sums so borrowed, a decree in equity, at the suit of the
mortgagee, requiring· the executrix to apply the proceeds of the probate sale to the payment of the sums due on his mortgage is proper.—
Curtis v. Schell, 129 Cal. 208, 220, 61 Pac. 951, 79 Am. St. Rep. 107. If
an heir of an estate execute an irrevocable power of attorney to receive
from the administrator the amount coming to him as such heir, and
receipt for the same, and to hold the same in trust as collateral, to
secure the donor's indebtedness to a bank, the instrument can not be
regarded as an equitable mortgage of real estate received thereunder
by the attorney in fact.—In re Springer's Estate, 97 Wash. 546, 551, 166
Pac. 1134.

15. Contracts with heirs in general.—A contract by a prospective
heir to transfer his inheritance can be specifically enforced in a court
of equity, if at all, and not in a probate court.—Dunn v. Wallingford,
47 Utah 491, 155 Pac. 347. If a corporation performs a contract, made
with the heirs of a decedent, whereby it was to redeem property of the
estate from execution sale, in consideration of their purchasing shares
of the company's capital stock, the company has no resort against the
estate on default by the heirs in respect to such consideration.—In re
Cooper's Estate, 95 Wash. 351, 163 Pac. 935.

16. Same. Contract relinquishment of right as heir.—Whatever interest the wife acquires in the community property, or in the husband's
separate property, she acquires as heir, and when she relinquishes her
rights as heir she relinquishes her right to a part of the community
property and to the subsequent acquisition of the separate property.—
Estate of Warner, 6 Cal. App. 361, 92 Pac. 191, 192. Where a woman,
in an antenuptial contract, releases all her rights in the property of her
intended husband, and as his heir, in consideration of his doing certain
things, if he fails to perform material covenants on his part, she may
show this, and still claim her rights as heir.—Estate of Warner, 6 Cal.
App. 361, 92 Pac. 191, 193. If an intended husband and wife make an
antenuptial agreement that, in consideration of the wife's receiving
from his estate, on his death, a certain sum of money, she will relinquish all claim to his property, she is entitled to such sum, not as an
heir, but under the terms of the contract.—Estate of Warner, 6 Cal.
App. 361, 92 Pac. 191, 192. The superior court, when sitting in matters
of probate, is the same as it is sitting in equity, in cases at law, or in
a special proceeding; and when it has jurisdiction of the subject-
matter of a case falling within either of these classes, it has power to
hear and determine, in the mode provided by law, all questions of law

and fact, the determination of which is necessary to a proper judgment in such case. Hence, where a widow's petition for letters of administration is contested on the ground that she was not entitled to succeed to any personal estate by reason of an antenuptial contract entered into by her and the deceased, and was not, therefore, entitled to letters, the superior court, sitting in probate, has jurisdiction to hear and determine an answer interposed by such widow, which alleges that the contract was procured by fraud; that it was entered into as the result of a mutual mistake; that the consideration was inadequate; that the contract was waived by the deceased; and that the decedent had failed to perform the same.—Estate of Warner, 6 Cal. App. 361, 92 Pac. 191, 192. If the other interested parties take advantage of the ignorance and innocence of a widow to strip her virtually of her rights in the estate through a contract she is induced to make, the situation is one where the rule of equity is applicable that relief should be granted if inadequacy of price is such as to demonstrate a gross imposition; although the rescission of a contract will not be adjudged for inadequacy of price at law.—Marker v. Van Gerpen, 39 S. D. 648, 166 N. W. 151.

17. Right of heirs to contest accounts. Jurisdiction to determine conflicting interests.—On the settlement of an account, the heirs have the right to question the allowance and approval of claims against an estate; but the presumption is in favor of the validity of the allowance, and the burden of showing its invalidity is cast on the heirs.—Estate of Swain, 67 Cal. 637, 642, 8 Pac. 497. Minor heirs are not estopped from questioning the correctness of the administrator's account by reason of proceedings in the probate court for the sale of real property to pay a claim alleged to be false.—Estate of Hill, 67 Cal. 238, 244, 7 Pac. 664. If heirs, by reason of certain conditions surrounding the estate, have been induced to advance their money to the estate, to acquiesce in the final account without examination, and to withhold their claims against the estate, and have thus been deprived of their rights in regard thereto, which results in a fraud being perpetrated upon them, they are entitled to have the final account vacated and the estate reopened, in order that they may have an opportunity to present their claims against the same, and that such other proceedings as may be proper may be had in the administration of the estate.—Johnson v. Savage, 50 Or. 294, 91 Pac. 1082, 1083. The fact that an administrator has chosen to neglect for many years the final settlement of the estate does not estop the heirs from contesting his final account, nor preclude them from seeking to charge him with rents, issues, and profits. —Estate of Misamore, 90 Cal. 169, 171, 27 Pac. 68. A decree settling the final account of an executor, reciting that he had paid and delivered all property of the estate to the persons entitled, and discharging him from his trust, is a bar to an action thereafter brought by a distributee to recover property alleged to have belonged to the estate, which he had refused to deliver.—Grady v. Porter, 53 Cal. 681, 686. While pro-

bate courts have all the powers of a court of equity in the settlement
of estates, the conflicting interests of heirs or lienors, no matter what
their nature or origin, can only be determined in appropriate proceedings under proper pleadings.—Estate of Heeney, 3 Cal. App. 548, 552,
86 Pac. 842. Where, during the lifetime of their father, children entered into an agreement between themselves to ignore their father's
will in the event he made one, and then share his estate equally as if
he had died intestate, such an agreement is not in the nature of an
attempted assignment of an expectant interest, and the determination
of the rights of the parties under the contract are not within the jurisdiction of the probate court which settled up the estate, but the
remedy to one of the children was an action for breach of the contract.
—Spangenberg v. Spangenberg, 19 Cal. App. 439, 126 Pac. 379. The
law gives to heirs, as such, no right to appear and contest the allowance of claims by the administrator or judge in probate in the first
instance or upon their original presentation; their recourse in such a
connection is to contest the administration's final account.—In re
Tamer's Estate, Clayton v. Elia (Ariz.), 179 Pac. 643.

REFERENCES.

Remedy of distributee as to accounting of which he had no notice,
and on which he did not appear.—See note 63 L. R. A. 95-108.

15. Not prejudiced by probating of will.—A testator devised and bequeathed his entire estate to his wife and minor son but omitted to
mention his children by his first wife. On the application for probate
the children of the first wife appeared and the court admitted the will
to probate. An appeal was taken by the children of the first wife to
the district court which affirmed the order of the county court admitting the will to probate subject to the rights of each and all of the
children of the first wife in and to the estate as might thereafter be
established by the county court. An appeal was then taken from that
judgment on the hearing of which the supreme court held that the
probating of the will was not final as to its validity and construction
which might be discussed and adjudicated at any time before the final
distribution and affirmed the judgment of the district court.—Lowery
v. Hawker, 22 N. D. 319, 37 L. R. A. (N. S.) 1143, 133 N. W. 918.

III. DISTRIBUTION.

1. In general.—If all debts and charges against the estate, including
the expenses of administration, have been paid, and there is in the
hands of the executor and administrator an ascertained balance of
assets subject to distribution, the estate is ready for distribution, and
the distribution can not be delayed. The court "must" then proceed
to make distribution. The command of the law, under such circumstances, is peremptory.—Estate of Ricaud, 57 Cal. 421, 422. But where
there is not an ascertained balance of assets, real or personal, in the
hands of the executor or administrator, or if the assets are merely

claimed to exist, and the right to them is involved in litigation, either by an action brought by the executor or administrator to recover them for the estate, or by an action against the executor or administrator to recover them from the estate, then the estate is not ready for distribution.—Estate of Ricaud, 57 Cal. 421, 423. The "distribution" of an estate includes the determination of the persons who by law are entitled thereto, and also the "proportion or parts" to which each of these persons is entitled; and the "parts" of the estate so distributed may be segregated or undivided portions of the estate. A proceeding for distribution is in the nature of a proceeding in rem, the res being the estate which is in the hands of the executor under the control of the court, and which he brings before the court for the purpose of receiving directions as to its final distribution.—William Hill Co. v. Lawler, 116 Cal. 359, 361, 362, 48 Pac. 323. The word "distributed" has reference to decrees of distribution in probate courts. It is not a technical word in conveyances, and is not usually found in deeds.—Estate of Heberle, 35 Cal. 328, 329 (March 24, 1903). It can not be contended that the petition for distribution is in one proceeding, and a settlement of accounts and decree of distribution in another, because of the fact that the clerk of the court filed the petition for distribution under a different number from the other papers in the estate, where all of the papers belong to the settlement of one and the same estate.—Estate of Sheid, 129 Cal. 172, 176, 61 Pac. 920, 921. Unless exceptional circumstances prevent it, an estate in the territory of Hawaii should be closed in about eight months.—Estate of Espinda, 9 Haw. 342, 344; Estate of Kaiu, 17 Haw. 514, 515. If an administrator receives his decedent's estate in the form of money, which is distributed, the estate is distributed "in kind," or in the form in which he received possession of it.—Estate of Davis, 8 Cal. App. 355, 97 Pac. 86, 89. A final decree of distribution, which describes land by a descriptive name, is sufficient, though it names two erroneous courses, apparent on their face, when applied to the land, for the reason that they do not answer the calls in the deed, as to following the boundaries of adjoining owners and the county road. Under such circumstances, the description being proved, without the erroneous courses, and the latter being apparent, they will be rejected as surplusage.—Bates v. Howard, 105 Cal. 173, 38 Pac. 715, 718. Distribution of the personal estate of a deceased person must come through the administrator.—Hadley v. Hadley, 73 Or. 179, 144 Pac. 80. The distribution of an estate includes the determination of the persons who by law are enti'. ed thereto, and also the proportion or parts to which each of these persons is entitled.—Estate of Schmierer, 168 Cal. 747, 145 Pac. 99. The law does not contemplate or provide for the distribution of property or money in the hands of the executor or administrator to persons who may claim adversely to the estate, but leaves all such questions to be determined by an action on behalf of or against the executor.—Estate of Wenks, 171 Cal. 607, 154 Pac. 24. An administrator can not distribute an estate except as prescribed in the order therefor.—Estate of Spitz, 24 Haw. 649. Contempt proceedings will lie against an administrator to compel him to distribute an estate in conformity with the order therefor, made on his petition for discharge.—Estate of Spitz, 24 Haw. 649. The law of a sister state, governing the distribution of estates of decedents, is presumed to be the same as the law of California.—Wills v. Wills, 166 Cal. 529, 137 Pac. 249. The statute providing for the distribution of the remainder of property of an intestate, after allowing to the widow and children the homstead and other allowances refers to property in Kansas, owned by any intestate at the time of his death, irrespective of his residence.— Williams v. Wessels, 94 Kan. 71, 74, 145 Pac. 856. Where there remains part of an estate, after all devisees and legatees have been fully paid, and no provision is made in the will for the contingency of there being an excess over the amounts therein bequeathed, such excess must be distributed to the heirs at law.—In re Seay's Estate, Marsh v. Seay (Cal.), 181 Pac. 58.

REFERENCES.

Distribution when domiciliary and ancillary administrators have been appointed.—See note 9 L. R. A. 219.

2. Petition for distribution.—A petition for distribution can not regularly be filed until after the final account is settled. A statutory provision permitting a petition for distribution to be filed "with" the final account is probably intended to enable the administrator to hasten the closing of the estate, and to make one notice and one hearing serve both purposes. But, whatever the reason may be, there is no authority for filing a petition for distribution at any time prior to the settlement of the final account, unless it is filed "with" it. If filed prior to that time, it is premature, and should be dismissed.—Estate of Sheid, 122 Cal. 528, 531, 55 Pac. 328. A petition for final distribution should not contain a prayer for an accounting.—Estate of Cook, 77 Cal. 220, 11 Am. St. Rep. 267, 1 L. R. A. 567, 19 Pac. 431, 437. A legatee may file his petition for distribution to him at any time after the lapse of one year from the issuance of letters testamentary, and the fact that a supplement to the will has been filed and probated as a part thereof, after the issuance of such letters, does not deprive petitioner of this right.— Estate of Mayhew, 4 Cal. App. 162, 87 Pac. 417, 419. It is proper to deny an application for the final distribution of an estate, which is not in a condition to be closed, and where no bond or security is given for the debts.—Estate of Washburn, 148 Cal. 64, 67, 82 Pac. 671. It is the duty of the petitioner for a decree of distribution to inform the court as to all heirs of the estate entitled to share in the distribution thereof; but if he claims to be sole heir, and follows the statute in giving notice, etc., he is not guilty of a fraud upon the court in not stating the names of others who claimed to be heirs.—Royce v. Hampton, 16 Nev. 25, 35. If a decree of distribution is not made upon the petition of the administrator, he is not bound to notify the court that there are other parties, besides the petitioner, who claim to be heirs of the estate.—Royce v. Hampton, 16 Nev. 25, 34. It is proper to deny a petition asking for a distribution to a distributee of his distributive share of an estate if there is pending an application for the sale of real estate to raise funds necessary to pay charges and funeral expenses.— Estate of Koppikus, 1 Cal. App. 88, 81 Pac. 733, 734.

3. Notice and evidence of relationship.—A decree of final distribution may be made without personal notice, where the statute does not require such notice to be given of the application for final distribution.— Daly v. Pennie, 86 Cal. 552, 554, 21 Am. St. Rep. 61, 25 Pac. 67. The statute does not require ten days' notice of the hearing of the final account and petition of an administrator for the distribution of an estate. It rests solely with the court to fix the day for hearing and the time of notice to be given; and where it was impossible to post the notice of the hearing for ten days, the court has power to settle the account and to render a decree of distribution, though only nine days intervened prior to the date set for the hearing.—Asher v. Yorba, 125 Cal. 513, 516, 58 Pac. 137. But the notice required by the statute must, of course, be given; and, by giving such notice, the entire world is called before the court, and the court acquires jurisdiction over all persons for the purpose of determining their rights to any portion of the estate.—William Hill Co. v. Lawler, 116 Cal. 359, 362, 48 Pac. 323; Crew v. Pratt, 119 Cal. 139, 149, 51 Pac. 38; Williams v. Marx, 124 Cal. 22, 24, 56 Pac. 603; More v. More, 133 Cal. 489, 495, 65 Pac. 1044. If there is no evidence in the record on appeal that notice was not properly given, and the decree of distribution recites that "it appears by proper evidence that the notice, as prescribed by law, had been given of the hearing of said petition, and of the settlement of said final account," this is sufficient, and conclusive evidence of the fact that the necessary notice was given.—Estate of Sbarboro, 70 Cal. 147, 11 Pac. 563, 564. The statute of Washington governing the decree of distribution in probate proceedings, by reference to the statute governing the sale of real estate by an executor or administrator, provides that the decree of distribution shall be made only after notice of hearing has been "personally served on all persons interested in the estate at least ten days before the time appointed for the hearing of the petition or shall be published at least four successive weeks in such newspaper as the court shall order." In this case though the notice was published four times, less than four weeks elapsed between the first and the fourth publication and the notice was held to be insufficient to give the court jurisdiction to make the order of distribution.—In re Hoscheid's Estate, 78 Wash. 309, 139 Pac. 63. An administrator who gives the statutory notice by publication of the hearing of the petition for distribution is not required to give a niece of the decedent special notice of the death and of the proceedings merely because he knows her to be illiterate and to reside in a foreign country.—Beltran v. Hynes (Cal. App.), 180 Pac. 540. Whatever may be the rule in other jurisdictions, the rule is settled in the State of California that evidence

of the declarations of a deceased brother of an intestate sister, as to the relationship between them are admissible in favor of his daughter as petitioner for distribution of the estate of the deceased sister, without requiring any independent proof as to the relationship between the deceased brother and sister.—Estate of Clark, 13 Cal. App. 786, 110 Pac. 828. In a proceeding for the distribution of the estate of an intestate, the burden of proof is upon the persons claiming distribution to establish their relationship to the deceased.—Estate of Fleming, 162 Cal. 524, 123 Pac. 284.

4. Limitations on distribution.

(1) In general.—Whether distribution is sought as a separate proceeding, or on the settlement of the final account, provided a petition therefor has been filed with said account, the power to distribute can be exercised only after the final accounts of the administrator have been settled.—Smith v. Westerfield, 88 Cal. 374, 379, 26 Pac. 206; Estate of Sheid, 129 Cal. 172, 61 Pac. 920. And the court can not distribute property charged with a lien in favor of the administrator on account of money expended by him for the benefit of the estate.—Huston v. Becker, 15 Wash. 586, 47 Pac. 10, 11. Nor can the court subject property distributed, to a lien for the administrator's compensation.—In re Sour's Estate, 17 Wash. 675, 50 Pac. 587, 589.

(2) Payment of taxes. Collateral-inheritance tax.—No distribution can be made until all taxes are paid. It will not be presumed that the taxes have been paid. It is the duty of the court to see that they are paid, and "taxes" include collateral-inheritance taxes.—Estate of Mahoney, 133 Cal. 180, 184, 85 Am. St. Rep. 155, 65 Pac. 389; Kerr's Cal. Cyc. Code Civ. Proc., § 1669; Kerr's Cal. Cyc. Pol. Code, § 3752. It is to be assumed that, before paying, or delivering to beneficiaries under the will any property given to them by the testator, the executors will deduct therefrom, or collect from the said beneficiaries, the amount of the collateral-inheritance tax upon their respective gifts.—Estate of Chesney, 1 Cal. App. 30, 33, 81 Pac. 679. Where legacies amounting, in the aggregate, to $15,000, have been given by the will, and the legatees have received a portion of the money, an order directing the executors to pay the whole of said legacies as shown by the will, with legal interest, less the inheritance tax thereon, is indefinite in not designating the sum of money to be paid to each of the legatees; and the uncertainty is not removed by reference to the will in the decree, where the will does not appear in the record. It is the better practice to specify, in the order, the sum to be paid by the executor, and the amount of collateral-inheritance tax to be deducted therefrom.—Estate of Mitchell, 121 Cal. 391, 53 Pac. 810, 811. As the court must be satisfied, before any decree of distribution of an estate is made, that any inheritance tax which is due and payable has been fully paid, it has power to direct the executor of an estate to deduct from legacies due the amount of a succession tax

thereon, and to pay said sums so deducted to the county treasurer.—Estate of Martin, 153 Cal. 225, 94 Pac. 1053, 1055. Where decree of distribution fixed residue in hands of representative at certain sum, "less amount of inheritance tax as required by law," but did not fix amount of tax, and distributees were not within inheritance tax law, they were entitled to whole residue without deduction of any tax.—Wirringer v. Morgan, 12 Cal. App. 26, 106 Pac. 425. The administrator with the will annexed, who succeeded the executor making a misappropriation, is expressly authorized and obligated by the Inheritance Tax Act, to deduct the tax on the value of the residuary estate misappropriated from the other property in its hands constituting part of the residuum of the estate and belonging under the provisions of the will to the residuary legatee.—Estate of Hite, 159 Cal. 392, Ann. Cas. 1912C, 1014, 113 Pac. 1072.

5. Delay of distribution.—When the estate is not ready for distribution, the probate court has power, in the exercise of its judicial discretion, to delay its distribution until the right to the assets has been judicially determined, and the balance of assets for distribution has been ascertained.—Estate of Ricaud, 57 Cal. 421, 423. The probate court has jurisdiction, as between the executor and those claiming the estate, to determine what belongs to the estate; but it does not have jurisdiction to determine the rights of those claiming adversely to the estate, and if serious questions upon such claims arise, the duty of the court might be to delay the final decree until such claims can be determined in another forum.—Estate of Burdick, 112 Cal. 387, 391, 44 Pac. 734. The distribution of an estate need not be postponed to await a contest of the will.—Estate of Pritchett, 51 Cal. 568, 570, 52 Cal. 94, 96. Where an estate consists almost wholly of an indivisible chose in action, actually in litigation, the very existence of the property as assets being uncertain and contingent upon the determination of the suits, it is improper to allow distribution of such estate pending litigation, even when the estate is but little indebted.—(See Cal. Code Civ. Proc., section 1661).—In re Colton's Estate, 164 Cal. 1, 127 Pac. 643.

6. Jurisdiction of courts.—The superior court has full chancery jurisdiction, and also probate jurisdiction, and a special proceeding in rem has been prescribed to it, in which it is required to administer estates, whether testate or intestate. There is no occasion to determine whether, while sitting in probate, it is acting as a court of equity or not. The distribution of estates, and the determination of interests of distributees in the property distributed, are matters clearly within its amended jurisdiction, and such jurisdiction is exclusive.—Toland v. Earl, 129 Cal. 148, 155, 79 Am. St. Rep. 100, 61 Pac. 914; Estate of Freud, 134 Cal. 333, 66 Pac. 476; Silva v. Santos, 138 Cal. 536, 541, 71 Pac. 703. The court should not assume to distribute property to those in whom it is already vested. All letters of administration are for purposes more or less temporary.

The primary object is the collection of the assets and the payment of the debts of the decedent. The distribution of the residue among those thereto by law entitled is only an incident, and, when the primary object of the administration is non-existent, when all debts against the estate have been paid or barred, when the estate has become vested in those entitled thereto by law, and especially when thirteen years have been allowed to elapse after the death of the testator, no courts should assume jurisdiction of the estate for the sole and only purpose of making a distribution thereof among those in whom the estate has already vested.—State v. Superior Court, 47 Wash. 508, 92 Pac. 942, 943. A probate court has no power, by an order of distribution, to create a lien upon the interest of the heirs in the property distributed.—Huston v. Becker, 15 Wash. 586, 47 Pac. 10, 11. Nor has it any authority to decree a distribution of real estate, subject to a lien for the fees of the administrator. This claim should be settled in the settlement of the estate, and the estate be distributed free from any lien therefor.—In re Sour's Estate, 17 Wash. 675, 50 Pac. 587, 589. The court can do no more than to pay the claims against the estate, and to distribute the remainder among the heirs and devisees, or direct the administrator to do so. It has no power to appropriate the share of an heir or devisee to the payment of his debts. That would be to administer upon his estate before he is dead in law or in fact.—Estate of Nerac, 35 Cal. 392, 397, 95 Am. Dec. 101. And a proceeding whereby the court directs that the distributed share of a non-resident heir at law shall be distributed among the other heirs, if the non-resident heir shall fail to appear and claim it within a year, is totally unauthorized.—Pyatt v. Brockman, 6 Cal. 418, 419, 65 Am. Dec. 521. A probate court has no jurisdiction to determine controversies between the estate in hand and adverse claimants, where there is no provision of law conferring such jurisdiction.—Guardianship of Breslin, 135 Cal. 21, 22, 66 Pac. 962. The probate court has jurisdiction to determine who are the legal heirs of a deceased person who died intestate, and who are the legatees or devisees of one who died testate; but its determination of such matters does not create any new title: It merely declares the title which accrued under the law of descents, or under the provisions of the will.—Chever v. Ching Hong Poy, 82 Cal. 68, 71, 22 Pac. 1081. On rendering ordinary decrees of distribution, probate courts deal only with issues and parties legitimately before them.—Chever v. Ching Hong Poy, 82 Cal. 68, 72, 22 Pac. 1081. The jurisdiction is merely to determine the persons entitled under the will, or by succession, or their grantees.—More v. More, 133 Cal. 489, 495, 65 Pac. 1044. In settling the accounts of an administrator the probate court has jurisdiction to determine the amount of money or property of the estate that has come into his hands and to charge him therewith. If he is improperly charged, his remedy is to appeal from the decree settling his final account.—Estate of Hall, 154 Cal. 527, 98 Pac. 269.

In the state of California the same presumption exists in favor of the acts of the superior court done in the exercise of its probate jurisdiction, as exists in favor of its acts done in ordinary litigation between parties.—Johnson v. Canty, 162 Cal. 391, 123 Pac. 263. A decree of the superior court of this state distributing the estate of a deceased person is in itself presumptive evidence of the jurisdiction of the court to render it, and by itself affords evidence of the transmission of the title of the deceased.—Johnson v. Canty, 162 Cal. 391, 123 Pac. 263.

REFERENCES.

Loss of jurisdiction.—See head-line 14, subd. 14, post.

7. Distribution with final accounting and settlement.

(1) In general.—The matter of settling the final accounts of an executor or administrator does not necessarily involve the matter of distribution at all. Distribution of the estate to the heirs or legatees may take place upon the settlement of the final account, or at any subsequent time. One or the other of these is the usual course, though the law allows, under certain conditions, a partial distribution before the settlement of the final account. Upon an order simply settling a final account, no matter concerning the distribution of the estate would be necessarily determined.—Estate of Thayer, 1 Cal. App. 104, 106, 81 Pac. 658. In this state the distribution of estates has been made, to some extent, a matter distinct from the settlement of accounts. But it is clearly made so merely for convenience.—McAdoo v. Sayre, 145 Cal. 344, 349, 78 Pac. 874. Upon the final settlement of the accounts of the executor or administrator, it is the peremptory command of the statute, without qualification, that the residue of the estate shall be distributed. The distribution is not to be postponed until after the time has elapsed within which the validity of the will may be contested, any more than until a minor heir shall have attained his majority, or an heir of unsound mind shall have recovered his reason.—Estate of Pritchett, 51 Cal. 568, 570, 52 Cal. 94, 96. If the executor or administrator has a large amount of money on hand, and there is no reasonable probability of any further collections, and it appears from the record that there are no debts outstanding against the estate, and that all moneys due the estate have been collected, except two outstanding claims, the collection of which is improbable, the court should decree a final settlement and distribution.—Bellinger v. Ingalls, 21 Or. 191, 27 Pac. 1038, 1039. The code authorizes a decree of distribution to be made at the same time that the final settlement is made.—Estate of Kennedy, 129 Cal. 384, 386, 62 Pac. 64. The allowance of the final account of an executor or administrator is not a decree of distribution.—McCrea v. Haraszthy, 51 Cal. 146, 151. An administrator, under the provisions of sections 1634 and 1665, Cal. Code Civ. Proc., and the decisions of the supreme court, is authorized to file a petition for final distribution with his

final account, and the court acquires jurisdiction, by the filing of said petition, and the giving of the notice prescribed by law, to entertain a proceeding to proceed with the distribution of the estate immediately upon the settlement of the final account, and such jurisdiction is unaffected by the fact that the administrator has no legal interest in any dispute between the respective claimants to the residue of the estate.—In re Ross' Estate, 179 Cal. 358, 182 Pac. 755, 757. The mere fact of the pendency of appeals from parts of the order settling the final account of the administrator affords no warrant for denying a petition for distribution filed simultaneously with the final account of the administrator, but the trial court may in its discretion continue the hearing upon the petition for distribution pending the determination of such appeals.—In re Ross' Estate, 179 Cal. 358, 182 Pac. 755, 757.

REFERENCES.

Petition for distribution can not be properly filed prior to settlement of final account, but may be filed "with" it.—See head-line 2, ante.

(2) **Waiver of settlement of account.**—Ordinarily, the settlement of the final account must precede the distribution of the estate.—Estate of Sheid, 122 Cal. 528, 531, 55 Pac. 328. But, where there is no real necessity for an accounting, this step preceding a distribution may be waived, as where the widow is the executrix and also the sole beneficiary under a will; where the entire estate has become vested in her, and she alone has the right to demand an accounting; and the accounting, when made, must have been made with her only, and for the purpose of settling the amount to which she, as sole distributee would be entitled. While an accounting in such a case might be convenient, there can be no doubt that she, the sole person interested, has the right to waive the rendition and settlement of such account, and to consent that the the distribution may be without such intermediate proceedings.—Middlecoff v. Superior Court, 149 Cal. 94, 84 Pac. 764, 765.

(3) **Settlement of accounts. Notice.**—It is not all accounts that must be settled before distribution. It is the settlement of the final account only which must precede the application for distribution. A statement of any receipts and disbursements of the executor or administrator, since the rendition of his final account, must be reported and filed at the time of such distribution, but this statement of receipts and disbursements is not the final account of the administrator. If all accounts or statements were required to be settled in advance of an application for distribution, it would, in most cases, result in preventing any distribution. Upon filing a petition for distribution, contests as to heirship may, and frequently do, arise, and months, and perhaps a year or more, may elapse before such contests are settled. In the mean time, receipts and expenditures go on, a state-

ment of which should be furnished to the court before distribution is made, and the executor or administrator discharged. The statute allows these statements, submitted after the decree of distribution is applied for, to be settled at the time the decree is made, without notice, or the court may order notice to be given, and refer the same for settlement.—Estate of Sheid, 129 Cal. 172, 175, 61 Pac. 920, 921. If the account be for a final settlement, accompanied by a petition for distribution, the notice must state those facts, and must be for at least the time prescribed by the statute.—Estate of Grant, 131 Cal. 426, 429, 63 Pac. 731. The court acquires jurisdiction of parties interested in the estate to hear the application for a final accounting and settlement, and distribution, where the notice prescribed by the statute has been given.—Estate of Ryer, 110 Cal. 556, 561, 42 Pac. 1082. An order made without the prescribed statutory notice is void. In such a case there can be no valid settlement of the account, and no valid order can be made for the payment of a claim.—Estate of Spanier, 120 Cal. 698, 701, 53 Pac. 357. Whether additional notice shall be given or not is a matter within the discretion of the court below, and, in the absence of anything to show that such discretion has been abused, the appellate court will not interfere, where such further notice was not given.—Estate of Jessup, 81 Cal. 408, 437, 6 L. R. A. 594, 21 Pac. 976, 22 Pac. 742, 1028.

(4) Distribution subsequent to final settlement. Power of court.—Distribution may be made, also, at any time subsequent to the final settlement of the account; but, whenever made, the court has power to inquire into and to determine who are the heirs of the deceased, and who are entitled to receive the estate.—Smith v. Westerfield, 88 Cal. 374, 380, 26 Pac. 206. The power to "distribute" an estate on the settlement of the final account of an executor includes the power to determine to whom distribution shall be made.—Reformed etc. Church v. McMillan, 31 Wash. 643, 72 Pac. 502, 503. It is the duty of the court upon final distribution to distribute all of the residue of the estate to the persons entitled thereto. The res over which the court acquires jurisdiction is not only the property described in the petition for distribution, but also the residue of the estate, and, notwithstanding the omission of the petition specifically to describe an undivided interest in a certain lot, the court has power to make a decree distributing not only the estate particularly described, but also "any other property not now known or discovered, which may belong to said estate, or in which said estate may have interest."—Humphrey v. Protestant Episcopal Church, 154 Cal. 170, 97 Pac. 187, 188. A decree of final distribution can be had only after settlement of the final account.—Estate of Spreckels, 165 Cal. 597, 133 Pac. 289.

REFERENCES.

Power of court on distribution.—See head-line 14, subd. 2, post.

8. What matters may be adjusted.

(1) In general.—The only items which are properly to be settled in an executor's account are items relating purely to his administration of the estate; charges of administration and payment of debts of decedent; but, upon the hearing for distribution, the court, in harmony with its general equitable powers, can adjust all matters between the legatees and distributees and the executors, and credit the latter against the estate distributed to the former for all advances which may have been made to either of them under the terms of a will.—Estate of Willey, 140 Cal. 238, 242, 73 Pac. 998. The decree of distribution has nothing to do with contracts or conveyances which may have been made by heirs, devisees, or legatees of or about their shares of the estate, either among themselves or with others; such matters are not before the probate court, and over them it has no jurisdiction. An heir may contract about or convey the title which the law cast upon him on the death of his ancestor; and the validity or force of such contract is not affected by the fact that a probate court afterward, by its decree of distribution, declared his asserted heirship and title to be valid.—Chever v. Ching Hong Poy, 82 Cal. 68, 71, 22 Pac. 1080; More v. More, 133 Cal. 489, 495, 65 Pac. 1044. Jurisdiction of "matters of probate" includes the ascertainment and determination of the persons who succeed to the estate of a decedent, either as heir, devisee, or legatee, as well as the amount or proportion of the estate to which each is entitled, and also the construction or effect to be given to the language of a will, but does not include a determination of claims against the heir or devisee for his portion of the estate arising subsequent to the death of the administrator, whether such claim arises by virtue of his contract or in invitum; nor is the determination of conflicting claims to the estate of an heir or devisee, or whether he has conveyed or assigned his share of the estate, a "matter of probate."—Martinovich v. Marsicano, 137 Cal. 354, 356, 70 Pac. 459. If it were not for the California statute providing that "although some of the legitimate heirs, legatees, or devisees may have conveyed their share to other persons, and such shares must be assigned to the person holding the same, in the same manner as they otherwise would have been to such heirs, legatees, or devisees" the only questions on distribution, in that state, would be as to who are the heirs, legatees, and devisees, and what property they are entitled to as such, and the court would be without authority to distribute to any person, other than heirs, legatees, or devisees. But, under such a statute, the court, on distribution, may determine disputes between heirs, legatees, or devisees, and persons claiming to be the grantees of their shares under conveyances made by them.— Estate of Ryder, 141 Cal. 366, 369, 74 Pac. 993. See also head-line 10, post. Where a wife, supposing her husband to be dead, married a second time, and her claim of widowhood was litigated upon issues joined as to her rights to family allowance and to a probate home-

stead, which issues were determined against her, such determination is res judicata, and she is estopped from claiming widowhood upon distribution of the estate.—Estate of Harrington, 147 Cal. 124, 128, 109 Am. St. Rep. 18, 81 Pac. 546. An antenuptial contract affecting the personal property of a deceased person should be proved, and the rights of the parties thereunder determined before the county court, which has exclusive jurisdiction over the distribution of the personal property of deceased persons.—Winkle v. Winkle, 8 Or. 193, 196. The question of title can not be determined in a proceeding for the distribution of a decedent's estate.—Estate of Rowland, 74 Cal. 523, 526, 5 Am. St. Rep. 464, 16 Pac. 315. Whether application for distribution is made as an independent proceeding, or in connection with the final account, the equitable claims of parties against the heirs or assignees of heirs is not a proper subject for the consideration of the court.—More v. More, 133 Cal. 489, 495, 65 Pac. 1044. On final distribution of a deceased wife's estate, a surviving husband is not entitled to have property held by her executor declared to be community property to which he is entitled, because his claim is not as heir or devisee, but is adverse to the estate, and, as such, will be no more concluded by the decree of distribution than would the claim of a third party who claimed adversely to the decedent.— In re Rowland, 74 Cal. 523, 525, 526, 5 Am. St. Rep. 464, 16 Pac. 315. Though property which is distributed to the successor in interest of a devisee is subject to any valid lien of mortgage created thereon by the devisee, the decree of distribution should not attempt to determine the rights between the mortgagee and distributee.—Estate of Lynn, 163 Cal. 803, 127 Pac. 75. The superior court, in proceedings for final settlement and distribution in probate, has power to determine, as between heirs, legatees, and devisees, the payment of debts, expenses, and interest on mortgaged property, and the application of rents and profits of real estate.—Estate of DeBernal, 165 Cal. 223, Ann. Cas. 1914D, 26, 131 Pac. 375. Executors who have been in possession of cash funds of an estate for many years, should be charged with the amount, and with interest and profit, if any, they may have received therefrom; they should also be charged on final distribution with interest on all sums paid out or advanced, without authority, on account of legacies under the will.—In re Hawgood's Estate, 37 S. D. 565, 584, 159 N. W. 117.

(2) Question of heirship.—The purpose of a statute which provides that the court may ascertain and declare the rights of all persons to an estate and all interests therein, and to whom distribution thereof shall be made, is to expedite the distribution of estates by enabling persons claiming interests therein to have their claims determined in advance of the application for distribution.—In re Oxarart, 78 Cal. 109, 111, 20 Pac. 367. The purpose of the proceeding is to determine the parties to whom the estate is to be distributed. It is therefore subsidiary to the proceeding for distribution, and the jurisdiction of the

court in the two cases is coextensive.—Móre v. More, 133 Cal. 489, 495, 65 Pac. 1044. The pendency of proceedings to determine heirship does not exclude the usual proceeding for the determination of that question at the hearing of the application for distribution. When, in advance of any determination of the court of the questions involved in a proceeding to determine heirship, an application is made for distribution, there is no reason why the court should not hear the latter application, determine all questions of heirship, and dismiss the other proceeding.—In re Oxarart, 78 Cal. 109, 111, 20 Pac. 367; Estate of Sheid, 129 Cal. 172, 176, 61 Pac. 920. If the petition for distribution has been filed at the proper time, all the questions made thereunder to determine heirship and title to the estate may be properly determined under it.—Estate of Sheid, 122 Cal. 528, 532, 55 Pac. 328. It is clearly the purpose of the California statute relating to determination of heirship to provide the means by which, where there are hostile claimants to an estate, all the conflicting rights thereto may be summarily and finally determined in one proceeding.—Estate of Burton, 93 Cal. 459, 29 Pac. 36; Blythe v. Ayres, 102 Cal. 254, 258, 36 Pac. 522. Where conflicting claims are made to the distributive share of an estate, it is not an imperative duty of the court, in proceedings for distribution, to decide the rights of the parties; it may make the decree of distribution so as to leave the parties free to have their dispute decided in a court of equity in a proper action.—Estate of Gamble, 166 Cal. 253, 135 Pac. 970.

(3) Advancements.—In the state of California the rules governing the subject of advancement are embraced in sections 1395-1399, 1309, and 1351 of the Civil Code. No special form, not even the signature of the decedent, is required to constitute a charge of the advancement in writing, as prescribed by section 1397. It is sufficient if it appears that the writing was done by the decedent and shows the intent to charge the money or property given as an advancement rather than a gift or loan.—Estate of Hayne, 165 Cal. 568, Ann. Cas. 1915A, 926, 133 Pac. 277. On the subject of advancements it is provided by statute merely that property given by way thereof shall be charged against the heir when the estate is divided; it is not prescribed how the fact shall be determined nor who shall have the burden of proof.— Packard v. Packard, 95 Kan. 644, 149 Pac. 404. A child that has received property from a parent during the latter's lifetime may, after his death, prove by outside and parol evidence that the disposition was not by way of advancement.—Packard v. Packard, 95 Kan. 644, 149 Pac. 404. ·

(4) Election to take under will.—The question whether one, upon whom the duty to elect rests, has or has not elected to take under a will, depends, upon the circumstances of each particular case.—In re Prerost's Estate, De Camp v. Prerost, 40 S. D. 536, 168 N. W. 631. If one, who asserts title to personal property as a purchaser through a person who has since died, is made a beneficiary as to the same

under the will of the deceased, and, as executrix, has it scheduled as assets of the estate there is thereby an election made to take under the will and not by reason of the purchase.—Truman v. Dakota Trust Co., 29 N. D. 456, 464, 151 N. W. 219.

9. Consideration of will.—Where a trust has been created by will, the validity of the trust is necessarily involved in the question of distribution; for, if invalid, the bequest fails. Hence, if necessary to distribution, it is within the province of the probate court to define the rights of all who have, legally or equitably, any interest in the property of the estate, derived from the will.—More v. More, 133 Cal. 489, 495, 65 Pac. 1044. For the purpose of enabling the court to distribute the estate of a testator in accordance with his will, it is required to consider the will, as well as the estate left by him, and to construe its terms for the purpose of determining his intention, and make its order or decree of distribution in accordance with such construction. But, as in the case of a judicial determination of any instrument, the will is but evidence upon which the court acts in rendering its judgment. The judgment is the final determination of the rights of the parties to the proceeding, and upon its entry their rights are thereafter to be measured by the terms of the judgment, and not by the will. A will can no more be used as evidence to impeach the decree of distribution, than can any other evidence upon which a judgment is rendered.—Goad v. Montgomery, 119 Cal. 552, 557, 51 Pac. 681; In re Trescony, 119 Cal. 568, 570, 51 Pac. 951. Where it has been attempted to create a trust by will, and there has been a decree of distribution, the rights of the parties are to be ascertained from the decree of distribution and not from the will. Such decree is the final and conclusive adjudication of the testamentary disposition made by the decedent. The decree supersedes the will and prevails over any provision therein which may be thought inconsistent with the decree. —Keating v. Smith, 154 Cal. 186, 97 Pac. 300, 302. In California, no independent action in equity lies to construe a will, whether it involves merely legal questions or the regulation of trusts created by the will. Such jurisdiction is vested exclusively in the probate court. Under the probate system of that state, all deraignment of the title of the property of deceased persons is through the decree of distribution, entered after a final account in the administration of an estate, whether testate or intestate, and this decree can not be made by any other court, or in any other proceeding. The probate court not only may, but should, and often must, construe the trusts created by the will. After the decree is made, the will practically drops out of existence. The law of the estate is the decree, and not the will, and all deraignments of title are through the decree.—Toland v. Earl, 129 Cal. 148, 152, 79 Am. St. Rep. 100, 61 Pac. 914. Upon distribution, questions may arise affecting the rights of beneficiaries, to whom payment has previously been made by the executor, to take at all under the will; and questions of the invalidity of general or partial trust provisions, lapsed legacies, excessive charitable bequests, omitted heirs, etc., are questions which may affect the entire or partial disposition under the will. It must be apparent, that, as these matters which may so radically affect the rights of the beneficiaries under any will can only be legally and effectively determined upon distribution, any effort to have them determined in settling accounts must, in the nature of things, be out of place. If an executor undertakes to construe the provisions of a will, or to make payment thereunder in anticipation of the decree of distribution, he does so at his peril, and can not, in an account, call upon the court, in advance of a distribution, to construe the provisions of the will, or determine the rights of the legatees, for the purpose of ascertaining whether the opinion of the court conforms to the judgment of the executor.—Estate of Willey, 140 Cal. 238, 242, 73 Pac. 998. After the probate court has distributed lands which belong to an estate, in the due course of administration, it has no further control of the same, in the exercise of its probate jurisdiction; and the circumstance that at a future time there is to be a division of the property among remaindermen, beneficiaries of the trust in a will, does not affect the rule.—Morffew v. San Francisco, etc., R. R. Co., 107 Cal. 587, 594, 40 Pac. 810. Where it is within the privilege of the widow to elect to take in accordance with the will, rather than to claim her right as surviving widow to the one-half of the estate, it will be assumed, for the purpose of sustaining the decree of distribution, that she made such election, or that she could have presented her claim for the undivided half of the estate, but failed to do so.— Cunha v. Hughes, 122 Cal. 111, 113, 68 Am. St. Rep. 27, 54 Pac. 535. A decree of final distribution is necessarily a judicial construction of the will, and of the several interests of the distributees, and can not be attacked collaterally.—Williams v. Marx, 124 Cal. 22, 24, 56 Pac. 603; McKenzie v. Budd, 125 Cal. 600, 602, 58 Pac. 199; Martinovich v. Marsicano, 137 Cal. 354, 359, 70 Pac. 459. The court, in determining whether the amount of personal property in the hands of executors is sufficient for the immediate payment of petitioner's legacy, is not required to take into consideration the amount that may be required for erecting tombstones authorized by the will. If the moneys in the hands of the executors, after making other payments, shall be insufficient therefor, they can resort to the realty.—Estate of Chesney. 1 Cal. App. 30, 81 Pac. 679, 680. Advancements made before the execution of the will can not be considered in distributing the estate unless specified in the will, since it is presumed that the testator had all previous advancements in his mind when he made his will, and acted accordingly so as to have the final division conform to his wishes.— Estate of Vanderhurst, 171 Cal. 553, 154 Pac. 5. Whether the beneficiary of a will has forfeited her right to take under the will by a violation of a contest clause contained therein properly arises on distribution, and can not be determined on an appeal from an order admitting the will to probate.—In re Bergland's Estate, 177 Cal. 227,

170 Pac. 400, 401. The admission of the testimony of an attorney who drew the various instruments as to what was intended by their terms was error, since the will, the contract, and the decree of distribution spoke for themselves.—Horton v. Winbigler, 175 Cal. 149, 165 Pac. 423, 427. For the purpose of making them a portion of its distributive terms, the will and an agreement may be incorporated in a decree of distribution.—Horton v. Winbigler, 175 Cal. 149, 165 Pac. 423, 427. If the will and contract were properly admitted, the error in admitting oral evidence as to what was intended should be the interest of the beneficiaries.—Horton v. Winbigler, 175 Cal. 149, 165 Pac. 423, 427. Where the decree of distribution is, in its terms contrary to the will, the decree prevails, since the will can not be used to impeach the decree of distribution.—Estate of Ewer, 177 Cal. 660, 171 Pac. 683. The rule to the effect that the decree of distribution prevails over the will, in cases where they do not conform with each other in their terms, is a rule of necessity; the terms must be made to conform if possible.—Estate of Ewer, 177 Cal. 660, 171 Pac. 683. If a testator leaves a wife, a daughter, and two brothers, and directs that no distribution be had until after the brothers shall have died, and disposes of the estate so that the wife shall have a life estate in one-half, and at her death his "children" shall take this half in fee, on the death of the brothers, the child having died previously and never having married, the whole property is to be distributed to the widow.—Estate of Glann, 177 Cal. 347, 170 Pac. 833. Where a will makes no disposition of one certain piece of the testator's property and the decree distributes the estate, without specifically mentioning this piece, to the person, or institution, named in the will as sole and residuary devisee and legatee, but provides also that there shall be distributed to this person, or institution, any other property, not now known or discovered, which may belong to the estate, this provision carries that piece of property.—Victoria Hospital Assn. v. All Persons, etc., 169 Cal. 455, 147 Pac. 124.

10. Objections to distribution.—The fact that a proceeding is pending for the adjudication of heirship is not a good ground for the continuance of a petition for the distribution of the estate, as the question of heirship may be determined on the hearing of the petition for distribution.—In re Oxarart, 78 Cal. 109, 112, 20 Pac. 367. One who has no interest in the estate has no right to object to its distribution.—Estate of Walker, 148 Cal. 162, 82 Pac. 770, 771. An objector has no independent right to complain of a distribution, in full accord with the terms of a will, the probate of which has not been revoked, and which is unassailable, either by proceedings to revoke the probate, or in an equitable action to have the distributees thereunder decreed to be trustees for him.—Tracy v. Muir, 151 Cal. 363, 121 Am. St. Rep. 117, 90 Pac. 832, 833. Assignments of error based upon objections to the jurisdiction of the court to decree a final distribution, for the reason that there is litigation pending, involving property belonging to the estate, can not be sustained, where the record shows that whatever litigation there had been concerning the estate has been finally determined.—Drasdo v. Jobst, 39· Wash. 425, 81 Pac. 857, 858. The sureties of the administrator can not, in an action by a distributee to recover the sum distributed to him, be heard to question the validity of the decree, where notice was given as required by statute.—McClellan v. Downey, 63 Cal. 520, 523. The opinions of the supreme court of California are not entirely harmonious as to the authority of the court, on distribution, to determine, against the objection of an heir, legatee, or devisee, as to the rights of a third person claiming under a conveyance alleged to have been made by such devisee, legatee, or heir. It may, however, be conceded, that, under the provisions of section 1678 of the Code of Civil Procedure of that state, the court, on distribution, may determine disputes between heirs, legatees, and devisees and persons claiming to be the grantees of their shares under conveyances made by them, although the determination of such disputes would not ordinarily be within the functions of the probate court. If such authority exists, however, it rests solely upon the provision of that section, and is limited by its terms. But that section includes only conveyances of their shares made by "heirs, legatees, or devisees," and has no reference to conveyances made prior to the death of the deceased, by persons who were not, at the time of the conveyance, either heirs, legatees, or devisees, and who then had no interest in the property that was capable of being conveyed.—Estate of Ryder, 141 Cal. 366, 369, 74 Pac. 993. If the distributee of an estate has assigned his share, and such assignment has been recognized by the court, and is not disputed by the assignor, neither the administrator nor others can object to distribution made to such assignee, or that such share shall be paid to the assignee.—Estate of Davis, 27 Mont. 490, 71 Pac. 757, 760. The validity of disputed assignments of a distributive share, or legacy, or devise, can not be tried or determined by a court sitting in a probate proceeding. This is a collateral question; but when there is no dispute, as where the party entitled gives his consent, there is no reason, on principle, why the court may not recognize and give it effect.—In re Davis' Estate, 27 Mont. 490, 71 Pac. 757, 759. Where a person, at the time of his death, has no interest in property, having conveyed the same during his lifetime, his heirs have no interest in the estate, and have no right to object to a distribution thereof to the grantee.—Estate of Conroy, 6 Cal. App. 741, 93 Pac. 205, 206. Persons who have no interest in an estate have no standing to question the manner of its distribution.—Estate of Spreckels, 165 Cal. 223, 133 Pac. 289. On a proceeding for the distribution of the estate of a decedent, the court is not bound to comply with a written statement filed by a person entitled to distribution, purporting to withdraw his petition therefor, if he was represented in such proceeding by an attorney of record and the statement was neither signed nor agreed to by such attorney.—Estate of Cowell, 167 Cal. 228, 139 Pac. 84. In California, while there is an attorney of record representing a party, the court is not bound to observe or follow the directions of the party himself as to the disposal of the case, made in his absence and without the consent of his attorney.—Estate of Cowell, 167 Cal. 228, 139 Pac. 84. Under the law of this state, as it now stands, a motion for a new trial of any issue of fact actually made and determined in any proceeding in probate will lie when the law expressly authorizes issues of fact to be framed in such proceeding, and the provisions authorizing written objections on the part of persons interested in the estate and providing for the hearing and determination of those objections do expressly authorize issues of fact to be framed.—Carter v. Waste, 159 Cal. 23, 112 Pac. 727. Section 1668 of the Code of Civil Procedure of California, as amended in 1907, expressly authorize the framing of issues of fact in a proceeding for final distribution of the estate of a deceased person, by the filing of written objections to the petition for distribution, and a motion for a new trial in such proceeding is authorized.—Carter v. Waste, 159 Cal. 23, 112 Pac. 727. It is the duty of any person who desires to dispute the final settlement of an administrator's account to appear in the court and file or make his objections and a failure to do so constitutes laches and prevents a plea that the proceedings were taken against him through excusable neglect.—Chandler v. Probate Court, 26 Ida. 173, 141 Pac. 638. If, on a man's death after his divorcing his second wife, of whom there has been no issue born, the only child by the first wife becomes administratrix, and, on filing her first and final account, files with it her petition for a distribution to her as sole heir, the divorced wife, as guardian of twins she has since borne, but whose legitimacy is in controversy, can not admit, in a counter petition, the heirship, although joint with that of the wards, and then conduct the cause on the theory that these wards are the only persons interested in the proceeding; vague and weak objections to the application for distribution will not avail.—Estate of Walker, 176 Cal. 402, 168 Pac. 689. A widower, having a son living, took a second wife, and some time subsequently conveyed to her a piece of real property. He died and no administration was had upon his estate. The widow sold the property and invested the proceeds, and after her death the son appeared and filed a protest in the matter of the final distribution of her estate, alleging that the property conveyed to her by his father was community property. He was not successful. It was held that he should have raised his point on the death of his father, and that his claim was now a claim of title adverse to that of the estate.—Estate of Wenks, 171 Cal. 607, 154 Pac. 24. Parties to a compromise agreement, who in person or by counsel knew, or had the means of knowing the terms of a decree of distribution, which was a contemporary interpretation of the agreement, can not object to the distribution decreed.—Heydenfeldt v. Osmont, 178 Cal. 768, 175 Pac. 1. The submission of a proceeding for the distribution of the estate of a deceased person, in pursuance of a stipulation and an agreed statement of facts which set out the claim of the appellants to a distributive share of the estate operated as a waiver of the necessity, if any existed, for the appellants to file formal written objections to the petition for distribution.—Estate of Davidson, 21 Cal. App. 118, 131 Pac. 67.

REFERENCES.

As to right of attorney to control cause.—See note in 93 Am. St. 169.

11. Kinds of property.—If the widow dies, pending administration of her husband's estate, there seems to be no objection to the distribution of her share of the estate to her heirs, as being the persons entitled thereto, if the creditors do not object. It would, perhaps, be more orderly to have her interest in the estate distributed in terms, in administration of her estate, to her heirs, and that such heirs go with the decree to have distribution in the husband's estate; or, to have distribution, if personal property, to her administrator for the purposes of administration; but such course would not materially change the relation of the parties, where it appears that her estate was administered upon and that she left no heirs other than those mentioned in the decree.—McClellan v. Downey, 63 Cal. 520, 524. The homestead right attaches in favor of the widow and children, if the estate is insolvent or below the homestead limit in value; but where the estate is solvent and above the homestead allowance in value, such part of the homestead as may be set aside to the widow must be deducted from her distributive share of the real estate falling to her under the statute.—In re Little, 22 Utah 204, 61 Pac. 899, 901. In adjusting the respective shares of heirs and devisees, if it appears that the homestead was conveyed to an heir in pursuance of an arrangement between the heirs and devisees, the value which such heir received by reason of the conveyance should be charged against such heir, and the others be given their pro rata share.—Haines v. Christie, 28 Colo. 502, 66 Pac. 883, 887. If a foreigner dies in this state, leaving property here, and children, the former must, in the absence of an antenuptial contract, be distributed in the manner required by the statute of the state. —Estate of Baubichon, 49 Cal. 18, 28. It is the place of the actual domicile of the person at the time of his death which determines the distribution of his personal estate; hence, where a testator died in Europe, and it is found as a fact that the domicile at the time of his death was in the state of Nevada, and that he left property in the state of California, the probate court of the latter state should decree distribution of the personal assets of the estate of the decedent according to the law of the state of Nevada.—Estate of Apple, 66 Cal. 432, 441, 6 Pac. 7. Where money has been distributed to a non-resident minor heir at law of the intestate, who does not appear, and who does not claim it, the money should be paid into the state treasury, where it must remain until claimed by the owner, or, in case of his death, by his representatives.—Pyatt v. Brockman, 6 Cal. 418. It may be said, not, of course, as a proposition of law, but as a statement of fact for the guidance of courts in probate, that, generally speaking, claims in litigation should not be distributed unless with the full assent of all the parties interested, and under circumstances where it is apparent to the court that no embarrassment will result to the administrators, or to the administration, in the orderly effort to reduce such a claim to judgment and possession.—In re Colton's Estate, 164 Cal. 1, 127 Pac. 643. Future testamentary interests, as to time of enjoyment, are distributed by decree, same as property as to which there is immediate right of possession.—Hardy v. Mayhew, 158 Cal. 95, 139 Am. St. 73, 110 Pac. 113.

REFERENCES.

Law governing distribution of fund collected or recovered for the negligent killing of a person.—See note 4 L. R. A. (N. S.) 814, 815. Distribution of community property on death of wife.—See § 32, ante. Distribution of common property on death of the husband.—See § 33, ante.

12. Distributees.

(1) In general.—The only persons whose claims to distribution can be considered are those who claim directly from the deceased, as heirs, devisees, or legatees, and those who claim as their assignees, under conveyance made by them subsequent to the death of the deceased.—Estate of Ryder, 141 Cal. 366, 371, 74 Pac. 993. A trustee takes only such estate as is necessary for the performance of the trust, and a decree which distributes the trust property to the trustee "for the period, and for the use, trust, and purpose hereinafter in this decree specified," is proper; and this gives to the trustee only an estate for years.—Estate of Reith, 144 Cal. 314, 320, 77 Pac. 942. A decree of distribution should dispose of the property, and the whole title thereto, and of all the estates therein. So where, by a will, the title in fee is vested in several children, subject to a trust and to the possession of the property by the trustee during the trust period, such title in fee, subject to said trust, should be distributed to the children.—Estate of Reith, 144 Cal. 314, 320, 77 Pac. 942. Where the whole title to property passed from the testatrix by the will, and the title in fee vests in the children at the death of the testatrix by virtue of a direct testamentary gift to them, subject only to trusts, it is erroneous to decree that the property would go to her heirs upon the death of one of the children before arriving at the age mentioned in the will. In the event of the death of one of said children, his or her share in the property would vest in fee in his or her heirs.—Estate of Reith, 144 Cal. 314, 321, 77 Pac. 942. There is no law or practice, however, which requires the courts, in making distribution of an estate, to determine by its decree whether an alleged mortgage upon the interest of an heir is valid, or that the debt has not been paid, or whether there is not some defense to it. An estate should not be distributed to a mortgagee, but he has a right to be heard in the matter of the distri-

bution, where he has an interest which may be affected by the decree. But no intervention should be allowed on his part unless sustained by some pleading or statement of the grounds upon which he claims the right to be heard.—Estate of Crooks, 125 Cal. 459, 461, 58 Pac. 89. The court has jurisdiction to distribute only the estate of which the decedent was possessed at the time of his death, and it is only a claim against that estate, or some portion of it, for which it can make provision in its decree. There is no provision authorizing the court to assign a share of the estate to a person who holds a mortgage or judgment lien, or other encumbrance thereon, made or suffered by the heir, subsequent to the death of the ancestor. A judgment creditor of the heir, therefore, is not entitled to receive any portion of the estate, and the court could not, upon distribution, assign to him any share thereof. A statute, making the order or decree of distribution conclusive, does not include the judgment creditor, and his lien is no more affected by the order of distribution than would be a lien upon the property of the heir created prior to the death of the decedent. The owner of a judgment lien is not required to appear in court, or to present his lien at the time of distribution, at the peril of having the land distributed free from his lien.—Martinovich v. Marsicano, 137 Cal. 354, 357, 358, 70 Pac. 459. Where a deceased widow's estate is entitled to one-half of the community property, and one-fourth of the remainder devised by her husband's will, it is error for the court to distribute to such estate only one-fourth of the whole.—Estate of Wickersham, 138 Cal. 355, 363, 70 Pac. 1076. A suit by persons interested in an estate to determine their distributive shares therein is not a condition precedent to an order of distribution, where all parties interested have agreed as to the share each is to receive, and a decree has been entered in pursuance of such agreement.—In re Day's Estate, 27 Mont. 490, 71 Pac. 757, 760. Ordinarily, a legatee or devisee, or an heir, is entitled, as a matter of right, to receive his share of the estate at the time fixed by the statute, if the same can be given to him without loss to creditors, regardless of the fact that it might be better for all interested in the estate that the property should be held in administration for a longer period.—Estate of Glenn, 153 Cal. 77, 94 Pac. 230, 231. Under section 1386, subdivision 5, and section 1393 of the Civil Code of California, a cousin once removed of a deceased person does not stand in the same degree of kinship as the nephews and nieces of the deceased, and is not entitled with them to succeed to the estate.—Estate of Moore, 162 Cal. 324, 122 Pac. 844. A person who appears, prima facie, to have a right to one-third of an estate, the distribution of which, under the terms of the will, must deplete the fund so that, on the successful prosecution of the right, there may not remain sufficient to satisfy the judgment, may require a bond of the distributees for his protection. —Oles v. Macky's Estate, 58 Colo. 295, 144 Pac. 891. One who claims a share of the estate of a deceased person, who is prima facie entitled thereto, has the right to a stay of a distribution of the estate by the

court of administration, so that her interest may not be impaired by
a reduction of the estate until her claim thereto may be adjudicated,
and a denial by the county court of such stay is a gross abuse of
discretion.—Oles v. Macky's Estate, 58 Colo. 295, 298. If shares of
stock in a water company, originally issued to a married woman are,
after her death, distributed to her husband in the settlement of her
estate, he gets no rights additional to those that she possessed therein.
—Riverside Land Co. v. Jarvis, 174 Cal. 316, 163 Pac. 54.

REFERENCES.

Conflict of laws as to legitimacy of distributee.—See note 65 L. R. A.
178-182. Binding effect of settlement, by sole heir or distributee, of
claim belonging to estate, upon administrator.—See note 11 L. R. A.
(N. S.) 148-151. Settlement by sole distributee of claim in favor of
the deceased, binding effect of an administrator.—See note 10 Am. &
Eng. Ann. Cas. 555.

(2) Assignees. Shares "conveyed." Grantee.—If it were not for
a statute providing that, "although some of the original heirs, legatees,
or devisees may have conveyed their shares to other persons, such
shares must be assigned to the person holding the same, in the same
manner as they would have been to such heirs, legatees, or devisees,"
the only questions on distribution would be as to who are the heirs,
legatees, or devisees, and what property they are entitled to as such,
for the court would then be without authority to distribute to any
persons other than heirs, legatees, or devisees, where such statute is
the only provision of law that authorizes distribution to any other
person.—Estate of Ryder, 141 Cal. 366, 369, 74 Pac. 993. Under such
a statute, the court is authorized to assign the share of an original
heir or devisee to another only when such heir or devisee has "conveyed" his share to such other person; and the provision in such a
statute, that such share must be assigned to the person holding the
same in the same manner as they otherwise would have been to such
heirs, legatees, or devisees, instead of implying that the distributee
takes the share distributed, discharged of any mortgage, or judgment
lien thereon, made or suffered by the heir or devisee in favor of third
persons, clearly indicates that he takes it subject to such lien or encumbrance.—Martinovich v. Marsicano, 137 Cal. 354, 357, 70 Pac. 459. The
only section of the code of California authorizing distribution to the
grantee of an heir, or a devisee, is section 1678 of the Code of Civil
Procedure of that state, and this does not justify the court in distributing the estate of a deceased person to the mortgagee of an heir or
devisee or to an assignee as security, who is not a grantee of the heir or
devisee. If the devisee has mortgaged his interest, the court, at most,
can only distribute to such devisee, subject to the mortgage.—Estate
of Crooks, 125 Cal. 459, 461, 58 Pac. 89. There is no provision in the
code authorizing the court to assign a share of the estate to a person
who holds a mortgage or judgment lien or other encumbrance thereon

made or suffered by the heirs subsequent to the death of the ancestor. A judgment creditor of the heir, therefore, is not entitled to receive any portion of the estate, and the court can not, upon distribution, assign to him any share thereof.—Martinovich v. Marsicano, 137 Cal. 354, 357, 70 Pac. 459. Upon petition for final distribution, the petitioner, where he has acquired all the interest of the heirs of the decedent to the decedent's estate, is entitled to have the property distributed to him, and it is error for the court to distribute to the heirs of the decedent, upon the hearing of such petition, if not contested by them.—Estate of Vaughn, 92 Cal. 192, 194, 28 Pac. 221. If a legatee assigns his legacy as security, a bona fide assignee thereof is entitled on distribution to the amount due him.—Estate of Phillips, 71 Cal. 285, 12 Pac. 169. But, in Oregon, the assignee of an heir or legatee is a stranger in the probate proceedings in an estate, and can not have an order distributing to him the share of his assignor.—Harrington v. La Rocque, 13 Or. 344. A power of attorney to receive the distributive share of an heir in an estate, although irrevocable, is not a conveyance of such share; and if the holder of such a power fails to appear on final distribution, and allows such share to be distributed to the heir, he can not enjoin a creditor of the heir in an attempt to apply the property in payment of his debt.—Freeman v. Rahm, 58 Cal. 111, 115. Property may properly be distributed to a distributee's assignee.—Estate of Conroy, 6 Cal. App. 741, 93 Pac. 205, 206. The assignee of the assignee of a distributee's interest in an estate is entitled on distribution to have such distributive share set apart to him notwithstanding the pendency of a suit against the original assignee, brought a few days before the hearing for distribution to have the assignment set aside, but in which suit there had been no service, or appearance entered, before said hearing.—Estate of Phillips, 71 Cal. 285, 12 Pac. 169, 171. If a testator devises real property to his widow and a son, the interest devised to the widow vests in her immediately upon the death of the testator, subject only to the right of administration; and, upon the docketing of a judgment rendered against her, pending the administration, it becomes a lien upon her interest in the real estate so devised, which continues for the time prescribed by statute; and her assignment of her interest to the son subsequent to the rendition of the judgment against her, and the distribution of the estate to the latter, does not affect the rights of the holder of the judgment lien. The court is not authorized to make distribution of real estate to others than the heirs, legatees, or devisees, except in cases where the heir or devisee has "conveyed" his share to some other person. The judgment creditor, therefore, is not entitled to receive any portion of the estate, and the court could not, upon distribution, assign him to any share thereof. But he is not required to appear in court and present his claim at the time of the distribution, at the peril of having the land distributed freed from his lien, and he does not forfeit his lien by reason of his failure to so present his claim.—Martinovich v. Marsicano, 137 Cal. 354, 357,

70 Pac. 459. Assignment by a legatee under a will of certain money "which may be coming to me as an heir at law of the said . . . deceased, under the terms of his will" will be construed as intended to transfer portions of the interest of the assignor as a "beneficiary under the will."—Estate of Rankin, 164 Cal. 138, 127 Pac. 1034. Where the interest of an heir in an estate is assigned to another and the estate is subsequently settled by decree of distribution, the interest so acquired by assignment is merged in the decree of distribution, and the title of such assignee is referable to and he holds under the decree and not under the assignment.—Hopkins v. White, 20 Cal. App. 234, 128 Pac. 780, 782. Upon a proceeding for the distribution of the estate of a deceased person, where one claiming as an execution purchaser of the interest of an heir asks distribution to himself, and the heir raises an issue as to the validity and legal effect of such sale, and sets up a prior assignment of his interest to a third person, it is proper for the court in probate to refuse to determine such conflicting claims and to decree distribution to the heir, subject to the rights, if any of the adverse claimants.—Estate of Howe, 161 Cal. 152, 118 Pac. 515. The provisions of section 1678 of the Code of Civil Procedure of California, authorizing the court, upon the distribution of the estate of a deceased person, to distribute the shares of heirs, legatees, or devisees to those who have received conveyances thereof, only apply where no question arises on distribution as to such conveyances having been made. When the fact of conveyance is in dispute, or where its validity or effect is an issue upon the distribution, the determination of that question is not a matter within the probate jurisdiction of the superior court.—Estate of Howe, 161 Cal. 152, 118 Pac. 515. Although the probate court has jurisdiction to consider and determine the right of distribution of a person claiming as an assignee of an heir, devisee, or legatee under a conveyance made subsequent to the death of the decedent, it has not jurisdiction to adjudicate the claim to distribution of the assignee or, grantee of an heir apparent under a conveyance made prior to the death of the decedent.—Spangenberg v. Spangenberg, 19 Cal. App. 439, 126 Pac. 379.

(3) Retention of distributee's share for debt.—A probate court, having jurisdiction to make a settlement and distribution of a decedent's estate, may determine the share of each distributee, and, to that end, can inquire into and determine the indebtedness of the distributee to the estate, and order a deduction of the same from his share.—Holden v. Spier, 65 Kan. 412, 70 Pac. 248. The equitable right to retain the debt of a distributee from his distributive share is not affected by the lapse of time, and the deduction of the debt should be made, although an action to recover the same would be barred by the statute of limitations.—Holden v. Spier, 65 Kan. 412, 70 Pac. 348, 350. The distributive share due an heir from personal property may be applied by the administrator in payment of a debt due the estate by that heir.—Stenson v. H. S. Halvorson Co., 28 N. D. 151, 159, L. R. A. (N. S.)

1915A, 1179, Ann. Cas. 1916D, 1289, 147 N. W. 800. The debtor who by the death of his creditor becomes an heir of the latter is subject to having the debt retained by the estate on final settlement, and the rights of his co-heirs are superior to a judgment recovered by an outside person before the death.—Wilson v. Channell, 102 Kan. 793, 175 Pac. 95.

REFERENCES.

Deduction of debt from distributee's share.—See head-line 14, subd. 2, post.

(4) **Equitable lien on distributive share.**—An indebtedness owing by an heir to his ancestor, remaining unpaid on the final settlement of the estate, constitutes an equitable lien upon such heir's distributive share of the real property belonging to the estate, superior to the lien of a judgment existing and docketed against him at the time of the death of his ancestor; and, after such final settlement, the interests of the other heirs in the real property are paramount to the lien of the judgment creditor; furthermore, the claim of the estate against the debtor heir is not affected by the statute of limitations.—Wilson v. Channell, 102 Kan. 793, 175 Pac. 95.

(5) **Right of action to recover property.**—An action may be brought against a surviving executor of the will of a deceased person to recover a sum of money due to a trustee for certain beneficiaries, under the terms of the decree of distribution of the estate.—Le Mesnager v. Variel, 144 Cal. 463, 464, 103 Am. St. Rep. 91, 77 Pac. 988. All the distribution amounts to, in any case, is a conveyance from the deceased to the distributee, who manifestly gets no better title than the deceased had, and the title of the deceased not having been traced to the government, a grantor's possession, or to a common source of title, no title is shown in the distributee. The distribution of an estate that has escheated does not convey a warranted title, any more than the distribution of any other estate, and does not entitle the distributee, having no title, to maintain an action of ejectment.—Helm v. Johnson, 40 Wash. 420, 82 Pac. 402, 403. In an action by a distributee to recover the sum distributed to him, the surety of the administrator, after proper notice given, is bound by the decree of distribution and can not be heard to question its validity.—McClellan v. Downey, 63 Cal. 520, 523. Though an heir's property has been distributed under a void decree of distribution, void because of notice essential to jurisdiction to make the appointment of an administrator not having been given, the heir may maintain a suit to recover his share of the estate; a purchaser from the distributee is chargeable with notice of everything appearing on the face of the judgment-roll in the probate proceedings; if that record fails to disclose jurisdiction to appoint an administrator, such purchaser is charged with notice thereof.—Carter v. Frahm, 31 S. D. 379, 400, 141 N. W. 370.

Enforcement of decree, contempt, and execution.—See head-line 14, subd. 12, post. Action to recover estate.—See head-line 14, subd. 15, post. Indebtdeness of heir to estate as counterclaim or set-off against distributive share in proceeds of real estate.—4 L. R. A. (N. S.) 189.

A decree of distribution giving the property to the bona fide purchaser "subject, however, to any rights" of a person claiming under a deed absolute in form but in fact simply a mortgage, is erroneous, since if the rights under the mortgage really existed, the decree would, as a matter of law, be subject to it.—Estate of Lyon, 163 Cal. 803, 127 Pac. 75. Where a widow was at the same time both a beneficiary under, and an executrix of, a will, and had purchased the interests of the other legatees and devisees thereunder, but there is no evidence that the consideration for such purchase was inadequate, nor that any of the beneficiaries so disposing of their interests were dissatisfied with their bargain, a decree of distribution confirming title to the property in such widow will be conclusive of the rights therein declared.—French v. Phelps, 20 Cal. App. 101, 128 Pac. 772, 777.

13. Distribution to non-residents.—While each state will deal with the property of a decedent within its jurisdiction, so far as creditors are concerned, according to its pleasure, the universal rule is, that distribution of the decedent's personal estate must be governed by the law of his actual domicile at the time of his death.—Estate of Apple, 66 Cal. 432, 434, 6 Pac. 7; Whitney v. Dodge, 105 Cal. 192, 198, 38 Pac. 636. All the authorities agree that the residuum of the foreign assets must finally be collected and distributed by the domiciliary executor.—Estate of Ortiz, 86 Cal. 306, 316, 21 Am. St. Rep. 44, 24 Pac. 1034; Joy v. Elton, 9 N. D. 448, 457, 83 N. W. 875; and see note to 45 Am. St. Rep. 668, 670. "There is no reason why the courts of a state other than the domicile of a decedent could not, after the payment of costs and debts, administer and distribute the personal estate within their jurisdiction according to the laws of the state of such domicile. Indeed, in the exercise of a proper discretion, this would, under some circumstances, be a duty required of them. 'As a general rule assets remaining in the hands of an ancillary representative, after paying the claims of local creditors, will be transferred to the place of the domicile for distribution. This rule, however, is not absolute or inflexible, but, on the contrary, the transfer will or will not be made as the court may deem proper in the exercise of a sound judicial discretion according to the circumstances of the case. The court may, in its discretion, order that the residue of the assets remaining in the hands of an ancillary representative, after paying the claims of local creditors, be retained and distributed by him, instead of being transmitted to the principal representative; and, in a number of cases, it has been held that, under the circumstances of the particular case, a retention of the assets was proper. But since the distribution of and succession to personal property, wherever situated, is governed by the laws of the state or country where the owner had his domicile at the time of his death, the distribution, when made by the ancillary representative, must be according to the law of the domicile.' "—Rader v. Stubblefield, 43 Wash. 334, 10 Ann. Cas. 20, 86 Pac. 560, 565. The personal property of a non-resident is subject to distribution under the laws of this state if located in this state at the time of the owner's death.—Estate of Sloane, 171 Cal. 248, 152 Pac. 540. Under section 1691 of the Code of Civil Procedure of California, the power of the former probate court, or of the present superior court, to appoint agents for non-resident distributees, to take possession of their distributive shares, neither was nor is limited to orders therefor made prior to the decree of distribution. That section authorizes the appointment of such agent after such decree, upon a showing of the necessity therefor.—Bell v. Wilson, 159 Cal. 57, 112 Pac. 1100. In order to warrant the appointment of an agent it must appear to the court that a particular distributee is a non-resident having no agent in this state. This showing is jurisdictional, but these facts appearing, it is not necessary to the validity of the order that it designate the agent as appointed for the distributee by name. The agent appointed holds the property distributed for any one who subsequent to the order of appointment may show that he is entitled to it, whether it be the distributee or some third person claiming under him.—Bell v. Wilson, 159 Cal. 57, 112 Pac. 1100. The validity of an order appointing an agent for a non-resident distributee is not affected by the fact that the same person was by such order appointed as agent for an assignee of such distributee. If the court had no jurisdiction to appoint an agent for the assignee, the order would still be valid as an appointment of an agent for the distributee.—Bell v. Wilson, 159 Cal. 57, 112 Pac. 1100. The necessity for the appointment of an agent for a non-resident distributee proceeds from the fact that the executor or administrator can not have the estate closed and obtain a final discharge and release of his sureties until the entire estate is turned over to the distributees and their receipts therefor presented to the court. It is to accomplish this purpose that the "necessity" for the appointment of an agent arises, and could generally only arise after distribution, and upon the failure of such distributee to receive and receipt for his share.—Bell v. Wilson, 159 Cal. 57, 112 Pac. 1100. It is not the duty of the court, under section 1666 of the Code of Civil Procedure of California, in making the decree of distribution, to enter into any investigation as to whether a distributee is or is not a resident of the state, or if a non-resident, whether he has or has not an agent there. Whether he is a resident or not only becomes of real importance after the distribution is made, and is then only important in so far as it may affect the closing of the administration of the estate.—Bell v. Wilson, 159 Cal. 57, 112 Pac 1100. The purchase price of land in the state of California which a testatrix domiciled in another state had contracted to sell in her lifetime, and which was collected by her administrator with the will annexed in the state of California, is personal property, the distribution of which is governed by the law of the domicile of the testatrix.—Estate of Dwyer, 159 Cal. 680, 115 Pac. 242. Under section 1691, Code of Civil Procedure of California, the power of the former probate court, or of the present superior court to appoint agents for non-resident distributees, to take possession of their distributive shares, neither was nor is limited to orders therefor made prior to the decree of distribution. That action authorizes the appointment of such agent after such decree, upon a showing of the necessity therefor.—Bell v. Wilson, 159 Cal. 57, 112 Pac. 1100. The court having jurisdiction of the matter of the estate in which the order was made appointing the agent for a non-resident distributee, had jurisdiction of a proceeding instituted in such matter by an assignee of such distributee to compel the agent to account for the property of which he took possession. A final judgment rendered in such accounting is binding on the agent and is equally binding and conclusive upon his sureties.—Bell v. Wilson, 159 Cal. 57, 112 Pac. 1100.

14. Decree.

(1) In general.—A decree of distribution is not a judgment or order directing the payment of money, nor does it direct the assignment or delivery of documents or personal property. It is an adjudication as to rights only. It is simply evidence of title, and not a judgment that the heir or legatee recovery money or other property from another.— Estate of Kennedy, 129 Cal. 384, 387, 62 Pac. 64. The decree of distribution must name the persons entitled under the will, or by succession, or their grantees.—Martinovich v. Marsicano, 137 Cal. 354, 358, 70 Pac. 459; Estate of Crooks, 125 Cal. 459, 461, 58 Pac. 89. A decree of distribution must simply name the persons and the proportion or parts to which each is entitled.—Estate of Kennedy, 129 Cal. 384, 387, 62 Pac. 64. Orders made relative to the distribution of estates are properly made in accordance with the statutes in force at the time.—In re Thorn's Estate, 24 Utah 209, 67 Pac. 22, 23. The ordinary and usual way in which the title of the ancestor descends to the heir, in such a shape as to make it available to him, is by a decree of distribution. The intervention of the probate court, and an adjudication and distribution thereunder, are essential to the passing of the title of the ancestor to the heir, so perfected as to make it beneficial to him.— Balch v. Smith, 4 Wash. 497, 30 Pac. 648, 650. A trustee takes only such estate as is necessary for the performance of the trust; and the decree properly distributes the trust property to the trustees "for the uses, trusts, and purposes, hereinafter in this decree specified." But a decree of distribution should dispose of the property, and the whole title thereto, and all the estates therein. If, by a will in question, the title in fee is vested in certain children, subject to a trust, and to the possession of the property by the trustees during the trust period, such title in fee, subject to said trust, should be distributed to the children.—Estate of Reith, 144 Cal. 314, 77 Pac. 942, 944. A decree

of distribution has, in most respects, all the efficacy of a judgment in law, or a decree in equity.—Melone v. Davis, 67 Cal. 279, 281, 7 Pac. 703. Before the court allows to a legatee a portion of his legacy under the statute, it is its duty to protect the executor or administrator, so that he shall receive his commissions upon the "amount of his estate accounted for by him." But such protection can be afforded without depriving the court of its discretion to make an order for the payment of a legacy, although the actual money in the hands of the administrator or executor may be no more than the amount of his commissions.— Estate of Dunn, 65 Cal. 378, 381, 4 Pac. 379. A decree of distribution is not void for want of description, if, under the test of the application of the ordinary rules of evidence to the subject, it can be readily shown to represent a specific and certain piece of land.—Smith v. Biscailuz, 83 Cal. 344, 361, 21 Pac. 15, 23 Pac. 314. See De Sepulveda v. Baugh, 74 Cal. 468, 5 Am. St. Rep. 455, 16 Pac. 223. If the probate court has ordered property to be sold to pay the debts and expenses of administration, it is improper to decree a distribution of such property.—Estate of Freud, 134 Cal. 333, 337, 66 Pac. 476. The rule that all presumptions must be indulged which are favorable to the regularity of the proceedings leading to the rendition of a judgment and in support thereof is to be applied with no less rigor to a decree of distribution than to any other kind of judgment, and it is therefore to be presumed that the evidence upon which the decree was predicated was in all respects sufficient and competent, and that any legal objections that could have been made against it were made by the party objecting to the granting of the petition, and were decided by the court at the hearing.—French v. Phelps, 20 Cal. App. 101, 128 Pac. 772, 776. It is held in this case that a minute entry was not intended as a decree of distribution.—Estate of Spreckels, 165 Cal. 597, 133 Pac. 289.

(2) Power of court.—A court has no jurisdiction to make distribution where the petition for final distribution was not filed with the final account, but was filed afterwards and before the final account was settled. Where the decree is for final distribution, statutory provisions which relate wholly to partial distribution are not applicable.— Estate of Sheid, 122 Cal. 528, 55 Pac. 328; Estate of Coursen, 6 Cal. Unrep. 756, 65 Pac. 965, 967. An order of distribution is final, and the court has no power, after such a decree is made, to make a different disposition of a portion of the estate pending an appeal perfected from such final decree.—Estate of Garraud, 36 Cal. 277, 280. It is within the province of the probate court to define the rights of all who have legally or equitably any interest in the property of the estate derived from the will, whether they are entitled to any present enjoyment, or their interests are contingent.—Goad v. Montgomery, 119 Cal. 552, 558, 63 Am. St. Rep. 145, 51 Pac. 681. For the purpose of enabling the court to distribute the estate of the testator in accordance with his will, it is required to consider the will as well as the estate left by him, and to construe its terms for the purpose of determining his intention, and to make its order or decree of distribution in accordance with such construction.—Goad v. Montgomery, 119 Cal. 552, 557, 51 Pac. 681. A decree of distribution that property be distributed "subject to the claim of said administrator" for a designated sum is, in effect, declaring that the property is charged with the payment of the sum named. It creates a lien on the property by operation of law, and the court has the right and power to so charge the property.—Finnerty v. Pennie, 100 Cal. 404, 407, 34 Pac. 865. A mortgage is not a conveyance, but only a contract by which property is hypothecated for the performance of an act. Hence, no distribution of the estate of a deceased person can be made to the mortgagee of an heir or devisee. or to an assignee, as security.—Estate of Crooks, 125 Cal. 459, 460, 461, 58 Pac. 89. Where one has succeeded to the interest of a widow, and petitions for a distribution to him of such interest, the court has power to make the distribution of such interest, but any further than that the decree is a nullity.—Estate of Grider, 81 Cal. 571, 22 Pac. 908, 910. While the statute authorizes the probate court to assign shares of real estate only to the heirs, or to persons to whom they have "conveyed," that court has no authority to assign the share of an heir to another who does not hold a valid conveyance of the title.—Maconchy v. Delehanty (Delehanty's Estate), 11 Ariz. 366, 21 Ann. Cas. 1038, 17 L. R. A. (N. S.) 173, 95 Pac. 109, 111; Martinovich v. Marsicano, 137 Cal. 354, 358, 70 Pac. 459; Estate of Ryder, 141 Cal. 366, 369, 74 Pac. 993. Property may be distributed, though not in the possession of the administrator, and even although adversely held and claimed under title.—Estate of Kennedy, 129 Cal. 384, 387, 62 Pac. 64. If advances have been made by an administrator to a distributee, and latter's share of the estate distributed to him is not sufficient to pay such advances, the court should distribute his share subject to the payment of the amount found to be due from him to the administrator.—Estate of Moore, 96 Cal. 522, 530, 32 Pac. 584. A court has power to distribute a trust for charitable purposes to trustees, subject to limitation, to hold the legal title to part of the property and the remainder in trust for heirs.—Estate of Hinckley, 58 Cal. 457, 517. If the same person is executor and also a trustee under the will, the court, in ordering a distribution of the estate, may direct him to credit his account as executor with so much of the estate as may be ordered transmuted to his account as trustee.— In re Higgins' Estate, 15 Mont. 474, 28 L. R. A. 254, 39 Pac. 506, 517.

REFERENCES.

Power of court as to distribution.—See head-line 7, subd. 4, ante. Retention of distributee's share for debt.—See head-line 12, subd. 3, ante.

(3) Not an escheat.—An order of the probate court that the county treasurer pay into the state theasury "all moneys and effects in his hands belonging to said estate," does not distribute the fund in question to the state as being entitled thereto, under the law of succession, or otherwise. The decree or order is not in the nature of an escheat of the funds so deposited to the state; it is rather an order that such moneys and effects be held on deposit as the property of said estate, subject to the claims of heirs of said decedent, who may come forward to claim the same within the time allowed by law.—Estate of Miner, 143 Cal. 194, 197, 76 Pac. 968.

(4) Notice.—A decree of distribution can be made only after notice, but the notice is sufficient where it appears to be in due form, was signed by the clerk of a proper court through his deputy, was posted according to law by a person qualified by law so to do, and there is no evidence in the record that he did not act for said clerk, or that said notice did not remain where posted for the time required by law, and the final decree of distribution contains a recital that "it appears by proper evidence that the notice, as prescribed by law, had been given of the hearing of said petition and of the settlement of said final account." This is sufficient and conclusive evidence of the fact that the necessary notice was given.—Estate of Sbarboro, 70 Cal. 147, 149, 11 Pac. 563; McClellan v. Downey, 63 Cal. 520. In a case where the testator provided in his will that his wife should manage his estate as trustee, but she subsequently renounced her trust and consented to the substitution of her son as trustee, the order of substitution was not void for want of notice to minor trustees who were not beneficiaries, where, during the life of the wife, she and those persons who were beneficially interested in the property and its management, were alone affected by the order made and in the question as to who should act as such manager.—Moore v. Superior Court, 86 Cal. 495, 496, 25 Pac. 22.

(5) Annulling will after distribution.—Whether an instrument propounded as a will was executed in the manner prescribed by law, is what it purports to be, the last will and testament of the deceased, are facts that the probate court is called upon to determine in the exercise of the jurisdiction it has acquired over the subject-matter and over the parties in interest, and when that court decides that such instrument was properly executed, and that it is the last will and testament of the deceased, and proceeds to administer the estate, its acts, and those of the executor under its authority and pursuant to the statute, are valid and binding as to all dealings with third parties had in good faith and for value. Precisely the same reason that protects a purchase consummated from an executor or administrator before his administration is revoked or superseded, protects the purchaser from the distributee of the estate. When the probate of the will has been annulled upon a contest instituted by an heir subsequent to an entry of a decree of distribution, the heir may undoubtedly pursue the property, and perhaps its proceeds, in the hands of the distributee, but, for the reason already given, he can not follow the property into the hands of one who bought in good faith and for value from the executor, administrator, or distributees prior to the revocation, and at a time when the pro-

ceedings appeared to be, and were, valid and binding.—Thompson v. Samson, 64 Cal. 330, 333, 30 Pac. 980.

(6) **Error. Irregularity. Nullity.**—A decree of the probate court discharging an executor, before a decree of distribution has been made, is premature, but not void, as there is nothing in the decree to show that any part of the estate still remains in the hands of the executors. The decree of distribution and discharge may take effect contemporaneously.—Dean v. Superior Court, 63 Cal. 473, 474, 475, 477. A decree of distribution which does not dispose of all the assets is erroneous. Thus, if the will of the testatrix devises to her son all her interest in the estate owned by his father, her first husband, at his death, and the decree distributes the residue of the said estate "hereinafter particularly described" to the second husband of the testatrix and to her surviving children by him, describing the property, "and any other property not now known or discovered, which may belong to the said estate, or in which the said estate may have any interest," there is at least a question whether this provision would not carry any after-discovered property belonging to the testatrix's first husband at his death, and would bind her legatee, where he is a party to the proceeding. And this doubt is strengthened by the fact that the decree makes no mention of his right to any such property. The decree, in such a case, should make some disposition of this asset of the estate.— Estate of Coursen, 6 Cal. Unrep. 756, 65 Pac. 965, 967. Error by the clerk of the court in indorsing different numbers upon the petition for distribution, and upon the statement of account and decree of distribution, is not material where there is but one estate and the papers all belong to the settlement of one and the same estate.—Estate of Sheid, 129 Cal. 172, 176, 61 Pac. 920. If a legatee has no interest in property distributed, the fact that an improper distribution thereof was made by the final decree, does not prejudice him.—Estate of Coursen, 6 Cal. Unrep. 756, 65 Pac. 965, 967. Neither does a false designation prejudice other particulars of a description of land contained in a decree of distribution, if the land described is capable of identification by extrinsic evidence.—Wheeler v. Bolton, 66 Cal. 83, 86, 4 Pac. 981. It is error to make distribution to an insane person who does not appear by guardian for, in such a case, there is no competent person asking for it in his behalf.—In re Davis' Estate, 27 Mont. 490, 71 Pac. 757, 761. No distribution of the estate prior to final settlement by administration can be had except as provided in the statute; and a distribution made without such steps having been taken, is void.—Abile v. Burnett, 33 Cal. 658, 666. A decree of distribution, entered without notice of the proceeding to distributees, is void as to them, where they did not appear in such proceedings; and it makes no difference that the court recites in its decree that notice was given to all parties. Such a recital, in the absence of notice, can not give jurisdiction to the court. The court can not, by declaring it has jurisdiction, invest itself with jurisdiction.—Estate of Grider (Cal.), 21 Pac. 532, 533; 81 Cal. 571, 22 Pac.

908. A decree of distribution is intended to be a final disposition of the estate, and not contingent upon the establishment, at some future time, of the existence of a condition. A clause inserting a condition in the decree should not be included therein.—Estate of Garrity, 108 Cal. 463, 474, 38 Pac. 628, 41 Pac. 485. Though the court makes an order construing a will and declaring certain persons entitled to a legacy bequeathed therein, such order, if erroneous, is not conclusive, but may be corrected by the court on making final distribution.—Estate of Casement, 78 Cal. 136, 141, 20 Pac. 362. Where on a petition for the settlement of a final account of an administrator the court undertook to make a decree of final distribution it was held that the distributee took nothing under such decree and could not transfer any title to a purchaser.—Carter v. Frahm, 31 S. D. 399. The omission of a devise over is inconsequential if the will itself is made part of the decree. Rule applied where decree by reference embodied in itself entire will.—In re Blake's Estate, 157 Cal. 448, 108 Pac. 287.

(7) **Effect of decree.**—Upon the entry of the decree of distribution, such decree becomes the measure of the rights of the parties interested in the estate, and the will is entitled to no further consideration for that purpose, except upon a direct appeal from the decree.—In re Trescony, 119 Cal. 568, 570, 51 Pac. 951; Jewell v. Pierce, 120 Cal. 79, 83, 52 Pac. 132; Cunha v. Hughes, 122 Cal. 111, 112, 68 Am. St. Rep. 27, 54 Pac. 535; Williams v. Marx, 124 Cal. 22, 24, 56 Pac. 603; McKenzie v. Budd, 125 Cal. 600, 602, 58 Pac. 199. An order of distribution protects the administrator, if he disposes of the property in accordance with its terms; and, if the court had jurisdiction to hear the petition, the order of distribution will be a complete protection against any claim that may be made against him by reason of his compliance therewith.—Estate of Williams, 122 Cal. 76, 77, 54 Pac. 386. As against the estate the rights of the distributees are fully adjudicated by the decree of distribution.—St. Mary's Hospital v. Perry, 152 Cal. 338, 92 Pac. 864, 865. But the utmost effect of a decree of distribution, with respect to strangers, is to render the decree binding as to all property before the court, and subject to administration and distribution by it. It has no effect as to property beyond the court's jurisdiction, and is not evidence against a stranger when the action concerns property beyond its jurisdiction.—Mace v. Duffy, 39 Wash. 597, 81 Pac. 1053. A decree of distribution by the probate court will not defeat an action of one who was not an heir, and who was not a party to any of the proceedings in that court, when it was settling the estate of the deceased person.—Coats v. Harris, 9 Ida. 458, 75 Pac. 243. A decree of distribution of the estate of the decedent settles the question of heirship.—Mulcahey v. Dow, 131 Cal. 73, 76, 63 Pac. 158; and the grantee of an heir or devisee, or any person who claims under an heir or devisee, is bound by the decree as fully as would be the heir or devisee himself, if he had not made the conveyance.—William Hill Co. v. Lawler, 116 Cal. 359, 362, 48 Pac. 323. The final distribution of an entire estate, is an investi-

ture of the absolute right and title thereto in the distributees.—Estate of Garraud, 36 Cal. 277, 280; but the title of the heirs does not originate in the decree of distribution. It comes to them from their ancestor, and the settlement of the estate in the probate court; and the final decree of distribution in that court, only serves to release their property from the conditions to which, as the estate of a deceased person, it is subject.—Bates v. Howard, 105 Cal. 173, 38 Pac. 715, 718. A decree of distribution which purports to distribute undivided interests in all of the property of the decedent, and all other property not known or discovered, which may belong to the deceased, or in which his estate may have an interest, will pass title to lands of the decedent omitted from the particular description in the decree.—Smith v. Biscailuz, 83 Cal. 344, 360, 21 Pac. 15, 23 Pac. 314. But if a son, pending administration of his father's estate, makes a deed of his interest therein, such deed does not carry an after-acquired title distributed to the son under a decree of distribution of the estate of his mother who, as widow, was the sole distributee in fee of the father's estate, where the deed did not purport to convey title in fee, and could not therefore carry an after-acquired title.—McKenzie v. Budd, 125 Cal. 600, 602, 58 Pac. 199. A person can not be considered as holding in trust for his adversary property which has been awarded him, as against the other, by a decree of distribution rendered on due notice.—Davis v. Seavey, 95 Wash. 57, Ann. Cas. 1918D, 314, 163 Pac. 35; Doble v. State, 95 Wash. 62, 163 Pac. 37. A person who stands by and allows a final decree of distribution to be entered in a county court, without in any way claiming the exemptions provided for by the statute, and who does not seek to have said judgment set aside or modified by the said county court, and does not appeal therefrom, can not afterwards question the validity of such judgment on grounds which could have been presented in such appeal.—Fischer v. Dolwig, 29 N. D. 561, 151 N. W. 431, 166 N. W. 793. A decree of distribution reciting that certain land "be and the same is set over unto" a person named in the connection, "her heirs and assigns as provided in and by the terms of the will aforesaid, the same to be to her and her heirs and assigns forever," adjudges such person to have received a fee simple estate.—Thompson v. Lake Madison C. Assn. (S. D.), 170 N. W. 578. Where a decree of distribution was rendered on due notice, and two years have passed, a person who might have appeared at the hearing can not have the executor held as his trustee because of a codicil to the will, which codicil the executor failed to produce to the court.—Davis v. Seavey, 95 Wash. 57, Ann. Cas. 1918D, 314, 163 Pac. 35. A decree of distribution which by its terms distributes a residue, known or unknown, is sufficient to pass title to lands omitted from particular description.—Heydenfeldt v. Osmont, 178 Cal. 768, 175 Pac. 1. A decree of distribution releases the title of heirs from conditions of administration, and furnishes the heirs with legal evidence to establish title.—Carter v. Frahm, 31 S. D. 379, 392, 141 N. W. 370. Where a decree in final settlement distributes property to a person named "to have and to hold, during her natural life, and full power to sell and dispose of the same as in her discretion may seem advisable," with remainder over to other persons named, the first taker may convey so as to vest a fee simple in the grantee.—Parker v. Bower, 172 Cal. 436, 156 Pac. 869. A decree of final distribution issuing out of the county court can not originate title, but only releases it, in the hands of the heirs, from the condition of administration to which it was subject, and to furnish the heir with legal evidence of such release.—Jacquish v. Deming (S. D.), 167 Pac. 157. One who obtains title to a note and mortgage through a decree of distribution is entitled to sue therein.—West v. Mears, 17 Cal. App. 718, 121 Pac. 700. An interested party instituted a proceeding for the appointment of himself as administrator of an estate, alleging fraud in a similar and earlier proceeding, in which another had been appointed administrator, and received, in distribution under final decree, the property of the estate; a decree adverse to the plaintiff was made in the later proceeding, and such decree renders the matter res judicata; hence, any further similar proceeding will be dismissed on motion for a nonsuit.—O'Brien v. Reardon, 29 Cal. App. 703, 155 Pac. 534.

REFERENCES.

Conclusiveness of decree of distribution and power of chancery to correct or to set aside the settlement of accounts in probate courts.— See note 48 Am. Dec. 744-751. Effect of decree of distribution.—See note, ante, on the law of succession, following table after § 41.

(8) **Conclusiveness of decree as to persons.**—Upon an application for the distribution of an estate, after the notice prescribed by the statute has been given, the entire world is notified to be present at the hearing and, to make known their claims, if any they have, to the estate of the decedent or any portion thereof, and the decree of distribution becomes a judicial determination of their claims, which, unless reversed, set aside, or modified upon appeal, is conclusive of their rights, the same as is a final judgment in any other action or proceeding. By giving the notice in the manner prescribed by the statute, the court acquires jurisdiction of all persons entitled to assert any claims to the estate, and, whether they appear and present their claim for adjudication, or fail to appear and suffer default, the judgment is conclusive, not only as to the persons who had any rights in the estate, but also as to the extent and limitation of their rights.—William Hill Co. v. Lawler, 116 Cal. 359, 362, 48 Pac. 323; Crew v. Pratt, 119 Cal. 139, 149, 51 Pac. 38; Goad v. Montgomery, 119 Cal. 552, 558, 63 Am. St. Rep. 145, 51 Pac. 681; In re Trescony, 119 Cal. 568, 570, 51 Pac. 951; Cunha v. Hughes, 122 Cal. 111, 113, 68 Am. St. Rep. 27, 54 Pac. 535; Jewell v. Pierce, 120 Cal. 79, 83, 52 Pac. 132; McKenzie v. Budd, 125 Cal. 600, 58 Pac. 199; Toland v. Earl, 129 Cal. 148, 152, 79 Am. St. Rep. 100, 61 Pac. 914; Mulcahey v. Dow, 131 Cal. 73, 77, 63 Pac. 158; Estate of Miner, 143 Cal. 194, 204, 76 Pac. 968; Estate of Murphy, 145 Cal. 464, 468, 78 Pac.

960; St. Mary's Hospital v. Perry, 152 Cal. 338, 92 Pac. 864; Lewis v. Woodrum, 76 Kan. 384, 92 Pac. 306. A decree of settlement made by a probate court, an apportionment of the residue of the estate among those entitled to share in it, and an order of distribution are binding and conclusive upon all having notice of the proceedings unless they are vacated or set aside upon the grounds and by the methods prescribed by statute.—Lewis v. Woodrum, 76 Kan. 384, 92 Pac. 306. In Kansas it is not necessary that the administrator give any other notice than that of final settlement, provided for in the statute, to make an order of distribution of the estate of a decedent, made by the probate court, effective and binding upon persons claiming a right to share in such distribution as heirs, or otherwise.—Scrubbs v. Scrubbs, 69 Kan. 487, 77 Pac. 269. As the court can exercise jurisdiction over the persons only to whom the estate is to be distributed, it is these persons only who can be affected by the notice for distribution, or be required to give it any attention. The notice is necessarily limited in its effect to those who are entitled to have the property distributed to them.— Martinovich v. Marsicano, 137 Cal. 354, 359, 70 Pac. 459. The administrator or executor is bound by the decree of settlement and distribution of an estate.—McNabb v. Wixom, 7 Nev. 163. It is the duty of everyone interested in a decree of distribution to appear at the hearing and to assert his rights in the court having jurisdiction of the estate; and poverty and poor health is not a sufficient excuse to shield a person who claims an interest in the estate from being charged with laches, if he makes no effort to appear and assert his rights.—Royce v. Hampton, 16 Nev. 25. A proceeding to obtain a decree of distribution is essentially a proceeding in the nature of one in rem, the all-important question upon the hearing is, who are the heirs entitled to the estate, and the statute makes the decree, subject to appeal, conclusive on that question.—Mulcahey v. Dow, 131 Cal. 73, 76, 77, 63 Pac. 158. Under section 1666 of the Code of Civil Procedure of California, a decree of distribution is conclusive as to the rights of heirs, legatees, or devisees, but it is conclusive against them only as heirs, legatees, or devisees, that is only so far as they claim in such capacities. Its determination of such matters does not create any new title; it merely declares the title which accrued under the law of descents or under the provisions of the will.—Cooley v. Miller & Lux, 156 Cal. 510, 105 Pac. 981. A decree distributing an estate to the heirs is not conclusive against one claiming as grantee from such heirs by an instrument executed after the death of the ancestor, and before the decree. Nor does it bind third parties who claim an interest adverse to that of the testator or intestate.—Archer v. Harvey, 164 Cal. 274, 128 Pac. 410, 412. An unassailed decree of distribution to the widow of a testator of all of his real property in fee is conclusive against the existence of any trust in favor of a son of the testator under the will.—Wills v. Wills, 166 Cal. 446, 137 Pac. 249. The will can not be resorted to in such a case to show that the property was distributed in trust, as it is only where by apt language the will is incorporated into the decree that this may be done.—Wills v. Wills, 166 Cal. 446, 137 Pac. 249. In a proceeding under section 1664 of the Code of Civil Procedure of California to determine and declare the rights of all persons in the estate of a testator, in advance of distribution, the decree rendered therein is conclusive in the matter of the distribution of the estate and the fact that one of the interested parties dies pending such proceeding does not make her interest subject to administration, where it is provided by the decree that her heirs are entitled to have such interest distributed to them.—Estate of Horman, 167 Cal. 473, 140 Pac. 11. While a will was void under the statute of the state of Washington as to children not named or provided for, a decree of distribution assigning the whole property to the husband of the testatrix became final and conclusive after the time for appeal had expired, the court having jurisdiction and there being no suggestion of fraud.—In re Ostlund's Estate, 57 Wash. 359, 135 Am. St. Rep. 990, 106 Pac. 1117. A formal administration was not void or ineffective, because of the fact that the record therein shows that the court declared that the property as to which administration was had was the community property of the decedent and her surviving husband, and distributed it all accordingly. This does not make the proceedings or decree void. At the most it was a mere error and mistake injurious to the person who would have inherited the property from the deceased, if it had been her separate estate, and which they could correct only by moving for a new trial or by taking an appeal from such decree. In the absence of such proceedings for a review of that decree it became final and conclusive upon all heirs, legatees, and devisees. (See Cal. Code Civ. Proc., section 1668.)—O'Brien v. Nelson, 164 Cal. 573, 129 Pac. 985. After failure to appeal, within the time allowed by statute, from a decree of distribution establishing possession or title in one person solely of two having or claiming joint property rights, the other persons, and such as might claim under him, are bound by the decree.—Furman v. Brewer, 38 Cal. App. 687, 177 Pac. 495. In a proceeding instituted under section 1664 of the California Code of Civil Procedure to determine and declare the rights of all persons in the estate of a testator, in advance of distribution, the decree rendered therein is conclusive in the matter of the distribution of the estate and the fact that one of the interested parties dies pending such proceeding does not make her interest subject to administration where it is provided by the decree that her heirs are entitled to have such interest distributed to them.—Estate of Horman, 167 Cal. 473, 140 Pac. 11. A decree of distribution is a judgment in rem, and, although erroneous, is as conclusive against one who fails to appear, when having the opportunity, as it is against the party whose fault produced the error.—McGavin v. San Francisco P. O. Asylum Co., 34 Cal. App. 168, 167 Pac. 182. A decree in probate, made after a hearing to which all parties concerned had been cited by due and legal notice, which decree declared what share a widow is entitled to in the estate of her deceased husband under the terms of his will, is an adjudication of the effect of the will in that respect and on appeal is binding upon those parties.—Estate of Hartenbower, Weiss v. Hartenbower, 176 Cal. 400, 168 Pac. 560, 561. The decree of distribution, if not appealed from, is a final and conclusive adjudication of the rights which might be claimed by any person as legatee or devisee under the will.—Estate of Schmierer, 168 Cal. 747, 145 Pac. 99. By a decree of distribution, made agreeably to a compromise agreement between the parties, the court is required to distribute all the residue to the persons entitled, and, under the statute, its order and decree are conclusive in this regard as to the rights of all distributees.—Heydenfeldt v. Osmont, 178 Cal. 768, 175 Pac. 1. Where pretermitted heirs having invoked the jurisdiction of the United States court for the Indian Territory, sitting in probate, against certain orders made in the probate proceedings in which they were interested, and having obtained an order of distribution, though not the character of relief sought, but being such as the court had, upon proper showing, authority to make, and it not appearing that any exceptions thereto were saved and it further not appearing what was done with regard to complying with the order of distributions, held that such heirs were barred by the decree of distribution.—Steele v. Kelley, 32 Okla. 547, 122 Pac. 935. While a decree of distribution does not create the title in the distributees, it is a solemn adjudication of who acquired the title of the deceased, and, if rendered upon due process of law, is final and conclusive upon that question.—In re Ostlund's Estate, 57 Wash. 359, 135 Am. St. Rep. 990, 106 Pac. 1118.

REFERENCES.

Conclusiveness of decree.—See, also, head-line 12, subd. 4, ante. Conclusiveness of decrees of distribution and power of chancery to correct or to set aside a settlement of accounts in probate courts.—See note 48 Am. Dec. 744-751.

(9) **Conclusiveness of decree as to subject-matter.**—The fair and legitimate interpretation of the statute is, that a judgment or order respecting the administration of the estate is conclusive upon the administration as to all matters directly involved in such judgment or order.—Howell v. Budd, 91 Cal. 342, 349, 27 Pac. 747. The decree of distribution is final and conclusive as to the legacies.—Hill v. Den, 54 Cal. 6, 23. If a party has been properly brought before the court, at the hearing, upon the application for a distribution of the estate, he has an opportunity to make objections, and, whether he makes them or not, he is equally bound by the decree.—Smith v. Vandepeer, 3 Cal. App. 300, 302, 85 Pac. 136, 137. The right of a legatee is finally and conclusively established by the decree of distribution; and, in the absence of appeal therefrom, it is the duty of the executor or administrator simply to deliver the property distributed to the distributees.—St. Mary's Hospital v. Perry, 152 Cal. 338, 92 Pac. 864, 866. A decree

of distribution is conclusive as to the rights of heirs, legatees, or devisees in regard to the proportions or parts to which each is entitled.—Estate of Kennedy, 129 Cal. 384, 387, 62 Pac. 64. If a court has jurisdiction to take the management and control of property, and to determine the amount of charges thereon, and to direct their payment out of the property, and to return the surplus to the parties entitled thereto, its judgment in determining the amount of such surplus, and designating the persons to whom it is to be given, is necessarily conclusive upon them and they take their portions of the surplus under and by virtue of the judgment, and not adversely thereto.—Estate of Burdick, 112 Cal. 387, 400, 44 Pac. 734. A decree of distribution is conclusive as to the rights of heirs, legatees, or devisees only so far as they claim in such capacity.—Chever v. Ching Hong Poy, 82 Cal. 68, 71, 22 Pac. 1081. Such decree is conclusive only as to the matter actually litigated. It is conclusive only as to succession or testamentary rights.—More v. More, 133 Cal. 489, 495, 65 Pac. 1044. The decree is conclusive only as to heirs.—Estate of Burdick, 112 Cal. 387, 392, 395, 44 Pac. 734; Estate of Young, 123 Cal. 337, 346, 55 Pac. 1011. If land is distributed in general language, such as "all of the land to which the decedent had title at the time of his death," a description by metes and bounds in the decree would not defeat the claims of the distributee under the general description.—Marcone v. McDowell, 178 Cal. 396, 173 Pac. 465. Where the settlement of an administrator's account and the decree of distribution have resulted from false testimony presented to the court, the adjudication must stand unless appealed from.—Benning v. Superior Court, 34 Cal. App. 296, 167 Pac. 291. A decree of distribution is the final determination of the rights of the parties to a proceeding and upon its entry their rights are thereafter to be exercised by the terms of the decree. It constitutes not only the law of the personalty, but also of the real estate. A decree of distribution has, in most respects, all the efficacy of a judgment at law or decree in equity. When a decree of distribution has been made the probate court has no longer jurisdiction of the property distributed, and the distributee thenceforth has an action to recover his estate, or, in proper cases, its value.—Sjoli v. Hogenson, 19 N. D. 82, 122 N. W. 1008. A decree of distribution, after due and legal notice, by a court having jurisdiction of the subject-matter is conclusive as to the fund items, and matters covered by and properly included therein, until set aside or modified by the court or until reversed on appeal.—In re Evans, 22 Utah 366, 83 Am. St. Rep. 794, 130 Pac. 234. If a county court in Oregon admits to probate the will of a non-resident testator, who left shares of stock in an Oregon corporation, which stock is distributed by that court to legatees named in the will, the decree in that respect is conclusive in interpleader proceedings to determine title; the legatees have a vested title to such shares.—Thomas Kay Woolen Mill Co. v. Sprague (Or.), 259 Fed. 338. A decree of distribution is conclusive as a muniment of title and controls any language of the will inconsistent with it.—Drexler v. Washington Dev. Co., 172 Cal. 758, 159 Pac. 166.

(10) Decree is not conclusive as to whom, and what.—A decree of distribution is not conclusive as to one not an heir.—Estate of Rowland, 74 Cal. 523, 526, 5 Am. St. Rep. 464, 16 Pac. 315; Finnerty v. Pennie, 100 Cal. 404, 407, 34 Pac. 869. As the decree is conclusive only as to the rights of heirs, legatees, and devisees, the claimant, in his own right, antagonistic to the estate, is not concluded thereby. A decree of distribution is not conclusive as to antagonistic claims.—Estate of Rowland, 74 Cal. 523, 526, 16 Pac. 315; Finnerty v. Pennie, 100 Cal. 404, 407, 5 Am. St. Rep. 464, 34 Pac. 869. It does not conclude a legatee under a will, who claims certain property in the hands of the executor in his own right, from asserting his adverse claim against the distributee.—Estate of Rowland, 74 Cal. 523, 526, 5 Am. St. Rep. 464, 16 Pac. 315. It does not conclude the rights of the administrator as an adverse claimant of a lien upon the estate.—Finnerty v. Pennie, 100 Cal. 404, 407, 34 Pac. 869. It does not conclude the claims of a surviving husband to certain property, in the possession of the executors of the will of his deceased wife, as community property.—Estate of Rowland, 74 Cal. 523, 525, 5 Am. St. Rep. 464, 16 Pac. 315. A decree of settlement and distribution, subject to bonds given by distributees, does not conclude the sureties until they have a right to be heard in a regular action in which they are made parties.—Noble v. Witten, 34 Wash. 507, 76 Pac. 95, 96. A decree of distribution of the estate of a deceased person which has been administered on as in intestate's estate, although it has become final, is not a bar to the subsequent admission to probate of the will of the deceased. The admission of such will to probate is not an attack, direct or collateral, upon the decree of distribution, and is authorized to establish the status of that instrument as a will, in order that the devisees and legatees claiming under it may be in a position to assert their rights in equity against the distributees as involuntary trustees of the rightful owners of the property of the estate.—Estate of Walker, 160 Cal. 547, 117 Pac. 510. A finding in the decree of distribution of the grantor's estate that the purchaser under execution of the interest of one of the heirs has not yet acquired the legal title to such interest and is not entitled to have it distributed to him, is not an adjudication that he has acquired no right that may not ripen into a legal title, the period of redemption from the execution sale not having yet expired, and the probate court having no authority to distribute to an execution purchaser.—Sherran v. Dallas, 21 Cal. App. 405, 132 Pac. 454. Where a statutory notice of an application for a decree of distribution provided that if any of the persons interested are minors they must have a guardian appointed to receive notice and appear for them, a minor who has no general guardian and for whom no guardian ad litem had been appointed and who claimed as heir was not bound by the decree and sale, even though his interest as such heir did not appear of record.—Horton v. Barto, 57

Wash. 477, 135 Am. St. Rep. 999, 107 Pac. 193. Where a person agreed with an attorney to give him by way of compensation for his services a one-half interest in certain water rights upon the settlement of the question to be litigated, and pending litigation the client died, a decree of distribution distributing the estate of such client to the heirs is not conclusive against such attorney, and he may specifically enforce his agreements for the transfer of the water rights upon a showing that he has performed his part of the contract.—Archer v. Harvey, 164 Cal. 274, 128 Pac. 410, 412. While a decree of distribution, duly made, is conclusive upon those who may thereafter claim the property as heirs of the person whose estate is thereby distributed, it is not conclusive as to the facts on which such heirship depends when they arise collaterally in another action.—Estate of Walden (Monro v. Latimer), 166 Cal. 446, 137 Pac. 35. It is held that the question whether the decree rendered under section 1723 of the Code of Civil Procedure of California was conclusive upon such heirs as appeared before the court and submitted themselves to its jurisdiction, was not argued or decided, and that this court will not modify the decree in that respect upon petition for rehearing, but that there is nothing in the opinion that can be taken as foreclosing this question in future proceedings in the cause.—King v. Pauly, 159 Cal. 549, 115 Pac. 210, Ann. Cas. 1912C, 1244.

(11) **Enforcement of decree, contempt, execution.**—Disobedience of an order of final distribution of an estate may be enforced by proceedings for contempt.—Ex parte Smith, 53 Cal. 204, 208; Wheeler v. Bolton, 54 Cal. 302, 305; Estate of Clary, 112 Cal. 292, 294, 44 Pac. 569; Ex parte Cohn, 55 Cal. 193, 196; Estate of Kennedy, 129 Cal. 384, 387, 62 Pac. 64; Estate of Wittmeier, 118 Cal. 255, 256, 50 Pac. 393. But while the court in probate may, through the medium of contempt proceedings, compel an executor or administrator to deliver to a distributee property distributed by its order or decree, the statute in terms authorizes distributees to demand, sue for, and recover their respective shares from the executor or administrator, or any person having the same in possession.—St. Mary's Hospital v. Perry, 152 Cal. 338, 92 Pac. 864, 865. If an administrator has a personal claim against the distributee of an estate, and has been directed to pay to such distributee his share of the estate, the administrator can not defeat the distributee on the ground that a garnishment has been served by the assignee upon such administrator against the distributee on the claim assigned. An administrator can not be permitted to juggle with funds belonging to a distributee, nor to avail himself of his trust relationship to secure a personal advantage in the collection of a claim against the cestui qui trust.—McLaughlin v. Barnes, 12 Wash. 373, 41 Pac. 62, 63. A decree of distribution of the estate of a deceased person is an adjudication as to rights only, and can not be executed by any form of process.—Estate of Kennedy, 129 Cal. 384, 387, 62 Pac. 64. Hence, no execution can issue for the enforcement of an order of distribution.—Ex parte Smith, 53 Cal. 204, 208. If a decree of distribution orders the executor to pay

a specified sum of money to distributees, his failure to comply with such order is a contempt of court, for which he may be punished as for a contempt.—Ex parte Smith, 53 Cal. 204, 208. When a decree of distribution has been made, the probate court has no longer jurisdiction of the property distributed, unless to compel delivery; and the distributee thenceforth has an action to recover his estate, or, in proper cases, its value.—Wheeler v. Bolton, 54 Cal. 302, 305.

REFERENCES.

Right of action to recover property.—See head-line 12, subd. 4, ante. Suits against an executor or administrator individually, to recover a distributee's share of an estate.—See division II, head-line 4, subd. 2, ante.

(12) Termination of authority as to property.—Upon the entry of a decree of distribution the right of possession in the administrator terminates and his authority relative to the property ceases; such property is no longer a part of the estate intrusted to the care of the administrator; touching it, both his rights and his obligations are at an end.—Cardoner v. Day, 253 Fed. 572.

(13) No right to participate in decree, when.—Where an insurance company, during the administration of an estate, agrees with certain designated persons, individually, to perfect the title to the real estate of their ancestor, such heirs agreeing to purchase stock in the company, and the contract is made irrespective of any rights that such persons may have in the estate, which estate is not mentioned in the contract, neither the insurance company nor its assignee is entitled to participate in the decree of distribution.—In re Cooper's Estate, 95 Wash. 351, 163 Pac. 935.

(14) Collateral attack.—A decree of distribution can not be attacked collaterally on the ground of error or irregularity in the proceedings as to matters adjudicated therein.—William Hill Co. v. Lawler, 116 Cal. 359, 364, 48 Pac. 323; Lynch v. Rooney, 112 Cal. 279, 287, 44 Pac. 565; Crew v. Pratt, 119 Cal. 139, 152, 51 Pac. 38; In re Trescony, 119 Cal. 568, 570, 51 Pac. 951; Jewell v. Pierce, 120 Cal. 79, 83, 52 Pac. 132; Williams v. Marx, 124 Cal. 22, 24, 56 Pac. 603; Middlecoff v. Superior Court, 149 Cal. 94, 84 Pac. 764. Thus when it is made to appear by the record that no account was really necessary, and that it had been waived, the irregularity in not filing an account is effectually cured as to the distributee, who has acquired the right to have the whole residue distributed to her absolutely, and, there being no objection, or appeal by any other person, the decree of distribution is thereby rendered valid and secure against collateral attack.—Middlecoff v. Superior Court, 149 Cal. 94, 84 Pac. 764, 766. A court is also bound by the order of distribution, and commits error by allowing the widow, in a collateral proceeding, to take anything but the estate allotted to her by will.—Webster v. Seattle Trust Co., 7 Wash. 642, 33 Pac. 970,

971. An order distributing an estate can not be collaterally attacked except for fraud.—Ryan v. Kinney, 2 Mont. 454. Where an heir assigned her interest in the estate, and by subsequent decree of distribution the assignee was declared entitled to all rights under the assignment, the assignment is not open to attack in a subsequent action on the ground that it is a fraud on creditors. To allow such attack would be to allow a collateral attack on the decree, which must be deemed conclusive as to the rights conferred.—Hopkins v. White, 20 Cal. App. 234, 128 Pac. 780, 782. When the decree of distribution determines matters, although the determination may be incorrect, it is conclusive as to the rights of heirs, legatees, and devisees unless corrected on appeal. It is not subject to collateral attack or to be impeached by resort to the terms of the will, and the rights of the parties must thereafter be determined by a resort to the decree of distribution alone as a final and conclusive adjudication of the testamentary disposition.— Luscomb v. Fintzelberg, 162 Cal. 433, 123 Pac. 247. Where a decree of distribution provides that a partition shall not be had before the children of —— "or" —— (naming the two life tenants) shall reach majority, and afterwards partition is had at the suit of the children of one of these life tenants, all of whom are of age although the children of the other life tenant are not so, it will be assumed after the partition, that the court had the decree of distribution before it and put its own construction upon it, and whether that construction be right or wrong it is not subject on this point in a suit for specific performance, to successful collateral attack.—Hall v. Brittain, 171 Cal. 424, 153 Pac. 906. The provision of section 1666 of the Code of Civil Procedure of California, that "such order or-decree (of distribution) is conclusive as to the rights of heirs, legatees, or devisees, subject only to be reversed, set aside or modified on appeal," is only intended to make such decree final and conclusive as against collateral attack, and not as expressly excluding any remedy except direct appeal from the order or decree.—Carter v. Waste, 159 Cal. 23, 112 Pac. 727. A county court's decree of distribution is final and conclusive as against a collateral attack.—Stenson v. H. S. Halvorson Co., 28 N. D. 151, Ann. Cas. 1916D, 1289, L. R. A. 1915A, 1179, 147 N. W. 800. An adjudication effected by the making of a decree of distribution is not subject to collateral attack.—Estate of Schmierer, 168 Cal. 747, 145 Pac. 99. A decree of distribution is not subject to collateral attack, no matter how erroneously it may appear to depart from the terms of the will devising and bequeathing the estate distributed, if all the interested parties have had due notice of the petition.—Miller v. Pitman, — (Cal.) —, 182 Pac. 50, 51, A decree of a probate court distributing an estate is binding upon the world until set aside in a direct proceeding, and can not be attacked in a collateral proceeding except for fraud in its procuring, or want of jurisdiction appearing on the face of the record. —Doble v. State, 95 Wash. 62, 163 Pac. 37. Where a final decree of distribution has been rendered upon due notice, it is not to be avoided

because of the presenting of false proof touching the merits of the question of who is entitled as distributee; such an attack is collateral. —Davis v. Seavey, 95 Wash. 57, 163 Pac. 35. Section 7754, Compiled Statutes of Idaho, of 1919, furnishes the proper remedy when other property of the deceased is discovered; the existence of such property does not justify the setting aside of a final decree of distribution; the remedy is a subsequent issuance of letters testamentary, or of administration with the will annexed.—Chandler v. Probate Court, 26 Ida. 173, 180, 141 Pac. 635. If one of several heirs, while administrator of the estate, purchases at foreclosure sale, with his private means, land mortgaged by his decedent, and takes, after being discharged as administrator, a sheriff's deed in his own name, and has the same at once duly recorded, this heir, after holding the land subsequently for seventeen years succeeding the transfer, and paying the taxes thereon regularly throughout that time, can not be disturbed in his legal possession by the other heirs, although two of these were but ten years old at the time of the issuance of the letters of administration; such other heirs are estopped by laches, and their action is barred by the statute of limitations.—Stianson v. Stianson (S. D.), 167 N. W. 237.

(15) **Presumption in favor of decree.**—A decree of distribution is presumed to have been regularly rendered on duly published notice; it is a final adjudication as against one who seeks to impeach it, unless fraud on the part of the person benefited is disclosed.—Davis v. Seavey, 95 Wash. 57, 163 Pac. 35. A final decree of distribution entered by a county court is of equal rank with judgments entered in other courts of record, and the same presumptions exist in its favor.—Fischer v. Dolwig, 29 N. D. 561, 151 N. W. 431, 166 N. W. 793, 796.

(16) **Vacating decree. Fraud. Equity.**—A probate court has no jurisdiction, after a decree of distribution and discharge, and after the time specified in the statute for giving relief from judgments obtained through "mistake, inadvertence, surprise, or excusable neglect," to entertain a petition to set aside a decree for fraud, or because the court had been imposed upon by false testimony. In such cases, however, courts of equity have jurisdiction to afford proper relief.—Estate of Hudson, 63 Cal. 454, 457; Wheeler v. Bolton, 54 Cal. 302, 305; Moore v. Superior Court, 86 Cal. 495, 496, 25 Pac. 22; Morffew v. San Francisco, etc., R. R. Co., 107 Cal. 589, 594, 40 Pac. 810. The probate court has power, at any time within six months after the entry of a decree of distribution, to set it aside on a proper showing of "mistake, inadvertence, surprise, or fraud."—De Pedrorena v. Superior Court, 80 Cal. 144, 145, 22 Pac. 71. After the statutory period for obtaining relief against a decree of distribution on the ground of "mistake, inadvertence, surprise, or fraud," the decree can be attacked and set aside only by a proceeding in equity.—Estate of Cahalan, 70 Cal. 604, 607, 12 Pac. 427; Dean v. Superior Court, 63 Cal. 473. It may be that the probate of a will can not be reviewed in equity, but the proposition that a decree of distribution is subject to reversal in equity, upon a show-

ing that it was procured by fraud or mistake, is settled. The general rule that all final judgments are subject to attack for fraud or mistake does not apply to decrees probating wills. Such decrees are universally admitted to be an exception to the general rule, however unsatisfactory and illogical may be the reasons given to support such exception; and a decree of distribution is not such a part of the same probate proceeding as the decree probating a will, that it must be governed by the same rule.—Bacon v. Bacon, 150 Cal. 477, 483, 89 Pac. 317, 319. A suit in equity may be maintained to set aside a decree of distribution which shows the result of a mistake, not of the court, but of the parties interested in the estate, where plaintiff has not been guilty of laches, and such a suit is a direct attack on the order of distribution, in which the probated will is competent evidence to prove the error.—Bacon v. Bacon, 150 Cal. 477, 89 Pac. 317, 324. Where a decree of distribution is obtained by extrinsic fraud, as where the executrix connived with a false claimant to make it appear that he was a child of decedent when in fact he was not so, and allowed distribution to be made to him of a portion of the estate, in fraud of the minor children of the decedent, whose rights it was her duty to protect, such decree of distribution may be relieved against in equity and the fraudulent distributee be held as a trustee for the rightful heirs.—Sohler v. Sohler, 135 Cal. 323, 330, 87 Am. St. Rep. 98, 67 Pac. 282. If a decree of final distribution is erroneous as to the law or the facts, the remedy is by appeal. Mere error is not a ground for relief in equity.—Daly v. Pennie, 86 Cal. 552, 553, 21 Am. St. Rep. 61, 25 Pac. 67; Smith v. Vandepeer, 3 Cal. App. 300, 85 Pac. 136, 137. But if a direct attack is made upon the ground of fraud, the fact that the fraud was discovered in time for plaintiffs to have availed themselves of it in the probate court does not affect their right to relief in a court of equity.—Olivas v. Olivas, 61 Cal. 382, 387. A decree of distribution can not be set aside in equity for want of personal notice to the heirs, because the statute does not require personal notice.—Daly v. Pennie, 86 Cal. 552, 21 Am. St. Rep. 61, 25 Pac. 67. But it may be set aside by a court of equity, at the instance of the party injured thereby, where no notice was given of the hearing of the petition for distribution.—Baker v. Riordan, 65 Cal. 368, 4 Pac. 232, 234; In re McFarland's Estate, 10 Mont. 586, 27 Pac. 389. The statute of limitations does not commence to run against an action to set aside a decree of distribution for mistake until the mistake is discovered.—Bacon v. Bacon, 150 Cal. 477, 89 Pac. 317, 323. A decree of final distribution once filed can, after the lapse of six months, be assailed only in an independent suit and for proper cause.—Moyes v. Agee (Utah), 178 Pac. 753. A decree of distribution, entered by a superior court upon notice, or publication, in harmony with the statute, is upon due process of law and conclusive; it can not be vacated by another superior court.—Bayer v. Bayer, 83 Wash. 430, 145 Pac. 433. A decree of distribution, rendered on due notice given, can not be set aside after the lapse of two years, on a showing that a codicil to the will was, by the executor, withheld from the court's notice.—Davis v. Seavey, 95 Wash. 57, 163 Pac. 35. The probate court may, three years after its final decree in probate proceedings, begun by the appointment of the divorced wife of the decedent as administratrix on a petition setting forth that she was the widow, set aside the proceedings, on being presented with the facts, and appoint a new administrator.—Paul v. Paul (S. D.), 170 N. W. 658. Proceedings whereby a person not entitled to administration has been appointed administrator through practicing fraud upon the court may, three years after final decree, be set aside, although the moving party, being a son of the decedent, was of age during all the time; provided, the wrongful administrator kept him quiet by fraudulent representations and promises, and by practicing upon his ignorance.—Paul v. Paul (S. D.), 170 N. W. 658. If the court, having jurisdiction, makes a decree of distribution before payment has been made of all the claims against the estate, which decree incorrectly states that all the claims have been paid, the adjudication is merely erroneous and subject to appeal; it gives no right to the assignee of an unpaid claimant to have the decree vacated.—Benning v. Superior Court, 34 Cal. App. 296, 167 Pac. 291. To avoid, for fraud, the final effect of a decree of distribution rendered upon due notice, the alleged fraud must relate to matters which prevented the plaintiff from appearing and setting up his claim during the course of administration of the estate, or at the final distribution hearing.—Davis v. Seavey, 95 Wash. 57, 163 Pac. 35. A decree of distribution after becoming final can be vacated only because of extrinsic fraud, and the title of a distributee under such decree can not be affected by a suit to set the decree aside. —Warren v. Ellis (Cal. App.), 179 Pac. 544. The failure of the widow as administratrix to include in the inventory of her husband's estate, property standing in his name, but claimed by her, is a fact having no proper place in a controversy to set aside for extrinsic fraud the decree of final distribution and a decree quieting her title to the property.—Fresno Estate Co. v. Fiske, 172 Cal. 582, 593, 157 Pac. 1127. A distributee under an erroneous judgment may, in a proper case, be held as an involuntary trustee; but the fraud or mistake, forming the basis of that relation and warranting that equitable relief be granted by setting aside a decree, must be extrinsic or collateral to the matter which was tried and determined by the court.—McGavin v. San Francisco P. O. Asylum Co., 34 Cal. App. 168, 167 Pac. 182. If distribution is made agreeably to a will whereby the bulk of the testator's estate was left to trustees for an orphan asylum the heirs can not, after having neglected to raise the question that the instrument was executed within thirty days of the testator's death, successfully ask that the decree be set aside.—McGavin v. San Francisco P. O. Asylum Co., 34 Cal. App. 168, 167 Pac. 182. The complaint in a suit to set aside a final decree of distribution need not allege the facts showing jurisdiction in the county court, but is sufficient if it sets forth

in general terms that the final decree was made; it will be presumed
that the petition for the appointment of an administrator alleged the
proper jurisdictional facts.—Fischer v. Dolwig, 29 N. D. 561, 151 N. W.
431, 166 N. W. 793, 796.

(17) **Vacating premature decree.**—An order of distribution may be
set aside and vacated by the court where the same was prematurely
made, and where requirements of the statute in the administration of
the estate were not complied with, such as making an inventory and
appraisement of the estate, the giving of due notice to heirs at law
by the mailing of notices in addition to the publication, and setting
the time required by statute before ordering the distribution of
the estate; and where it further appears that the distribution of the
estate made under the will of decedent was not in accordance with
the provisions of law applicable to the facts before the court when
the order was made. In such a case the decree of the court below
construing the will of decedent, ordering distribution of the estate,
and approving the final account of said administrator, and discharging him and his bondsmen, and declaring said estate closed, will be
set aside and wholly annulled, and the court below will be ordered to
reopen the administration of the estate, and to proceed with the administration, settlement, and distribution thereof, subsequent to the issuance of letters of administration with the will annexed, in the manner
provided by law.—In re McFarland's Estate, 10 Mont. 586, 27 Pac. 389,
391.

(18) **Loss of jurisdiction.**—When a decree of distribution is made,
the probate court has no longer jurisdiction of the property distributed, unless to compel delivery, and the distributee thenceforth has a
right of action to recover his estate, or, in proper cases, its value.—
Wheeler v. Bolton, 54 Cal. 302, 305; Buckley v. Superior Court, 102
Cal. 6, 10, 41 Am. St. Rep. 135, 36 Pac. 360; Morffew v. San Francisco,
etc., R. R. Co., 107 Cal. 587, 594 40 Pac. 810. And as the court, after
issuing a decree of distribution of an entire estate, loses jurisdiction
of the property distributed, it can not afterwards make a different
disposition of a portion of the property so distributed.—Prefontaine
v. McMicken, 16 Wash. 16, 47 Pac. 231, 232. The probate court loses
jurisdiction of the property distributed after decree rendered, for all
purposes whatever except that of enforcing the order.—Prefontaine
v. McMicken, 16 Wash. 16, 47 Pac. 231. Until there has been a final
settlement of the estate, and a distribution of the property, or some
other act equivalent thereto, the jurisdiction of the probate court over
the estate has not been determined.—Hazleton v. Bogardus, 8 Wash.
102, 35 Pac. 602, 603.

15. Payment. Duty of executors.—An executor should not go beyond his duty and trench upon the jurisdiction of the court by assuming, in advance of a decree of distribution, to construe the terms of
the will, the validity of particular bequests, who are beneficiaries

thereundér, or to make payments of the funds of the estate upon his own judgment as to these matters. This is not only trenching upon the jurisdiction of the court, but is infringing the rights of all persons interested in the estate to have these matters disposed of solely on distribution, partial or final.—Estate of Willey, 140 Cal. 238, 241, 73 Pac. 998. Executors are liable for wrongfully making payment of the shares of certain distributees to their pretended attorney. —Bryant v. McIntosh, 3 Cal. App. 95, 96, 84 Pac. 440. It is the duty of the executor or administrator to deliver the property distributed to the distributees; and, unless the decree expressly provides otherwise, he is entitled to nothing more than a receipt for the property from such distributees. If the decree gives the property in trust for certain purposes, the mere acceptance of the property under the decree by the distributees, with knowledge of the provisions of the decree, is an acceptance of the trust, under all the terms and conditions declared by the decree, and no other acceptance is required. If the legatee having accepted the trust by acceptance of the legacy under the decree declaring it, and therefore, subject to the terms and conditions imposed, refuses to carry it out, or diverts the money to other purposes, the law may afford a remedy to any one beneficially interested. But the executor has no supervisory power with respect to that. He is called upon by the decree simply to deliver the property distributed. He has no right to require from the distributee any agreement as to the performance of the trust as a condition precedent to delivery, and any statement by the distributee to the executor as to his intention in the matter of such performance is absolutely immaterial.—St. Mary's Hospital v. Perry, 152 Cal. 338, 92 Pac. 864, 866. The administrator is a wholly indifferent party. It is for the court to say to whom the residue of the estate shall go, and under what conditions it shall go, and it is the duty of the administrator to deliver the residue of the estate to the parties designated by the court.—McCabe v. Healy, 138 Cal. 81. 90, 70 Pac. 1008. A decree of distribution of an estate to a fraudulent grantee, as successor of the defrauded party, is not conclusive of the equities between the parties, or of the constructive trust raised by the fraud, as such matter was not actually litigated in the matter of the estate.—More v. More, 133 Cal. 489, 495, 65 Pac. 1044. An executrix, in her representative capacity, has no right to object to paying legatees on the ground that they have forfeited their rights to legacies by an alleged violation of a provision in the will.—Estate of Murphy, 145 Cal. 464, 78 Pac. 960, 961.

16. Distribution without decree.—A disposition of the property of a decedent, without decree of court authorizing it, is not necessarily void. When the claims of creditors are paid, or are barred, and the costs and charges of administration are satisfied, the estate is for all practical purposes fully administered upon, the right of possession in the administrator terminates, and the right of the heirs to the residue of the estate in his hands becomes absolute. The heirs are then en-

titled to have this residue delivered over to them, as their own property under the law; and it is made the duty of the administrator, by the statute, to surrender the property to them. This duty they can enforce by obtaining a decree of the court directing its performance. As such a decree, however, neither creates their title nor their rights of possession to the property, a distribution made without it can not be invalid. And especially is this so where the distributees are of adult age and otherwise competent to contract, and they agree among themselves, and with the administrator, upon the terms of distribution, and enter into the possession of the property after the distribution is made. The heirs but come into the possession of their own property with the consent of the only person who can rightfully withhold possession from them, and they are not to be disturbed in such possession because of informality in obtaining it. Nor can an administrator be charged with maladministration for distributing property without a decree of the court authorizing it, if it is done after the debts of the estate and the costs and charges of administration have been paid, and it is made to those having the right to the property. After the creditors are paid, or are barred, the distributees alone are interested in the estate. And when they are estopped from objecting, as thy are, either by agreeing to distribution, or by accepting the property when distributed, there is no one left who can lawfully complain, and the administrator is entitled, on the settlement of his final account, to have his act approved.—Griffin v. Warburton, 23 Wash. 231, 62 Pac. 765, 767. Where land is devised by will to trustees, with a valid power to sell and apply the proceeds to certain valid trusts, the legal title vests in them, and they have power to convey that title subject to administration, without obtaining a prior order of the court in probate authorizing the conveyance. The fact that the deed from the trustees erroneously recites that it was made in pursuance of an order of court would not prevent the legal title from passing to the grantee, subject to administration.—Blair v. Hazzard, 158 Cal. 721, 112 Pac. 298. A contract between six out of seven heirs apparent during the lifetime of their father, reciting a consideration of love and affection, was to the effect that if he should devise or bequeath to any of said parties more or less than one-seventh of the total amount of his property, whatever they received from his estate upon partial or final distribution should be pooled, and divided equally among them. Under the father's will the plaintiff had received upon partial distribution of his estate a one-twentieth part thereof, whilst the executor, who was a residuary legatee of over one-fourth of the estate, has refused for considerably over one year to distribute the same, purposely to' evade responsibility to plaintiff and other heirs similarly situated. Held that though the contract is susceptible of the narrow construction that its enforcement depends upon a distribution, yet it will not be so construed, as against the plaintiff, under the facts of the case.— Spangenberg v. Spangenberg, 19 Cal. App. 439, 126 Pac. 379.

17. As affected by partial distribution.—A decree of partial distribution which has become final prior to the beginning of a partition, and fixes and determines the rights of the distributees, is, in the absence of fraud, available as a muniment of title.—Broome v. Broome, 179 Cal. 638, 178 Pac. 525. Where an order of the superior court denying partial distribution of the estate in accordance with the terms of the will on the ground that the trusts created thereby were invalid, is reversed on appeal, the judgment of the appellate court becomes conclusive as to the parties to the proceedings for partial distribution, and is res judicata as to who were entitled to take the estate on distribution, and subsequent decrees of partial and final distribution in conformity with the judgment of the supreme court are correctly made.—Estate of Spreckels, 165 Cal. 597, 123 Pac. 371. Where orders or decrees made in partial distribution of the estate were wholly unauthorized and void, final distribution should be made as in the case of the making of no partial distribution.—In re Hawgood's Estate, 37 S. D. 565, 574, 159 N. W. 117.

18. Rights of creditors. Set-off. Garnishment.—The share of a distributee does not come within the reach of creditors until after it has been distributed by the court, but, after such distribution, the share of an heir or devisee may be garnished by his creditor or may be reached by proceedings supplementary to execution.—Estate of Nerac, 35 Cal. 392, 398, 98 Am. Dec. 111; Dunsmoor v. Furstenfeldt, 88 Cal. 522, 528, 22 Am. St. Rep. 331, 12 L. R. A. 508, 26 Pac. 518; Harrington v. La Rocque, 13 Or. 344, 10 Pac. 498, 499. When the distributive share of an heir has been ascertained, and ordered to be paid by the court, it is no longer regarded as in the "custody of the law." The right to it has become fixed, and the executor ceases to hold it in his representative capacity. After such distribution and order he holds it in his personal capacity.—Harrington v. La Rocque, 13 Or. 344, 10 Pac. 498, 499. In Washington, after the administrator has been directed by the court to pay a distributee, the representative can not set off a personal claim against the distributee; nor can he avoid such payment by the plea that he has been garnished for such distributive share.—McLaughlin v. Barnes, 12 Wash. 373, 41 Pac. 62, 63. But in California an unpaid judgment of the estate against a surviving wife may be set off against her share in the estate, irrespective of the fact of her insolvency.—Estate of Angle, 148 Cal. 102, 82 Pac. 668, 670. After distribution a creditor can not maintain an equitable action, on the ground of fraud, to annul all the proceedings in the matter of an estate, where he was charged with constructive notice of the proceedings, and was chargeable with inexcusable laches in not obtaining relief, if a fraud was being perpetrated.—Tynan v. Kerns, 119 Cal. 447, 451, 51 Pac. 693. The court, upon petition of the distributees, and over the objections of the creditors, or without their consent, will not arrest the course of administration, charge the assets with a lien for the unpaid debts, legacies, and expenses, discharge the administrator

from further duties respecting the estate, and deliver the property
of the estate to the heirs, residuary legatees, or devisees, burdened
only with the charge of the sums due, to be paid at the will of the
distributees, or when they are compelled to do so by a suit to enforce
the lien, particularly where the estate is not a condition to have the
administration closed. Each creditor is entitled to have the proceeding kept on foot, and the property kept in legal custody, until
his debt is paid or secured in some manner provided in the statute;
and he can not be required to yield this right, or to accept a lien
or charge on the property, to be enforced in some new and independent
proceeding.—Estate of Washburn, 148 Cal. 64, 82 Pac. 671, 672. Under
the Kansas statute which gives the surviving wife one-half of the
husband's real estate, the undivided share thus allotted to her by the
law may be levied upon and sold for the payment of her indebtedness.
—Trowbridge v. Cunningham, 63 Kan. 847, 66 Pac. 1015. A judgment
recovered by an administrator against a legatee may be set off, upon
distribution, against an assignee of the legatee's distributive share.—
Estate of Gamble, 166 Cal. 253, 135 Pac. 970.

REFERENCES.

Garnishment of husband's interest in wife's legacy or distributive
share.—See note 47 L. R. A. 360. Garnishment of distributive shares
and residuary legacies before settlement.—See note 59 L. R. A. 387-389.
Levy on interest of heir in ancestor's land.—See note 23 L. R. A. 643.
Indebtedness of heir to estate as counter-claim or set-off against distributive share in proceeds of real estate.—See note 4 L. R. A. (N. S.)
189-191. Distributive share of heir in real estate as chargeable with
heir's indebtedness to estate either as against land itself or the proceeds of a sale thereof.—See note 7 Am. & Eng. Ann. Cas. 563.

19. Actions by transferees of choses in action.—In respect to choses
in action, an executor or administrator is invested with, and has
authority to sell or to dispose of them by indorsement to another,
or to a distributee, without an order of the probate court. Such a
transfer is valid, and passes the title, so as to enable the transferee or
distributee to maintain an action thereon, and the payers or makers
of them, in the absence of fraud or collusion between the administrator and the person to whom he transferred them, can not abate the
action on the ground of a want of authority to make such transfer.—
Weider v. Osborn, 20 Or. 307, 25 Pac. 715. The transferee of a chose
in action, upon distribution of the estate, and in payment of his
share of the estate, may maintain an action thereon in his own name.—
Weider v. Osborn, 20 Or. 307, 25 Pac. 715. Purchasers or indorsees
of choses in action, sold or transferred by the administrator, may
maintain an action on them in their own name, whereever an assignee
is permitted to sue in his own name.—Weider v. Osborn, 20 Or. 307,
25 Pac. 715.

20. Appeal.

(1) **In general.**—Appeals may be taken from judgments and orders made in probate proceedings.—In re Tuohy's Estate, 23 Mont. 305, 58 Pac. 722, 723; In re Klein's Estate, 35 Mont. 185, 88 Pac. 798, 801; In re Kelly's Estate, 31 Mont. 356, 79 Pac. 244. If a final decree of distribution is erroneous whether as to the law or as to the facts, the remedy is by appeal.—Daly v. Pennie, 86 Cal. 552, 553, 21 Am. St. Rep. 61, 25 Pac. 67. On appeal it will be assumed that the probate court had jurisdiction of the subject-matter of the controversy where all the parties interested were before the court, and, without objection to the jurisdiction, asked for the distribution of the property in controversy.—Estate of Apple, 66 Cal. 432, 433, 6 Pac. 7. An appeal by a person who does not show himself to be an "aggrieved party" will be dismissed; as, where a mortgagee appeals, and his interest in no way appears f om the record.—Estate of Crooks, 125 Cal. 459, 462, 58 Pac. 89. It is the duty of an executor or administrator to guard against the error of a distribution without some ample provision for all known obligations of the estate; and he has, therefore, a right to appeal from a decree of distribution.—In re Sullivan's Estate, 48 Wash. 631, 94 Pac. 483, 487. In Montana an appeal may be taken from a decree of distribution by the district court in a probate proceeding pending before it within one year from the rendition of the judgment.—In re McFarland, 10 Mont. 445, 26 Pac. 185, 189; In re Dewar's Estate, 10 Mont. 422, 25 Pac. 1025. A decree of distribution may be modified on appeal.—In re Sullivan's Estate, 48 Wash. 631, 94 Pac. 483, 487. If a decree of distribution is made at the same time that a final settlement is made, and the decree of final settlement is reversed on appeal, the distribution may be disregarded, and a new distribution be made.—Estate of Kennedy, 129 Cal. 384, 386, 62 Pac. 64. Pending an appeal from a decree of final distribution of an estate, made by a probate court, such court has no power to make any further disposition of the estate, and any order by which it attempts to do so, and which operates upon the same subject-matter as the former order, is null and void.—Estate of Garraud, 36 Cal. 277, 280. The public administrator who makes and has no claim upon the estate beyond his commissions, and who did not file the petition for distribution therein, or take any part at its hearing, is not a necessary party to an appeal from the decree of distribution.—Jones v. Lamont, 118 Cal. 499, 503' 62 Am. St. Rep. 251, 50 Pac. 766. If a decree of distribution is erroneous, the remedy is by appeal. —Estate of Schmierer, 168 Cal. 747, 145 Pac. 99.

(2) **Notice of appeal.**—Notice of appeal served after sixty days from entry of decree of final distribution held too late, section 1715, Code of Civil Procedure of California not having been affected by the Act of March 20, 1907, relating to appeals in general and applying to probate proceedings where not inconsistent with the statute relating thereto.—In re Brewer's Estate, 156 Cal. 89, 103 Pac. 486.

(3) Stay of proceedings.—The perfecting of an appeal from a decree of distribution, by filing the undertaking mentioned in the statute, stays proceedings in the court below on the judgment appealed from.—Estate of Schedel, 69 Cal. 241, 10 Pac. 334, 335. Thus where the court has allowed a sum of money to the executors for services rendered up to the date of the decree, an appeal by the widow from this decree suspends its execution, and, until the determination of such an appeal, the executors are not only precluded from distributing the estate in accordance with the terms of the decree, but are required to retain the property in their care and custody.—Firebaugh v. Burbank, 121 Cal. 186, 190, 53 Pac. 560.

(4) Reviewable orders.—An appeal lies from the district court to the supreme court from the final judgment of the district in a proceeding for distribution in the same manner as from the judgment of said court in other probate proceedings.—In re Barnes' Estate, Barnes v. Barnes, 47 Okla. 117, 147 Pac. 504. An order of the county court denying a petition to modify an order of distribution is reviewable by writ of error on the application of petitioner who became a party to the administration proceedings on the presentation of her petition to modify the order.—Oles v. Macky's Estate, 58 Colo. 295, 298.

(5) Non-appealable orders.—The following are non-appealable orders. An order refusing to postpone the decree of final distribution.—Estate of Burdick, 112 Cal. 387, 396, 44 Pac. 734; an order declaring who is entitled to a legacy in advance of a final judgment or order of distribution of the money which is the subject of the legacy.—Estate of Casement, 78 Cal. 136, 138, 141, 20 Pac. 362; an order vacating an order of final distribution.—Estate of Murphy, 128 Cal. 339, 60 Pac. 930, 931; an order refusing to set aside and to vacate a former order of distribution, and settlement of the final account of an executor.—Estate of Lutz, 67 Cal. 457, 8 Pac. 39; In re Kelly's Estate, 31 Mont. 356, 79 Pac. 244; and an order committing an executor or administrator to jail until he complies with the terms of a decree of distribution. The statute relative to appeals from orders made after final judgment, are not applicable to probate proceedings.—Estate of Wittmeier, 118 Cal. 255, 256, 50 Pac. 393.

(6) Who can not appeal.—A decree of distribution will not be reviewed, on appeal by an executor or administrator, where he, as such, has no interest in the matter sought to be reviewed.—Merrifield v. Longmire, 66 Cal. 180, 4 Pac. 1176, 1177; In re Dewar's Estate, 10 Mont. 422, 25 Pac. 1025, 1026; he has a right to appeal, if authorized by the statute.—In re Phillip's Estate, 18 Mont. 311, 45 Pac. 222; but if not authorized, his appeal from a decree of distribution must be dismissed. He can not, in any case, litigate the claims of one legatee as against others at the expense of the estate.—Jones v. Lamont, 118 Cal. 499, 503, 62 Am. St. Rep. 251, 50 Pac. 766; McCabe v. Healy, 138 Cal.

81, 90, 70 Pac. 1008. Under statutory authority an executor and legatees may appeal from a decree of distribution of an estate, or from any part thereof which adjudges that certain persons are entitled to share in the estate.—In re Klein's Estate, 35 Mont. 185, 88 Pac. 798, 801. An executor and legatees may appeal from on order denying a motion for a new trial, in probate proceedings, on issues that others are entitled to distribution.—In re Kelly's Estate, 31 Mont. 356, 79 Pac. 244; In re Klein's Estate, 35 Mont. 185, 88 Pac. 798, 801. Trustees who claim funds in the hands of the executor adversely to the estate, but who are not named in the will, and who have presented no claim against the estate, are not persons "aggrieved," who are authorized to appeal from a decree distributing the funds of the estate to the heir.—Estate of Burdick, 112 Cal. 387, 396, 44 Pac. 734. An "adverse party" is every party whose interest in the subject-matter of the appeal is adverse to, or will be affected by, the reversal or modification of the judgment or order from which the appeal has been taken.—Estate of Young, 149 Cal. 173, 85 Pac. 145. An executor is a mere stakeholder, having no interest in the manner of distribution of the assets; and therefore is not "a party interested" so as to contend, on appeal, that the court was without jurisdiction to distribute save as directed in the will.—Estate of Carr, 175 Cal. 387, 165 Pac. 958. An administrator or executor is not a party aggrieved by a decree determining the proportions in which various claimants shall share in the residue of an estate available for distribution, and can not appeal therefrom.—In re Ross' Estate, 179 Cal. 358, 182 Pac. 303, 304. A party can not enjoy the benefits of a distribution agreement, ratified by a decree of court, and then appeal from a judgment that rests on the same basis as the decree.—Ayers v. Ross, 175 Cal. 191, 165 Pac. 529. A party can not, as a rule, appeal from a judgment after availing himself of its benefits, unless he aims thereby to have such benefits added to.—Estate of Ayers, 175 Cal. 187, 165 Pac. 528. A disinterested claimant, on an appeal from an order denying her a new trial of the proceeding for distribution, and after the appellate court has approved the finding that she was in no way related to the deceased and had absolutely no interest in his estate, is not an aggrieved party as to findings made on any other issue, or as to the disposition of the estate made by the decree, and can not question their correctness.—Estate of Fleming, 162 Cal. 524, 123 Pac. 284.

(7) Dismissal.—An appeal from a decree of distribution will be dismissed where it appears that the appellants have received payment in full of the distributive shares allotted to them in and by such decree.—Estate of Baby, 87 Cal. 200, 202, 22 Am. St. Rep. 239, 25 Pac. 405. An executor's appeal from a decree of settlement and distribution must be dismissed, for he has no right to litigate the claim of one legatee as against the other at the expense of the estate.—Estate of Marrey, 65 Cal. 287, 3 Pac. 896.

(8) Distribution pending appeal.—The distribution of an estate will be prohibited, pending an appeal. The court will not allow the general administrator to dissipate the fruits of the appeal before the appeal can be determined. The status of the parties litigant should be preserved so as to prevent the fruits of litigation from being lost pending the appeal, and, when it becomes necessary in aid of the appellate jurisdiction, proper orders or writs will be issued to secure that end.— State v. Superior Court, 28 Wash. 677, 69 Pac. 375, 377. If the administrator takes an appeal from the decree of final settlement, and, pending the appeal, a decree of distribution is made, such a decree of distribution may perhaps be disregarded, and a new distribution made, if the decree of final settlement is so modified, on appeal, as to show that the administrator has nothing in his hands whatever.—Estate of Kennedy, 129 Cal. 384, 386, 62 Pac. 64. A decree of distribution does not fall within the provisions of the statute authorizing or requiring stay bonds. Hence, if an appeal is taken from a decree of distribution, a special stay bond, given upon such appeal, is void for want of consideration, and no recovery can be had against the sureties.— Estate of Kennedy, 129 Cal. 384, 388, 62 Pac. 64.

(9) Record. Bill of exceptions.—Usually record on appeal from decree of distribution is sufficient without bill of exceptions, but, when determination depends wholly or in part on facts established by evidence, appellant may embody in bill so much as is pertinent.—In re Benner's Estate, 155 Cal. 153, 99 Pac. 715. Devisee claiming in opposition to petitioner for distribution as heir is entitled to bill of exceptions where decree is in favor of petitioner, though he did not appear at hearing of petition.—In re Benner's Estate, 155 Cal. 153, 99 Pac. 715.

(10) Same. Judgment-roll.—On appeal from a decree of final distribution the judgment-roll consists of "the petition for distribution, the opposition thereto, if any written opposition was filed, the counter petitions filed, if any there were, or any other papers in the nature of pleadings, filed at or before the hearing, purporting to set forth the claims of the parties who appeared and claimed distribution, with the answers thereto, also the findings of the court, if any, upon the issue formed, any orders or other papers of like character to those mentioned in section 670 of the Code of Civil Procedure, and the decree of distribution itself."—Estate of Broome, 169 Cal. 604, 147 Pac. 270.

(11) Review. Certiorari. Writ of review.—On appeal from a decree of distribution, the appellate court has jurisdiction to settle the rights of all interested parties.—Estate of Mayhew, 4 Cal. App. 162, 164, 87 Pac. 417. Items in the will may be considered.—Estate of Mayhew, 4 Cal. App. 162, 165, 87 Pac. 417; Estate of Merchant, 143 Cal. 537, 77 Pac. 475; but questions respecting the separate estate of the deceased, and community property belonging to him and his wife, which had finally been determined in the course of the administration of the estate, in special proceedings for that purpose, will not be reviewed on findings made on the application for distribution, which merely recite the ultimate facts so previously found.—Drasdo v. Jobst, 39 Wash. 425, 81 Pac. 857, 859. So on appeal from a decree of final distribution, an objection to the jurisdiction of the court, on the ground of unsettled litigation, is not sustainable, where it appears from the record that whatever litigation there had been concerning the estate had been finally determined.—Drasdo v. Jobst, 39 Wash. 425, 81 Pac. 857, 858. And a decree of distribution will not be disturbed upon appeal, unless the appellants show that their own interests in the estate have suffered by reason of the findings of the decree of the court. Appellants can not be heard to complain that they have received some part of the estate that should have gone to the surviving wife or her legal representatives.—Estate of Kasner, 1 Cal. App. 145, 147, 81 Pac. 991. A judgment committing an executor or administrator to jail until he complies with the terms of a decree of distribution can not be reviewed upon a writ of certiorari, as a review under that writ extends only to the question whether the court regularly pursued its authority.—Ex parte Smith, 53 Cal. 204. It is not a proper function of the writ of review to add to or modify the record with respect to jurisdictional facts determined therein, but to test the question of jurisdiction on the facts appearing on the face thereof. In a proceeding on certiorari to review a decree of distribution, a recital of the order vacating a decree that all persons interested "were duly served with due notice" of the motion to vacate, is conclusive of that fact.—De Pedrorena v. Superior Court, 80 Cal. 144, 146, 22 Pac. 71. On appeal from a decree of distribution it was held that the record furnished no means of ascertaining whether the computation of the amount of the net proceeds of a certain lot applicable to the legacy in question was correct or not.—Estate of Gamble, 166 Cal. 253, 135 Pac. 970.

(12) **Review. Presumptions.**—On appeal the presumptions of law are all in favor of the action of the court below. If error is claimed the record on appeal must contain sufficient legal evidence of it, or the claim must be disregarded.—Estate of Broome, 169 Cal. 604, 147 Pac. 270. On appeal by an executor from a decree of distribution, in the absence from the record of a bill of exceptions the court must assume that the proof before the trial court was ample to uphold its conclusions.—Estate of O'Hare, 178 Cal. 114, 172 Pac. 385.

(13) **Review. What can not be considered.**—The fact that the findings made in a proceeding for distribution do not support the judgment does not render the judgment void, but only erroneous, a condition warranting a reversal on an appeal therefrom by an aggrieved party. Such a point can not be considered on an appeal from an order denying a motion for a new trial, but only on direct appeal from the judgment. —Estate of Fleming, 162 Cal. 524, 123 Pac. 284. If the right to succeed to the property of a deceased is submitted for decision upon an agreed statement of facts, the respondents can not contend on appeal that the appellant should not be heard because he filed no formal objections

to the petition for distribution to the respondents.—Estate of David-son, 21 Cal. App. 118, 131 Pac. 67. On appeal from a decree of final distribution, when the purpose is to have the will construed otherwise than as construed by the decree, the court can not lend itself to this purpose without having before it the will itself, duly authenticated by the court below. In the absence of the will thus authenticated, the reviewing court will consider nothing but the judgment-roll.—Estate of Broome, 169 Cal. 604, 147 Pac. 270. If a testator's son takes, under a distribution agreement, personal and real property not properly his under the will, and mortgages the realty, he can not, on appeal, assail the agreement as invalid.—Estate of Ayers, 175 Cal. 187, 165 Pac. 528. Where a decree of final distribution, made agreeably to a stipulated compromise of a contest of the will, affirmatively shows that a party's attorney was in court during the hearing and interposed no objection to the manner or sufficiency of the proof of compromise, such party can not raise these questions on appeal.—Estate of Carr, 175 Cal. 387, 165 Pac. 958.

(14) **Review. Of evidence.**—On an appeal from an order distributing an estate, the evidence is reviewed and held sufficient to support the finding that the distributee was a niece and an heir of the testator.—Estate of Hartman, 157 Cal. 206, 21 Ann. Cas. 1302, 36 L. R. A. (N. S.) 530, 107 Pac. 105. In a suit for the distribution of an entire estate to the petitioner, as being the daughter and only child of a testator, and yet not mentioned in the will, evidence examined and found insufficient to show the petitioner to be the testator's child.—Estate of Keith, 175 Cal. 26, 165 Pac. 10. The finding that the persons to whom the estate was distributed were the nieces of the deceased is held sustained by the evidence.—Estate of Moore, 162 Cal. 324, 122 Pac. 844. In a pro-ceeding for the distribution of the estate of an intestate to persons claiming to be a half sister and the children of a deceased half brother of the deceased, the evidence is reviewed and, although con-flicting, is held sufficient to sustain the findings of the trial court that neither of such claimants was in any way related to the deceased nor one of his heirs at law.—Estate of Fleming, 162 Cal. 524, 123 Pac. 284.

(15) **Reversal and its effect.**—If a decree of distribution is reversed, the executors are entitled to restitution of the whole estate. The mat-ter then stands as if no decree had ever been made.—Ashton v. Hey-denfeldt, 124 Cal. 14, 17, 56 Pac. 624; Ashton v. Heggerty, 130 Cal. 516, 520, 62 Pac. 934. An executor can not appeal from a final decree of distribution, even though the property has been improperly distributed. —Estate of Coursen, 6 Cal. Unrep. 756, 65 Pac. 965, 967. Where a decree of distribution receives an unqualified reversal on appeal, it is ineffectual to prevent the recovery of property delivered under it by the executrix.—Ashton v. Heggerty, 130 Cal. 516, 520, 62 Pac. 934.

(16) **Damages for frivolous appeal.**—Damages may be imposed for taking a frivolous appeal; as, from a judgment of nonsuit rendered

against a plaintiff, who held a claim for money against a third person, which claim had been distributed to an heir or legatee as part of the estate of the creditor, and where the plaintiff had sued such third person to enforce the claim on the theory that the decree of distribution of itself operated as a money judgment.—Lapique v. Plummer, 168 Cal. 310, 142 Pac. 1079.

CHAPTER III.

DISTRIBUTION AND PARTITION.

PARTITION IN CONNECTION WITH DISTRIBUTION.

§ 751. Estate in common. Commissioners.

When the estate, real or personal, assigned by the decree of distribution to two or more heirs, devisees, or legatees, is in common and undivided, and the respective shares are not separated and distinguished, partition or distribution may be made by three disinterested persons, to be appointed commissioners for that purpose by the court, who must be duly sworn to the faithful discharge of their duties, a certified copy of the order of their appointment, and of the order or decree assigning and distributing the estate, must be issued to them as their warrant, and their oath must be indorsed thereon. Upon consent of the parties, or when the court deems it proper and just, it is sufficient to appoint one commissioner only, who has the same authority and is governed by the same rules as if three were appointed.—*Kerr's Cyc. Code Civ. Proc.,* § 1675.

ANALOGOUS AND IDENTICAL STATUTES.

The * indicates identity.

Arizona*—Revised Statutes of 1913, paragraph 1043.
Idaho*—Compiled Statutes of 1919, section 7734.
Montana*—Revised Codes of 1907, section 7678.
Nevada—Revised Laws of 1912, section 6075.
North Dakota—Compiled Laws of 1913, section 8849.
Oklahoma*—Revised Laws of 1910, section 6468.
South Dakota*—Compiled Laws of 1913, section 5929.
Utah—Compiled Laws of 1907, section 3958.
Wyoming*—Compiled Statutes of 1910, section 5710.

§ 752. Partition, and notice thereof. Time of filing petition.

Such partition may be ordered and had in the superior court on the petition of any person interested. But before commissioners are appointed, or partition ordered by the court as directed in this chapter, notice thereof must be given to all persons interested who reside in this state, or to their guardians, and to the agents, attorneys, or guardians, if any in this state, of such as reside out of this state, either personally or by public notice, as the court may direct. The petition may be filed, attorneys, guardians, and agents appointed, and notice given at any time before the order or decree of distribution, but the commissioners must not be appointed until the order or decree is made distributing the estate.—*Kerr's Cyc. Code Civ. Proc.*, § 1676.

ANALOGOUS AND IDENTICAL STATUTES.
The * indicates identity.
Arizona*—Revised Statutes of 1913, paragraph 1044.
Idaho*—Compiled Statutes of 1919, section 7735.
Montana*—Revised Codes of 1907, section 7679.
Nevada—Revised Laws of 1912, section 6076.
Oklahoma*—Revised Laws of 1910, section 6469.
South Dakota*—Compiled Laws of 1913, section 5930.
Utah—Compiled Laws of 1907, section 3957.
Wyoming*—Compiled Statutes of 1910, section 5711.

§ 753. Estate in different counties, how divided.

If the real estate is in different counties, the court may, if deemed proper, appoint commissioners for all or different commissioners for each county. The estate in each county must be divided separately among the heirs, devisees, or legatees as if there was no other estate to be divided, but the commissioners first appointed must, unless otherwise directed by the court, make division of such real estate wherever situated within this state.— *Kerr's Cyc. Code Civ. Proc.*, § 1677.

ANALOGOUS AND IDENTICAL STATUTES.
The * indicates identity.
Arizona*—Revised Statutes of 1913, paragraph 1045.
Idaho*—Compiled Statutes of 1919, section 7736.

Montana*—Revised Codes of 1907, section 7680.
Nevada—Revised Laws of 1912, section 6079.
North Dakota—Compiled Laws of 1913, section 8855.
Oklahoma—Revised Laws of 1910, section 6470.
South Dakota—Compiled Laws of 1913, section 5931.
Utah—Compiled Laws of 1907, section 3960.
Wyoming*—Compiled Statutes of 1910, section 5712.

§ 754. Partition or distribution after conveyance.

Partition or distribution of the estate may be made as provided in this chapter, although some of the original heirs, legatees, or devisees may have conveyed their shares to other persons, and such shares must be assigned to the person holding the same, in the same manner as they otherwise would have been to such heirs, legatees, or devisees.—*Kerr's Cyc. Code Civ. Proc.*, § 1678.

ANALOGOUS AND IDENTICAL STATUTES.
No identical statute found.
Arizona—Revised Statutes of 1913, paragraph 1046.
Idaho—Compiled Statutes of 1919, section 7737.
Montana—Revised Codes of 1907, section 7681.
Nevada—Revised Laws of 1912, section 6080.
North Dakota—Compiled Laws of 1913, section 8852.
Oklahoma—Revised Laws of 1910, section 6471.
South Dakota—Compiled Laws of 1913, section 5932.
Utah—Compiled Laws of 1907, section 3961.
Wyoming—Compiled Statutes of 1910, section 5713.

§ 755. Shares to be set out by metes and bounds.

When both distribution and partition are made, the several shares in the real and personal estate must be set out to each individual in proportion to his right, by metes and bounds, or description, so that the same can be easily distinguished, unless two or more of the parties interested consent to have their shares set out so as to be held by them in common and undivided.—*Kerr's Cyc. Code Civ. Proc.*, § 1679.

ANALOGOUS AND IDENTICAL STATUTES.
The * indicates identity.
Arizona*—Revised Statutes of 1913, paragraph 1047.
Idaho*—Compiled Statutes of 1919, section 7738.
Montana*—Revised Codes of 1907, section 7682.
Probate Law—118

Nevada—Revised Laws of 1912, section 6081.
North Dakota*—Compiled Laws of 1913, section 8853.
Oklahoma*—Revised Laws of 1910, section 6472.
South Dakota*—Compiled Laws of 1913, section 5933.
Utah—Compiled Laws of 1907, section 3957.
Wyoming*—Compiled Statutes of 1910, section 5714.

§ 756. **Whole estate may be assigned to one, in certain cases.**
When the real estate can not be divided without prejudice or inconvenience to the owners, the court may assign
the whole to one or more of the parties entitled to share
therein, who will accept it, always preferring the males to
the females, and, among children, preferring the elder to
the younger. The parties accepting the whole must pay
to the other parties interested their just proportion of
the true value thereof, or secure the same to their satisfaction, or in case of the minority of such party, then to
the satisfaction of his guardian; and the true value of
the estate must be ascertained and reported by the commissioners. When the commissioners appointed to make
partition are of the opinion that the real estate can not
be divided without prejudice or inconvenience to the
owners, they must so report to the court, and recommend
that the whole be assigned as herein provided, and must
find and report the true value of such real estate. On
filing the report of the commissioners, and on making or
securing the payment as before provided, the court, if it
appears just and proper, must confirm the report, and
thereupon the assignment is complete, and the title to
the whole of such real estate vests in the person to whom
the same is so assigned.—*Kerr's Cyc. Code Civ. Proc.,*
§ 1680.

ANALOGOUS AND IDENTICAL STATUTES.
The * indicates identity.

Arizona*—Revised Statutes of 1913, paragraph 1048.
Idaho*—Compiled Statutes of 1919, section 7789.
Montana*—Revised Codes of 1907, section 7683.
Nevada—Revised Laws of 1912, section 6082.
North Dakota*—Compiled Laws of 1913, section 8857.
Oklahoma*—Revised Laws of 1910, section 6473.

South Dakota*—Compiled Laws of 1913, section 5934.
Utah*—Compiled Laws of 1907, section 3962.
Wyoming*—Compiled Statutes of 1910, section 5715.

§ 757. Payments for equality of partition. By whom and how made.

When any tract of land or tenement is of greater value than any one's share in the estate to be divided, and can not be divided without injury to the same, it may be set off by the commissioners appointed to make partition to any of the parties who will accept it, giving preference as prescribed in the preceding section. The party accepting must pay or secure to the others such sums as the commissioners shall award to make the partition equal, and the commissioners must make their award accordingly; but such partition must not be established by the court until the sums awarded are paid to the parties entitled to the same, or secured to their satisfaction.— *Kerr's Cyc. Code Civ. Proc.*, § 1681.

ANALOGOUS AND IDENTICAL STATUTES.
The * indicates identity.

Arizona*—Revised Statutes of 1913, paragraph 1049.
Idaho*—Compiled Statutes of 1919, section 7740.
Montana*—Revised Codes of 1907, section 7684.
Nevada—Revised Laws of 1912, section 6083.
North Dakota*—Compiled Laws of 1913, section 8858.
Oklahoma*—Revised Laws of 1910, section 6474.
South Dakota*—Compiled Laws of 1913, section 5935.
Utah*—Compiled Laws of 1907, section 3963.
Wyoming*—Compiled Statutes of 1910, section 5716.

§ 758. Estate may be sold.

When it appears to the court, from the commissioners' report, that it can not otherwise be fairly divided, and should be sold, the court may order the sale of the whole or any part of the estate, real or personal, by the executor or administrator, or by a commissioner appointed for that purpose, and the proceeds distributed. The sale must be conducted, reported, and confirmed in the same manner and under the same requirements provided in article four, chapter seven of this title.—*Kerr's Cyc. Code Civ. Proc.*, § 1682.

ANALOGOUS AND IDENTICAL STATUTES.
The * indicates identity.

Arizona*—Revised Statutes of 1913, paragraph 1050.
Idaho*—Compiled Statutes of 1919, section 7741.
Montana*—Revised Codes of 1907, section 7685.
Nevada—Revised Laws of 1912, section 6084.
North Dakota*—Compiled Laws of 1913, section 8860.
Oklahoma*—Revised Laws of 1910, section 6475.
South Dakota*—Compiled Laws of 1913, section 5936.
Utah*—Compiled Laws of 1907, section 3964.
Wyoming—Compiled Statutes of 1910, section 5717.

§ 759. Partition. Notice. Duties of commissioners.

Before any partition is made or any estate divided, as provided in this chapter, notice must be given to all persons interested in the partition, their guardians, agents, or attorneys, by the commissioners, of the time and place when and where they shall proceed to make partition. The commissioners may take testimony, order surveys, and take such other steps as may be necessary to enable them to form a judgment upon the matters before them.— *Kerr's Cyc. Code Civ. Proc.*, § 1683.

ANALOGOUS AND IDENTICAL STATUTES.
The * indicates identity.

Arizona*—Revised Statutes of 1913, paragraph 1051.
Idaho*—Compiled Statutes of 1919, section 7742.
Montana*—Revised Codes of 1907, section 7686.
Nevada—Revised Laws of 1912, section 6087.
North Dakota*—Compiled Laws of 1913, section 8856.
Oklahoma*—Revised Laws of 1910, section 6476.
South Dakota*—Compiled Laws of 1913, section 5937.
Utah—Compiled Laws of 1907, section 3958.

§ 760. Commissioners to make report, and decree of partition to be recorded.

The commissioners must report their proceedings, and the partition agreed upon by them, to the court, in writing, and the court may, for sufficient reasons, set aside the report and commit the same to the same commissioners, or appoint others; and when such report is finally confirmed, a certified copy of the judgment, or decree of partition made thereon, attested by the clerk under the seal of the court, must be recorded in the office of the recorder of the county where the lands lie.—*Kerr's Cyc. Code Civ. Proc.,* § 1684.

ANALOGOUS AND IDENTICAL STATUTES.
The * indicates identity.

Arizona*—Revised Statutes of 1913, paragraph 1052.
Idaho*—Compiled Statutes of 1919, section 7743.
Montana*—Revised Codes of 1907, section 7687.
Nevada—Revised Laws of 1912, section 6088.
North Dakota—Compiled Laws of 1913, section 8859.
Oklahoma*—Revised Laws of 1910, section 6477.
South Dakota*—Compiled Laws of 1913, section 5938.
Utah—Compiled Laws of 1907, section 3959.
Wyoming—Compiled Statutes of 1910, section 5718.

§ 761. When commissioners to make partition are not necessary.

When the court makes a judgment or decree assigning the residue of any estate to one or more persons entitled to the same, it is not necessary to appoint commissioners to make partition or distribution thereof, unless the parties to whom the assignment is decreed, or some of them, request that such partition be made.—*Kerr's Cyc. Code Civ. Proc.,* § 1685.

ANALOGOUS AND IDENTICAL STATUTES.
The * indicates identity.

Arizona*—Revised Statutes of 1913, paragraph 1053.
Idaho*—Compiled Statutes of 1919, section 7744.
Montana*—Revised Codes of 1907, section 7688.
North Dakota—Compiled Laws of 1913, section 8851.
Oklahoma*—Revised Laws of 1910, section 6478.
South Dakota*—Compiled Laws of 1913, section 5939.
Wyoming*—Compiled Statutes of 1910, section 5719.

§ 762. Advancements made to heirs.

All questions as to advancements made, or alleged to have been made, by the decedent to his heirs, may be heard and determined by the court, and must be specified in the decree assigning and distributing the estate; and the final judgment or decree of the court, or in case of appeal, of the supreme court, is binding on all parties interested in the estate.—*Kerr's Cyc. Code Civ. Proc.,* § 1686.

ANALOGOUS AND IDENTICAL STATUTES.
The * indicates identity.

Arizona*—Revised Statutes of 1913, paragraph 1054.

Colorado—Mills's Statutes of 1912, section 8025.

Idaho*—Compiled Statutes of 1919, section 7745.

Montana*—Revised Codes of 1907, section 7689.

Nevada—Revised Laws of 1912, section 6089.

North Dakota*—Compiled Laws of 1913, section 8850.

Oklahoma*—Revised Laws of 1910, section 6479.

South Dakota*—Compiled Laws of 1913, section 5940.

Utah*—Compiled Laws of 1907, section 3955.

Wyoming*—Compiled Statutes of 1910, section 5720.

§ 763. Form. Petition for partition.

[Title of court.]

[Title of estate.]   ⎰No. ——.1 Dept. No. ——.
                                       ⎱   [Title of form.]

To the Honorable the ——2 Court3 of the County4 of ——, State of ——.

This petition, presented by the undersigned, one of the heirs at law of said ——, deceased, respectfully represents:

That on the —— day of ——, 19—, letters of administration on the estate of ——, deceased, were duly issued to ——, and that he, the said ——, immediately entered upon his duties as such administrator;

That said estate has been fully administered, and that a petition for distribution has been filed and is now pending therein;

That the property of said estate will vest in and be assigned by decree of distribution, to be made herein, to two or more heirs5 hereinafter named, in common and undivided, and the respective shares will not be separated and distinguished by such decree of distribution.

The following are the names and residences of all persons interested in said estate, and the names and residences of all guardians, agents, and attorneys residing in this state, representing any of such persons.

Your petitioner therefore prays that this court make, and cause to be entered, a decree of partition setting off to each person interested in said estate his share thereof in severalty; and that an order be made herein appointing commissioners to make partition and to segregate and assign to each of said heirs [6] his share of said real estate in severalty, and for such other or further order as may be meet.

———, Attorney for Petitioner.　　———, Petitioner.

Explanatory notes.—1 Give file number. 2 Title of court. 3 Or, to the judge, etc., as provided by statute. 4 Or, City and County. 5, 6 Or, devisees or legatees.

§ 764. Form. Order for notice of application for partition on distribution.

[Title of court.]

[Title of estate.]　　{No. ——.1　Dept. No. ——.
　　　　　　　　　　　　[Title of form.]

A petition having been filed herein by ——, a person interested in the estate of said ——, deceased, praying for the partition, and the appointment of commissioners to make partition, of all that portion of the said estate which may be assigned by the decree of distribution herein, in common and undivided,—

It is ordered by the court, That ——,[2] the —— day of ——, 19—, at —— o'clock in the forenoon of said day, at ——, at the court-room of said court,[3] be, and they are hereby, appointed as the time and place for the hearing of said petition; and that public notice of the time and place of said hearing be given, by the clerk of this court, to the persons by law required to be notified, by posting notices thereof [4] in at least three public places in said county [5] for at least ten days before said time appointed for hearing.

Dated ——, 19—.　　———, Judge of the —— Court.

Explanatory notes.—1 Give file number. 2 Day of week. 3 Give location of court-room. 4 Or in such other manner as the court may direct. 5 Or, city and county. The petition for this order can not be filed by an executor or administrator, because an executor or administrator has no such interest in the land of the deceased as to entitle him to institute partition proceedings. Ryer v. Fletcher Ryer Co., 126 Cal. 482, 58 Pac. 908. Furthermore, the petition must be filed and notice given before distribution. Buckley v. Superior Court, 102 Cal. 6, 41 Am. St. Rep. 135, 36 Pac. 360.

§ 765. Form. Notice of time of hearing on petition for partition and appointment of commissioners.

[Title of court.]

[Title of proceeding.]

{ No. ——.1 Dépt. No. ——.
  [Title of form.]

Notice is hereby given: That —— has filed in this court, in the above-entitled proceeding, his petition praying for partition of the property of said estate among the parties entitled thereto, and for the appointment of commissioners to make such partition.

And further notice is given: That ——,2 the —— day of ——, 19—, at —— o'clock in the forenoon of said day, at the court-room of said court ——,3 have been fixed by the court as the time and place for the hearing of said petition, when and where all persons interested in said estate may appear and be heard on the matter of the granting of said petition.   ——, Clerk.

Dated ——, 19—.   By ——, Deputy Clerk.

Explanatory notes.—1 Give file number. 2 Day of week. 3 Give location of court-room, etc.

§ 766. Form. Order appointing commissioners to make partition.

[Title of court.]

[Title of estate.]

{ No. ——.1 Dept. No. ——.
  [Title of form.]

Now come —— and ——, the petitioners applying for partition herein, by ——, their attorney, and prove to the satisfaction of the court that due and legal notice of the said petition, and of the time and place of hearing the same, has been given as required by law and by the order of the court; and the same now coming regularly on for hearing upon the said petition and the records and files herein;[2] and it further appearing that an order and decree of distribution of said estate has been duly made herein, the court, after hearing the evidence, finds that partition ought to be made herein as hereinafter set forth.

It is therefore ordered by the court, That ——, ——, and —— be appointed commissioners herein,[3] and that, as such commissioners, they proceed, after giving notice as required by law, to make partition and division of the property hereinafter described, and segregate and set off the same in severalty as follows, to wit: To —— the equivalent of an undivided ——[4] part thereof; to —— the equivalent of an undivided ——[5] part thereof, etc., and that the part allotted to each be ascertained, marked, and described, so that the same can be easily distinguished, and that the partition so made be forthwith reported to this court.

The property to be so partitioned is described as follows, to wit: ——.[6]

Dated ——, 19—.   ——, Judge of the —— Court

Explanatory notes.—1 Give file number. 2 If any contest is made, say, "and —— also appearing by ——, his attorney, in opposition thereto, and the issues being joined." 3 Or, if but one commissioner is appointed, say, "the parties having consented to the appointment of only one commissioner, that —— be appointed commissioner herein." 4, 5 Designate fractional part. 6 Describe the property. A suit for partition, in a probate court, is a "special proceeding," and minors may be represented by an attorney appointed by the court. Robinson v. Fair, 128 U. S. 53, 32 L. Ed. 415, 9 Sup. Ct. 30.

§ 767. Form. Oath to be indorsed on commission.

[Title of court.]

[Title of estate.]   { No.——.1 Dept. No.——.
                            {   [Title of form.[

State of ——,   } ss.
   County[2] of ——, }

——, ——, and ——, commissioners appointed to make

partition of the property of the estate of ——, deceased,
being duly sworn, each for himself, and not one for the
other, says that he will support the constitution of the
United States and the constitution of the state of ——,
and that he will faithfully discharge his duties as such
commissioner according to law.

Sworn and subscribed to before me this —— day of
——, 19—.   ——, Clerk of the —— Court.[3]
                           By ——, Deputy Clerk.

Explanatory notes.—1 Give file number. 2 Or, City and County. 3 Or
other officer taking the oath.

§ 768. Form. Report by commissioners, assigning all estate to one interested.

[Title of court.]

[Title of estate.]   ⎰No. ——.1   Dept. No. ——.
                                   ⎱   [Title of form.]

To the Honorable the —— [2] Court of the County [3] of
——.

We, the undersigned, commissioners appointed by this
court to make partition of the real estate of ——, deceased, in pursuance of an order of distribution made and
entered herein, having each been sworn to the faithful
discharge of his duties before an officer duly authorized
to take and administer oaths and to certify the same;
and a certified copy of the order appointing us, and of
such order of distribution, having been issued to us as
our commission [4] to act; and the oath of each commissioner having been properly certified and indorsed upon
such commission, all of which will more fully appear by
the said commission annexed hereto, respectfully make
report of our proceedings as follows:

That we, in pursuance of due and legal notice given
by us to all persons interested in said partition, of the
time and place when and where we would proceed to
make such partition, and after hearing the allegations
and proofs of said persons, and after viewing said prop-

erty, find that it can not be divided without prejudice to the owners thereof; and that ——, one of said interested persons, is willing to accept the whole thereof and pay or secure its value.

Hence we recommend that the whole of said real estate be assigned to the said —— upon his paying or securing the value thereof as provided by law;

The following is a true description, and statement of the value of each separate parcel of said property: ——.[5]

Dated ——, 19—.

—— } Commissioners. ——

Explanatory notes.—[1] Give file number. [2] Title of court. [3] Or, City and County. [4] Such commission consists of a certified copy of the order of appointment, and of the order or decree assigning or distributing the estate. [5] Give description and value of each parcel.

§ 769. Form. Order confirming report of commissioners, and assigning the whole estate to one.

[Title of court.]

[Title of estate.]   { No. ——.[1] Dept. No.——.
                      {   [Title of form.]

The report of ——, ——, and ——, the commissioners heretofore appointed by this court to make partition of the property of the above-named estate, having been filed herein, and it appearing from said report that said commissioners are of the opinion that the real estate of such estate can not be divided without prejudice or inconvenience to the owners thereof; that the true value of said real estate is —— dollars ($——); and that such commissioners have recommended that the whole estate be assigned to one or more of the parties entitled to share therein, who will accept it; on motion of ——, attorney for ——, due notice thereof having been given to all persons interested, the court proceeds to hear the parties, and, after due consideration, finds:

That ——, one of the parties entitled to share in said

estate, will accept the whole thereof, if assigned to him, and will pay to the other parties interested their just proportion of the true value thereof, or secure the same to their satisfaction: and it appearing to be just and proper that such report should be confirmed,—

It is hereby ordered, That such report be confirmed; and that the whole of said estate be assigned to the said —— upon his making or securing the payment to the other parties interested of their just proportion of the true value of such property.

The property so assigned as aforesaid is particularly described as follows, to wit: ——.[2]

Dated ——, 19—.　　　——, Judge of the —— Court.

Explanatory notes.—1 Give file number. 2 Describe the property.

§ 770. Form. Notice by commissioners before partition.

[Title of court.]

[Title of estate.]　　　　{ No.——.1　Dept. No.——.
　　　　　　　　　　　　{ 　　[Title of form.]

To ——, ——, and ——.[2]

You are hereby notified: That the undersigned, commissioners heretofore appointed to make partition of the estate above named, will meet at ——,[3] on ——,[4] the —— day of ——, 19—, at —— o'clock in the forenoon [5] of said day, to make such partition, at which place and time you may be heard in the premises.

Dated ——, 19—.

　　　　　　　　——⎫
　　　　　　　　——⎬Commissioners.
　　　　　　　　——⎭

Explanatory notes.—1 Give file number. 2 Give names of all persons interested in the partition, their guardians, agents, and attorneys. 3 Name the place. 4 Day of week. 5 Or, afternoon.

§ 771. Form. Report, by commissioners, of partition.

[Title of court.]

[Title of estate.]　　　　{ No.——.1　Dept. No.——.
　　　　　　　　　　　　{ 　　[Title of form.]

To the Honorable the —— [2] Court of the County [3] of ——.

We, the undersigned, commissioners appointed by this

court to make partition of the real estate of ——, deceased, in pursuance of an order of distribution made and entered herein, having each been sworn to the faithful discharge of his duties before an officer duly authorized to take and administer oaths and to certify the same; and a certified copy of the order appointing us, and of such order of distribution, having been issued to us as our commission [4] to act; and the oath of each commissioner having been properly certified and indorsed upon such commission, all of which will more fully appear by the said commission annexed hereto, respectfully make report of our proceedings as follows:

That we, in pursuance of due and legal notice given by us to all persons interested in said partition, of the time and place when and where we would proceed to make such partition,[5] and after hearing the allegations and proofs of said persons and viewing said property did make partition of said property as follows: .

We assigned to —— the parcel particularly described as follows, to wit: ——.[6]

We assigned to —— the parcel particularly described as follows, to wit: ——.[7]

Dated ——, 19—.

$$\left.\begin{matrix} —— \\ —— \\ —— \end{matrix}\right\}\text{Commissioners.}$$

Explanatory notes.—[1] Give file number. [2] Title of court. [3] Or, City and County. [4] Such commission consists of a certified copy of the order of appointment, and of the order or decree assigning or distributing the estate. [5] Although the statute does not require any proof of notice by the commissioners, yet, as it does require notice, it would seem proper that either an admission or proof of service of such notice be furnished. [6],[7] Where the payment of money is necessary to equalize the difference in value between parcels respectively assigned, add, after the description in one parcel, "the amount of money to be received by the distributee," and after the description of the other parcel, "the amount of money to be paid by such distributee."

§ 772. Form. Order confirming commissioners' report and directing partition.

[Title of court.]

[Title of estate.]
{ No. ——.1   Dept. No. ——.
      [Title of form.]

The report of ——, ——, and ——, the commissioners heretofore appointed by this court to make partition of the property of the above-entitled estate, having been filed herein, and it appearing therefrom that said commissioners have performed their duties as required by law, on motion of ——, attorney for ——, due notice thereof having been given to all parties interested,—

It is ordered, That said report be, and the same is hereby, confirmed, and that said property be partitioned, as agreed upon by such commissioners, as follows, to wit: ——.2

Dated ——, 19—.   ——, Judge of the —— Court.

Explanatory notes.—1 Give file number. 2 Give name of person to whom each parcel is assigned, with description of such parcel, following the partition reported by the commissioners. Asking for partition in the same proceeding by which final settlement and distribution are sought does not render the decree of partition void, if the record shows that the question of partition was not considered until after the decree of final settlement and distribution; and the omission of the names of minor children does not affect jurisdiction, where the petition and order appointing an attorney to represent the minors contain the names of all interested in the proceedings. Robinson v. Fair, 128 U. S. 53, 32 L. Ed. 415, 9 Sup. Ct. 30.

§ 773. Form. Decree of partition.

[Title of court.]

[Title of estate.]
{ No. ——.1   Dept. No. ——.
      [Title of form.]

Now comes ——, by ——, his attorney, and presents to the court the report of ——, ——, and ——, commissioners appointed by the court to make partition herein, and moves the court to confirm the report accordingly, and shows to the court that notice of the time and place of making the partition so made and reported by said commissioners was given by the said commissioners to all parties interested in said partition as required by law; that notice of the time and place of making said motion has been duly served on the attorneys of record of all parties interested herein;[2] and no person appearing to object to said partition,[3] the court, having examined said report and heard the evidence offered, grants said motion, and confirms said partition.

It is therefore ordered, adjudged, and decreed by the court, That said pa..ition, so made by said commissioners, be confirmed, and that the same be firm and effectual forever between said parties, and that, in accordance therewith, there be vested in —— in severalty, in lieu of his undivided share of said estate, the property described as follows, to wit: ——.[4]

The property to be so partitioned is described as fol· lows, to wit: ——.[5]

Dated ——, 19—.   ——, Judge of the —— Court.

Explanatory notes.—[1] Give file number. [2] Or, has been duly given by posting notice thereof in three of the most public places in this county, or city and county, at least ten days prior to said time. [3] Or, —— and ——, appearing by ——, their attorney, and filing and presenting their written objections to said report and partition. [4] Describe the property, and proceed with other shares in the same manner. [5] Describe the property.

§ 774. Form. Report, by commissioners, recommending sale.

[Title of court.]

[Title of estate.]   { No. ——.[1] Dept. No. ——.
                          [Title of form.]

To the Honorable the —— [2] Court of the County [3] of ——.

The undersigned, commissioners appointed by this court to make partition of the real estate of ——, deceased, in pursuance of a decree of distribution entered herein, respectfully report:

That, after having received our warrant, consisting of a certified copy of the order of our appointment and of said decree distributing said estate, and having been duly sworn to faithfully discharge our duties, which oath is indorsed on said warrant, and which said warrant and

oath are hereto annexed, we gave due and legal notice
to all persons interested in said partition, and to the
guardians, agents, and attorneys of all so represented, of
the time when and place where we would proceed to make
such partition; and in pursuance of such notice, after
hearing the allegations and proofs of such persons and
their representatives, and after viewing said property,
we are of the opinion and find that the real estate can not
be divided without prejudice [4] to the owners thereof; and
that no one of said owners is willing to accept the whole
thereof and pay or secure to his co-owners the value of
their respective shares; and that said property can not
otherwise be fairly divided and should be sold.

Wherefore we recommend that said real estate be sold
and the proceeds distributed among the parties entitled
thereto.

Dated ——, 19—.

Respectfully submitted.

——⎫
—— ⎬Commissioners.
——⎭

Explanatory notes.—[1] Give file number. [2] Title of court. [3] Or, City
and County. [4] Or, inconvenience.

§ 775. Form. Order of sale of estate and distribution of
proceeds.

[Title of court.]

[Title of estate.]   { No. ——.[1] Dept. No. ——.
                                      {   [Title of form.]

The report of ——, ——, and ——, the commissioners
heretofore appointed by this court to make partition of
the property of the above-entitled estate, having been
filed herein; and it appearing therefrom that the property of said estate can not be divided without prejudice [2]
to the owners; that no person interested in said estate is
willing to take the whole thereof, and make or secure payment as provided by law; and that a sale is necessary to
secure a fair and equitable division of said property,—

It is ordered, That the whole of said property be sold, and the proceeds distributed according to law; and that before the making of such sale the administrator [3] of said estate file an additional bond in the sum of —— dollars ($——).[4]

The following is a description of the property hereby ordered to be sold: ——.[5]

Dated ——, 19—.   ——, Judge of the —— Court.

Explanatory notes.—1 Give file number. 2 Or, inconvenience. 3 Or, executor. 4 Where the statute requires an additional bond. 5 Describe the property.

PARTITION IN CONNECTION WITH DISTRIBUTION.

1. Partition.
    (1) Is authorized only in what cases.
    (2) In general.
    (3) By agreement.
    (4) Commissioners and reference.
2. Limited power of court.
3. Petition and proceedings preliminary to decree.
4. Requirement as to notice.
5. Limit as to whose interests may be recognized.
6. Same. Who entitled to distribution.
7. Decree of partition.
    (1) Essentials and conclusiveness of.
    (2) Matters that will be adjusted.
    (3) Effect of.
    (4) Setting aside.
8. Power of court after decree. Notice.
9. Partition suits.
    (1) In general.
    (2) Right to maintain.
    (3) Jurisdiction.
    (4) Judgment.
    (5) Appeal.
10. Sale and setting aside.
11. Decree of distribution.
    (1) Construction.
    (2) Consideration of advancements.
    (3) Objections to.
    (4) Attack on.
    (5) Validity.
12. Equitable distribution.

1. Partition.

(1) Is authorized only in what cases.—Section 1675 of the Code of Civil Procedure of California, conferring upon the probate department of the superior court power to partition estates held in common and undivided, applies only to cases before the court in which it is possible to set aside property to be held in severalty. Partition necessarily results in the termination of the cotenancy, and vests in each person a sole estate in a specific purparty or allotment of the lands. Partition can not be made in probate unless the interest of the decedent is an estate in severalty. The probate court is authorized to make partition only in cases of joint tenure. Its action must be confined to a single estate. Under such a statute partition is had only because the land was the property of the decedent, not because it is the land of the heirs. The fact that jurisdiction of all undivided interests of a decedent is given, does not evince a purpose to intrust the court with the power to make

Probate Law—119

partition or allotment of property in which strangers have an interest. —Buckley v. Superior Court, 102 Cal. 6, 8, 41 Am. St. Rep. 135, 36 Pac. 360. In statutes concerning the distribution of the estate of a decedent, the word "estate" is clearly used as the equivalent of "distributable assets."—Estate of Hinckley, 58 Cal. 457, 515.

REFERENCES.

Partition in connection with the distribution of estates of deceased persons.—See note 41 Am. St. Rep. 140-151.

(2) In general.—The power of partition is not necessarily involved in the proof or contest of wills, or the distribution of the estate; any estate, whether testate or intestate, may be open to partition in courts of general jurisdiction where the partition has not been adjudicated by the probate court as a part of its duties in effecting the distribution of the estate.—Burke v. Bladine, 99 Wash. 383, 169 Pac. 811. The partition of real estate is, in New Mexico, regulated by statute, and is not dependent upon the common law or general provisions of equity.—Field v. Hudson (N. M.), 176 Pac. 73. From the earliest times the power to award owelty has been regarded as necessary to the act of partitioning property.—Gonzalez v. Gonzalez, 174 Cal. 588, 163 Pac. 993. Proceedings for the partition of real estate are summary and in rem, and a party objecting to the report of commissioners may not offer evidence in support of his or her objections.—Field v. Hudson (N. M.), 176 Pac. 73. There is nothing improper in the act of agents, employed to partition property, seeking the opinion of some other person better versed than they in estimating values.—Gonzalez v. Gonzalez, 174 Cal. 588, 163 Pac. 993.   •

(3) By agreement.—In the state of Washington it is not essential to a valid partition of property of an estate between the persons entitled thereto that an order of the probate court be had for that purpose. If the heirs are adults and the claims of creditors are satisfied a valid partition can be made by agreement.—Thatcher v. Copeca, 75 Wash. 249, 134 Pac. 925. When two holders of common property which they wish partitioned between them, agree in writing to submit the matter to "arbitrators," each to name one of these and the two so named to agree upon a third, these "arbitrators," although so called by the property holders, are not such in legal contemplation, but merely agents.—Gonzalez v. Gonzalez, 174 Cal. 588, 163 Pac. 993. Where all the heirs of an intestate have agreed in writing on a scheme of partition, the enjoyment of their portions severally should not be delayed until quitclaim deeds shall have passed between them.—McCabe v. McCabe, 96 Kan. 702, 153 Pac. 509. The fact that persons, chosen by the property holders concerned to conduct a partition of the property, are sworn in accordance with the law relative to arbitration, does not make these persons arbitrators.—Gonzalez v. Gonzalez, 174 Cal. 588, 163 Pac. 993.

(4) Commissioners and reference.—If commissioners appointed to partition land conclude that it can not be divided in kind, it is the duty of the administrator to aid them in appraising it by revealing everything that in any way bears upon the appraisement, even though such revelation may prejudice his individual interest; if the statute requires the land to be appraised at its "true value," the court should reject an appraisement of from $5 to $10 per acre less than that value; it is the administrator's duty to get as much for the land as possible.—In re Ketcham's Estate, Anderson v. Ketcham (S. D.), 171 N. W. 764. Where it has been submitted to commissioners to make partition of real estate, these commissioners transcend their authority in awarding a portion to one of the parties on such party's paying the other a sum of money.—Field v. Hudson (N. M.), 176 Pac. 73. Commissioners appointed in a partition proceeding can, not err in their report, in respect to form, if they follow the words of the statute.—Field v. Hudson (N. M.), 176 Pac. 73. In respect to the method to be pursued by commissioners, in a partition proceeding, in the performance of their office, the statute makes no provision for their taking evidence, but contemplates that the partition shall be the result of their going personally upon the premises and viewing them.—Field v. Hudson (N. M.), 176 Pac. 73. The law of New Mexico regulating the partition of real estate contains nothing by which the court is authorized to instruct the commissioners.—Field v. Hudson (N. M.), 176 Pac. 73. If the commissioners, appointed in a proceeding for partition of real estate, make an unauthorized report, it is in the power of the court to refer the matter to them for renewed consideration or else to dismiss them and appoint new commissioners.—Field v. Hudson (N. M.), 176 Pac. 73. The report of a referee, in a partition suit, is merely advisory to the court, and the decree rendered may be in disregard of the basis used therein for estimating values.—MacDonald v. Bernal, 34 Cal. App. 431, 167 Pac. 902.

2. **Limited power of court.**—The superior court, while sitting as a court of probate, has no other powers than those given to it by statute, and such incidental powers as pertain to it to enable it to exercise the jurisdiction which is conferred upon it. It has no power to determine disputes between heirs and devisees, and strangers, as to the title of property.—Buckley v. Superior Court, 102 Cal. 6, 8, 41 Am. St. Rep. 135, 36 Pac. 360. The subject-matter of the jurisdiction of the court in partition, in connection with distribution, is the property of the deceased only, and this jurisdiction can not be extended, even by consent of all parties interested in the property.—Buckley v. Superior Court, 102 Cal. 6, 8, 41 Am. St. Rep. 135, 36 Pac. 360. Probate courts have power, in connection with, and as ancillary or supplementary to the settlement and distribution of estates, to make partition of undivided real property among the heirs at law of a deceased person.—Robinson v. Fair, 128 U. S. 53, 86, 32 L. Ed. 415, 9 Sup. Ct. 30. The probate court in California never had jurisdiction to make partition of real estate,

except in the course of a settlement of the estates of deceased persons, and for the purpose of distribution to the heirs or devisees of such estates.—Richardson v. Loupe, 80 Cal. 490, 496, 22 Pac. 227. If a widow, being the head of a family, dies, leaving children, some of whom are minors, who continue to occupy the homestead, partition of such homestead can not be made, against the objection of such minor children, before they become of age.—Trumbly v. Martell, 61 Kan. 703, 60 Pac. 741.

3. Petition and proceedings preliminary to decree.—Under sections 1675 and 1676 of the Code of Civil Procedure of California, partition may be made by three disinterested persons when the estate assigned by the decree of distribution to two or more heirs, devisees, or legatees is common, and the respective shares are not separated. The partition can be ordered on the petition of any person interested in the estate, but said petition must be filed, and the attorneys, guardians, and agents representing absent parties must be appointed and notice be given before the order or decree of distribution is made. The provision that the petition "may" be filed, and notice given at any time before the decree, was evidently intended to mean that the petition "must" be filed before the decree of distribution.—Buckley v. Superior Court, 102 Cal. 6, 10, 41 Am. St. Rep. 135, 36 Pac. 360. But an executor or administrator of the estate of a deceased person, though such estate is shown to be insolvent, has no such interest in the land of the deceased as will entitle him to institute an action for the partition thereof.—Ryer v. Fletcher Ryer Co., 126 Cal. 482, 485, 58 Pac. 908.

4. Requirement as to notice.—If a petition for the partition of a decedent's real property may be filed at any time after the decree of distribution is entered, it is not apparent how the parties could have notice of the intended proceedings, if they are not required to watch the record for years at their peril. The notice required by section 1676 of the Code of Civil Procedure of California is confined to "all persons interested who reside in this state, or to their guardians, and to the agents, attorneys, or guardian, if any in this state, of such as reside out of this state." Everyone interested in the settlement of an estate is supposed to be before the court, and to take notice of its proceedings; but when the estate has been settled and the interests of all parties have been ascertained by the decree of distribution, and the property has been set over to them absolutely and unconditionally, without any previous proceedings indicating an intention to divide the property, the jurisdiction of the court is exhausted.—Buckley v. Superior Court, 102 Cal. 6, 10, 11, 41 Am. St. Rep. 135, 36 Pac. 360. Sections 1676 and 1683 of the Code of Civil Procedure of California require that notice be given to all parties interested, residing in the state, before the commissioners are appointed or partition is ordered, stating the time, and place, and where the commissioners will proceed to make the partition; but the probate court can inquire only as to who are parties in interest claiming under the decedent, and whether the proper notice

has been given to them; and, as it has no jurisdiction of anyone except those interested in the estate, it is clear that it can not determine whether proper notice has been given to others, and that it can not bring them within its jurisdiction.—Buckley v. Superior Court, 102 Cal. 6, 9, 41 Am. St. Rep. 135, 36 Pac. 360. If land can not be divided in kind, all of the heirs are entitled to notice of the appraisement made by the commissioners appointed to partition it, so that each may have an opportunity, in the light of such appraisement, to determine whether he desires to take the land; but a surviving husband is not entitled to preference, under the statutes of South Dakota, in the purchase of his deceased wife's land, as that statute does not give the oldest male heir preference, except as between children.—In re Ketcham's Estate, Anderson v. Ketcham (S. D.), 171 N. W. 764. Under the statute of Washington, requiring notice to be given to all persons interested in a partition, and providing that it may be served personally, notice of partition proceedings, in which minor heirs are interested, is sufficient as to a non-resident party, where it was served, personally, outside of the state, upon such party and upon the agent of such party, at least thirty-three days before the time partition was made.—Ponti v. Hoffman, 87 Wash. 137, 151 Pac. 249. A court does not have jurisdiction to make an order of distribution before less than the statutory time of notice has elapsed between the time set for hearing and the time of making such order.—In re Hoscheid's Estate, 78 Wash. 309, 313, 139 Pac. 61.

5. Limit as to whose interests may be recognized.—Section 1678 of the Code of Civil Procedure of California is expressly confined to persons who have purchased from heirs, legatees, or devisees an interest in the estate, and then places them simply in the shoes of their grantors in the matter of such partition and distribution.—Richardson v. Loupe, 80 Cal. 490, 497, 22 Pac. 227. This section applies particularly to cases of partition between heirs or devisees, where commissioners are appointed to make division, etc.; and merely gives the right to the grantee of an heir or devisee to have the share of his grantor set off to him.—Chever v. Ching Hong Poy, 82 Cal. 68, 71, 22 Pac. 1081.

6. Same. Who entitled to distribution.—The partition can be ordered on the petition of any person interested in the estate, and it is only "parties interested" whom the court will recognize. But the grantee of an heir of the deceased is a person interested in the estate and is entitled, on a distribution thereof, to the share so conveyed to him.—Buckley v. Superior Court, 102 Cal. 6, 9, 10, 41 Am. St. Rep. 135, 36 Pac. 360; Estate of Vaughn, 92 Cal. 192, 28 Pac. 221; Chever v. Ching Hong Poy, 82 Cal. 68, 22 Pac. 1081; Estate of De Castro v. Barry, 18 Cal. 96; Demaris v. Barker, 33 Wash. 200, 74 Pac. 362, 364. Purchasers from heirs, legatees, or devisees are placed simply in the shoes of their grantors in the matter of the partition and the distribution of the estate.—Richardson v. Loupe, 80 Cal. 490, 497, 22 Pac. 227. The pendency of administration of an estate does not bar the right of the heirs

to an immediate partition of the realty.—Mackey v. Mackey, 99 Kan. 433, 163 Pac. 465.

REFERENCES.

Right to partition among remaindermen pending life estate.—See note 28 L. R. A. (N. S.) 125.

7. Decree of partition.

(1) **Essentials and conclusiveness of.**—The county courts of Oregon have no authority to determine what persons are entitled to the realty, and to make partition of the real estate of the decedent.—Hanner v. Silver, 2 Or. 336, 338. The decree must name the person entitled under the will, or by succession, or their grantees.—Estate of Crooks, 125 Cal. 459, 461, 58 Pac. 89; Martinovich v. Marsicano, 137 Cal. 354, 358, 70 Pac. 459; Buckley v. Superior Court, 102 Cal. 6, 9, 41 Am. St. Rep. 135, 36 Pac. 360. The grantee of an heir or devisee, or any person who claims under an heir or devisee, is bound by the decree as fully as would be the heir or devisee himself if he had not made the conveyance. The provisions of section 1678 extend to the distribution as well as to the partition which is provided in chapter XI of the Code of Civil Procedure of California, being sections 1658-1703½, and render the decree as conclusive upon those to whom the heirs have conveyed the estate as it otherwise would have been upon such heirs, legatees, or devisees, and the decree is equally conclusive whether the estate is distributed to the persons in segregated parts, or in undivided proportions.—William Hill Co. v. Lawler, 116 Cal. 359, 362, 48 Pac. 323; Snyder v. Murdock, 26 Utah 233, 73 Pac. 22. Under the statute, proceedings of the probate court are construed in the same manner and with like intendments as those of courts of general jurisdiction; hence, a decree of distribution made in a partition proceeding in that court is, unless appealed from, conclusive.—Thompson v. Lake Madison C. Assn. (S. D.), 170 N. W. 578.

(2) **Matters that will be adjusted.**—The court, in decreeing partition, may adjust the equitable rights of all the parties interested, so far as they relate to and grow out of the relation of the parties to the common property, and will make allowance for the payment of money made on account of the property.—Advance-Rumely Thresher Co. v. Judd, 104 Kan. 757, 180 Pac. 763. Where the claims against the personal estate have been determined and adjusted before the entering of a decree in a partition suit between the heirs, there is no reason why credits due an interested party from the personal estate should not be balanced against claims due from such party for rental collections in the partition suit.—Mackey v. Mackey, 99 Kan. 433, 163 Pac. 465.

(3) **Effect of.**—A decree or judgment in partition has no other effect than to sever the unity of possession, and does not vest in either of the cotenants any new or additional title; after the partition each has precisely the same title that he had before.—Potrero Nuevo Land Co. v. All Persons, etc., 29 Cal. App. 743, 748, 156 Pac. 876.

(4) Setting aside.—A decree in partition will not be set aside on the ground of fraud, where the court had jurisdiction of the proceedings, and there was neither collusion nor fraud, although there was an honest mistake as to the extent of the interest held by one of the parties, and an interested person was appointed guardian ad litem for one of the parties, who was an infant.—Howell v. Howell, 77 Or. 539, 152 Pac. 217.

8. Power of court after decree. Notice.—Ordinarily, the court has no power over the property, or the rights of the distributees, after the entry of a decree of distribution of the estate of a deceased person, and courts of equity alone can afford relief; but the statute gives to the court the power to reserve its jurisdiction to proceed beyond the making of the decree so as to make partition and to compel delivery. For this purpose the parties in interest must be kept before the court, and must be given an opportunity to protect themselves in the proceedings looking to a division of their property. There may be a partition in connection with the distribution of the estate, but proceedings indicating an intention to divide the property should be instituted before the distribution, for after the distribution, the court would have no power over the property, or the rights of the distributees.—Buckley v. Superior Court, 102 Cal. 6, 11, 41 Am. St. Rep. 135, 36 Pac. 360. The delivery provided for by section 7675 of the Revised Codes of Montana, when the property is ready for distribution, serves all the purposes of distribution, and the power to direct the delivery is tantamount to the power to order distribution directly to the persons entitled to take.—State v. District Court, 41 Mont. 357, 365, 109 Pac. 438.

9. Partition suits.

(1) In general.—In a partition suit, non-resident wives of the parties to the partition, are not necessary parties.—Cunningham v. Friendly, 70 Or. 222, 227, 139 Pac. 928, 140 Pac. 989. If the petition, in an action for partition, fails to show that dower has been assigned to the widow, and that she is in possession of the homestead, these matters, if relied upon as a defense, must be set up by way of answer.—Chouteau v. Chouteau, 51 Okla. 744, 152 Pac. 373. Whether a wife was unduly influenced or not to make a deed of her property to her children without her husband's consent is immaterial in a suit for partition brought by him after her death for partition; for, whether unduly influenced or not, she could not convey his interest in her land without his consent.—Murray v. Murray, 102 Kan. 184, 185, 170 Pac. 393.

(2) Right to maintain.—A wife living with her husband in this state deeded to her children certain land owned by her, the husband not joining. Shortly thereafter the wife died, and fourteen years later the surviving husband brought this action for partition, the land not having been the homestead of either, nor judicially sold, nor necessary to the payment of debts. No application was made by the husband to the probate court for allotment. Held, that he was entitled to maintain the action.—Murray v. Murray, 102 Kan. 184, 185, 170 Pac. 393. Where a wife occupies as a home the homestead set apart by order of the probate court from the estate of her deceased husband for the use of herself as a home, the same is not liable to partition at the suit of the heirs of the deceased husband. Holmes v. Holmes, 27 Okla. 140, 30 L. R. A. (N. S.) 920, 111 Pac. 220. A will left a life estate in land to the testator's two children with remainder to their children, and the decree in distribution provided that there should be no partition "until the youngest child of —— or of —— (naming the life tenants) shall have reached its majority." The court held that the use of the disjunctive indicated that when all the children of one of the life tenants reached majority those children could bring proceedings for partition even if the children of the other were still infants.—Hall v. Brittain, 171 Cal. 424, 427, 153 Pac. 906.

(3) **Jurisdiction.**—In partition suits in Oregon, a court of equity has jurisdiction to pass upon the question of title as well as that of possession.—French v. Goin, 75 Or. 255, 146 Pac. 91.

(4) **Judgment.**—Under the statute of New Mexico, Code of 1915, Art. 19, the court has no power to enter a judgment partitioning real estate without the intervention of commissioners, and the judgment of the court must be based on the report of the commissioners.—Field v. Hudson (N. M.), 176 Pac. 73.

(5) **Appeal.**—A suit arising out of a partition between heirs of an intestate, and to give effect to the same, forms no exception to the rule that the findings of fact by the trial court, when there is conflicting testimony, is final, if based on substantial evidence.—McCabe v. McCabe, 96 Kan. 702, 153 Pac. 509. It can not be a matter for presumption that, of cotenants, one has excluded the other from occupancy, but a finding of fact to that effect by the trial court is final.—Mackey v. Mackey, 99 Kan. 433, 163 Pac. 465.

10. **Sale and setting aside.**—One who purchases at a partition sale of property of heirs of an intestate, takes subject to the right of creditors of the deceased, whose claims have been approved, in case of an insufficiency of personalty to pay the debts.—Rippe v. Welters, 96 Kan. 738, 153 Pac. 536. Where land can not be divided in kind, and the commissioners appointed to partition it, make an appraisement thereof and, without notifying the heirs, outside of the administrator, who was the husband of the deceased, make a sale of the land to such administrator, at from $5 to $10 per acre below its true value; and where the administrator, before the report of the commissioners is filed, negotiates a sale of the land, at its appraised value, to a sister of one of the commissioners, the sale will be set aside upon the ground of fraud in law.—In re Ketcham's Estate, Anderson v. Ketcham (S. D.), 171 N. W. 764, 766.

11. Decree of distribution.

(1) Construction.—A decree of distribution which disposes of "all of said property," after particularly describing property as the "residue of the estate," is held to meet the requirements of section 1666, Code of Civil Procedure of California, and has the effect of distributing all of the estate without limitation.—Miller v. Pitman (Cal.), 182 Pac. 50, 51.

(2) Consideration of advancements.—Advancements are recognized by statute and must be considered in the final distribution of the estate of the deceased person.—Wilson v. Channel, 102 Kan. 793, 175 Pac. 95. Advances made by an administrator to an heir on account of his distributive share can not be considered upon the hearing of an account, but are to be allowed only as a credit against the heir's distributive share upon final distribution.—In re Ross' Estate, 179 Cal. 358, 182 Pac. 303, 305.

REFERENCES.

Advancements.—See note 80 Am. Dec. 559-565.

(3) Objections to.—If distribution of an estate be made to the heirs of an heir, the latter having died before final decree and no proceedings in probate having been taken in relation to that particular death, a creditor of the deceased heir may object, but not a person who has taken a conveyance from such heir prematurely.—In re Blackinton's Estate, Woodward v. Utter, 29 Ida. 310, 158 Pac. 492.

(4) Attack on.—The law does not require personal notice to be given of the presentation and pendency of a petition for final distribution, and where a complaint attacking the decree of distribution fails to allege that the notice required by law was not given, it will be presumed that such notice was given.—Miller v. Pitman (Cal.), 182 Pac. 50, 51.

(5) Validity.—If a want of jurisdiction of proceedings for the final distribution of an estate affirmatively appears upon the face of the record of a probate court, its judgment must be held void upon collateral attack as well upon direct attack.—Teynor v. Heible, 74 Wash. 222, 133 Pac. 1, 46 L. R. A. (N. S.) 1033.

12. Equitable distribution.—A memorandum which is found among the papers of an intestate and which closes with the statement, "I have left no will, the court will distribute equitably," may be read as indicating in its earlier portions, what the deceased had in mind as an equitable distribution, considering what he had already done for one heir.—Sanford v. Sanford, 31 N. D. 190, 193, 153 N. W. 412.

CHAPTER IV.

AGENTS FOR ABSENT INTERESTED PARTIES. DISCHARGE OF EXECUTOR OR ADMINISTRATOR.

DISCHARGE OF EXECUTOR OR ADMINISTRATOR.

§ 776. Court may appoint agent to take possession for absentees.

When any estate is assigned or distributed, by a judgment or decree of the court, as provided in this chapter, to any person residing out of, and having no agent in, this state, and it is necessary that some person should be authorized to take possession and charge of the same for the benefit of such absent person, the court may appoint an agent for that purpose and authorize him to take charge of such estate, as well as to act for such absent person in the distribution; provided, that if such estate be in money when so assigned or distributed, the executor or administrator of such estate may deposit the share of each person, and in the name of said person, as far as known, as designated in said assignment or decree of distribution, with the county treasurer of the county in which said estate is being probated, who shall give a receipt for the same, and be liable upon his official bond therefor; and said receipt shall be deemed and received by the court, or judge thereof, as a voucher in favor of said executor or administrator, with the same force and effect as if executed by such assignee, legatee, or distributee; and said section as amended shall be applicable to any and all estates now pending in which a decree of final discharge has not been granted.—*Kerr's Cyc. Code Civ. Proc.,* § 1691.

ANALOGOUS AND IDENTICAL STATUTES.
The * indicates identity.

Arizona—Revised Statutes of 1913, paragraphs 1060, 1066.
Idaho—Compiled Statutes of 1919, section 7746.
Montana—Revised Codes of 1907, section 7690.
Nevada—Revised Laws of 1912, section 6090.
New Mexico—Statutes of 1915, section 1839.
North Dakota—Compiled Laws of 1913, section 8867.
Oklahoma—Revised Laws of 1910, section 6480.
South Dakota—Compiled Laws of 1913, section 5941.
Utah*—Compiled Laws of 1907, section 3970.
Washington—Laws of 1917, chapter 156, page 690, section 165.
Wyoming—Compiled Statutes of 1910, section 5721.

§ 777. Agent to give bond, and his compensation.

The agent must execute a bond to the state of California, to be approved by the court, or a judge thereof, conditioned that he shall faithfully manage and account for the estate. The court appointing such agent may allow a reasonable sum out of the profits of the estate for his services and expenses.—*Kerr's Cyc. Code Civ. Proc.*, § 1692.

ANALOGOUS AND IDENTICAL STATUTES.

The * indicates identity.

Idaho—Compiled Statutes of 1919, section 7747.
Montana*—Revised Codes of 1907, section 7691.
Nevada*—Revised Laws of 1912, section 6091.
North Dakota—Compiled Laws of 1913, section 8868.
Oklahoma—Revised Laws of 1910, section 6481.
South Dakota—Compiled Laws of 1913, section 5942.
Utah—Compiled Laws of 1907, section 3971.
Washington—Laws of 1917, chapter 156, page 691, section 166.
Wyoming*—Compiled Statutes of 1910, section 5722.

§ 778. Unclaimed estate, how disposed of.

When personal property remains in the hands of the agent unclaimed for a year, and it appears to the court that it is for the benefit of those interested, it shall be sold under the order of the court, and the proceeds after deducting the expenses of the sale, allowed by the court, must be paid into the county treasury. When the payment is made, the agent must take from the treasury duplicate receipts, one of which he must file in the office of the auditor, and the other in the court. Where any agent has money in his hands as such agent, and it appears to the court upon the settlement of his account as such agent that the balance remaining in his hands should be paid into the county treasury, the court may direct such payment and upon such agent filing the proper receipt showing such payment, the court shall enter an order discharging such agent and his sureties from all liability therefor.—*Kerr's Cyc. Code Civ. Proc.*, § 1693.

§ 779. Account by agent of absentee. Sale of property. The agent must render the court appointing him, annually, an account, showing:

1. The value and character of the property received by him, what portion thereof is still on hand, what sold, and for what.

2. The income derived therefrom.

3. The taxes and assessments imposed thereon, for what, and whether paid or unpaid.

4. Expenses incurred in the care, protection, and management thereof, and whether paid or unpaid. When filed the court may examine witnesses and take proofs in regard to the account; and if satisfied from such accounts and proofs that it will be for the benefit and advantage of the persons interested therein, the court may, by order, direct a sale to be made of the whole or such parts of the real or personal property as shall appear to be proper, and the purchase-money to be deposited in the state treasury.—*Kerr's Cyc. Code Civ. Proc.*, § 1694.

§ 780. Liability of agent on his bond.

The agent is liable on his bond for the care and preservation of the estate while in his hands, and for the payment of the proceeds of the sale as required in the preceding sections, and may be sued thereon by any person interested.—*Kerr's Cyc. Code Civ. Proc.,* § 1695.

ANALOGOUS AND IDENTICAL STATUTES.
The * indicates identity.
Arizona—Revised Statutes of 1913, paragraph 1069.
Idaho*—Compiled Statutes of 1919, section 7750.
Montana*—Revised Codes of 1907, section 7694.
Nevada*—Revised Laws of 1912, section 6093.
North Dakota*—Compiled Laws of 1913, section 8871.
Oklahoma*—Revised Laws of 1910, section 6484.
South Dakota*—Compiled Laws of 1913, section 5945.
Washington—Laws of 1917, chapter 156, page 691, section 168.
Wyoming—Compiled Statutes of 1910, section 5725.

§ 781. Certificate to claimant.

When any person appears and claims the money paid into the treasury, the court making the distribution must inquire into such claim, and being first satisfied of his right thereto, must grant him a certificate to that effect, under its seal; and upon the presentation of the certificate to him, the controller must draw his warrant on the treasurer for the amount.—*Kerr's Cyc. Code Civ. Proc.,* § 1696.

ANALOGOUS AND IDENTICAL STATUTES.
The * indicates ident.:y.
Arizona—Revised Statutes of 1913, paragraph 1070.
Idaho*—Compiled Statutes of 1919, section 7751.
Montana*—Revised Codes of 1907, section 7695.
Nevada—Revised Laws of 1912, section 6094.
North Dakota*—Compiled Laws of 1913, section 8872.
Oklahoma*—Revised Laws of 1910, section 6485.
South Dakota*—Compiled Laws of 1913, section 5946.
Utah—Compiled Laws of 1907, section 3974.
Wyoming—Compiled Statutes of 1910, section 5726.

§ 782. Final settlement, decree, and discharge.

When the estate has been fully administered, and it is shown by the executor or administrator, by the production of satisfactory vouchers, that he has paid all sums of money due from him, and delivered up, under the order of the court, all the property of the estate to the parties entitled, and performed all the acts lawfully required of him, the court must make a judgment or decree discharging him from all liability to be incurred thereafter.—*Kerr's Cyc. Code Civ. Proc.*, § 1697.

ANALOGOUS AND IDENTICAL STATUTES.
The * indicates identity.

Arizona*—Revised Statutes of 1913, paragraph 1071.
Colorado—Mills's Statutes of 1912, section 8030 (Rev. Stats. 1908, section 7241); as amended by Laws of 1913, chapter 81, page 274 (relating to settlement of estates of deceased persons).
Idaho*—Compiled Statutes of 1919, section 7753.
Kansas—General Statutes of 1915, section 4662.
Montana*—Revised Codes of 1907, section 7696.
Nevada*—Revised Laws of 1912, section 6095.
North Dakota—Compiled Laws of 1913, section 8704.
Oklahoma*—Revised Laws of 1910, section 6486.
South Dakota*—Compiled Laws of 1913, section 5947.
Utah*—Compiled Laws of 1907, section 3965.
Washington—Laws of 1917, chapter 156, page 689, section 163.
Wyoming*—Compiled Statutes of 1910, section 5702.

§ 783. Discovery of property.

The final settlement of an estate as in this chapter provided, shall not prevent a subsequent issue of letters testamentary or of administration, or of administration with the will annexed, if other property of the estate be discovered, or if it become necessary or proper for any cause that letters should be again issued.—*Kerr's Cyc. Code Civ. Proc.*, § 1698.

ANALOGOUS AND IDENTICAL STATUTES.
The * indicates identity.

Arizona*—Revised Statutes of 1913, paragraph 1072.
Idaho—Compiled Statutes of 1919, section 7754.
Montana*—Revised Codes of 1907, section 7697.
Nevada*—Revised Laws of 1912, section 6096.
North Dakota*—Compiled Laws of 1913, section 8873.
Oklahoma*—Revised Laws of 1910, section 6487.
South Dakota*—Compiled Laws of 1913, section 5948.
Washington—Laws of 1917, chapter 156, page 694, section 180.
Wyoming*—Compiled Statutes of 1910, section 5703.

§ 784. Form. Order appointing agent to take possession for non-resident distributee.

[Title of court.]

[Title of estate.]   { No. ——.1   Dept. No. ——.
                                       {   [Title of form.]

It appearing to the court from the records and papers on file in this case, and from testimony given before the court upon settlement of the final account of the administrator 2 of the said ——, deceased, that —— is an heir at law of the said deceased; that the said —— is a non-resident of this state; and that on the —— day of ——, 19—, a decree of distribution was duly given, made, and entered herein, by the terms of which the property hereinafter described was distributed to the said ——; and it further appearing that the said —— has no agent in this state to receive the said property; that said property is of the value of —— dollars ($——), and is in danger of destruction unless protected and preserved; and that it is necessary for an agent to be appointed to take possession and charge of said property for the benefit of the said ——, —

It is ordered, That —— be, and he is hereby, appointed an agent to take possession and charge of the property hereinafter described for the benefit of the said ——, and to act for him in respect to said distribution, upon the said agent's execution of a bond to the state of —— in the sum of —— dollars ($——), to be approved by this court, and conditioned that he will faithfully manage and account for such estate.

The following is a description of the property referred to herein: ——.3

Dated ——, 19—.   ——, Judge of the —— Court.

Explanatory notes.—1 Give file number. 2 Or, executor, etc., as the case may be. 3 Give description.

§ 785. Form. Bond of agent appointed for non-resident distributee.

[Title of court.]

[Title of estate.]   { No. ——.¹ Dept. No. ——.
                              {   [Title of form.]

Know all men by these presents: That we, —— as principal, and —— and —— as sureties, are held and firmly bound unto the state of —— in the sum of —— dollars ($——), lawful money of the United States of America, to be paid to the said state of ——, for which payment well and truly to be made we bind ourselves, our and each of our heirs, executors, and administrators, jointly and severally, firmly by these presents.

The condition of the above obligation is such, that whereas by an order of the ——² court of the county ³ of ——, state of ——, duly made and entered on the —— day of ——, 19—, the above-named principal, ——, was appointed an agent to receive and take charge of the distributive share of ——, one of the distributees of the estate of ——, deceased, and to faithfully manage and account for such estate, for the benefit of such absent distributee, —

Now, therefore, if the said principal shall well and faithfully perform the duties of his said trust and agency, then this obligation is to be void; otherwise to remain in full force and effect.

Dated, signed, and sealed with our seals this —— day of ——, 19—.   —— [Seal]
                                          —— [Seal]
                                          —— [Seal]

Explanatory notes.—¹ Give file number. ² Title of court. ³ Or, city and county. Justification of sureties. See form, § 723, ante.

§ 786. Form. Petition, by agent of non-resident distributee, for sale of unclaimed personal property.

[Title of court.]

[Title of estate.]　　　　　{ No.——.¹ Dept. No.——.
　　　　　　　　　　　　　　　{ 　　[Title of form.]

To the Honorable the ——² Court of the County ³ of ——, State of ——.

Your petitioner respectfully shows to this court:

That on the —— day of ——, 19—, he was, by an order of this court duly made and entered, appointed an agent to receive and take charge of the distributive share of ——, one of the heirs at law of ——, deceased;

That, in pursuance of said order, he qualified as such agent, is now the duly qualified and acting agent of the said ——, and has in his possession certain personal property so received, particularly described as follows, to wit: ——,⁴

That said personal property has remained in the hands of your petitioner unclaimed for a year; that it is not only unproductive, but is an object of constant expense, and is steadily deteriorating in value;⁵ and

That it is for the benefit of those interested in said personal property that it be sold.

Your petitioner therefore prays that this court order such property to be sold in such manner as it shall deem best for those interested therein.

——, Attorney for Petitioner.　　　　——, Petitioner.

Explanatory notes.—¹ Give file number. ² Title of court. ³ City and County. ⁴ Insert description. ⁵ Or other reasons why it should be sold.

§ 787. Form. Order of sale of personal property in possession of agent for non-resident distributee.

[Title of court.]

[Title of estate.]　　　　　{ No.——.¹ Dept. No.——.
　　　　　　　　　　　　　　　{ 　　[Title of form.]

Now comes ——, the petitioner herein, by Mr. ——, his attorney, and shows to the satisfaction of the court that his petition for an order of sale of the personal property remaining in his hands as agent for ——, a non-resident distributee of the estate of ——, deceased, was filed herein on the —— day of ——, 19—; that said property has remained in the hands of such agent for more than a year last past; that it has not been claimed; and that it is for the benefit of those interested in such personal property that it be sold.

It is therefore ordered, That said personal property, hereinafter described, be sold [2] by said agent, after such notice and in such manner as the law provides respecting the sale of personalty by administrators and executors.

The property to be sold as aforesaid is particularly described as follows, to wit: ——.

Dated ——, 19—.   ——, Judge of the —— Court.

Explanatory notes.—[1] Give file number. [2] At public auction or private sale, as directed.

§ 788. Form. County treasurer's receipt to agent for non-resident distributee.

[Title of court.]

[Title of estate.]   { No.——.[1] Dept. No.——.
                                                [Title of form.]

Received of ——, the duly appointed, qualified, and acting agent of ——, a non-resident distributee of the estate of ——, deceased, the sum of —— dollars ($——), being the proceeds, less expenses, of the sale of his distributive share of such estate heretofore ordered by the ——[2] court of the county [3] of ——, state of ——.

Dated ——, 19—.

——, Treasurer of the County [4] of ——.

Explanatory notes.—[1] Give file number. [2] Title of court. [3,4] Or, city and county.

§ 789. Form. Account of agent for non-resident distributee.

[Title of court.]

[Title of estate.] {No. ——.1 Dept. No. ——.
. [Title of form.]

Property Received by ——, Agent.

The real property, hereinafter described in Schedule A, attached hereto and made a part of this account, has been received by me, and is of the value of —— dollars ($——). A portion thereof, to wit, ——, has been sold for the sum of —— dollars ($——), and the remainder thereof is still on hand.

The personal property, hereinafter described in Schedule B, attached hereto and made a part of this account, has been received by me, and is of the value of —— dollars ($——). A portion thereof, to wit, ——, has been sold for the sum of —— dollars ($——), and the remainder thereof is still on hand.

The income derived from said real property amounts to the sum of —— dollars ($——); and the income derived from said personal property amounts to the sum of —— dollars ($——).

Taxes and assessments have been imposed upon said property as shown in Schedule C hereto annexed and made part hereof, all of which taxes and assessments have been paid.

The following expenses, hereinafter described in Schedule D, attached hereto and made a part of this account, have been incurred in the care, protection, and management of said property, and the same have been paid.

Recapitulation.

Amounts Chargeable to Agent.

Real property sold, value of................$——
Real property less part sold, value of........ ——
Personal property sold, value of............. ——
Personal property less part sold, value of.... ——

Income derived from real property......... ——
Income derived from personal property...... ——
    Total .... $——
       Amounts to be Credited to Agent.
Taxes and assessments paid...............$——
Expenses incurred and paid............... ——
    Total .... $——
Total amount chargeable to agent...........$——
Total amount to be credited to agent........ ——
    Remainder chargeable to agent.......... $——
           Schedule, A.

The following is a particular description of the real property which has come into my hands as agent of ——, a non-resident distributee of the above-entitled estate, to wit: ——.[2]

           Schedule B.

The following is a particular description of the personal property which has come into my hands as agent of ——, a non-resident distributee of the above-entitled estate, to wit: ——.[3]

           Schedule C.

The following is an itemized statement of the taxes and assessments which have been levied or imposed on the property of said distributee in my hands: ——.[4]

           Schedule D.

The following is an itemized statement of expenses incurred and paid by me in the care, protection, and management of the distributive share of ——, a non-resident distributee of the estate of ——, deceased, which has come into my hands as agent, to wit: ——.[5]

Explanatory notes.—[1] Give file number. [2,3] Insert description. [4,5] Give items and amount.

§ 790. Form. Verification of account.

State of ——,   }
  County [1] of ——, } ss.

——, being duly sworn, deposes and says: That he has

read the foregoing account, knows the contents thereof, and that the same is true of his own knowledge, except as to the matters therein stated on his information and belief, and that as to those matters, he believes it to be true.   ⸺

Subscribed and sworn to before me this ⸺ day of ⸺, 19⸺.   ⸺, Notary Public, etc.²

Explanatory notes.—1 Or, City and County. 2 Or other officer taking the oath.

§ 791.   Form.   Report of agent for non-resident distributee.

[Title of court.]

[Title of estate.]   {No. ⸺.¹   Dept. No. ⸺.
                            {   [Title of form.]

To the Honorable the ⸺² Court of the County ³ of ⸺, State of ⸺.

The undersigned, agent of ⸺, a non-resident distributee of the estate of ⸺, deceased, respectfully renders the foregoing, his first annual account for the said ⸺, and reports as follows:

That on the day of his appointment, to wit, on the ⸺ day of ⸺, 19⸺, he took charge of all the real estate and personal property described in the order appointing him;

That he has sold a portion of said real property, to wit, ⸺, for the sum of ⸺ dollars ($⸺); and that he has sold a portion of said personal property, to wit, ⸺, for the sum of ⸺ dollars ($⸺);

That a net income of ⸺ dollars ($⸺) has been derived from said real and personal property;

That he has paid state, county, and city taxes on said real and personal property to the amount of ⸺ dollars ($⸺);

That he has made expenditures on said property, as itemized in Schedules C and D, contained in the account hereinbefore stated;⁴

And that because of ⸺⁵ it will be for the benefit and

advantage of the person interested in such real and personal property that the same be ordered sold by this court, and the purchase-money be deposited in the county treasury.

Wherefore petitioner prays that a day be appointed for the hearing of said account, and that upon said hearing said account be allowed, approved, and settled, and that an order of this court be entered directing the sale of the whole or such parts of the said real and personal property as shall appear to the court proper, and that the purchase-money be deposited in the county treasury.

——, Agent for Non-Resident Distributee.

——, Attorney for Agent.

Explanatory notes.—1 Give file number. 2 Title of court. 3 Or, City and County. 4 See § 789, ante. 5 State reasons why sale should be made.

§ 792. Form. Order directing sale, by agent, of property of non-resident distributee.

[Title of court.]

[Title of estate.]

{ No.——.1 Dept. No.——.
{   [Title of form.]

Now comes ——, agent of ——, a non-resident distributee of the estate of ——, deceased, and shows to the court that on the —— day of ——, 19—, he filed, as provided by law, his annual account as such agent, together with a report of his proceedings concerning the property placed in his charge; and the court being satisfied from the examination of witnesses and proofs taken in regard to said account that it will be for the benefit and advantage of the persons interested that all of the property both real and personal in the hands of such agent be sold, —

It is ordered, That the said account be, and the same is hereby, allowed, confirmed, and approved; that the whole of the property hereinafter described, and now in the hands of ——, as such agent, be sold by him at public auction,2 the real property to be sold by him after such notice and in such manner as is provided by law for the sale of real property by executors and administrators, and the personal property to be sold by him after such notice and in such manner as is provided by law for the sale of personal property by executors and administrators; and that said ——, the agent aforesaid, report his proceedings under this order to this court.

The property to be sold under this order is particularly described as follows, to wit: ——.[3]

Dated ——, 19—.   ——, Judge of the —— Court.

Explanatory notes.—[1] Give file number. [2] Or otherwise, as directed. [3] Describe the property.

§ 793.   Form.   Order confirming sale of property by agent.

[Title of court.]

[Title of estate.]   { No. ——.[1]   Dept. No. ——.
                       {   [Title of form.]

——, agent of ——, a non-resident distributee of the estate of ——, deceased, having made to this court a return of his proceedings under the order of sale herein, and it being shown to the court that such sale was made in the manner directed by this court, and after such notice as is provided by law; and that, at such sale, —— became the purchaser of the property sold, to wit, ——, for the sum of —— dollars ($——), he being the highest and best bidder, and the said sum being the highest and best sum bid, —

It is ordered, adjudged, and decreed by this court, That said sale be, and the same is hereby, confirmed, approved, and declared valid;[2] and that the purchase-money be deposited in the state treasury.

Dated ——, 19—.   ——, Judge of the —— Court.

Explanatory notes.—[1] Give file number. [2] Where personal property is sold. If the sale is of real property, say, "that the said sale be, and the same is hereby, confirmed and approved; that said —— execute to said purchaser all proper and legal conveyances of all of said real estate; and that the purchase-money be deposited in the county treasury"; and the order should contain the same recitals required in an order confirming a sale by an executor or administrator.

§ 794.   Form.   Petition claiming money paid into treasury by agent.

[Title of court.]

[Title of estate.]   {No. ——.1   Dept. No. ——.
                      {   [Title of form.]

To the Honorable the ——² Court of the County³ of ——, State of ——.

Now comes ——, by his attorney, Mr. ——, and respectfully shows to this court that on the —— day of ——, 19—, this court, in the matter of said estate, made and entered its decree distributing to your petitioner certain property of the estate of ——, deceased, to wit, ——;⁴ but that petitioner was not, at the date of said decree, a resident of this state; that thereupon this court, as provided by law, appointed —— as agent to take charge of said property for petitioner; that, under the direction and order of this court, said ——, on the —— day of ——, 19—, made a sale of said property, and subsequently, on the —— day of ——, 19—, deposited the proceeds of such sale in the state⁵ treasury of this state;⁶ and that your petitioner is the identical person mentioned as the distributee in said decree, and in all proceedings herein subsequent thereto, and is entitled to the money so paid into the treasury of this state.⁷

Your petitioner therefore prays that this court grant him a certificate showing his right to said money.

——, Attorney for Petitioner.   ——, Petitioner.

Explanatory notes.—1 Give file number. 2 Title of court. 3 Or, City and County. 4 Give description of both real and personal property. 5 Or, county. 6, 7 Or, county, or city and county.   ·

§ 795.   Form.   Certificate entitling claimant to money paid into treasury by agent.

[Title of court.] ·

[Title of estate.]   {No. ——.1   Dept. No. ——.
                      {   [Title of form.]

It being shown to the court that a decree was made and entered herein on the —— day of ——, 19—, dis-

tributing to ——, a non-resident distributee of the estate
of ——, deceased, certain property of said estate, to wit,
——; that —— was appointed agent for the said —— to
take charge of said property; that, under the direction
and order of this court, the said agent made a sale of
said property, and deposited the proceeds of such sale
in the state [2] treasury; and it appearing from the petition of —— filed herein that petitioner now claims the
money so paid into the state [3] treasury,—the court proceeds to make inquiry into said claim, and finds that said
—— is the same person mentioned herein by said name;
that the said —— is a distributee of said estate; that
the money representing his share of such estate has, after
due and legal proceedings, been deposited in the state.[4]
treasury; and that the said —— is entitled to such money.

It is therefore certified and ordered by this court, under
its seal, That said —— has a right to said money,
amounting to the sum of —— dollars ($——), and is
entitled to withdraw the same, and the controller of
state [5] is hereby authorized and directed to draw his warrant therefor in favor of the said ——.

Dated ——, 19—.   ——, Judge of the —— Court.
[Seal]   Attest: ——, Clerk of the —— Court.
                    By ——, Deputy Clerk.

Explanatory notes.—1 Give file number. 2-4 Or, county. 5 Or, auditor,
county clerk, or other officer whose duty it is to draw such warrant.

§ 796. Form. Receipt on distribution.

[Title of court.]

[Title of estate.]   { No. ——.[1] Dept. No. ——.
                          {   [Title of form.]

Received of ——, administrator [2] of the estate of ——,
deceased, the sum of —— dollars ($——),[3] being in full
of my distributive share of said estate.

Dated ——, 19—.

——, Heir at law [4] of ——, Deceased.

Explanatory notes.—1 Give file number. 2 Or, executor, etc., according to the fact. 3 Insert description here of any other property re-

ceived; or, all property distributed to me under decree of distribution in the above-entitled estate, made on the —— day of ——, 19—. 4 Or, devisee or legatee, according to the fact.

§ 797. Form. Petition for final discharge.

[Title of court.]

[Title of estate.] ⎰ No. ——.1 Dept. No. ——.
⎱ [Title of form.]

To the Honorable the ——2 Court of the County 3 of ——, State of ——.

Your petitioner, ——, administrator 4 of the estate of ——, deceased, respectfully shows to this court: That said estate has been fully administered; that he has paid all sums of money due from him, and has delivered up, under the order of this court, all property of the said estate to the parties entitled thereto; that he has performed all acts lawfully required of him; and that he has filed in this court the vouchers required by law.

Wherefore he prays that he be discharged as such administrator,5 and that he be discharged from all liability to be hereafter incurred.

——, Attorney for Petitioner. ——, Petitioner.

Explanatory notes.—1 Give file number. 2 Title of court. 3 Or, City and County. 4, 5 Or, executor, etc., according to the fact.

§ 798. Form. Decree of final discharge.

[Title of court.]

[Title of estate.] ⎰ No. ——.1 Dept. No. ——.
⎱ [Title of form.]

——, administrator 2 of the estate of ——, deceased, having this day shown to this court, by the production of satisfactory vouchers, that he has paid all sums of money due from him, and has delivered up, under the order of this court, all the property of said estate to the parties entitled thereto; that he has performed all the acts lawfully required of him; and that no further acts remain to be performed by him as such administrator,3 —

It is ordered, adjudged, and decreed, That said ——,

administrator [4] of the estate of said ——, deceased, be,
and he is hereby, discharged from all liability to be hereafter incurred as such administrator,[5] and his sureties
are likewise released from further liability.

Dated ——, 19—.   ——, Judge of the —— Court.

Explanatory notes.—1 Give file number. 2-5 Or, executor.

DISCHARGE OF EXECUTOR OR ADMINISTRATOR.

1. Representative is entitled to
when.
2. Prerequisites to discharge.
3. Jurisdiction of court until discharge.
4. What amounts to discharge.
5. Validity of order.

6. Unauthorized procedure on distribution.
7. Effect of discharge. Conclusiveness.
8. Power of court to set aside.
9. After-discovered property.
10. Appeal.

1. Representative is entitled to when.—When it appears. upon the
settlement of the accounts of the representative, at the end of the
year, that the entire property of the estate is exhausted by payment
or distribution made as required by the statute, such account shall be
considered as a final account, and the executor or administrator shall
be entitled to his discharge on producing and filing the necessary
vouchers and proofs.—Estate of Isaacs, 30 Cal. 105, 111. The code does
not provide that the discharge can only be made "after" the decree of
distribution, but after the estate "has been fully administered"; and
there is no reason why the decree of distribution and discharge should
not take effect contemporaneously.—Dean v. Superior Court, 63 Cal.
473, 476, 477. An executor or administrator is not entitled to his discharge until after the estate has been fully administered. He is not
entitled to it immediately after the decree of distribution, unless the
estate has been settled. Admitting that there must be an order of distribution, however, to support the judgment of discharge, the two may
take effect contemporaneously.—Dean v. Superior Court, 63 Cal. 473,
476. Nor is the mere allowance of the final account the legal equivalent
of a decree of discharge. Until the entry of a decree discharging the
executor or administrator from liability, he is not discharged from his
trust.—McCrea v. Haraszthy, 51 Cal. 146, 151. The estate is deemed
to be pending until the entry of the decree discharging the administrator or executor from all liability, after the production by him of satisfactory vouchers that he has performed all the acts lawfully required
of him in the administration of the estate.—Dohs v. Dohs, 60 Cal. 255,
260. Property passes, on the death of its owner, to the latter's heirs
or devisees, they taking by inheritance or the terms of the will; their
title does not originate in the decree of distribution, although such, on
becoming final, constitutes a muniment of title, which will prevail
over contrary provisions of the will or of the statutes of descent.—
Estate of Yorba, 176 Cal. 166, 167 Pac. 854. An executor or ad-

ministrator, on having made distribution agreeably to the decree of distribution, is not required to await discharge until after the expiration of the time within which the decree may be appealed from.—Nason v. Superior Court (Cal. App.), 179 Pac. 454. An administrator is not entitled to a final discharge and to have his sureties exonerated from liability on his bond where he has paid claims of a lower class, leaving other legally established claims of a preferred class unpaid, there being insufficient moneys of the estate to pay in full all valid claims against it.—In re Estate of Keppelman, International Harvester Co. v. Algie, 101 Kan. 654, 658, 168 Pac. 876.

2. Prerequisites to discharge.—If property has been distributed by the decree of a probate court, and the executor or administrator has possession thereof, his duty is not ended until he has delivered the property in accordance with the decree, and not till then can he have his discharge.—Wheeler v. Bolton, 54 Cal. 302, 305. If the representative pays the shares of the distributees to the wrong person, his liability is not affected by the judgment or decree discharging him from all liability to be incurred thereafter.—Bryant v. McIntosh, 3 Cal. App. 95, 84 Pac. 440, 441. It is only after the payment and delivery of all the property of the estate to those entitled, and the production of satisfactory proof of the fact, that the representative is entitled to his final discharge.—Estate of Clary, 112 Cal. 292, 294, 44 Pac. 569. When, after the debts have been paid, the balance still remaining has been ordered distributed by the court, the executor or administrator is not entitled to a discharge until he has further accounted to the court for this balance by showing that he has paid or delivered the property to the parties entitled thereto.—McAdoo v. Sayre, 145 Cal. 344, 349, 78 Pac. 874. If the representative has been directed to deposit certain money in bank for the use and benefit of an heir, he is not entitled to be released, and his bondsmen discharged, until he has fully complied with the decree of the court.—Ehrngren v. Gronlund, 19 Utah 411, 57 Pac. 268; and, if he has taken deeds to himself as executor or administrator, he must, as a condition precedent to his discharge and the liberation of his bondsmen, execute to the legatees, as tenants in common, quitclaim deeds to the property.—In re Roach's Estate, 50 Or. 179, 92 Pac. 118, 127.

3. Jurisdiction of court until discharge.—Jurisdiction of the probate court over an executor or administrator does not cease until his final discharge.—Estate of Clary, 112 Cal. 292, 294, 44 Pac. 569. Until the entry of a judgment or decree discharging the representative, the trust still continues, in contemplation of law, and the representative remains clothed with the duty and authority of his office.—Dean v. Superior Court, 63 Cal. 473, 475; Dohs v. Dohs, 60 Cal. 255, 260. Until final discharge, the probate court retains jurisdiction, not alone of the representative, but of the property of the estate in his hands, and may compel the proper disposition of the latter, in accordance with its decree, by punishing the delinquent trustee, as for contempt.—Estate of Clary,

112 Cal. 292, 294, 44 Pac. 569; Wheeler v. Bolton, 54 Cal. 302; Ex parte Smith, 53 Cal. 204. The probate court does not lose its jurisdiction upon the entry of the decree of distribution.—Estate of Clary, 112 Cal. 292, 294, 44 Pac. 569. A decree of distribution is not a mere order for the payment of money, because the representative can not get his final discharge without showing that he has paid to the heirs all the money in his hands. The court discharges him from his trust upon proof that it has been fully performed, and payment to the heirs happens to be the last duty in the order of time to be performed.—Estate of Kennedy, 129 Cal. 384, 387, 62 Pac. 64.

4. What amounts to discharge.—An executor or administrator may obtain an order or decree that he has fully accounted for, and paid over to the proper parties the entire residue of the estate, after payment of debts and expenses. Such a decree is called a discharge, and the effect is to exonerate him and his sureties on his bond.—Cook v. Ceas, 143 Cal. 221, 228, 77 Pac. 65; but the allowance of a final account is not a discharge of the representative from his trust. Until the entry of a decree discharging him from liability, he is not discharged from his trust.—McCrea v. Haraszthy, 51 Cal. 146, 151.

5. Validity of order.—A decree discharging an executor or administrator is not void on its face, unless it affirmatively appears therefrom that it was shown to the court that the representative had not complied with the prerequisites to the judgment; but, if it does appear from the decree that it was not shown to the probate court "by satisfactory vouchers" that the executor "had paid all sums due from him," or that it was not shown, to the satisfaction of the court, that he had delivered up all the property of the estate to the persons entitled, etc., the decree, in so far as it attempts to "discharge" the representative, would be void, because in excess of the jurisdiction of the court.—Dean v. Superior Court, 63 Cal. 473, 475, 476. After settling the account and apportioning the money in the hands of the representative of a decedent, it is error for the court to direct that, "upon the payment into court and to the clerk thereof" of a designated sum by the representative, "the last-mentioned sum is to be paid out and distributed as hereinbefore directed"; and that the "said administrators shall thereupon be entitled to their discharge." The representative, so long as he remains in office, is entitled to retain the assets of the estate in his possession until disposed of to the parties entitled thereto under the direction of the court.—Estate of Sarment, 123 Cal. 331, 55 Pac. 1015, 1017.

6. Unauthorized procedure on distribution.—An application for final distribution of all the property of a decedent's estate, without bond or security for the debts, can not be entertained by the court where the real proposition of the petitioner is that all the property be turned over to the distributees, subject to the debts, legacies, and expenses, that the executors be discharged, and that said distributees shall undertake to

complete the process of the administration of the estate by paying the
said debts, legacies, and expenses. The court has no power, upon
petition of the distributees, and over the objection of the creditors, or
without their consent, to arrest the course of administration, charge
the assets with the lien for the unpaid debts, legacies, and expenses,
discharge the administrator from further duties respecting the estate,
and deliver the property of the estate to the heirs, residuary legatees,
or devisees, burdened only with the sums due, to be paid at the will of
the distributees, or when they are compelled to do so by a suit to
enforce the lien.—Estate of Washburn, 148 Cal. 64, 66, 82 Pac. 671.

7. Effect of discharge. Conclusiveness.—The discharge of the representative from the estate he represents separates him from its business
as completely as if he were dead.—Willis v. Farley, 24 Cal. 490, 502.
A decree of the probate court settling an executor's or administrator's
final account, and discharging him from his trust, after due, legal
notice, and in the absence of fraud, is conclusive upon all matters or
items which come directly before the court, until reversed. It will be
presumed that such decree was founded upon proper evidence, and that
every prerequisite to a valid discharge was complied with. The decree
can not be impeached in any collateral proceeding. It is conclusive,
however, only as to matters embraced in the account. It is no bar to
the claims of the creditors or heirs, that did not, in any manner, form
the subject of it.—Hartsel v. People, 21 Colo. 296, 40 Pac. 567, 568,
quoting from Black on Judgments, § 644; and see Reynolds v. Brumagim, 54 Cal. 254, 257; Grady v. Porter, 53 Cal. 680, 685.

8. Power of court to set aside.—A probate court has jurisdiction to
set aside its order or decree discharging an administrator from his
office, upon the ground that such decree had been inadvertently made
and entered.—Wiggin v. Superior Court, 68 Cal. 398, 9 Pac. 646, 648;
Estate of Noah, 88 Cal. 468, 472, 26 Pac. 361. In the state of Washington, a conditional order discharging an executor or administrator is
not effective until the order has been made absolute. The court still
has jurisdiction of the proceeding, and may set aside the conditional
order upon the motion of one who claims that full distribution has not
been made.—State v. Superior Court, 13 Wash. 25, 42 Pac. 630, 631.
After the expiration of the time limited by the statute in which one
may petition to be relieved from a judgment taken against him through
his "mistake, inadvertence, surprise, or excusable neglect," a decree
settling the final account of the representative of a decedent, and discharging him from his trust, if regular upon its face, can not be set
aside by the probate court on the ground that it had been inadvertently
and prematurely entered, or on the ground of fraud. The remedy in
such cases is exclusively in equity.—Dean v. Superior Court, 63 Cal. 473,
477; Estate of Cahalan, 70 Cal. 604, 607, 12 Pac. 427. A writ of prohibition is not the proper remedy to correct an inadvertent order or decree
discharging an executor or administrator from his office.—Wiggin v.
Superior Court, 68 Cal. 398, 9 Pac. 646, 648.

9. After discovered property.—After final settlement of the estate of an intestate the court is not bound to issue further letters unless there still remains property of the estate not finally disposed of. This rule is implied by section 1698, California Code of Civil Procedure.— O'Brien v. Nelson, 164 Cal. 573, 129 Pac. 985.

10. Appeal.—A decree discharging an administrator having been irregularly and improvidently made, that fact takes the case out of the general rule that there is no appeal from a decree discharging an administrator.—Mason v. Superior Court (Cal. App.), 179 Pac. 454.

CHAPTER V.

ACCOUNTS OF TRUSTEES. DISTRIBUTION.

TRUSTS, TRUSTS UNDER WILLS, TESTAMENTARY TRUSTEES, AND
DISTRIBUTION TO TRUSTEES.

I. Trusts.

II. Trusts under wills, testamentary trustees, and distribution to trustees.

Probate Law—121

§ 799. Superior court not to lose jurisdiction by final distribution.

Where any trust has been created by or under any will to continue after distribution, the superior court shall not lose jurisdiction of the estate by final distribution, but shall retain jurisdiction thereof for the purpose of the settlement of accounts under the trusts. And any trustee created by any will, or appointed to execute any trust created by any will, may, from time to time, pending the execution of his trust, or may, at the termination thereof, render and pray for the settlement of his accounts as such trustee, before the superior court in which the will was probated, and in the manner provided for the settlement of the accounts of executors and administrators. The trustee, or, in case of his death, his legal representatives, shall, for that purpose, present to the court his verified petition, setting forth his accounts in detail, with a report showing condition of trust estate, together with a verified statement of said trustee, giving the names and post-office addresses, if known, of the cestui que trust, and upon the filing thereof, the clerk shall fix a day for the hearing and give notice thereof of not less than ten days, by causing notices to be posted in at least three public places in the county, setting forth the name of the trust estate, the trustee, and the day appointed for the settlement of the account. The court, or a judge thereof, may order such further notice to be given as may be proper. Such trustee may, in the discretion of the court, upon application of any beneficiary of the trust, or the guardian of such beneficiary, be ordered to appear and render his account, after being cited by service of citation, as provided for the service of summons in civil cases, and such application shall not be denied where no account has been rendered to the court within six months prior to such application. Upon the filing of the account so ordered, the same proceedings for the hearing and settlement thereof shall be had as hereinabove provided.—*Kerr's Cyc. Code Civ. Proc.,* § 1699.

ANALOGOUS AND IDENTICAL STATUTES.
No identical statute found.
Arizona—Revised Statutes of 1913, paragraph 1055.
Idaho—Compiled Statutes of 1919, section 7721.
Montana—Revised Codes of 1907, section 7698.
Utah—Compiled Laws of 1907, section 3977.

§ 800. Compensation of trustees.
On all such accountings the court shall allow the trustee or trustees the proper expenses and such compensation for services as the court may adjudge to be just and reasonable, and shall apportion such compensation among the trustees according to the services rendered by them respectively, and may in its discretion fix a yearly com-

pensation for the trustee or trustees to continue as long as the court may judge proper.—*Kerr's Cyc. Code Civ. Proc.,* § 1700.

ANALOGOUS AND IDENTICAL STATUTES.

The * indicates identity.

Arizona*—Revised Statutes of 1913, paragraph 1056.
Idaho—Compiled Statutes of 1919, section 7722.
Montana*—Revised Codes of 1907, section 7699.
Utah—Compiled Laws of 1907, section 3978.

§ 801. Appeal from decree settling account of trustee.

From a decree settling such account appeal may be taken in the manner provided for an appeal from a decree settling the account of an executor or administrator. The decree of the superior court, if affirmed on appeal or becoming final without appeal, shall be conclusive.— *Kerr's Cyc. Code Civ. Proc.,* § 1701.

ANALOGOUS AND IDENTICAL STATUTES.

The * indicates identity.

Arizona*—Revised Statutes of 1913, paragraph 1075.
Idaho*—Compiled Statutes of 1919, section 7723.
Montana*—Revised Codes of 1907, section 7700.

§ 802. Trustee under will may decline. Resignation of executor. Appointment by court.

Any person named or designated as a trustee in any will which has been or shall hereafter be admitted to probate in this state may, at any time before final distribution, decline to act as such trustee, and an order of court shall thereupon be made accepting such resignation;

EXECUTOR, RESIGNATION OF, TO BE IN WRITING.—But the declination of any such person who has qualified as executor shall not be accepted by the court, unless the same shall be in writing and filed in the matter of the estate in the court in which the administration is pending, and such notice shall be given thereof as is required upon a petition praying for letters of administration.

APPOINTMENT OF TRUSTEE OR EXECUTOR BY COURT.—The court in which the administration is pending shall have power at any time before final distribution to appoint some fit and proper person to fill any vacancy in the office of trustee under the will, whether resulting from such declination, removal, or otherwise; provided, it shall be required by law or necessary to carry out the trust created by the will, that such vacancy shall be filled; and every person so appointed shall, before acting as trustee, give a bond such as is required by section one thousand three hundred and eighty-eight of this code, of a person to whom letters of administration are directed to issue.

SAME. UPON WRITTEN APPLICATION OF PERSON INTERESTED. —Such appointment may be made by the probate judge upon the written application of any person interested in the trust filed in the probate proceedings, and shall only be made after notice to all parties interested in the trust, given in the same manner as notice is required to be given of the hearing upon the petition for the probate of a will. In each of the preceding cases the court may order such further notice as shall seem necessary. In accepting a declination under the provisions of this section, the court may make and enforce any order which may be necessary for the preservation of the estate. This section shall be applicable to any and all estates now pending in which a final distribution and discharge has not been granted.— *Kerr's Cyc. Code Civ. Proc.*, § 1702.

ANALOGOUS AND IDENTICAL STATUTES.

The * indicates identity.

Arizona*—Revised Statutes of 1913, paragraph 1058.

Kansas—General Statutes of 1915, section 11820.

§ 803. Form. Petition for appointment of trustee under will.

[Title of court.]

[Title of estate.]   { No. ——.1   Dept. No. ——.
                       {   [Title of form.]

To the Honorable the ——² Court of the County ³ of ——.

The petition of —— respectfully shows:

That he is interested in the trust created by the last

will of said ——, deceased, which will was duly admitted to probate herein on the —— day of ——, 19—, and petitioner is a beneficiary named in said trust;[4]

That ——, the trustee named in said will to execute said trust died[5] on or about the —— day of ——, 19—, and there is now a vacancy in the office of trustee under said will;

That it is necessary,[6] in order to carry out the trust created by said will, that said vacancy be filled, and a trustee be appointed in place of said ——, deceased,[7] as above stated;

That —— is a fit and proper person to fill the office of trustee under said will and is willing to accept the position and perform the duties of such trustee.

Wherefore petitioner prays that, after due notice given, a hearing be had hereon, and an order be made appointing said —— trustee to carry out the provisions of the above-named trust, and for such other or further order as may be meet.

Dated ——, 19—.   .   ——, Petitioner.

——, Attorney for Petitioner.

Explanatory notes.—1 Give file number. 2 Title of court. 3 Or, City and County. 4 Or show the interest of the petitioner. 5 Or, resigned as trustee, or removed from the state. 6 Or, will be required by law. 7 Or, resigned, or removed.

§ 804. Form. Order appointing trustee.
[Title of court.]

[Title of estate.]   { No. ——.1 Dept. No. ——,
                                      {   [Title of form.]

Now comes ——, a person interested in the trust created by the last will of said deceased, and shows to the court that on the —— day of ——, 19—, he filed his application for the appointment of ——[2] as trustee herein; that thereupon the clerk appointed the —— day of ——, 19—, as the day for hearing said application; and that due notice of said hearing has been given to all parties interested in said trust, as required by law and by the order of the court;[2] and the court being satisfied that the law requires, and that in order to carry out said trust, it is necessary that a trustee be appointed,—

It is therefore ordered by the court, That —— be appointed as trustee under the will of said deceased, to fill the vacancy in said trusteeship caused by the death [4] of ——, the person named as such trustee in said will;[5] that before acting as trustee he shall give a bond in the sum of —— dollars ($——), in form as required by law; and that thereupon he shall have power as such trustee to.[6]

Dated ——, 19—.   ——, Judge of the —— Court.

Explanatory notes.—1 Give file number. 2 Name the person. 3 If the matter has been continued, say, "and said hearing having been regularly postponed to this time." 4 Or, removal from the state of ——; or, resignation. 5 Or, by the failure of said testator in said will to appoint any person as trustee to carry out said trust. 6 Designate the powers as stated in the will or decree of distribution.

§ 805. Form. Order accepting resignation of testamentary trustee.

[Title of court.]

[Title of estate.]   { No. ——.1   Dept. No. ——.
                            {   [Title of form.]

The declination, in writing, of ——, who was named in the will of said deceased as trustee of certain property therein disposed of, having been filed herein on the —— day of ——, 19—, and the clerk having thereupon fixed the —— day of ——, 19—, as the time for hearing said resignation, and having given notice of said hearing as required by law,[2] the court now accepts said resignation.

It is therefore ordered by the court, That the resignation of —— as trustee of certain property under the will of said deceased be accepted.

Dated ——, 19—.   ——, Judge of the —— Court.

Explanatory notes.—1 Give file number. 2 And the hearing having been regularly postponed to this date.

§ 806. Jurisdiction.

The provisions of the next preceding section shall apply in all cases where a final decree of distribution has not been made; but the jurisdiction given by said section shall not exclude, in cases to which it applies, the jurisdiction now possessed by the courts of this state.—*Kerr's Cyc. Code Civ. Proc., § 1703.*

ANALOGOUS AND IDENTICAL STATUTES.
No identical statute found.
Arizona—Revised Statutes of 1913, paragraph 1059.

§ 807. Distribution of estate. Deposit with county treasurer when.

When any estate is distributed by the judgment or decree of the court or a judge thereof, as provided in this chapter, to a distributee who can not be found and his or her place of residence is unknown, or to a minor or incompetent person, who has no lawful gnardian to receive the same, or person authorized to receipt therefor, the portion of said estate consisting of money shall be paid to and deposited with the county treasurer of the county in which the estate is being probated, who shall give a receipt for the same, and shall be liable on his official bond therefor; and said receipt shall be deemed and received by the court or judge thereof as a voucher in favor of said executor or administrator, with the same force and effect as if executed by the distributee thereof. And this section shall be applicable to any and all estates now pending in which a final decree of discharge has not been granted. Said moneys so paid into the county treasury, shall be paid out upon petition to, and the order of the superior court or judge thereof to the person entitled to receive the same.—*Kerr's Cyc. Code Civ. Proc., § 1703½.*

ANALOGOUS AND IDENTICAL STATUTES.
The * indicates identity.
Alaska—Compiled Laws of 1913, section 1712; as amended by Laws of 1917, chapter 24, page 46.

Arizona*—Revised Statutes of 1913, paragraph 1060.
Kansas—General Statutes of 1915, sections 4663 and 9243; as amended
by Laws of 1917, chapter 187, page 237.

TRUSTS, TRUSTS UNDER WILLS, TESTAMENTARY TRUSTEES, AND
DISTRIBUTION TO TRUSTEES.

I. Trusts.

1. Creation of trusts.
  (1) In general.
  (2) Express parol trust.
  (3) Trust, not a mortgage.
  (4) Joint bank account.
2. Validity.
  (1) In general.
  (2) Statute of frauds.
3. Distinction as to legal title.
  Powers and trusts.
4. Resulting trusts.
  (1) In general.
  (2) Burden of proof.
5. Constructive trusts.
6. Involuntary trusts.
7. Deeds of trust.
  (1) In general.
  (2) Legal title.

  (3) Transfer of fee.
  (4) Setting aside.
8. Power of appointment.
9. Suit to have trust declared.
10. Partition. Res judicata.
11. Statute of limitations.
12. Laches.
13. Construction of instrument.
14. Dealing with trust property.
15. Compensation of trustee.
16. Powers of trustee.
17. Liability of trustee.
18. Removal of trustee and substitution.
19. Termination of trust.
20. Enforcement of trust.
21. Appeal.

II. Trusts under wills, testamentary trustees, and distribution to trustees.

1. Trusts under wills.
  (1) In general.
  (2) Creation of trusts. In general.
  (3) Same. As to income.
  (4) Same. As to spendthrifts.
  (5) Same. Because of fraud.
  (6) Same. Burden of proof.
  (7) Same. Number of trustees.
  (8) Construction of trusts. In general.
  (9) Same. In personal property.
  (10) Same. Joint will.
  (11) Judgment construing trust.
  (12) Law of situs governs.
  (13) Validity of trusts.
  (14) Void trusts.
2. Probate jurisdiction of trusts.
  (1) To determine whether valid trust has been created.
  (2) Retention of, for purpose of settling accounts.
  (3) Exclusiveness of jurisdiction.
  (4) To determine what questions.
  (5) Over trustees, to prevent mismanagement.

3. Executor and testamentary trustee.
  (1) Object of law.
  (2) Testamentary trustees. In general.
  (3) Executors who are trustees under will. Distinct and separate capacities.
  (4) Duty, power, and liability of testamentary trustee. In general.
  (5) Same. Investments.
  (6) Same. Distribution of bequeathed property.
  (7) Same. Power under non-intervention will.
  (8) Same. Authority as to lease.
  (9) Same. Release of surety company.
  (10) Duties of trustee can net be assumed until when.
  (11) Duty of testamentary trustee before distribution.
  (12) Discharge of executor acting as trustee.
  (13) Trust with power to sell under will.
  (14) Testamentary guardians.
4. Jurisdiction in equity.

I. TRUSTS.

1. Creation of trust.

(1) **In general.**—A trust is created in judicial intendment whenever the legal and equitable interests in property are separated.—Keeney v. Bank of Italy, 33 Cal. App. 515, 165 Pac. 735. While it is competent by a trust deed to create a trust which shall take effect after the death of the grantor, nevertheless, there must be some interest or estate which passes at the time of the execution of the deed.—Niccolls v. Niccolls, 168 Cal. 444, 143 Pac. 712. A declaration of trust contained in a written instrument is presumed to express the intention of the person making it, and the presumption is to be overcome only by strong, clear and convincing proof to the contrary.—Welsh, Driscoll & Buck v. Buck, 48 Utah 653, 161 Pac. 455. On grounds of public policy, and because of the right a donor has to attach what conditions he pleases to his gift, so long as he takes away from creditors of the donee nothing that they have the right to look to for payment, one can not, by any disposition of his own property, put the same or the income thereof beyond the reach of his creditors, so long as he himself retains the right to receive and use it.—McColgan v. Magee, 172 Cal. 182, Ann. Cas. 1917D, 1050, 155 Pac. 995.

(2) **Express parol trust.**—If a person, who is indebted to another, indorses, while on his death bed, a number of post-office department warrants and money orders to his creditor, causes them to be inclosed in an envelope, sealed, and addressed to the creditor, and delivered to a third person, with instructions to send them to the addressee in case he dies, the transaction is not a gift inter vivos, and is not a donatio causa mortis, but rather the creation of an express parol trust.—O'Brien v. Bank of Douglas, 17 Ariz. 203, 205, 149 Pac. 747.

(3) **Trust, not a mortgage.**—If a husband convey community property to his creditor with the oral understanding that the latter shall sell the same and out of the proceeds pay himself and others, to whom the grantor is intended, and divide the balance between the grantor and

his wife, the transaction creates a trust arising by operation of law and not a mortgage.—Bier v. Leisle, 172 Cal. 432, 156 Pac. 870.

(4) Joint bank account.—If a bank depositor writes to the cashier of the bank: "Will you please add my sister's name (giving it), to my bank account, which will make it more convenient to me," and the cashier then enters the account on the pass book as subject to the check of either, or to the survivor of them, and the depositor seeing this expresses her approval, such sister is entitled to the deposit on the death of the depositor.—See McCarthy v. Holland, 30 Cal. App. 495, 158 Pac. 1045; Williams v. Savings Bank, 33 Cal. App.. 655, 166 Pac. 366; Williams v. Savings Bank, 33 Cal. App. 659, 166 Pac. 368.

'   REFERENCES.

Language necessary to create a trust.—34 Am. St. Rep. 195. Trust in favor of wards.—See note on Guardian and Ward, ante, following § 160, subd. 6. Investments by guardian.

2. Validity.

(1) In general.—In the creation of a trust, the legal title may remain in the trustor or may be transferred to a trustee, but to constitute a valid trust, the beneficial or equitable estate must be irrevocably vested in the cestui que trust by the instrument or declaration creating the trust.—O'Gorman v. Jolley, 34 S. D. 26, 37, 147 N. W. 78. A trust, whereby the trustee is required to pay specified sums of money to Roman Catholic churches for the celebration of masses in line with the pious intention of the author of the trust, is valid.—Rutherford v. Ott, 37 Cal. App. 47, 173 Pac. 490. An express trust will be held void if not sufficiently certain in its terms, and, a fortiori, a trust created by parol, uncertain in its terms, as proved, will be held void.—Souza v. First Nat. Bank, 36 Cal. App. 384, 172 Pac. 175.

(2) Statute of frauds.—A trust agreement concerning land must be in writing.—Stewart v. King, 85 Or. 14, 166 Pac. 55. In the state of Oregon, trusts arising by operation of law are excepted from the statute of frauds.—Martin v. Thomas, 74 Or. 206, 219, 144 Pac. 684. Though the statute requires the creation of a trust in relation to real property to be in writing, yet, if an oral trust is created by the promise of sons at the sickbed of their father to convey to their mother property of the father, that would descend to them after their father's death, the subsequent execution of a conveyance takes the transaction out of such statute.—Arnston v. First Nat. Bank (N. D.), 167 N. W. 760.

3. Distinction as to legal title. Powers and trusts.—In every true trust, the legal title is vested in the trustee; but powers in trust differ from trusts in this, that in the case of such powers the legal title is vested, not in the trustee, but in a third person; the donee of the power in trust can, however, convey the title and dispose of the property to or for the beneficiaries; the donee of a power in trust can

execute the power without the interposition of any court.—Crystal Pier Co. v. Sneider (Cal. App.), 180 Pac. 948.

4. Resulting trusts.

(1) **In general.**—If real property has been conveyed without consideration, and the circumstances unequivocally rebut the presumption of a gift, equity will charge the grantee with a resulting trust in favor of the grantor.—Toney v. Toney, 84 Or. 310, 165 Pac. 221. A letter written by a holder of real estate, in which the latter is declared to have been bought with the money of another person, is sufficient basis for an adjudication that such person is the beneficiary of a resulting trust.—Tuckerman v. Berry (Colo.), 164 Pac. 721. Where a niece collected rents from property belonging to her aunt and deposited the same in a joint account standing in both their names, a resulting trust might arise in favor of the aunt.—Kelly v. Woolsey, 177 Cal. 325, 170 Pac. 837, 843. A father who, being guardian of the estate of his children, uses their money to pay off a mortgage on the farm which is the family homestead thereby creates a resulting trust in favor of the children.—Hicks v. Sage (Kan.), 180 Pac. 780. Facts which, were the parties to the transaction other than husband and wife, would attach to one the character of trustee for the benefit of the other under a resulting trust, have not that effect necessarily where the husband furnishes the money and the property is bought in the name of the wife; in such a case, a gift to the wife is presumed, though the presumption is rebuttable.—Anderson v. Cercone (Utah), 180 Pac. 586.

(2) **Burden of proof.**—If a man buys property in his wife's name, and there are children of the wife by a former husband, he has the burden of proving by satisfactory evidence that he intended her to be his trustee as to such property, and did not intend to provide for her support and comfort.—Bucknell v. Johnson, 39 S. D. 212, 163 N. W. 683. To establish a resulting trust, the burden is upon the one who asserts the trust, and the evidence must be clear, cogent, and convincing.—Brucker v. DeHart, 106 Wash. 386, 180 Pac. 397, 398. The burden which rests, under the rule, upon one who asserts a resulting trust, to establish the same by evidence that is clear, cogent, and convincing is not shifted where the suit is against him to cancel the deed by which the property has been conveyed to him.—Brucker v. DeHart, 106 Wash. 386, 180 Pac. 397, 398.

5. Constructive trusts.—Where a party obtains the legal title to property, not only by fraud or by violation of confidence or of fiduciary relations, but in any other unconscientious manner, so that he can not equitably retain it against the rightful owner, equity carries out its theory of a double ownership, equitable and legal, by impressing a constructive trust upon the property in favor of the one who is in good conscience entitled to it, and who is considered in equity as the beneficial owner.—Hayden v. Dannenberg, 42 Okla. 776, Ann. Cas.

1916D, 1191, 143 Pac. 859. A constructive trust may be established by poral evidence, but it must be clear, unequivocal, and decisive.—Hayden v. Dannenberg, 42 Okla. 776, Ann. Cas. 1916D, 1191, 143 Pac. 859. If money is obtained by fraud and invested in land, the title to which is taken in the name of the wrongdoer, a constructive trust results in such land in favor of the person wronged, and follows the land in which the money was invested, unless the land has passed to a purchaser for value, without notice of the trust.—Success Realty Co. v. Trowbridge, 50 Okla. 273, 150 Pac. 898. If there exists a confidential relation between parties to a deed, such as husband and wife, or parent and child, its betrayal raises a constructive trust as to the property involved.—Meek v. Meek, 79 Or. 579, 156 Pac. 250. In a case where a woman, on her deathbed, desiring that property of hers shall be devoted to the maintenance and support of her grandchildren, makes a deed absolute in form, to her son, in accepting which he orally agrees to hold in trust for these grandchildren, a declaration of trust, thereafter prepared, and signed by this son, to the same effect as the oral agreement, is subject to the rule that a written instrument is to be construed most strongly against the maker; the circumstances create a constructive trust in favor of the grandchildren.—Willats v. Bosworth, 33 Cal. App. 710, 166 Pac. 357. If a husband receives a deed from his dying wife, promising that he will in turn execute a conveyance of the property to one of her relatives, to be delivered upon the grantor's death, his failure to make such deed impresses the property with a constructive trust in favor of such relative.—Hillyer v. Hynes, 33 Cal. App. 506, 165 Pac. 718.

REFERENCES.

Impressing share of heir, devisee, or legatee with a constructive trust because of his fraud in frustrating the decedent's intention to give the property to a third person.—8 L. R. A. (N. S.) 698, 31 L. R. A. (N. S.) 176. Heir, devisee, or legatee as trustee ex maleficio.—106 Am. St. Rep. 94. May a constructive trust be based upon an undertaking to hold, for the benefit of another, property received through devise or inheritance, where no actual testamentary intention was frustrated.—33 L. R. A. (N. S.) 996.

6. **Involuntary trusts.**—If a father, sick unto death, calls his children, and says to them in substance: "I want mother (his wife) to have all of my property; and I want you boys to deed it to her when I am gone; this will be as good as a will"; and the boys agree to this, so telling their father, and the father dies without having made a will; there is created, according to the ordinary rules of equity, a constructive trust; and, under the statute, an involuntary trust, which seems to include both a constructive trust, and a resulting trust, is thereby created; such a trust may be enforced against the sons; it is superior to the liens of the judgments of their individual creditors.—Arntson v. First Nat. Bank (N. D.), 167 N. W. 760.

7. Deeds of trust.

(1) In general.—The person to whom a deed runs as grantee is presumed to hold the property for his own benefit, but the presumption may be overcome by proof that the intention of the grantor was that his title should be that of a trustee.—Sanford v. Sanford, 31 N. D. 190, 199, 153 N. W. 412. Under a deed creating a trust to hold during the life of the beneficiary and apply the rents to his use, and after his death to convey the property to the survivors of the grantees, but to sell before the beneficiary's death if they deem that to be advisable, there can not be, at time prior to the life beneficiary's death, a merger of the equitable and of the legal title.—Estate of Aldersley, 174 Cal. 366, 163 Pac. 206. If one makes a deed whereby the grantees become trustees to use the rents for the benefit of a beneficiary during his lifetime, and then the life beneficiary and these grantees join in conveying the property, the result is a passing of the equitable life estate and of the reversionary interest therein.—Estate of Aldersley, 174 Cal. 366, 163 Pac. 206. The holder of a deed asserted by him to have been made by the trustee of a resulting trust to have as the beneficiary of the trust, is controlled by the general rule that the burden of proof is on the person who asserts the trust, and, the evidence must be clear, cogent, and convincing; if the case be one where it is sought by the administrator of the grantor to set aside the deed as being a conveyance of the community property of the grantor and her deceased husband.—Brucker v. De Hart, 106 Wash. 386, 180 Pac. 397. A conveyance in trust for the management, investment, and reinvestment of the property, and the payment of the income thereof to the trustor for life, and that upon the death of the trustor the property shall go to and vest in her heirs at law or as she shall provide by last will and testament, does not create a mere dry, naked trust terminable at the option of the trustor, but creates an equitable life estate in the trustor, with equitable remainders to trustor's heirs at law, subject to divestment only upon the exercise of the power of nomination by will reserved to the trustor.—Gray v. Union Trust Co., 171 Cal. 637, 154 Pac. 306. The survivor of three persons to whom a deed has been made as trustees for a cemetery, can not, as an individual, convey the premises at all and, as a trustee, can convey them only for the purposes named in the deed.—Bitney v. Grim, 73 Or. 257, 144 Pac. 490. Where a mother made a deed of land to her son, admitting that the intention was that he should have the property at her demise, but claiming that she was to have "a home" while she lived, a finding, in an action to quiet title, that she executed the deed to him is inconsistent with the further finding, that it was understood and agreed between the parties that the deed should not be delivered until the mother's last sickness; the term "executed" includes delivery.—Worthley v. Worthley, 33 Cal. App. 473, 165 Pac. 714.

(2) Legal title.—A deed to a mother, as trustee, if executed for the benefit of her son when he shall reach the age of majority, clothes her

with an executor trust which does not become executed while the son
is a minor, and so long as a trust is executory the legal title can not
vest in the beneficiary.—Ransau v. Davis, 85 Or. 26, 158 Pac. 279, 165
Pac. 1180.

(3) Transfer of fee.—A conveyance of property in trust, to sell,
transfers an estate in fee.—Robison v. Hicks, 76 Or. 19, 146 Pac. 1099.
Inasmuch as "heirs," or other words of inheritance, are not necessary
in a deed in order to convey a fee, and inasmuch as the statute of
uses has never been adopted in Oregon, a conveyance, without the
word "heirs" or other words of inheritance, may vest trustees with
possession, and impose upon them active duties relating to the estate's control and management until the contingency arises which
terminates the trust.—Crown v. Cohn, 88 Or. 642, 172 Pac. 804. A deed
in trust to take possession of, lease, sell, and convey the land, and
so to invest the proceeds as to enable the trustees to furnish a support for the grantor during life, and thereafter "to hold all the rest
and residue of the property or the proceeds thereof" for the use of
persons specified, is to be construed as empowering the trustees, after
as well as before the grantor's death, to sell so as to convey a valid
estate in fee.—Crown Co. v. Cohn, 88 Or. 642, 172 Pac. 804.

(4) Setting aside.—In a suit to set aside a deed of trust, after the
death of the grantor, on the ground of undue and improper influence
exerted by the beneficiaries, the court may find that a relation of
friendship and confidence existed between the grantor and grantee
and yet adjudge that there had been no undue influence exerted.—
Whiteley v. Watson, 93 Kan. 671, 145 Pac. 568. If the wife of a dying
man accedes to the latter's entreaties to join with him in executing
a trust deed, she can not afterwards set aside the deed on the ground
of undue influence; undue influence rests on fraud and never on fear
lest refusal to execute may hasten the death of the person requesting.—
Hayward v. Tacoma Savings B. & Tr. Co., 86 Wash. 542, 153 Pac. 352.

8. Power of appointment.—When a power of appointment is reserved in a trust conveyance, to be exercised by will alone, the fact
does not prevent the vesting of the future estate in remainder, when
everything that the law contemplates shall exist for the creation
of equitable remainders or remainders in trust, whether vested or
contingent, since in either case estate and interest are alienable.—
Gray v. Union Trust Co., 171 Cal. 637, 642, 154 Pac. 306. The trust
in this case considered and held to create vested remainders subject
to divestiture only upon the exercise of the power of nomination by
will reserved to the trustor.—Gray v. Union Trust Co., 171 Cal. 637,
642, 154 Pac. 306. While the grantor of a trust can not delegate a
judicial function to any court, such function being created by law,
the naked power of appointing in succession the trustees under a
trust is not a judicial function but a power which may be designated
by the grantor.—Estate of Bishop, 23 Haw. 575, 583.

9. Suit to have trust declared.—The rights of executors and administrators, under the statute, in respect to the estates of their decedents do not include the right of suit to establish a resulting trust and to compel a conveyance of the land.—Cook v. Elmore, 25 Wyo. 393, 171 Pac. 261. A fiduciary relation on the part of those securing the probate of a will is not essential to the making of a sufficient case of extrinsic fraud to sustain an action for a decree in equity charging the executor, legatee, or devisee with a trust in favor of the defrauded party.—Nicholson v. Leatham, 28 Cal. App. 597, 155 Pac. 98. Where a woman purchased tracts of land from time to time with her own money and these were deeded to one and another of her children, and there was evidence of oral declarations as to such deeds, inconsistent with absolute ownership, also written evidence of like tendency, and one of the children, administering her mother's estate treated the tracts as part of the estate, the court properly decreed a resulting trust in favor of the estate.—Womach v. Sandygren, 96 Wash. 12, 164 Pac. 600. Where a widow, having living children, marries again and, after title to real estate has been taken in her name, dies intestate, the husband can not, as against these children, claiming as heirs, have a decree declaring the decedent to have been a trustee of a resulting trust, on the ground that he furnished the money with which the property was bought.—Bucknell v. Johnson, 39 S. D. 212, 163 N. W. 683. A person who, for thirty-three years has known that a second person, holding the title of land belonging to both, has divested himself of such title in favor of third persons, can not, on the second person's death, require his executors to enforce the terms of a trust respecting the land, he is barred by laches.—Ewald v. Kierulff, 175 Cal. 363, 165 Pac. 942. The facts were examined and it was held that a purchase of land by one person with the money of another gave rise to a trust; that from the purchase of the land until his death the cestui que trust was in possession, individually and as copartner with the trustee, and collected rent from the partnership for said land; that the trustee had done nothing inconsistent with a recognition of the trust, nor asserted any adverse claim in himself until after the death of the cestui que trust; held that the statute of limitations did not bar an action by his administrator against the trustee to recover the rents and profits pending the settlement of the estate.—Cook v. Elmore, 25 Wyo. 393, 403, 171 Pac. 261. In a suit to have the executor and heirs of the plaintiff's co-owner in a mining claim declared trustees for his benefit, declarations made by the decedent, after issuance of patent, that the plaintiff was still the owner of an interest in the claim, when in fact his name had been omitted from the patent, and evidence, that the decedent at one time joined with the plaintiff in a lease of the property, are admissible in evidence.—Delmoe v. Long, 35 Mont. 139, 154, 88 Pac. 778. If a man purchases real estate and, in order to defeat his wife's inchoate right of dower in it, has the deed made to his brother, such brother, if the purchaser then dies, will, upon these facts being shown, be decreed to hold in trust for the estate of the deceased.—Griffith v. Griffith, 74 Or. 225, 145 Pac. 270. In a suit to have the executor and heirs of the plaintiff's co-owner in a mining claim declared trustees for his benefit, declarations made by the decedent, after issuance of patent, that the plaintiff was still the owner of an interest in the claim, when in fact his name had been omitted from the patent, and evidence that the decedent at one time joined with the plaintiff in a lease of the property, are admissible in evidence. —Delmoe v. Long, 35 Mont. 139, 154, 88 Pac. 778.

10. Partition. Res judicata.—Where, under the terms of a trust, a partition can be had only by agreement of the survivors of the named beneficiaries and of the issue of those that have died, the widow of the decedent, on the occurrence of such a death, before such an agreement can not ask for a partition where she had never acquired any interest in the property.—Sweinhart v. Plant Inv. Co., 178 Cal. 125, 172 Pac. 386. A decree, establishing a trust, which provides that none of the property can be sold without the written agreement of the surviving children of a testator and of the heirs of the body of those who have died, can not be questioned in a suit for partition brought by the widow of one of the children who has left no issue.—Sweinhardt v. Plant Inv. Co., 178 Cal. 125, 172 Pac. 386. Where a court in Illinois had acquired jurisdiction of all the parties to partition proceedings, and jurisdiction of the property involved, and had determined in advance of the sale that certain of the heirs might become purchasers, and the sale having been made has confirmed it, the matter is res judicata and binding upon parties in this state.—Plant v. Plant, 171 Cal. 765, 154 Pac. 1058.

11. Statute of limitations.—The statute of limitations does not run in favor of a trustee of an express trust until he has taken some action which amounts to a repudiation of the trust.—Cook v. Elmore, 25 Wyo. 393, 402, 171 Pac. 261. In the case of resulting and constructive trusts the statute of limitations commences to run from the time the act occurs which creates the trust, or, in other words, when the cestui que trust could bring an action to enforce, and no repudiation of the trust by the trustee is necessary to start the statute running.— Cook v. Elmore, 25 Wyo. 393, 402, 171 Pac. 261. The well defined and recognized exception to the rule that the statute of limitations starts to run in favor of the trustee in a resulting, and in a constructive trust, at the time of its creation, and that no repudiation is necessary to start the statute running, is when the cestui que trust is in possession and the trustee has done nothing inconsistent with a recognition of the trust, nor asserted an adverse claim.—Cook v. Elmore, 25 Wyo. 393, 402, 171 Pac. 261. If a woman, when dying, executes deeds of property to her husband, he promising that he will execute a deed of it to her niece, to be delivered on his death, the husband takes the property burdened with a constructive trust; if the niece brings an action against the husband's administrator to enforce such a promise, it is one to recover real property and is governed by the five-year statute of limitation.—Hillyer v. Hynes, 33 Cal. App. 506, 165 Pac. 713.

12. Laches.—Where a married woman dies intestate and an adult son, of some education, executes a deed of his share of her community property, thereby vesting the same in his father, the son can not afterwards claim that the father holds merely as his trustee, on the ground that the deed was executed under duress, unless the claim is asserted within a reasonable time after removal of the duress.—Durazo v. Durazo, 19 Ariz, 571, 173 Pac. 350, 352.

13. Construction of instrument.—A deed absolute in terms, like a devise absolute in terms, is not susceptible of being constructed as vesting in the taker an express trust, even though the grantor may have had that in mind when making it.—Lanigan v. Miles, 102 Wash. 82, 172 Pac. 894. A trust providing for the payment to a cemetery association, or to some person or persons who have charge of the upkeep of a cemetery does not involve a perpetuity.—Rutherford v. Ott, 37 Cal. App. 47, 173 Pac. 490.

14. Dealing with trust property.—It can not be made an inflexible rule that a trustee or executor may not charge the estate with the commissions of a broker employed to find a purchaser for property.—Rutherford v. Ott, 37 Cal. App. 47, 173 Pac. 490.

15. Compensation of trustee.—The compensation of a trustee is confided to the discretion of the trial court, and such discretion is not abused when the court fixes at $200 the compensation of a trustee of a $200,000 estate for fourteen months of service.—In re Prescott's Estate, Appeal of Fredericks, 179 Cal. 192, 175 Pac. 895. The trust estate, consisting of a farm held in trust for a minor until he is of age, is answerable for services rendered in cultivating the property and caring for crops raised thereon, where the trustee is insolvent; such services were of benefit to the estate.—Ranzau v. Davis, 85 Or. 26, 158 Pac. 279, 165 Pac. 1180.

16. Powers of trustee.—A trustee can not lease trust real estate and, instead of accounting for cash rentals, retain these as repayments to him of advances, made by him in his private capacity, to the lessee. —Purdy v. Johnson, 174 Cal. 521, 163 Pac. 893. If a deed of trust of land, to hold for the lifetime of a beneficiary, but with power to sell before his death if the trustees deem it advisable to do so, containes a provision authorizing the trustees to use the "rents, issues, and profits, of the land in the performance of their duties, such provision empowers them to utilize in lieu of the rents, issues, and profits interest on money received from a sale, if one is made, but it does not authorize them to use any part of the principal for the purposes of the trust.—Estate of Aldersley, 174 Cal. 366, 163 Pac. 206. A trustee may purchase at his own sale in a case where a court of equity has determined that he may, and the sale is made under the court's direc-

tion by officers appointed by it.—Plant v. Plant, 171 Cal. 765, 154 Pac. 1058. It is not only where the trusteeship is coupled with a power of sale that a trustee himself may purchase at a sale under the court's direction, the sale being made by officers appointed by the court to make it.—Plant v. Plant, 171 Cal. 765, 154 Pac. 1058.

17. Liability of trustee.—A person to whom shares of stock in a family estate corporation are actually issued, and in whose name these are duly registered on the books of the company, is individually liable for an assessment on the stock, even though he in fact holds in trust for another.—Webster v. Bartlett Estate Co., 35 Cal. App. 283, 169 Pac. 702.

18. Removal of trustee and substitution.—A court of equity may remove a trustee who has violated his trust, and, in order that the trust may not fail for want of a trustee, may substitute another person to preserve the trust property.—Hartnett v. St. Louis Min. & Mill. Co., 51 Mont. 395, 153 Pac. 437.

19. Termination of trust.—Where a deed of trust conveys property to a trustee to manage, invest, and reinvest and pay the income to the trustee for life, and upon her death the trust property shall go to the heirs at law of trustor or to and vest in as she shall provide by last will and testament, and no power of revocation is reserved, and no termination provided for, a court of equity can not decree a termination of the trust in a suit in which the trustor and trustee are alone parties before the court.—Gray v. Union Trust Co., 171 Cal. 637, 154 Pac. 306. A complaint in a suit to compel a reconveyance of trust property on the ground that the purposes of the trust have been fully accomplished, alleges facts from which it is fairly inferable that the trustee has been fully reimbursed for all advancements made by him, and hence is sufficient as against a general objection to the introduction of evidence.—Willoburn Ranch Co. v. Yegen, 49 Mont. 101, 140 Pac. 231.

20. Enforcement of trust.—Where property is adjudged to a person by decree of the probate court such person can not be sued as a trustee of the property.—Doble v. State, 95 Wash. 62, 68, 163 Pac. 37. A trust can not be impressed upon property or funds in the hands of the executor of the estate of the alleged trustee, when the person aggrieved admits the impossibility of tracing or identifying the fund in either its original or its substituted form.—Kent v. Kent, 50 Utah 44, 48, 165 Pac. 271. A bequest of "all the rest, residue and remainder of" the testator's property to a named person, with a "desire" following that this person "shall distribute the same or the proceeds thereof among" the testator's "nephews and nieces, and to such of them and in such proportions as he shall deem just and proper," is enforceable as a trust.—Estate of Dewey, 45 Utah 98, Ann. Cas. 1918A, 475, 143 Pac. 124. A parol agreement, between a woman and her husband, who, relying thereon, subsequently wills to her his real estate, can not be enforced as effecting an express trust to make an impartial division between their children.—Brown v. Kansche, 98 Wash. 470, 167 Pac. 1075. A complaint for the enforcement of an alleged express trust is, if laches on the part of the plaintiff appear therefrom, subject to demurrer.—Ewald v. Kierulff, 175 Cal. 363, 165 Pac. 942. Where the owner of mortgaged land conveys to a trustee for a corporation, reserving a certain number of acres thereafter to be selected by him, the grantee agreeing to pay off the mortgage with the proceeds of sales of the land, the acres, when selected thereafter, are held by the trustee as a naked trust and the trustee can be compelled to convey them to such owner.—Fogarty v. Hunter, 83 Or. 183, 162 Pac. 964. A trust may be created and enforced where a filial relationship is actually assumed, and a man may make a contract whereby he agrees to leave to one, although not legally adopted, a child's share of his estate at his death; services and companionship will constitute a valuable consideration for the promise.—Price v. Wallace (Or.), 242 Fed. 221, 223, 155 C. C. A. 61. Equity will not aid the enforcement of a trust, where a filial relationship was alleged to have been assumed, or aid the enforcement of a contract whereby a man agreed to leave to a young woman, although not legally adopted, a child's share of his estate at his death, unless it is clearly and satisfactorily shown that the agreement relied on was made; that is was clear and specific in its terms; and that by enforcing it, the true intent of the parties is being carried out.—Price v. Wallace (Or.), 242 Fed. 221, 223, 155 C. C. A. 61. The owner of land had, in anticipation of death, conveyed to a brother with the understanding, not expressed in the deed, that he was to sell, and divide the proceeds between his brothers, a surviving sister, and himself. The grantee had then himself died, after conveying to his wife with the same understanding. The brothers and sister then brought suit against the wife and the suit was compromised, she agreeing to hold the property in trust and they allowing judgment to be given in her favor. Held that equity would regard the judgment as impressed with the trust and would enforce the latter notwithstanding its resting in parol.—Lamb v. Lamb, 171 Cal. 577, 153 Pac. 913. A deed creating a trust, among other things, to convey property after the death of the life beneficiary could not be enforced, as to such trust, prior to the act of 1913, page 438, amending section 857 of the Civil Code.—Estate of Aldersley, 174 Cal. 366, 163 Pac. 206. If a person forms an investment company for the management of his properties, and then transfers his shares therein to a trust company with directions that, after his death it shall pay, out of the dividends, a designated sum per month to a beneficiary, the receipt whereof shall constitute a waiver by him of monthly compensation for services performed by him for the investment company, the payment by this company to the beneficiary, after such death, of the same sum per month, under an agreement that it is in lieu of dividends, and the receipt of the same without question for nearly six years, deprives the beneficiary of the right to sue the trust company for the dividends.—Howard v. Anglo-California Trust Co., 34 Cal. App. 164, 167 Pac. 177.

21. Appeal.—It is the duty of a trustee sued for the dissolution of the trust to appeal from a judgment dissolving the trust if the rights of other persons than the plaintiff are believed to be impaired or destroyed thereby, even though its sole interest therein is a fixed compensation for performing its duties as such trustee.—Gray v. Union Trust Co., 171 Cal. 637, 639, 154 Pac. 306. Where a court by its order refuses to remove a trustee an appeal from the order will not be considered on the merits unless supported by an authenticated record.—Estate of Davis, 175 Cal. 198, 165 Pac. 525. On appeal from a judgment adverse to parties suing to set aside a deed of trust, as having been procured by the beneficiaries through the exercise of fraud and undue influence, objection can not be made to a conclusion of law as not conforming to a particular finding of fact, when there are other findings that justify the conclusion.—Whiteley v. Watson, 93 Kan. 671, 145 Pac. 568. The trial court in an action to declare and enforce a trust in real property, determined from the evidence that a mother, holding under a deed of gift from her son, to whom she had given the property in the first place, was not a trustee, although she made no pretense of holding otherwise than for his protection; on appeal, it was held that there was substantial evidence to support the trial court's determination, and therefore that it ought not to be disturbed.—Citizens' T. & S. Bank v. Tuffree, 178 Cal. 185, 172 Pac. 586. It is not permissible to reverse a judgment on one finding alone, disregarding all others.—Whiteley v. Watson, 93 Kan. 671, 145 Pac. 568.

II. TRUSTS UNDER WILLS, TESTAMENTARY TRUSTEES, AND DISTRIBUTION TO TRUSTEES.

2. Trusts under wills.

(1) In general.—The subject of trusts is not within the scope of this work. That will be found discussed in the annotations to Kerr's Cyc. Civ. Code, §§ 2250-2289. It is our purpose here simply to discuss a few general principals of trusts in connection with trusts under wills, and the limited jurisdiction of the probate court respecting the same as conferred by the California Code of Civil Procedure, §§ 1699-1703½. The author of a trust may devise property subject to the execution of the trust, and such a devisee acquires a legal estate in the property as against all persons except the trustee.—Estate of Barclay, 152 Cal. 753, 93 Pac. 1012. A decree in an action to close and settle a trust respecting lands does not affect the independent interest of a widow in such land as a tenant in common.—Estate of Kennedy, 120 Cal. 458, 463, 52 Pac. 820. A bequest to be held in trust for the benefit of children until they reach the age of 25 years is not a trust void for undue suspension of the power of alienation, under the statute providing that the power of alienation shall not be suspended beyond the existence of lives in being.—Estate of Hendy, 118 Cal. 656, 50 Pac. 753. A trust created by a will, to continue during the lives of persons in being at the time, is not forbidden under the provisions of the statute relating to perpetuities and "trusts to convey," but is valid.— Estate of Lux, 149 Cal. 200, 85 Pac. 147, 149. A bequest giving and bequeathing to a designated person as follows: "I give and bequeath to Rev. James Collins for mass for his grandfather's and grandmother's souls," is a gift direct, with the performance of a duty enjoined. It is not a void trust, nor uncertain as to the beneficiaries, and is not repugnant to the law against bequests for "superstitious uses."—Harrison v. Brophy, 59 Kan. 1, 40 L. R. A. 721, 51 Pac. 883.

REFERENCES.

Effect of trust upon death of donor, without exercising power of revocation.—See note 6 Am. & Eng. Ann. Cas. 189. Effect of executor's promise, as to payment of legacy, upon trust relations with legatee.— See note 9 L. R. A. (N. S.) 214-216.

(2) Creation of trusts. In general.—As a general proposition, every person competent to make a will, to enter into a contract, or to hold a legal title to property has the power to create a trust, even in himself, and to dispose of his property in that way.—Skeen v. Marriott, 22 Utah 73, 61 Pac. 296. No particular form or expression in a will is necessary to constitute a valid trust. It is sufficient that, from the language used, the intention of the testator is apparent, and that the disposition of the trust which he endeavors to make of his estate is consistent with the rules of law. The intent of the testator is the matter for primary consideration, and it is immaterial what method of expression is employed, so long as that intention can be ascertained.—Estate of Heywood, 148 Cal. 184, 82 Pac. 755, 757; Estate of Walker, 149 Cal. 214, 217, 85 Pac. 310, 311. An acknowledgment of a trust, with specific reference to the will creating it, and from which the terms of the trust can be ascertained, is sufficient to create a voluntary trust, and the executor who holds the control of the funds creating such trust is estopped from disputing the receipt of the money as a trustee.—Elizalde v. Elizalde, 137 Cal. 634, 636, 66 Pac. 369, 70 Pac. 861. A trust may be created in a will to "manage" property, and to collect the income, issues, and profits thereof, and to pay them to specified persons.—Estate of Heywood, 148 Cal. 184, 82 Pac. 755, 757. But, where property is devised absolutely to devisees named, a mere direction in the will to the executors "to invest the proceeds," without mentioning any trust or trustee, other than such as would arise out of the office of executor, does not create a trust, and the court has no power or jurisdiction to carve out a trust from the will.—McCloud v. Hewlett, 135 Cal. 361, 367, 67 Pac. 333. So where the testator has not devised land to his executors in trust for the purposes of his will, but has merely given them certain directions to be observed in carrying out its provisions, the will does not create an

express trust in real property.—Estate of Pforr, 144 Cal. 121, 125, 77
Pac. 825. A devise in a will to the members of a church in trust for
their benefit, "whether it be for schools, parks, watering cities, plant-
ing forests, acclimatizing foreign plants, or anything else whereby
the members may be benefited," is a valid trust. The persons to be
benefited are distinguished therein and are identified by their church
membership.—Staines v. Burton, 17 Utah 331, 70 Am. St. Rep. 788, 53
Pac. 1015. Construction of will as reposing in the mother a trust
created for the purpose of protecting and preserving the property for
the use of the daughter as devisee, without otherwise limiting or
decreasing her title thereto, and not for the purpose of affecting the
ownership.—See Kinkead v. Maxwell, 75 Kan. 50, 88 Pac. 523, 525.
Creation, by will, of valid devises and bequests of real and personal
property in trust, with designation of particular powers of trustees.—
See Estate of Dunphy, 147 Cal. 95, 81 Pac. 315, 316. A direction to the
executors of a will to collect the rents and to maintain the estate for
two years is not a restraint upon its alienation during that period,
nor is the provision for its sale at the expiration of two years a prohibition against its sale prior to that time.—Estate of Pforr, 144 Cal.
121, 126, 77 Pac. 825. No particular words are necessary to create a
trust by will, provided language is used from which a trust may be
implied.—Estate of Dewey, 45 Utah 98, Ann. Cas. 1918A, 475, 143 Pac.
124. An instrument in the nature of a testamentary disposition of
property, which must be proved in a court of probate, but by reason
of imperfect execution can not be proved as a last will and testament,
will not create a trust in favor of donees named therein.—O'Gorman v.
Jolley, 34 S. D. 26, 38, 147 N. W. 78. A memorandum of deceased
accompanying a deposit of money in bank made by him to the effect
that in case of his death the deposit should be divided between his
four children; was not a will but merely the creation of a trust in
the moneys deposited.—Estate of Seiler, 176 Cal. 771, 775, 170 Pac.
1138. If a trust has been established in property standing in the name
of a husband, his wife has, prima facie, no dower; she can have it
only by showing a want of notice.—Huffine v. Lincoln, 52 Mont. 585,
160 Pac. 820. The strictness of the law in relation to the execution
of wills is not due to any solicitude for the creditors of the heirs,
but to a desire that the real intention of the testator shall be ascertained and prevail; a personal creditor of the heirs, therefore, can
not complain that the deceased, instead of making a will of his property to his wife, created a trust by which his children agreed to convey it to her.—Arntson v. First Nat. Bank (N. D.), 167 N. W. 760.
In order to escape the doctrine that a trust to convey can not be
created by will it is not sufficient that words are to be found in the
will which, not being in themselves dispositions in meaning or effect,
show a knowledge had by the testator of the dispositions.—Estate of
Willson, 171 Cal. 449, 153 Pac. 927. An executor is a prima facie
trustee for the next of kin, but is not necessarily a trustee for the

testator's estate; though a devise to an executor, coupled with a power to sell real property for any specified purpose without an order of court creates a trust.—Thorson v. Hooper, 57 Or. 75, 109 Pac. 389. A husband, while he may create a valid trust in community personalty during his life, can not, by an instrument in writing, hold the equitable title thereof during his lifetime and dispose of the fee and subject the property to another trust after his death, in violation of the spirit of the law; at his death the property becomes subject to the law of descent.—Stewart v. Bank of Endicott, 82 Wash. 106, 143 Pac. 453.

REFERENCES.

Effect of creation of testamentary trust for payment of debts.— See note 5 L. R. A. (N. S.) 355-372. Necessity of word "heirs," in deed or devise in trust, to pass fee to trustee.—See note 2 L. R. A. (N. S.) 172-183. Precatory trusts, general rule as to creation of.— See note 2 Ann. Cas. 593.

(3) Same. As to income.—There is nothing in our law to forbid a man from declaring a trust, either by will or deed, whereby the income of certain property shall be paid to a son until he attains the age of 25 years, when the corpus of the trust property shall be made over to him.—Estate of Yates, 170 Cal. 254, 149 Pac. 555. Facts showing a resulting trust in a will, as to the income of property, in favor of a daughter as sole heir; that there was no gift of the income by implication; and that the testator did not intend that the income should accumulate.—Von Holt v. Williamson, 23 Haw. 201, 206. As to trusts created by a will, whereby the body of the estate and the accumulations of income, in each case, are to be handed over to the beneficiary on his arriving at the age of 25, these still continue for the period of time in them specified, and as each of the legatees attains his majority he is entitled to the accumulations and to the later accruing income of the trust fund. Each legatee has a disposable interest in the corpus of the trust, but the corpus is to be given him when, and only when, he reaches the years named in the trust.— Estate of Yates, 170 Cal. 254, 149 Pac. 555.

(4) Same. As to spendthrifts.—The general doctrine that spendthrift trusts, inalienable by the beneficiary and inaccessible to his creditors during his life or for a term of years, are valid in this state, is well established.—McColgan v. Magee, 172 Cal. 182, Ann. Cas. 1917D, 1050, 155 Pac. 195. The statute law of Kansas contains nothing to prevent the creation, by a testator, of what is known as a "spendthrift trust."—Sherman v. Havens, 94 Kan. 654, 659, Ann. Cas. 1917B, 394, 146 Pac. 1030. The doctrine that property may be made inalienable by the declaration of a spendthrift trust rests upon the theory that a donor has the right to give his property to another on any conditions he may see fit to impose, and that, inasmuch as such a gift takes nothing from the prior or subsequent creditors of the beneficiary to which they previously had the right to look for payment, they can

not complain that the donor has provided that the property or income shall go or be paid personally to the beneficiary, and shall not be subject to the claims of creditors.—McColgan v. Magee, 172 Cal. 182, Ann. Cas. 1917D,*1050, 155 Pac. 195. Where the beneficiary of a spendthrift trust contracted for the rebuilding of the dwelling house on the trust premises, exhausted thereon the money received on fire policies, taken out by him, and left unpaid a bill for lumber, the trustees taking no part in the transaction, the lumber contractor was not allowed to enforce a mechanic's lien as against the revenue of the property.—Pond v. Harrison, 96 Kan. 542, L. R. A. 1916B, 1264, 152 Pac. 655. A specific provision in a will held not to amount to the creation of a spendthrift trust, whereby the testator betrays an intention to secure the bequest against the claims of the legatee's creditors.—Sherman v. Havens, 94 Kan. 654, Ann. Cas. 1917B, 394, 146 Pac. 1030.

(5) Same. Because of fraud.—Where an intended testamentary disposition has been changed or thwarted by the promise or engagement of one having a confidential relationship with the intending donor, and to the advantage of the promisor, the latter takes his advantage subject to the performance of his promise, and his subsequent repudiation of the promise is a fraud; this fraud warrants a declaration of trust, regardless of the intention when the promise was made, or it will be presumed that in the making of the promise there was no intention to perform.—Huffine v. Lincoln, 52 Mont. 585, 160 Pac. 820.

(6) Burden of proof.—A will may be absolute in its terms whereby property is devised by a man to his wife, and yet there may be a bona fide understanding between the two that, when circumstances shall become propitious, she will make a distribution among their children; to establish a trust in such a case the children have the burden of proof and the evidence required must be very clear and convincing.— Holler v. Arnodt, 31 N. D. 11, 27, 153 N. W. 465.

REFERENCES.

Implied trust arising from testamentary gift secured by promise of donee to hold for benefit of another.—See note 21 Ann. Cas. 1384.

(7) Number of trustees.—It is of little moment how many successive trustees may be provided for to administer the fund, disposed of by a will creating a trust, or that the different trustees may have different duties; the important points are whether the trust intended was one and indivisible and did it vest upon the death of the testator.—In re Galland's Estate, Galland v. Seattle Trust Co., 103 Wash. 106, 173 Pac. 740. Where the number of trustees was fixed in a will and it was provided that vacancies should be filled by the "choice" of the majority of the justices of the supreme court, the word "choice" is synonymous with the word "appoint," and an appointment so made is not subject to confirmation or rejection by the circuit court having original jurisdiction in matters relating to trusts.—Estate of Bishop, 23 Haw. 575,

583. A will named five trustees to execute a certain trust created therein, and provided that the number of trustees should be kept at five and that vacancies should be filled by a majority of the justices of the supreme court. Held, in construing the will that it was the intention of the testatrix to vest the power of filling vacancies in the justices as individuals and not in the court having original jurisdiction in matters of trust, and when such original jurisdiction was transferred by law to another tribunal, it did not transfer the power of appointment conferred by the will to fill vacancies.—Estate of Bishop, 23 Haw. 575, 578. A will dated in 1889 and probated in 1891, named two trustees to execute the trust therein created, and provided that whenever the beneficiaries of the trust or a majority of them should apply to a justice of the supreme court, a third trustee should be appointed. Held, that by the judiciary act of 1892 all original equity jurisdiction having been taken from the several justices of the supreme court and reposed in the circuit judges of the islands, the power to appoint a third trustee is now exercisable by a circuit judge and not by a justice of the supreme court.—In re Estate of Carter, 24 Haw. 536.

(8) Construction of trusts. In general.—In ascertaining the intention of the testator as to the source from which payments under a trust created by will shall be made, the court is not restricted solely to an examination of the particular subdivisions of the will concerning such payments. Resort may be had to all the provisions of the will which tend to disclose his intention in that particular.—Estate of Heywood, 148 Cal. 184, 82 Pac. 755, 757. A trust to "manage" property implies, by force of the term used, that the trustees are to retain it under their control, and is inconsistent with the idea that they have authority to sell or otherwise to dispose of it.—Goad v. Montgomery, 119 Cal. 552, 560, 63 Am. St. Rep. 145, 51 Pac. 681; and see Estate of Heywood, 148 Cal. 184, 82 Pac. 755, 757. A clause in the will providing for the payment of annuities, as soon as the trustees shall have sufficient funds available for that purpose, is to be construed as relating only to the date when the annuities begin to run.—Crew v. Pratt, 119 Cal. 131, 137, 51 Pac. 44. Where the legal title to land is vested in the trustee, who is "to have and hold" and "manage" the property during the continuance of the trust which is not to vest in the beneficiaries until the happening of a future event named, the trustee is authorized to receive the rents and profits, whatever may be the right of the beneficiaries at the termination of the trust to the accumulated incomes, should there be any.—Blackburn v. Webb, 133 Cal. 420, 65 Pac. 952, 953. The language of a will setting aside a trust fund must govern the intention of the testator, and if the intention can not be ascertained from the will itself, resort must be had to the recognized rules of interpretation in such cases; but, where the testator, by the same clause of the will, disposes of the income after the death of a trustee, and finally of the fund itself, this bequest is complete in itself, and has no dependence on any other portion of the will for its construction or execution, where the language used by the testator is too plain to admit of construction. —Morse v. Macrum, 22 Or. 229, 29 Pac. 615. In an action to construe a will in which the testator gave to his said "executors" all his property real and personal," etc., but used the qualifying words, "intrust, nevertheless, to and for the following uses and purposes," etc., it was held that the devise was in trust to the executors, not as executors, but purely and simply as trustees.—Smith v. Smith, 15 Wash. 239, 46 Pac. 249, 250. Construction of devises to trustees in general and use of the phrase "to transfer and convey," in making a testamentary devise.— See Estate of Fair, 132 Cal. 523, 84 Am. St. Rep. 70, 64 Pac. 1000, 1003. The rule is that courts go further in stretching the language of a will than of a deed in order to give effect to the intention; in the case of a conveyance creating a trust, and operating inter vivos, the intention to make a gift by implication would be less readily found than in a will, where it would be supported by the presumption against intestacy.— Chater v. Carter, 22 Haw. 34, 49. Where there is manifestly a clear intent on the part of a testator to give the sums named in his will as legacies to the beneficiaries, as where there is no bequest over in the event of death, such legacies vest in the legatees an absolute, indefeasible, and disposable interest.—Estate of Yates, 170 Cal. 254, 149 Pac. 555. When words used by a testator indicate a purpose to educate, maintain, and nourish his three children until the youngest arrives at full age, and in the same connection it is said, referring to the widow, who is named as executrix, "I direct and request that she use such or all of the money which may be the proceeds of any property she may sell," the effect intended is that there shall be a trust for the benefit of the children and, in a residuary sense, in favor of her.—Beakey v. Knutson, 90 Or. 574, 174 Pac. 1149, 177 Pac. 955. Under a will creating a trust and providing, at its expiration, for a contingent remainder to go to the testator's grandchildren, in case there be any in being, and, in the contrary case, then to the issue of his brothers and sisters, the body of the estate when the trust ends, goes to the testator's heirs as in a case of intestacy, if there be living at the time neither such grandchildren nor such issue of brothers and sisters.—Lee v. Albro, Lee v. Murphy, 91 Or. 212, 178 Pac. 784. On the death, without heirs, of one of five children, of a testator before his own death a devise to a trustee, directed by the will to divide the estate between the five, lapses as to a one-fifth portion, and as to such portion the father dies intestate.—Estate of Davis, 175 Cal. 198, 165 Pac. 525. Where property was given by will in trust to be held until the death of the last survivor of a number of annuitants and for twenty-one years thereafter to pay certain annuitants and to accumulate the unapplied income, and then divide the trust estate "among those persons entitled at the time to the aforementioned annuities," an annuity payable to the children of S. P. "for life and then to their heirs," the interest of the heirs in the annuity was for the entire period of the trust, and upon the death of one his share became payable to his heirs.—Hawaiian Trust Co. v. McMullan, 23 Haw. 685, 690.

REFERENCES.

Implied trust arising from testamentary gift secured by promise of donee to hold for benefit of another.—21 Ann. Cas. 1384.

(9) Same. In personal property.—A trust, created under a will, in personal property for the benefit of the testator's wife during her life, and directing the trustee after her death, to pay over the residue to two grandchildren named, is not invalid as suspending the power of alienation, under sections 769 and 1344 of the Civil Code. Those sections apply only to trusts in real property; and a trust in personal property is subject to no statutory restriction. The grandchildren named have a vested remainder in the residue of the personal property after the death of the wife.—Estate of Gregory, 12 Cal. App. 309, 107 Pac. 566. An estate, consisting of personal property alone, was left to a trustee, the trust to cease at the death of the testator's son; the trustee to have full management, to pay out of the income $10 a month to an old servant and the rest to the son for his support, and if this should be not sufficient for such support, to use so much of the principal therefor as he should deem necessary. On the termination of the trust the property was to go as further provided in the will. It was held that if these further provisions were invalid, the effect was not to alter the trust estate, so far as the son was concerned, but only to vest general heirs with the property on the termination of the trust.— Estate of Campbell, 175 Cal. 345, 165 Pac. 931.

(10) Same. Joint will.—A father and mother, each owning property, made a joint will, in effect providing that their respective estates should be kept together as an entirety, and upon the death of either, the survivor should take the entire estate with full power to invest it or to dispose of it to parties other than the beneficiaries, and that upon the death of the survivor the property should vest in trustees, who were authorized to invest, change or convert the property of the estate and to manage and control it for a period of fifteen years, after which time it was to be distributed equally among living children and the heirs of the body of deceased children. Held, the wife of a deceased child took nothing under the will except a personal legacy, and the estate did not vest in the beneficiaries until the expiration of the fifteen year period after the death of the survivor.—In re Brown's Estate, Brown v. Brown, 101 Kan. 335, 340, 166 Pac. 499.

(11) Judgment construing trust.—A judgment and decree construing a trust created by will is final and conclusive upon all parties then before the court.—Toland v. Earl, 129 Cal. 152, 61 Pac. 914, 79 Am. St. Rep. 100; and where a trust is accepted, and the fund is segregated and may be identified, the trust, upon the death of such person, devolves upon his personal representatives.—Kauffman v. Foster, 3 Cal. App.

741, 745, 86 Pac. 1108; Tyler v. Mayre, 95 Cal. 160, 27 Pac. 160, 30 Pac. 196.

. (12) Law of situs governs.—The validity of a trust in real estate, attempted to be created by will, must be determined by the law of the situs of the real estate.—Campbell-Kawannanakoa v. Campbell, 152 Cal. 201, 92 Pac. 184, 188. See Penfield v. Tower, 1 N. D. 216, 46 N. W. 413. A trustee, under a will declaring an express trust, has, although the will may have been executed in another state, a vested interest in property in this state as to which the trust relates. Such trustee may oppose a sale of the property petitioned for by a local administrator, and may appeal from an order made in the petitioner's favor.—Estate of Rawitzer, 175 Cal. 585, 166 Pac. 581. A trustee of an express trust, made such by and under the terms of a will, executed in another state by a testator residing therein, becomes, on the testators death, at once vested with property in this state, as to which the trust is declared; if the will contains a direct devise and bequest to such trustee empowering him to take the property immediately for the purposes of the trust.—Estate of Rawitzer, 175 Cal. 585, 166 Pac. 581.

(13) Validity of trust.—It is the universally accepted rule that the title and disposition of real estate is governed by the lex loci rei sitae. This necessarily includes the proposition that the validity of a trust in real estate attempted to be created by a will must be determined by the law of the situs of the real estate.—Campbell-Kawannanakoa v. Campbell, 152 Cal. 201, 92 Pac. 184, 186; Penfield v. Tower, 1 N. D. 216, 46 N. W. 413. Where a trust over absolutely depends upon a trust to convey, the trust to convey being invalid, the trust over must fall with it; and where real and personal property are all part and parcel of the trust scheme, and the trust as to real property is invalid, and there is nothing in the record to show that money, which is the subject of the trust, is not the accumulation of the real estate, the trust is void as to all of the property.—Estate of Dixon, 143 Cal. 511, 77 Pac. 412, 413. It is only when the language actually used by the testator will admit of no other reasonable construction than that it creates an invalid trust, that a court will declare this to be its effect.—Estate of Heywood, 148 Cal. 184, 191, 82 Pac. 755, 758. A trust in a will will not be declared invalid because a large discretion is vested in the trustee. Where a testamentary trust authorized a trustee, who was the husband of the testatrix, to sell the property of the estate, and to invest the proceeds as he might deem best, and to appropriate so much of the estate to the education and maintenance of the children of the testatrix as the trustee might deem necessary, and also provided that no bond should be required of the trustee; that no report of his doings should be made to the court; and that he should have full power to sell and to dispose of the trust property as his judgment might dictate, so long as the proceeds should be applied to the purposes of the trust; such provisions furnish no reason for declaring the trust invalid.—Keeler v. Lauer, 73 Kan. 388, 85 Pac. 541, 543. The will should not be construed as creating an

illegal trust by implication. An illegal trust must clearly and necessarily appear before the will, for such reason, can be upset.—Estate of Dunphy, 147 Cal. 95, 81 Pac. 315, 318. It is settled by the great weight of authority in America that the author of a trust to pay, or to apply for the benefit of another, the income of property, or a portion of such income, may lawfully provide that the interest of the beneficiary shall not be assignable, or shall not be subject to the claims of his creditor; and such provision need not be expressed, but may be implied from the general intention of the donor, to be gathered from the terms of the trust in the light of all the circumstances.—Seymour v. McAvoy, 121 Cal. 438, 442, 41 L. R. A. 544, 53 Pac. 946, 947. A trust created by will, which can by no possibility suspend the power of alienation beyond the duration of lives in being at the death of the testator, is not unlawful under section 715 of the Civil Code.—Estate of Heberle, 156 Cal. 723, 102 Pac. 935. When trusts created by a will or deed are, some valid and some not, a valid one stands unless so blended with the others that it can not be eliminated without destroying the main intent of the trustor or working manifest injustice to beneficiaries of a trust other than the one in question.—Estate of Whitney, 176 Cal. 12, 167 Pac. 399.

(14) Void trusts.—A trust in a will which suspends the power of alienation for any fixed period of years, not depending upon the duration of life, is void, however short the period may be, because, during the time of such limitation, the persons capable of conveying the interest might die.—Crew v. Pratt, 119 Cal. 139, 147, 51 Pac. 38. In California a trust in a will which prohibits the suspension of the power of alienation for a longer period than during the continuance of lives in being at the time of the death of the testator, is void in its creation as to real property situated within that state. So a trust in a will which devises the title to real property in fee simple to the trustees to be conveyed by them to the beneficiaries is also void.—Campbell-Kawannanakoa v. Campbell, 152 Cal. 201, 92 Pac. 184, 185. Where the creation of a trust as to real property is attempted in a will, but such trust is void in its creation, and there are no apt words in the will disposing of the property upon the failure of such trust, intestacy as to the property must be the result.—Estate of Heberle (Cal.), 95 Pac. 41, 42. A trust to convey real estate to beneficiaries named, or which attempts to illegally restrict the power of alienation, is void from its creation.— Estate of Heberle, 153 Cal. 275, 95 Pac. 41, 42; Estate of Walkerly, 108 Cal. 628, 41 Pac. 772, 49 Am. St. Rep. 97; Estate of Cavarly, 119 Cal. 408, 51 Pac. 629; Estate of Fair, 132 Cal. 523, 60 Pac. 442, 64 Pac. 1000, 84 Am. St. Rep. 70; Estate of Dixon, 143 Cal. 511, 77 Pac. 412; Estate of Sanford, 136 Cal. 97, 68 Pac. 494. Where a devise of property to trustees is made by a will, "to transfer and convey," etc., and provides no way by which the property may vest in any other person, except by a conveyance by said trustees; and, moreover, the testator clearly expresses his intent that it should

so vest only by a conveyance by the trustees, such trust is invalid and void under the laws of California.—Estate of Fair, 132 Cal. 523, 533, 60 Pac. 442, 64 Pac. 1000, 84 Am. St. Rep. 70 (Temple J., Harrison J., and Beatty J., dissenting and maintaining that the devisees under such a will are the donees of a power in trust to convey the property when the trust estate ends, and that while a trust to convey can not be created, such a power in trust is perfectly valid). If real property is devised to trustees, and the will clearly contains a trust to convey such property to designated persons, and there is no devise to such persons, the will is invalid, and the property, not being disposed of by the will, vests at the death of the testator in the heirs at law, and should be distributed to them.—Estate of Picholr, 139 Cal. 682, 685, 73 Pac. 606. An express trust to convey real property is void, but the purpose may be carried out where, in the will creating the trust, words are to be found constituting in themselves a disposition of the property to the beneficiaries intended, without aid from the conveyance to be made by the trustees.—Estate of Willson, 171 Cal. 449, 153 Pac. 927. Though a direction, in a trust created by will, for accumulations beyond the age of minority of the legatees is void, that fact does not in law operate to destroy the trust in its creation; it merely avoids the provision for the illegal accumulations, with the result that the legatees after maturity would be entitled to receive the incomes of the trust funds.— Estate of Yates, 170 Cal. 254, 149 Pac. 555. A direction in a trust, created by a will, for accumulations beyond the age of the minority of a legatee is void, but this fact does not, in law, operate to destroy the trust in its creation, but merely to avoid the provision for the illegal accumulations.—Estate of Yates, 170 Cal. 254, 256, 149 Pac. 555.

2. Probate jurisdiction of trusts.

(1) To determine whether valid trust has been created.—It is within the province of a probate court to determine whether a valid trust has been created by will, but the power to regulate and direct its subsequent administration lies with the court possessed of general equity jurisdiction.—Estate of Hinckley, 58 Cal. 457, 518; Morffew v. San Francisco, etc., R. R. Co., 107 Cal. 587, 594, 40 Pac. 810. When a trust vests, under the will, in the trustees, although they are named as executors, they are subject to equity and not to probate jurisdiction.— Jasper v. Jasper, 17 Or. 590, 22 Pac. 152, 155. Where an interested party would claim that certain letters, sent by a testator to the person named in the will as residuary legatee, were lost in the mail, and would establish these letters as lost codicils to the will making out a trust in his favor, he must proceed in the probate court.—Francoeur v. Beatty, 170 Cal. 740, 151 Pac. 123. It is the duty of the court in probate, upon proceedings for the distribution of a testator's estate, to determine whether or not a valid trust had been created by the will, and to determine and declare in the decree the scope and terms of such trust as it found valid; to select the trustees and to make dis-

tribution to them of the trust property, and also to determine what
other persons had legal or equitable rights to the distributable property of the estate, and the extent and nature of their interests.—Luscomb v. Fintzelberg, 162 Cal. 433, 123 Pac. 247.

(2) Retention of, for purpose of settling accounts.—By section 1699
of the Code of Civil Procedure of California, jurisdiction is retained by
the superior court "for the purpose of the settlement of accounts under
the trusts," where the trust created by will continues after the distribution. "Pending the execution of his trust," or at its determination, the
trustee may "render and pray for the settlement of his accounts as such
trustee, before the superior court in which the will is probated."—
McAdoo v. Sayre, 145 Cal. 344, 350, 78 Pac. 874; Estate of O'Connor,
2 Cal. App. 470, 84 Pac. 317. The probate court retains jurisdiction,
however, only for the one purpose of settling the accounts of the trustees. It was no doubt intended by the legislature that the trustees,
without any independent proceeding, or without being called upon by
the beneficiaries, might file their accounts in the court in which the
estate was administered and have it settled as a matter of convenience.
—Mackay v. San Francisco, 128 Cal. 678, 684, 61 Pac. 382. The statute
provides that the report accompanying the account must give the names
and post-office addresses, if known, of the cestuis que trust. But if the
report fails to do this, a writ of prohibition will not lie to prevent
further action of the court on the ground that the proceeding is void.
An appeal lies from any order that may be made in the proceeding, and
it will furnish a sufficient remedy to any person, aggrieved by the
action of the court, in attempting to proceed without jurisdiction.—
McAdoo v. Sayre, 145 Cal. 344, 350, 78 Pac. 874.

(3) Exclusiveness of jurisdiction.—A court of equity can not remove
a person who is named as executor, and also as trustee under a will,
from the executorship, for courts of probate have exclusive jurisdiction
over the appointment and removal of administrators and executors.—
In re Higgins' Estate, 15 Mont. 474, 28 L. R. A. 116, 39 Pac. 506, 515.
When a person has been appointed by a testator to execute the requests
of a will, and has also been vested by such testament with an interest
or a power over the property which, after the testator's death, he is to
perform for the benefit or to the use of another, it seems that the probate tribunal alone has jurisdiction.—In re Roach's Estate, 50 Or. 179,
92 Pac. 118, 121; McAdoo v. Sayre, 145 Cal. 344, 78 Pac. 874; Estate of
O'Connor, 2 Cal. App. 470, 84 Pac. 317; but see Mackay v. San Francisco, 128 Cal. 678, 685, 61 Pac. 382. When an executor lawfully secures
possession of the property of a decedent's estate, any intermeddling
therewith by a testamentary trustee, until the executor has been discharged, may be regarded by the probate court as the usurpation of
its authority; for, as the testator's debts, funeral expenses, etc., must
be paid before any trust can attach to the property, under a devise or
bequest thereof, the jurisdiction of such court necessarily precedes that

of an equity tribunal, and is therefore exclusive.—In re Roach's Estate, 50 Or. 179, 92 Pac. 118, 121.

REFERENCES.

Jurisdiction of probate court to administer testamentary trust.—See note 21 Ann. Cas. 255.

(4) **To determine what questions.**—In the settlement of a trustee's account, where the same person is named as trustee in the will, and is also the executor thereof, the probate court, having been invested by statute with a limited equitable jurisdiction, has the power, and it is its duty, whenever the power is invoked, to ascertain who is entitled to the trust estate already delivered by the trustee, and also that which yet remains to be delivered, and to make such orders as may be necessary to enable the trustee to make final settlement with the beneficiary, in safety, and to secure a final settlement of his account which will entitle him to a discharge.—McAdoo v. Sayre, 145 Cal. 344, 350, 78 Pac. 874, 876; Estate of O'Connor, 2 Cal. App. 470, 84 Pac. 317. The executors named as trustees in the will of deceased hold the property of the estate as executors until distribution thereof, and must account to the probate court for all property of the estate of said deceased received by them as such executors, and for their management of the same prior to distribution under the will of deceased; and it is for the court to determine what, if any, commissions they are entitled to receive for their services as executors of the will, and also to determine, in the settlement of their accounts, what moneys were properly expended by them in the discharge of their duties, and so chargeable to the estate represented by them, and whether they have exercised ordinary care in the management of the property of said estate, or whether they have mismanaged the same, or permitted waste thereof. It is also a question solely for the consideration of the probate court, whether an attorney should be appointed to represent absent or minor heirs, and, if so appointed, the amount of compensation to be allowed. That court also has jurisdiction to make an order setting apart a homestead for the widow, and to make an order for family allowance.—Dougherty v. Bartlett, 100 Cal. 496, 499, 35 Pac. 431.

REFERENCES.

Jurisdiction in equity.—See head-line 4, post.

(5) **Over trustees, to prevent mismanagement.**—Notwithstanding the powers and discretion given to a testamentary trustee, he is subject to the direction and control of a court of equity, which will have full power to prevent mismanagement of the estate and to correct any abuse of the trust.—Keeler v. Lauer, 73 Kan. 388, 85 Pac. 541; and the probate courts in California, in the exercise of their equitable jurisdiction, have undoubtedly the same power.—Estate of O'Connor, 2 Cal. App. 470, 84 Pac. 317, 319; Mackay v. San Francisco, 128 Cal. 678, 685, 61 Pac. 382. In the state of Washington, where trustees of the property of an estate, instead of executors, have been appointed by a

non-intervention will, the probate court has no jurisdiction of the questions involving the management of the estate; but the same are cognizable in equity, particularly where the complaining party is not a creditor of the estate, nor an heir within the meaning of that term as used in the statute.—City of Seattle v. McDonald, 26 Wash. 98, 66 Pac. 145, 147.

3. Executor and testamentary trustee.

(1) Object of law.—The object of section 1699 of the Code of Civil Procedure of California was to provide a convenient and effective method of procedure by which to secure a judicial determination, binding on all persons interested, that the estate is all accounted for, the accounts fully settled, and the trust executed.—McAdoo v. Sayre, 145 Cal. 344, 348, 78 Pac. 874. The policy of the probate law is to reach final settlement and distribution of the estate as soon as may be, whether the deceased died testate or intestate, and this should be no less the policy where the trustees are made by the will devisees in trust.—Estate of O'Connor, 2 Cal. App. 470, 84 Pac. 317, 320.

(2) Testamentary trustees. In general.—A testamentary trustee does not take by virtue alone of the decree of distribution. He takes as trustee under the will at the death of the testator.—Estate of O'Connor, 2 Cal. App. 470, 84 Pac. 317, 319. The estate which a trustee under a will takes is not necessarily a fee, but only such an estate as is required for the execution of his trust. He may be given an estate expressly limited in duration to the minority of the children.—Keating v. Smith, 154 Cal. 186, 97 Pac. 300. The trustees under a will may maintain an action for partition of the lands devised to them in trust, inasmuch as the devise carries the title, with the power to sell.— Noecker v. Noecker, 66 Kan. 347, 71 Pac. 815, 816. As to the execution of the trusts by trustees under a will, after distribution, the trustees are governed by the decree, and not by the will.—Goldtree v. Thompson, 79 Cal. 613, 20 Pac. 414. (Thornton J., dissenting.) See Goldtree v. Thompson, 79 Cal. 613, 22 Pac. 50. Where, under a will, certain trusts are created, performable within the state of Washington, and the trustees therein have in their possession within that state funds belonging to said trusts, and are in that state, using the same in strict compliance with the terms of such trust, all of the parties and all of the property involved are, for all the purposes of an action brought to restrain one of the executors from further prosecuting a proceeding in another state in relation to such trust, deemed to be personally within the jurisdiction of the trial court in which such proceedings to restrain are instituted, and jurisdiction to enjoin proceedings in such foreign state exists in the courts of the state of Washington. A distinction is drawn between a court of equity interfering with the action of courts of a foreign state, and restraining persons within its own jurisdiction from using foreign tribunals as instruments of wrong and oppression.—Rader v. Stubblefield, 43 Wash. 334, 10 Ann. Cas. 20, 86 Pac. 560, 566. A testamentary trustee is usually subject to the

directions of the court, and is freed from the statutory limitations imposed upon executors and administrators.—Jones v. Ross, 82 Or. 706, 162 Pac. 974. Where a married woman, dangerously ill, is intent upon conveying her property to her daughter, but is induced by her husband to forego this purpose and convey to him, promising that in that case he will devise to the daughter and a son all the property, both this and his own, the effect is that the husband becomes trustee for the daughter.—Huffine v. Lincoln, 52 Mont. 585, 160 Pac. 820.

REFERENCES.

Power of corporation to act as trustee.—See note 8 Am. & Eng. Ann. Cas. 1181.   .

(3) **Executors who are trustees under will. Distinct and separate capacities.**—One chosen to execute the directions of a will may be given two characters, that of an executor, and that of a trustee; but the duties of the one are separate and distinct from, and independent of, the other. When a person has been appointed by a testator to execute the requests of a will, and is also vested by such testament with an interest in, or a power over the property which, after the testator's death, he is to perform for the benefit of, or to the use of, another, the relation of the person so appointed to the estate, when legally committed to him, must, upon principle, be the same as if a branch of the duties were delegated to one person as executor and the remaining part to another as trustee. When the same person has been appointed by a will to perform such dual duty in respect to the property of an estate, no service is demanded of him as testamentary trustee, until he has fully performed his executorial obligation, and secured an order of the probate court discharging him, and liberating his bonds-. men. Where the same person is executor and trustee, he must give a bond in his character of trustee before he can exonerate himself from his liability as executor.—In re Roach's Estate, 50 Or. 179, 92 Pac. 118, 122. The relation of the testamentary trustee of the trust property is different from that of an executor.—Estate of O'Connor, 2 Cal. App. 470, 84 Pac. 317, 320. The fact that the two offices of trustee and of executor are held successively by the same individuals, does not give to them, in the exercise of one office, the power that had been conferred for the exercise of the other.—Goad v. Montgomery, 119 Cal. 552, 561, 63 Am. St. Rep. 145, 51 Pac. 681. It is the duty of the personal representative to preserve the trust funds, in common with the other funds which have come into his possession.—Elizalde v. Elizalde, 137 Cal. 634, 638, 66 Pac. 369, 70 Pac. 861; but executors, as such, are not trustees of an express trust, and the authority conferred upon them as such by the direction of the will, creates only such a trust as pertains to the office of executor.—Estate of Pforr, 144 Cal. 121, 125, 77 Pac. 825. If an executor, who is also appointed as trustee for the purpose of converting assets into cash and paying the proceeds over to a guardian, never assumes, as trustee, to perform such duty, but does assume to

perform it in the capacity of executor, the sureties on his bond are estopped from questioning the capacity in which he was acting.—Bellinger v. Thompson, 26 Or. 320, 37 Pac. 714, 718. Where the same person is named in a will both as executor and as trustee, and is by the terms of the will required to execute certain trusts created by the will, the two capacities, those of executor and trustee, are distinct and independent of each other, and his power and duty as a trustee does not begin until, as executor, he has ceased to have any control over the property.—Joy v. Elton, 9 N. D. 428, 83 N. W. 875; Goad v. Montgomery, 119 Cal. 552, 561, 63 Am. St. Rep. 145, 51 Pac. 681. As the duties of executors and trustees are separate and distinct, and as separate, distinct bonds must be given, the bonds given by executors will not protect the estate against the nonfeasance or misfeasance of the trustees, though they be the same individuals.—In re Higgins' Estate, 15 Mont. 474, 28 L. R. A. 116, 39 Pac. 506, 514.

(4) Duty, power, and liability of testamentary trustee. In general.— Where trust duties are imposed upon trustees as devisees and legatees under a will, such duties can not properly be assumed by the same persons who were named as executors under the will, and who have qualified as such executors, until the court has approved their accounts and ordered a distribution of the estate, in which order the executors may be directed to credit their accounts, as executors, with such of the estate as may be ordered transmuted to their accounts as trustees, or are otherwise authorized by the court to transfer the residue of the estate in their hands as executors to themselves as trustees.—In re Higgins' Estate, 15 Mont. 474, 28 L. R. A. 116, 39 Pac. 506, 517. If the same persons are named in the will as its executors and as trustees, their powers and duties as trustees do not begin until, as executors, they have ceased to have any control over the property, and the decree of distribution is to be considered for the purpose of ascertaining their powers.—Goad v. Montgomery, 119 Cal. 552, 561, 63 Am. St. Rep. 145, 51 Pac. 681. They do not become trustees, however, by virtue alone of the decree of distribution, but take as trustees under the will at the death of the testator; and while fuller and more complete powers and duties are devolved upon them by the decree of distribution, they have the same rights and powers, where they are devisees, as any other devisee, prior to distribution.—Estate of O'Connor, 2 Cal. App. 470, 84 Pac. 317, 319. Under the statutes of Washington, and where the will so provides, trustees appointed by the will are legally authorized to manage and settle the testator's estate, in the manner directed in his will, without the intervention of the court having probate jurisdiction. —Newport v. Newport, 5 Wash. 114, 31 Pac. 428. But in that state, if a non-intervention will makes the executor trustee of the estate for the purpose of paying creditors, it means such creditors only as qualify by proving their claims within the proper time as in other estates, and thereby making themselves beneficiaries of the trust.—Foley v. McDonnell, 48 Wash. 272, 93 Pac. 321, 323. A release of one's person from

legal guardianship does not imply the duty of a trustee to surrender, or of a married female minor to demand from such trustee, a legacy intrusted to his care and control for delivery to beneficiaries as soon as they severally attain lawful age.—Montoya De Antonio v. Miller, 7 N. M. 289, 19 L. R. A. 353, 34 Pac. 40. If a will commits to trustees the whole estate bequeathed to minor children, with directions to pay them the income for life, the petition of a guardian for the payment of the income to him will be dismissed, for the reason that the entire control of such estate is in the trustees.—In re Young's Estate, 17 Phila. 511. Where co-trustees are appointed by a testator for purposes set forth in the will, it is not competent for one of them to act alone.—In re Cornett's Estate, Cornett v. West, 102 Wash. 254, 173 Pac. 44. A testamentary trustee, where he is negligent or unfaithful, is answerable for the amount that the property coming into his hands ought to have yielded.—Candelaria v. Miera, 18 N. M. 107, 134 Pac. 820.

(5) Same. Investments.—Where a will requires the trustee to invest the funds of a trust created thereby in securities of the United States, the investment of such funds in Mexican bonds by the trustee was unauthorized and a violation of the terms of the will, and the amount so invested was property surcharged to the trustee.—International Trust Co. v. Preston, 24 Wyo. 163, 176, 156 Pac. 1128. Where an unauthorized investment of trust funds by the trustee was made long before the appointment of the guardian of minor cestui que trusts, the approval of such guardian of such unauthorized investment was without consideration and without authority from the court; such approval could not bind the minors, and would not release the trustee from liability.—International Trust Co. v. Preston, 24 Wyo. 163, 179, 156 Pac. 1128. To establish a ratification by the remainderman of an unauthorized investment of the trust estate by the trustees, such ratification must have been made with full knowledge of all the facts, as well as apprised of the law as to how those facts would be dealt with by the court.—International Trust Co. v. Preston, 24 Wyo. 163, 179, 156 Pac. 1128. It is not within the power of the court to change the terms of a trust created by will by approving unauthorized investments, and such approval through the approval of the annual reports of the trustees containing references to such unauthorized investment is not res judicata.—International Trust Co. v. Preston, 24 Wyo. 163, 180, 156 Pac. 1128.

(6) Same. Distribution of bequeathed property.—If property is bequeathed to a nephew, to distribute among such of the testator's nephews and nieces, and in such proportions as he shall deem proper, the distribution is to be made equally among all the nephews and nieces on failure of the nephew named to make the distribution.— Estate of Dewey, 45 Utah 98, Ann. Cas. 1918A, 475, 143 Pac. 124. If a testator makes a bequest to a nephew to distribute the subject-matter, or its proceeds, among "my nephews and nieces, and to such of them and in such proportions as he shall deem just and proper," the

legatee can not himself be a beneficiary of the distribution.—Estate of Dewey, 45 Utah 98, Ann. Cas. 1918A, 475, 143 Pac. 124.

(7) Same. Power under non-intervention will.—Whenever a non-intervention will reposes a trust in the executor beyond the mere proving of the will and procuring the order of solvency, the executor is in fact and essentially a trustee for all the purposes necessary to execute the terms of the will, whatever he may be called.—In re Cornett's Estate, Cornett v. West, 102 Wash. 254, 260, 173 Pac. 44. . A trustee in a non-intervention will possesses only the powers of a trustee, and those only in conjunction with his co-trustee, and he has no authority to borrow money in the name of the estate without the concurrence of his co-trustee, and where he does so he should be required personally to take up the loan and relieve the estate from all apparent obligation therefor.—In re Cornett's Estate, Cornett v. West, 102 Wash. 254, 261, 173 Pac. 44.

(8) Same. Authority as to lease.—Where by the terms of a trust created under a will, the trustees were not authorized to make a lease to extend beyond the expiration of their trust, a lease executed by them for a fixed term with the privilege of renewal, which extended beyond the expiration of such trust, becomes upon its termination void as to the residue of the term of the lease, and can not be enforced thereafter by the lessee against the person entitled to the estate.— South End Warehouse Co. v. Lavery, 12 Cal. App. 449, 107 Pac. 1008.

(9) Same. Release of surety company.—A surety company upon the bond of trustees under a will can not be relieved of further liability thereon upon its arbitrary demand to be so released, and without showing any fault, dereliction, or misconduct on the part of its principal.—Maryland Casualty Co. v. Klaber's Estate, 84 Or. 115, 164 Pac. 574.

(10) Duties of trustee can not be assumed until when.—The duties of an executor and trustee are separate and distinct from and independent of each other; and, until one is discharged from the former, and assumes the duties of the latter, his liability as executor still continues. —In re Roach's Estate, 50 Or. 179, 92 Pac. 118, 122.

(11) Duty of testamentary trustee before distribution.—While the testamentary trustee, who is a devisee under the will, may not, prior to distribution, deal with the property as fully as he may after distribution, there seems to be no reason why he may not exercise the rights and powers that any other devisee may exercise, in a proper case and under justifiable circumstances. That a duty respecting the trust property may devolve upon the trustee before distribution, and that a liability may attach to him for a failure to discharge that duty, rests both upon reason and authority. Whatever may have been the object of the testator in creating a testamentary trust and appointing one of the trustees as executrix, certain it is that he would not have appointed

trustees at all if he had intended to commit the management of the estate exclusively to the executrix, and that it should reach his heirs at law, or the beneficiaries of the trust, directly through distribution by the executrix, and the administration then to cease. The testator, having devised his estate to trustees, it becomes their duty, having accepted their trust, to obtain control of the trust property. When the trustees should take that step, where the will names one of them as executrix, or under what circumstances, it is not necessary to stipulate, as the court would be the ultimate judge on the case presented. But clearly it is the duty of the trustees to take such action, under all proper circumstances, and a failure to do so renders them liable to the beneficiaries, if loss of the estate or damage thereto ensues.— Estate of O'Connor, 2 Cal. App. 470, 84 Pac. 317, 320.

(12) Discharge of executor acting as trustee.—Where the same person is appointed both executor and trustee, it is difficult, though sometimes of importance, to determine when the office of executor has ceased and that of trustee has commenced. The rule appears to be that, if a part of the assets have clearly been set apart and appropriated by the executor to answer a particular trust, he will be considered to hold the fund as the trustee for that trust, and no longer as mere executor.—In re Higgins' Estate, 15 Mont. 474, 28 L. R. A. 116, 39 Pac. 506. But, where the same person is named as executor and also as trustee under a will, he is, as executor, chargeable until he gives a bond as trustee (unless exempted from giving such a bond), and settles his account in his administration, and charges himself as trustee. If a testator in his will appoints his executor to be a trustee, it is as if different persons had been appointed to each office. Executors must act, and executorial responsibility can only terminate after a compliance with the statute, and after a settlement, approved by the court, has been made, and a distribution and delivery up has been ordered by the court.—In re Higgins' Estate, 15 Mont. 474, 28 L. R. A. 116, 39 Pac. 506, 515, 517. An executor, who is also named in the will as trustee, after taking possession of assets belonging to the estate as executor, can not relieve himself and his bondsmen, with respect to such assets, by his own mere mental operations, and thereby cross the line dividing the two capacities in which he is acting, those of executor and trustee. To be discharged from his liability as an executor, he must take some affirmative action of a character which is open and notorious, such as would be an accounting in the court from which he received his letters as executor, and a discharge as executor.—Joy v. Elton, 9 N. D. 428, 83 N. W. 875.

(13) Trust with power to sell under will.—A will which does not confer upon executors the power to make any sale or disposition of the testator's estate, other than that they "shall have the property sold" at the expiration of two years after his death, and shall distribute the proceeds among his designated beneficiaries, does not devise the land to his executors in trust for the purposes of his will, but merely gives

them certain directions to be observed in carrying out its provisions. Such authority given by the testator creates only such a trust as pertains to the office of executor; and the sale which is thus directed is to be made by them as executors of his will, and as a part of their administration of the estate, and not as the trustees of an express trust, and is ineffective without a confirmation by the court.—Estate of Pforr, 144 Cal. 121, 125, 126, 77 Pac. 825. A will authorizing the executrix to sell any property of the estate at public or private sale, with or without notice, and without any order from the court, and which contains provisions for certain of the property not otherwise specifically disposed of, to go to the wife in trust for the children, and to be held by her until one of the daughters has arrived at the age of twenty-one years, does not, by the effect of these provisions, prevent an absolute disposition of the property until after the time the daughter° arrives at the required age, unless in the meantime, it can be sold at the prices fixed in the will. Nor does a will of this character devise the lands in trust with power to sell in execution of such trust, nor create any trust in her except such as pertains to her office as executrix.—Estate of Campbell, 149 Cal. 712, 715, 87 Pac. 573, 574; Bank v. Rice, 143 Cal. 265, 101 Am. St. Rep. 118, 76 Pac. 1020.

REFERENCES.

Sales under power in will.—See note § 592, head-line 38, ante.

(14) **Testamentary guardians.**—Where a general guardian is named as testamentary guardian in the purported will, he has, upon his appointment, authority to conduct litigation over the purported will, and where the will appears to be legal and fair upon its face, it is within the scope of his power and authority to pursue reasonable methods for the proof and probate of the instrument, and to incur expenses in connection therewith.—In re Brady's Estate, 10 Ida. 366, 79 Pac. 75, 76.

4. Jurisdiction in equity.—If the office of trustee is separate from, and independent of, the office of executor, a court of equity may remove the incumbent from the office of trustee, and leave him to act as executor; or, if he has completed his duties as executor, and is holding and administering the estate simply as trustee, a court of equity may remove him.—In re Higgins' Estate, 15 Mont. 474, 28 L. R. A. 116, 39 Pac. 506, 515. In an action against the trustee for an accounting and for fraud, a court of equity, and not the probate court has jurisdiction.—Courrier v. Johnson, 19 Colo. App. 94, 73 Pac. 882. In a case where extrinsic or collateral fraud upon the probate court has prevented a fair submission of the controversy, equity may give relief. Thus in an action to obtain a decree adjudging persons to hold property as trustees for heirs, the title to which they are alleged to have fraudulently procured in the administration of a decedent's estate as trustees of a void trust in the will; and, where the complaint is that the former proceedings were wholly sham, a mere fraudulent contrivance designed solely to give the appearance of legality and protection against attack to what was, in fact nothing but the taking of plaintiff's property without consideration and without any authority of law, and that they were carried through by means of false representations, and the real facts and purposes of the transaction were concealed from the probate court, such an imposition upon the jurisdiction of the probate court, to the injury of the absent property owners, from whom the nature of the transaction was concealed, and who were wholly in ignorance thereof, and could not have learned concerning the same from anything appearing on the face of the purported proceedings, clearly constitutes what is known as extrinsic fraud warranting equitable relief.—Campbell-Kawannanakoa v. Campbell, 152 Cal. 201, 92 Pac. 184, 187. In Dougherty v. Bartlett, 100 Cal. 496, 35 Pac. 431, the court expressed no opinion upon the question whether a suit in equity could be maintained, prior to the distribution of the estate, to compel executors named in the will, who were also appointed as trustees therein, to enforce the performance of a special trust, and for the accounting of the trust estate by the trustees thereof. A probate court has no power to require trustees, as such, to act. A court of equity alone can do that.—Gibson v. Kelly, 15 Mont. 417, 39 Pac. 506, 516. The superior court has jurisdiction to make an allowance to testamentary trustees for counsel fees in obtaining a distribution of the estate to the trustees.—Estate of O'Connor, 2 Cal. App. 470, 84 Pac. 317, 321. Where an ancestor, for a valuable consideration, orally promises that a descendant shall at his death receive the share of his estate indicated by the statute of descents and distributions, but dies leaving all his property to others by will, a court of equity may grant relief by impressing a trust upon the property in the hands of the beneficiaries of the will, which trust must be regarded as arising by implication of law, and therefore as not within the operation of the statute forbidding the creation of express trusts in real property otherwise than by writing.—Stahl v. Stevenson, 102 Kan. 844, 847, 171 Pac. 1164, 1168. A court of equity has no jurisdiction to construe a will where no trust is involved and the claims of the parties are of strictly legal interests in land.—Parks v. Boynaems, 21 Haw. 196. The title to trust funds is to be adjudicated in the district court, notwithstanding that the estate to which they relate is still in course of settlement in the probate court.—Yockey v. Yockey, 95 Kan. 519, 148 Pac. 665. It is a rule of equity that a legatee, that has become such by reason of having promised the testator to take and use the property for a certain purpose, may, on proof, be forced by the court to devote the legacy to that purpose, if a lawful one, and, if otherwise, to hold the property for the heirs.—Garner v. Purcell, 173 Cal. 495, 160 Pac. 682. One asserting that a legacy under a will is charged with a secret trust has the burden of establishing his assertion by evidence, either direct or circumstantial.—Garner v. Purcell, 173 Cal. 495, 160 Pac. 682. Equity will not permit a trust to fail for want of a trustee; and where the trust is not of such a nature that the performance of its duties is confined to the testamentary trustee because of the peculiar and personal confidence reposed in him by the testator, and where it appears that the main intention of the testator was that his estate should be administered according to the terms of the trust as created in his will, and that the duties thereof can be performed by a trustee other than the person named in the will, should a vacancy occur, the court may, and should, appoint a suitable person for that purpose.—Hill v. Hill, 49 Okla. 424, 152 Pac. 1122.

REFERENCES.

Jurisdiction of probate courts.—See head-line 2, subd. 4, ante.

5. Jurisdiction. Sale by trustees.—Where the persons named in a will as its executors are the same as those to whom the testator directed the property to be distributed in trust for his children, a power of sale conferred upon them as executors is not applicable to the property distributed to them as trustees under the will. Such a power terminates with their discharge as executors. The testator may have been willing to give this power of sale to the executors since he knew that every sale by them must be confirmed by the court before the title to the land would pass from his estate, while he might have been unwilling to vest the same persons with a power whose exercise would be without his supervision and control.—Goad v. Montgomery, 119 Cal. 552, 561, 63 Am. St. Rep. 145, 51 Pac. 681. But, while the law charges courts with the exercise of special care and control over proceedings involving the estates of deceased persons, and while the statute expressly provides for, and requires, the confirmation of the court in sales by executors and administrators of property belonging to the estates of deceased persons, yet, in the case of trust property, no such duty is expressly imposed upon the court by the law, and the court can not acquire jurisdiction to exercise or perform such duties in such a case by the mere agreement of the parties. There is no rule of law by which a court may or may not refuse to confirm a sale made by a trustee, and in the absence of express law requiring the confirmation of the sale by testamentary or other trustees of an express trust, the court must look to the instrument creating such officer and defining his duties for the purpose of ascertaining his authority over the trust property.—Murphy v. Union Trust Co., 5 Cal. App. 146, 89 Pac. 988, 990. Words in a will that direct, as to a sale, only "that all my property be sold by my executor as soon as conveniently after my decease," confer upon the executor the naked power to sell, which power must be exercised as executor and not as testamentary trustee.—Jones v. Ross, 82 Or. 706, 162 Pac. 974.

6. Discretionary trusts.—A trust is not void for the reason that it leaves to the discretion of the trustees the question as to how much income shall be used to support and educate the children of the testator.—Estate of Reigh, 144 Cal. 314, 77 Pac. 942, 944. Where a husband bequeathed all of his estate to his wife, and in the will made the following provision: "I recommend to her the care and protection of my mother and sister, and request her to make such provision for them as in her judgment will be best," it was held that a trust was imposed on the wife to make suitable provision for the mother and sister.— Colton v. Colton, 127 U. S. 300, 32 L. Ed. 138, 8 Sup. Ct. 1164. (Appealed from the circuit court of the United States for the district of California.) But where the trustees are to receive land and the profits of land, and apply the net proceeds of the same to the use and benefit of the beneficiaries to such extent and at such time as in their judgment shall be proper, such discretionary clause renders the trust void, because it is, in its main feature, not imperative, but merely discretionary.—Estate of Sanford, 136 Cal. 97, 100, 68 Pac. 494.

7. **Devises in trust.**—No general rule can be stated that will determine when a conveyance will carry with it the whole beneficial interest, and when it will be construed to create a trust; but the intention is to be gathered in each case from the general purpose and scope of the instrument.—Estate of Reigh, 144 Cal. 314, 318, 77 Pac. 942, 943. A devise in a will of personal and real property to the executor, "in trust for the execution of my will," following a bequest to the children of the testator providing that "one-half of all the moneys that may be realized from the sale of all my personal and real property of whatsoever kind, shall be paid to them respectively when they attain the age of 21," is a devise to the children, and each of them, and not to the executor; the right to the property passes to the children, but the right of immediate possession to the executor.—Rogers v. Strobach, 15 Wash. 472, 46 Pac. 1040, 1041. Under a will in which the residuum is bequeathed to trustees in trust,—"first, to pay over the income to the parties mentioned during the periods prescribed, and, whenever such proportions cease; then, second, in trust (not to pay over) for his or her children"; the children take the corpus of the property held in trust and not the revenue only.—Goldtree v. Thompson, 79 Cal. 613, 22 Pac. 50, 51. Where a testator devised property to his children and directed that the same be held by the executors in trust for them until they became of legal age, and where one of the children married before attaining legal age, it was held that, in the absence of an express intention in the will to the contrary, marriage can not change the status of minority, in the absence of statutory enactment, and that, under the terms of the will, such child is not entitled to her portion of the estate until arriving at legal age in the sense as employed by the testator.—Montoya De Antonio v. Miller, 7 N. M. 289, 19 L. R. A. 353, 34 Pac. 40. Where a provision was made in a will for a trust, reposing in the mother the control of the property devised to a daughter, and which was not created for the purpose of affecting the ownership of the lands, its sole object being to protect and preserve the property for the use of the devisee, such provision can not be held to change the character of the estate.—Kinkead v. Maxwell, 75 Kan. 50, 88 Pac. 523. A testator may set apart out of the money of his estate a reasonable amount with which to erect a monument over his grave.—Estate

of Koppikus, 1 Cal. App. 84, 81 Pac. 732, 733. A devise to trustees, to
convey and transfer property "absolutely" to a person named, is not
operative by reason of the presence of the word "absolutely" any more
than if such word was not used, since it is no word of conveyance and
means only that the transfer is unconditional, and of the entire estate.
Estate of Willson, 171 Cal. 449, 153 Pac. 927. Under a will whereby
on the expiration of a named trust a remainder shall go to the testator's grandchildren, in case there be such then in being, and in the
contrary case, to the living issue of his brothers and sisters, the devise
is one of alternative contingent remainders, primary and secondary,
and of expectancies rather than estates.—Lee v. Albro, Lee v. Murphy,
91 Or. 212, 178 Pac. 784.

8. Purposes of trust communicated orally.—Independently of the
statute of wills, where a testator bequeaths property in trust to a
legatee, without specifying in the will the purposes of the trust, and
at the same time communicates those purposes to the legatee orally, or
by unattested writings, and the legatee, either expressly or by silent
acquiescence, promises to perform the trust, and the trust itself is not
unlawful, a court of equity will raise a constructive trust in favor of
the beneficiaries intended by the testator.—Curdy v. Berton, 79 Cal.
420, 12 Am. St. Rep. 157, 5 L. R. A. 189, 21 Pac. 858.

9. Accounting.

(1) Distinction between accounts.—The court, upon the final accounting of a testamentary trustee who is a devisee under the will,
has the power to dispose of the entire matter of the trust by determining who is entitled to the property, and directing the trustee to
turn it over to the persons entitled thereto. But the accounts thus
settled are the accounts of the trustee acting in that capacity, and are
separate and distinct from the accounts of the executor, which latter
are settled before, or at the time of the final distribution.—Estate of
O'Connor, 2 Cal. App. 470, 475, 84 Pac. 317, 319.

(2) Duty and liability to account.—Every trustee who, by the terms
of the instrument creating the trust, has possession or control of the
trust property, is chargeable in his accounts with the whole of the
estate thus committed to his hands. Aside from his allowance for compensation and expenses, he can not, in his account, obtain credit against
this charge, except as he may dispose of the trust property to a beneficiary in the lawful execution of the trust, in which case he is
entitled to credit thereon for the property so disposed of; and when
he has thus disposed of all, his account then stands balanced and then
only has he fully accounted and become entitled to his discharge. He
may, if he chooses, exercise his own judgment as to the beneficiary,
and, upon the termination of the trust, deliver the property to such
person before presenting his accounts for settlement, or he may present
his account for compensation and expenses, and obtain settlement to

that extent before proceeding to make a settlement with the beneficiary, and then present for settlement a supplementary account for the balance. But, in either case, he has not fully accounted until he has thus disposed of the entire estate, and he will remain subject to be called on to account until this is done, and until the court, having jurisdiction of the accounts, has, upon a hearing, declared the account correct and the trust fully executed.—McAdoo v. Sayre, 145 Cal. 344, 348, 78 Pac. 874; Estate of O'Connor, 2 Cal. App. 470, 84 Pac. 317. Where a trustee under a will has advanced money, from time to time, to the beneficiary for living expenses, the burden is on him to prove the propriety and correctness of the items, and not on the beneficiary to disprove the correctness of the account.—Purdy v. Johnson, 174 Cal. 521, 163 Pac. 893. A trustee under a will who fails to keep and to render to beneficiaries full and true accounts of his dealings with the funds in his hands will have, on a settlement, all the presumptions against him.—Purdy v. Johnson, 174 Cal. 521, 163 Pac. 893.

(3) Same. For Interest.—While trustees under wills are not ordinarily liable for interest on moneys coming into their hands, unless they have improperly failed to invest them, they are not justified in borrowing more money than they need and charging the trust estate with interest on the borrowed amounts.—Purdy v. Johnson, 174 Cal. 521, 163 Pac. 893. Where a trustee under a will overdraws the trust bank account, so that interest accrues in the bank's favor which is compounded monthly, the trustee should not on making collections, withhold these, instead of depositing them as collected in order to keep down the interest account.—Purdy v. Johnson, 174 Cal. 521, 163 Pac. 893. Where notes are distributed to persons as trustees of a beneficiary of a will, it is their duty to collect them, and they are liable for the amount of them with interest unless they make it to appear that the failure to collect has been through no fault of theirs.—Purdy v. Johnson, 174 Cal. 521, 163 Pac. 893.

(4) Involves what determination. Power of court.—The settlement of the final account of the testamentary trustee, in accordance with the provisions of section 1699 of the Code of Civil Procedure of California, will necessarily involve a decision as to the effect of the instrument by which the trust was created, in order to ascertain who is entitled to the trust estate, and to determine whether or not the trustee has properly disposed of it in the execution of the trust. In many cases a determination of this question will be necessary upon the settlement of the current accounts, but in the case of a final account, showing complete execution of the trust, it will be necessary in every case. Furthermore, in the case of bills for an accounting in equity, the proceeding has always been to ascertain who was entitled to the balance found on hand, and to give judgment accordingly in his favor against the trustee. The forms of interlocutory decrees, in such cases, include a judgment of this character, to become effective on the approval of the account. These methods of procedure in probate and

in equity were obviously not established arbitrarily, but from the
necessities of the case, and because there could be no complete
accounting without establishing the right of the parties entitled to the
property accounted for when it was passed from the control of the
trustee.—McAdoo v. Sayre, 145 Cal. 344, 350, 78 Pac. 874; and see
Estate of O'Connor, 2 Cal. App. 470, 84 Pac. 317.

(5) **Calling trustees to account.**—Under section 1699 of the Code of
Civil Procedure of California, one who has no interest in the trust has
no standing in court to assail the account presented by the trustees,
or to move the court to require an account of them. The section in
question gives the right to apply for an order on the trustees for an
accounting exclusively to the beneficiary or his guardian. Even if this
provision were omitted, such right would still be limited to those
having some interest in the trust, or in the trust property. The trustee
then has the right, when an account presented by him is attacked by
objections at the hearing, or when he is cited to appear and to render
an account, to make the preliminary objection that the person who
thus invokes the action of the court with respect to himself, has no
interest in the property, and hence can not be heard to make his objection, or to demand an accounting. This objection of the trustee may
be disputed, and thereupon the court must determine whether or not
such party is a beneficiary, or is interested in the trust. So, also, there
may be two or more parties, each claiming to be beneficiaries. In such
a case the trustee may be justly entitled to credits if one of these
parties is the real beneficiary, which he could not have if the other
were the party interested. The account can not be settled without a
determination of the question as to which party is entitled. Considered as a mere matter of power, therefore, the court must have the
authority, in such a proceeding, whenever the necessity properly
arises, to determine who are the parties entitled as beneficiaries.—
McAdoo v. Sayre, 145 Cal. 344, 346, 78 Pac. 874. An accounting may
be ordered by the court.—In re Higgins' Estate, 15 Mont. 474, 28
L. R. A. 116, 39 Pac. 506, 517.

(6) **Compensation of trustee. In general.**—It is altogether too narrow a view of the testamentary trustee's relation to the trust property,
to say that it begins at distribution, and not before, and that his
expenses, incurred in the discharge of a duty he owes to the trust, are
limited to such as arise after distribution, and under no circumstances
to any expenses incurred prior to distribution. Whether the action of
the trustee in seeking distribution is reasonable or unreasonable, and
whether justified by the circumstances under which he acts, is a matter
for the court to determine. But, when he has been compelled to act,
and the necessity for action finds justification by his success, there is
neither justice nor reason in denying to the court the power to determine whether or not he should be paid for necessary expenses out of
the trust fund; and the court has jurisdiction to determine what, if
any, allowance should be made out of the trust estate for the services

of the trustee's counsel in procuring distribution of the property to the trustee; and where a claim is fairly before the court, the court does not lose jurisdiction by passing upon other items of the account of the trustee.—Estate of O'Connor, 2 Cal. App. 470, 84 Pac. 317, 319, 321. It is a principle of equity that one having a common interest with others in a trust fund, who successively maintains his suit to prevent diversion of the trust fund, may be reimbursed for costs and expenses, including attorneys' fees.—Estate of O'Connor, 2 Cal. App. 470, 84 Pac. 317, 321; Mitau v. Roddan, 149 Cal. 1, 6 L. R. A. (N. S.) 275, 84 Pac. 145. Where a declaration of trust is silent upon the subject of the trustees' compensation, the regulation or fixing thereof is controlled, by express authority of section 2274 of the Civil Code of California, by section 1618 of the Code of Civil Procedure of that state. If the sole duties of the trustee are to attend to the collection of rents, payment of taxes and insurance, and to keep the trust property insured, he is not entitled, upon the termination of the trust, to commissions upon the corpus of the trust property. Under such circumstances the proper basis of compensation ought properly to be the commissions upon the sums of money, or their equivalent, received or paid out by the trustee; and, in the case of successive trustees of the same trust estate, each one's claim to compensation must be adjusted with reference to the rights of his predecessors in the office of trustee.—In Matter of Leavitt, 8 Cal. App. 756, 97 Pac. 916. Where the court has already and correctly determined that the fixing of the trustee's fees must be deferred till the final settlement of the trust, the court which must finally pass upon the matter should not be hampered by a decree forestalling any phase of the question, by which the court attempts to determine what part of the trust period the fees should be fixed pursuant to the old and what part pursuant to the new statute, and that clause should have been omitted from the decree.—In re Cornett's Estate, Cornett v. West, 102 Wash. 254, 262, 173 Pac. 44.

(7) **Same. Under non-intervention will.**—The trustees under a nonintervention will are not entitled to fees as executors nor to anticipate the performance of the trust by paying themselves fees as trustees in advance of such performance.—In re Cornett's Estate, Cornett v. West, 102 Wash. 254, 261, 173 Pac. 44. Where a trustee under a nonintervention will personally performs services in their nature properly chargeable as current expenses of the estate, and for which he might have employed another, he is entitled to receive reasonable pay for his services when and as they are performed, and this rule is properly applied to the management by such trustee of an apartment house belonging to the trust estate.—In re Cornett's Estate, Cornett v. West, 102 Wash. 254, 262, 173 Pac. 44. A person named as "executor and trustee" in a non-intervention will, "in trust to pay the debts and funeral expenses" of the testator, and to hold the property until his youngest child should reach the age of twenty-one, is not entitled to

fees as an executor, his character being rather that of a trustee.—In re Cornett's Estate, Cornett v. West, 102 Wash. 254, 173 Pac. 44.

10. Distribution to trustees.

(1) **Power of court.**—A decree of distribution to trustees named in will, and who are also its executors, is the instrument by virtue of which the trustees receive the property in trust, and the powers and duties in regard to such property are to be measured by the terms of the decree. For the purpose of enabling the court to distribute the estate of a testator in accordance with his will, it is required to consider the will, as well as the estate left by him, and to construe its terms for the purpose of determining his intention, and to make its order or decree of distribution in accordance with such construction; but, as in the case of a judicial determination of any other instrument, the instrument is but evidence upon which the court acts in rendering its judgment. The judgment, however, is the final determination of the rights of the parties to the proceeding, and, upon its entry, their rights are thereafter to be measured by the terms of the judgment, and not by the instrument. Whether the distribution is to individuals, in their own right, or to hold for others under specified trusts, the rights of all parties interested in the estate are determined by the decree, and thereafter it becomes immaterial to consider whether the will has received a proper construction. The court may incorporate the provisions of the will in its decree, either in express terms, or by reference thereto. In such a case the terms of the will become the language of the decree, but it is still the decree, and not the will by which the rights of the parties are to be determined.—Goad v. Montgomery, 119 Cal. 552, 63 Am. St. Rep. 145, 51 Pac. 681. If the estate is distributed to the trustees appointed under the will, the decree of distribution is a determination of the validity of the trust and of the right of the trustees to take under the will.—Goldtree v. Allison, 119 Cal. 344, 346, 51 Pac. 561. The probate court has exclusive jurisdiction of the final distribution of the estate of a decedent, and such a decree of distribution, after due notice by the probate court, is conclusive upon a person who might have claimed that a share of the estate belonged to him, and this applies to a decree of distribution to trustees as well as to others.—Crew v. Pratt, 119 Cal. 139, 149, 51 Pac. 38; Goad v. Montgomery, 119 Cal. 552, 63 Am. St. Rep. 145, 51 Pac. 681. Whatever may be the rights of the devisee under the will, the decree of distribution becomes the law of the estate. The court having construed the trust created by the will, that judgment and decree is final and conclusive upon all parties and the court.—Kauffman v. Foster, 3 Cal. App. 741, 86 Pac. 1108, 1109.

(2) **Effect and validity of decree.**—A decree of distribution of an estate to trustees named in a will, upon certain trusts, is a conclusive adjudication of the validity of the disposition made by the testator.

interest under the will; the decree supersedes the will, and prevails over any provision therein which may be thought inconsistent with the decree.—Keating v. Smith, 154 Cal. 186, 97 Pac. 300. If a court, independently of the provisions of a will, has no power to create a valid trust, a decree, in so far as it may attempt to raise a trust, must be treated as a nullity.—McCloud v. Hewlett, 135 Cal. 361, 368, 67 Pac. 333. Where trust property is distributed to trustees "for a period, for the uses, trusts, and purposes hereinafter in this decree specified," such decree gives to the trustee an estate only for years.—Estate of Reith, 144 Cal. 314, 320, 77 Pac. 942.

(3) On death, trust devolves on whom.—A trust having devolved upon a devisee in his lifetime, by a decree of distribution, which trust has been accepted by him, devolves, in case of his death, upon his personal representatives.—Kauffman v. Foster, 3 Cal. App. 741, 86 Pac. 1108, 1110.

11. Removal of trustee.—Where the settlement of the matters out of which developed the spirit of antagonism between two trustees of a non-intervention will, has been disposed of by legal decree, and there is nothing to indicate that the offending trustee acted otherwise than in good faith on advice of counsel, it is not an abuse of discretion on the part of the court to refuse to remove such trustee.—In re Cornett's Estate, Cornett v. West, 102 Wash. 254, 264, 173 Pac. 44. In a proceeding by a trustee under a non-intervention will to have his co-trustee removed, the court has discretionary powers, if the point of difference has been already judicially passed upon.—In re Cornett's Estate, Cornett v. West, 102 Wash. 254, 173 Pac. 44.

12. Termination of trust.—Where three of the cestuis que trust, in a valid, active trust created by will, are minors, and the purposes of the trust are not impossible of fulfilment, and are not fully accomplished, the cestuis que trust can not by agreement terminate the trust, and thereby take title to and possession of the property, prior to the time fixed by the terms of the will.—Hill v. Hill, 49 Okla. 424, 152 Pac. 1122. Where a will creates a valid, active trust, and where the title to the property has passed to the trustee and not to the beneficiaries, the trustee and beneficiaries can not by agreement entered into, to terminate the trust features of the will and to divide the property, avoid the trust provisions of the will; the trust features of the will must be respected.—Hill v. Hill, 49 Okla. 424, 152 Pac. 1122. A trust in a will, to pay the principal and accumulated income to the beneficiary upon reaching the age of twenty-five years does no violence to the rule against perpetuities and the undue suspension of the power of alienation; though a limitation of years is fixed by the terms of the trust, its ultimate duration is manifestly based upon a life in being; should the beneficiary die, the trust absolutely determines for lack of a beneficiary.—Estate of Yates, 170 Cal. 254, 149 Pac. 555.

Probate Law—124

13. Discharge of trustees.—The power of the court is not exhausted when it has adjusted all disputes as to the correctness of any items of the account, and has allowed compensation and expenses to the trustee and declared the balance due; it still has power, and it is its duty, whenever the power is invoked, to ascertain who is entitled to the trust estate already delivered by the trustee, and also that which yet remains to be delivered, and to make such orders as may be necessary to enable the trustee to make final settlement with the beneficiary in safety, and to secure a final settlement of his account which will entitle him to his discharge.—McAdoo v. Sayre, 145 Cal. 344, 346, 350, 78 Pac. 874.

14. Actions. In general.—Any person having an interest in a trust under a will, or in the trust property, has the right to insist, in a proper proceeding, that the trust shall be maintained and executed according to the wishes of the settlor, as expressed by the terms of the will.—Hill v. Hill, 49 Okla. 424, 152 Pac. 1122.   In an action by judgment creditors to subject the personal interest of a trustee under a will, to the payment of their judgments, where such trustee sought without avail to interplead as such trustee, it was held, that, as in none of the proceedings, including the present action, were the grandchildren of the testator, who were the real beneficiaries under the will as to the land sought to be subjected to the payment of the said judgments, made parties, the defendant as trustee should have been permitted to show the actual facts concerning the title.—Niblack v. Knox, 101 Kan. 440, 444, 167 Pac. 741.   In an action by judgment creditors to subject the personal interest of a trustee under a will, to the payment of their judgment while as between the plaintiffs and the defendant personally, the latter might be deemed the owner of the land sought to be so subjected, his duties as trustee precluded him from acquiring any interest adverse to his trust or placing himself in any position where his self interest might conflict with his duties as trustee, and this would apply to a personal interest acquired under a decree in a suit in equity in which minor beneficiaries under the trust were not made parties.—Niblack v. Knox, 101 Kan. 440, 444, 167 Pac. 741.   The plaintiffs in an action by judgment creditors to subject the personal interest of a trustee under a will to the payment of their judgments, have no right to look to any interest in the land belonging to the grandchildren of the testator, who are the real beneficiaries under the will, but the latter should, if necessary, be made parties in order that their rights may be protected.—Niblack v. Knox, 101 Kan. 440, 444, 167 Pac. 741.   Where a married woman, owning separate property, was anxious, during a dangerous illness, to convey to her daughter, but consented to convey to her husband instead, on his promising to devise both this property and his own to the daughter and a son, the husband, on the death of the woman and the repudiation of his own promise, is in the position of the daughter's defaulting trustee, and the daughter is the real party in interest on whom devolves the privilege of maintaining appropriate action.—Huffine v. Lincoln, 52 Mont. 585, 160 Pac. 820. In such a case, the son can not, after the husband shall have repudiated the promise, waive, deny, and defend the wrong, in a suit brought by the daughter against her father as a defaulting trustee, and yet claim that, by the granting of relief to her, he will be cut off from sharing in his mother's estate.—Huffine v. Lincoln, 52 Mont. 585, 160 Pac. 820.

15. Same. Costs and expenses.—In a controversy over the income of the corpus of a trust estate created by a will, where it is adjudged that such income is a separate trust arising by operation of law in favor of one of the claimants, the costs, and expenses of such claimants, including attorneys' fees incurred in a suit to settle such controversy, are not allowable out of the principal or corpus of the trust estate.—Von Holt v. Williamson, 23 Haw. 245, 247. In a contest between various trusts created by a will, each particular trust should be charged with its own costs and attorneys' fees, which should not be charged to the residuary estate; this is particularly applicable to an unsuccessful claimant; he is not entitled to costs and expenses out of the corpus of the estate.—Von Holt v. Williamson, 23 Haw. 245, 247. In a contest between the trustees of a non-intervention will, which was one mainly personal to themselves, it was proper to refuse to order the costs thereof to be paid from the trust estate.—In re Cornett's Estate, Cornett v. West, 102 Wash. 254, 264, 173 Pac. 44.

16. Same. Appeal.—If one having the double capacity of executor and trustee, under the terms of a will, appeals from an order, made in a cause in which he appeared and could appear only as trustee, the fact that the notice of appeal is taken by him in the other capacity does not invalidate the appeal.—Estate of Rawitzer, 175 Cal. 585, 166 Pac. 581. Where a majority of the justices of the supreme court acting under a power of appointment in a will and without reward or pecuniary benefit, fill a vacancy among the trustees under such will, they are not thereby disqualified from sitting in a case on appeal involving the validity of the appointment.—Estate of Bishop, 23 Haw. 575, 578.

PART VIII.

ORDERS, DECREES, PROCESS, RECORDS, RULES OF PRACTICE, TRIALS, PROCEEDINGS TO TERMINATE LIFE ESTATES OR HOMESTEADS, OR COMMUNITY PROPERTY, ON OWNER'S DEATH IN CERTAIN CASES, NEW TRIALS AND APPEALS.

CHAPTER I.

ORDERS, DECREES, PROCESS, ETC.

(1972)

§ 834. Service of process on guardian.

§ 835. Disposition of life estate, or homestead, or community property, on owner's death, in certain cases.

§ 835.1 Death before patent is issued.

§ 836. Form. Petition for decree of termination of life estate.

§ 837. Form. Order for notice of hearing of petition.

§ 838. Form. Notice of petition for termination of life estate, and of time and place for hearing same.

§ 839. Form. Decree declaring life estate terminated.

§ 840. Form. Petition for decree vesting homestead or community property in survivor.

§ 841. Form. Decree declaring homestead vested in survivor

§ 842. Form. Decree declaring estate community property.

PROBATE PRACTICE AND PROCEDURE.

1. Notice of proceedings.
2. Same. Appearance and waiver of notice.
3. Citation.
   (1) Purpose of statute.
   (2) Petition for.
   (3) Order for.
   (4) Sufficiency of.
   (5) Compared with summons.
   (6) Service of.
   (7) Same. By publication.
   (8) Personal notice and service.
   (9) Obedience to, how enforced.
   (10) Trial after response.
4. Publication.
5. Rules of practice.
   (1) In general.
   (2) Nature of procedure.
   (3) Rescission of contracts.
   (4) Suit upon claim.
6. Attorney for absent heirs.
7. Trial.
   (1) In general.
   (2) Evidence.
   (3) By jury.
8. Orders and decrees.
   (1) In general.
   (2) Form of, signing, filing, etc.
   (3) To contain description when.
   (4) Failure to recite jurisdictional facts.

   (5) Correction of errors.
   (6) Signing of minutes.
   (7) Misleading entries. Clerk's register. Effect of.
   (8) Presumptions.
   (9) Entry of, in records.
   (10) Effect of. Protection of administrator.
   (11) Conclusiveness.
   (12) Are void when.
   (13) Vacating orders.
   (14) Collateral attack.
   (15) Obedience to, how enforced.
9. Costs.
   (1) In general.
   (2) Preliminary fees and charges.
   (3) Are statutory.
   (4) Discretion of court.
   (5) Do not include attorneys' fees.
   (6) No amendment of judgment to include.
   (7) Contesting probate of will.
   (8) Action against co-executor.
   (9) Presumption on appeal.
   (10) To be borne by estate, when.
10. Disposition of life estates, etc.
11. New trial and appeal.
12. Relief in equity.

§ 808. Orders and decrees to be entered in minutes.

Orders and decrees made by the court, or a judge thereof, in probate proceedings, need not recite the existence of facts, or the performance of acts, upon which the

jurisdiction of the court or judge may depend, but it shall
only be necessary that they contain the matters ordered
or adjudged, except as otherwise provided in this title.
All orders and decrees of the court or judge must be
entered at length in the minute-book of the court.—
Kerr's Cyc. Code Civ. Proc., § 1704.

ANALOGOUS AND IDENTICAL STATUTES.
The * indicates identity.
Arizona—Revised Statutes of 1913, paragraph 1073.
Colorado—Mills's Statutes of 1912, section 8052.
Idaho—Compiled Statutes of 1919, section 7755.
Montana*—Revised Codes of 1907, section 7701.
Nevada—Revised Laws of 1912, section 6103.
North Dakota—Compiled Laws of 1913, section 8582.
Oklahoma—Revised Laws of 1910, section 6489.
South Dakota—Compiled Laws of 1913, section 5949.
Utah—Compiled Laws of 1907, sections 4036, 4039.
Wyoming—Compiled Statutes of 1910, section 5458.

§ 809.   **Form.   Order fixing time for hearing.**
[Title of court.]

[Title of estate.]   No. ——.[1] Dept. No. ——.
                                      [Title of form.]

——, the administrator [2] of the estate of ——, deceased, having this day filed in this court his ——,[3]—
    It is ordered, That ——,[4] the —— day of ——, 19—,
at —— o'clock in the forenoon [5] of said day, and the
court-room of said court, at the court-house [6] in said
county [7] of —— be, and the same are hereby, fixed as the
time and place for the hearing upon said ——.[8]
    Dated ——, 19—.   ——, Judge of the —— [9] Court.

Explanatory notes.—1 Give file number. 2 Or, executor. 3 State what.
4 Day of week. 5 Or, afternoon. 6 Giving location. 7 Or, city and
county. 8 State what. 9 Title of court.

§ 810.   **Form.   Order continuing hearing**
[Title of court.]

[Title of estate.]   No. ——.[1] Dept. No. ——.
                                      [Title of form.]

    The hearing of —— [2] in said estate is continued to

——,³ the —— day of ——, 19—, at —— o'clock in the forenoon⁴ of said day.

Dated ——, 19—.   ——, Judge.

Explanatory notes.—1 Give file number.   2 State what.   3 Day of week.   4 Or, afternoon.

§ 811. How often publication to be made.

When any publication is ordered, such publication must be made daily, or otherwise as often during the prescribed period as the paper is regularly issued, unless otherwise provided in this title. The court, or a judge thereof, may, however, order a less number of publications during the period.—*Kerr's Cyc. Code Civ. Proc.*, § 1705.

ANALOGOUS AND IDENTICAL STATUTES.
The * indicates identity.

Arizona*—Revised Statutes of 1913, paragraph 1074.
Idaho*—Compiled Statutes of 1919, section 7756.
Montana*—Revised Codes of 1907, section 7702.
Oklahoma*—Revised Laws of 1910, section 6490.
South Dakota*—Compiled Laws of 1913, section 5950.
Utah—Compiled Laws of 1907, section 4027.

§ 812. Form. Affidavit of publication.

[Title of court.]

[Title of estate.]   { No. ——.1   Dept. No. ——.
                                       {   [Title of form.]

State of ——,   }
                     } ss.
County² of ——,   }

——, of said county³ and state, having been first duly sworn, deposes and says:

That he is, and at all times embraced in the publication herein mentioned was, the principal clerk of the printers and publishers⁴ of ——, a newspaper⁵ printed and published daily (Sundays excepted) in said county;⁶

That deponent, as such clerk,⁷ during all times mentioned in this affidavit, has had, and still has, charge of all the advertisements in said newspaper; and

That a notice, of which the annexed is a true printed

copy, was published in the above-named newspaper on the following dates, to wit, ——;[8] being for a period of once a week for four (4)[9] weeks; and further deponent saith not.   ——

Subscribed and sworn to before me this —— day of ——, 19—.   ——, Notary Public,[10] etc.

Explanatory notes.—1 Give file number. 2 Or, City and County. 3 Or, city and county. 4 Or, printer or foreman. 5 "Of general circulation," if the statute requires it. 6 Or, city and county. 7 Or, printer or foreman. 8 Give date of each publication. 9 "Successive" weeks, if such is the fact. 10 Or other officer taking the oath.

§ 813. Recorded decree or order to impart notice from date of filing.

When it is provided in this title that any order or decree of the court, or a judge thereof, or a copy thereof, must be recorded in the office of the county recorder, from the time of filing the same for record, notice is imparted to all persons of the contents thereof.—*Kerr's Cyc. Code Civ. Proc.*, § 1706.

ANALOGOUS AND IDENTICAL STATUTES.
The * indicates identity.

Arizona*—Revised Statutes of 1913, paragraph 1075.
Idaho*—Compiled Statutes of 1919, section 7757.
Montana*—Revised Codes of 1907, section 7703.
Oklahoma*—Revised Laws of 1910, section 6491.
South Dakota*—Compiled Laws of 1913, section 5951.
Utah—Compiled Laws of 1907, section 4040.
Wyoming*—Compiled Statutes of 1910, section 5459.

§ 814. Citation, how directed and what to contain.

Citations must be directed to the person to be cited, signed by the clerk, and issued under the seal of the court, and must contain:

1. The title of the proceeding;

2. A brief statement of the nature of the proceeding;

3. A direction that the person cited appear at a time and place specified.—*Kerr's Cyc. Code Civ. Proc.*, § 1707.

ANALOGOUS AND IDENTICAL STATUTES.

The * indicates identity.

Arizona*—Revised Statutes of 1913, paragraph 1076.
Idaho*—Compiled Statutes of 1919, section 7758.
Montana*—Revised Codes of 1907, section 7705.
North Dakota—Compiled Laws of 1913, sections 8549, 8550.
Oklahoma—Revised Laws of 1910, section 6492.
South Dakota—Compiled Laws of 1913, section 5952.
Utah—Compiled Laws of 1907, section 4034.
Washington—Laws of 1917, chapter 156, page 643, section 3.
Wyoming*—Compiled Statutes of 1910, section 5460.

§ 815. Form. Citation.

[Title of court.]

[Title of estate.]   {No. ——.1 Dept. No. ——.
                              {   [Title of form.]

The People of the State of ——.

To ——, Greeting.

By order of this court, You are hereby cited and required to appear before the judge of this court, at the court-room of Department No. —— thereof, at the court-house [2] in the county [3] of ——, on ——,[4] the —— day of ——, 19—, at —— o'clock in the forenoon [5] of that day, then and there to show cause, etc., ——.

Witness, the Honorable ——, judge of the —— [6] court, in and for the county [7] of ——, state of ——, with the seal of said court affixed, this —— day of ——, 19—.

[Seal]   Attest: ——, Clerk.

                                By ——, Deputy Clerk.

Explanatory notes.—1 Give file number. 2 Designate its location.
3 Or, city and county. 4 Day of week. 5 Or, afternoon. 6 Title of court.
7 Or, city and county.

§ 816. Form. Citation to show cause why letters should not be revoked for neglect to make return of sale.

[Title of court.]

[Title of estate.]   .   {No. ——.1 Dept. No. ——.
                              {   [Title of form.]

The People of the State of ——.

To ——, Greeting.

By order of this court, You, the said ——, administrator [2] of the estate of ——, deceased, are hereby cited to appear before the ——[3] court of the county [4] of ——, state of ——, at the court-house,[5] on ——,[6] the —— day of ——, 19—, at —— o'clock a. m.,[7] of that day, to show cause, if any you have, why your letters [8] should not be revoked for neglecting to make a return of sale of the property of such estate within thirty (30) days [9] after the making of such sale.

In witness whereof, I, ——, clerk of the court aforesaid, have hereunto set my hand and affixed the seal of. said court, this —— day of ——, 19—.

[Seal]   ——, Clerk of the —— Court.

                     By ——, Deputy Clerk.

Explanatory notes.—1 Give file number. 2 Or, executor, etc., according to the fact. 3 Title of court and department thereof, if any. 4 Or, city and county. 5 Give location of court-house. 6 Day of week. 7 Or, p. m. 8 Of administration, or letters testamentary, according to the fact. 9 Or other time prescribed by the statute.

§ 817. Citation, how issued.

The citation may be issued by the clerk upon the application of any party, without an order of the judge, except in cases in which such order is by the provisions of this title expressly required.—*Kerr's Cyc. Code Civ. Proc.*, § 1708.

ANALOGOUS AND IDENTICAL STATUTES.
The * indicates identity.
Arizona*—Revised Statutes of 1913, paragraph 1077.
Idaho*—Compiled Statutes of 1919, section 7759.
Montana*—Revised Codes of 1907, section 7706.
Oklahoma—Revised Laws of 1910, section 6492.
Utah—Compiled Laws of 1907, section 4034.
Washington—Laws of 1917, chapter 156, page 643, section 8.
Wyoming—Compiled Statutes of 1910, section 5461.

§ 818. Citation, how served.

The citation must be served in the same manner as a summons in a civil action.—*Kerr's Cyc. Code Civ. Proc.*,

ANALOGOUS AND IDENTICAL STATUTES.

The * indicates identity.

Arizona*—Revised Statutes of 1913, paragraph 1078

Idaho*—Compiled Statutes of 1919, section 7760.

Montana*—Revised Codes of 1907, section 7707.

Nevada—Revised Laws of 1912, section 6105.

North Dakota—Compiled Laws of 1913, sections 8551, 8554, 8556.

Oklahoma*—Revised Laws of 1910, section 6493.

South Dakota*—Compiled Laws of 1913, section 5953.

Utah—Compiled Laws of 1907, section 4034.

Washington—Laws of 1917, chapter 156, page 644, sections 4 and 5.

Wyoming*—Compiled Statutes of 1910, section 5462.

§ 819. Form. Certificate of service of citation.

[Title of court.]

[Title of estate.]   {No. ——.¹ Dept. No. ——.
                                       {   [Title of form.]

I, ——, sheriff of the county ² of ——, do hereby certify:

That I served the within citation on the within-named —— on the —— day of ——, 19—, by delivering to him personally, in said county ³ of ——, a copy of said citation.

Dated ——, 19—.   ——, Sheriff.

Fees, $——.

Explanatory notes.—1 Give file number. 2, 3 Or, city and county.

§ 820. Form. Proof of personal service of citation.

[Title of court.]

[Title of estate.]   {No. ——.¹ Dept. No. ——.
                                       {   [Title of form.]

——, being duly sworn, says:

That he is over twenty-one years of age, not interested in the above-entitled estate, and is competent to be a witness in the matter of said estate; that on the —— day of ——, 19—, he served the citation, directed by this court to be served, upon ——, ——, and ——, the persons named in said citation, by delivering to each of them per-

sonally, in said county[2] and state, a copy of said citation, the original of which is hereto annexed.

Subscribed and sworn to before me this —— day of
——, 19—.

——, County Clerk of said County[3] of ——.[4]

Explanatory notes.—1 Give file number. 2, 3 Or, city and county. 4 Or
other officer authorized to take the oath.

§ 821. Personal notice, when to be given by citation.

When personal notice is required, and no mode of
giving it is prescribed in this title, it must be given by
citation.—*Kerr's Cyc. Code Civ. Proc.*, § 1710.

ANALOGOUS AND IDENTICAL STATUTES.

The * indicates identity.

Arizona*—Revised Statutes of 1913, paragraph 1079.
Idaho*—Compiled Statutes of 1919, section 7761.
Montana—Revised Codes of 1907, section 7708.
Oklahoma*—Revised Laws of 1910, section 6494.
South Dakota*—Compiled Laws of 1913, section 5954.
Utah—Compiled Laws of 1907, section 4034.
Washington—Laws of 1917, chapter 156, page 643, section 3.
Wyoming*—Compiled Statutes of 1910, section 5463.

§ 822. Citation to be served five days before return.

When no other time is specially prescribed in this title,
citations must be served at least five days before the return day thereof.—*Kerr's Cyc. Code Civ. Proc.*, § 1711.

ANALOGOUS AND IDENTICAL STATUTES.

The * indicates identity.

Arizona*—Revised Statutes of 1913, paragraph 1080.
Idaho*—Compiled Statutes of 1919, section 7762.
Montana*—Revised Codes of 1907, section 7709.
Nevada—Revised Laws of 1912, section 6107.
North Dakota—Compiled Laws of 1913, sections 8550, 8559.
Oklahoma*—Revised Laws of 1910, section 6495.
South Dakota*—Compiled Laws of 1913, section 5955.
Utah—Compiled Laws of 1907, section 4034.
Washington—Laws of 1917, chapter 156, page 644, section 5; Reming-
ton's 1915 Code, section 1283.
Wyoming—Compiled Statutes of 1910, section 5464.

§ 823.   One description of realty is sufficient.

When a complete description of the real property of an estate sought to be sold has been given and published in a newspaper, as required in the order to show cause why the sale should not be made, such description need not be published in any subsequent notice of sale, or notice of a petition for the confirmation thereof. It is sufficient to refer to the description contained in the publication of the first notice, as being proved and on file in the court.—*Kerr's Cyc. Code Civ. Proc.,* § 1712.

ANALOGOUS AND IDENTICAL STATUTES.

The * indicates identity.

Arizona*—Revised Statutes of 1913, paragraph 1081.
Idaho*—Compiled Statutes of 1919, section 7763.
Montana*—Revised Codes of 1907, section 7710.
Oklahoma*—Revised Laws of 1910, section 6496.
South Dakota*—Compiled Laws of 1913, section 5956.
Wyoming*—Compiled Statutes of 1910, section 5465.

§ 824.   Rules of practice generally.

Except as otherwise provided in this title, the provisions of part two of this code are applicable to and constitute the rules of practice in the proceedings mentioned in this title.—*Kerr's Cyc. Code Civ. Proc.,* § 1713.

ANALOGOUS AND IDENTICAL STATUTES.

The * indicates identity.

Arizona*—Revised Statutes of 1913, paragraph 1082.
Idaho*—Compiled Statutes of 1919, section 7764.
Montana*—Revised Codes of 1907, section 7711.
Utah—Compiled Laws of 1907, section 3778.
Wyoming—Compiled Statutes of 1910, section 5466.

§ 825.   New trials and appeals.

The provisions of part two of this code, relative to new trials and appeals, except in so far as they are inconsistent with the provisions of this title, apply to the proceedings mentioned in this title; provided, that hereafter a motion for a new trial in probate proceedings can be made only in cases of contests of wills, either before or

after probate, in proceedings under section one thousand
six hundred and sixty-four of this code and in those cases
where the issues of fact, of which a new trial is sought,
were tried by a jury or were of such character as to
entitle the parties to have them tried by a jury whether
or not they were so tried.—*Kerr's Cyc. Code Civ. Proc.*,
§ 1714.

ANALOGOUS AND IDENTICAL STATUTES.
The * indicates identity.

Arizona—Revised Statutes of 1913, section 1083.
Colorado—Mills's Statutes of 1912, paragraph 8043.
Idaho*—Compiled Statutes of 1919, section 7765.
Montana—Revised Codes of 1907, section 7712.
North Dakota—Compiled Laws of 1913, sections 8595-8598.
South Dakota—Compiled Laws of 1913, section 5966.
Wyoming—Compiled Statutes of 1910, section 5467.

§ 826. Appeal must be taken when.

The appeal may be taken at any time after the order,
decree, or judgment is made or rendered, but not later
than sixty days after the same is entered in the minute-
book of the court as provided in section one thousand
seven hundred and four.—*Kerr's Cyc. Code Civ. Proc.*,
§ 1715.

ANALOGOUS AND IDENTICAL STATUTES.
No identical statute found.

Arizona—Revised Statutes of 1913, paragraph 1233.
Colorado—Mills's Statutes of 1912, section 8043.
Idaho—Compiled Statutes of 1919, section 7766.
Kansas—General Statutes of 1915, section 4676.
Montana—Revised Codes of 1907, section 7713.
North Dakota—Compiled Laws of 1913, section 8601.
Oklahoma—Revised Laws of 1910, section 6504.
South Dakota—Compiled Laws of 1913, section 5965.

§ 827. Issues joined, how tried and disposed of.

All issues of fact joined in probate proceedings must
be tried in conformity with the requirements of article
two, chapter two, of this title, and in all such proceedings
the party affirming is plaintiff, and the one denying or
avoiding is defendant. Judgments therein, on the issue

joined, as well as for costs, may be entered and enforced by execution or otherwise by the court as in civil actions. —*Kerr's Cyc. Code Civ. Proc.,* § 1716.

ANALOGOUS AND IDENTICAL STATUTES.

The * indicates identity.

Arizona*—Revised Statutes of 1913, paragraph 1084.
Colorado—Mills's Statutes of 1912, section 8043.
Idaho*—Compiled Statutes of 1919, section 7767.
Montana*—Revised Codes of 1907, section 7714.
Nevada—Revised Laws of 1912, section 6109.
North Dakota—Compiled Laws of 1913, section 8576.
Oklahoma—Revised Laws of 1910, section 6497.
South Dakota—Compiled Laws of 1913, section 5957.
Utah—Compiled Laws of 1907, section 4041.

§ 828. Court to try case when. Trial of issues.

If no jury is demanded, the court must try the issues joined, and sign and file its decision in writing, as provided in sections six hundred and thirty-two and six hundred and thirty-three. If, on written demand, a jury is called by either party, and the issues are not sufficiently made up by the written pleadings on file, the court, on due notice to the opposite party, must settle and frame the issues to be tried, and submit the same, together with the evidence of each party, to the jury, on which they must render a verdict.

NEW TRIAL.—Either party may move for a new trial, upon the same grounds and errors, and in like manner, as provided in this code for civil actions.—*Kerr's Cyc. Code Civ. Proc.,* § 1717.

ANALOGOUS AND IDENTICAL STATUTES.

No identical statute found.

Arizona—Revised Statutes of 1913, paragraph 1085.
Colorado—Mills's Statutes of 1912, section 8043.
Idaho—Compiled Statutes of 1919, section 7768.
Montana—Revised Codes of 1907, section, 7715.
Nevada—Revised Laws of 1912, section 6109.
North Dakota—Compiled Laws of 1913, section 8576.
Oklahoma—Revised Laws of 1910, section 6497.
South Dakota—Compiled Laws of 1913, section 5957.
Utah—Compiled Laws of 1907, section 4042.
Wyoming—Compiled Statutes of 1910, section 5468.

§ 829.   Form.   Order appointing attorney.

[Title of court.]

[Title of estate.]   { No. ——.¹   Dept. No. ——.
                                      {   [Title of form.]

It being shown to the court, That an instrument which purports to be the last will of ——, deceased, has been filed herein; that probate of the same has been petitioned for; and that there are minor heirs who are interested in said estate, —

It is ordered, That —— be, and he is hereby, appointed as an attorney to represent —— and ——,² who are the minor heirs of said deceased, in all proceedings of said estate.

Dated ——, 19—.   ——, Judge of the —— Court.

Explanatory notes.—1 Give file number. 2 Give names.

§ 830.   Decrees, what to be recorded.

When a judgment or decree is made, setting apart a homestead, confirming a sale, making distribution of real property, or determining any other matter affecting the title to real property, a certified copy of the same must be recorded in the office of the recorder of the county in which the property is situated.—*Kerr's Cyc. Code Civ. Proc.*, § 1719.

ANALOGOUS AND IDENTICAL STATUTES.
The * indicates identity.
Arizona*—Revised Statutes of 1913, paragraph 1086.
Idaho*—Compiled Statutes of 1919, section 7770.
Montana*—Revised Codes of 1907, section 7717.
Oklahoma*—Revised Laws of 1910, section 6499.
South Dakota*—Compiled Laws of 1913, section 5959.
Utah—Compiled Laws of 1907, section 4040.

§ 831.   Costs, by whom paid in certain cases.

When it is not otherwise prescribed in this title, the superior court, or the supreme court, on appeal, may, in its discretion, order costs to be paid by any party to the proceedings, or out of the assets of the estate, as justice may require.   Execution for the costs may issue out of the superior court.—*Kerr's Cyc. Code Civ. Proc.*, § 1720.

ANALOGOUS AND IDENTICAL STATUTES.
The * indicates identity.
Alaska—Compiled Laws of 1913, sections 1600, 1602, 1603.
Arizona*—Revised Statutes of 1913, paragraph 1087.
Idaho*—Compiled Statutes of 1919, section 7771.
Montana*—Revised Codes of 1907, section 7718.
Nevada—Revised Laws of 1912, section 6109.
North Dakota—Compiled Laws of 1913, sections 8586, 8623.
Oklahoma—Revised Laws of 1910, section 6513.
Oregon—Lord's Oregon Laws, section 1137.
South Dakota—Compiled Laws of 1913, section 5979.
Utah—Compiled Laws of 1907, section 4045.
Wyoming*—Compiled Statutes of 1910, section 5470.

§ 832. Commitment for contempt. Removal. Appointment.

Whenever an executor, administrator, or guardian is committed for contempt in disobeying any lawful order of the court, or a judge thereof, and has remained in custody for thirty days without obeying such order, or purging himself otherwise of the contempt, the court may, by order reciting the facts, and without further showing or notice, revoke his letters and appoint some other person entitled thereto executor, administrator, or guardian in his stead.—*Kerr's Cyc. Code Civ. Proc.*, § 1721.

ANALOGOUS AND IDENTICAL STATUTES.
The * indicates identity.
Arizona*—Revised Statutes of 1913, paragraph 1088.
Idaho*—Compiled Statutes of 1919, section 7772.
Montana*—Revised Codes of 1907, section 7719.
Oklahoma*—Revised Laws of 1910, section 6500.
South Dakota*—Compiled Laws of 1913, section 5960.
Utah*—Compiled Laws of 1907, section 3840.

§ 833. Form. Order revoking letters for contempt, and appointing some other person administrator, executor, or guardian.

[Title of court.]

[Title of estate.] 　　　　{ No. ——.1　Dept. No. ——.
　　　　　　　　　　　　　 { 　　[Title of form.]

It appearing that this court,[2] on the —— day of ——, 19—, made an order directing the administrator [3] of said

Probate Law—125

estate to file ——[4] within ——,[5] which order was disobeyed; that said ——, the administrator[6] aforesaid,
was cited to answer for contempt of this court[7] because
of such disobedience; that, after a full hearing, he was
committed to the custody of the sheriff of said county
until he obeyed such order; and that he has remained in
such custody for thirty (30) days[8] without obeying said
order, or otherwise purging himself of the contempt, —

It is ordered, That the letters[9] issued to said ——, as
such administrator,[10] be, and they are hereby, revoked,
and that ——, be appointed administrator[11] of said
estate in his stead; and the clerk of this court is directed
to issue letters[12] to the said —— upon his filing a bond
as required by law, in the sum of —— dollars ($——),
to be approved by the judge of this court.

Dated ——, 19—.   ——, Judge of the —— Court.

Explanatory notes.—1 Give file number. 2 Or, a judge thereof. 3 Or,
the executor, or guardian, etc., according to the fact. 4 State what
order directed. 5 State time within which act was to have been done.
6 Or, executor, or guardian, as the case may be. 7 Or, a judge thereof.
8 Or, other time prescribed by the statute. 9 Of administration, guardianship, or letters testamentary, according to the fact. 10, 11 Or, executor, or guardian, as the case may be. 12 Of administration, guardianship, or letters testamentary, as the case may be.

§ 834.   Service of process on guardian.

Whenever an infant, insane, or incompetent person has
a guardian of his estate residing in this state, personal
service upon the guardian of any process, notice, or order
of the court concerning the estate of a deceased person in
which the ward is interested, is equivalent to service
upon the ward, and it is the duty of the guardian to attend to the interests of the ward in the matter. Such
guardian may also appear for his ward and waive any
process, notice, or order to show cause which an adult or
a person of sound mind might do.—*Kerr's Cyc. Code Civ.
Proc.*, § 1722.

ANALOGOUS AND IDENTICAL STATUTES.
The * indicates identity.
Arizona*—Revised Statutes of 1913, paragraph 1089.
Idaho*—Compiled Statutes of 1919, section 7773.
Montana*—Revised Codes of 1907, section 7720.
North Dakota—Compiled Laws of 1913, section 8552.
Oklahoma*—Revised Laws of 1910, section 6568.
South Dakota*—Compiled Laws of 1913, section 5961.
Utah*—Compiled Laws of 1907, section 4046.
Wyoming*—Compiled Statutes of 1910, section 5471.

§ 835. Disposition of life estates or homesteads, or community property, on owner's death in certain cases.

If any person has died or shall hereafter die who at the time of his death was the owner of a life estate which terminates by reason of the death of such person; or if such person at the time of his death was one of two or more persons holding land in joint tenancy, which land by reason of his death vests absolutely in the surviving joint tenant or tenants; or if such person at the time of his death was the spouse of a person owning land upon which either spouse had declared a homestead, the home-stead interest of which deceased person absolutely terminated by reason of his death.

INTERESTED PERSONS MAY PETITION.—Any person interested in the land, or in the title thereto, in which such estate or interest was held, may file in the superior court of the county in which the land or any part thereof is situated, his verified petition setting forth such facts, and thereupon and after such notice by publication or otherwise as the court may order.

DECREE OF COURT.—Provided, that notice shall be given in each county where any part of said land is situated in the same manner as in the county where said petition is filed, the court shall hear such petition and the evidence offered in support thereof, and if upon such hearing it shall appear that such estate or interest so terminated or vested, the court shall make a decree to that effect, and thereupon a certified copy of such decree shall be recorded in the office of the county recorder of each county in which any part of said land is situated, and thereafter shall have the same effect as a decree of final distribution so recorded.

INHERITANCE TAX.—Provided, that if such estate or interest was a joint tenancy, any inheritance tax which is due and payable by reason of the death of such deceased person, must be fully paid before such decree is made; and the amount of said inheritance tax shall be fixed, and said tax shall be paid, in the same manner as in the case of an administration upon the estate of a decedent.— *Kerr's Cyc. Code Civ. Proc., § 1723.*

ANALOGOUS AND IDENTICAL STATUTES.

No identical statute found.

Idaho—Compiled Statutes of 1919, section 7774.
Montana—Revised Codes of 1907, section 7721.
Oregon—Laws of 1915, chapter 247, page 357; act giving effect to certain conveyances to life tenant.
Wyoming—Compiled Statutes of 1910, section 5472.

§ 835.¹ Death before patent is issued.

In any case where a person has entered, or shall have entered, any lands in the United States and has died, or shall die, before patent for the same was issued, or shall have been issued, and patent thereafter was, or shall have been issued to the heirs of such decedent, any person interested in such lands as heir at law, or the successor in interest of such heir at law or the administrator, or executor, or heir at law of any of them if deceased, may file a petition in the superior court of the state of California in and for the county wherein said land or any part thereof is situate, setting forth the date of the death of such deceased entryman, the date and the issuance of such patent, and that the same was issued to the heirs at law of such deceased entryman, and the land described therein and the names, ages, and residences, if known, of the heirs at law of such deceased entryman (or if any such heirs are dead, or their residence is unknown, such facts shall be stated), and a request that a decree be entered in said court establishing who are or were the heirs at law of such deceased person.

Notice of the time and place for the hearing of said petition must be given by the clerk by posting notices thereof in three or more public places in said county at least ten days prior to the date fixed for said hearing.

At any time before the date fixed for such hearing any person interested in said lands may answer said petition and deny any of the matters contained therein.

At the time fixed for such hearing or at such time thereafter as may be fixed by the court, the court must hear the proofs offered by the petitioner and the person answering the same, if there be any answer thereto, and must make a decree conformable to the proofs. Such decree shall have the same force and effect as decrees entered in accordance with the provisions of part iii, title xi of this code.—*Kerr's Cyc. Code Civ. Proc.,* § 1724.

§ 836. Form. Petition for decree of termination of life estate.
[Title of court.]

[Title of proceeding.] 　　　{ No. ——.¹   Dept. No. ——.
　　　　　　　　　　　　　　　　{ 　　[Title of form.]

To the Honorable the —— Court of the County ² of ——.

The petition of —— respectfully shows:

That he is interested in the real property hereinafter described and in the title thereto; and is now the owner in fee ³ thereof;

That heretofore and during the life of such life tenant, one ——⁴ was the owner of a life estate in said property which terminated at his death; and

That said ——⁵ died on or about the —— day of ——, 19—, at ——,⁶ and thereupon his life estate in said property ceased and terminated.

Said real property is situated in the county ⁷ of ——, state of ——, and is described as follows: ——.⁸

Wherefore petitioner prays for a decree of this court to the effect that the life estate formerly held by the said ——⁹ in the real property above described, absolutely terminated at his death on the —— day of ——, 19—.

——, Attorney for Petitioner.   ——, Petitioner.

[Add usual verification.]

Explanatory notes.—1 Give file number. 2 Or, City and County. 3 Or, state other interest of petitioner. 4, 5 Give name of deceased life tenant. 6 Give place of death. 7 Or, city and county. 8 Give description. 9 Give name of life tenant. The petition is addressed to the superior court—not the probate court.

§ 837.   Form.   Order for notice of hearing of petition.

[Title of court.]

[Title of estate.]   { No. ——.1   Dept. No. ——.
                          {   [Title of form.]

It is ordered, That notice of the hearing and pendency of the petition filed herein for a decree determining a life estate ² be given by a summons to be issued by the clerk in the form of a summons in a civil action directed to —— and ——, etc.,³ heirs of said deceased, and, generally to all other persons interested in the estate of said deceased, and to be served upon said heirs in the same manner and for the same time as a summons in a civil action is required to be served, and to be published for two successive weeks in a newspaper published in said county ⁴ for notice to those interested other than said heirs.

And it appearing to the court that said ——, above-named, resides out of the state of ——, at ——,⁵ ——

It is ordered, That service of said summons be made on him by publishing the same at least once a week for two months in the ——, the newspaper most likely to give him notice.⁶   ——, Judge of the —— Court.

Dated ——, 19—.

Explanatory notes.—1 Give file number. 2 Or, to determine the disposition of a homestead, or of community property where the same has, by reason of death, vested in a surviving husband or wife. 3 Give the names of persons named as heirs in the petition. 4 Or, city and county. 5 Name the place; or, that his residence is unknown; or, that he can not, after due diligence, be found within the state; or, that he has departed from this state; or, that he conceals himself to avoid the service of summons. 6 And, if ordered, where residence is known, that a copy of said summons be mailed, postpaid, directed to said —— at his said place of residence.

§ 838. **Form. Notice of petition for termination of life estate, and of time and place for hearing same.**

[Title of court.]

[Title of matter.]1   { No. ——.2 Dept. No. ——.
                        {   [Title of form.]

Notice is hereby given, That —— and ——, who are persons interested in the title to and in the real property hereinafter described, have filed a verified petition in said court and matter, setting forth that said —— was the owner of a life estate in said real property, which absolutely terminated by reason of her death on ——, 19—, and praying the court to make a decree to that effect; and that the court has fixed ——,3 the —— day of ——, 19—, at —— o'clock in the forenoon 4 of said day, and the court-room of said court,5 as the time and place for the hearing of said petition.

The said real property is situated in the county 6 of ——, state of ——, and is particularly described as follows, to wit: ——;7 and said petition is here and hereby specially referred to for all particulars thereby shown.

Dated ——, 19—.   ——, Clerk.

                              By ——, Deputy Clerk.

——, Attorneys for Petitioners.8

Explanatory notes.—1 As, In the Matter of the Life Estate of Mary Stiles in Certain Real Property Terminated by Reason of Her Death. 2 Give file number. 3 Day of week. 4 Or, afternoon. 5 Designate location of court-room. 6 Or, city and county. 7 Describe the property. 8 Give address.

§ 839.   Form.   Decree declaring life estate terminated.

[Title of court.]

[Title of estate.]   { No. ——.¹   Dept. No. ——.
                                                     {   [Title of form.]

Now comes ——, the petitioner herein, by ——, his attorney, and proves to the satisfaction of the court that he filed his petition herein on the —— day of ——, 19—, for an order declaring a life estate terminated; that thereupon the court by order prescribed the notice to be given of the pendency and hearing thereof; and that in compliance with said order, notice of the pendency and hearing of said petition was duly given by ——;² and the time of notice prescribed having elapsed, and no person having appeared to contest or oppose said petition, the court, after hearing the evidence, finds that the allegations of said petition are true, and that the prayer thereof ought to be granted.

It is therefore adjudged, decreed, and determined by the court, That the said —— died on the —— day of ——, 19—, and that his life estate, right, title, and interest in the land hereinafter described, has, by reason of his death, absolutely terminated; that neither the heirs of said deceased, namely, ——, and ——,³ nor any other person or persons claiming under said deceased, by descent, succession, or otherwise, have any right, title, interest, or estate in said land; and that the same is now vested in fee simple in ——, free from any and all right, title, or claim, by or on account of any person claiming under said deceased.

The said land is situated in the county of ——,⁴ state of ——, and is particularly described as follows, to wit: ——.⁵

Entered ⁶ ——, 19—.   ——, Clerk.

                                         By ——, Deputy.

Explanatory notes.—1 Give file number. 2 Insert manner of notice as prescribed in order therefor and as proved. 3 Give the names. 4 Or, city and county. 5 Describe the land. 6 Orders or decrees need not be signed. See § 77, ante.

§ 840. **Form. Petition for decree vesting homestead or community property in survivor.**

[Title of court.]

[Title of proceeding.] $\Big\{$ No. ——.¹ Dept. No. ——.
[Title of form.]

To the Honorable the —— .Court of the County ² of ——.

The petition of —— respectfully shows:

That he is interested in the real property hereinafter described and in the title thereof as hereinafter stated;

That prior to the ——³ day of ——, 19—, petitioner and his wife, ——,⁴ had intermarried and had become husband and wife and so remained until the death of said wife ⁵ as hereinafter stated;

That the real property hereinafter described was acquired by said spouses during said marriage relation and was community property of said spouses;

That on or about said —— day of ——, 19—, said real estate was duly selected and recorded as a homestead by declaration of homestead duly executed, acknowledged, and recorded in volume —— of Homesteads, at page ——, in the office of the county recorder of the county ⁶ of —— ;⁷

That on or about the —— day of ——, 19—, said —— died at ——,⁸ and thereupon said homestead ⁹ and all title thereto vested and now remains in your petitioner as surviving spouse of said marriage;

That the following is the name and residence of each of the persons who would be an heir at law of the separate property of the deceased, to wit:

Name.   Residence.   Relationship.

——   ——   ——

——   ——   ——

That the following is a statement of all claims of creditors against the deceased with the name and residence of each creditor, namely:

Name.	Residence.	Statement of claim.
——	——	——
——	——	——

Said real property is situated in the county of ——,
state of ——, and is described as follows, to wit: ——.[10]

Wherefore petitioner prays for a decree of this court to
the effect that the title to said homestead [11] vested in the
petitioner on said —— day of ——, 19—, and for such
other or further order as may be meet.

——, Attorney for Petitioner. ——, Petitioner.

[Add usual verification.]

Explanatory notes.—1 Give file number. 2 Or, City and County.
3 Give date of recording homestead; or, if application is for community
property, give date of deed by which earliest parcel was acquired.
4 Or, husband, giving name of deceased spouse. 5 Or, husband. 6 Or,
city and county. 7 In case the application is for community property,
not homestead, this entire paragraph should be omitted. 8 Give place
of death. 9 Or, community property. 10 Give description. 11 Or, community property.

Notice of the filing of such petition should be given as the court may
order; and it would not be improper to order that notice be given by
the personal service of a citation upon all persons residing within the
state, who are named in and shown by the petition filed to be interested
therein, including creditors, at least ten days prior to the hearing of
said petition, and by publication, etc.

§ 841. Form. Decree declaring homestead vested in survivor.

[Title of court.]

| [Title of estate.] | { | No. ——.1 Dept. No. ——. |
| | { | [Title of form.] |

Now comes ——, the petitioner herein, by ——, her [2]
attorney, and proves to the satisfaction of the court that
she filed her [3] petition herein on the —— day of ——,
19—, for an order declaring the homestead vested in the
survivor; that thereupon the court by order prescribed
the notice to be given of the pendency and hearing
thereof; and that in compliance with said order, notice of
the pendency and hearing of said petition was duly given
by ——;[4] and the time of notice prescribed having
elapsed, and no person having appeared to contest or

oppose said petition, the court, after hearing the evidence, finds that the allegations of said petition are true and that the prayer thereof ought to be granted.

It is therefore adjudged, determined, and decreed by the court, That the said —— died on the —— day of ——, 19—; that at the time of his [5] death the said petitioner was the wife [6] of said ——, deceased; that upon the death of said deceased all his [7] right, title, interest, and estate in the lands hereinafter described became vested in the said —— as surviving wife [8] of said deceased, the said land constituting a homestead duly selected and recorded in the lifetime of said deceased by said ——, and being the community property [9] of said deceased, and his [10] said wife,[11] ——; and that neither of the other heirs at law, namely, ——,[12] nor any person interested in said estate, other than said petitioner did, upon the death of said deceased, receive or become vested by descent, succession, or otherwise, of any right, title, interest, or estate in said land, and that the same is now vested in fee simple in ——,[13] free from any and all right, title, or claim, by or on behalf of any other person claiming under said deceased.

The said land is situated in the county [14] of ——, state of ——, and is particularly described as follows: ——.[15]

Entered [16] ——, 19—.   ——, Clerk.

                                                    By ——, Deputy.

Explanatory notes.—1 Give file number. 2, 3 Or, his. 4 Insert manner of notice as prescribed in order therefor and as proved. 5 Or, her. 6 Or, husband. 7 Or, her. 8 Or, husband. 9 Or, the separate property of the person selecting or joining in the selection of the same. 10 Or, her. 11 Or, husband. 12 Give the names. 13 The survivor. 14 Or, city and county. 15 Describe the land. 16 Orders or decrees need not be signed. See § 77, ante.

§ 842. Form. Decree declaring estate community property.

[Title of court.]

[Title of estate.]   { No.——.[1] Dept. No.——.
                                     {   [Title of form.]

Now comes ——, the petitioner herein, by ——, his at-

torney, and proves to the satisfaction of the court that
he filed his petition herein on the ——— day of ———, 19—,
for a decree declaring an estate to be community property; that thereupon the court by order prescribed the
notice to be given of the pendency and hearing thereof;
and that in compliance with said order, notice of the pendency and hearing of said petition was duly given by
———;[2] and the time of notice prescribed having elapsed,
and no person having appeared to contest or oppose said
petition, the court, after hearing the evidence, finds that
the allegations of said petition are true, and that the
prayer thereof ought to be granted.

It is therefore ordered, adjudged, and decreed by the
court, That the land hereinafter described was, during
the lifetime of said deceased, and at the time of her death,
the community property of ———,[3] deceased, and said
———, her husband, who were then, and at the time the
same was acquired by said deceased, husband and wife;
and that the said land became, at the death of the said
deceased, the property of said husband, and is now
vested in the said ———, free of all right, title, claim, or
demand of any other person claiming under the said ———,
deceased, as heir or otherwise.

The said land is situated in the county [4] of ———, state
of ———, and is particularly described as follows: ———.[5]

Entered [6] ———, 19—.   ———, Clerk.

By ———, Deputy.

Explanatory notes.—1 Give file number. 2 Insert manner of notice
as prescribed in order therefor and as proved. 3 Give name of deceased
wife. 4 Or, city and county. 5 Describe the land. 6 Orders or decrees
need not be signed. See § 77, ante.

PROBATE PRACTICE AND PROCEDURE.

1. Notice of proceedings.	(4) Sufficiency of.
2. Same. Appearance and waiver of notice.	(5) Compared with summons.
	(6) Service of.
3. Citation.	(7) Same. By publication.
(1) Purpose of statute.	(8) Personal notice and service.
(2) Petition for.	(9) Obedience to, how enforced.

1. Notice of proceedings.—All persons who are interested in the disposition of estates are entitled to some kind of notice of proceedings which affect their interests, and to a hearing or an opportunity to be heard; but, if the statute provides for reasonable notice and an opportunity to be heard, it is not open to the objection that it does not provide "due process of law."—State v. District Court, 41 Mont. 357, 366, 109 Pac. 438. The giving of notice required by section 7645, Rev. Codes of Montana, is necessary to clothe the court with jurisdiction of the person of those interested in the estate; the giving of the notice is indispensable, and, if not observed, the order of allowance will not be binding.—Estate of Davis, 35 Mont. 273, 280, 88 Pac. 957. On the hypothesis that probate proceedings are proceedings in rem, parties interested in the res are entitled to notice, and, without the opportunity thus given them to be heard, they can not be deprived of legitimate property rights.—Estate of Davis, 22 Haw. 436, 439.

2. Same. Appearance and waiver of notice.—Service of summons is waived by a general appearance; and where the notice required in probate proceedings serves the purpose of a summons in ordinary actions, it follows, by analogy, that the giving of notice in such proceedings may be rendered unnecessary by the appearance of the parties and their participation in the proceedings. In such case, the purpose of the notice has been served, and one who has appeared and taken part in the hearing will not be heard to say that the court had no jurisdiction to determine his rights.—In re Davis' Estate, 33 Mont. 539, 88 Pac. 957, 958. The giving of notice in probate proceeding may be rendered unnecessary by the appearance of the parties and their participation in the proceedings.—Estate of Davis, 35 Mont. 273, 280, 88 Pac. 957. A paper which is, in effect, a petition for administration, if signed by others interested besides the petitioner and containing their express consent to the appointment and also their waiver of notice or citation in respect to the proceedings, "from the commence-ment to the final disposition thereof," amounts to an appearance by such persons.—Fischer v. Dolwig, 29 N. D. 561, 151 N. W. 431, 166 N. W. 793, 796. A person interested in an estate may, in advance of another's filing a petition for administration, consent to such filing and waive all notice and citation.—Fischer v. Dolwig, 29 N. D. 561, 151 N. W. 431, 166 N. W. 793, 796.

3. Citation

(1) **Purpose of statute.**—The statute providing for citations by the probate court for the discovery of assets of estates of decedents, con-templates the examination of persons, but not the adjudication of rights or claims of right which may be asserted or involved; juris-diction in that regard is confined to the district court, in an action brought for the purpose.—State (ex rel. Cohen) v. District Court, 53 Mont. 210, 162 Pac. 1053.

(2) **Petition for.**—A petition, for a citation under section 7505, Rev. Codes of Montana, is fatally defective if it fails to allege that any one of the persons cited has, in his possession, or has knowledge of, any deeds or writings which contain evidences of the right, title, interest, or claim of the decedent.—State v. District Court, 35 Mont. 318, 320, 89 Pac. 62. (Citing Code Civ. Proc., § 2571.)

(3) **Order for.**—An order directing a citation to issue to heirs is good and valid, though it is silent as to the number of weeks that it shall be published; in that case, the statutory time would be implied.—Finley v. Morrison, 87 Or. 160, 169 Pac. 781.

(4) **Sufficiency of.**—The statute whereby the citation, to be served upon the person for whom it is proposed to have a guardian appointed as being of unsound mind, must contain "a brief statement of the nature of the proceeding," is sufficiently complied with by a citation, to show cause why a guardian should not be appointed according to "petition on file."—In re Espinosa's Estate and Guardianship, 179 Cal. 189, 175 Pac. 896. If a citation to heirs informs them when and where they are required to appear, and the time so designated is at a day of the regular term of the county court, an order based thereon is not void though the citation may be irregular in the particulars men-tioned.—Stadelman v. Miner, 83 Or. 348, 155 Pac. 708, 163 Pac. 585, 163 Pac. 983. It is not fatal to a citation, intended to bring an executor into court, though there is therein no designation of the representa-tive capacity of the person cited.—In re Murphy's Estate, 98 Wash. 548, 168 Pac. 175. A citation that does not give the required time for appearance is insufficient.—Smith v. Whiting, 55 Or. 393, 400, 106

Pac. 791. A citation to appear on the day that publication thereof is completed is not in accord with the statute; it is less than the required statutory time after the service.—Smith v. Whiting, 55 Or. 393, 402, 106 Pac. 791.

(5) **Compared with summons.**—The object of a citation, in probate proceedings, is to secure the attendance of parties, but, if this is accomplished by voluntary appearance, the object of the statute is fully subserved.—Rutenick v. Hamakar, 40 Or. 444, 67 Pac. 196, 201. It is simply a notice, which may be molded to suit the occasion, and not a process which a party may sue out or not, and which, having sued out, he can serve when he pleases, provided it be done within the statutory time for the service of process. The citation notifies the parties to appear at a time mentioned to show cause. As the court has the power to set the hearing, the citation may of course issue; but there is no alias citation like an alias summons. Unlike a summons, the length of the notice may be prescribed by the court. Otherwise it is five days; and, as a rule, its functions are very unlike those of a summons. The statute in reference to citations shows on its face that no provision in regard to summons applies to citations; and it has been held, in a proceeding to revoke the probate of a will, where the contest was commenced within one year from the probate, by the filing of a valid petition for the revocation thereof, and the issuance of a citation, but which was defectively served, that the court had jurisdiction of a motion to dismiss the proceeding, after the lapse of one year, for want of service of the citation, and that a new citation could issue to the party upon whom the defective service was made, notwithstanding the lapse of one year.—San Francisco, etc., Asylum v. Superior Court, 116 Cal. 443, 453, 48 Pac. 379. Compare Bacigalupo v. Superior Court, 108 Cal. 92, 40 Pac. 1055.

(6) **Service of.**—A citation is to be served in the same manner as a summons:—Ashurst v. Fountain, 67 Cal. 18, 6 Pac. 849. A citation, like a summons, is properly served by delivering a copy thereof to the defendant personally.—Hannah v. Green, 143 Cal. 19, 21, 76 Pac. 708. If an administrator has been cited to render his final account, the sureties on his undertaking can not be held liable, unless service of the citation has been made on him.—Ashurst v. Fountain, 67 Cal. 18, 6 Pac. 849. Where the order admitting a will to probate, and appointing an executor, recited, among other things, that due proof was made to the satisfaction of the court; that notice had been given of the time appointed for proving said will and for hearing said petition; that citations had been duly issued and served, as required by previous order of the court; and that it appeared to the court that notice had been given according to law to all parties interested, etc.; these recitals, in the absence of any other record evidence of an order that a citation issue to the heirs residing in the county, or of its service, are sufficient to warrant the presumption that such order had been regularly made and that the citations had been duly issued and served.

It might be otherwise, if it appeared of record, that an insufficient order relating to the citation had been made, or that the citation issued was not in substantial compliance with the order, or that the mode of service was fatally defective, for, in such a case, it is not to be presumed that a different order was made, or a different citation issued, or that service was made in a different mode, where the record does not show, or purport to show, the form or substance of the order, or of the citation, or the mode of service. Hence the presumption that the order to issue and to serve a citation was regularly made, and that the citation was regularly issued and served, does not contradict the record, in any respect, but is in perfect accord with the recitals of the order admitting the will to probate.—Moore v. Earl, 91 Cal. 632, 635, 27 Pac. 1087.

(7) Same. By publication.—A citation may be served by publication, on one who has departed from the state, in the same manner as a summons in a civil action.—Spencer v. Houghton, 68 Cal. 82, 8 Pac. 679; Trumpler v. Cotton, 109 Cal. 250, 41 Pac. 1033; Heisen v. Smith, 138 Cal. 216, 94 Am. St. Rep. 39, 71 Pac. 180. In probate or guardianship proceedings, the citation itself issues only on the order of the court.—Heisen v. Smith, 138 Cal. 216, 218, 94 Am. St. Rep. 39, 71 Pac. 180. In a proceeding in a probate court to compel an accounting by a guardian, who has left the state, and who can not be personally served, neither the guardian nor the sureties are bound by the decree rendered upon the account in the absence of service by publication.— Spencer v. Houghton, 68 Cal. 82, 8 Pac. 679. But upon such service being made, a settlement, in the guardian's absence, is binding on his sureties.—Trumpler v. Cotton, 109 Cal. 250, 41 Pac. 1033. A citation to a guardian, to make a "report" of his administration, will be construed as requiring the rendition of a final account, where the ward has become of age.—Heisen v. Smith, 138 Cal. 216, 218, 94 Am. St. Rep. 39, 71 Pac. 180. Delay of the clerk in issuing a citation does not affect the validity of the proceedings, provided it is issued before the publication is commenced. If a citation has already been issued, and a new citation is the same in terms as the old one, except as to the change of the return day, it is simply an amendment of the original citation, and is to be so regarded.—Heisen v. Smith, 138 Cal. 216, 217, 218, 94 Am. St. Rep. 39, 71 Pac. 180. The omission of the word "seal" in the copy of a citation published is not material. From the nature of things, the seal itself can not be copied in a printed publication, and hence all that is required is that its presence on the original should be sufficiently indicated. This is usually done by writing the word "seal" in the margin; but it may be otherwise sufficiently indicated, as by the certificate of the clerk contained in the published copy that the seal was attached to the original.—Heisen v. Smith, 138 Cal. 216, 218, 94 Am. St. Rep. 39, 71 Pac. 180. While, in this state, the transaction of "judicial business" on Sundays, or holidays, is forbidden, the publication of a citation in a weekly newspaper

issued only on Sundays does not come within such prohibition, because such publication is a ministerial act, and not a transaction of "judicial business." Hence such publication does not affect the jurisdiction of the court.—Heisen v. Smith, 138 Cal. 216, 218, 94 Am. St. Rep. 39, 71 Pac. 180. The statute which provides for the publication of a citation to heirs, on petition of the administrator to sell the real estate to pay the debts of the estate, makes the period to be "not less than four weeks, or for such further time as the court or judge may prescribe"; but, provided the day fixed for hearing is after the four weeks, it is immaterial if the time of publication stated in the order extends beyond that day.—Finley v. Morrison, 87 Or. 160, 169 Pac. 781.

(8) **Personal notice and service.**—When personal notice is required to be given, and no mode of giving it is otherwise prescribed by the statute, it must be given by citation. Personal notice is distinguishable from notice given by publication.—Ashurst v. Fountain, 67 Cal. 18, 19, 6 Pac. 849; Spencer v. Houghton, 68 Cal. 82, 86, 8 Pac. 679; San Francisco, etc., Asylum v. Superior Court, 116 Cal. 443, 451. Personal service of a citation upon resident heirs can not be shown by parol testimony.—Smith v. Whiting, 55 Or. 393, 402, 106 Pac. 791.

(9) **Obedience to, how enforced.**—A citation may be issued to require the performance of an act, and disobedience may sometimes be enforced by arrest and imprisonment.—San Francisco, etc., Asylum v. Superior Court, 116 Cal. 443, 451, 48 Pac. 379, referring to various sections of the Code of Civil Procedure of California. Whenever the executor or administrator of an estate fails to perform any duty required by law, the probate court has the power, by proper orders, to direct and compel the performance of it; and any person interested in the estate as a creditor, or otherwise, may invoke the aid of the court to compel the performance of the duties required by law of executors or administrators.—Stratton v. McCandliss, 32 Kan. 512, 4 Pac. 1018, 1021.

(10) **Trial after response.**—Under the liberal practice in Washington, as to the form of actions, where a citation has been issued upon a petition, and response is made thereto, and a dismissal of the proceeding asked for, upon the ground that the court can not hear it as a probate proceeding, it is not necessary to sustain a demurrer and to dismiss the proceeding on that ground, but the petition may be treated as in the nature of a complaint, issues may be framed thereunder, and the cause be tried without requiring another statement of the same facts, under some other form or name. And, if it develops that it is not a probate proceeding, it will not be treated as such.—In re Murphy's Estate, 30 Wash. 1, 70 Pac. 107, 108.

4. **Publication.**—The statute making provision as to how often publication is to be made applies not only to publications directed by the court, but to those ordered in probate proceedings by the statute, and the word "ordered," in the statute, was probably intended to

Probate Law—126

have the same meaning as the word "required."—Estate of Cunningham, 73 Cal. 558, 559, 15 Pac. 136. The phrase, "three weeks successively," in a statute which directs that notice shall be published in a newspaper for three weeks successively, evidently means the same thing as "three successive weeks." In respect to a sale, it simply indicates the time during which the sale must be advertised, and not the manner of publication, as that it shall be published "successively" during the period. The word "successively" refers to weeks, and not to the publication of the paper. Such a case, requiring a notice of the sale of real estate of a decedent to be so published, is, therefore, within the provisions of the statute, one in which the court or judge may order a publication for a less number of times than each issue of the paper in which the notice is to be published.—Estate of Cunningham, 73 Cal. 558, 559, 15 Pac. 136; Estate of O'Sullivan, 84 Cal. 444, 447, 24 Pac. 281. It must be observed that the number of publications is not provided by the statute. Section 1705 of the Code of Civil Procedure of California declares, in effect, that the notices provided for by section 1549 of that code must be published as often as the paper is published during the time over which the notice is extended, unless otherwise directed by the court or judge. This mandatory requirement equally applies to both weekly and daily papers. If the publication of a notice is directed to be made in a daily paper, and the court or judge does not otherwise direct, the notice must be published every day that the paper is issued prior to the time fixed, and if not so made, the publication is invalid. But where a publication was to be made for four weeks next preceding the hearing of a designated petition, which hearing was fixed for January 3, 1872, and it appeared that the publication was made on the fifth, twelfth, nineteenth, and twenty-sixth days of December, and January 2, there would be no doubt, if such publication had been made in a weekly newspaper published in the county, that it would have come strictly within the requirements of the statute; but the question before the court was, did the fact that the publication was had in a daily newspaper, once a week for the required time, satisfy the law; and it was held, after a consideration of the authorities, that publications of notice in daily papers once a week, for the time prescribed by the notice, is a sufficient compliance with the law.—People v. Reclamation District, 121 Cal. 522, 524, 50 Pac. 1068, 53 Pac. 1085. An affidavit of publication of a notice of probate proceedings sufficiently shows that the notice was published every day the paper was regularly issued, as required by section 1705 of the Code of Civil Procedure of California, where the affidavit of the publication made is that the notice was published "fourteen consecutive times, to wit, from the 18th day of October, 1889, to and until the 2d day of November, 1889, both days inclusive, on the 18th, 19th, 21st, 22d, 23d, 24th, 25th, 26th, 28th, 29th, 30th, 31st of October, and 1st and 2d days of November, 1889, every day said newspaper was published during said time, Sundays and holidays excepted," where it is admitted

that the paper in which said notice was published was not issued on
Sundays or holidays, and that therefore the publication in fact complied
with the statute.—Estate of Hamilton, 120 Cal. 421, 430, 52 Pac. 708.
The statute does not require an order to show cause why a sale of real
estate of the decedent should not be made to contain a description of
the property. There is no necessity for its containing a description
which is given in the petition, and which fully apprises all interested
parties, at that stage of the proceedings, of the land proposed to be
sold. It is sufficient for the order to refer to the petition on file, where
that fully describes the property.—Estate of Roach, 139 Cal. 17, 20,
72 Pac. 393. Under section 1491a of the Code of Civil Procedure of
California, within thirty days after the first publication of notice to
creditors of a deceased person, the executor or administrator must file
in court a printed copy of said notice, accompanied by a statement
setting forth the date of the first publication thereof and the name of
the newspaper in which the same is printed.—Hawkins v. Superior
Court, 165 Cal. 743, 134 Pac. 327. A newspaper is a "newspaper of
general circulation," if it satisfies the statutory requirements, notwithstanding that the actual printing of it may be done occasionally at a
locality other than the place of circulation.—In re Lefavor, Lefavor v.
Ludolph, 35 Cal. App. 145, 169 Pac. 412. A "newspaper of general
circulation" is not changed in character, nor is its identity destroyed,
by the mere dropping of a part of the wording in its name.—In re
Lefavor, Lefavor v. Ludolph, 35 Cal. App. 145, 169 Pac. 412.

5. Rules of practice.

(1) In general.—In Oregon, the proceedings in the county court, when
exercising jurisdiction in probate matters, are required to be in writing,
and, though no particular pleadings or forms are prescribed, the practice is in the nature of a suit in equity, as distinguished from an action
at law.—In re Morrison's Estate, 48 Or. 612, 87 Pac. 1043, 1044. Section
1713 of the Code of Civil Procedure of California provides that: "Except as otherwise provided in this title, the provisions of part 2 of this
code are applicable to and constitute the rules of practice in the proceedings mentioned in this title." The title referred to, §§ 1294-1810,
contains the entire procedure in probate matters; and part 2, §§ 307-
1059, the procedure in civil cases.—San Francisco, etc., Asylum v.
Superior Court, 116 Cal. 443, 450, 48 Pac. 379. By §§ 1713 and 1714, the
provisions of part 2 of the California Code of Civil Procedure—relating
to proceedings in ordinary actions—do not constitute the rules of practice in probate proceedings when "it is otherwise provided"; and the
provision of part 2—relating to new trials and appeals—are not applicable when "inconsistent" with the provisions of the title in which the
sections are found. Hence, the particular mode of settling accounts of
executors or administrators, specially provided for, being inconsistent
with the provisions relating to new trials must be followed.—Estate
of Sanderson, 74 Cal. 199, 205, 15 Pac. 753. In a proper case, a change

of venue may be had from one probate court to another on a trial of an
issue of fact.—People v. Almy, 46 Cal. 245, 248. And, in such a case,
the clerk of the court to which the case is sent may certify a transcript of the proceedings and result of the trial back, and the court from
which the case was sent can then enter the appropriate judgment with
proper recitals.—People v. Almy, 46 Cal. 245, 248. If a guardian applies
for letters of administration against one already appointed as administrator, such guardian is plaintiff and the administrator is defendant.—
Estate of Wooten, 56 Cal. 322, 325. Under the probate practice of California, no such officer as an executor de son tort is recognized.—Dow-
den v. Pierce, 73 Cal. 459, 463, 14 Pac. 302, 15 Pac. 64. If an administrator has been cited to appear and defend against the allowance of a
claim against the estate, but makes default, a return filed twenty days
after the hearing, and two days after the entry of the order of default,
does not change the character of such order.—In re Carver's Estate,
10 S. D. 609, 74 N. W. 1056. It is competent for counsel to stipulate
that the order of the county court appointing an administrator may be
affirmed on appeal by the circuit court.—In re Skelly's Estate, 21 S. D.
424, 113 N. W. 91, 94. A stipulation that a probate order, judgment, or
decree was actually entered at a date prior to its actual entry does not
estop the appellant from showing the contrary to sustain his appeal,
where the respondents have parted with no right by reason of the
stipulation.—Estate of Scott, 124 Cal. 671, 676, 57 Pac. 654. The termination of probate proceedings in another state can be shown only
by competent evidence, and this evidence must be the records of the
probate court, which can be proved only by a properly exemplified or
examined copy of such records.—Mears v. Smith, 19 S. D. 79, 102
N. W. 295, 297. It is a rule of construction and practice that when
a writing requires explanation, and where the circumstances of its
creation, as disclosed by the evidence, are undisputed, it becomes a
question of law for the court and not of fact for the jury, to determine
what the proper construction of the writing should be.—Bragg v.
Martenstein, 25 Cal. App. 199, 143 Pac. 79. Section 7141, Revised Codes
of Montana, relative to giving written notice of a motion, is inapplicable to the trial of an issue raised by a petition for the distribution
of an estate and objections thereto.—In re Estate of Peterson, Chell-
quist v. Eustance, 49 Mont. 96, Ann. Cas. 1916A, 716, 140 Pac. 237.
Where the state has prevailed in a proceeding to recover certain
property as upon an escheat, and an order has been made, upon the
motion of the district attorney, respecting the payment of counsel fees
and expenses, and this culmination of the case is resisted by the
original defendants, as well as by their counsel, the fact that they
assumed the role of amicus curiae does not affect the proceeding, as
it is not a proper case for the appearance of a friend of the court.—
State v. McDonald, 63 Or. 467, 471, Ann. Cas. 1915A, 201, 128 Pac. 835.
A revivor of an action to cancel deeds and mortgages and to quiet title
to allotted Seminole Indian lands made without notice upon the sug-

gestion of the plaintiff's father, by summary order of court, and without
the consent of defendants, assuming that such revivor was an irregularity, and that the father was not plaintiff's heir and successor, the
irregularity was waived by the general appearance of the defendants.—
Dickinson v. Abb (Okla.), 176 Pac. 623, 525. The legislative attempt in
Oregon to transfer all probate business and jurisdiction of the county
court in Multnomah county to the circuit court was held to be violative
of the constitution, in that it was local and special legislation, and was
an attempt to regulate the practice of courts of justice in a particular
county.—In re McCormick's Estate, Branch v. McCormick's Estate, 72
Or. 608, 611, 143 Pac. 915, 144 Pac. 425. Where a probate code is a
complete and comprehensive act upon the subject-matter of its title,
the whole constitutes a general system which must be respected as
such in all attempts at construction; the sections and subdivisions are
in pari materia, and by the well established rule must be harmonized,
real, and construed together, thus forming a complete statutory structure enacted all at the same time.—First Security & L. Co. v. Englehart (Wash.), 181 Pac. 13, 15. If an executor brings ejectment, and
his complaint fully avers his status as an executor, it is not necessary
for a subsequent complaint by another in intervention, which in its
essence is defensive to the executor's assertion of title in and right to
the possession of the land, to aver such status.—Cameron v. Ah Quong,
175 Cal. 377, 165 Pac. 961.

(2) Nature of procedure.—The administration of an estate under the
probate jurisdiction of a court, which involves the appointment of an
administrator and culminates in a final decree of distribution, is a
proceeding in rem.—Carter v. Frahm, 31 S. D. 379, 392, 141 N. W. 370.
When a county court of Oregon exercises jurisdiction in probate matters, the mode of procedure is in the nature of a suit in equity as
distinguished from an action at law.—Hillman v. Young, 64 Or. 73,
81, 127 Pac. 793, 129 Pac. 134.

(3) Rescission of contracts.—Where the statute authorizes the rescission of a contract for mental incapacity, a reference in such statute
to the chapter on rescission is merely for the purpose of subjecting
the rescission to the general rules governing the operation of this
remedy; the various code sections relating directly to the rescission
of contracts are applicable to rescission for mental incapacity, as
authorized by a specific section of the code.—Thronson v. Blough, 33
N. D. 574, 166 N. W. 132.

(4) Suit upon claim.—A suit upon a claim against a decedent's
estate can not be brought before a circuit court of Oregon, under section 1241, L. O. L., and make the practice of the county court the
practice of the circuit court.—In re McCormick's Estate, Branch v.
McCormick's Estate. 72 Or. 608, 611, 143 Pac. 915, 144 Pac. 425. The
word "proceeding" as used in the California statute, authorizing the
amendment of any pleading by adding or striking out the name of

any party, or by correcting a mistake in the name of a party, or a
mistake in any other respect, if the relief is sought within six months,
does not refer exclusively to an action at law; such statute is applicable to probate proceedings, and may be invoked to amend a claim
filed against the estate of a decedent.—Davis v. Superior Court, 35
Cal. App. 473, 170 Pac. 437. A complaint in an action to recover on a
claim against an estate fails to state a cause of action unless it expressly alleges that the claim as made was first duly presented to the
executor or administrator.—Vanderpool v. Vanderpool, 48 Mont. 448,
138 Pac. 772. An averment in plaintiff's complaint against an administratrix to recover the reasonable value of services rendered her
intestate, that on a certain day and "before the time for presentation
of claims against the said estate had expired" he had presented his
claim to the defendant, etc., is not open to the objection that, as to
the fact that the claim had been presented within the time prescribed
in the notice to creditors of the estate, it states a mere conclusion of
law; and, in the absence of a special demurrer or motion, such an
inferential allegation will support proof.—Gauss v. Trump, 48 Mont.
92, 135 Pac. 910. If exceptions and objections are filed to the allowance
of a claim against an estate, in the manner directed by statute, the
issue thus presented should be heard and tried by the probate judge,
and, until heard and tried, is pending in such court.—Estate of Coryell,
16 Ida. 201, 215, 101 Pac. 723. Evidence, in an action to recover from
an estate on a quantum meruit for services performed for decedent,
under an alleged agreement by the terms of which she agreed to
devise her ranch to plaintiff in consideration of his managing the same
during her lifetime, sufficient to warrant the jury in finding in favor of
plaintiff.—Gauss v. Trump, 48 Mont. 92, 135 Pac. 910. While a claim
presented to defendant as executrix did not purport to be based upon
a promissory note, the complaint alleged, and the evidence showed,
that it was; it was therefore held to be such a variance as amounted
to a failure of proof.—Vanderpool v. Vanderpool, 48 Mont. 448, 138 Pac.
772.

6. Attorney for absent heirs.—The section of the California statute
respecting this matter was repealed in 1903, but as some of the states
considered in this work may still have such a section in their codes,
we refer to a few of the California cases upon that subject. The
appointment of an attorney for absent heirs, and the allowance to
him of a fee, are matters entirely within the discretion of the probate
court, and if such allowance be improvident or indiscreet, the court
may vacate it on the suggestion of anyone, or on its own motion.—
Estate of Rety, 75 Cal. 256, 257, 17 Pac. 65; Estate of Lux, 134 Cal. 3,
66 Pac. 30. The allowance of a fee of $50 for the services of an attor-
ney for absent heirs, appointed by the court to represent them in proceedings to obtain an order for the sale of real estate, is not unusual
or excessive.—Estate of Simmons, 43 Cal. 543, 547. The fee of the
attorney shall be paid from the portion of the heir, legatee, or devisee

represented, as a necessary part of the expenses of administration, and until the payment of the general expenses of the administration of the estate and the debts of the deceased, there can be no portion, of the party represented, from which such payment can be made. The attorney so appointed stands in no better position than the person whom he represents, and his compensation is dependent upon the existence of a fund or property belonging to such person. Until the payment of the general expenses of administration, and the debts of the deceased, there can be no such fund or property.—Estate of Carpenter, 146 Cal. 661, 666, 80 Pac. 1072. The charge for the services of such an attorney is to be made against the interest represented by the attorney, and the statute authorizes payment out of the estate only where the estate can be reimbursed by retaining the amount from the portion of the heir represented.—Estate of Lux, 134 Cal. 3, 8, 66 Pac. 30. When an attorney has been appointed to represent an absent heir, nothing should be paid to such attorney, if such person does not turn out to be an heir.—Estate of Lux, 134 Cal. 3, 8, 66 Pac. 30. It is evident that an attorney can not be appointed for an absent heir, who is already represented by an attorney. As soon as the absent heir is represented by an attorney employed by himself, the functions of an appointee cease. The order of appointment must specify the names of the parties, so far as known, for whom the attorney is appointed, who is thereby authorized to represent such parties in all such proceedings had subsequent to his appointment. The appointment is authorized only for a devisee, legatee, heir, or creditor. Before the appointment can be made, the court must be satisfied that such persons exist, and the order must designate who they are, or otherwise the fee allowed can not be charged to the person represented by the attorney. If the names are not known, they must still be identified, in some way, in the order.—Estate of Lux, 134 Cal. 3, 6, 7, 66 Pac. 30. The attorney for minor heirs can represent them only in a proceeding which has been duly inaugurated, and in which the court has already jurisdiction of the minors, by such summons or notice as the code provides. He can not waive their rights, or, by any of his acts, invest the courts with jurisdiction of their persons, which it had not already acquired.—Campbell v. Drais, 125 Cal. 253, 258, 57 Pac. 994. The attorney for minors in probate proceedings is to "represent" them. The general provisions in relation to guardians ad litem, in the chapter on parties to civil actions, do not apply to probate proceedings. The matter is governed by special proceedings as to attorneys for minors.—Carpenter v. Superior Court, 75 Cal. 596, 599, 19 Pac. 174.

7. Trial.

(1) In general.—In Idaho, the statute provides for a trial "de novo" in the district court, on appeal from the probate court, in probate matters; and this requires that appeals be tried upon the original papers, and upon the same issues had below. If there is no issue, there can

be no case made, and it is axiomatic that a cause or an issue can not be tried de novo that has never been tried.—In re McVay's Estate, 14 Ida. 56, 64, 93 Pac. 28, 32. In California, findings of fact are proper whenever issues of facts are tried by the probate court.—Haffenegger v. Bruce, 54 Cal. 416; Estate of Crosby, 55 Cal. 574. It is not incumbent upon the court, in the settlement of the accounts of an executor or administrator, to make and file express findings, still, when the account is assailed, in any particular, for matters not appearing upon its face, the court may properly make express findings upon such issues. —Miller v. Lux, 100 Cal. 609, 613, 35 Pac. 345, 639. It has never been definitely determined by the supreme court of California that findings are necessary, on the decision of a motion for a probate order, to set apart a homestead, or upon a probate order of sale of real property belonging to the estate of the decedent, and the intimations have rather been that they are not necessary.—Estate of Turner, 128 Cal. 380, 388, 57 Pac. 569, 60 Pac. 965; Estate of Arguello, 85 Cal. 151, 152, 24 Pac. 641. It is clear, however, that no findings are required upon the hearing of ex parte applications for letters of administration which are heard together, where no issues are joined upon either petition.— Estate of Heldt, 98 Cal. 553, 554, 33 Pac. 549. In Washington, the statute which requires findings of fact and conclusions of law made by the trial court to be separately stated applies only to actions at law tried without a jury. It does not apply to equitable proceedings or, by analogy, to probate proceedings.—In re Farnham's Estate, 41 Wash. 570, 84 Pac. 602, 603. The rules of pleading and practice in civil cases are applicable to proceedings in the probate courts. Issues joined in such proceedings are to be tried and determined by that court as in civil cases; and, upon trial by the court without a jury, parties to the proceedings are entitled to findings unless they are waived; and, it the findings are not waived, it is error to enter judgment without them. —Estate of Burton, 63 Cal. 36, 37. The court, in every stage of an action, must disregard any defect or error in the proceedings which does not affect the substantial rights of the parties.—In re McVay's Estate, 14 Ida. 56, 64, 93 Pac. 28. A transfer of the final determinations of a county court, in probate matters, removes the entire cause to the circuit court, where it is tried as if it had been originally instituted therein, expect that the review is confined to an examination of the transcript sent up.—In re Roach's Estate, 50 Or. 179, 92 Pac. 118, 122. Where there has been a postponement of the hearing on the administrator's report and account, it is the duty of the court, at the time to which the postponement has been made, to try and determine the issues of law and fact presented by such report and account.— Kent v. Dalrymple, 23 Ida. 694, 704, 132 Pac. 301.

(2) Evidence.—In proceedings to settle the estate of one who was a German by birth, and who at the time of his death had many near relatives in Germany, it was proper for the court, as against relations in the fifth degree, to sustain the motion of a party, claiming relation-

ship in the fourth degree, for a continuance until communication with Germany was re-established, in order that proof might be forthcoming to support the claim of the moving party.—In re Henrich's Estate, Ahrens v. Aston (Cal.), 179 Pac. 883. Probate court documents, filed, signed, and sworn to by a person as administrator of the estate concerned, and as guardian of the estates of the minor children of the decedent, are record evidence of a very high grade of the facts pertinent to the estate and to which they relate.—Cunningham v. Costello, 19 Ariz. 512, 172 Pac. 664, 669. The provisions of section 2047, Cal. Code Civ. Proc., allowing a witness to testify from a writing, although he may retain no recollection of the particular facts, are mandatory, and the allowance of such testimony is not discretionary; but if it were otherwise, it is held in the instant case that, under the revealed circumstances, the exclusion of such testimony would have been an abuse of such discretion.—In re Moore's Estate (Cal.), 182 Pac. 285, 291. The testimony of testator's former attorney as to witness' recollection of facts upon the issue of mental capacity, testifying from a document in the form of a bill of exceptions prepared by him while the contents were fresh in memory, using the court reporter's notes to check its accuracy as to the testator's testimony in a former action, was improperly excluded, in view of the provisions of section 2047, Cal. Code Civ. Proc., whether all or only a part of such testimony was included in such instrument.—In re Moore's Estate (Cal.), 182 Pac. 285, 291.

REFERENCES.

Admissibility of declarations of relationship to decedent in behalf of relative of declarant who is claimant of decedent's estate.—See note 21 Ann. Cas. 1305.

(3) **By jury.**—Exceptions to an account of an executor or administrator do not create "issues of fact joined," such as must be submitted to a jury on demand of a party in interest.—Estate of Sanderson, 74 Cal. 199, 209, 15 Pac. 753. Without the provisions of sections 1716 and 1717 of the Code of Civil Procedure of California, parties to a contest in the probate courts of that state would never be entitled to a jury trial; and the statute is not to be construed as granting an absolute right to a jury trial in cases in which, according to the course of the common law, a jury trial was denied as inappropriate, and especially upon the settlement of accounts of executors or administrators, where so much is left to the mere discretion of the judge, and in the face of the language of the code, in many sections, implying that the settlement shall be by the court.—Estate of Moore, 72 Cal. 335, 340, 13 Pac. 880. But, in that state, the issue of heirship is a proper one to submit to a jury.—Estate of Sheid, 122 Cal. 528, 532, 55 Pac. 328. And error in the impanelment of a jury and the submission to it of special issues upon such a question, is not prejudicial, where the court itself has found upon all of the issues submitted to the jury.—Estate of Westerfield, 96 Cal. 113, 115, 30 Pac. 1104. Under the statute of Washington,

there is no escape from the position that, in a proceeding for the recovery of specific real or personal property, the issues of fact shall be tried by a jury; and this applies to a proceeding by an executor or an administrator to recover from his successor the possession of property, the title of which is put in issue.—In re Murphy's Estate, 30 Wash. 1, 70 Pac. 107, 108. In Montana, where objection is made to proceedings for a sale of land of the decedent to pay his debts, those who object are not entitled to a jury trial, unless the issues have first been made up and a written demand made and filed three days prior to the day set for the hearing. Under the statute of that state, it is clearly the duty of the court or judge to try the issues joined without a jury, unless one is demanded in the manner, and within the time, prescribed therein. Those requirements presuppose issues joined before a demand for trial by jury is made. The policy of the law is that proceedings of this nature should progress as speedily as they may, to the end that the affairs of the estate may be closed up, and the parties in interest discharged from the supervision of the court. The presiding judge is not supposed to know what issues, if any, are to be made, until the pleadings are filed, and not then until attention is called to them. If, in any case, no issue of fact is presented, the presence of a jury is unnecessary. The statute, therefore, not only requires the issues to be made up before the demand is made, but, also, that the demand be made a sufficient length of time before the hearing, to secure the attendance of a jury.—In re Tuohy's Estate, 33 Mont. 230, 83 Pac. 486, 489. In probate proceedings, issues are tried by a jury only where it is so provided by statute; in Colorado, the constitutional provisions for trial by jury do not apply.—Stratton v. Rice (Colo.), 181 Pac. 529, 531. The court, in Colorado, does not err in refusing a jury trial to a woman who, in a proceeding for the probate of a will and the settlement of an estate, sets up that she is the widow of decedent and entitled to one-half of his estate, the issue to be tried being that of her marriage to the decedent; there is no statute of that state giving the right to a jury trial in such a case.—Stratton v. Rice (Colo.), 181 Pac. 529, 531. An issue in a probate matter is to be tried and determined as an ordinary civil action, except that a jury trial is a privilege, and not a matter of right.—In re Peterson's Estate, 49 Mont. 96, 97, Ann. Cas. 1916A, 716, 140 Pac. 237. Under sections 1716 and 1312 of the Code of Civil Procedure of California, either party to any probate proceeding, in which the statute authorizes the formation of issues of fact, may ask for a jury.—Estate of Baird, 173 Cal. 617, 160 Pac. 1078. A jury trial is not demandable as a matter of right in an action in a probate court to set aside the appointment of an administrator upon the alleged ground that the deceased was not at the time of his death a resident of the county in which the appointment was made.—In re Holloway's Estate, 100 Kan. 368, 164 Pac. 298. Proceedings, in which, under statute, the framing of issues of fact is authorized, include a proceeding for a partial distribution of the estate of a decedent.—

Estate of Baird, 173 Cal. 617, 160 Pac. 1078. When issues, triable by a jury, are joined in the probate court, and no demand for a jury is made, the court will try such issues; but, if a jury is demanded and the court is of the opinion that the issues are not sufficiently made, it is directed by the statute of Idaho, and perhaps of some other states, to settle, frame, and submit them, with the evidence to the jury.—Miller v. Kettenbach, 18 Ida. 253, 262, 138 Am. St. Rep. 192, 109 Pac. 505. Probate proceedings, in so far as the right of trial by jury is concerned, are not, in Oregon, included in the category of "civil cases."—Stevens v. Myers, 62 Or. 372, 408, 121 Pac. 434, 126 Pac. 29.

8. Orders and decrees.

(1) In general.—The order authorized by section 7506, Rev. Codes of Montana, can go no further than to require a disclosure which may be used in an action pending or to be brought in behalf of the estate.— In re Roberts' Estate, 48 Mont. 40, 42, 135 Pac. 909.

(2) Form of, signing, filing, etc.—There is no statute expressly authorizing the making of the memorial of the terms of an order of the superior court by the method of writing it on a separate piece of paper, and having the judge attach his signature thereto. It has become customary to do so, in many instances, and the courts have often recognized such a memorial as competent evidence of the terms of the order. But the code expressly requires probate orders to be entered in the minute-book of the court. It is the order there entered which is the order of the court, and it is the date of the entry of this order which sets the time running for an appeal. In making entries in the minute-book, it is neither necessary nor customary to begin the entries of each order with the statement of the name of the court in which it is made. Slight discrepancies between the entry of the order in the minute-book, and an order signed by the judge, and filed in the case, will not extend the time of appeal. Such time will commence to run from the entry of the first minute order.—Tracy v. Coffey, 153 Cal. 356, 95 Pac. 150, 151. There is no uniformity of the manner in which different judges sign or attest proceedings in the settlement of estates before them; sometimes they use their simple signature without any designation of their official character; sometimes they add such designation; but it has never been held or supposed that the validity of the orders or proceedings was, in any respect, affected by the absence of the official designation from the signature, or the presence of the designation, "county judge," instead of "probate judge." It has always been considered sufficient that the papers disclosed on their face the character in which the judge acted.—Touchard v. Crow, 20 Cal. 150, 159, 81 Am. Dec. 108. A paper is filed when delivered to the proper officer; and endorsing it with the time of filing is not a part of the filing.— Smith v. Biscailuz, 83 Cal. 344, 358, 21 Pac. 15, 23 Pac. 314. A paper or document is filed, within the meaning of the statute, when it is delivered to and received by the clerk to be kept among the files of

his office, subject to the inspection of the parties. The indorsement required to be made thereon by the clerk is intended merely as a memorandum, and as evidence of the time of the filing, but is not essential thereto. The act of filing consists of presenting the paper to the proper officer, and of its being received by him, and disposed of by him among the records of his office. A paper may be filed without being marked or indorsed by the clerk.—In re Conant's Estate, 43 Or. 530, 73 Pac. 1018, 1020. The indorsement, upon papers, of the fact of filing, does not constitute a part of the filing, but is only evidence that such filing has been made; and, while it is usual and proper for the officer with whom a paper has been filed, to indorse upon the same the fact and time of such filing, such indorsement is not absolutely essential to the validity of the filing, if the paper has been in fact delivered to the proper officer, at the proper place, for the purpose of being filed.—Starkweather v. Bell, 12 S. D. 146, 80 N. W. 183, 185. If a notice of appeal and undertaking are in fact filed with the county judge, and placed on the files of the county court by the ex officio clerk of that court, the law as to filing is complied with, notwithstanding the indorsements of such filing are not made upon the papers by inadvertence, or otherwise, of the county judge, and notwithstanding the fact that the clerk of the circuit court and ex officio clerk of the county court, also by inadvertence, have indorsed the papers as having been filed in the circuit court instead of the county court.—Starkweather v. Bell, 12 S. D. 146, 80 N. W. 183, 185.

(3) **To contain description when.**—As the statute requires all orders and decrees of the court or judge in probate proceedings to be entered at length in the minute-book of the court, it is obvious that an order or decree, providing for the distribution of an estate, must describe the property distributed.—Estate of Sheid, 122 Cal. 528, 529, 55 Pac. 328.

(4) **Failure to recite jurisdictional facts.**—The orders and decrees of a probate court are not required to recite the existence of facts or the performance of acts upon which the jurisdiction of the court depends; and the failure to recite such facts does not raise a presumption of their non-existence.—Holmes v. Holmes, 27 Okla. 140, 30 L. R. A. (N. S.) 920, 111 Pac. 220. If a probate order or decree, not reciting the jurisdictional facts, is directly attacked, such facts may be shown by any competent evidence, whether appearing by the judgment-roll or not.—Carter v. Frahm, 31 S. D. 379, 398, 141 N. W. 370.

REFERENCES.
Presumption in favor of regularity of probate orders and decrees.— See infra, 1 (8).

(5) **Correction of errors.**—A probate court has power to amend its records to make them speak the truth.—Brooks v. Brooks, 52 Kan. 562, 35 Pac. 215. It may correct its own errors in the settlement of estates, either in regard to matters of law, or of fact, at any time before final settlement, provided it can be done from the record, without opening

proof in the case.—Lucich v. Medin, 3 Nev. 93, 106, 93 Am. Dec. 376; In re Millenovich, 5 Nev. 161, 187. The court may correct an error in the names of petitioners in a case pending and undetermined.—Lucich v. Medin, 3 Nev. 93, 106, 93 Am. Dec. 376. The substantial rights of parties are not to be affected by mere errors in the formation of the jury, or in the giving of instructions.—Estate of Moore, 72 Cal. 335, 339, 13 Pac. 880. But an error in the judgment itself can not be corrected, after the term at which it was rendered, under the statute authorizing courts of record to modify or vacate their own judgments for "irregularity in obtaining a judgment or order."—Lewis v. Woodrum, 76 Kan. 384, 92 Pac. 306. A decree of the probate court settling a guardian's final account may be amended in respect to errors pointed out by persons interested; but errors appearing in a judgment, which the court itself fell into, can be corrected only by motion for a new trial or appeal.—State (ex rel. McHatton) v. District Court, 55 Mont. 324, 176 Pac. 608. A probate court may, by a nunc pro tunc entry, correct, or add to, the record of its proceedings when discovered to have been incorrectly or not fully entered at the time of such proceedings; a party's appearance may be so entered.—Faler v. Culver, 94 Kan. 123, 146 Pac. 333.

(6) **Signing of minutes.**—A statute requiring the orders and decrees of the probate court to be entered at length in the minute-book, and to be signed by the judge, but which is entirely silent as to the consequences to follow upon the failure of the judge to sign the minutes as therein provided, is merely directory.—McCrea v. Haraszthy, 51 Cal. 146, 150.

(7) **Misleading entries. Clerk's register. Effect of.**—Where it appears, without conflict, that an entry in the register upon which the appellant relied for his information had, in truth, no reference to the fact of the entry, at length, of a decree of distribution in the minute-book, and was not intended to record that fact, but that it referred to a wholly different step—an entry by the court-room clerk, in his rough daily minutes of proceedings, of the fact that the decree had been made and filed on a designated date; and the fact that appellant was misled by said entry, through his failure to make inquiry, where it appears that he could have obtained the true signification of such entry by inquiry in the clerk's office, can not give him any rights which he does not otherwise have.—Estate of Pearsons, 119 Cal. 27, 29, 50 Pac. 929.

(8) **Presumptions.**—No presumption of the regularity of a probate order arises if a lack of jurisdiction appears.—Territory v. Mix, 1 Ariz. 52. But every presumption, not upset by the record itself, is to be indulged in support of the regularity and validity of orders and decrees in probate. This presumption of regularity applies to the orders and decrees of probate courts, made within the limits of their restricted powers, the same as it does to proceedings of courts of general jurisdiction.—Estate of Twombley, 120 Cal. 350, 351, 52 Pac. 815. In Wyom-

ing, the presumption of regularity of the proceedings of a district court
of that state applies to its proceedings in probate matters.—Lethbridge
v. Lauder, 13 Wyo. 9, 76 Pac. 682, 685. Where a section of a probate
code provides that orders and decrees need not recite the existence
of jurisdictional facts, it does not mean that such jurisdictional facts
need not exist or that they should not be shown by the judgment-roll,
but it does mean that such orders and decrees are valid without the
recital of jurisdictional facts. When such an order or decree is entered without such recitals, the jurisdictional facts will be presumed
as against a collateral attack, which presumption can be overcome
only by the judgment-roll itself.—Carter v. Frahm, 31 S. D. 398, 141
N. W. 370. After jurisdiction acquired by proper notice, superior court
though sitting in probate, is court of general jurisdiction in acting on
administrator's petition for sale of land, and entitled to same presumptions that attach to its action in other cases on collateral attack.—
Dane v. Layne, 10 Cal. App. 366, 101 Pac. 1067.

REFERENCES.

Presumption where order or decree fails to recite jurisdictional
facts.—See supra, 1 (4).

(9) **Entry of, in records.**—The proper place for the entry of a probate order is in the minute-book of the court.—Tracy v. Coffey, 153
Cal. 356, 95 Pac. 150, 151. For the purposes of an appeal, an order,
decree, or judgment is "entered" when it is entered at large upon the
minutes.—Estate of Sheid, 122 Cal. 528, 529, 55 Pac. 328. To say that
the court "made, entered, and filed" an order does not show that the
"clerk" entered the order at length on the minute-book of the court.
What the court does is one thing, and what the clerk does is quite
another. When the court has entered its judgment, or filed its probate order, the function of the judge in that connection is ended.
The duty of entering the judgment or order in the judgment-book is
a mere ministerial duty, devolving upon the clerk, and it is the performance of that duty by the clerk, which gives the right of appeal,
and constitutes the test of appellate jurisdiction.—Estate of Pichoir,
139 Cal. 694, 696, 70 Pac. 214, 73 Pac. 604. The entry of probate orders,
decrees, or judgments, in the book prescribed by the statute is no part
thereof. They are perfect and complete, and have full force and effect
before they are entered.—Estate of Hughston, 133 Cal. 321, 323, 65 Pac.
742, 1039. The action of the court, outside of probate matters, does not
depend upon the entry of its orders by the clerk, but upon the fact that
the orders have been made, and whenever it is shown that an order
has been made by the court, it is as effective as if it had been entered
of record by the clerk.—Niles v. Edwards, 95 Cal. 41, 47, 30 Pac. 134;
Von Schmidt v. Widber, 99 Cal. 511, 515, 34 Pac. 109. The requirement of the statute, that probate orders and decrees must be entered
in the minutes, implies that the date of entry should be affixed to the
record; and if the entry, in the judgment-book, of an order or decree,
bears no date, and there is no provision of the law for the authentica-

tion of the date of entry, the question as to such date must be decided upon evidence aliunde, that is to say, the testimony of the clerk or copyist, etc. The court can not know that the entry has been made, and, above all, it can not know when the copying was begun or completed, without taking evidence and determining its effect.—Estate of Pichoir, 139 Cal. 694, 697, 70 Pac. 214, 73 Pac. 604. The register and the docket should be kept by the clerk with a regard for truth as to dates. In the whole range of the duties of the clerk, there is none more important than the duty of keeping a true history of the time when his "clerical" work was actually done. Under our practice, it is the initial point of many rights; and willfully to make a false certificate as to these matters is a violation of official duties. If the officers, whose duty it is to keep a correct record, are unable to remember when a judgment was actually entered, the moving party, to correct an alleged mistake as to the date of the entry of the judgment, may possibly become a loser through the vicious practice, in the clerk's office, of keeping an inaccurate account of dates.—Menzies v. Watson, 105 Cal. 109, 112, 38 Pac. 641. The superior court, acting as a court of probate, can not conclude the jurisdiction of the supreme court by a statement, in the bill of exceptions, that the clerk's entry of a judgment or order was made at a particular date.—Estate of Pichoir, 139 Cal. 694, 697, 70 Pac. 214, 73 Pac. 604. If the transcript on appeal shows only the date of the rendition of judgment, but does not show when it was entered, it does not appear from the record that the appellate court has jurisdiction.—Estate of Moore, 143 Cal. 493, 495, 77 Pac. 407.

(10) Effect of. Protection of administrator.—Under the constitution of the state of Idaho, the probate courts are given sole and exclusive, "original jurisdiction" in all matters of probate. As to those matters, the probate court is a court of record, to the judgment, records, and proceedings of which, in such matters, absolute verity is attached in every respect, as fully and completely as can attach to the records, judgments, and proceedings of district courts, or other courts of record. —In re McVay's Estate, 14 Ida. 56, 64, 93 Pac. 28, 31. But a probate order, reciting jurisdictional facts, is not conclusive if the record fails to show them affirmatively.—In re Charlebois, 6 Mont. 373, 12 Pac. 775, 778. It has been held in Nevada, that if a probate order is lost from the files, and is not recorded in the minutes of the court, through carelessness of the clerk, proof of such order may be made dehors the record, and that such order will protect the executor or administrator who has paid out money under it.—In re Millenovich, 5 Nev. 161, 187; but an unauthorized or void order is no protection to the representative; as, where the court attempted to make a disposition of moneys other than those belonging to the trust.—Estate of Kennedy, 120 Cal. 458, 461, 52 Pac. 820; or, where the court has settled an account and apportioned the money in the hands of the administrator; directed that a designated sum be paid into court; and that the administrator shall thereupon be entitled to his discharge.—Estate of Sarment, 123

Cal. 331, 337, 55 Pac. 1015; or, where the court attempts to authorize the administrator to replenish a stock of goods of decedent by the purchase of other goods.—In re Osburn's Estate, 36 Or. 8, 58 Pac. 521, 523.

(11) **Conclusiveness.**—A decree in California, under the McEnerny act, which is based on a final decree in probate proceedings, binds a distributee concerned in such proceedings and all persons claiming under him, even though it be asserted that the final decree was procured by fraud.—Estate of Daughaday, 168 Cal. 63, 141 Pac. 929. A final decree in pobate proceedings, if not appealed from, is conclusive on all the world, as to all matters mentioned in it having reference to the estate; unless fraud can be shown.—Estate of Daughaday, 168 Cal. 63, 141 Pac. 929. Orders and decrees of distribution made by superior courts in administering estates, when made upon due notice as provided by our statutes, are final adjudications, conclusive and binding upon all the world; such adjudications have all the force and effect of judgments in rem.—Krohn v. Hirsch, 81 Wash. 222, 142 Pac. 647. Where claims against a decedent's estate have been presented to the administrator and approved by the probate judge; where the administrator has rendered an account as to all claims except those reserved for future consideration; and where it has come on for hearing, everything contained in such account, including the listed claims, also comes on for hearing; and, when an order is entered approving the account, such order approves everything contained in the account; hence, where the account contains listed claims, and no appeal is taken from the order of approval, such order is final and conclusive as to such claims. —Miller v. Lewiston Nat. Bank, 18 Ida. 124, 136, 141, 108 Pac. 901. Where all the proceedings during the administration of an estate, and especially the allowance and approval of the final account, the distribution of the estate, and the discharge of the administrator, are all based upon and obtained by extrinsic and insufferable fraud of the administrator, while acting as such, the orders, decrees, and discharge have no further effect and do not require to be vacated or set aside to bind the surety in a suit in equity leased upon such fraud.—Weyant v. Utah Sav. & Trust Co., — (Utah) —, 182 Pac. 189, 201. When a complaint made under section 1723 of the Code of Civil Procedure of California states a case in equity to quiet title to alleged community property held in the wife's name, if all necessary parties had appeared before the court, the decree therein would be conclusive; but where there was no personal representative of the deceased wife before the court, and not all of the heirs were before the court, this court is bound to consider the decree relied on solely as one given in the special proceeding provided by that section and to give to it, in the event that proceedings had were all in strict accord with the requirements of that section, only such effect as upon a proper construction of the section must be given to a decree under its provisions.—King v. Pauly, 159 Cal. 529, 115 Pac. 210.

(12) Are void when.—An order of a probate court made without authority of the statute is void.—Estate of Kennedy, 120 Cal. 458, 461, 52 Pac. 820; Estate of Sarment, 123 Cal. 331, 337, 55 Pac. 1015; In re Osburn's Estate, 36 Or. 8, 58 Pac. 521, 523; Andrus v. Blazzard, 23 Utah 233, 63 Pac. 888, 894; Erwing v. Mallison, 65 Kan. 484, 93 Am. St. Rep. 299, 70 Pac. 369, 372. Thus an order appointing an administrator and granting letters of administration is void where the probate court, without jurisdiction, assumes to act in the matter.—Erwing v. Mallison, 65 Kan. 484, 93 Am. St. Rep. 299, 70 Pac. 369, 372; and it is obvious that an executor or administrator can not shield himself from personal liability, by refuge under an order which is absolutely void.—Andrus v. Blazzard, 23 Utah 233, 63 Pac. 888, 894. A county court sitting in probate in Colorado is without jurisdiction over real estate in Nebraska and its order for sale of such land is not merely voidable, but void, and gives an administrator no jurisdiction in his representative capacity to sell the land, and every one is bound to take notice thereof.—People v. Parker, 54 Colo. 604, 132 Pac. 57.

(13) Vacating orders.—A probate court or judge has the power to set aside an order which has been inadvertently made.—Raine v. Lawlor, 1 Cal. App. 483, 82 Pac. 688, 689; Clarke v. Baird, 98 Cal. 642, 644, 33 Pac. 756. It may set aside an order made without authority.— Mallory v. Burlington, etc., R. R. Co., 53 Kan. 557, 36 Pac. 1059, 1060. Thus letters of administration, issued without authority, may be set aside by the court in which they are issued, upon its own motion; or, such action may be taken at the instance of any one interested in the administration.—Mallory v. Burlington, etc., R. R. Co., 53 Kan. 557, 36 Pac. 1059, 1060. The allowance of a claim made on an ex parte application may be set aside without notice to the claimant.—Estate of Sullenberger, 72 Cal. 549, 552, 14 Pac. 513. As the court has no jurisdiction to order the administrator to make payment of a claim, after an appeal has been perfected by other claimants, such order, if made, will be annulled upon certiorari.—Pennie v. Superior Court, 89 Cal. 31, 26 Pac. 617. Section 473 of the Code of Civil Procedure of California, which provides that a court may relieve a party from a judgment, order, or proceedings taken against him, through his "mistake, inadvertence, surprise, or excusable neglect," is applicable to probate matters, provided application be made within a reasonable time, not in any case to exceed six months; and the court has power, at any time within six months after the entry of the decree, to set it aside on a proper showing.—Dean v. Superior Court, 63 Cal. 473; De Pedrorena v, Superior Court, 80 Cal. 144, sub nom. In re Pedrorena, 22 Pac. 71; Levy v. Superior Court, 139 Cal. 590, 73 Pac. 417; Cahill v. Superior Court, 145 Cal. 42, 78 Pac. 467. An order for the sale of real estate to pay debts is properly vacated, before confirmation of the sale, when it appears that it was made before the time for filing claims had expired, with no showing that the personalty had proved insufficient, upon insufficient jurisdictional allegations and with no notice to

the heirs.—Estate of Kamaipiialii, 19 Haw. 163. As prescribed in the juvenile court law, any order made by the court, in the case of any person subject to its jurisdiction under such statute, may be changed, modified, or set aside, upon due consideration of the effect thereof upon the system of parol and discharge provided by law, or by rule of the board of trustees of the particular institution to which the juvenile was committed.—Ex parte Johnson, 36 Cal. App. 319, 171 Pac. 1074. A defendant, against whom a default decree has been taken on publication of summons, and who would avail himself of the statute allowing defendants in such cases to file answers within a year after default, must tender his answer along with his petition to vacate the judgment; the same rule applies where it is sought to vacate an order allowing an administrator to sell, the order having been made on a published citation.—In re Marks' Estate, 81 Or. 632, 639, 160 Pac. 540, 542.

(14) **Collateral attack.**—The judgment of a probate court imports absolute verity, and can not be collaterally attacked. It may, however, be impeached by evidence which appears on the face of the record, and which shows a want of jurisdiction. In other words, the decrees of such a court can not be attacked collaterally for want of jurisdiction, unless the same appears on the face of the proceedings, or because of any error or irregularity. The decree, if not totally void, is conclusive on collateral attack, so long as it remains in force.— Lethbridge v. Lauder, 13 Wyo. 9, 76 Pac. 682, 685; Wiggins v. Superior Court, 68 Cal. 398, 9 Pac. 646; Clark v. Rossier, 10 Ida. 348, 3 Ann. Cas. 231, 78 Pac. 358, 360; Hubbard v. Hubbard, 7 Or. 42, 44; Tustin v. Gaunt, 4 Or. 305, 309; Holmes v. Oregon, etc., R. R. Co., 6 Saw. 262, 5 Fed. 75. "If it be found that the tribunal is one competent to decide, whether the facts in any given matter confer jurisdiction, it follows, with inexorable necessity that, if it decides that it has jurisdiction, then its judgment within the scope of the subject-matter over which its authority extends, in proceedings following the lawful allegation of circumstances requiring the exercise of its power, are conclusive against all the world, unless reversed on appeal, or avoided for error or fraud in a direct proceeding. It matters not how erroneous the judgment. Being a judgment, it is the law of that case, pronounced by a tribunal created for that purpose. To allow such judgment to be questioned or ignored collaterally would be to ignore practically, and logically to destroy, the court, and it is not necessary that the facts and circumstances upon which the jurisdiction depends shall appear upon the face of the proceedings because, being competent to decide, and having decided, that such facts exist by assuming the jurisdiction, this matter is adjudicated, and can not be collaterally questioned."— Lethbridge v. Lauder, 13 Wyo. 9, 76 Pac. 682, 685, quoting from 1 Woerner on Law of Administration, § 145. The remedy for one aggrieved by an order or judgment of a probate court, concerning matters in said court, is by a proper motion, or by appeal.—Clark v.

Rossier, 10 Ida. 348, 3 Ann. Cas. 231, 78 Pac. 358. A decree of distribution of a probate court is of like force and effect as a judgment in a civil case and can not be set aside on collateral attack. If erroneous the remedy is by appeal.—Alaska, etc., Co. v. Noyes, 64 Wash. 672, 117 Pac. 493.

REFERENCES.

Probate judgments.—See notes 33 Am. Dec. 242, 94 Am. Dec. 194, 95 Am. Dec. 115, 44 Am. St. Rep. 127.

(15) Obedience to, how enforced.—When an executor or administrator refuses to pay to a distributee, money found to be in his hands, he may be punished for contempt. This, however, is based upon the proposition that the representative is an officer of the court, and may be so dealt with whenever he refuses to perform a plain duty enjoined upon him as such officer.—Estate of Kennedy, 129 Cal. 384, 388, 62 Pac. 64; Ex parte Cohn, 55 Cal. 193; Ex parte Smith, 53 Cal. 204. It is true that the court has jurisdiction over the executor or administrator until his final discharge; but no special or express order that the executor or administrator pay over to distributees the money in his hands is authorized or required. The court discharges him from his trust upon proof that it has been fully performed, and payment to the heirs happens to be the last duty in the order of time to be performed. Upon the entry of the decree, the law fixes upon him the duty to pay over, and the court may compel performance as in the case of any other plain duty resting upon him by virtue of his office.— Estate of Kennedy, 129 Cal. 384, 387, 388, 62 Pac. 64.

9. Costs.

(1) In general.—The priority of the United States attaches only to the net proceeds of the property of the deceased, after proper charges and expenses of administration are satisfied; but the costs and expenses of defending an action, where the claim should have been allowed, are not to be included in the expenses of administration.— United States v. Eggleston, 4 Saw. 199, 25 Fed. Cas. No. 15,027. In a contest over the accounts of an executor, the contestants are entitled to their costs, where the court below deducted a considerable sum, and then allowed the balance of the accounts.—In re Millenovich, 5 Nev. 161, 188. Costs can not be allowed, except as an incident to some judgment or order of the court.—Henry v. Superior Court, 93 Cal. 569, 572, 29 Pac. 230. Where there was a trifling balance due on a note and mortgage, of the exact amount of which defendant was uncertain, a deposit of the approximate amount, though made after the complaint was filed, justified the court in believing that he was willing to pay, and it was proper to award him his costs.—Bailey v. Moshier, 35 Cal. App. 345, 347, 169 Pac. 913.

REFERENCES.

Liability of executors and administrators for costs.—See note § 655, division I, head-line 1, subd. 4.

(2) Preliminary fees and charges.—The North Dakota act of 1909, amending section 2589 of the Revised Codes of that state, relating to the fees of county court, which act provides for an initial fee of $5 and an additional charge of $5 for each and every $1000 or fraction thereof in excess of the first $1000 on the value of the estates, to be paid by the petitioner for letters testamentary, of administration, or of guardianship is unconstitutional in so far as the additional charge or fee is concerned; it violates that provision of the constitution, which declares that all laws of a general nature shall have a uniform operation; it also violates other provisions of the constitution; even the prior law as to the initial fee of $5, was invalid, as it was not imposed upon all estates equally, but according to the value thereof.—Malin v. Lamoure County, 27 N. D. 140, 50 L. R. A. (N. S.) 997, 145 N. W. 582. A part of section 2589 of the Revised Codes of North Dakota of 1905, as amended in 1909, providing for an initial fee of $5 to be paid by the petitioner for letters testamentary, of administration, or of guardianship, is invalid as to the provision therein contained as to additional fees, but that fact does not authorize a court to declare the remainder of the act void, as the invalid part is not so essentially and inseparably connected in substance with the remainder of the act as to require a rejection of the whole statute; hence, the initial fee of $5, as well as the expenditures for publishing and sending out notices, can be sustained as reasonable court charges, being levied uniformly upon all estates; the imposition of such fees is not a denial or sale of justice, provided that they are uniform, are reasonable, and have a reasonable relation to the services rendered.—Malin v. Lamoure County, 27 N. D. 140, 50 L. R. A. (N. S.) 997, 145 N. W. 582.

(3) Are statutory.—The superior court, acting in probate proceedings, obtains its authority to award costs from the statute, and not by virtue of its general probate jurisdiction. Its power to award costs is confined to the terms of the statute.—Henry v. Superior Court, 93 Cal. 569, 571, 29 Pac. 230; Estate of Olmstead, 120 Cal. 447, 453, 52 Pac. 804.

(4) Discretion of court.—The probate court is clothed with discretion to order costs to be paid "by any party to the proceedings, or out of the assets of the estate, as justice may require." This discretion can not be exercised until there is something upon which it may be based; and all the provisions of the code bearing upon the subject of probate contests, indicate that good faith and reasonable cause are the things to be inquired into by the court in the exercise of its discretion.—Henry v. Superior Court, 93 Cal. 569, 572, 29 Pac. 230.

(5) Do not include attorneys' fees.—Attorneys' fees are not, in any proper sense, a part of the costs in a probate case.—Henry v. Superior Court, 93 Cal. 569, 29 Pac. 230; Estate of Olmstead, 120 Cal. 447, 454, 52 Pac. 804. A later statute as to costs, must prevail in probate proceedings, especially where such statute is included in the provisions which relate specifically to proceedings in probate.—Estate of Olmstead, 120 Cal. 447, 452, 52 Pac. 804.

(6) No amendment of Judgment to Include.—If a probate decree is silent as to the matter of costs, such judgment can not afterwards be amended nunc pro tunc, by the court, so as to include costs.—Estate of Potter, 141 Cal. 424, 426, 75 Pac. 850. The principle is such cases is that, if the court has not rendered a judgment that it might or should have rendered, or if it has rendered an imperfect or improper judgment, it has no power to remedy such error by ordering an amendment, nunc pro tunc, of a proper judgment.—Estate of Potter, 141 Cal. 424, 426, 75 Pac. 850.

(7) Contesting probate of will.—Until a will has been admitted to probate, or probate has been denied, the court has no power to appropriate the funds of an estate to aid either the proponent or contestant.—Henry v. Superior Court, 93 Cal. 569, 573, 29 Pac. 230; Estate of McKinney, 112 Cal. 447, 453, 44 Pac. 743. When there is a successful contest after probate, the court, in its discretion, may allow to the executors, out of the estate, their reasonable costs and expenditures in endeavoring to uphold the will of which they had been appointed the executors.—Estate of McKinney, 112 Cal. 447, 44 Pac. 743. And where there is a successful contest before probate, and the legatees or executors acted in good faith, and upon probable grounds in proposing the will for probate, the court may, in its discretion, allow to the unsuccessful proponents all ordinary costs incurred in endeavoring to establish the will and make the same a charge against the assets of the estate.—Estate of Olmstead, 120 Cal. 447, 52 Pac. 804. So there may be cases in which the duty of a widow, or other person entitled to administration of an estate, in case of intestacy, to contest the probating of an alleged will, might be as plain and urgent, under the circumstances known to such person, as would be the duty of an executor already appointed, or one nominated as executor in a will offered for probate, or a legatee thereunder, to oppose a contest and endeavor to establish such will; and the broad and comprehensive terms of the provision of the code which provides that in probate proceedings in general a superior court, "may, in its discretion, order costs to be paid by any party to the proceeding, or out of the assets of the estate as justice may require," applies as well to a party contesting a will as to one opposing it. The statute puts the entire matter of costs within the sound discretion of the court, and such discretionary power extends to and includes the case of an unsuccessful contestant. It is only in rare and extreme cases, however, that the court is justified in ordering the costs of an unsuccessful contestant to be paid out of the estate.—Estate of Bump, 152 Cal. 271, 92 Pac. 642. The court may direct costs to be paid out of the funds of the estate, where an executor or administrator, on the complaint of an heir, has been removed for mismanagement.—Estate of Mullins, 47 Cal. 450, 452.

(8) Action against co-executor.—If an heir brings an action against a surviving executor to compel him to make good the default of a deceased co-executor, the defendant in such action can not recover his costs incurred therein from the sureties on the bond of his deceased co-executor.—Hewlett v. Beede, 2 Cal. App. 561, 83 Pac. 1086, 1089.

(9) Presumption on appeal.—Where a case is presented upon the proposition that the power does not exist, in any way, or under any circumstances, to make the costs of an unsuccessful contest of a will payable out of the assets of the estate, the presumptions are all in favor of the action of the court below. The power does exist, and in the absence of any showing to the contrary, it must be presumed that it was properly exercised.—Estate of Bump, 152 Cal. 271, 92 Pac. 642, 643.

(10) To be borne by estate, when.—Costs of litigation affecting an estate, expended by the executor or administrator in good faith, are to be taxed against the estate, whether the litigation be successful or not.—Stahl v. Schwartz, 81 Wash. 293, 142 Pac. 651. Where in a probate proceeding, and in a suit brought in connection with it to construe the will, it is manifest that an honest effort has been made for a proper administration according to the legal tenor of the will, the costs should be borne by the estate.—In re Wilson's Estate, 85 Or. 604, 167 Pac. 580; Mackin v. Noad, 86 Or. 221, 165 Pac. 585. On the failure of his suit brought by one member of a decedent's family, as executor, against another in respect to a financial dealing with the decedent, the estate should bear the costs, where the plaintiff was prompted in the matter by official zeal and had as his purpose the estate's interest. —Gorsline v. Gore, 90 Or. 389, 176 Pac. 603.

10. Disposition of life estates, etc.—The proceedings under sections 1723 of the Code of Civil Procedure of California for a decree adjudging that a life estate, created under the will of a deceased person, has been terminated by reason of the death of the one to whom it was granted, partake of the nature of proceedings in rem. The petition is addressed to the superior court, and not to the probate court, and is similar to a complaint or petition in equity.—Matter of Tracey, 136 Cal. 385, 388, 69 Pac. 20; Estate of De Leon, 102 Cal. 537, 541, 36 Pac. 864. But, although the proceeding is improperly entitled as a probate cause, yet if the facts stated in the petition, notwithstanding its title, are such as entitle it to be treated as a complaint in equity, it will be so treated, and, if the allegations thereof are sufficient in all respects to justify the relief granted, the court having jurisdiction of the subject-matter and of the parties may grant the proper relief.— Estate of De Leon, 102 Cal. 537, 541, 36 Pac. 864. The jurisdiction of the court to render the decree, in such case, so as to bind all persons interested in the property, depends upon notice being given to them as required by the statute; and, in all cases in which the statute allows a contructive service, or in which jurisdiction may be obtained of a thing by a prescribed form of notice, in which the real party in interest had no actual notice, and did not appear or subject himself to the jurisdiction of the court, the mode of service prescribed by the statute must be strictly pursued.—Matter of Tracey, 136 Cal. 385, 390, 69 Pac. 20. Where a petition was filed under the section above named, setting up an alleged right of homestead, and praying that it be decreed that the said alleged homestead property vested in petitioner by reason of the death of her husband, and the court made an order fixing a certain time and place for the hearing of the petition, and that "notice of said hearing be given by the posting of this order in three of the most prominent places in said county," naming them, more than ten days prior to the day fixed for the hearing, but there was no notice directed to any person or to any class of persons, such notice given was radically defective and did not give to the court any jurisdiction to hear the proceeding or to render a decree.—Hansen v. Union Sav. Bank, 148 Cal. 157, 160, 82 Pac. 768. The said section 1723 was only intended as a proceeding to have it determined that a certain person is dead, upon whose death the asserted right of another person depends, and not to have the validity of the right conclusively adjudicated. The decree in the proceeding merely determines that, if the party petitioning has any asserted right or title accruing on the death of another person, such asserted right or title has accrued. The court is not given power under that section to declare in whom, upon the termination of a life estate, title is vested absolutely. It is empowered to make a decree that the life estate of a deceased party has absolutely terminated.—Hansen v. Union Sav. Bank, 148 Cal. 157, 160, 82 Pac. 768. But the statute seems to contemplate a difference in the terms of a decree between cases where a life estate has terminated, and homestead or community property has vested in the survivor of a marriage, by reason of death.

11. New trial and appeal.—New trials, in probate proceedings, are proper only in cases involving issues arising upon authorized pleadings.—In re Antonioli's Estate, 42 Mont. 219, 223, 111 Pac. 1033. An affidavit, to be effective in accompanying a motion for a new trial, must show that the evidence, claimed to be newly discovered, could not, with reasonable diligence have been produced at the trial, and that it is not merely cumulative.—Estate of Jepson, 178 Cal. 257, 172 Pac. 1107. The Idaho statute, relative to new trials and appeals, is applicable to probate proceedings.—In re Blackinton's Estate, Woodward v. Utter, 29 Ida. 310, 158 Pac. 492. Section 1714 of the Code of Civil Procedure of California, as amended, merely fixes the procedure in probate cases by doing away with the cumbersome process of a motion for a new trial; it does not deprive the supreme court of the right to examine the record and to direct the lower court to do anything which may be proper in the exercise of its probate jurisdiction.—Estate of Vanderhurst, 171 Cal. 553, 154 Pac. 5. The supreme court of Utah is committed to the doctrine that probate proceedings are

in rem, and that where the statutory notice has been given all who are interested in the estate are bound by all orders or decrees duly entered in a particular case, and that, ordinarily, the remedy is by appeal, not by separate suit in equity for relief against such orders and decrees.—Weyant v. Utah Sav. & Trust Co., — (Utah) —, 182 Pac. 189, 197. Where the record on appeal contains no proof of notice, but the order finds "that the clerk had given notice of the settlement of said account in the matter and for the time heretofore ordered by the court," this meets the requirement of the section, and is conclusive upon the parties on appeal.—Estate of Davis, 35 Mont. 273, 280, 88 Pac. 957. If a court, having discretion in a matter moved for, denies the motion as being outside its jurisdiction, and at the same time intimates that the grounds of the motion are good, it can not be said that it has exercised its discretion, in a case where appeal can be had only for abuse of discretion.—Estate of Simmens, 168 Cal. 390, 393, 143 Pac. 697. Where the record fails to disclose that any evidence was suppressed, it was error to give the familiar instruction with respect to the presumption of law that such evidence would be adverse.—In re Moore's Estate, — (Cal.) —, 182 Pac. 285, 292. The admission of secondary evidence as to the contents of a check, conceded to be error, but harmless in view of the stipulation of counsel that such evidence was to be considered only for the purpose of fixing the date of the return of the check.—Bailey v. Moshier, 35 Cal. App. 345, 349, 169 Pac. 913. Where the testimony is positive and unequivocal and there is nothing improbable or suspicious about it, it can not be ignored, and a finding based thereon can not be said to be unsupported.—Bailey v. Moshier, 35 Cal. App. 345, 346, 169 Pac. 913.

12. Relief in equity.—Persons who obtain conveyances from heirs before the estate is settled are required to establish their rights in a court of equity if the conveyances are questioned in the probate court.—In re Blackinton's Estate, Woodward v. Utter, 29 Ida. 310, 158 Pac. 492. Where the statutory notice has not been given, and where there is extrinsic as contradistinguished from intrinsic fraud, orders and decrees in probate proceedings may be relieved against by persons interested in the estate of a decedent in a court of equity.—Weyant v. Utah Sav. & Trust Co., — (Utah) —, 182 Pac. 189, 197.

REFERENCES.

Relief in equity from orders and decrees of probate and other courts having exclusive jurisdiction over the estates of decedents and of minors and other incompetent persons.—See note 106 Am. St. Rep. 639-647.

CPSIA information can be obtained
at www.ICGtesting.com
Printed in the USA
BVHW05*1753060818
523683BV00019B/1471/P

9 780331 663914